W9-DAW-585

The SCRIBNER ENCYCLOPEDIA *of*
AMERICAN LIVES

The SCRIBNER ENCYCLOPEDIA *of*

AMERICAN LIVES

THE 1960s

VOLUME TWO

M–Z

WILLIAM L. O'NEILL
VOLUME EDITOR

KENNETH T. JACKSON
SERIES EDITOR IN CHIEF

CHARLES SCRIBNER'S SONS®

New York • Detroit • San Diego • San Francisco • Cleveland • New Haven, Conn. • Waterville, Maine • London • Munich

Charles Scribner's Sons
An imprint of The Gale Group
300 Park Avenue South, 9th floor
New York, NY 10010

Library of Congress Cataloging-in-Publication Data

The Scribner encyclopedia of American lives. The 1960s / edited by William L. O'Neill.
     p.   cm.
    Includes bibliographical references and index.
    ISBN 0-684-80666-5 (set : alk paper)
    ISBN 0-684-31221-2 (v. 1)   ISBN 0-684-31222-0 (v. 2)
    1. United States—Biography—Dictionaries. 2. Biography—20th century.
  I. O'Neill, William L.
CT213.S374   2003
920.073'09'046—dc21   2002012581
                                          CIP

1 3 5 7 9 11 13 15 17 19 20 18 16 14 12 10 8 6 4 2
PRINTED IN THE UNITED STATES OF AMERICA

The paper in this publication meets the minimum requirements of the American National Standard for Information Services—Permanence of Paper for Printed Library Materials, ANSI Z39.48–1992.

CONTENTS

VOLUME 1

VOLUME 2

The SCRIBNER ENCYCLOPEDIA *of*

AMERICAN LIVES

M

McCAIN, John Sidney, Jr. (*b.* 17 January 1911 in Council Bluffs, Indiana; *d.* 22 March 1981 over the Atlantic Ocean), U.S. Navy admiral who served as Commander in Chief of the Pacific Fleet in the late 1960s and early 1970s during the final phases of the Vietnam War.

McCain was the youngest of three children born to Admiral John Sidney McCain, Sr., and Katherine Vaulx, a homemaker. He graduated from Central High School in Washington, D.C., in 1927 and entered the U.S. Naval Academy at Annapolis, from which he graduated with a B.S. degree in 1931. From 1931 to 1933 he served as an ensign on the battleship *Oklahoma,* and on 21 January 1933, he married Roberta Wright. They had three children, one of whom, John Sidney McCain III, became a U.S. Navy pilot and later a senator from Arizona.

After attending the U.S. Navy Submarine School in New London, Connecticut, in 1933, McCain served on three submarines before returning to Annapolis in 1938 to teach electrical engineering and physics. In 1940 he returned to submarine service as a commanding officer on various submarines in the Atlantic and Pacific theaters during World War II. His achievements during the war earned him a Bronze Star and a Silver Star for distinguished service.

Following the war McCain spent three years at the Pentagon, as director of records in the Bureau of Naval Personnel, and then served as commander of two submarine divisions and a heavy cruiser. By 1950 he was back at the Pentagon, directing undersea warfare research development for the chief of naval operations during the Korean War. For the remainder of the 1950s McCain alternated between naval commands and service at the Pentagon. Promoted to rear admiral in 1959, McCain became the chief congressional liaison for the navy. From 1960 to 1962 he directed amphibious warfare training for the North Atlantic Treaty Organization (NATO), after which he returned to the Pentagon as chief of information. Another promotion followed in 1963, when McCain became a vice admiral and was appointed commander of the Atlantic fleet amphibious forces.

The most significant events during this period occurred in April and May of 1965, when U.S. forces invaded the Dominican Republic. The country had seen several changes of government following the assassination of the dictator Rafael Trujillo in 1961, and when a group of army officers attempted to reinstate Juan Bosch—earlier overthrown, with U.S. support, for his willingness to permit Communist participation in government—Washington sent in the marines. McCain, as operational commander of the invading force, earned the Legion of Merit. Members of the Organization of American States opposed the invasion, which sowed lasting rancor between the United States and various Latin American countries. McCain, however, maintained that the invasion was necessary to prevent Communist aggression directed by Cuba's leader Fidel Castro.

John S. McCain, Jr. *(right)*, and John S. McCain III. NATIONAL ARCHIVES AND RECORDS ADMINISTRATION

By late 1965 McCain had been appointed military adviser to Arthur Goldberg, the U.S. delegate to the United Nations. He served in this capacity for nearly two years; then, in May 1967, he was designated a full admiral and became commander in chief of U.S. naval forces in Europe. A year later on 11 April 1968, President Lyndon B. Johnson appointed McCain as Commander in Chief, Pacific Fleet (CINCPAC), to replace Admiral Ulysses S. Grant Sharp. Meanwhile, on 26 October 1967, McCain's son John McCain III was shot down and captured during a bombing raid over North Vietnam. When the North Vietnamese learned of the younger McCain's prominent father, they quickly recognized the propaganda value of their new captive. During the years that followed, as they held him prisoner in various locations—including the infamous "Hanoi Hilton"—the Vietnamese made much of the younger McCain's status, broadcasting news about him on their English-language Voice of Vietnam. They even offered him an early release from prison, but he followed the code of conduct for U.S. prisoners of war, which states that prisoners should accept release only in the order of their capture. In part because of this act of defiance toward his captors, the younger McCain suffered repeated tortures, along with the other deprivations of a North Vietnamese prison: dysentery, malnutrition, and a mixture of terror, loneliness, and boredom. As for the elder McCain, he bore his son's imprisonment stoically, sending terse but gracious notes of thanks back to friends who inquired after his son or expressed their sympathies.

In early 1969 McCain said in a *Reader's Digest* interview that the Vietnam War was the "testing ground" of a Communist plan "to extend their domination over the world's peoples through wars of national liberation." Despite the defeat of U.S. forces in the 1968 Tet offensive, a series of battles launched by the Vietnamese Communists to capture cities in South Vietnam, he asserted, "We have the enemy licked now. He is beaten." The U.S. State Department, however, cautious against sounding a strident tone, disavowed McCain's comments.

McCain supported and recommended President Richard M. Nixon's plan to enlarge the war through a joint U.S. and South Vietnamese invasion of Cambodia in 1970. Unfortunately, the invasion failed to achieve its military objectives and instead produced a number of negative, unintended consequences—at home, extensive rioting on college campuses, and in Southeast Asia, a coup that toppled Cambodia's hereditary ruler, Prince Norodom Sihanouk, in favor of Lon Nol's unstable dictatorship. Attempting to salvage a bad situation, McCain set about aiding and supporting Lon Nol militarily. He proceeded with this effort in spite of the Cooper-Church Amendment, whereby Congress had prohibited the use of traditional military advisory groups in Cambodia. When General Theodore Mataxis, chief of the U.S. military aid team in Cambodia, disregarded the advice of the U.S. ambassador to that country (his nominal superior) McCain supported Mataxis.

On 1 November 1972 McCain retired and was succeeded as CINCPAC by Admiral Noel Gaylor. McCain moved with his wife to Washington, D.C., where he embarked on a second career as president of the U.S. Strategic Institute, a think tank focusing on issues of national security. He also served as publisher of the journal *Strategic Review* and chaired the Monuments and Cemeteries Commission of the U.S. Veterans Administration.

During his time in Vietnam, McCain had arranged to spend each Christmas at the demilitarized zone bordering North Vietnam as a way of honoring his imprisoned son. He did so once more at Christmas 1972; then, on 17 March 1973, following the signing of the Paris peace accords that ended U.S. involvement in the war, John McCain III and the other prisoners of war were released. The younger McCain returned to a hero's welcome and numerous military decorations, but five and a half years in Vietnamese prison camps had reduced his weight by sixty pounds and rendered his hair permanently white.

Even as he celebrated the release of his son, McCain was the target of a congressional investigation. A few months later, a report from Congress revealed that the admiral and General Creighton W. Abrams (who had replaced William Westmoreland as chief of ground forces in Vietnam at the same time that McCain took over as CINC-PAC) had violated the Geneva Convention. Specifically, the two military leaders, acting under authorization from the Joint Chiefs of Staff, had ordered nighttime bombing raids against hospitals in North Vietnam and Cambodia.

Despite the reprimand he received from Congress, McCain remained active in public life. In particular, he was an outspoken opponent of President Jimmy Carter's plan to turn the Panama Canal over to Panamanian control. In 1981 McCain was returning from a vacation in Europe aboard a military transport from London to Loring Air Force Base in Maine when he died of a heart attack. He is buried at Arlington National Cemetery. In 1989 the U.S. Navy commissioned the destroyer USS *John S. McCain,* named after McCain and his father.

Members of a distinguished military family, McCain and his father became the first father and son admirals in U.S. Navy history. They are depicted on the cover of the 1999 book *Faith of My Fathers,* by John S. McCain III, who was destined to eclipse both of his namesakes in fame and influence. Like his father, McCain, Jr., represented an old order, an order dedicated to discipline, obedience, self-sacrifice, and commitment—values that, by the end of the 1960s, were in retreat across the American landscape. One may question many of McCain's actions during the Vietnam War, including some that many would label as unethical or even immoral, yet one cannot doubt the sincerity of his belief in the rightness of his cause. He made difficult decisions in defending the country he loved during a time of profound change and moral ambiguity.

★

McCain's memoirs are contained in *Reminiscences of Admiral John S. McCain, Jr., U.S. Navy (Retired),* a document housed at the U.S. Naval Institute in Annapolis. Other naval records and some correspondence are at the Naval Historical Center in Washington Navy Yard, Washington, D.C., while correspondence with Abrams is in the Abrams Collection, Center of Military History, Washington, D.C. A great deal of information about McCain, his father, and his son is in John S. McCain III, *Faith of My Fathers* (1999). Obituaries are in the *New York Times* and *Washington Post* (both 24 Mar. 1981).

JUDSON KNIGHT

McCARTHY, Eugene Joseph (*b.* 29 March 1916 in Watkins, Minnesota), U.S. senator and author who challenged President Lyndon Johnson in the 1968 Democratic presidential primaries as an anti–Vietnam War candidate, winning fervent support from college students, liberal activists, and others before ultimately losing his party's nomination to Vice President Hubert Humphrey.

McCarthy was born and raised in a rural area of central Minnesota. One of two sons of Michael J. McCarthy, a

Eugene J. McCarthy. THE LIBRARY OF CONGRESS

farmer, and Anna (Baden) McCarthy, a homemaker, he showed both an intellectual streak and athletic prowess (in baseball and ice hockey) while growing up. He attended Saint John's Preparatory School and Saint John's University, receiving a bachelor's degree in 1935, followed by graduate studies at the University of Minnesota, where he received a master's degree in sociology in 1941. From 1936 to 1940 he taught social science in high school and then returned to Saint John's University as a professor of economics and education. A brief stint as a civilian technical assistant with army intelligence in 1942 interrupted his academic career. After flirting with the idea of taking monastic vows, he married a teacher, Abigail Quigley, in 1945 and became a sociology instructor at the College of Saint Thomas, in Saint Paul. He and his wife had four children and later divorced.

Becoming active in the Democratic Farmer–Labor Party in the Saint Paul area, he received its nomination for U.S. Congress in 1948. McCarthy was elected and went on to serve five terms; he was best known there as the leader of McCarthy's Marauders (a caucus of young midwestern liberals) and for debating the much feared Senator Joseph McCarthy in 1952. (Joseph McCarthy was best known for his heavy-handed and wide-ranging investigation of Communism in the U.S. government and in society at large.) In 1958 McCarthy was elected to the U.S. Senate. His national profile was raised when he nominated Adlai Stevenson for president at the 1960 Democratic National Convention. Increasingly, he gained a reputation as a loner, although he generally voted with his party's liberal faction. Briefly considered as Lyndon Johnson's vice presidential running mate in 1964, he went on to win reelection to the Senate by a record-setting margin that year.

Over the next two years McCarthy emerged as a critic of Johnson's Vietnam War policies, voting in 1966 to repeal the Gulf of Tonkin Resolution, which effectively gave the president unlimited authorization to use American military forces in Southeast Asia. Beyond the war itself, McCarthy objected to the Johnson administration's disregard for the Senate's role in shaping foreign policy. He was likewise critical of the Central Intelligence Agency's influence in policy-making and sought to reduce U.S. arms sales abroad. In 1967 he detailed his views in *The Limits of Power,* a thoughtful, yet scathing book that condemned reckless American intervention in other nations' affairs.

For all his anger and frustration, McCarthy was slow to emerge as the leader of the "dump Johnson" movement. Initially, he considered Senator Robert F. Kennedy to be the strongest potential challenger. A deliberate, cerebral man with a penchant for writing poetry, McCarthy never saw himself at the head of a radical campaign to seize the Democratic Party. Thanks to the urgings of the liberal activist Allard K. Lowenstein and his own daughter Mary, he

finally decided to accept the backing of antiwar activists and enter the 1968 presidential primaries. McCarthy explained his candidacy in clear-cut moral terms. In a December 1967 speech, he called the Vietnam War "central to all the problems of America . . . diplomatically indefensible" and the source of the country's growing disillusionment with government.

Although the experts dismissed his chances, McCarthy's campaign attracted impressive numbers of college students as volunteers. Young people were encouraged to get "Clean for Gene," that is, to spruce up and canvass door-to-door for votes. The efforts of this "Children's Crusade" proved decisive in the campaign's first primary, held in New Hampshire on 12 March. Winning a surprising 42 percent of the vote, McCarthy demonstrated that Johnson was vulnerable. The shock waves from New Hampshire led to Johnson's withdrawal from the race on 31 March. Two days later McCarthy decisively won the Wisconsin primary, only to face new opposition from Robert Kennedy (who had decided to enter the primaries) and Vice President Hubert Humphrey (who courted delegates outside the primary system). Running against these opponents proved more difficult than taking on the unpopular president. Losing his stride, McCarthy came in third in the Indiana primary on 7 May and was beaten by Kennedy in Nebraska a week later.

Lacking a stark contrast over issues, the Democratic primary race began to focus on more personal charges. The Kennedy forces portrayed McCarthy as an aloof intellectual; the McCarthy supporters painted Kennedy as a ruthless opportunist. Against his opponent's flash and charisma, McCarthy presented a subdued reasonableness that held considerable appeal in affluent suburban areas. It worked well for him in the Oregon primary—backed by a strong local volunteer organization, he scored an impressive victory there, becoming the first candidate ever to defeat a Kennedy brother in an election. This win set up the two men for a showdown in California on 4 June.

The bitterness between the McCarthy and Kennedy campaigns reached new heights during the California contest. At a San Francisco appearance, McCarthy charged that Kennedy "played a prominent role in formulating policies which resulted in disastrous adventures," including the Vietnam War. He also criticized his opponent for relying too much on private enterprise to reduce poverty in America's inner cities, favoring a more activist government approach that included job-linked housing programs outside the ghetto. This latter issue became a point of contention during the two candidates' televised debate on 1 June. Kennedy accused his foe of proposing to "take 10,000 black people and move them into Orange County [a Los Angeles suburb]," a charge with decidedly racist overtones. McCarthy failed to respond to these and other jabs with much vigor, turning in a lackluster performance. Three days later Kennedy defeated McCarthy by five percentage points, only to be assassinated shortly after claiming victory. The tragedy effectively ended the McCarthy campaign as well, although McCarthy continued to search for delegates and engage in credentials challenges up until the Democratic convention.

After winning the New York primary on 18 June, McCarthy conducted what some supporters viewed as an erratic, indifferent campaign. He appeared downbeat and self-absorbed, uncertain of how to proceed against Humphrey, who was rolling up enough delegates to secure the Democratic presidential nomination. Despite the fact that political polls indicated that McCarthy, rather than Humphrey, was the strongest candidate against the likely Republican nominee, Richard Nixon, old-guard Democratic professionals remained opposed to his candidacy. The late entrance of Senator George McGovern into the race as a second antiwar candidate complicated matters further. As the convention approached, McCarthy bristled at the notion that he had become a halfhearted, passive candidate who lacked compassion and feeling. At one delegate gathering, he noted, "A little passivity in that office [the presidency] is all right, a kind of balance. . . . I have never quite known what active compassion is. . . . Compassion, in my mind, is to suffer *with* someone, not in advance of him."

On the eve of August's Democratic convention in Chicago, McCarthy acknowledged that his chances were all but hopeless. Humphrey easily triumphed over McCarthy on the first ballot but never recovered from the ill-will between his party's factions. The violence committed by Chicago police against demonstrators outside the convention hall further soured McCarthy's supporters from casting their lot with Humphrey. Although he discouraged his supporters from launching an independent campaign on his behalf, McCarthy refused to endorse the Democratic ticket until Humphrey turned away from Johnson's war policies. He finally gave his support on 29 October, after the vice president announced his willingness to suspend bombing in North Vietnam. This last-minute gesture failed to save Humphrey from a narrow defeat by Nixon.

Before Election Day, McCarthy had announced his intention not to seek reelection to the U.S. Senate. Returning to the political wars in 1972, he ran a limited campaign for the Democratic nomination. Four years later he sought the presidency as an independent, polling less than 1 percent of the vote (although arguably drawing enough votes from the Democratic contender, Jimmy Carter, nearly to elect the Republican nominee, Gerald Ford). Further unsuccessful bids for office followed, including a run for the U.S. Senate in 1982 and a small-scale effort as the presidential nominee of the Consumers Party in 1988. He had trouble attracting notice for his third try for the Democratic pres-

idential nomination in 1992. Ever the maverick, he opposed federal election reform and championed a shorter work week during this campaign, which garnered few votes. Besides seeking office, he spent his post-Senate years lecturing at universities and writing books. His published works have included everything from political studies to children's stories and collections of poetry.

An unusual mixture of freethinker and traditionalist, McCarthy spent much of his public career trying to reform existing American institutions. His 1968 campaign was an attempt to restore the balance of power between Congress and the presidency and to curb the excesses of the military. As an articulate spokesman for the antiwar forces, McCarthy made opposition to U.S. involvement in Vietnam seem reasonable and morally compelling. More conservative than many of his followers, he served to bring many young activists into the political system before embarking on his own idiosyncratic path in the 1970s.

★

Books by McCarthy relating to the events of 1968 include *The Limits of Power* (1967), *The Year of the People* (1969), and *Up 'Til Now: A Memoir* (1987). Valuable studies of the campaign by former McCarthy aides include Arthur Herzog, *McCarthy for President* (1969), and Jeremy Larner, *Nobody Knows* (1969). Lewis Chester, Godfrey Hodgson, and Bruce Page, *An American Melodrama: The Presidential Campaign of 1968* (1969), provides an excellent overview of the politics of that year.

BARRY ALFONSO

McCARTHY, Mary Therese (*b.* 21 June 1912 in Seattle, Washington; *d.* 25 October 1989 in New York City), novelist, literary critic, and essayist who, despite her reputation as an anti-Communist, wrote admiringly of the Communist Hanoi government during the Vietnam War.

McCarthy was the eldest of four children born to Roy Winfield McCarthy and Therese Preston. Soon after her birth, her father entered law school, but health problems forced him to close his law practice in 1918 and move the family to his parents' home in Minneapolis. Her parents died in the 1918 influenza epidemic, leaving the children to be raised by their great-aunt and great-uncle. In 1923 McCarthy's maternal grandparents took her back to Seattle.

After graduating in 1929 from Annie Wright Seminary, a boarding school for girls in nearby Tacoma, Washington, McCarthy entered Vassar College as an English major. She graduated with a B.A. in 1933, the same year she moved to New York City and embarked on the first of four marriages, to the actor Harold Johnsrud. Divorced in 1936, she married the renowned literary critic Edmund Wilson in 1938. With Wilson she had her only child, a son, the same year.

By that point McCarthy had developed a formidable reputation as a literary critic for the *Nation* and *New Republic* and as drama critic for the *Partisan Review,* but Wilson persuaded her to try her hand at fiction. The result was *The Company She Keeps* (1942), often regarded as the finest of McCarthy's seven novels.

She divorced Wilson in October 1945, and on 6 December 1946 she married a schoolteacher, Bowden Broadwater. During the 1940s and 1950s McCarthy distinguished herself as a critic and author of both fiction and nonfiction. Notable works from this period include the novel *The Groves of Academe* (1952), in which she satirized what would today be termed the "political correctness" of liberal academicians, as well as the first of three memoirs, *Memories of a Catholic Girlhood* (1957). After divorcing Broadwater in 1960, McCarthy married James Raymond West, a diplomat, on 15 April 1961. The romantically restless McCarthy had met her match in West, a man completely removed from the New York intellectual circles that had dominated her professional and social life for three decades. The two, who divided their time between two spacious residences—a Paris apartment and a house in Castine, Maine—remained together for the rest of McCarthy's life.

Ever the memoirist, McCarthy in 1963 published a novel, *The Group,* based on her experiences at Vassar. The story, which chronicles the lives of eight young women over a period of seven years following their graduation, was made into a motion picture starring Candice Bergen and Joan Hackett in 1966. McCarthy's next novel, *Birds of America* (1971), is the story of a young bird-watcher deeply affected by the intrusion of technology into the natural environment. At one point the protagonist, Peter Levi, reacts to news of the bombing of North Vietnam by fleeing to a zoo.

McCarthy herself became deeply concerned over the American involvement in the Vietnam War. This was a major theme of her nonfiction during the 1960s and early 1970s, presented in *Vietnam* (1967), *Hanoi* (1968), and *Medina* (1972) as well as in a series of articles for the *New York Review of Books.* The first two books, as well as the magazine articles, were the product of trips to Saigon in 1967 and Hanoi in 1968, and the 1972 volume chronicled the trial of Captain Ernest Medina for war crimes associated with the 1968 massacre of South Vietnamese civilians at the village of My Lai. Many Americans opposed the war, but McCarthy was part of a much smaller faction—a group that included both the actress Jane Fonda and the linguist Noam Chomsky—who came to lend active support to the Communist North Vietnamese regime. In the case of McCarthy, aspects of her career both before and after the 1960s make this affinity for Hanoi a rather surprising choice.

Carol Brightman, author of *Writing Dangerously: Mary McCarthy and Her World* (1992), referred approvingly to

Mary McCarthy. THE LIBRARY OF CONGRESS

1930s radicals as the "granddaddy generation." The appellation reflected a sentiment expressed often by the student radicals of the 1960s, who saw in the Stalinism of earlier intellectuals a model for their own extreme brand of activism. Still, McCarthy was not a true member of the "granddaddy generation": during the decade of the Spanish Civil War and the Moscow show trials (in which Soviet dictator Josef Stalin used a semblance of legality to facilitate the arrest and murder of his rivals for Communist Party leadership), she had remained impervious to Stalinism and ridiculed its humorless dogmatism at every possible opportunity.

During the anti-Communist backlash of the 1950s, McCarthy condemned the tactics of Senator Joseph McCarthy (no relation to her), who had launched investigations of Communists and alleged Communists in the government and society at large, yet she maintained the position that Stalinism was an even greater evil. In so doing, she made many foes, not the least of whom was the playwright Lillian Hellman, who in 1980 filed a $2.25 million lawsuit against McCarthy for disparaging her honesty in a television interview with Dick Cavett. (Hellman died in 1984 without the case ever coming to trial.)

This backdrop provides a means for understanding McCarthy's writings during the 1960s, when she became an advocate for a government openly aligned with Stalinist principles—a government that practiced indoctrination and imprisonment on a scale far beyond the power, much less the desire, of the United States or South Vietnam. In McCarthy's view, however, the Hanoi government represented peasant nationalists striving for self-determination against the destructive tactics of the U.S. war machine and its puppets in Saigon.

Typical of her antipathy to the American war effort was her "Report from Vietnam I: The Home Program," published in the *New York Review of Books* on 20 April 1967. "I confess that when I went to Vietnam early in February," she began, "I was looking for material damaging to the American interest and that I found it, though often by accident or in the process of being briefed by an official." Her attitude toward North Vietnam was quite different, as revealed in a 6 June 1968 *New York Review of Books* article entitled "Hanoi II": "In glaring contrast to Saigon," she wrote, "Hanoi is clean—much cleaner than New York, for example. The sidewalks are swept, there is no refuse piled up, and a matinal sprinkler truck comes through, washing down the streets."

In another article she actually praised the North Vietnamese for not allowing her to see the combat zones and condemned American officials for encouraging visitors "in blustery, hectoring tones" to see the fighting firsthand. Rather than suspect the honesty of her hosts, she suggested that by preventing her from glimpsing anything of their war machinery, they were acting in her best interests. In any case, citing Homer and Leo Tolstoy as authorities, she maintained: "I do not feel it as a deprivation that I failed to see the front lines. The meaning of a war, if it has one, ought to be discernible in the rear." All of this proved a bit too much for many critics reviewing *Vietnam* and *Hanoi* and for noted intellectuals such as Diana Trilling and Daniel Bell, who wrote her open letters in the pages of the *New York Review of Books*. Bell, for instance, commented in an 18 January 1968 letter on her "renewed desire to be 'Left,'" and her use of "the shards and detritus of radical stereotypes she learned thirty years ago."

Noted for her acerbic wit and her ability to defend herself when challenged, McCarthy responded to many of her critics. In her answer to Bell, she indicated that her views on the Soviet Union had changed since the refutation of Stalinism by Prime Minister Nikita Khrushchev at the Twentieth Party Congress in the 1950s. Even her appreciation of Soviet dissidents, such as the writer Aleksandr Solzhenitsyn, was tinged with admiration for the system that provided them with a constant source of tension: "To feel solidarity with them . . . is to imagine yourself in their life and to see that it has some rewards."

McCarthy's other works from the 1960s include the essay collections *On the Contrary* (1961) and *The Humanist in the Bathtub* (1964). During the 1970s she wrote *The Mask of State* (1974) about the Watergate hearings, conducted to investigate a break-in at the Democratic Party headquarters

that was traced to supporters of President Richard Nixon. McCarthy published her final novel, *Cannibals and Missionaries*, in 1979. The 1980s saw two more essay collections as well as the memoirs *How I Grew* (1987) and the posthumous *Intellectual Memoirs: New York, 1936–1938* (1992). McCarthy died of cancer in New York City and is buried in Castine, Maine.

With a career that spanned the better part of six decades, from the height of the depression to the eve of Communism's downfall, McCarthy was a quintessential twentieth-century figure, gifted with both the insight and the myopia common among those who witnessed one of history's most turbulent times. In the 1930s she showed an almost flawless ability to detect the deception to which Stalinist intellectuals, in their quasireligious faith, had succumbed. Three decades later, however, she, too, gave in to some of the century's great vices: the assumption that different standards should be applied in evaluating Western and non-Western governments and the belief that the foe of what she considered an evil force—the United States in Vietnam—must necessarily be virtuous. Still, her writing on other subjects showed her to be a fiercely penetrating critic, and her defiance of the vastly more wealthy and more powerful Hellman illustrated the courage that she displayed throughout much of her career.

★

McCarthy's papers are housed at Vassar College. Johns Hopkins University in Baltimore has a much smaller collection of papers dating from 1979 to 1987. In additional to semiautobiographical fictional works, such as *The Group* (1963), McCarthy wrote three memoirs: *Memories of a Catholic Girlhood* (1957), *How I Grew* (1987), and *Intellectual Memoirs: New York, 1936–1938* (1992). Notable biographies, all of which combine literary criticism, include Irvin Stock, *Mary McCarthy* (1968); Carol W. Gelderman, *Mary McCarthy: A Life* (1988); Carol Brightman, *Writing Dangerously: Mary McCarthy and Her World* (1992); and Frances Kiernan, *Seeing Mary Plain: A Life of Mary McCarthy* (2000). An obituary is in the *New York Times* (26 Oct. 1989).

JUDSON KNIGHT

McCLOY, John Jay (*b*. 31 March 1895 in Philadelphia, Pennsylvania; *d*. 11 March 1989 in Stamford, Connecticut), prominent Wall Street attorney and civil servant who during the 1960s was a leading presidential adviser and negotiator in disarmament matters and other foreign-policy issues.

McCloy was born John Snader McCloy, the second of two sons of John Jay McCloy, an actuarial clerk with Penn Mutual Life Insurance Company, and Anna May Snader, a homemaker. He attended Amherst College, Massachusetts, graduating cum laude in 1916, and then attended Harvard

John J. McCloy *(right)*, with President John F. Kennedy, October 1961. © BETTMANN/CORBIS

University, graduating in 1921 and passing the New York bar examination. In New York City he worked at several law firms until, after World War II, Nelson Rockefeller suggested that McCloy join Milbank, Tweed, Hope and Hadley, the firm representing the Rockefellers. McCloy was accepted as partner into the firm (renamed Milbank, Tweed, Hadley and McCloy in January 1946), becoming a full-time senior partner in 1963. The dominant international banking and oil interests of his practice required overseas travel, knowledge of U.S. foreign policy, and negotiating skills. McCloy married Ellen Scharmann Zinsser on 25 April 1930; they had two children.

When the 1960s began, McCloy assisted President Dwight D. Eisenhower on disarmament matters and advocated a U.S.–Soviet Union test-ban treaty, summit meeting, and disarmament talks. President-elect John F. Kennedy named McCloy his special adviser on disarmament and in 1961 appointed McCloy head of the United States Disarmament Administration. McCloy soon drafted legislation to establish the Arms Control and Disarmament Agency, testifying before Congress to ensure passage of the bill. When the Soviets conducted open-air nuclear testing, McCloy advised Kennedy likewise to break the three-year American moratorium on such tests. The McCloy-Zorin "Joint Statement of Agreed Principles for Disarmament Negotiations," which furnished the first American-Russian foundation for future nuclear disarmament talks, was adopted by the United Nations. McCloy had achieved two of Kennedy's three objectives—the establishment of the Arms Control and Disarmament Agency and a skeletal base for future disarmament discussions—but no test-ban

treaty. In April 1962 McCloy was sworn in as part-time chairman of the General Advisory Committee to the Arms Control and Disarmament Agency.

McCloy was one of the handful of personal advisers to the Kennedy administration who was summoned to Washington during the Cuban Missile Crisis (October–November 1962) to analyze whether to invade Cuba and, if so, how to avert nuclear confrontation between the United States and the Soviet Union. As chairman of the three-man committee communicating with the Soviets, McCloy negotiated with Vasily Kuznetsov, the Soviet deputy foreign minister, a face-saving compromise to avoid the immediate threat of nuclear conflict. The compromise agreed to the U.S. withdrawal of Jupiter missiles in Turkey and Soviet "disengagement" of its bombers from Cuba.

While traveling on legal business in the Middle East, McCloy learned that he would receive the Presidential Medal of Freedom from Kennedy; but it was President Lyndon B. Johnson who presented the award on 6 December 1963. Johnson also appointed McCloy to the Warren Commission, which soon began its investigation of Kennedy's assassination. McCloy did not attend all of the commission hearings, but he and the former head of the Central Intelligence Agency, Allen Dulles, traveled in the spring of 1964 to Dallas, the site of the assassination, for an on-site inspection. In its final report of September 1964, the commission concluded that there had been no conspiracy to assassinate the president. (Later, between 1976 and 1978, McCloy testified before the House of Representatives Select Committee on Assassinations, which investigated concerns that the Warren Commission had failed to investigate all of the evidence.) Concerning the growing unrest and military action in Vietnam during the mid-1960s, McCloy cautioned Johnson against becoming militarily involved in Southeast Asia, but as long as U.S. troops remained in harm's way, McCloy publicly supported the president's policies.

During the 1960s McCloy worried about the viability of the North Atlantic Treaty Organization (NATO), which he perceived as a permanent commitment of the United States to lead a definitive military strike back against any Soviet bloc threat in Europe. He believed that crises within NATO and on the European continent were potentially more threatening to U.S. security and international peace than any other problem at the time, including Vietnam and the uncertain worldwide economy. At his own urging, in April 1966 he became the president's special consultant on NATO. He was troubled by the rise of nationalism in Europe, especially French president Charles de Gaulle's efforts to erode U.S. influence in Europe; de Gaulle carried out his threat to withdraw French troops from NATO and cautioned that France would assist NATO only in the event of an unprovoked attack.

Since McCloy considered the Federal Republic of Germany as pivotal for East-West balance, one of his priorities was to convince the British not to withdraw their troops from the Federal Republic of Germany. The British worried about the strategic shift in U.S. war-planning from "massive retaliation" (nuclear attack at the start of hostilities) to "flexible response" (use of conventional NATO troops prior to any nuclear strike against the enemy), and the West Germans themselves did not appreciate this change of strategy, which seemed to offer less assurance of their survival in case of a Soviet bloc attack. The Americans, who at the time were committing more troops and economic resources to Vietnam, complained about the cost of keeping troops in West Germany, especially as the arrangement whereby the West German government compensated for the millions of dollars paid by U.S. soldiers to German businesses by purchasing U.S. arms was being challenged by a growing number of nationalistic Germans. Even Erhard's pro-NATO and pro-American stance was insufficient to prevent the challenges within his own country that forced an end to this arrangement. In December 1966 Erhard was defeated by Kurt Kiesinger, who developed a somewhat more relaxed attitude toward East Germany.

All of this signaled a surprising change in direction to McCloy, who successfully labored on trilateral agreements among the Americans, British, and Germans. The United States offered extensive bond sales to the British in order to assure the maintenance of British troops in West Germany and also offered bonds to the Germans to replace the German purchase of arms. In order to maintain a top-level troop strength committed to the defense of NATO (i.e.,

West Germany), the United States enacted "dual-basing," or keeping two brigades of a division in the United States (where soldiers would make purchases on U.S. bases) and one brigade in West Germany; the United States periodically rotated these brigades that were intended for NATO defense in West Germany. McCloy's determination and flexibility helped to assure NATO's survival.

By the end of 1967 McCloy had become more cautious about his public support of the Vietnam conflict. Although he did not join those criticizing the Johnson administration's war effort, McCloy realized that the military campaign was not progressing as it should toward a decisive U.S. victory. Many felt that when the Council on Foreign Relations (of which McCloy was chairman, from 1953 to 1970) and its quarterly, *Foreign Affairs,* began debating Vietnam during 1967 and 1968 the role of the establishment began to diminish rapidly. This was especially true after the January 1968 Tet Offensive, an assault launched by the North Vietnamese against cities in South Vietnam, the short-term success of which undermined American popular support for the war effort. Other negotiating activities, especially from 1965 to 1968, included McCloy's efforts as New York State's chairman of the Modern Courts Committee to work on judge-selection reform.

When Richard M. Nixon was elected president in 1968, he included McCloy on his foreign policy transition team. After the inauguration, McCloy was consulted less frequently; even his authority as chairman of the president's General Advisory Committee on Arms Control and Disarmament declined. The administrations of Presidents Jimmy Carter and Ronald W. Reagan, however, actively sought McCloy's advice. In March 1985 President Reagan honored him on his ninetieth birthday in the Rose Garden of the White House, and Richard von Weizsächer, president of the Federal Republic of Germany, there conferred upon McCloy honorary German citizenship. McCloy, who in 1982 suffered a heart attack and was diagnosed with congestive heart failure in the mid-1980s, died of pulmonary edema at home. He is buried in Arlington National Cemetery in Arlington, Virginia.

McCloy's impact on the 1960s was somewhat more subtle than his influence upon the previous two decades, perhaps because much of his public service then was carried out behind closed doors. During the 1960s he worked with certain sets of priorities, such as placing the economic well being of the nation over sectional conflict (especially in regard to oil and the Middle East) or patiently working out delicate treaty-type negotiations sensitive to the pride of both sides (such as disarmament discussions and his advice during the Cuban missile crisis). Sometimes he veered away from his initial instincts, such as his attitude toward Vietnam, in order to support apparently superior presidential insight; at other times he convinced the executive branch of the need for action, such as his role in NATO and his concern for the Federal Republic of Germany.

McCloy's knowledge, capabilities, energy, and longevity enabled him to serve his country, the legal profession, and banking interests throughout almost seven decades; hold numerous official or consulting positions; secure seats on commercial and philanthropic boards; and receive American and foreign accolades and honorary degrees. Although he identified himself as a Republican, his unique legal and business sense, realistic and flexible negotiating capabilities, and honorable ethical standards, reflecting his Presbyterian heritage, made him a meaningful asset to all administrations—Republican and Democrat—from World War II up until shortly before his death.

★

McCloy's papers are housed at Amherst College. Biographies include Walter Isaacson and Evan Thomas, *The Wise Men: Six Friends and the World They Made—Acheson, Bohlen, Harriman, Kennan, Lovett, McCloy* (1986), and Kai Bird, *The Chairman: John J. McCloy—The Making of the American Establishment* (1992). Short biographical pieces on McCloy include Benjamin Frankel, ed., *The Cold War, 1945–1991: Leaders and Other Important Figures in the United States and Western Europe*, vol. 1 (1992); Dieter K. Buse and Juergen C. Doerr, eds., *Modern Germany: An Encyclopedia of History, People, and Culture, 1871–1990*, vol. 2 (1998). An obituary is in the *New York Times* (12 Mar. 1989). There are numerous oral history collections, including those at Princeton University (1965), the Lyndon Baines Johnson Library at the University of Texas at Austin, Texas (1969), and Columbia University (1973). "Conversation with John McCloy" (13 July 1957) is in Eric Sevareid, *Conversations with Eric Sevareid: Interviews with Notable Americans* (1976).

MADELINE SAPIENZA

McCOVEY, Willie Lee (*b.* 10 January 1938 in Mobile, Alabama), Major League Baseball player who gained fame as a record-setting power hitter and a talented first baseman with the 1960s San Francisco Giants, was elected to the Baseball Hall of Fame, and was admired as one of the most courageous, honest, and gentlemanly of America's athletes.

McCovey was the seventh of ten children of Frank Mc-Covey, a railroad worker, and Ester (Jones) McCovey, a homemaker. He grew up in segregated Mobile, where discrimination against African Americans such as McCovey's family was deeply institutionalized. The African-American schools could not field baseball teams.

McCovey's father provided a powerful moral compass for his children. As a youngster, McCovey played baseball, football, and basketball on city youth teams. He was always the first baseman on his baseball teams, a flanker on his

school football team, a quarterback in night football leagues, and the center on his basketball team. He and his friends formed the nucleus of a baseball team that was so good it moved into a city adult league when McCovey was still a preteen; the team won the league's championship.

In 1950 McCovey left school and began working to help support his family; in 1954 he moved to Los Angeles to look for full-time employment. One of the youth sports directors in Mobile told a New York Giants scout about McCovey's extraordinary athletic ability, and in January 1955 the Giants invited McCovey for a tryout in Florida, giving him the bus fare for the journey. He was signed by the ball club and sent to the minor leagues. At the time he was six feet, two inches tall and weighed only 165 pounds; when he reached his full size in the 1960s, he was six feet, four inches tall and weighed 210 pounds. By 1958 he had climbed through the minor leagues to the Phoenix Giants, an AAA franchise in the Pacific Coast League. While there, he electrified the team's fans with titanic performances that included a .372 batting average for the 1959 season. That year, he joined the San Francisco Giants (recently relocated from New York) with about fifty games left and performed so well that he was voted the Rookie of the Year for the National League.

The immensely popular Orlando Cepeda played first base for the Giants and was putting up great numbers as a hitter. The Giants manager, Alvin Dark, sometimes alternated between placing McCovey and Cepeda at first base and in left field, but mostly put McCovey in left field, where fans derided his weak fielding. Although he eventually made himself into a passable major league outfielder, fans never forgot how bad he had been during his early days in the big leagues.

During the early 1960s, even as McCovey's fame and popularity were growing, he was becoming gravely ill. He had arthritis in his knees that made every movement agonizingly painful. Even more alarming, his right hip was calcifying and actually bled when he moved. Compounding McCovey's miseries was the death of his father in 1964; his chief source of moral support was gone.

By 1968 McCovey was at the top of his game. He won the National League batting title for three consecutive years, 1967–1969. He had become the full-time Giants first baseman (following Cepeda's 1966 trade to St. Louis), and fans and players alike were dazzled by his fielding, giving him the nickname "Stretch" because of his ability to snare wild throws and still tag first base in time to retire batters. In 1969 he had a fabulous season, leading the National League in home runs (45), runs batted in (126), intentional walks (45, a major league record), slugging percentage (.656), and on-base percentage (.453), resulting in his being voted the National League's Most Valuable Player. But in

Willie McCovey. AP/WIDE WORLD PHOTOS

1970 he developed blurred vision and, although he still played well, his performance declined.

In 1972 McCovey suffered a horrendous injury. In a game against the San Diego Padres, he pivoted to field a bad throw, pointing his right (gloved) arm directly down the line between home plate and first base. The San Diego batter failed to run in the runner's box along the line as he was supposed to, instead charging on the line itself and slamming into McCovey's arm, shattering its bones so they were protruding from his skin. Surgeons placed several pins in the arm, and McCovey's career seemed over. But the already immensely popular player became a legend that season by returning to the lineup in a couple of months and performing well. Even more remarkable was his continued ability to hit home runs, because slow-motion photography revealed that when swinging, McCovey always let go of the bat with his left hand, generating all of his enormous force from his right, shattered arm.

Thereafter, fans always applauded McCovey whenever he came to bat, in any ballpark; even opposing fans cheered him, whatever he did. In 1974 he was traded to the San Diego Padres. Eventually the Oakland Athletics traded for him in 1976, but hardly played him. Then in 1977 he returned to the San Francisco Giants, receiving a standing ovation more than five minutes long when he came to bat. He was named the Comeback Player of the Year for 1977 and cemented his reputation as one of the best fielding first basemen ever. He retired during the 1980 season and was

elected to the Baseball Hall of Fame in 1986. Following his retirement from professional baseball, McCovey became a sales manager for a linen manufacturer and also provided public relations and management support to the Giants organization.

The major league manager Gene Mauch described McCovey as "the most awesome hitter I've ever seen," and there were many who held the same opinion. In the early 2000s McCovey still was cheered whenever he was introduced at a ballpark, and he occasionally joined the Giants broadcasters for a ball game. Until Barry Bonds surpassed his record in 2001, McCovey held the National League record for home runs by a left-handed hitter (521). McCovey hit eighteen grand slams, third behind Lou Gehrig and Eddie Murray, and was probably one of the three best clutch hitters ever (along with Gehrig and Hank Aaron). In addition, most baseball historians rank McCovey as the National League's best-ever first baseman, and perhaps as the all-time best, behind only Gehrig and Jimmie Foxx. In the 1960s McCovey was admired by his fellow players not only for his athletic achievements but for his friendly, quiet personality and his integrity; these qualities have earned him the continuing admiration of fans.

★

Nick Peters, *Willie McCovey: Stretch* (1988), is the only readily available full-length biography of McCovey and is intended for general and young audiences. George Sullivan, *Sluggers: Twenty-*

seven of Baseball's Greatest (1991), provides details about how McCovey batted. Donald Dewey and Nicholas Acocella, *The Biographical History of Baseball* (1995, rev. ed. 2002), offers an account of why McCovey is esteemed. *Current Biography Yearbook* (1970) provides additional details about his youth.

KIRK H. BEETZ

McCULLERS, Carson   (*b.* 19 February 1917 in Columbus, Georgia; *d.* 29 September 1967 in Nyack, New York), novelist, short-story writer, and playwright who in 1961 published her last major work, *Clock Without Hands,* completing a small but important body of fiction known for its sensitive portrayals of social outcasts and misfits.

McCullers was born Lula Carson Smith, the oldest of three children of Lamar Smith, a jewelry store owner, and Vera Marguerite Waters. McCullers showed an early aptitude for the piano, but after moving to New York City in 1934, she studied creative writing at Columbia University and New York University. In 1937 she married James Reeves McCullers, Jr., a serviceman and would-be writer. Their relationship was tumultuous, fueled in part by their excessive alcohol use. They divorced in 1941 but remarried in 1945. In 1953 Reeves McCullers committed suicide. They had no children.

Carson McCullers published her best-known works well before 1960. She established her literary career at age twenty-three with her first novel, *The Heart Is a Lonely Hunter* (1940), a haunting drama centering on an enigmatic deaf-mute and four loners who tell him their deepest thoughts. A year later she published *Reflections in a Golden Eye,* a short novel about sexual obsessions at a southern army base. It was followed by *The Ballad of the Sad Café* (1943), a novella about a bizarre love triangle between a mannish woman, a hunchback, and an ex-convict. *The Member of the Wedding,* chronicling a lonely twelve-year-old girl's desperate attempt to escape her hometown, was published in 1946. The stage version of this novel, adapted by McCullers herself, had a successful Broadway run from 1950 to 1951.

Despite her accomplishments, which included two Guggenheim Fellowships, McCullers entered the 1960s in a precarious state. She had suffered respiratory and heart ailments since childhood, and two strokes in 1947 had partially paralyzed her left side. She had not had a major publication in over a decade. When her semiautobiographical second play, *The Square Root of Wonderful,* failed on Broadway in 1957, she was devastated. Moreover, she was emotionally needy. During her marriage and afterward, McCullers had a series of crushes on men and women, including the writer Katherine Anne Porter. McCullers also

Carson McCullers. AP/WIDE WORLD PHOTOS

experienced depression and in 1948 attempted suicide. She was in constant physical pain. Many friends did not expect that she would live to finish *Clock Without Hands*.

McCullers had conceived of the idea for *Clock Without Hands* in the 1940s and began writing it in 1951. She worked on it from 1952 to 1953, while she and her husband were living in France, and in 1954, during one of her several stays at Yaddo, a writers' retreat in Saratoga Springs, New York. With the encouragement of her friends, most notably her physician Mary Mercer, McCullers finally finished the manuscript in December 1960. Although some, including McCullers's longtime friend the playwright Tennessee Williams, did not deem the manuscript ready for publication, those closest to her feared that she could not work on it any longer. The novel was published in September 1961.

Whereas McCullers's earlier fiction focuses on the private agonies of people on the fringe, *Clock Without Hands* plays out on a more public stage. The novel is set in a small Georgia town on the eve of *Brown* v. *Board of Education*, the landmark 1954 Supreme Court decision to desegregate public schools. As in *The Heart Is a Lonely Hunter*, there is a large network of loosely connected characters. Chief among them are Judge Fox Clane, a hidebound politician who tries to roll back time through ludicrous schemes; Jester Clane, his liberal but naive grandson; and Sherman Pew, an impetuous young man troubled by his mixed-race parentage. Together they embody the changing attitudes toward race relations in the postwar South as well as the continuing obstacles and tragedies in the fight for justice. Another key character is J. T. Malone, the town pharmacist, who on the opening pages of the novel discovers that he is dying of leukemia. The novel, which closes with his passing, is also a meditation on life's meaning and on death, a theme that preoccupied McCullers in her own life.

Coming fifteen years after McCullers's last major book publication, *Clock Without Hands* was eagerly anticipated—it remained on best-selling lists for months—and was widely reviewed. It received decidedly mixed notices. Those who found the book disappointing cited insufficient character and plot development and a weakening of McCullers's craft. *Clock Without Hands* is generally considered the least successful of McCullers's longer works of fiction. It is also the only one not to have been dramatized.

McCullers endured more health setbacks in the 1960s, including breast cancer, a broken hip and elbow, and several corrective surgeries for her atrophied limbs. For most of her last years she was wheelchair-bound or bedridden in her Nyack, New York, home, where she had lived for the most part since 1945. Despite her near paralysis, she traveled to England in October 1962 and Ireland in April 1967, the latter trip at the invitation of John Huston, who had just directed a film version of *Reflections in a Golden Eye*.

As McCullers's health further declined in the 1960s, so did the volume of her literary output. Following *Clock Without Hands*, she published only a handful of short stories and articles in magazines, and a collection of children's verses titled *Sweet as a Pickle, Clean as a Pig* (1964) was published posthumously in 1971. A musical version of *The Member of the Wedding*, a collaborative effort with Mary Rogers, was not realized. But if McCullers herself produced little in the 1960s, others kept her works alive in the public mind. In addition to Huston's film, McCullers saw two of her other works take on a life of their own. Edward Albee's adaptation of *The Ballad of the Sad Café* played on Broadway from 1963 to 1964. In 1965 Thomas Ryan completed his screenplay for *The Heart Is a Lonely Hunter*, which was directed by Robert Ellis Miller and released in 1968. In 1966 McCullers began dictating her autobiography to her assistants and friends. Left incomplete when she died from a cerebral hemorrhage the next year, it was published in 1999 as *Illumination and Night Glare*. McCullers is buried in Oak Hill Cemetery in Nyack.

In a sense, McCullers's fiction is prophetic. Her novels are populated with blacks agitating for equal rights, men and women struggling to redefine unconventional love, and people unhappy with the status quo—all themes that came to the forefront in the 1960s. Some scholars have suggested that illnesses kept McCullers from fully realizing her talents, but what she did write has given an eloquent voice to the alienated, the oppressed, and those who simply do not fit in.

★

A major collection of McCullers's manuscripts, correspondence, and other papers is at the Harry Ransom Humanities Research Center, University of Texas at Austin. Additional correspondence is held at the Robert Flower Collection at Duke University. Virginia Spencer Carr, *The Lonely Hunter: A Biography of Carson McCullers* (1975), is the definitive book-length study. Josyane Savigneau, *Carson McCullers: A Life* (2001), which was written with the cooperation of McCullers's estate, including permission to quote from unpublished materials and an interview with Mary Mercer, presents a more sympathetic portrait. An obituary is on the front page of the *New York Times* (30 Sept. 1967).

JEFFREY H. CHEN

MACDERMOT, (Arthur Terence) Galt (*b.* 18 December 1928 in Montreal, Quebec, Canada), composer, church organist/choirmaster, and pianist who wrote the score for the innovative 1967 rock musical *Hair*, which achieved the fourth-longest run of any 1960s musical.

MacDermot was the son of Terence W. L. MacDermot, an educator and diplomat, and Elizabeth Savage MacDermot, a homemaker. MacDermot was the middle child; he had

Galt MacDermot, September 1968. HULTON/ARCHIVE BY GETTY IMAGES

two sisters. As a boy he played violin and piano, and as a teenager he discovered boogie-woogie and jazz and became a fan of Pete Johnson, Duke Ellington, and Meade Lux Lewis. As a youngster MacDermot was schooled throughout Canada wherever his father was a principal. He attended kindergarten at Montreal High School, and then attended the next eight years at Upper Canada College, Toronto. At twelve years of age, he attended the University of Toronto for one year; returned to Montreal High School for two more years; entered Lisgar Collegiate, Ottawa, for two years, and received his high school diploma there in 1948. He attended Bishop's University, Quebec, and received a B.A. in history and English in 1950.

MacDermot then moved with his family to South Africa, where he earned a B.A. in music composition and organ at the University of Cape Town in 1953. He was inspired by the rich musical sounds he heard in the black African urban ghettos. In a 1969 *New York Times* interview, he said, "They'd be playing what was really rock and roll. What they called *quaylas*—like a South African version of High Life— . . . you don't hear it anywhere else." While in South Africa, MacDermot began writing operas.

In 1954 MacDermot married Marlene Bruynzeel, a clarinetist of Dutch descent, and the couple returned to Montreal; they later had four daughters and a son. From 1954 to 1961 he worked for the Westmount Baptist Church as an organist and choirmaster. He also played piano with a

jazz trio. In 1961 MacDermot moved his family to England, where his jazz composition "African Waltz" (recorded by Johnny Dankworth) had become a best-seller. When it was released in the United States on Riverside, MacDermot won two Grammy Awards for best jazz composer of the year and best instrumental theme. He played piano in London for two-and-one-half years, and then moved to the United States. MacDermot became an American citizen in August 1994.

MacDermot rented a house on Staten Island, New York, and later purchased a modest home there after *Hair*'s success. For several years he supported his family by making demonstration records for music publishers, but his goal was to write a stage show. In 1967 he had that opportunity when the music publisher Nat Shapiro introduced him to Gerome Ragni and James Rado, two actors who had written a book and lyrics for a musical. They were in search of someone to write the score. MacDermot applied his skills, and *Hair* was born.

Hair (described in playbills as the "American Tribal Love-Rock Musical") reflects the hippie culture of the 1960s. Thematically it is an antiestablishment protest, set amid a celebrated life of psychedelic drugs and uninhibited sexuality. It exhibits the free lifestyle of assorted Greenwich Village hippies, portraying a world of social dropouts. They reject materialistic culture, oppose the draft, and hate the war in Vietnam. *Hair* satirizes racism, sexual repression, and other societal problems. The play's original posters depicted a male wearing long hair, protesting parental values, hence the title of the musical.

Hair opened on 17 October 1967, presented by Joseph Papp and directed by Gerald Freedman, at the off-Broadway New York Shakespeare Festival's Public Theater. The intention was that *Hair* would run for a limited engagement of eight weeks, with ninety-four performances. Not willing to let his off-Broadway hit expire, Papp (with Michael Butler) moved *Hair* to Cheetah, a large discotheque. That version was the same as the original in direction, design, and casting. *Hair* moved to the Biltmore Theatre on 29 April 1968 with a new director, Tom O'Horgan, and MacDermot as the music director. The play closed in December, completing 1,742 performances. It achieved a breakthrough by having the cast totally nude at the first-act finale. *Hair* was a milestone in Broadway musical history, playing to approximately four million people in the first two years and eventually grossing $80 million.

The critic Stanley Richards said of *Hair,* "It shattered Broadway's conventions." Clive Barnes of the *New York Times* described it as "so likable, so new, so fresh and so unassuming, even in its pretensions. It is the first Broadway musical . . . to have the authentic voice of today rather than . . . yesterday." Others were offended. The composer Leonard Bernstein walked out on the show, saying, "The songs are just laundry lists." Richard Rodgers, who could hear only the beat, described it as "one-third music."

At one time, seven road companies were performing *Hair* throughout the United States. The musical was performed worldwide; it produced eleven original cast record albums in as many languages. *Hair* was a unique rock musical. Forty others opened after 1967, but none had the same appeal as *Hair.* As one Broadway observer said, "I loved *Hair,* I thought it was marvelous, but there was only one *Hair.* You don't create that kind of thing a second time." The original Broadway cast recording of *Hair* (on RCA Victor) won a Grammy for the best long-play recording of 1968.

In 1969 the critic Robert Berkvist described MacDermot as "Almost Ivy League. . . . You'd buy insurance from him, you'd buy a used car, you'd trust him with your wife. He gets haircuts. And get this, kids—he's 40." In fact, when MacDermot was first exposed to the script for *Hair,* he claimed to be unaware of the hippie culture. Some of the subject matter bothered MacDermot when the play was first performed. He was concerned about audience reaction to racial comments, especially to the song "Colored Spade." Overall, MacDermot was pleased with *Hair.* He said, "I liked the lyrics, and I thought the play was funny." MacDermot, the man behind the scenes, said, "I'm not very interested in publicity."

MacDermot continued to write musical scores. He received the Tony and New York Drama Critics' Circle Awards for the score of *Two Gentlemen of Verona* in 1971, and was named by both Drama Desk and *Variety* Poll as the year's outstanding theater composer. Following the success of *Hair,* MacDermot wrote more than a dozen other stage and film productions and produced an impressive folio of oratorios and sacred music. The composer said it best: "I just want to go on writing music."

★

For a biographical sketch of MacDermot, see Durrell Bowman, contrib., *The Encyclopedia of Music in Canada* (1992). Abe Laufe, *Broadway's Greatest Musicals: 1977 Revised Edition* (1969), discusses audience reaction to *Hair*; Stanley Green, *Encyclopedia of the Musical Theater* (1976), gives facts about the play; Stanley Richards, *Great Rock Musicals* (1979), provides its entire script. Barbara Lee Horn, *The Age of Hair* (1991), covers the origins of the hippie movement and its transformation in the 1970s. Kurt Ganzl, *The Encyclopedia of Musical Theater* (1994), explains the evolution of *Hair*; and Kurt Ganzl, *Ganzl's Book of the Broadway Musical* (1995), describes acts one and two of the play. Helpful articles on MacDermot's work include "From Hair to Hamlet," *New Republic* (18 Nov. 1967); "He Put 'Hair' on Broadway's Chest," *New York Times* (11 May 1969); and "Galt MacDermot Offers New Music with a Pulse," *New York Times* (8 May 1981).

SANDRA REDMOND PETERS

MACDONALD, Dwight (*b.* 24 March 1906 in New York City; *d.* 19 December 1982 in New York City), literary and social critic who was both a conservative defender of high-culture literary values and a radical foe of the U.S. government's policies toward poverty and war.

Macdonald was one of two sons born to Dwight Macdonald, a lawyer, and Alice Hedges, a homemaker. He had an elite education, graduating from Phillips Exeter Academy in 1924 and receiving a B.A. in history from Yale University in 1928. He wrote for Yale's newspaper and literary magazine and edited its humor magazine. Macdonald then went to work as a staff writer for *Fortune* magazine. The more he studied and wrote about capitalism, the less he liked it, and he began associating with political radicals, including Nancy Rodman, whom he married in 1934. The couple had two sons.

Macdonald left *Fortune* in 1936 and the following year became editor of the revived *Partisan Review.* In 1938 Macdonald's revulsion with the political system in the United States led him to examine the communism of the Soviet Union, but he soon found the regime of Josef Stalin equally offensive. He considered a number of political alternatives, including Trotskyism and pacifism, the latter of which inspired him to burn his draft card in 1948. He eventually described himself with the seemingly self-contradictory phrase "conservative anarchist."

Macdonald edited *Partisan Review* from 1938 to 1943. He then started his own magazine, *Politics,* which was published until 1949. From then on he wrote articles and columns, most notably for *The New Yorker,* for which he was a staff writer from 1951 to 1966, and *Esquire,* for which he wrote film reviews and later a political column in the 1960s.

At the same time, Macdonald became known as something of a lifestyle radical, holding nude parties at his home as early as the late 1940s. He had a number of extramarital affairs, which eventually strained his marriage. In 1954 he and Nancy divorced, and he married Gloria Lanier, with whom he remained for the rest of his life.

Although his political views changed over the years, Macdonald remained true to the ideals of high literary culture he had absorbed at Yale. This was highlighted in his well-known essay "Masscult and Midcult," which appeared in two parts in *Partisan Review* in 1960. Perhaps harking back to his days in radical politics, where the bitterest feuds were often with those of fairly similar views, Macdonald claimed that the greatest foe of high culture was not the mass culture that more or less admitted its trashiness (he praised Zane Gray as an example); rather, the danger came from what he called "midcult," writing that seemingly aimed for high literary goals but fell far short. In this category he listed Nobel laureates Pearl S. Buck and John Steinbeck, as well as such popular favorites as Irwin Shaw and Herman Wouk, charging them with sentimentality and middle-class nostalgia. He insisted, however, that his literary elitism was compatible with political democracy.

In the same vein Macdonald published "The String Untuned," a savage review of *Webster's Third International Dictionary* and its efforts to report popular usage of words instead of trying to set standards, in *The New Yorker* in 1962. In the same year, "Masscult and Midcult" and "The String Untuned" were published in a collection, *Against the American Grain,* in which the theme was further addressed by sharp-edged dissections of two midcult favorites, James Gould Cozzens and Colin Wilson. Macdonald's dry wit was notable, as when he said of the novel that brought Cozzens fame and fortune, "*By Love Possessed* has enriched my vocabulary, or, more precisely, added to it."

In 1965, when the journalist Tom Wolfe published a slashing attack on *The New Yorker,* Macdonald leapt to the magazine's defense, describing Wolfe's efforts to enliven journalism with the devices of fiction as an inferior genre, which he dubbed "parajournalism."

Despite his focus on literary standards, Macdonald had not forgotten politics. In 1962 Michael Harrington published *The Other America,* a startling exposé of continuing poverty in a nation that considered itself well-to-do. Early in 1963, *The New Yorker* published Macdonald's long essay-

Dwight Macdonald. CORBIS CORPORATION (BELLEVUE)

review of the book, "Our Invisible Poor." Historians believe it was Macdonald's review that brought the book to the attention of President John F. Kennedy, thus leading to the creation of the War on Poverty program.

Macdonald remained dubious about the government. He was horrified by the Cuban Missile Crisis and the way (he believed) Kennedy had brought the world to the brink of atomic war. He rejoiced at Lyndon Johnson's victory over Barry Goldwater in the 1964 presidential election, then watched in dismay Johnson's escalation of the hostilities in Vietnam. In 1965 the White House invited about four hundred intellectuals, including Macdonald, to a festival of the arts. The poet Robert Lowell declined, as a way of stating his opposition to the administration's policy on Vietnam. After some consideration Macdonald decided to attend the festival, but he issued a statement insisting that his presence was not to be treated as approval of the war and solicited signatures for an antiwar petition from his fellow invitees (he received seven).

From then on Macdonald was a committed opponent of the war, appearing at the 1968 March on the Pentagon and other protests. He took public radical stands on other issues, supporting the Columbia University student take-over in 1968 and appearing at their "countercommencement." When the largely African-American school boards in Ocean Hill–Brownsville demanded local control over their schools in 1969, he supported them against the largely white United Federation of Teachers, though this caused a break with his old ally Michael Harrington.

In 1969 and 1970 Macdonald wrote to a number of universities, saying, "I'm tired of writing and might enjoy teaching." Indeed, he took a few visiting professorships and wrote little more. Macdonald was elected to the National Institute of Arts and Letters in 1970, and in 1971 retired from *The New Yorker*. He died of heart failure in 1982.

Macdonald remains a controversial figure. His literary views are seen by today's postmodernists as the kind of "dead white male elitism" that has been supplanted (although it might be added that the midcultists he criticized have been treated no better by literary history). Macdonald never constructed a comprehensive political theory of his own, but his critiques of established authority remain relevant, and his eloquence and wit keep him worth reading.

★

Macdonald's papers are kept at the Sterling Library, Yale University, New Haven, Connecticut. Michael Wreszin published *A Rebel in Defense of Tradition,* a full-length biography of Macdonald (1994), and *A Moral Temper: The Letters of Dwight Macdonald* (2001). Stephen J. Whitfield, *A Critical American: The Politics of Dwight Macdonald* (1984), and Gregory D. Sumner, *Dwight Macdonald and the Politics Circle* (1996), concentrate on Macdonald's political views. An obituary is in the *New York Times* (20 Dec. 1982).

ARTHUR D. HLAVATY

McGILL, Ralph Emerson (*b.* 5 February 1898 near Soddy, Tennessee; *d.* 3 February 1969 in Atlanta, Georgia), reporter, editor, publisher, nationally syndicated political columnist, and civil rights campaigner.

McGill was the eldest of six children born to Benjamin Franklin McGill, a coal miner, and Mary Lou Skillern, a homemaker, on a farm in Igou's Ferry, Tennessee. A sickly child, he began his formal education at the age of eight, when he attended the Fourth District School of Highland Park, Chattanooga. As his health improved, McGill was made captain of the football team at the McCallie Preparatory School, Chattanooga, where he studied between 1913 and 1917. He attended Vanderbilt University between 1917 and 1922, taking time off between 1918 and 1919 to serve in the U.S. Marine Corps during World War I. During his college years McGill was a member of the Reserve Officer Training Corps (ROTC) and the Sigma Chi fraternity. He played tackle on the football team, joined a literary group called the Fugitives (along with future nov-

elist Robert Penn Warren and poets Allen Tate and Merrill Moore), and ran bootleg liquor to make extra money. He was a cub reporter for the Nashville *Banner* and wrote for the university paper the *Hustler*, where his talent for challenging authority began to emerge. One of his editorials for the *Hustler* accused the university trustees of embezzlement and won McGill a suspension. Although he did not graduate from Vanderbilt, over the course of his life McGill received fourteen honorary degrees, thirteen of which were awarded in the 1960s.

McGill continued to write for the Nashville *Banner* after college, and in 1929 he married Mary Elizabeth Leonard, with whom he had two daughters and a son. That same year he became assistant sports editor at the *Atlanta Constitution*, eventually progressing to executive editor in 1938. His first act as executive editor was to rule that the *Constitution* would always print the word Negro with a capital N, to give the title its proper authority. McGill was appointed editor in chief in 1942. The *Atlantic Monthly* called the *Constitution* under his leadership "one of the most influential newspapers on the Atlantic seaboard."

In the 1930s and 1940s McGill built a reputation as a staunch advocate for civil rights, becoming known as the "conscience of the South." He was critical of the "baronial autocrats" he saw corrupting and dominating the political

Ralph McGill. THE LIBRARY OF CONGRESS

systems of the South, using the position of "states' rights" to keep the South in "a backward and isolationist position." Yet although many southern readers found his editorials offensive, northern liberals thought McGill was timid and predictable. His reputation in the North was perhaps damaged by his technique of interspersing campaigns for civil rights and racial equality with lighthearted editorials. It was a technique that kept McGill in work, enabling him to become, by the late 1950s, one of the most influential and respected newspapermen in the United States. In 1959 he received a Pulitzer Prize for an editorial about the bombing of an Atlanta synagogue and was cited for his "long, courageous and effective editorial leadership."

By the 1960s McGill's influence on American politics and public life was profound. To avoid mandatory retirement as the editor of the *Constitution*, he became the publisher of the paper in 1960, a position that allowed him to continue writing his editorial column. By then he was directly involved in politics and a well-known figure in political and civil rights circles. In 1960 he accompanied Vice President Richard M. Nixon to Russia, met President-elect John F. Kennedy, received the Lauterbach Award "for distinguished service in the field of civil liberties," and was named a member of the Pulitzer Prize Advisory Board. In 1961 he was awarded an honorary LL.D from Harvard University. It was inscribed, "In a troubled time his steady voice of reason champions a New South."

McGill's wife died in 1962, leaving him to raise their only surviving child Ralph, Jr., then aged seventeen. They traveled to Japan on a trip funded by the Asian Foundation so that McGill could attend a series of seminars with Japanese university and newspaper people. He married Dr. Mary Lynn Morgan, a dentist twenty-three years his junior, in 1967.

In 1963 McGill received seven honorary degrees, served on presidential committees in the Kennedy Administration, and traveled to West Africa for the State Department to speak about race relations in America. He also published his fourth compilation of columns, *The South and the Southerner*.

In 1963 Dr. Martin Luther King, Jr., began his nonviolent demonstrations in Birmingham, Alabama, and it was a great embarrassment to McGill that the *Constitution* did not lead with coverage of these events. McGill was as widely known among black leaders as he was among white politicians. He had connections among journalists who kept him informed about groups such as the Student Nonviolent Coordinating Committee (SNCC), the Congress of Racial Equality (CORE), and the Council of Federated Organizations (COFO), where the rhetoric of the Black Power movement was gaining support. After the bombing of an Alabama church that killed four children, McGill took a new, harder line with segregationists in his columns, raising

his profile still further as a champion of civil rights and an outspoken critic of racial injustice in all its forms. In 1964 McGill was awarded the Presidential Medal of Freedom by President Lyndon B. Johnson, the highest civilian honor in the United States, and in the following year received the Eleanor Roosevelt Humanities Award.

In the mid-1960s McGill became a committed supporter of U.S. involvement in Vietnam. In characteristically direct style, McGill traveled to Vietnam in 1966 to talk with the authorities and visit the front line, an experience that confirmed his belief that the war was justified. On his return to the United States he spoke out in favor of continuing U.S. commitment to the war.

The assassinations of Dr. Martin Luther King, Jr., and Senator Robert F. Kennedy in 1968 fell as heavy blows for McGill. A personal friend of Kennedy's, McGill saw his assassination as "but another exhibit of the steady growth of violence as part of the mosaic of our national culture." He traveled to Russia for a second time, returning to cover both political conventions of 1968.

McGill's career as a journalist covered some of the most turbulent years of American social history. As an outspoken advocate of liberty and freedom, he became one of the key commentators and campaigners of the 1950s and 1960s. His column was nationally syndicated for over twenty years. McGill summarized the ups and downs of the civil rights movement since 1954, "The critical national problems are our poor and our unprepared. Apartheid is not the answer. We have tried that already." McGill died of heart failure and is buried in Westview Cemetery in Atlanta.

★

McGill's papers are in the Woodruff Library, Emory University. His fourth book, *The South and the Southerner* (1963), is largely autobiographical. A biography of McGill by one of his colleagues at the *Constitution* is Harold H. Martin, *Ralph McGill, Reporter* (1973). McGill published several compilations of columns during the 1950s, including *A Church, A School* (1959), containing his Pulitzer Prize–winning editorial. Obituaries are in the *Atlanta Constitution* and *New York Times* (both 4 Feb. 1969).

ANNMARIE B. SINGH

McGINNISS, Joseph ("Joe") (*b.* 9 December 1942 in New York City), journalist and writer whose book *The Selling of the President, 1968,* an exposé of the media strategy of Richard M. Nixon's presidential campaign, topped the best-seller lists in 1969 and forever changed public understanding of how politicians use the media to influence the electorate.

McGinniss, the only child of Joseph Aloysius McGinniss, a construction-specifications engineer who later opened a travel agency in a Manhattan hotel, and Mary Leonard, grew up in the affluent suburb of Rye, New York. Raised a Catholic, McGinniss was a solitary child who made up his own elaborate games and considered becoming a priest. He attended the Resurrection School run by the Sisters of Charity during his elementary years, and Archbishop Stepinac High School from 1956 to 1960, where he wrote for the school newspaper. After receiving praise from a teacher for an essay written when he was in the eleventh grade, McGinniss realized he might have a gift for writing.

He chose to pursue journalism as an avocation during his time in college and was a reporter and editor for the *Crusader,* the student newspaper of the College of the Holy Cross in Worcester, Massachusetts, which he attended from 1960 to 1964. In the summer of 1963 he began working for the *Port Chester Daily Item.* In 1964, after graduating with a B.S. degree in English and being rejected by the Columbia Graduate School of Journalism, he went to work for the *Worcester Telegram.* McGinniss's career progressed quickly. After just nine months at the *Telegram* he became a sportswriter for the *Philadelphia Bulletin.* He married Christine Cook on 25 September 1965; they had three children before divorcing. He married Nancy Doherty on 20 November 1976; they had two children.

Within two years of his divorce from his first wife, McGinniss was writing a regular column for the *Bulletin*'s competitor, the *Philadelphia Inquirer.* In those columns he commented on the U.S. involvement in Vietnam, the assassinations of Dr. Martin Luther King, Jr., and Senator Robert F. Kennedy, and the 1968 presidential election. Of his writing McGinniss has said that his goal is to "go someplace that the reader couldn't go . . . to give the reader the feeling of what it would be like to be there." He became known for his informed, insightful, and independent commentary on issues that were timely, if not controversial.

McGinniss stumbled across the lead for his first book, *The Selling of the President, 1968,* in June of that year. He had fallen out with the publisher of the *Philadelphia Inquirer,* Walter H. Annenberg, over an editorial apology Annenberg published for a column McGinniss wrote stating that Robert Kennedy's assassination was a product of the violent nature of U.S. society. While cooling off on vacation, and working on a profile of sports personality Howard Cosell for *TV Guide,* McGinniss learned that a member of Cosell's carpool had landed the advertising account for Hubert Humphrey's presidential campaign. Intrigued at the coupling of advertising and politics, McGinniss approached the campaign. "I had heard . . . [them] say they were going to make Humphrey into Lincoln. I thought it might be fun to watch." The Humphrey campaign turned McGinniss away, but the strategists for Humphrey's opponent Richard M. Nixon welcomed him. In fact, the campaign organizers allowed him to observe firsthand the process of packaging Nixon for the electorate.

McGinniss left his job at the *Philadelphia Inquirer* and for the next five months traveled with the Nixon organization. He gained intimate access to the highest level media-strategy meetings and attended tapings of commercials and hour-long panel shows with candidate Nixon. "This is the beginning of a whole new concept. . . . This is the way [presidents] will be elected forevermore. The next guys up will have to be performers." So predicted Roger Ailes, media strategist for Nixon's campaign. From interviews with the top media strategists, including Frank Shakespeare from the Columbia Broadcasting System (CBS), Harry Treleaven of the famed J. Walter Thompson advertising agency, and Ailes, a former executive producer of *The Mike Douglas Show,* McGinniss recounts the events and personalities involved with an authenticity that is both engaging and compelling. *The Selling of the President, 1968* is supplemented with reprints of notes and memos from the media advisers and presents the media as "insidious" and "trite," the electorate as malleable and television-addled, and Nixon as a pragmatic and consummate politician.

McGinniss's account exhibited a timely cynicism and presented the American public with its first glimpse of the lengths to which Nixon would go to secure his political agenda. The book spent seven months on the *New York Times* best-seller list, four of those months in the number-one position. Critics were divided generally along political lines. Described as "witty and insightful," "a bit frightening," and a "hatchet job," it was noted for the "unobserved but overheard and intimately quoted Nixon." One critic even suggested that Nixon should hire McGinniss to manage his image.

At age twenty-seven McGinniss found himself a celebrity, and was pursued by publishers, theatrical producers, network-news producers, and broadcast executives to write on topical issues, write Broadway plays, anchor newscasts, and host radio talk shows. Instead McGinniss chose to write a novel. *The Dream Team* was published in 1972 and flopped. He returned to nonfiction with two works, *Heroes* (1976) and *Going to Extremes* (1980), which were much admired by critics. In 1983 McGinniss published yet another work that put him on the best-seller list, *Fatal Vision,* a true crime recounting of the murder of a young pregnant mother and her two daughters. He continued in this genre with the best-sellers *Blind Faith* (1989) and *Cruel Doubt* (1991). His 1993 biography of Teddy Kennedy, *The Last Brother,* was also a best-seller, though critics considered it not up to McGinniss's standards in his previous work. *The Miracle of Castel di Sangro* (1999) is a nonfiction work that capitalizes on his passion for soccer.

★

McGinniss is discussed in Barbara Lounsberry, *The Art of Fact: Contemporary Artists of Nonfiction* (1990). Articles and reviews about McGinniss and his writing are in *Life* (10 Oct. 1969), *New Republic* (11 Oct. 1969), *The New Yorker* (27 Dec. 1969), and *Holy Cross Magazine* (winter 2002).

ANNMARIE B. SINGH

McGOVERN, George Stanley (*b.* 22 July 1922 in Avon, South Dakota), Democratic senator who led opposition against President Lyndon B. Johnson's Vietnam policy during the mid- to late 1960s and who was responsible for rewriting the rules governing the Democratic presidential primaries following the 1968 election.

McGovern was the second of four children born to Joseph C. McGovern, a Methodist minister, and his wife, Frances McLean. He was shy as a child and enjoyed reading. "He very nearly failed the first grade," wrote Robert Sam Anson in *George McGovern: A Biography,* "because his teacher interpreted his reluctance to read aloud in class as lack of intelligence." Despite his shyness, he joined the debating team as a sophomore in high school and excelled. He attended Dakota Wesleyan University, only a few blocks from his home, and married Eleanor Faye Stegeberg on 31 October 1943. They have five children. During World War II, McGovern served as a bomber pilot for the U.S. Air Force from 1943 to 1945, flying thirty-five combat missions. After the war McGovern returned to South Dakota and continued his college education, receiving his B.A. in 1946. He taught history and political science at Dakota Wesleyan from 1949 to 1953 and received an M.A. in 1949 and a Ph.D. in 1953 from Northwestern University.

McGovern served as a delegate for Henry Wallace's Progressive Party in 1948 but had little political experience. After listening to Adlai Stevenson's acceptance speech for the Democratic presidential nomination in 1952, he wrote a letter to the local newspaper expressing his admiration. When members of the South Dakota Democratic Party read the letter, they invited the young history professor to become the state party's executive secretary. For the next three years he traveled throughout the state, building South Dakota's almost nonexistent Democratic Party. In 1956 McGovern ran for Congress and became the first Democrat to win a representative seat in South Dakota in twenty-two years. In 1958 he won again. As a representative McGovern supported federal aid to public schools and farmers and medical insurance for the elderly.

In 1960 President John F. Kennedy appointed McGovern to the Food for Peace program, a program that was designed to support allies with surplus U.S. crops. McGovern had developed the idea, believing that it would benefit U.S. farmers while also providing needed food around the world. During his two years as the program's director, he

George McGovern. THE LIBRARY OF CONGRESS

became an authority on world hunger and wrote *War Against Want: America's Food for Peace Program.* In 1962 McGovern resigned his position to run for a senate seat against the Republican Joseph H. Bottum. During the campaign McGovern became ill when he was infected with hepatitis through a dirty needle used during a vaccination. Because he was unable to campaign, his wife, Eleanor McGovern, made public appearances for him. McGovern won the race by 597 votes, becoming South Dakota's first Democratic senator in twenty-six years. In 1968 he would garner 56 percent of the vote to defeat the challenger, Archie M. Gubbard.

McGovern fought for numerous liberal causes as a senator during the 1960s. He supported a nuclear test ban treaty, antipoverty legislation, and the Housing and Urban Development Act. As a member of the Committee on Agriculture, Nutrition, and Forestry, he became one of the strongest proponents for the nation's farmers. He advocated for an increase in agriculture exports, even into Communist countries. He believed that the cold war should be brought to an end and that both Cuba and China should be formally recognized.

By 1963 the Kennedy administration had stationed sixteen thousand advisers in Vietnam, and McGovern made history as the first person to confront the administration's policy from the Senate floor. He believed that France's presence in Indochina had been a debacle, and he was ready to accept Ho Chi Minh's leadership of a reunited Vietnam. McGovern objected to the United States' support of the repressive South Vietnamese government and alleged that the governing body lacked the popular support necessary to win the war. McGovern repressed his views, however, following Kennedy's assassination, and he remained silent through 1964. He reluctantly voted for the Gulf of Tonkin resolution in August 1964, a bill that empowered the president to respond to North Vietnamese aggression. McGovern was assured that the measure was designed only to provide political cover for Lyndon Johnson in the presidential race against Senator Barry Goldwater.

Later, McGovern learned from a friend, the vice presidential candidate Hubert Humphrey, that Johnson actually planned to escalate the war following the election. On 15 January 1965, before Johnson's second inauguration, McGovern delivered his first major policy statement on Vietnam. "We are not winning in South Vietnam," he stated. "We are backing a government there that is incapable of winning a military struggle or of governing its people." McGovern's dovishness came to national attention when he debated two well-known hawks, Hanson Baldwin, military editor of the *New York Times,* and Senator Gale McGee of Wyoming, in March 1965 on the Columbia Broadcasting System. After McGovern visited Vietnam in November, his dissent became more vocal. By 1968 he declared that he might consider backing another candidate against Johnson and, eventually, began his own short-lived presidential campaign in August 1968. When McGovern learned that President Richard M. Nixon was escalating the war in 1969, he began to call for a complete withdrawal of U.S. troops. His continued dissent led to his decision to seek the Democratic presidential nomination in 1972.

At the beginning of 1969 McGovern became the chairman for the Democratic Reform Commission, the committee responsible for reviewing the rules of delegate selection. Few people, including McGovern, wanted the job, but once he accepted it, he was determined to initiate real reform within the Democratic Party. There had been much dissatisfaction within the party over Hubert Humphrey's nomination in 1968. One-third of the delegates had been chosen two years before the convention, and women and minorities had been underrepresented. The reforms enacted by the commission addressed these concerns by creating specific rules for delegate selection, including quotas for underrepresented groups and primaries in the selection of a presidential candidate.

In 1972 McGovern ran as the Democratic presidential candidate and was defeated in a landslide by the Republi-

can Richard Nixon. He continued to serve in the Senate until 1980, at which time he temporarily left public life. In the mid-1990s McGovern wrote *Terry: My Daughter's Life-and-Death Struggle with Alcohol* and became a member of the National Advisory Council on Alcohol Abuse and Alcoholism. (Terry Jane McGovern, who had battled depression and alcoholism from an early age, froze to death in 1994 following a drinking binge.) McGovern was appointed by President Bill Clinton in the 1990s as the U.S. ambassador to the United Nations' Food and Agriculture Administration and remained in the position following the election of George W. Bush in 2000.

★

McGovern's view on the Vietnam War can be found in his book *A Time of War, A Time of Peace* (1968), and an account of his life appears in *Grassroots: The Autobiography of George McGovern* (1977). Biographical information can be found in Robert Sam Anson, *McGovern: A Biography* (1972), and Theodore H. White, *The Making of the President, '72* (1973).

RONNIE D. LANKFORD, JR.

MacLAINE, Shirley (*b.* 24 April 1934 in Richmond, Virginia), dancer, actor, political activist, and writer who developed from a quirky, kooky antistar into a well-versed actor and influential activist in the 1960s.

MacLaine was born Shirley MacLean Beaty, the daughter of Ira O. Beaty, a bandleader, high school principal, and real-estate broker, and Kathlyn MacLean Beaty, an actor. MacLaine's younger brother followed her into show business and became known as Warren Beatty. MacLaine's early life consisted of conforming to a conservative, upper-middle-class lifestyle and learning to be a lady. However, MacLaine was a mischievous, outspoken tomboy who never fit the mold.

Born with weak bone structure in her ankles, MacLaine had difficulty walking and was enrolled in ballet lessons at age two-and-a-half "for therapeutic reasons." As she states in her autobiography *Don't Fall Off the Mountain* (1970), "I loved it from the beginning." In 1945 the family moved to Arlington, Virginia, where MacLaine continued ballet classes at the Washington School of the Ballet. It became apparent that at five feet, seven inches MacLaine was too tall to be a ballerina, so she shifted her focus to musical comedy.

After graduating from Washington and Lee High School in 1952, MacLaine moved to New York City to continue dance lessons and find a job. She was picked out of a line of girls at an audition for dancers for the Servel Ice Box traveling trade show because of her long legs and red hair. When her new employer could not pronounce her

Shirley MacLaine. ARCHIVE PHOTOS, INC.

last name, he asked for her middle name: "Okay, Shirley MacLaine, you're hired." With a job and a new name, she was on her way. After a stint in the chorus of *Me and Juliet* (1952), MacLaine joined the chorus of *Pajama Game*. She was also the understudy to the dance lead Carol Haney, who "never got sick." In May 1954, on the fourth day of the run, Haney broke her ankle, and MacLaine went on with no rehearsal. She was a hit, and a film contract from the producer Hal Wallis followed. Before relocating to Hollywood, MacLaine was interviewed by Alfred Hitchcock, who offered her a part in *The Trouble with Harry* (1955).

On 17 September 1954, before leaving for location in Vermont, MacLaine married Steve Parker, an actor twelve years her senior. They had one child, Stephanie Sachiko (later the actor Sachi Parker), born in 1956, and divorced in 1982. In Vermont, MacLaine, who had been living "cheap," was astounded at the amount of free food available for the cast, and gained twenty-five pounds in three weeks. After the film finished shooting in Hollywood, MacLaine rented a one-room shack on Santa Monica beach. She refused to be refashioned in the glamour-girl image popular at the time. She cut her own hair, showed complete indifference to her clothes, never dieted, and would not consider posing for "cheesecake" pictures.

Her first film for Wallis was *Artists and Models* (1955);

other films followed, none notable until she played the role of Ginny Moorehead, a pathetic hooker, in *Some Came Running* (1958), starring Frank Sinatra, and received her first nomination for an Academy Award. Working with Sinatra resulted in MacLaine's becoming the mascot of "The Clan," also called the "Rat Pack." It was Sinatra who got her the lead in *Can-Can* (1960). During a rehearsal attended by Nikita Khrushchev, the premier of the Soviet Union, MacLaine welcomed him in Russian. Khrushchev was pleased by her speech but thought her dancing was "immoral" and stated, "The face of humanity is more beautiful than its backside."

Other notable films MacLaine made during the 1960s were *The Apartment* (1960), for which she received a second Academy Award nomination, and *My Geisha* (1962), produced in Japan by her husband. In 1962 she starred with Audrey Hepburn in *The Children's Hour*, which, due to fear of censorship, was rewritten to remove the playwright's lesbian scenario. MacLaine felt the moral climate of America was changing and regretted that she didn't fight to have the film reflect the playwright's exploration of the relationship between the two women. A battle she did fight was against Wallis, in an attempt to be released from her contract. This battle went to court but also was tried in the press. The gossip columnist Mike Connolly published a number of lies about MacLaine, who reacted by slapping him in public. Many applauded her efforts, including President John F. Kennedy, who telegraphed, "CONGRATULATIONS ON YOUR FIGHT STOP NOW IF YOU HAD REAL GUTS YOU'D SLUG WALLACE—GOVERNOR NOT HAL."

For her title role in *Irma la douce* (1963), MacLaine spent hours interviewing prostitutes in Paris. Many were scandalized, but MacLaine received her third Academy Award nomination. Her other films in the 1960s included *The Bliss of Mrs. Blossom* (1968), *Sweet Charity* (1969), another movie that, according to MacLaine, suffered due to an excess of prudery, and *Two Mules for Sister Sara* (1969), with MacLaine once again playing a prostitute, this time disguised as a nun.

Reflecting the decade's involvement in activism and self-discovery, MacLaine devoted time to political campaigning and a number of causes. She campaigned for Adlai Stevenson and John F. Kennedy, was a delegate to the 1968 Democratic National Convention, and campaigned for Robert Kennedy. After Senator Kennedy's assassination, she threw herself into George McGovern's U.S. Senate campaign in 1968 and in 1972 worked tirelessly on his presidential campaign. MacLaine, always outspoken, was vocal in her efforts to save the convict-author Caryl Chessman from execution. During the mid-1960s she traveled throughout the South to register African-American voters. MacLaine was against U.S. involvement in the Vietnam War. She was named the national chair for the Dooley Foundation, which operates medical clinics, hospitals, and orphanages in Vietnam, Laos, Thailand, India, and Nepal. In November 1969 she participated in the huge peace rally held in Times Square.

To educate herself about different lifestyles, MacLaine went to a number of exotic spots during the 1960s. In addition to frequent trips to Japan to see her husband and daughter, she traveled throughout Russia, exercising her facility to "talk to anyone about anything," despite language barriers. In 1964, in the Himalayan kingdom of Bhutan during a coup, she was detained overnight and threatened by guns and bayonets. She went to East Africa, lived with the Masai tribes and became a "blood sister," and in 1967 spent six weeks in India, studying the principles of yoga. Reflecting on her travels, MacLaine stated, "I think I've logged more miles than the secretary of state."

In 1965, to alleviate boredom during filming, MacLaine started to write reflections on her life. Her book *Don't Fall Off the Mountain* took five years to complete. Since then she has written seven more autobiographical books. All have been immensely popular. MacLaine continues to appear in films and won the Oscar for best actress for her work in *Terms of Endearment* (1983).

During the 1960s MacLaine was one of the first show business stars to realize the potential of Hollywood actors to be agents for change. Providing funds and stimulating media coverage, in addition to physically campaigning for people and causes, MacLaine used her notoriety to influence the political process.

★

Good sources for information about MacLaine are her autobiographies, particularly *Don't Fall Off the Mountain* (1970). Other sources include Roy Pickard, *Shirley MacLaine* (1985), and James Spada, *Shirley and Warren* (1985). MacLaine's political activities are detailed in Ronald Brownstein, *The Power and the Glitter: The Hollywood-Washington Connection* (1990). Articles include Joseph Roddy, "New-Style Star Tries a Rough Role," *Look* (29 Jan. 1963), on her work in *Irma la douce;* Howard Thompson, "Far from Ol' Virginny with Miss MacLaine," *New York Times* (24 May 1964); and William A. Henry III, "The Best Year of Her Lives; Shirley MacLaine, at 50, Is Still a Rising Star," *Time* (14 May 1984). An overview of her films can be found in Molly Haskell, "Shirley MacLaine: Still Here," *Film Comment* 31 (May to June 1995): 20–26.

MARCIA B. DINNEEN

McLUHAN, (Herbert) Marshall (*b.* 21 July 1911 in Edmonton, Alberta, Canada; *d.* 31 December 1980 in Toronto, Ontario, Canada), professor of English literature and media analyst whose controversial theories had a strong impact on views of the expanding media in the 1960s.

McLuhan was one of two sons of Herbert Ernest McLuhan, a real estate agent and insurance salesman, and Elsie

Naomi, an actress. He grew up in Winnipeg, Canada, and attended the University of Manitoba, from which he earned both a B.A. in English (1933) and an M.A. in English (1934). McLuhan then enrolled at Cambridge University in England, where he received a bachelor's degree in 1936, a master's degree in 1939, and a doctorate in English literature in 1942. He married Corinne Keller Lewis in 1939; they had two sons and four daughters. McLuhan began his teaching career at the University of Wisconsin–Madison in 1936 and taught at various colleges and universities in the United States and Canada for the next four decades.

If McLuhan needed a catalyst to move him toward media analysis, it came from the shock he experienced in his first teaching post. The students he faced at the University of Wisconsin were his juniors by no more than five to eight years, but he felt he was teaching them across a gap. He sensed this had something to do with ways of learning and understanding, and he felt compelled to investigate it. The investigation led him back to the subtlest of lessons on the training of perception from his Cambridge professors, such as I. A. Richards (*The Meaning of Meaning, Practical Criticism*), and forward to James Joyce's experiments in literature (*Finnegans Wake*), then back to antiquity and the myth of Narcissus, the beautiful youth who so admired his reflection in a pool that he took root on the bank and became a flower. Along the way he detoured through the workaday world of the comic-strip character Dagwood and the rich linguistic world of the Trobriand Islanders of the South Pacific.

Understanding Media: The Extensions of Man, written in 1960 and first published as a report to the U.S. Office of Education, focuses on media effects in all areas of society and culture, but McLuhan's starting point is always the individual, because he defines *media* as technological extensions of the body. McLuhan often puts both his inquiry and his conclusions in terms of the ratio between our physical senses (the extent to which we depend on each relative to the others) and the result of modifications to that ratio. This inevitably involves a psychological dimension. For example, when the alphabet was invented, thus intensifying the role of the visual sense in the communication process, sight took such precedence over hearing that the effect carried over from language and communication to reshape literate society's conception and use of space.

McLuhan stresses sense ratios and the effects of altering them. In Africa the introduction of radio distorted the sensory balance of oral culture, produced an inevitable disorienting effect, and rekindled tribal warfare; in dentistry a device called an *audiac* consists of headphones bombarding the patient with enough noise to block pain from the dentist's drill; in Hollywood the addition of sound to silent pictures impoverished and gradually eliminated the role of mime, with its emphasis on the sense of touch.

Marshall McLuhan. CORBIS CORPORATION (BELLEVUE)

These examples involve the relationships among the five physical senses, which may be ranked in order of the degree of fragmentation of perceptions received through them. Sight comes first, because the eye is such a specialized organ. Then come hearing, touch, smell, and taste, progressively less specialized senses. In contrast to the enormous power of the eye and the distances from which it can receive a stimulus, the tongue is thought capable of distinguishing only sweet, sour, bitter, and salt, and only in direct contact with the substance providing the stimulus.

Western culture, with its phonetic literacy, when transplanted to oral, nonliterate cultures, fragments their tribal organization and produces the prime example of media hybridization and its potent transforming effects. At the same time electricity has transformed Western culture, dislocating its visual, specialist, fragmented orientation in favor of oral and tribal organization. McLuhan retains the metaphors of violent energy in speculating on the final outcome of these changes—the fission of the atomic bomb and the fusion of the hydrogen bomb.

The hybridization of cultures occupies McLuhan's writing most fully, but he offers other examples, such as electric light restructuring existing patterns of social and cultural organization by liberating the activities of that organization from dependence on daylight.

McLuhan emphasizes that media, as extensions of the body, not only alter the ratios among our physical senses but also, when combined, establish new ratios among themselves. This happened when radio changed the way news stories were presented and the way film images were presented in the talkies. Then television came along and brought big changes to radio.

When media combine, both their form and use change. So do the scale, speed, and intensity of the human endeavors affected, and so do the environments surrounding the media and their users. The hovercraft is a hybrid of the boat and the airplane. As such, it eliminates not only the need for the stabilizing devices of wings and keels but the interfacing environments of landing strips and docks.

These are some of the basic lessons of *Understanding Media*, the book that brought McLuhan to prominence in the same year that the global village first heard the name Haight-Ashbury and a year before San Francisco hosted the first McLuhan Festival, featuring the man himself. The saying "God is dead" was much in vogue in the counterculture that quickly adopted McLuhan's ideas but missed the irony of giving a man of deep faith—he was an adult convert to Roman Catholicism—the status of an icon.

Spectacular sales of *Understanding Media,* in hardback and then in paperback editions, and the San Francisco symposium brought McLuhan a steady stream of speaking engagements. He addressed countless groups, from the American Marketing Association and the Container Corporation of America to American Telephone and Telegraph (AT&T) and International Business Machines (IBM). In March 1967 the National Broadcasting Company (NBC) aired "This Is Marshall McLuhan" in its *Experiment in TV* series. He played on his own famous saying, publishing *The Medium Is the Massage* (coproduced with Quentin Fiore and Jerome Agel, 1967) even as he was signing contracts for *Culture Is Our Business* and *From Cliché to Archetype* (with the Canadian poet Wilfred Watson) with publishers in New York. Dozens of universities awarded McLuhan honorary degrees, and he secured the Albert Schweitzer Chair in the Humanities at Fordham University in 1967. At the University of Toronto's Center for Culture and Technology, where McLuhan was director, a steady stream of visitors arrived from around the world to absorb his lessons on media or just to see him and be seen with him. The artist and filmmaker Andy Warhol was scheduled to visit but did not show (when McLuhan finally met Warhol, he pronounced Warhol a "rube"); the singer John Lennon and his wife, Yoko Ono, arrived unannounced. *Understanding Media,* which was eventually translated into more than twenty languages, overshadowed the only McLuhan booklength publication from the 1960s that took him back squarely to his roots as a professor of English literature, the two-volume *Voices of Literature* (1964–1965, edited with Richard J. Schoeck). By the time the decade ended, he had collaborated with the Canadian artist Harley Parker on *Through the Vanishing Point: Space in Poetry and Painting*

(1968) and once more with Fiore and Agel on *War and Peace in the Global Village.* This popular paperback, exploding at every page with McLuhan's observations juxtaposed with a visual chronicle of twentieth-century happenings, bore the improbable subtitle *an inventory of some of the current spastic situations that could be eliminated by more feedforward.* The book looks and feels light-years away from the Cambridge University of the 1930s where he trained, but that was just where McLuhan had picked up the idea of *feedforward* from his teacher I. A. Richards.

On 21 July 1969 *Apollo 11,* the first manned spacecraft to land on the Moon, was on the launchpad, and McLuhan was blithely ignoring his camera cue at the American Broadcasting Company (ABC) studios in New York. He explained to the whole world how the space exploration program had for all practical purposes scrapped Earth and "turned it into planet Polluto." Nature, he observed, had ended with *Sputnik,* the first Earth-orbiting satellite, launched by the Soviet Union in 1957. Here the lesson he had been teaching about technology as a new environment was clear. Everyone could understand that the old environment of Planet Earth was now surrounded by Earth-orbiting satellites. The symbolism of the Moon shot seemed to have more importance for McLuhan than the actual journey of three men a quarter of a million miles from Earth. In private he spoke of the necessity for humans to learn to laugh at the pomposity of Moon shots. The *Apollo 11* astronauts set foot on the moon on McLuhan's fifty-eighth birthday. He died of a stroke at the age of sixty-nine.

McLuhan wrote with no knowledge of galvanic skin response technology, terminal node controllers, or the Apple Newton. He might not have been able to imagine what a biomouse is. But he pointed the way to understanding all of these, not in themselves but in their relation to each other, to older technologies, and above all in relation to ourselves—our bodies, our physical senses, our psychic balance. When he published *Understanding Media* in 1964, McLuhan was disturbed about mankind shuffling toward the twenty-first century in the shackles of nineteenth-century perceptions. He might be no less disturbed today. And he would continue to issue the challenge that confronts the reader on every page of his writings to cast off those shackles.

★

W. Terrence Gordon's *McLuhan for Beginners* (1997), a documentary comic book, brought the author the invitation to write McLuhan's biography, *Escape into Understanding: A Biography of Marshall McLuhan* (1997). Arthur Kroker, *Technology and the Canadian Mind: Innis, McLuhan, Grant* (1984) offers an excellent discussion of McLuhan's thought in relation to that of the political economist Harold Innis and the philosopher George Grant. Other books on McLuhan include Sam Neill, *Clarifying McLuhan*

(1993), which discusses aspects of McLuhan's work that are all but ignored by other commentators; Barrington Nevitt and Maurice McLuhan, eds., *Who Was Marshall McLuhan?* (1995), an eclectic overview of McLuhan by numerous authors; Judith Stamps, *Unthinking Modernity: Innis, McLuhan, and the Frankfurt School* (1995), which seeks to locate McLuhan's place in intellectual history in relation to Walter Benjamin and Theodor Adorno; and Glen Willmott, *McLuhan, or Modernism in Reverse* (1996), an interesting discussion of the thesis that McLuhan's place in intellectual history is at the break point between modernism and postmodernism. Obituaries of McLuhan are in the *Chicago Tribune* and *New York Times* (both 1 Jan. 1981).

W. TERRENCE GORDON

McMURTRY, Larry Jeff (*b.* 3 June 1936 in Wichita Falls, Texas), Pulitzer Prize–winning novelist, essayist, teacher, and screenwriter, best known for his novels set in 1960s Texas and about legends of the West.

McMurtry grew up on a ranch near Archer City, Texas, the son of William Jefferson McMurtry and Hazel Ruth McIver, a homemaker. Both his father and grandfather were cattle ranchers, and as a child McMurtry was immersed in the stories, myths, and histories of the West. He graduated from Archer City High School in 1954 and then attended North Texas State College in Denton, graduating with a B.A. in 1958. He went to Rice University in Houston, graduating with an M.A. in 1960. On 15 July 1959 he married Josephine Ballard; they had one son, James, who became an actor and musician. The couple divorced in 1966.

McMurtry wrote stories from an early age, and his first novels, *Horseman, Pass By* (1961) and *Leaving Cheyenne* (1963), were published while he was working as an English instructor at Texas Christian University in Fort Worth. His novel *The Last Picture Show* (1966) established him as the Southwest's most popular writer. Much of McMurtry's work is set in the southwestern United States. Most of his novels describe a post-frontier society struggling to find an identity for itself and its citizens. His first three books, published between 1961 and 1966, are set around the town of Thalia, which bears a resemblance to Archer City. They are concerned with the problems of small-town life and an existence dominated by the heroic presence of pioneering ancestors. Set in the mid-1950s, these early novels address the way rapid cultural change affects life in small-town Texas, and they struck a chord with many readers in the 1960s. McMurtry's characters are stifled by conventions and troubled by their isolation, and they face conflicts between old and new ways of life, and he offended many Texans with his bleak portrayal of their home state.

McMurtry's first novel, *Horseman, Pass By,* successfully

Larry McMurtry. MR. JERRY BAUER

filmed as *Hud* in 1963, tells the story of Lonnie Bannon, growing up in the harsh environment of his grandfather's ranch near Thalia in the mid-1950s. Bannon struggles with the idea that the family's way of life is coming to an end; in particular, he finds himself torn between the old-fashioned honesty and modest graft of his grandfather and the materialism and ambition of his amoral half brother Hud. Set against the background of an outbreak of foot-and-mouth disease that threatens the ranch's survival, the novel exposes hypocrisies present in both sets of values. *Horseman, Pass By* set the tone for much of McMurtry's later output in that it is unsentimental about the past, yet avoids being idealistic about the future. A *New York Times* review of 10 June 1961 describes McMurtry as "among the most promising first novelists" of the year, but identified another common feature of McMurtry's work, its tendency to overdramatize situations and stretch "the law of probability." Perhaps for this reason, though generally well reviewed, McMurtry never really gained acceptance as a "literary" novelist.

Leaving Cheyenne followed the success of *Horseman, Pass By*. In it, three characters each tell the first-person story of a love triangle that spans a generation. Also set in Thalia, *Leaving Cheyenne* continues McMurtry's examination of cultural change in small-town America and was filmed as *Loving Molly* (1973). McMurtry's third novel, *The Last Picture Show* (1966), is also his best known. Here his description of the bleakness of small-town life is at its most intense. With its young people being drawn away to the cities,

Thalia is a town of boarded-up storefronts and empty landscapes. The traditions of cattle ranching can no longer sustain its economy, while the traditions of prom queens and high school sports are no longer important to its young. *The Last Picture Show* was praised for its realism as a description of the Texas landscape and of the lives of the people who lived there. McMurtry accurately describes the sense of change and loss experienced in many rural American communities in the late 1950s and early 1960s.

Through a series of broken relationships and the symbolic closure of the town's movie theater, *The Last Picture Show* also describes the transition to adulthood of Jacy and her admirers Duane and Sonny, and is considered McMurtry's finest achievement as a novelist. Its satirical sequel, *Texasville,* appeared in 1987. In 1971 *The Last Picture Show* was made into an acclaimed film by the director Peter Bogdanovich. McMurtry's story managed to capture the mood of a particular moment in the history of the West. Later novels, including the lengthy *Moving On* (1970) and the urban-based *Terms of Endearment* (1975), continue exploring the themes of changing identity, dislocated lives, and dysfunctional relationships.

Although he was a successful novelist by his late twenties, McMurtry continued to teach throughout the 1960s, including English and creative writing at Rice (1963–1965), at George Mason College (1970), and at American University, Washington, D.C. (1970–1971). In 1971 he opened Booked Up Inc. in Washington, D.C., an antiquarian bookshop that soon had branches in Archer City and Tucson, Arizona. He has received many awards, including the Wallace Stegner Fellowship (1960), the Guggenheim Fellowship (1964), and a Pulitzer Prize for his frontier novel, *Lonesome Dove* (1985).

By the mid-1960s McMurtry had emerged as an important voice of disaffected small-town youth, yet by the 1980s he was best known as a writer of Westerns. This was largely because of the success of *Lonesome Dove* (1985), which is set in nineteenth-century Texas. But, in fact, only a handful of his more than twenty novels are Westerns in the generic sense. As well as writing screenplays for television and movie versions of his novels, McMurtry also has been a regular reviewer for the *Washington Post* and became president of PEN (which originally stood for "Playwrights, essayists, editors, and novelists") American Center in 1989. Since the 1990s, after a heart bypass operation, he has concentrated on bookselling in his hometown of Archer City.

★

McMurtry's papers are held in the Albert B. Alkek Library at Southwest Texas State University, and at the University of Texas Permian Basin and the University of North Texas (formerly North Texas State), while his views on Texas are expressed with characteristic frankness in *In a Narrow Grave: Essays on Texas* (1968).

McMurtry's early career is described in Thomas Landess, *Larry McMurtry* (1969), and an introduction to McMurtry and his work is in Mark Busby, *Larry McMurtry and the West: An Ambivalent Relationship* (1995). A useful collection of writings about McMurtry from the 1960s to the 1980s is Clay Reynolds, ed., *Taking Stock: A Larry McMurtry Casebook* (1989).

CHRIS ROUTLEDGE

McNALLY, Terrence   (*b.* 3 November 1939 in Saint Petersburg, Florida), playwright and author of screenplays who, in the 1960s, was noted as a writer of "antiestablishment" plays in both form and content that included anti–Vietnam War and homosexual themes.

McNally, the only child of Hubert Arthur McNally and Dorothy Katharine Rapp, grew up and attended school in Corpus Christi, Texas. After graduating from high school, he went to New York City in 1956 to attend Columbia University, where he received the Henry Evans Traveling Fellowship. McNally received his B.A. in English in 1960 and graduated Phi Beta Kappa. As a struggling young play-

Terrence McNally. AP/WIDE WORLD PHOTOS

wright, he worked as a stage manager for the Actors Studio in New York City and tutored the novelist John Steinbeck's children during 1961 and 1962. He also served as a film critic for the publication *Seventh Art* (1963–1965) and as an assistant editor for *Columbia College Today* (1965–1966).

McNally was already writing plays while in college, and his play *The Roller Coaster* was published in the *Columbia Review* in 1960. In 1962 he received the Stanley Drama Award, which is presented in support of aspiring playwrights, for his play *This Side of the Door.* In that same year, at the age of twenty-four, McNally had his first play produced in New York. Originally called *There Is Something Out There,* the revised version was titled *And Things That Go Bump in the Night* and was staged in Minneapolis in 1964, in New York in 1965, and in London in 1977. The play received considerable attention for its bizarre style in telling the tale of an emotionally crippled and demented family engulfed by fear, who lock themselves in the basement in anticipation of some sort of apocalypse. Placed within a subtext of the 1960s civil rights problems and cold war paranoia, it shocked many with its bad-boy presentation of a bisexual son who brings home his transvestite boyfriend.

In 1963 *The Lady of the Camellias,* which McNally adapted from a play by Giles Cooper, was staged at New York's Winter Garden Theatre but closed in only ten days and after thirteen performances. McNally's play *Next* was staged in Connecticut in 1967 and in New York in 1969 at the Greenwich Mews Playhouse. The off-Broadway play starred James Coco in a comedy about a shy, overweight theater manager in his forties who mistakenly gets drafted and has to report for his army physical. To make matters worse, the individual conducting the physical is a tough woman sergeant who enjoys embarrassing Coco's character, who is nearly nude, representing his final humiliation of having nothing left to expose. The play's subtext is an antiwar statement about U.S. involvement in Vietnam.

McNally carried on the Vietnam War theme in his one-act play *Botticelli,* which was first performed for television in 1968. The play focuses on seemingly educated and intelligent American soldiers in Vietnam who play an erudite word game while standing guard and appear to have little feeling as they "kill a gook" ("gook" being the soldiers' epithet for the North Vietnamese during the war). In *Tour,* which was first produced in Los Angeles in 1967 and then staged the following year in New York, McNally provides a humorous look at an American couple traveling abroad.

Several other plays written by McNally made it to the New York stage in 1968, including *Sweet Eros,* in which a poet delivers a monologue that is continually interrupted, at first by sobs, then by muffled protests, and finally by a song, all coming from a young woman he has kidnapped and who is gagged and tied to a chair. In *Witness,* which was staged with *Sweet Eros,* the gagged captive is a man who must listen to the raving speeches of a young man who has been driven to madness by newspapers and television and who wants to assassinate the president during a motorcade (much like the real assassination five years earlier of President John F. Kennedy). Also staged in 1968 were the plays *Cuba Si!* and *Noon,* which were produced in New York as part of the trilogy *Morning, Noon, and Night* (*Morning* was written by Israel Horovitz and *Night* by Leonard Melfi). In *Noon,* McNally presents a farce about five people who respond to a personal ad to participate in an orgy in a Greenwich Village apartment. He also authored the 1968 book for the musical *Here's Where I Belong,* which was based on his former employer Steinbeck's book *East of Eden* (1952).

In 1969 McNally's play *Last Gasps* was televised, and the play *Bringing It All Back Home* was produced in New Haven, Connecticut. He began the 1970s with the play *Where Has Tommy Flowers Gone?,* which was staged in New York in 1971. Throughout the 1960s, McNally's plays were primarily situation comedies with a message. But in *Where Has Tommy Flowers Gone?* McNally portrays the life and attitude of a character who is disturbingly angered and alienated and who wants to blow up the world. The play captures the social aura of the late 1960s and early 1970s through its depiction of "flower children," the "now generation," and violent revolutionaries via a series of vignettes, skits, and brief incidents.

McNally, who received Guggenheim Fellowships in 1966 and 1969, never let the limited success of his early plays, which were mostly financial flops, inhibit his artistic vision. He continued to write plays with controversial political and sexual themes throughout the 1960s, mirroring the decade's growing political consciousness and movement toward sexual freedom. McNally's plays were produced throughout the 1970s, but it was not until later in his career that he garnered wide critical acclaim. Between 1993 and 1996 he received four Tony Awards, three for best play (*Love! Valour! Compassion!, Master Class,* and *Ragtime*) and one for best book of a musical (*Kiss of the Spider Woman*). As a result, McNally gained a reputation as one of America's leading dramatists. He certainly did not mellow with the years. Keeping with his antiestablishment mindset of the 1960s, he created a controversy with his 1997 play *Corpus Christi,* a modern-day retelling of the life of a Jesus character who, along with his disciples, is homosexual.

★

Several comprehensive critical studies of McNally's work are available, including Toby Silverman Zinman, ed., *Terrence McNally: A Casebook* (1997), and David Roman, "Negative Identifications: HIV-Negative Gay Men in Representation and Performance: A Center for Lesbian and Gay Studies Book," in *Queer Representations: Reading Lives, Reading Cultures* (1997). See also Benilde Montgomery, "*Lips Together, Teeth Apart:* Another Version of Pastoral," *Modern Drama* (Dec. 1993), and an interesting assessment of McNally by Jan Stuart, "Terrence McNally Gets Naked," *Newsday* (6 Nov. 1994).

DAVID PETECHUK

McNAMARA, Margaret Craig   (*b.* 22 August 1915 in Seattle, Washington; *d.* 3 February 1981 in Washington, D.C.), teacher, tutor, and goodwill worker who in 1966 founded Reading Is FUNdamental, a national organization that promotes literacy among disadvantaged children and their families.

McNamara was one of two daughters born to Thomas J. Craig, an insurance executive, and Margaret McKinstry. She grew up in Alameda, California, where she cultivated a love for the outdoors. At the University of California at Berkeley, where her idealism was honed, McNamara met her future husband, Robert Strange McNamara, who later became the secretary of defense in the presidential administrations of John F. Kennedy and Lyndon B. Johnson. After graduating in 1937, McNamara taught biology and physical education at a high school in San Rafael, California. In August 1940 the McNamaras married and moved to Cambridge, Massachusetts, where Robert taught at Harvard University. The couple had three children.

In the summer of 1945 both McNamaras contracted poliomyelitis. Her husband's case was very mild, but McNamara was paralyzed. Even so, by early 1946 she was walking again. Polio is rare among adults, and her rehabilitation took place at the Children's Hospital in Baltimore, Maryland, where she was surrounded by paralytic children. In the next fourteen years in Ann Arbor, Michigan, where her husband worked for the Ford Motor Company, McNamara did volunteer tutoring and was active in civic affairs. Although McNamara retained a permanent limp, she resumed her favorite outdoor activities, mountain climbing and skiing.

In December 1960 Robert McNamara accepted Kennedy's nomination as the secretary of defense. The family settled in the Kalorama neighborhood of Washington, D.C. Among the glittering Kennedy set from the East Coast, people observed that the McNamaras were "bright and straight" and that Margaret McNamara was "so innocent," "so fine and natural." McNamara immersed herself in goodwill work, which she already had taken up actively in national organizations. The most publicized of all her projects was her founding of Reading Is FUNdamental (RIF).

When she resumed tutoring in Washington, D.C., McNamara saw that her young inner-city students had few books at home. On a spring day in 1966 she brought the children a Jules Verne adventure book. They became interested instantly. One boy wanted to have the book, and McNamara agreed, realizing that given the opportunity to choose and keep the books they liked, children would be more likely to establish a lifelong interest in reading. The books also could serve to reach an entire family through one child. McNamara launched RIF on 3 November 1966. It quickly flourished in inner-city schools, reaching disadvantaged children and their families in a wide range of settings. With McNamara's vigorous efforts to raise funds and organize support, RIF went beyond Washington, D.C., and became a national organization that operated in all fifty states, on Native American reservations, and on far-flung island territories of the United States.

As the 1960s wore on, anti–Vietnam War sentiment intensified, and people with connections to the Johnson administration, including the McNamaras, became a target for hostility and threats. McNamara worked hard to support her husband and family through these difficult times. She also had other obligations, including work with cabinet wives. In July 1967 McNamara had an operation for ulcers, yet the family was still able to enjoy vacationing at their second home in Snowmass, Colorado, and abroad.

In the late 1960s and throughout the 1970s, McNamara traveled extensively in developing countries with her husband, who had become the president of the World Bank. McNamara sowed the seeds of RIF along the way. She also advised her husband on global education and health issues. With her tireless efforts, McNamara convinced many members of Congress that RIF deserved the nation's full and steadfast support. In 1976 Congress passed the Inexpensive Book Distribution Program, matching individual community-raised funds with federal government funding, three to one.

President Jimmy Carter awarded McNamara the Presidential Medal of Freedom on 15 January 1981 for her work in Reading Is FUNdamental. Although she was dying from cancer and appeared extremely weak, McNamara sat in a wheelchair with her back straight, looking up at the president with her typical direct gaze. McNamara died at home in Washington, D.C. That summer, her ashes were scattered at Buckskin Pass, near Snowmass, on a peaceful mountainside meadow with a creek and a blanket of wildflowers.

McNamara, "one of God's loveliest creatures," as her husband called her, was always unaffected and selfless to a fault. Throughout her life as a career goodwill worker, a loving wife and mother, a fearless fighter of her illnesses, and an avid mountain climber and skier, McNamara's perseverance and intelligence were extraordinary. She left her legacy in Reading Is FUNdamental, which became the nation's largest children and family literacy organization. In

2002 RIF ran a program to put 200 million books in the hands and homes of children who need them most.

★

Information about McNamara can be found in Henry L. Trewhitt, *McNamara* (1971); Deborah Shapley, *Promise and Power: The Life and Times of Robert McNamara* (1993), which contains the most in-depth account of McNamara; Robert S. McNamara with Brian VanDeMark, *In Retrospect: The Tragedy and Lessons of Vietnam* (1995); and Paul Hendrickson, *The Living and the Dead: Robert McNamara and Five Lives of a Lost War* (1996). An obituary is in the *New York Times* (4 Feb. 1981).

SHAOSHAN LI

McNAMARA, Robert Strange (*b.* 9 June 1916 in San Francisco, California), secretary of defense during the administrations of Presidents John F. Kennedy and Lyndon B. Johnson (1961–1968) who became known as one of the leading architects of the war in Vietnam.

The son of Robert James McNamara, sales manager for a wholesale shoe company, and Claranell Strange, McNamara was a frail child with a bright mind. The hallmarks of his persona—a first-rate intellect matched with unwavering discipline—were apparent early in his life. He was reading at a high school level when he entered first grade, and was active in student government at Piedmont High School. He studied economics and philosophy at the University of California, Berkeley, where he was elected to Phi Beta Kappa at the end of his sophomore year. He received a B.A. with honors in 1937, and married Margaret McKinstry Craig, a schoolteacher and fellow Berkeley student, on 13 August 1940. They had three children.

McNamara attended the Harvard School of Business and received an M.B.A. in 1939. He studied the principle that a company would be more efficient and therefore successful if its managers could master the flow of information—in a corporate setting, this meant statistics. In his 1995 book *In Retrospect,* McNamara wrote: "To this day, I see quantification as a language to add precision to reasoning about the world." This philosophy would shape his public life, and not always for the better. When the United States entered World War II, McNamara was rejected for active duty owing to nearsightedness. He remained at Harvard as an assistant professor until 1943, when he took a leave of absence and went to England. There he set up a statistical system for the Eighth Air Force to manage the flow of personnel and equipment. Within the year he earned a captain's commission and eventually rose to the rank of lieutenant colonel. He was a natural at planning, logistics, and operational analysis, able to digest massive quantities of information that would have choked a lesser intellect.

Robert McNamara, 1962. HULTON-DEUTSCH COLLECTION/CORBIS

After the war McNamara was recruited to join a team of nine other statistical experts, known as the "Whiz Kids," who were hired by Ford Motor Company in 1946. They addressed the company's slipshod management and accounting practices, implementing their statistical control methods and reviving Ford's ailing fortunes. McNamara earned a reputation for "knowing where every buck is spent." Rising rapidly through the company, he succeeded Henry Ford II as president on 9 November 1960—becoming the first head of Ford Motors from outside the Ford family.

Yet McNamara would lead Ford for only one month. In late 1960, when President-elect John F. Kennedy asked the legendary Washington power broker Bob Lovett for cabinet recommendations, the first name that came up was McNamara's. Before agreeing to the position of secretary of defense, McNamara made it clear to Kennedy that he had no intention of being a passive observer. He intended to coordinate the services, reducing waste and duplication. This was music to Kennedy's ears; he wanted to run foreign policy and military affairs from the White House. For the position of secretary of defense, he wanted someone who could hold the reins on the world's largest bureaucracy.

McNamara clearly understood his charge, telling a *New York Times* reporter in January 1961 that his main task was "to bring efficiency to a $40 billion enterprise." On 21 January 1961 McNamara was sworn into office, and his first act as secretary was to streamline the Pentagon leadership, eliminating some assistant secretary posts and creating a new office of management planning. He used systems analysis to determine the cost-effectiveness of new weapons systems and insisted on allocating budget funds based on functionality rather than branch of service, stressing "commonality" when possible. In the past, civilian control of the military had been true only in theory; McNamara made it a reality. This added to his legend in Washington—the man who saved Ford Motors had now tamed the roaring military. He was, in the words of the journalist and historian David Halberstam, the "can-do man in the can-do society in the can-do era."

The determination of McNamara and Kennedy to treat the Pentagon as just another organization, however, turned out to be appallingly shortsighted. As secretary of defense, McNamara inevitably would become a top adviser on foreign affairs and the man who would orchestrate any U.S. military action—the government's "general-in-chief." However, nothing in McNamara's background prepared him for these tasks; indeed, his almost evangelical belief in the power of fact and reason was poorly suited to the swirling ideological passions of the cold war era. In retrospect, it appears inevitable that McNamara would fail. McNamara was also a victim of domestic political machinations. Although it had been seven years since the Senate censured Senator Joseph McCarthy for his anti-Communist crusades, the issue was still alive as far as Kennedy was concerned—owing in large part to his narrow victory over Republican Richard M. Nixon in 1960. Both Kennedy and his vice president, Lyndon B. Johnson, were wary of being labeled "soft on Communism."

Shortly after his election, Kennedy was briefed by the Central Intelligence Agency (CIA) about an operation initiated by President Dwight D. Eisenhower to undermine the Cuban regime of Fidel Castro. Determined to show muscle on the Communism issue, Kennedy decided to proceed with plans to launch a small invading force comprising CIA-trained Cuban exiles. McNamara agreed to the plan. On 17 April 1961 nearly 1,500 Cuban expatriates stormed the beaches at the Bay of Pigs. The mission was a tactical and political disaster. The insurgents were defeated in three days, and the Cuban populace rallied around Castro. When he left office in 1967, McNamara told reporters that his greatest regret was the Bay of Pigs, a policy that "could have been recognized as an error at the time."

Failure in Cuba necessitated an even harder line for the new administration, both to fend off domestic critics and to demonstrate toughness to the Soviet Union. As Halberstam wrote, the Bay of Pigs was "a shattering event" that would go on to "seriously disturb the balance of the first two years of the Kennedy Administration." In Vienna, in June 1961, the Soviet premier Nikita Khrushchev blustered his way through a meeting with Kennedy, making it clear that he thought the U.S. president was weak and indecisive. On 13 August 1961, seeking a solution to the dramatic flow of refugees out of Communist East Berlin to capitalist West Berlin, Khrushchev erected the Berlin Wall. Kennedy was forced to accept this unilateral action as a fait accompli.

The attention of the U.S. government then fell squarely on the previously obscure nation of Vietnam. Kennedy believed that the cold war would be fought and won, not in direct conflict with the Soviet Union but indirectly, in the Third World. He favored a military policy known as "flexible response," which would allow the United States to confront Communist aggression on a smaller scale, anywhere in the world. McNamara implemented this policy for Kennedy, strengthening conventional fighting capacity, expanding troop levels dramatically, and creating a counterinsurgency force, known as the Green Berets, that could stamp out revolution whenever and wherever it arose. Vietnam would be the ultimate test of this policy.

Vietnam turned out to be a poor test case. While North Vietnam was Communist, the opposition to Ngo Dinh Diem, the nationalist leader of South Vietnam, was an ambiguous mix of Communists and nationalists. Nevertheless, Diem referred to his opposition as "Vietcong," or Vietnamese Communists. This analysis was dubious at best. As the historian Stephen Ambrose writes, "Diem was incapable of distinguishing between Communist and anti-Communist opposition to his government." McNamara, like others in the administration, repeatedly fell prey to poor analysis of Southeast Asia generally and Vietnam specifically. McCarthy's "Red" baiting had another lingering effect on Kennedy's foreign policy—the State Department was purged of most of its experts on China. Compounding the problem, Vietnam policy had always been seen through a French prism. Until 1954 the U.S. Embassy in Paris had handled U.S. policy in Vietnam; afterward, French speakers with backgrounds in European affairs staffed the embassy in Saigon and the Vietnam desk at the State Department.

Finally, there was a tendency in the Kennedy administration to close ranks among senior officials when important decisions were made—thereby banishing country or regional experts, who resided at lower levels of government. McNamara was no doubt comfortable with this arrangement; describing his theory of corporate management, he once said, "I have always believed that the more important the decision, the fewer people should be involved in the decision." As a result, the administration seized on the so-called domino theory—in which South Vietnam was the linchpin to preventing a Chinese Communist takeover of Asia—without considering that Vietnam and China had been rivals for hundreds of years before the introduction of Communist theory.

McNamara made the first of many visits to Vietnam in 1962. By that time the United States had more than 10,000 military "advisers" there. (In 1954 President Dwight D. Eisenhower had declined to intervene in Vietnam, but had sent the first wave of U.S. military and economic advisers.) McNamara saw nothing to dissuade him from the belief that superior troops, training, and firepower inevitably would win the battle, presumably without much difficulty. On that first trip, when U.S. involvement was still at a minimum, McNamara said, "Every quantitative measurement we have shows we're winning the war." He failed to take into account intangible, human factors, such as the presence of a more determined foe, fighting to defend home soil—the elements that the German theorist Carl von Clausewitz had called the "friction" of war more than a century earlier. This failure was to be McNamara's Achilles' heel.

In August 1962 the Soviets began to build ballistic missile sites in Cuba. Like most Kennedy administration foreign policy decisions, the response to this development was handled in the White House, with the president surrounded by a relatively small circle of senior advisers. In this case, the results were a textbook example of how to manage foreign policy in a crisis. The president's team, known as the Executive Committee, or Ex Comm, patiently and deliberately debated their alternatives while the fate of the world hung in the balance and events on the ground shifted constantly. McNamara sided with the president in advocating a blockade of Soviet ships carrying offensive weapons to Cuba in October 1962. Over the more hawkish advice of the generals, who felt that the Soviets would understand only force, the blockade was ordered, and a standoff on the high seas ensued. The Kennedy administration was criticized for its confrontational, "warlike" attitude. Yet in the end, Khrushchev blinked first, ordering Soviet ships back to Russia. It was a great victory for the Kennedy administration, a decisive escape from the most dangerous crisis the world had ever known.

On 22 November 1963 President Kennedy was assassinated in Dallas. The newly inaugurated president Lyndon Johnson urged McNamara to remain at the Pentagon. Johnson accelerated the pace of events in Vietnam with his determination to "win the war." On 2 August 1964 the president received reports that North Vietnamese forces in the Gulf of Tonkin had attacked U.S. destroyers. Johnson seized the opportunity and pushed a resolution through Congress—the Gulf of Tonkin Resolution—that effectively gave him a blank check to broaden the war effort as he saw fit, without congressional interference. McNamara was one of the key lobbyists on the resolution and later admitted that he misled Congress about administration war aims.

In late 1964 McNamara supported the administration's determination to conduct an air war against North Vietnam—the systematic bombing lasted into early 1965. On 8 June 1965 Johnson authorized U.S. troops to engage in ground combat. Public opinion began to turn against the war. In this growing crisis, McNamara relied on what he knew best, data. Many of the photographs of McNamara in this period show him poring over endless volumes of statistics. He was constantly in the country, talking to soldiers, conferring with commanders, assessing the situation. Yet in gathering his research, he was too willing to accept military reporting that conformed to his relentless optimism. If he was played for a fool, he played right along. McNamara never sought independent corroboration of data. He went before the country and reported that indicators were good. While Johnson had his domestic policies to insulate him from Vietnam, McNamara had nowhere to hide. He became a focal point for antiwar protesters, vilified as a "murderer" and a "baby burner." Senator Wayne Morse of Oregon, one of two dissenting votes on the Gulf of Tonkin Resolution, referred to the escalating conflict in Vietnam as "McNamara's war." These charges deeply hurt him and contributed to his growing disenchantment with the war effort.

McNamara began to focus his energies on a negotiated settlement to end the conflict. Hoping to draw the North Vietnamese to the table, he proposed, and Johnson reluctantly accepted, a thirty-seven-day pause in bombing during December 1965 and January 1966. Nothing came of it, and McNamara began to fall out of favor with Johnson, who wanted a decisive victory. The president began to rely more and more on the hawkish advice of generals in the field. McNamara began to think about leaving the Pentagon, finding a position that would allow him to test his evolving theory that "security is not military hardware" but rather "development." In April 1967 he requested that Johnson nominate him for president of the World Bank, a position that would be vacant at the end of the year. Johnson accommodated his wishes. McNamara assumed the presidency of the World Bank in January 1968 and held the position until 1981. McNamara received the Presidential Medal of Freedom with Distinction from Johnson in 1968 for service to his country.

The legacy of McNamara is long but decidedly mixed. One of the best minds of his generation, a corporate titan, and chief architect of the turnaround at Ford Motor Company, he was also responsible in part for the escalation of the Vietnam War, an ill-conceived and poorly executed endeavor that cost more than 58,000 American lives. The specter of this war still hangs over U.S. public life and U.S. foreign policy. His legacy is one of great potential gone awry. At the first cabinet meeting for the incoming Kennedy administration, Vice President Lyndon Johnson was immediately taken with the men that would make up Kennedy's brain trust, the men whom Halberstam ironically labeled "the Best and the Brightest." Johnson was dazzled; each one was smarter than the next. The most impressive was McNamara, "the fellow from Ford with the Stacomb on his hair." Johnson passed his impressions on to Speaker of the House Sam Rayburn. His response was prophetic: "Well, Lyndon, you may be right and they may be every bit as intelligent as you say, but I'd feel a whole lot better about them if just one of them had run for sheriff once."

★

McNamara reflected on his role in Vietnam in *In Retrospect: The Tragedy and Lessons of Vietnam* (1995). There are several full-length biographies, including Henry L. Trewhitt, *McNamara: His Ordeal in the Pentagon* (1971), and Deborah Shapley, *Promise and Power: The Life and Times of Robert McNamara* (1993). Works about McNamara's political beliefs include William W. Kaufmann, *The McNamara Strategy* (1964), and James Roherty, *Decisions of Robert S. McNamara: A Study of the Role of the Secretary of State* (1970). McNamara also features prominently in the vast literatures of the Kennedy presidency, the Cuban Missile Crisis, and the Vietnam War, including such classics as Arthur M. Schlesinger, Jr., *A Thousand Days: John F. Kennedy in the White House* (1965); Robert F. Kennedy, *Thirteen Days: A Memoir of the Cuban Missile Crisis* (1969); David Halberstam, *The Best and the Brightest* (1972); and Stanley Karnow, *Vietnam: A History* (1983). Articles about McNamara's work in the 1960s include "Confessing the Sins of Vietnam," *Newsweek* (17 Apr. 1995), "McNamara's Final Surrender," *National Review* (25 Dec. 1995), and "McNamara's Vietnam War Reconsidered," *Society* (1 Sept. 1998).

TIMOTHY KRINGEN

McQUEEN, Steve (*b*. 24 March 1930 in Indianapolis, Indiana; *d*. 7 November 1980 in Juarez, Mexico), the highest-paid actor of the 1960s and 1970s, whose rugged, intense, and brooding on-screen and off-screen persona made him an icon of rebellion, action, and the style of the era.

McQueen was born Terence Stephen McQueen to William McQueen and Julia (Crawford) McQueen. His father, a former stunt pilot, deserted the family when McQueen was six months old, leaving a wound that never healed. McQueen's mother left her son to be raised on an uncle's ranch in Slater, Missouri, where he worked the fields, herded pigs, and fantasized about being a cowboy. He began his racing career at age four—on his tricycle. Racing motorcycles and sports cars became an obsession for McQueen, who claimed it curbed his aggression. His mother took him back to Indianapolis when he was nine, but he never adjusted to the move. He was a terrible student, joined a street gang, and spent his time stealing hubcaps and shooting pool. Having lost his uncle, the one person who he felt loved him, McQueen was often in trouble with the law and had to

Steve McQueen, 1961. THE KOBAL COLLECTION

endure his stepfather's beatings after his mother remarried. His mother finally sent him to the California Junior Boys' Republic, a reform school in Chino, California, when he was fourteen. There he found a mentor who helped him channel his rebellious energy and build his self-esteem. McQueen left the school in 1946 with only a ninth-grade education. After he became a star, he set up a scholarship program at the school and visited the facility often.

Following a brief and bitter reunion with his mother after his stepfather's death, McQueen drifted. He worked as a deckhand aboard the S.S. *Alpha,* a towel boy in a Texas brothel, a "grunt" laborer on Texas oil rigs, a carnival barker, and a member of a lumber crew in Canada. Only a year after leaving his mother at seventeen, he enlisted in the U.S. Marines. Upon receiving an honorable discharge, McQueen went to New York City. At a girlfriend's suggestion, he studied acting on the GI Bill. Although, at first, acting seemed to him "a silly game, a waste of time and energy," he soon discovered that he had a talent for it and that it gave him a sense of self-respect. McQueen entered Sanford Meisner's Neighborhood Playhouse in 1952. He also studied with Herbert Berghof and was accepted into the Actors Studio by Lee Strasberg. He progressed as a stage actor, earned several minor television roles, and had parts

in such films as *Somebody up There Likes Me* (1956), *Never Love a Stranger* (1958), *The Great St. Louis Bank Robbery* (1958), *The Blob* (1958), and *Never So Few* (1959). He married the dancer Neile Adams in November 1956, with whom he remained for a tumultuous fifteen years and had two children.

Despite his initial distaste for westerns, they were McQueen's bread and butter for several years. Playing the bounty hunter Josh Randall on the television series *Wanted—Dead or Alive* (1958–1961) launched McQueen's career. He gave his best cinematic performance to date in the legendary western *The Magnificent Seven* (1960). McQueen was ecstatic when his television series was cancelled, as it freed him to pursue his film career. By this time, McQueen himself saw that he had a "real chance to grab that big brass ring." For him, stardom meant financial success and the stability that had been missing from his life.

McQueen turned in a self-conscious performance in the comedy *The Honeymoon Machine* (1961). *Hell Is for Heroes* (1962), a grim World War II drama and his eighth film, brought him more solid critical reviews but did nothing to advance his career. Frustrated, he went to Europe to film *The War Lover* (1962). McQueen once again played a dangerous loner, the headstrong pilot Buzz Rickson, who betrays his best friend for a woman and then crashes his plane. The film was produced entirely in England, the hub of international racing. Upon hearing of his plans to race some of Britain's top circuits, studio lawyers informed McQueen that he would be sued for the entire cost of the film—$3 million—if an injury postponed production. He ignored them and began to pal around with the legendary racing champion Stirling Moss. The friendship led to numerous high-profile driving seats for McQueen, including an impressive run in the twelve-hour Sebring, Florida, race for the British Motor Corporation (BMC). He fared so well in racing that he was forced to choose between his acting career and accepting an offer to race for BMC in Europe.

By this time the father of two, McQueen opted—narrowly—to take a role in what became his "big picture," *The Great Escape* (1963), based on the true story of the greatest Allied prison break in World War II history. Upon the film's release, McQueen became a white-hot Hollywood property. He followed it up with a turn in his most romantically appealing role to date, playing opposite Natalie Wood in the tough and tender love story *Love with the Proper Stranger* (1963). That year McQueen won the best actor award at the Moscow Film Festival for *The Great Escape,* and *Newsweek* called his performance in *Love with the Proper Stranger* "brilliant . . . deserving of an Academy Award." He was featured on the cover of *Life* magazine. Men and women alike found something compelling about the quiet, moody man of honor that the actor seemed to be both onstage and off. After eleven years, McQueen had achieved international stardom. He then formed Solar Productions, through which he could also produce some of his pictures and exert more creative control.

Soldier in the Rain (1963), a comedy, fared poorly at the box office—the film's dramatic elements undermined its comic scenes. His next film, the downbeat drama *Baby, the Rain Must Fall* (1965), proved another disappointment. To escape the frustrations of acting, McQueen threw himself into a heavy schedule of cycling events, taking home five trophies in 1964 alone and turning down several films so that he could race. Determined to prove himself internationally, he accepted a spot on the American team for the International Six-Day Trials in East Germany, a prestigious event. Notoriously averse to the favored attention he received in Hollywood, McQueen was just another competitor in the field, holding his own against world-class riders.

McQueen returned to acting after a year-long break to shoot *The Cincinnati Kid* (1965), about a young poker player trying to defeat the game's champion. The director, Norman Jewison, guided a superb performance from the actor; the poker-table scenes are electric with tension, and McQueen's romantic scenes with the actresses Tuesday Weld and Ann-Margret are equally powerful. The film was an international hit. He next starred in and produced *Nevada Smith* (1966), his first western in years, about a man seeking to avenge his parents' murders. The film's many action scenes involved fist-, gun-, and knife fights as well as chases through swamps. It was a rugged and demanding role for McQueen, who always performed his own stunts.

McQueen's most ambitious film to date, the monumental production *The Sand Pebbles,* was released in 1966. In it he played another loner, a cranky gunboat engineer in 1920s China who dies to save the life of the schoolteacher with whom he has fallen in love. Among the many international honors for his role, McQueen was nominated for the Academy Award for best actor in 1966. The ordinarily scruffy actor then underwent some refining to portray a suave, wealthy intellectual who plans a robbery in *The Thomas Crown Affair* (1968), playing opposite Faye Dunaway. After years of performing his own daredevil stunts, McQueen crashed a sky glider during filming, though only his pride was injured. The film was a hit and broadened his range as an actor.

McQueen went from criminal to cop for the title role in *Bullitt* (1968), which he also produced. In the action-packed film, which became his fifth box-office hit in a row, he played a tough cop investigating a mobster's death. The film's edgy car-chase scene, in which McQueen himself careens through the streets of San Francisco, is a classic. Although he had sworn off comedies after *Soldier in the Rain,* McQueen wanted to do "something fresh," and so

he took a role in the film based on William Faulkner's lighthearted novel *The Reivers* (1969). Again he regretted doing a comedy, though the film was popular. In 1969 McQueen attended the Le Mans twenty-four-hour race in France with his Solar camera crew. They shot thirty thousand feet of footage for a prospective film about the famous event. He had lost the opportunity to do a racing film, *Day of the Champion,* years before, but he had more clout now and was hungry to "make the best damn racing movie ever." *Le Mans* (1971) was a bad decision that cost McQueen millions as well as his marriage—Adams had long disapproved of McQueen's dangerous racing and stunt driving. After years of fighting about the subject, she finally left him.

The 1960s were McQueen's best years. By 1970 he was ranked with John Wayne and Paul Newman as one of the top box-office stars. He went on to make a spate of box-office hits and misses, including *On Any Sunday* (1971), *Junior Bonner* (1972), *The Getaway* (1972), *Papillon* (1973), *The Towering Inferno* (1974), *An Enemy of the People* (1977), *Tom Horn* (1980), and *The Hunter* (1980). In 1971 he married his *Getaway* costar, Ali McGraw; they divorced in 1978. In January 1980 he wed his third wife, Barbara Minty, a model. During the last decade of his life, McQueen gave no interviews. He died of a heart attack while undergoing experimental treatment in Mexico for mesothelioma, a rare lung cancer. McQueen was cremated, and his ashes were scattered over the Pacific Ocean.

★

Biographies of McQueen include William F. Nolan, *McQueen* (1984); Penina Spiegel, *McQueen: The Untold Story of a Bad Boy in Hollywood* (1986); and Neile McQueen Toffel, *My Husband, My Friend* (1986). Obituaries are in the *New York Times* and the *Los Angeles Times* (both 8 Nov. 1980).

BRENNA SANCHEZ

MAILER, Norman Kingsley (*b.* 31 January 1923 in Long Branch, New Jersey), major American writer who became an influential and controversial public figure during the 1960s.

Mailer was one of two children born to Isaac Barnet Mailer, an accountant, and Fanny Schneider, a housekeeper. Mailer's parents immigrated to the United States from the same small Lithuanian town, although his father's family went first to South Africa. After Mailer's birth, the family moved to Brooklyn, settling first in Flatbush and then in Crown Heights. Mailer graduated from Boys' High School in 1939 and went on to Harvard University, receiving a B.S. degree in engineering in 1943. At Harvard he met Beatrice Silverman, who became the first of his six wives when they eloped in January 1944. They had one child, but divorced in 1952.

Norman Mailer. ARCHIVE PHOTOS, INC.

Mailer was drafted into the U.S. Army in 1944 and served as a rifleman in the South Pacific during World War II. Discharged in 1946, he took advantage of the GI Bill and spent two years at the Sorbonne in Paris, focusing on writing. *The Naked and the Dead,* a novel informed by Mailer's combat experience, appeared in 1948 to critical acclaim and became a best-seller. His next two novels, the politically charged *Barbary Shore* (1951) and the sexually charged *Deer Park* (1955), did not fare as well. During the late 1950s Mailer turned to the essay as the narrative form that best allowed him to express his increasingly extreme social and political views. This move galvanized his career, propelling him to the fore of the nation's cultural consciousness during the 1960s.

Mailer's first essay collection, *Advertisements for Myself* (1959), included fragments of fiction, interviews, and polemics, as well as a running autobiographical commentary that offered a no-holds-barred account of his opinions and ambitions. Mailer's audacious autobiographical voice struck a nerve, as did his essays. "The White Negro," originally published in *Dissent* in 1957, generated controversy for defining the "hipster" as a philosophical psychopath who had absorbed the most brutal aspects of black urban experience and could invigorate an otherwise enervated postwar culture. Readers balked at the essay's premises and

violence, but it had a profound influence. In 1967 Eldridge Cleaver, the writer and Black Panther leader, claimed in his book *Soul on Ice* that the essay contained a "solid kernel of truth" that allowed him to "forgive Mailer for his excess of esoteric verbal husk."

In another essay, "Evaluations: Quick and Expensive Comments on Talent in the Room," Mailer ruthlessly evaluated his literary contemporaries, many of them friends, judging their capacity to become "major" American writers. For Mailer, a major writer was one who occupied a prominent place in public life and who could have an impact on the culture in which he or she lived and worked. He dismissed nearly all of his contemporaries according to these criteria, including such highly regarded writers as James Jones, William Styron, Truman Capote, Jack Kerouac, Saul Bellow, J. D. Salinger, Gore Vidal, Ralph Ellison, James Baldwin and—in a footnote—Mary McCarthy. Although he did not hesitate to expose his shortcomings, Mailer was more generous about his own literary talent. Becoming a major writer was his consuming ambition, he announced, and as a writer he would "settle for nothing less than making a revolution in the consciousness of our time." *Advertisements for Myself* was prescient, capturing the social and political tensions that defined the 1960s along with the desire for self-realization that fueled the countercultures to which those tensions gave rise. It also defined Mailer as an unapologetic and politically driven literary contender.

During the early 1960s Mailer honed his journalistic skills, his autobiographical voice, and his flair for public controversy with a series of essays for *Esquire* magazine. His relationship with the magazine was one of his most productive, lasting throughout the decade. Mailer's early essays for *Esquire* covered such diverse topics as the 1960 Democratic National Convention, the suicides of the screen star Marilyn Monroe and the novelist Ernest Hemingway (Mailer's literary idol), the Cuban Missile Crisis (when the Soviets positioned missiles in Cuba), and the 1962 Sonny Liston–Floyd Patterson boxing match in Chicago. Mailer abandoned the journalist's traditionally distanced, objective stance in these essays, choosing instead to report on himself as an active participant in the events he covered. In so doing, he revolutionized the field of journalism, influencing a new generation of writers that eventually came to be known as the "New Journalists." Mailer collected many of the early *Esquire* essays in *The Presidential Papers* (1963), which he published as "open letters" to President John F. Kennedy. With one or two exceptions, the essays were not addressed to the president explicitly, but concerned either "topics a President ought to consider and rarely does" or "topics he considers every day, but rarely in a fashion which is fresh." Mailer's list of such topics included, on the one hand, capital punishment, censorship, the press, the Mafia, the cold war, and totalitarianism and, on the other, architecture, witchcraft, cannibalism, and scatology.

Imbroglios in Mailer's personal life contributed to his growing fame and infamy. During the early 1960s he lived a wild social life in New York and Provincetown, Massachusetts, with his second wife, Adele Morales, an artist whom he had married on 19 April 1954. They had two daughters. In 1960 the couple made headlines and Mailer was committed briefly to Bellevue Hospital after he stabbed Adele with a penknife following a party. They divorced in 1962. In early 1962 Mailer married Lady Jeanne Campbell, who gave birth to a daughter that August. Jeanne divorced Mailer in 1963. In December of that same year, he married for the fourth time, to actress Beverly Bentley. They had two sons. Continuing public squabbles with such writers as James Baldwin, Jim Jones, Norman Podhoretz, William Styron, and Gore Vidal also helped define Mailer's public persona. Not all these squabbles were literary or political in nature. Mailer followed professional boxing and was himself an amateur boxer, often challenging his friends, houseguests, and rivals (both male and female) to spar with him.

In 1964 Mailer returned to fiction with *An American Dream*. The novel was published serially in *Esquire*, requiring Mailer to write eight installments against a deadline. It documents the rise and fall of the fictional Stephen Rojack, a war hero, former congressman, television personality, professor, and public intellectual, who murders his wife and then embarks on a long, odyssean run from the police. The *Esquire* series was a success, in part because some of its more sensational elements corresponded to scandals in Mailer's own life, but *An American Dream* received very mixed reviews when it appeared in book form in 1965. By then, however, Mailer was once again immersed in public life, covering the 1964 Republican National Convention and electrifying an audience of more than 15,000 with his speech during the 1965 antiwar protest organized by the activist Jerry Rubin at the University of California, Berkeley. In 1966 Mailer published a third collection of essays, *Cannibals and Christians*, followed the next year by *Why Are We in Vietnam?*, a short work of experimental fiction that explored the indirect causes of the Vietnam War. Both were generally well received, although some critics complained about the latter's obscenity and violence (exacerbated by the original cover photograph, in which Mailer sports a black eye).

During the mid-1960s Mailer also experimented with drama and film. He staged theatrical productions of *The Deer Park*, including an off-Broadway production that was poorly received by critics but ran for almost 150 performances. Mailer also directed and starred in several films, through which he continued his lifelong exploration into the nature of American masculinity and its relationship to violence. His first film, *Wild 90*, in which Mailer played the leader of a group of gangster hoods, had no script and was shot without retakes over the course of two days and nights in the spring of 1967. In his next film, *Beyond the Law*, he portrayed an Irish police lieutenant whose precinct comes under investigation for brutality. The film, more carefully produced than *Wild 90*, was screened at the New York Film Festival in the fall of 1968 and was generally well received by critics, although it did very poorly in distribution. Mailer's other projects were more arcane. In 1965, for example, he had begun to build an imaginary utopian city in his living room out of Lego blocks, a project he publicized widely in advance in such serious periodicals as *Architectural Forum*. The massive and time-consuming project harked back to Mailer's training as an engineer and reflected his ongoing concerns about how contemporary institutional architecture contributed to social and political ills.

In October 1967 several of Mailer's passions converged when he participated in the anti-Vietnam march on the Pentagon, one of the nation's most symbolic examples of institutional architecture, a formidable structure that the marchers planned to levitate through sheer revolutionary mind power. The night before the march an intoxicated and inspired Mailer appeared at a rally with the poet Robert Lowell, and the next day he was arrested and imprisoned along with hundreds of others. The entire experience formed the basis of one of his most celebrated and important works, *The Armies of the Night* (1968). The first section of the book, titled "The Steps of the Pentagon," originally appeared in the March 1968 issue of *Harper's*, subtitled "The Novel as History." The second section, "The Battle of the Pentagon," was first published in the April 1968 issue of *Commentary*, subtitled "History as Novel." *The Armies of the Night* is in equal parts detailed historical reportage and moving autobiographical meditation, with the overall effect being a relentless inquiry into the boundaries that traditionally separate history from fiction and personal from political experience. Although typically brash and unapologetic, the novel is also a remarkably poignant study of revolutionary protest and the generational ruptures that defined America's self-identity during the 1960s and early 1970s, and won the Pulitzer Prize and the National Book Award. Mailer followed this success with a disastrous third film (the debauched *Maidstone*, which appeared in 1968), but more literary awards followed quickly for *Miami and the Siege of Chicago*, about the violent 1968 Democratic National Convention.

Nevertheless, the decade ended on a sour note for Mailer. In 1969 he ran a spirited but doomed race for mayor of New York, campaigning under the often-censored slogan "No More Bullshit." Mailer's platform was ahead of his time, calling for the establishment of New York City as the nation's fifty-first state, the banning of private automobiles in Manhattan, the legalization of gambling, the institution of state-subsidized day-care centers and nurseries, the provision of free bicycles in city parks and methadone to heroin addicts, and perks for police officers who chose to live in the areas they patrolled. That same year Mailer separated from Bentley, although they did not divorce until 1980.

The turmoil caused by the loss of the election and the failure of his marriage left Mailer in a funk. In his next major work, *Of a Fire on the Moon* (1970), about the Apollo 11 mission, Mailer described his fallen mood, referring to himself in the third person: "He had in fact been left with a huge boredom about himself. He was weary of his own voice, own face, person, persona, will, ideas, speeches, and general sense of importance." Mailer's dissatisfaction was reflected in his unhappiness with his work; although it captivated the nation, the Apollo 11 Moon shot did not fully engage Mailer as a writer.

Nevertheless, the 1960s were arguably Mailer's most productive years, during which he vigorously fused personal experience with public life in ways that not only revolutionized narrative form, but also shaped the nation's cultural and political climate. For Mailer, as for much of the United States, the turbulent decade culminated in January 1970, when he appeared as a witness for the defense in the conspiracy trial of the Chicago Eight—the individuals who had helped staged the general protest at the 1968 Democratic National Convention, which Mailer had covered to grand acclaim in *Miami and the Siege of Chicago.* In 1971 Mailer published *The Prisoner of Sex,* which served as his public response to the women's liberation movement. Throughout the remainder of the 1970s, however, his publication pace slowed, and the focus of his writing altered as he concentrated on a massive novel set in ancient Egypt, which finally appeared in 1983 as *Ancient Evenings.* By the turn of the century Mailer's body of writing spanned more than three dozen books of fiction and nonfiction (with many that continued to trouble the distinction), including the Pulitzer Prize–winning *Executioner's Song* (1979), the celebrated *Harlot's Ghost* (1991), and *The Time of Our Time* (1998), an anthologized survey of his work, life, and times, which are inextricably linked.

Mailer was married to his fifth wife and longtime mistress Carol Stevens for only one day, 7 November 1980. They married to honor their relationship and to publicly acknowledge their daughter, but two hours after the civil ceremony, Mailer flew to Haiti to obtain a divorce, returning the next day. Four days later, on 11 November 1980, he married his sixth wife, the artist Norris Church; they have one child.

Mailer's literary brilliance, coupled with his personal exploits and his outspoken criticism of politics and popular culture, earned him a lasting reputation as one of the twentieth-century America's most notorious talents.

★

Mailer's official biographer is Robert Lucid, whose biography is forthcoming. For a good overview of how Mailer and his work were perceived in the 1960s, see Lucid's compilation *Mailer: The Man and His Work* (1971), as well as Richard Poirier, *Norman Mailer* (1972). Unauthorized biographies include Jennifer Bailey, *Norman Mailer: Quick Change Artist* (1979); Peter Manso, *Mailer: His Life and Times* (1985); Carl Rollyson, *The Lives of Norman Mailer* (1991); and Mary Dearborn, *Mailer: A Biography* (1999).

SHALEANE GEE

MALCOLM X (Malik El-Shabazz) (*b.* 19 May 1925 in Omaha, Nebraska; *d.* 21 February 1965 in New York City), African-American nationalist leader who became the most prominent spokesman of the black separatist Nation of Islam in the early 1960s and later emerged as one of the decade's most militant champions of human rights for black Americans.

Malcolm X was born Malcolm Little, the seventh of itinerant Baptist preacher and black nationalist organizer Earl Little's eight children. The fourth child of his fair-skinned mother, Louise Norton, Malcolm had a similarly light complexion and reddish hair. After white racists torched the

Malcolm X, March 1964. ASSOCIATED PRESS AP

family's house in Lansing, Michigan, the Littles settled in East Lansing in 1929. Two years later Earl Little died after reportedly being attacked by a group of whites. After her husband's death, Louise's mental health gradually deteriorated. In 1939 she suffered a nervous breakdown and was committed to a mental hospital.

Between 1940 and 1941 Malcolm lived in various foster homes in the Lansing area. In early 1942, discouraged by the racist and all-white environment of rural Michigan, he left school after completing the eighth grade and moved to Boston to live with his half-sister Ella Collins. In the following two years Malcolm wandered from job to job and became involved with the underworlds of both Boston and New York City, earning his living peddling drugs, gambling, and pimping. In late 1944 Malcolm organized a burglary gang in Boston. Arrested and convicted of burglary in 1946, he was sentenced to ten years in prison.

While in prison Malcolm converted to the religious teachings of Elijah Muhammad, whose Nation of Islam (NOI) sect merged elements of Islam, Christianity, and black nationalism. Condemning whites as "devils" and calling for a separate African-American state, Muhammad preached black pride, moral uplift, and economic self-reliance. Malcolm adopted the black Muslims' strict rules of moral conduct and began to read ravenously, devouring philosophy, history, and many other subjects. Having become a fervent and highly articulate follower of Muhammad, he was paroled and released from prison in 1952.

After his release Malcolm moved to Detroit, where he became a member of the local NOI's Temple Number One. Shortly thereafter Malcolm received his X, which stood for the lost name of black Muslims' African ancestors. Treated by Muhammad like a son, Malcolm revered the sect's spiritual leader and was determined to spread his pro-black gospel among African Americans. In 1954 he assumed the responsibility for New York's Temple Number Seven. Over the next ten years Malcolm became the NOI's most successful organizer, establishing numerous new Muslim temples across the country. In 1958 Malcolm married Betty Sanders, a member of the New York temple. That same year the first of their six daughters was born.

In July 1959 a Columbia Broadcasting System television (CBS-TV) documentary about the NOI suddenly brought the obscure sect to the attention of the American public. Entitled "The Hate That Hate Produced," the documentary horrified white Americans and triggered a deluge of news stories about Muhammad's organization. *Life, Look, Newsweek,* and *Time* reported extensively about the sect and about Malcolm, its most articulate spokesman. Droves of reporters besieged the young minister, asking him to participate in radio and television panels to discuss the black Muslims' controversial message.

While a nonviolent, student-led sit-in movement ush-

ered in the turbulent 1960s, Malcolm plunged into a marathon of press, radio, and television interviews, talking to *Playboy* journalists as well as to academic audiences at Harvard and Yale. By 1961, chiefly because of Malcolm's tireless recruiting efforts, the NOI's membership had soared from a few hundred to tens of thousands. More than fifty temples—or mosques, as they came to be called after 1961—had been established across the country. Malcolm assumed more and more responsibility within the NOI and became the organization's first National Minister in 1963. Although the black Muslims became increasingly popular among poor African Americans, among whites they conjured up images of a racial Armageddon.

Critical of the black freedom movement of the 1960s, Malcolm denounced the nonviolent philosophy of the civil rights leader Martin Luther King, Jr. In his famous 1963 "Message to the Grass Roots" speech, he attacked King and other civil rights leaders as "modern Uncle Toms" whom the white man manipulated to keep black Americans passive. Rather than loving their enemy, he argued, blacks should rely on the tradition of "an eye for an eye, and a tooth for a tooth" to attain their freedom. Similarly, Malcolm blasted King's goal of integrating African Americans into American society as impractical and unnatural.

Although Malcolm worshipped Muhammad as Allah's messenger, political and doctrinal differences between the two men had become apparent as early as 1960. Despite his attacks on the tactics of the civil rights movement, Malcolm believed that black Muslims ought to participate in demonstrations or at least lend support to the emerging freedom struggle. However, black Muslims were not allowed to engage in politics, and Muhammad had explicitly instructed Malcolm not to assist in civil rights organizations' efforts. The increasing resentment of Muhammad's family toward Malcolm, whom they perceived as a potential threat to Muhammad's power, further intensified the tensions between the two leaders.

Malcolm's faith in Muhammad was seriously shaken in early 1963, when two former secretaries of the NOI's spiritual leader filed paternity suits against him. Prior to these revelations Muhammad had repeatedly excommunicated members of the sect for marital infidelity or similar violations of the NOI's strict moral code. Unsurprisingly, Malcolm felt betrayed by Muhammad, whom he had always believed to be a symbol of morality and spirituality among black Americans, and he began repeatedly to defy Muhammad's orders. At the same time the NOI's leader sought to curtail the increasing power of his National Minister.

Malcolm's comments about the assassination of President John F. Kennedy in late 1963 finally led to the split with the NOI. On 1 December 1963, while speaking to a crowd in New York, Malcolm remarked about Kennedy's death that the slain president "never foresaw that the chickens would come home to roost so soon." Although his statement had referred to the atmosphere of hatred that had made Kennedy's death possible, the mourning American public was outraged. Three days later Muhammad suspended Malcolm from the NOI for ninety days and forbade him to speak to the press or to teach in his New York mosque. Malcolm believed that his suspension was part of a deliberate plot to eliminate him from the Muslim organization. On 1 March 1964 his fears seemed to be confirmed by Muhammad's announcement that his suspension would be indefinite. Seven days later Malcolm disclosed his break with the NOI.

Freed from the shackles of Muhammad's restrictive doctrines, Malcolm intended to use his popularity among poor African Americans and international audiences to assume a leadership position in the black freedom struggle. On 12 March 1964 Malcolm announced the formation of the Muslim Mosque, Inc., designed as the spiritual base of the struggle. Continuing his criticism of the nonviolent civil rights movement, Malcolm told the press that he would attempt to convert African Americans to active armed self-defense against white supremacist terror. Nevertheless, he stressed his organization's willingness to cooperate in local civil rights projects in the South. In addition, the Muslim Mosque would launch a voter registration drive among northern blacks to facilitate black community control.

Malcolm's militant statements articulated the sentiment of many frustrated African Americans in the 1960s, but they frightened white America. His announcement that black men did not "intend to turn the cheek any longer," together with his call upon African Americans to form defensive rifle clubs, led the *New York Times* to denounce him as an "irresponsible demagogue." According to Malcolm nonviolence was simply nonsensical as long as white Americans continued their brutal reign of terror against the southern black freedom movement. He repeatedly declared that blacks should fight for their freedom "by any means necessary." King, whom Malcolm met only once, in late March 1964, disagreed but refused to debate him on this question.

In April 1964, during a pilgrimage, or Hajj, to Mecca, Saudi Arabia, Malcolm began to reconsider some of his convictions. In letters that he sent to friends and fellow black leaders in America, he announced his conversion to orthodox Islam and explained his changed perception of whites. "True Islam," Malcolm wrote to astonished readers, "removes racism" and leads people to "accept each other as brothers and sisters, regardless of differences in complexion." Abandoning Muhammad's "white devil" theory, he began to define whiteness primarily as attitudes and actions, a shift that opened new avenues for cooperation between blacks and certain whites.

After leaving Mecca, Malcolm, or El-Hajj Malik El-Shabazz, as he began to call himself, toured several African

countries. Malcolm was received like a diplomat in Ghana, where he addressed the Ghanian parliament and had a private audience with President Kwame Nkrumah. Crisscrossing the African continent, Malcolm increasingly interpreted the problems of African Americans in the context of a worldwide, Pan-African struggle for human rights and stressed the bonds between black Americans and Africa.

Upon his return to the United States in May 1964, Malcolm announced his intention to bring the case of African Americans before the United Nations. Accusing the United States government of violating black Americans' human rights, he called for an official censure by the United Nations. One month later he declared the formation of another black nationalist organization, the Organization of Afro-American Unity (OAAU), whose secular program encouraged blacks to control their own educational, cultural, economic, and political institutions. Redefining black nationalism, Malcolm had abandoned separatism and instead called for African Americans' philosophical and cultural return to Africa in America.

In July 1964 Malcolm returned to Africa and attended the African summit conference in Cairo, Egypt, as an official representative of his new organization. During the conference Malcolm appealed to the delegates of thirty-four African nations to indict the United States before the United Nations and to pass a strong denunciation of American racism. During his five-month lobbying trip Malcolm had private meetings with numerous African leaders such as President Gamal-Abdel Nasser of Egypt and Kenya's revolutionary leader Jomo Kenyatta.

Despite the failure of Malcolm's campaign, the U.S. government grew increasingly concerned about the outspoken militant, whose verbal assaults tarnished America's reputation in the cold war rivalry with the Soviet Union. The Federal Bureau of Investigation (FBI) and the Central Intelligence Agency (CIA) stepped up their surveillance of Malcolm, which had begun in the 1950s. Infiltrating the Muslim Mosque and the OAAU, the FBI eventually compiled over 2,300 pages of material on the controversial black leader.

After his return from the second Africa trip in November 1964, Malcolm attempted to establish a working relationship with the civil rights movement. He often spoke with activists from the Student Nonviolent Coordinating Committee, and on 4 February 1965 he made a speech in Selma, Alabama, where King and his Southern Christian Leadership Conference were staging nonviolent demonstrations for new voting rights legislation.

While Malcolm was still redefining his ideas and beliefs in early 1965, his relations to the NOI grew more hostile. His repeated revelations about Muhammad's extramarital affairs and the black Muslims' secret contacts with the Ku Klux Klan made Malcolm a major target for constant harassment and death threats by the NOI. On the night of 14 February 1965 Malcolm and his family survived a fire-bomb attack on their house in East Elmhurst, Queens. Amid this atmosphere of daily threats, an exhausted Malcolm told reporters of his feeling that his death was near.

On 21 February 1965, during an OAAU meeting in the Audubon Ballroom in New York City's Harlem neighborhood, Malcolm was murdered by several gunmen. Over three decades after the conviction of three assailants for Malcolm's murder, scholars continue to debate whether the NOI or the American government, in particular the FBI and CIA, were responsible for his death. He is buried at Ferncliff Cemetery in Hartsdale, New York.

The significance of Malcolm became apparent only after his death. While still incomplete by the time of his murder, his black nationalist philosophy became the most important reference point for the emerging Black Power movement, which dominated the second half of the 1960s. His ideas on black pride, black political and economic advancement, and Pan-Africanism influenced an entire generation of militant African-American activists. Even beyond the 1960s many young blacks revered Malcolm as the epitome of black self-respect. The African-American actor Ossie Davis spoke for many when he remarked during the slain leader's funeral, "And if you knew him you would know why we must honor him: Malcolm was our manhood, our living, black manhood!"

★

The Autobiography of Malcolm X (1965) remains one of the most impressive accounts of the life of Malcolm X. Useful biographies include Peter Louis Goldman, *The Death and Life of Malcolm X* (2nd ed., 1979); Eugene Wolfenstein, *The Victims of Democracy: Malcolm X and the Black Revolution* (1981); and the controversial Bruce Perry, *Malcolm: The Life of a Man Who Changed Black America* (1991). Robert L. Jenkins and Mfanya Donald Tryman, eds., *The Malcolm X Encyclopedia* (2002), provides information on virtually every aspect of his life. Clayborne Carson, *Malcolm X: The FBI File* (1991), contains additional biographical information and reveals the extent of governmental surveillance.

SIMON WENDT

MANCHESTER, William Raymond (*b.* 1 April 1922 in Attleboro, Massachusetts), reporter, historian, and biographer best known for his controversial and award-winning book *The Death of a President: November 20–November 25, 1963* (1967), which examines the days surrounding the assassination of John F. Kennedy.

Manchester was the first of two sons of William Raymond Manchester, a social worker, and Sallie E. R. Thompson Manchester, a homemaker. After graduating from high school in

1940, Manchester attended the University of Massachusetts, majoring in English. World War II interrupted his studies, and he served with the U.S. Marine Corps from 2 July 1942 until 24 October 1945, achieving the rank of sergeant. He was decorated with the Purple Heart. After discharge Manchester returned to his studies and graduated with a B.A. in 1946; he was the class valedictorian.

Following graduation Manchester enrolled at the University of Missouri and completed an M.A. in English, devoting his thesis to the life and works of H. L. Mencken, the newspaper columnist and essayist. Working on the thesis necessitated a correspondence with Mencken that grew into a friendship. The thesis was the basis of Manchester's first book, *Disturber of the Peace: The Life of H. L. Mencken* (1951). After graduating in 1947 Manchester, with Mencken's support, went to work at the *Baltimore Sun,* initially as a police reporter. Manchester married Julia Brown Marshall, a newspaperwoman, on 27 March 1948; they had three children.

At the *Sun,* Manchester was promoted to Washington correspondent, then foreign correspondent, traveling in England and throughout Europe, the Middle East, and Southeast Asia, interviewing a number of heads of state. In 1953 he was a war correspondent with the French in North Vietnam. Manchester left the *Sun* in 1954 to serve as a confidential secretary to Mencken, who had become an invalid due to a stroke. After Mencken's death, Manchester relocated to Middletown, Connecticut, to work as the managing editor of Wesleyan University Press.

Manchester wrote four novels, but only the first, *The City of Anger* (1953), was well received. With the biography *A Rockefeller Family Portrait: From John D. to Nelson* (1959), Manchester was more successful, but it was his *Portrait of a President: John F. Kennedy in Profile* (1962) that achieved critical success. In *The Writer's Voice* (1973), Manchester comments on the importance of finding the right questions to intrigue the subject of an interview. His first interview with Kennedy was supposed to last for ten minutes; it took three-and-a-half hours. The fact that Kennedy enjoyed Manchester's company and respected him as a historian was important to the Kennedy family in the selection of who would write a historical account of the president's death.

Following Kennedy's assassination in November 1963, it became apparent to the Kennedy family that one complete and undistorted record of the event would be preferable to several historically inaccurate accounts. Manchester was not their first choice for the project. It was Theodore H. White, who wrote about Kennedy's campaign in *The Making of the President, 1960* (1961), but he declined. Their next choice was Walter Lord, the author of *A Night to Remember* (1955), about the sinking of the *Titanic,* and *Day of Infamy* (1957), about the attack on Pearl Harbor; Lord said he would think about it. On 5 February 1964 Man-

William Manchester, January 1969. © BETTMANN/CORBIS

chester was asked to write the book, and he jumped at the opportunity. Before beginning the project, Manchester was required to sign a memorandum stipulating that both the president's wife, Jacqueline, and his brother Robert had the right to review the manuscript, and that it would not be published without their approval.

In researching the book, Manchester conducted more than 1,000 interviews. Marina Oswald refused to be interviewed, but Jacqueline Kennedy spoke with Manchester for ten hours. Using a tape recorder, he was able to extract information, facts, thoughts, and emotions still fresh in people's minds. He read a year's worth of Dallas newspapers to research the attitude of Texans toward Kennedy. Writing in longhand, working 100 hours a week, massing detail upon detail, Manchester built his book. On 8 March 1966 the first draft was completed, and the problems began. Rather than reading the book themselves, Robert and Jacqueline Kennedy had others read it on their behalf. A legal battle ensued that finally ended with two out-of-court settlements: one with *Look* magazine, which had purchased the rights to serialize the book for $665,000 (the highest bid to date for serialization rights to a book), and the other with the book's publisher, Harper and Row. Claiming breach of contract, the Kennedys did not want the book published in any form. Nevertheless, after Manchester deleted 1,600 words from the text (about seven pages), the book was published on 7 April 1967.

Some critics were disturbed by the massive accumulation of detail and Manchester's idolization of President Kennedy, but the public loved the book. It sold 1.3 million copies. The reviewer Eliot Fremont-Smith of the *New York*

Times wrote, "As a historical document the value of *The Death of a President* cannot seriously be challenged. Never before has the family of a slain leader been so willing to serve history as the Kennedys have." Manchester donated the bulk of his profits from the book to the Kennedy Library.

Following the publication of *The Death of a President,* Manchester resumed work on a previous project, a biography of the Krupps, *The Arms of Krupp, 1587–1968* (1968). Since childhood Manchester had been intrigued by men of power, which was apparent in his choice of biographical subjects. Notable examples, in addition to his books on Kennedy and Mencken, are *American Caesar: Douglas MacArthur, 1880–1964* (1978), *The Last Lion: Winston Spencer Churchill, Volume 1: Visions of Glory: 1874–1932* (1983), and *The Last Lion: Winston Spencer Churchill, Volume 2: Alone: 1932–1940* (1987). The planned volume three on Churchill was not written. After the death of his wife in 1998, Manchester suffered two strokes that affected his ability to write. In an interview Manchester said, "Language for me came as easily as breathing for fifty years, and I can't do it any more."

Manchester's book on the assassination of President Kennedy recaptures the events of the 1960s. It brings to life not only the facts but the emotions shared by those glued to their television sets or on their knees in churches and outside U.S. embassies around the world. The book is history, but it is also a reflection of a nation in mourning.

★

Full coverage of *The Death of a President,* both the writing of the book and the legal problems with the Kennedys, is covered in

John Corry, *The Manchester Affair* (1967). A discussion of Manchester's writing techniques is in George Garrett, ed., *The Writer's Voice: Conversations with Contemporary Writers* (1973), conducted by John Graham. Reviews of *The Death of a President* are Eliot Fremont-Smith, "At Last, the Whole Book—And Worth Having," *New York Times* (3 Apr. 1967), and Tom Wicker, "November 22, 1963," *New York Times* (9 Apr. 1967). More recent biographical material is Dexter Filkins, "No End in Sight," *Sydney Morning Herald* (11 Oct. 2001).

MARCIA B. DINNEEN

MANCINI, Henry Nicola (*b.* 16 April 1924 in Cleveland, Ohio; *d.* 14 June 1994 in Los Angeles, California), composer, conductor, and arranger who brought new styles to film and television music; successful recording artist and concert performer; and winner of numerous awards for his compositions during the 1960s.

Born Enrico Nicola Mancini, his first name anglicized to Henry, Mancini was the son of Italian immigrants Quinto Mancini, a steelworker, and Anna Pece, a homemaker. He grew up in Aliquippa, Pennsylvania, where his father, an amateur musician, taught him to play the piccolo and flute. By his teens Mancini was studying music seriously, and upon graduating from high school he briefly attended the Juilliard School of Music in New York City, in 1942, al-

Henry Mancini, 1963. CORBIS CORPORATION (BELLEVUE)

though his academic career was cut short by World War II. After serving in the U.S. Army in Europe he joined the Glenn Miller Orchestra in 1946 as a pianist and arranger. There he met Virginia (Ginny) O'Connor, a singer with the band, whom he married on 13 September 1947; they had a son and twin daughters.

Based in Los Angeles, Mancini spent the late 1940s and 1950s studying music at the Westlake School of Music and privately with Ernst Krenek, Dr. Alfred Sendry, and Mario Castelnuovo-Tedesco, working his way up as a composer for film studios. In 1958 the director Blake Edwards hired him to write the score for a new television series, *Peter Gunn;* this inaugurated a long, productive relationship between the two. Mancini's themes mixed in elements of jazz and rock and roll, attracting immediate attention for their contemporary feel, and Ray Anthony had a Top Ten hit with the show's theme in February 1959. Meanwhile, Mancini signed a contract with RCA Victor Records that turned out to be a major coup. While other film and television composers saw their work released on a soundtrack album that prominently displayed the title but not the name of the composer, Mancini's screen work began to appear on albums under his name. The first of these, *The Music from Peter Gunn,* won the Grammy Award for album of the year in 1958, hit number one in February 1959, and earned a gold record. It was quickly followed by *More Music from Peter Gunn,* a Top Ten hit.

This was the beginning of a long string of 1960s successes for Mancini. *Mr. Lucky,* a television series that premiered during the 1959–1960 season, led to the Top Ten *Music from Mr. Lucky* album, a Top Forty "Mr. Lucky" single, and two more Grammy Awards. Mancini wrote exclusively for film for the rest of the decade. In addition to the albums of his film music, he recorded music written by others. Many of these albums reached the charts, but his own compositions were much more successful. In 1961 Mancini scored Edwards's *Breakfast at Tiffany's,* and his album of the film's music topped the charts and went gold. "Moon River," its theme song, cowritten with lyricist Johnny Mercer, was a Top Ten hit for both Mancini and Jerry Butler (who recorded separate versions of the song). The song became better known as the signature song of Andy Williams, who sang it under the film's credits and at the Academy Awards ceremony, where it won the Oscar for best song. Mancini also won for best score. In addition, "Moon River" won the Grammy Award for song of the year, and Mancini's recording of the song won record of the year in 1961.

In 1962 Mancini reached the Top Ten with his album of music from the film *Hatari!* and in 1963 he continued his success with his and Mercer's theme song from Edwards's *Days of Wine and Roses,* which won both the Academy Award for best song and the Grammy for song of the year, while his single recording won the Grammy for record of the year. Mancini did not record an album for *Days of Wine and Roses,* but Andy Williams did, and it hit number one and went gold.

Mancini focused more on recordings in 1963, reaching the Top Ten with *Our Man in Hollywood* and *Uniquely Mancini.* But his and Mercer's theme from *Charade* was another Oscar nominee, and his *Charade* album was another Top Ten hit. He scored five films released in 1964, among them Edwards's first two movies in the *Pink Panther* series (*The Pink Panther* and *A Shot in the Dark*), and his delightful "*The Pink Panther* Theme" became one of his best-known compositions; his recording of it, a Top Forty hit, won three Grammys, and his *Pink Panther* album reached the Top Ten and went gold. Another 1964 release was *Dear Heart,* with a title song, cowritten with lyricists Jay Livingston and Ray Evans, that produced Top Forty hits for Andy Williams and Jack Jones and earned Grammy and Oscar nominations. Mancini's album *Dear Heart and Other Songs About Love* was another Top Ten entry.

With the ascendance of rock in the wake of the Beatles, Mancini's record sales began to dip in the mid-1960s, but he maintained a busy schedule of scoring, recording, and live performances that resulted in more chart entries and numerous award nominations. In June 1969 he returned to the top of the charts with his million-selling recording of Nino Rota's "Love Theme from *Romeo and Juliet*," from the album *A Warm Shade of Ivory,* which hit the Top Ten and went gold. *Six Hours Past Sunset,* released that fall, was his twenty-fifth album to reach the charts in the decade.

Mancini continued to work prolifically for the rest of his life. By the end of the 1960s his film scores were starting to appear on conventional soundtrack albums, while he continued to record an average of three albums a year. In 1970, counting soundtracks, he released eight new albums. That year he won his twentieth Grammy, a total second only to Quincy Jones's among nonclassical recording artists. Mancini won his fourth Academy Award in 1982 for his song score to *Victor/Victoria,* directed by Edwards and starring Edwards's wife Julie Andrews. In the early 1990s Mancini cut back on his film and television work as he and Edwards prepared a stage adaptation of *Victor/Victoria,* which was incomplete when Mancini died of pancreatic cancer. The show opened on Broadway in 1995, again starring Andrews, and had a healthy run, the cast album posthumously earning Mancini his seventy-third Grammy nomination.

★

Mancini's autobiography is *Did They Mention the Music?* (1989), written with Gene Lees. A good critical appreciation of Mancini as a film composer is in William Darby and Jack Du Bois, *American Film Music: Major Composers, Techniques, Trends,* *1915–1990* (1990), in which he rates his own chapter and his photo on the cover. An obituary is in the *New York Times* (1 June 1994).

WILLIAM RUHLMANN

MANSON, Charles Milles (*b.* 12 November 1934 in Cincinnati, Ohio), musician, lifetime criminal, and charismatic leader of a group of hippies known as the Family, who, after a series of murders in 1969, became a symbol of the decade's dark side.

Manson was the illegitimate child of a promiscuous sixteen-year-old alcoholic girl—perhaps a prostitute—named Kathleen Maddox. In a 1937 child-support suit, the court of Boyd County, Kentucky, named Colonel Scott (no other name given) as his legal father. Maddox's brief marriage to an older man, William Manson, gave Manson his name. When Maddox was jailed in 1939 for robbing a service station, Manson went to stay with his religious aunt and uncle. After his mother's parole in 1942, he lived rootlessly with her and her alcoholic lovers. In 1947 Manson was sent to the Gibault School for Boys in Terre Haute, Indiana; after ten months he ran away, beginning his own life of crime and incarceration.

Manson was inescapably shaped by years in penal in-

Charles Manson. ARCHIVE PHOTOS, INC.

stitutions, beginning with a conviction for burglary at age twelve and progressing through auto theft, forgery, and pimping. Small and weak-looking, Manson learned to manipulate others. Between prison sentences, he married twice: to seventeen-year-old Rosalie Jean Willis in January 1955 (divorced 1958) and to a prostitute named Leona in late 1959 (divorced 10 April 1963). He had one child by each marriage. Manson was released from Terminal Island in Los Angeles County on 21 March 1967 into a world that had changed a great deal during his incarceration. With permission, he relocated to San Francisco, which was just entering the "Summer of Love," a supposed counterculture new dawn that brought the young and innocent to San Francisco from all over the world in the summer of 1967. Although he was already in his thirties and a career criminal, Manson was otherwise as naive as the teenagers to whom he gravitated. In prison an aging member of Ma Barker's gang of robbers and kidnappers, Alvin ("Creepy") Karpis, had taught Manson to play guitar. In the Haight-Ashbury district of San Francisco, a hippie haven, Manson was stunned and delighted to find that playing the role of a gentle musician could bring him food, a place to stay, and all the sex he wanted.

With the methods of a pimp and the goals of a messiah, Manson developed a hodgepodge philosophy. Many values were clear: freedom, spirituality, self-expression, and a genuine if simplistic dedication to Earth's ecology. The details were vague enough to be applied as needed. Thus, Manson assembled what has been called "the Family." Playing guitar on the Berkeley campus of the University of California, Manson met Mary Brunner and immediately moved in with her. Near Venice Beach, he picked up Lynnette Fromme, also known as "Squeaky." Manson received a suspended sentence for helping Ruth Ann Morehouse, then fourteen, leave her family.

Doubtless, Manson controlled those he attracted, but he also learned from them. For instance, the writer Ed Sanders mentions Manson's fondness for *Stranger in a Strange Land,* a satirical science-fiction novel by Robert A. Heinlein. Actually, Manson barely read at the seventh-grade level, though certainly he incorporated many ideas when he heard them. Manson also learned from religious groups throughout California, from Scientology to the Process Church. He was changed by taking LSD, and he learned to use the drug to influence others. Manson also maintained contact with fellow criminals. At the home of one, he met Patricia Krenwinkle, age eighteen, who soon quit her job to join Manson and "Charlie's girls," traveling throughout the Pacific Coast in a Volkswagen van. In September 1967, twenty-five-year-old Bruce Davis became Manson's first male follower.

If ever there was a true hippie movement, by this time it was considered to be dying, turned into a media shuck at precisely the time that Manson's group grew and took shape. They exchanged the van for a black school bus. Soon Bobby Beausoleil, Susan Atkins (also known as Sadie Mae Glutz), Dianne ("the Snake") Lake, Sandra Good, Cathy ("Gypsy") Share, and others joined the traveling commune. Manson and his group also made wealthy and famous friends—though exactly who these friends were is often a matter of dispute and a subject of gossip. Certainly, he befriended both Dennis Wilson of the Beach Boys and Terry Melcher, a record producer and the son of Doris Day. Manson sought help for his music career, but the only concrete result was one song on the Beach Boys' album *20/20.* The entire troupe stayed with Wilson for months in 1968, where they met and were joined by Charles ("Tex") Watson.

After travels in the school bus and various stopovers, in August 1968 the group settled at the Spahn Movie Ranch in Chatsworth, California. The owner, George Spahn, elderly and mostly blind, was pacified by Squeaky Fromme as his private attendant. Life was both tough and idyllic: living in shacks, eating food from dumpsters, using stolen credit cards. The group also sang and made polymorphous perverse love every night. Some four children were born, at least one fathered by Manson. Manson and others spent time elsewhere—including Canoga Park and Death Valley—but were living at the Spahn ranch when they committed their infamous murders.

Just after midnight on 9 August 1969, Tex Watson drove a car, also containing Linda Kasabian, Patricia ("Katie") Krenwinkle, and Susan Atkins, to 10050 Cielo Drive. Manson knew the house from his friendship with Terry Melcher, though the inhabitants were new: Sharon Tate, an actress and the wife of the director Roman Polanski, and her friends, Abigail Folger, Wojtek Frykowski, and Jay Sebring. A visitor named Steve Parent also was killed, though the caretaker Bill Garretson, in another building, survived. The murders went beyond gruesome— a symphony of stabbings and shootings—the killers wrote "PIG" on the wall in blood.

The next night, the group attacked 3267 Waverly Drive, the home of Leno and Rosemary LaBianca. Manson himself joined Watson, Atkins, Krenwinkle, Kasabian, Leslie Van Houten, and Steven Grogan, also known as "Clem," though it is uncertain whether he actually participated in the violence. They used the LaBiancas' carving knife and left the carving fork stuck in Leno's abdomen. They also carved "WAR" in his stomach and again wrote on the wall in blood: "DEATH TO PIGS," "RISE," and "HEALTER SKELTER." (The last phrase was a misspelling of "Helter Skelter.") Afterward, they ate from the LaBiancas' refrigerator.

Commentators still debate the group's motivation. The

prosecutor Vincent Bugliosi later convinced a jury that Manson planned to ignite a race war, after which the blacks would turn power over to Manson. His inspiration allegedly had come from the Beatles' eponymous 1968 release, best known as "the White Album," which contained such songs as "Helter Skelter," "Blackbird," "Piggies," and the frightening "Revolution 9." More practically, Bobby Beausoleil had just been arrested for killing Gary Hinman over a drug deal, and some of the women thought that other murders, blamed on blacks, could help Beausoleil seem innocent. Certainly, the murders were an ultimate expression of the group's togetherness and their hatred of Earth-destroying corporate America; they were also Manson's revenge on the world of celebrity that represented the success he hoped his own music would bring.

The trial—a media circus and the longest trial in California history at the time—dragged on for over nine months. Manson's shenanigans in the courtroom included holding up a newspaper with the headline "MANSON GUILTY, NIXON DECLARES" so that the jury could see it, thus very nearly bringing about a mistrial. On 25 January 1971 Manson was found guilty of first-degree murder. He and others received death sentences, commuted to life imprisonment when California law changed. Theoretically eligible for parole, Manson settled in for permanent incarceration. In 1985 a fellow inmate, Jan Holmstrom, doused Manson with paint thinner and set him ablaze, but Manson recovered. After transfer from San Quentin in 1989, Manson continued to write letters and give television interviews from Corcoran State Prison in Corcoran, California.

Many social critics see Manson's group as an inevitable dark outgrowth of counterculture life and goals. While Manson found a ready pool of followers among the runaways and the stoned revolutionaries of love, his actions were as determined by the lessons of prison life and basic human nature as they were by his times. Most important, the murders crystallized fears concerning class struggle and the revolt of the young, putting a leering face to the general discomfort among the middle class and wealthy and helping increase the cultural climate of division and fear between the classes and generations.

★

Nikolas Schreck, ed., *The Manson File* (1988), provides original writing and art by Manson, a useful (and opinionated) annotated bibliography, and information on Manson's life and impact since the murders. Manson himself has criticized *Manson in His Own Words,* as told to Nuel Emmons (1986), but its insights are invaluable. The two major books by others have their own agendas and complement each other: Ed Sanders, *The Family: The Story of Charles Manson's Dune Buggy Attack Battalion* (1971), and Vincent Bugliosi, *Helter Skelter: The True Story of the Manson Murders*

(1974). Susan Atkins and Tex Watson each wrote an account of life with Manson as well as their conversion to Christianity in prison: respectively, *Child of Satan, Child of God* (1977) and *Will You Die for Me?* (1978).

BERNADETTE LYNN BOSKY

MANTLE, Mickey Charles (*b.* 20 October 1931 in Spavinaw, Oklahoma; *d.* 13 August 1995 in Dallas, Texas), baseball player and sportswriter who won three Most Valuable Player awards and a Triple Crown during an eighteen-year career with the New York Yankees. Mantle was an outstanding center fielder who was considered the best switch-hitter in the history of Major League Baseball.

Mantle was the eldest of five children of Elvin Clark Mantle, a miner, and Lovell Richardson Mantle, a homemaker. Named after his father's favorite baseball player, the major league catcher Mickey Cochrane, Mantle, as a little boy, learned to switch-hit (hit from either side of home plate) by batting left-handed against pitches thrown by his grandfather and right-handed against pitches thrown by his father. Mantle graduated from Commerce High School in 1949 and quickly signed with the New York Yankees. He began his minor league career as a shortstop; although his

Mickey Mantle. ARCHIVE PHOTOS, INC.

fielding was poor, his hitting was superb. When he went to spring training in 1951 with the Yankees, Mantle was placed in right field. He was sent down to the minors for striking out too often, only to be brought back up because he hit well in the minors; he played in ninety games during the regular season. On 23 December 1951 Mantle married Merlyn Louise Johnson; they had four sons.

In 1952 Mantle became the regular center fielder for the Yankees, replacing the legendary Joe DiMaggio. Expectations for him were high, and the pressure unnerved him. When he failed to live up to expectations, the hometown fans booed him. In center field his swiftness enabled him to make spectacular plays, and he had a strong throwing arm. Mantle struck out 111 times that season, but his batting average was .311. In 1953 he scored 105 runs, for the first of nine straight seasons in which he scored more than 100 runs. By that year Mantle was drinking heavily, going out to bars after games with friends, usually the shortstop Billy Martin and the pitcher Whitey Ford. Martin helped Mantle a great deal by explaining the strategies of baseball, but their long nights of drinking took a heavy toll on Mantle. Sometimes he would not sleep at all and would show up for a game barely able to stand up. Furthermore, injuries took their toll: damaged knees, torn muscles, and osteomyelitis (infection within the bone) slowed him down and made every game painful.

Despite all these obstacles and handicaps, Mantle had one of the greatest seasons ever in 1956, when he won the American League Triple Crown with fifty-two home runs, 130 runs batted in, and a .353 batting average. He also led the league with 132 runs scored and a slugging average of .705. It was a season in which Mantle challenged the best years of Babe Ruth, and it established him as one of the best players of his era. In 1957 Mantle had another outstanding season, scoring 122 runs, with a batting average of .365 and an on-base percentage of .512, figures that challenged those of Ted Williams, the Boston Red Sox Hall-of-Famer. Mantle was elected the American League's Most Valuable Player (MVP) for 1956 and 1957. Even so, fans continued to boo him. He had developed a reputation for surliness, because he shied away from reporters as well as from the crowds he drew almost everywhere he went.

His teammates saw Mantle in a different light: he was witty and fun loving, and they knew he lived with constant pain. As the 1960s dawned, Mantle was losing the cartilage in his knees. He played in several World Series for the Yankees, and he was among the players most responsible for winning the league championships. During one World Series, he had an abscess on his hip and underwent surgery that cut a four-by-two-inch hole all the way down to the bone. He insisted on playing, even though his teammates could see blood seeping from his wound. After hitting a home run and hobbling around the bases, even the fans could see the blood soaking his uniform.

In 1960 the Yankees traded with the Kansas City Athletics to acquire Roger Maris. Maris was a big left-handed batter who threw right-handed and who was even more withdrawn in public than Mantle. Mantle had a fine year, but the American League's MVP award that year went to Maris. In 1961 the two men staged one of the greatest competitions in the history of baseball. By the middle of the season, both Mantle and Maris were hitting home runs at a furious pace, and sportswriters speculated on whether the men would break Babe Ruth's record of sixty home runs in a season, set in 1927. Fans now cheered Mantle, but booed Maris. Then Mantle was injured, and the race belonged to Maris. Mantle took Maris under his wing and tried to help him relax, but Maris started losing his hair from the stress. Mantle led the league with 132 runs scored and hit fifty-four home runs. Maris hit sixty-one home runs and was voted MVP once again.

Although he played only 123 games in 1962, Mantle received the MVP award that year for a batting average of .314, a slugging average of .622, and an on-base average of .486. In spring 1962, in a game against the Minnesota Twins, Mantle hit a hard bouncer to the shortstop and ran toward first base like a bat out of hell; about halfway to first base he collapsed. Witnesses say that he did not slow down at all before falling, that one moment he was running and the next he dropped straight down. He had torn the upper hamstring in his right leg and, while falling, had torn ligaments in his left ankle. Although it could have been a career-ending injury, in weeks Mantle was back in the lineup, toughing out the pain.

By 1964 it was becoming clear that Mantle's athletic skills were eroding. Although he was only thirty-two years old, his speed had declined, and every swing of the bat caused him pain. He compensated by using the baseball savvy he had picked up over the years. Moreover, he was team leader, quietly explaining strategy to young players and making a point of knowing the names of the rookies to help them feel comfortable in the major leagues. Before the beginning of the 1966 season Mantle was playing touch football with a couple of his brothers and injured his right shoulder. Bone chips were removed from Mantle's shoulder, enabling him to play during the 1966 season, but he could no longer throw well. Opposing players soon realized this and would try to take an extra base when Mantle threw the ball. In 1967 Mantle was made the Yankees' first baseman, where his weak arm would be less of a liability. He struggled to master the position, and became a fine fielder at first base.

After the 1968 season Mantle took his time deciding whether to play in 1969. The pain had become too much for him, and he chose to retire. In 1974, during Mantle's first year of eligibility, he was elected unanimously to the Baseball Hall of Fame, inducted along with his friend Whitey Ford. Mantle had not spent his money wisely while he was a ballplayer, and he needed to work. He made television commercials and, with Whitey Ford, wrote the popular *Whitey and Mickey: A Joint Autobiography of the Yankee Years,* published in 1977. He also wrote articles for *Sports Illustrated.* In 1979 Mantle took a job as a greeter at a gambling casino, for which he was suspended from organized baseball for several years. Organized baseball had a strict rule against anyone affiliated with the game associating with gamblers of any kind. His suspension meant that Mantle was no longer allowed to coach baseball or to attend any baseball functions, including old-timers games and reunions of ballplayers. During the 1980s he often expressed regret about how he had conducted himself while playing in the major leagues. As great a player as he was, he believed that he could have been even better had he taken better care of his physical condition.

In the early 1990s Mantle stopped drinking alcohol; he remarked that he liked being sober. Nonetheless, his many years of alcohol abuse gave him cirrhosis of the liver and probably led to the liver cancer that eventually killed him. Although he underwent a liver transplant, the liver cancer came back; he died at the age of sixty-three. Mantle is buried in Sparkman-Hillcrest Cemetery in Dallas. No other switch-hitter has hit as well as Mantle. He had a powerful stroke from both sides of the plate, and he hit for high batting averages and home run totals. He was a smart base runner who managed to steal a base when needed, even though his injured knees cost him speed.

During his years with the Yankees, Mantle was one of baseball's best-loved players, and his Oklahoma drawl became familiar from numerous radio interviews, helping to generate the image that baseball was pastoral, played by country children, although baseball really was an urban game through most of its history. In the years after his retirement, Mantle became an example of what not to do if a player hopes to have a long career. Mantle himself admitted that he could have been an even better player if he had tried to stay in good physical shape, not overindulged in alcohol, and paid attention to his manager to improve his understanding of the game.

★

Mantle's autobiography, *The Education of a Baseball Player* (1967), emphasizes a recurring theme in Mantle's writings and interviews: his feeling that he was chronically unprepared for events in his career. *Whitey and Mickey: A Joint Autobiography of the Yankee Years* (1977), written with Edward (Whitey) Ford and Joseph Durso, tells of the happy times Whitey Ford and Mantle spent together. Herb Gluck, *The Mick* (1985), is the most satisfying biography. Mickey Merlin, Jr., Dan Mantle, and Mickey

Herskowitz, *A Hero All His Life: A Memoir by the Mantle Family* (1996), is a tribute to Mantle that records his private life, with information on Mantle's last several years not to be found elsewhere. David Falkner, *The Last Hero: The Life of Mickey Mantle* (1995), is a good account of how Mantle the private man and Mantle the public man were often in conflict. An obituary is in the *New York Times* (14 Aug. 1995).

KIRK H. BEETZ

MARCUSE, Herbert (*b.* 19 July 1898 in Berlin, Germany; *d.* 29 July 1979 in Starnberg, Germany), philosopher, social theorist, educator, and author whose doctrines advanced the radical social theory of the 1960s, contributing to the revolutionary impetus for the cultural and political radicalism of the New Left and the anti-imperialistic revolts of the Third World.

Marcuse was born into an upper-class German-Jewish family. His father was Carl Marcuse, a businessman, and his mother was Gertrud Kreslawsky, a homemaker. Although alienation from one's authentic self represented the essence of Marcuse's philosophy, he described his childhood as free from alienation. Marcuse's radicalism appeared early in his

Herbert Marcuse. CORBIS CORPORATION (BELLEVUE)

life. During World War I, from 1916 to 1918, Marcuse served in the German army. Poor eyesight kept him in the homeland without seeing military action. He joined the Social Democratic Party in 1917 but resigned in 1918 following allegations that the German government, led by Social Democrats, was responsible for the murder of the Communist leaders Rosa Luxembourg and Karl Liebnecht.

The year 1918 had a major impact on both modern Germany and the young Marcuse. Social upheaval swept the country. Near year's end Marcuse joined a soldier's council, his initial encounter with political activism. While he was sympathetic to the council's intentions, Marcuse spoke of personal disillusionment because of the reticence of younger soldiers to assume leadership. Their passivity allowed the reelection of the old guard. Also in 1918 Marcuse began studying at the University of Berlin, later transferring to the University of Freiburg, where he received his Ph.D. in literature in 1922 and, continuing until 1928, in postgraduate studies in philosophy under Martin Heidegger. Marcuse's early ideas on politics, art, and philosophy developed into those valued by a 1960s counterculture, and he became a visionary for the New Left.

In 1932 Marcuse's first major book in German, *Hegel's Ontology and Theory of Historicity,* garnered respect from contemporary European philosophers. The following year he joined the Institute of Social Research in Frankfurt, founded in 1923 by his lifelong friends Theodor Adorno and Max Horkheimer. Owing to Nazi repression, the institute closed that year, and Marcuse fled to Geneva. In 1934 Marcuse immigrated to the United States, reopened the institute at Columbia University in New York City, and lectured until 1940, the year in which he became a naturalized U.S. citizen. He published *Reason and Revolution: Hegel and the Rise of Social Theory* in 1941, providing an explanation of the concepts of the idealist philosopher Georg Wilhelm Hegel for American students. Hegel's ideas emphasized reason, rather than romantic intuitionism.

From 1941 to 1944, during World War II, Marcuse worked in intelligence on the staff of the U.S. Department of State. From 1946 to 1950 he served as the chief of the Central European section for the Office of Intelligence Research. Marcuse viewed his efforts as retaliation against the repression generated by fascism. He resumed teaching after his civil service and was a respected and popular philosophy professor. He held posts at Columbia University (1951–1952); Harvard University in Cambridge, Massachusetts (1952–1953); Brandeis University in Waltham, Massachusetts (1954–1965); and the University of California, San Diego, at La Jolla (1965–1970), where he retired.

During the civil rights and antiwar movements against the Vietnam conflict in the 1960s, Marcuse's "power of negative thinking" became the standard for revolutionary speech in the movement he called the "Great Refusal." His devotees included the African-American radical Angela Davis, from Brandeis University. Countless students read his books. New Left marchers carried posters of his face, along with images of the Chinese communist leader Mao Tse Tung, the Argentinean guerrilla leader Che Guevara, and the Vietnamese president Ho Chi Minh. Marcuse shared a healthy criticism of the Nazi period with West German students.

Underground newspapers touted Marcuse. The *Los Angeles Free Press* described him as one of the most beautiful men in the world. In 1969 Frankfurt students cranked out leaflets advocating alternative courses on leftist radicalism. On Roman streets, one of Marcuse's devotees declared, "We see Marx as the prophet, Marcuse as his interpreter, and Mao as the sword." Later that year Marcuse insisted that the frenzy over his ideas was a misunderstanding of his philosophy and its application, saying, "I am deeply committed to the movement of 'angry students,' but I am certainly not their spokesman." Marcuse was enigmatic—a noncombative whose tenets advocated countercultural revolution. While he condoned student protests, he disapproved of particular demonstrations. He criticized the students' priorities during the 1968 rebellion at Columbia University, when students protested against certain university policies and plans by seizing five buildings and three hostages. Marcuse commented, "I don't think that university administrations should be the prime targets. I still consider the American university an oasis of free speech and real critical thinking in the society."

Philosophically, Marcuse advocated social revolution and change in any existing system, wherever human societies suffer repression, regardless of its political form. His book *Soviet Marxism: A Critical Analysis* (1958) unleashed discussion criticizing Soviet Communism. Three of Marcuse's works proved most influential for the New Left: *Eros and Civilization: A Philosophical Inquiry into Freud* (1955); *One-Dimensional Man: Studies in the Ideology of Advanced Industrial Society* (1964); and an essay, "Repressive Tolerance," published in the book *A Critique of Pure Tolerance* (1965). In *Eros and Civilization,* Marcuse outlined his neo-Freudian ideology on repression and liberation, arguing that the more advanced the industrial society, the less willingly its political structure corrects problems. The book, an insightful theoretical study on Sigmund Freud and Karl Marx, proved marginally useful for dissident radicals, offering only a sketchy framework for change within the existing system. After *One-Dimensional Man,* Marcuse's books and articles furthered leftist politics. He argued for individual liberation through art, the direction in his final book, *The Aesthetic Dimension: Toward a Critique of Marxist Aesthetics* (1978).

One-Dimensional Man, held up against "the system" by protesters, proclaimed Marcuse's thesis that society is irrational. Technology within any advanced industrial society (whether capitalistic or communistic) denies liberation for its workers. No humane society can claim to be rational when the ultimate technological machines—nuclear weapons—exist for human destruction. Marcuse, a self-professed philosophical Marxist who was widely described as a neo-Marxist, argued for revitalization of Marxist theory actualized by "phenomenological," or concrete, experience. He said, "The best students are Socialist, but not Marxist. They don't want a Stalinist bureaucracy. They want a transvaluation of values."

In 1968 Marcuse received written threats from the John Birch Society and other right-wing groups, demanding that he desist from spreading his radical views. He also drew criticism from other conservative sources. The *National Review* described him as an "apostle of chaos," and *Pravda,* the official Communist newspaper of the Soviet Union, called Marcuse a "false prophet." The former Republican vice president Spiro T. Agnew, former Republican governor Ronald Reagan of California, and American Legion all verbally condemned him. Marcuse himself denounced the title "Father of the New Left," given to him by the press and by some political activists. Following a death threat, radical students and government guards monitored his home and office.

In October 1968 an agent for the Federal Bureau of Investigation frisked an interviewer from the *Saturday Evening Post* before he entered the Marcuse home. Once the interviewer was inside, Marcuse discussed contemporary society. "Society is insane," he began. Marxists would shudder when organized labor supported the war in Vietnam, and big business wanted it to be over because "there are more profits in private enterprise than in war production." A family man, Marcuse chuckled when asked about free love. Although he said it might be fun, he noted that his friend Norman O. Brown (in *Life Against Death* and *Love's Body*) misconstrued Freud's discussion of "polymorphous perverse" sexuality when he endorsed unrepressed, unrestricted adult sex. An advocate for students, Marcuse said, "Repression of the students will get more serious if the war continues. But it won't stop them. They are deeply disappointed in the democratic process. They will keep up the struggle."

Marcuse was portrayed as the epitome of continental charm. He was affable, spoke with a thick German accent, and appeared nonplussed by his extensive media notoriety as the philosophical guru of the radicals. During the 1960s an interviewer described him as "a calm, amused, cigar-smoking, white-haired old German professor, a gentleman with an energetic, alert, powerful head and a delightful boyish laugh." Conversely, a critic in the *National Review* derided him as "stuffy, Germanic, ultra-academic, a herr-doktor-professor." More than appearance, it was Marcuse's ideas (particularly his idea about one-dimensional man, mesmerized by materialism, apathetic to underprivileged

classes, and denying his own repressive state) that fueled student uprisings.

Marcuse was described as a kind husband and father in his three marriages. His first wife, Sophie, died in 1951; they had one son. On 19 February 1955 he married Inge Werner, whose two sons he helped to raise; she died in 1974. He married his third wife, Erica Sherover, on 21 June 1976. A music lover, Marcuse received an honorary degree from the New England Conservatory of Music. He enjoyed swimming, good food, and reading at home. Marcuse was quiet, relaxed in his private life, and deeply committed to his work—a model of propriety.

By the late 1970s, when Marcuse was no longer the beloved prophet and symbol of the 1960s, he appeared content to continue lecturing and writing. The *Daily Telegraph* claimed that he became disillusioned with the new era. Still, public approval or disapproval did not diminish his devotion to his work. Marshall Cohn, a philosopher at the City University of New York, described Marcuse's change from folk hero to someone now passé: "He became the public representative of a certain radicalism, and when that moment left, his celebrity left. He was a substantial figure in a school of philosophy that is not that potent in this country."

The political climate had altered by the 1970s. In 1979, facing conservatism at home and abroad, he retreated to the German countryside as the guest of the Max Planck Society. With a group of social researchers, the retired professor engaged in his favorite pastimes: political and social analysis. Marcuse died in Starnberg at age eighty-one, following a stroke. Marcuse once reflected on the 1960s, "You see the heroic period was that of the hippies and yippies. They did an indispensable job. There were heroes . . . but we have moved into a different period."

★

For Marcuse's papers see Douglas Kellner, ed., *Collected Papers of Herbert Marcuse* (1998–). Alasdair Macintyre, *Herbert Marcuse: An Exposition and a Polemic* (1970), offers a critical interpretation of Marcuse's work. Douglas Kellner, *Herbert Marcuse and the Crisis of Marxism* (1984), provides a rationale for Marcuse's rejection of Marxist orthodoxy, an explanation for his radicalism, and an extensive and detailed bibliography. Among the best magazine and newspaper articles covering Marcuse and his work are "The Metaphysics of Rebellion," *Ramparts* (29 June 1968); "Mao, Marx, et Marcuse!" *Saturday Evening Post* (19 Oct. 1968); "Marcuse Defines His New Left Line," *New York Times Magazine* (27 Oct. 1968); "Marcuse: The Prophet of the New Left, Our Era's Prime Advocate of Violence, Is Here Assassinated," *Horizon* (summer 1969); "Correspondence on the Student Revolutionaries," *New Left Review* (spring 1979); "Marcuse, Hero of the Left," *Daily Telegraph* (31 July 1979); "The Revolution Never Came," *Time* (13 Aug. 1979); "On *The Aesthetic Dimension:* A Conversation with Marcuse, Hero of the Left," *Contemporary Literature* (fall

1981); and "One-Dimensional Man," *New Republic* (1 Feb. 1999). An obituary is in the *New York Times* (31 July 1979).

SANDRA REDMOND PETERS

MARIS, Roger Eugene   (*b.* 10 September 1934 in Hibbing, Minnesota; *d.* 14 December 1985 in Houston, Texas), record-setting baseball slugger of the 1960s and businessman.

Maris, the younger of two sons, had his name changed officially when he began to play professional baseball. His name was originally "Maras," and as a young man he was taunted with plays on his name. The entire family, of Austrian ethnicity, changed their name as well. His father, Rudolph, was a foreman for the Great Northern Railroad and an avid hockey player well into his middle age. His mother was Anne Corinne (Connie) Sturbitz, a housewife. The family moved from Hibbing to Grand Forks, North Dakota, and then to Fargo, where Maris attended Fargo High School and then Bishop Shanley Catholic High School. He set a national high school football record by running back four kicks for touchdowns in 1951.

There was no baseball team at the Catholic high school, so Maris played on the American Legion teams, which went on to win state titles. Upon his high school graduation, the University of Oklahoma offered Maris an athletic scholarship, but he decided against it. Instead, he entertained offers from both the Chicago Cubs and the Cleveland Indians. The Cubs felt he was too small, but Cleveland offered him $5,000 with an extra $10,000 incentive if he made the majors in five years. He insisted that he be assigned no lower than a C league, so that he could play with the Fargo/Moorhead team close to his hometown. He got his wish and became rookie of the year his first year of professional baseball. On 13 October 1956 Marris married his high school sweetheart, Patricia Ann Carvell; they had seven children.

Maris made it to the majors within five years but was traded to Kansas City (Missouri) in 1958 and then to the New York Yankees in 1959. New York was a team bent on winning; after all, they had the great Mickey Mantle at center field. Maris fit perfectly with his five-tool abilities of speed, defense, throwing arm, hitting ability, and power. He was central to the Yankees' winning five straight pennants and was center stage in baseball in the 1960s. He won the Most Valuable Player award in the American League in 1960 and led the Yankees to the World Series.

After the first eleven games of the 1961 season, Mantle and Maris broke out, with home run matching home run, the one hitting after the other in the batting order. Except for their talents, the two men could not have been more different. Mantle, the darling of the Yankees, was a fun-

Roger Maris. CORBIS CORPORATION (BELLEVUE)

loving playboy always willing to test the nightlife of the big city, while Maris was stolid, sensitive, quiet, and even surly. Although the two were close friends, the media pitted them against each other. Maris and Mantle went deep into September 1961, chasing Babe Ruth's elusive 1934 record of sixty home runs, but Mantle went on the disabled list in the last three weeks owing to bad treatment of a bruised hip, and Maris continued the quest alone. The baseball commissioner was implored not to recognize the breaking of Ruth's record if it was not accomplished within 154 games. (In 1961 the American League had expanded the number of teams to ten and the length of the season from 154 to 162 games.)

Maris had sixty home runs after 159 games and almost broke the record in Baltimore, but it was not until the 162nd game that he hit his sixty-first and thus earned an asterisk designating that the record was not achieved in the same number of games as those of Ruth. It was a humiliating gaffe on the part of baseball and an insult to Maris. His season was filled with grief, however, as fans hurled taunts and threw objects at him from the stands. The press was of no help. To them, if anyone were to challenge Ruth, then it must be Mantle, the golden boy. Maris lost weight, and clumps of his hair fell out as he internalized his frustrations. Even winning a second consecutive Most Valuable

Player award did nothing to salve his wounded pride. He again led the Yankees to a World Series, but it appeared that New York wanted no more of Maris.

The following year was worse, for now everyone wanted to see if he was a fluke. They insisted on more, despite his respectable thirty-three home runs that year. The Yankees went to the World Series for a third time, while Maris retreated within himself. Suffering back and leg pains, he played only ninety games in 1963 and hit twenty-three home runs. He followed with twenty-nine home runs in 1964. That was the end of the Yankees' run of pennants. Maris suffered a hand injury in a slide at home plate, but the Yankees demanded that he play. He went to a private physician, who discovered a chipped bone in his hand. The Yankee management was furious that he had gone outside the system for treatment. His play diminished, as did the Yankees', and in the winter of 1966, he learned that he had been traded to the St. Louis Cardinals.

For Maris, who had kept a home in Raytown, Missouri, and later had bought one in Independence, it was like going home, and the Cardinals were delighted to have him. They needed another left-hander at bat, and Maris fit perfectly. He helped the Cardinals to two World Series, and St. Louis fans embraced Maris's instinctive grasp of the game. He wanted to retire after 1967, but August Busch, the Cardinals' owner, offered him a beer distributorship in an area of his choosing if he played a second year. Maris and the Cardinals went to the World Series again in 1968. He retired and chose Gainesville, Florida, a university town, for his business. He was successful beyond expectations, and he brought his entire family into the operation.

In 1983, after he had come down with lymphatic cancer, the Yankees held a Roger Maris day on which they retired his number 9 and put a bronze plaque in the memorial section of center field alongside Ruth and the other Yankee greats. Redemption had come at last for Maris, but cancer would take his life. He volunteered for radical experimental treatments, but they were not effective. He died in a Houston hospital. The death of Maris, who was a defining baseball personality of the 1960s, brought the baseball world to Fargo, North Dakota, where Maris was buried in Holy Cross Cemetery. "This is our home and these are our people," said his wife. "We moved away in 1957, but our hearts were always here." Five days later in New York, a funeral mass for Maris, conducted by John Cardinal O'Connor, was held in Saint Patrick's Cathedral. The dignitaries of the city, including former president Richard Nixon, George Steinbrenner, and his old Yankee teammates, were in attendance.

Maris was both a hero and antihero of baseball. He harbored all the virtues of traditional middle America at a time when society was undergoing social upheaval and liberation from the constraints of the past. Maris adhered to the independent thinking that allowed him to challenge

authority while pursuing excellence as a baseball player. His record of sixty-one home runs was to last thirty-seven years, until Mark McGwire broke it in 1998 with the Maris family in attendance. Maris's bat is in the Hall of Fame, but he is not.

★

Maris's own story told to Jim Ogle, *Roger Maris at Bat* (1962), gives personal insight into Maris's 1961 year. Maury Allen, *Roger Maris: A Man for All Seasons* (1986), is a laudatory biography. Harvey Rosenfeld, *Roger Maris: A Tale of Fame* (1991), is an uncritical study. David Halberstam, *October 1964* (1994), assesses the Maris era with the Yankees and Cardinals and the decline of Yankee dominance. Ron Smith, *1961* (2001), dissects that pivotal year and was developed into a made-for-cable motion picture of the same title. *The Sporting News* (23 Dec. 1985) reviews Maris's career. An obituary and a tribute to Maris highlighting his career in the 1960s are in the *New York Times* (15 Dec. 1985).

JACK J. CARDOSO

MARISOL (Marisol Escobar) (*b.* 22 May 1930 in Paris, France), sculptor whose mysterious beauty and large wood block figures in assemblages caused a sensation during the 1960s.

Born Marisol Escobar, Marisol was the daughter of Gustavo Escobar, a real estate mogul, and Josefina Hernandez Escobar, a housewife. Her first name derives from Spanish words (*mar y sol*) meaning "sea and sun." Marisol and her brother Gustavo, who later became an economist, lived very comfortable and nomadic lives, constantly traveling with their parents throughout the Americas and Europe. Her mother died when she was eleven, during World War II.

After the war the family moved to Los Angeles, where Marisol attended the Westlake School for Girls. Always interested in art, she decided to become a painter, and she studied with Howard Warshaw at the Jepson School in Los Angeles. Earlier, during her childhood education in Catholic schools, she had won prizes for drawing very realistic copies of icons representing saints.

After a year spent studying painting at the Académie des Beau-Arts in Paris in 1950, Marisol moved permanently to New York City. She studied painting briefly at the Art Students League, then, for three years (1950–1953) at the Hans Hofmann School of Art. She considered Hofmann a fine teacher, but felt she was not adept in his abstract style.

In 1953 Marisol experienced her breakthrough. While visiting a primitive art gallery in New York, she was spellbound by pre-Columbian pottery and Mexican folk art boxes with small, carved figures. She immediately abandoned painting and became a self-taught carpenter and carver, soon developing considerable aptitude at these crafts. "It started as a kind of rebellion," she told a reporter in 1965. Instead of the

Marisol poses behind two of her sculptures, one depicting a man, the other a woman. AP/WIDE WORLD PHOTOS

existential aura of 1950s New York abstract painting, Marisol's new work emphasized the whimsical.

For the next several years her playful sculptures featured roughly carved wooden figures of people and animals, or small, often erotic, bronze or clay figurines. Sometimes she combined the materials, as with *Figures in Type Drawer* (1954). In 1957 her work appeared at the prestigious Leo Castelli Gallery and was discussed in *Life* magazine. By then she had dropped her last name so that she would "stand out from the crowd," as she later commented.

During the 1950s New York artists held intense panel discussions at a meeting hall. At these discussion group meetings, called "the Club," emerging artists were often grilled mercilessly about their work. When Marisol was invited she wore a stark, white Japanese mask. There ensued a deafening cry for her to remove it, and she did—only to reveal that she had on makeup exactly the same as the mask. Similar stunts garnered much publicity, and she became legendary by the early 1960s, when pop art began to be noticed beyond the glut of then-current abstract painting.

A natural beauty, her chic bones-and-hollows face was complemented by her long, glossy black hair. Marisol wore designer clothes at the newest discotheques, or simple sweaters, jeans, and boots at art openings. Her whispery voice, natural reserve, and marathon silences lent a mysterious allure. It was not for nothing that she became known in the 1960s as the "Latin Garbo."

The scale of her work changed, from tiny figurines in the 1950s to full human-height wooden blocks in the 1960s. The block figures of mahogany or pine would be painted or penciled, and she began to use discarded objects as props. Her inspiration for using found objects came from the Spanish artist Pablo Picasso, as well as from the proto–pop artist Robert Rauschenberg, who was famous for his mixed media assemblages from the mid-1950s. Marisol's props ranged from a stuffed dog's head for *Woman with Dog* (1960) to real trumpets and a saxophone for *Jazz Musicians* (1964). "I do my research in the Yellow Pages," she once commented. "You could call them a new palette for me."

By the mid-1960s Marisol had become a naturalized United States citizen. Her work was associated with pop art, but though she believed her style was similar to the ironic use of popular culture in pop art, she also considered it fundamentally different. Confusion then was compounded, since she was a frequent escort at parties with the "pope of pop," Andy Warhol, and she made several appearances in his avant-garde films of the mid-1960s. Throughout her career she has told interviewers that her work never had the dimensions of political or social criticism associated with pop art.

In 1962 her best known works were a sixty-six-inch-high portrait called *The Kennedy Family,* and another, called *The Family,* which stood eighty-three inches tall and represented a farm family from the 1930s' dust bowl era. By the mid-1960s her works were of larger groups of figures, of which the most critically acclaimed was an environmental group called *The Party* (1966), consisting of life-size wood block figures, mostly of elegantly gowned and coifed high society wives whose penciled-in faces resemble Marisol. One figure's forehead has a small, working television set. In the midriff of another one is a lit-up slide of a Harry Winston diamond necklace. Figures of a butler and a maid bear trays of real glasses. The aura seems slightly sinister and confrontational because all of the figures face forward toward the viewer. It is as if the viewer has just entered a high-society cocktail party and the figures are evaluating, mask-like, the viewer's social status.

During the later 1960s Marisol received many commissions for portrait figures of patrons and of heads of state. Her portrait of *Playboy* magazine founder Hugh Hefner appeared on the 3 March 1967 cover of *Time* magazine. In 1968 she traveled to the Far East and South America and decided to forgo figures of others for what she then called her "quest for self" in many self-portraits. During the 1970s her sculpture was of fish, animals, and flowers with erotic, often violent, overtones. Beginning in the 1980s she returned to large-scale figural assemblages and portrait-homages to well-known contemporary artists and personalities.

Marisol's sculpture in the 1960s combined found objects and wooden blocks as figures. Arranged into complex, life-size figure arrangements, they galvanized the art public of that era.

★

Marisol's work from the 1960s is examined in Roberta Bernstein, *Marisol* (1970). Also see Grace Gluck, "It's Not Pop, It's Not Op—It's Marisol," *New York Times Magazine* (17 Mar. 1965). An informative interview is in Cindy Nesmer, *Art Talk: Conversations with 12 Women Artists* (1975).

PATRICK S. SMITH

MARSHALL, Thurgood (*b.* 2 July 1908 in Baltimore, Maryland; *d.* 24 January 1993 in Bethesda, Maryland), pioneering civil rights attorney who fought tirelessly for the equal treatment of all Americans under the law and who was the first African-American justice to sit on the U.S. Supreme Court.

Marshall was the elder of two sons of William Canfield Marshall and Norma Williams. His father, a waiter at a

"whites only" yacht club on Chesapeake Bay, and his mother, a teacher at a segregated elementary school, instilled in Marshall an appreciation for the importance of pride, humility, justice, equality, and the pursuit of excellence. From his father, Marshall learned the value of a rebellious spirit. Later in his life, Marshall recalled his father's admonishment to both his sons: "If anyone calls you a nigger, you not only got my permission to fight him, you got my orders to fight him." Thankfully, Marshall was largely insulated from the sting of racism during his childhood in Baltimore, where his family lived in a modest but comfortable home on Druid Hill Avenue. As a boy, he routinely played with both black and white children.

An undistinguished scholar in the public schools of Baltimore, Marshall later described himself as something of a "cutup" who was often punished by being banished to the school's basement to memorize a passage from the U.S. Constitution. After graduation from high school, he enrolled at Lincoln University in the rolling countryside of Pennsylvania's Chester County, not far from Philadelphia. Graduating with honors in 1930, Marshall was denied admission to the University of Maryland Law School on the basis of race, a policy he later challenged successfully on behalf of another black student. He enrolled instead at Howard University Law School in Washington, D.C., from which he graduated first in his class in 1933. Marshall married Vivian Burey in 1929; she died in 1955 after a long illness. They had no children. He remarried a year later to Cecilia A. Suyat, a secretary for the National Association for the Advancement of Colored People (NAACP), with whom he had two sons.

Returning to his hometown after graduation, Marshall set up a private practice specializing in civil rights and criminal law. He also served as counsel to the Baltimore chapter of the NAACP, a position that soon brought him to the attention of Arthur Springarn, the organization's national president. In 1936 he moved to New York City to serve as assistant to the NAACP's chief counsel, two years after which he was named to replace the retiring chief counsel. From 1940 until 1961, Marshall served as director of the NAACP's legal defense and educational fund. During this period he was the chief strategist of the organization's legal assault against racial discrimination, winning twenty-nine of thirty-two such cases argued before the Supreme Court. Marshall captured national attention in the mid-1950s when he successfully argued *Brown* v. *Board of Education* before the high court. The Court's decision struck down the legal justification for "separate but equal" public school facilities and, more than any other single event, laid the groundwork for the civil rights struggle of the late 1950s and 1960s.

In 1961 President John F. Kennedy nominated Marshall for a federal judgeship on the U.S. Court of Appeals for

Thurgood Marshall prior to being sworn in for his first session on the U.S. Supreme Court, October 1967.
© Bettmann/Corbis

the Second Circuit (an area covering New York, Vermont, and Connecticut). Southern segregationists in the Senate pulled out all the stops in their unsuccessful effort to block Marshall's confirmation, a process that took nearly a year. In 1965 President Lyndon B. Johnson named Marshall solicitor general, in which position he argued cases on behalf of the federal government before the Supreme Court. Of the nineteen cases he argued before the high court over the next two years, Marshall won fourteen. Thurgood's most famous case as solicitor general was *Miranda* v. *Arizona,* in which he argued successfully that law enforcement officers must inform all criminal suspects of their constitutional rights.

President Johnson in 1967 nominated Marshall to fill a Supreme Court vacancy created by the retirement of Justice Tom Clark. Despite violent opposition from four southern members of the Senate Judiciary Committee, Marshall eventually was confirmed by a vote of sixty-nine to eleven in the full Senate. He took his seat on the high court on 2 October 1967 and quickly established himself as the Court's most outspoken member on matters of racial justice. Juan Williams, writing in *Ebony* magazine, said of Marshall: "Throughout his time on the Court, Marshall has remained a strong advocate of individual rights. . . . He has remained a conscience on the bench, never wavering in his devotion to ending discrimination." Former Justice William Brennan, one of Marshall's liberal allies on the Court, later told *Ebony:* "The only time Thurgood may make people uncomfortable, and perhaps it's when they should be made uncomfortable, is when he'll take off in a given case

that he thinks . . . is another expression of racism." Six years after his nomination of Marshall to the high court, Johnson said of his decision that it was "the right thing to do, the right time to do it, the right man, and the right place."

In his early years on the Supreme Court, liberals dominated the nation's highest judicial panel, a comfortable environment for Marshall, who was an avowed liberal on most issues. He developed a particularly close relationship with some of his fellow liberals on the bench, namely Brennan and William O. Douglas. For his first several years on the high court, Marshall cast few dissenting votes. Among the more important of Marshall's majority decisions during the 1960s were *Amalgamated Food Employees Union* v. *Logan Valley Plaza* in 1968 and *Stanley* v. *Georgia* in 1969. In the former case, the majority ruled that striking union members could not be barred from picketing at a shopping center, which the Court held was a "public forum." In *Stanley* v. *Georgia,* the Court held that the private possession of pornography could not be subject to prosecution. In his written contribution to the majority opinion, Marshall observed: "If the First Amendment means anything, it means that a state has no business telling a man, sitting alone in his own house, what books he may read or what films he may watch."

Marshall ruled with the majority in *Roe* v. *Wade* that a woman has the right to an abortion without interference from the government in the first trimester of pregnancy, contending that it is part of her "right to privacy." Years after the Court's landmark decision legalizing abortion, internal Court memos revealed an exchange between Marshall and Justice Harry A. Blackmun in which Marshall expressed concern that Blackmun's proposal focused too much attention on the end of the first thirteen weeks of pregnancy, thus allowing the states too much control after the first trimester. In response Blackmun modified the majority opinion somewhat, altering it to say that after approximately the first trimester, states could regulate abortion to protect the mother's health.

Throughout his years on the Supreme Court, Marshall fought vigorously against capital punishment. During one notable death penalty argument, Justice William H. Rehnquist suggested that the repeated appeals of an inmate had cost taxpayers too much money. Marshall interrupted Rehnquist's argument to say: "It would have been cheaper to shoot him right after he was arrested, wouldn't it?" Outside the courtroom of the high court, Marshall enjoyed a reputation as a master storyteller with an earthy sense of humor. Of his colleague's storytelling skills, Justice Brennan wrote in the *Harvard Law Review:* "The locales are varied—from dusty courtrooms in the Deep South, to a confrontation with General MacArthur in the Far East, to the drafting sessions for the Kenyan Constitution." According to Brennan, Marshall's stories, while designed to entertain, served a deeper purpose. Brennan saw the tales as Marshall's way to preserve the past while removing some of the period's less pleasant memories. "They are also a form of education for the rest of us. Surely, Justice Marshall recognized that the stories made us—his colleagues—confront walks of life we had never known."

According to Marshall's obituary in the *New York Times,* many of his stories recounted the dangers and hostility that he had experienced as a civil rights lawyer, traveling thousands of miles throughout the American South representing indigent black clients and unpopular causes. In one such story, Marshall told of being arrested in Tennessee on trumped-up drunk-driving charges shortly after he and a colleague had won acquittal for a black defendant. According to Marshall's story, he was brought before a magistrate who told him: "If you're not drunk, will you take my test? Will you blow in my face? I'm a teetotaler, and I can smell the least bit of whiskey." Marshall, who stood six feet, two inches tall and weighed more than two hundred pounds, said of the magistrate: "He was a short man. I put my hands on his shoulders and breathed just as hard as I could into the man's face." The case against Marshall was quickly dismissed. In a postscript to his story, Marshall added, "We drove to Nashville. And then, boy, I really wanted a drink!"

In 1973 Marshall dissented from the Court's majority opinion in *San Antonio School District* v. *Rodriguez,* which held that the property tax system used by Texas and a number of other states to finance public education did not vi-

olate the Constitution's guarantee of equal protection. Under such systems, school districts with generous tax bases can afford to provide better schools than less wealthy districts. In his dissent Marshall accused the majority of an "unsupportable acquiescence in a system which deprives children in their earliest years of the chance to reach their full potential as citizens." Arguing that the right to an education should be considered a "fundamental" constitutional right, Marshall contended that state policies that have the effect of discriminating on the basis of wealth should be subject to especially searching judicial scrutiny. He wrote: "In my judgment, the right of every American to an equal start in life . . . is far too vital to permit state discrimination on grounds as tenuous as those presented by this record."

The 1980s saw marked changes in the makeup of the Court, as Republican administrations added more conservative justices to the judicial panel. Despite finding himself in the Court's ever-shrinking liberal minority, Marshall publicly declared his intention to serve out his lifetime appointment. As time went on, however, he grew increasingly unhappy with the policies of the administrations of Ronald Reagan and George Bush and new rulings that he felt seriously eroded earlier civil rights gains. Even more frustrating to Marshall was what he saw as a lack of understanding among his fellow justices about the effects of racism on American society as a whole. Failing health finally forced Marshall to step down from the Supreme Court in 1991. He died of heart failure at the age of eighty-four.

A major figure in American public life for more than half a century, Thurgood Marshall was responsible for mapping out the legal strategy that brought to an end the era of government-sanctioned segregation in the United States. In 1967 he became the first African American to sit on the Supreme Court, a position in which he remained for twenty-four years. During more than two decades as director and counsel of the NAACP's legal defense and educational fund, Marshall decided to take the struggle for equal rights to the courts. It was before the Supreme Court in 1954 that Marshall won his greatest legal victory in *Brown* v. *Board of Education.* That unanimous decision by the high court struck down the "separate but equal" system of racial separation in effect in the public schools of twenty-one states. Even more important, it laid the groundwork for the civil rights movement of the late 1950s and 1960s.

An unabashed liberal during his quarter century as a Supreme Court justice, Marshall was a strong advocate of individual rights, never wavering in his dedication to the elimination of discrimination in all its varied forms. Interviewed by *People,* Benjamin Hooks, the former executive director of the NAACP, said of Marshall: "It's my belief that without Thurgood Marshall, we would still be riding in the back of the bus, going to separate schools, and drinking 'colored' water."

★

Further insight into the life and career of Thurgood Marshall may be found in Lisa Aldred, *Thurgood Marshall* (1991); Randall Walton Bland, *Private Pressure on Public Law: The Legal Career of Justice Thurgood Marshall, 1934–1991* (1993); Joseph Nazel, *Thurgood Marshall: Supreme Court Justice* (1993); Mark V. Tushnet, *Making Constitutional Law: Thurgood Marshall and the Supreme Court, 1961–1991* (1997), and, as editor, *Thurgood Marshall: His Speeches, Writings, Arguments, Opinions, and Reminiscences* (2001); and Mark Rowh, *Thurgood Marshall: Civil Rights Attorney and Supreme Court Justice* (2002). An obituary is in the *New York Times* (25 Jan. 1993).

DON AMERMAN

MARTIN, Dean (*b.* 7 June 1917 in Steubenville, Ohio; *d.* 25 December 1995 in Los Angeles, California), popular singer, film actor, television host, and comedian who formed one of the most successful comedy acts of the 1940s and 1950s with Jerry Lewis, then used it as a springboard for a broader career as an entertainer in the 1960s and 1970s.

Born Dino Paul Crocetti, Martin was the son of Italian immigrants Gaetano Crocetti, a barber, and Angela Barra, a homemaker. After dropping out of high school Martin worked at several professions, including boxing and as a

Dean Martin. THE KOBAL COLLECTION

croupier, but by 1940 he was singing professionally. On 2 October 1941 he married Elizabeth Ann MacDonald, the first of his three wives, who bore him four children before they divorced in 1949. He married Jeanne Beiggers, with whom he had three children, in 1949, and Catherine Mae Hawn in 1973; both of these marriages also ended in divorce.

Martin's career did not take off until July 1946, when he formed a partnership with comedian Jerry Lewis. The team of Martin and Lewis spent the next ten years enjoying remarkable success in personal appearances, radio shows, television, and a series of popular films. Martin also launched a career as a recording artist during this period, releasing such major hits as "That's Amore" and "Memories Are Made of This" on Capitol Records.

In 1956 Martin struck out on his own, and after an initial rough patch began to score in films and on records. By the start of the 1960s he was well established as a handsome, easygoing, and somewhat self-mocking leading man in the movies, making two or three pictures a year. In 1960 he appeared in the comedy *Who Was That Lady?*, the screen adaptation of the Broadway musical *Bells Are Ringing*, and the caper film *Ocean's 11*, in which his costars were friends Frank Sinatra, Sammy Davis, Jr., and other members of what was called the Rat Pack. The group continued to team up in various combinations for film projects over the next several years. *Sergeants 3* (1962) was a remake of *Gunga Din* set in the Old West; *4 for Texas* (1963) was another Western comedy; and *Robin and the 7 Hoods* (1964) was a musical set in Chicago during the 1920s gangster era. During this period Martin also appeared with Sinatra and Davis in several live performances marked by outrageous hijinks, and video and audio recordings of them began to turn up, first illegally and then as legitimate releases many years later, contributing to the Rat Pack legend. Among Martin's other films of this period are the original movie musical *What a Way to Go!* (1964), with music by Jule Styne and screenplay and lyrics by Betty Comden and Adolph Green, and *Kiss Me, Stupid* (1964), produced, directed, and cowritten by Billy Wilder, in which Martin deliberately parodied himself.

With the rise of rock and roll, Martin's career as a recording artist dimmed. At the start of 1962 he left Capitol Records and signed with Reprise Records, a new label founded by Sinatra. At first Reprise was able to improve his fortunes only slightly. Then, in 1964, producer Jimmy Bowen had Martin cut a version of the 1948 song "Everybody Loves Somebody" in an arrangement by Ernie Freeman that employed piano triplets in a style derived from 1950s rock and roll. The result was a surprising success. In August, the single replaced the Beatles' "A Hard Day's Night" at the top of the charts, and Martin's recording career was revitalized. The *Everybody Loves Somebody* album also hit number one and was certified gold, and Martin quickly followed with a series of albums and singles that performed well over the rest of the decade. "The Door Is Still Open to My Heart," a revival of a 1955 rhythm-and-blues hit by the Cardinals, became a Top Ten hit and, like "Everybody Loves Somebody," a number-one hit on the easy listening charts, and an album of the same name reached the Top Ten and went gold. "You're Nobody Till Somebody Loves You," a revival of a 1946 hit by Russ Morgan, made the pop Top Forty and gave Martin his third consecutive easy-listening chart topper before 1964 was over. In total he scored twelve gold albums, eleven Top Forty pop hits, and twenty Top Ten easy-listening hits between 1964 and 1969.

Martin's renewed success on records and his continuing work in films brought the television networks calling, and on 16 September 1965 he launched a comedy-variety series, *The Dean Martin Show,* which won a Golden Globe Award in 1967. Viewers were highly entertained by the seemingly inebriated host dressed in a tuxedo, appearing to work largely off the cuff, and the show was one of television's highest rated programs until 1971. It remained on the air regularly until 1974, after which Martin continued to do occasional specials.

Even with his recording, television, and personal appearance work, Martin still found time to make movies, and in 1966 he began a series of four films in which he portrayed secret agent Matt Helm, sending up the popular James Bond series: *The Silencers, Murderers' Row, The Ambushers,* and *The Wrecking Crew.* He also continued to appear in Westerns (*Bandolero!* and *Five Card Stud*) and comedies (*How to Save a Marriage and Ruin Your Life*) during the late 1960s.

Martin's casual, seemingly spontaneous work appears to have been genuine. Notoriously, he did not show up on the set of his television show until the day of taping; he left to others the choice of songs and arrangements on his record albums, which were cut in a minimum number of sessions; and many of his movies were star vehicles that made relatively low demands on him. But the sheer amount of work he accomplished in various media belies the charming, irresponsible drunk persona Martin often affected.

Martin worked less frequently after the early 1970s and by the mid-1980s was virtually retired. He died of acute respiratory failure and is buried at Westwood Memorial Park in Los Angeles.

★

Nick Tosches, *Dino: Living High in the Dirty Business of Dreams* (1992) is a major biography, but a highly sensationalized one. John Chintala, *Dean Martin: A Complete Guide to the "Total Entertainer"* (1998), is thorough, and his extensive liner notes (actually books in themselves) to the boxed sets *Memories Are Made of This* and *Return to Me,* issued by the German label Bear Family,

are the most objective accounts of Martin's life and career. An obituary is in *Time* (8 Jan. 1996).

WILLIAM RUHLMANN

MARTIN, John Bartlow (*b.* 4 August 1915 in Hamilton, Ohio; *d.* 3 January 1987 in Highland Park, Illinois), journalist, diplomat, and, throughout the 1960s, a political adviser and speechwriter to Democratic presidential candidates

Martin, the oldest of three sons, was born in Hamilton, Ohio, to John Williamson Martin, a building contractor, and Laura (Bartlow) Martin. The family moved to Indiana, and Martin graduated with a degree in political science from DePauw University in 1937. He then worked as a reporter for the *Indianapolis Times,* covering city hall and the police beat. On 23 January 1937 Martin married Barbara Bruce, a wealthy Chicago socialite. Martin moved to the city in 1937 and attempted to earn a living as a freelance writer. The marriage failed, but Martin discovered that he could earn an income by writing articles for such magazines as *Official Detective* and *Actual Detective.* Martin began to write for magazines with greater circulation, such as *Harper's* and *Esquire,* on such subjects as the frame of mind during World War II in Muncie, Indiana, a city that had gained fame as "Middletown" in a 1920s sociological study. He married Frances Smethurst on 17 August 1940 and enjoyed a happy marriage until his death in 1987. They had one daughter and two sons.

The first of Martin's sixteen books, *Call It North Country: The Story of Upper Michigan,* was published in 1944. Following a short stint in the army, Martin traveled the Midwest in 1946 researching a *Life* article on the postwar mood. He also wrote another regional book on Indiana history. His coverage of the 1947 Centralia, Illinois, mine accident that caused 111 deaths brought Martin to the attention of Adlai Stevenson, a Democratic candidate for the Illinois governorship. When Stevenson sought the presidency in 1952, he recruited Martin to edit a collection of speeches for publication. Martin joined Stevenson's campaign as part of a group of speechwriters dubbed the "Elks Club," so called because the Stevenson campaign rented the Elks Club building in Springfield, Illinois. Other prominent members of this prestigious group included Arthur M. Schlesinger, Jr., a Pulitzer Prize–winning historian; John Kenneth Galbraith, the famed economist; and Archibald MacLeish, a future poet laureate of the United States. In both Stevenson's 1952 and 1956 presidential campaigns, Martin served as an editorial advance man and speechwriter.

Throughout the 1960s Martin served as a behind-the-scenes adviser and speechwriter to Democratic presidential candidates, beginning with John F. Kennedy's 1960 presidential campaign. Following Kennedy's victory, Martin was appointed ambassador to the Dominican Republic but waited almost a year to assume his office because of political unrest within the country. In the interim, Martin served as a speechwriter for members of the Kennedy administration, including Newton Minow, chairman of the Federal Communications Commission. Martin penned Minow's May 1961 speech to the National Association of Broadcasters. Engaged in writing a *Saturday Evening Post* article on television, Martin had watched twenty straight hours of programming, and in the speech he invited television viewers to watch their televisions from the time a station goes on the air until it signs off. He declared, "I can assure you that you will observe a vast wasteland of junk." Minow edited out "of junk," and the phrase "vast wasteland" entered the lexicon and continues to be used today to describe television programming. Ironically, Martin attempted to use television as an educational tool to combat the high illiteracy rate in the Dominican Republic, only to see his efforts thwarted by a military coup.

As the U.S. ambassador to the Dominican Republic, Martin worked ceaselessly to support that country's first democratically elected government. He traveled to the United States to consult with Kennedy in late 1963, but when Kennedy was assassinated in November, he was heartbroken and resigned from government service. Martin returned to journalism with a new appreciation for the rigors of politics, "less zealous about attacking the failings of our public officials and arrogating all virtue to the vigilant press. I found out just how hard it [governing] really is."

Martin reentered politics in 1968 when Robert F. Kennedy entered the race for the Democratic Party presidential nomination. Martin became Kennedy's main adviser in Indiana, a key primary battleground. He also advised the candidate on the nature of his native state, stating, "Indiana is a state suspicious of foreign entanglements, conservative in fiscal matters, and with a strong overlay of Southern segregationist sentiment. Hoosiers are phlegmatic, skeptical, hard to move, with a 'show me' attitude." Kennedy, following Martin's advice to talk conservatively while campaigning in the Hoosier state, won the Democratic primary, giving his campaign momentum heading into the crucial California primary. Martin accompanied to Kennedy to California, where Martin's worst fears of another Kennedy assassination came true when Robert Kennedy was murdered in Los Angeles by Sirhan Sirhan in June 1968. Afterward, Martin campaigned for the Democratic nominee Hubert Humphrey more out of a desire to defeat Republican Richard Nixon than from any faith in the liberalism of Humphrey. After Humphrey's defeat, Martin left politics behind, becoming a professor at the Medill School of Jour-

nalism at Northwestern University in Chicago, a position he held for ten years.

After Martin left politics for academia, he attempted to dissuade his students from the "new journalism" practiced by Tom Wolfe, Norman Mailer, and Hunter Thompson, decrying what he perceived as the growing inability to write simple, proper sentences and these writers' invention of characters and situations in the name of dramatic license. Despite his seemingly old-fashioned views, the Medill School created the John Bartlow Martin Award for Public Interest Magazine Journalism to honor his work. Martin's admiration for Stevenson led him in the 1970s to write a two-volume biography of the Illinois statesman. Martin also wrote a record of his service in the Dominican Republic and a memoir, *It Seems Like Only Yesterday*. He died of throat cancer and is buried in his beloved Upper Michigan.

★

Martin's papers are in the Manuscript Division of the Library of Congress. A special collection relating to Adlai Stevenson is in the Seeley G. Mudd Library at Princeton University. Martin's memoir is *It Seems Like Only Yesterday: Memoirs of Writing, Presidential Politics, and the Diplomatic Life* (1986). Obituaries are in the *Chicago Tribune* and the *New York Times* (both 5 Jan. 1987).

STEPHEN McCULLOUGH

MARTIN, William McChesney, Jr. (*b*. 17 December 1906 in St. Louis, Missouri; *d*. 27 July 1998 in Washington, D.C.), dedicated public servant best remembered for his leadership of the Federal Reserve Board during the 1950s and 1960s.

Martin was the elder of two sons of William McChesney Martin, an attorney and banker, chief executive officer of the St. Louis Federal Reserve Bank for twenty-seven years. His mother was Rebecca Woods. After a diverse early career that included prominent positions at the New York Stock Exchange, the Export-Import Bank, the U.S. Treasury Department, and the International Bank for Reconstruction and Development, Martin became chairman of the Federal Reserve System in April 1951, appointed by President Harry Truman. Serving as America's central banker for nineteen years, until his retirement in 1970, Martin shaped notions about the proper role and function of the Federal Reserve Board. In a famous speech in 1956, Martin declared that the agency's purpose was "to lean against the winds of deflation or inflation, whichever way they are blowing." During most of the inflationary 1960s, Martin interpreted this to mean that the Federal Reserve Board should adopt a tight monetary policy. Martin was flexible, however, easing policy during the economic crisis of 1967 and 1968 but tightening it again in 1969. Insisting that the Federal Reserve play a critical role in managing the nation's economy,

William McChesney Martin, Jr. ARCHIVE PHOTOS, INC.

and that the board of governors, not the reserve banks, have primary authority in wielding policy, Martin continued the work of his predecessor, Marriner S. Eccles.

In a way, Martin also built upon the legacy established by his father. William McChesney Martin, Sr., a well-respected banker, had helped draft the original Federal Reserve Act of 1913 upon the request of President Woodrow Wilson. After the passage of the act, the elder Martin became president of the Federal Reserve Bank in St. Louis. Martin followed in his father's footsteps. Upon graduating from Yale University with a B.A. in English and Latin, he briefly considered becoming a Presbyterian minister but entered the banking world instead. Martin first worked as a bank examiner in the Federal Reserve Bank of St. Louis and then became a stockbroker at a St. Louis brokerage firm, where he quickly became a partner. In the early 1930s Martin moved to New York City. After acquiring a seat on the New York Stock Exchange (NYSE), he became involved with Wall Street politics on the side of the Reformers, a group that battled against the reactionary Old Guard, led by the NYSE president Richard Whitney. The Reformers, who eventually gained control of the Exchange, strove to make the institution more open and responsive to the needs of the public. Among various other reforms, they enlarged the duties of the Exchange president and converted that position into a paid, full-time post. The first person to occupy this newly restructured job was Martin.

Assuming the job in 1938 at the age of thirty-one, Martin became not only the Exchange's first paid president but also the youngest person ever to occupy this top post. He became known as the "boy wonder of Wall Street."

As president of the NYSE, Martin earned the nickname Mr. Chocolate for his sober, levelheaded leadership style (as well as his preference for hot chocolate). He served for only three years; in 1941, upon the entry of the United States into World War II, he stunned Wall Street by declining the opportunity to receive a military deferment and instead allowing himself to be drafted. He resigned the presidency in order to enlist as a private in the U.S. Army. After the war concluded, Martin served as president of the U.S. Export-Import Bank from 1945 to 1948. He then served as the assistant secretary of the Treasury from 1949 until his appointment to the Federal Reserve Board in 1951. Martin married Cynthia Davis in 1942; they had three children.

As Federal Reserve chairman, Martin solidified his reputation as a man of personal integrity and financial conservatism. As the U.S. economy expanded and the stock market boomed in the mid-1960s, Martin consistently warned of the dangers of excess speculation and high inflation. On 1 June 1965, in a particularly blunt address at Columbia University on commencement day, he warned that unless stricter restraints on money and credit were enacted, the economy was headed for disaster. He paralleled the reckless speculation of the current "go-go years" with the euphoria of the 1920s. In reaction to this disturbing speech, the stock market dropped significantly. Wall Streeters derided the downturn as the Martin Market. The depressed market conditions, however, did not last long; the bull period resumed by autumn, making it appear that the chairman's warnings were unsubstantiated. In the wake of his gloomy prediction that the sky was going to fall, Martin received a new nickname; no longer Mr. Chocolate, he was now William McChicken Little Martin. Eventually Martin was proved right; the market tumbled in the ensuing 1968 economic crisis.

For his blunt style and commitment to a restrictive monetary policy, Martin was often unpopular, especially with many politicians whose constituencies favored easy money and low interest rates—the opposite of Martin's prescription for the economy. Despite pressure to do otherwise, Presidents Dwight Eisenhower, John F. Kennedy, and Lyndon Baines Johnson all reappointed Martin to the chairmanship, respecting his prudence and financial wisdom. Their decisions to keep Martin as head of the Federal Reserve had many effects on the economy and consequently may have influenced the results of at least one presidential election.

In 1960 Richard M. Nixon, campaigning for president, unsuccessfully urged President Eisenhower not to reappoint Martin. Influenced by his economic adviser, Arthur Burns, Nixon worried that a recession would occur by the fall of 1960 unless the Federal Reserve reversed its restrictive monetary policy. Martin would never consent to such a change in course, and President Eisenhower refused to force the issue by appointing a new chairman who was more receptive to an easy-money policy. True to Nixon's fears, a recession ensued, and he narrowly lost the election to John F. Kennedy. When Nixon finally won the presidency in 1968, he immediately tried to shift Martin from head of the Federal Reserve to U.S. Treasury secretary, so that Nixon could appoint his friend Arthur Burns to the chairmanship position. Martin refused to leave the Federal Reserve before his term expired. As Dr. Andrew Brimmer, who served on the board of governors under Martin, contends, "By deciding to serve out the balance of his Federal Reserve term, Martin prevented the system from being politicized by a president for whom that was a major goal." Indeed, Martin was committed to keeping the Federal Reserve independent of political control.

Upon leaving the Federal Reserve in 1970, Martin reentered the private business world. He left behind a strong legacy, a vision of the Federal Reserve as an institution that should be nonpartisan, independent, and committed to a flexible monetary policy. He thus is referred to often as the father of the modern Federal Reserve Bank.

★

Biographical information on Martin can be found in Andrew F. Brimmer, "William McChesney Martin," *Proceedings of the American Philosophical Society* 44, no. 2 (June 2000). For information on the era, see William McChesney Martin, Jr., "Monetary Policy and International Payments," *Journal of Finance* (Mar. 1963): 1–10, and *The Securities Markets: A Report, with Recommendations by William McChesney Martin, Jr.* (1971); John Brooks, *The Go-Go Years: The Drama and Crashing Finale of Wall Street's Bullish 60s* (1973); and Donald F. Kettl, *Leadership at the Fed* (1986). See also James J. Needham, *The Threat to Corporate Growth* (1974). Obituaries are in the *New York Times* (29 July 1998), *The Economist* (8 Aug. 1998), and *Time* (10 Aug. 1998).

JANICE TRAFLET

MASTERS, William Howell (*b.* 27 December 1915 in Cleveland, Ohio; *d.* 16 February 2001 in Tucson, Arizona), and **Virginia Eshelman JOHNSON** (*b.* 11 February 1925 in Springfield, Missouri), sex researchers and therapists whose jointly written best-seller, *Human Sexual Response* (1966), provided popular yet empirically rigorous scientific support for the sexual revolution of the late 1960s and early 1970s.

Masters, the son of Francis Wynne Masters and Estabrooks Taylor, graduated from the Lawrenceville School, Law-

William Masters *(left)*, and Virginia Johnson *(right)*. CORBIS CORPORATION (BELLEVUE)

renceville, New Jersey, in 1934 and received a B.S. degree from Hamilton College, Clinton, New York, in 1938. When he was a medical student at the University of Rochester School of Medicine and Dentistry, Masters's mentor was the anatomist and endocrinologist George Washington Corner (1889–1981). Corner had discovered the hormonal basis of menstruation in 1928, codiscovered the hormone progesterone in 1929, and chaired the National Research Council's Committee for Research in Problems of Sex from 1947 to 1956. After receiving his M.D. degree in 1943, Masters moved to St. Louis, Missouri, where he did a series of internships and residencies in obstetrics, gynecology, pathology, and internal medicine at St. Louis Maternity Hospital and Barnes Hospital. In 1947 he joined the clinical faculty of obstetrics and gynecology at the Washington University School of Medicine in St. Louis and established a private practice in gynecology. Influenced by the work of Alfred C. Kinsey, Masters began conducting sex research under laboratory conditions at Washington University in 1954.

Virginia Eshelman was the daughter of Hershel Eshelman, a conservative farmer, and Edna Evans, a Republican committeewoman. She became proficient at piano and voice as a child, skipped two grades, and graduated from the public high school in Springfield, Missouri, in 1941. Raised to believe that marriage and children were the ultimate goal of every woman, she had two early short-lived marriages, the first in the early 1940s to a Missouri politician, which lasted two days, and the second to an attorney. From 1941 to 1947 she attended Drury College in Springfield, the University of Missouri at Columbia, and the Kansas City Conservatory of Music, but never earned a degree. She made her living as a country singer, a mezzo-soprano in a vocal quartet, an insurance clerk, a business reporter, and a market researcher. In 1950 she married her third husband, the bandleader George Johnson, with whom she had two children. They divorced in 1956, and shortly afterward she applied for a clerical job at Washington University. About that time Masters was seeking a woman to interview volunteers for his research. Despite Johnson's lack of formal credentials, he hired her as his assistant on 2 January 1957, because of her maturity, her practical expertise in psychology, and the fact that she was a mother.

With funding from the United States Institutes of Health (now the National Institutes of Health), for the next nine years Masters and Johnson recorded photographic, electrocardiographic, electroencephalographic, biochemical, metabolic, and other scientific data on hundreds of paid volunteers masturbating and copulating in their laboratory. In 1964 in St. Louis, they cofounded the Reproductive Biology Research Foundation, which they renamed the Masters and Johnson Institute in 1973. They described and analyzed the sex act in four chronological phases: excitement, plateau, orgasm, and resolution. After writing only a few professional journal articles, they published their results as a book, *Human Sexual Response*. Released on 18 April 1966, it sold more than 300,000 hardcover copies in the next four years. The book fostered a new frankness about sex, a willingness to discuss it openly in mixed company, and a relaxing of social inhibitions that eventually led to the publication of such popular manuals as Alex Comfort's *Joy of Sex* (1972).

Masters and Johnson always claimed that they wrote *Human Sexual Response* for a medical and scientific audience, but that assertion could be questioned. Its publisher was Little, Brown and Company, a prominent commercial trade publisher that did not specialize in medical books. Although it was advertised originally only to the medical and scientific community, the book immediately crossed over to the general public and became a best-seller. There is strong prima facie evidence that its popular appeal was planned. Several factors distinguish *Human Sexual Response* from most medical books. It contains a glossary, useful and typical in popular medical works but unnecessary and rare in works for physicians and scientists. Its illustrations are

noticeably less detailed than those in most medical texts. It contains some peculiar euphemisms and neologisms, such as "automanipulation" for masturbation, which may reflect a superficial attempt to avoid the appearance of targeting prurient book buyers. The book's language is unadorned and technical, but its nontechnical style is readily accessible to intelligent general readers.

Critics applauded *Human Sexual Response,* scientists praised its originality and thoroughness, and physicians and psychologists welcomed its insights into their clinical practices. Its descriptions helped married couples better understand each other's physical and psychological feelings. The book's only significant attackers were religious moralists, who accused Masters and Johnson of trivializing, dehumanizing, despiritualizing, and demystifying sex. *Human Sexual Response* superseded both "Kinsey Reports," *Sexual Behavior in the Human Male* (1948), and *Sexual Behavior in the Human Female* (1953). Its main advance over these earlier studies was that Kinsey only interviewed his subjects, but Masters and Johnson actually observed human sexual action and measured its phenomena. Their perspective was quantitative, physiological, and psychological, while Kinsey's was qualitative and sociological.

Besides their laboratory research, Masters and Johnson were concerned with clinical therapy and psychological healing. In 1959 they began to develop a method of sexual counseling that emphasized the teamwork of a male therapist, a female therapist, and the sexually dysfunctional couple, integrating medical diagnosis, laboratory tests, and round-table discussion. Masters and Johnson preferred a two-week program of co-therapy, with a five-year follow-up. They described this program in their second book, *Human Sexual Inadequacy* (1970). Masters and Johnson also wrote *The Pleasure Bond* (1975), *Homosexuality in Perspective* (1979), *Textbook of Sexual Medicine* (with Robert C. Kolodny, 1979), *Human Sexuality* (1982), *Masters and Johnson on Sex and Human Loving* (1986), *Crisis: Heterosexual Behavior in the Age of AIDS* (1988), *Biological Foundations of Human Sexuality* (1993), and *Heterosexuality* (1994).

Masters and Johnson married in 1971, following Masters's divorce from his first wife, Elisabeth Ellis, with whom he had two children. They divorced in 1993, but the divorce did not end their professional partnership. Masters married his third wife, Geraldine Baker Oliver, the same year. He closed the Masters and Johnson Institute when he retired in 1994. Masters died at the Tucson Medical Center Hospice from complications of Parkinson's disease.

★

Vern L. Bullough, *Science in the Bedroom* (1994), is the standard work on the history of sex research in the United States and includes a study of Masters and Johnson. The feature stories on Masters in *Newsweek* (10 June 1966) and *Life* (24 June 1966) provide interpretations of the impact of *Human Sexual Response*. An obituary of Masters is in the *New York Times* (19 Feb. 2001).

ERIC V.D. LUFT

MATTHAU, Walter (*b*. 1 October 1920 in New York City; *d*. 1 July 2000 in Santa Monica, California), comic character actor best known for playing grumpy old men in such movies as *The Odd Couple* (1966) and *The Fortune Cookie* (1967), playing alongside Jack Lemmon.

Matthau, who is listed in some sources with the surname Matthow or Matuschanskayasky, was the son of Jewish Russian immigrants. His father, Milton, was a street peddler in New York City, and his mother, Rose Berolsky, was a garment worker. After his father left the family, from the age of three Matthau lived with his mother and older brother Henry in a Ukrainian ghetto on New York's Lower East Side. He began acting at age eleven at the New York Yiddish Theater and also became a proficient boxer. After graduating from Seward Park High School he served in the Army Air Corps during World War II, receiving six battle stars, and then attended the New School's Dramatic Workshop on the GI Bill. He studied under Erwin Piscator, alongside Tony Curtis and Rod Steiger. Matthau was well known for misleading interviewers. He was fond of ex-

Movie still of Walter Matthau from Neil Simon's *The Odd Couple*, 1968. © BETTMANN/CORBIS

plaining that his father was a defrocked Russian Orthodox priest, while Matthau apparently invented the elaborate surname Matuschanskayasky in revenge for having been given more work than expected on the 1974 disaster movie *Earthquake.*

Matthau's acting career began with a part in an off-Broadway production of *The Aristocrats* in 1946 and continued when he was the understudy for the role of an octogenarian bishop in *Anne of a Thousand Days* on Broadway in 1948. He married Grace Johnson in 1948, and they had two children, but the couple divorced in 1958. In 1959 Matthau married Carol Marcus Saroyan, with whom he had a son, Charles, who is a film director. Matthau made his screen debut in *The Kentuckian* (1955) and by the late 1950s was combining regular stage appearances with minor character roles in movies. In particular he gave picture-stealing performances as villains in Westerns such as *Ride a Crooked Trail* (1958) and *Lonely Are the Brave* (1962). With his sagging, bloodhound face, Matthau always struggled to win leading roles on the stage or in movies, but by the 1960s he was an established Hollywood character actor. By 1965 he had appeared in more than twenty movies, 150 television shows, and twenty Broadway plays. Even so, he was in his late thirties before his name and his face became well known.

Interviewed in 1971, Matthau said, "Every actor looks for a part that will combine his talents with his personality." Disheveled sportswriter Oscar Madison was the part that did this for him. He first took the role in Neil Simon's play *The Odd Couple* on Broadway in 1965, winning a Tony Award for best actor and a New York Drama Critics' Award. The following year Matthau teamed up with Jack Lemmon for the first time in Billy Wilder's *The Fortune Cookie* (1966), and the pair began an on-screen double act that became one of the most successful in movie history. After the success of the stage version of *The Odd Couple*, *The Fortune Cookie* was something of a return to Matthau's movie origins, in which he often played crooked lawyers. But this time, as an attorney who persuades his brother-in-law to fake a sports injury to win damages in a lawsuit, Matthau found himself alongside an actor who complimented his deadpan comic delivery to perfection. Reviews of the film were mixed, but Matthau won an Academy Award for best supporting actor, and the obvious chemistry between the two male leads made a repeat performance inevitable. He was nominated for Oscars twice more, for *Kotch* (1971), directed by Lemmon, and *The Sunshine Boys* (1975), in which he starred with George Burns.

The Matthau-Lemmon partnership surfaced for the second time in 1968, in the form of the movie version of *The Odd Couple,* probably Matthau's best-known film appearance. Reprising his part as Oscar Madison, Matthau slouches around the apartment he has agreed to share with his newly separated friend Felix Ungar, played by Lemmon. In the 1960s, as divorce rates rose, *The Odd Couple* provided sharp comic commentary on an increasingly common temporary domestic arrangement. As the plot progresses Oscar and Felix begin to argue incessantly about their living arrangements. Oscar is a disorganized slob, while Felix is excessively clean and tidy. At one point Oscar complains that Felix keeps leaving him reminder notes such as "We are all out of cornflakes, F.U." He explains, "It took me three hours to figure out that F.U. was Felix Ungar." While Oscar and Felix squabbled on screen, Matthau and Lemmon became close friends. After Matthau's death in 2000, Lemmon said, "I have lost someone I loved as a brother, a closest friend, and a remarkable human being. We have also lost one of the best damn actors we'll ever see."

In the 1960s Matthau and Lemmon formed one of the most enduring screen partnerships in movie history. They worked together many times between 1966 and Matthau's death in 2000, often revisiting their *Odd Couple* characters in all but name. Best known for playing irascible, obstinate slobs, Matthau was in fact a versatile actor, as appearances in Sidney Lumet's *Fail Safe* (1964) and Edward Dmytryk's *Mirage* (1965) show. In *Plaza Suite* (1971) he convincingly played multiple characters.

A heavy smoker and gambler, Matthau suffered his first major heart attack in 1966, while making *The Fortune Cookie,* and estimated that he had gambled away over $5 million during his lifetime. Though generally good-humored, he was inclined to tell tall tales and to make life difficult for anyone he disliked. One of his favorite jokes was to speak to movie executives only in Yiddish. After appearing in over seventy films in his forty-five-year career, Matthau died at the Saint John's Health Center in Santa Monica, California, following a heart attack. He is buried at Westwood Memorial Park in Los Angeles.

★

A full-length biography of Matthau is Allan Hunter, *Walter Matthau* (1984). Carol Matthau is candid about her life with Matthau in her book *Among the Porcupines: A Memoir* (1993). Allen Eyles, "Walter Matthau," *Focus on Film* (spring 1972) is also useful. Among the best interviews with Matthau is Karen Duffy, "Genius," *Interview* (1 Dec. 1994). Obituaries are in the *Times* (London) (3 July 2000) and *Time* (10 July 2000).

CHRIS ROUTLEDGE

MAULDIN, William Henry ("Bill") (*b.* 29 October 1921 in Mountain Park, New Mexico), cartoonist, most famous for commentary on army life during World War II, who resurfaced as a potent and challenging political cartoonist in the late 1950s.

Mauldin was the son of Sidney Mauldin, who "collected careers as an Eagle Scout accumulates merit badges" (as

Mauldin wrote in *The Brass Ring*) and Edith Bernis. Mauldin's father took his wife and two children throughout the southwestern United States and Mexico, working as a miner, salesman, apple farmer, and subsistence homesteader. His parents divorced when he and his brother were teenagers. Mauldin attended high school in Alamogordo, New Mexico, where his first published cartoon appeared in the school paper. His style improved vastly after a $20 mail-order course in cartooning with the Landon School in Cleveland, Ohio. In 1937 Mauldin moved to Phoenix, Arizona, and attended Phoenix Union High School; he did not graduate, but he did join the Reserve Officers Training Corps and was encouraged by the cartoonist Reg Manning. With $500 from his grandfather for tuition, Mauldin went to Chicago to take life drawing and political cartooning courses for a year at the Chicago Academy of Fine Arts.

Mauldin moved back to Phoenix in 1940, living with his mother and stepfather. A friend in Phoenix helped shape Mauldin's life, suggesting that they join the National Guard together. Company D of the Forty-fifth Division became part of the standing army immediately after Mauldin joined. Mauldin served as staff cartoonist of the *45th Division News,* beginning his career as soldier and cartoonist. Wanting more authentic action, he was transferred to K Company, 180th Infantry, as a rifleman; meanwhile, he continued to create cartoons, and his work was reprinted in the *Daily Oklahoman* and other papers. In February 1942 he married Norma Jean Humphries, with whom he had two children.

Just as a court jester safely makes fun of the king, Mauldin's cartoons tweaked the noses of the brass but showed deep respect and empathy for the foot soldiers. The major paper of the U.S. armed forces, *Stars and Stripes,* began carrying Mauldin's cartoons in 1943, despite complaints by General George S. Patton that Mauldin's characters were too scruffy and disrespectful. Even in the army, sentiment was on Mauldin's side. In 1945 he won a Pulitzer Prize for his Willie and Joe cartoons, was featured in a *Time* magazine cover story, and had his best-known book published—*Up Front,* a collection of World War II cartoons and reminiscences. Mauldin made a short tour of Korea, covering the war for *Collier's* magazine, and this resulted in a book in 1952. Some of his short stories were published, and he had a minor role in the 1951 movie *The Red Badge of Courage.*

At the suggestion of Herbert Block, Mauldin was hired as a political cartoonist by the *St. Louis Post-Dispatch* in 1958. From the first, he tackled issues that would disturb and divide the country during the coming decade: racial equality, capital punishment, environmental damage, union scandals, and the war in Indochina. Some of his cartoons in the late 1950s and early 1960s seem decades ahead of their time, as Mauldin took on the overzealous antibiotic

Bill Mauldin at the Pulitzer Prize awards ceremony, May 1966. © BETTMANN/CORBIS

industry, television violence, the cigarette manufacturers, the censoring of the word "nigger" in *Huckleberry Finn,* and world overpopulation. In 1959 he won another Pulitzer Prize for a cartoon decrying the banishment of Russian intellectuals to Siberia, while the National Cartoonist's Society gave him an award for best editorial cartoon of the year in 1960 and the Reuben Award as cartoonist of the year in 1961. United Features syndicated his work to newspapers nationwide.

In his 1960s work Mauldin became the court jester of a nation. Like his army cartoons, his political cartoons show deep affection and pride mixed with a keen sense of egos that needed reducing and problems that deserved public attention. For instance, the cartoon that gave its title to his 1965 collection, *I've Decided I Want My Seat Back,* shows a determined American Eagle about to take back the top of a flagpole from a huffy bird labeled "Jim Crow." Mauldin's most famous cartoon from the 1960s, on the occasion of President John F. Kennedy's assassination, is pure poignancy: a picture of the Lincoln Memorial statue, its head in its hands, weeping.

In 1962 Mauldin moved to the *Chicago Sun-Times,* his home newspaper for the rest of his career. One controversial cartoon showed a dark form labeled "Black Muslims" as the shadow of a hooded figure representing the Ku Klux Klan. Pieces critical of U.S. involvement in Vietnam appeared as early as 1962, but Mauldin also produced many cartoons supportive of America's actions in Cuba and elsewhere. Mauldin visited South Vietnam, where his oldest

son was serving as a member of the U.S. Army, as a correspondent for the *Sun-Times* in January 1965. He later wrote in a 1973 article that as the bombs fell, he was "hollering [his] head off in approval," and the resultant cartoons earned "Americanism awards from Legion posts." He was persuaded back to the opinion of his "long-haired offspring," however, and "the plaques dribbled off and the familiar old protests began again." By 1965 he and his first wife had divorced and he was married to his second wife, Natalie; they had four children. In 1967 he went to Israel to report on the Six-Day War.

Mauldin's cartoons continued in the *Sun-Times* and over 250 other newspapers until 1992, when he retired and moved to Santa Fe, New Mexico. However, his fame was at its peak in the early 1960s. *The Brass Ring,* a memoir published in 1971, ends in 1945. Mauldin occasionally made the news—for example, when he taught a course in political cartooning at Yale University in 1974; when *Up Front* was reissued in 1984; and when he traveled to Saudi Arabia in 1991. He divorced again and married a third time, but in 2002 he was alone, divorced once more, and incapacitated, in a nursing home in Orange County, California.

Perhaps only a cartoonist as familiar and loved as Mauldin was could have taken on the issues he did, creating such controversy, while retaining his wide public platform. Another part of his success, in the early 1960s as well as during World War II, was that he always drew what his mind and heart determined, and was neither guided by fashion nor deterred by it.

★

The Archives of American Art at the Smithsonian Institution in Washington, D.C., has collected Mauldin's published cartoons from 1946 to 1987, as well as memorabilia and correspondence. Mauldin's memoir, *The Brass Ring* (1971) only covers his life until 1945, but presents photos, cartoons, his early history, and a strong sense of his personality. His cartoons from 1958 through 1961 are collected in *What's Got Your Back Up?* (1961), and those from 1961 through 1965 in *I've Decided I Want My Seat Back* (1965). Mauldin's article, "Ain't Gonna Cover Wars No More: Evolution of a Dove," appeared in the *New Republic* (10 Feb. 1973). Bob Greene, "Bill Mauldin Is in Need of His Buddies Now," *Chicago Tribune* (11 Aug. 2002), describes the elderly cartoonist's problems.

BERNADETTE LYNN BOSKY

MAY, Elaine (*b.* 21 May 1932 in Philadelphia, Pennsylvania), comedian, writer, director, performer, and a founding member of the Chicago improvisational comedy theater group Second City, who achieved recognition in the early 1960s for her dry, witty technique in the comedy duo Nichols and May, and went on to write, direct, and perform on Broadway and in motion pictures.

Elaine May (*left*), with Mike Nichols. ASSOCIATED PRESS AP

May is the daughter of Jack Berlin, who directed, wrote, and performed for a Yiddish traveling theatrical group, and actress Jeannie Berlin. She married Marvin May in 1949 and divorced young, giving birth to a daughter while still in her teens. In 1950 May attended the University of Chicago, where she first met her later comedy partner Mike Nichols. In 1955 she joined the Compass Theatre, where she and Nichols, along with a number of notable comedians, performed improvisational comedy. The group of talented young performers, which included Shelly Berman, Alan Arkin, and Barbara Harris, formed the Second City improvisational comedy group. It was while in Second City that May and Nichols decided to form a comedy duo and take their act on the road.

They eventually took their act to Greenwich Village in the lower part of Manhattan, where they performed at Village Vanguard and Blue Angel. The improvisational comedy of Nichols and May was a perfect fit for the intellectual, counter-culture attitudes of the Village in the 1960s. Their success was almost immediate. In contrast to the Catskills humor of Red Skelton, Jack Benny, Henny Youngman, Buddy Hackett, and other popular comedians of the 1950s and 1960s, Nichols and May did not tell traditional jokes. Their humor was based on an exchange of dialogue that brilliantly employed understatement and acerbic wit. The targets of their humor were previously sacrosanct institutions, such as political bureaucracies, and they calmly

broached formerly off-limits topics such as adultery, which contributed to their popularity with a generation in the process of recreating itself. Like the Beat poets, modern artists, and new musicians who also frequented the village, Nichols and May's original, satiric examination of the human condition helped forge a new type of comedy.

Shortly after arriving in New York City, Nichols and May appeared on the *Steve Allen Show*. By 1960 they had their own show on Broadway—*An Evening with Nichols and May*, which ran for 306 performances from 8 October 1960 to 1 July 1961. Howard Taubman, in his *New York Times* review of the show, observed, "Miss May and Mr. Nichols combine perception with an air of genial relaxation." May wrote other plays for the stage in the 1960s, including *A Matter of Position* and *Not Enough Rope* (both produced in 1962) as well as *Adaptation* and *Next,* which debuted off-Broadway in 1969. The duo released several successful record albums of their comedy; the first, *An Evening with Mike Nichols and Elaine May* (1960), won a 1961 Grammy Award for best comedy performance.

After the duo broke up in 1961, May focused on writing for theater, but she still found time to perform. In 1962 she married the lyricist Sheldon Harnick; the couple divorced in 1963. From 1964 to 1965 May appeared on the satiric news program *That Was the Week that Was*. In 1966 she was cast in *The Office*, a Broadway comedy that closed in previews after only ten performances. In 1967 she appeared with Jack Lemmon and Peter Falk in the Clive Donner film *Luv* and with José Ferrer and Shelley Winters in Carl Reiner's *Enter Laughing*.

In 1971 May became one of the first women to write, direct, and star in her own motion picture, *A New Leaf*, in which May plays a naive heiress pursued by an egocentric bachelor (played by Walter Matthau) who has depleted his trust fund. Although the film was not a financial success and the final edit was completed without May's input, it is still a well-crafted comedy, and May's unique comedy style is prevalent throughout the film. In 1972 she found success on the big screen directing *The Heartbreak Kid*, based on a Neil Simon script.

May continued to work in film, earning two Academy Award nominations for her screenwriting: the first in 1978 when she and Warren Beatty updated *Here Comes Mr. Jordan* (1941) into *Heaven Can Wait*, and the second when she adapted the Joe Klein novel *Primary Colors* for the screen in 1998. In 1987 May wrote and directed *Ishtar*. The film was widely panned and considered one of the biggest Hollywood bombs of all time, but most criticism of the film was unjustified. *Ishtar* stars Warren Beatty and Dustin Hoffman as two untalented, would-be songwriters who inadvertently become entangled in international intrigue. The film is a brilliant exercise in understatement and dry wit. Unfortunately for May early publicity on the film prior to its release started a snowball of bad press that ultimately sank the film. In 1996 May adapted *La Cage Aux Folles* into *The Birdcage* for her old partner Mike Nichols. Throughout her work in movies, May has continued to write for and perform on Broadway, and in the 1990s she combined her talents with fellow writers David Mamet and Woody Allen to produce the long-running hit play *Death Defying Acts*.

May's comedy work as half of Nichols and May in the early 1960s set the tone for many who followed, particularly those concerned with satire. May and Nichols redefined the comedy duo and were instrumental in bringing quirky, off-beat, and intelligent wit to a new generation of comedians.

★

No full-length biography of May exists, but articles about her appear in numerous publications; of particular relevance to May in the 1960s are articles in the *New York Times* (10 Oct. 1960), *Village Voice* (20 Feb. 1969), *New Yorker* (22 Feb. 1969), and *Saturday Review* (1 Mar. 1969).

KEVIN ALEXANDER BOON

MAYER, Maria Goeppert. *See* Goeppert-Mayer, Maria.

MAYS, William Howard, Jr. ("Willie") (*b.* 6 May 1931 in Westfield [some sources say Fairfield], Alabama), Major League Baseball player and coach whose all-out emotional and physical commitment transformed the game and whose record-setting play in the 1950s and 1960s earned him recognition from baseball historians as one of the greatest players of all time.

Mays's father, William Howard Mays, worked in a tool room for a steel mill and also played center field for a local semiprofessional baseball team. His mother, Anna Sattlewhite Mays, had been a high-school track star. Mays's parents divorced when he was three years old, and he was raised by his father. His mother remarried and had ten children, who were half-brothers and -sisters to Mays.

Although he worked hard, long hours, Mays, Sr., made time for his son and encouraged the boy's athletic interests and natural talent, trying to steer him in the direction of professional baseball as a means of escaping the life of a manual laborer. He was a pitcher for the Negro amateur leagues himself.

At Fairfield Industrial High School, which did not have a baseball team, Mays was the quarterback of the football team and the highest scorer on the basketball team. Outside

Willie Mays. ARCHIVE PHOTOS, INC.

of school he began playing baseball with the semiprofessional Gray Sox at age thirteen. By 1948 he had joined the professional Birmingham Black Barons of the Negro Leagues as a center fielder at the request of the manager, Piper Davis. In spite of playing professional baseball and traveling around the country, Mays stayed in high school and earned his diploma in 1950.

Mays was spotted by a New York Giants scout and signed with that organization in 1950. A minor league team in Sioux City, Iowa, refused to accept Mays because he was African American, and he instead went to the Trenton, New Jersey, Giants of AA ball, where he performed well. The Giants management wanted to bring Mays along gradually, because he seemed unprepared for the rough treatment he would receive in the major leagues.

In 1951 Mays was moved to the Minneapolis, Minnesota, Millers, a AAA club. He had a .477 batting average and was beloved by the fans when he was called up to the major leagues. He performed poorly at first in New York and was unhappy with the racism he encountered. Mays asked to be sent back to Minneapolis, but the Giants manager, Leo Durocher, persuaded Mays to stay, insisting the young man was the best player he had ever seen. Mays's performance improved, and he was voted the National League Rookie of the Year for 1951.

In 1952 Mays was drafted into the U.S. Army. He served stateside, playing a great deal of baseball and learning his famous "basket catch." Mays was discharged from the army in 1954 and returned to the Giants. That year, in the first game of the World Series, Mays made a basket catch over his shoulder while running to dead center field off a tremendous blast by Vic Wertz of the Cleveland Indians. "The Catch" is often cited as the best ever made, but fans of Mays knew it was only one of many amazing plays. In 1954 Mays was named as the National League's Most Valuable Player, and he began his twenty-year run as a member of their All-Star team.

In 1955 Mays hit fifty-one home runs, stole twenty-four bases, and distinguished himself with consistently great play. The next year he stole forty bases and, at age twenty-four, secured his reputation as the greatest all-around offensive threat in the history of baseball. Soon after, he also was deemed the best defensive center fielder in the game's history. A favorite with Giants fans, Mays earned the nickname "Say Hey Kid" because of his enthusiasm on the diamond. In May 1956 he married Marguerite Wendell; they adopted a baby boy in 1958. The couple had a messy, public divorce in 1963.

The Giants moved to San Francisco for the 1958 season and saw their attendance at a minor league park double from that of the previous season in New York. By then, Mays was generally regarded by baseball fans as the game's best player; many argued that he was better than Babe Ruth. Even so, Mays was going through dark times: his marriage was foundering, fans in San Francisco seemed slow in taking a liking to him, and racists in Dublin, California, politely told him not to buy a house there. Mays experienced the sort of petty, cruel racism that he had hoped not to find in California.

His wonderful play in 1962, during which the Giants won the National League pennant, brought him the adulation he had missed since leaving New York. Overcoming the damp, cold, shifting winds of Candlestick Park—the worst hitter's park in baseball, especially for home-run hitters—Mays bashed long balls at such a ferocious pace that journalists thought he would beat Hank Aaron to Babe Ruth's career record of 714 major league home runs. Mays also managed to maintain a high batting average that year and to set a career-high record of 141 runs batted in. In 1965 he hit fifty-two home runs, with an incredible average of 9.3 at bats per home run, while leading the league with a .645 slugging average. Mays received the league's Most Valuable Player award for 1965.

On 27 November 1971 Mays married Mae Louise Allen, a Howard University graduate who knew sports. Mays was traded on 11 May 1972 to the New York Mets, supposedly so he could close out his career in the city where he had first become famous. He did not want to leave the Giants and resented the trade. In 1973 Mays retired from the major leagues. In 1979, his first year of eligibility, he was voted into the Baseball Hall of Fame. From 1986 to 1998 he rejoined the Giants organization to assist with coaching and public relations.

To most baseball historians, Mays remains the best of all players. He had the greatest range and throwing arm of any center fielder. As a base stealer and runner, he was astoundingly cunning and intimidating. He hit for high batting averages and a multitude of doubles (523, lifetime), triples (140), and home runs (660). As a power hitter, he ranks only behind Babe Ruth and Mark McGwire. Further, he was a master of all the strategies of baseball. When they played the Giants, opposing teams prepared three sets of signs for each game, because Mays would figure out the first and second sets of signs (maybe the third, too) and tell his manager, who would then know the opposition's strategy. The combination of Mays's great talent, immense dedication, and superior intelligence established him as the model of the perfect ball player, both in the 1960s and for following generations.

★

Mays and Lou Sahadi, *Say Hey: The Autobiography of Willie Mays* (1988), is an excellent sports autobiography, with Mays telling about both his good and bad experiences, from the racism in his early days of playing baseball to his induction into the Hall of Fame. Donald Dewey and Nicholas Acocella, *The Biographical*

History of Baseball (1995, rev. ed. 2002), provides a helpful summary of the essentials of Mays's life. George Sullivan, *Sluggers: Twenty-seven of Baseball's Greatest* (1991), offers statistics and other facts to explain Mays's greatness as a hitter.

KIRK H. BEETZ

MEADER, (Abbott) Vaughn   (*b.* 20 March 1936 in Waterville, Maine), Grammy award–winning comedian, singer, and satirist known for his uncanny mimicry of President John F. Kennedy; his career never fully recovered after Kennedy's assassination.

Meader was the only child of Charles Vaughn Meader, a millworker, and Mary Ellen Abbott. After Meader's father broke his neck in a diving accident and drowned when Meader was only eighteen months old, his mother moved to Boston to work as a cocktail waitress, leaving Meader behind with relatives. A sometimes unruly and troubled child, Meader was sent to live with his mother in Boston at the age of five, but she had become alcohol-dependent and placed him in a children's home. After shuttling among several schools in Massachusetts and Maine, Meader eventually graduated from Brookline High School in Boston in 1953 and joined the U.S. Army. While stationed in Mannheim, West Germany, as a laboratory technician, he formed a country music band (the *Rhine Rangers*) with fellow soldiers, later adding impressions of popular singers to his

Vaughn Meader, November 1962. ASSOCIATED PRESS AP

repertoire. Meader married the German-born Vera Heller in 1955.

After his discharge in 1957 at the rank of private first class, Meader sold sewing machines door to door in Maine, before moving to New York City in 1959 to study at the School of Radio Technique under the GI Bill. While performing as a singer, musician, and comic in small nightclubs, Meader began impersonating Senator John F. Kennedy during the 1960 presidential campaign. The audience reaction was so favorable that Meader ended every performance with a "JFK press conference." Although Meader was not, strictly speaking, an impressionist—the Kennedy routine was just five minutes of his thirty-minute act, which included original songs, parodies, and jokes—he mastered all of Kennedy's mannerisms (such as jabbing his forefinger for emphasis) and phrases (among them, "Let me say *this* about *that*"). Meader's physique was similar to Kennedy's, and he even adopted Kennedy's hairstyle. The Kennedy bit became popular enough for Meader to appear on *Celebrity Talent Scouts* on the Columbia Broadcasting System (CBS) during the summer of 1962 (the show was taped on 25 June and broadcast on 3 July) and to have a full-page captioned photograph in *Life* magazine as part of a feature on Kennedy mimics.

After seeing Meader's stage act, the producers Bob Booker and Earle Doud, who had been planning a comedy album based on the Kennedy family, quickly signed him up. *The First Family* was recorded on 22 October 1962 before a live audience—the same night that President Kennedy himself was on television announcing that the Soviet Union had nuclear missiles in Cuba. Rejected by a dozen labels, the album was released on Cadence Records on 7 November 1962, and it became a sensation, helped also by the fact that Kennedy's popularity had soared as a result of his strong stand against the Soviets during the Cuban Missile Crisis.

The First Family mostly consisted of short segments gently satirizing the Kennedys by putting the president in nonpresidential situations, such as sorting out children's bathtub toys, as well as presidential ones, such as humorous press conferences. Record distributors could barely keep up with demand, and it became the fastest-selling record in history (about 4 million copies sold in four weeks). On 15 December 1962 the album went to the top of the charts and remained there for twelve weeks, eventually selling more than 7.5 million copies. Meader, only twenty-six years old, appeared on numerous television programs, including *The Ed Sullivan Show, The Jack Paar Program, The Steve Allen Westinghouse Show,* and *The Andy Williams Show,* and went from earning $7.50 a show in nightclubs to more than $5,000 per appearance.

Meader's mimicry was so good—*Playboy* lauded him as a "carbon copy of the President"—that even Arthur M.

Schlesinger, Jr. (a special assistant to the president) was startled when he heard "Kennedy" make some impolitic comments on the radio. Although First Lady Jacqueline Kennedy did not appreciate the record, Kennedy himself was amused, even playing it for the cabinet and purchasing 100 copies to send as Christmas gifts. Officially asked at a press conference if the album annoyed him, Kennedy quipped, "I actually listened to Mr. Meader's record, but I thought it sounded more like Teddy than it did me—so *he's* annoyed."

After the cast went on a successful tour (opening at Carnegie Hall), Meader began to grow weary of the act. Although the Kennedy routine had been very profitable—he earned seven cents in royalties for every album sold, and women threw themselves at him as if he really were Kennedy—he feared being typecast, and initially resisted participating in *The First Family, Volume Two*. That album was released in March 1963 and sold about 2 million copies. He signed with Verve Records and began working on an album of new material, *Have Some Nuts*, which was released in early 1964.

On 22 November 1963 Meader was in Milwaukee for an appearance before a group of Wisconsin Democrats, when a cabdriver asked him if he had heard that Kennedy had been shot in Dallas. Meader, thinking he was being set up for a punch line, replied, "No, how does it go?" Because of Kennedy's assassination, Meader's television and nightclub appearances were immediately postponed or canceled, and any remaining copies of both *First Family* albums were re-called and destroyed by Cadence. Meader announced that he would never do Kennedy's voice again and went into seclusion. The comedian Lenny Bruce later observed that they put two graves in Arlington National Cemetery, one for Kennedy and one for Meader. Strangers came up to Meader on the street to offer their condolences, as if he were a member of the Kennedy family. Oddly enough, although the material he had taped for December's Grammy Awards telecast was cut out, *The First Family* won the Grammy for album of the year, and Meader won for best comedy performance.

Kennedy's assassination effectively ended Meader's career, since (as he put it in 1977), he was "a living reminder of a tragedy." The public was not interested in any of his new albums or routines, and he went through what he described as his "wine, women, song, and drugs period." He drank heavily, his wife left him (they divorced in 1965), and by 1965 he had squandered all the money from the original album. Meader briefly quit the music business and lived in seclusion in a log cabin in Maine with his second wife, Susan Hannah (they married in 1969 and divorced in 1973), before giving away all his possessions and moving to San Francisco in 1967, where he began to use LSD and eventually cocaine and angel dust. After moving back to

New York, he recorded *The Second Coming* (1971), an album about Christ's reappearance in the rock-music age, which received no airplay due to perceived offensive religious content.

Meader continued to work throughout the 1970s and 1980s as a saloon singer (reverting to his given name Abbott), forming various country and bluegrass groups in Kentucky and Maine. He even tried his hand at film music and acting, starring briefly in a play in Los Angeles about a man obsessed with John Kennedy. Meader married his third wife, Christine Surma, in 1979; they divorced in 1984. After marrying his fourth wife, Sheila Colbath, in 1986, Meader managed a restaurant, the Wharf, in Hallowell, Maine, and continued to perform original songs, although he suffered from emphysema. He never had any children.

Meader's talents as a satirist and singer were always overshadowed by his impression of John F. Kennedy, with whom he was perpetually linked, both in life and death.

★

Although there is no full-length biography of Meader, aspects of his career are discussed in Richard Lamparski, *Whatever Became of . . . ?* (1974), in *Joe Franklin's Encyclopedia of Comedians* (1979), and in Ronald L. Smith, *Who's Who in Comedy* (1992). An interesting profile of Meader is Andrew Goldman, "Vaughn Meader Is Alive and . . . *Well*, He's Still Alive," *Boston Magazine* (Mar. 1997). Other informative articles are Rudy Maxa, "Camelot's Comedian: Getting Ready for Teddy with Vaughn Meader," *Washington Post Magazine* (4 Nov. 1979); David Lamb, "A Long Way from Camelot: Vaughn Meader's JFK Impersonation Made Him a Star. Then An Assassin's Bullet Took Everything Away," *Los Angeles Times* (20 Apr. 1997); and Stephen Nohlgren, "From Camelot to Gulfport," *St. Petersburg Times* (21 Mar. 2000). An early article about the *First Family* album is Peter Bunzel, "A Kennedy Spoof Full of 'Vigah,'" *Life* (14 Dec. 1962). Reactions to Meader's record by Kennedy and his advisers is in Nicholas J. Cull, "No Laughing Matter: Vaughn Meader, the Kennedy Administration, and Presidential Impersonations on Radio," *Historical Journal of Film, Radio and Television,* 17, no. 3 (Aug. 1997): 383–399. An interview with Meader is "Vaughn Meader," *New York Times Magazine* (21 Nov. 1999).

JOHN A. DROBNICKI

MERCER, John Herndon ("Johnny") (*b.* 18 November 1909 in Savannah, Georgia; *d.* 25 June 1976 in Los Angeles, California), one of the leading popular music lyricists of the mid-twentieth century and winner of four Academy Awards for best song, including "Moon River" (1962) and "Days of Wine and Roses" (1963); cofounder of Capitol Records.

Mercer was the son of George A. Mercer, an attorney and real estate salesman, and Lillian Ciucevich. Mercer's fam-

Johnny Mercer *(left)*, with Henry Mancini after receiving the Academy Award for best song for "Days of Wine and Roses," 1963. © BETTMANN/CORBIS

ily, which included a sister and three older half-brothers from his father's first marriage, was fairly well to do, living in one of Savannah's more prosperous neighborhoods. Mercer attended Woodberry Forest Preparatory School in Orange, Virginia, from 1922 to 1927, where he showed an intense interest in poetry and music. At the age of fifteen he wrote his first song, a jazz number he called "Sister Suzie, Strut Your Stuff."

After graduation Mercer returned to Savannah, where he worked briefly in his father's failing real-estate business. At his mother's urging, he joined the Savannah Little Theater in 1927. Later that year he traveled with the theater group to participate in a one-act play competition in New York City. After the competition he made his Broadway debut in a production of Ben Jonson's *Volpone* in 1928. Lured by musical theater, he auditioned unsuccessfully for a role in *Garrick's Gaieties of 1930,* but managed to place one of his songs in the show. Mercer married Ginger Meehan, a dancer in *Gaieties,* in June 1931, and the couple settled in Brooklyn, where Mercer began to focus his energies on songwriting. They had two children.

From the beginning Mercer collaborated with some of the leading composers of the day. "Lazybones," his first big hit in 1933, was written with Hoagy Carmichael. That same year he went to work for orchestra leader Paul Whiteman, serving as a vocalist, emcee, and songwriter for Whiteman's popular radio show. In 1935 he headed to Hollywood after landing a songwriting and acting contract with RKO Studios. Although his acting career was relatively

brief, over the next several decades Mercer wrote hundreds of songs for the movies. In the early 1940s the songwriter joined music-store owner Glenn Wallich and fellow songwriter Buddy DeSylva in founding Capitol Records, at which he served as president and talent scout. In 1946 Mercer won his first Academy Award for best song, for "On the Atchison, Topeka, and the Santa Fe," written with composer Harry Warren for the film *The Harvey Girls*.

Mercer won his second Academy Award in 1951 for his lyrics to Hoagy Carmichael's "In the Cool, Cool, Cool of the Evening," written for the film *Here Comes the Groom*. Although Mercer was a songwriter for several decades, he produced perhaps his greatest musical contributions during the 1960s. He did some of his most memorable work, and earned two more Oscars, during the last full decade of his career as a lyricist. A major factor in Mercer's work during the 1960s was his rewarding collaboration with composer/orchestra leader Henry Mancini.

Mercer's greatest fame came for his lyric writing, but he did create both the words and music for two musical films, *Daddy Long Legs* (1954) and *Top Banana* (1951). He also supplied both the lyrics and the melody for a handful of popular hits, including "Something's Gotta Give" (1955), "I'm an Old Cowhand" (1936), and "Dream" (1944).

Early in the decade Mercer and Mancini wrote "Moon River" for the film *Breakfast at Tiffany's,* starring Audrey Hepburn and George Peppard. The song, an instant classic, won Mercer his third best-song Oscar in 1962. A masterful marriage of words and music, the song is particularly memorable for the wistfulness of Mercer's lyrics.

The Mercer-Mancini collaboration hit pay dirt once again in 1963, with the Academy Award–winning song for "Days of Wine and Roses," the theme song for the movie of the same name, starring Jack Lemmon and Lee Remick. Mercer also worked with Mancini on songs for two other films, *The Great Race* (1965) and *Darling Lili* (1970).

Another 1960s hit for Mercer was "I Wanna Be Around" (1959), first made popular by vocalist Tony Bennett, and later covered by dozens of artists, including a sizzling live version presented by rhythm-and-blues artist James Brown at the Apollo Theater. An interesting story surrounds the genesis of this song, the idea for which was first suggested to Mercer in a letter from Ohio cosmetician Sadie Vimmerstedt. She sent him a single line, "I want to be around to pick up the pieces when somebody's breaking your heart," and with that as his inspiration, Mercer wrote the rest of the lyrics. He never forgot Vimmerstedt's contribution, however, and he gave her a coauthor credit that earned her about $3,000 a year once the song became a big hit.

In 1965 Mercer wrote English lyrics to revise a popular French song, creating "Summer Wind," a big hit for Frank Sinatra and Wayne Newton. Two years later, collaborating with composer Neal Hefti, Mercer wrote the title song for the film version of Neil Simon's *Barefoot in the Park.*

In the late 1960s, when music publishers Howard Richmond, Abe Olman, and Al Brackman founded the Songwriters Hall of Fame (SHOF), Mercer seemed a natural choice as founding president of the organization, which had been created to give songwriters some well-deserved visibility. Mercer served in that post from 1969 until 1973, when he passed the torch to Sammy Cahn, his hand-picked successor. Mercer remained active into the mid-1970s. In late 1975 he was diagnosed with a brain tumor and died at the age of sixty-six. Mercer is buried in Bonaventure Cemetery in his hometown of Savannah.

One of the most prolific American lyricists of the twentieth century, Mercer will be remembered for far more than the sheer volume of his output and the speed with which he turned out songs. According to the SHOF Web site, Mercer's unique place in songwriting history cannot be traced to either "the hip sophistication of his lyrics" or "his Southern charm." As captivating as these qualities may have been, they fail to capture the real Mercer. "Ask anyone who writes lyrics, Johnny Mercer was a genius."

Mercer helped to shape the face of American popular music through more than four decades. His quintessentially American lyrics served as themes for such classic jazz and ballad singers as Frank Sinatra, Billie Holiday, and Tony Bennett. According to fellow songwriter Oscar Brand, "Johnny Mercer had a panache quality that was beyond celebrity. You wanted to cherish this man."

★

A permanent Mercer exhibit is at the Pullen Library on the campus of Georgia State University in Atlanta. A portrait of Mercer, along with the lyrics that are his greatest legacy to American popular music, is in Bob Bach and Ginger Mercer, eds., *Our Huckleberry Friend: The Life, Times, and Lyrics of Johnny Mercer* (1982). Further information can be found in Gene Lees, *American Film* (Dec./Jan. 1978); and Warren Craig, *The Great Songwriters of Hollywood* (1980). An obituary is in the *New York Times* (26 June 1976).

DON AMERMAN

MEREDITH, James Howard (*b.* 25 June 1933 in Kosciusko, Mississippi), civil rights leader who came to national attention when he successfully applied to be the first African American to enroll in the University of Mississippi, spawning civil unrest and riots.

Meredith's father, Moses ("Cap") Meredith, was a strict disciplinarian who insisted that his children stand up to racism and discrimination. Cap was ingenious in his methods: he named his son "J. H." to thwart local whites, who

James Meredith appearing on *Meet the Press,* May 1963. ASSOCIATED PRESS AP

insisted on referring to all blacks disrespectfully by their first names, in contrast with the treatment generally accorded white residents. When he replied to inquiring whites that J. H. stood for nothing, that it was "just J. H.," they were visibly frustrated. The Meredith family was relatively well off, compared with the average African-American family of 1930s Mississippi. Cap Meredith was the first member of his family to become a landowner, purchasing an eighty-four-acre farm in Attala County, approximately four miles from Kosciusko. Roxie (Patterson) Meredith (some sources say her maiden name was Smith), Meredith's mother, raised both her own children and those from Cap's previous marriage, in an eleven-room house. The thirteen children (Meredith was the seventh) were obedient to their father, accepting his dictate that they would never work in domestic or servile positions.

In August 1950 Meredith left Mississippi for Gibbs High School in Saint Petersburg, Florida, where he graduated in 1951. A month later Meredith enlisted in the U.S. Air Force. On the application, he was asked to provide his full name, so he chose "James Howard," names he would not use again until he applied to the University of Mississippi. Meredith's time in the air force was productive. He earned a good wage, traveled, and met Mary June Wiggins, who was working on the base. They married on 16 December

MEREDITH

1956 (in later years they had three sons) and were both stationed at the Tachikawa Air Force Base in Japan, where Meredith was able to attend the Far Eastern Division of the University of Maryland. As a sergeant first class and a clerical trainee supervisor for Japanese civilians, Meredith also acted as an educator. While in Japan, however, he and his wife decided to return to Mississippi to pursue formal university training.

In July 1960 Meredith left the service. He and and his wife purchased Cap's farm, and Meredith, determined to break the color barrier, applied to the University of Mississippi. On 7 February the Board of Trustees formally altered policies to prevent Meredith's enrollment and posted plainclothes policemen on campus to ensure his exclusion. Meredith expressed his "disappointment" with the new deadlines the registrar's office had informed him of and promptly applied for the summer session, only to have the registrar return his deposit. Meredith, faking obtuseness, continued to write the university registrar, asking about transfer credits he might receive and, in April, wrote the dean to request a review of his file to determine what, if anything, might be lacking. His letters went unanswered, and that month the admissions committee met to revise, once again, the rules for transfer students to further discourage Meredith's application. The committee demanded that any applicant provide a letter from five alumni of the historically all-white institution, a difficult obstacle for African Americans in the state to overcome.

The same month that the university returned his deposit, Meredith registered to vote in Mississippi. On 31 May, he filed a federal suit against the University of Mississippi, which charged that the demand for alumni recommendations placed an unfair burden on blacks and was therefore in defiance of the U.S. Constitution. A trial ensued, but Judge Sidney C. Mize did not rule until December 1961, when he denied Meredith's request for admission to the university. Meredith's lawyer immediately filed an appeal with the U.S. Fifth Circuit Court of Appeals. After additional posturing from Mize, on 25 June the appeals court ordered that Meredith be allowed to attend the University of Mississippi.

Unfortunately, the matter was not resolved. When the court dismissed the case, Governor Ross Barnett of Mississippi stepped in and refused to let Meredith enroll, defying the federal government and even going so far as to meet Meredith and his lawyers at the registrar's office on 20 September to deny Meredith admission. But Meredith's public speeches about these events and the black press coverage of him made him a popular figure among African Americans, and by September 1962 the entire nation was riveted by Meredith and his attempts at integration.

Finally, on 30 September, under the order of President John F. Kennedy, twenty-four federal marshals escorted Meredith on campus. Kennedy timed his national address on the matter to coincide with Meredith's safe arrival, telling white Mississippi that "the eyes of the nation and all the world are upon you and upon all of us." Kennedy's address was never heard by those to whom it was directed, however. By the time it aired, a full-scale riot was developing at the campus. Federal marshals armed with tear gas faced more than two thousand students and protestors armed with rifles. In the ensuing chaos, 150 marshals were injured, twenty-eight of whom were shot, and two white bystanders were found dead from bullet wounds. One was a French correspondent, Paul Guihard, who had been shot in the back. In what was to be his final dispatch he wrote: "It is in these moments you feel there is a distance of a century between Washington and the segregationists of the South. The Civil War has never ended." The following day Meredith, escorted by government troops, became the first African American to enroll at the University of Mississippi.

A nation watched as Meredith completed his degree at "Ole Miss," graduating on 18 August 1963. At the height of the tension twenty-three thousand soldiers were on campus, and Meredith was constantly under guard. Nonetheless, he had the support of many in the nation and reported receiving as many as two hundred letters of encouragement a day. His movements and observations were reported in the black press, in newsletters of the Ku Klux Klan, and in mainstream newspapers. His press releases and conferences likewise were attended. Meredith's graduation received national and international coverage, and African Americans reported being inspired by his example of strength and tenacity, drawing on it to apply to university in greater numbers and defy segregation in all aspects of life.

After graduation, Meredith attended the University of Ibadan in Nigeria from 1964 to 1965, returning to America to pursue a law degree at Columbia in 1966. In June of that same year he also led the "March against Fear," which traveled from Memphis to Jackson to encourage African Americans to register to vote. It was successful, resulting in the voter registration of 300,000 blacks. During the march, however, Meredith was shot by a would-be assassin. Meredith survived and was released from the hospital in time to complete the event.

Part of Meredith's appeal was that, unlike the Little Rock Nine, he appeared to be relentlessly steering his own charge at educational integration, resulting in his being a subject of both hatred and celebration in ways other educational reformers were not. Since graduating from Columbia in 1968 Meredith has become a controversial figure among African Americans for his increasingly conservative politics.

★

Meredith's personal papers, most of which relate to his enrollment experience and subsequent career, are in the James H. Meredith Collection, Department of Archives and Special Collections, University of Mississippi. For an autobiographical account of the Mississippi experience, see James Meredith, *Three Years in Mississippi* (1966). Outside observations of the integration events include Walter Lord, *The Past That Would Not Die* (1965), and Nadine Cohodas, *And the Band Played Dixie: Race and Liberal Conscience at Ole Miss* (1977), which includes a chapter on Meredith.

JENNIFER HARRIS

MIES VAN DER ROHE, Ludwig (*b.* 27 March 1886 in Aachen, Germany; *d.* 17 August 1969 in Chicago, Illinois), architect whose work in the 1940s and 1950s established the modernist style that came to dominate design in the 1960s and 1970s.

Born Maria Ludwig Michael Mies, Mies van der Rohe was the only child of Michael Mies, a stonemason, and Amalie Rohe, a homemaker. After studying in the local cathedral school from 1897 to 1900, he attended a craft school for the better part of two years before going to work as a carpenter's apprentice and later as a journeyman brickmason. Mies van der Rohe's formal experience as an architect began in 1905, when he went to work in the office of Bruno Paul in Berlin. A later employer, Peter Behrens, counted among his stu-

Ludwig Mies van der Rohe. AP/WIDE WORLD PHOTOS

dents Walter Gropius and Le Corbusier. In 1910 Behrens took his protégés to see a Berlin exhibition of the American Frank Lloyd Wright's work, an event that had a profound effect on Mies van der Rohe.

Mies van der Rohe remained with Behrens until 1912, at which point he established his own practice. He married Adele Auguste Bruhn on 10 April 1913 and had three children, but theirs was not a happy marriage, and they separated in 1921. Drafted into the army engineer corps late in 1915, Mies van der Rohe saw no action in World War I. For him, the true action lay afterward, as his modernist style first came into its own during the years of the postwar Weimar Republic. Nonetheless, he was stymied somewhat by the inflationary German economy of the 1920s and launched his more memorable projects—the Weissenhofsiedlung project (1927) and the Tugendhat House in Brno, Czechoslovakia (1928–1930), toward the end of the decade. Also in the late 1920s he became involved with the designer Lilly Reich, who would remain his professional and personal companion for the rest of his life. By this point he had added his mother's maiden name to his own, becoming known as Ludwig Mies van der Rohe from the 1920s onward.

Though he did not suffer under the Nazis—he even won a competition to design the new Berlin Reichsbank in 1933—Mies van der Rohe nonetheless immigrated to the United States in 1938 and became a U.S. citizen in 1944. For twenty years, until his retirement in 1958, he served as director of the school of architecture at Armour Institute of Technology (today known as IIT, the Illinois Institute of Technology), in Chicago. During those two decades Mies van der Rohe largely defined the architectural styles that would prevail in the 1960s, creating a wide array of buildings that fell into one of two basic types: skyscrapers and large-scale, but low-slung structures dedicated to special uses.

Exemplary of the first type are the twin towers of the Lake Shore Drive apartment houses in Chicago (1948–1951) and the Seagram Building in New York City (1954–1958). In both cases, the idioms that Mies van der Rohe created—revolutionary as they were in the 1940s and 1950s—proved so influential that the structures now seem commonplace, which is ironically the greatest possible testament to their success. Both projects are of the type that might be easily dismissed as "glass boxes," a reflection of the fact that today it is hard to imagine a time when such architecture seemed unusual. Yet the projects were not only unusual but were also a necessary response to the ornate styles that continued to prevail through the middle of the twentieth century, despite the progress made by Wright in the articulation of his Prairie School, an architectural style marked by the use of natural textures and open planning.

Located at 860 and 880 Lake Shore Drive, gazing out over Lake Michigan, the Lake Shore Drive apartments site consists of two identical twenty-six-story apartments located so close to each other (just forty-six feet separate them) that from certain angles they appear to be a single, L-shaped building. The people of Chicago in the early 1950s nicknamed them the "glass houses," and at a glance, it is easy to see why. Each building is all steel and glass, based on twenty-one-foot grids in which four window units are separated by three mullions of steel, painted black. Like Le Corbusier, Mies van der Rohe viewed the job of the designer as a responsibility that extended far beyond the mere creation of a building to house the activities of human beings. Experienced in furniture design from his early days in Germany, Mies van der Rohe had a strong sense for the spaces that the residents and workers in his buildings would occupy, and a key feature of the Lake Shore Drive project is the attention to detail that extends to the lobby. There one finds furniture composed of simple, ascetic lines reflective of a mid-century modernism that today bears the taint of an outmoded futurism, but which was once daring in its audacious simplicity.

As important as interior spaces were to Mies van der Rohe, an equally important consideration was external space. The Seagram Building in New York, which many buildings in midtown Manhattan resemble, is at 375 Park Avenue. The building is a thirty-eight-story tower that became the model for office buildings of the 1960s. With the Seagram tower, Mies van der Rohe introduced American corporate architecture to an inherently American—that is, New World—concept that predates Columbus: the plaza. So influential were designs incorporating open space in front of buildings that in 1961 New York's political leaders rewrote zoning laws to encourage the development of similar spaces in other parts of the city.

With the Lake Shore Drive apartments and the Seagram Building, the latter completed in the year of his retirement, Mies van der Rohe set the tone for the architecture of the next quarter century. To a less noticeable extent, though still to a significant degree, he did the same with his low-rises, including the Farnsworth House in Plano, Illinois (1950); Crown Hall, on the IIT campus (1956); and the New National Gallery in West Berlin (1962–1968). These buildings, like his high-rises, exemplified his famous dictum—he seems to have coined the phrase, which has permeated modern culture—that "less is more." Rather than design these buildings to enhance a specific function, he intended them to be suitable for many activities. This innovation would prove highly influential on the designs of the 1960s, especially because it comported with clients' desires to cut costs and retain resale value.

Mies van der Rohe belonged to the 1960s inasmuch as his ideas sounded a keynote for the art of the decade in no less a way than that of Andy Warhol in the realm of the visual arts or the Beatles in music. That these visual and musical exemplars were men much younger than he, whose work bore the influence of psychedelia and later movements, says much about how architectural design's impact lagged behind that of other arts. To be an influential architect of the 1960s, given the costs and the time involved in erecting large skyscrapers, one must necessarily have begun work on the vision in the 1950s or even earlier. The architects of the 1960s, by contrast, among them Mies van der Rohe's student Philip Johnson, would have an impact on later decades.

Mies van der Rohe's activity in the 1960s seems confined primarily to finishing projects begun in the early part of the decade or even in the 1950s. Among these were the Bacardi Office Building in Mexico City (1957–1961); the American Federal Savings and Loan Association in Des Moines, Iowa (1960–1963); the Berlin National Gallery; and the Toronto Dominion Center in Canada (1963–1969). Additionally, the Federal Center in Chicago, begun in 1959, would not be completed until 1973, long after Mies van der Rohe's death. He spent much of his last decade collecting awards, of which there were many, including a Presidential Medal of Freedom from John F. Kennedy in 1963. Mies van der Rohe died in Chicago and was buried in Graceland Cemetery.

In appreciating the effect that Mies van der Rohe had on the architecture of the 1950s and the 1960s, it is important to understand that the great designing minds of that time—with Mies van der Rohe's among the greatest—were eager to develop a language that bore no relation to the past. The aim of these mid-twentieth-century designers, in other words, was almost the opposite of that which has permeated the twenty-first-century world, in which the rapid acceleration of technology has engendered a longing for the permanence of the past.

Mies van der Rohe, whose career bridged a period in which the Panama Canal and the space program represented the greatest technological triumphs, sought to create an ahistorical architecture. On the one hand, he rejected the creations of the past, but his work already was rooted deeply enough in the mid- to late twentieth century that he recognized the short shelf life of futurism. Reminiscing on the medieval buildings of his hometown that he had glimpsed in his youth, Mies van der Rohe told John Zukowsky of the Art Institute of Chicago, "I was impressed by the strength of these buildings because they did not belong to any epoch. . . . All the great styles passed, but . . . they were still as good as on the day they were built."

★

Most of Mies van der Rohe's correspondence is housed in the Manuscript Division of the Library of Congress, and collections of his drawings can be found in the Museum of Modern Art in New York City, the Bauhaus Archive in Berlin, the Canadian

Center of Architecture in Montreal, and the Art Institute of Chicago. Notable biographical and critical works include Arthur Drexler, *Mies van der Rohe* (1960); Franz Schulze, *Mies van der Rohe: A Critical Biography* (1985); and David Spaeth, *Ludwig Mies van der Rohe* (1985). Also significant are Peter Blake, *The Master Builders* (1960), which discusses Mies van der Rohe along with Le Corbusier and Wright; Philip Johnson, *Mies van der Rohe* (1978), an important work by a distinguished protégé; and Ludwig Mies van der Rohe and John Zukowsky, *Mies Reconsidered: His Career, Legacy, and Disciples* (1986). An obituary is in the *New York Times* (19 Aug. 1969).

JUDSON KNIGHT

MILLER, Arthur Asher (*b.* 17 October 1915 in New York City), author of *Death of a Salesman* and numerous other plays that captured the conscience of America in the decades following World War II; he took public positions on the moral and political issues of the 1960s.

The son of Isidore Miller, an uneducated Polish immigrant who ran a thriving coat-manufacturing business, and Augusta Barnett Miller, a homemaker who read voraciously, Miller had an older brother and a younger sister. Following graduation from Abraham Lincoln High School in 1933, Miller applied to the University of Michigan. Rejected, he

Arthur Miller. THE LIBRARY OF CONGRESS

worked for a time for his father in a newly established garment firm and wrote a short story. Then, after pleading his case in a letter to a dean professing that he had become "a much more serious fellow," he enrolled at the University of Michigan, from which he graduated in 1938.

Upon graduation Miller returned to New York City, where he participated in the Federal Theater Project and married Mary Grace Slattery on 5 August 1940. The couple had two children, a daughter and a son. Miller attempted to enlist in the armed services at the beginning of World War II but was rejected because of an old football injury. Following several years of apprenticeship writing, Miller enjoyed critical acclaim for *All My Sons,* a play that opened on Broadway in 1947 and won a New York Drama Critics Circle Award. *Death of a Salesman* (1949) was even more enthusiastically received, earning both a New York Drama Critics Circle Award and a Pulitzer Prize and establishing Miller as a major figure in American drama.

The fifties were turbulent years for Miller, both personally and professionally. In 1956 he and Slattery were divorced, and Miller married the nation's much-admired sex symbol and movie star, Marilyn Monroe. The couple had no children. That same year he was subpoenaed to appear before the House Un-American Activities Committee (HUAC), which was investigating Communism in America. Miller spoke honestly about his own leftist activities, but he refused to identify friends and acquaintances who may have been Communist sympathizers; on 31 May 1957 he was held in contempt of Congress. Although the conviction was later reversed, the phenomenon known as "McCarthyism" (after Senator Joseph McCarthy of Wisconsin, signifying the use of unsubstantiated accusations and cutthroat investigative techniques to compel conformity) became a significant influence in Miller's creative life. His major plays of the 1950s—*An Enemy of the People* (1950), *The Crucible* (1953), and *A View from the Bridge* (1955)— all explore issues of personal identity and honor in the face of communal pressure, with the Salem witch hunts of 1692, the subject of *The Crucible,* a transparent proxy for the HUAC hearings.

Life was no less settled for Miller in the sixties. Monroe committed suicide on 5 August 1962, a year and seven months after she had applied for a Mexican divorce from Miller and six months after the playwright married Ingeborg Morath (17 February 1962), an Austrian-born photographer. The couple had one child, a daughter. Miller had withdrawn from the theater for eight years when he was blacklisted in the 1950s. In 1964, when he returned with *After the Fall,* critics reacted sharply. The introspective protagonist, they assumed, was Miller himself, and Maggie was an obvious stand-in for Marilyn; the play was embarrassingly confessional. Still, audiences listened with interest and pain to the playwright's newest and most personal effort to dramatize a postlapsarian world in which no one, whether oppressor, oppressed, or observer, is without culpability. Against this moral backdrop, Quentin, the central character, embarks on an odyssey of individual anguish, searching to place himself, individually and professionally, within a historical context of evil.

Miller's own Jewish background and his efforts to understand the distinction between guilt and responsibility prompted *Incident at Vichy* (1965). This play takes readers from the private landscape of Quentin's mind to the historical venue of World War II France, where Jews and other "undesirables" were rounded up by a government that had yielded to German racial laws. As each of the detainees is interviewed, the others anxiously converse, expressing the misgivings and the assurances of a people who refused to believe in the death camps. Miller judges all harshly: as in *After the Fall,* there are no innocents.

Miller's third important play of the sixties, *The Price* (1968), recalls the years of the Great Depression, when two brothers made choices that sealed their lives and careers. Dominated by an elderly Jewish junk dealer and sage named Gregory Solomon, the play examines the nature of individual, family, and social commitment as Solomon negotiates with the brothers for the sale of their parents' furniture, in storage since their father died. The play is an exercise in self-justification, with each brother refusing to invalidate his life by admitting that his choice, years earlier, was wrong. As the action unfolds, it becomes symbolic of the transactional nature of all experience and the power of individual choice.

Indirectly, each play connects earlier national and individual failures of courage, denials, and guilt to key events of the sixties: the war in Vietnam; the assassinations of President John F. Kennedy, the Reverend Martin Luther King, Jr., and Senator Robert F. Kennedy; and the chronic and then explosive problem of race and ethnicity. By the 1960s Miller had become very much a public figure. He spent more time at home in Roxbury, Connecticut, but he did not remove himself from the public eye.

Ever the spokesperson for liberal democratic values, Miller published stories and essays in widely circulated magazines and took public stands on numerous political issues, from the treatment of Vietnamese peasants by American soldiers to teenage gangs, the arms race, the shooting of Robert Kennedy, and the nation's guilt. In "The Bored and the Violent," published in *Harper's* (November 1962), he addressed juvenile delinquency, a problem much in the public mind. Observing that the phenomenon of youthful criminal behavior is worldwide and present across economic classes, Miller challenged the prevailing perspective: these marauding gangs, he claimed, were not "rebels" protesting social norms but young people reacting to boredom. In "The Writer and Society," a 1969 interview with the writer Richard Evans, he voiced his fear that we were capable of dropping another atom bomb, this time on Vietnam. Noting with disapproval U.S. actions in Central America, Cuba, and the Philippines, Miller criticized America's tendency to put people in power who have no popular following. Anxious about the prospect of total war, he discoursed on America's political bankruptcy in Vietnam.

In 1964 Miller became special commentator for the *New York Herald-Tribune* at the Nazi trials in Frankfurt, Germany. Concerned not only about the disposition of the case against twenty-two of the German dictator Adolf Hitler's SS troops at Auschwitz, site of an infamous concentration camp, Miller asked key moral and political questions: Can such a movement rise again in Germany—or elsewhere? These men were unspeakably brutal, yet they had families, held positions of respect, and could pass for "anybody's uncle." What is the point of such trials, almost twenty years after the war? Once again, Miller seized the occasion to speak of individual conscience and complicity.

In 1968 Miller participated as a delegate for Senator Eugene McCarthy in the Democratic National Convention in Chicago, an event that spawned violence from antiwar protestors in the streets and disgruntled delegates in the convention hall. Writing about the experience in "The Battle of Chicago: From the Delegates' Side" (1968), Miller speaks not only of the "hippies" outside the International Amphitheater but also, more pointedly, of the delegates within. They, with the demonstrators and the police, were "sharers in the common breakdown" of a process that should have accommodated conflicting interests. His analysis of the violence within the convention hall focused on the opposing ideas of politics held within the Democratic Party. With both Hubert Humphrey and McCarthy supporters in the room, the convention, he said, was "the closest thing to a session of the All-Union Soviet that ever took place outside of Russia."

Throughout his career freedom of expression was a first principle for Miller. During a four-year term (1965–1969) as president of the writers organization International PEN, Miller publicly supported that principle by petitioning the Soviet government to lift the ban on the works of Aleksandr Solzhenitsyn, by refusing to allow his own work to be published in Greece in protest of that government's oppression of writers, and by urging the release of writers held throughout the world for political reasons. His international activism for freedom of expression, along with the publication of *In Russia* (1969), a book on which he and Morath collaborated, prompted the Soviet Union to ban all of his work. In 1967 Miller published an article entitled "It Could Happen Here—and Did" before the Columbia Broadcasting System (CBS) television production of *The Crucible;* the lessons of that play, he cautioned, go beyond the Salem and McCarthy witch hunts to a general warning about social paranoia and governmental brutality.

The 1960s saw two landmark events for Miller the playwright, both related to *Death of a Salesman*. In 1968 sales of the 1949 play, reissued in several editions, reached one million. In 1966 CBS screened *Death of a Salesman* to an audience of seventeen million viewers. The event prepared the way for another television revival in 1985, which, like the earlier presentation, stimulated viewers to recognize in Willy Loman—salesman, father, participant in the debilitating game of success—a range of coincidences in circumstance and character. Here was an aging man, filled with self-pity and misplaced pride, who had spent his life pursuing the wrong dream. There is a collective guilt in Willy's failure, occasioned by the knowledge that a society that relentlessly demands success does not accommodate failures. In a televised conversation with Miller in 1985, the broadcast journalist Forrest Sawyer acknowledged in *Death of a Salesman* a "voice that cuts across time, continents, and cultures"—the formula, simply identified yet painfully realized, of a classic. Clearly, Miller had perfected the art of domestic realism, admirably recreating the daily lives of American families within an insistent and moralizing liberalism that had become his signature. Just as clearly, Miller's voice appealed to the conscience of Americans, bringing together the concerns of intellectuals and the "common man."

Miller frequently wrote commentary on the New York theater, and in the 1960s his concern was plain. Broadway was no longer a place for serious drama; the new Lincoln Center, though initially promising, would not present repertory theater after all; and the off-off-Broadway movement, begun in Greenwich Village cafés and lofts, had not yet gotten past the "incubation stages of self-expression." Despite his own success, Miller was disillusioned by a theater that had ceased to honor a serious, relevant art form that, as he put it in "What Makes Plays Endure" (1965), captures "a tonality which marks the present from the past" and prompts audiences to understand that the theater, like self-knowledge, "seems necessary again."

In later years the veteran playwright witnessed numerous revivals of his works, among the most celebrated a production of *Death of a Salesman* in China in 1983. For a time in the 1980s the British seemed more appreciative of Miller's work than did Americans, but the tide eventually turned, with New York openings of new works and a continuing schedule of revivals in regional theaters. On 30 January 2002 Miller's wife of forty years died of cancer, just as a revival of *The Man Who Had All the Luck*, Miller's first Broadway play, was gaining the attention of theatergoers in New York. Miller's many essays on the theater and on a range of political issues, his novels and short stories, his nonfiction, and his films have received wide attention. Both

The Crucible and *A View from the Bridge* have been adapted for the operatic stage.

In Miller's chronologically scattered account of his life and beliefs, *Timebends: A Life* (1987), the dramatist returns repeatedly to his early years in Brooklyn and to the McCarthy years, which, along with the depression and the Holocaust, morally framed his writing and his politics into the 1960s and beyond. An international figure whose plays are staged around the world, Miller nonetheless remains a distinctly American voice, a playwright who has earned the encomium "elder statesman of the American theater."

★

Although there is no definitive biography, Miller's own *Timebends: A Life* (1987) captures the moral center of the writer's life, documenting a wide range of events and providing Miller's interpretation of them. June Schlueter and James K. Flanagan, *Arthur Miller* (1987), which offers critical analyses of the plays, also includes a substantial biographical introduction. Further insight into Miller's artistic and political thought may be found in his essays, a selection of which was edited by Steven R. Centola as *Echoes Down the Corridor: Collected Essays, 1944–2000* (2000). Also helpful in understanding the playwright are Matthew C. Roudané, ed., *Conversations with Arthur Miller* (1987), and Christopher Bigsby, ed., *The Cambridge Companion to Arthur Miller* (1997), the latter containing a comprehensive bibliographic essay by Susan Haedicke.

JUNE SCHLUETER

MILLS, C(harles) Wright (*b.* 28 August 1916 in Waco, Texas; *d.* 20 March 1962 in Nyack, New York), leading sociologist in the 1950s and early 1960s, completing *White Collar: The American Middle Classes* (1951) and *The Power Elite* (1956), books that critiqued the excesses of American capitalism and influenced the development of the New Left during the 1960s.

Mills was the son of Charles Grover Mills, an insurance salesman, and Frances Ursula Wright. He was raised by his mother and older sister and, at an early age, developed a love of reading. The family moved frequently, finally settling in Dallas, where Mills entered Dallas Technical High School in 1930. He was forced to attend Catholic mass and later wrote, "I never revolted from it; I never had to. For some reason, it never took." He graduated in 1934 and, at the insistence of his father, enrolled in Texas A&M, a military college. Mills suffered at the hands of the upperclassmen and later claimed that the hazing he had received turned him into a rebel. After a year at Texas A&M, he transferred to the University of Texas at Austin, where he studied sociology, earning a B.A. in 1938 and an M.A. in philosophy in 1939.

In 1937 Mills married Dorothy Helen Smith. They would divorce (1940) and remarry (1941) and then divorce again (1947). The day after the second divorce, on 10 July 1947, Mills married Ruth Harper. They divorced in 1959. On 11 June 1959 Mills married Gloria Yaroslava Surmach. They had a son, adding to Mills's two daughters, one from each of his previous marriages. Mills left the University of Texas in 1939 for doctoral studies in sociology and anthropology at the University of Wisconsin, where he received his Ph.D. in 1942. Although Mills, like his grandfather, was an imposing figure physically, he was disqualified for military service during World War II because of hypertension. "If anything," wrote the historian David Halberstam in *The Fifties,* "this heightened his alienation from the American political mainstream, for it put him on the sidelines at what was the defining moment for most members of his generation." He taught at the University of Maryland during World War II, and in 1946, at the age of twenty-nine, he became an assistant professor of sociology at Columbia University in New York City.

Mills separated himself from his colleagues in both dress and decorum. "Mills seemed determined to provoke and antagonize his colleagues," wrote Halberstam. "He dressed as a lumberjack—in khaki pants, flannel shirts, and combat boots—and would arrive for class from his house in the country (which he had built himself)—astride his BMW motorcycle." In New York, Mills met intellectuals like Dwight Macdonald, Philip Rahv, and Irving Howe but formed few close relationships. His combativeness alienated friends and critics alike.

During the 1950s Mills wrote two influential books, *White Collar: The American Middle Classes* (1951) and *The Power Elite* (1956), and both would have a profound impact on the New Left during the 1960s. "Mills eventually became the critical link between the old left, Communist and Socialist, which had flourished during the Depression," noted Halberstam, "and the New Left, which sprang up in the sixties to protest the blandness of American life." In *White Color* he decried the loss of individualism in the United States; in *The Power Elite* he gave expression to a growing swell of discontent with the years in which Dwight Eisenhower was president. "Mills's reconceptualization of America as mass society," wrote Andrew Jamison and Ron Eyerman in *Seeds of the Sixties,* "culminated with the publication of *The Power Elite*, a book that many would later see as a bible for the student movement of the 1960s."

In August 1960 Mills visited Cuba for two weeks to gather information for *Listen Yankee: The Revolution in Cuba.* He interviewed the guerrilla leader Che Guevara and spent a great deal of time with Cuba's leader, Fidel Castro, who expressed admiration for *The Power Elite.* In *Listen Yankee,* published in 1960, Mills worried that the United States' aggressive policy would have negative consequences.

C. Wright Mills. ARCHIVE PHOTOS, INC.

"He suggested that overt hostility and the development of sanctions against Cuba would drive the new, independent, socialist state out of a neutralist stance and into the Soviet bloc," wrote John Eldridge in *C. Wright Mills,* "which, as we now know, is precisely what happened." Mills's positive overview of the Cuban revolution also brought scrutiny from the Federal Bureau of Investigation (FBI) and a death threat. Despite the controversial nature of the book, *Listen Yankee* sold more than 400,000 copies.

Mills's "Letter to the New Left" appeared in the September–October 1960 issue of *New Left Review.* "Many prophetic movements have their John the Baptists," Irwin and Debi Unger wrote. "For the New Left, this figure was C. Wright Mills." In his "Letter to the New Left" and other writings, Mills began to rethink the political assumptions left over from the 1930s and offered fresh perspectives. Whereas the Old Left had invested its faith in the working class, Mills believed that labor, like government and business, had been co-opted by bureaucratic forces. He argued that, to solve society's problems, individuals would have to circumvent the system with direct democracy, organizing voluntary groups at offices, factories, and schools to generate and implement ideas. In the 1960s New Left organizations, such as Students for a Democratic Society (SDS), implemented direct democracy by moving into poor neighborhoods and attempting to improve living conditions. As the founder of SDS, Tom Hayden, recalled in

Reunion: A Memoir, Mills "seemed to be speaking to us directly when he declared in his famous 'Letter to the New Left' that all over the world young radical intellectuals were breaking the old molds, leading the way out of apathy."

Mills's rhetoric caught on with the student movement because of his willingness to take a radical stance and write in a popular style. While many academics strove to become more objective following World War II, Mills attempted to revive the idea of the partisan intellectual from the 1930s. The intellectual, he believed, should raise questions, take sides on issues, and play an active role in public debate. As Theodore Roszak noted in *The Making of a Counter Culture,* Mills was not unique in pointing out the current state of affairs in America. "But it was Mills who caught on. His tone was more blatant; his rhetoric, catchier."

In December 1960, days before a scheduled debate with A. A. Berle, Jr., on U.S. policy in Cuba, Mills suffered a major heart attack. He remained in the hospital for two weeks and then checked himself out. He traveled throughout Russia and Europe with his family during the latter half of 1961 and returned to the United States in January 1962. Mills died of a second heart attack at the age of forty-five. *The Marxists* was posthumously published in 1962. "When he died," wrote Halberstam, "he had already become something of a mythic figure to a new generation of young American radicals and it would turn out that his posthumous influence was to be even greater." Mills is buried in Oak Hill Cemetery in Nyack, New York. His epitaph reads, "I have tried to be objective. I do not claim to be detached."

★

A number of Mills's letters appear in *C. Wright Mills: Letters and Autobiographical Writings* (2000). Irving Horowitz, *C. Wright Mills: An American Utopian* (1983), offers a full-length biography, and David Halberstam, *The Fifties* (1993), provides a short sketch. Howard Press, *C. Wright Mills* (1978), and John Eldridge, *C. Wright Mills* (1983), analyze Mills's writings. Mills's influence on the 1960s is discussed in Theodore Roszak, *The Making of a Counter Culture* (1969); Tom Hayden, *Reunion: A Memoir* (1988); Andrew Jamison and Ron Eyerman, *Seeds of the Sixties* (1994); and Irwin and Debi Unger, eds., *The Times Were a Changin': The Sixties Readers* (1998). Articles on Mills's theories and legacy are in the *Nation* (9 Oct. 2000) and *Texas Monthly* (Mar. 2001): 80–90. An obituary is in the *New York Times* (21 Mar. 1962).

RONNIE D. LANKFORD, JR.

MINOW, Newton Norman (*b.* 17 January 1926 in Milwaukee, Wisconsin), attorney and Democratic Party activist appointed by President John F. Kennedy as chairman of the Federal Communications Commission (FCC); inextricably linked to the 1960s as the person who called television "a vast wasteland."

Minow, son of Jay A. Minow, who operated a profitable chain of laundries, and Doris Stein Minow, grew up and attended public schools in Milwaukee. During World War II he enlisted in the U.S. Army and earned a certificate in engineering at the University of Michigan as part of the army's specialized training program. Later he served with the Signal Corps and helped string the first telephone line connecting India and China. He attained the rank of sergeant and was honorably discharged in 1946.

Minow married Josephine Baskin in 1949, the same year he received his B.S. degree in speech and political science from Northwestern University. The couple had three daughters. In 1950 Minow was awarded his J.D. from Northwestern University Law School. The following year he was appointed law clerk to Fred M. Vinson, then chief justice of the U.S. Supreme Court.

Minow's public career began in 1952 as an administrative aide to Adlai Stevenson, then governor of Illinois. He became an important member of the governor's staff and a key figure in Stevenson's presidential campaigns in 1952 and 1956. In 1960 he worked for John F. Kennedy's presidential campaign.

Appointed chairman of the FCC in 1960 at age thirty-

Newton Minow, January 1961. ASSOCIATED PRESS AP

four, Minow quickly sent shock waves through the broadcast industry with his agenda for television reform. On 9 May 1961, in his first address to the National Association of Broadcasters, the bespectacled, slightly pudgy bureaucrat declared, "If you want to stay on as trustees, you must deliver a decent return to the public—not only to your stockholders." The chairman invited those in his audience to watch their own television stations for one full day. "I can assure you," he warned, "that you will observe a vast wasteland."

To the broadcast community, this speech ushered in a troubling new era of strict regulation with a controversial emphasis on program content. In the popular press, though, the coverage of the "Vast Wasteland" speech was widespread and favorable. The phrase *vast wasteland*, inspired by the T. S. Eliot poem *The Waste Land,* entered the nation's lexicon, and Minow became a celebrity. Never before or since has an FCC chairman been a household name.

The Associated Press's annual poll of editors voted Minow the Top Newsmaker of 1961 in the field of entertainment (the runners-up were Jack Paar, Gary Cooper, and Elizabeth Taylor). Political cartoonists capitalized on the chairman's unusual name and easily caricatured looks. Minow cartoons were not limited to the editorial pages. The proof positive of his ascension to celebrity was that the comic sections of newspapers frequently carried cartoons that used his name or cause in their gag lines.

Minow sparked a national debate over the public-service responsibilities of the television industry. His two years on the FCC created unrelenting headaches for broadcasters, who had grown accustomed to a cozy relationship with the regulatory agency during the Eisenhower administration. During Minow's tenure the proverbial rubber stamp used in the past for FCC renewal applications was replaced with a fine-tooth comb.

Even though the broadcast industry resented Minow's stance, the result of the regulatory pressure was noticeable change. At the same time that the trade press and various industry leaders were attempting to prove that the FCC's new ardor was inherently wrong—in fact unconstitutional—television programming was being adjusted to meet new standards. Attempts at appeasement to ward off government regulation were conspicuous. Violence receded on prime-time programming, educational offerings for children increased, and Minow's influence made it easier for the network news divisions to rise in stature.

Despite his high visibility in matters related to program content, Minow's most significant contributions to U.S. broadcasting produced little public sensation. He championed the All Channel Receiver Bill (enacted 1962), which required all television sets to be capable of receiving ultra-high frequency (UHF) stations and changed the landscape for independent and public television stations in the fol-

lowing decade. Minow pushed for legislation to aid educational television and supported the formation of the Communications Satellite Corporation, or COMSAT (enacted 1962), which ultimately led to greater choice and program diversity.

Minow resigned from the FCC in May 1963 and became executive vice president, director, and general counsel for the *Encyclopaedia Britannica.* The following year the creators of the television show *Gilligan's Island* tweaked the legacy of the former chairman by naming the castaways' ill-fated chartered vessel the *Minnow.* In 1965 Minow began a long partnership with the Chicago law firm Sidley and Austin.

In the decades after the "Vast Wasteland" speech, issues of mass media continued to be the focus of Minow's interest. From 1973 until 1980 he was a director on the Board of the Public Broadcasting Service, including a stint as chair from 1978 to 1980. Minow was also a trustee of Chicago Educational TV from 1964 to 1991 and retains the title of life trustee. In 1976 and 1980 he served as cochair of the televised presidential debates sponsored by the League of Women Voters. In 1987 Minow was named a professor of communications law and policy in the Annenberg Program at Northwestern University and has directed the Annenberg Washington Program Communications Policy Studies since that time.

True to the idealism of the "New Frontier," a term used to describe the adventurous and uplifting philosophy of the Kennedy administration, Minow always believed that doing well and doing good are not irreconcilable. His goading of the broadcast industry for its lack of social conscience never faltered. In 1995, with coauthor Craig Lamay, Minow wrote *Abandoned in the Wasteland: Children, Television, and the First Amendment.* The book urges broadcasters, parents, advertisers, and lawmakers to work together in a commitment to the education of children in the United States.

On the fortieth anniversary of the "Vast Wasteland" speech, Minow reflected on the longevity of his characterization of television: "I wanted the best remembered words to be 'public interest.' I paid very little attention to 'vast wasteland.' I was astonished people picked up on those two words . . . . But 'vast wasteland' struck a nerve."

Some have mistakenly interpreted Minow's 1961 speech to be a broad-based denunciation of television, when, in fact, what he articulated to the U.S. public was a hopeful vision of what television could become. The public interest has been the constant and unifying theme of Minow's career, which always embraced the classic liberalism that flourished in the United States in the early 1960s.

★

Minow's papers, including his FCC files, are housed at the State Historical Society of Wisconsin. His tenure on the commission is examined in Mary Ann Watson, *The Expanding Vista: American Television in the Kennedy Years* (1990). Contemporaneous news accounts of the "Vast Wasteland" speech were abundant in the trade press, notably *Broadcasting* magazine and *Variety,* including "Black Tuesday at the NAB Convention," *Broadcasting* (15 May 1961). Stephanie B. Goldberg, "The Warrior and the Wasteland," *Chicago Tribune Magazine* (29 Oct. 1995), is a detailed retrospective on Minow's life and career.

MARY ANN WATSON

MITCHELL, John Newton (*b.* 15 September 1913 in Detroit, Michigan; *d.* 9 November 1988 in Washington, D.C.), lawyer, attorney general of the United States, and naval officer.

Mitchell was the only child of Joseph Charles Mitchell, a businessman, and Margaret Agnes (McMahon) Mitchell, a homemaker. When Mitchell was about three years old, he and his family moved from Michigan to Long Island, New York, where he attended elementary schools in Blue Point and Patchogue. At Jamaica High School in Jamaica (Queens), New York, he received the nickname "Big John." An athlete who excelled at ice hockey, he was, he said, an unexceptional student. He graduated from high school in 1931 and then entered Fordham University in the Bronx, New York, graduating in 1931. He earned his law degree in 1938 from Fordham Law School.

In 1936, while still in law school, Mitchell worked as a

John N. Mitchell. ARCHIVE PHOTOS, INC.

clerk for the law firm Caldwell and Raymond. After passing the bar exam in 1938, he joined the staff. His assignment was to find ways for state governments to circumvent laws that required voters to approve the issuance of bonds so that the governments could finance public housing developments. His solution was to create nonprofit organizations that could back their bonds with the rent they would receive from residents of the housing developments. He quickly became in demand for his skill in writing bond proposals. In April 1942 Mitchell was made a partner in the firm.

From 1943 to 1946 Mitchell served as an officer in the U.S. Navy, commanding squadrons of torpedo boats. He received the Silver Star for his achievements. When he returned to his law firm in 1946, it was renamed Caldwell, Trimble, and Mitchell. He became known for his expertise in government funding for the construction of housing, colleges, and hospitals. In December 1957 he divorced his first wife, Elizabeth Katherine Shine, with whom he had two children. Later that month he married Martha Beall Jennings, and they later had one daughter.

Mitchell's steadiness and his skill at organization gave him a solid career in government law, and through the 1960s, he might have been remembered best for helping create low-income housing throughout the country. In his private life, he seems to have been a relaxed husband who enjoyed his wife's outspoken behavior. But both his law practice and his marriage were shaken when his law firm merged with another and became Nixon, Mudge, Rose, Guthrie, Alexander, and Mitchell. Former vice president Richard Nixon's office was next to Mitchell's, and they consulted with one another often.

In 1968 Mitchell helped draft the Housing and Urban Development Act. By then, he had become close friends with Nixon, but when Nixon asked him to become campaign manager for his second run for the presidency, Mitchell demurred. He was a private man and disliked being in the public eye. Eventually Nixon prevailed, and Mitchell brought organization to a campaign staff that was in disarray. Although some staff members complained that Mitchell was inflexible, Nixon gave him a free hand in running the campaign. He developed the "southern strategy" that helped Nixon win the presidency by a narrow margin over Hubert Humphrey.

Nixon then asked Mitchell to serve as U.S. attorney general. He did not want the job but yielded to Nixon's persuasion. When he took office on 22 January 1969 he said, "I am first and foremost a law enforcement officer." Nixon had emphasized that Mitchell's primary task would be to fight crime. He moved into a Watergate apartment, which was said to be grandly appointed. In 1969 he helped write anticrime bills, and he had wiretaps placed on mobsters. He believed he was implementing the actions that Nixon wanted him to take, but many of his espionage techniques were eventually ruled illegal in the 1970s. For example, in *United States* v. *U.S. District Court,* the Supreme Court in June 1972 ruled that the government cannot place a wiretap on anyone other than foreign espionage agents.

During 1970, leaks of White House discussions to the press angered Nixon. Mitchell had wiretaps placed on at least thirteen staffers for the National Security Council to find out who was leaking information about the Vietnam War. In addition, he filed suit to prevent the publication of the Pentagon Papers that Daniel Ellsberg had leaked. In 1971, in the case of *New York Times* v. *United States,* the Supreme Court ruled against him, allowing the Pentagon Papers to be published. In his effort to end violent demonstrations on college campuses and on public property, Mitchell authorized mass arrests of demonstrators. In the case of a May 1971 antiwar march in Washington, D.C., about 13,400 people were arrested, though they were never successfully prosecuted.

Nixon was up for reelection in 1972, and he wanted his friend to run the campaign. Mitchell resigned as attorney general on 15 February 1972 to take over Nixon's reelection campaign. The campaign was doing well until 16 June 1972, when an attempted break-in at the Democrats' office in the Watergate office building was discovered, resulting in the arrests of White House aides E. Howard Hunt and G. Gordon Liddy. On 1 July 1972 Mitchell resigned as manager of Nixon's campaign, perhaps because he was dismayed by the break-in or perhaps because he was connected to it.

During 1973 Mitchell was under great stress as the conspiracy to cover up the details of the Watergate break-in was slowly revealed. It seemed as though the White House was working to convince people that Mitchell was the one responsible for ordering the break-in. In May 1973 a grand jury indicted Mitchell for obstruction of justice, perjury, and conspiracy. Besides that, his marriage was falling apart. In interviews she gave at the time, Martha Mitchell insisted that she knew her husband was conspiring in a cover-up, sometimes even holding conspiracy meetings in their own home. That and her husband's effort to have her discredited as mentally ill prompted their separation in 1973. By 1974 Martha Mitchell was telling anyone who would listen that her husband had conspired in the cover-up.

On 1 January 1975 Mitchell was convicted on all the counts in the indictment. His sentence was two-and-a-half to eight years in prison. In July 1975 he was disbarred. His appeals delayed his serving time in prison until June 1977. After nineteen months, he was paroled in January 1979. Thereafter, he sought to live in private and enjoy the company of his children. He died of a heart attack in Washington, D.C., on 9 November 1988 and is buried in Arlington National Cemetery in Arlington, Virginia.

Mitchell made a significant contribution to the 1960s by showing how public works could be safely and legally financed; his work facilitated the construction of urban low-income housing and helped financially restricted communities improve or build schools. As the U.S. attorney general, he was responsible for enlarging the scope of the Justice Department's powers, only to see those powers curtailed by congressional reforms during the 1970s.

★

Mitchell reportedly agreed to write an account of the Watergate scandal, but he apparently never did. His martyred wife Martha has been the subject of full-length biographies, but Mitchell has not. The entry on Mitchell in *Current Biography Yearbook 1969* is noteworthy for describing Mitchell's achievements before the scandals of the Nixon administration. For his role in the Watergate scandal, see Richard Ben-Veniste and George Frampton, *Stonewall: The Legal Case Against the Watergate Conspirators* (1977) and Michael A. Genovese, *The Nixon Presidency: Power and Politics in Turbulent Times* (1990). Winzola McLendon's *Martha: The Life of Martha Mitchell* (1979) discusses Mitchell's second marriage. An obituary is in the *New York Times* (10 Nov. 1988).

KIRK H. BEETZ

MOMADAY, N(avarre) Scott (*b.* 27 February 1934 in Lawton, Oklahoma), Native-American writer whose Pulitzer Prize–winning novel *House Made of Dawn* (1968) focused attention on Native-American literature and foreshadowed the rekindling of Native-American activism.

Momaday is the only child of Alfred Morris Momaday, an artist and art teacher of Kiowa descent, and Mayme Natachee Scott, a teacher and writer whose great grandmother was Cherokee. In 1936 the college-educated couple found work in New Mexico, where they lived among Navajo and Pueblo Indians. Their son absorbed tribal culture and lore from these Southwestern Indians as well as from his Kiowa relatives in Oklahoma. His parents' artistic and literary interests also shaped his development. Momaday considered stories related by his parents "more exciting than anything . . . at school." In 1946 his parents accepted positions in a two-teacher day school on the Jemez Pueblo northwest of Albuquerque, New Mexico, and Momaday later declared that his "most vivid and deeply cherished boyhood memories [were] centered upon that place." In addition to attending the Franciscan Mission School in Jemez, Momaday studied in New Mexico at the Santa Fe Indian School and a high school in Bernalillo, and at the Augusta Military Academy in Fort Defiance, Virginia.

Six years after completing high school in 1952, Momaday earned a B.A. in political science from the University of New Mexico in Albuquerque, but still seemed uncertain of his future. From 1956 to 1957 Momaday was enrolled in the law program at the University of Virginia in Charlottes-

N. Scott Momaday. AP/WIDE WORLD PHOTOS

ville, where he met William Faulkner, later an influence on Momaday's "The Bear."

While teaching on the Jicarilla Apache reservation in Dulce, New Mexico, Momaday submitted samples of his poetry and received a Wallace Stegner Creative Writing Fellowship at Stanford University in California. In 1959 Momaday was chosen by Yvor Winters, a professor interested in Native-American poetry, for admission to Stanford's graduate program in English, and Momaday completed his M.A. the following year. Winters helped Momaday to hone his poetry, and, seeking greater latitude, the aspiring writer turned to another Stanford English professor, Wallace Stegner, for assistance in shaping his prose. On 5 September 1959 Momaday married Gaye Mangold. The couple had three daughters and later divorced.

After earning a Ph.D. in 1963 Momaday accepted a position teaching English at the University of California, Santa Barbara. Two years later Oxford University Press published his dissertation, a study of the reclusive nineteenth-century Massachusetts poet Frederick Goddard Tuckerman. Although his formal training had emphasized American literature, at Santa Barbara, Momaday developed a graduate course in American Indian studies. He also worked on a multidimensional account of the Kiowas' past and a novel exploring the identity crisis confronting Native Americans caught between two cultures. At least half a decade before mainstream academe "discovered" Native Americans, Momaday was exploring their oral tradition in his classes and concentrating on Indian themes in his own work. A Guggenheim Fellowship in 1966 enabled the young professor to devote a year to research and writing in Amherst, Massachusetts, the home of Emily Dickinson, whose poetry gave him "deep insights into life."

Momaday's efforts resulted in two books, *House Made of Dawn* (1968) and *The Way to Rainy Mountain* (1969).

The former is a complex, widely misunderstood novel that received positive comments from many reviewers, some of whom lacked knowledge of the tribal tradition on which the book's imagery was based. When *House Made of Dawn* received the 1969 Pulitzer Prize in fiction, the author initially dismissed the news; some senior editors at the publishing company could not even remember the work, and the literary world was shocked. The Pulitzer jury explained that their selection was based in part on "the arrival on the American literary scene of a matured, sophisticated literary artist from the original Americans." The novel follows the struggles of a Jemez Indian trying to bridge the gulf between the cultural conflict of his past and his hope of finding meaning as part of his tribe's future. *The Way to Rainy Mountain* imaginatively traces the 300-year odyssey of the Kiowa from the upper Yellowstone valley to their reservation on the southern plains. The book was Momaday's attempt to discover his tribal roots and record the saga of the Kiowa before time obliterated their oral history. His blend of tribal lore, family stories, and historical perspective firmly connected the Indian to the American landscape, and stood in sharp contrast to the one-dimensional savage so often depicted by Hollywood.

Momaday's timing could not have been better. The Native-American community had been without a voice since the end of the Indian wars in the late nineteenth century. Although African Americans had made major strides in asserting their rights for several decades, Native Americans had remained passive. At the close of the 1960s, beneath an apparently tranquil surface, massive discontent roiled in the nation's Indian communities. Although he was young enough to storm the barricades of white indifference, Momaday was not an activist firebrand. Introspective and thoughtful, he was more comfortable with the measured, written word than incendiary rhetoric. Nonetheless, his literary success seemed to ignite the imagination of the Native-American community and to energize voices more strident than his own. Although Momaday deliberately distanced himself from the activists of the American Indian movement and their confrontations with the "establishment" at Alcatraz, Wounded Knee, and the Bureau of Indian Affairs in Washington, D.C., his reputation as a writer was enhanced by the revitalization of Native-American pride that his words helped to inspire.

In autumn 1969 Momaday moved to the University of California, Berkeley, where he remained until accepting a position as an English professor at Stanford in 1973. He acknowledged, "I found it very difficult to write after that [receiving the Pulitzer] for a long time." Momaday spent the dreary and frustrating winter of 1974 in the Soviet Union teaching American literature at Moscow State University to students more interested in hearing a Native American criticize his country's government than discussing American poets. His loneliness and distance from home apparently focused his attention on the U.S. Southwest and rekindled his creativity. The lonely semester abroad also stimulated a dormant interest in art; Momaday's drawings illustrate many of his books, and his paintings have been displayed in galleries throughout the world. On 21 July 1978 Momaday married Regina Heitzer, whom he met at the University of Regensburg in Germany. They had one daughter and later divorced. In 1982 Momaday left Stanford for the University of Arizona in Tucson, where he continued to serve as a Regents Professor of English through the turn of the century. Much of his post-1960s writing revisited themes explored in his early works, even recycling some of their passages.

The literary trail blazed by Momaday in the 1960s widened dramatically in the following decades as other Native-American writers found their voices. His subsequent work, honors, and public presentations secured his position in what has been called the American Indian literary renaissance. The expectations raised by his work in the 1960s have not been fulfilled to the satisfaction of some critics, who have been frustrated by his restraint or reluctance to explore new topics and expand his horizons. Momaday insists, however, that he writes to satisfy himself rather than the critics. Nonetheless, he looks fondly back to his days of widest acclaim, the 1960s, which he considers the greatest decade of the twentieth century and a "good time in which to have lived."

★

Momaday's autobiography is *The Names: A Memoir* (1976), which includes tales from his childhood and a family genealogy. Biographical works include Martha Scott Trimble, *N. Scott Momaday* (1973); Alan R. Velie, *Four American Indian Literary Masters: N. Scott Momaday, James Welch, Leslie Marmon Silko, and*

Gerald Vizenor (1982); and Matthias Schubnell, *N. Scott Momaday: The Cultural and Literary Background* (1985), which contains the most comprehensive biographical sketch of Momaday and a literary criticism of his early writings. Charles L. Woodard, ed., *Ancestral Voice: Conversations with N. Scott Momaday* (1989), is one of several lengthy interviews in which Momaday explains his views on many topics related to his writing.

BRAD AGNEW

MONK, Thelonious Sphere (*b.* 10 October 1917 in Rocky Mount, North Carolina; *d.* 17 February 1982 in Englewood, New Jersey), jazz composer and pianist, discovered by the public during the 1960s, known for his innovative rhythm, chord voicing, melody, and distinctive piano style.

Monk was born in North Carolina, but his mother, Barbara Batts, a civil service worker, left his father, Thelonious Monk, Sr., a manual laborer, when her three children were young and relocated to New York City. The family moved into a two-room apartment in Manhattan's San Juan Hill section. Monk lived at that apartment for most of his life, first with his mother, and then, when he married in 1947, with his wife, Nellie Smith, and their two children, until

Thelonious Monk performing at the Newport Jazz Festival, 1959. TED WILLLIAMS/CORBIS

the building was demolished. Their son, Thelonious Monk, Jr. (T. S. Monk), is a drummer and head of the Thelonious Monk Institute; their daughter Barbara's early death from cancer cut short her promising career in the arts.

Monk attended Public School 141 and Peter Stuyvesant High, where he excelled in physics and math, but he dropped out at sixteen years of age during his sophomore year. He was only five years old when he first began playing the piano, and eleven when he started taking lessons. He eventually began entertaining at Harlem rent parties, diverse events at which people would raise money to pay their rent. He also accompanied his mother in church solos, led a neighborhood trio, spent two years touring in a quartet with an evangelist, and studied briefly at the Julliard School of Music.

As a child, Monk spent time listening to jazz on the radio. During his teenage years, his influences were Louis Armstrong, Duke Ellington, Fats Waller, Earl Hines, and especially James P. Johnson, a neighborhood jazz hero. When Art Tatum moved to New York in 1932, Monk described him as "the greatest pianist I had ever heard."

Monk did not serve in the armed forces during World War II, as he had been classified as physically unfit for duty. He instead spent the decade developing his style—he played with the Coleman Hawkins sextet and the Dizzy Gillespie band—and recording some of the most important jazz compositions of the twentieth century. From 1947 to 1952 he recorded such works as "'Round Midnight," "Ruby, My Dear," "Straight, No Chaser," "Epistrophy," and several other jazz classics for Blue Note Records.

Beginning in the 1940s Monk continued writing instrumentation influenced by the pianist Teddy Wilson and the Harlem "stride" tradition (a single note on the first and third beats of the bar, a chord on the second and fourth). His early moniker was "High Priest of Bebop," but his musical creativity stretched beyond bop to provocative chording and strident voicing. John Coltrane said, "Playing with Monk is sometimes like walking into an empty elevator shaft."

Following an erroneous arrest on a narcotics charge in 1951, Monk was barred from playing in New York nightclubs for six years, but he continued recording and performing in various venues. While the majority of the innovations for which Monk is famous occurred prior to the 1960s, he was professionally active throughout the decade. In fact, the 1960s is the time when Monk finally became famous. In 1957 Monk led a seven-month engagement at the Five Spot. His quartet included the jazz newcomer Coltrane; from this experience came a legendary album, *Monk with Coltrane,* released in 1957. Their association was short-lived, however. By the time of their appearance at Town Hall in 1959, Monk had begun working with his lifelong associate and saxophonist Charlie Rouse, who un-

derstood Monk's stylistic nuances and worked with him through 1970. Known for his dry humor, Monk once told his band, "All ways know, always night, all ways know—and dig the way I say 'all ways.'"

From 1955 to 1961 Monk recorded for the Riverside label. His albums *Monk in Italy* and *April in Paris/Live,* both released in 1961, were live recordings from his European tour that same year. His success and growing fame led to a 1962 contract with Columbia Records. In 1963 he performed at Lincoln Center and toured Japan; his concert in Tokyo was memorialized in a double album. Monk also was elected to the *Down Beat* Hall of Fame that year. In 1964, the year his career reached its apex, he appeared at the Monterey Jazz Festival and was the subject of an extensive cover story in *Time* magazine. He toured Europe again in 1967.

Monk's piano performances during the 1960s were legendary. He dominated the stage, a tall, rugged, 200-pound man who wore assorted eccentric hats and left the piano bench during riffs to shuffle across the stage in a "Monkish" manner. Monk deviated from the stride with a marked ability to express rhythmic spontaneity. His lively rubato and varied articulation provided an element of surprise to his listeners. Monk reinterpreted his best-known tunes in the 1960s, including "Round About Midnight," "Straight, No Chaser," "Ruby, My Dear," and "Epistrophy," and became noted for his instrumental masterpieces "Evidence," "Misterioso," and "Criss Cross." His compositions, which were associated with harmonic clusters and dissonance, demanded attention from both listeners and performers.

Jazz did not exist in isolation from the turmoil that marked the 1960s. During this period, when other musical genres overshadowed jazz, there was a dearth of work opportunity. Jazz, an art form in transition, emphasized "free" jazz. Competing musicians in the country's twenty or so clubs often resented artists who got gigs. Caught in racial bias, which contributed to resentment, African-American musicians accused whites of lacking talent. In contrast, white musicians complained of "Crow Jim" (a phrase meant to suggest reverse prejudice) when African Americans got work.

Unaffected by racial fervor, Monk said, "My music is not a social comment on discrimination or poverty or the like. I would have written the same way even if I had not been a Negro." His manager Harry Colomby quoted Monk as saying, "When I was a kid, some of the guys would try to get me to hate white people for what they've been doing to Negroes, and for a while I tried real hard. But every time I got to hating them, some white guy would come along and mess the whole thing up." Monk was exceptional in the 1960s. He continued writing and performing his music and lacked resentment toward his fellow artists. It was his time to shine in the sun, but he was saddened by the jealousies he felt all around him. At one point Monk quietly allowed, "I was friends to lots of musicians, but looks like they weren't friends to me."

When Monk was not on stage, he relaxed at home with Nellie—what he called "layin' dead." Their two-room apartment featured a Steinway baby grand piano by the sink, a small kitchen table, and a crowded living room and bedroom. Monk was clothes conscious. Before evening performances, Nellie shuffled through assorted piles to help him dress in proper suits and silk shirts. Monk reported that he once had been asked to pose in a monk's habit, on a pulpit, holding a glass of whiskey. He said no with wry humor, "Monks don't even stand in pulpits."

Having reached his musical apex in 1964, Monk retired from concert tours and recording in the 1970s. He suffered from chronic liver damage brought about by years of drugs and drinking and spent his final years in Weehawken, New Jersey, with Nellie, or in the home of his patron, Baroness Pannonica de Koenigswarter. He died of a cerebral hemorrhage and is buried in Ferncliffe Cemetery in Hartsdale, New York.

Although Monk's albums had been in the marketplace for twenty years, it was not until the 1960s that the general jazz audience took notice. Even within the jazz milieu, his piano style, with its phrasing, cadences, and dissonant chords, was often puzzling to critical ears. Monk was impressive as a pianist but even more significant as a composer. The jazz critic Martin Williams hailed him as the greatest composer since Duke Ellington. Andre Hodeir compared Monk with Gerry Mulligan and Charley Parker, writing, "Only in Monk's music do asymmetry and discontinuity enhance one another, thereby assuming their full, symbiotic significance." Monk described his music more tersely: "All you're supposed to do is lay down the sounds and let the people pick up on them. If you ain't doing that, you just ain't a musician." The decade of the 1960s was rife with change. In his musical genius, Monk exemplified that mood and came into his own as a public figure, acknowledged as the greatest jazz composer of his generation.

★

For information about Monk's life, see Laurent De Wilde, *Monk* (1997), translated from the French by Jonathan Dickinson; and Thomas Fitterling, *Thelonious Monk: His Life and Music* (1997), translated from the German by Robert Dobbin. Many magazine articles describe aspects of Monk's life. Among the best are Nat Hentoff, "The Private World of Thelonious Monk," *Esquire* (Apr. 1960); "Thelonious Monk: Arrival Without Departure," *Saturday Review* (13 Apr. 1963): 32–37; and "Loneliest Monk," *Time* (28 Feb. 1964). For information about Monk's place in the world of jazz, see Andre Hodeir, *Toward Jazz* (1962), translated from the French by Noel Burch; and Len Lyons and Don Perlo, *Jazz Portraits: The Lives and Music of the Jazz Masters* (1989),

which details Monk's misunderstood jazz reputation. Ian Carr, Digby Fairweather, and Brian Priestley, *Jazz: The Rough Guide* (1995), offers information on Monk's career and albums. For a list of compositions, see L. Bijl and F. Cante, *Monk on Records: A Discography of Thelonious Monk* (1985). An essential film is Charlotte Zwerin's acclaimed documentary, *Thelonious Monk: Straight, No Chaser* (1988), which was edited from footage shot entirely in the 1960s. An obituary is in the *New York Times* (18 Feb. 1982).

SANDRA REDMOND PETERS

MONROE, Marilyn (*b.* 1 June 1926 in Los Angeles, California; *d.* 5 August 1962 in Brentwood, California), actress, model, and legendary sex symbol who, after reaching a career peak in the late 1950s, entered a downward spiral that culminated with her death by drug overdose.

Monroe was born Norma Jean Mortensen, the only child of Gladys Pearl Baker, a film technician, and Edward Mortensen, a mechanic. They were together only briefly, and Mortensen had deserted his wife by the time Monroe was born. When she entered school, Monroe was going by the name of Norma Jean Baker. As revealed in numerous bi-

Marilyn Monroe. ARCHIVE PHOTOS, INC.

ographies written after she became famous, Monroe's childhood was as bleak as her stardom was glamorous. Both her mother's parents had been committed to mental institutions, and Gladys herself spent so much time in and out of mental hospitals that her daughter had to be raised in a succession of foster homes and orphanages.

Though she attended Van Nuys High School, the sixteen-year-old Monroe dropped out to marry James Edward Dougherty, an aircraft production worker, on 19 June 1942. Her career in modeling began while Dougherty was away in the merchant marine during World War II, a period when Monroe supported herself partly by posing for covers of minor photo magazines. She divorced Dougherty in 1946, cut her hair and bleached it blonde, changed her name to Marilyn Monroe, took a screen test with Twentieth Century–Fox, and signed her first movie contract. After several forgettable pictures, Monroe appeared in John Huston's *Asphalt Jungle* (1950), her first important film. She studied acting with Natasha Lytess in the late 1940s and early 1950s and survived a scandal involving a nude calendar photo taken during a period when she had no acting work. Instead of ending her career, news of the photo only added to her sexual mystique.

By the mid-1950s Monroe was a star, enjoying popular and sometimes critical success with such films as *Niagara* (1953), *Gentlemen Prefer Blondes* (1953), *How to Marry a Millionaire* (1953), and *The Seven-Year Itch* (1955). After the last of these movies, Monroe grew weary of the "dumb blonde" image she had long cultivated, an image that had as much to do with her breathy voice and hourglass shape as with her platinum hair. Eager to grow artistically, she studied with Lee and Paula Strasberg at the Actors Studio in New York City during 1956, and her efforts paid off in the most impressive performances of her career, including *Bus Stop* (1956) and *Some Like It Hot* (1959).

Professional changes accompanied personal ones, as Monroe left one man noted for his athletic prowess and married another who earned his living with his intellect. The first of these husbands was Joe DiMaggio, the great New York Yankees slugger, whom she wed on 14 January 1954 and divorced just nine stormy months later. The other was the playwright Arthur Miller, whom she married on 29 June 1956. (Though she was married three times, Monroe had no children.) She adopted Miller's faith, Judaism, and cultivated an interest in literature: from this period comes a photograph of Monroe reading James Joyce's ponderous *Finnegan's Wake*.

The Monroe of the late 1950s had reached the pinnacle of her career, but the decline that followed in the early 1960s was almost surreal in its haste. By the time *Let's Make Love* appeared in 1960 to a tepid critical reception, she had long since begun displaying signs of the behavior that would send her life and career into a tailspin. A sufferer

from insomnia, Monroe had become addicted to sleeping pills and compounded the dangers associated with these and other barbiturates by combining them with alcohol, which she had begun increasingly to abuse by the early 1960s. At the encouragement of the Strasbergs, Monroe had entered into psychoanalysis during the late 1950s, a move that initially yielded benefits both professional and personal. As a subscriber to the ideas embodied in the Stanislavski acting method (named for the famed Russian actor and director), Monroe believed in inhabiting a character's personality as fully as possible; in order to do this, it was necessary to understand one's own personality to the fullest. On a more personal level, psychoanalysis helped her confront the pain and loneliness of her childhood as well as the pressure and sense of exploitation that came from being Hollywood's most acclaimed starlet—and from being a subject of the male sexual fantasy.

Although psychoanalysis helped Monroe at first, ultimately it became a crutch. As her personal and professional life spun out of control, Monroe relied on her therapist more and more to get her through each day. Examining and reexamining the painful details of her past was like overscratching an itch: by dwelling on the tendency toward mental illness in the Baker family, Monroe began to fear that she, too, might be mentally imbalanced, or at least that she might be judged so.

The 1950s had been Monroe's decade, so it was fitting that the beginning of her career's end occurred in 1960. First there was *Let's Make Love,* a dismal picture compounded by a troubled off-screen romance with her costar, Yves Montand. The affair served only to pinpoint the troubles in her marriage to Miller, with whom she had little more than a professional relationship by 1960. Even that would come to an end, along with their marriage, in the aftermath of Monroe's last completed film.

Based on a script by Miller, *The Misfits* (1961) is the story of a beautiful divorcee and the men who clamor for her affections. Because Miller repeatedly revised scenes while on location, the resulting plot is a mishmash. Despite the challenges, however, John Huston, with whom Monroe had worked on *The Asphalt Jungle,* turned in an exemplary performance as director. So, too, did Monroe's costars Clark Gable, Eli Wallach, and an actor who rivals Monroe as a great tragic figure, Montgomery Clift. As for the star of the film, however, her contribution was uneven at best. Outward signs of Monroe's disintegration first became apparent during the filming of *The Misfits,* when she regularly showed up late to the set and sometimes failed to turn up at all.

Gable's death on 16 November 1960, just twelve days after completion of *The Misfits,* upset Monroe deeply. Two months later Monroe divorced Miller. The film was released the following month, on 1 February, to abominable reviews. Monroe had approximately eighteen months left to live, and she would spend little of it actually filming. Her fears of mental instability came to fruition when, in late 1961, she was confined briefly to an institution. Early in 1962 she moved into a modest bungalow in the Brentwood section of Los Angeles and on 23 April began work on the prophetically titled *Something's Got to Give.* Monroe's erratic behavior on the set of *The Misfits* carried over to her current picture, and this time Fox ran out of patience. After only twelve days of shooting, the studio fired her. They even took legal action against Monroe, suing her for $500,000. (She is estimated to have earned $200 million for Fox over the course of her career.)

Nonetheless, they had to finish the film—the first that would contain nude scenes with Monroe—so the studio agreed to reinstate her. Before shooting could resume, however, Monroe was found dead in her Brentwood bungalow. An autopsy showed a deadly quantity of barbiturates in her system, and though her death is widely regarded as a suicide, she left behind no note. DiMaggio made the funeral arrangements, and for three decades, until his own death in 1999, he regularly placed flowers on her grave. Monroe is buried at Westwood Village Memorial Cemetery in Los Angeles.

Part sex goddess, part little girl, Monroe made herself the most popular actress in history by cultivating an on-screen style that seemed natural, though, in fact, it was the result of considerable effort on her part. She excelled at comedy, as in *Some Like It Hot,* but could render performances that smoldered with a latent intensity and sense of the tragic, as in *Bus Stop.* Her persona in that movie seems closest to the popular image of Monroe as at once vulnerable and a paragon of sexuality. Monroe was unquestionably a tragic figure, both at the beginning and at the end of her life. At the start of her long journey was a miserable childhood, with all its horrors in the form of insanity, abandonment, abuse, and poverty. At the conclusion was a death as lonely as her girlhood. Painful as all this tragedy is, it is essential to the Marilyn Monroe story and explains the power she continues to hold over the imagination. The agony at both ends of her existence only makes the glamour in between all the more luminous; without Norma Jean Baker, Marilyn Monroe could never shine as bright as she still does.

★

There are more than a hundred books on Monroe, including *My Story* (1974), which Monroe cowrote with the playwright and novelist Ben Hecht a few months before her death, and a series of interviews in *Marilyn Monroe in Her Own Words* (1983). Among biographies, one of the most reliable is Fred Guiles, *Norma Jean* (1969), and one of the most popular is Norman Mailer, *Marilyn* (1973), which draws on the factual information in the Guiles

book. Another important source, one that includes photocopies of vital documents, is Robert F. Slatzer, *The Life and Curious Death of Marilyn Monroe* (1974). An obituary is in the *New York Times* (6 Aug. 1962).

Judson Knight

MOORE, Francis Daniels (*b.* 17 August 1913 in Evanston, Illinois; *d.* 24 November 2001 in Westwood, Massachusetts), and **Thomas Earl STARZL** (*b.* 11 March 1926 in Le Mars, Iowa), surgeons who pioneered human organ transplant operations and, although they did not directly collaborate, together led the way in the 1960s toward making kidney and liver transplants standard surgical procedures.

Moore was the youngest of three children of Philip Wyatt Moore, a businessman, and Caroline Seymour Daniels. He graduated cum laude with an A.B. degree in general studies from Harvard University in 1935 and earned his M.D. from Harvard Medical School in 1939. He married Laura Benton Bartlett on 24 June 1935; they had five children. Following Laura's death in 1988, Moore married Katharyn Watson Saltonstall on 13 May 1990. During his surgical internship and residency at Massachusetts General Hospital from 1939 to 1943, especially through treating victims

Thomas E. Starzl. Corbis Corporation (Bellevue)

of the 1942 fire at the Cocoanut Grove nightclub in Boston, he became interested in the occasional need to replace body parts. From 1943 to 1981 he taught surgery at Harvard Medical School. From 1948 until he retired from practice in 1976 he was surgeon in chief at Peter Bent Brigham Hospital, which merged in 1980 with Robert Breck Brigham Hospital and the Boston Hospital for Women to form Brigham and Women's Hospital. As his health declined, he chose to commit suicide rather than suffer the debilitating effects of chronic heart failure.

Starzl was the second of four children of Roman Frederick Starzl, a newspaper publisher, and Anna Laura (Fitzgerald) Starzl, a nurse. Starzl earned his B.A. degree in biology in 1947 from Westminster College, Fulton, Missouri, his M.A. degree in anatomy in 1950, his Ph.D. degree in neurophysiology in 1952, and his M.D. degree in 1952, all from Northwestern University Medical School (since 2002 the Feinberg School of Medicine). He was surgical intern, fellow, and assistant resident at Johns Hopkins Hospital in Baltimore from 1952 to 1956, chief resident in surgery at Jackson Memorial Hospital in Miami from 1956 to 1958, and resident in thoracic surgery at the Veterans Administration Research Hospital in Chicago from 1958 to 1959. He taught surgery at Northwestern from 1958 to 1961, at the University of Colorado School of Medicine from 1962 to 1980, and at the University of Pittsburgh School of Medicine from 1981 until he retired in 1998. On 27 November 1954 Starzl married Barbara June Brothers, with whom he had three children. The couple later divorced, and he married Joy D. Conger on 1 August 1981. Starzl wrote prolifically and is among the most widely cited of all medical authors.

When Moore and Starzl entered medicine, human organ transplantation was a future prospect and a fond hope. Bioscientists believed that transplanted bone marrow could cure leukemia, transplanted kidneys could substitute for the inconvenience of dialysis, and transplanted livers, hearts, and lungs could save patients from many fatal chronic conditions. The ground was broken on 17 June 1950 when Richard H. Lawler performed the world's first successful human organ transplant at Little Company of Mary Hospital in Chicago. The patient, Ruth Tucker, a forty-four-year-old victim of congenital polycystic renal failure, received one kidney from a forty-nine-year-old woman of the same blood type and survived until 30 April 1955. The first successful bone marrow, liver, heart, and lung transplants all occurred in the 1960s.

Moore, Charles Stuart Welch, and several other surgeons performed experimental liver transplants on dogs in the 1950s and early 1960s. Following the pioneer work of Alexis Carrel in animal kidney transplantation, David Milford Hume and John Putnam Merrill at Brigham achieved limited success with human kidney transplants in the 1950s. As surgical chief at Brigham, Moore vigorously promoted organ and tissue transplantation research, enabling Joseph Edward Murray to perform the world's second successful human organ transplant, a kidney from one monozygotic twin to another, on 23 December 1954. Murray won the 1990 Nobel Prize in physiology or medicine for this work.

Moore and Starzl began corresponding about liver transplantation in the late 1950s and met at the 1960 conference of the American Surgical Association. Starzl wanted to work for Moore in Boston, but since Moore believed that Starzl would do better in a less competitive environment, he helped to arrange Starzl's appointment in Colorado, where, under William Rhoads Waddell, Starzl flourished.

A great uncertainty in transplantation is whether the recipient's body will tolerate or reject the transplanted organ. This problem is lessened when the donor is a blood relation, especially a twin, but since such donors are seldom available, pharmaceutical means are necessary to improve tolerance and fight rejection. Starzl's experiments with azathioprine, corticosteroids, other immunosuppressants, and supplement drugs enabled him to perform many successful transplants of allogenetic (genetically different) kidneys in 1962 and 1963.

Starzl performed the world's first three human liver transplants on 1 March, 5 May, and 24 June 1963 at the University of Colorado Hospital in Denver. The first patient, a three-year-old boy with congenital liver defects, died on the operating table. The second, a forty-eight-year-old man with cirrhosis and cancer, survived twenty-two days after the operation. The third, a sixty-seven-year-old man with jaundice and cancer, survived seven days. Moore also tried a liver transplant in 1963, but the patient died of pneumonia caused by the immunosuppressants.

Over the next several years, the most productive research on liver transplantation was conducted by Moore in Boston, Starzl in Denver, and Roy Calne in England. Moore's classic text *Metabolic Care of the Surgical Patient* (1959) did not deal specifically with transplant cases but offered biochemical and physiological principles that proved germane throughout the 1960s and early 1970s in the management of transplant patients. It helped surgeons reduce rates of transplanted tissue rejection and thus ensured longer and less complicated survivals for transplant recipients until the advent of cyclosporin A and other powerful immunosuppressive drugs in the 1970s.

Using prednisone and azathioprine, Starzl performed the world's first successful liver transplant on 23 July 1967. The patient, a nineteen-month-old girl with primary liver cancer, died 400 days after the operation, not from tissue rejection or any complications of the surgery but from metastases of the cancer throughout her body. Until the 1970s she remained the longest liver transplant survivor. Complications, such as liver gangrene, late rejection, and jaundice, killed many liver recipients between 1967 and 1970, but her case gave Starzl and Moore and their colleagues new optimism that bore fruit in the next decade.

Paradoxically, the advent of major organ transplants limited rather than expanded the physician's traditional paternalistic power over patients. As workable health care options became more varied, patients began in the 1960s to demand more freedom of choice over their personal health care decisions. Patient autonomy began to take its place among physician beneficence, physician nonmaleficence, compassion, confidentiality, competence, and social distributive justice as the primary principles of medical ethics.

★

Moore's autobiography, *A Miracle and a Privilege: Recounting a Half Century of Surgical Advance* (1995), and Starzl's autobiography, *The Puzzle People: Memoirs of a Transplant Surgeon* (1992), each provide detailed personal observations and analysis. Starzl's article, "Transplantation of the Liver," in *Progress in Liver Disease* 3 (1970): 495–542, describes the history of this procedure up to that time. Transcripts of interviews with Moore recorded in 1991 and 1992 by the Harvard Medical School Oral History Committee are in the Countway Library of Medicine, Boston. Starzl donated his papers to the University of Pittsburgh Library in 2001. Manuscript material on Starzl is also available at the National Library of Medicine, History of Medicine Division, Bethesda, Maryland, in the archives of the American Surgical Association. An obituary of Moore is in the *New York Times* (29 Nov. 2001).

ERIC V. D. LUFT

MOORE, Garry (*b.* 31 January 1915 in Baltimore, Maryland; *d.* 28 November 1993 in Hilton Head Island, South Carolina), radio and television performer and writer. One of television's first "stars of the ordinary," Moore was not an actor, comedian, or performer in any traditional sense, yet he made a name for himself as host of *I've Got a Secret* (1952–1964) and *The Garry Moore Show* (1958–1964; 1966–1967).

Born Thomas Garrison Morfit, son of the wealthy Baltimore attorney Mason P. Morfit and Mary Louise Harris, Moore rebelled against a country-club upbringing and dropped out of high school in 1933. Hoping to become a playwright, he joined the Vagabonds, a local amateur theater company, penning dialogue for musical comedy revues and sketches. Among the troupe's members, he encountered Zelda Sayre Fitzgerald, wife of the writer F. Scott Fitzgerald. The two became friends and collaborated on several one-act plays. When it became apparent that these were not likely to be produced, Fitzgerald used family connections to secure a job for Moore at a radio station, as a temporary measure while he continued to work on his writing.

Garry Moore. CORBIS CORPORATION (BELLEVUE)

From this beginning, he plunged headlong into commercial broadcasting, moving from a local job to network radio and from daytime talk to a prime-time variety series in which he costarred with Jimmy Durante. CBS, initiating television operations after World War II, struck up a relationship with Moore that would make him a star of the small screen for two decades. By the late 1950s he occupied more hours of national broadcast time than any other performer. His work schedule included a daily radio program, a daily daytime TV program, and hosting duties on a weekly prime-time game show. The latter, *I've Got a Secret*, was a Mark Goodson–Bill Todman panel show modeled after *What's My Line?* It featured a group of four celebrities chatting their way toward a guess at the "secret" that a contestant had whispered in the host's ear. Moore had it canceled in 1964, apparently out of sheer exhaustion. It was the twelfth most popular show on television when it left the air.

If *I've Got a Secret* was his biggest hit, Moore's comedy-variety hour was probably his best work. In 1958 CBS asked the star to give up his daily daytime show in favor of a weekly prime-time series. Choosing to produce it in New York at a time when most such series had moved to Los Angeles, he introduced a number of Broadway stars and cabaret acts to the small screen, including Carol Burnett,

Dorothy Loudon, Jonathan Winters, and Alan King. Burnett, who was a regular on the show, would model her own long-running comedy-variety show after it. Other regulars on *The Garry Moore Show* included the brilliant doubletalk artist Marian Lorne, and Durward Kirby, Moore's "sidekick" announcer.

With a dozen or more comedy-variety shows on the air at the turn of the 1960s, Moore gave his program a distinct identity by including several recurring features that were not part of the variety show's music hall tradition. In a regular segment entitled "Candid Camera," the conceptual auteur Allen Funt, late of radio's *Candid Microphone*, showed short films of people who had been set up for various types of embarrassment and humiliation. In 1960 *Candid Camera* spun off as a separate series hosted by Funt and Kirby and became one of the decade's biggest hits.

While most comedy-variety hours ended with some sort of ensemble sketch or musical number, Moore concluded his show each week with a grand finale titled "That Wonderful Year." About seven minutes in length, the segment examined music, fashion, and current events (the latter from a lighthearted perspective) during a particular year in American pop-culture history, culminating in a costumed ensemble musical production. Its focus on style expressed through loosely structured montage rather than on conventional documentary voice anticipates the direction that filmed commercials were taking by the late 1960s. Andy Warhol, who rarely had much to say about specific television content, called "That Wonderful Year . . . the best thing on television during the black-and-white period." He also lauded the show's spoofs of old genre films. Both Moore and Burnett received Emmy awards for their performances on the show during the 1961–1962 season.

Noting that he had "said everything I ever wanted to say three times already," Moore left television at the end of the 1966–1967 season. At the age of fifty-two he was one of the medium's wealthiest personalities. After spending several years sailing around the world on his yacht, he returned to daytime television, hosting a syndicated daytime revival of *To Tell the Truth* (1969–1977), a panel show similar to *I've Got a Secret*. In 1977, in a planned media event, Moore was one of fifty-six celebrities, including the astronaut Edwin "Buzz" Aldrin and the congressman Wilbur Mills, who publicly "came out" as recovering alcoholics for the purpose of encouraging others to seek treatment.

Moore survived a bout with throat cancer in the late 1970s and spent much of his ensuing retirement at his favorite activity, sailing, dividing his time between seaside homes at Hilton Head Island, South Carolina, and Northeast Harbor, Maine. Moore married Eleanor Little, with whom he had two sons, on 5 June 1939. She died in 1974. A second marriage, to Mary Elizabeth "Betsy" De Chant,

took place on 16 January 1975, and the couple had a daughter. Moore died of emphysema.

★

Tom Shales, "Garry Moore: A Host of Talents; The Genial Genius of TV's Infancy," *The Washington Post* (30 Nov. 1993), provides a review of Moore's career with attention to his impact on early television. Some four hours of taped, transcribed interviews with Betsy Palmer, a colleague and close personal friend of Moore, contain factual information and personal anecdotes; the interviews are held by the Center for the Study of Popular Television at Syracuse University. Obituaries are in the *Los Angeles Times* and *New York Times* (both 29 Nov. 1993).

DAVID MARC

MOORE, Mary Tyler (*b.* 29 December 1936 in New York City), multiple-award-winning actress who created two of the most memorable characters in comedic television history: the beloved housewife Laura Petrie on *The Dick Van Dyke Show* (1961–1966) and the spunky single career woman Mary Richards on *The Mary Tyler Moore Show* (1970–1977).

Moore was the oldest of three children of George Moore, a utilities company auditor, and Marjorie Hackett, a homemaker who suffered from alcoholism, a disease that plagued all her children. The family moved to Los Angeles when Moore was eight; she attended Catholic school in California, graduating in 1955 from Immaculate Heart High School. At eighteen Moore married a neighbor, a twenty-seven-year-old food salesman, Richard (Dick) Meeker, and quickly became pregnant with her son. By then, she had begun making forays into show business, appearing as a dancing elf in commercials for Hotpoint appliances. She landed her first television series role in 1959, playing Sam the switchboard operator on *Richard Diamond, Private Eye*. Only her legs were shown on-screen, and Moore quit after three months.

Her big break came in 1961 with the television series built around the appealing Everyman comedian Dick Van Dyke. Audiences immediately responded to the casting of the pert, sensitive Moore opposite Van Dyke, finding strong chemistry between the two as they portrayed a loving husband and wife—albeit a couple forced by the strict TV standards of the day to sleep in twin beds. The show was innovative in many respects. Up until then, situation comedies had focused almost exclusively on domestic life, but *The Dick Van Dyke Show* spent as much time at the lead character's workplace, where he was a writer for a variety show. The series creator and supporting actor Carl Reiner drew on his own real-life experiences as a writer for *The Sid Caesar Show* and in the process cast a revealing behind-the-scenes light on the magic of show business.

While Moore's character, Laura Petrie, was in most re-

Mary Tyler Moore. ARCHIVE PHOTOS, INC.

spects a traditional suburban housewife, she did break one television barrier: she was the first homemaker to wear pants on-screen. Most comedies featured perfectly attired women in dresses and pearls, which they wore even while vacuuming, but Moore insisted that pants were more realistic. Her Capri-pants-and-flats look became a fashion benchmark. Moore first demonstrated her comic potential in an early episode entitled "Blond-Haired Brunette," in which a botched dye job leaves her half-blond. She explains the disaster to Van Dyke through sobs, rolled eyes, and gulping speech as the audience roars with laughter. After that, she was no longer confined to the role of "straight man" to Van Dyke's antics. Other memorable episodes featured her sliding down a pile of walnuts in a dream sequence and gamely enduring as her toe remains stuck in a bathtub faucet for an entire show.

As Moore shaped her character, she looked to her two role models, Lucille Ball and Katharine Hepburn. Ball owned the studio where the show was filmed and dropped by the set occasionally. She often laughed at funny moments during filming—the ultimate compliment to Moore and the rest of the cast. A high point for Moore came when Ball one day stopped her to say, "You're very good." The series brought Moore lead-actress Emmy Awards in 1964 and 1966 and a Golden Globe Award in 1965.

In 1961 Moore divorced her husband after six years of marriage. Two years later she married the television executive Grant Tinker—a relationship that later assured her the chance to take on her most groundbreaking television role. First, however, Moore tried her hand at feature films. She found that she was upstaged by Julie Andrews and Carol Channing in 1967's *Thoroughly Modern Millie* and then tep-

idly received in several other movie roles, including her 1969 portrayal of a nun opposite Elvis Presley in the critically panned *Change of Habit*. Her personal life was also rocky: she suffered a miscarriage in 1966 and then was diagnosed with diabetes, a disease that eventually led her to become a spokeswoman for the Juvenile Diabetes Foundation.

Finally, Moore favorably caught the attention of audiences and television executives in a 1969 television variety show that reunited her with Dick Van Dyke. The Columbia Broadcasting System (CBS) gave the green light to the development of a new television series built around Moore; she and her husband co-founded the production company MTM Enterprises to work on the project, with Moore as chairwoman. The development of the new show reflected the emerging women's liberation movement of the 1960s and 1970s. Women were increasingly pursuing careers instead of stay-at-home marriages, as they demanded more political and social rights along with sexual freedom. The television series *That Girl* starring Marlo Thomas (1966–1971) had paved the way for a show about a single career woman. In 1970 Moore became Mary Richards, a producer climbing the ranks at a Minneapolis television news station, in *The Mary Tyler Moore Show*.

The show's development ran afoul of CBS executives when they learned that Richards was to play a divorcee. Fearing that audiences would associate the divorce with the popular Van Dyke, executives insisted that she instead simply be on the rebound from a serious relationship. Unlike *That Girl*, there was no steady boyfriend in the lead character's life; *The Mary Tyler Moore Show* became increasingly bold in suggesting that Richards had an active sex life. Distinguished by its insightful writing and memorable supporting characters, the series ran for seven seasons and won twenty-nine Emmys. Moore herself was nominated in the lead-actress category every year and won in 1973, 1974, and 1976.

Moore's career never again hit the same comedic stride. For several years she enjoyed a growing reputation as a skilled dramatic actress, winning praise with her portrayal of a paralyzed sculptor in the Broadway play *Whose Life Is It, Anyway?* in 1980. Also in 1980 she was nominated for an Academy Award for her portrayal of a cold mother in the film *Ordinary People,* a role for which she won a Golden Globe Award. Despite her success as an actress, Moore was entering the most trying period in her life. Her only son died in 1980 from a self-shooting that was ruled accidental, and she divorced Tinker in 1981. In 1983 she married her third husband, Robert Levine, a cardiologist eighteen years her junior. The following year Moore checked herself into the Betty Ford Clinic for treatment for alcoholism. The disease already had claimed the life of her younger sister, who died of an alcohol-and-drug overdose in 1978; her brother died of cancer in 1991 while in recovery from alcoholism.

Moore's attempts to return to series television flopped in quickly canceled shows during the 1980s and 1990s. She was named to the Television Hall of Fame in 1985. During the 1990s she made varyingly successful television movie appearances; her portrayal of an illegal adoption trafficker in *Stolen Babies* (1993) won her another Emmy Award. Even as the twentieth century ended, the enduring legacy of the Mary Richards role continued with television retrospectives, specials, and even a commemorative statue built in downtown Minneapolis depicting the famous *Mary Tyler Moore Show* opening: Moore tossing her hat into the air to celebrate "making it after all."

In *The Complete Directory to Prime Time TV Stars,* Moore was equated with Lucille Ball and Carol Burnett and dubbed "one of the great comediennes of American television." *People* magazine, naming Moore one of its top twenty-five stars in 1989, put it another way: "More than any other TV performer, Mary used charm to win us: She became America's sweetheart."

★

Moore's autobiography, *After All,* was published in 1995. A biography is Jason Ponderoff, *Mary Tyler Moore* (1986). She was profiled in the *New York Times Magazine* (26 Nov. 1995).

LEIGH DYER

MORENO, Rita (*b.* 11 December 1931 in Humacao, Puerto Rico), dynamic actress, singer, and dancer who in the 1960s was the first Latina actress to win an Academy Award and who also received a Grammy, a Tony, and two Emmys.

Moreno, born Rosa Delores Alverio, immigrated with her divorced single mother, Rosa María Marcano Alverio, to New York City in 1936, leaving her father, Paco Alverio, a farmer, and a brother behind. Moreno and her mother settled on the Upper West Side of Manhattan, where her mother did piecework as a seamstress. This neighborhood was a Puerto Rican enclave and the setting of Moreno's greatest cinema triumph in the 1960s, *West Side Story,* a musical that satirized life in America. She studied dancing and, at the age of seven, appeared in a Greenwich Village nightclub with her teacher, Paco Cansino, the uncle of the movie star Rita Hayworth. When Moreno was eight her mother began taking her to radio auditions and talent agencies. From the time she was eleven Moreno was the Spanish-speaking voice of such performers as Elizabeth Taylor and Judy Garland in dubbed movies. Moreno attended Public School 132 in Brooklyn during this time. She dropped out of high school at age sixteen.

On 13 November 1945 Moreno made her Broadway debut at the Belasco Theater as Angelina, the youngest sister of an Italian soldier, in *Skydrift,* a World War II drama that lasted only seven performances. It was at this time she adopted her stepfather's surname, Moreno. Later, in Hollywood, her studio suggested Rita as a first name. Moreno's first film appearance was in *So Young, So Bad* (1950), and she played minor roles in more than two dozen films through the 1950s. She also appeared on the cover of *Life* magazine on 1 March 1954.

In 1961 the choreographer Jerome Robbins cast her in the film version of *West Side Story.* Hailed by movie critics "the finest film musical ever made" and "a cinema masterpiece," *West Side Story* is a drama of New York City's juvenile gang wars. It tells the story of two nice kids, a Puerto Rican girl (Maria) and a Polish boy (Tony), who meet and fall in love despite the hatred and rivalry of their respective ethnic groups. The lovers come to a tragic end, just like Shakespeare's Romeo and Juliet. Moreno played Anita, Maria's faithful friend. A year after her stellar 1956 performance in *The King and I,* Moreno had been asked by Robbins to try out for the lead role of Maria in the original theater production. Moreno, busy as well as intimidated, did not, and by the time the movie version was being produced her face had matured and she was better suited to the character of Anita.

When she arrived for the audition, Moreno found five other actresses vying for the role of Anita. Even though Robbins had requested that she audition for the role, Moreno was sure she would not get it. She was asked to do a scene where Anita is nearly raped in a drugstore. When she read the lines and the epithets they contained—"Ya lyin' Spic, gold tooth, garlic breath, and pierced ear"—she was transported back some twenty years to the tenements of her youth where, on her way to kindergarten, she ducked snowballs thrown with all the hatred of racial prejudice. When the reading was over she ran from the room, collapsed on a couch, and wept. She got the part.

On 9 April 1962 *West Side Story* swept the Academy Awards, winning ten Oscars, including one for Moreno for best supporting actress. She received glowing reviews for what one critic called "her stormy, sexy, funny, and first-rate performance." Another critic wrote, "Miss Moreno emerges as a first-rate dramatic talent. Some people claim she steals the picture." Despite her Oscar win, studios offered her only limited roles, pandering to the public's image of Moreno as a spitfire Latina. So, on 15 October 1964, Moreno returned to the stage in Lorraine Hansberry's *Sign in Sidney Brustein's Window.*

Moreno voiced her concern for Hispanic causes in numerous public service announcements. On 9 August 1963 she participated in a march through downtown Los Angeles to protest the city's failure to integrate its school system. She also supported the civil rights campaign led by the Reverend Martin Luther King, Jr., briefly working for his Southern Christian Leadership Conference in 1964.

Rita Moreno *(center)*, in a scene from *West Side Story*. AP/WIDE WORLD PHOTOS

In a 1965 interview Moreno spoke out about prejudice against Puerto Ricans and claimed that Puerto Ricans were a more isolated community than African Americans. She asserted that because Puerto Ricans did not want to address the color problem in America, it was difficult to involve the Puerto Rican community in civil rights issues. In the mid-1960s there was no strong Puerto Rican presence in middle-class America. No Puerto Rican community leader had the charisma of Dr. King. In the turbulent 1960s Moreno became increasingly active in politics and civil rights issues, declaring, "Hollywood Jim Crowism must end now in all its aspects."

In 1964 Moreno met a New York cardiologist and internist named Leonard I. Gordon. On 18 June 1965 they married, and in 1967 their only child, a daughter, was born. Gordon suffered from serious congenital heart problems, so in 1970 he retired to manage Moreno's career. With the help of the actor Marlon Brando, with whom she had had a tempestuous relationship from 1953 to 1961, Moreno returned to films in *The Night of the Following Day* (1969). A critic for *The New Yorker* wrote that Moreno did "the only acting in the picture." Additional films of the period include *Popi* (1969), *Marlowe* (1969), and *Carnal Knowledge* (1971). Onstage, Moreno's role as Serafina in Tennessee Williams's *Rose Tattoo* won her the Joseph Jefferson Award from Chicago's critics on 4 April 1968.

In 1972 Moreno, along with the rest of the cast, won a Grammy for a soundtrack recording made by television's *Electric Company*. Opening on 20 January 1975, *The Ritz,*

a Broadway play based on the Hispanic character Googie Gomez, whom Moreno had invented at Hollywood parties, was a hit and earned her a Tony Award. In 1977 she won an Emmy for her work as a guest artist on a television episode of the children's program *The Muppets*. She won another Emmy in 1978 for her portrayal of a vulnerable prostitute on *The Rockford Files*. Moreno is in the *Guinness Book of World Records* as the only woman to have won all four of show business's top awards. She participates in artistic and civic organizations, such as the Third World Cinema, and continues her acting career, matching her art with a concern for others.

★

A biography of Moreno is Susan Suntree, *Rita Moreno* (1993). Biographical information about Moreno is in *Current Biography Yearbook* (1985); *Notable Hispanic American Women* (1993); Diane Telgen and Jim Kamp, *Latinas! Women of Achievement* (1996); and Nicolas Kanellos, ed., *The Hispanic American Almanac* (1996). An in-depth interview is in *Harper's* (Apr. 1965), and another article of interest is "Rita Moreno and Other Latin Trailblazers," *Latina Style* (fall 1995).

DOROTHY L. MORAN

MORRIS, Robert (*b.* 9 February 1931 in Kansas City, Missouri), sculptor, artist, and writer whose sculptural works are more about the perception of an object, or the process involved in its making, than about the object itself.

Morris studied engineering at the University of Kansas City while taking art classes at the Kansas City Art Institute from 1948 to 1950. In 1951 he went on to the California School of Fine Arts in San Francisco. After serving in the U.S. Army Corps of Engineers in Arizona and Korea from 1951 to 1952, Morris continued his art studies at Reed College in Portland, Oregon, between 1953 and 1955. He then returned to San Francisco, where he spent his time painting and then sculpting in the abstract expressionist style. He also became involved in theater improvisation, and he and his wife, the dancer and choreographer Simone Forti, started a workshop "exploring the relations of the body's movement to sound, text, props, rules and tasks." Morris's interest in all forms of art increased during this era, and he explored film, theater, and multimedia. In 1961 he and his wife moved to New York City, where, for two years, he took art history courses at Hunter College in New York City, writing his master's thesis on the Romanian sculptor Constantin Brancusi.

In New York, Morris's eclectic, diverse, and influential career in art began to blossom and grow. He continued his interest in dance and theater. He and Forti participated in a loose-knit confederation of dancers called the Judson Dance Theater, for which Morris choreographed numerous works, including *Arizona* (1963), *21.3* (1963), *Site* (1963), and *Waterman Switch* (1965). During the 1960s Morris played a central role in defining three principal artistic movements of the period: minimalism (which stresses the idea of reducing a work of art to the minimum number of colors, values, shapes, lines and textures), conceptual art (in which the idea for a work is considered more important than the finished product, if any), and process art (which emphasizes the "process" of making art rather than any predetermined composition or plan, and the concepts of change and transience). One of Morris's earliest minimalist works, *The Column* (1961), was used in a performance of the Judson Dance Theater. Another object made for one of the performances was converted into a sculpture—*Box for Standing* (1961). Morris had solo exhibits in New York City at the Green Gallery in 1964 and 1965 that displayed this influential work.

One of Morris's first and best-known works is his innovative *Box with the Sound of Its Own Making* (1961), in which he displayed a wooden box that emits the tape-recorded sounds of its construction, a process that took three and a half hours. Morris was also a respected art critic and scholar, writing several influential critical essays. Four of these essays show a chronology of some of his most important work: task-oriented dance in *Some Notes on Dance* (1965); minimalist sculpture in *Notes on Sculpture* (1968); process art in *Anti Form* (1968); and earthworks in *Aligned with Nazca* (1975).

Much of Morris's work in the 1960s has been classified as neo-dada. The unifying element of neo-dada art is its reinvestigation of dada's irony and its use of found objects or banal activities (or both) as instruments of society. Dada was an early-twentieth-century art movement that ridiculed contemporary culture and traditional art forms. Such dadaist artists as Marcel Duchamp and Max Ernst produced works that were antitraditional or reflected a cynical attitude toward social values. At the same time, dadaism was irrational and often cryptic. Dadaists typically produced art objects in unconventional forms made with unconventional methods.

As an art form, neo-dada attacked the lofty aspirations of high art and was very much a part of the art culture of the 1960s. Morris extended and distorted modernism's tendency toward the concept that art should represent the structure or terms of its own medium. He introduced the use of found objects, industrial materials, and mixtures of text and image that infused his works with a "skeptical irreverence and sociopolitical significance." The elements of his compositions interact, either through the process of their making or in the viewer's interaction with them. As the 1960s progressed, he explored more elaborate industrial processes in his sculpture, using materials such as aluminum and steel mesh.

In the late 1960s and 1970s Morris moved from the rigid plywood and steel of his minimalist works to the soft materials of his experiments with process art. Felt became his primary material. He designed a series of works that were piled, stacked, and hung from the wall, to explore the effects of gravity and stress on ordinary materials. The Leo Castelli Gallery in New York City exhibited a variety of these felt works in 1968. Morris continued to experiment with other unorthodox materials in his inside exhibits. He used such materials as dirt and threadwaste (recycled fibers from textile manufacturers), which resist deliberate shaping into predetermined forms. He promoted breaking down traditional ideas that link the work of an artist with a studio, advancing instead the idea of letting the materials take their own position. His work in the early 1970s in the earthworks art form was also a major contribution. Morris further challenged the "myth of artistic self-expression." The pieces that show this form include ironic "self-portraits" consisting of sculpted brains and electroencephalogram readouts, as well as other works that were considered "investigations of perception and measurement." Since the 1970s Morris has explored such varied mediums as blindfolded drawings, mirror installations, encaustic paintings (using a paint made of wax), and hydrocal (a brand of gypsum cement) and fiberglass castings. His themes range from nuclear holocaust to Ludwig Wittgenstein's *Philosophical Investigations* (the work of a postmodern philosopher).

During his career, Morris has had more than seventy-five solo exhibitions and ten group exhibitions. His solo exhibits include those at New York's Whitney Museum of American Art in 1970, the Art Institute of Chicago in 1980, the Chicago Museum of Contemporary Art in 1986, and the Corcoran Gallery of Art in Washington, D.C., in 1990. In 1994 the Solomon R. Guggenheim Museum, New York City, organized a major retrospective of his work. This exhibit traveled to the Deichtorhallen in Hamburg, Germany, and the Musée National d'Art Moderne in Paris.

Well-respected museums, such as the Museum of Modern Art, the Whitney Museum, and the Guggenheim (all in New York City); the National Gallery of Canada, Ottawa; the Tate Gallery, London, and many more, have his works in their permanent collections. He has received numerous awards, among them, First Prize, International Institute, Torcuato di Tella, Buenos Aires (1967); Guggenheim International Award (1967); Guggenheim Fellowship (1969); Sculpture Award, Society Four Arts (1975); and the Skowhegan Medal for Progress and Environment, Maine (1978). At the opening of the twenty-first century, Morris lived in New York City and Gardiner, New York, and continued to develop as an artist.

Morris is difficult to assess on the basis of any individual piece he has produced. His contribution to contemporary art must be based upon his entire body of work—past, present, and future. His work and influence challenge the historical concept of a single artistic masterpiece and put the emphasis on a "connected and evolving artistic discourse." As Morris himself has indicated, his is "a continuous project altered daily." Implicit in his work is the idea that art can be made of anything and should be "experienced."

Morris has taken his ideas of minimalism, conceptualism and process art and made it part of the American art world. His entire body of work allows new and experienced artists to become part of their own work and be as individualistic as they wish to be. He believes all artists should be part of the "art" that they do, no matter what the medium, style, or thought.

★

There is no full-length biography of Morris. His own books and articles give insights into his thoughts, but contain little autobiographical information. Morris also is known as a scholar and an excellent art critic; his works appear in numerous art journals and other publications including *Artforum, Art* magazine, and *Artweek*. A good basic book is Morris, *Continuous Project Altered Daily: The Writings of Robert Morris* (1993). Most material written about Morris is in exhibit catalogues or books on a specific type of art, including Gregory Battcock, ed., *Minimal Art: A Critical Anthology* (1968); E. C. Goosen, *The Art of the Real: USA, 1948–1968* (1969); Marti Mayo, *Robert Morris: Selected Works 1970–1980* (1982); Pepe Karmel and Maurice Berger, *Robert Morris: The Felt Works* (1989); and Rosalind Krauss, Maurice Berger, David Anin, et al., *Robert Morris: The Mind/Body Problem* (1994).

JOAN GOODBODY

MORRISON, James Douglas ("Jim") (*b.* 8 December 1943 in Melbourne, Florida; *d.* 3 [possibly 2] July 1971 in Paris, France), singer, songwriter, and poet, whose songs of rebellion and desire electrified audiences and whose largely wasted and tragic life came to represent the dark side of the creative spirit for generations after.

Morrison was the eldest of three children of George Stephen Morrison, a naval officer, and Clara Clarke, a homemaker. Morrison's father had a distinguished career, rising to become captain of an aircraft carrier by the time his son had moved to Los Angeles in the mid-1960s, and eventually becoming a rear admiral. Morrison attended high school in Alameda, California, but graduated from George Washington High School in Alexandria, Virginia, in 1961. He was an exceptional student in English, amazing his teachers with his knowledge of the lore of literature, including even obscure writers. In high school he filled himself with the writings of Friedrich Nietzsche, William Blake, and the Greek poets. After graduating from high school in 1961, Morrison attended St. Petersburg Junior College; then from 1962 to 1963 attended Florida State University. During these years his ambition was to become a filmmaker. At Florida State, and later at the University of California, Los Angeles (UCLA), where he earned a B.A. in theater arts in 1965, Morrison astounded his teachers with the wide scope of his reading and the deep retention of what he read.

In 1964 Morrison entered the motion picture school at UCLA. He did not find a place to live, preferring to sleep in the seamier parts of Los Angeles, seldom bathing, with a few clothes stored in the trunk of a car. Even when famous and rich, he tended to sleep outside or live in motel rooms, changing motels daily. At UCLA he met Ray Manzarek, a talented keyboardist. One day, while at the beach, Morrison showed Manzarek some songs he was writing, and Manzarek was impressed enough to suggest they form a band. Manzarek recruited the other band members—drummer John Densmore and guitarist Robbie Krieger—from a Maharishi Yogi meditation class he attended. Morrison drew the band's name, the Doors, from Aldous Huxley's book *The Doors of Perception* (1964), which had been inspired by Morrison's favorite poet, William Blake. The lines from Blake that Morrison drew on are disputed by biographers, but "There are things that are known and things that are unknown; in between are the doors," seems likeliest, although "If the doors of perception were cleaned, everything would appear to man as it truly is, infinite" is a close runner-up.

The Doors wanted to become a club band in Los Angeles; they nearly broke up just before landing a gig as the house band of an upscale nightclub, the Whiskey-a-Go-Go. In September 1965 Morrison met eighteen-year-old

Jim Morrison. MR. JACK VARTOOGIAN.

Pamela Susan Courson, who was later described as either his common-law wife or his girlfriend. He abused her, perhaps even beat her. She became hooked on heroin by 1969 and died of an overdose on 25 April 1974. By 1965 Morrison was already trying every drug, licit or illicit, he could lay his hands on. His capacity for taking drugs amazed even other addicts.

In January 1967 the Doors became a headliner with the release of their first album, *The Doors*. Their first hit single, "Light My Fire," written by Krieger, sold over 1 million copies in 1967. The single exemplified the Doors sound: Morrison with deep-throated, fiery delivery; Manzarek's rich, deep, sophisticated keyboard work, Krieger's clear, crisp chords; and Densmore's underlying drumming, blending in with the keyboard, guitar, and singing.

In November 1967 the band's second album, *Strange Days,* was released to both critical and commercial success, especially among young teens, who flocked to hear the band. By this time, Morrison was almost perpetually strung out on drugs, sometimes unable to stand while performing. He experimented with his onstage behavior, trying to find what limits his audience would put on his performance; his awkward, silly hopping about became sexually suggestive acts. On 9 December 1968 he was arrested for supposedly exposing himself during a performance in Miami, Florida. At the time he seemed almost certainly guilty; from a perspective of decades later, the charges were quite likely bogus. His trial was a sham, and the judge prevented his defense team from presenting evidence that would have exonerated Morrison.

Even so, Morrison showed contempt for his audiences; he cursed them and even spit on the girls who crowded the edge of the stage. Offstage, he demanded that fans give him oral sex in public (and someone almost always complied), and he slept with many women, giving rise to seemingly endless paternity lawsuits. Morrison seemed as much disgusted with himself as with his fans, whom he thought did not pay enough attention to what his lyrics meant. Despite his drug habit, he put on weight, developing a paunch. The other members of the Doors were heartily sick of his rudeness and his lack of responsibility. After releasing a couple of mediocre albums, they made one last good one, *Morrison Hotel,* named after a seedy Los Angeles establishment and released in February 1970.

For Morrison the album came too late. He tried to sober up, and for a time he seemed a thoughtful, gracious man, but by the end of 1970 he was drinking every day and working his way through the bars of Los Angeles. On or about 21 June 1970 he married Patricia Kennealy, editor of *Jazz and Pop,* in a witch's wedding ceremony. (Kennealy claimed to be a white witch.) Shortly afterward he left for Europe, but with Courson, not his new wife. The couple found an apartment in Paris, where Morrison hoped to heal himself. Instead, he began touring the bars there, becoming perpetually drunk. On either 2 July or 3 July 1971 he died while taking a bath. Courson discovered his body in the early morning hours of 3 July and called for help. No autopsy was performed; Morrison's body was sealed in a casket, and no one was allowed to view it. The coroner ruled that the cause of death was a heart attack, but it was almost certainly due to an overdose of heroin and alcohol.

Morrison is buried in Père Lachaise cemetery in Paris. His gravestone has been defaced by graffiti, but by the 1990s it was the third most popular tourist destination in Paris. The name on the gravestone is James Douglas Morrison, the name he preferred. His legacy exists in two forms—image and music. In image, Morrison became the archetypal tragic rock star, burned out at twenty-seven, all rebellion and sullenness. His onstage antics, such as throwing himself into an audience, have become the stock-in-trade of rock singers. Musically, the sound of the Doors has been often imitated; glimmers of the rich sound of Manzarek's keyboarding and the anguished howling of Morrison's singing can be heard in numerous groups and singers such as David Bowie and Alice Cooper.

★

Dylan Jones, *Jim Morrison: Dark Star* (1990) assembles the elements of Morrison's life into a critical, coherent narrative. David Dalton, *Mr. Mojo Risin': Jim Morrison, the Last Holy Fool*

(1991), notes how Morrison role-played in his life the romantic image of the mad poet. Ray Manzarek, the keyboardist for the Doors, has written two memoirs. In *Riders on the Storm: My Life with Jim Morrison and The Doors* (1990), he looks hard at Morrison and delves into the dynamics of making the music that made them famous. *My Life with the Doors* (1998), does not exploit his relationship with Morrison so much as it fills in the lives of the other people who made the Doors a renowned rock group. An obituary is in the *New York Times* (9 July 1971).

KIRK H. BEETZ

MORSE, Wayne Lyman   (*b.* 20 October 1900 near Madison, Wisconsin; *d.* 22 July 1974 in Portland, Oregon), author, educator, and United States senator from Oregon from 1945 to 1969 who was best known for his opposition to the Vietnam War.

Morse, one of six children of Wilbur Frank Morse, a livestock farmer, and Jessie (White) Morse, a homemaker and farm wife, grew up in Madison under the populist political tradition of Wisconsin Senator Robert LaFollette. After attending Madison public schools and graduating from Madison High School, he earned a B.A. degree in labor economics in 1924 and an M.A. degree in speech in 1925 from the University of Wisconsin. Morse married Mildred Martha Downie, a home economics instructor, on 18 June 1924. They had three daughters. Morse completed a four-year military training course at the University of Wisconsin

Wayne Morse. CORBIS CORPORATION (BELLEVUE)

in 1922 and was commissioned as a second lieutenant in the U.S. Army Reserves, in which he served from 1923 to 1929.

Morse taught speech at the University of Minnesota from 1924 through 1926, earning a bachelor of law degree in 1928. He received a doctor of jurisprudence from Columbia University in 1932. He joined the University of Oregon as assistant professor of law in 1929 and became dean of its law school in 1931. The University of Oregon has since endowed the Wayne Morse Chair of Law and Politics in his honor.

In 1938 Secretary of Labor Frances Perkins appointed Morse Pacific coast labor arbitrator. Morse arbitrated labor disputes between ship owners and the International Longshoreman's and Warehousemen's Union. In 1942 President Franklin D. Roosevelt selected him to represent the public on the War Labor Board.

In 1944 Morse ousted Republican incumbent Rufus Holman in the Oregon primary for the United States Senate and defeated Democrat Edgar Smith in the general election. He quickly exhibited liberalism, independence, outspokenness, and courage, antagonizing Republican leaders. Morse served on the Senate Labor Committee, supported trade unionism, opposed the Taft-Hartley Act of 1947, and backed the containment policies of President Harry Truman, designed to prevent the spread of Communism.

Morse was reelected to the Senate in 1950 as a Republican, but he clashed with party leaders on economic issues and broke with the 1952 Republican presidential candidate Dwight D. Eisenhower for his conciliatory policies towards conservative Republicans. When the Senate convened in January 1953, Morse became an Independent. He carried a folding chair into the Senate chamber and placed it in the aisle between the two parties. The Republican leadership stripped him of his Labor Committee position. Morse opposed Eisenhower's policy of promoting private ownership of tidelands oil and private development of dams by electric power companies. On 24–25 April 1953 Morse engaged in a record twenty-two-hour, twenty-six-minute filibuster against the tidelands oil legislation. The previous Senate filibuster record had been held by Morse's mentor, LaFollette.

Morse in 1954 aligned with the Democrats, who regained control of the Senate and appointed him to the Foreign Relations Committee. He was elected to the Senate in 1956 as a Democrat and fought with Eisenhower over civil rights, the promotion of private ownership of the public domain, and foreign policy issues. Morse backed civil rights legislation, increased price-support payments for farmers, and federal aid to education.

Morse in 1961 became chairman of the Subcommittee on Education. He supported the New Frontier programs of President John F. Kennedy and the Great Society programs of President Lyndon B. Johnson. Morse voted for the War on Poverty, the Civil Rights Act of 1964, federal aid to elementary and secondary education, Medicare and Medicaid, and the Voting Rights Act of 1965. Johnson appointed Morse to two emergency labor boards, but Morse angered the labor unions involved in both cases, causing them to oppose his reelection in 1968.

Morse concentrated increasingly on foreign policy issues. He traveled to most Latin American countries and supported the Alliance for Progress, a massive economic aid program for Latin America, but his opposition to the Vietnam War cemented his place in political history. Morse disapproved of increasing the American role in Vietnam as early as 1961, but he became a more vocal critic after Johnson expanded American involvement there. In 1964 North Vietnamese torpedo boats attacked American destroyers in the Gulf of Tonkin. At Johnson's request the Senate passed a joint resolution authorizing him to take all necessary steps, including the use of armed force, against aggression in Southeast Asia. Morse and Ernest Gruening of Alaska were the only two dissenting senators.

Morse voted against every measure, including appropriations, that would keep American troops in Vietnam. Besides harassing public officials who would not release information, Morse spoke against the Vietnam War in the Senate and across the nation. He argued that American intervention violated international law, described the conflict largely as a Vietnamese civil war, stressed mounting American casualties, and denied that the war was winnable.

Morse's stance on Vietnam hindered his quest for reelection to a fifth Senate term in 1968. He fervently supported Eugene McCarthy when the Minnesota Democrat sought the presidency on an antiwar platform in 1968. Morse lost his reelection bid by just over 3,000 votes to Republican Robert Packwood. His controversial decisions on the emergency labor relations boards contributed to his defeat.

Morse retired to his twenty-nine-acre farm in Eugene, Oregon, to raise saddle horses and cattle. He sought to regain his Senate seat, but lost to Republican Mark Hatfield in 1972. Morse tried again in 1974, winning the May primary and preparing to campaign against the incumbent Packwood. He died in Eugene after developing a urinary infection that led to blood poisoning and kidney failure. He is buried in the Rest Haven Memorial Park in Eugene.

The extraordinarily hardworking Morse influenced the Senate as the consummate outsider. The independent maverick crossed political lines to vote his conscience. Unfazed by criticism, Morse was guided by unequivocal conscience and integrity, and he spoke his mind and pursued his goals with relentless, self-righteous conviction. His colorful, often provocative rhetoric upbraided his opposition without re-

gard to party membership. Morse, a legal and legislative scholar, championed untamed, fiery liberalism; fought for civil rights, civil liberties, and trade unionism; and opposed special interest groups seeking to limit the public domain.

Morse's stormy relations with fellow senators and presidents Truman, Eisenhower, and Johnson earned him the nicknames the "Lone Ranger" and the "Tiger of the Senate." Senators admired his profound intellect and feared the whiplash of his scorn. He infuriated his colleagues with brash, bold speeches, yet managed to educate the public with his liberal views. As a debater, Morse exhibited shrewdness, agility, and enormous energy. He searched for truth at the expense of his personal popularity.

★

Morse's papers are located at the University of Oregon, Eugene. Lee Wilkins, *Wayne Morse: A Bio-Bibliography* (1985), summarizes Morse's life and works by and about him. Works on Morse and his political career include A. Robert Smith, *Tiger in the Senate: The Biography of Wayne Morse* (1962); Harrison E. Spangler, *The Record of Wayne Morse* (1962); and Edward N. Fadeley, *Wayne Morse Remembered* (1974). Obituaries are in the *New York Times* (23 July 1974), the *Washington Post* (27 July 1974), and *Time* and *Newsweek* (both 5 Aug. 1974).

DAVID L. PORTER

MOSES, Robert Parris (*b.* 23 January 1935 in New York City), educator, author, philosopher, civil rights advocate, and founder of the Algebra Project, best known for his work as field secretary for the Student Nonviolent Coordinating Committee, in which he led the effort for voter registration among the black population of Mississippi.

Moses, the son of Gregory Moses, a janitor, and Louise Parris Moses, grew up with his two brothers in New York City's Harlem neighborhood. Both parents encouraged academic achievement in their children. Moses's paternal grandfather, William Henry Moses, had been an educated man, a well-known Southern Baptist preacher and fundraiser for the National Baptist Convention, and his parents wanted their children to continue a tradition interrupted by economic deprivation during the Great Depression.

Moses took a citywide competitive examination as a teenager and scored so high that he was accepted into Manhattan's Stuyvesant High School, a center for gifted students. In his senior year he received a scholarship to attend Hamilton College, a small liberal arts institution in upstate New York. He received his B.A. degree in philosophy and mathematics from Hamilton in 1956. Moses entered Harvard University and began his graduate study with an emphasis on analytic philosophy in the fall of 1956. He completed requirements for the Master of Arts degree and began doctoral studies in 1957. He was forced to abandon

Robert Parris Moses. THE LIBRARY OF CONGRESS

his graduate work in early 1958, however. His mother had died of cancer, and his father's health was poor, so he returned to New York City to help his family. He accepted a teaching position at the Horace Mann School, a noted private institution. To supplement his income Moses tutored a fourteen-year-old popular black singer by the name of Frankie Lyman, leader of a group called the Teenagers.

Moses's activist work began in 1959, when he helped organize the second Youth March for Integrated Schools in Washington, D.C. As the 1960s began he took his first trip to the Deep South, visiting his uncle, William Henry Moses, a professor at the Hampton Institute. While he was in Newport News, Virginia, a town near Hampton, he participated in a demonstration and met Wyatt Tee Walker and Bayard Rustin, associates of the Reverend Martin Luther King, Jr. Moses volunteered his spare time to work for Rustin, who was coordinating the Committee to Defend Martin Luther King, a legal defense organization necessary due to King's frequent arrests because of his civil rights work. In June 1960 Rustin persuaded Moses to go to Atlanta and work with the Southern Christian Leadership Conference on the voter registration campaign. He emphasized that he should work with a youth group, the Student Nonviolent Coordinating Committee (SNCC). With a letter of introduction, Moses met with Ella Baker, the primary force behind the newly formed student organization.

As a committed member of SNCC, Moses worked tirelessly on the picket lines. His longtime interest in the Chinese philosophy (called Taoism) of the philosopher Lao-tzu greatly influenced his pacifist thought and contemplative demeanor. His commitment to Eastern philosophy resulted in his being wrongfully accused of favoring Communism. He left the home office in Atlanta and volunteered to go to Mississippi to take on the challenge of registering black Mississippians to vote. Baker befriended Moses and directed him to Amzie Moore, a local leader of the National Association for the Advancement of Colored People (NAACP) in Mississippi. Moore believed that blacks could improve their lot with political power, starting with enfranchisement, and convinced Moses of the empowerment that voting could engender. They agreed that political power would more likely address the economic concerns of blacks than the direct action, confrontational techniques of sit-ins or freedom rides. The new direction toward attempts at voter registration proved to be a major shift for the civil rights movement in Mississippi, one that Moses led.

Moses went home to New York to complete his teaching contract but returned to Mississippi in the spring of 1961. He became SNCC's first full-time voter registration worker. Once committed, Moses did not waver, despite being harassed, beaten, jailed, and threatened with his life. From 1961 until spring 1963 Moses worked with a fervor unmatched by other leaders. Years later, in an interview with *Emerge* magazine, Moses explained, "The issue was whether you were going to commit to the work and what that meant was that they would have to gun you down to [get you to] leave." Moses arrived in McComb, Mississippi, in July 1961 and began his duties as the first field secretary for the SNCC. The new approach was to build a community base for voter registration efforts that included "Freedom Schools," where African Americans would be instructed on how to vote, educated about current events, and taught methods by which the community could be empowered against segregation and discrimination.

Moses developed a coalition with other civil rights organizations working in the area. He came into contact with what Peter B. Levy called "an assortment of pre-existing networks of activism in the African American community." The networks gave Moses and his coworkers entrée into their homes and meeting places, access to vital resources in order to keep the movement going, and encouragement in the face of the so-called Mississippi justice. Once segregationist, white Mississippians became aware of Moses's activity, they threatened him and his coworkers with physical violence and economic reprisal. The whites killed one of the local black workers assisting Moses. Acts of intimidation served only to mobilize and strengthen resistance in the black community. On 25 September 1961 one hundred black students staged a freedom march to McComb City

Hall. Violence broke out, and several civil rights workers were injured. Even though the white mob had incited the violence, authorities arrested the students for disturbing the peace and sentenced them to prison terms of four to six months. Moses himself spent the last three months of 1961 in a Mississippi jail.

After he was released Moses spent the winter and spring strategizing for the summer of 1962. The Council of Federated Organizations (COFO) was mobilized, and Moses was named director and given funds to develop the Voter Education Project. At this time all the efforts for voter registration came from grassroots organizations. The federal government offered neither assistance nor protection to black Mississippians until the media brought the injustices to the public's attention. Moses's leadership and participation in the voters' rights work of the civil rights movement was vital. He proposed that SNCC and COFO shift tactics in the Mississippi delta, one of the poorest parts of the United States. Their collective effort was to mount a campaign known as the "Mississippi Freedom Summer." The plan was for Freedom Summer activities to take place before the Democratic National Convention began in Atlantic City, New Jersey, in 1964.

The COFO recruited one thousand students, many of whom were white, from elite colleges and universities. Local Mississippian activists disagreed on the strategy of using educated whites to come in and work. They felt that it would be business as usual, and local control would not be realized. But the plan moved ahead, with noted activists throwing their support to Moses, especially two key Mississippians, the political and civil rights activist Fannie Lou Hamer and Aaron Henry, the leader of the Mississippi chapter of the NAACP. In December 1963 SNCC committed itself to planning and executing Freedom Summer. The summer of 1964 was a violent one. Three student workers were murdered. White nightriders bombed and burned numerous local civil rights sites, including thirty-five churches, and Mississippi authorities arrested one thousand activists. In spite of the murders, jail terms, and violence, Moses and the student workers continued to train workers for the Freedom Schools. The curriculum consisted of the three R's, citizenship skills, and African-American history.

Freedom Summer came to a climax at the Democratic Party's convention in August 1964. The black Mississippi voters' struggle was now the center of public attention. Moses had encouraged the development of a new political party, the Mississippi Freedom Democratic Party (MFDP). The MFDP sought legitimate recognition for their members, and in a historic speech before the Credentials Committee, Hamer argued the rationale for seating MFDP delegates alongside the official Mississippi delegation. She told of the oppressive actions taken toward her, the murders and death

threats imposed on blacks who tried to register to vote, and the loss of property suffered by people who tried to exercise their right of participation in the political process.

President Lyndon B. Johnson, under pressure from all sides and fearful of losing the southern vote, offered the MFDP the compromise of seating two at-large delegates. The MFDP rejected the compromise and walked out of the convention. For once, Moses expressed his anger and broke his famous reserve, vowing never to speak to a white person again. After the Democratic convention he was thoroughly disenchanted with politics and the lack of support from the federal government. Because of continued threats against his life, he felt that he had become too visible, and so he changed his name to Robert Parris.

The convention proved to be a pivotal point for the civil rights movement. The struggle was no longer about civil rights; it became one of liberation. The voter registration efforts in Mississippi and the Freedom Summer of 1964 lent impetus to Congress's passing of the Voting Rights Act of 1965, believed by many activists to be the most powerful tool available to bring down injustice. Moses's civil rights activity took a toll on his marriage to Dona Richards, who was also involved in the struggle. The couple had no children and divorced in 1966.

In 1965 Moses began speaking out against the Vietnam War. When his application for conscientious objector status was denied, he failed to report to the draft board as ordered in August 1966. He fled to Canada and lived there for two years. While in exile in Canada, Moses married Janet Jemmott, who had served as the SNCC field secretary in Natchez, Mississippi. The couple moved to Tanzania in 1968 and settled in a small village. In East Africa, Moses worked for the Ministry of Education as director of the mathematics department at the Same' School, where his wife taught English. The Carter Amnesty Program of 1977 (put in place by President Jimmy Carter) provided a way for Moses to return to the United States without being imprisoned. He settled in Cambridge, Massachusetts, and returned to Harvard to pursue his doctoral studies, support his wife as she returned to medical school, and raise their four children.

In 1982 Moses became the recipient of a MacArthur Fellowship, which provided him with funds for five years to use as he saw fit. He identified mathematics literacy as a primary need for the coming century and used his fellowship to develop and implement the Algebra Project. The program serves more than forty thousand students in rural areas of the South and in schools in inner cities throughout the United States. It is designed to engage students intellectually in the field of mathematics. Moses attributes his methodology to Ella Baker, for his work with the Algebra Project is based on the voter registration programs in the South that he led during the 1960s. Moses has received numerous awards and honorary degrees for his work with the civil rights movement and the Algebra Project, including the Heinz Award for the Human Condition (2000), the Nation-Puffin Prize for Creative Citizenship (2001), the Margaret Chase Smith American Democracy Award from the National Association of Secretaries of State (2002), and the James Bryant Conant Award of the Education Commission of the States (2002).

Moses was one of the most important yet most elusive personalities of the 1960s. Like many other activists of the era, his efforts have been overshadowed by those of King, Malcolm X, Stokely Carmichael, and others. Nonetheless, his work to extend voting rights to African Americans during the 1960s has had a lasting effect on the country.

★

There are numerous books published about the civil rights movement, but few focus on Moses. Two leading biographical sources are Eric Burner, *And Gently He Shall Lead Them: Robert Parris Moses and Civil Rights in Mississippi* (1994), and David DeLeon, ed., *Leaders from the 1960's: A Biographical Sourcebook of American Activism* (1994). Other biographical sources include Richard W. Leeman, ed., *African-American Orators: A Bio-critical Sourcebook* (1996), and Peter B. Levy, *The Civil Rights Movement* (1998).

JOHNNIEQUE B. (JOHNNIE) LOVE

MOTT, Stewart Rawlings (*b.* 4 December 1937 in Flint, Michigan), philanthropist, political activist, and businessman whose avant-garde philanthropic work in the 1960s focused on controversial issues ranging from population control, abortion reform, and sex research, to government reform and arms control.

Mott was the son of the industrialist Charles Stewart Mott and his fourth wife, Ruth Rawlings, a former teacher. He had three older half-siblings, and two sisters. As a child Mott was overweight and lacked coordination; he nearly drowned at age nine after trying to skate on what proved to be thin ice. His relationship with his father, who was sixty-two when Mott was born, was strained, partly because of the elder Mott's work habits and myriad business interests, which kept him away from his family. Mott's parents often traveled, leaving the children in the care of governesses.

Educated at public schools in Flint, Mott spent summers at camp, which he reportedly detested. After running away from one at age eleven, Mott and his father reached a compromise wherein he would divide his time between camp and working at various odd jobs. Between 1951 and 1955 he attended Deerfield Academy in Massachusetts and then enrolled at the Massachusetts Institute of Technology as an engineering student. Following his junior year, Mott went

on a tour of Europe, fell in love with a woman he met in Greece, and then "disappeared" in Afghanistan. He was "located" after his family used its influence with government agencies.

With a broken engagement and strained family relations, Mott settled in Manhattan and enrolled at Columbia University's General Studies School, eventually earning two B.A. degrees, one in business administration and the other in comparative literature, in 1961. He remained at Columbia pursuing an M.A. degree in Greek drama, but left the school just short of meeting the requirements for the degree. In 1962 Mott returned to Flint and spent one year working as an apprentice at various family holdings. The following year, he taught English at Eastern Michigan University, but soon decided that he was not cut out for the life of an academic.

Once again returning to Flint, Mott intended to join the Charles Stewart Mott Foundation, but instead became active with Planned Parenthood. In 1963 he founded a branch of the organization in Flint and, based on that success, was asked to serve as an emissary on a national level. This marked the beginning of his long association with Planned Parenthood and his focus on the subjects of population control, family planning, and reproductive rights. Mott made his first gifts to the charity and over the next four years donated in excess of $1.2 million of his own money.

A conscientious objector to U.S. involvement in the Vietnam War, Mott further developed interests in arms control, peace initiatives, and government reform. He asked to join the Mott Foundation as a consultant, with the aim of reorganizing the grantmaker to move away from its local emphasis into broader areas in which he was more interested. When his conservative father declined the proposals, Mott moved back to New York City and eventually established his own charity Spectamur Agendo, which took its name from the family motto "Let us be known by our deeds." He volunteered at the Manhattan office of Planned Parenthood to hone his fund-raising skills. It was a task at which he proved more than successful, raising over $3 million in 1966 alone.

Mott achieved national prominence in 1968 when he ran full-page advertisements in the *New York Times* and several Michigan newspapers that urged New York governor Nelson A. Rockefeller to run for the presidency as an antiwar candidate. He even established a volunteer organization for the proposed campaign and began raising funds, but Rockefeller seemingly ignored him. When President Lyndon B. Johnson announced his plans not to seek reelection, Mott shifted his support to Senator Eugene McCarthy, donating more than $200,000 to his presidential campaign. Additionally, he made contributions to several other candidates who were running on platforms that advocated an end to the Vietnam conflict.

Continuing his support for reproductive rights, Mott organized the First National Conference on Abortion Laws, which was held in Chicago in 1969. The following year he visited the Soviet Union with the Fund for Peace as an advocate for both family planning and arms control. Mott was less successful funding the Summer Festival for Peace, a series of concerts that failed to attract large crowds. In 1972 he established the political advocacy group People Politics, which was charged with raising funds to reform the Democratic Party by pushing for stronger representation by African Americans, women, and youth.

Although in a 1971 *New Yorker* interview Mott had said, "I don't especially wish to get married, because that could lead to divorce and alimony and property settlements, and I'd like to keep my assets unencumbered for charity," eight years later the confirmed bachelor married the sculptor Kappy Wells, with whom he had one son. The couple divorced in 1999.

His liberal stances landed Mott on the White House "Enemies List" in the 1970s, which proved somewhat ironic, as his personal financial interests were represented by Milton Rose, a partner in President Richard M. Nixon's New York law firm. In 1974 Mott purchased 122 Maryland Avenue NE, a historic building in Washington, D.C. Although he intended to live in the dwelling and use it as an office, Mott soon discovered that it had far more room than he needed. He began to rent out office space to the Fund for Peace and later to the American Civil Liberties Union. In 1989 he reorganized his own charitable foundations into the Stewart Mott Charitable Trust, and it became headquartered in the building. The trust continues to fund projects in the four major areas that have always been of interest to Mott: peace, arms control, and foreign policy; population issues, international family planning, and reproductive rights; government reform and public policy; and human rights, civil rights, and civil liberties.

★

For more information on Mott's life, see *Who's Who in America,* vol. 2 (2001), and *Current Biography* (1975). For a profile of Mott and his business career, see "Blue Chip off the Old Block," *The New Yorker* (27 Nov. 1971).

TED MURPHY

MOYNIHAN, Daniel Patrick (*b.* 16 March 1927 in Tulsa, Oklahoma), scholar and political adviser whose work on the problems of the inner city and the African-American family sparked controversy in the mid-1960s.

Despite the fact that he is commonly associated with the northeastern United States, Moynihan was actually born in Oklahoma, the first of three children of John Henry Moynihan, a journalist and advertising copywriter for RKO Pictures, and Margaret Ann Phipps, a homemaker. The family made its way to New York City when Moynihan was still a small child, and by 1937 Moynihan was living in a middle-class suburb. In that year, however, Moynihan's father deserted the family. Suddenly in poverty, the family drifted from one bad neighborhood to another, living for a time above a bar in Hell's Kitchen, one of the seedier neighborhoods in midtown Manhattan.

After graduating first in his class from Benjamin Franklin High School in 1943, Moynihan enrolled at City College (now City College of the City University of New York). A year later he joined the U.S. Naval Reserve and enrolled in the navy's V-12 program at Middlebury College in Vermont, where he underwent officer training. The navy then sent him to Tufts University in Medford, Massachusetts, where he earned four degrees: a bachelor of naval science (1946), a bachelor of arts (1948, cum laude), a master of arts (1949), and a Ph.D. Though he began work on the latter degree in 1949, two years after leaving the navy, Moynihan did not actually earn his doctorate until 1961.

In the meantime, Moynihan spent two years (1950–1951) at the London School of Economics and Political Science on a Fulbright scholarship; gained his first practical political experience by volunteering in the New York mayoral and gubernatorial campaigns of Robert Wagner and Averell Harriman, respectively, in 1953; and, on 29 May 1955, married the painter and sculptor Elizabeth Brennan. Brennan, with whom he had three children, later served as his adviser during his campaigns for the U.S. Senate.

After serving the city and state of New York in various capacities during the late 1950s, Moynihan went to Washington, D.C., with the administration of the newly inaugurated president, John F. Kennedy, in 1961. He served in the office of the secretary of labor from that year until 1965, first as special assistant (1961–1962) to Secretary of Labor Arthur Goldberg; then as executive assistant (1962–1963) to Goldberg and W. Willard Wirtz, who became the new secretary in 1962; and, finally, as Wirtz's assistant secretary of labor for policy planning and research (1963–1965).

Moynihan's own experience with poverty gave him a deep sense of compassion for the poor, while his Irish Catholic background instilled in him an awareness of ethnicity and ethnic marginalization not common among most Americans of white western European extraction. Furthermore, his father's absence had given him firsthand experience with the connection between poverty and the breakdown of the family. These concerns motivated not only his work with the labor department but also his writing as a scholar on policy issues.

A prolific author with more than two dozen books to his name by the beginning of the twenty-first century, Moynihan first established a reputation as a writer and com-

Daniel Patrick Moynihan. ARCHIVE PHOTOS, INC.

mentator in the 1960s. Among the books he wrote or co-wrote during that decade were *Beyond the Melting Pot: The Negroes, Puerto Ricans, Jews, Italians, and Irish of New York City* (1963, with Nathan Glazer; second edition, 1970); *The Negro Challenge to the Business Community* (1964, with Eli Ginzberg and others); *The Assault on Poverty* (1965); *Poverty in America* (1965, with Margaret S. Gordon and others); *The Negro Family: The Case for National Action* (1965, with Paul Barton and Ellen Broderick); and *Maximum Feasible Misunderstanding: Community Action in the War on Poverty* (1969).

One of these books, *The Negro Family,* would bring upon Moynihan a firestorm of disapprobation that constituted the greatest crisis of his career. The book was actually a Department of Labor pamphlet published at a time when the administration of President Lyndon B. Johnson was poised to launch the "Great Society," a set of government programs by which Johnson intended to declare "war on poverty." It is hard to imagine two approaches more different.

The war on poverty and its attendant programs, which had the enthusiastic support of many, if not most, white liberals, African-American leaders, and social scientists, were based on the implicit assumption that problems in the black community, such as poverty, drug abuse, crime, and out-of-wedlock births, could be solved by providing mem-

bers of that community with the things they had hitherto lacked. These deficits included the opportunity for an education, effective political participation through the vote, an end to discrimination, and an infusion of funds to close the economic gap between blacks and other groups within the nation.

The Negro Family, on the other hand, treated poverty as a symptom rather than a cause of problems within the black community. The real issue, Moynihan and his coauthors maintained, was the disintegration of the black family: without solid two-parent homes, their research indicated, no amount of money, jobs, and other cosmetic cures could save the black underclass. These conclusions were based not on preconceptions but on analysis of data. In studying Labor Department statistics, for instance, Moynihan had discovered a predictable pattern: when unemployment was high, the welfare rolls swelled, but when unemployment dropped, so did the number of people on the dole. Beginning in 1963, however, the unemployment rate had gone down, but the number of people on the welfare rolls was increasing. Obviously, then, the problem was not a lack of jobs but what Moynihan called a "tangle of pathologies."

Black leaders reacted to Moynihan's book by calling him a racist, while white detractors accused him of "blaming the victim." However, *The Negro Family* actually places much of the blame for the "tangle of pathologies" on slavery and the Jim Crow laws, though in the final analysis it is not a book directed so much toward placing blame as toward identifying the problem. This did not stop a harsh reaction to the report, even on the part of such figures as James Farmer of the Congress of Racial Equality or Bayard Rustin of the A. Philip Randolph Institute—men of such stature that their good faith is not a matter of question.

Perhaps as an outgrowth of the response to *The Negro Family,* Moynihan left Washington and the Johnson administration in 1965. Later that year he conducted an unsuccessful campaign for president of the New York City Council and served as codirector of policy and planning for the mayoral campaign of Abraham Beame. After a stint as fellow at the Wesleyan University Center for Advanced Studies in Middletown, Connecticut (1965–1966), Moynihan served as director of the Massachusetts Institute of Technology and Harvard University Joint Center for Urban Studies in Cambridge, Massachusetts (1966–1969). He was also a professor of education and urban politics at Harvard from 1966 to 1973.

As a conservative Democrat, Moynihan was not necessarily averse to Republicans, nor they to him, and so it was that President-elect Richard M. Nixon asked him to join the administration in 1968. Nixon had been reading Moynihan's work, which, as he later recalled in his *R.N.: The Memoirs of Richard Nixon* (1978), he found "refreshing and stimulating." Nixon invited him to serve in a number of capacities: assistant to the president for urban affairs, counselor to the president, and executive secretary of the newly created Urban Affairs Council. Moynihan held these positions from 1969 to 1970, during which time another politically incorrect observation brought him into the crosshairs once again. Maintaining that the government should quit interfering in the black community and should allow African Americans more of a free hand to work out their problems, he coined the unfortunate phrase "benign neglect." Opponents of both Moynihan and Nixon seized on this expression as supposed evidence of a declining commitment to civil rights.

Following his reelection in 1972 Nixon appointed Moynihan ambassador to India, and in 1975 President Gerald R. Ford named him ambassador to the United Nations. Late in the following year, Moynihan won the first of four elections to the U.S. Senate. In Washington he soon made a name for himself as a Democrat capable of working with Republicans, while his sharp criticism of President Bill Clinton's sexual and ethical peccadilloes showed him as a leader unwilling simply to maintain the party line. Moynihan retired from the Senate at the end of his fourth term, in 2001.

White-haired and known for quirky speech patterns, Moynihan has remained a public figure of wide renown, and respect for his work has only increased with time. This is particularly the case with regard to his observations on family, poverty, welfare, and social problems expressed in *The Negro Family*. The enthusiasm driving the War on Poverty has long ago evaporated, and poverty is far worse than it was when Johnson launched the Great Society in 1965. Not surprising, from the perspective of Moynihan's report, is the concurrent disintegration of the underclass black family—and this despite the trillions of dollars that have been directed toward solving the problem. By the mid-1990s all but the most committed demagogues had come to recognize that the old ways of solving the problem of poverty were not working, and they were forced to admit (however grudgingly) that Moynihan had been right all along.

★

Insights on Moynihan's work in the late 1960s and early 1970s may be found in Richard Nixon, *R.N.: The Memoirs of Richard Nixon* (1978). Robert A. Katzmann, *Daniel Patrick Moynihan: The Intellectual in Public Life* (1998), offers a view of the subject from the perspective of numerous colleagues. Moynihan's own *A Dangerous Place* (1975), written with Suzanne Weaver, chronicles his time at the United Nations. Also of note are Douglas Schoen, *Pat* (1979), and Godfrey Hodgson, *The Gentleman from New York* (2000).

MUHAMMAD, Elijah (*b*. 7 October 1897 in Bold Springs, Georgia; *d*. 25 February 1975 in Chicago, Illinois), black nationalist and founder of the Nation of Islam, known as "Messenger of Allah to the Lost-Found Nation of Islam in North America."

Born Elijah Poole, Muhammad was one of thirteen children of Wali, a Baptist minister and sharecropper, and Mariah (Hall) Poole, a domestic servant. When he was fifteen years old, Muhammad witnessed the lynching of his friend Albert Hamilton, falsely accused of the rape of a white woman. After having completed only a formal fourth-grade education, Muhammad married Clara Evans on 17 March 1919. When he was twenty-four, he left Georgia with his extended family for Detroit, Michigan.

In Detroit Muhammad joined the Moorish Science Temple of America, becoming affiliated in 1931 with Wallace D. Fard (David Ford), a Detroit clothing merchant and the founder of the Allah Temple of Islam. Fard, who gave Muhammad the name of Elijah Karriem, changed the name of his organization from the Allah Temple of Islam to the Nation of Islam. Muhammad claimed leadership of the organization, but his position was contested by other members, and both men fled from Detroit after a murder was connected to the Allah Temple. Elijah Karriem (by that time given the name of Muhammad) ended up in Washington, D.C., where he read extensively at the Library of Congress. Muhammad rejoiced in the American defeat at Pearl Harbor. In 1942, refusing the draft, he was charged with sedition and draft evasion and spent three years in jail. Muhammad began calling himself the "Messenger of Allah to the Lost-Found Nation of Islam in North America." He was under police and Federal Bureau of Investigation (FBI) surveillance from 1930 until his death, and the FBI alone holds over a million pages of records on him.

Much controversy surrounded the origins of Fard, who either died or disappeared in 1934. Many years later, a 28 July 1963 article in the *Seattle Post-Intelligence* claimed that Fard was alive and well in New Zealand. Muhammad, by then the leader of the Nation of Islam, offered a $100,000 reward to anyone who could prove it. The FBI determined that Fard, a white ex-convict from San Quentin, was born in Portland, Oregon, in 1891, and not in Mecca of a black and white couple. His former common-law wife claimed Fard was really Fred Dodd, born in New Zealand in 1891 of Polynesian and English parents. Another claimed he was really Arnold Josiah Ford, a black rabbi from New York.

After 1934, Muhammad claimed that Allah himself had appeared in the person of Fard, and that he, Muhammad, was a prophet of Allah. His message that whites were devils from whom the blacks must remain separate and over

Elijah Muhammad, February 1966. ASSOCIATED PRESS AP

whom the blacks would gain ultimate victory in the battle of Armageddon (in reference to the biblical story of the final struggle between good and evil) offered many poor blacks a sense of hope in a time when such hope was not available elsewhere.

While some claimed that between 100,000 and 250,000 African Americans were affiliated with the Nation of Islam during the 1960s, Muhammad's son, Warith (Wallace) D. Muhammad in the 1990s claimed the number was more like ten thousand. Some claim that the Nation of Islam had eighty thousand members in 1960, but others report that the group's seventy temples had 100, 000 members at the time of Muhammad's death.

Muhammad played an important role in African-American literature of the 1960s. James Baldwin based his book *The Fire Next Time* (1963) upon his interviews with Muhammad.

The most famous member of the Nation of Islam remains Malcolm Little, better known as Malcolm X, who converted to Islam while held in federal prison in 1947 at Concord, Massachusetts. Released in 1952, he went to work for Elijah Muhammad and continued with the Nation of Islam until 1964. Named national spokesman for the Nation of Islam by Elijah Muhammad, Malcolm X and Muhammad started the weekly newspaper *Muhammad Speaks*. In his *Autobiography* (1964) Malcolm X calculated that he had "either directly established, or I had helped to establish, most of the one hundred or more mosques in the fifty states."

By January of 1960 Muhammad had fathered the first of thirteen illegitimate children. His legendary affairs may have included at least one that was incestuous. Flying in executive jets and wearing a $150,000 diamond-studded fez, Muhammad lavished material goods upon himself. When George Lincoln Rockwell, head of the American Nazi Party, called Muhammad the black Adolf Hitler, Muhammad took the remark as a compliment.

All this put strains on the Nation of Islam, and at the same time threatened the relationship between Muhammad and Malcolm X. Because of various paternity charges against Muhammad, Malcolm X—already censured by Muhammad for making controversial public statements after the assassination of President John F. Kennedy—dissociated himself from the Nation of Islam.

In 1965 Louis Farrakhan (Louis Eugene Walcott), minister of Harlem Temple, denounced Malcolm X in *Muhammad Speaks*. Nation of Islam members who opposed Muhammad were often killed or injured, and some believe that Muhammad ordered the assassination of Malcolm X that year.

In 1967 Farrakhan became the Nation of Islam's national representative. Muhammad was no longer in a leadership position because he was under critical scrutiny for his extramarital activities. That same year W. Deen Muhammad, Elijah Muhammad's son, renamed the Nation of Islam as the World Community of Al-Islam in the West.

After Muhammad's death from congestive heart failure, he was buried in Glenwood Cemetery in Chicago. Leadership in the organization was divided between Farrakhan, who married his daughters to Muhammad's nephew and grandson, and the considerably more moderate W. Deen Muhammad. In February of 2000, the two men agreed to work together for the betterment of the Nation of Islam. Elijah Muhammad left an estate of $5.7 million, which he divided between his twenty-one heirs, including eight legitimate and thirteen illegitimate children.

★

For biographical information on Muhammad, see Claude Andrew Clegg, *The Original Man: The Life and Times of Elijah Muhammad* (1997), and Karl Evannz, *The Messenger: The Rise and Fall of Elijah Muhammad* (1999). Also see Zafar Ishaq Ansari, "W. D. Muhammad: The Making of a 'Black Muslim' Leader (1933–1961)," *American Journal of Islamic Social Sciences* 2 (1985): 245–262. Information on the Black Muslim movement can be found in Clifton E. Marsh, *From Black Muslims to Muslims: The Transition from Separatism to Islam, 1930–1980* (1984), and Harold Bloom, *The American Religion: The Emergence of the Post-Christian Nation* (1992).

LARRY D. GRIFFIN

MULLIKEN, Robert Sanderson (*b.* 7 June 1896 in Newburyport, Massachusetts; *d.* 31 October 1986 in Arlington, Virginia), chemist and physicist who received the 1966 Nobel Prize in chemistry for his fundamental work concerning chemical bonds and the electronic structure of molecules.

Mulliken was the son of Samuel Parsons Mulliken, a renowned organic chemist, and Katherine Wilmarth Mulliken. He studied at the Massachusetts Institute of Technology in Cambridge, Massachusetts, graduating in 1917 with a B.S. in chemistry. After graduation he worked as a junior chemical engineer for the U.S. Bureau of Mines, and conducted research on poison gases at the American University in Washington, D.C., for the war effort during World War I. After the war he worked as a chemist for the New Jersey Zinc Company.

In 1919 Mulliken entered the graduate program in chemistry at the University of Chicago, where he earned his Ph.D. in 1921 under the direction of Robert A. Millikan. His dissertation was on the partial separation of mercury isotopes by evaporation and other processes. Mulliken stayed another year at the university working as a National Research Council postdoctoral fellow on an extension of his previous research in an attempt to obtain greater isotope separation. In the process he built an apparatus based on the different behavior of isotopes under the processes of evaporation and diffusion through a membrane.

In 1923, while still a National Research Council fellow, Mulliken moved to the Jefferson Physical Laboratory at Harvard University in Cambridge, Massachusetts. There he assisted in the preparation of the 1926 comprehensive report on the spectra of diatomic molecules (molecules containing two atoms) for the National Research Council.

Robert S. Mulliken. THE LIBRARY OF CONGRESS

From 1926 to 1928 he taught at Washington Square College of New York University, where he started as an assistant professor of physics. An active research group soon gathered around him, and he was recognized as an international leader on the characterization of molecular band spectra.

Mulliken joined the faculty of the University of Chicago in 1928, where he started as an associate professor of physics. The next year he married Mary Helen von Noe; they had two daughters. In 1931 he was made a full professor. While at Chicago, Mulliken's work on diatomic molecules ended with the publication of three review articles, in which he introduced the now-famous correlation diagrams relating the state of a molecule to its constituent atoms. In 1930 he secured an international agreement on notation for diatomic molecules and in 1955 accomplished the same for polyatomic molecules, or those containing more than two atoms.

In 1932 Mulliken suggested an entirely new approach to the process of molecule formation and chemical bonding. This approach theoretically systematized the electron states of molecules in terms of "molecular orbitals." An orbital is a pattern of probability for finding an electron at a given energy state in its movement around the atomic nucleus. Previously it had been assumed that electron orbitals for atoms were static, even after atoms bonded with one another to form molecules. However, electrons at the highest energy states rearrange to make this chemical bonding possible. Mulliken's achievement was to propose that when molecules are formed, the atoms' original electron configurations are changed into an overall molecular configuration. In other words, molecules are separate entities in which the atoms have lost their individual characteristics. The molecular orbital theory was basic to almost every succeeding development in molecular science and paved the way for fundamental advances in the study of electronegativity (the relative attractive force exerted by atoms of a given element) and other aspects of chemical structure.

From 1932 to 1935 Mulliken extended the idea of molecular orbitals to small polyatomic molecules. This concept brought about some important results. He argued that mathematical group theory was necessary to understand individual molecular orbitals, especially in the electronic states of highly symmetrical molecules. He also introduced an absolute scale of electronegativities, suggesting that the electronegativity of an atom can be calculated as the difference between the average of its ionization potential and its electron affinity.

During World War II he worked as the director of the information division of the Plutonium Project (part of the Manhattan Project) at the metallurgical laboratory of the University of Chicago. His postwar contributions included the development of the charge-transfer interpretation of spectra of donor-acceptor molecular complexes, calculation of spectral intensities, explanation of selection rules in molecular spectra, theory of hyper conjugation, and concept of population analysis.

In 1955 Mulliken served as a scientific attaché at the U.S. embassy in London. From 1956 to 1961 he was the Ernst Dewitt Burton Distinguished Service Professor of Physics, and from 1961 to 1985 the distinguished service professor of physics and chemistry at the University of Chicago. From 1964 to 1971, while living in Chicago, he was also a distinguished research professor of chemical physics at Florida State University, where he spent the winter months. He retired from the University of Chicago in 1985.

Mulliken was a member of the International Academy of Quantum Molecular Science, American Physical Society, American Association for the Advancement of Science, American Chemical Society, National Academy of Sciences (elected in 1936), and the Royal Society. He received Guggenheim Fellowships for Europe in 1930 and 1932, and was a Fulbright Fellow for England in 1952. Mulliken also received several honorary degrees. He published more than 200 papers and was the coauthor of various books and monographs, including *Molecular Complexes* (1969), *Diatomic Molecules* (1977), and *Polyatomic Molecules* (1981).

Although he was recognized as an authority in this field from early on, most of the awards Mulliken received for his work came in the 1960s: the Theodore Williams Richards Gold medal (1960), Gilbert N. Lewis Medal (1960), Peter Debye Award (1961), J. G. Kirkwood Award (1964), Willard Gibbs Medal (1965), and Nobel Prize in chemistry (1966). Mulliken received the Nobel for his fundamental work concerning chemical bonds and the electronic structure of molecules by the molecular orbital method. The award was in chemistry and not in physics due to the fact that during his career he refocused his research from one realm to the other.

Mulliken is credited with creating the terms "orbital," "sigma electron," and "pi electron," as well as making many observations on weak intermolecular forces. His work, although primarily carried out during the decades preceding the 1960s, is nonetheless considered to have been a major influence in the field of chemistry during that decade.

★

Robert S. Mulliken, Life of a Scientist: An Autobiographical Account of the Development of Molecular Orbital Theory, edited by Bernard J. Ramail (1989), includes a chronology, photographs, and illustrations. For additional biographical information on Mulliken, see *Current Biography* (1967); John A. Garrety and Mark C. Carnes, *American National Biography* (1999); and *Notable Scientists: From 1900 to the Present* (2001). Obituaries are in Patricia Burgess, ed., *The Annual Obituary* (1986), and in the *New York Times* (2 Nov. 1986).

MARIA PACHECO

MURROW, Edward Roscoe (*b.* 25 April 1908 near Greensboro, North Carolina; *d.* 27 April 1965 in New York City), government official, author, newscaster, and television and radio host who lent integrity and intelligence to broadcast journalism in the 1950s and 1960s.

Egbert Roscoe Murrow was one of three sons born to Roscoe Murrow, a North Carolina farmer, and Ethel Lamb, a homemaker and former schoolteacher. Murrow spent his early years in a log cabin in Polecat Creek, North Carolina, on a 120-acre farm in an area that had not changed in more than a hundred years. His parents were both storytellers, and he and his brothers, Dewey and Lacey, were also blessed with that talent.

In 1912 the Murrows moved to the state of Washington to make a better life for themselves. His father worked at whatever jobs were available, from farmhand to lumberjack. Murrow's brother Dewey described the intense religious and moral tutelage of their mother and father. The guidelines of his upbringing were an integral part of what made Edward R. Murrow so true to the broadcasting industry's highest standards of public service.

Murrow's formal education began in the Blanchard grammar school, near his home in Washington state, a two-room shack in the countryside near Edison, Washington. He started working at the age of twelve as a field hand. He attended Edison High School, and in his senior year he was elected senior class president, president of the student body, and most popular student athlete. During his high school and college years, Murrow spent his summers working in lumber camps in Washington, where he developed both his ability to get along easily with other people and his love of cigarettes. He changed his name to Ed because, he said, "it was safer" and protected him from being teased by his coworkers.

Murrow graduated from Washington State College in Pullman in 1930. He was president of the National Student Federation of America during his senior year at Washington State (1929) and held the position until 1932.

In 1932 he became the assistant director of the Institute of International Education, at that time located in New York City, in charge of the foreign office. He married Janet Huntington Brewster on 28 October 1934, and they had one son.

In September of 1935 Murrow left the institute to be-

Edward R. Murrow. ARCHIVE PHOTOS, INC.

come the director of talks and education for the Columbia Broadcasting System (CBS), a job he held until 1961. As director of the CBS European Bureau in London during World War II, he hired and trained some of the most notable war correspondents. A distinguished correspondent in his own right, he became "the voice of London," a symbol of the fight to overcome the Axis powers.

Murrow returned to the United States in 1946 as a CBS vice president and director of public offices. In 1947 he resigned to return to radio broadcasting. In 1951 he started his television career with the show *See It Now,* an offshoot of his radio program, *Hear It Now.* Often controversial, a daring 1954 edition of the program scrutinized Senator Joseph McCarthy and criticized his devastating effect on free speech and freedom of the press. Murrow's other television programs included *Person to Person* (1953–1959), *Small World* (1958–1960), and *CBS Reports,* an acclaimed, sixty-minute series dealing with contemporary issues. One of Murrow's most notable documentaries for *CBS Reports* was "Harvest of Shame," which vividly portrayed the exploitation of migrant workers in America.

By 1960 Murrow's career in broadcasting exemplified the struggle between the era of autonomous news broadcast personalities and corporate news-gathering and reporting departments.

Murrow used his radio and television broadcasts to revive and popularize many democratic ideas, including free speech, citizen participation, the pursuit of truth, and the sanctification of individual liberties and rights. Recognizing these attributes as well as his popularity, visibility, and abilities, President John F. Kennedy appointed Murrow to head up the U.S. Information Agency (USIA) in 1961. Murrow took the job as an acceptable way out of his difficulties with CBS. (In a time when the networks were determined not to be confrontational, Murrow's hard-hitting journalistic style made executives try to reduce his profile.)

Thomas Sorensen, USIA adviser, listed the qualifications for the director of the agency: "Experience in world affairs and knowledge of foreign peoples . . . should comprehend the 'revolution of rising expectations' throughout the world, and its impact on U.S. foreign policy. . . ." Furthermore, the USIA director should be "pragmatic, open-minded, and sensitive to international political currents, without being naïve. Understand the potentialities of propaganda while being aware of its limitations." This is an excellent description of Murrow.

Murrow's appointment to the USIA was controversial. J. Edgar Hoover, the director of the Federal Bureau of Investigation (FBI), did not like or trust Murrow. The FBI finally turned over the summarized reports they had accumulated on the journalist and let President Kennedy decide whether or not to finalize Murrow's appointment. The political focus of the USIA under the Kennedy administration was directed to so-called country teams and objectives that included regularly drafted country plans and a direct and immediate connection of agency products to radio, television, film, and publications. From the beginning, Murrow had no problem adopting an activist role. He shared Kennedy's view of the world and spent much of his time recommending to the president that the Foreign Service Institute be revamped and expanded. The Institute is the federal government's primary training institution for officers and support personnel of the U.S. foreign affairs community, preparing American diplomats and other professionals to advance U.S. foreign affairs and interests both overseas and in Washington, D.C. In Murrow's time the USIA provided the materials and conducted some of the training. Murrow helped reshape the institute into the organization it is today. Even though he was unsympathetic to the "Ban the Bomb" movement, Murrow, along with his policy people, spearheaded the USIA drive to link nuclear testing with disarmament and to halt the development and spread of nuclear weapons. The project occupied much of his time during his last two years as director.

Murrow, though not excluding the happy possibility of dialogue, accepted the administration's view of the agency job as that of psychological warfare with the Soviets and other hostile forces—of political, not military battles, and words instead of weapons. This stance puzzled many who knew him as a newsman. But having taken on the job, he pursued it vigorously, with what Joseph E. Persico called "puritanical consistency." Therefore, he could easily testify against legislation threatening a cutoff of mail service between the United States and Eastern Europe on the grounds that the flow of information went both ways, or he could urge that "Red China" not be barred from access to American-developed communications satellites.

Murrow's parting words as USIA director were especially meaningful to those who remained in the agency under President Lyndon B. Johnson: "Communications systems are neutral. They have neither conscience nor morality, only a history. They will broadcast truth or falsehood with equal facility." His influence continued long after he left his leadership position with the USIA. McGeorge Bundy believed that Murrow left "a lot of your friends wiser than you found them," and Arthur Schlesinger, Jr., once wrote that Murrow was "always the Voice of America."

By the fall of 1963 Murrow had developed lung cancer but had not reduced his activities, although it became obvious he would soon have to stop working. His friend Pat Smithers described Murrow's appearance at a meeting: "There was something a bit shadowy about what had been substance. Physically, not intellectually or mentally." Soon after that, his poor health, as well as the desire to express his own ideas and concerns, persuaded him that he was ready to move back to radio or television. He arranged a

meeting with Elmer Lower, the newly appointed president of American Broadcasting Company (ABC) News, but went into the hospital instead. Following his death his body was cremated, and the ashes were scattered in a glen at Glen Arden Farm in Pawling, Dutchess County, New York.

Murrow died almost twenty years to the day of the euphoric gathering in the Scribe bar in a liberated Paris, where he commented to his colleagues "We've shown what radio can do in war. Now let's go home and show what we can do in peace!" During his life he earned nine Emmy Awards and received the Freedom House Award in 1954; was trustee at the Institute of International Education and a member of the Council on Foreign Relations; and belonged to the Association of American Correspondents, London, Phi Beta Kappa, and Kappa Sigma. He received numerous honorary degrees from Oberlin College, Hamilton College, Rollins College, and Temple University.

"Broadcasting gave fame and fortune to Mr. Murrow, but it remains in debt to the man," according to Jack Gould. Many of Murrow's biographers initially believed in his persona of perfection, but after their research they discovered his public and private lives to be distinct from one another, and his inner self a mystery. Murrow exemplified what is best in journalism: curiosity, independence, and principles. He remains an inspiration to his fellow craftsmen.

★

The Murrow Papers are at the Fletcher School of Law and Diplomacy, Tufts University. For biographical information, see Alexander Kendrick, *Prime-Time: The Life of Edward R. Murrow* (1969); Robert Lichello, *Edward R. Murrow, Broadcaster of Courage* (1971); Robert Smith, *Edward R. Murrow: The War Years* (1978); David Halberstam, *The Powers that Be* (1979); A. M. Sperber, *Murrow, His Life and Times* (1986); and Joseph E. Persico, *Edward R. Murrow: An American Original* (1988). Murrow was the author of many works, including *This Is London* (1941); *In Search of Light: The Broadcasts of Edward R. Murrow, 1938–1961* (1967); and "Call in Courage: Act on your Knowledge," a speech published in *Vital Speeches* (1993). An obituary is in the *New York Times* (28 Apr. 1965).

JOAN T. GOODBODY

MUSKIE, Edmund Sixtus (*b.* 28 March 1914 in Rumford, Maine; *d.* 26 March 1996 in Washington, D.C.), governor and U.S. senator who led the passage of key environmental legislation.

Muskie was the second of six children born to Stephen Muskie, a tailor, and Josephine (Czarnecka) Muskie, a homemaker, in Rumford, a mill town in western Maine. Like other Maine communities, Rumford was dominated by a paper factory (Oxford Paper Company), which fouled the air with smoke and the local water source with industrial pollutants. Growing up, Muskie could hardly have been oblivious to these environmental abuses or to the town's dependence on the paper mill as its chief employer. A shy youngster, Muskie became an avid reader, a practice encouraged by his Polish-born father, who had taught himself to read and write English. His father's intense interest in contemporary politics also impressed his son, who later explained that he was prepared to run for the Maine legislature in part "because of my father's general interest in public affairs." Muskie's concern for the environment stemmed initially from fishing expeditions with his father in the Maine wilderness. Muskie attended the Pettingill School and Stephens High School and won a scholarship to Bates College, a small liberal arts college in Lewiston, Maine. He graduated in 1936 with a B.A. in history, having been class president and a member of Phi Beta Kappa. He attended Cornell Law School, earning his LL.B. in 1939, and returned to Maine to open a practice in Waterville. In 1942 he joined the U.S. Navy as a junior officer and served abroad the USS *Brackett* in the Atlantic and Pacific. He

Edmund S. Muskie (*right*) accepting the vice presidential nomination at the Democratic National Convention, 1968. © BETTMANN/CORBIS

was discharged in 1945, and in 1948 he married Jane Gray, with whom he would have five children.

Although he was a first-generation Polish-American Catholic in a state dominated by a Protestant Republican establishment, Muskie ran for the state legislature in 1946. Surprisingly, he was elected and was again in 1948 and 1950. Between 1951 and 1952 he was state director of the Office of Price Stabilization and in 1954, after an arduous campaign, convincingly defeated the incumbent Republican to become governor of Maine. Muskie served two terms (1955–1959), during which he was associated prominently with the issue of "water improvement." He insisted on the importance of upgrading Maine's compromised water quality; at the same time, however, he was equally conscious of industry's place in the state's economic life.

Already a widely popular figure in Maine, Muskie decided to run for the U.S. Senate in 1958 and easily defeated the Republican incumbent. He would remain a senator until 1980. Shortly after his arrival in Washington, D.C., in 1959, Muskie angered the Senate majority leader, Lyndon B. Johnson, by refusing to support his strategy to modify Senate filibustering rules. Johnson punished Muskie by appointing him to the Public Works Committee. In 1963, however, the Public Works chairman, Pat McNamara, created a new subcommittee on Air and Water Pollution and named Muskie as chairman. Rather than complain about ill treatment, Muskie made the most of his appointment, focusing at first on clean air, a subject that none of the mainstream environmental organizations had incorporated into its agenda. Muskie built a clean air constituency by holding hearings in major cities across the country, including Los Angeles, where a serious smog problem had developed. He became the preeminent authority on clean air and on other environmental issues. His first success came with the 1963 Clean Air Act, a noncontroversial measure that provided federal matching grants to states and localities to develop air pollution control programs.

The 1965 Clean Air Act was more controversial, as it established federal carbon monoxide and hydrocarbon standards for motor vehicles. And the 1970 Clean Air Act set still more stringent federal standards. Automobile manufacturers complained that developing the required technology would make new cars prohibitively expensive, if indeed such technology were possible. Muskie was unmoved by the automakers' lamentations; he was convinced that they could comply with the law and that they could do so at a reasonable cost. The automotive industry responded by using the catalytic converter. In short, Muskie recognized his and Congress's responsibility to protect the physical environment without endangering the American economy.

Muskie's reputation as "Mr. Clean" was enhanced further by the passage of the 1965 Water Quality Act and the 1966 Clean Water Restoration Act, which together mandated that states enforce water-quality standards for interstate waterways within their boundaries. The 1968 Clean Water Restoration Act also provided federal funds for the construction of sewage-treatment plants and established water-quality standards for the noninterstate waters.

In 1968 Muskie stepped away briefly from his Senate position to become the running mate of Hubert Humphrey, the Democratic Party's presidential nominee. Together they waged a strong campaign while enduring the damaging fallout from divisions over the Vietnam War, the stormy and riotous Democratic convention in Chicago, strident student protestors, and the difficulty of supporting President Johnson's hard line toward North Vietnam, not to mention the shortage of funding for television commercials. Muskie made scores of appearances in urban ghettos, union halls, and college campuses. His quiet manner, Lincolnesque demeanor, and understated sense of humor won supporters for the Democratic ticket. In November, however, Richard M. Nixon, the Republican presidential candidate, prevailed by a narrow margin.

After the 1968 campaign Muskie resumed his duties in the Senate, although he did launch an ill-fated run for the presidency in 1972 that was undermined by "dirty tricks" engineered by the Nixon White House. In 1980, at the request of President Jimmy Carter, he left the Senate to replace Secretary of State Cyrus Vance, who had resigned to protest an abortive raid to rescue American hostages held in Iran. Muskie appeared once more on the national scene in 1986 to join a three-person commission appointed by President Ronald Reagan to investigate the Iran-Contra scandal, a covert operation to gain the release of American captives in the Middle East by the sale of arms to Iran. He died of a heart attack a decade later and was buried in Arlington National Cemetery in Arlington, Virginia.

Muskie's major legislative accomplishments in the 1960s were the Clean Air and the Clean Water Acts that he shepherded through the Senate between 1965 and 1970. Was he himself satisfied with these laws? To a certain extent he was, declaring in *Journeys* that "we've written some good legislation." Nonetheless, he was not deluded about the limitations of his handiwork, for he also acknowledged that Americans "have produced pollution faster than we have [moved against it]." In a sense, that bluntly honest and unsettling assessment is as important a contribution to the environmental movement as the legislation itself.

★

The Edmund S. Muskie Archives is located at Bates College in Lewiston, Maine. The archives also maintains a Muskie oral history project. Edmund S. Muskie, *Memorial Tributes Delivered in Congress: Edmund S. Muskie, 1914–1996* (1996), contains Muskie's mixed review, a generation after their passage, of the effectiveness of the Clean Water and Clean Air Acts. Muskie's memoir, *Journeys* (1972), provides the fullest account of the origins of his environmental conscience. Theo Lippman and Donald C. Hauser, *Muskie* (1971), offers a satisfactory account of his governorship and Senate career until 1970. Bernard Asbell, *The Senate Nobody Knows* (1978), is a richly detailed study of the passage of the 1975 Clean Air Act. Obituaries are in the *New York Times* and *Washington Post* (both 27 Mar. 1996).

RICHARD HARMOND

N

NABOKOV, Vladimir (*b.* 23 April 1899 in Saint Petersburg, Russia; *d.* 2 July 1977 in Montreux, Switzerland), novelist, critic, and poet known as a brilliant prose stylist and experimenter, whose novel *Lolita* (1955) became an emblem of the new sexual openness in the 1960s; also a renowned lepidopterist.

The eldest of five children, Nabokov published his first book of poems in 1916. He was born to Vladimir Dmitrievich, a prominent local politician in the Saint Petersburg city duma, or council, and Elena Ivanovna Rukavishnikov, a homemaker. Nabokov attended Tenishev Academy in Saint Petersburg beginning at age twelve. Nabokov's father, an outspoken opponent of the Bolshevik takeover, escaped with his young family to London in 1919. After fleeing Russia, Nabokov enrolled at Trinity College, Cambridge, to study Romance and Slavic languages. He graduated in June 1922, just a few months after his father's assassination in Berlin. In his early career Nabokov wrote in Russian, using the name Vladimir Sirin.

Nabokov married Vera Evseevna Slonim, a Russian Jew, on 25 April 1925 and published his first novel, *Mashen'ka* (*Mary*) in 1926. Living in Berlin, Nabokov worked as a tutor, translator, and movie extra to supplement his small income from writing. The couple's only child, Dmitri, was born on 10 May 1934. In 1937 the Nabokovs moved to Paris, and in 1940, when France became occupied by the Nazis during World War II, they fled to New York. Nabokov took with him the manuscript of *The Real Life of Sebastian Knight* (1941), his first novel in English and his first to be published under his given name. Once in the United States, Nabokov's work in lepidoptery, the study of butterflies and moths, won him a research fellowship at Harvard University's Museum of Comparative Zoology. Nabokov became a naturalized U.S. citizen on 12 July 1945; at about the same time, he heard that his brother Sergei, who had remained in Berlin during World War II, had died in a Nazi concentration camp.

By the late 1940s Nabokov already saw himself as an American writer, but the works that gained him the reputation as one of the most inventive writers of the twentieth century were produced in the 1950s and 1960s. Among the most important are *Pnin* (1957), *Pale Fire* (1962), and *Ada or Ardor: A Family Chronicle* (1969). His best-known and most influential novel is *Lolita*. Although *Lolita* first appeared in France in 1955, its full impact was not felt until the 1960s, largely because it was banned in many countries until then. Chronicling a middle-aged man's sexual obsession with a twelve-year-old girl, *Lolita* contributed to the relaxation of attitudes toward sex in the 1960s and triggered revisions to obscenity laws around the world.

Nabokov himself anticipated problems with *Lolita* and initially hoped to publish under a pseudonym to protect his position as a professor at Cornell. Five major American publishers rejected the novel, and a reader at Simon and Schuster called it "sheer pornography." *Lolita* finally was

Vladimir Nabokov. AP/WIDE WORLD PHOTOS

accepted by Olympia Press in France, the publisher of such "difficult" avant-garde writers as Samuel Beckett, Henry Miller, and William S. Burroughs. In 1957 U.S. Customs seized but later released the Olympia Press edition, and it was banned in France until 1958. When Putnam published the novel in the United States that year, it sold 100,000 copies in just three weeks. A British edition appeared in 1959, after a relaxation of the obscenity laws. The public response to the novel was a strange mixture of popular trivializing and moral outrage. By 1960 the words "Lolita" and "nymphet" had been adopted widely into the language, and Nabokov himself was alarmed to discover that girls were dressing up as Lolita to go trick-or-treating on Halloween. The comedian Groucho Marx said that he had put off reading Nabokov's novel for six years, when Lolita would be eighteen.

The income from *Lolita* enabled Nabokov to resign his post at Cornell and become a full-time man of letters. The director Stanley Kubrick planned to make a movie of the novel, and Nabokov, by this time in hiding in Europe, was offered $75,000 to write the screenplay. Kubrick later said that it was the best screenplay ever written for a Hollywood movie. The idea of a film about Humbert Humbert's sexual obsession was too much for Americans campaigning against the relaxation of Hollywood's moral standards. Kubrick took refuge in England, where he made the film and where he stayed for the rest of his life. When the movie appeared in 1962, the flames of notoriety were fanned still further. Kubrick's film challenged establishment views about good taste and decent behavior and made Nabokov a household name.

Nabokov was uneasy with his fame and sought protection from interviewers, journalists, moralists, and fans, all of whom mobbed him whenever he appeared in public. He lived at the Palace Hotel in Montreux, Switzerland, from 1959 onward, though he retained his American citizenship. It was there that he wrote *Pale Fire* (1962), a long poem about an exiled king, with a critical commentary by the poem's subject, a fictionalized, satirical representation of an exiled Balkan monarch. Despite its controversial subject matter, *Lolita* is perhaps the most conventional of Nabokov's works from the 1950s and 1960s. Both *Pale Fire* and *Ada or Ardor* are ambitious, experimental works that emphasize Nabokov's view of literature as a game. At the same time as he tells his stories, Nabokov exposes their construction with puns, word games, and tricks. By the 1960s Nabokov had become a major influence on the cultural and literary climate of the United States and Europe. With the help of his son, he translated novels originally published in Russian and made pronouncements on other major figures, calling Sigmund Freud the "Viennese witch doctor" and attacking the sloppiness of modern scholarship.

Nabokov was a reluctant celebrity. He turned down honorary degrees and memberships of learned societies on the grounds that he could not be an active member of any organization. In fact, the only society he joined was the American Lepidopterists' Society, but he asked that his name be left off the membership lists. By the end of the twentieth century Nabokov was widely regarded as one of the finest postwar writers and one whose influence reached far beyond literature. He died from a viral infection at the age of seventy-eight and is buried in Montreux.

★

Nabokov's papers are divided between the Vladimir Nabokov archive in Montreux, Switzerland, and the Library of Congress. He published an autobiography based on sketches of life in pre-revolutionary Russia, *Speak, Memory* (1966), and his *Selected Letters: 1940–1977* was published in 1989. The definitive biography of Nabokov is by Brian Boyd and comes in two parts, *Vladimir Nabokov: The Russian Years* (1990) and *Vladimir Nabokov: The American Years* (1991). Obituaries are in the *New York Times* and the *Washington Post* (both 5 July 1977).

CHRIS ROUTLEDGE

NADER, Ralph (*b.* 27 February 1934 in Winsted, Connecticut), reformer and public citizen whose landmark book on automobile safety, *Unsafe at Any Speed* (1965), helped launch the consumer movement of the 1960s.

Nader was the youngest of four children of the Lebanese immigrants Nathra, a baker and restaurant owner, and Rose Bouziane Nader. Nader graduated magna cum laude from Princeton University in 1955 and from Harvard Law School in 1958. In 1958 and 1959 he served as a cook in the U.S. Army. From his parents, Nader and his siblings learned that it was a citizen's duty to be educated about public affairs, to be engaged in community activities, and to speak out. Nader began that civic involvement early: at age eleven he was an avid reader of the *Congressional Record*. As a student at Princeton, he protested the use of the pesticide DDT, which he believed was killing birds. While in law school, he began researching automobile safety, a subject that occupied him for several years. His article, "The Safe Car You Can't Buy," appeared in the *Nation* in April 1959.

Nader opened a law office in Hartford, Connecticut, that same year, while continuing his advocacy journalism. A visit to the Scandinavian countries in 1961 left Nader impressed with their governments' responsiveness to citizen's complaints. Returning to the United States, he introduced both a concept and a word, *ombudsman,* a person who responds to citizens' complaints about government officials or agencies. He helped the Connecticut legislature draft an ombudsman bill, the nation's first. Nader moved

to Washington, D.C., in 1963 and was soon hired as a consultant to Daniel Patrick Moynihan, the assistant secretary of labor. He also served as an unpaid adviser to a Senate subcommittee that was investigating automobile safety.

During the twentieth century, 1.5 million Americans had died in automobile accidents—more than were killed in war. Conventional wisdom held that drivers were primarily to blame. Nader disagreed. In 1965 he published *Unsafe at Any Speed,* a scathing critique of the automobile industry. The book's subtitle, *The Designed-in Dangers of the American Automobile,* reflected his central point: that the greatest threat to highway safety came not from reckless drivers but from the faulty designs of the cars themselves. Unencumbered by government regulation—there had never been federal oversight of automobile design—manufacturers built cars that were unnecessarily dangerous. Badly designed cars had a tendency to roll after a collision, increasing the risk of injury. Inside the car, there was often a deadly "second collision," when passengers hit unyielding steering columns, gear shifts, glove compartment doors, dashboards, or mirrors—all dangerous instruments in vehicles unequipped with safety belts.

Nader's chief target was the Corvair, a sporty car manufactured by General Motors (GM), whose faulty rear sus-

Ralph Nader, March 1966. ASSOCIATED PRESS AP

pension system made it more likely than most models to skid and roll over. The car's design, he declared, was "one of the greatest acts of industrial irresponsibility in the present century." Nader charged that GM had designed and marketed a car that it knew to be unsafe. Corporate profit had taken precedence over consumer safety. By its neglect, the federal government was guilty of complicity. The result, in Nader's phrase, had been "highway carnage." Alarmed by Nader's charges, GM hired an investigator to find information that might be used to discredit him. The investigator trailed Nader and asked his friends and associates about his politics, sex life, and prejudices. He found nothing damaging. The escapade backfired on GM when outraged senators learned of the corporation's attempt to silence Nader. The company's president publicly apologized at a Senate hearing.

GM's harassment had three important results: First, it brought enormous publicity for Nader's book. Sales for *Unsafe at Any Speed* increased, and Nader became a national figure. GM's misguided attempt to discredit Nader gained him sympathy and a public forum he would not otherwise have had. Second, Congress became more determined than ever to regulate, for the first time, the design of automobiles. One result was passage of the National Traffic and Motor Vehicle Safety Act in 1966. Third, Nader sued GM for invasion of privacy. The case was settled for $425,000, money that Nader used to help launch numerous consumer advocacy projects. *Unsafe at Any Speed* and the controversy surrounding it also helped doom the Corvair. GM stopped production in 1969. Nader later claimed that "tens of thousands of people" had been saved every year because of the highway safety program that began in the mid-1960s.

After *Unsafe at Any Speed,* Nader was much in demand as a public speaker. He funneled speaking fees, book royalties, and voluntary contributions to new consumer advocacy projects. He soon made it clear that his interests went well beyond a single issue. In 1967 he turned his attention from automobile safety to meat safety, working for passage of the Wholesome Meat Act, which brought intrastate meatpacking under inspection.

In 1968 Nader founded the Center for the Study of Responsive Law, which examined numerous issues, including food safety, corporate welfare, pensions, age discrimination, and air and water pollution. Young volunteers attracted to Washington by Nader's example began investigating federal agencies to verify that they were serving the public interest. The first group of "Nader's Raiders," as they were called, published a report in 1969 that was critical of the Federal Trade Commission. In 1970 Nader created the Public Interest Research Group (PIRG) in Washington, D.C. Later in the year, state groups were founded in Oregon and Minnesota, the first of many across the country. With the national and state PIRGs, Nader sought to marry the energy and commitment of student volunteers to the expertise of full-time professional advocates, including lawyers, economists, and scientists. The PIRGs drew more than 500,000 college volunteers in the early 1970s. In 1971 Nader founded Public Citizen, an umbrella organization whose divisions worked for safe foods and drugs, consumer control over personal health decisions, universal access to quality health care, nuclear safety, conservation, and the use of renewable energy sources.

Nader was not without his critics. Some viewed him as a nuisance. Even his allies occasionally were frustrated by his incessant demands. Many in the business community claimed that the costs of government regulation often outweighed the benefits. Nader's fiercest opponents charged that his ultimate goal was to destroy the free enterprise system altogether. Even if his goals were not always realized in practice, and although Nader himself was frequently dissatisfied by the results of his efforts, few Americans of the 1960s had as much continuing impact as did he. In addition to his work on highway safety, his most obvious contribution, Nader was involved in passage of freedom of information laws (which provided greater public access to government information), mining safety laws, and workplace safety legislation. Many of these laws led to the creation of new federal agencies, such as the Occupational Safety and Health Administration and the Consumer Product Safety Administration.

In 1980 Nader resigned from Public Citizen, but he continued his involvement in several areas of public policy. In the 1990s he was an outspoken opponent of free trade, arguing that the merger of governments and multinational corporations threatened workers' rights and the environment. Skeptical of globalization, he opposed the North American Free Trade Agreement, the World Trade Organization, the World Bank, and the International Monetary Fund. In 2000 Nader was the Green Party candidate for president.

One of the central impulses of the 1960s, given voice by President John F. Kennedy when he invited Americans to ask what they could do for their country, was active citizenship tinged with idealism. A related impulse seen, for example, in the civil rights movement and the attempt of the Students for a Democratic Society to foster participatory democracy, was the conviction that responsive institutions—true democracy, in other words—required the full and equal participation of the many, not control by the few. Undergirding all of Nader's crusades in the 1960s were the same impulses. Whether going after GM, the Federal Trade Commission, or Congress itself, Nader was acting as he believed all American citizens should act.

He was also—and he was hardly alone in this in the 1960s—deeply suspicious of authority and of institutions. What the system needed, he maintained, was not good leaders at the top, but engaged citizens at all levels, or what he called "initiatory democracy." "Power," he insisted, "comes from the people." With Nader, such ordinary words, the stuff of civics textbooks, became real. His personal version of public citizenship—researching, speaking, writing books, lobbying—became his life. Nader lived frugally, owning neither an automobile nor a television set. He was not motivated by money. He worked long hours. He never married. A man in his thirties who wore conservative suits, Nader little resembled those members of a younger generation who demanded "power to the people." What he offered was not a slogan but a plan—one that required deep engagement with one's fellow citizens and promised to remake the world. Thousands of young Americans in the 1960s were uplifted by the message and answered the call.

★

Nader has written or sponsored dozens of books and reports. *Unsafe at Any Speed* (1965) remains the most significant. See also Ralph Nader and Donald Ross, with Brent English and Joseph Highland, *Action for a Change: A Student's Manual for Public Interest Organizing* (1971), which presents the philosophy behind his Public Interest Research Groups and offers guidelines for creating them. Charles McCarry, *Citizen Nader* (1972), covers Nader's life and career through the 1960s. Also useful is Robert F. Buckhorn, *Nader: The People's Lawyer* (1972). Thomas Whiteside, *The Investigation of Ralph Nader* (1972), provides a detailed discussion of General Motors' efforts to discredit Nader after the publication of *Unsafe at Any Speed*.

FRED NIELSEN

NAGEL, Ernest (*b.* 16 November 1901 in Nové Mesto, Bohemia; *d.* 20 September 1985 in New York City), one of the United States' most prominent philosophers of science, whose 1961 book *Structure of Science* was considered a defining work in the logic of scientific explanation.

Nagel, one of two children in an immigrant family, was born in an area that is in today's Czech Republic. His parents were Isadore Nagel, a businessman, and Frida Weiss Nagel. The family arrived in the United States in 1911, and Nagel became a U.S. citizen in 1919. In 1923 he received his bachelor of science degree in social studies from the City College of New York. He pursued his master's and doctoral degrees in philosophy at Columbia University, receiving them in 1925 and 1931 respectively. Between 1923 and 1929 he taught physics in New York City public schools. Nagel moved on to City College of New York as an instructor in 1930, and in 1931 he began teaching philosophy at Columbia University. In 1935 Nagel married the physicist Edith Haggstrom, with whom he had two sons.

Ernest Nagel. THE LIBRARY OF CONGRESS

With the exception of the year 1966–1967, when he taught at Rockefeller University, Nagel stayed at Columbia until his retirement in 1970. He continued to give seminars at Columbia and remained strongly connected to it until his death in 1985.

At Columbia, Nagel became part of a core group of naturalists, philosophers who believed that only nature, without the assistance of supernatural powers, was responsible for the laws of science and society. At City College he was trained by Morris R. Cohen, with whom he published *Introduction to Logic and Scientific Method* in 1934. The book was immensely successful and remained one of the most influential in the field well into the 1950s. Following a year of study in Europe, Nagel published "Impressions and Appraisals of Analytic Philosophy in Europe" in the *Journal of Philosophy* (1936). This work introduced logical positivism—the marriage of empiricism and linguistics—to American philosophers.

In 1961 Nagel published his most famous and widely read book, *The Structure of Science*. This book, which discusses the logic of scientific explanation, is still considered one of the most definitive works in this area of the philosophy of science. Nagel first discussed four types of scientific explanation: *deductive*, where the explanation follows logically from the premises of the argument; *probabilistic*, where the explanation is probable given the premises; *tel-*

eological (functional), where the explanation defines the function or goal of what is explained or studied; and *genetic*, meaning historical, where the explanation relies on earlier knowledge to explain the studied object. *The Structure of Science* clearly and methodically examined the problems in the logic of the various methods of scientific explanation. The book also examined the nature of scientific theories and attempted to show that all scientific theories, including those in the social sciences, can be explained by the same empirical methods usually associated with the physical sciences.

The 1960s were a tumultuous time. Conflict raged around the globe, while in countries such as the United States and England student movements were calling for a change. Science itself was swiftly changing, with new discoveries and better understanding of the living world. In that climate of radicalism, philosophy itself was undergoing a fundamental transformation. It is a testament to Nagel's clarity of style and logic that his book remained as respected as it did. The philosophy of logical positivism was fast becoming outdated in people's minds. A year after *Structure of Science* was published, Thomas S. Kuhn published *The Structure of Scientific Revolutions* (1962). The book became a best-seller.

Like the decade in which it was published, Kuhn's book departed radically from traditional thought. While Nagel and others saw science as progressing in a logical fashion, each discovery building on previous knowledge gained, Kuhn espoused the idea that science progresses in fits and starts, "a series of peaceful interludes punctuated by intellectually violent revolutions . . . the tradition-shattering complements to the tradition-bound activity of normal science." Following these revolutions, "one conceptual world view is replaced by another." Kuhn referred to each worldview as a paradigm. His use of the term *paradigm* popularized it for generations to come. Kuhn opened the floodgates of the New Philosophy of Science, a modern school of thought whose main proponents were Paul Feyerabend, Norwood Russell Hanson, and Imre Lakatos. The New Philosophy was fast replacing logical positivism and naturalism.

In a decade that saw a growing antagonism toward traditional philosophies often perceived as intolerant, the respect in which Nagel was held speaks to his open-mindedness. Kuhn's book was more appealing in a world filled with scientific revolutions and political unrest, but Nagel's willingness to criticize, as Patrick Suppes points out, "ill-conceived notions from whatever quarters they might come" made him an inspiration to students not only of philosophy but of other disciplines as well. It did not hurt that Nagel also was involved in the changing world around him, writing for the *Nation* and *Partisan Review*. While his brand of philosophy was falling out of favor in the 1960s, he himself remained relevant.

Nagel's vast knowledge of science set him apart from other philosophers of science. He had an intense interest in physics, which he continued to pursue after retirement, and he conducted a regular seminar on methodology in social sciences. In 1978 he was elected to the National Academy of Sciences, not a common occurrence among philosophers. In his long and distinguished career he won numerous honors and awards. Among them were Columbia University's Nicholas Murray Butler Medal in Gold (1980); an honorary doctor of science degree from Brandeis University; and doctor of letters degrees from Rutgers University (1967), Case Western Reserve University (1970), and Columbia University (1971). He served as president of the American Academy of Arts and Sciences from 1961 to 1963. In addition to publishing in various philosophical journals, Nagel was editor of the *Journal of Symbolic Logic* (1939–1945), *Journal of Philosophy* (1940–1956), and *Philosophy of Science* (1956–1959). He died of pneumonia and is buried in South Wardsboro, Vermont.

★

Biographies of Nagel include Patrick Suppes, "Ernest Nagel," *Biographical Memoirs of the National Academy of Sciences*, vol. 65 (1994): 257–273; Antony Flew, "Nagel, Ernest," in *The Encyclopedia of Unbelief* (1985); and Andrew Reck, *The New American Philosophers: An Exploration of Thought Since World War II* (1968).

ADI R. FERRARA

NAMATH, Joseph William ("Joe") (*b.* 31 May 1943 in Beaver Falls, Pennsylvania), Hall of Fame quarterback who, perhaps more than any other athlete, captured the rebellion, anti-establishment tone, glitz, glamour, and style of the 1960s.

Like dozens of other collegiate and professional quarterbacks, Namath is a product of the fertile high school gridirons of western Pennsylvania. His parents, both of Hungarian heritage, are John Andrew Namath, a millwright, and Rosal ("Rose') (Juhasz) Namath Szolnoki, a homemaker and later a sales clerk. Namath's parents separated eventually, but not before having three other sons and adopting a daughter.

Namath played all sports—often with African-American teammates—in their respective seasons, but he was cut from the Beaver Falls High School football team when he first tried out, because he was too small. Growing three inches and adding twenty pounds in each of his last two years in high school, Namath earned All-State honors in football and baseball in his senior year, with the football team going undefeated. He also starred in basketball. Thinking he would join the U.S. Air Force after graduation, he also considered other options, including professional baseball (he was offered a $25,000 signing bonus)

Joe Namath. AP/WIDE WORLD PHOTOS

and college football (he received close to fifty athletic grant-in-aid offers). His mother insisted that he go to college. Just missing the minimum scholastic score to enter the University of Maryland, he was touted to coach Paul ("Bear") Bryant of the University of Alabama by Maryland coaches who did not want Namath beating them while playing for another school on the Terrapins' schedule.

Although Tuscaloosa, Alabama, was still segregated and vastly different from Pennsylvania, Namath—helped by his extraordinary athleticism and easygoing personality—fit in nicely. He even acquired and retained something of a southern accent. Freshmen were not eligible for varsity competition in 1961, but as a sophomore in 1962 Namath contributed to the Crimson Tide's stellar 9–1 season and a 17–0 Orange Bowl victory over the Oklahoma Sooners. Disciplined by Bryant for a drinking incident, Namath sat out the last game of the 1963 season and Alabama's 12–7 Sugar Bowl victory over the Mississippi Rebels. Namath's senior season was bittersweet. In 1964 Alabama won the national championship, but Namath was injured in the fourth game of the season. Rolling out on an option, untouched, he tore ligaments and cartilage in his right knee. It would be a hallmark of the rest of his playing career. His knee was injured twice more that season, for the final time in preparation for the postseason Orange Bowl. Even limping, Namath played superbly, as he threw two touchdown passes and completed eighteen passes for 256 yards in a

21–17 loss to the Texas Longhorns. Inexplicably, Namath left Alabama without a degree, having missed out on All-America honors; he was not among the top ten Heisman Trophy vote-getters. Namath did, however, take a reputation as a hot professional prospect with him. The pro scouts loved his quick passing release, "football smarts," and leadership. Statistically, Namath, who experienced only three losses in his three varsity seasons, completed 203 of 373 passes for 2,714 yards and 25 touchdowns.

While the Vietnam War raged, a less deadly war between the American Football League (AFL) and the National Football League (NFL) was in progress. Bidding for talented players was escalating. The six-foot, two-inch and two-hundred-pound Namath was a first-round draft choice of the St. Louis (now Arizona) Cardinals (NFL) and the New York Jets (AFL). It is sometimes erroneously stated that he was the overall first pick in the AFL draft. The wide receiver Lawrence Elkins of Baylor had that honor. Fortunately for Namath, the entertainment mogul David ("Sonny") Werblin owned the Jets, and he understood the value of having a star player.

Before playing a game, Namath's dark good looks graced the cover of *Sports Illustrated*. Borrowing the sobriquet from the New York Yankees' first baseman Joe Pepitone, Namath became "Broadway Joe." His unprecedented three-year, $427,000 contract, at a time when established NFL quarterbacks were earning well under $100,000 annually, only added to Namath's aura. Flush with money and fame, Namath basked in New York City's glitz and glamour. Much was made of his playboy image, complemented by a "swingin' bachelor pad" with a six-inch-deep white llama rug. Namath helped the perception by saying, "I like my Johnnie Walker [scotch] Red and my women blond." Gossip columnists linked him with numerous starlets.

When it came time to perform on the football field, Namath—wearing white football shoes in a decidedly black shoe era—put up impressive numbers. As AFL Rookie of the Year in 1965, he passed for a respectable 2,200 yards and eighteen touchdowns. The next season he led the AFL in passing yards (3,379). In 1967 he fully matured as a player and exploded for 4,007 yards, becoming the first pro quarterback to surpass 4,000 yards in a single season, a fourteen-game season. By this time the Jets were AFL contenders and "Joe Willie White Shoes," as he was called by some, was a media darling. He grew a Fu Manchu mustache and collected $10,000 for shaving it in a television commercial for Schick. Despite surgically scarred legs and knees, he even appeared in a panty-hose commercial. Other endorsements followed.

The pinnacle of Namath's career came on 12 January 1969. After "guaranteeing" a victory in Super Bowl III, Namath backed up his boast in Miami's Orange Bowl, leading the Jets to a 16–7 victory over the heavily favored Baltimore (now Indianapolis) Colts; Namath was named Most Valuable Player (MVP) of the game. It was the first Super Bowl victory for the fledgling AFL, and it added an aura of legitimacy to the younger league. If anything, Namath became an even bigger cult figure. People on the fringe of pro football fandom, especially those under age thirty, became willing converts, thanks to the counterculture quarterback and his maverick image.

Namath "retired" briefly and tearfully on 6 June 1969 when NFL Commissioner Pete Rozelle deemed unsavory a club (Bachelors III) in which Namath had a financial interest, because of alleged connections to gambling and organized crime. He divested himself of the club on 18 July 1969 before the 1970 season and returned to playing. Unfortunately, Namath would never again reach the heights of Super Bowl glory. Knee injuries that further robbed him of his mobility cut into his overall effectiveness. In 1970, 1971, and 1973 he averaged playing in only five games a season. In 1972 Namath led the NFL in passing yardage and touchdowns and was named to the Pro Bowl. In 1977 the Jets traded Namath to the Los Angeles (now St. Louis) Rams. Namath retired from professional football in 1978.

Respected by teammates and opponents alike, Namath was elected to the Pro Football Hall of Fame in 1985, the same year that the Jets franchise retired Namath's number-twelve jersey. He engaged in sporadic stage and screen acting during and after his playing days and logged two seasons (1985 and 1986) in the broadcast booth on *Monday Night Football* on the American Broadcasting Company (ABC). Namath gave up his bachelor's ways in 1984, when he married a petite brunette, Deborah Lynn ("Tatiana") Mays. They had two daughters. Namath filed for divorce on 19 March 1999. He owns restaurants in New York City; Tuscaloosa, Alabama; and Fort Lauderdale, Florida. He also has served as a chairperson for the Leukemia Society Coin Campaign and is a national spokesperson for the Arthritis Huddle, an advocacy group for osteoarthritis sufferers.

Namath left the game having thrown for a franchise-record 27,663 yards and 173 touchdowns. He is remembered as much for his image and panache as for his flawless passing mechanics. Namath's Alabama friend Jimmy Walsh, who became his agent, said, "Eventually, Joe Namath the football player will not be as significant as the idea of him."

★

Namath, with Dick Schaap, wrote an autobiography, *I Can't Wait Till Tomorrow, 'Cause I Get Better Looking Everyday* (1969). Namath also wrote, with Bob Oates, Jr., *Joe Namath: A Matter of Style* (1973), which discusses his playing days with the Jets. Biographical information is in David Lipman, *Joe Namath: A Football Legend* (1968); Robert B. Jackson, *Joe Namath: Superstar* (1968); Phil Berger, *Joe Namath: Maverick Quarterback* (1969); Larry Borstein, *Super Joe: The Joe Namath Story* (1969); Marshall and Sue Burchard, *Sports Hero Joe Namath* (1971); John Devaney, *Joe Namath* (1972); Rose Namath Szolnoki and Bill Kushner, *Namath: My Son Joe* (1975); Jim Burke, *Joe Namath: The Story of Joe Namath* (1975); Rick Telander, *Joe Namath, and the Other Guys* (1976); and Martin Ralbovsky, *The Namath Effect* (1976).

JIM CAMPBELL

NASH, Graham. *See* Crosby, Stills, and Nash.

NEUSTADT, Richard Elliott (*b.* 26 June 1919 in New York City), political scientist and consultant to Presidents Harry Truman, John F. Kennedy, and Lyndon B. Johnson.

Neustadt was born to Richard Mitchells Neustadt, a U.S. Social Security official and presidential adviser, and Elizabeth Neufeld, a social worker. He attended the University of California, Berkeley, where he earned his A.B. in 1939. Two years later he received his M.A. from Harvard University, and in 1951 he earned his Ph.D. from the same institution. In 1942 Neustadt worked as an assistant economist with the U.S. Office of Price Administration in Washington, D.C., before joining the U.S. Naval Reserve. After finishing his active tour of duty, he married Bertha Frances Cummings, an educator, on 21 December 1945. They had two children.

Following a stint with the Bureau of the Budget (1946–1949), Neustadt, a lifelong Democrat, received an appointment as special assistant to President Harry Truman. Those years, from 1950 to 1953, mark the origins of Neustadt's almost legendary knowledge of matters relating to the U.S. presidency. He never again would serve a president so directly, but his insights, both as a scholar and a political insider, would stand him in good stead during two Democratic administrations in the 1960s.

Neustadt's primary vocation was that of educator. From the mid-1950s to the mid-1960s he taught public administration at Cornell University (1953–1954) and government at Columbia University (1954–1964). Also during this period he served as a visiting professor at Princeton University (1957) and at Nuffield College, Oxford University (1960–1961). In 1961 he received the Woodrow Wilson Foundation Award from the American Political Science Association.

His first book, *The Presidency at Mid-Century,* appeared in 1956 and was followed in 1960 by *Presidential Power: The Politics of Leadership.* These and other accomplishments brought Neustadt to the attention of a new president, John F. Kennedy, who called on him as a consultant from the time of his election in 1960 until his assassination three years later. Most notably, Neustadt wrote a series of memos for Kennedy, mapping a successful order of transition into the highest office in the land. (So great was his stature that in later years Neustadt was asked to do the same by President Ronald Reagan, a Republican, Democratic presidential candidate Michael Dukakis, and President Bill Clinton.) Kennedy's successor, Lyndon B. Johnson, also relied on Neustadt's expertise from 1964 to 1966.

Destined to become Neustadt's most influential work, *Presidential Power* concerns three broad aspects of the presidential office and the men who have held it: their power of persuasion, their professional reputations, and their public prestige. Later editions gave Neustadt the opportunity to analyze presidents who came after Truman and Dwight D. Eisenhower, the focal points of the original edition. An updated version (with an afterword by Kennedy) in 1968 gave Neustadt an opportunity to appraise the performance of that president, who by then had been dead for five years.

Neustadt cited Kennedy as a president who remained true throughout his administration to the goals with which he had gone into office—in this case, containing nuclear warfare and advancing civil rights. He also used Kennedy as an example of a president whose style of response to situations was consistent: in the case of the cold war, for instance, from the Bay of Pigs (the ill-fated and U.S.-sponsored attempted invasion of Cuba) to the Cuban Missile Crisis (when the Soviets moved missiles into Cuba) to the Vietnam War, Kennedy's aim was to strike against any source of Communist-influenced sabotage.

In addition to consulting with Kennedy and Johnson, Neustadt served as special consultant to the U.S. Senate Subcommittee on National Policy Machinery (1959–1961), the U.S. Bureau of Budget (1961–1971), the U.S. Senate Subcommittee on National Security Staffing and Operations (1962–1967), the U.S. Atomic Energy Commission (1962–1968), and the U.S. Department of State (1962–1969). He was also a member of the advisory board for the U.S. Commission on Money and Credit (1960–1961) and a consultant to the Rand Corporation (1964–1978).

Fittingly, given his admiration for Kennedy, Neustadt spent the two remaining decades of his full-time career at Harvard University's John F. Kennedy School of Government, where he worked as a professor of government (1965–1978) and served as associate dean (1965–1975) and director of the Institute of Politics (1966–1971) before becoming Lucius N. Littauer Professor of Public Administration in 1978. Appointed Douglas Dillon Professor of Government in 1987, Neustadt retired two years later. His first wife died on 5 May 1984, and in December 1987 he married Shirley Williams, a cofounder of the British Social Democratic Party.

Over the years, *Presidential Power* has been revised and updated, usually with new titles to reflect the passage of time. The first fully updated version appeared in 1976 under the title *Presidential Power: The Politics of Leadership, with Reflections on Johnson and Nixon.* Four years later, Neustadt reissued the book as *Presidential Power: The Politics of Leadership from FDR to Carter* and in 1990 as *Presidential Power and the Modern Presidents: The Politics of Leadership from Roosevelt to Reagan.*

In addition to his most famous work, Neustadt wrote *The Presidency and Legislation: The Growth of Central Clearance* (1962) and contributed to *The Secretary of State and the Ambassador* (1964) and *The Congress and America's Future* (1965). His works since the 1960s include *Alliance Politics* (1970), *The Swine Flu Affair: Decision-Making on a Slippery Disease* (1978, with Harvey V. Fineberg), and *Thinking in Time: The Uses of History for Decision-Makers* (1986, with Ernest R. May). He also cowrote the afterword to Robert F. Kennedy's *Thirteen Days: A Memoir of the Cuban Missile Crisis* (1971).

When questioned in the 1990s as to his role advising present and future administrations, Neustadt quipped that he had "reached that advanced age where presidents-elect are most unlikely to seriously come to old geezers to be told how to keep out of trouble." Still, any aspirant to the challenging job would do well to study *Presidential Power.* From Truman through Clinton, Neustadt has been an influential voice among the world's most powerful men. The fact that he has chosen to remain removed from direct involvement in White House affairs has lent his work a perspective and clarity of vision that make *Presidential Power* as vital today as it was in 1960.

★

Papers reflecting Neustadt's work as a staff member in the Truman administration can be found at the Harry S Truman Library in Independence, Missouri. Assorted documents relating to Neustadt also are located at the John Fitzgerald Kennedy Library in Boston, Massachusetts, and the Lyndon Baines Johnson Library and Museum in Austin, Texas. A critique and appreciation of Neustadt's ideas, with a contribution by Neustadt, is Robert Y. Shapiro, Martha Joynt Kumar, and Lawrence R. Jacobs, eds., *Presidential Power: Forging the Presidency for the Twenty-first Century* (2000).

JUDSON KNIGHT

NEVELSON, Louise (*b.* 23 September 1899 in Kiev, Russia; *d.* 17 April 1988 in New York City), acclaimed abstract sculptor whose long maturation period culminated in a rich body of work in the 1960s that exemplified the creative energy of the medium at that moment in the art world.

Nevelson, born Leah Berliawsky, was one of four children of Isaac and Minna Zeisel (Smolerank) Berliawsky. The

Louise Nevelson standing below one of her sculptures. AP/WIDE WORLD PHOTOS

later in Boston on 12 June 1920. The couple moved to New York City, where Nevelson studied voice, drama, and art. She later observed, "I had the foresight to understand that all of these arts were pretty much one. All of them were essential; one supported the other."

In 1922 her son was born and, as a result, it was not until 1929 that she pursued art as a career, beginning by enrolling at the Art Students League. In 1931, finding marriage too restrictive, she separated from her husband (they divorced in 1941) and left her son with her family in Maine in order to study with the renowned artists Hans Hofmann and Diego Rivera. From 1933 to 1958 Nevelson gradually developed the style for which she became famous in the 1960s, drawing heavily on cubism and surrealism.

In 1958 her painted black wood environment, *Moon Garden + One*, exhibited at Grand Central Moderns in New York, demonstrated the theatricality of her work and also confirmed the debt her work owed to cubism. Always at the forefront, she was the first artist to create a whole environment, proving her affinity with drawing, collage, and architecture. *Sky Cathedral,* an important piece mounted in that exhibition, was an extravagant composition of stacked wooden boxes overflowing with found objects. The Museum of Modern Art acquired it in 1958, and this proved to be a significant breakthrough. As a result, in 1959, at the age of sixty, Nevelson was invited by the Museum of Modern Art to create a full exhibition. For that setting, she installed a sensational all-white environment, *Dawn's Wedding Feast,* and the critics deemed it "colossal."

Nevelson flourished in the dynamic 1960s. Her work continued to be exhibited in prestigious galleries, and these years were crammed with commissions, exhibitions, and honors. She started to work with gold in 1961, and her exhibition *The Royal Tides* was shown at the Martha Jackson Gallery in New York. In 1963 Nevelson became the first woman artist to have a one-person show at the selective Sidney Janis Gallery in New York, and in 1964 she began her affiliation with the prestigious Pace Gallery in New York. The Whitney Museum presented the first major retrospective of her work in 1967.

During the 1960s major international collectors became aware of her innovative work. In July 1962 she won the grand prize in the First Sculpture International at the Instituto Torcuato Di Tella in Buenos Aires, and that same summer she represented the United States at the thirty-first Venice Biennale. Her three rooms of "wall furniture," painted in black, white, and gold, greeted visitors to the U.S. pavilion; her exhibition was one of the few real sensations of the entire biennale.

Nevelson's growing prestige led to her involvement with various artists' associations. In 1962 Nevelson became the first woman president of the National Artists' Equity, and she succeeded in increasing the membership, especially

family immigrated to the United States in 1905, settling in the small coastal town of Rockland, Maine, where her father prospered in the lumber business and her mother was a homemaker. Because of her Russian-Jewish heritage, Nevelson always felt like an outsider in the provincial New England town. She once remarked, "I never made friends because I didn't intend to stay in Rockland, and I didn't want anything to tie me down." Nevelson inherited her parents' passionate belief in freedom and independence of thought, a radical orientation in politics, and a crusader's attitude toward women's rights. For most of her life she felt different from her peers, and she took pleasure in accentuating this difference through her unconventional fashion style. Thick sable eyelashes and distinctive headwear that framed her beautifully contoured face became Nevelson's personal trademarks.

Nevelson had little interest in school except for her art classes, where she excelled. Her art teachers, who were quick to recognize her talent, dubbed her "the artist." In 1918, shortly before her graduation from Rockland High School, Nevelson met a wealthy shipping company executive, Charles Nevelson, and they were married two years

among younger and avant-garde artists. In 1966 the socially conscious Nevelson joined with other artists to produce the Los Angeles Tower for Peace. The exhibition was a sixty-foot tower covered with pictures donated by artists from Los Angeles, New York, and Europe to protest the United States' policies in Vietnam.

In later years Nevelson's prominence attracted impressive commissions for public environments. Princeton University commissioned her monumental Cor-ten steel outdoor sculpture in 1969, and during the late 1970s Nevelson left her personal mark on the city she loved. In December 1977 her beautifully decorated Chapel of the Good Shepherd for Saint Peter's Lutheran Church on Park Avenue was dedicated. In 1979 the Louise Nevelson Plaza was installed in the canyons of lower Manhattan on Maiden Lane.

Nevelson's early life presaged the fight for women's rights in the 1960s. Long before the antiestablishment mood of the 1960s, Nevelson had freed herself of social conventions. In the 1960s women were demanding equality and recognition, but Nevelson had used her prodigious energy to insert herself into the male-dominated world of sculpture much earlier. Fame had come late to this self-proclaimed "original creation," and Nevelson savored it until the end. She worked until her death from lung cancer in April 1988; her body was cremated. On 11 September 2001 one of Nevelson's massive sculptures, *Sky Gate,* which had hung in the mezzanine of One World Trade Center since 1978, was destroyed in the terrorist attacks that took place on that day.

★

Biographies of Nevelson include Colette Roberts, *Nevelson* (1964); Arnold B. Glimcher, *Louise Nevelson* (1972); Laurie Wilson, *Louise Nevelson: Iconography and Sources* (1981); Jean Lipman, *Nevelson's World* (1983); and Laurie Lisle, *Louise Nevelson: A Passionate Life* (1990). Other useful sources are Nicholas and Elena Calas, *Icons and Images of the Sixties* (1971), and Diana MacKown, *Dawn and Dusk: Taped Conversations with Diana MacKown* (1976). Significant articles written about Nevelson's life during the 1960s include "All That Glitters," *Time* (31 Aug. 1962), and "Los Angeles: Tower for Peace," *Art News* (Apr. 1966). An obituary is in the *New York Times* (18 Apr. 1988).

MARGARET GARRY BURKE

NEWHART, George Robert ("Bob") (*b.* 5 September 1929 in Chicago, Illinois), stand-up comedian and comic actor who first came to public attention for the sophisticated monologues of his comedy record albums, especially *The Button-Down Mind of Bob Newhart.* He began a television career in the 1960s that included a short-lived variety show and two hit situation comedies, all of them favorites among urbane viewers.

Newhart was born on the West Side of Chicago, the second of four children and the only son of George Newhart, a self-employed plumber and heating repairman, and Julia Pauline (Burns) Newhart, a homemaker. He graduated from Loyola University of Chicago in 1952 with a B.S. degree in business. After spending two years in the U.S. Army, he earned a credential as a certified public accountant in 1958. "Sometimes I wonder how I ever got to be a comedian," he later told an interviewer. "I didn't come from a broken home."

While working as an accountant, Newhart enjoyed killing time with a friend during the business day by chatting out comedy routines over the telephone. The pair hatched a scheme to sell tape recordings of the calls to radio stations. Though the plan was unsuccessful, it opened a back door into show business for Newhart. Dan Sorkin, a Chicago disc jockey, found Newhart's satiric barbs at contemporary life funny and fresh. Sorkin helped Newhart get his earliest professional exposure, which included a comedy spot on a local television morning show. At the turn of the 1960s the long-playing (LP) record was transforming stand-up comedy from a leftover relic of the vaudeville age into a form of artistic expression. The growing audience of young, upscale LP-buyers particularly appreciated the social com-

Bob Newhart, 1961. ASSOCIATED PRESS AP

mentary found in record album humor. Sorkin took Newhart's audiotapes of the "telephone call" routines to contacts at Warner Bros. Records, where the talent director George Avakian signed the unknown comedian to a recording contract. Although Newhart had no professional experience before a live audience, Avakian booked him into the Tidelands, a Houston, Texas, nightclub, with the idea of making a live comedy album.

Newhart's performances were recorded during the two-week gig in February 1960, and these were edited into an LP, which was released on April Fool's Day. *The Button-Down Mind of Bob Newhart* was the first comedy LP ever to reach number one on Billboard's charts, outselling the cast album of *The Sound of Music* and several titles by Elvis Presley. It won three Grammy Awards: Album of the Year, Best Comedy Performance, and Best New Artist. Sequels, *The Button-Down Mind Strikes Back* and *Behind The Button-Down Mind,* soon followed.

The Chicago accountant became an instant star. His "button-down" humor—a reference to the style of shirt collars worn by the swelling ranks of urban office workers in the early 1960s—hit home, with jokes about office tyrants lecturing on paper clip theft and bus drivers trained in the art of leaving elderly ladies in their exhaust fumes. In June 1960, just two months after the release of the album, Newhart made his national television debut on *The Tonight Show Starring Jack Paar,* followed by appearances in prime time on *The Garry Moore Show* and *The Ed Sullivan Show.*

While other young club comics of the period made sponsors skittish with their reputations for political or sexual material, Newhart's low-key style and focus on "everyday life" put them at ease. His plaintive tagline, "Same to you, fella!" with which he ended his telephone routines, bespoke the resignation of a victim rather than the anger of a radical. When Mike Nichols and Elaine May, the hippest comedy team of the period, quit the 1961 Emmy Awards show over a censorship issue just days before the April telecast, Newhart was brought in to replace them. Needing someone that could perform topical material without causing sponsor problems, the producer Bob Finkel thought of Newhart. "Bob did an airplane bit on landing in Miami at the same time that [the Soviet premier Nikita] Krushchev was coming in," recalls Finkel. "The day after the show, Bob Newhart was the biggest thing in show business."

The first *Bob Newhart Show* premiered on the National Broadcasting Company (NBC) in fall 1961. Network executives had been trying to "modernize" the variety format, which had gone into a steep decline since its popularity in the 1950s, and Newhart seemed like the comedian who might be able to save the genre. The show was a critical triumph but a failure in the ratings. "It got an Emmy, a Peabody, and a pink slip from NBC—all in the same year,"

Newhart said. The comedian wrote much of the material, which dealt with some subjects that were considered too daring for TV audiences, including right-wing extremists and restrictive immigration policies.

For the balance of the 1960s Newhart gradually paid the show business dues that he had bypassed with his sudden stardom, playing the club circuit as well as college campuses in the new, concert-style format being developed by other stand-up comedians of the day. He got his first roles as a comic actor during the decade, winning small parts in a handful of Hollywood films, including *Hot Millions* (1968) and *Catch-22* (1970). Considered more appropriate for late-night television than prime time following the cancellation of his variety show, he substituted as host of *The Tonight Show Starring Johnny Carson* eighty-seven times.

Just as Newhart had ridden the wave of a new, more sophisticated style of stand-up comedy to launch his career, his return to prime-time television was part of a similar phenomenon in situation comedy a decade later. MTM Enterprises, the studio responsible for *The Mary Tyler Moore Show,* was at the center of the revitalization of the genre. Its second series to reach television was *The Bob Newhart Show* (1972–1978), which aired between *The Mary Tyler Moore Show* and *All in the Family* on the Columbia Broadcasting System's (CBS) famed lineup of Saturday night "sophisticoms" during the 1970s. Newhart played the role of Dr. Bob Hartley, a Chicago psychologist.

Having achieved series stardom, the comedian collaborated in developing his next sitcom, *Newhart,* which aired on CBS from 1982 to 1990. Newhart fans particularly appreciated the grand punch line of the final episode of *Newhart,* in which the innkeeper Dick Loudon wakes up as Dr. Bob Hartley, revealing the entire second sitcom series to have been a dream of Newhart's first sitcom character.

Newhart married Virginia Quinn in 1963, and the couple has four children. In 1993 Newhart was inducted into the Academy of Television Arts and Sciences' Hall of Fame. His other interests include a radio station, KZBN in Santa Barbara, California, which he purchased in 1995.

★

A biography is Jeff Sorenson, *Bob Newhart* (1988). Details of the comedian's early success appear in articles in the *New York Times Magazine* (7 Aug. 1960) and *Current Biography 1962.* A ninety-minute interview, available on audiotape and in transcription, was conducted by Daniel Nussbaum in 1998 and is held in the Steven H. Scheuer Television History Collection at Syracuse University Library.

DAVID MARC

NEWMAN, Paul Arthur (*b.* 26 January 1925 in Cleveland, Ohio), Oscar-winning motion picture actor whose looks, charm, and disaffected persona helped define the 1960s existential antihero in a series of highly successful films.

Newman was the second of two sons of Arthur S. Newman, a German-descended Jew and part owner of a sporting-goods store, and Theresa Fetzer Newman, a Hungarian Catholic who became a Christian Scientist when Newman was five. By then the family had moved from Cleveland Heights to an eleven-room home in Shaker Heights, a prosperous suburb of Cleveland. Newman does not remember being close to either parent, nor was he raised to have any particular faith.

Newman had a comfortable, upper-middle-class childhood. He played pool, raced bikes, and enjoyed practical jokes. His mother encouraged him to play the part of a court jester in *Robin Hood,* a school play in which he sang a song written by his uncle. At Shaker Heights High School he was an uninspired student. He dreamed of becoming a professional athlete but was not big enough to make the junior varsity football team. Girls noticed the lad with the extraordinary good looks and ocean blue eyes, but he paid little attention to them. He made money by working in his father's store and by selling encyclopedias door to door. In September 1942 he enrolled at Ohio University and appeared as a boxer in a college production of *The Milky Way.*

Bored and restless, Newman left school. He enlisted in the navy in June 1943 and was sent to Yale University to train for the Navy Air Corps. Tests revealed that he was color-blind. In the service during World War II he served

Paul Newman. ARCHIVE PHOTOS, INC.

as radio operator on torpedo planes in the South Pacific, spending his time off "drinking and reading." He had grown and filled out during his years in the service but was "just as dumb as when I went in" when he was mustered out in 1946. Newman flunked out of business courses at Kenyon College in Gambier, Ohio, and was kicked off the football team after busting up a local bar with some friends. He was arrested three times on minor offenses. The drama school at Kenyon corralled his belligerent energy. Newman won leads in *The Front Page, R.U.R.,* and *Charlie's Aunt,* even though he was "terrorized by the emotional requirement of being an actor." He found safety in writing, producing, and directing.

Newman did summer stock in Plymouth, Massachusetts, after his junior year at Kenyon, appearing at the Priscilla Beach Theater in *All My Sons* and *Dear Brutus.* After graduation from Kenyon in 1949 with a B.A. in English he worked summer stock for room and board in Williams Bay, Wisconsin, seeing it as "a paid vacation." His roles in *John Loves Mary* and *The Glass Menagerie* deepened his interest in acting and directing. That interest was extended to the company player Jacqueline Witte, who accompanied him into the Woodstock Players, outside Chicago. They married in December 1949. His work on *Our Town, Mister Roberts,* and *Born Yesterday* reflected a growing passion for the theater, but in April 1950 Newman returned to Cleveland because his father was gravely ill. Arthur Newman died in May, leaving Paul with the impression he had never earned his approval. It was, he later admitted, "one of the great agonies of my life."

Newman sold his father's business and moved his wife and infant son, born September 1950, to New Haven, Connecticut, where he enrolled in Yale's graduate school of drama. There he met the agent Bill Liebling, who urged the attractive young actor to go to New York City. Bit parts on live television followed. Walk-ons for *The March of Time* and *Tales of Tomorrow* were followed by speaking roles on *The Web, The Mask, You Are There,* and *The Aldrich Family.* Newman learned method acting at the Actors Studio in New York City, even though he found it difficult to "get in touch with" his feelings. At the end of 1952 he won the part of the second lead in William Inge's Pulitzer Prize–winning play, *Picnic.* The understudy for the female lead was twenty-two-year-old Joanne Woodward.

Newman's success on Broadway won him a contract with Warner Bros. His screen debut in the costume drama *The Silver Chalice* (1954) was an embarrassing failure. He returned to Broadway, appearing in *The Desperate Hours* and on live television in *Our Town* and *The Battler.* When Newman's friend the actor James Dean was killed in an automobile accident, his role as Rocky Graziano in MGM's *Somebody Up There Likes Me* (1956) went to Newman, giving him his first screen success.

The Newmans separated, and Jackie and the couple's

three children, including daughters born in 1953 and 1955, stayed on Long Island as Newman made his way in Hollywood. A series of inferior films followed until his work with Woodward and the director Martin Ritt in *The Long, Hot Summer* (1958). Newman's portrayal of Ben Quick, a lean and mean Mississippi redneck with a reputation for barn burning, won him the best actor award at the Cannes Film Festival and foreshadowed the emergence of his antisocial persona in the 1960s. Newman and Woodward were married on 29 January 1958, shortly after Newman's divorce was finalized. Later that year his part as the invalid husband of Elizabeth Taylor in Tennessee Williams's *Cat on a Hot Tin Roof* (1958) was nominated for an Oscar. Williams and the writers Gore Vidal and Christopher Isherwood became frequent guests in the tiny apartment the Newmans kept on the Upper East Side of Manhattan. Newman began the 1960s in Israel, filming *Exodus* (1960) for Otto Preminger. Critics found his portrayal of a freedom fighter earnest but unsympathetic.

Newman's next role, as Fast Eddie Felson in Robert Rossen's movie *The Hustler* (1961), captured the determination of a young drifter who lives to beat his pool-playing idol, Minnesota Fats, superbly played by Jackie Gleason. The cinematographer Gene Shufton won an Academy Award for converting a smoke-filled, claustrophobic set into the setting of a modern-day Greek tragedy. In the movie Newman is a gifted and flawed player. To become the best at his game he accepts money and protection from Bert Gordon, a sleazy promoter played to perfection by George C. Scott. Piper Laurie, a cripple who takes Felson in after he is badly beaten and has had his thumbs broken, completes the ensemble. Newman's Oscar-nominated performance had an "intensity," critics claimed, that allowed him "to look inside his character." What he discovers is Eddie's essential arrogance and vulnerability, qualities that make him a sympathetic outsider who lives according to his own code in a world that is determined to brutalize the talented nonconformist.

In Tennessee Williams's *Sweet Bird of Youth* (1962) Newman's character is beaten up again, and this time has it coming to him. Chance Wayne is the ambitious beach bum Newman had successfully played three years earlier on Broadway. In the screen version he is a parasitic self-promoter who becomes the lover of a fading movie star to advance his own interests as an actor. In the Hollywood ending he becomes obstinately defenseless and is horribly disfigured in pursuit of a true love.

Newman had become one of Hollywood's biggest stars. Long free from his Warner Bros. contract, he could pick his own projects and supporting teams to execute them. Dissatisfied with the mawkish finish to his previous film, he had the screenwriters Irving Ravetch and Harriet Frank develop a character called Hud Bannon, from a novel by

Larry McMurtry, who consciously "doesn't give a damn about anyone." Martin Ritt directed *Hud,* the story of an amoral, opportunistic rancher at war with his father and idolized by a nephew. It is Hud's view that "if you don't look out for yourself, the only helping hand you get is when they lower the box." Newman relished the part because Hud's callousness "reflected the dilemma of our time." In the role of Hud he represented the coldly indifferent people who "grow up at the tragic expense of other people." Audiences and critics were enthralled. Arthur Knight, writing in the *Saturday Review,* noted that Newman's Hud was "a charming monster," whose "scornful smile" was "a threat poised over every scene." Bosley Crowther of the *New York Times* thought Newman's performance was "tremendous" in its depiction of "a potent, voracious man, restless with all his crude ambitions and arrogant with his contempt" for all the old values his father seemed to represent. Stanley Kauffmann, writing for the *New Republic,* was certain that the film would "confirm Newman's place in the front rank of American film actors." The part won Newman his third nomination for an Academy Award.

The Newmans and their three daughters settled in a converted carriage house in Westport, Connecticut, where Newman became involved in Democratic Party politics and the civil rights movement. He later announced his opposition to the Vietnam War. He told interviewers he was no sex symbol but rather "an absolute square" who could not stand "dishonesty and idiocy." He was going public with his social concerns, he said, because "I'm not going to be disenfranchised just because I'm an actor."

Newman's role as the cynical private eye in the crime writer Ross MacDonald's *Harper* (1966), which costarred Lauren Bacall, drew inevitable comparisons to Humphrey Bogart's portrayals of the private eyes Sam Spade and Phillip Marlowe and revived Newman's career after a series of mediocre efforts. Harper tracks a missing millionaire into the tawdry Southern California twilight, exposing the underside of the 1960s, an urban landscape, as *Life*'s critic Richard Schickel observed, where he finds "the conscienceless climate of modern America." Newman's next film, *Torn Curtain* (1966), his only teaming with Alfred Hitchcock, proved a plodding hodgepodge of cold war spy clichés that Newman plowed through grimly.

Hombre and *Cool Hand Luke,* released months apart in 1967, were critical and box-office triumphs that celebrated Newman's image as the decade's leading iconoclast. Each updated familiar material. In *Hombre,* Newman plays a self-sufficient man who reluctantly becomes a hero when stagecoach passengers are terrorized by bandits. The character, John Russell, is alienated from both white and Indian cultures, and the film, directed by Ritt and scripted by Ravetch and Frank, suggests that civilization as well as personal nobility are possible only when one overcomes disengagement and takes responsibility for others.

America's youth culture embraced the forty-two-year-old actor as one of their own with the release of *Cool Hand Luke*. Luke Jackson is sent to a Southern chain gang for a minor offense—unscrewing the tops of parking meters during a drunken spree. There he encounters opposition within the prison population and among its guards for his independent spirit. He refuses to give up when he is badly beaten by Dragline, a chain-gang leader, and this defenseless obstinacy endears him to the hearts of fellow inmates and the film's audience. The warden tries to beat the defiance out of Cool Hand, who delivers the film's classic line, "What we have here is a failure to communicate." His character's success in resisting the state and its utter inability to violate his fundamental humanity made Newman an icon to many 1960s moviegoers. The intractable and increasingly unpopular war in Vietnam was soon joined by a credibility gap that separated the nation's youth from an older generation that tended to defend war and racism. Their anger and disillusionment found expression in what the critic Judith Crist called Newman's depiction of "the triumphant anti-hero," which won him his fourth Oscar nomination.

Before the 1960s were over Newman successfully made his directorial debut, starred in one of Hollywood's all-time hits, and appeared in a picture that intensified his enthusiasm for racing. *Rachel, Rachel* (1968) starred Woodward as a spinster schoolteacher in a small New England town who is approaching middle age as an emotional recluse before she learns to open herself to experience. Woodward's performance and Newman's direction won awards from the New York Film Critics for capturing the texture and loneliness of everyday life in 1960s America. In *Winning* (1969) the two starred in an unremarkable movie about race car drivers that thrilled fans, and Newman began spending his time away from the cameras racing hot cars. *Butch Cassidy and the Sundance Kid* (1969), his highly successful teaming with Robert Redford, is a seriocomic period piece, complete with an Oscar-winning score written by Burt Bacharach. The film reinterprets the lives of two Western bad men for the tastes of 1960s audiences, who by this time expected Newman's characteristic irritation with those in authority. The film's freeze-frame ending catches the two men aggressively advancing, although hopelessly outnumbered, against their would-be captors. Its iconography of the individual bravely facing annihilation at the hands of an obdurate collective became Newman's constant theme in the thirty years of filmmaking that followed.

Newman never again achieved the level of fame and cultural status he had enjoyed in the 1960s, even though his subsequent work was not without success. *The Sting* (1973), a re-teaming with Redford, won seven Oscars and

was a huge hit. *The Towering Inferno* (1974), costarring Steve McQueen, William Holden, and Fred Astaire, helped spark a cycle of all-star wide-screen spectacles. His work as a foul-mouthed minor league hockey coach in *Slap Shot* (1977) became an unexpected cult classic. *Fort Apache, The Bronx* (1981) was an update on the urban crime drama. Acclaimed roles in consecutive films—*Absence of Malice* (1981) and *The Verdict* (1982)—won Newman his fifth and sixth Oscar nominations. The award eluded him until Newman reprised his role as Fast Eddie Felson in Martin Scorsese's *The Color of Money* (1986), opposite Tom Cruise. The previous year he had been awarded a rare honorary Oscar "in recognition of many and memorable compelling screen performances" and for his "personal integrity and dedication to his craft." But it was the Scorsese film that finally won him an Oscar for best performance.

In November 1978 Newman's son, Scott, died of a drug and alcohol overdose. Newman created the Scott Newman Foundation in his memory, specializing in the treatment of alcohol and drug abuse. Newman lent his name and image to Newman's Own, a product line of foods ranging from salad dressing to popcorn. Millions of dollars in profits are directed toward the arts and toward charities helping children, including camps for kids with cancer. The Kennedy Center honored Newman and Woodward with lifetime achievement awards in 1992. The Academy of Motion Picture Arts and Sciences gave him the Jean Hersholt humanitarian award in 1993. The man who had become a screen legend by playing men who went it alone and lived outside the system told interviewers "the greatest thrill of my career is to take what I have and spread it around a little bit."

★

Newman has been the subject of several biographies, among them four entitled *Paul Newman*—by Charles Hamblett (1975), J. C. Landry (1983), Elena Oumano (1989), and Lawrence J. Quick (1996); also see Lionel Godfrey, *Paul Newman, Superstar: A Critical Biography* (1979). Eric Lax, *Paul Newman: A Biography* (1996), is richly illustrated and contains interviews with Newman. Joe Morello and Edward Z. Epstein, *Paul and Joanne: A Biography of Paul Newman and Joanne Woodward* (1988) analyzes the relationship of Newman and Woodward and their careers in moviemaking and on the stage. Two filmographies carefully chronicling his early work in Hollywood are Lawrence J. Quick, *The Films of Paul Newman* (1971), and Michael Kerbel, *Paul Newman* (1987). Stewart Stern, *No Tricks in My Pocket* (1989), is a behind-the-scenes look at Newman's work as a director. Two volumes of Newman's own writing on healthy eating are *The Hole in the Wall Gang Cookbook* (1998) and *Newman's Own Cookbook* (1985). Major articles on his life can be found in *Current Biography* (1959) and (1985).

BRUCE J. EVENSEN

NEWTON, Huey Percy (*b.* 17 February 1942 in Monroe, Louisiana; *d.* 22 August 1989 in Oakland, California), cofounder, with Bobby Seale, of the Black Panther Party for Self-Defense in Oakland, California, in October 1966.

Newton, the youngest of seven children born to Walter and Armelia (Johnson) Newton, spent a troubled childhood in depressed neighborhoods of Oakland, California. His father worked at as many as three jobs at a time—he was a longshoreman, a handyman, a truck driver, and a Baptist preacher—but he was unable to keep his youngest son

Huey Newton. AP/WIDE WORLD PHOTOS

from feeling rage at the oppression he sensed all around him. Newton was expelled from various schools in the Oakland system but finally graduated from Oakland Technical High School in 1959. Though his reading skills were poor, he matriculated at Oakland City College (now Merritt College), a two-year school. Eventually, through a special arrangement with the university, Newton earned a Ph.D. from the University of California, Santa Cruz, though he had no other college or university degrees.

Newton met Bobby Seale while both were students at Oakland City College (now Merritt College). Together they created the Black Panther Party for Self-Defense, a revolutionary organization that continues to be among the best known of the 1960s. The purpose of the Black Panther Party was complex; even the Panthers have not always agreed. Originally, their main activity was the observation of police interaction with African-American residents of Oakland, with the intent of ending police brutality. On the other hand, on the day they founded the party, Newton and Seale drew up a list of ten demands, along with the reasons for them, entitled "What We Want" and "What We Believe." Among their goals were education relevant to the lives of oppressed black people, an end to the economic exploitation of the black community by white businessmen, freedom for all black prisoners (on the grounds they had not been tried before juries of their peers), decent housing for blacks, and an end to police brutality. The founders drew a direct connection between the Ten-Point Program and street engagements with police. Newton always insisted on a holistic perception that did not permit the separation of theory from practice, the military from the theoretical. The task of changing the situation of African Americans even in the smallest degree was seen as so huge that almost any activist program could be made relevant to one of the ten points or goals. Perhaps the most remarkable facet of the Ten-Point Program is that two young men from a community college attempted such a project as part of a fully conceived, long-range plan of action that required many years to accomplish.

In February 1967 Newton and Seale met Eldridge Cleaver, who had been released from prison only three months earlier, at a neighborhood meeting of activist groups in San Francisco. In an essay entitled "Meeting the Panthers," Cleaver described his awe of the fully armed pair and their command of the attention and respect, especially of the women in the room. He almost immediately became a member of the group and accepted the responsibility of serving as chief author of its newspaper, the *Black Panther,* which was published from 1967 to 1970. These three men formed the triumvirate of the Black Panther Party, with Seale as chairman, Newton as defense minister, and Cleaver as minister of information. In May 1967 the party received national publicity when Seale and Cleaver, together with twenty-eight other members of the party, showed up at the California legislature in Sacramento to protest a proposed gun control law they assumed was aimed at themselves. Wearing uniforms of black leather jackets, black berets, baby blue shirts, and bandoliers, they were a menacing and fearsome sight.

As the party grew in numbers and influence, so did the hostility of the local police. In October 1967 Newton and a Panther friend were stopped by an Oakland police officer, John Frey, at approximately 4:00 A.M. Frey called for backup from an Officer Heanes. Certain that the two officers were about to kill him, Newton pulled his gun out of his jacket, fired at Frey, and wounded him. Then he took Frey's gun, shot him again, this time fatally, and spun to shoot Heanes in the right arm. Heanes, who had pulled out his own gun, switched it to his left hand and shot Newton in the abdomen. Cleaver cut the guns up with a hacksaw and scattered the pieces throughout the city so there could be no conclusive tests performed on these weapons. (Later, Newton's lawyer, Charles Garry, insisted that Frey had been killed by his partner's gun.) Newton stood three trials for the murder of Officer Frey; the first two ended in a hung jury, and the third, in a decision for involuntary manslaughter, for which he received a sentence of two to fifteen years. He spent three years in prison; the appellate court threw out his conviction because improper instructions were given to the jury. He was freed in August 1970.

Newton's own writings provide the best possible insight into the meaning of the 28 October shootout for the Black Panthers and their sympathizers. Earlier in 1967 he had written and published in the party newspaper three essays: "Fear and Doubt: May 15, 1967," and two columns under the general heading of "In Defense of Self-Defense." These two were later published in *To Die for the People* (1972) as "In Defense of Self-Defense, I: June 20, 1967," and "In Defense of Self-Defense, II: July 3, 1967." In these he elucidated the political and social attitudes of the person he identified in the first essay, "Fear and Doubt," as "the lower socio-economic Black male." Newton's way of dealing with his own fear was self-defense. His way of dealing with self-doubt was through Marxism and revolutionary doctrine— no black person can succeed because the system is created to serve whites and exclude blacks; but no self-respecting African American should want to succeed, because capitalism is morally corrupt anyway.

Newton elaborated on these ideas in "In Defense of Self-Defense I." The essay invokes the Declaration of Independence, which had been embraced by the Black Panther Party when Newton and Seale adopted its Preamble as the summary of their party's platform and program. Whenever citizens are dissatisfied with their government,

as African Americans are with the government of the United States, he stated, they have the right to withdraw their consent and change that government.

Newton's logic is revealed quite clearly here. He wrote that the colonist decided to write this Declaration when he finally "felt he had no choice but to raise the gun to defend his welfare." Today, however, "these same" people deny the right of "the colonized Black man" to abolish "this oppressive system." It is Newton's use of the then-popular mother country–black colony dichotomy that makes this analogy possible. By insisting that the relationship between black ghettos and the government of the United States is analogous to the relationship between the colonies and that of England, Newton drew a parallel between white reluctance to alter or abolish the United States government and the refusal of King George to permit self-rule in the distant American colonies.

Youthful leftists made Newton a celebrity after his shooting and arrest in 1967, mostly as a result of the efforts of Eldridge Cleaver, who was perhaps Newton's most devoted follower. The cries "Free Huey" and "Free Huey or the sky's the limit" became political statements as well as expressions of rejection of the police and the establishment they protected.

Newton's intelligence and leadership were distorted by racism and violence; he was a classic romantic, a 1960s version of the Hero of the People—defiant, dedicated unto death to the cause he espoused, resolutely antiauthority, antiwealth, antiprivilege. He demanded respect for his intelligence; from his college years on, he could not tolerate being thought of as ignorant or brutish. On the other hand, he grew up fighting because he was small and baby-faced. He respected the iron-handed authority of Mafia dons, was severe and even authoritarian in his own judgments, and wanted above all to be admired by the streetwise youth among whom he grew up. To be admired by gang members and professors alike is a challenging and complex goal; in addition to that, to wish to be "the Soul Servant" and "Shield" of one's people is perhaps demanding more than can be accomplished. Like many 1960s activists, Newton wanted to stand for something noble, even and maybe especially if it meant he would have to die for what he believed. Martin Luther King, Jr., too moderate to be a Panther hero, had nonetheless said that a person who sees nothing worth dying for has "nothing to live for." A 1968 James Brown song, "Say It Loud, I'm Black and I'm Proud," states that "We'd rather die on our feet than be livin' on our knees." In such an atmosphere, it was easy for an idealist like Newton to rationalize sacrifice as "revolutionary suicide," the title of Newton's autobiography.

During the Black Panther Party's years of ascendancy, Newton remained single, though he reportedly engaged in a long-term relationship with Elaine Brown, a fellow Black

Panther. In 1977 he married his secretary, Gwen Fontaine, who left him in 1982. Newton married Fredericka Slaughter in 1984. Though Newton had no biological children, he adopted his first wife's two children and his second wife's son. Following Newton's murder outside an Oakland crack house in 1989, Fredericka Newton established a foundation in honor of her husband and his beliefs. Newton's funeral service was held at the Allen Temple Baptist Church in Oakland.

Although Newton suffered from alcohol and cocaine dependency and allegedly practiced embezzlement, fraud, and extortion in his later years, his dream of an African-American community whose members have opportunities equal to those of other citizens has begun to be realized. His leadership, though tragically flawed, helped pave the way for improvement in the lives of many black citizens. The tragedy of Newton is in part a result of his conflicted self-image, in part a result of his substance abuse, and in part a result of his spending the crisis years of the 1960s movements, 1968–1970, in prison and out of the action. He was a cultural icon during that time, but he had wanted to be first a leader and then a martyr, and he failed.

★

Newton's personal papers dating from 1968 to 1994 can be found in the Department of Special Collections and University Archives of the Stanford University Libraries. His autobiography *Revolutionary Suicide* (1973) discusses his early life and experiences in the 1960s. A biography is J. L. Jeffries, *Huey P. Newton: Radical Theorist* (2002). Bobby Seale's *Seize the Time: The Story of the Black Panther Party and Huey P. Newton* (1970) provides another view of Newton's controversial life. Newton's *To Die for the People* (1972) contains key documents and speeches related to the Black Panther Party. An obituary is in the *New York Times* (23 Aug. 1989).

KAY KINSELLA ROUT

NICHOLS, Mike (*b.* 6 November 1931 in Berlin, Germany), award-winning director of stage and screen responsible for some of the most memorable productions of the 1960s, including *Barefoot in the Park* and *The Odd Couple* in the theater and *Who's Afraid of Virginia Woolf?* and *The Graduate* on film.

Nichols was born Michael Igor Peschkowsky. The son of Pavel Nicolaievitch Peschkowsky, who had fled the Russian Revolution, and Brigitte (Landauer) Peschkowsky, a housewife, he spent the first eight years of his life in Berlin, the city of his birth. Alarmed by the rise of Nazism in Germany, his father, a physician, immigrated to the United States in 1938 and was joined there by Nichols and his younger brother the following year. Because of illness, Brigitte Peschkowsky did not come to America until 1941. The fam-

Mike Nichols *(right)*, receiving his Academy Award for best director from Leslie Caron, April 1968. The award was for Nichols's film *The Graduate*. © BETTMANN/CORBIS

ily settled in the New York metropolitan area, living first in New York City and moving later to suburban Connecticut. His father Americanized his name to Paul Nichols. Mike Nichols became a naturalized U.S. citizen in 1944.

Gifted intellectually, Nichols studied at New York's distinguished Dalton School, as well as the Cherry Lawn School in the exclusive Connecticut enclave of Darien. When Nichols was just twelve, his father died, leaving his mother to raise Nichols and his brother. The loss of his father, however, did little to slow his academic progress. He skipped a few grades, and after completing high school enrolled in 1950 in the premedical program at the University of Chicago, supporting himself with a variety of odd jobs. Bored with college, he returned to New York but had little success finding work. Becoming more and more intrigued with the theater, he studied acting for about two years with the coach Lee Strasberg.

Back in Chicago, Nichols teamed up with Elaine May and joined the Compass Theater Company, which had been known as the Playwright's Theatre Club until 1954 and in 1959 became Second City. Nichols and May developed satirical comedy routines that soon had audiences exploding with laughter. The duo appeared in most of the leading entertainment venues nationwide and finally came to Broadway with *An Evening with Mike Nichols and Elaine*

May (1960–1961). Shortly after the hit show closed, Nichols took a role in *A Matter of Position,* a play directed by May. This critical change in their relationship proved the undoing of their professional collaboration. They split up shortly thereafter.

The breakup proved traumatic for Nichols. He later told Barbara Gelb, the author of a profile of Nichols for the *New York Times Magazine,* "When Elaine and I split up, that was a shattering year for me. . . . I didn't know what I was. I was the left-over half of something." When a Broadway producer friend suggested he try his hand at directing, Nichols jumped at the idea, quickly landing the job of directing Neil Simon's *Barefoot in the Park* in 1964. Suddenly, it seemed, he had found his bearings. He told *Vanity Fair,* "This is what all my experience . . . —[my work with the famed teacher Lee] Strasberg, Elaine, Compass, reading every word of Eugene O'Neill at fourteen— was leading up to. This is what I've been waiting for." The Simon comedy was a smashing success, winning Nichols a Tony Award for best director, and it was quickly followed by a string of other Broadway hits, including *The Knack, Luv,* and *The Odd Couple* in 1965. Nichols also won Tony Awards for his work on *Luv* and *The Odd Couple.*

Trading on his spectacular success in the theater, Nichols took on his first major Hollywood project, the film version of the playwright Edward Albee's devastating black comedy *Who's Afraid of Virginia Woolf?* (1966). Starring Elizabeth Taylor, who had personally asked Nichols to direct, and her then-husband Richard Burton, the film was both a critical and popular success. It also proved a breakthrough for Hollywood, demonstrating clearly that films could deal sensitively with adult themes and still do well at the box office. *Virginia Woolf* put yet another nail in the coffin of the badly dated Motion Picture Production Code. For Nichols, it was a total-immersion study in filmmaking. Looking back on the project, Nichols told *Film Comment,* "When I see *Virginia Woolf,* I can see me learning as I go, because it was shot in sequence. And I can see that I get better at it as I go." Nichols was nominated for a best director Oscar, no small accomplishment for a first-time film director. He lost, however, to Fred Zinnemann, who took the directing honors for his work on *A Man for All Seasons.* In all, *Virginia Woolf* was nominated for a total of thirteen Oscars and won five, including a second best actress Oscar for Taylor.

Next up for Nichols in Hollywood was *The Graduate,* the satirical, coming-of-age tale of the confused college graduate Benjamin Braddock, played winningly by Dustin Hoffman in his screen debut. The 1967 film also starred Anne Bancroft as the man-eating Mrs. Robinson, who sets her sights on the innocent young Ben. A latter-day Holden Caulfield, Hoffman's character quickly became the spokesperson for a generation of young Americans who had lost their trust for anyone over the age of thirty. The film firmly established Nichols's reputation as a film director, winning for him an Academy Award, Golden Globe Award, and New York Film Critics Award for best director.

In *The Films of the Sixties* (1980), the film writer Douglas Brode observed that *The Graduate* had made Nichols, at least for a while, "the most powerful and influential of those people who were reshaping the American motion picture product." After his triumph with *The Graduate,* Nichols returned to Broadway to direct another Neil Simon comedy, *Plaza Suite,* for which he won the 1968 Tony Award for best director. His next project, directing the film version of Joseph Heller's popular cult novel *Catch-22* (1970), was far less successful, however. Opening to mixed critical reviews, the film failed to catch fire at the box office. Nichols quickly bounced back, directing Jack Nicholson, Art Garfunkel, and Ann-Margret in *Carnal Knowledge* (1971), a film Nichols later described as "the darkest movie I ever made." Nichols returned to Broadway in 1972, where he directed Simon's comedy *The Prisoner of Second Avenue,* for which he again received the Tony Award for best director. The director's next film projects, *The Day of the Dolphin* (1973) and *The Fortune* (1975), were major disappointments. Peter Bart of *Variety* described them as "ordinary studio films." For the next few years, Nichols stayed away from films altogether. His work in the theater also dwindled to almost nothing.

In 1977, however, Nichols returned to Broadway in a big way as the producer of the hit musical *Annie,* which earned the Tony Award as best musical. Later that year, Nichols and his coproducer Hume Cronyn staged *The Gin Game,* starring Cronyn and his wife, Jessica Tandy, at the Long Wharf Theater in New Haven, Connecticut, before bringing it to Broadway. The play was eventually staged in London in 1979. Nichols directed *Drinks Before Dinner,* a production of the New York Shakespeare Festival, at New York City's Public Theater in 1978. Returning to the role of producer, this time with Allen Lewis, Nichols in 1980 staged *Billy Bishop Goes to War* off Broadway at the Theatre de Lys before moving uptown to the Morosco. He directed *Lunch Hour* in 1980 and *Fools* in 1981 on Broadway, and he continued to be active in the theater as both a director and producer for most of the 1980s.

After an absence of more than seven years, Nichols returned to Hollywood with a vengeance, directing *Silkwood* (1983), the fact-based story of the mysterious death of Karen Silkwood, a worker at a plutonium plant who publicly questioned safety conditions. He worked again with the *Silkwood* star Meryl Streep in *Heartburn* (1986), and then he directed Matthew Broderick in the film version of *Biloxi Blues* (1988). Nichols remained active as a film director through the 1990s, turning out *Working Girl* (1988), *Postcards from the Edge* (1990), *Wolf* (1994), *The Birdcage*

(1996), and *Primary Colors* (1998). Nichols also reunited with May during the 1990s, playing engagements in a number of cities.

In his personal life, Nichols married the jazz singer Patricia Scott in 1957; they had a daughter before divorcing in 1960. Nichols married Margot Callas in 1963, and they broke up in 1974. His third marriage was to Annabel Davis-Goff, a screenwriter; the couple had two children. On 19 April 1988 Nichols married the television journalist Diane Sawyer.

A director of uncommon insight and talent, Nichols brought to the stage and screen some of the most culturally significant creations of the late twentieth century. His early years as half of the comedy duo of Nichols and May endowed him with "a sharp eye for the foibles of male-female relationships and a bitingly satirical attention to contemporary social pressures," according to *Cinemania*. In films such as *Who's Afraid of Virginia Woolf?* and *The Graduate,* Nichols got in touch with the hopes, fears, and aspirations of his audience as few directors have ever managed to do. Nichols continues to turn out films in the new millennium that may define their time equally as well as some of his earlier work.

★

For a valuable overview of Nichols and his early career, see H. Wayne Schuth, *Mike Nichols* (1978). For further information about both his life and work, see the *New York Times Magazine* (1 July 1967 and 27 May 1984); *Time* (9 May 1988); *Vanity Fair* (June 1994); *Interview* (Apr. 1998); and *Film Comment* (May 1999).

DON AMERMAN

NICHOLSON, Jack (*b.* 22 April 1937 in Neptune, New Jersey), actor, director, and screenwriter often described as the most charismatic and talented actor of his generation, winner of two Academy Awards for best actor and one for best supporting actor; recipient of several Academy Award nominations and other prestigious international prizes for his performances.

Nicholson's family background was recently defined as "a mystery with as many false clues as *Chinatown*," the 1974 Roman Polanski film in which Nicholson starred. Nicholson, the son of June Nicholson, an unwed, teenaged mother, was raised by his grandparents, Ethel May, a beauty parlor owner, and John Nicholson, a sign painter. He had one half-sister. When Nicholson was very young, his grandfather left the family. Nicholson attended high school in Neptune, New Jersey. At the age of seventeen, he traveled to California. Despite his plans to return East to attend college, he landed a job as an office boy in MGM's

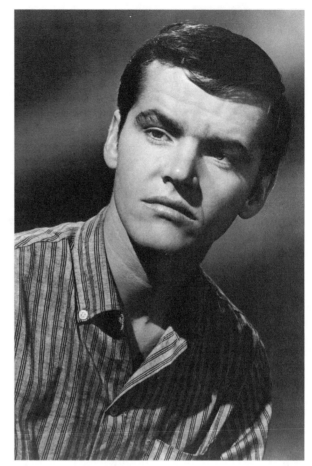

Jack Nicholson, 1963. THE KOBAL COLLECTION

animation department. In 1957, while in Los Angeles, Nicholson studied acting with Jeff Corey, one of the foremost acting instructors in Hollywood at that time; Nicholson also worked as an actor with the Players Ring Theatre.

Nicholson's debut as an actor happened on the fringes of the American film industry, where he was confined for the whole decade of the 1960s. He played alienated bikers or psychotic characters in horror films, a genre to which he later returned as an established star with Stanley Kubrick's *The Shining* (1980) and more grotesquely with George Miller's *The Witches of Eastwick* (1987) and Mike Nichols's *Wolf* (1994). Only when the values of the counterculture became more widely disseminated in American society was Nicholson able to achieve celebrity status. He was in his thirties when he finally became a star, a relatively late age for an actor endowed with his magnetism.

Nicholson's first film appearance is connected to the legendary producer and director of low-budget films, Roger Corman, who cast him in the title role of *Cry Baby Killer* (1958). After appearing in Irving Lerner's *Studs Lonigan*

(1960), an unsuccessful adaptation of James T. Farrell's radical immigrant saga, Nicholson continued to star in Corman's features for the next few years. He played a masochistic dental patient in *Little Shop of Horrors* (1960), followed by the role of Peter Lorre's troubled son in *The Raven* (1963), and finally costarred in *The Terror* (1963) with Boris Karloff. Nicholson subsequently acted in three features by Monte Hellman, another cult figure on the periphery of American cinema. He also wrote the script for Corman's hallucinogenic classic, *The Trip* (1968), and cowrote the cult movie, *The Head.* On 17 June 1962 Nicholson married Sandra Knight; the couple had one daughter before divorcing on 8 August 1968.

The films of the 1960s did little to enhance Nicholson's reputation, which underwent a major upsurge when, after turning down a role in *Bonnie and Clyde,* he replaced Rip Torn to play the character of George Hanson, a southern lawyer, in another countercultural cinematic manifesto, *Easy Rider* (1969). The incredible success of this road movie, enhanced by Nicholson's captivating, Academy Award–nominated performance as a drop-out lawyer, made Nicholson an icon of nonconformity for the Beatles-generation audiences who flocked to see this landmark feature of the New Hollywood. After the disappointing experience of Vincente Minnelli's *On a Clear Day You Can See Forever* (1970), in which his role was almost completely edited out, Nicholson starred in Bob Rafelson's *Five Easy Pieces* (1970), the film that assured his stardom. In this ideal epilogue to *Easy Rider* and the whole 1960s decade, Nicholson played the role of the former musician, Bobby Eroica Dupea, an older dropout than the other characters portrayed in *Easy Rider,* alienated from his own family and society as a whole. Dupea's journey northward to Alaska ends not in self-discovery but in a metaphorical death, making him yet another contemporary American male character marked by lack of identity and impotence. Nicholson revisited such depictions in many of his later films, from Mike Nichols's *Carnal Knowledge* (1971) to Michelangelo Antonioni's complex *Professione Reporter* (*The Passenger,* 1975). Costarring Karen Black and Susan Anspach (with whom Nicholson had a relationship and allegedly a son, born in 1970), *Five Easy Pieces* earned Nicholson his second Academy Award nomination, and his diner scene is a classic in film history.

By the end of the 1960s, which he began in relative obscurity, Nicholson had become an embodiment of the decade's dissatisfaction with the status quo. However, the challenges that Nicholson's characters bring to social conventions prove unsuccessful because of a typically American individualism and a consequent unwillingness to form attachments. In this light Dupea's final journey to Alaska in *Five Easy Pieces* should be read as an inversion of the myth of the road, a reestablishment of the American fascination

with the frontier, to which Nicholson had contributed the year before, with *Easy Rider.* Although Dupea invokes Huck Finn, "lighting out for the territory," he is no adolescent, and his final journey is intended as an illustration of his own failures.

Nicholson's best performances of the 1970s were built on his maverick persona established at the end of the 1960s, climaxing with his first Academy Award as the asylum patient Randall McMurphy in Milos Forman's *One Flew Over the Cuckoo's Nest* (1975). Like the private eye Jake Gittes in Polanski's stylish *Chinatown* (1974) or the sailor Billy Budduskey in Hal Ashby's *The Last Detail* (1973), ex-marine McMurphy is able to grasp the social injustices of his world but unable to confront them effectively.

In the early 1970s Nicholson started a seventeen-year relationship with Anjelica Huston, with whom he starred in John Huston's successful Mafia comedy, *Prizzi's Honor* (1985). The relationship ended in 1990 when Nicholson had a daughter with actress Rebecca Broussard. Broussard and Nicholson also had a son in 1992.

Even when his films were critical and commercial disasters and disappointed expectations, as in the case of Arthur Penn's *The Missouri Breaks* (1976), Nicholson's encounter with his role model Marlon Brando, Nicholson always remained immune to damage. Over the decades he has continued to exert his charisma on different generations of moviegoers, in spite of his turning down roles in important films such as *The Godfather* (1972), *The Sting* (1973), and *Apocalypse Now* (1979). Through the decades his cinematic persona has undergone a considerable change from the one he created during the 1960s and used so successfully during the early 1970s. *Terms of Endearment* (1983) and *As Good As It Gets* (1997), both directed by James L. Brooks, epitomize this shift. The two films, which gave Nicholson his second and third Academy Awards, portray a disreputable, middle-aged hero who is a significant departure from Nicholson's psychotic characters and alienated rebels. Both Garrett Breedlove (*Terms of Endearment*) and Melvin Udall (*As Good as it Gets*) are comic figures, devoid of the pathos of Nicholson's early characters. They are outsiders at the beginning of the filmic narrative, yet by the conclusion of both movies, they have been transformed into sensitive and more functional human beings.

Much like his characters, Jack Nicholson has successfully moved from the margins to the very center of the American film industry. Patrick McGilligan's biography of Nicholson speaks of the transition he has undergone, from the hero of the rebellious 1960s to the embodiment of social upward mobility and the rags-to-riches myth: "Jack Nicholson, one of the most accomplished actors and greatest motion picture stars of our time, is a success story as American as that of the log-splitter who became President."

★

Nicholson has been the subject of several biographies, including Robert David Crane and Christopher Fryer, *Jack Nicholson—Face to Face* (1975); David Downing, *Jack Nicholson: A Biography* (1984); two film biographies, Didier Sandre, *Jack Nicholson* (1981) and John Parker, *The Joker's Wild: The Biography of Jack Nicholson* (1991); Donald Shepherd, *Jack Nicholson: An Unauthorized Biography* (1991); and Patrick McGilligan, *Jack's Life: A Biography of Jack Nicholson* (1996). Critical studies include Norman Dickens, *Jack Nicholson: The Search for a Superstar* (1975); Bruce Braithwaite, *The Films of Jack Nicholson* (1977); Douglas Brode, *The Films of Jack Nicholson* (1990); and Mikita Brottman, ed., *Jack Nicholson: Movie Top Ten* (2000).

LUCA PRONO

NICKLAUS, Jack William (*b.* 21 January 1940 in Columbus, Ohio), prominent golfer who established himself during the 1960s as one of the sport's all-time greatest players at both the amateur and professional levels, as he won eight of the major championships and numerous other tournaments during the decade.

Nicklaus was one of two children born to Louis Charles Nicklaus, a pharmacist, and Helen Schoener, a housewife.

Jack Nicklaus posing with his World Series of Golf trophy, 1970. ARCHIVE PHOTOS, INC.

He began taking golf lessons at the age of ten, and just two years later he won the Ohio State Junior Championship. He qualified for his first United States Amateur tournament in 1955. At the age of sixteen Nicklaus won the Ohio State Open with scores of sixty-four and seventy-two on the final day, and he qualified for his first United States Open at the age of seventeen. In 1958, after his freshman year at Ohio State University, Nicklaus won the prestigious Trans-Mississippi Amateur tournament and also played in his first Professional Golf Association (PGA) event, the Rubber City Open in Akron, Ohio, where he finished in twelfth place. In 1959 Nicklaus was ready to begin establishing himself among golf's elite players, and that summer he won his first major championship, capturing the United States Amateur with a one-up victory over Charley Coe in the final match. Also that season Nicklaus played for the United States Walker Cup team in Scotland, reached the quarter-finals of the British Amateur, and successfully defended his title at the Trans-Mississippi.

On 23 July 1960 Nicklaus married his college sweetheart, Barbara Bash, and the couple eventually raised five children. That season he played inconsistently, being eliminated from the U.S. Amateur in the fourth round after finishing just two strokes behind the winner, Arnold Palmer, at the U.S. Open. But in September, Nicklaus set the tone for the rest of the 1960s as he won the individual title at the World Amateur Team Championship at the Merion Club near Philadelphia. Pacing the United States team to a runaway victory, he posted a stunning four-round score of 269, which was eighteen strokes lower than the mark previously posted there by Ben Hogan while winning the 1950 U.S. Open.

In 1961 Nicklaus compiled an impressive record in his last season as an amateur. He capped off his days of college golf by winning the Big Ten Conference title by twenty-two strokes in pacing Ohio State to the team championship, and followed this up by winning the individual championship at the National Collegiate Athletic Association (NCAA) tournament. Nicklaus also posted top ten finishes at the Masters (seventh place) and the U.S. Open (fourth), won the Western Amateur, and then finished off the year by sweeping to his second U.S. Amateur title, defeating Dudley Wysong eight and six in the final.

In November 1961 Nicklaus (who was five feet, eleven inches tall and weighed approximately 195 pounds at his peak) decided to leave Ohio State and become a full-time professional golfer on the PGA tour. He made his debut as a professional at the Los Angeles Open, the first event of the 1962 tour, and he finished in a tie for fiftieth place, which brought him a check for $33.33. His first good tournament as a pro came at the Phoenix Open, where he finished in a tie for second place and won $2,300, and later that spring he tied for first place in the Houston Classic before losing the play-off. Nicklaus then won the U.S. Open in an eighteen-hole play-off against Arnold Palmer, and in the fall he tacked on titles at the Seattle and Portland tourneys. Nicklaus finished as the third highest money winner for 1962 with $61,868, and he was voted the PGA's Rookie of the Year.

In 1963 Nicklaus notched five tournament championships and finished second on the money-winning list with $100,400. His highlights for 1963 included winning the Masters (shooting 286) and the PGA (279), along with a third place finish at the British Open. In 1964, now being referred to as "Fat Jack" by the media because of the weight he had put on, Nicklaus notched four tournament wins on the tour and also captured the Australian Open and Canada Cup titles. He finished as the tour's top money winner and scoring champion for 1964, despite his frustration at finishing in second place or tied for second in the Masters, British Open, and PGA tournaments.

With Arnold Palmer and Gary Player, Nicklaus was now regarded as one of the world's premier golfers. From 1964 to 1967 he joined his two rivals in the television series *The Big Three,* in which the trio played competitive matches on some of the world's most famous courses. Meanwhile, Nicklaus posted another of his best seasons of the decade in 1965 as he won five tournaments, including the Masters, in which he set a new scoring record with a total of 271, while also finishing on top of the money-winning and scoring average lists. That season he posted an amazing twenty top ten finishes in twenty-four tournaments.

Nicklaus captured three tournaments on the 1966 PGA tour while finishing second in money winnings, but the highlights of the season came with his victories in two major championships—the Masters (288) and the British Open (282). In his last blockbuster season of the decade in 1967, Nicklaus piled up another five tournament championships while finishing on top of the money-winning list, along with garnering the PGA's Player of the Year award. He also won another U.S. Open championship in 1967 after shooting a blistering sixty-five in the final round.

The 1968 season began a frustrating run of four years during which Nicklaus played well and won some tournaments on the tour yet struggled in the all-important major championships, winning just the 1970 British Open and the 1971 PGA. In 1968 he won two tournaments on the tour, along with the Australian Open, yet he had good chances to win at least six other events. Three tournament wins on the tour and third place in money winnings marked his 1969 season, but his tie for sixth place at the British Open was easily his top finish in the majors.

In 1970, frustrated by the past two seasons, Nicklaus began to lose weight; the "Fat Jack" image was soon gone forever. In the early 1970s he quickly reestablished himself as professional golf's most dominant player on his way to a career total of twenty major championships before joining the Senior PGA tour in 1990. With a powerful swing that allowed him to hit the ball a long way, while also blending in a deft touch that made him one of the best players around the greens, Nicklaus unquestionably established himself during the 1960s as one of golf's all-time great players.

★

Relatively early in his career, Nicklaus coauthored an autobiography with Herbert Warren Wind, *The Greatest Game of All: My Life in Golf* (1969), and then advanced the story with *On and Off the Fairway: A Pictorial Autobiography* (1978). Additional information can be found in the entry "Jack Nicklaus" in Peter Alliss, *The Who's Who of Golf* (1983). Throughout his career Nicklaus has authored or coauthored an extensive list of golf instructional books, including such titles as *Golf My Way* (1974) and *Jack Nicklaus' Playing Lessons* (1981).

RAYMOND SCHMIDT

NIEBUHR, Reinhold (*b.* 21 June 1892 in Wright City, Missouri; *d.* 1 June 1971 in Stockbridge, Massachusetts), influential theologian known for his application of Christian doctrine to contemporary social and political conditions.

The son of Gustav and Lydia (Hosto) Niebuhr, Reinhold moved with his family to Lincoln, Illinois, in 1902, where

Reinhold Niebuhr. ARCHIVE PHOTOS, INC.

his father, an immigrant preacher in the German Evangelical Synod of North America, had accepted a pastorate. In 1907 Niebuhr enrolled in Elmhurst College and then studied for the ministry at Eden Theological Seminary. Upon graduating from Eden in 1913, Niebuhr was ordained and planned to attend Yale Divinity School. But his father's unexpected death, his limited mastery of English, and Yale's refusal to accept his degree from Eden temporarily dimmed his prospects. Niebuhr overcame these disadvantages and graduated with a master's degree in June 1915.

That same year he began his tenure as pastor at Bethel Church in Detroit. By the time he left Bethel in 1928 to join the faculty at Union Theological Seminary in New York City, Niebuhr, with the help of his mother and his sister Hulda, had transformed the church from the smallest in the synod to a flourishing, vigorous congregation. While teaching at Union, Niebuhr elaborated and refined a theology of "Christian realism" in such major works as *Moral Man and Immoral Society* (1932), *The Nature and Destiny of Man* (two volumes, 1941 and 1943), and *The Irony of American History* (1952).

Niebuhr argued that Christians were obligated to engage in the affairs of the world and even to resist evil by force and violence if necessary. At the same time, they had to realize that human progress was limited by the reality of sin. Individuals, classes, and nations, however confident of their virtue, repeatedly succumbed to arrogance, venality, and the will to power. To think that any one person or government possessed a monopoly on truth and, therefore, had the right to impose their vision on society was a treacherous and destructive manifestation of pride that Niebuhr called "utopianism."

A stroke in 1952 curtailed Niebuhr's activities and brought a steady decline in his health. By the early 1960s he had developed a chronic colon ailment, for which doctors never identified a physical cause. In addition, he endured severe bladder frequency. His slow recovery from a prostate operation in the fall of 1963 further darkened his mood. Yet, through the ongoing efforts of his wife, Ursula (née Keppel-Compton), whom he had married in December 1931, Niebuhr maintained as much a semblance of an active life as his health permitted.

Following his retirement from Union in 1960, Niebuhr held visiting appointments at Harvard during 1961–1962, at Princeton during the autumn of 1962, and at Barnard in the spring of 1963. Although he added nothing significant to the corpus of his writings during the 1960s, he offered extensive commentary on the major figures, issues, and events of the day. Niebuhr remained ambivalent about the Kennedy administration. Kennedy's sense of the responsibilities of power endeared him to Niebuhr, but some of Kennedy's policies did not. Niebuhr, for example, thought the Cuban embargo a mistake because, as he wrote, it "has enabled Castro to blame all his economic problems" on the United States.

Niebuhr's steadfast anticommunism was unwavering during the 1960s, even as he modified his position on the use of nuclear weapons. In the 1950s Niebuhr entertained the possibility of deploying nuclear weapons to halt Soviet expansion in Europe. By the 1960s, however, he declared that "the first use of the nuclear weapon is morally abhorrent and must be resisted." After unleashing the murderous power of nuclear weapons, Niebuhr asked, would a civilization, even in victory, "have enough moral health to survive?"

Tragedy haunted Niebuhr during the 1960s. The sudden death of his brother, Richard, in July 1961, only days before the wedding of Niebuhr's daughter, Elisabeth, left him distraught. Exhausted and sad, he abandoned in August 1963 the book about communism and democracy on which he had been at work for several years. Kennedy's assassination in November compounded his grief, even as it awakened him from his personal sorrows.

Niebuhr was consoled only that "Kennedy's sacrificial death" would promote the cause of civil rights, which for Niebuhr marked a crucial turning point in American history. Never preoccupied with race, Niebuhr nonetheless pleaded throughout the 1960s for an end to discrimination, insisting that blacks be accorded the respect to which all human beings were entitled. When in the mid-1960s black militants intensified their demands for justice and equality, Niebuhr cautioned against "violent rebellion" and championed the civil disobedience of the Reverend Martin Luther King, Jr., as an alternative to the revolutionary ardor of Stokely Carmichael and H. Rap Brown. Niebuhr predicted, however, that the "despair and hopelessness" overwhelming young blacks would thrust American society into decades of racial tumult.

Regarding Barry Goldwater as a reckless fanatic, Niebuhr endorsed Lyndon Johnson for president in 1964 and that September received from Johnson the Presidential Medal of Freedom. But as early as 1965 Niebuhr began to admonish Johnson for escalating American involvement in Vietnam, a war Niebuhr believed the United States could not win. He considered "the policy of restraining Asian Communism by sheer military might . . . fantastic" and damaging to the "moral prestige" of the United States.

Niebuhr entered into one final public controversy in 1969, when Richard Nixon instituted Sunday worship services at the White House and invited ministers from various faiths to preside. In "The King's Chapel and the King's Court," which appeared in *Christianity and Crisis* on 4 August 1969, Niebuhr satirized political self-satisfaction and religious complicity. "It is wonderful," he wrote, "what a simple White House invitation will do to dull the critical faculties." Hate mail poured in from the disciples of Billy

Graham, whom Niebuhr had singled out for special reproof and, at the insistence of Nixon aide John Ehrlichman, the FBI opened a dossier on Niebuhr.

Weakened by pneumonia and a pulmonary embolism, Niebuhr died peacefully at home at the age of seventy-eight. The moral life, he once suggested, was neither tranquil nor gratifying. "For me," he wrote, summarizing a lifetime of study, reflection, and prayer, "the experience of faith is a total attitude toward the mystery of God and life, which includes commitment, love, and hope . . . beyond the conscious designs and contrivances of men."

★

In addition to the sources mentioned in the text, see Ursula M. Niebuhr, ed., *Remembering Reinhold Niebuhr: Letters of Reinhold and Ursula M. Niebuhr* (1991). Richard Wightman Fox, *Reinhold Niebuhr: A Biography* (1985), is indispensable. Hans Hoffman, *The Theology of Reinhold Niebuhr* (1956), Gordon Harland, *The Thought of Reinhold Niebuhr* (1960), June Bingham, *Courage to Change: An Introduction to the Life and Thought of Reinhold Niebuhr* (1961), Ronald Stone, *Reinhold Niebuhr: Prophet to Politician* (1972), Paul Merkley, *Reinhold Niebuhr: A Political Account* (1975), and Dennis McCann, *Christian Realism and Liberation Theology: Political Theologies in Conflict* (1981), remain useful if flawed accounts of Niebuhr's life and thought. Two anthologies, Nathan Scott, ed., *The Legacy of Reinhold Niebuhr* (1975), and Charles W. Kegley, ed., *Reinhold Niebuhr: His Religious, Social, and Political Thought* (rev. ed. 1984), contain essays of great value. For a thoughtful analysis of Niebuhr's continuing relevance, see Wilfred M. McClay, "The Continuing Irony of American History," in *First Things* (Feb. 2002). An obituary is in the *New York Times* (2 June 1971).

MARK G. MALVASI

NIKOLAIS, Theodore Alwin ("Nik") (*b.* 25 November 1910 in Southington, Connecticut; *d.* 8 May 1993 in New York City), choreographer whose theory of decentralization and imaginative use of projected lights, costumes, and props were hallmarks of his theatrical productions.

Nikolais, the youngest of six siblings, began to study piano at an early age. In 1929 he launched his career in theater as an accompanist at the Westport Movie House, but talking pictures soon forced him to look elsewhere for work, so he began to accompany dance classes in nearby Hartford, Connecticut. In 1933 he attended what he later termed a "life-changing" dance performance by the German choreographer Mary Wigman, who inspired him to study dance. From 1935 to 1937 he served as the director of the Hartford Parks Marionette Theatre. His work with the puppets provided him with the foundation for what he would later call his theory of decentralization: that "art is motion, not emo-

tion." In 1937 he founded his first dance company and school in Hartford.

Nikolais served overseas in the Army Signal Corps from 1942 until the end of World War II, and in 1948 he became director of Henry Street Playhouse in New York City. One year later he formed the Playhouse Dance Company in a studio on the Lower East Side. Though in a location somewhat removed from the center of the dance community, this suited Nikolais's tastes. This group later became the Nikolais Dance Theatre.

Nikolais met Murray Louis at Colorado College in 1949, and the two began a lifetime partnership, which included choreographing works together. Louis was also a dancer in the Nikolais Dance Theatre, even after he formed his own company in 1953. Also at Colorado College, Nikolais served as dance assistant for the German expressionist Hanya Holm.

In his choreography, Nikolais moved away from what he considered the self-absorption, and the tendency for dances to be allegorical, that had prevailed in the 1940s. He championed the idea of abstract gestures, unique and defensible in and of themselves, and neither interpretive nor derived from ballet or jazz. He emphasized the difference between movement and motion, defining motion as intentional movement, or the act of moving with purpose. Therefore, any action could constitute dance.

Nikolais also maintained that dance need not be accompanied by, and would not even be enhanced by, emotion. This he learned from working with puppets while at the Hartford Parks Marionette Theatre. It was an aspect of his work that did not always sit well with the early critics, who often deemed his creations "inhuman." However, his piece *Kaleidoscope* (1956) was considered "evidence of a new force in the modern dance world."

Nikolais continuously explored the concepts of space and time in his work. Unrestricted by allegory or realism, time took on new dimension and offered new possibilities. Key to his works was his theory of decentralization, in which man was part of, but not central to, his environment. His dancers did not represent human characters on stage. The dancer was one aspect in the interdependent relationship—Nikolais labeled it a *polygamy*—between the props, the sets, the lights, the music, and the motion.

He designed intricate sets and costumes to challenge the dancers and to further remove an audience's temptation to view them as humans. The props and costumes required his dancers to overcome obstacles as they explored space and time through pure motion. Often the costumes extended or distorted the dancers' forms, and occasionally completely obscured them.

In *Imago* (1963) the dancers were clad in small cylindrical headpieces reminiscent of helmets and had long articulated arm extensions ending in flat discs. Thus attired, they danced to a score of dissonant electronic sounds against a backdrop of cobalt blue. The music Nikolais used was all recorded: with the aid of a Guggenheim Fellowship, he purchased Robert Moog's first synthesizer in the 1960s.

Sanctum (1964) opens with a man swinging from a trapeze. Later, dancers appear inside stretchy fabric ovals, which flex open and shut suggestively as they move. In another section, the dancers maneuver across the stage, carrying long silver poles. Finally, several dancers seem to be trapped inside open-sided, cage-like boxes with flexible sides from which they struggle to free themselves.

In *Tower* (1965) the dancers emerge with sections of metal fence, which they proceed to hitch together to form a tower. Then the tower, in a flash of light and sound, is destroyed.

Nikolais was considered a pioneer in the fields of lighting as well as costumes. He was interested in lighting the movement, not the dancers themselves, so he generally lit the dances from below, and often projected images (which he painted himself) onto them. His use of projected lights is considered by some to have been a precursor for the discotheque scene that emerged in the 1970s.

In *Tent* (1968) a large expanse of white cloth is at once a set, a prop, and a dancer. The dancers carry the cloth on stage, assist in raising it, dance beneath it, around it, and under it, and finally appear above it wearing masks with just their legs showing beneath the cloth "like a grove of swaying stalks with heads," according to Don McDonogh. As the tent lifts, projected stripes and colors on the dancers' bodies make them appear naked and vulnerable. The tent occupies the same level of humanness as the dancers, and is thus equal to them in their environment.

The Nikolais Dance Theatre performed infrequently in the 1960s in New York City but toured extensively throughout the United States. Nikolais's 1968 tour of France catapulted him to world fame and ultimately led him, at the invitation of the French National Ministry of Culture, to form the Centre Nationale de Danse Contemporaine in Anger, France. Although he had retired as a dancer in 1950, Nikolais continued to choreograph until 1992, the year his last piece, *Aurora,* with music by John Scoville, premiered at the Joyce Theatre in New York City. He died of cancer at Cabrini Medical Center in New York City.

Nikolais took the crisp lines of Wigman and Holm, clothed them in stretch jersey, bathed them in projected images, and surrounded them in synthesized sound. An evening with the Nikolais Dance Theatre was an experience unlike any other.

★

Marcia B. Siegel, ed., "Nik: A Documentary," in *Dance Perspectives* (1971), offers some background information on Nikolais and is richly illustrated with color photos of his works, along with many personal sketches. Don McDonogh, *The Complete Guide to Modern Dance* (1976), gives detailed descriptions of some of Nikolais's dances. Elinor Rogosin, "Discovering Alwin Nikolais," in *Conversations with American Choreographers* (1980), explores his theory of decentralization and motion versus emotion.

KATHARINE FISHER BRITTON

NIN, Anaïs (*b.* 21 February 1903 in Neuilly, France; *d.* 14 January 1977 in Los Angeles, California), noted writer best known for her infamous *Diary of Anaïs Nin,* the first volume of which appeared in 1966.

Nin's official name at birth was Angela Anaïs Juana Antolina Rosa Edelmira Nin y Culmell, but everyone called her Anaïs. She was the only daughter and oldest of three children of Joaquin Nin y Castellanos, a Spanish composer and pianist, and Rosa (Culmell) de Nin, a singer of French and Danish descent. Nin spent her early childhood in France, but after her father abandoned the family, she moved with her mother and brothers to New York City in 1914. During the journey to America, Nin began recording her thoughts, feelings, and observations in a collection of letters she intended to send to her father to lure him to America. Her mother dissuaded her from sending them,

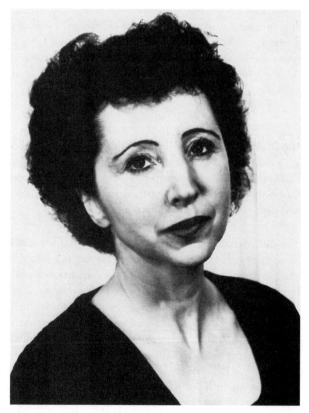

Anaïs Nin. AP/WIDE WORLD PHOTOS

saying they were too valuable. These letters would eventually form the basis for her *Diary.*

Once settled in the United States, Nin enrolled in public school but disliked its rigid structure and discipline. She dropped out in her teens after a teacher suggested that she use less literary and more colloquial language. She continued her self-education by reading voraciously. After a brief stint as a model, Nin married the banker Hugh Guiler in 1923 and moved to Louveciennes, a suburb of Paris. There she wrote her first book, *D. H. Lawrence: An Unprofessional Study* (1932), which attracted the attention of the novelist Henry Miller, a man who would leave an indelible mark on her life and writings. After reading her *Diary,* Miller recognized its literary potential. When World War II began, Nin and her husband returned to the United States, where she continued writing. No publisher would print her works, so she bought a printing press and published them herself. The critic Edmund Wilson praised *Under a Glass Bell* (1944), but except for that plaudit Nin struggled to gain recognition. In 1952 Nin became a naturalized U.S. citizen.

Her luck changed in the early 1960s when Alan Swallow, an independent publisher, agreed to reprint several of her novels in an omnibus edition. While this effort went virtually unnoticed by critics and sold few copies, her *Collages,* which appeared in 1964, fared better with readers and was even chosen by *Time* magazine as one of the best books of that year. That same year Nin's work created quite a stir on the international front. The French translation of one of her early novels, *A Spy in the House of Love,* appeared, and Nin became an overnight celebrity. Marguerite Duras, a French novelist and filmmaker, expressed an interest in adapting the novel for the screen, but the project never materialized, leaving Nin disappointed and in need of money. *A Spy in the House of Love* appeared in English as one of five parts of *Cities of the Interior* (1961), Nin's most ambitious and critically admired work besides her *Diaries.*

Nin then turned her energy and attention to her diaries and submitted a heavily edited draft of part of the document to publishers. This time Harcourt Brace showed interest, agreeing to publish the first volume, which covered Nin's years in Paris from 1931 to 1934. Her editor insisted that she edit the work yet more extensively, and she complied. But editing was never an easy task for Nin, and this time her job was complicated because many people, her husband included, objected to being mentioned in the text and asked to be removed. When the first volume appeared in 1966, it was hailed by many critics as a significant literary achievement. Jean Garrigue, writing for the *New York Times Book Review,* was particularly impressed. She described it as a "rich, various and fascinating work." Readers agreed and were attracted to the work's poetic fluidity, vivid descriptions of the Parisian art scene of the 1930s, insightful portraits of friends and acquaintances, and the delicate expression of Nin's preoccupations and feelings and her journey toward self-discovery.

Nin's life took on new meaning after *Diary* appeared. The fame and recognition in America, for which she had so desperately yearned, finally had become a reality. People all over the country asked her to give lectures, grant interviews, and attend book signings. She honored many of these requests, but she also spent time socializing and responding to the massive amount of mail she received. The rest of Nin's time was spent traveling. She commuted regularly between her homes in New York and Los Angeles, trying to maintain two separate existences. This double life was necessary because Nin was a bigamist, having secretly married Rupert William Pole in 1955. She had kept this secret from her unsuspecting husbands for more than a decade, but now her celebrity and the strain of duplicity became too much. Nin told Pole the truth, and their marriage was officially annulled in 1966. Their relationship remained intact, however, and Pole lived with Nin until she died. (Nin never had children by either husband.)

In 1967 and 1969 Nin saw the second and third volumes of her *Diary* printed. With each volume, critical opinion was increasingly unfavorable, and sales were poor at best. Nin's enthusiasm and commitment to her art remained constant, however, and she tirelessly promoted her *Diary* at every opportunity. When the paperback edition of the *Diary* appeared in 1973, sales were brisk. The public, it seemed, was still intrigued by Nin and wanted to know more about her. They were given more that same year in the documentary film *Anaïs Observed,* produced by Robert Synder.

Although she had cancer in the last years of her life, Nin kept up a frenetic schedule. She traveled, made personal appearances, granted interviews, gave talks, and even taught, and her work and literary accomplishments did not go unrecognized. In 1974 she was inducted into the American Academy and Institute of Arts and Letters. In 1976 the *Los Angeles Times* named her Woman of the Year, and several of her friends—the writers Henry Miller, Lawrence Durrell, and Christopher Isherwood—endorsed her for the Nobel Prize in literature. On 14 January 1977 Nin succumbed to cancer at the Cedars-Sinai Hospital in Los Angeles, California. Memorial services were held in her honor in several cities in the United States. Following her request, she was cremated, and her ashes were scattered at sea.

Nin's novels, which often were filled with strong female protagonists, explored issues as varied as biological impulses, sexual entanglements, psychological angst, self-identity, and the place of women in contemporary society. Her writings struck a resonant chord in the 1960s with many readers. Feminists could identify with Nin and her female protagonists, who tried to find personal and artistic fulfillment in a male-dominated society. The overtly erotic nature of Nin's writings also attracted readers whose sexual attitudes and mores were changing in light of the nascent sexual revolution.

★

A collection of Nin's diaries, correspondence, manuscripts, and related papers dating from 1903 to 1977 are located at the Department of Special Collections, University Research Library, University of California, Los Angeles. Correspondence and some writings dating from 1969 to 1992 (including correspondence between her publisher and literary agent after her death) are housed at the Department of Special Collections, McFarlin Library, University of Tulsa. Many of Nin's fiction manuscripts are located at the Department of Special Collections, Deering Library, Northwestern University, in Evanston, Illinois. An excellent biographical work is Deirdre Bair, *Anaïs Nin* (1995). See also Jean Garrigue, "The Self behind the Selves," *New York Times Book Review* (24 Apr. 1966). An obituary is in the *New York Times* (16 Jan. 1977).

LARRY SEAN KINDER

NIRENBERG, Marshall Warren (*b.* 10 April 1927 in New York City), biochemist who won the 1968 Nobel Prize in physiology or medicine for his role in deciphering the genetic code. This key research, done in the 1960s, allowed biologists to begin to manipulate genes and thus opened the field of genetic engineering that blossomed at the end of the twentieth century.

Nirenberg's parents, Harry and Minerva (Bykowsky) Nirenberg, moved to Florida when he was ten years old. Nirenberg attended the University of Florida, receiving a B.S. in 1948 and a master's degree in biology four years later. He earned a doctorate in biochemistry at the University of Michigan in 1957. In the same year he began research at the National Institutes of Health (NIH) in Bethesda, Maryland. There he met Perola Zaltzman, a Brazilian biochemist, whom he married on 14 July 1961. In 1962 he was appointed head of the Section of Biochemical Genetics at NIH. Nirenberg has remained at NIH his entire career; he eventually became chief of the Laboratory of Biochemical Genetics in the National Heart, Lung, and Blood Institute.

In the late 1950s Nirenberg became one of the group of biochemists exploring the question of how the information in the molecule of heredity, deoxyribonucleic acid (DNA), is used by the body to make protein. Scientists were just realizing that another molecule, ribonucleic acid (RNA), was a go-between in this process, but the particulars were still unknown. DNA is a long, double-stranded molecule made up of four kinds of building blocks called *nucleotides*. The nucleotide sequence in DNA determines that in RNA, which is made up of four slightly different nucleotides. RNA, however, is often single-stranded, as Nirenberg demonstrated in his research.

Marshall W. Nirenberg. THE LIBRARY OF CONGRESS

In 1960 a German postdoctoral student, Heinrich Matthaei, joined Nirenberg, and together they studied RNA and how it is used in making protein. They devised a "cell-free" system by purifying bacteria of all the chemical components needed for protein synthesis, which is the process by which the information in the RNA nucleotide sequence is used to create the bonded string of amino acids that forms a protein. Protein synthesis involves using the information in one linear molecule, RNA, to make another linear molecule, protein. The simple system in a test tube that Nirenberg and Matthaei created was key to their further progress. They originally used RNA obtained from cells, but then they created a synthetic RNA molecule that was just a string of molecules of one nucleotide, uracil, rather than a molecule containing all four nucleotides. They found that using this synthetic RNA resulted in the creation of a protein containing only one of the twenty amino acids, namely phenylalanine. For theoretical reasons, biochemists had predicted that the genetic code would be a triplet code and that a string of three nucleotides would code for one amino acid. Subsequent work by Nirenberg and others verified this prediction. This meant that the RNA triplet of UUU (a string of three uracil nucleotides) was the code for phenylalanine.

Published in 1961, this momentous research showed it is possible to decipher the genetic code, and it put Nirenberg, a shy man, in the limelight. Over the next several years he and his colleagues synthesized a large number of other synthetic RNA molecules containing various combinations of nucleotides and thus painstakingly worked out much of the rest of the genetic code. Mathematically, positing four nucleotides in groups of three, taking into account the order within each triplet, there are sixty-four possible combinations, each a different nucleotide triplet code. Because there are only twenty amino acids, it is not surprising that most correspond with more than one triplet code. It turns out that two of the triplets do not code for any amino acid; instead, they are "stop" messages that signal the end of the sequence.

Nirenberg was joined in the deciphering effort by a number of researchers working in other laboratories. Most notable among these were the biochemist Har Gobind Khorana, who later shared the Nobel Prize with Nirenberg, and Severo Ochoa, who had already won the Nobel Prize for other research. By 1966 all sixty-four triplets had been deciphered. Nirenberg and Khorana were awarded the Nobel Prize a mere two years later, indicating the significance of the work. In fact, at the time, the work was considered the most important research performed in molecular biology since James Watson and Francis Crick had identified the structure of the DNA molecule in 1953. Robert W. Holley, who had discovered the role of another type of RNA in protein synthesis, shared the prize with Nirenberg and Khorana.

Like many of those who made important contributions to molecular biology, Nirenberg soon abandoned work on bacteria, figuring that the major discoveries in the field had been made. He then investigated what he considered the next great frontier in biological research: the development of the nervous system. In the late 1980s he studied fruit fly development, a major focus of research at the time. *Drosophila homeobox* genes are important in setting down the basic structure of the fly in early development; Nirenberg discovered four new ones. He moved on to studying molecular mechanisms that regulate gene expression during embryonic development, particularly with fruit flies and mice.

In the years after receiving the Nobel Prize, Nirenberg lent his support to a number of causes he saw as important to the future of science and of society. He advocated strong governmental support for research, and in 1992 he joined with an international group of 1,500 scientists in signing the "World Scientists' Warning to Humanity," which dealt with the dangers of the global environmental problems.

Nirenberg's careful dissection of the process of protein synthesis in the early 1960s and his first steps in breaking the genetic code were crucial to the development of the field of genetic engineering. His work was an essential contribution to the goal of manipulating genes, so in a very real sense the efforts of twenty-first–century scientists to engineer crops and genetic therapies for human disease are a direct outcome of his research.

★

Nirenberg's papers are held by the National Library of Medicine (NLM). Many are digitally available on the Marshall Nirenberg Papers Web site, part of the Profiles in Science Web site of NLM (2000), which can be found at <http://profiles.nlm.nih.gov/>. Biographical essays on Nirenberg appear in *Current Biography* (1965) and *Modern Scientists and Engineers* (1980). Carla Mecoli-Kamp's "Marshall Warren Nirenberg" is in *Notable Twentieth-Century Scientists* (1995).

Maura C. Flannery

NIXON, Richard Milhous (*b.* 9 January 1913 in Yorba Linda, California; *d.* 22 April 1994 in New York City), thirty-seventh president of the United States, who enjoyed success during his first term, particularly in foreign affairs, but was forced to resign in 1974 because of his involvement in the Watergate scandal.

Nixon was born in the small town of Yorba Linda in Orange County, California, in 1913, the second of the five sons of Francis Anthony (Frank) Nixon, a farmer and grocery store owner, and Hannah Milhous Nixon, a homemaker whose Quaker religion the family adopted.

Nixon grew up in a small, Sears kit house without electricity or running water. His father experienced failure in several businesses until he settled down in nearby East Whittier as proprietor of a service station and grocery store. Nixon began working at an early age both inside and outside the home to help support the family. Nonetheless, he was able to find time for his studies, earning valedictorian status in eighth grade and finishing third in his high school class, second at Whittier College (1930–1934), and third at Duke University Law School (1934–1937), which he attended on scholarship. He was also a successful school politician, widely admired for his leadership abilities, prize-winning debate skills, and photographic memory. Paradoxically, he was a shy and bookish fellow who had difficulty forging intimate relationships.

After failing to secure a position in New York City with

President Richard M. Nixon. CORBIS CORPORATION (BELLEVUE)

the Federal Bureau of Investigation (FBI) in 1937, Nixon returned to Whittier to work in the law firm Wingert and Bewley, where he was made a partner within a year, and began to dabble in Republican politics. In 1938, while acting in a community theater production, he met Patricia Ryan, a schoolteacher; for him it was love at first sight. Born Thelma Catherine Ryan in a miner's shack in Ely, Nevada, in 1912, Pat was a graduate of the University of Southern California who had worked in New York City and as an extra in Hollywood films. After being pursued by a dogged Nixon for two years, she married him in 1940. They had two children—Tricia, who was born in 1946, and Julie, born in 1948. Although Pat worked loyally and quite effectively in campaigns and later as first lady, she was never happy with the rough-and-tumble of politics and the glare of publicity that fell on her private life. On several occasions her husband promised her he would take up a new profession.

After serving in the Office of Price Administration for several months in 1942, where he developed a strong distaste for government bureaucracy, Nixon enlisted in the U.S. Navy, where he was commissioned as a lieutenant and eventually rose to the rank of lieutenant commander. During World War II he served in the Pacific theater in Bougainville and Green Island. Even though he did not see combat, he took on the sobriquet the "Fighting Quaker"

when he ran for Congress in 1946. He answered the call from Republicans in his old Twelfth Congressional District in Orange County for a candidate to challenge the veteran Democratic representative, Horace Jeremiah ("Jerry") Voorhis. Nixon ran in support of "practical liberalism" as an "antidote to . . . New Deal idealism." In a very controversial campaign full of dirty tricks and mudslinging that blemished Nixon's reputation forever, he defeated Voorhis by a 57 percent to 43 percent margin. His defenders contended that Voorhis gave as good as he got and that, in any event, Nixon's tactics were not that unusual in the blood sport of California politics.

As a first-term congressman Nixon served on the House Committee on Un-American Activities (HUAC), where he was a voice of relative moderation, and the House Education and Labor Committee, where he was one of the architects of the Taft-Hartley Act. More important was his fact-finding mission to war-torn Europe in 1947, during which he developed a lifelong interest in foreign affairs and a belief in internationalism that stood in sharp contrast to the isolationism and unilateralism of many of his Republican colleagues. The energetic young congressman became famous in 1948 through his sensational work on HUAC investigating Alger Hiss, a former State Department official who was charged with espionage for the Soviet Union. Hiss was ultimately found guilty of perjury and sentenced to a five-year prison term. For many years the case was a cause célèbre among liberals and radicals who, it now appears erroneously, accused Nixon and the FBI of railroading an innocent Hiss.

Unopposed for reelection to the House in 1948, Nixon ran against Helen Gahagan Douglas for the U.S. Senate in 1950 in another famously scurrilous campaign during which opponents began calling him "Tricky Dick," a nickname that dogged him throughout his career. As in 1946, both sides played rough, but many Americans later remembered Nixon's celebrated attack on the liberal Douglas as a "Pink Lady" who was implicitly close to being a full-blown "Red" or Communist. Nixon won by almost 700,000 votes, the largest plurality of any senatorial candidate in 1950. The second youngest senator at the time, he generally supported President Harry Truman's foreign policy of containment, especially in Europe, while opposing Fair Deal domestic politics and assailing corruption in the executive branch. In 1952, because of his popularity among Republicans, his perceived conservatism and fervent anticommunism, his youth, and his western background, Nixon emerged as the ideal vice-presidential candidate to serve as a counterpoint to the older, more moderate, and eastern-oriented party standard-bearer, General Dwight D. Eisenhower.

In the 1952 campaign Nixon took the partisan low road while Eisenhower stayed above the fray. Nixon labeled the Democratic candidate, Adlai Stevenson, "Adlai the appeaser . . . who got a Ph.D. degree from [Secretary of State Dean] Acheson's College of Cowardly Containment." During the campaign he became involved in a potentially career-ending scandal when journalists discovered that he had a private "slush fund" from wealthy backers to help support his campaigning. With many Republican leaders calling for his resignation from the ticket and with Eisenhower wavering, Nixon took the unusual tack of going on live television to defend himself in what came to be called the "Checkers Speech" because of his reference to the little dog his daughters received as a gift that he refused to return to his benefactors. Although highbrow critics lambasted the performance as maudlin and mawkish, most of the public loved it, especially the Republicans, who convinced Eisenhower to retain Nixon on the ticket. They took 55 percent of the popular vote in 1952 and swept the electoral college by a 442 to 89 margin.

Nixon was an unusually active vice president, especially helpful to Eisenhower as a liaison between the White House and the Republicans in Congress. During Eisenhower's three major illnesses, a heart attack in 1955, ileitis in 1956, and a stroke in 1957, Nixon handled his potentially awkward position diplomatically. In 1958 he and the president worked out formal procedures for future presidential disabilities that looked to some degree like the Twenty-fifth Amendment to the Constitution, which was ratified in 1967.

Yet despite Nixon's generally exemplary performance, Eisenhower contemplated dropping him from the ticket in 1956 because his fierce partisanship and rough political style made him a lightning rod for attacks by Democrats, and also because the president believed that he needed a running mate with more experience in government. Nor was Eisenhower especially impressed with his vice president's leadership abilities or his personal maturity. But Nixon remained on the ticket in 1956, and he and Eisenhower beat Stevenson again with an impressive 57 percent of the vote and swept the electoral college by a 457 to 73 margin. During the second term Nixon made headlines with his activities in the international arena, bravely confronting violent demonstrators in Latin America in May 1958, standing in for the president in April 1959 in a meeting with the new Cuban leader, Fidel Castro, and trading rhetorical jabs in a much-publicized "kitchen debate" with Soviet premier Nikita Khrushchev in Moscow in July 1959.

Although the leading candidate for the Republican presidential nomination in 1960, Nixon faced stiff competition from the moderate branch of the party led by New York governor Nelson Rockefeller and from the fast-growing conservative branch led by Arizona senator Barry Goldwater. He won the nomination on the first ballot at the Chicago convention in July after earlier making a deal with Rockefeller called "the Compact of Fifth Avenue," in which

he moved toward the moderates' positions on many issues. His selection of a running mate, former Massachusetts senator Henry Cabot Lodge, Jr., was ill-advised, as Lodge turned out to be a weak and indifferent campaigner. Eisenhower was not entirely happy with Nixon's campaign, in which the vice president suggested that he would do things differently from his mentor when he reached the White House. For his part Nixon confronted a recession that he thought might have been eased had Eisenhower adopted different economic strategies. In addition, he was not helped when the president, who was asked in August to name one policy that his vice president initiated, responded flippantly, "If you give me a week, I might think of one. I don't remember."

Nixon's opponent, Massachusetts senator John F. Kennedy, was a charismatic candidate burdened by his Catholic faith and his relatively undistinguished résumé based upon his role as a backbencher in the House, which he entered the same year as Nixon, and the Senate, to which he was elected in 1952. Nixon unwittingly helped Kennedy establish his gravitas by agreeing to an unprecedented series of four televised debates during which the intelligent and media-savvy Democrat demonstrated that he could hold his own with the more experienced, though far less photogenic, vice president. On the eve of the election Kennedy picked up the support of many Republican African Americans after he intervened publicly to try to protect Dr. Martin Luther King, Jr., who had been arrested during a civil rights demonstration. He needed all the votes he could get, since he won the popular vote by the slimmest of margins, 49.7 to 49.5 percent, and the electoral vote by 303 to 219. The Republicans cried foul, contending that there had been widespread ballot-box stuffing in two close states, Texas and, especially, Illinois, which had been expected to go for Nixon. For a while Nixon considered demanding a recount, but he feared that such an action would "tear the country apart."

Accepting defeat, Nixon returned to California to work in a Los Angeles law firm and to write his memoirs, *Six Crises* (the Hiss investigation, the "Checkers" speech, Eisenhower's heart attack, the Latin American trip, the Khrushchev debate, and the presidential election), which became a best-seller in 1962. California Republicans drafted him to run for governor that year against incumbent Democrat Edmund "Pat" Brown. After he lost the election by almost 300,000 votes, his political career appeared to be over. On the morning after his defeat, a bleary-eyed Nixon offered bitter comments to the press, most famously, "You won't have Nixon to kick around anymore, because, gentlemen, this is my last press conference."

Soon after, he left California for New York City to work in the law firm Mudge, Stern, Baldwin, and Todd. Although he had been hired primarily as a "rainmaker" to bring in influential clients, he did a highly professional job in a losing cause arguing an important case, *Time, Inc.* v. *Hill*, before the Supreme Court in 1966. By 1964 Nixon returned to national politics as a Republican leader, waiting in the wings for the presidential nomination in case the candidacy of Barry Goldwater faltered. But Goldwater received the nomination, much to the dismay of the eastern Republican establishment. Unlike many Republicans who were appalled by what they perceived to be Goldwater's extremism, Nixon worked loyally in a losing cause and thus secured his support among leaders of the conservative wing of his party. Given President Lyndon B. Johnson's landslide victory over the Arizona senator, Nixon, a centrist, found himself in a strong position for the next round of presidential politics.

Preparing for the contest for the 1968 nomination, Nixon began building a political staff, hiring the journalist Pat Buchanan in 1965 and touring the country on the rubber-chicken circuit, speaking to some six hundred groups of the party faithful in forty states over a two-year period. In addition, he made several well-publicized international trips and wrote articles about foreign affairs that burnished his image as a statesman. Although few recognized it at the time, Nixon was something of a closet intellectual who read widely and thought deeply about history and diplomacy. After the front-running Republican candidate for president, Michigan governor George Romney, self-destructed in 1967, Nixon assumed his position, opposed by supporters of Rockefeller and the new conservative leader, California governor Ronald Reagan. He beat back their challenge on the first ballot at the Miami Beach convention in August, owing in good measure to his promise to southern conservatives to slow the pace of desegregation in their region.

He also appealed to southerners with his vice-presidential candidate, Governor Spiro T. Agnew of Maryland, a onetime Rockefeller Republican who moved to the right after a celebrated conflict with African-American leaders in his state. He was Nixon's Nixon in the campaign, offering tough partisan speeches dominated by a call for "law and order." The Republicans (and third-party candidate George Wallace, the former governor of Alabama) were responding to the unprecedented wave of urban rebellions in U.S. cities since 1965, the increasingly obstreperous antiwar protestors, the countercultural movement that advocated sexual liberation and the legalization of marijuana, and the general assault against middle-class values promoted by hippies, the New Left, and liberal intellectuals. For many Americans these forces represented all that was wrong with their country during the turbulent 1960s.

That turbulence was underscored by the infamous Democratic convention in Chicago in August, where the police and Mayor Richard J. Daley confronted ten thousand protestors in the streets and hundreds of delegates inside the convention hall who opposed the nomination of Johnson's handpicked candidate, Vice President Hubert H. Humphrey. All of the primaries had been won by antiwar senators Eugene McCarthy from Minnesota and Robert F. Kennedy from Massachusetts, but most states did not have primaries in 1968, and, in any event, the stronger of the two candidates, Kennedy, had been assassinated in Los Angeles in June. The violence in Chicago, which a government panel later labeled a "police riot," weakened the Democratic Party considerably.

Eschewing debates with Humphrey as well as press conferences, Nixon's campaign manager, John Mitchell, ran one of the most carefully managed campaigns in history, relying especially on tightly controlled, televised town meetings that looked more spontaneous than they really were. Both Humphrey and Nixon promised to end the war in Vietnam, but both were vague about their policies. Although he never said it directly, Nixon implied that he had a secret plan to end the war. Such a plan did not exist. Moreover, Nixon claimed that it would be unseemly for him to discuss the specifics of the phantom plan while Johnson was trying to arrange peace talks with the Vietnamese Communists. Nixon led during the entire campaign with Humphrey closing the gap as the election neared, in part because many blue-collar northerners returned to the Democrats after flirting with the idea of voting for the populism and racism of George Wallace, who promised to be even tougher on protestors and rioters than Nixon had been.

Fearing the election of their old foe, Nixon, the Russians pushed the North Vietnamese to accept Johnson's terms for opening peace talks. One week before the election an agreement was reached, the announcement of which led many voters to make a last-minute move toward Humphrey. However, the trend was reversed on the weekend before the election when the South Vietnamese government publicly quashed the deal. In activities that came close to treason, a Republican operative had urged the South Vietnamese, who did not need much urging, to reject the deal, promising a better arrangement when Nixon became president. The Johnson administration knew about this violation of the Logan Act since it had been wiretapping the operative, Anna Chennault, as well as South Vietnam's embassy in Washington and government offices in Saigon itself. Because the president did not want to reveal the wiretapping, and also because he lacked a specific smoking gun linking Chennault to the Nixon campaign, he and Humphrey chose not to reveal the illegal Republican meddling in official U.S. diplomacy. Nixon won the popular vote with 43.4 percent to Humphrey's 42.7 percent and Wallace's 13.5 percent, and the electoral vote of 301 to 191 to 46. Several weeks after being elected, Nixon quietly urged

Saigon to accept the deal that Johnson had crafted in his "October Surprise."

Nixon promised in his campaign to "Bring Us Together," no mean feat for any president in 1969, let alone the intensely partisan Nixon. He had won in good measure through the politics of polarization, an approach that continued throughout his administration. Nixon's cabinet was made up of white males, at least seven of whom were millionaires, albeit self-made men. But in this administration the cabinet was far less important than at any other time in American history, with Nixon operating his foreign and domestic policy through his White House staff. National Security Adviser Henry Kissinger, Chief of Staff H. R. Haldeman, and domestic policy chief John Ehrlichman, along with their aides, played key policy-making roles in all aspects of the administration, and in Kissinger's case, executed policy as well. Nixon chose this course because in the foreign-policy field he felt that he could not trust the State Department to keep a secret. As for the domestic arena, he correctly concluded that the permanent bureaucracies in the departments were dominated by Democrats and liberals who would oppose his attempts to dismantle parts of the welfare state, and especially the Great Society reforms of Johnson. Among the most suspicious, secretive, and even paranoid of all presidents, Nixon, the quintessential micromanager, tried to centralize all government activities in the White House, where he could control access to information about his strategies and initiatives.

Nixon was far less interested in domestic politics than he was in foreign policy, where he knew he had more freedom from Congress to operate. He was able to control access to his foreign policies through Kissinger's National Security Council (NSC) so thoroughly that an agent for the Joint Chiefs of Staff in the White House had to steal thousands of documents to keep the admirals and generals informed about what the president was up to in the international arena. Nixon wanted to demonstrate to his "enemies" that he could operate a secret diplomacy just as they did and that he would not be pushed around by antiwar mobs in the streets, Congress, and his special enemy, the media.

His first order of business was to end the Vietnam War. To accomplish "peace with honor," he adopted Vietnamization, the slow but steady withdrawal of U.S. troops from Vietnam, to relieve the antiwar and antidraft pressure at home. At the same time, under loopholes in the agreement Johnson made with the Communists, he increased the bombing of North Vietnam and secretly began bombing areas in neutral Cambodia used by Hanoi to send supplies and cadres south. When a journalist ran a story about the covert bombing, Nixon ordered illegal wiretapping to find the person responsible for leaking the information, the first of many such surveillance operations that became part of

the bill of particulars of impeachment against the president five years later.

Despite a 1 November 1969 ultimatum to Hanoi and the increased bombing, the Communists clung to their bargaining position. They forced the United States to make concessions because of the timetable for the inevitable withdrawal of all U.S. troops and because of the power of the antiwar movement. The movement's clout was demonstrated on 15 October 1969, when more than two million people turned out for the Moratorium in two hundred U.S. cities to express their opposition to the slow pace of withdrawal from Vietnam. During the Moratorium, the movement's most successful demonstration, the participants—most of whom were middle-class adults—took time off from work or college to attend rallies and prayer sessions and to picket and distribute leaflets.

Nixon's attempt to weaken the Communists with incursions into Cambodia in May 1970 and Laos in February 1971 were failures. The Cambodian invasion created the greatest violence and instability in history on American campuses, including the killing of four students by National Guardsmen at Kent State University in May 1970 and strong opposition in the Democratic-controlled Congress. Ultimately, Nixon had to agree to permit North Vietnamese troops to remain in South Vietnam after American troops left to move negotiations along before the 1972 election. When in October 1972 the Communists backed off on their demand that South Vietnamese president Nguyen Van Thieu had to resign before they would agree to a ceasefire, a provisional agreement was signed. But that came undone when the South Vietnamese rejected the deal, an action that Nixon attributed to North Vietnamese obstructionism—obstructionism that led to the B-52 "Christmas bombing" of Hanoi and Haiphong to bring the Communists back to the peace table. The Americans and the Vietnamese Communists finally signed a treaty on 27 January 1973, which closely resembled the treaty originally initialed the previous October and which so favored Hanoi that it easily conquered all of Vietnam in April 1975. Nixon thought he had made the best deal that he could and counted upon his promise to return with military force if the Communists refused to abide by the terms of the treaty, particularly those that related to the political process in South Vietnam. He never expected that his presidency would soon be emasculated by the trials and tribulations of the Watergate scandal, which did not become a crisis for him until April 1973.

Nixon was far more successful with his brilliant triangular diplomacy that led to detente with the Soviet Union and the Strategic Arms Limitation Treaty (SALT) in May 1972 and his celebrated, mediagenic, ten-day visit to China in February 1972. Pressured by anticommunists like Nixon, successive American governments since the Communist takeover of China in 1949 had refused to recognize Beijing. By cleverly playing off China and the Soviet Union's mutual fears that the United States would ally with their enemy against them, the now apparently amoral Nixon was able to establish relatively friendly relations with Moscow and Beijing, thus providing a salutary reduction in his country's cold war tensions and insecurities.

In many ways, despite later ups and downs, the normalization of relations with the two Communist giants led to the ending of the cold war. One of those ups and downs had to do with the Yom Kippur War of 1973, begun when Egypt and Syria attacked Israel to regain the territories Israel had conquered in 1967. During that war the United States went on full nuclear alert when it appeared that the Soviet Union was going to intervene to aid Egypt. Despite that scare, Nixon's policies of relative evenhandedness toward the Arabs, particularly Anwar Sadat's Egypt, paved the way for the Camp David accords of 1978.

The Nixon administration's destabilization of the democratically elected government of Chile's Marxist president Salvador Allende contributed to conditions that resulted in Allende's overthrow in 1973 by General Augusto Pinochet, who established a brutal, authoritarian regime. In other areas of the Third World, his administration was not as sympathetic to or interested in liberation movements as had been the Democrats.

Although elected to rein in big government and the welfare state that had grown under Democratic leadership, Nixon's domestic record includes either active or passive support for so many liberal programs that he could be considered the last liberal president of the twentieth century. His attorney general, John Mitchell, explained, "watch what we do, rather than what we say." Nowhere could this be seen as clearly as in the contentious area of school desegregation. Despite his promises to the South to slow the pace of desegregation, Nixon deftly moved the issue out of the executive branch to the judicial branch of government so that he would not be blamed for what happened in the region. The courts then moved swiftly to desegregate more southern school districts during Nixon's tenure than during the previous eight years of Democratic rule. The president did appeal to the South, which with the election of 1968 finalized its transition from a Democratic to a Republican stronghold. He spoke out against busing, one of the remedies for segregation recommended by the courts, and failed in an attempt to emasculate the Voting Rights Act and to appoint two conservative southerners to the Supreme Court, Clement F. Haynsworth, Jr., and G. Harrold Carswell, both of whom the Senate rejected.

Nixon did leave a conservative imprint on the court with the appointment of Chief Justice Warren Burger in 1969, Harry Blackmun in 1970, and Lewis Powell and William Rehnquist, both in 1971. However, Blackmun and Powell

did not turn out to be as conservative as the president expected, with the former writing the majority opinion in the 1973 case of *Roe* v. *Wade* that legalized abortion. Serving as president during the heyday of the women's liberation movement, Nixon supported passage of the Equal Rights Amendment. More importantly, he strengthened the Equal Employment Opportunity Commission to deal with issues of gender discrimination and, under Title IX, broadened the power of the Civil Rights Commission to prohibit gender discrimination in educational institutions receiving federal funds, an initiative that led to a revolution in university programs for female athletes.

Nixon was also the greatest environmental president since Theodore Roosevelt, even though he considered the burgeoning movement "crap." Because of the popularity of that movement (the first Earth Day was in 1970) and the environmental credentials of his likely chief opponent in the 1972 presidential campaign, Maine senator Edmund Muskie, Nixon signed legislation establishing the Environmental Protection Agency and approved Clean Air Act amendments, the Endangered Species Act, the Coastal Zone Management Act, and the Marine Mammal Protection Act, among many other measures.

He did not succeed in reforming the welfare program. Nixon's revolutionary Family Assistance Plan, a centerpiece of his first administration, was attacked by liberals who thought it too harsh and by conservatives who thought it too weak. It had been paired with a more successful project, the New Federalism, which returned billions of tax dollars from the federal government to the states in a massive decentralization program.

Among other examples of progressive legislation that Nixon did get approved were the ending of the Selective Service System and the adoption, in 1973, of an all-volunteer army; lowering the voting age from twenty-one to eighteen; removing the Post Office from the cabinet to become the independent U.S. Postal Service; establishing AMTRAK, the Occupational Safety and Health Administration, and the Consumer Product Safety Act; increasing federal expenditures for the arts; and establishing wars against cancer and drugs. Although he was not happy signing off on all of those bills, he had little choice considering their popularity among the public and the Democratic Congress. If he hoped to be reelected in 1972, Nixon had to meet the liberals halfway.

That reelection was also endangered by the shaky economy he inherited from the Johnson administration, with spiraling inflation figures and growing unemployment ("stagflation") causing a good deal of pain among Americans. In August 1971, going against every economic principle in which he had once believed, Nixon approved wage and price controls that temporarily stabilized the economy. But it was a quick fix that fell apart in 1973, with the situation made even worse when the Organization of Petroleum Exporting Countries (OPEC) both embargoed oil to the United States in the wake of the Yom Kippur War and raised the price per barrel as much as fourfold. The wage-and-price decision in 1971 was coupled with an even more dramatic announcement: the U.S. all but abandoned the gold standard by permitting the dollar to float against other currencies.

Nixon began his campaign for reelection in 1969 with a private slush fund of $2 million that could be used by his Committee to Re-Elect the President (CREEP) for legal and extralegal political espionage and under-the-table payoffs to people like the Democratic Alabama politician who challenged George Wallace for governor in 1970. Using such funds Nixon also set up a secret, investigatory agency in the White House, called the Plumbers (to find leaks). Among other crimes, the group was involved in the 1971 break-in of the office of Daniel Ellsberg's psychiatrist. Ellsberg was the man who leaked the Defense Department's history of the Vietnam War, the "Pentagon Papers," to the press. Some of those same operatives were involved in the 17 June 1972 break-in at Democratic Party headquarters at the Watergate complex in Washington. Nixon and his aides successfully covered up the White House's ties to the burglars until after the election.

Owing to reforms in the Democratic Party nomination procedures and CREEP's extralegal and illegal political machinations, Nixon wound up running against his "favorite" opponent in the 1972 election, Senator George McGovern of South Dakota, the most liberal of his potential rivals. Republicans labeled McGovern the AAA candidate for his support of amnesty for draft dodgers, abortion on demand, and appeasement toward the Vietnamese Communists. McGovern's campaign almost self-destructed at the start when he first supported and then removed from the ticket his vice-presidential candidate, Missouri Senator Thomas Eagleton, after news reports about Eagleton's earlier psychological illness. When on 26 October 1972 Henry Kissinger announced in his October Surprise that "Peace is at hand," McGovern lost his only winning issue. A week later he lost the election in a landslide, 61 percent to 38 percent in the popular vote, while capturing the electoral votes of only Massachusetts and the District of Columbia. Armed with that strong mandate from the voters and uncomfortable about being a "liberal" president, Nixon and his aides began planning a rightward shift during his second administration.

But in January 1973 everything began coming undone as the judge in the Watergate trial, the conservative Republican John J. Sirica, pressured the burglars with long jail terms until one of them, James McCord, began to talk about his links to the White House. Congress soon got into the act with a Senate investigation, during which White House

counsel John Dean presented damning details about the president's involvement in the cover-up of the break-in. Even more important, during those same hearings another White House aide revealed that from 1971 through 1973 the president had secretly taped all of his conversations. A battle soon ensued between the president and Congress, mediated by the courts, about access to those soon-to-be incriminating tapes. During the same period investigative journalists, particularly Bob Woodward and Carl Bernstein of the *Washington Post,* began discovering other evidence of illegal and unconstitutional acts in which the president had a direct hand. And as if he did not have enough troubles, the president had to demand the resignation of Vice President Agnew in the fall because of Watergate-unrelated crimes connected to accepting kickbacks from contractors. Nixon selected and Congress approved Agnew's replacement, Michigan representative Gerald R. Ford, whom Nixon privately thought so unpresidential as to represent an insurance policy for him against impeachment.

But that did not stop the House, whose judiciary committee had begun hearings on Watergate that led to investigations and even more revelations about illegal operations in the White House. During the same period independent prosecutors, first Archibald Cox and then Leon Jaworski, ran parallel investigations.

After the courts made Nixon release transcripts and then the tapes themselves, few in Congress, or in the nation in general, doubted that he had committed crimes worthy of impeachment. And it was not just the obvious criminal activity surrounding the cover-up of the break-in that concerned them. In many ways the White House appeared to be undermining American democracy. Nixon himself claimed that he was just playing the same hardball politics practiced by his predecessors, but although some of his shady activities had precedent, many did not, and those that had been practiced before were unprecedented in their scope. As if this was not bad enough, many Americans were astonished by the discovery that the proper, almost Victorian, public Nixon was caught on tape as profane and vulgar, anti-Semitic, racist, and mean-spirited.

Even before it received the famous "smoking gun" tape in early August 1974, the House Judiciary Committee voted late in July, twenty-seven to eleven, to impeach Nixon for obstruction of justice, twenty-eight to ten for abuse of power, and twenty-one to seventeen for contempt of Congress. Among the abuses uncovered, aside from the original cover-up, were Nixon's political uses of the Internal Revenue Service, illegal wiretaps of political enemies, illegal campaign contributions, threats to the media, cheating on his personal taxes, selling ambassadorships, and a host of other acts that John Mitchell labeled the "White House Horrors." The accumulation of evidence led the president to resign on 9 August 1974, just before he certainly would have been impeached by the House of Representatives and then removed from office by the Senate. Those crimes also led to the conviction and imprisonment of Mitchell, Haldeman, Ehrlichman, Dean, and several other members of the administration and CREEP. Nixon himself escaped prosecution and potential imprisonment when President Ford pardoned him on 8 September 1974, an act that may have cost Ford the presidential election in 1976. Worried about Nixon's precarious health and concerned about putting the nation through another year of trauma as the former president prepared for several trials, Ford thought it best to end the "long national nightmare."

After recovering from a life-threatening attack of phlebitis and serious depression, Nixon began to campaign one more time, this time for "ex-president." And in a political comeback even more unlikely than the one he made after losing the California gubernatorial election in 1962, Nixon did achieve that status by the middle 1980s. He attained it through carefully planned public appearances and, especially, through writing first his memoirs in 1978, and then, in an incredible flurry, eight more best-selling books between 1980 and 1994 that outlined his views on diplomacy and evaluations of foreign leaders he had met. He had become a wise, elder statesman whose experience and allegedly brilliant record in foreign affairs made him a national asset. People had not forgotten Watergate, but they began to compartmentalize Nixon's career into unsavory domestic doings and distasteful personality traits caught on tape and his successful foreign-policy exploits. President Bill Clinton echoed this theme at Nixon's funeral in Yorba Linda, following his death from a stroke in 1994 in New York City, when he generously proclaimed, "May the day of judging President Nixon on anything less than his entire life and career come to a close." Nixon is buried in Yorba Linda.

★

Nixon's presidential papers and the infamous Watergate tapes can be found in the National Archives in College Park, Maryland. Most of his pre-presidential papers are located at the National Archive's regional facility in Laguna Niguel, California, while the privately operated Richard M. Nixon Presidential Library and Birthplace in Yorba Linda contains fragmentary pre- and post-presidential papers. Nixon's memoir *RN* (1978), though self-serving, is useful, but it needs to be read with three balanced studies, Stephen Ambrose's *Nixon* (three volumes, 1987, 1989, and 1991), Herbert S. Parmet's *Richard Nixon and His America* (1990), and Tom Wicker's *One of Us: Richard Nixon and the American Dream* (1995). Most favorable to Nixon are Jonathan Aitken, *Nixon: A Life* (1993), and Irwin Gellman, *The Contender* (1999), a revisionist approach to the period up to 1952. For the presidency itself the main monographs are Michael A. Genovese, *The Nixon Presidency* (1990); Joan Hoff, *Nixon Reconsidered* (1994); Melvin Small, *The Presidency of Richard Nixon* (1999); and Richard

Reeves, *President Nixon: Alone in the White House* (2001). For Watergate, Stanley I. Kutler, *The Wars of Watergate* (1992), is encyclopedic, and for Nixon's run for the ex-presidency, see Robert Sam Anson, *Exile* (1984). Obituaries are in the *Chicago Tribune*, *New York Times*, and *Washington Post* (all 24 Apr. 1994).

MELVIN SMALL

NIZER, Louis (*b.* 6 February 1902 in London, England; *d.* 10 November 1994 in New York City), possibly the most celebrated trial lawyer of the 1960s, who gained fame for both his courtroom work as well as his best-selling autobiographical books.

Nizer's family moved from England when he was three years old, and although he attended high school in Brooklyn, he retained a bit of a British manner. His father, Joseph Nizer, owned a dry-cleaning store in Brooklyn, and his mother, Bella Bialestock Nizer, was a homemaker. Nizer graduated from Columbia University in 1922 with a B.A. and then studied at Columbia Law School, where he was awarded the LL.B. He was admitted to the New York Bar in 1924. From 1924 to 1928 he worked as an attorney in New York City. In 1926 he established a partnership with Louis Phillips that evolved into the firm of Phillips, Nizer, Benjamin, Krim, and Ballon in 1928. Nizer embarked on a career that never shrank from the combative. He wrote, "I would pray, O Lord, never to diminish my passion for a client's cause, for from it springs the flame which leaps across the jury box and sets fire to the conviction of the jurors."

Nizer married Mildred Mantel Wollins in 1939 and became a stepfather to her two sons. Besides his celebrated oratorical, legal, and authorial abilities, Nizer also excelled as a painter and a composer. He was a member of the American Society of Composers, Authors, and Publishers as well as a prize-winning artist.

Early in his career Nizer became involved in the motion picture industry; one of his first books discussed movie codes during the New Deal era. During World War II he authored a book, *What to Do with Germany* (1944), which Dwight Eisenhower reportedly circulated to his staff and insisted they report on in writing. Nizer's book recommended that the Allies assume control of the German government, at least for a brief period, and that Nazi leaders within the German hierarchy face trial. At the end of the war Nizer's ideas were put into action. Nizer also supported the aims of the 1945 United Nations Conference on International Organization, a San Francisco meeting that resulted in the creation of the United Nations.

Nizer counted among his clients many people associated with the motion picture industry, and these famous people became the focus of his books. In 1961 he wrote *My Life in Court,* which remained at the top of best-seller lists for more than a year. In it he recounted his experience representing the journalist Quentin Reynolds in his libel suit against a fellow reporter, Westbrook Pegler, who had called Reynolds an absentee war correspondent. The jury found malice on Pegler's part, and Reynolds received a large punitive damage award. The incident became the basis of a popular play, *A Case of Libel.* Nizer also described a movie industry proxy fight and a medical malpractice suit in which a woman's family received a large award after a doctor failed to perform an emergency cesarian section on her, resulting in the deaths of both the woman and her child.

A later book, *The Jury Returns* (1966), discussed the John Henry Faulk libel case, in which Faulk sued broadcasters for blacklisting him after reports linked him with an alleged Communist conspiracy. *The Jury Returns* also described Nizer's efforts to obtain clemency for a prisoner whom Nizer viewed as a reformed killer. A reviewer in the *American Bar Association Journal* wondered if the convict was a proper subject for rehabilitation, considering that he had never admitted his guilt despite having been granted at least two appeals.

While Nizer's books often retold trials and included what would usually be considered dry excerpts from transcripts, they also relied on both Nizer's ego and his knowledge of the law. Nizer interspersed long discussions of the weaknesses of current divorce law, corporate law, and medical malpractice. In his discussion on divorce he noted that states sometimes chose to ignore the decrees of other states (like Nevada, which had a particularly lax divorce statute) or "divorce mill" nations in the Caribbean. Nizer took his readers through the legal technicalities while relating the story of his clients' divorce proceedings.

Likewise, he informed readers of the difficulty of successfully prosecuting a medical malpractice action because it was nearly impossible to find experts willing to testify that a doctor had failed to exercise reasonable care in performing medical procedures. In the case of the botched obstetrical case that Nizer tried, he found an inexperienced family member who was willing to testify. Although this witness's testimony probably had little effect on the jury, it prevented the defense from dismissing the suit. Nizer went on to establish his case on the basis of his cross-examination of the incompetent physician. (This expert testimony problem eventually led law firms to hire staff doctors to testify in medical malpractice proceedings, a development that greatly angered practicing physicians.)

By writing his own opinions about various legal matters in language accessible to lay people, Nizer became a major force in the movement for legal reform. His books were read widely at the same time that the United States Supreme Court under Chief Justice Earl Warren was reform-

ing constitutional law; moreover, the public viewed positive images of the legal profession every week in hit television shows like *The Defenders* and *Perry Mason.* Nizer and attorneys like him, however, created the impression that wise, objective lawyers could solve any social evil—a notion that was repeatedly challenged in later decades.

Nizer's ego was a prominent feature of *My Life in Court.* As *Time* magazine noted, "For all the book's courtroom lore and legal pyrotechnics, it also has one theme that is something of a bore: Louis Nizer. Often he seems only an ego with a law degree." *Time* went on to complain that Nizer saw courtroom battles only in terms of good against evil.

In 1972 Nizer was himself the subject of an unsuccessful libel and copyright suit brought by Julius and Ethel Rosenberg's sons in response to his book, *The Implosion Conspiracy* (1973), on the famous trial and execution of the atomic secrets spies. Nizer's long list of celebrated clients included Johnny Carson, Charlie Chaplin, Salvador Dali, Eddie Fisher, Mae West, and Governor James Rhodes of Ohio. He wrote many articles aimed at the practicing lawyer and was considered an expert not only in trial strategy but also in copyright and commercial contracts. Nizer continued active in the law firm he cofounded until his death of kidney failure at age ninety-two. He is buried in Washington Cemetery in Brooklyn.

★

Nizer's memoirs include *My Life in Court* (1961) and *Reflections without Mirrors: An Autobiography of the Mind* (1979). He also wrote *New Courts of Industry: Self-Regulation under the Motion Picture Code, Including an Analysis of the Code* (1935); *What to Do with Germany* (1944); and *The Jury Returns* (1966). An obituary is in the *New York Times* (11 Nov. 1994).

JOHN DAVID HEALY

NOYCE, Robert Norton (*b.* 12 December 1927 in Burlington, Iowa; *d.* 3 June 1990 in Austin, Texas), inventor of the silicon computer chip, cofounder of Fairchild Semiconductor and Intel, and originator of a decentralized management style that ultimately became the dominant corporate culture of Silicon Valley.

Noyce was the third of four sons, all high academic achievers, of Ralph Noyce, Sr., a Congregationalist minister, and Harriett Norton. He did not leave home until he started graduate work. He went to Grinnell College, where his most outrageous act was stealing a pig in order to have a barbecue. (He called the farmer the next day to confess the crime, and his honesty nearly earned him an expulsion from school.) Noyce graduated with a B.A. in physics in 1949. He then went to the Massachusetts Institute of Technology (MIT), where he gained his Ph.D. in physical elec-

Robert Noyce. AP/WIDE WORLD PHOTOS

tronics in 1953. He began his professional career with the Philco Corporation, where he designed better ways of etching germanium crystals, the basis for early transistors.

After three years Noyce applied for a position at Shockley Semiconductor Laboratory. So confident was he that he would get the job, a story alleges, he moved his family to Palo Alto, California, and made a down-payment on the house where they would live before he even had his job interview. But Noyce would not stay at Shockley for long: the company, one of the pioneers of the transistor, was committed to germanium as the basis of transistor technology, while Noyce and a number of his colleagues had become convinced that silicon held the key to all future semiconductor development.

A natural leader, Noyce in 1957 was asked to head a group of eight Shockley engineers in the creation of a new company, Fairchild Semiconductor, which would make silicon transistors. Wiring such tiny components was expensive, especially when working with silicon, so late in 1958 Noyce and Gordon E. Moore began working on a cluster of transistors, all laid down on a single chip. A few months later, however, the engineers at Fairchild were shocked to see Jack Kirby of Texas Instruments announce the creation of a similar "integrated circuit," based on the traditional germanium. Within weeks Noyce, Moore, and Jean Hoerni, another of what Shockley called the "traitorous eight," had worked out a planar production process that allowed Fairchild to take its silicon-based integrated circuits to market first. Ultimately, the race was decided at the U.S. Patent Office, which awarded Noyce and Fairchild Patent #2,981,877 for the planar silicon chip, but gave Kirby and Texas Instruments Patent #3,138,743 for the miniaturized electronic circuit; the companies finally settled their decade-long dispute with a cross-licensing agreement in the summer of 1966. Royalties paid to the two companies had already reached $100 million by the early 1980s. Noyce eventually recorded a dozen important patents in his name.

In 1959 Fairchild Camera, which had put up the original money for Noyce and his colleagues to incorporate, exercised its option to buy the company outright, although they kept Noyce as general manager. Noyce and his friends were now wealthy men. By 1968 Fairchild Semiconductor had yearly sales of some $130 million and had grown from twelve employees to twelve thousand. But it never lost the management style that Noyce created for it from the start: open, egalitarian, with complete responsibility and complete autonomy (balanced by complete accountability) for all employees. It was Noyce, at Fairchild Semiconductor, who created the corporate culture that has characterized the entirety of Silicon Valley ever since.

By 1968 Noyce was casting around for new worlds to conquer, and he found it in the quest for a large-scale integrated circuit, or LSI. But Fairchild was too cumbersome an entity to pursue such a visionary goal; therefore, Noyce, along with Moore and Arthur Grove, who had joined Fairchild in 1963, decided to found yet another start-up semiconductor company. The self-effacing Nocye and Moore rejected their initial name for the company, N M Electronics, in favor of the less-boastful Integrated Electronics, immediately shortened to Intel. To demonstrate their seriousness, each man put the $250,000 he had received from the sale of Fairchild Semiconductor nine years before into the start-up costs of the new business. They also allowed Grinnell College, Noyce's alma mater, to invest an equal amount, an investment that would prove a wise one for the small Iowa school.

Noyce's first great accomplishment at Intel was the creation of the 1103 memory chip, which fit four thousand transistors into the same space as two lowercase *M*s (mm) would occupy on this page. It could do the work of a thousand industry-standard memory cores, and do it faster. Intel grew from about $3,000 in revenues in 1969 to $23.4 million in 1972, and to $66 million the next year, continuing its exponential growth for many years thereafter. During this period Ted Hoff, one of Noyce's researchers, discovered how to transform each chip into a computer, or "microprocessor." The result was a series of microcomputer chips that have become the standards of the industry, from 1974's 8080 chip, with 4,500 transistors running at two megahertz, to 2002's Pentium 4 chip, with fifty-five million transistors running at two gigahertz (gigahertz is 1,000 times the speed of megahertz).

Noyce's other great accomplishment was his "councils," as he called them, in which staff members from every division would meet to resolve the kinds of divisional conflicts that paralyzed companies relying on a more formal management structure. In the 1990s, when Japanese "quality circles" were introduced into the United States, observers discovered that Intel had been applying this methodology all along.

Noyce retired from day-to-day operations at Intel in 1975, and in 1978 agreed to become head of the Semiconductor Industry Association. In 1988 he became president of SEMATECH (*SE*miconductor *MA*nufacturing *TECH*nology), an industry-government consortium, and moved to Austin, Texas. He served on the board of trustees at Grinnell from 1962 until his death, and on the University of California board of regents from 1982 on. His awards included the National Medal of Science, and medals from the Franklin Institute, the Institute of Electrical and Electronic Engineers (IEEE), and the American Federation of Information Processing Societies.

Noyce met Elizabeth Bottomley in 1953, just after he had completed his Ph.D., and married her that fall. They had four children, but divorced in 1974, and Noyce married Ann Bowers, Intel's personnel director, the next year. A champion diver in college, Noyce was an avid hang glider, pilot, and skier. Ironically, all his physical activity could not save him from a fatal heart attack at the age of sixty-two.

Noyce was a skilled engineer, a successful entrepreneur, and the most charismatic leader the semiconductor industry has had. Most people would be content with fame gained in a single field, but Noyce is remembered as the coinventor of the integrated circuit and creator of the silicon microchip as well as the creator of an innovative—and wildly successful—management style at the two companies he cofounded, Fairchild Semiconductor and Intel.

★

Biographical information on Noyce appears in T. R. Reid, *The Chip: How Two Americans Invented the Microchip and Launched a Revolution* (1984). A profile by a distinguished colleague is Gordon E. Moore, "Robert N. Noyce," *National Academy of Engineering Memorial Tributes* 6 (1993): 154–159. Also notable is Tom Wolfe, "The Tinkerings of Robert Noyce," *Esquire* (Dec. 1983): 346–374. An obituary is in the *New York Times* (4 June 1990).

HARTLEY S. SPATT

O

OATES, Joyce Carol (*b.* 16 June 1938 near Millersport, New York), prolific novelist, short-story writer, playwright, essayist, college professor, and lecturer widely regarded as one of the best American writers of her era.

Although neither of Oates's parents graduated from high school and both had endured great hardship, they encouraged their daughter's academic aspirations and writing abilities. During the Great Depression, Frederic Oates worked sporadically for a radiator manufacturer; he was also a skilled sign painter and practiced his craft to bring in money during periods of unemployment. The family lived on a farm in northern New York State, where Oates and her mother, Carolina (Bush) Oates, took care of the chickens, and Frederic took care of the harvest. Oates has a younger brother and sister, both of whom were born after the difficult years of the depression.

Oates attended a one-room school and spent her free time reading. At about age nine, she read Lewis Carroll's *Alice's Adventures in Wonderland* and was inspired to write. In the fourth grade she was sexually molested by a group of boys, an experience that has affected her emotionally all her life. When she entered high school at age fourteen, her grandmother gave her the typewriter that she used constantly until she bought an electric typewriter in the mid-1960s. In 1956, when she graduated from high school, Oates received a New York State Regents Scholarship that nearby Syracuse University matched dollar for dollar, thus

enabling her to attend college. While at Syracuse, Oates wrote and studied tirelessly; one professor recalls her writing a novel per semester. In 1957, her sophomore year, Oates won *Mademoiselle* magazine's prestigious college fiction competition. She majored in English, minored in philosophy, and was class valedictorian in 1960.

Oates went on to graduate school at the University of Wisconsin, and in October 1960 she met Raymond J. Smith, a thirty-year-old graduate student who was studying for his doctorate in English. They married on 23 January 1961; later that year, she received her M.A. in English. Oates then briefly attended Rice University with an eye to earning her doctorate but soon left school to focus on her writing. She and her husband were miserable in Texas, finding the overt racial discrimination disheartening. When Smith accepted a position in Detroit, Michigan, Oates found a job teaching freshman English at the University of Detroit.

Oates published her first book, a collection of short stories entitled *By the North Gate,* in 1963. It received mostly friendly reviews. In 1964 a friend put Oates in touch with the literary agent Blanche Gregory, a sharp businesswoman, who not only found publishers for Oates's stories but also managed to persuade publishers to pay top dollar for them. Oates remembers payments for her stories trebling, seemingly overnight. Also in 1963 Oates's absurdist play *The Sweet Enemy* was performed at New York City's Actors Playhouse. Although she was extremely shy and had

difficulty interacting with the cast and director during rehearsals, she managed to make changes in the script when
needed; both critics and fellow playwrights admired the
work.

Oates's first published novel, *With Shuddering Fall*
(1964), was criticized for the harshness of its worldview and
the unpleasantness of its characters. Oates insisted that she
wrote about reality, not wishful thinking. Given her hard
life in an impoverished rural community at the end of the
Great Depression, the deprivations of World War II, her
sexual molestation as a very young girl, and her experience
of racial segregation in Texas, it should not be surprising
that much of her writing is an unflinching examination of
human suffering. By 1967 Oates had been promoted to
assistant professor at the University of Detroit, and she applied for and received a grant from the Guggenheim Foundation to fund her writing from May to September that
year. She accepted a teaching position at the University of
Windsor, to begin in the fall, and apparently in retaliation
the University of Detroit gave her an 8:00 A.M., five-days-
a-week schedule of composition courses for her final spring
semester that left her exhausted and miserable. The year
1967 also marked a great upward swing in her literary career; her novel *A Garden of Earthly Delights* was published,
the first of a trilogy that includes *Expensive People* (1968)
and *them* (1969). In contrast to what Oates believed had
been insufficient promotion of her earlier books, her publisher, Vanguard, took out large advertisements for *A Garden of Earthly Delights.*

The novel, instantly controversial, established her as a
major writer. Set in rural New York, the book reflects some
of her own real-life experiences. It covers the Great Depression and World War II, with its deep-running themes
of poverty and prosperity, while examining the idealization
of America as the great land of opportunity for all. These
themes struck a chord in a society dealing with issues of
racism, an unpopular war in Vietnam, and a seemingly
permanent stratum of poor people. Yet Oates's greatest accomplishment in *A Garden of Earthly Delights* is her char-
acterizations, especially that of the main character, Clara,
whom the novel follows from her birth to her untimely
death. Like Oates, Clara attends a one-room school and is
sexually molested. She is a sensitive person and mostly likable, which makes the awful cruelties inflicted on her all
the more painful to read. Even though Clara's talent would
seem to merit her rising in American society, she cannot
escape her impoverished and battered past. Oates remembered having been inspired to construct a novel of epic
scope after reading the German writer Thomas Mann's
Buddenbrooks; A Garden of Earthly Delights, a sweeping account of four decades of American history, is such a work.

In 1968 Oates published a collection of poetry, *Women
in Love and Other Poems,* but it was the publication of *Ex-*

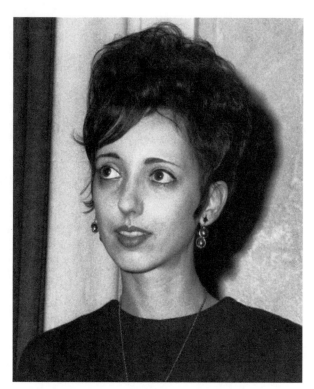

Joyce Carol Oates. CORBIS CORPORATION (BELLEVUE)

pensive People that received the most critical and public
attention. Where *A Garden of Earthly Delights* focuses on
rural life, *Expensive People* concentrates on suburbia. It is a
satiric novel with an experimental narrative structure. The
character Nada ("nothing") might be an analogue for
Oates herself. Nada is a serious writer who looks much like
the thin, large-eyed Oates, and the narrative even includes
a short story supposedly written by Nada that was actually
a story that Oates had earlier published in a magazine.
According to Oates, the idea of the novel originated in her
own thinking about whether she wanted to have children.
(She never did.) She then imagined one such child narrat-
ing the story. This child is Richard, an obese teenager with
a dyspeptic view of his life. He is an inherently untrust-
worthy narrator but often a funny one, and his murder of
Nada is horrifying.

Expensive People was a popular success, selling tens of
thousands of hardbound copies and hundreds of thousands
of paperback copies. Oates followed *Expensive People* with
a great novel, the work that established her as a leading
American writer, *them.* The novel received the 1970 National Book Award; Oates is one of the youngest authors
ever to be so honored. This book completed the trilogy by
moving its focus to the inner city of Detroit. In *them,* Oates
tries to capture the humanity and desperation of working-
class people in the inner city, trying to make Detroit symbolic of all of America's inner cities. The narrative follows

the life of Loretta and her children, Maureen and Jules. The characterization of these characters is brilliant—their depth of personality is extraordinary. They are sensitive, intelligent people, trapped in an environment of brutality, cruelty, and racism. Loretta ends up marrying a man who sexually assaulted her, the police officer Howard Wendall, and the plot then follows the events in the lives of the Wendall family. Loretta and Maureen become hardened, misanthropic figures, using their outward cynicism as shells to protect them from the evils they cannot avoid. Maureen becomes a prostitute, feeling stronger because of the money she receives. Only Jules has any hope of escape by the novel's end. He is a thief and a murderer, and he is brutalized for most of his life, possibly including being raped, but during his adventures outside the law, he reveals a romantic idealism under his criminality. His leaving for California may represent the only escape from the misery of inner city life for any of the novel's characters.

With the publication of *them,* Oates became a celebrity, and each of her books thereafter was widely reviewed. In 1978 she became a writer in residence at Princeton University and was elected to the American Academy of Arts and Letters. Feminist critics complained that Oates's women characters were too weak or that her themes were not politically correct, even though *A Garden of Earthly Delights* would seem to be a feminist novel. Other readers continued to complain about the harshness of her fiction, although by the twenty-first century, her novels were becoming more positive. Nearly every critic has agreed that she is a major writer.

★

Oates's "My Father, My Fiction," *New York Times Book Review* (11 July 1989): 1, 15–16, is a beautiful account of her relationship with her parents and their relationship to her writings. A good, in-depth biography is Greg Johnson's *Invisible Writer: A Biography of Joyce Carol Oates* (1998). In "The Producer: Joyce Carol Oates Used to Be Dismissed as a Human Word Processor (Though She Doesn't Use One). But after 94 Books, She Sells Better than Ever—and Gets Raves," *Newsweek* (17 Sept. 2001): 64, Susannah Meadows assesses Oates's stature as of 2001.

KIRK H. BEETZ

O'BRIEN, Lawrence Francis, Jr. ("Larry") (*b.* 7 July 1917 in Springfield, Massachusetts; *d.* 28 September 1990 in New York City), Democratic political strategist, government official, and congressional liaison in the Kennedy and Johnson administrations, who as postmaster general developed a plan to reorganize the United States Post Office as a quasi-government corporation.

O'Brien, a Roman Catholic of Irish descent, was the older of two children of Lawrence Francis O'Brien, Sr., a café owner and local Democratic politician, and his wife, Myra (Sweeney) O'Brien. Lawrence, Sr., and Myra were immigrants from County Cork in Ireland. O'Brien was born to politics because the Roland Hotel, the boardinghouse and restaurant his father owned, was the informal Democratic headquarters in western Massachusetts. Politicians like James Michael Curley, the mayor of Boston, and David I. Walsh, the first Irish-American U.S. senator from Massachusetts, came to the Roland to meet with local Democratic leaders.

While helping with the family business and assisting with his father's political activities, O'Brien enrolled in the night extension program of Northeastern University in 1937. He completed an LL.B in 1942, although he never practiced law. The U.S. Army drafted him, but because of his poor eyesight he was assigned as a clerk at Camp Edwards, Massachusetts. In 1944, while still in the army, he married Elva Brassard. Shortly after being discharged in 1945 he managed the first of two congressional campaigns for his friend Foster Furcolo. In 1946 Furcolo was narrowly defeated, but in 1948 he was elected, and O'Brien became his administrative assistant in Washington, D.C. O'Brien returned to Springfield in 1950 after breaking with Furcolo. In 1952 a young congressman, John F. Kennedy, asked O'Brien to organize a statewide campaign against the Republican senator from Massachusetts, Henry Cabot Lodge. Kennedy was elected with O'Brien's organizational assistance, but O'Brien refused an opportunity to move to Washington, D.C., as a Senate aide. He remained in contact with Kennedy, working to maintain the senator's stature in Massachusetts.

In 1959 O'Brien joined the Kennedy for President campaign. He exhibited a gift for turning finite campaign resources into a large number of votes. The classic example is the West Virginia primary in which Kennedy faced Minnesota Senator Hubert Humphrey. O'Brien devised a plan to use the state's housewives to mobilize primary voters. Because these women were at home during the day, he gave volunteers lists of 300 names, a short statement, and allowed them to use their own phones to call voters. The campaign was able to reach thousands of voters at little cost. O'Brien wrote two campaign manuals for the Democratic National Committee: *Citizens for Kennedy and Johnson: Campaign Manual* (1960) and *The Democratic Campaign Manual 1964* (1964). In reviewing the 1960 primary campaign, Kennedy named O'Brien "the best election man in the business."

Kennedy asked O'Brien to become special assistant to the president for congressional relations, the president's lobbyist to Congress. O'Brien applied many of the techniques he used to win campaigns in developing the Office

Lawrence F. O'Brien announces his resignation as postmaster general in order to join Robert F. Kennedy's presidential campaign, 1968. © BETTMANN/CORBIS

of Congressional Relations. The office kept track of members of Congress, their constituencies, and pet projects. With this information O'Brien disbursed presidential patronage efficiently and effectively. After President Kennedy's assassination in Dallas, Texas, on 22 November 1963, the new president, Lyndon B. Johnson, asked O'Brien to stay on as congressional liaison. O'Brien also managed Johnson's successful 1964 reelection campaign.

The Johnson administration had a full agenda of domestic policy programs as well as foreign policy issues, especially the war in Vietnam. O'Brien was given significant latitude to shepherd the domestic legislation, known as the Great Society, through Congress. In 1965, for example, the Office of Congressional Relations was able to secure passage of the Higher Education Act over the objections of conservative members of Congress. Conservatives were concerned that the law gave scholarships to students who would otherwise have to work to pay for their education. Other bills that passed during O'Brien's tenure as congressional liaison included those creating the Peace Corps and the Alliance for Progress, Medicare, the model cities program, the Civil Rights Act of 1964, various voting rights legislation, and a nuclear test ban treaty.

By 1965 O'Brien was ready to return to the private sector. Johnson convinced him to stay in Washington, D.C., by appointing him postmaster general, a cabinet position. He was able to continue his legislative work as well as develop a new direction for the Post Office. As postmaster general, O'Brien suggested to Congress that the Post Office become a quasi-governmental corporation. Congress

balked at the suggestion until 1969, but he was able to introduce greater mechanization as one way to reduce costs at the Post Office.

O'Brien resigned from the Johnson cabinet in April 1968 in order to manage Senator Robert F. Kennedy's campaign for president. After Kennedy was assassinated in June 1968, O'Brien returned to Springfield "with nothing to do and nothing I wanted to do." Vice President Hubert Humphrey convinced him to lead the Humphrey for President campaign through the primary and general election as well as serve as chairman of the Democratic National Committee. Richard Nixon defeated Humphrey in November 1968.

For the remainder of the decade O'Brien managed his own public relations and management consulting firm, O'Brien Associates. Among the firm's clients was Hughes Enterprises, the conglomerate owned by the reclusive billionaire Howard Hughes. O'Brien returned to politics in 1970 as the chairman of the Democratic National Committee. A target of President Nixon's reelection apparatus, he endured three audits by the Internal Revenue Service. On 17 June 1972 five men were arrested while replacing listening devices in O'Brien's Democratic National Committee office in the Watergate complex. These men were eventually determined to be agents of Nixon's reelection campaign committee; the subsequent cover-up and investigation led to Nixon's resignation in 1974.

Retiring as Democratic National Committee chairman after the Democratic Convention in July 1972, he returned to O'Brien Associates. He also wrote his memoir, *No Final Victories: A Life in Politics—From John F. Kennedy to Wa-*

tergate (1974). In 1975 O'Brien became the commissioner of the National Basketball Association and lent his organizational talents to the growth and stabilization of the league. Retiring from that position on 1 February 1984, O'Brien spent the last years of his life in New York City, where he died of cancer. His wife and their son survived him. He is buried in St. Michael's Cemetery in Springfield, Massachusetts.

★

O'Brien's political papers can be found at the John F. Kennedy Library in Boston, Massachusetts, and at the Lyndon Baines Johnson Library in Austin, Texas. His memoir, *No Final Victories: A Life in Politics—From John F. Kennedy to Watergate* (1974), provides insight into his role as presidential adviser and Democratic Party operative. Nigel Bowles, *The White House and Capitol Hill: The Politics of Presidential Persuasion* (1987) is a scholarly examination of O'Brien's role as a congressional liaison. Patrick Anderson examines O'Brien's role as a presidential adviser in *The President's Men: White House Assistants of Franklin D. Roosevelt, Harry S Truman, Dwight D. Eisenhower, John F. Kennedy, and Lyndon B. Johnson* (1968). Obituaries are in the *New York Times* and the *Washington Post* (both 29 Sept. 1990). The Lawrence F. O'Brien Oral History Interview is available at both the Kennedy and Johnson presidential libraries.

JOHN DAVID RAUSCH, JR.

OCHS, Philip David ("Phil") (*b.* 19 December 1940 in El Paso, Texas; *d.* 9 April 1976 in Far Rockaway, New York), folk musician whose pointed political songs about the Vietnam War, the civil rights movement, American foreign policy, and other controversial issues made him one of the most influential singers and songwriters of the 1960s.

Ochs was the son of Jacob Ochs, an itinerant doctor, and Gertrude Phin Ochs, a homemaker and Scottish immigrant; he had one brother and one sister. After seeing combat at the Battle of the Bulge, Jacob Ochs was diagnosed with manic depression (now called bipolar disorder) and spent most of his son's childhood in and out of mental institutions. When not institutionalized he took whatever medical jobs he could find, moving his family at various times to New Mexico, Texas, New York, and Ohio. When Ochs was in the fifth grade he began playing the clarinet and soon demonstrated extraordinary musical aptitude. By age sixteen he was the lead clarinet soloist for Capital University's Conservatory of Music in Columbus, Ohio. In 1956, at his own request, he was sent to the Staunton Military Academy in Virginia, and after graduation he enrolled at Ohio State University in 1958. There he majored in journalism, became obsessed with Elvis Presley and James Dean, adopted a radical political philosophy, abandoned

Phil Ochs. AP/WIDE WORLD PHOTOS

the clarinet for the guitar, began composing folk songs, and started his own newspaper when the student paper refused to publish his leftist writings.

After winning local acclaim as a folksinger, Ochs dropped out of college one semester short of graduation and moved to New York City. On 15 March 1963 he performed his first paid concert at Gerde's Folk City in Greenwich Village and soon was playing at a variety of clubs and writing for the folk music magazine *Broadside*. That year he married Alice Skinner, with whom he had a daughter; they separated in 1965. Ochs's first exposure to a large audience came in July 1963 at the Newport Folk Festival, a performance that brought him widespread acclaim. As his fame grew, Ochs's Bleecker Street apartment became a frequent hangout for other folk singers, including the emerging Bob Dylan, who became a close friend. In 1964 Ochs's first album, *All the News That's Fit to Sing,* was released. Its title and contents reflected his songwriting process, which consisted largely of scouring newspapers for material. "Every newspaper headline is a potential song," he said. Like Dylan's early work, Ochs's songs were anything but subtle. They were harsh, witty, and pointed attacks on war, racism, and the establishment. The melodies were simple; the lyrics, Ochs felt, were the important part. Though well received by critics, the first album sold poorly, in part because radio stations refused to air its controversial songs. The album did, however, bring Ochs to the attention

157

of the Federal Bureau of Investigation (FBI), which monitored his movements, tapped his phone, and began compiling a file that numbered hundreds of pages by the time of his death.

In 1964 Ochs traveled to Mississippi for a series of concerts; he had just arrived when the bodies of three murdered civil rights workers were found in a nearby swamp. "I'm afraid they're going to kill me while I'm singing on stage," he told a friend. But he survived, and the experience led him to write one of his most significant songs, "Here's To the State of Mississippi," a scathing attack on white southerners. The song included the chorus "Here's to the land you've torn out the heart of / Mississippi, find yourself another country to be part of." In 1965 Ochs released his second album, *I Ain't Marching Anymore,* a brilliant collection of fourteen biting political songs. Among them were the clever satire "Draft Dodger Rag" and "That Was the President," an elegy to John Kennedy. But the undisputed masterpiece was the album's title track, a defiant declaration of pacifism that became an anthem of the antiwar movement. "The fact that you won't be hearing this song on the radio," Ochs wrote, "is more than enough justification for the writing of it."

In 1965 one of Ochs's most poignant songs, "There But for Fortune," became a Top Forty hit for Joan Baez. Always an aggressive self-promoter, Ochs had enough of a following by 1966 to sell out Carnegie Hall for a concert appearance that later became part of a live album, *Phil Ochs in Concert.* By this time Dylan had converted to rock music, and Ochs also began writing songs that were less overtly political. His best songs from 1966 and 1967, including "Changes," "When I'm Gone," and "Crucifixion," were more personal and abstract than his previous work, and more musically intricate. But to his dismay none of them became hits.

On 23 June 1967 Ochs organized and performed at an antiwar demonstration in Los Angeles, where he was living. Dubbed the War Is Over Rally, after the title of one of his songs, the event made national news when police attacked the peaceful demonstrators. Later that year Ochs released *Pleasures of the Harbor,* the first album to exemplify his new, subtler sound. In 1968 he became, along with Abbie Hoffman and Jerry Rubin, one of the founders of the Youth International Party (YIP). At the Democratic National Convention in Chicago the Yippies mocked the political process by nominating a pig for president. Chicago police, not amused, arrested Ochs, Hoffman, and four others for possession of livestock inside city limits. Ochs was released after a few hours in jail, but he later became a key witness for the defense in the infamous Chicago Seven trial of 1969. Ochs's next album, the prophetically named *Rehearsals for Retirement,* drew on his Chicago experience. Though it is now considered one of his best albums, it sold poorly at the time.

As the 1970s began Ochs seemed lost both artistically and personally. The public did not respond to his new style of songwriting, and two more albums flopped. So did an ill-conceived concert tour in which he wore a sparkling gold suit and sang Elvis Presley songs. He became an alcoholic and a Valium addict and began believing he had stomach cancer and was a member of the Central Intelligence Agency (CIA). He tried to hire Colonel Tom Parker, who managed Presley, as his manager, and when that failed, he tried to hire Colonel Harlan Sanders, the fast food entrepreneur, instead. He assumed a new identity, calling himself John Butler Train, lashing out at anyone who referred to him as Phil Ochs. He was arrested at various times for assault, driving under the influence, and weapons possession. Friends convinced Ochs to commit himself to a mental institution, but he left after one day. On 9 April 1976 Ochs hanged himself in the bathroom of his sister's apartment, where he had been living while trying to recover. The body was found by his fourteen-year-old nephew. Ochs was cremated and his ashes scattered around Edinburgh Castle in Scotland, his mother's homeland.

Throughout his career Ochs seemed to be tormented by his apparent inferiority to Dylan and that he was nowhere near as commercially successful. "It never ceases to amaze me how the American people allow the hit parade to hit them over the head with a parade of song after meaningless song about love," he wrote in 1963. Still, at his peak from 1963 through 1965, Ochs was arguably as influential as any folksinger in the nation, Dylan included. Songs like "I Ain't Marching Anymore" and "Here's To the State of Mississippi" helped drive a social movement that redefined American society. Like many whose lives revolved around the social movement of the 1960s, Ochs seemed to fall apart after that movement degenerated into chaos.

★

Ochs is the subject of two full-length biographies: Marc Eliot, *Death of a Rebel: A Biography of Phil Ochs* (1979; expanded ed. 1989), and Michael Schumacher, *There But for Fortune: The Life of Phil Ochs* (1996). David Cohen, *Phil Ochs: A Bio-Bibliography* (1999) contains biographical information, a bibliography, a discography, and an analysis of Ochs's work. Significant articles are in *Esquire* (Oct. 1976) and the *Austin Chronicle* (18 Aug. 1997).

ERIC ENDERS

O'CONNOR, Flannery (*b.* 25 March 1925 in Savannah, Georgia; *d.* 3 August 1964 in Milledgeville, Georgia), writer of bizarre novels and short stories focusing on the rural South and peopled with misfits and prophets, matriarchs and the maimed.

O'Connor was born Mary Flannery O'Connor; she dropped her first name for professional purposes. She was the only child of Edward Francis O'Connor, Jr., owner of a real estate business, and Regina L. Cline, a homemaker. When O'Connor was twelve, her father began to experience symptoms of disseminated lupus erythematosus, a fatal disease. The family moved into Regina O'Connor's family home in Milledgeville, Georgia. Witnessing her father's illness until he died in 1941 strengthened O'Connor's Roman Catholic faith. After graduating from high school in 1942, she enrolled in Georgia State College for Women (later Georgia College) in Milledgeville. Initially working on a degree in sociology, O'Connor shifted her focus to writing.

After graduating with a B.A. in 1945, O'Connor went to the Graduate School of Fine Arts at the University of Iowa, where she joined the Writer's Workshop. In 1946 she sold her first story, "The Geranium," to *Accent* magazine. During her second year at Iowa she was awarded the Rinehart Prize for part of what was to become her first novel, *Wise Blood* (1952). In June 1947 O'Connor received her M.F.A. in literature and accepted an invitation to Yaddo, a writer's colony in Saratoga Springs, New York. There she worked on *Wise Blood,* with different chapters published in *Mademoiselle, Sewanee Review,* and the *Partisan Review.* She also met lifelong friends. When her Yaddo friends Robert and Sally Fitzgerald moved to Ridgefield, Connecticut, in the summer of 1949, she moved in with them. O'Connor planned to stay in the North, but in late 1950, on her way home for Christmas, she became gravely ill. Doctors in Atlanta diagnosed her condition as lupus, the disease that had killed her father. O'Connor almost died, but the disease was arrested by massive injections of ACTH, a cortisone derivative.

It was not until the summer of 1951 that O'Connor was able to leave the hospital, too weak to climb stairs. O'Connor and her mother moved to Andalusia, the site of a dairy farm, a few miles outside Milledgeville. With her mother managing the farm, O'Connor went back to writing. When *Wise Blood* was published in 1952, it created a stir. Set in the rural South, it is a story of a quest for faith, full of dark comedy, violence, and religious symbolism. The characters are best described as grotesque. O'Connor's next book, *A Good Man Is Hard to Find and Other Stories* (1955), was critically acclaimed.

As a result of the massive doses of ACTH, O'Connor's bones were weakened to the extent that her hipbones could not support her weight, and she was forced to use aluminum crutches. Although it was difficult for her to get around, during the late 1950s and early 1960s O'Connor traveled to colleges and universities, lecturing to students and faculty and participating in symposia on writing. The lectures were informative and entertaining and covered a variety of topics. For example, "Some Aspects of the Grotesque in Southern Fiction" discusses the function of the grotesque, a major feature of her writing. Her lectures were often explanations of her novels and stories given to a bemused public.

In 1958 she was persuaded to travel to Lourdes, France, to seek a miraculous cure for her disease. In a letter to the poet Elizabeth Bishop she wrote, "We went to Europe, . . . but my capacity for staying at home has now been perfected, sealed & is going to last me the rest of my life."

Flannery O'Connor. CORBIS CORPORATION (BELLEVUE)

Although O'Connor initially had left home to become a writer, being at home did not mean that she became a recluse. O'Connor had many visitors, and she corresponded continually with the famous and the not so famous. She was particularly generous with her time and advice for aspiring writers.

O'Connor's masterpiece, *The Violent Bear It Away* (1960), is the story of the initiation of a reluctant prophet. Again using a bizarre set of characters, the concept of a journey to find faith, and religious symbolism and violence, O'Connor shows that humans must destroy and suffer to find themselves. The novel focuses on Protestant fundamentalism, appropriate because the author is from the Bible Belt but unusual since she is a Roman Catholic. O'Connor explained in one of her lectures that Protestants are in closer contact with God without the mediation of the church and, therefore, subject to more intensity. Although the hero, a young adolescent, tries to fight his fate, it overtakes him. The hardships of his journey, which include experiencing death, committing murder, and being raped, cause him to be reborn into the life of the spirit.

In early 1964, while at work on a third novel, O'Connor had an abdominal tumor removed. It was benign, but the procedure reactivated the lupus, and her kidneys were affected. O'Connor knew that she was dying and discontinued the novel. (A fragment of it, entitled "Why Do the Heathens Rage?" had been published in *Esquire* in 1963.) She focused instead on finishing enough short stories for another book. O'Connor slipped into a coma and died of kidney failure in Milledgeville. She is buried in Memory Hill Cemetery there. *Everything That Rises Must Converge* was published posthumously in 1965. As in her previous work, the setting and subject are of the contemporary South, and social issues are part of the fabric of the stories. In the title story, the serious subject of integration has moments of high comedy when a white woman, indignant at the presence of a black woman sitting opposite her on a bus, realizes that both of them are wearing the same hat. Although O'Connor believed in integration and recognized the plight of blacks in the South, she was reluctant to criticize her community openly.

"Revelation" is another story that alludes to social issues. Here, a self-righteous matriarch busies herself placing people into social classes until a college student, home from Wellesley College, throws a book at her, tries to strangle her, and calls her a pig. Violence leads to revelation. The final story in the volume, "Judgement Day," is a reworking of an old story first written at Iowa in 1946, and the subject of death and symbolic resurrection is particularly poignant as the dying author labored to complete her work.

Although O'Connor did not publish a large number of books, she became a major figure in the literary world. Her writing was critically acclaimed and translated into a dozen languages. Writing about the rural South in a contemporary time frame, O'Connor's focus on the spiritual condition of modern humanity has a universal appeal. She detected an attitude of smugness and self-righteousness in people that she believed needed to be changed. In addition, the deeply religious O'Connor saw the shallow complacency of an increasingly highly rationalized and technological society and felt people's need to rediscover faith. But O'Connor rejected a return to the past. There was no desire to hark back to the Old South and its traditions. Those characters who yearned to return to so-called better days usually provoke some type of death or destruction. To urge her readers toward new insight, O'Connor used humor, violence, and the grotesque. She juxtaposed comedy and murder, the intensity of belief with the despair of those who had no faith. Her techniques often upset readers, but to be disturbed and repulsed can lead people to view their world in new ways.

★

O'Connor's papers are at the Georgia College Library in Milledgeville. Her lectures and essays are collected in Sally and Robert Fitzgerald, eds., *Mystery and Manners: Occasional Prose* (1969). Sally Fitzgerald selected and edited the *Letters of Flannery O'Connor: The Habit of Being* (1979). Numerous studies of O'Connor have biographical material and criticism of her work, including Stanley Edgar Hyman, "Flannery O'Connor," in *Seven American Women Writers of the Twentieth Century: An Introduction* (1963); James A. Grimshaw, Jr., *The Flannery O'Connor Companion* (1981); Jill P. Baumgaertner, *Flannery O'Connor: A Proper Scaring* (1988); and Richard Giannone, *Flannery O'Connor, Hermit Novelist* (2000). An obituary is in the *New York Times* (4 Aug. 1964).

MARCIA B. DINNEEN

ODETTA (*b.* 31 December 1930 in Birmingham, Alabama), singer, noted for her versatility, penetrating voice, and showmanship, who revived many almost forgotten folk songs through dedicated research and relentless practice.

Known almost all her life by her first name only, Odetta was born Odetta Holmes. Her father, Reuben Holmes, worked in a steel mill; her mother, Flora Sanders, worked as a domestic servant. Reuben died soon after his daughter's birth. Upon her mother's remarriage to Zadock Felious, Odetta called herself Odetta Holmes Felious. The family moved to Los Angeles in 1937. Odetta learned to play her grandmother's piano and developed an interest in classical music. By her tenth birthday her exceptional voice was in evidence at the Congregational Church near her home, and at thirteen Odetta began classical training. The range of her voice was amazing, varying from contralto to baritone to basso.

Odetta performing at the Berkeley Community Center, 1958. TED STRESHINSKY/CORBIS

In 1947 Odetta graduated from Belmont High School in Los Angeles and worked as a housekeeper. She attended night classes at Los Angeles City College, from which she earned a degree in classical music and musical comedy. In 1949 she landed a job with the chorus for the road company of the musical *Finian's Rainbow*. While in San Francisco with the company, she became the resident singer at the Tin Angel nightclub in 1953. A club owner in New York City read of Odetta's voice and hired her for a gig at the Blue Angel. It was there that the singers Pete Seeger and Harry Belafonte heard her and began helping her with her career.

In the 1950s Odetta performed in motion pictures and became singer in residence at the Turnabout Theater in Los Angeles. During those years she studied folk music and developed her unique manner of blending from one song into the next without breaking. In 1956 her first album, *Odetta Sings Ballads and Blues*, was released to positive reviews. She was compared favorably to Bessie Smith and Leadbelly, two people she credited with influencing her style. In 1959 Odetta broke into television by appearing with the writer Langston Hughes on the series *Lamp unto My Feet*. She also recorded songs with Belafonte and performed with the Count Basie Orchestra at New York City's Hunter College, then with Seeger at Yale University. Her ability to sing not only folk music but the blues and opera made her much in demand as a singer, and her acting skills were also sought. On 1 May 1959 Odetta married Dan Gordon and settled in Chicago. They later divorced, and she remarried twice (to Gary Sheed in the late 1960s and to Iversen "Louisiana Red" Minter in 1997). In 1960 she

landed the role of Nancy in the film version of William Faulkner's *Sanctuary*, a role she played with emotive power. Thereafter she took parts in many television series episodes.

The album *Odetta Sings Christmas Spirituals* was released in 1960, revealing the deeply spiritual aspect of her performances. She said that she assumed different characters for the songs she sang. This theatrical aspect of her performances was hard to capture on records, but *Sometimes I Feel Like Crying* (1962) and *Odetta Sings the Blues* (1968) came close. Her singing on these albums ranged from brassy to operatic to scratchy nasal, making the spirit of the songs come alive. Such performances influenced a host of singers, from Bob Dylan to Janis Joplin. Odetta taught herself to play the guitar, accompanying herself by playing by ear; in the 1960s she became almost as noted for her hard-driving, bold guitar playing as for her singing.

During the 1960s Odetta was involved in the civil rights movement. Her albums had already blurred the color line in music, erasing it altogether in *Christmas Spirituals*, but for all her acclaim from people of all races, she was still an African American in an era of racial revolution. She participated in the protest in Selma, Alabama, and in 1963 was in the historic march and rally in Washington, D.C., where the Reverend Martin Luther King, Jr., gave his "I Have a Dream" speech. Remarkably, just two years later, Birmingham, Alabama, which had seen much racial unrest, honored Odetta with a ceremony and the key to the city.

In the meantime Odetta's albums came out rapidly, each meeting with an eager audience: *One Grain of Sand* (1963), *It's a Mighty World* (1964), *Odetta Sings of Many Things* (1964), *Odetta Sings Dylan* (1965), *Ballads for Americans*

(1965), *Odetta in Japan* (1965), *Odetta* (1967), *Best of Odetta* (1967), *Odetta at Carnegie Hall* (1967), and *Odetta Sings the Blues* (1968). Never again would she make as many recordings in so short a time. In them, her mature style is evident; in *Odetta at Carnegie Hall*, in particular, her free-flowing approach to her program, in which she could shift to any of the songs in her vast repertoire at any time, is most in evidence. This unpredictable shifting of songs made it hard for bands and other performers to work with her; therefore she usually performed on her own.

After the 1960s Odetta's painstaking scholarship grew more in evidence. She frequented the Library of Congress, digging up old, perhaps forgotten, songs from chain gangs, field workers, cowboys, and many other sources, and practiced them for months at a time before she thought they were ready for performance. In so doing she became not only one of America's most remarkable singers but one of its greatest music historians, bringing to life the words and tunes of the country's past and its working people.

★

The entry on Odetta in *Current Biography 1960* is brief but laden with facts about her early career. Wilfred Mellers, *Angels of the Night: Popular Female Singers of Our Time* (1986), offers relevant data. Laura C. Jarmon, "Odetta," in *Notable Black American Women*, edited by Jessie Carney Smith (1992), is the fullest article on the singer. Toby Bielawski's interview, "The Wisdom and Music of Odetta," for *Radiance* magazine (winter 1999), is an excellent resource for Odetta's views of her music.

KIRK H. BEETZ

O'HAIR, Madalyn Murray (*b.* 13 April 1919 in Pittsburgh, Pennsylvania; *d.* 1995 [body found in January 2001] near Austin, Texas), founder and president of American Atheists, Inc., who was instrumental in securing the landmark Supreme Court ruling in 1963 prohibiting school prayer.

Born Madalyn Mays, O'Hair was the daughter of John Irvin Mays, a wealthy building contractor who could afford all the best for his child and his wife, Lena Scholle Mays, a homemaker. O'Hair remembered her early childhood with fondness, from rides in chauffeured limousines to making mud pies. She attended Sunday school at a Presbyterian church. The 1929 stock market crash, however, ruined her father's business, and he became one of millions of men moving about the United States looking for work as a carpenter, electrician, and repairman.

According to O'Hair, she came to despise God at the age of thirteen, when she read the Bible for the first time, and found the Old Testament to be horribly cruel, the New Testament to be "too mystical," and the miracles to be beyond belief. She developed a general contempt not only

Madalyn Murray O'Hair, 1969. AP/WIDE WORLD PHOTOS

for Christian beliefs, but for people in general. For example, she described herself as knowing little, "But compared to most cud-chewing, small-talking, stupid American women, I'm a brain." O'Hair attended the University of Toledo from 1936 to 1937 and the University of Pittsburgh from 1938 to 1939. She eloped with a man named J. Roths in 1941; the two were separated while they were both serving in the armed forces. During World War II she enlisted in the United States Women's Army Corps and became a cryptographer on General Dwight D. Eisenhower's staff. She became involved with William J. Murray during the war. At the end of World War II, she divorced Roths and married Murray, with whom she already had one son, William J. Murray III. Later they had a second son, Jon Garth Murray, before they divorced in the mid-1950s.

She entered Ashland College in Ohio in 1948, earning a B.A. She then attended graduate school at Western Reserve University (later renamed Case Western Reserve University) from 1948 to 1949, then Ohio Northern University from 1949 to 1951. She attended South Texas College of Law, receiving an LL.D. in 1953. On a scholarship from the National Institutes of Health, she studied social work at Howard University in 1954.

O'Hair found employment as a social worker in Baltimore. In October 1960 her son William came home from junior high school complaining about how he was treated. One complaint was that he was uncomfortable with religion in the school. O'Hair wrote to the school board to complain about her son having to be part of school prayers, and the school board responded that state law mandated the prayer at the start of each day at school. She took her complaint to the state government, and the state attorney general issued a finding that school prayer and reading the Bible in school were constitutional, but students should be allowed to excuse themselves from participation in these activities.

O'Hair's efforts drew public attention, and she received hate mail. O'Hair believed that teachers discriminated against her sons, and this motivated her lawsuit, filed 7 December 1960. Superior Court Judge J. Gilbert Prendergast dismissed the suit in April 1961, saying that finding in O'Hair's favor would force students to submit to her atheist beliefs. She appealed to the Maryland Court of Appeals, where she again lost, and then to the United States Supreme Court on 15 May 1962. Soon afterward she was fired from her job for incompetence.

The Supreme Court, asserting that public schools must be neutral in matters of religion, issued a ruling on 17 June 1963 in which it declared that the Maryland statute requiring prayer in public schools violated the First Amendment to the U.S. Constitution. O'Hair spent much of the next decade filing suits to outlaw tax exemptions for churches and clerics, as well as tax deductions for donations to churches. She sued to eliminate mandatory periods of meditation in schools and to remove "In God We Trust" from American currency. All of these lawsuits failed.

On 18 October 1965 she married Richard Franklin O'Hair, variously described as an intelligence agent and an artist, settling in Austin, Texas. By this time O'Hair was famous and much in demand for interviews. She tried to capitalize on her notoriety by writing hate-filled, anti-Christian tracts, but publishers would not accept them, so she founded her own publishing company, the American Atheist Press, and published her writings herself, beginning with *Why I Am an Atheist* (1965; second edition 1991). Sometimes she claimed that Jesus was a myth and the New Testament a gathering of folk tales; other times she said that Jesus was evil and an advocate of bizarre sexual practices.

She apparently loved being the center of attention and would say anything to be noticed. When participating in debates, sometimes on television, whenever another participant would begin to speak, she would shout at the top of her lungs, "There is no god! There is no god!" repeatedly, drowning out the other speakers until all efforts to debate were surrendered. When it was her turn to speak, she continued shouting, "There is no god!" By 1970 journalists were calling her a "clown." She referred to herself as "the

most hated woman in America" and appeared to take pleasure in the confusion and unhappiness she caused.

By the mid-1970s she had given up filing lawsuits, asserting that the courts were biased against her. She continued writing and publishing tracts into the 1990s, titling one *Jesus Christ: Super Fraud* (1984), but her bigotry had worn thin and her hatred too predictable to hold the public's interest. Further, her son William, suffering from alcoholism and with two failed marriages behind him, declared that atheism was an unfulfilling way of life. By 1980 the young man who had once helped instigate the school-prayer lawsuit was publicizing his conversion to Christianity and his membership in the Baptist church, facts that reputedly disheartened his mother.

Sometime in 1995 O'Hair, her other son, Jon, and her granddaughter, Robin Murray-O'Hair, disappeared. About $600,000 was missing from the atheist organizations she ran, and journalists speculated that she had run away with the money. The Austin police thought otherwise—the money was later found in the form of gold coins she kept in her house—and by 1998 had managed to identify three kidnappers, including an employee O'Hair had fired for embezzling funds from her organizations. In 2001 this employee led police to the graves of O'Hair, Jon, and Robin. Her son William had her remains cremated and provided no religious services, as his mother had wished. Her ashes were interred secretly somewhere in or near Austin.

★

See O'Hair, *An Atheist Epic: Bill Murray, the Bible, and the Baltimore Board of Education* (1970; rev. ed., 1989) for information on her lawsuit that brought the Supreme Court ruling banning forced prayer in public schools. Keith Demaret, "Once the Boy Behind the Ban on School Prayers, Bill Murray Now Prays for a National Change of Heart," in *People Weekly* (26 Mar. 1984) gives a good account of William Murray's efforts to allow religion in public schools. Don Feder, "Fallout from Secular Revolution Still Clouds America's Public Square," in *Insight on the News* (5 Mar. 2001) discusses O'Hair's legacy. An obituary is "O'Hair Case Solved, but Legends Linger" in *Christian Century* (21 Feb. 2001).

KIRK H. BEETZ

O'HORGAN, Thomas ("Tom") (*b.* 3 May 1926 in Chicago, Illinois), composer and director who directed avant-garde, antiestablishment plays in the 1960s, most notably the musical *Hair*.

O'Horgan was encouraged in his theatrical pursuits by his father, Foster, a talented singer who loved the theater but who went into the printing business instead of pursuing his dream. An only child, O'Horgan was, as he once said in an interview, "spoiled rotten" by his parents. In grade school O'Horgan told his teacher he wanted to be a stage manager and played with a puppet theater his father had made for him. In the fourth grade his teacher, Robert Sheehan, introduced O'Horgan to a version of the opera *Hansel and Gretel*, and O'Horgan began singing the part of Hansel.

From that time on, theater and music were synonymous to him. After graduating from high school O'Horgan attended DePaul University in Chicago, where he studied music composition, dabbled in writing operas, and formed his own opera group. He eventually earned his B.A. and M.A. and began working on a doctorate. He eventually moved to New York City and sang in a male quintet. Returning to Chicago, O'Horgan worked with the Second City theater group, which was called the Playwright's Theatre Club until 1954 and The Compass Players from 1955 to 1959. The group included Barbara Harris, Mike Nichols, and Elaine May. While there, O'Horgan wrote nearly two dozen musical scores for various productions. He then developed a bizarre nightclub act in which he played the harp and sang.

After traveling around the country performing in nightclubs, O'Horgan returned to New York and began directing plays off-off Broadway, most notably at a downtown experimental theater club called Cafe LaMama. His directorial debut at Cafe LaMama was Jean Genet's play *The Maids*, in which O'Horgan followed Genet's staging instructions and cast two men in the roles of the two sinister maids. O'Horgan directed plays at Cafe LaMama over a period of eight years, from 1961 to 1968. He also acted and composed music there. At one point O'Horgan decided he did not want a normal home and possessions. He moved out of his loft apartment and stayed with Ellen Stewart, who owned Cafe LaMama. "This was all really part of a movement," O'Horgan said in a *New York Times Magazine* article in 1972. "The whole materialistic thing seemed ridiculous to a lot of us."

O'Horgan directed his first off-Broadway production, called *6 from LaMama*, at the Martinique Theater on 11 April 1966. In a review in the *New York Times*, critic Stanley Kauffmann wrote, "The major contribution here is by the director, . . . O'Horgan. . . . [He] shows a fundamental . . . gift: the ability to see in a script the physical unfolding that will articulate its essences and rhythms."

O'Horgan worked tirelessly on what appeared to be an endless series of plays, including Rochelle Owens's black pastorale *Futz*, for which he won an Obie in 1967. He also directed the film version in 1969. In his *New York Times* review of the play critic Clive Barnes noted, "Mr. O'Horgan has evident talent, and wherever it's leading him, it's leading him fast."

It soon became apparent where O'Horgan's talent was leading him. As part of the experimental underground New York theater world, O'Horgan knew two members of the Open Theater group who had cowritten an off-Broadway musical slated to go to Broadway. Gerome Ragni and James Rado, along with their collaborator, Galt MacDermot, asked O'Horgan to direct it. The musical *Hair*, a trenchantly topical production about race, politics, and war, opened on Broadway in May 1968. Referred to as the hippie antiestablishment musical, the play focused on antiwar and other philosophies espoused by the 1960s longhaired, counterculture youth. *Hair* also included explicitly physical and profane segments, including a scene in which the actors disrobe, marking the first time full frontal nudity by a group of actors occurred on a Broadway stage.

Outrageous and daring for its day, *Hair* was a hit. Michael Smith, writing in the 2 May 1968 issue of the *Village Voice*, summed it up succinctly when he wrote, "Instead of reviewing *Hair* I should simply report that something downtown, dirty, ballsy, and outrageous has hit Broadway at last, . . . and hopefully Broadway will never be the same."

Hair's notoriety grew so quickly that productions opened in Europe in both Munich and London in the fall of 1968. Productions in Hamburg, Germany; Belgrade, Yugoslavia; and Sydney, Australia, quickly followed. With his 1968 off-Broadway directorial hits of *Futz* and *Tom Paine*, which was originally conceived for the LaMama troupe and taken to Europe first, O'Horgan's reputation was growing rapidly. He was hailed as Director of the Year in a 1968 *Newsweek* article. O'Horgan's success continued into the 1970s with his direction of the plays *Lenny* and Andrew Lloyd Webber's *Jesus Christ Superstar*, both appearing on Broadway in 1971. He also directed the restaging of *Hair* in 1977.

Although O'Horgan's work reflected the 1960s in terms of its rebellious and antiestablishment nature, his directorial efforts were sometimes lambasted for presenting work in a way that was more campy than relevant. Nevertheless, O'Horgan was one of the primary avant-garde directors who took New York theater, which many critics believed was in its death throes, and injected it with imagination and vision. Although his vision could be bizarre and heavy-handed in terms of visual and physical tricks, O'Horgan had a knack for getting the most from his actors. One technique he devised for his prerehearsals involved using sensory techniques to help actors integrate their mind and body and then channel the resultant "energy" into an unfettered performance. One critic noted, "O'Horgan does not so much direct actors as 'tune' them."

O'Horgan, the only director ever to have had four productions running simultaneously on Broadway (*Hair, Lenny, Jesus Christ Superstar,* and *Inner City*), has continued to direct plays by authors such as Sam Shepard and Lanford Wilson. He has also been involved in staging operas and numerous other projects. Additionally, he has written more than forty musical scores for operas, plays, drama, films, and television.

★

Howard Junker, "Director of the Year," *Newsweek* (3 June 1968) provides a look at O'Horgan and his work just as he was rising to prominence. Also see two other profiles of O'Horgan: "The Cerebral Trip Is Over," *Time* (25 Oct. 1971), and Maggie Paley, "Superstar Becomes a Circus," *Life* (Oct. 1971). An especially interesting article about O'Horgan that describes making the rounds with the director as he visits productions of several of his plays is John Gruen's "Do You Mind Critics Calling You Cheap, Decadent, Sensationalistic, Gimmicky, Vulgar, Overinflated, Megalomaniacal?" *New York Times Magazine* (2 Jan. 1972).

DAVID PETECHUK

OLDENBURG, Claes Thure (*b.* 28 January 1929 in Stockholm, Sweden), pop sculptor and painter who endowed his soft sculpture and monuments with a humor and fantasy unique in the pop style of the 1960s.

The older of two sons of Swedish diplomat Goesta Oldenburg and concert singer Sigrid Elisabeth (Lindforss) Oldenburg, Oldenburg was brought to the United States as an infant, moved to Oslo in 1933, then settled in Chicago in 1936. In his late teens and early twenties he frequented the seedy environment along Rush Street's burlesque row. He studied literature and art at Yale University, earning a

B.A. in 1950. In 1953 he became a naturalized U.S. citizen. In June 1956 he moved to Manhattan, settling at 330 East 4th Street, which served as his studio until June 1961. On 13 April 1960 he married Patricia Joan Muschinski; they divorced in 1970.

Through his friendship with Allan Kaprow and Red Grooms, Oldenburg cofounded a gallery in the Judson Memorial Church, where in May–June 1959 he held his first public one-man show; it featured fragile sculptures made by dripping newspaper into wheat paste and setting this on a chicken wire armature. In early 1960 he staged six group performances, or "happenings," in the Judson Gallery. In December 1961 and January 1962 Oldenburg set up his *Store*, which he had incorporated as a business called the Ray Gun Manufacturing Company, in two versions at the Judson Gallery and then the Reuben Gallery. He put up for sale brightly painted three-dimensional plaster sculptures in lumpy shapes of food and apparel items, the kinds that he saw about him in delicatessens and bargain basements. A plate of meat was priced at $399.98 and a man's sock at $199.95.

In the summer of 1962 the show was expanded at the Green Gallery on 57th Street to include gargantuan soft sculptures made of sewn pieces of canvas that were painted and stuffed with foam rubber. These included a five- by seven-foot hamburger and a ten-foot ice cream cone. In a sense, these evoked the human condition more poignantly than the hard sculpture of a person because, like flesh, they

Claes Oldenburg in his studio. ARCHIVE PHOTOS, INC.

yielded to the prodding of a finger. Beginning in 1963 Oldenburg made soft white vinyl works, "ghost" versions of appliances, such as fans and typewriters, and that year prepared an entire environment, his *Bedroom Ensemble*. In March–April 1965 came the first drawings of his monuments, works to be set in the outside environment rather than in a gallery or other enclosed space. In 1965 Oldenburg moved from the Chelsea Hotel, where he had been staying, to a new studio loft at 404 East 14th Street.

Oldenburg's soft sculptures are richly allusive. The sexual component is strongly present in the *Bedroom Ensemble* and in works associated with it, where the light switches are like giant nipples and the plugs and wall sockets evoke sexual intercourse. But the allusions, which are often set forth in elaborate notes and drawings, can be multiple and many-faceted. Of his *Giant Soft Drum Set* (1967) he observed, among other points, that it would not have developed without his experience as artist in residence at Aspen; he compared the piece to architecture, "with the wooden sticks being the poles and the metal cymbals the roofing." Noting that his first and only musical instrument was a set of drums, he described the drum set as "the image of the human body of both sexes, a bisexual object." The drooping *Giant Soft Fan* (1966–1967) is more than a flaccid inept apparatus (as are all his apparatuses—telephones, toilets, etc.). He finds in this object connections we would never suspect. He pointed out, for instance, that the blades represent a banana with its skin peeled back, that the motion of the blades recalls that of windmill flails, and that the word *fan* means Satan in Swedish.

Some of the monuments were exercises of fantasy, never meant to be erected. These included a Good Humor bar with a bite taken out, for a tall building on New York's Park Avenue (1965); moving giant pool balls that would shoot across Central Park at random times, crushing the unfortunate pedestrian who happened to be in the way (1967); and huge toilet float balls to be floated down the Thames River (1967). Actually set up on the campus of Yale University in 1969 was the aluminum tube with steel body of his *Lipstick (Ascending) on Caterpillar Tracks*, joined images of warfare and female consumerism, with the lipstick resembling a red-tipped warhead.

In 1961 Oldenburg set forth a manifesto consisting of proclamations beginning with the phrase "I am for an art that. . . ." The world described was chaotic, dangerous, unpredictable, and exciting, one filled with things in constant motion that were messy and noisy and ridiculous. Examples include: "I am for an art that comes out of a chimney like black hair and scatters in the sky"; "I am for an art that spills out of an old man's purse when he is bounced off a passing fender"; "I am for the art of red and white gasoline pumps and blinking biscuit signs"; "I am for an art of old plaster and new enamel." Major accom-

plishments after the 1960s included the forty-five-foot-high Cor-Ten and stainless steel clothespin installed opposite Philadelphia's City Hall on 25 June 1976, the bicentennial year. In the spring of the Clothespin (Oldenburg always preferred the old-fashioned wooden clothespins to hold together canvas sections) one can see the number "76." The clothespin form can be perceived as that of two lovers; a sexually aggressive advancing female, her legs spread; a bird of flight; or a missile.

Oldenburg married Coosje Van Bruggen on 22 July 1977. Together they set up the *Batcolumn* (a 100-foot-tall column in the shape of a baseball bat) beside the U.S. Social Security Administration Building in Chicago in 1977, and a *Spoonbridge and Cherry* (a metal bridge in the form of a spoon with a cherry resting in it) in the Walker Art Center in Minneapolis (1985–1988).

Oldenburg kept the wittiness of pop art but replaced its typical hardness and distancing and occasional social commentary with objects that seemed more accessible because they projected a variety of anthropomorphic qualities.

★

Barbara Rose, *Claes Oldenburg* (1970), includes many drawings and statements by the artist. Other works about Oldenburg are Barbara Haskell, *Claes Oldenburg: Object Into Monument* (1971); Guggenheim Museum and National Gallery of Art, *Claes Oldenburg: An Anthology* (1995), with essays by Germano Celant, Dieter Koepplin, and Mark Rosenthal and excellent full-page color photos from the early work, some with audience observing and participating; and Richard H. Axsom and David Platzker, *Printed Stuff: Prints, Posters, and Ephemera by Claes Oldenburg: A Catalogue Raisonné 1958–1996* (1997).

ABRAHAM A. DAVIDSON

OLIPHANT, Patrick Bruce ("Pat") (*b.* 24 July 1935 in Adelaide, Australia), journalist, fine artist, and one of the world's most influential political cartoonists, noted for his caricatures of seven American presidents, including Lyndon B. Johnson and Richard M. Nixon.

Oliphant is the son of Donald Knox Oliphant, who was a cartographer for the Ministry of Lands of Australia, and Grace Lillian (Price) Oliphant, a homemaker. The family's home was located up in the hills, about an hour from Adelaide by train. Oliphant disliked the lonely, solitary life his family's home imposed, although it encouraged him to develop his imagination. During the early 1940s he attended a one-room schoolhouse, but at age eleven he began commuting to Adelaide to go to school. His father encouraged his interest in drawing.

In 1953 Oliphant took a job as a copyboy for the *Adelaide News,* where he was able to observe the political cartoonist

Patrick Oliphant. AP/WIDE WORLD PHOTOS

Norman Mitchell at work. Cartooning looked like fun. After four months at the *Adelaide News,* he took a job at the *Adelaide Advertiser.* For a year he worked as a copyboy in the photographic department and then became a press artist, working on images for advertisements and illustrations for articles. He also touched up photographs and drew weather maps for the newspaper's agricultural supplement, the *Chronicle.*

When the *Adelaide Advertiser*'s political cartoonist left the newspaper in 1955, Oliphant got the chance to be the new political cartoonist. He quickly chafed under the conservative policies of the newspaper's management. He found that he was not supposed to offend people with his cartoons. Therefore, he invented Punk, a little penguin who always appeared in a corner of an Oliphant cartoon, making barbed comments about the subject of the cartoon. Punk quickly became a favorite of readers, and through Punk's asides Oliphant was able to insert caustic commentary in his cartoons without running afoul of the tastes of his bosses. On 11 January 1958 Oliphant married Hendrika DeVries, with whom he had three children. They later divorced.

In 1964 one of America's most admired political cartoonists, Paul Conrad, left his job at the *Denver Post* to work for the *Los Angeles Times.* Oliphant, who had immigrated to the United States that same year, applied for and got Conrad's old job. He found working for the *Denver Post* to be liberating, and his work soon showed signs of maturing into the classic form that would make him one

of the world's most influential cartoonists. He eschewed labels and trite symbols; he expected his caricatures of public figures to be good enough to be recognized by the public without labeling them. Oliphant's drawings of President Lyndon B. Johnson began with Johnson appearing as a tall, strong, erect figure. In Oliphant's cartoons, Johnson might be the only fully drawn character, with all other figures flat, giving the effect of Johnson's personality dominating whatever else was depicted in a cartoon. Oliphant almost immediately opposed U.S. involvement in the Vietnam War, and as the country became more deeply enmeshed in the conflict, his depictions of Johnson became more savage. Yet unlike most of his contemporaries, he sometimes captured the sad, injured humanity of Johnson. His sharply biting commentary can be seen in a cartoon called "Frazzled," in which a standing Johnson holds several phones to his ears, while others ring, and he says, "Yes, General Westmoreland, we're working on your quota—Hello Detroit, how many hundred thousand troops?—hold it, there—Hello, Minneapolis? . . . " At the time, race riots had broken out in American cities, and the cartoon depicts Johnson desperately trying to keep up with events that have spun out of his control. This portrayal contrasts with another Oliphant cartoon of the same period, "Night Reading," in which Johnson is carefully drawn, his face deeply careworn, his body slumping over a desk, his big hands holding open Dr. Benjamin Spock's book, *Baby and Child Care* (1957), while on his desk are scattered official reports on crime, the Middle East, and Vietnam. Johnson's first grandchild was about to be born, and Oliphant's cartoon is a reminder of the humanity of Johnson. Johnson's hunched, sad figure holds in it the president of the Great Society, who had wanted to be the president who did the most for the helpless since Abraham Lincoln. Punk stands beside the desk and asks, "Isn't Dr. Spock in the Peace Moveme . . .?" Another little figure holds out his hands to Punk and cries out, "Shaddup!" It is as if Oliphant is telling himself to lay off Johnson for this one moment of humanity. Oliphant won the 1967 Pulitzer Prize for editorial cartoons, possibly for his consistent ability to go beyond the joke or gag in his drawings to convey the deeper meaning of the toll government policies, bureaucracy, and leaders exacted from humanity. Upon winning the Pulitzer Prize, he criticized the awards committee for favoring cartoons that depicted America in a favorable light (they had liked his cartoon of Ho Chi Minh's unwillingness to make peace), probably killing his chances of winning another award.

The election of Richard M. Nixon to the presidency in 1968 was a boon to political cartoonists; his bushy eyebrows, shifty eyes, and prominent jowls were captured by many cartoonists, including Oliphant. Nixon's administration seemed filled with eccentric characters to be caricatured in cartoons. In Oliphant's cartoons Nixon started out as a boldly drawn figure, a master at political infighting, a man skilled at handling the powers of the presidency. In one early Nixon cartoon—"Low Profile?"—Oliphant depicts the president as a big, scowling bomber dropping explosives over North Vietnam, with Punk saying, "Please! Don't call it bombing—call it protective reaction," a sly comment on Nixon's penchant for manipulating the English language to soften the impression his actions would have on the public. By 1970 Oliphant's depictions of Nixon used fewer lines than before, and the lines were thin, not thick, even for Nixon's eyebrows, and like Johnson before, Nixon appeared increasingly overwhelmed by events; in "Security Blanket," Nixon sucks his thumb and holds the blanket "Sensitive National Secrets" around him while menacing eyes glare out of darkness at the president; Punk, too, hides in the blanket.

Oliphant's style was imitated by innumerable cartoonists in the 1970s and beyond; sharply drawn figures with detailed faces and clothing, the use of a little figure like Punk to make additional comments on the subject of a cartoon, and the uncompromising criticism of public figures all became parts of American cartooning. Oliphant always said he disliked being imitated, that younger cartoonists should find styles of their own, but no one can be blamed for using the devices of an acknowledged master of the art. Besides, few cartoonists managed to combine Oliphant's biting commentary with the depth of humanity found in his best cartoons.

★

Oliphant's papers are in the Library of Congress. Oliphant and Wendy Wick Reaves, *Oliphant's Presidents: Twenty-five Years of Caricature* (1990), includes a memoir by Oliphant and an appreciation of his art by Reaves. Jean W. Ross, "Oliphant, Patrick (Bruce)," in *Contemporary Authors*, vol. 101 (1981), includes an interview with Oliphant. Patrick Butters, "A Serious Side: America's Premier Political Cartoonist Also Is a Fine, If Mischievous, Sculptor," in *Insight on the News* 14, no. 17 (11 May 1998): 38, offers an appreciation of Oliphant's fine art.

KIRK H. BEETZ

ONASSIS, Jacqueline Lee Kennedy ("Jackie") (*b.* 28 July 1929 in Southampton, Long Island, New York; *d.* 19 May 1994 in New York City), first lady and widow of the thirty-fifth president of the United States, Onassis led America and the world through the dark days of mourning after the assassination of her husband, President John F. Kennedy.

Born Jacqueline Lee Bouvier, Onassis was named for her father, John Vernou "Black Jack" Bouvier III, and for her mother's family surname. Her mother, Janet Norton Lee, was of a prominent family in Hamptons society, the daughter of a bank chairman. Onassis's father, from a family of financiers, was himself a stockbroker. Onassis was the elder of the couple's two daughters. When her parents separated

Jacqueline Kennedy Onassis. CORBIS CORPORATION (BELLEVUE)

in 1936 Onassis was seven years old; the marriage dissolved in a bitter divorce in 1940. Her mother married Hugh D. Auchincloss in 1942. Onassis, upset by the antics of her parents, turned for comfort to her sister and to their assorted pets. She studied ballet and attended posh schools. While working in Washington, D.C., as a reporter after graduating from George Washington University in 1951, she met her future husband, John F. Kennedy, then a U.S. congressman.

Jack and Jackie Kennedy were married on 12 September 1953 in Newport, Rhode Island. They rented a home in Georgetown. After the stillbirth of their first child in 1956, a daughter, Caroline, was born in 1957. Kennedy was elected to the U.S. presidency in 1960. Their son, John F. Kennedy, Jr., was born just weeks before the inauguration, and the new first family created a stir—a handsome, young war-hero president, a beautiful socialite first lady, and their two small children. As the wife of the president, the charming Onassis captivated the world's leaders.

Soon after settling into the White House, Onassis began planning to restore the building as a monument for the American people. She formed the White House Historical Association and secured a $50,000 contribution from *Life* magazine to fund a major restoration project of the mansion. Congress responded positively to her request to declare White House furnishings government property. She hired contractors, revived the structure and its interior, and scoured the basement of the residence for discarded antiques of historical significance. "Everything in the White House . . . must have a reason for being there," she said. In 1962 she arranged for a televised tour of the newly redecorated residence.

Onassis instituted many more informal evenings at the White House than her predecessors had hosted. Washington society eagerly sought invitations to these events, which often featured entertainment by a famous musician or other artist. Onassis lent her support to the arts throughout her years as first lady.

In August 1963 Onassis gave birth to another son, Patrick Bouvier Kennedy. He was the first child born to a sitting president in more than six decades, but he was born prematurely and died two days later. Onassis went into seclusion. She ventured forth publicly for the first time three months later to accompany her husband on a trip to Dallas, Texas, where on 22 November 1963, against the wishes of the U.S. Secret Service, the president and first lady traveled in a motorcade in an open convertible. When the motorcade entered Dallas's Dealey Plaza, three rifle shots sounded within seconds of each other. The first shot missed the motorcade altogether, a second bullet pierced the back of Kennedy's neck, and a third and fatal bullet shattered the back of his skull. The motorcade rushed to Parkland Hospital, where President John F. Kennedy was

pronounced dead at 1:00 P.M. Onassis refused to change from her blood-stained suit as she returned to Washington, D.C., with her husband's body.

Upon her return Onassis gave instructions to the White House chief of protocol to "find out how [Abraham] Lincoln was buried." At the funeral the thirty-four-year-old widow wore a heavy mourning veil as she walked behind the flag-draped casket, borne on a horse-drawn caisson and accompanied by a riderless horse. During the burial ceremony she lit an eternal flame at her husband's gravesite at Arlington National Cemetery. She spent her time in the days and weeks after the funeral distributing mementos of the slain president to those who knew him. When she moved from the White House she left a plaque that reads, "In this room lived John Fitzgerald Kennedy with his wife Jacqueline—during the two years, ten months and two days he was President of the United States—January 20, 1961–November 22, 1963." The new president, Lyndon Baines Johnson, wrote to her after the funeral, "Jackie, you have been magnificent and have won a warm place in the heart of history."

Onassis remained in Washington and eventually purchased a home on N Street. In 1964, unable to shake her grief, she bought a cooperative apartment on Fifth Avenue in New York City overlooking Central Park, near the residences of her sister and her stepbrother as well as several of her in-laws. That year she assembled an exhibit of presidential effects, which she sent on tour to raise funds for a presidential library for her late husband. She made an appearance at the 1964 Democratic National Convention in Atlantic City and lent her support to the senatorial campaign of her brother-in-law, Robert Kennedy, that year. She worked on a project to restore historic colonial mansions of the Old South and another to preserve the Metropolitan Opera building in New York City. She traveled extensively—to London in 1965, to Switzerland and Rome in 1966, and to Mexico in 1967. She visited eastern Asia and South America, and suffered through the publication of numerous books about the untimely death of her husband as well as books about her and their children. Her every move was scrutinized in the press; she was hounded by the media and was known to withdraw emotionally.

In widowhood Onassis was pursued aggressively by Aristotle Onassis, an aging Greek shipping tycoon. By the end of 1968 the two were married, and the former first lady had moved with her new husband and children to the Ionian island of Skorpios. Her decision was clearly spurred by the assassination of Martin Luther King, Jr., in April of that year, followed by the assassination of Robert Kennedy in June. The latter incident led her to comment openly that she no longer cared to live in the United States. After the death of her second husband in 1975 she returned to New York City, where she worked for Doubleday Publishers.

Onassis died of cancer on 19 May 1994 in New York City. She is buried beside President Kennedy at Arlington.

★

C. David Heymann explores the life of Onassis in depth in *A Woman Named Jackie: An Intimate Biography of Jacqueline Bouvier Kennedy Onassis* (1989). *Remembering Jackie: A Life in Pictures* (1994), by the editors of *Life*, is a compilation of intimate pictures, text, and quotes from the woman who appeared on eighteen *Life* covers. An obituary is in the *New York Times* (20 May 1994).

GLORIA COOKSEY

ONSAGER, Lars (*b.* 27 November 1903 in Oslo, Norway; *d.* 5 October 1976 in Miami, Florida), physical chemist who received the 1968 Nobel Prize in chemistry for his derivation of a set of equations known as the *Law of Reciprocal Relations*, which is sometimes described as the *Fourth Law of Thermodynamics* because it makes possible a study of irreversible processes.

Onsager was the son of Erling Onsager, a barrister of the Supreme Court of Norway, and Ingrid Kirkeby. He had a liberal early education that was a combination of private school and his mother's tutoring, followed by high school in Oslo. The combination gave him an extraordinary background in literature and fine arts. Onsager then entered the Norwegian Institute of Technology as a student in chemical engineering. However, in his first year at the institute

he became interested in the theory of electrolyte solutions, an interest that was the beginning of a scientific curiosity and ultimately led to his receiving a Nobel Prize. Onsager soon mastered the new theory, and detected a flaw in it. He studied in a stimulating environment under professors who encouraged his efforts in studying theory.

After graduation in 1925 Onsager went with one of his professors on a trip to Denmark and Germany that included a stay of a couple of months at Zurich University with Peter Debye, coauthor with Erich Hückel of the new theory of electrolyte solutions. Onsager later described his first encounter with Debye, which started with his solemn statement, "Professor Debye, your theory of electrolytes is incorrect." He based his comment on a puzzling discrepancy between the theory and the actual results in experiments. Debye and Hückel had assumed that a central ion in solution would move uniformly in a straight line while all the other ions were randomly undergoing Brownian motion. Within a few years Onsager had developed the theory to include mobilities of all ions in equal proportions.

Onsager immigrated to the United States in 1928, embarking on a dubious career as a college instructor, first at Johns Hopkins University, where he lasted only a year, and next at Brown University. Following that he was at Harvard, where students called his science courses "advanced Norwegian." Onsager was described by a colleague as a contender for the title of world's worst lecturer. At Brown

Lars Onsager *(right)*, receiving his Nobel Prize from King Adolf Gustav of Sweden, 1968. ARCHIVE PHOTOS, INC.

University he did the classic work on irreversible processes that ultimately led to the Nobel Prize, without the advantage of a Ph.D. He presented a thesis for a Ph.D. on this work to Brown, where the highly theoretical work was not doubted but regarded as too incomprehensible.

Yale was kinder. Onsager went to Yale as the Sterling and Gibbs Fellow in 1933, was made an assistant professor of chemistry in 1934, and was granted a Ph.D. in 1935. His dissertation was on the mathematical background for his interpretation of deviations from Ohm's law in weak electrolytes. Interestingly, Brown awarded him an honorary doctor of science in 1962 when he had become widely acclaimed for his research, most of it at Yale. In the early 1960s he was also reworking his "incomprehensible" discovery of "reciprocal relations," which had been ignored at Brown but was recognized with a Nobel Prize in 1968.

At Yale, Onsager's research covered a wide range of subjects that included colloids, superconductivity, turbulence, ice, electrons in metals, and dielectrics. Onsager also found a firm statistical basis for the theory of liquid crystal ordering, which led the way for the research that ultimately produced liquid crystal displays, better known as LCDs. Although he served as visiting professor in many prestigious universities during the years that followed, he officially stayed with Yale until retirement in 1972. In 1968, the year he received the Nobel Prize, he was a visiting professor at the University of Göttingen in Germany. Onsager became a United States citizen in 1945; his Nobel Prize lists him as an American.

In the presentation speech for the Nobel Prize in 1968, Professor S. Claesson of the Royal Swedish Academy of Sciences noted that the award to Onsager was a more than usual application of a special rule of the Nobel Foundation. The rule reads: "Work done in the past may be selected for the award only on the supposition that its significance has until recently not been fully appreciated." Also recognized in the speech was the fact that Onsager's contributions on irreversible thermodynamics have numerous applications not only in physics and chemistry but also in biology and technology.

From 1954 to 1971 Onsager received a total of nine honorary doctorate degrees, plus many prestigious medals and prizes in addition to the 1968 Nobel Prize. In the 1960s two conferences were based on Onsager's work: an international conference at Brown University in 1962, "Irreversible Thermodynamics and the Statistical Mechanics of Phase Transitions," and in 1965 at the National Institute of Standards near Washington, D.C., "Phenomena in the Neighborhood of Critical Points."

Onsager had difficulty communicating with people of lesser intellect throughout his life. Not only did his students find him difficult to understand, but many of his colleagues had the same problem. He had the reputation of being enigmatic and verbally obscure. Onsager simply did not recognize this and would continue lectures and conversations with what biographers describe as the Onsager grin and twinkling Nordic blue eyes, as if he were fully understood by all.

He is also described as having had a mischievous sense of humor. The chair of the department at Brown suggested he do some experiments rather than spend all his time on theoretical work. Onsager replied that he would like to do that, but he must have the equipment he needed: a tube that would stretch from the basement to the third floor of the chemistry building. Also, the tube must be made of platinum. Actually, such an experiment had already been performed—as part of the Manhattan Project for the atomic bomb. The chair never mentioned doing experiments again to Onsager.

Onsager married Margarethe Arledter on 7 September 1933. They had four children. Onsager died, presumably from a heart attack, at age seventy-two. He is buried in Grove Street Cemetery in New Haven, Connecticut.

★

Bibliographies of Onsager include Nobel archives, *Lars Onsager—Biography* (1968); H. Christopher Longuet-Higgins and Michael E. Fisher, *Lars Onsager November 27, 1903–October 5, 1976* (1991); and Harriet Zuckerman, *Scientific Elite: Nobel Laureates in the United States* (1995). An obituary is in the *New York Times* (6 Oct. 1976).

M. C. NAGEL

ORBISON, Roy Kelton (*b.* 23 April 1936 in Vernon, Texas; *d.* 6 December 1988 in Hendersonville, Tennessee), popular singer and songwriter with a remarkable voice, who scored many Top Ten hits in the 1960s with songs blending the melancholy sound of country music and the rhythmic drive of rhythm and blues.

Orbison was the second of three sons of Orbie Lee Orbison, a car mechanic, and Nadine Schultz, a nurse. He played the guitar from age six and began his singing career in high school in Wink, Texas, formed his first band, the Wink Westerners, a quintet made up of members of the high school orchestra. After graduation in 1954 Orbison enrolled at North Texas State University in Denton, but dropped out of college after two years.

Orbison was deeply impressed by Elvis Presley, then at his peak as a performer, and began to perform rockabilly music, a hybrid of country and rhythm and blues. After adding some new personnel, Orbison changed the name of his band to The Teen Kings. In his sophomore year in college he met Claudette Hestand, whom he married in 1956. She inspired Orbison's hit song "Claudette," which was recorded by the Everly Brothers in late March 1958. By then Orbison already had a "hit" as a performer. "Ooby Dooby," released on the legendary Sun label in May 1956, reached number fifty-two on the Billboard Chart. Subsequent releases with Sun performed only marginally, and in 1958 Orbison shifted to RCA Victor. In September 1959 he signed with Monument Records, and his career took off.

His first significant hit for Monument was "Uptown," released in February 1960. A blues-based strut about the great ambitions of a bellhop, the song rose to number seventy-two on the charts, raising hopes that future songs would be hits. Orbison's dreams were realized in April 1960 with the release of "Only the Lonely," a song that takes full advantage of Orbison's bel canto eloquence and deeply emotional vocal cry. The song spoke to huge numbers of people, from street corner gangs singing a cappella, to solitary teenagers, to romantics everywhere. Orbison had found his voice and his niche. "Only the Lonely" went to number two on the charts, but although Sun Records tried to capitalize on his new fame by releasing a lesser song entitled "Devil Doll," Orbison's next hit with Monument in October 1960, called "Blue Angel," cemented his popularity. He now had a highly recognizable style, which helped differentiate him in an era of pop music when past giants were in decline or exile, and the charts were full of insipid teen ballads, cover songs by singers like Pat Boone, and movie themes.

Orbison's songs appealed to heartfelt melancholy, fears that love's dreams would not work out, and the belief that loneliness was a certain future. Such was the attraction of his May 1961 hit, "Running Scared," a bolero-influenced tune about the fear that the singer's new amour would be unable to resist the charms of a former lover. As the drumbeat paces faster and faster, Orbison's voice soars to an unintelligible denouement. Orbison's appearance only added to the song's mournful appeal. A naturally shy and polite man, he wore thick prescription sunglasses, had a pallid, puffy face, and always dressed entirely in black.

Another hit, "Crying," released in September 1961, heightened Orbison's reputation for performing songs with a lachrymose quality. In it the singer tells of his crushed feelings, despair over the future, and dread at seeing his love happy with someone else. Orbison's developing and highly popular work now provided a counterpoint to the happy endings of contemporary ballads. His next hit, the lovely "Dream Baby" (1962), added a psychological longing to his lyrics. Writing most of these songs alone, Orbison continued to mine the anxieties of his own youth, and in doing so captured the sexual uncertainties of his times. "The Crowd," issued on Monument in June 1962, expressed the loneliness of the brokenhearted, separated from the familiarity of friends. His next hit, "Workin' for the Man" (October 1962), returned to the class ambitions of

Roy Orbison. AP/WIDE WORLD PHOTOS

"Uptown." After that brief moment of social investigation, Orbison returned to more psychological probing. "In Dreams," released in February 1963, began almost as a soothing child's song, then broke into an agitated moderato, with pleasant dreams broken by the dawn's realization that one's love has gone. Orbison's firm, five-octave pitch, delivered with impressive confidence and phrasing, gave the song a deeper and inescapable realism.

On the strength of this powerful single, Orbison toured England for a second time in 1963, with the Beatles second on the bill. New to the charts but packed with ambition, the Beatles asked Orbison if they could close the show, even though his name was the reason for the tour's success. Orbison generously agreed, but repaid the Beatles for their arrogance with intensely powerful performances that were hard to follow. Orbison befriended the Beatle George Harrison and returned to the United States with predictions about a British invasion of pop. The next year his releases with Monument fared well, with an outstanding highlight in September 1964, the release of "Oh, Pretty Woman," a strong rocker about a lonely man's desire for a prostitute.

After Orbison's contract with Monument expired, he signed a lucrative deal with Metro-Goldwyn-Mayer (MGM). Beginning with the August 1965 release of "Ride Away," the combination of big studio music and Orbison never realized any worthwhile hits. The loss of his wife to a motorcycle accident in June 1966 left Orbison with three sons. In 1968 two of his sons died tragically in a house fire. He married Barbara Wellnoener-Jacobs in 1969; the couple had two sons.

Orbison's contract with MGM ended in 1974, followed by uneventful years with Mercury Records. Monument released Orbison's hit songs in the United Kingdom, where his popularity never sagged, a second time. He was elected to the Rock and Roll Hall of Fame in 1987. Orbison's career had a major revival in 1988 with his lead participation in an ensemble tour, album, and movie about a group called The Traveling Wilburys, which featured Bob Dylan, former Beatle George Harrison, Jeff Lynn of the Electrical Light Orchestra, and Tom Petty. The album expressed the adoration many younger pop stars felt toward Orbison. At the same time, Orbison released a virtuoso album of songs entitled *Mystery Girl,* including the hit "You Got It." In the midst of this revival, Orbison died of a heart attack while visiting his mother in Tennessee. He is buried at Westwood Memorial Park, in Los Angeles, California. In the media aftermath "You Got It" became his first Top Five song since the early 1960s.

Orbison remains popular at the start of the twenty-first century. His songs are featured on movie sound tracks and are favorites on nostalgia radio. Many singers from the generation immediately after his have listed Orbison as an inspiration, including Springsteen and Bono, lead singer of the Irish rock band U2.

★

There are two major biographies of Orbison: Alan Clayson, *Only the Lonely: Roy Orbison's Life and Legacy* (1989), and Ellis Amburn, *Dark Star: The Roy Orbison Story* (1991). An obituary is in the *New York Times* (8 Dec. 1988).

GRAHAM RUSSELL HODGES

ORR, Robert Gordon ("Bobby") (*b.* 20 March 1948 in Parry Sound, Ontario, Canada), Hall of Fame hockey player who was the first and only defenseman to win the National Hockey League (NHL) scoring championship and who was also responsible for improving the fortunes of the Boston Bruins organization virtually on his own, leading them to two Stanley Cup championships within four years of joining the team.

Orr was the fourth of five children of Douglas and Arva Orr. His father was a packer of explosives in a munitions factory and was a fine amateur hockey player himself. Orr became involved in organized hockey before he was six years old, but his skills were often overlooked because of his small size. Even though he always played in leagues with boys several years his senior, the dissenters were not convinced. He continued to hone his abilities on the frozen

Bobby Orr, 1966. © BETTMANN/CORBIS

waters of the Sequin River, developing puck handling by playing a game called "shinny."

Eventually he attracted the attention of a local celebrity, "Bucko" McDonald. "If I've ever seen an NHL prospect, this kid is one," McDonald boasted. He encouraged Orr to utilize his fine skating and great shot as a defenseman. Controlling the play from that vantage point, he caught the eye of the scouting staff of the Boston Bruins. At the age of fourteen he was admitted to the training camp of the team's Junior "A" affiliate in Oshawa, Ontario. Still small in comparison to his contemporaries, he was almost laughed out of orientation when he responded to the roll call, declaring that his position was "defense," but he made the team. Even though he had one year of junior eligibility remaining at the conclusion of his fourth schedule, Orr's All-Star selections, broken scoring records, and ever-improving hockey savvy assured that he would be promoted to the parent Bruins. Stories abound concerning Orr's uncanny skating and puck-handling skills. One of his coaches, Don Cherry, described how, when killing a penalty one night, Orr lost one of his hockey gauntlets (gloves) at mid-ice. Calmly he wheeled around behind his own net and moved up-ice carrying the puck. Almost as an afterthought, he suddenly reached down, scooped up the empty glove, never breaking stride, and continued in the same direction. Orr's hockey skills were not all that was impressive about him, however. He was unusually polite and respectful toward teachers, employers, and tutors. When he arrived at the Boston training camp in the fall of 1966, he insisted upon addressing his older teammates as *mister* or *sir*. When a photographer asked him to pose for a picture, he refused to stand alone, stating that he had done nothing to deserve that honor.

Recognition came almost immediately. Peter Axthelm of *Newsweek* observed, "The rest of the players seemed to be coming to the rink just to stand around and watch him." Stan Fischler wrote of his early exploits, "No rookie ever overwhelmed the NHL the way Orr did in 1966–1967." Orr amassed an amazing forty-one points in sixty-one games, even though he was a defenseman, and was chosen for the Second All-Star Team. He easily won the Calder Trophy as the best first-year skater in the league. In the following season he was selected as winner of the Norris Trophy as the league's top defenseman, a feat he accomplished eight seasons in a row. Twice he won the scoring championship, something no other defenseman in NHL history has ever done. When he earned the Art Ross Trophy during the 1969–1970 season, it was but one of seven major awards he earned that year. He was also voted Most Valuable Player (MVP), best player in the playoffs, and best defenseman that season. Moreover, he was placed on the First All-Star Team once more and recorded the best plus/minus statistics as well. He was also recognized as Canada's top male athlete.

At his peak Orr stood six feet tall and weighed 197 pounds, and in his early Bruins career he was required to handle some of the opposing team's toughest players. He was unselfish in his attitudes toward his fellow players, and his 102 assists in the 1970–1971 season stand as a record for a defenseman. Orr totaled 270 goals and 915 points in just 657 games.

Orr's career was cut short by troublesome knees. During a charity match in the summer of 1967 he fell and hurt his right knee, missing five weeks, and then he spent ten days in the hospital when he was hit on it again in mid-season. Not long afterward a check by Toronto's Bobby Baun badly tore the ligaments in Orr's left knee. He had surgery on that damaged joint several times and either missed long stretches of schedules or played in pain. Often he returned to the action too quickly, endangering his long-term health. In the early 1970s his career was plagued with injury, and though he set a record for goals by a defenseman in the 1974–1975 season, he could only compete in ten games during the following one. Orr signed with the Chicago Blackhawks in 1976, but after only twenty contests he realized he needed to completely rest his ailing leg, which he did for almost two full years. After only six games at the beginning of the 1978 season, he retired from the game.

Orr remained active in his post-playing days. He worked as a special assistant to the league president, served on the advisory board of the Hartford Whalers, and become part owner of the American Hockey League Lowell Hockey sextet in Massachusetts. He acted as a player agent for several years in the late 1990s and also became a successful businessman. He and his wife, Peggy (Wood) Orr, have two sons. He was inducted into the Hockey Hall of Fame in 1979, the youngest player ever to be so honored.

★

Orr is the coauthor of two books about hockey and his career: with Dick Grace, *Orr on Ice* (1970), and with Mark Mulovy, *Bobby Orr: My Game* (1974). Books about Orr include Stan Fischler, *Bobby Orr and the Big Bad Bruins* (1969), and Al Hirschberg, *Bobby Orr: Fire on Ice* (1975). He is also the subject of many magazine and newspaper articles, including Tom Dowling, "The Orr Effect," *Atlantic* (Apr. 1971).

GLENN R. GOODHAND

OSWALD, Lee Harvey (*b.* 18 October 1939 in New Orleans, Louisiana; *d.* 24 November 1963 in Dallas, Texas), American Marxist and presumed assassin of President John F. Kennedy.

Oswald was born in the Old French Hospital in New Orleans, Louisiana. His father, Robert E. Lee Oswald, was an insurance collector who died in August 1939, just before Oswald's birth. Oswald spent much of his childhood moving from one residence to another with his mother, Marguerite (Claverie) Oswald, a nurse. At age three he joined his brother and half-brother at the Evangelical Lutheran Bethlehem Orphan's Asylum, where the older boys had been living for one year. In 1945 Marguerite, after remarrying, reclaimed them. She was divorced in 1948 and thereafter moved frequently. Oswald never graduated from high school but was of slightly higher than average intelligence; his diary and other writings suggest that he suffered from dyslexia.

Oswald enlisted in the U.S. Marine Corps in 1956, at age seventeen, and spent a three-year tour of duty involved in radar operations for the U-2 spy plane. A vocal critic of capitalism, he spent his free time studying the Russian language and vowed to emigrate to Russia upon his discharge. In 1959 he secured entry to Russia through Finland by posing as a student, arriving on 15 October 1959 on a six-day visa. He was detained in Moscow when he announced his desire to renounce his U.S. citizenship and become a Soviet citizen. The American correspondent Priscilla J. McMillan later suggested that he was a "pitiful, slightly un-

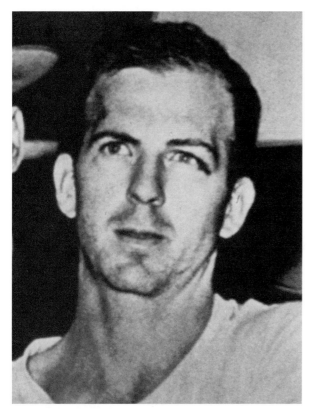

Lee Harvey Oswald. ARCHIVE PHOTOS, INC.

balanced boy" who was allowed to remain in Russia if only to disprove the international criticism of Soviet intolerance of outsiders. His request for citizenship was denied, however, and he was assigned the status of a stateless person.

Oswald settled in Minsk, Byelorussia, where he worked in a radio-television factory. On 30 April 1961 he married Marina Nikolaevna Prusakova. Their first daughter was born in Minsk in February 1962. Oswald tired quickly of the drab, proletariat lifestyle. In May 1962 he and his family boarded a train to Moscow. There they booked passage on the Dutch liner *Maasdam,* set to leave Rotterdam on 4 June for America. Their trip, including rail passage to the Netherlands, was funded with $435.71 loaned to them by the American Embassy.

The Oswalds arrived in Hoboken, New Jersey, on 13 June. Two days later they flew to Fort Worth, Texas, where Oswald found employment at the Leslie Welding Company. In August he rented a furnished duplex at 2703 Mercedes Street and set out to foster friendships among other Russian émigrés, in part for the sake of Prusakova, who spoke no English. Oswald, who had become secretive and erratic, then walked off his job without notice in early October 1962. He moved to Dallas and worked as an apprentice cameraman at Jaggars-Chiles-Stovall Graphic Arts, living at the Young Men's Christian Association and visiting

his family in Fort Worth on weekends. Early in November he rented an apartment at 604 Elsbeth Street and sent for Prusakova and their daughter. After learning of his wife's pregnancy, he moved in March to a larger apartment, at nearby 214 West Neely Street.

Oswald repaid his State Department loan on 25 January 1963. Two days later, under the alias of A. J. Hidell, he ordered a .38 caliber Smith and Wesson revolver from Seaport Traders, Incorporated. On 12 March, using the same alias, he ordered a high-powered rifle and scope from Klein's Sporting Goods in Chicago, Illinois. In receipt of his purchases, Oswald posed on 31 March for two photos; these so-called backyard photographs taken by Prusakova depict Oswald dressed in black and bearing his newly purchased firearms. He holds two left-wing publications: the *Militant* and the *Worker.* Six days later he was fired from his job.

On the evening of 10 April he took his rifle and rode by bus to the Dallas home of Edwin Walker, a retired U.S. Army Major General and a prominent leader of the right-wing John Birch Society. There Oswald made an attempt on Walker's life, but the bullet missed its mark. Two weeks later Oswald left by bus for New Orleans, where he secured a job with a coffee distributor for $1.50 an hour. He rented an apartment and sent for his family on 9 May but sent them back to Dallas within weeks, because he wanted to go to Cuba to join forces with the Communist regime of Fidel Castro. Oswald attempted to enter Cuba through Mexico at the end of September but was denied entry. He returned to Dallas, where he rented a room at 1026 North Beckley Street under the alias of O. H. Lee. He secured employment at the Texas School Book Depository, and on 20 October, Prusakova gave birth to a second daughter in Dallas.

On 8 November sources confirmed that President John F. Kennedy would visit Dallas; a motorcade route was released on 19 November, showing that the presidential limousine would pass in front of the depository at 411 Elm Street. For the next three days, history lay in wait for the actions of Oswald, a theretofore inconsequential twenty-four-year-old man with no political power, privilege, or means. On 22 November 1963, the morning of the assassination, Oswald went to work at the book depository after spending the night away from his apartment. In his hands he carried a long package wrapped in brown paper, which he told friends contained curtain rods for his apartment. Investigators believe that Oswald's package contained his rifle, because no curtain rods were ever found in the depository or in Oswald's apartment.

After the assassination, police uncovered a sniper's nest on the sixth floor of the book depository building. Further investigation uncovered Oswald's Mannlicher-Carcano rifle tucked between piles of books, also on the sixth floor. An eyewitness to the assassination, a person who later identified Oswald in a police lineup, placed Oswald in the sniper's nest on the sixth floor of the book depository during the time when the shots were fired. Oswald, according to the witness, stood at the window with a rifle and fired at least two shots at the motorcade during the moments when Kennedy was hit. After the shooting Oswald was seen riding a city bus. He returned on foot to North Beckley Street, entered his residence, and emerged within minutes on the streets of Dallas in the midst of a high-profile dragnet. When confronted by Officer J. D. Tippit, Oswald shot the policeman repeatedly at pointblank range in front of multiple witnesses. Oswald then forced his way into a movie theater, where police arrested him.

On the morning of 24 November, after two days of interrogation by Dallas police, Oswald was en route to a federal facility when he was confronted and shot by Jack Ruby, a Dallas nightclub owner who had been outraged over the Kennedy assassination. Oswald died at Parkland Hospital at 1:07 P.M., forty-eight hours and seven minutes after Kennedy was pronounced dead at the same facility. Oswald's funeral on 25 November posed a stark contrast to the elaborate state funeral of the dead president, held that same day. Because no cemetery in Dallas would accept Oswald's body, it was interred under heavy guard at Rose Hill Cemetery in Fort Worth. The Reverend Louis Saunders officiated at the hurried graveside ceremony, and volunteers from the press corps served as pallbearers.

Oswald was twenty-four years old in 1963 when he allegedly shot Kennedy, after which the details of Oswald's adult life were scrutinized by both the U.S. Federal Bureau of Investigation and the Central Intelligence Agency (CIA) in an effort to discern Oswald's motive. Investigators have scoured the evidence, including Oswald's employment history, his residences, and his associates. His diary has been examined, and casual conversations reconstructed. But the full truth about the Kennedy assassination lies buried with Oswald, leaving his story to remain one of the unsolved mysteries of the twentieth century.

While in Russia he kept a diary; in it he expressed disillusionment not with Communism but instead with the bungling of the Soviet bureaucracy, which he compared to the government of the United States. According to McMillan, Oswald is an interesting character, because he experienced both the American and Soviet ways of life, and yet, despite being in Russia and thus isolated from American antiwar activists, his ideas were, McMillan writes, similar to the ideas of "a generation of American activists in the later 1960s. . . . Oswald was . . . a lonely American anti-hero a few years ahead of his time."

Many conspiracy theories have proliferated. Among them is a supposed Soviet-Cuban connection based on a rumored CIA coup against Castro. Another theory is that a domestic crime cartel ordered the assassination of Kennedy and hired Oswald as a decoy assassin to protect the identity of the real shooter or shooters. This organized crime connection relies heavily on the belief that Oswald's killer, Jack Ruby, was a member of the cartel and was ordered to permanently silence Oswald by killing him. Ruby, who was convicted of Oswald's murder, died of cancer four years later, while awaiting appeal.

★

Writing about Oswald has been less about his life than about the crime of which he was accused. The journalist Priscilla Johnson McMillan tells an eloquent story of Oswald from the privileged vantage point of Marina Prusakova in *Marina and Lee* (1977). Edward Jay Epstein, *Legend: The Secret World of Lee Harvey Oswald* (1978), presents a theory based on the Cuban connection but remains noncommittal. Gerald Posner, *Case Closed* (1993), supports the results of the Warren Commission, which concluded that Oswald acted alone, and Ronald Lewis, *Flashback* (1993), alludes to the author's own foreknowledge of a Castro-based assassination conspiracy and exonerates Oswald from complicity in the plot.

GLORIA COOKSEY

P-Q

PACKARD, David. *See* Hewlett, William Redington, and David Packard.

PAIK, Nam June (*b.* 20 July 1932 in Seoul, Korea), performance and video artist who, during the 1960s, transformed the formal properties of television and video into an electronic art form by using combinations of music, actions, images, and objects.

Little is known about Paik's early years. While in high school, he discovered the post-romantic, atonal music of the Viennese composer Arnold Schoenberg. In 1949 the war between the communists and noncommunists in Korea compelled Paik's family to relocate from Seoul to Hong Kong, where the seventeen-year-old attended Rayden School. A move to Tokyo in 1950 presented Paik the opportunity to study music, art history, and aesthetics at Tokyo University (1952–1956). There he submitted his thesis on Schoenberg, theories of serial composition, and Western modernism.

In 1956 Paik moved to Germany to further investigate the traditions of European music at the University of Munich and the Academy of Music in Freiberg. He met Karlheinz Stockhausen, a vanguard German composer of electronic compositions, at a New Music event, as well as the American innovator John Cage, who invented the "prepared piano" and believed that all noise was music.

Inspired by these musical mavericks, Paik in 1959 explored the electronic studio of a Cologne radio station, experimenting with the equipment to produce various sounds.

Paik's transformation from audio artist to video artist was motivated by his involvement in the burgeoning scene of "Happenings" that grew out of the avant-garde culture of the late 1950s and early 1960s. He became part of the Fluxus anti-art movement, and was influenced by its founder, George Maciunas. Experimenting with audiotape, Paik recorded piano, screaming, classical music, and sound effects, then edited them into an aural collage. Paik's invitation to join the Fluxus Group came when Maciunas witnessed a performance of one of Paik's cut-up sound montages. As the tape played, Paik threw beans at the ceiling, covered his face with a roll of paper, screamed, cried, and hurled the paper into the audience while two tape recorders blared bursts of radio news. He smeared shaving cream onto his hair, face, and suit, poured flour over his head, and then jumped into a bathtub. Later, Paik played a salon piece on the piano, then banged his head repeatedly on the keyboard. Paik quickly developed a reputation as the "wild man" of the Fluxus movement.

During the early 1960s Paik continued to explore the outer realms of music, performance, and interactivity. *Symphony for 20 Rooms* (1961) involved audio collages interspersed with players kicking objects around a room. In *One for Violin Solo* (1962), Paik raised a violin over his head and smashed it to the ground. In 1963 visitors to the Exposition of Music, Paik's first single-artist show, interacted with performances, actions, and objects located in different rooms. Paik contributed to the anti-art movement of the "prepared piano" by decorating the instrument with barbed wire, dolls, photographs, and a bra.

Paik quickly became frustrated by the limitations of audio expression and introduced increasingly spontaneous actions into his audio work. In 1963 he created an installation that was both pre-video and pre-digital. For *Random Access,* strips of audiotape were secured to the exhibition space walls. When the tapes were rubbed with a magnetic tape head, they produced sounds. In March of that year Paik devoted himself to research into video. His early work in the new medium began as an installation at the Exposition of Music–Electronic Television. Paik placed thirteen television sets in non-traditional positions, on their backs and sides. He manipulated the horizontal and vertical controls, breaking the compositional form of the standardized television image.

Zen for TV (1963) featured a television set placed on its side, displaying a horizontal line transmission while the other sets faced the floor. For *Rembrandt Automatic* (1963), Paik positioned a TV face-down so its flickering light seeped out and caused reflections on the floor. The results altered the viewer's attitudes toward television solely as a deliverer of entertainment and information. *Point of Light* (1963) featured a television wired to a radio pulse generator. When the viewer turned the volume knob, the light in the screen's center grew larger, communicating the fact that a video image could be modified and controlled by the participant. Paik experimented further with participation television. He wired a microphone into a set, and when a viewer spoke, the voice was translated into explosive point-of-light patterns.

In 1965 Paik met the experimental filmmaker Jud Yalkut, who recorded Paik's video images on film with his handheld 16-mm Bolex camera. In turn, Paik incorporated Yalkut's film footage into his videotapes.

At his first one-man show as a video artist at the New School for Social Research in New York City, Paik's *Magnet TV* (1965) utilized a magnetic force to alter a video image. Later, he used a degausser, an industry tool employed to erase videotape, to creatively manipulate video images.

Also in 1965, the first Sony portable half-inch videotape recorder and player became available to consumers. This development expanded the reach of television and put the medium into the hands of artists such as Paik, who bought his first video camera at the Liberty Music Shop in New York City. His first recording was in the store, where he captured the repetitive action of buttoning and unbuttoning his coat on videotape.

Paik's most significant collaboration was with the avant-garde cellist Charlotte Moorman, with whom he partici-

Nam June Paik in his studio. Associated Press AP

pated in the historic *TV as a Creative Medium Show* at the Howard Wise Gallery in New York City in 1969. An all but topless Moorman played cello wearing a bra that housed two small television monitors designed by Paik. The live performance was a scandal and further demonstrated the fact that television was a versatile and diversified medium connected to life, not just an impassive object to be watched at home.

Paik altered the color of his work with the Paik–Abe Video Synthesizer, which he developed with the engineer Shuga Abe in 1964. They refined their invention at WGBH in Boston, as well as two New York facilities, WNET-TV in New York City and the Experimental Television Center in Binghamton.

During the 1960s Paik was responsible for the introduction of a new artistic medium into global culture. His bold experiments inspired a cadre of video artists in the 1970s, many of whom were first-generation video creators. In the new millennium, video art is an established and accepted medium, and Paik continues to exercise his protean talents to explore the electronic and digital properties of the medium he helped create. His work has evolved in size and scope as sculpture installations, environments, and images.

★

John G. Handhardt, *The Worlds of Nam June Paik* (2000), is a comprehensive overview of Paik's work. Aspects of his career in video art are examined in Wulf Herzogenrath, *Nam June Paik:*

Fluxus, Video (1983); Edith Decker-Phillips, *Paik Video* (1988); and Nam June Paik, *Nam June Paik: Video Works, 1963–88: 29 September–11 December 1988, Hayward Gallery* (1988).

VINCENT LoBRUTTO

PAPP, Joseph (*b.* 22 June 1921 in New York City; *d.* 31 October 1991 in New York City), among the most innovative producers and directors in the history of American theater, founder of the New York Shakespeare Festival and the Public Theater.

Born Yosl Papirofsky, Papp was the second of four children of Samuel Papirofsky, a trunk maker and peanut peddler, and his wife, Yetta Morris Papirofsky, a seamstress. Papp was raised in the slums of Brooklyn; his first exposure to the theater came at age eight, when he played Scrooge in a school production of *A Christmas Carol.* By the time he was in junior high school, Papp had discovered Shakespeare, and although he never went beyond high school, he could recite every Shakespearean soliloquy.

In 1935, at the age of fourteen, Papp became involved with the Federal Theater Project, a New Deal program for artists. Here he first encountered theater that was politically and socially charged. Papp graduated from Eastern District High School in 1938. He enlisted in the U.S. Navy during World War II; among other duties, he staged shows in locations as varied as aircraft carriers and officers clubs, from the North Atlantic to the South Pacific. Papp left the service with the rank of chief petty officer. After the war he

Joseph Papp *(left)*, with his wife, 1960. © BETTMANN/CORBIS

made his way to Hollywood, where, between 1946 and 1948, he studied acting and directing at the Actors Laboratory Theater, eventually becoming the managing director. In 1950 he took a position as assistant stage manager with the national touring company for Arthur Miller's *Death of a Salesman.*

By 1952 Papp had begun working as a stage manager for the Columbia Broadcasting System television network in New York City. At the same time he began producing free performances of Shakespeare's plays, which he staged in church basements. Later, using his own funds, Papp staged the productions on flatbed trucks. He founded the New York Shakespeare Festival, originally known as the Shakespeare Workshop, in 1954. By 1956 this institution, unique in New York theater, had found a permanent home in Central Park. Papp's involvement with the Actors Lab, which was thought to be a Communist front organization, brought him to the attention of the House Un-American Activities Committee in 1958. Although he admitted that he once had been a member of the Communist Party, Papp invoked his Fifth Amendment rights when asked to identify other members. The investigation did not impede Papp's career, but it did leave him determined to use theater as a "social force," not merely as a form of entertainment. During the 1960s, therefore, Papp set out to create a truly public theater that was accessible to all people.

In 1962 the New York Shakespeare Festival was given a permanent home in Central Park at the newly constructed Delacorte Theatre. Papp's free productions of Shakespeare's works, dubbed Shakespeare in the Park, were the prototype for a series that have since sprung up throughout North America. Working tirelessly and taking little or no salary for several years, Papp produced and directed the majority of the plays himself. Among the most dynamic and respected off-Broadway producers of his generation, Papp also showcased many innovative playwrights, including David Rabe, Sam Shepard, and John Guare. George C. Scott, Colleen Dewhurst, James Earl Jones, and Meryl Streep were just a few of the actors who, early in their careers, took roles in Papp's productions. Even established film stars, such as Robert DeNiro and Morgan Freeman, who needed neither the experience nor the exposure, accepted union scale pay just for the opportunity to work with Papp.

In 1966 Papp received permission from the New York City authorities to house his nonprofit group, the New York Shakespeare Festival, in the old Astor Library, which was slated for demolition. Papp transformed the property, to be called the Public Theater, into a multi-theater complex, the largest of its kind in the United States. The repertoire of Papp's new venture was relentlessly contemporary and experimental. In fact, the Public Theater opened with the world premier of the rock musical *Hair* on 17 October

1967. With its memorable musical score and unstructured format, the play broke new ground for the American theater. Its vitality and songs, many of which were recorded by artists the world over, marked a shift in musical tastes, a fact that few critics noticed at the time. The musical also emerged as one of the most potent symbols of the antiwar movement.

Both critics and conservative theatergoers were dismayed by Papp's detour from Shakespeare. The reviewer for the *Village Voice* noted that "*Hair* is bald opportunism. It exploits every obvious up-to-date issue—the draft, the war . . . in a crass effort to be both timely and tidy. . . . Let the Public Theater begin again." Nevertheless, the play went on to become one of the biggest hits of the 1967–1968 season. Over time the play generated more than $1.5 million for the Public Theater alone.

In creating public theater Papp charted a new course in American stagecraft. While most plays on Broadway during the 1960s featured predominantly white actors, with minority group members in supporting roles, if they appeared at all, Papp was casting African-American and Hispanic actors. Never fearful of addressing controversial subjects, Papp produced plays that dealt with the Vietnam War, free love, and drug use. He later took on such topics as AIDS, urban poverty, and prison life. Not surprisingly, Papp was not afraid to risk shocking and even alienating middle-class audiences. Papp expressed no qualms, however, about taking his shows to the more conservative Broadway stage to make money. The profits from his Broadway successes, most notably *A Chorus Line* (1975), enabled him to fund more daring theatrical experiments and to promote various educational initiatives. In the process he introduced countless Americans to the world of theater.

Papp had a reputation for arrogance, independence, and pique, and he had little use for the elite of the theater world. He was, on occasion, known to escort critics from his productions. But for all his disdain of the theater establishment, Papp was amply rewarded throughout his long career. He won three Pulitzer Prizes and garnered twenty-eight Tony Awards. During his last decade, Papp's finances were in disarray and his personal life tumultuous. He had to draw on the endowment of the Public Theater and the box office receipts from the Shakespeare Festival to meet operational expenses. Married four times, Papp was the father of five children. His son's death from AIDS in the spring of 1990 hastened the decline of his own health. Papp died from cancer in 1991 at the age of seventy.

Armed with nothing more than "moral authority and his big mouth," Papp spent forty years building his company into one of the most important and influential in American theater. Perhaps his most enduring legacy, however, is his lifelong effort to bring theater to the masses.

★

Papp's papers are archived as part of the New York Shakespeare Festival Archive, now part of the Billy Rose Theater Collection of the New York Public Library for the Performing Arts. Biographies of Papp include Stuart W. Little, *Enter Joseph Papp: In Search of a New American Theater* (1974), and Helen Epstein, *Joe Papp: An American Life* (1994). Obituaries are in the *New York Times* (2 Nov. 1991) and the *New Republic* 205 (16 Dec. 1991): 36–39.

MEG GREENE

PARKS, Gordon, Sr. (*b.* 30 November 1912 in Fort Scott, Kansas), prominent photographer who became an autobiographer, novelist, musician and composer, essayist, and an award-winning photojournalist and film director.

Parks was born Gordon Roger Alexander Buchanan Parks, the son of Andrew Jackson, a Kansas dirt farmer, and Sarah (Ross) Parks, a homemaker and mother of fifteen children, Parks being the youngest. At age sixteen Parks's life changed drastically with the death of his mother and the illness of his ailing father. Parks moved to Minneapolis, Minnesota, to live with his older sister and her husband. An argument between him and his sister's husband caused him to be thrown out of the house and forced to live on his own. He dropped out of high school and struggled to support himself with a variety of odd jobs, including mop-

Gordon Parks. AP/WIDE WORLD PHOTOS

ping floors in a slum hotel, playing piano in a brothel, working as a busboy in a Saint Paul hotel, and playing semiprofessional basketball. He eventually secured a position with the Northern Pacific Railroad. While working and traveling he read voraciously, wrote music, and developed an eye for photography after purchasing his first camera in a pawnshop.

Lacking technique and training but gifted with an eye for composition, Parks's big break came when he convinced a women's clothing store owner in Saint Paul to let him try fashion photography. His work eventually came to the attention of Marva Louis, wife of heavyweight boxer Joe Louis. She encouraged him to come to Chicago, where he would have greater exposure to the fashion world. Fashion photography enabled him to earn enough money to support his family as well as have the freedom to explore documentary photographic techniques in the slums of Chicago. Parks had married Sally Alvis in 1933; the couple had three children, one of whom, before dying young in a 1979 plane crash, worked as a film director.

Many of Parks's milestone achievements took place prior to the 1960s. Winning the Julius Rosenwald Foundation fellowship in 1941 for documentary photographs marked the beginning of his professional career. He broke racial barriers in a profession typically not open to African Americans. It is said that his creative output from 1944 to 1978 was more than extraordinary. Parks's photography in the United States dealt with many substantive issues, from politics and entertainment to the lives of ordinary men and women in their struggles to survive. This intertwining of real life and photography became a distinctive characteristic of Parks's work throughout his career.

In 1944 Parks applied for a position with *Harper's Bazaar,* published by Hearst Publishing, a company that refused to hire him because of his race. However, the famed photographer Edward Steichen understood the quality of Parks's work and sent him to Alexander Lieberman, director of *Vogue* magazine. Lieberman contacted the senior editor of *Glamour* magazine, and from that point on Parks's work appeared in both publications.

In 1942 Parks began working for *Life* magazine as a photojournalist and essayist. He served as a European correspondent in France, Italy, Spain, and Portugal. Parks stayed with *Life* until 1972, covering more than three hundred assignments ranging from high fashion layouts to crime, gangs, the civil rights movement, and black activist organizations. Parks's photo-essay on Harlem gang leader Red Jackson of the Midtowners revealed a perceptive and extraordinary understanding of the culture of gang life. Parks had a way of getting his subjects to talk about their lives.

By the 1960s Parks was enjoying his status as one of the country's most influential photojournalists. In 1961 he was assigned to create a documentary on poverty in Brazil, con-

trasting it with the cosmopolitan life in Rio de Janeiro. As with his essays about Harlem gangs and segregation, he centered his piece around one individual. Parks met a young asthmatic boy named Flavio Da Silva, who became his primary subject. Parks photographed Flavio's parents, brothers, and sisters, all of whom lived together in a one-room shack. He wrote how the entire family depended on Flavio in spite of his deteriorating health. The story became a classic example of photojournalism and is still used widely to illustrate the concept.

Parks's work on the Flavio story stirred the hearts of people around the world, and thousands of dollars poured into *Life,* money that was to be used to bring Flavio to the United States for medical treatment, which was successful. In 1964 Parks produced a short documentary, *Flavio.* Flavio remained in touch with Parks at the beginning of the twenty-first century.

In 1961 Parks divorced his first wife and married Elizabeth Campbell in 1962. The couple had one child, but they were divorced in 1973. Parks married editor Genevieve Young in 1973, but this union, too, ended in divorce in August 1979.

In 1963 Parks published his first novel, *The Learning Tree.* It is a saga of a black family living on a farm in Kansas during the 1920s. It is Parks's own story based on recollections of his early years growing up, covering his life from the time of his mother's death to 1944. *The Learning Tree* is a significant piece of literature in that it contributes to a positive image of black Americans.

Parks's coverage of the civil rights movement for *Life* lasted from the early 1950s through the late 1960s. He profiled Martin Luther King, Jr., Malcolm X, Muhammad Ali, Stokely Carmichael, the Black Panthers, and others. One of his most controversial pieces of journalism concerned Malcolm X and the Nation of Islam. His coverage included their activities in Chicago, Illinois, New York City, and Los Angeles, California, and detailed the development of education and self-reliance among members of the Nation of Islam. In *To Smile in Autumn,* Parks describes Malcolm X as having charm and the remarkable ability to captivate an audience. He stated that Malcolm X was brilliant, ambitious, honest, and fearless and that he had the temerity to say publicly what every other African American wanted to say.

As the study of Malcolm X began, Parks recognized a visible change in Malcolm X's attitude when discussing the "brotherhood of mankind." He also observed the agonizing break between Malcolm X and Elijah Muhammad. Also, Parks had been with Malcolm X two days prior to his assassination. Information Malcolm X shared with him caused his own life to be threatened; the destruction of the Time-Life building in New York City was feared as well. Parks and his family were placed under the protection of the Federal Bureau of Investigation for two months until

Parks decided to meet with one of the black Muslim leaders to end the standoff. An assistant managing editor of *Life,* Dee Dee Moore, stated that it was Malcolm X's trust of Parks that made it possible for the one-time documentary to be developed.

In the summer of 1966 Parks began his study of Muhammad Ali. This was a difficult time in Ali's career because of his stand on the Vietnam War and because of his heavyweight title being revoked. Ali revealed to Parks his concerns about growing up poor in Kentucky and not being able to fulfill his dream of getting a good education. In 1967 Parks began his coverage of several black nationalists and the culture of the Black Panthers. Covering Stokely Carmichael, Parks found himself in harm's way once again, this time in the Watts area of Los Angeles.

In the mid-1960s Parks ventured into Hollywood as the first black director for a major studio. He produced, directed, and composed the musical score for the feature film adaptation of *The Learning Tree* (1968). The Library of Congress placed the film on the National Film Register. *A Choice of Weapons,* published in 1966, details Parks's life as fictionalized in the *The Learning Tree* film. For Metro-Goldwyn-Mayer (MGM) he directed *Shaft* (1971), *Shaft's Big Score* (1972), and *The Super Cops* (1974). *Shaft* is viewed as the forerunner of the blaxploitation genre.

The second volume of Parks's memoirs, *To Smile in Autumn* (1979), begins in 1944, with his fashion photographs appearing in *Vogue* and *Glamour,* and ends in 1978, when he had accomplished almost everything he had identified as a goal. *Voices in the Mirror: An Autobiography,* the third memoir, was published in 1990 and shows Parks's strength and vitality in his later years. His autobiographical film *Moments Without Proper Names* aired on Public Broadcasting Service (PBS) in 1988.

In 1988 Parks added to his repertoire a ballet titled *Martin.* He completed the musical score and libretto, and PBS began filming in 1989. It was shown in January 1990 in honor of Dr. Martin Luther King, Jr.

Critics view Parks's films as a revealing statement about the portrayal of black characters. Parks created assertive, sexual black heroes instead of "foot shuffling servants." Although *Shaft* brought MGM back from dire financial straights, it did not secure him a position in Hollywood as a director.

Parks's multifaceted career opened doors for other African-American artists who followed him in the 1960s and beyond. In *Visions* he wrote, "I've known both misery and happiness, lived in so many different skins it is impossible for one skin to claim me."

★

Autobiographical sources on Parks include *A Choice of Weapons* (1966), *To Smile in Autumn: A Memoir* (1979), and *Voices in the Mirror: An Autobiography* (1990). Other selected biographical sources include Donald Bogle, *Blacks in American Films and Television: An Encyclopedia* (1988); *Contemporary Authors* (1989), vol. 26; *Contemporary Black Biography* (1993), vol. 1; and *Black Literature Criticism* (1994), vol. 1. Parks's literary contributions include *Flash Photography* (1947); *Camera Portraits: The Techniques and Principles of Documentary Portraiture* (1948); *A Poet and His Camera* (1968); *Gordon Parks: Whispers of Intimate Things* (poetry and photographs, 1971); *Born Black* (essays and photographs, 1971); *In Love* (poetry and photography, 1971); *Moments Without Proper Names* (1975); *Flavio* (1978); and *Shannon* (1981).

JOHNNIEQUE B. (JOHNNIE) LOVE

PATTERSON, Floyd (*b.* 4 January 1935 in Waco, North Carolina), 1952 Olympic gold medalist in boxing, the youngest heavyweight champion in history, and the first boxer to lose and subsequently regain the world heavyweight title. He was best known during the 1960s for his fights against Ingemar Johansson, Sonny Liston, and Muhammad Ali.

The third of eleven children born to Thomas Patterson, a construction worker and longshoreman, and Annabelle (Johnson) Patterson, a homemaker, Patterson moved with his family to Brooklyn, New York, in 1936 when he was barely a year old. As a child Patterson was so backward and withdrawn that his mother feared he was mentally retarded. His father had gone north in search of work but found the streets of Bedford-Stuyvesant detrimental to his son, who early became involved with gangs. After several arrests for truancy, shoplifting, and other petty crimes, Patterson was consigned to the Wiltwyck School for Boys in Esopus, New York, an institution identified as being for emotionally disturbed boys. At Wiltwyck he learned to read and write, and perhaps just as important, acquired the boxing skills that ultimately became the source of his livelihood and his fame. Not until his release from Wiltwyck, however, did Patterson consider boxing as a career.

Patterson's journey to the heavyweight championship began in 1949 at the Gramercy Park Gym of legendary trainer and manager Constantine "Cus" D'Amato. In January 1950 Patterson won the Amateur Athletic Union (AAU) tournament in the 147-pound weight class. After winning the New York Golden Gloves light heavyweight title in 1951 and 1952 Patterson, fighting as a middleweight, captured a gold medal at the 1952 Olympic Games in Helsinki, Finland, when he took only seventy-four seconds to knock out Vasile Tita of Romania. Patterson won forty of his forty-four amateur bouts, thirty-seven by knockout.

Patterson made his professional debut as a light heavyweight on 12 September 1952, scoring a fourth-round technical knockout over Eddie Godbold. He won his first twelve professional contests before losing to Joey Maxim on

Floyd Patterson, 1966. ARCHIVE PHOTOS, INC.

7 June 1954 and then enjoyed a string of twenty-three consecutive victories, broken by his loss to Johansson in 1959. Patterson's first shot at the heavyweight championship came in 1956 when the retirement of Rocky Marciano vacated the title. On 30 November, Patterson made short work of the heavily favored veteran Archie Moore, knocking him out in the fifth round. At the age of twenty-one years and five months, Patterson became the youngest heavyweight champion in history.

On 20 June 1960 Patterson made history when he knocked out Ingemar Johansson in the fifth round of their bout for the world heavyweight title, becoming the first man to regain the championship after having relinquished it. Nine months earlier, on 26 June 1959, Johansson had taken the crown from Patterson when he caught him with a powerful right cross that sent him to the canvas in the third round.

Because D'Amato refused to match Patterson against any fighter associated with the promoter James Norris and his corrupt International Boxing Club, Patterson fought a series of inferior opponents and meaningless exhibitions until his first confrontation with Johansson. Patterson battled Johansson a third time, a six-round melee on 13 March 1961 that Patterson won by knockout. After defeating Tom McNeeley on 4 December 1961 to retain the heavyweight title, Patterson had to defend it against the man whom critics suggested he had been avoiding: Charles "Sonny" Liston.

Patterson's title fight with Liston, held in Chicago on 25 September 1962, was among the shortest on record. Liston demolished Patterson two minutes, six seconds into the first round. Deeply humiliated, Patterson wore a false beard and mustache in public for months to conceal his identity. In the rematch on 22 July 1963 the results were the same, except that Patterson lasted four seconds longer than in the first meeting. Although no longer the champion, Patterson continued to box. After falling to Liston, he scored an eighth-round technical knockout over Dante Amonti on 6 January 1964 and went on to defeat in turn Eddie Machen, Charles Powell, George Chuvalo, and Tod Herring, though only Chuvalo posed a serious challenge. During the 1960s Patterson also fought twice more for the heavyweight championship, losing by technical knockout to Muhammad Ali, who had earlier taken the title from Liston, and by decision to Jimmy Ellis.

The fight between Ali and Patterson on 22 November 1965 was overshadowed by racial and religious tension, assuming the character of a holy war of Christian against Muslim. A convert to Roman Catholicism, Patterson said, "The image of a Black Muslim as the world heavyweight champion disgraces the sport and the nation. Cassius Clay [Patterson refused to call his opponent Muhammad Ali] must be beaten and the Black Muslims' scourge removed from boxing." To shame Patterson, Ali taunted him with racial slurs and needlessly prolonged the fight until the referee at last called a halt to the mismatch in the twelfth round.

Following the loss to Ali, Patterson's advisers urged him to stop fighting. When he refused, his wife, the former Sandra Hicks, whom he had married in a civil ceremony on 11 February 1956 and, after his conversion, remarried in a religious ceremony on 13 July 1956, filed for divorce. (They had four children.) On 29 September 1966 Patterson, still regarded as a leading heavyweight contender, knocked out Henry Cooper in the fourth round. He defeated Willie Johnson and Bill McMurray in his first two bouts of 1967 before battling Jerry Quarry to a draw on 9 June and subsequently losing the rematch in October.

When Ali was stripped of his title for draft evasion, Patterson got a final opportunity to reclaim the heavyweight championship. He lost a close decision to Ellis on 14 September 1968 in a bid for the World Boxing Association (WBA) title, a fight that many at ringside believed him to have won. Following the match with Ellis, Patterson at last announced his retirement. Yet two years and one day later, on 15 September 1970, he returned to the ring, knocking out Charlie Green in the tenth round.

Patterson continued boxing until 1972; the finale came on 20 September with a second loss to Muhammad Ali in a bout for the North American Boxing Federation (NABF) heavyweight championship. In a career that spanned twenty years Patterson compiled a record of fifty-five wins, eight losses, one draw, and forty knockouts in sixty-four professional fights.

Retiring to New Paltz, New York, with his second wife, Janet, and their three children, Patterson opened the Huguenot Boxing Club in 1973. Elected to the Olympic Hall of Fame in 1987 and the International Boxing Hall of Fame in 1991, Patterson served on the New York State Boxing Commission between 1977 and 1985 and as director of the New York Off-Track Betting Commission. In 1995 Governor George Pataki appointed Patterson chairman of the New York State Athletic Commission, a position from which he resigned in 1998 after disclosing that he suffered from acute memory loss, to which injuries sustained during his career undoubtedly contributed.

Among the smallest of the modern heavyweight champions, the six-foot tall Patterson never exceeded a fighting weight of two hundred pounds. A gracious demeanor concealed the ferocity he displayed in the ring, earning him a reputation as one of the true gentlemen in his sport.

★

With coauthor Milton Gross, Patterson wrote his autobiography, *Victory Over Myself* (1961). Jack Newcombe, *Floyd Patterson: Heavyweight King* (1961), remains the standard biography. Although somewhat dated, John D. McCallum, *The World Heavyweight Boxing Championship: A History* (1974), contains a useful chapter on Patterson. Profiles of Patterson during his years as heavyweight champion include Gay Talese, "Portrait of the Ascetic Champ," *New York Times Magazine* (5 Mar. 1961), and Pete Hamill, "Floyd's Fight to Save His Pride," *Saturday Evening Post* (27 June 1964). More recent essays on Patterson are "Boxing's Last Gentleman," *New Yorker* (31 July 1995), and Steve Pinto, "Patterson 'Very Involved' Despite Memory Loss," in the Middletown, New York, *Times Herald-Record* (3 Apr. 1998). James B. Roberts and Alexander G. Skutt, *The Boxing Register: International Boxing Hall of Fame Official Record Book* (1997), offers a brief but informative overview of Patterson's career, including a detailed summary of his professional bouts.

MARK G. MALVASI

PAULING, Linus Carl (*b.* 28 February 1901 in Portland, Oregon; *d.* 19 August 1994 in Big Sur, California), chemist, physicist, and biologist who won the 1954 Nobel Prize in chemistry and a Nobel Peace Prize in 1962—the only person who has won two undivided Nobel Prizes; he revolutionized both inorganic chemistry and organic chemistry, identified how sickle-cell anemia works, and was an outspoken advocate for nuclear disarmament and appeasement of the Soviet Union.

Pauling was the first of three children born to a druggist, Herman W. Pauling, and a homemaker, Lucy Isabelle ("Belle") Darling Pauling, descendants of frontier settlers. Herman Pauling died in June 1910. Pauling attended Washington High School in Portland but left without graduating, already having enough high school credits for admission to Oregon Agricultural College (OAC), which he entered in September 1917. In 1919 his mother died. He met the greatest influence on his life and career, Ava Helen Miller, during his senior year at OAC. She was only a sophomore in 1922, when he left for graduate school at the California Institute of Technology (Cal Tech). They married on 17 June 1923.

Family life placed new demands on Pauling with the birth of Linus, Jr., in March 1925. After receiving his doctorate summa cum laude in 1925, Pauling received a Guggenheim Fellowship to study in Munich, Germany, where he worked on chemical bonding with top researchers. His numerous papers on the subject in the 1920s and 1930s opened new fields of research. However, his relationship with his wife became strained during the years he was in Germany (1925–1927) because she remained in California. It was a relief to both of them when he accepted an assistant professorship at Cal Tech in 1928, and they settled down to raise their three sons and one daughter. Pauling even-

Linus Pauling. THE LIBRARY OF CONGRESS

tually became chairman of the division of chemistry and chemical engineering, a post he held from 1936 to 1958. In the mid-1930s his work began to shift from inorganic chemistry to biochemistry. In 1939 he published *The Nature of the Chemical Bond* (revised in 1967), which became the seminal, revolutionary work in the field.

It was during World War II that Pauling began to take a strong interest in politics. The physician who saved his life from nephritis was a Communist and suffered government reprisals, eventually losing his practice, and the government wanted to intern the Japanese-American gardener the Paulings employed. J. Robert Oppenheimer asked Pauling to join the Manhattan Project, which was charged with creating the first nuclear weapons; Pauling refused, but he became interested in nuclear weapons at this time. In the late 1940s his insights into sickle-cell anemia led to treatments for the disease while shedding new light on genetic diseases in general. In 1954 Pauling was awarded the Nobel Prize in chemistry for his work on chemical bonding, and there were those in the scientific community who thought he should receive the Nobel Prize in physiology or medicine for the application of his discoveries to sickle-cell anemia as well.

Meanwhile, matters at Cal Tech were not going well. During the 1930s and 1940s Pauling had joined with other atheists at the school to deny employment or promotions to any professor who had a spiritual life. In so doing, in the fierceness of his commitment, he crossed the line from bias to outright bigotry. Eventually he also worked to discriminate against anyone who was not politically left wing. Yet he did not agree with Cal Tech's late-1950s decision to add courses in the humanities, many of which were taught from a left-wing point of view, to the curriculum. He considered them a waste of time.

By the 1960s Pauling seemed exhausted, and he canceled some of his scientific projects. The only issue that seemed to galvanize him was the testing of nuclear weapons, and he became a leading advocate of nuclear disarmament, writing articles about the effects on people of radiation from nuclear tests. On 10 October 1962 he was awarded the Nobel Peace Prize for his work in communicating the dangers posed by radiation from testing nuclear weapons. People on both sides of the issue seemed to misunderstand why he merited the prize, with those on the left praising his political correctness and those on the right complaining that he was merely trying to appease the Soviets. In fact, his political views were controversial; it was his science that was important in that his work showing that radiation and residue from nuclear tests were harmful to humans and their environment helped lead to test ban treaties. A major test ban treaty was signed on the very day that Pauling received the Peace Prize; many observers were convinced of the relationship between the two events.

Pauling was heavily criticized for his radical politics in many magazines and newspapers around the world, although he received support from leftist publications. He advocated the unilateral disarmament of the United States and the United Kingdom, arguing that the Soviet Union would then disarm because it would no longer feel threatened. This point of view ignored the obvious aggression by the Soviet Union in Europe and China as well as fears in the United States and Western Europe that the Soviet Union posed a serious and continuing threat. By the mid-1960s Pauling had formed the habit of suing for libel any publication that suggested he might be a Communist or "fellow traveler" who favored the Soviet Union over his own country. (That a disarmed Western world would be easy pickings for a nuclear-armed Soviet Union was often pointed out by publications such as the *National Review*.) Nearly always, the publications he sued settled out of court.

On 17 July 1962 the conservative *National Review* suggested Pauling was a "collaborator," and Pauling threatened to sue. The editor of the *National Review* was William F. Buckley, Jr., who relished the prospect of a fight and refused to settle Pauling's claim. The resulting court battle damaged Pauling's reputation because the *National Review* showed that Pauling had broken American law by corresponding with Ho Chi Minh while the United States was at war with North Vietnam. The lawsuit resulted in a landmark ruling that changed how journalists were allowed to write about famous people. On 19 April 1964 Judge Samuel J. Silverman ruled that all public figures, not only politicians, had to prove actual "malice" to win a libel suit; "defamation" was insufficient. This ruling has allowed American journalists to write with almost unfettered freedom about anyone who is in the public eye—even lying—as long as "malice" cannot be proven. On 30 June 1964, tired and demoralized, Pauling resigned from Cal Tech because of the faculty's resentment concerning both his politics and his continuing habit of taking credit for work done by others. For the next few years he worked on a new edition of *The Nature of the Chemical Bond*.

Pauling served as professor of chemistry at the University of California, San Diego, from 1967 to 1969. He found working at San Diego congenial, but in 1969 Stanford University offered him more money, more spacious and up-to-date laboratories, and more research assistants as well as the opportunity to live at his beloved home in Big Sur. He accepted the Stanford position, and during the next five years tried to apply his knowledge of chemistry, physics, and genetics to unlock treatments for diseases. Somewhere in the intricacies of chemical bonding and the double helix, he believed, were answers not only for sickle-cell anemia but also for viral infections such as colds and for some cancers, especially those linked to viruses. He thought he had found an answer in vitamin C, which seemed to reinforce the structure of DNA, thus having the potential to fend off mutations that seemed to be at the heart of cancer.

In 1970 the most widely influential of Pauling's books, *Vitamin C and the Common Cold*, was published. In it Pauling argued that taking vitamin C as a dietary supplement could protect people from colds and other viral diseases. Later he argued that megadoses of vitamin C could cure some kinds of cancer. A majority of specialists in viruses and cancer disagreed. For a lifetime of achievement in science, however, Pauling received the National Medal of Science from President Gerald Ford on 18 September 1975.

Pauling and the researcher Arthur Robinson founded the Pauling Institute in the 1970s to further pure research. Robinson was marvelous at raising money, but he aroused Pauling's deeply held prejudices when he publicly declared he was a capitalist and in his writings suggested that vitamin C taken in large quantities could be carcinogenic. Pauling was outraged at Robinson's political views and took it as a personal insult that Robinson's laboratory work should seem to disagree with his theories. He and his partner dissolved their relationship, and Pauling erased him from his life.

On 7 December 1981 Pauling's wife died of stomach cancer. Pauling continued writing scientific papers until his death from prostate cancer on 19 August 1994. He was cremated and his ashes were scattered.

Pauling's was an exceptionally productive life. Neither his mean-spiritedness, his tendency to take credit for other people's work, nor his politics detract from his greatness as a scientist. His work in several scientific fields is an example of how a true scientist applies his mind and skill to problems. Out of his dogged and brilliant work emerged new scientific disciplines as well as solutions to fundamental chemical, physical, and biological questions that laid the groundwork for expanding research and knowledge. He may have been his era's greatest chemist; he may be the greatest of all biochemists; and his work on sickle-cell anemia and on the effects of nutrition on diseases opened new avenues for understanding and treating illness.

★

The Ava Helen and Linus Pauling papers are housed in Special Collections, The Valley Library, Oregon State University, in Corvallis. Probably the most objective account of Pauling's life is Anthony Serafini's *Linus Pauling: A Man and His Science* (1989), which not only describes Pauling's strengths and weaknesses but offers good, clear explanations of his scientific work. An interesting, although short, account of Pauling's science is Francis Crick's "LP + C + 2NP Is Not Equal to DNA" in the *New York Times Magazine* (1 Jan. 1995): 18. An obituary is in the *New York Times* (21 Aug. 1994).

KIRK H. BEETZ

PEALE, Norman Vincent (*b*. 31 May 1898 in Bowersville, Ohio; *d*. 24 December 1993 in Pawling, New York), prominent clergyman and prolific religious writer who touted *The Power of Positive Thinking* and tapped into mass media; considered by many to have launched the twentieth-century self-help movement.

Peale was the son of Charles Clifford Peale, a physician and Methodist minister, and Anna DeLaney, a homemaker. He was profoundly influenced by his father's gift for public speaking and admiration and enthusiasm for God. A small-town "country boy," Peale earned his B.A. from Ohio Wesleyan University, a Methodist-founded college, in 1920, and hesitated slightly before committing to his own career as a Methodist clergyman. He studied theology and earned his M.A. and S.T.B. from Boston University in 1924. The faculty at Boston were religious liberals, many interested in the ties between psychology and religion, which would become a life-long interest for Peale. His flair for compelling ministry became apparent early on as he served parishes in Rhode Island, New York, and New Jersey and his congregations grew. He married Loretta Ruth Stafford, a church worker, on 20 June 1930; they had

Norman Vincent Peale. THE LIBRARY OF CONGRESS

two daughters and a son. In 1932 Peale converted his denomination from Methodist to Dutch Reformed to take his place at the 300-year-old Marble Collegiate Church in Manhattan. The church became his home parish for the next fifty years. The congregation was only a few hundred strong when Peale assumed its leadership; by the time he retired, his Sunday worship service was broadcast to thousands over closed-circuit television on big screens.

Peale established a religio-psychiatric clinic next door to the church. He started a radio program called *The Art of Living* (which later moved to television), edited the magazine *Guideposts,* and wrote books, including *The Art of Living* (1937), *A Guide to Confident Living* (1948), and *The Power of Positive Thinking* (1952). *The Power of Positive Thinking* was a resounding hit; it stayed atop the *New York Times* best-seller list for a record-breaking three years. In the book Peale applied the techniques he himself had used to overcome his early shyness and self-doubt. The post–World War II religious boom bolstered his success, and the book was translated into thirty-three languages. *The Power of Positive Thinking* established Peale as a significant force in American popular religion. Many see it as the first self-help book. In 1953 *Life* counted Peale among the nation's twelve great preachers. His biography, *Norman Vincent Peale: Minister to Millions,* was made into a Hollywood movie, *One Man's Way,* in 1963.

Peale's audience continued to grow after 1960, but not as dramatically as in the previous decade, fueled as it was by the religious revival. During the 1960s he wrote *The Tough-Minded Optimist* (1961), *Adventures in the Holy Land* (1963), *Sin, Sex and Self-Control* (1965), *Jesus of Nazareth: A Dramatic Interpretation of His Life from Bethlehem to Calvary* (1966), *The Healing of Sorrow* (1966), and *Enthusiasm Makes the Difference* (1967). Some of Peale's religious colleagues disapproved of the liberal and psychological emphasis of these writings and of Peale's popular ministry. His critics regarded his message as too simplistic and more humanistic than distinctly Christian—some considered it a watered-down version of Christianity. Others considered his teachings, which included "fifteen-minute formulas," a "three-point program," "seven simple steps," "eight practical formulas," and "ten simple rules," far too formulaic and easy to be valid. Many could not reconcile his methods of success in the material world with the church's pious teachings. But Peale himself never claimed to be profound or intellectual. Rather, he was deeply interested in the everyday issues that ordinary people faced.

Peale also was seen to have made compromises in order to increase numbers at his church and to make his message more accessible. He avoided the more solemn messages of the church, those about sin, guilt, and suffering. Peale never spoke on social injustice, never addressed the Holocaust, and avoided discussing racism as a social issue, except for occasional stories about discrimination. His ever-optimistic sermons sometimes seemed out of place in a century that included two world wars, the Holocaust, and the advent of nuclear weapons. In a decade marked by the beginnings of the war in Vietnam and often-violent unrest over civil rights, the minister kept mum on hot-button topics. Peale faced such criticism by maintaining that he could not be all things to all people. He humbly admitted that while he had many worse qualities, his best quality was his love for Jesus Christ and his belief that Christ was the "greatest thing to ever happen to this world."

Though Peale's theology was liberal, his politics were not. He was chairman of the ultraconservative Committee for Constitutional Government, which lobbied against the New Deal reforms of Democratic President Franklin D. Roosevelt's administration. He stepped up for 150 Protestant clergymen in 1960 and publicly opposed presidential candidate John F. Kennedy, fearing the influence of the Catholic Church on the White House under a Catholic president. "Faced with the election of a Catholic," he said, "our culture is at stake." The resulting uproar caused the pastor to avoid any further political commitments, for fear he might offend the fans of his popular religio-psychiatric message. He was, however, a Republican, and was personally and politically close to the Nixon and Eisenhower families. It has been said that his beliefs—that all problems essentially are personal—were, in fact, quite conservative.

The harsh criticism Peale suffered for opposing Kennedy plagued him for years. His own son was forced to listen to professors' tirades against "Pealeism" in seminary. By 1965 Peale had become alienated from the institutional church but, paradoxically, he was enthusiastic when offered two prestigious positions in the church hierarchy. He survived a contested election to serve the first of four terms as president of the Protestant Council of the City of New York, and was president of the Reformed Church in America from 1969 to 1970.

In the itinerant Methodist tradition Peale traveled widely, extending the reach of his ministry and message. He received several honorary degrees and numerous awards throughout his career, including five Freedoms Foundation awards and the Presidential Medal of Freedom. Peale died after a stroke in 1993 at age ninety-five. All told, Peale wrote forty-one books in his lifetime. His wife carried on his ministry, speaking to business leaders and students about "positive thinking." Motivational speakers from Dale Carnegie to Zig Ziglar owe a debt to Peale, according to his biographer Carol V. R. George.

★

Biographies of Peale include Arthur Gordon, *Norman Vincent Peale—Minister to Millions, a Biography* (1958), and Carol V. R.

George, *God's Salesman* (1993). Peale wrote an autobiography, *The True Joy of Positive Living* (1984). Obituaries are in the *Los Angeles Times, New York Times,* and *Washington Post* (all 26 Dec. 1993).

BRENNA SANCHEZ

PECKINPAH, David Samuel ("Sam") (*b.* 21 February 1925 in Fresno, California; *d.* 28 December 1984 in Inglewood, California), actor, television and motion picture scriptwriter, and film director whose 1969 film *The Wild Bunch* reflected the violence and social upheaval of the late 1960s.

Peckinpah was one of three children born to David Edward Peckinpah, an attorney and later a judge, and Fern Louise Church-Peckinpah, a homemaker. Peckinpah married four times, wedding his second wife, the actress Begonia Palacio, twice. He sired five children, four of them by his first wife, Marie Selland, whom he divorced in 1964. He also fathered a daughter with Palacio, whom he divorced in 1972. He married his third wife, Joie Gould, later that year.

Peckinpah attended Fresno High School but in 1943 enlisted in the U.S. Marine Corps; he saw limited duty in China. After World War II he enrolled in Fresno State College, from which he received a B.A. In 1947 he married Marie Selland, who introduced him to the theater, and in 1948 Peckinpah enrolled in the graduate drama program at the University of Southern California, from which he

Sam Peckinpah. CORBIS CORPORATION (BELLEVUE)

received an M.A. After the birth of his first child Peckinpah dropped out and worked at the Huntington Park Civic Theater near Los Angeles, where he was both an actor and director in residence for two years.

In 1954 Peckinpah was hired as a dialog coach for the film *Riot in Cell Block 11* (1954) and was subsequently cast for a small part in *Invasion of the Body Snatchers* (1956). In 1955 he wrote episodes for the television series *Gunsmoke,* one of which earned him a Writer's Guild nomination. Peckinpah's subsequent television assignments during the 1950s included *Have Gun Will Travel* (1957) and the critically acclaimed *The Westerner* (1960).

During the 1960s Peckinpah established himself in films. His first feature film assignment was *The Deadly Companion* (1961), an unremarkable western but one that marked his debut as America's "bad boy" director, due to recurring battles with producers. His reputation as a director of considerable talent, however, was established in his next film, *Ride the High Country* (1962). Set in the early twentieth century, when automobiles were replacing horses and uniformed police were replacing the swaggering lawmen who had tamed the West, the film, starring Joel McCrea and Randolph Scott, is an action tale of two aged gunfighters well past their prime and out of place in a world that no longer needs them. Addressing salvation and loneliness, themes to which Peckinpah would return, *Ride the High Country* was not recognized by Metro-Goldwyn-Mayer (MGM) as the classic it later would become. Nevertheless, the film did catch the attention of critics, who subsequently would place it among Peckinpah's finest films. *Newsweek,* for example, declared it the best American film of 1962.

Peckinpah's career lagged during the mid-1960s due as much to a dearth of westerns (in 1960 forty-six westerns were shown on television as compared to eleven in 1964) as to his repeated conflicts with his studio employers. For example, Columbia executives thought Peckinpah's 1965 western *Major Dundee,* starring Charlton Heston, was an overlong and confused story and confronted him about the problem. Peckinpah wouldn't cooperate with the studio's request to alter the film, so eventually outside parties had to be brought in to edit the footage, a move that angered Peckinpah so much that he disowned the film. Despite the movie's failure, Peckinpah became a living legend, as the press magnified his confrontation with the Hollywood power structure. But Peckinpah's feud with Columbia executives resulted in his being barred from the studio's lot. He subsequently was also fired from MGM after disagreements with studio executives over his assignment to direct *The Cincinnati Kid.*

For the next several years Peckinpah found it difficult to find work in Hollywood. He returned to television in 1966, when the American Broadcasting Company (ABC) hired him to adapt and direct Katherine Anne Porter's novella *Noon Wine* for a new hour-long dramatic anthology series, *ABC Stage 67*. Starring Jason Robards, Jr., *Noon Wine* was a critical success, and Peckinpah received a Writers Guild nomination for best television adaptation and a Directors Guild nomination for best television direction. *Noon Wine*'s success helped rehabilitate Peckinpah's career.

In 1969 Peckinpah returned to Hollywood, where Warner Bros. employed him to direct what many critics consider his best film, *The Wild Bunch*. The epic western was made in a decade witnessing Vietnam War protests, political assassinations, and violent opposition to the civil rights movement. Peckinpah was not apologetic about the excessive violence that characterizes much of the film and defended the brutality depicted in *The Wild Bunch* when he said, "the whole underside of our society has always been violent . . . everybody seems to think that man is a noble savage. But he's only an animal, a meat-eating, talking animal." One critic wrote of *The Wild Bunch*, "I'd never laid eyes on a western like that. It seemed to me to be so much a film about the Vietnam war, a film about guys . . . going to foreign countries and murdering people."

Starring William Holden, the film tells the story of embittered and aging gunfighters who realize that their time has passed. Nevertheless, they are hired to "make one last score" and subsequently become entangled in the Mexican Revolution, where they engage in some of film history's most relentless carnage before finding redemption. Peckinpah told the film critic Pauline Kael that he wanted the picture to be so ferocious that "it would rub people's noses in the ugliness of violence." The film established Peckinpah as one of the most imaginative filmmakers in Hollywood. His use of slow motion to depict graphic scenes of blood and gore sparked controversy among critics and audiences alike. Peckinpah received an Oscar nomination for the film's screenplay.

The Wild Bunch elevated Peckinpah to the A-list of Hollywood directors, and he continued to make high-quality films that were generally reviewed favorably. *The Ballad of Cable Hogue* (1970) was followed by his first nonwestern, *Straw Dogs* (1971), then by *Junior Bonner* (1972), *The Getaway* (1972), *Pat Garrett and Billy the Kid* (1973), *Bring Me the Head of Alfredo Garcia* (1974), *The Killer Elite* (1975), *Cross of Iron* (1977), *Convoy* (1978), and his last film, *The Osterman Weekend* (1983).

Peckinpah suffered from both a severe drinking problem and a strong addiction to cocaine, as well as other health problems. He suffered a heart attack in 1984 and died at Centinela Hospital Medical Center at age fifty-nine. His body was cremated and his ashes scattered over the Pacific Ocean at Paradise Cove, California.

By the end of the 1960s Peckinpah had established himself among the top rank of directors in Hollywood. *The Wild Bunch* became an instant classic, and Peckinpah's name became synonymous with excessive violence in films that were viewed by critics as mirroring the turbulent 1960s.

★

Biographies of Peckinpah include Garner Simmons, *Peckinpah: A Portrait in Montage* (1982); Marshall Fine, *Bloody Sam: The Life and Films of Sam Peckinpah* (1991); and David Weddle, *"If They Move . . . Kill 'Em!": The Life and Times of Sam Peckinpah* (1994). Obituaries are in the *Los Angeles Times* and *Washington Post* (both 29 Dec. 1984).

JACK FISCHEL

PEI, I(eoh) M(ing) (*b.* 26 April 1917 in Canton [now Guangzhou], China), award-winning architect known in the 1960s for his large-scale glass, cast-in-place, and concrete-clad buildings.

Pei, the second of five children, grew up in Hong Kong and later in Shanghai. His father, Tsuyee Pei, was a senior banker with the Bank of China, while his mother, Lien Kwun (Chwong) Pei, was a musician and devout Buddhist. Pei attended Saint John's Middle School in Shanghai before moving to the United States in 1935 to study briefly at the University of Pennsylvania before transferring to the Massachusetts Institute of Technology (MIT), where he received a B.Arch. in 1940. He served with the National

I. M. Pei, 1964. © BETTMANN/CORBIS

Defense Research Committee in Princeton, New Jersey, from 1943 to 1945 during World War II. On 20 June 1942 Pei married Eileen Loo, a Harvard architecture student. They have four children. Pei graduated with an M.Arch. from the Harvard University Graduate School of Design in 1948. He and his wife became American citizens in 1954.

In the early 1950s Pei worked for William Zeckendorf's real estate development firm, Webb and Knapp. There he learned the practicalities of design on important developments such as the Kips Bay Plaza apartments in New York City (1957–1962). It was on this building that, along with engineer August E. Kommendant, Pei developed the unique window truss load-bearing wall. Pei's talent for design was obvious. With these early projects he established his trademark style of blending buildings with their surroundings for mutual enhancement. Pei's ideas about urban design fit perfectly with the trend in the 1960s for large-scale, integrated urban planning, and many of his designs from that decade have become architectural classics.

Though it was personally rewarding, Pei's work for Zeckendorf did not help his reputation with other designers, who saw working as the employee of a developer as a form of selling out creative freedom. Perhaps with this in mind, in 1955 Pei established the firm of I. M. Pei and Associates with Henry N. Cobb and Eason H. Leonard. As the 1960s progressed Pei acquired a reputation as one of the finest architects of his generation. The years at Zeckendorf taught him the importance of adhering to formulas, and much of his early work is considered conservative. He was, however, also left with a distrust of theorizing. Unlike architects such as Walter Gropius, with whom he is sometimes compared, Pei has expressed a preference for developing ideas through his designs rather than in theoretical writings. For example, the National Center for Atmospheric Research in Boulder, Colorado (1961–1967), which Pei has called his "breakout" project, has twin cylindrical towers that contrast powerfully with the mountains behind. The project effectively announced his arrival as a world-class architect, and did so through visual impact and functionality alone. Unlike Gropius and others, Pei saw no need to explain the building's place in a grand scheme for the future of architecture and design.

In 1964 Pei's rising status was reflected in his selection to design the John F. Kennedy Library at Columbia Point, Boston, Massachusetts. The project took over a decade to complete and was eventually dedicated in 1979, having gone through three design incarnations for three different sites. Yet Pei remained true to the ideas explored in earlier buildings, especially in his efforts to allow the building and the landscape to enhance one another.

In the second half of the 1960s Pei began to move away from his modernist origins. Abandoning the cool efficiency of Gropius and Ludwig Mies van der Rohe, Pei's design

for the Everson Art Museum at Syracuse University in Syracuse, New York (1966–1968), is bold and dramatic. Four rectangular concrete blocks contain the gallery spaces and tower over a plaza. Pei became a specialist at designing museums and other municipal buildings and proved especially skilled at creating gallery spaces and entrances. But it was not just the buildings and their interiors that were impressive. In the case of the Kennedy Library, for example, outstanding views to the outside were also a key feature of the design.

In 1966 Pei's firm changed its name to I. M. Pei and Partners to recognize the collaborative nature of its projects. The Dallas Municipal Center (1966–1977) brought Pei and the firm international recognition. Built from concrete in the shape of an upside-down pyramid embedded in the ground, the Dallas Municipal Center combines two of the characteristic features of Pei's buildings: high drama and a fascination with geometric shapes. The Dallas pyramid is an early example of many Pei pyramids, including the Grand Louvre project in Paris (1989). Other key buildings designed by Pei and his collaborators in the 1960s include the standardized model for air traffic control towers around the United States (1967–1970); the Canadian Imperial Bank of Commerce Complex, Toronto (1967–1973); the Herbert F. Johnson Museum of Art at Cornell University, Ithaca, New York (1968–1973); and the east wing of the National Gallery of Art, Washington, D.C. (1968–1978). The last of these revolutionized museum design with its entrance hall and galleries designed to maximize visitor flow in combination with usable display space.

In 1979 Pei won the gold medal for architecture from the American Academy of Arts and Letters, and by the 1980s had become one of America's most respected architects. He won the prestigious Pritzker Architecture Prize in 1983 and used the $100,000 award to fund a scholarship for Chinese students to study architecture in the United States. On 4 July 1986 he became one of only twelve naturalized Americans to be awarded the Medal of Liberty, and in 1990 President George H. W. Bush awarded him the Medal of Freedom.

Pei designed some of the most important public buildings of the 1960s, transforming many American cityscapes in the process. He also experimented with materials, helping make possible the glass-clad tower blocks characteristic of the 1970s and becoming a major influence on the design of museums and other public buildings. Throughout the 1960s he pushed the limits of materials such as glass and concrete, but he managed to be innovative and flamboyant without overembellishing his designs. For example, the Chinese influence evident in Pei's design for the Henry Luce Chapel at Taunghai University, Taida, Taiwan (1954–1963), is achieved without resorting to obvious, superficial Chinese motifs. Perhaps the most important feature of Pei's designs in the period is his sensitivity to making each design fit with its surroundings and intended use. The best of Pei's buildings, including the Dallas Municipal Center, add a dramatic, sculptural presence to their setting.

★

Pei explains his ideas about urban design in the article "The Nature of Urban Space" in Harry S. Ransom, ed., *The People's Architects* (1964). Biographies of Pei include Bruno Suner, *Ieoh Ming Pei* (1988), and Carter Wiseman, *I. M. Pei: A Profile in American Architecture* (1990). Biographical information is also found in Paul Heyer, *Architects on Architecture* (1966); *Contemporary Architects*, 3rd ed. (1987); Pamela Dell, *I. M. Pei: Designer of Dreams* (1993); Michael T. Cannell, *I. M. Pei: Mandarin of Modernism* (1995); Aileen Reid, *I. M. Pei* (1995); and Gero von Boehm, *Conversations with I. M. Pei: Light Is the Key* (2000). Among the best articles about Pei's work in the 1960s are "Paeans for Pei," in *Progressive Architecture* (Oct. 1963), and Peter Blake's "I. M. Pei and Partners," in *Architecture Plus* (Feb. 1973 and Mar. 1973).

CHRIS ROUTLEDGE

PENN, Arthur Hiller (*b.* 27 September 1922 in Philadelphia, Pennsylvania), stage, television, and film director whose *Bonnie and Clyde* (1967) proved to be one of the most influential films of the 1960s.

Penn was the second of two sons born to Harry Penn, a watch repairman, and Sonia (Greenberg) Penn, a nurse. His parents divorced when he was three years old. From 1925 to 1936 Penn lived with his mother, who struggled financially during the depression, in New Jersey and New York. His mother had to move frequently, and Penn attended thirteen different schools. When he was fourteen Penn returned to Philadelphia to assist his ailing father in the running of his watch-repair shop. His parents' divorce was traumatic for Penn, and he credits an affinity for alienated heroes in his films to his youthful identity crisis as the product of a broken home. Penn later asserted that the French filmmaker François Truffaut's movie *The 400 Blows* stunned him, because it so resembled his own childhood.

During his youth, however, he was not a particular fan of the cinema, after being terrified by a horror film when he was just five years old. Penn, instead, was more drawn to the stage. At Olney High School in Philadelphia he did some acting and was attracted to the technical aspects of theatrical production. He was also active in the Neighborhood Playhouse, located near his home. Following the death of his father in 1943, Penn was drafted into the U.S. Army. Stationed at Fort Jackson in South Carolina, he spent considerable time in nearby Columbia at the Civic Theatre, where he met Fred Coe (who would later bring

Arthur Penn. BRADLEY SMITH/CORBIS

Penn into the television industry). He joined the Soldiers Show Company to entertain American occupation troops in Europe. After his discharge from the military, Penn used the GI Bill benefits to study art and literature at Black Mountain College in North Carolina. From 1947 to 1950 he studied literature in Italy and took acting lessons from the Russian actor and director Michael Chekhov in Hollywood.

Penn was working as a floor manager and assistant director for the television division of the National Broadcasting Company (NBC) and living in California in 1953, when Coe invited him back to New York City to direct live teleplays for such series as *Philco Television Playhouse* and *Playhouse 90*. Penn's distinguished television work included *The Miracle Worker*, William Gibson's dramatization of the teacher Anne Sullivan's efforts to open the world of sight and sound to the deaf and blind Helen Keller. In the late 1950s and early 1960s Penn gave his attention to the New York stage and directed a string of Broadway hits: *Two for the Seesaw* (1957–1958); *The Miracle Worker* (1959–1960), which won the Antoinette Perry (Tony) Award; *Toys in the Attic* (1959–1960); *Fiorello!* (1959–1960); *All the Way Home* (1960–1961); *Golden Boy* (1964–1965); and *Wait Until Dark* (1965–1966).

Meanwhile, Penn tried his hand at film direction. His first feature was *The Left-Handed Gun* (1958), starring Paul

191

Newman as a neurotic Billy the Kid. The film contained elements, such as identification with an alienated hero and critique of the violence in the American frontier and society, that would characterize Penn's outstanding cinematic work in the 1960s. Penn, however, was disappointed with his initial incursion into Hollywood. Warner Bros.' editing of the film distorted Penn's more pessimistic conclusion, and the film was panned by both film critics and audiences, although in Europe the film was well received. A disillusioned Penn returned to the New York stage until an opportunity to do a cinematic adaptation of *The Miracle Worker* (1962) drew him back to Hollywood. The film was a critical and box office success, earning Penn an Academy Award nomination for best director and Oscars for Anne Bancroft as best actress and Patty Duke as best supporting actress.

After he was inexplicably fired and replaced with John Frankenheimer on *The Train* (1963), Penn vowed to take personal control of his next film. *Mickey One* (1965), featuring Penn's friend Warren Beatty, explores the theme of an alienated individual at the mercy of forces beyond his control. The story concerns a nightclub comedian who is on the run from underworld forces attempting to kill him for committing a transgression of which he has no knowledge. The film borrows from the work of the Austrian writer Franz Kafka and was criticized by some critics for its pretentious symbolism. According to Penn the paranoia in *Mickey One* was representative of the continuing impact of McCarthyism and government surveillance upon the lives of American citizens. (Named for Senator Joseph McCarthy, McCarthyism referred to the unsubstantiated claims and witch-hunting tactics that colored the investigation of purported Communists in the U.S. government in the early 1950s.) While audiences were cool in their response to *Mickey One,* it was a film of which Penn was proud.

For his next film project Penn collaborated with the playwright and screenwriter Lillian Hellman on an adaptation of Horton Foote's novel *The Chase*. Hellman viewed the film as an examination of American violence in microcosm through the dissection of a small Texas town. Penn had high hopes for the 1966 film starring Marlon Brando, Jane Fonda, and Robert Redford. Penn's artistic vision, however, clashed with the perception of the producer Sam Spiegel, who made the final cut. A dejected Penn regretted making the film and again vowed to maintain control over his projects.

Bonnie and Clyde (1967) offered such an opportunity. Working with the stars Estelle Parsons, Faye Dunaway, Gene Hackman, Michael J. Pollard, and Warren Beatty (also the film's producer); the writers David Newman and Robert Benton; the special consultant Robert Towne; and the cinematographer Burnett Guffey, Penn directed a film

that baffled executives at Warner Bros. Initially, the studio believed that the film would work only with drive-in audiences, and they targeted the picture for a limited release. Also, many critics were upset that the film glorified the violent behavior of the real-life depression-era bank robbers and killers Clyde Barrow and Bonnie Parker. Influenced by the French New Wave films of Truffaut and Jean-Luc Godard, Penn crafted a film that was experimental in narrative structure and undermined audience expectations with rapid shifts in mood. While he drew on European influences, Penn's focus was definitely on the American experience and the role of violence in the nation's history. Responding to critics of the film's violence, Penn observed, "I think violence is part of the American character. . . . America is a country of people who act out their views in violent ways—there is not a strong tradition of persuasion, of ideation, and of law."

Against the background of the Vietnam War, coupled with urban and campus unrest, Penn's film of two young people rebelling against an oppressive establishment that repossessed people's homes struck a responsive chord with many filmgoers, especially young people. The film's unexpected popularity led many critics to revise their initial negative assessments, praising the film's artistic merits as well as its social relevance. *Bonnie and Clyde* received ten Academy Award nominations, including best picture and best direction, and won three Oscars.

Penn continued to express his affinity for young people with his next screen project, *Alice's Restaurant,* a film adaptation of the folksinger Arlo Guthrie's popular narrative song detailing his avoidance of conscription because of an arrest for the heinous crime of littering. Penn was attracted to the film owing to his empathy for rebellious youth in the 1960s and because it was set in his adopted home of Stockbridge, Massachusetts. When contrasting the counterculture youth to his own generation, Penn asserted, "These kids are on to something much more genuine, much more tender, and loving. . . . I'm hoping that the film will be able to elucidate that part of their subculture." The youth culture, as well as the critics, responded favorably to *Alice's Restaurant,* making it one of the major box office hits of 1969.

Penn next turned his questioning gaze to the history of the American West with his cinematic adaptation of Thomas Berger's comic novel *Little Big Man* (1970). The traditional heroic depiction of western settlement is turned on its head in this film narrated by Jack Crabb (played by Dustin Hoffman), the 121-year-old survivor of the Battle of the Little Bighorn. The film and novel are an indictment of American history, drawing an analogy between nineteenth-century expansionism into the West and American involvement in the Vietnam War. *Little Big Man* was a box office and critical success, gaining Penn his third Oscar nomination for best director.

After the acclaim for *Bonnie and Clyde, Alice's Restaurant,* and *Little Big Man,* all of which reflected Penn's support for the antiestablishment values of the 1960s youth generation, the director took a break from making films, but he was never able to regain the momentum of his film career fully. In 1975 Penn made the detective film *Night Moves* with Hackman, followed by the Western *The Missouri Breaks,* with Marlon Brando and Jack Nicholson, in 1976. The films were highly anticipated but were panned by critics and avoided by filmgoers. Both films are better appreciated today than when they were originally released. Penn's few films since the 1970s, such as *Four Friends* (1981), *Target* (1985), *Dead of Winter* (1987), and *Inside* (1996), have found only limited release and reception. In a 1986 interview Penn retorted, "It's not that I've drifted away from film. I'm very drawn to film, but I'm not sure that film is drawn to me."

In 1955 Penn married the actress Peggy Maurer, and they had two children. While Penn's cinematic vision waned after 1970, his films of the 1960s well represent the artistic and political questioning of American society and institutions during that tumultuous decade.

★

For background information on Penn and a discussion of his artistic vision, see Robin Wood, *Arthur Penn* (1969); Robert Phillip Kolker, *A Cinema of Loneliness: Penn, Kubrick, Coppola, Scorsese, Altman* (1980; rev. ed., 1988); and Joel Zuker, *Arthur Penn: A Guide to References and Resources* (1980). Analysis of *Bonnie and Clyde* may be found in Sandra Wake and Nicola Hayden, eds., *The Bonnie and Clyde Book* (1972); John Cawelti, ed., *Focus on Bonnie and Clyde* (1973); and Lester D. Friedman, *Arthur Penn's Bonnie and Clyde* (2000).

RON BRILEY

PERCY, Walker (*b.* 28 May 1916 in Birmingham, Alabama; *d.* 10 May 1990 in Covington, Louisiana), physician and author whose novels of alienation and society made him one of the few authors to integrate Christian faith with a coherent view of modern science and technology.

Percy was born into a wealthy family. His father, LeRoy Pratt Percy, a lawyer, committed suicide in 1927; two years later his mother, Martha Susan (Phinizy), was killed in an auto accident. His father's first cousin, William Alexander Percy, took Percy and two of his brothers to live in Greenville, Mississippi.

By high school Percy was writing poetry, and at Greenville High School he wrote a column for the school's newspaper. He majored in chemistry at the University of North

Walker Percy. MR. JERRY BAUER

Carolina, Chapel Hill, graduating with a B.A. in 1937. He next attended the College of Physicians and Surgeons at Columbia University. After receiving his M.D. in 1941 he interned at New York City's Bellevue Hospital, where he worked as a pathologist.

Dealing with cadavers of homeless people who had died of various diseases, he himself caught pulmonary tuberculosis. He spent two years in Trudeau Sanitarium in Saranac Lake, New York, and had further recovery time in Wallingford, Connecticut. He found mental exercise in reading the works of the philosophers Søren Kierkegaard and Martin Heidegger, the Russian writer Fyodor Dostoyevsky, and the French existentialists Jean-Paul Sartre and Albert Camus. These writers stirred in him a process of thought that included the existentialist conundrum of how an individual person may find meaning in an impersonal universe.

Preoccupied by his studies of philosophy and his own efforts to penetrate the mysteries of the human condition, he moved to Sewanee, Tennessee, to think. There he met Mary Bernice "Bunt" Townsend, whom he married on 7 November 1946. They moved to New Orleans. By 1947 he had concluded that, while society may be corrupt and without meaning, the universe had meaning in the presence of a personal God, and that year he converted to Roman Catholicism. After his conversion Percy moved to Covington, Louisiana, where he spent the rest of his life. There he and Bunt brought up their two daughters.

During the 1950s Percy expressed his pondering of the human condition in articles about philosophy and psychiatry. Some of these essays were reprinted in Percy's collection *The Message in the Bottle: How Queer Man Is, How Queer Language Is, and What One Has to Do with the Other* (1975). Alienation is an important theme running through these pieces; this idea preoccupied him through the 1960s.

In 1961 Knopf published Percy's novel *The Moviegoer*, which attracted only modest attention from reviewers, partly because the publisher thought it was a minor work and did not publicize it extensively. *The Moviegoer* did not win its ultimate place as an American masterpiece easily. Percy had originally submitted a long manuscript about a southern man who was alienated from both southern culture and American society as a whole. Instead of giving up on it, the Knopf editor Stanley Kauffmann, who thought only about forty pages of it were worth publishing, told Percy to revise it. It went through four drafts before Kauffmann found it satisfactory. Both the editors of Knopf and Percy himself were surprised when *The Moviegoer* received the 1962 National Book Award for fiction and thereafter sold well. The novel eventually became the work on which Percy's reputation primarily rested.

The novel's main character is Binx Bolling, a stockbroker obsessed with the valuelessness of his own life. To Binx, everyone he knows is "dead," even if they do not realize it. He is a "moviegoer" because motion pictures offer him solace, structure, and meaning. This parallels Percy's own experiences while working in New York; he had spent much of his free time in movie theaters. Binx is alienated from everyone, from himself, and from God, and he represents a condition that transcends the era of technology's alienation from self and culture; in the worldview of *The Moviegoer*, Binx represents the perpetual state of humanity: fallen because of original sin. In *The Moviegoer* and subsequent novels the central solution to alienation is to reconcile oneself with God; human society has always alienated people, even if they do not realize it, but societies are inherently corrupt and will always fail to fulfill human aspirations, even America's culture of liberty.

In the fiction of Sartre and Camus, Percy had seen a way to pull together the ideas about philosophy he had explored in the 1950s by expressing them in fiction, and there are hints of Camus's *Stranger* in *The Moviegoer*. In Camus's novel the protagonist Meursault is alienated by a society that denies his individuality; like Binx, he finds himself set apart, as if observing events around him from an objective distance, as if not truly participating. Whereas *The Stranger* ends with Meursault refusing to believe in life beyond death, Percy takes his themes in another direction, insisting that there is a life after death and that, through God, a person can have the individual identity society would otherwise deny him or her, as it is denied for Camus's Meursault.

The Moviegoer reflects Percy's effort to present Kierkegaard's ideas and his own about how religious faith can apply to people who are alienated by a society that cannot meet their needs for fulfillment and happiness. The ending of the novel is difficult to understand because it carries Binx from his existentialist misery to his mother's Roman Catholic faith. What Percy seemed to hope to achieve was a revelation in which Binx as an Everyman figure discovers that, in a relationship with God, the imperfections in his personality and his alienation cease to matter because he has transcended the creations of humanity and placed himself philosophically and spiritually in the domain of God's perfection.

During the 1960s Percy was impressed by the civil rights movement, as were many American writers. His view seems to have been that slavery had denied the American South the fullness of God's blessing. "One little test: here's a helpless man in Africa, all you have to do is not violate him. That's all," he wrote. "One little test: you flunk!" (Dr. Thomas More, in *Love in the Ruins* [1971]). This may be one reason for the alienation Percy's characters feel as they try to reconcile their upbringing in the Old South with their experiences in the new America.

On the basis of his one published novel Percy became a celebrity, and his next novel, *The Last Gentleman* (1966), was greeted with much serious critical attention as well as a large audience. The events in *The Last Gentleman* occur amid the racial upheavals of the 1960s, with protagonist Williston Bibb Barrett ("Will") moving through the conflict while trying to understand what he sees and relate it to his personal life. He falls in love with Kitty McVaught and moves with her to Alabama, where he is to tutor her sixteen-year-old brother Jamie, while trying not to run afoul of her dysfunctional, socially alienated family. The book is religious in the sense that Will senses God's hand in events; through his belief in God he finally perceives his own unique identity, which allows him to feel, absorb, and comprehend the craziness taking place around him rather than just observing without understanding. The ending is meant to be a triumph, a turning of literary convention on its head by having the dying Jamie baptized: the death is sad, but Jamie's conversion and blessing mean that he has triumphed in the great conflict of good versus evil and has, by dying, transcended death.

The Last Gentleman did not disappoint many readers, even though it lacked the revolutionary punch of its predecessor. Will's search for his identity, complicated by bouts of amnesia, was the means whereby Percy looked at the American South of the 1960s while placing events in the larger context of the United States as a whole. Love seems to be crucial in the story of death and hardship, and the novel, more overtly than *The Moviegoer*, examines religion in a society that is without life or hope. In the end, death becomes grace.

Will Barrett reappeared in *The Second Coming* (1980), a novel in which the ideas are tough and demanding. Unsatisfied with what he has experienced, Will decides to force God to manifest Himself in person. It seems that Will has failed to understand the lessons of faith, although he embodies the doubts about God that logically arise out of the modern world.

Percy proved remarkably consistent in the quality of his work. Each subsequent novel seemed worthy of its predecessors. In *Love in the Ruins* (1971), alienation is again explored, although, curiously, the main character seems fine, and it is society that seems alienated from him. In *Lancelot* (1977), *The Second Coming* (1980), and *The Thanatos Syndrome* (1987), alienation is still present, but the narratives involve ideas about how society may be improved, with the understanding that full redemption may not be possible.

Percy died of cancer at the age of seventy-three and is buried in the Saint Joseph Abbey Cemetery (Saint Tammany Parish) in Covington. He is considered the greatest southern writer of the second half of the twentieth century, but he transcended southern literature by creating novels that spoke to the fundamental human condition that crosses cultures and ages, offering answers for the problem of individual human needs that conflict with social demands.

★

Percy's *Signposts in a Strange Land* (1991) is a posthumous gathering of essays that provide information about his early life and the inspirations for his novels. A biography of Percy is Patrick H. Samway, *Walker Percy: A Life* (1997); Samway also discusses Percy's search for a home in his fiction and the role Covington, Louisiana, played in his creative development in "Walker Percy's Homeward Journey," *America* 170, no. 17 (14 May 1994): 16–19. Edward J. Dupuy examines the relationship between Percy's life and his fiction in *Autobiography in Walker Percy: Repetition, Recovery and Redemption* (1996). In the obituary "Walker Percy, RIP," in *National Review* 42, no. 11 (11 June 1990): 17–18, Ben C. Toledano argues that Percy's work is mostly misunderstood because people have failed to recognize the depth of its themes.

KIRK H. BEETZ

PERKINS, James Alfred (*b*. 11 October 1911 in Philadelphia, Pennsylvania; *d*. 19 August 1998 in Burlington, Vermont), president of Cornell University (1963–1969) who in 1969 acceded to the demands of armed militant students to increase the admission opportunities for minorities and subsequently resigned amid controversy surrounding his actions.

Perkins, the son of H. Norman Perkins and Emily (Cramp) Taylor, graduated with honors from Swarthmore College in Pennsylvania with an A.B. in political science in 1934. He continued his education at Princeton University in New Jersey, earning his M.A. in 1936 and his Ph.D. in 1937, both in political science. As a young man he became a member of the Society of Friends, or Quakers, which may have influenced the decisions he later made as the chief administrator at Cornell University in Ithaca, New York. On 20 June 1938 Perkins married Jean Bredin.

From 1937 to 1941 Perkins taught college, but when World War II disrupted American life, Perkins served in the U.S. Office of Price Administration and the Foreign Economic Administration. After the war, Perkins returned to college life as an administrator until 1951, when he left to become an executive associate at Carnegie Corporation, an educational foundation. During the Kennedy and Johnson administrations, Perkins was involved in setting government policies. He served as deputy chairman of the Research and Development Board of the Department of Defense from 1951 to 1952, but returned to Carnegie Corporation.

Perkins was inaugurated as Cornell's seventh president on 4 October 1963. His prospects seemed bright, and he certainly had little inkling that he would be forced to resign only six years later. However, the 1960s were years full of strife in all areas of American society, including the arena

James A. Perkins. AP/WIDE WORLD PHOTOS

of higher education. University campuses were often unsafe as some students demonstrated, rioted, and agitated for change. Activists led protests opposing the Vietnam War, selective service, college curricula, lack of civil rights for minorities, and a host of other issues. Some of the protests, such as teach-ins, were relatively nonviolent, but as the decade wore on, violence increasingly became a tool of some activist groups.

Perkins's life was changed forever by events on the Cornell campus in 1969. Racial turmoil there resulted in the takeover of Willard Straight Hall, Cornell's student union, by 100 militant students in the Afro-American Society. At gunpoint, the activists demanded increased enrollment of minority students. Instead of refusing and attempting to end the takeover peaceably, or forcefully if necessary, for the protection of the entire faculty and student body, Perkins acceded to the students' demands. His decision to give in to the militants set a dangerous precedent for student takeovers; colleagues across the United States viewed Perkins's action as putting professors, administrators, and students everywhere at the mercy of disgruntled students who were willing to resort to violence.

Among the student revolts of the 1960s, the uprising at Cornell was considered pivotal, and Perkins was at the cynosure of public censure for allowing student threats to sway him. Educators asked themselves if they should remain at Cornell, and many questioned whether Perkins was worthy to retain his post. Even though the outcome of the president's actions was considered to be positive years later—minority enrollment increased from 10 students to more than 250 during the years he was president —Perkins lost the respect of his colleagues. His reputation was besmirched on a national level because he had tolerated, if not condoned, student threats. As a result Perkins resigned from Cornell on 31 May 1969.

Although his accomplishments at Cornell were eclipsed by the circumstances surrounding his resignation, Perkins had his successes. He was responsible for creating new departments in biological science and computer science and establishing new programs such as the Laboratory of Plasma Studies, Risley House (a residence hall for the arts), the Society for the Humanities, the Center for International Studies, and the Water Resources Institute. He secured funding for construction of the Herbert F. Johnson Museum of Art and oversaw the construction of the Space Sciences Building. Perkins also was responsible for two capital campaigns that raised more than $100 million for the construction of Cornell's Medical College in New York City.

Besides his accomplishments at Cornell, Perkins served in various advisory positions in the presidential administrations of both John F. Kennedy and Lyndon Johnson. He was the chairman of the Negro College Fund (1965–1969)

and a member of the Carnegie Commission on Higher Education (1967–1973). He also published *The University in Transition* (1966), a reproduction of three lectures delivered at Princeton in the Stafford Little Series. In the book, Perkins discusses the forces that endanger the halls of education, including internal disorder. He comments, "The modern university is, in one of those strange paradoxes of human affairs, dangerously close to becoming the victim of its own success" and warns that theory and doctrine must be governed by management and direction. Viewed retrospectively, these words seem particularly ironic.

When the 1960s came to a close, Perkins faced a future blighted by his response to the student takeover at Cornell. Many people never forgot that he had put academia at risk by giving in to armed militants. The reverberations were somewhat assuaged in 1995 when Thomas W. Jones, a leader of the students who staged the takeover, established the James A. Perkins Prize for Interracial Understanding and Harmony. Jones said he admired Perkins for his efforts to help African Americans attend Cornell: "He made a courageous decision and he deserves recognition for it."

Perkins's legacy at Cornell also lives on through the James A. Perkins Professorship of Environmental Studies in the College of Agriculture and Life Sciences. Established in 1992, the professorship was first awarded to Eloy Rodriguez, the first Chicano environmental biologist to hold an endowed chair in the United States.

After he left Cornell, Perkins founded the International Council for Educational Development. He also wrote several books, including *Higher Education: From Autonomy to Systems* (1972), *The University in a Restless Decade* (1972), and *The University as an Organization* (1973). Perkins contributed to popular magazines such as the *Saturday Review* and to scholarly journals, and he was on the editorial boards of both *Change* and *Higher Education*. He served as the vice chair of the National Council on Foreign Languages and International Studies and held many other prestigious positions in academe, government, and the private sector. After the death of his first wife in 1970, he married Ruth Begengren Dall on 30 January 1971. He raised nine children.

At age eighty-six Perkins died from complications following a fall. (Sources variously record the date of death as 19 or 20 August 1998.) The Cornell president Hunter Rawlings said in a press release following Perkins's death, "Jim Perkins represented the highest ideals of liberal education, and he left a permanent legacy not only on the Cornell campus but also in the foundation of our nation's dynamic postwar educational and research institutions."

In later years, that third week of April 1969 figured largely in how Perkins's memory lived on. Perkins was alternately remembered as a weak man who capitulated to activists or as a brave man who made a decision that caused political change. Forgotten were his many awards and honors; remembered was the way he responded to a short but critical crisis.

★

Perkins's papers (1941–1990) are held by the Division of Rare and Manuscript Collections at the Cornell University Library. There is a biographical article in the *Cornell News* (21 Aug. 1998). Scenes from the revolt at Cornell can be found in Donald Alexander Downs, *Cornell '69: Liberalism and the Crisis of the American University* (1999). An obituary is in the *Washington Post* (24 Aug. 1998).

A. E. SCHULTHIES

PEROT, H(enry) Ross (*b.* 27 June 1930 in Texarkana, Texas), businessman, philanthropist, and statesman who in the 1960s revolutionized the way services were delivered in the electronic data systems market and became a prominent advocate for U.S. prisoners of war held by the North Vietnamese government.

Perot, the son of the cotton broker Gabriel Elias Perot and Lulu May (Ray) Perot, a former secretary, spent his childhood and adolescence in Texarkana. He and his sister graduated from public schools in the northeast Texas town. Perot's charismatic personality, legendary leadership skills, and impatience with bureaucracy were already evident in high school. From 1947 to 1949 he attended Texarkana Junior College (later Texarkana Community College), where he was elected the class president in 1948. In 1949 Perot was appointed to the U.S. Naval Academy in Annapolis, Maryland. He served as the class vice president in his second year and the president in each of his final two years. He graduated from the academy in 1953 and married Margot Birmingham, a schoolteacher, on 13 September 1956. Their family grew to include five children. Perot served in the U.S. Navy from 1953 to 1957. His exemplary work on the USS *Leyte* brought him praise from his commanding officers and earned him ever more important duties. One day an International Business Machines (IBM) executive, who was also a naval reservist, was on the bridge while Perot was directing the movements of the *Leyte* and all of its support ships. Impressed with Perot's self-assurance and abilities, the executive offered him a job once he left the navy. Perot accepted, opting against reenlistment in 1957.

Working for IBM in Texas, Perot quickly became a top sales representative, finding new clients and markets for IBM's computers. One of his clients was Texas Blue Cross, where in 1960 he spent many hours learning about the databases the insurance industry used. His contacts at Texas Blue Cross and other corporations paid big dividends when he established his own company. Perot felt that IBM did not adequately compensate him for his superb sales abilities, and he grew frustrated with a bureaucracy he believed hindered employees with creative ideas. He developed a proposal that outlined a bold plan to develop software to meet the informational needs of both government and private industry clients. Convinced that the big money was in hardware, not software, IBM executives dismissed Perot's ideas.

Certain that he had glimpsed the future, Perot resigned from IBM. He envisioned a service company that would help clients achieve the maximum use and profit from their hardware investment and would supply data processing for small organizations that could not afford to purchase large computer systems. With only $1,000 he incorporated Electronic Data Systems (EDS) on 27 June 1962. Because few businesses at the time realized the value of EDS's services, the company was not an immediate success.

Early in 1963 Frito-Lay signed the first long-term facilities management (Perot's term for data processing and computing services) agreement in the technology industry. Perot's breakthrough idea was to offer his customers five-year, fixed-price contracts rather than the sixty- or ninety-day agreements that were then standard in the business. Calling on the clients he had served while selling hardware for IBM, Perot showed executives in these companies how they could make money by leasing out their computers during idle periods, usually in the middle of the night. He leased time himself and began developing the software that would make his fortune. Foreseeing a bright future in government contracting, he opened a small office in Washington, D.C., in 1963 and began lobbying to receive government contracts.

In 1964 EDS grossed $400,000, with a net of $4,100; in 1965 the gross was $865,000, with a net of $26,487. When the legislation establishing the federal Medicare and Medicaid health programs was signed into law on 30 July 1965, Perot saw his opportunity. He used his great powers of persuasion to have Texas Blue Cross hire EDS to develop the software required to keep track of the clients and money from Medicare and Medicaid; the money from the federal government began to flow in September 1967. Once the software was developed, Perot used it for other similar accounts throughout the United States. In 1968 EDS grossed $7.5 million, with a net of $2.4 million.

Under Perot's leadership, EDS developed a famously conservative corporate culture, including a strict dress code. Perot aggressively sought Vietnam veterans to work for EDS, reasoning that people who had just come from a place where they were under fire twenty-four hours a day would find the sixteen-hour days and codes of conduct at EDS a breeze. Although Perot reportedly had outbursts of temper at employees, they tended to accept his mercurial

H. Ross Perot, December 1969. © Bettmann/Corbis

behavior because he was a great motivator and teacher; moreover, many employees became rich by following Perot's lessons in salesmanship and customer service. They could not leave EDS, however, without forfeiting their valuable stock awards, and they could not go to work for a competitor without violating signed agreements. All of these characteristics made EDS formidable, even frightening, in the eyes of some outsiders, who called EDS employees "shock troops."

When Perot took EDS public on the New York Stock Exchange on 12 September 1968, both he and his employees benefited. The stock began trading at $16.50 per share. There was a buying frenzy, with a single share becoming worth $230; Perot personally held ten million shares. By 1970 Perot was worth $1.5 billion, and EDS was established as America's largest data processing company, with expansion beginning overseas. Perot had become wealthy enough to begin contemplating philanthropy.

Perot's early philanthropic efforts were directed at assisting U.S. prisoners of war (POWs) held in North Vietnam. In December 1969 Perot rented two commercial airliners, filled them with medicine, gifts, and letters from friends and families, and set out for North Vietnam. Perot's efforts, including an offer of $100 million to release the POWs, were rejected by the North Vietnamese government. He then flew across the world to different nations to try to gain entry to North Vietnam, offered to give supplies to North Vietnamese orphans, and arranged for the POWs' families to fly to Paris so they could appeal directly to the Vietnamese mission there. Although Perot was never able to deliver the supplies, when the POWs finally returned to the United States, they reported that his high-profile gestures had resulted in somewhat improved conditions for them. He had put his own life at risk in trying to help them.

Perot's daring mission to Iran was much more successful. On 28 December 1978 Iranians arrested two EDS employees and demanded $12 million as ransom, which Perot offered to pay. When the kidnappers refused to accept the payment, Perot went to Iran to personally negotiate for the employees' release and eventually organized a rescue operation that included military veterans working for EDS. The employees escaped and fled Iran under harrowing circumstances; Perot was waiting for them in Turkey and chartered a jet to fly them home safely to the United States. This tale of derring-do became the basis of Ken Follett's book *On Wings of Eagles* (1983), as well as a popular television movie.

In the 1960s Perot altered the American business landscape by showing that computer software services were a valid industry and that people would pay for ideas. He laid the foundation for the fortunes made by later entrepreneurs such as Bill Gates of Microsoft and for the service economy of the 1990s and beyond. His actions during the 1960s earned him fame as a business maverick, a self-made billionaire, and an advocate for prisoners of war.

★

Perot's autobiography is *My Life and Principles for Success* (1996). Biographies include Todd Mason, *Perot: An Unauthorized Biography* (1990), and Gerald Posner, *Citizen Perot: His Life and Times* (1996). Magazine articles include Roy Rowan, "The World According to Ross Perot: The Billionaire, Superpatriot, and Gadfly Speaks Out on What's Wrong with America," *Life* (Feb. 1988), which includes an account by Perot of how he became a successful entrepreneur, and Paul Burka, "Little Big Man," *Texas Monthly* (Oct. 2000), which offers a thoughtful analysis of how Perot changed the way of doing business in America.

KIRK H. BEETZ

PETER, Laurence Johnston (*b*. 16 September 1919 in Vancouver, British Columbia; *d*. 12 January 1990 in Palos Verdes Estates, California), author and lecturer best known for his philosophy known as "the Peter Principle," who made business theory accessible to the masses with wit, charm, and intellectual rigor.

Peter was the son of Victor C. Peter, an actor, and Vincenta Steves. Records of Peter's early life are scant, but apparently his father drowned when he was young. The family lived in a shack, and he spent his days working to help his family survive. Everything the Peter family had was functional, and Peter's lifelong interest in cutting waste in organizations and in streamlining tasks may stem from a childhood in which there could be no wasted motion and no wasted resources. Peter had to leave school for about four months because of "tuberculosis of the spine," which left him wearing a back brace for many years.

In 1938 Peter graduated from high school and enrolled in the University of British Columbia, where he took classes until 1954. From 1941 to 1947 he found jobs teaching industrial arts for schools in British Columbia. During this period he apparently began collecting the anecdotes that formed the cores of his best-selling books. He also married and divorced Nancy Bailey.

From 1947 to 1948 Peter worked for the provincial prison department, teaching youths who were in prison, and honing his skills at gaining and holding the attention of a reluctant audience. From 1948 to 1964 he was a mental health counselor for the Vancouver School district. From 1957 to 1958 he attended Western Washington State College (later named Western Washington University) in the United States, receiving a B.A. in 1957 and earning a M.Ed. in 1958. He then enrolled in the doctoral program in education at Washington State University, receiving his Ph.D. in 1963.

After receiving his doctorate, Peter was an assistant professor of education at the University of British Colombia, Vancouver, from 1964 to 1966. From 1966 to 1969 he was an associate professor at the University of California, Los Angeles (UCLA). In 1967 Peter became the director of the Evelyn Frieden Center for Prescriptive Teaching, a job he held until 1970. On 25 February 1967 he married Irene J. Howe, with whom he had four children.

In the late 1950s Peter had begun to lecture about organizations and hierarchies. He first spoke on the Peter Principle in 1960, to an audience of businessmen who were either outraged or amused by his discussion of incompetence in business and government. In 1963 author Raymond Hull first heard of the Peter Principle. He attended a badly done play with Peter, and during intermission Peter explained how the play failed because its director had reached his "level of incompetence." Hull sensed a book in the making, urged Peter to write it, and then happily discovered that Peter had already spent many years writing such a book. Hull took the substantial manuscript and revised it into *The Peter Principle: Why Things Always Go Wrong*.

Hull and Peter first submitted the manuscript to McGraw-Hill, which had published Peter's academic book *Prescription Teaching* (1965). The publisher rejected *The Peter Principle*, with an editor declaring, "I can foresee no commercial possibilities for such a book and consequently can offer no encouragement." Thirty more publishers rejected the manuscript. Meanwhile, Peter was making a name for himself in the Los Angeles area as a public speaker, and the *Los Angeles Times* published a piece about him and the Peter Principle. Someone sent this article to a publisher in England, who then sent the article to an editor for the New York publisher William Morrow.

By then Peter's collaboration with Hull was years behind him, so it must have surprised him when a representative from William Morrow flew to Los Angeles to meet him and ask him to write a book about the Peter Principle. Like Hull years before, the publisher's representative was delighted to learn that the book had already been written. Morrow, which paid Peter and Hull a $2,500 advance, published *The Peter Principle* in 1969, the same year Peter advanced to the position of full professor. The first printing was a respectable run of 10,000 copies. The book quickly became a best-seller, and Morrow went through several printings in 1969, eventually publishing millions of copies. *The Peter Principle* became one of the best-selling nonfiction books ever, selling eight million copies in English in thirty years and being translated into thirty-eight languages.

Hull had made the crucial contributions of shortening

the book to an acceptable length for a popular audience and of distilling Peter's considerable charm and satirical humor, making the book funny yet serious. Yet the essential appeal of *The Peter Principle* was the way it summed up the frustrations of millions of people who suffered with service employees who refused to serve, production workers who would not produce anything, teachers without enough sense to evacuate a room while it was flooding, and leaders who only followed—all because, as Peter wrote, "In a hierarchy every employee tends to rise to his level of incompetence."

Peter offered many examples from his experiences and firsthand observations to illustrate and support his principle. These examples were zany, but they were familiar to millions of readers. For example, he told of the time he sent a job application to a school, with every form filled out correctly, only to have it returned to him because there was a rule that it should be sent registered mail in order to be sure it arrived at the school intact.

For the rest of his life, Peter was offered jobs as a management consultant, but he turned them all down, saying that he chose not to rise to his own level of incompetence. He hoped that by understanding how one could advance beyond one's ability, one would choose to be happy by remaining at the job he or she felt best able to do. How to recognize that job when one had it was among the themes of subsequent books such as *The Peter Prescription and How to Make Things Go Right* (1972) and *The Peter Plan: A Proposal for Survival* (1975). Peter continued to publish more academically inclined works, such as the four-volume *Competencies for Teaching* (1975).

Although he made serious contributions to the study of teaching methods, Peter's reputation and fame stem primarily from his numerous books for general audiences, ending with *Why Things Go Wrong* in 1984. His sense of humor, his engaging storytelling, and his intelligence made his books long-term best-sellers that remained in print even after the start of the twenty-first century. In 1988 Peter suffered a stroke and soon afterward died at home from complications caused by the stroke.

★

All of Peter's books, even his most academic publications, are partly autobiographical, because they draw at least in part on his personal experiences. His book *The Peter Principle: Why Things Always Go Wrong* (1969), stems mostly from his firsthand experiences. His *Why Things Go Wrong: or, The Peter Principle Revisited* (1985) similarly offers autobiographical insights in the examples it presents. Obituaries are in the *Chicago Tribune, Los Angeles Times,* and *New York Times* (all 15 Jan. 1990); and the *Washington Post* (17 Jan. 1990).

KIRK H. BEETZ

PETER, PAUL AND MARY (Peter Yarrow, *b.* 31 May 1938 in New York City; Paul Stookey, *b.* 30 December 1937 in Baltimore, Maryland; and Mary Travers, *b.* 9 November 1936 in Louisville, Kentucky), left-leaning folk music trio who dominated popular music in the early 1960s, singing songs written by Bob Dylan and others and performing frequently at political events.

Mary Allin Travers, the daughter of two newspaper reporters, moved with her parents to New York in 1938 and grew up in Greenwich Village, where she became immersed in the growing folk music scene of the 1950s. In 1955, while still in high school, she became a member of the Song Swappers, a group of eight singers who accompanied the folksinger Pete Seeger on a batch of songs recorded for the expanded version of *Talking Union,* an album by the Almanac Singers originally recorded in 1941, which was released by Folkways Records. By the start of the 1960s, she was living in Greenwich Village and mingling with other folk musicians in the local clubs, where she met the other members of Peter, Paul and Mary.

Noel Paul Stookey showed an early interest in rhythm and blues and took up the guitar at age eleven. He led rock bands in high school and in college at Michigan State University. After leaving school without earning a degree, he worked as a production manager at a chemical company, but he began spending more and more time in Greenwich Village, where he worked as a singer, comedian, and master of ceremonies. By 1960 he had turned to performing full time.

Peter Yarrow first studied violin and then turned to the guitar. After graduating from New York's High School of Music and Art, he attended Cornell University, graduating in 1959. Initially, he stayed on at the school, working as an assistant instructor in folklore and folk music. By 1960 he was working in Greenwich Village, where his manager Albert Grossman convinced him that he would do better in a group than as a solo performer. Grossman put Yarrow together with Travers and Stookey (who used his middle name so that the group could be called Peter, Paul and Mary, a variant on the line about "I saw Peter, Paul, and Moses / Playing Ring-Around-the-Roses" in the folk song "I Was Born 10,000 Years Ago." They made their debut at Folk City in the fall of 1961.

In January 1962 Peter, Paul and Mary signed to Warner Bros. Records, which released their self-titled debut album in March. Drawn from the album, "Lemon Tree" became a Top Forty singles hit, and the album soared up the charts, eventually hitting number one and selling more than two million copies. A second single, "If I Had a Hammer (The Hammer Song)," written by Pete Seeger and Lee Hays, made the Top Ten and won Peter, Paul and Mary two

Paul Stookey *(left)*, Mary Travers *(center)*, and Peter Yarrow *(right)*.

Grammy Awards, for best performance by a vocal group and best folk recording. The trio's second album, *Moving,* released in January 1963, was another chart topper and, like their next four albums, went gold. It featured the enchanting children's novelty song "Puff, the Magic Dragon," a Top Five hit.

In June 1963 Peter, Paul and Mary released their version of Bob Dylan's civil rights anthem "Blowin' in the Wind." It reached the pop Top Five and earned them Grammy Awards in the same two categories they had won in the year before. It also went a long way toward establishing Dylan as a major songwriter. The trio followed with another single written by Dylan, "Don't Think Twice, It's All Right," a Top Ten hit released in August 1963, the same month that saw the release of their third album, *In the Wind,* which became their third consecutive number-one album. That same month, on 28 August 1963, they appeared at the celebrated March on Washington, now best remembered for the "I Have a Dream" speech by the civil rights leader Reverend Dr. Martin Luther King, Jr.

Between November 1963 and February 1964, there were many weeks when all three Peter, Paul and Mary albums were in the national Top Ten. The emergence of the Beatles and the British invasion of rock groups they led, starting in February 1964, diminished the trio's popularity, but it continued to be widespread for the rest of the decade. In July 1964 they released their double album *In Concert,* and it became a Top Five hit. The following month they sang "Blowin' in the Wind" at the funeral of Andrew Goodman, one of three men murdered in Mississippi while trying to register blacks to vote.

By 1965 Peter, Paul and Mary were touring internationally. In January their Top Forty single "For Lovin' Me" introduced the songwriter Gordon Lightfoot. It was featured on their Top Ten album *A Song Will Rise,* released in March. That same month, on 24 March 1965, they joined Dr. King on his march from Selma to Montgomery, Alabama, in support of voting rights. *See What Tomorrow Brings,* their album released in October 1965, was not as big a hit as its predecessors, but it still made the Top Twenty. By August 1966, when they released *The Peter, Paul and Mary Album,* they were beginning to follow trends in popular music by adding other instruments to their basic folk approach. Introducing such songwriters as Laura Nyro and John Denver, the album was a Top Forty hit but still marked a sales decline. The group made a commercial comeback in August 1967 with the novelty song "I Dig Rock and Roll Music," written by Stookey, a record on which they affectionately recreated the styles of the Beatles, the Mamas and the Papas, and Donovan. *Album 1700,* which contained the song, reached the Top Twenty.

By 1967 Peter, Paul and Mary were performing not only at civil rights demonstrations but also at anti–Vietnam War demonstrations, such as the one held in Washington, D.C., on 21 October. Meanwhile, they were growing apart musically; their 1968 album *Late Again,* which reached the Top Twenty, consisted largely of individual efforts. In 1969 they reached the Top Twenty with Yarrow's elegiac "Day Is Done" and their children's album, *Peter, Paul and Mommy,* which won the Grammy Award for best children's recording. That fall they enjoyed a surprising hit when their version of John Denver's "Leaving on a Jet Plane," which had appeared on *Album 1700* in 1967, was belatedly released as a single and became their only number-one hit.

Ironically, this hit came as the group was ready to split. Stookey's conversion to born-again Christianity added to aspirations for solo work, and Peter, Paul and Mary announced a sabbatical in the fall of 1970. They reunited for a tour and an album in 1978, however, and from 1980 on have been permanently reunited.

★

There is no biography of Peter, Paul and Mary. The most comprehensive account of their career is the author's, "Peter, Paul and Mary: A Song to Sing All Over This Land," published in *Goldmine* (12 Apr. 1996), which the group has adopted as its history and reprints on its official website at http://www.peterpaulandmary.com. Also useful are the group-written liner notes to the *Reader's Digest* triple-CD set *Greatest Hits and Finest Performances* (1998).

WILLIAM RUHLMANN

PHILLIPS, John Edmund Andrew (*b.* 30 August 1935 on Parris Island, South Carolina; *d.* 18 March 2001 in Los Angeles, California), singer, songwriter, and guitarist who founded the Mamas and the Papas, one of the most successful folk-rock groups of the 1960s.

Phillips was the youngest of three children of Captain Claude Andrew Phillips, a U.S. Marine, and Edna Gertrude Gaines, a homemaker who later ran a dress shop and worked in a department store, among other jobs. (In his autobiography, *Papa John,* Phillips writes that when he was eighteen, his mother confessed that he was actually the son of Roland Meeks, a doctor in the marines who died in a Japanese prison camp.) Phillips grew up primarily in Alexandria, Virginia, and became interested in music while he was in high school; he was taught to play the guitar by his brother-in-law and sang harmonies with a group of male friends. His childhood was tumultuous, in part because of tensions between his mother and his father, who was given a medical discharge from the marines after two heart attacks.

Phillips graduated from high school in 1954 and, despite a spotty school record, earned an appointment to the U.S. Naval Academy at Annapolis. He was given a medical discharge in March 1955, officially because of a childhood head injury, although he makes clear in his autobiography that this was just his excuse. He then enrolled briefly at several colleges before giving up higher education and becoming a salesman, primarily of cars, in the fall of 1956. In May 1957 he married Susan Adams, with whom he had two children, the second of whom, Laura Mackenzie Phillips, grew up to become the actress Mackenzie Phillips.

The Mamas and the Papas after a news conference in London, England, 1967. John Phillips is at the far right. ASSOCIATED PRESS AP

Phillips's interest in music led him to organize the vocal quartet the Abstracts in the spring of 1959; the group changed its name to the Smoothies when they signed with Decca Records in early 1960. Their recordings were not successful, and they split up by the end of the year. Phillips stuck with one member, Phil Blondheim, who had changed his name to Scott McKenzie, and adding the banjoist and guitarist Dick Weissman, they formed a Kingston Trio–like folk group called the Journeymen in early 1961. The Journeymen were more successful than the Smoothies, releasing three albums on Capitol Records and performing at the nation's most prestigious nightclubs. While they were appearing in San Francisco in the spring of 1961, Phillips met the teenager (Holly) Michelle Gilliam, with whom he fell in love. The following year, he divorced his wife. He and Gilliam married on 31 December 1962. Phillips and Gilliam had one daughter, Chynna, who went on to become a singer in the group Wilson Phillips and also had a career as a solo artist. They divorced in 1970.

The Journeymen broke up in the spring of 1964, and Phillips organized the New Journeymen, initially consisting of himself, his wife, and the banjoist and guitarist Marshall Brickman. In December, Phillips brought in Denny Doherty, formally of the Halifax Three, as lead singer, and Brickman quit soon after. Doherty introduced Phillips to

Cass Elliot, a former member of the Mugwumps, and the four singers spent much of the spring and summer of 1965 rehearsing on the island of Saint Thomas in the Virgin Islands. Moving to Los Angeles, they auditioned for record labels and were signed by Lou Adler's Dunhill Records. They named themselves the Mamas and the Papas.

The Mamas and the Papas' first single, released in late 1965, was "California Dreamin'," Phillips's plaintive lament about imagining the joys of West Coast living while being stranded in wintertime New York. The group's distinctive harmonies made the song a million-selling Top Five hit. It was followed by the debut album *If You Can Believe Your Eyes and Ears* in the winter of 1966. The album topped the charts and went gold, spawning a second hit, "Monday, Monday," which also hit number one and sold a million copies. Released in the spring, a third single, "I Saw Her Again," made the Top Five.

Meanwhile, the group was rent with dissension brought on by romantic troubles. Michelle Phillips had an affair with Doherty, and Phillips briefly had her drummed out of the group before relenting and reinstating her in time to work on the second album. Released as *The Mamas & the Papas* in late summer, it hit the Top Five and went gold. The next single, "Look Through My Window," only made the Top Twenty, but "Words of Love," with Elliot on lead vocals, drawn from the album, reached the Top Five, and "Dedicated to the One I Love," released in early 1967, just missed topping the charts. It was the advance single for the third album, *The Mamas & the Papas Deliver,* which hit number one and went gold. The album also included "Creeque Alley," a virtual biography of the group and another Top Five hit.

Phillips and Adler organized the Monterey Pop Festival, the first of the big rock festivals of the 1960s, which occurred in June 1967, with the Mamas and the Papas as the closing act. The group's next single, "Twelve Thirty (Young Girls Are Coming to the Canyon)," released that summer, was a Top Twenty hit. An even bigger hit was the Phillips-penned "San Francisco (Be Sure to Wear Flowers in Your Hair)," released by the former Journeyman Scott McKenzie, which reached the Top Five.

The Mamas and the Papas released a revival of the Rodgers and Hart show tune "Glad to Be Unhappy" as their next single (it reached the Top Forty) while preparing their fourth album. However, interpersonal relations had become so strained that they were unable to finish it in time for the Christmas season. The relatively disappointing *The Papas & the Mamas* finally appeared in the spring of 1968, and from it a revival of the 1931 hit "Dream a Little Dream of Me," billed to "Mama Cass with the Mamas & the Papas," made the Top Ten. The group split soon after.

Phillips attempted to launch a solo career with the album *John Phillips (John the Wolfking of L.A.)* in 1970, but it was a commercial failure. Dunhill then forced the Mamas and the Papas to reunite for an album to fulfill their contract, but *People Like Us* (1971) was another disappointment. Phillips married Genevieve Waite on 31 January 1972. They had two children before separating in 1985.

Phillips worked on other projects and became progressively more involved with drugs during the 1970s, finally being arrested in 1980. After cleaning up, he launched a new version of the Mamas and the Papas with Doherty, his daughter Mackenzie, and Spanky McFarlane, the former singer from the group Spanky and Our Gang. He was a coauthor of the 1988 number-one hit "Kokomo," recorded by the Beach Boys. Phillips died of heart failure and is buried in Palm Springs Mortuary and Mausoleum in Palm Springs, California.

★

Papa John: An Autobiography (1986), by John Phillips with Jim Jerome, tells, as its cover blurb proclaims, "a music legend's shattering journey through sex, drugs, and rock 'n' roll," placing particular emphasis on Phillips's drug problems of the late 1970s and 1980s. Michelle Phillips, *California Dreamin': The True Story of the Mamas and the Papas* (1986), gives her perspective. Obituaries are in the *Los Angeles Times* and *Washington Post* (both 19 Mar. 2001).

WILLIAM J. RUHLMANN

PHILLIPS, Kevin Price (*b.* 30 November 1940 in New York City), Republican political strategist, commentator, and writer who identified a new Republican majority in the late 1960s, propelling Richard M. Nixon to presidential victories in 1968 and 1972.

Phillips was born into a middle-class family that valued education and public service. His father, William Edward Phillips, was a career civil servant, working at one time as the chief executive officer of the New York State Liquor Commission. His father was raised a Catholic, but his mother, Dorothy Price, was a Protestant. Phillips said his own religion was "reading the Sunday papers." An intelligent and precocious youth, Phillips became interested in politics at an early age, supporting Dwight D. Eisenhower in the 1952 presidential election even though he was only eleven. At fifteen he was the chairman of the Bronx Youth Committee for Eisenhower and walked the streets campaigning for his reelection in 1956.

Phillips's parents sent him to the Bronx High School of Science, where he became a National Merit Scholar. At age sixteen Phillips entered Colgate University in Hamilton, New York, as a political science major. He spent his junior year studying history and economic history at the University of Edinburgh. Bored with Colgate when he returned from Scotland, he arranged to spend half his senior year in Washington, D.C., in a special academic project. He graduated in 1961 with a list of honors and joined the staff of the Republican U.S. Representative Paul Fino, becoming the youngest legislative assistant in the House of Representatives at the age of twenty. In between working in Washington, Phillips finished a J.D. from Harvard Law School in Cambridge, Massachusetts, in 1964, not because he had any particular affinity for law, but because he believed a law degree from Harvard would further his political career.

Phillips worked his way up to an administrative aide to Fino, but left his office in 1968. In September 1968 he married Martha Henderson, the Republican staff director of the U.S. House of Representatives Budget Committee; they had two sons. The lanky, bespectacled, dark-haired Phillips had used his time in Washington to make himself into an expert in ethnicity and voting patterns. "You could ask me about any congressional district in the country," Phillips said, "and I could tell you its ethnic composition, its voting history, and the issues that would appeal to its electorate." Putting his expertise into writing, in late 1967 Phillips finished the first draft of his influential book, *The Emerging Republican Majority*. Phillips argued that the Republican Party should present a conservative image in order to capture the votes of traditional Democratic strongholds in what he perceived as "battlegrounds." In essence, Phillips believed that traditional Democrats were upset with the liberalism of their party, and the Republican Party had a golden opportunity to sway these voters away from the Democrats.

After President John F. Kennedy was assassinated in 1963, the new Democratic president Lyndon B. Johnson promised a "Great Society" for everyone in the United States. The 1964 election pitted the liberal Johnson against the conservative Republican Barry Goldwater from Arizona. Goldwater was seen as too reactionary for many Americans, attacking civil rights legislation and government expansion, and even talking about using nuclear weapons in the Vietnam War. Johnson won the election with more than 61 percent of the popular vote, solidifying the triumph of liberalism. Despite Johnson's overwhelming victory, Goldwater's message did resonate with some voters, and he won a few southern states, a feat Republican candidates were seldom able to achieve. This accomplishment was not lost on Phillips, and he identified the South as a dominant conservative pool ready to be tapped. As Phillips saw it, the upper South had concerns that the Republican Party was able to address.

As Johnson committed combat troops to Vietnam in 1965, and urban riots lit up the night skies throughout the North, many Americans began to question whether liberalism and the Democratic Party were indeed working in

Kevin Phillips, August 1969. ASSOCIATED PRESS AP

their best interests. Traditional Democratic voters who were veterans, labor union members, ethnic Catholics, and hardworking, law-abiding citizens viewed Johnson's programs as helping only the few. Phillips correctly identified that these voters felt marginalized by the Great Society. As a result, building on Goldwater's momentum, the 1966 midterm elections witnessed a white backlash against the Democrats, and voters sent more Republicans to the House, destroying Johnson's liberal majority.

Richard M. Nixon was one Republican politician who benefited from this slowly growing conservative movement. After Goldwater's loss in 1964, Nixon began to court conservative southern Republicans such as South Carolina senator Strom Thurmond to build on Goldwater's success in the South, promising not to continue civil rights reforms if elected. This position fit with what Phillips believed: that the South, traditionally Democratic from the days of redemption during Reconstruction, was fed up with the Democratic Party and the liberalism that they felt helped African Americans, protected criminals, and bowed to special interests and the elite eastern establishment.

Sections of Phillips's book were circulated through

Nixon's presidential campaign, and Nixon's chief campaign manager asked Phillips to join the team in 1968 as the chief political and voting patterns strategist. When Nixon won the 1968 election, Phillips's proclamation of a new Republican majority was validated. As such, his publisher finally agreed to publish *The Emerging Republican Majority* in 1969. Phillips's work on Nixon's campaign and the success of his book launched him as one of the country's foremost political forecasters and analysts. In 1969 he was appointed as the special assistant to the U.S. Attorney General John Mitchell for sixteen months. He resigned in April 1970 to become a syndicated newspaper columnist.

Ironically, many Republicans distanced themselves from Phillips, calling him a "quack" and dismissing his book as "baloney." Even Nixon's administration disowned him. These criticisms were handed down in part because of the candidness of his message. Saying the Republican Party aimed to become the major party by campaigning against African Americans, Latinos, and other marginalized groups that the Democratic Party had courted was not politically wise.

After 1970 Phillips continued to write influential books, most dealing with how politics, parties, and money interrelate. His works include *Electoral Reform and Voter Participation* (1975); *The Politics of the Rich and Poor: Wealth and the American Electorate in the Reagan Aftermath* (1990), a 1991 National Book Critics Circle nominee; *Arrogant Capital* (1995); and *Wealth and Democracy* (2002). He contributed regularly to major national newspapers and served as a commentator for the Columbia Broadcasting System and National Public Radio. In 1971 he became the president of the American Political Research Corporation. He also served as the editor and publisher of *The American Political Report*.

Phillips's greatest contribution was perhaps his ability to assess changing political situations at the grass roots level and forecast those trends into larger national movements. He was able to identify a major shift in political alignments that placed Republicans in the forefront for more than twenty years. With *The Emerging Republican Majority* and Phillips's accurate strategies that identified this new majority, Nixon was able to attract three major groups away from the Democratic Party—urban ethnic voters, blue-collar working classes, and southern whites—in order to build a new Republican coalition that lasted through the remainder of the century.

★

James Boyd, "It's All in the Charts," *New York Times* (17 May 1970), reviews Phillips's *The Emerging Republican Majority* and offers biographical information on the young Phillips.

VALERIE ADAMS

PICKETT, Wilson, Jr. (*b.* 18 March 1941 in Prattville, Alabama), singer whose full-throated, sexually charged, impassioned soul music performances were wrapped in an explosive persona that symbolized the emergence in the 1960s of an assertive African-American identity while providing an evocative soundtrack for the turbulent decade.

Pickett was the fourth of eleven children born to Wilson Pickett, Sr., and a mother whose name is unknown. The family picked cotton for a living. Pickett's mother and father separated when he was very young, and for several years he lived with his mother. When he was fourteen Pickett moved to Detroit to live with his father and began singing in his local Baptist church choir. For a brief time in the mid-1950s he sang with the famed gospel group the Violinaires. Pickett married "Bonnie" (her surname is unknown) when he was seventeen, but the marriage did not last. He later had a fourteen-year domestic relationship with Dovie Hall, with whom he raised a son sired from another relationship.

In 1960 Pickett joined a vocal harmony group called the Falcons. Pickett wrote and sang lead in the group's 1961

Wilson Pickett, 1973. DAVID REED/CORBIS

recording "I Found a Love," which went to number seven on the Cash Box rhythm and blues chart the following year. The song represented the new sound of gospel-influenced rhythm and blues that came to be called soul music, and Pickett's screaming and exhortatory lead vocals represented the genre's most heavily gospelized approach. Pickett left the Falcons in 1962 to establish a solo career. His first single made no impact, but in spring 1963 he entered the charts for the first time with an original composition, "If You Need Me." He quickly followed with another strong offering, "It's Too Late."

In 1964 Pickett joined Atlantic Records, one of the leading producers of soul music. Atlantic believed the style of soul music for which Pickett was noted was being best recorded in studios in the South, so the company's producer, Jerry Wexler, took Pickett to Stax Records in Memphis, Tennessee, to record in its studio. The results were stunning, producing the biggest hit record of Pickett's career, "In the Midnight Hour." The record went to number one on the Billboard rhythm and blues chart and stayed there for an extraordinary twenty-three weeks. "In the Midnight Hour" was Pickett's most influential record, and it virtually defined the soul sound of the day. Thousands of bands, both black and white, made the song part of their repertoire in the 1960s. Three other hit singles during 1965 and 1966 came out of the Stax sessions: "Don't Fight It," which rose to number four on the Billboard rhythm and blues charts; "634-5789," a number-one hit; and "Ninety-nine and a Half (Won't Do)." These songs cemented Pickett's arrival as a major new soul talent. Atlantic also released an album that included these hits, *The Exciting Wilson Pickett* (1966), which is considered his most outstanding album.

In late 1966 Wexler took Pickett to the Fame Studio in Muscle Shoals, Alabama, where Pickett recorded another series of standout hit records. The first, "Land of a Thousand Dances," marked another number-one hit on the Billboard rhythm and blues charts. The song was a remake of a Chris Kenner hit from 1963, but Pickett's version was sung in a hard-driving, swaggering manner featuring screaming and grunting. It was the biggest pop hit of his career, rising to number six on the Billboard pop charts. Pickett closed out 1966 with "Mustang Sally," a faster and much improved version of Mack Rice's original from two years earlier.

In spring 1967 Pickett reprised his hit with the Falcons, "I Found a Love," and pushed it to sixth place on the charts. Pickett's other 1967 hits included "Soul Dance Number Three" and "Funky Broadway," another number-one hit, which was a remake of the Dyke and the Blazers' song from earlier in the year. Two outstanding albums from Pickett's Muscle Shoals sessions were *The Wicked Pickett* (1966), which established an evocative nickname for

the singer, and *The Sound of Wilson Pickett* (1966).

During 1968 Pickett entered into a fruitful collaboration with the songwriter Bobby Womack, who wrote "I'm in Love" and other songs on the *I'm in Love* album. Womack also wrote "I'm a Midnight Mover" and half of the other songs on Pickett's *The Midnight Mover* album. Pickett then began recording soul versions of rock hits, notably the Beatles' song "Hey Jude" in 1969 and the Archies' "Sugar, Sugar" in 1970.

Atlantic realized it could not sustain Pickett's career on remakes of rock hits forever, and in 1970 the company had Pickett record in Philadelphia, Pennsylvania, with the producers Kenny Gamble and Leon Huff. The two were fast making an impact on the soul market with a highly orchestrated, danceable music known as the Philadelphia Sound. The Philadelphia sessions produced two hugely successful singles, "Engine Number Nine" in 1970 and "Don't Let the Green Grass Fool You," which hit number two on the Billboard rhythm and blues charts and was a million-selling single in 1971. Another number-one, million-selling single, "Don't Knock My Love," was recorded in Muscle Shoals with the producer Brad Shapiro in 1971. It was the last Top Twenty pop hit in Pickett's career. While chronologically the record is in the 1970s, "Don't Knock My Love" in essence represents the last achievement of Pickett as a 1960s soul music artist.

Pickett signed with RCA Records in 1972 and tried to change his singing approach from a screaming and shouting style to a softer, more crooning manner to stay in tune with the times. The records, however—five albums and a load of singles—proved both commercial and artistic failures, and Pickett left RCA in 1975. Pickett's last rhythm and blues hit, "A Funky Situation" (1978), appeared on his own label, Wicked. Recordings during the 1980s failed to resurrect Pickett's career, and the 1990s saw the singer battling alcohol and cocaine addiction problems.

Election to the Rock and Roll Hall of Fame in 1991 and receipt of the Rhythm and Blues Foundation Pioneer Award in 1993 helped to immortalize Pickett's contribution to soul music. In 1999 Pickett's first album in twelve years, the aptly titled *It's Harder Now*, was released. It paled in comparison to the singer's glory years in the 1960s, when he effortlessly produced hit after hit of hard-driving, impassioned soul that broke down racial barriers in music and made him a cultural hero to the African-American community.

★

A number of pages are devoted to Pickett's life and career in Gerri Hirshey, *Nowhere to Run: The Story of Soul Music* (1984). A personal profile of Pickett at the height of his popularity is David Llorens, "Soulin' with 'Wicked' Pickett," *Ebony* (Oct. 1968). An essay on Pickett focusing on his musical output, written by Leo Sacks, is part of the liner notes for the compact disc collection *The Best of Wilson Pickett: A Man and a Half* (1992).

ROBERT PRUTER

PIKE, James Albert, Jr. (*b.* 14 February 1913 in Oklahoma City, Oklahoma; *d.* 3 September 1969 in the Judaean desert, Israel), attorney, Episcopal dean and bishop, iconoclast, and searcher who to some became a martyr upon his unusual death in a desert in the Middle East.

Pike was the only child of James Albert Pike, a salesman, and Pearl Agatha (Wimsatt) Pike, a homemaker. His father died of tuberculosis in 1915 when Pike was just two years old. He moved with his mother to California in 1921. In 1924 she married Claude McFadden, an attorney. Even as a child, Pike's curiosity was insatiable; he had read both the dictionary and the phone book from cover to cover by the time he was five and a whole set of the *Encyclopedia Britannica* before he was ten. Pike attended Hollywood schools and graduated from high school in 1930.

As long as he lived, Pike continued his formal education. When he entered the Jesuit College, University of Santa

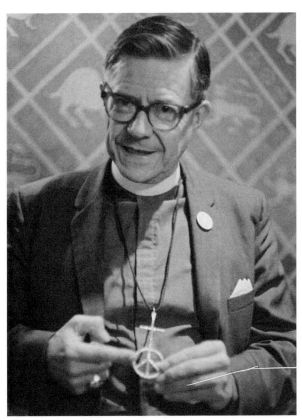

James A. Pike, 1967. © BETTMANN/CORBIS

Clara in California in 1930, he was a devout Roman Catholic headed for the priesthood. After two years he became an agnostic, dropped out of Santa Clara, and left the Catholic Church. For a year he attended the University of California, Los Angeles, finally transferring to the University of Southern California in Los Angeles where he got an A.B. in 1934 and a LL.B. in 1936. Pike received his J.S.D. from Yale (Sterling Fellow, 1936–1937) in New Haven, Connecticut, in 1938. He continued to earn degrees his entire life, including many honorary ones, ranging from a B.D. (magna cum laude, Union Theological Seminary, 1951) to an Honorary Fellow (University of Tel Aviv, 1956).

In 1938 Pike married his first wife, Jane Alvies, moved to Washington, D.C., as an attorney with the Securities and Exchange Commission, and established the law firm of Pike and Fischer. He divorced Alvies in 1940. Pike served from 1943 to 1945 in the U.S. Navy, first in naval intelligence and later as an attorney with the U.S. Maritime Commission. Just before entering the service, he married Esther Yanovsky on 29 January 1942; they had four children. During his time in Washington, Pike became involved in the Episcopal Church and studied for the ministry at the Virginia Theological Seminary in Alexandria. He was ordained as a deacon in the Episcopal Church in December 1944 and as a priest in November 1946.

Pike's career as a clergyman and scholar moved ahead rapidly. After two years as the curate of Saint John's Church and chaplain at George Washington University, he moved to Poughkeepsie, New York, as the rector of Christ Church and chaplain at Vassar College (1947–1949). Next he took a post at Columbia University in New York City, where he was the head of the religion department and chaplain. From 1952 to 1958 he was the dean of the Cathedral of Saint John the Divine in New York City, where his liberal sermons and television forum attracted much attention. In 1958, over conservative opposition, he was elected the bishop coadjutor of the Diocese of California in San Francisco, becoming the diocesan bishop (1958–1966) on the death of his predecessor a few months later.

Pike developed a controversial reputation through his passion, persistence, and public concern about political issues. He did this in an era when most ecclesiastics were devoting their energies to the problems and concerns of their own churches. He used his public image, including appearing on the cover of *Time* magazine, and public forum to bring his concerns for his church to the forefront. These issues included recovery of Christian origins, studies of the historical Jesus, the ordination of women, ecumenical renewal of the church, and the credibility of traditional dogmas. His call to "demythologize" the church was an expression of his view that the church was burdened by "theological baggage." He called for "more belief, fewer beliefs." A prolific author, Pike expounded his views in controversial books such as *A Time for Christian Candor* (1964) and *If This Be Heresy* (1967). He also wrote *The Church, Politics, and Society* (with H. W. Pyle, 1955), *What Is This Treasure?* (1966), *The Other Side* (1967), and *You and the New Morality: Seventy-four Cases* (1967).

Pike was an early advocate of women's ordination to the priesthood. In 1965 he recognized Phyllis Edwards as an ordained woman deacon, although it would be another two decades before the church's full acceptance of that concept. By 1966 Pike had become increasingly disenchanted with the Episcopal Church and institutional religion in general. In September of that year, the Episcopal House of Bishops called for a heresy trial that resulted in the formal censure of Pike's theological views as "offensive" and "irresponsible." He was vindicated at the 1967 General Convention, thus ending the heresy battle. These activities and his strong personal beliefs let him continue his favorite political sermon targets: abortion laws, capital punishment, apartheid, anti-Semitism, farm worker exploitation, and civil rights. He also engaged in such activities as marching for civil rights in Selma, Alabama, and being expelled from Rhodesia.

In 1966 Pike resigned as the bishop of California and joined the Center for the Study of Democratic Institutions, a liberal think tank in Santa Barbara. He soon left the center to continue his independent research and lectures. Personal problems caught up with Pike as the decade reached its turbulent end. After the suicide of his oldest son in 1966, and subsequent self-reported paranormal events, he started on a long and public search to reach and reconcile with his son. Noted psychics and mediums aided his quest. In July 1968 Pike divorced his second wife and on 20 December of that year he married his secretary, Diane Kennedy. He denounced the institutional church in April 1969. At this time he helped to form the Foundation for Religious Transition in Santa Barbara.

While Pike's brilliant and restless mind continued to lead him on a fast-paced search for truth and meaning, his Christian faith remained with him "in a radical and raw form," and he continued to explore its roots. On a visit to Israel's occupied West Bank in 1969 to research Christian origins, Pike and his wife apparently took a wrong turn in the desolate Judaean desert, southeast of Bethlehem. They left their car and became separated. Pike's wife managed to reach help at the Dead Sea shore. After an exhaustive four-day search by the Israeli army, Pike's body was found in the Wadi Duraja, a canyon amid rugged terrain. He is buried in the Protestant Cemetery in Jaffa, Israel.

Few American religious figures have matched Pike's lasting impact on modern theology and society. Pike always felt the search was more important than the discovery, the question more important than the answer. As he expressed in his sermons and writing throughout the 1960s, Pike en-visioned a church free of divisions, open to deep conversation and theological exploration, and fearless in the pursuit of individual and social justice. He was most at home as an outsider, an iconoclast, and a rebel. To some Pike was a heretic, to others a man decades ahead of his time.

★

The James A. Pike papers are housed at the Special Collections, Syracuse University Library in New York. In addition, some of his papers are in the archives of the Episcopal Church in Austin, Texas. Books on his controversial life include William Stringfellow and Anthony Towne, *The Bishop Pike Affair: Scandals of Conscience and Heresy, Relevance, and Solemnity in the Contemporary Church* (1967), and *The Death and Life of Bishop Pike* (1976); Merrill Unger, *The Mystery of Bishop Pike: A Christian View of the Other Side* (1968); Hans Holzer, *The Psychic World of Bishop Pike* (1970); and Michael Lawrence Mickler, *James A. Pike: Bishop and Iconoclast* (1989). "Death in the wilderness," *Time* (1969); "Man of faith, child of doubt," by J. Cogley, *Life* (1969); "Wrong turn in Judea," *Newsweek* (1969); a series in the *New York Times* (3 Sep. 1969–15 Sep. 1969) that looks at the search for, recovery of remains, burial, and memorial services for Pike.

JOAN GOODBODY

PLATH, Sylvia (*b.* 27 October 1932 in Boston, Massachusetts; *d.* 11 February 1963 in London, England), poet who achieved fame after her suicide with the 1965 publication of *Ariel;* her life and works resonated with feminists who saw her as a victim of patriarchal culture.

As a child Plath lived in coastal Winthrop, Massachusetts; she wrote of her enduring attraction to the geography of her youth in a 1963 essay, "Ocean 1212-W" (included in the 1977 prose collection *Johnny Panic and the Bible of Dreams*), in which her appreciation for the sea resides in part in its metaphoric potential: "like a deep woman, it hid a good deal, it had many faces, many delicate, terrible veils. it spoke of miracles and distances; if it could court, it could also kill."

Plath's father, Otto Plath, had immigrated to the United States from Prussia in 1901 and received a Ph.D. from Harvard University in 1928, becoming a professor of biology at Boston University (BU). Plath's mother, Aurelia Schober, was Otto's student in an advanced German-language course at BU. They were married in 1932. After Otto Plath's death in 1940, eight-year-old Sylvia and her younger brother moved inland to Wellesley, Massachusetts, where Aurelia Plath supported the family as a teacher of clerical skills.

The separation from her "seaside childhood" and the loss of her father are configured in Plath's later work with romantic emphasis: she was exiled from paradise. Those

Sylvia Plath. AP/WIDE WORLD PHOTOS

years, she states at the end of "Ocean 1212-W," "sealed themselves off like a ship in a bottle—beautiful, inaccessible, obsolete, a fine white flying myth."

After distinguishing herself at Gamaliel Bradford High School, from which she graduated in 1950, Plath entered Smith College in Northampton, Massachusetts, on a scholarship. A perfectionist, her obsessive will to succeed—academically, socially, and creatively—is evident from her college journal entries. She had begun writing poetry at an early age, and revered the form and its modernist practitioners such as W. H. Auden. She aspired to be a serious poet but relentlessly pursued the writing of popular fiction as a legitimate way to support herself as a writer.

Plath had success publishing her short stories in women's magazines while at Smith; work written to be salable, it gives little indication of her later distinction. In 1953 she won a guest editorship at *Mademoiselle* in New York City. Tall, blonde, and attractive, Plath modeled as a teenager. As an intern she was photographed for the magazine, a seemingly natural projection of its smart, all-American-girl mien. The images belie the fact that Plath suffered frequent bouts of self-doubt and depression at this time; after her return home she attempted suicide. The experience and her subsequent hospitalization in a psychiatric facility are recounted in the autobiographical novel *The Bell Jar* (1963). In this work the protagonist, Esther Greenwood, looks at the limited options available to her as a woman in 1950s America and concludes, "The last thing

I wanted was infinite security and to be the place an arrow shoots off from." Esther's psychic reintegration is largely effected in the novel through a throwing off of societal expectations; one way she does this is by taking control of her reproductive capabilities through birth control. Writing in *Life* magazine (21 November 1971), Martha Duffy called the novel "a major text for women's liberation" that revealed Plath to be "a kind of naive prophet" whose instincts were demonstrably feminist.

After her recovery Plath returned to Smith and graduated with honors in 1955 with a B.A. in English. She then traveled to England and attended Cambridge University on a Fulbright Fellowship. There she met the poet Ted Hughes, whom she married in London on 16 June 1956. She returned with Hughes to Massachusetts, where she taught English at her alma mater in 1957–1958. During this time she attended Robert Lowell's poetry workshop in Boston. The economic boom in the postwar United States had yielded to individuals the pleasures and torments of individual preoccupation, and during the 1950s and 1960s mainstream poetry moved from the restrained and objective (the formalist) to the personal and subjective (the confessional). Lowell is considered to have launched the confessional school with his 1958 book *Life Studies*; Plath's *Ariel* is perhaps the most famous text to issue from this school.

From 1959 Plath and Hughes lived in England; they had a daughter in 1960 and a son in 1962. Plath's first book, *The Colossus and Other Poems,* was released in Great Britain in 1960. Her letters and journal entries from this time show her as frequently subordinating her own poetic ambitions to those of Hughes. In October 1962 Plath separated from Hughes and moved with their children to London; the breakup was precipitated by Hughes's adultery. Most of the poems published posthumously in *Ariel* were written during Plath's estrangement from Hughes in the final months of her life, in a fever of productivity. "I am joyous . . . writing like mad—have managed a poem a day before breakfast. . . . Terrific stuff, as if domesticity had choked me," she wrote on 12 October 1962.

In her poetry Plath moved from the traditional verse forms that characterize *The Colossus* to free verse and a fuller, more idiosyncratic exploration of subject and an unleashing of a frequently dark emotional sensibility. Rage, rivalry, grief, and despair propel the poems in *Ariel*. Elizabeth Hardwick wrote of the book, "so powerful is the art that one feels an unsettling elation as one reads the lacerating lines." The poems issue from a distinctly female condition; the images presented are emanations of the predicaments and realities, as well as the emotional undercurrents, of Plath's life. They can be seen as partaking in the revolutionary ethos of the 1960s in their themes: the dismantling or abandonment of outmoded constructs; the shedding of externally imposed constraints that limit the self; the possibility—indeed, the necessity—of remaking and rebirth. The last lines of the title poem of *Ariel* are representative of the book's emotional thrust: "And I / Am the arrow, / The dew that flies / Suicidal, at one with the drive / Into the red / Eye, the cauldron of morning."

Duality is a commonplace in Plath's work; literary critics and biographers alike have explored the motif of psychic division that runs through her writings, the "true" self at variance with the "false." Such opposition becomes more than a literary conceit in Plath when one considers her in light of the women's movement, incipient in the late 1950s and early 1960s when Plath produced her mature work. Writing about the social and cultural milieu of the time, the author and activist Betty Friedan, in the introduction to *The Feminine Mystique* (1964), took note of the "strange discrepancy between the reality of [women's] lives and the image to which we were trying to conform." In her autobiographical works Plath would exemplify what Friedan referred to as the "schizophrenic split" in the female psyche of educated American women, the fault line underlying the conventional gender role.

The image of the father is primary in Plath's work, as suggested by the title of her most anthologized poem, "Daddy." The paternal image takes on historical and spiritual dimensions in the poetry, extending from father and husband to fascist, devil, and god. The harsh realities of the twentieth century—of a world, as she writes in "Daddy," "Scraped flat by the roller / Of wars, wars, wars"—seemed to preempt for Plath the state of grace for which she yearned. In a short story, "Mothers," written in 1962, the protagonist mourns the "irrevocable gap between her faithless state and the beatitude of belief." God, in his absence or profanation, is a precondition of the *Ariel* poems, which posit a "heaven / Starless and fatherless, a dark water" ("Sheep in Fog"). Critics have castigated Plath for her appropriation of Holocaust imagery in the *Ariel* poems, primarily "Daddy," in which the oppressor is portrayed as a Nazi and the speaker as a Jew bound for "Dachau, Auschwitz, Belsen."

Alone with her children in a London apartment during the brutally cold winter of 1962–1963, Plath ultimately enacted in real life the drama that unfolds in *Ariel*—she killed herself by inhaling the fumes from her gas oven. Thus sacrificed on the altar of domesticity, her work, including her life as she portrayed it in her prose writings, was seen as a rationale for feminists demanding a radical societal overhaul. In this view Hughes, who became the poet laureate of Great Britain in 1984, was the embodiment of patriarchy, reviled for his role in Plath's life and as the executor of her estate. Plath is buried in Heptonstall Churchyard in Heptonstall, Yorkshire, England. Her gravestone, repeatedly defaced by Hughes-bashing fans outraged that she was buried under her married name, was eventually replaced by a

simple wooden cross. In retrospect Hughes was an invaluable proponent of Plath's artistry, and her influence can be seen throughout his work.

Because the suicidal impulse in the *Ariel* poems was carried over into the poet's life with such seeming inevitability, the life and work became blurred. Plath's language, strikingly contemporary yet underpinned with archetype and myth, now issued from a woman dead at thirty, who had left behind a considerable autobiographical record in the form of letters and journals. Plath herself became a myth, the subject of cult-like obsession and the object of public consumption: books by and about Plath proliferated beginning in the late 1960s. Prurient interest in her suicide ensured her posthumous fame.

In his foreword to *Ariel,* Lowell stated that in her poems Plath "becomes herself . . . something imaginary, newly, wildly and subtly created." And in the end that is her legacy—poetry that both attests to and conveys the transforming power of art. *Ariel* is a singular creation, rooted in but transcending its time.

★

Plath's life and work have been the subject of endless commentary. Of the numerous biographies available are Anne Stevenson, *Bitter Fame: A Life of Sylvia Plath* (1989), and Linda Wagner-Martin, *Sylvia Plath: A Literary Life* (1999). See also Janet Malcolm, *The Silent Woman: Sylvia Plath and Ted Hughes* (1994). For the literary context see Robert Phillips, *The Confessional Poets* (1973); Elizabeth Hardwick, "Victims and Victors," in *Seduction and Betrayal: Women and Literature* (1974); and Leslie Ullman, "American Poetry in the 1960s," in *A Profile of Twentieth-century American Poetry* (1991). Critical takes on Plath's work are Paul Alexander, ed., *Ariel Ascending: Writings About Sylvia Plath* (1985), and Harold Bloom, ed., *Sylvia Plath* (1989). Feminist appraisals are Paula Bennett, "Sylvia Plath: Fusion and the Divided Self," in *My Life a Loaded Gun: Female Creativity and Feminist Poetics* (1986), and Janice Markey, *A New Tradition? The Poetry of Sylvia Plath, Anne Sexton, and Adrienne Rich* (1988). An epitaph by the literary critic A. Alvarez is in the *Observer* (London, 7 Feb. 1963).

MELISSA A. DOBSON

PODHORETZ, Norman Harold (*b.* 16 January 1930 in New York City), writer, editor, critic, neoconservative, and New York intellectual who in the 1960s promoted views of the New Left as the editor of *Commentary* and as the author of *Making It* (1966).

Podhoretz and his older sister were born to the European immigrants Julius Podhoretz, a milkman, and Helen (Woliner) Podhoretz, a homemaker, in the Brownsville section of Brooklyn. Podhoretz graduated from Boy's High School in Brooklyn in 1946 with an outstanding scholastic record.

Norman Podhoretz. © BETTMANN/CORBIS

He then enrolled in Columbia University in New York City, graduating with a B.A. in English in 1950. Upon being awarded a Kellert Fellowship and a Fulbright Scholarship, he attended Cambridge University in England, where he received a B.A. in 1952 and an M.A. in 1957. Podhoretz also attended the Jewish Theological Seminary in Manhattan in 1950, and again in 1980, where he earned a B.H.L. and subsequently was awarded an honorary doctor of letters. On 21 October 1956 he married Midge Rosenthal Decter, a writer; the couple raised a son and a daughter, in addition to two children from Decter's previous marriage.

At Cambridge, Podhoretz came under the influence of F. R. Leavis, who in 1951 published the New York scholar's first work of literary criticism in *Scrutiny*. Articles by Podhoretz subsequently appeared in the *Partisan Review*, *New Republic*, *New Yorker*, and other periodicals. After a four-year stint in the U.S. Army, he was discharged in December 1955 and became the assistant editor of *Commentary*, the publication of the American Jewish Committee. In 1960 Podhoretz was appointed its editor, following the death of Elliot Cohen. Under Cohen's editorship, *Commentary* had established a hard-line anticommunist policy, which Podhoretz was determined to change. His goal was to transform *Commentary* into a center for the revival of American social criticism.

Podhoretz's impact on the new *Commentary* was immediate. In the first three issues under his editorship he serialized Paul Goodman's book *Growing Up Absurd,* which, after being rejected by nineteen publishers, was published by Random House soon after its appearance in *Commentary*. Goodman's bristling indictment of U.S. society in the 1960s soon became one of the first "bibles" of the New Left. Podhoretz credited his publication of Goodman's book as an important reason for the rapidly growing interest in the new *Commentary*. The magazine during the 1960s became an important voice for the views of such major intellectuals as Lionel Trilling, Alfred Kazin, Leslie Fiedler, Dwight Macdonald, and Irving Howe. *Commentary* also shed its parochial image, becoming less of a venue for special Jewish concerns and embracing issues affecting the nation and the world at large.

Two books that Podhoretz wrote during the 1960s contributed to his reputation as one of America's most controversial intellectuals. His article "My Negro Problem—and Ours," which was published in the February 1963 issue of *Commentary* and in a collection of his essays in *Doings and Undoing: The Fifties and After in American Writing* (1964), turned out to be a milestone in his career. The essay relates his experiences growing up in "integrated" Brownsville, where, he stated, "It was the Negroes who persecuted the whites, and not the other way round." As Podhoretz later wrote in his autobiography *Making It* (1966), the essay grew out of his irritation with "all the sentimental nonsense that was being talked about integration by whites who knew nothing about Negroes and by Negroes who thought that all their problems could be solved by living next-door to whites."

In hundreds of letters to *Commentary,* Podhoretz was alternately criticized for his racism and praised for his courage. One critic, David Boroff, wrote of the essay, "Measured by the author's own touchstone for literature, 'to help the age became less chaotic and confused,' it is irresponsible, gratuitously confessional, and damaging to the most crucial struggle of our time." Given the emotional turmoil that enveloped the civil rights movement during the 1960s, it appears that much of the controversy over "My Negro Problem—and Ours" had less to do with the truth of Podhoretz's experiences than with the timeliness and social usefulness of the article.

Also controversial was *Making It* (1966), a confessional autobiography in which Podhoretz reveals how the drive for power, money, fame, and social status became the prime motivating factor throughout his career. He frankly admits that he strove to become rich, to be talked about, and to create constant intellectual controversy. Podhoretz explained that in writing this memoir, he was merely being honest about an attitude that pervades American society. He charged that, in his experience, indifference to success and achievement was a snobbish, puritanical pose or affectation.

Ambition, he concluded, had replaced sex as the "dirty little secret" of our time.

Reactions to *Making It* were mixed. Some critics praised the book for its candor and integrity, whereas others were put off by the book's almost embarrassing frankness. One critic accused Podhoretz of forfeiting his potential to become an important critic of contemporary literature and culture, settling instead "for the strongly expressed negative judgment, the devastating assault more likely to provide quick fame, quick power, quick money." *Making It* remains a classic work of its kind and reveals as much about the 1960s as it does about Podhoretz.

By the middle of the 1960s *Commentary*'s circulation was three times its 1960 figure, and along with *Partisan Review* it had become one of the leading periodicals among American intellectuals. However, Podhoretz had moderated his enthusiasm for leftist politics, noting that the New Left was as naive about Communist totalitarianism as the Old Left of the 1930s. He was particularly disappointed with the presidential candidacy of the Democrat George McGovern in 1972; the fallout from that election marked his break with liberalism and the New Left and the beginning of his journey toward a neoconservative ideology. In *Breaking Ranks: A Political Memoir* (1979), his candid second autobiographical work, Podhoretz explains how he grew to abhor liberal views. With this change in political perspective, Podhoretz restructured *Commentary* into a forum for neoconservatism, characterized by such positions as opposition to détente with the Soviet Union, support for a strong U.S. military, and firm backing for Israel.

During the 1970s Podhoretz moved farther away from literary criticism to address politics and social issues. This change can be found in his book *The Present Danger: Do We Have the Will to Reverse the Decline of American Power?* (1980), in which Podhoretz argues that a Soviet victory over America may not be the result of a military defeat, but of an increasing debilitation of culture, the economic system, and the standard of living. In *Why We Were in Vietnam* (1982), Podhoretz argues that the Vietnam War was moral because it was fought to free the Vietnamese from Communism, and thus U.S. involvement in the war should not be viewed as a national mistake.

Podhoretz edited *Commentary* until 1995, when he retired after thirty-five years to devote himself to writing. He remained associated with *Commentary* as an editor at large and became a senior fellow of the Hudson Institute.

By the end of the 1960s Podhoretz had established himself as an important voice among New York intellectuals. Specifically, his 1963 article "My Negro Problem—and Ours" provided Podhoretz with the great success and recognition that he had been waiting to achieve.

★

Podhoretz has written three autobiographies: *Making It* (1966), *Breaking Ranks: A Political Memoir* (1979), and *Ex-Friends: Falling Out with Allen Ginsberg, Lionel and Diana Trilling, Lillian Hellman, Hannah Arendt, and Norman Mailer* (1999). Biographical information is in D. J. Enright, *Conspirators and Poets: Reviews and Essays* (1966); Mark R. Winchell, *Neo-conservative Criticism: Norman Podhoretz, Kenneth S. Lynn, and Joseph Epstein* (1991); and Podhoretz, *My Love Affair with America: The Cautionary Tale of a Cheerful Conservative* (2000). Articles about Podhoretz include "Norman's Conquest: A Commentary on the Podhoretz Legacy," *Policy Review* (22 Sept. 1995), and "Norman Podhoretz: Making Enemies," *Publisher's Weekly* (25 Jan. 1999).

JACK FISCHEL

POITIER, Sidney (*b.* 20 February 1927 [some sources say 1927] in Miami, Florida), actor, civil rights activist, and motion picture director who in the 1960s became the first African-American film star in Hollywood history.

A native of Cat Island in the Bahamas, Poitier was born in Miami during a stopover by his parents, Reginald James and Evelyn (Outten) Poitier, who secured U.S. citizenship for him but little else. He was raised dirt poor with his seven siblings in Nassau, where his father barely made a living as a tomato farmer and his mother broke rocks to make gravel. In 1943, after a brief stay in Miami with his older brother, Poitier ran off to New York City. While Poitier, who had virtually no formal schooling, struggled to support himself by working as a dishwasher and tried to improve his reading skills, he strove to lose his Caribbean accent by listening to the radio. After an unhappy tour of duty in the army, he was discharged in December 1944, entered the American Negro Theater School, and began the daunting task of breaking the color line on the American stage. On 29 April 1950 Poitier married Juanita Hardy, a dancer; the couple raised four daughters.

A Hollywood screen test earned Poitier his first feature role as a doctor, not an orderly, who treats a racist patient in the film *No Way Out* (1950). Despite garnering good notices for his center-stage performances in *No Way Out* and *Cry, the Beloved Country* (1951), a tragedy set in South Africa, Poitier still had to hustle for supporting roles in other film projects and in live television drama. With *The Blackboard Jungle* (1955), where he played the most salvageable student in a rowdy classroom of urban delinquents, his luck changed for good. From the tense urban melodrama of *Edge of the City* (1957) to the songs and dances of *Porgy and Bess* (1959), he worked steadily throughout the 1950s, perhaps most memorably in *The Defiant Ones* (1958). In the latter film he and Tony Curtis portrayed escaped prisoners who must learn to put their

Sidney Poitier *(right)*, as he appeared in *A Raisin in the Sun,* 1961. ARCHIVE PHOTOS, INC.

prejudices aside to achieve liberation. Poitier and Curtis each earned Academy Award nominations as best actor for their culturally resonant face-offs (though neither of them won).

The civil rights revolution of the 1960s expanded Poitier's options and repertoire, even though the motion pictures tended to retread familiar screen territory rather than break new ground. In the Korean War film *All the Young Men* (1960), Poitier personifies the tensions of interracial command as a sergeant reluctant to assume leadership. More interesting and daring is *Paris Blues* (1961), which cast him against type as a moody expatriate jazzman performing in Paris to escape American racism and finally paired him with an African-American leading lady, Diahann Carroll. Personally if not professionally, the most meaningful film for Poitier during this period was the 1961 version of Lorraine Hansberry's searing play *Raisin in the Sun* (1959). *Variety* praised Poitier's "striking, commanding performance" as the son of a Chicago family fighting discriminatory housing patterns and oedipal pressures. The article went on to say, "There is a poetry in the very expression of his body movements . . . [which] convey physically but clearly the inner turmoil, the years of denial that the character has had to seal within himself."

In *Lilies of the Field* (1963), Poitier's quietly authoritative and immensely engaging performance as a handyman for a group of German nuns won him the Oscar as best actor. At the Academy Awards ceremony, a boisterous ovation greeted the reading of his name, recognition not only

of the actor but also of the representative value of the occasion. "It has been a long journey to this moment," said a somber Poitier with typical understatement. Backstage that same evening, Poitier found himself instantly anointed as a spokesperson for black America. "The reporters feel that because I won an Academy Award, I'm some kind of political expert," he said at the time. "I'm what I always wanted to be—an actor. Why don't they ask me some questions about acting?"

The Oscar win catapulted Poitier to the Hollywood A-list, but whether in cold war thrillers (as a reporter aboard a submarine in *The Bedford Incident,* 1965) or schmaltzy interracial romances (as a tutor to a blind girl in *A Patch of Blue,* 1965), Poitier's erotic energy was kept in neutral. Not until his discreet clinch with the actress Abby Lincoln in *For Love of Ivy* (1968) did a popular Hollywood film feature a love scene between two African-American stars. Ironically, perhaps Poitier's most culturally significant role in the mid-1960s was his cameo appearance as Simon Peter in the biblical epic *The Greatest Story Ever Told* (1965), which verified an African-American presence in the heretofore blue-eyed regions of the Hollywood Holy Land.

Poitier's golden year was 1967, when the *New York Times* film critic Bosley Crowther called him "the most conspicuous and respected exponent of the American Negro on the screen." Astonishingly, three of his films—*To Sir with Love, In the Heat of the Night,* and *Guess Who's Coming to Dinner?*—were the top box-office hits that year. In *To Sir with Love,* he stood on the other side of the blackboard jungle as a hip teacher ministering to London slum kids; the pop singer Lulu's plaintive title tune made achingly clear the romantic longing of a white girl for a black man.

Poitier's next two performances neatly expressed the African-American impulses to anger and assimilation during the 1960s. In *In the Heat of the Night,* he played the Philadelphia detective Virgil Tibbs, who, while traveling through a Dixie backwater, becomes first the suspect and then the solution to a local murder. The contrast of an aberrant, racist, Neanderthal South with an open-minded, idealistic, and integrationist North may have been a Hollywood conceit. When the redneck sheriff condescendingly addresses the detective as "Virgil" one too many times, however, an enraged Poitier spits out a rebuke that incited raucous cheers from audiences of all shades, "They call me *MISTER* Tibbs!"

In *Guess Who's Coming to Dinner?,* Stanley Kramer's then controversial treatment of interracial marriage, Poitier appears as a model future son-in-law except for one slight problem—his color. Tendentious and preachy in rhetoric and modest and discreet in imagery, the film was nonetheless a landmark in its time. Perhaps, too, compared with the ill-scrubbed, ill-mannered swains some daughters were bringing home to meet the folks, not a few 1960s parents would have been thrilled to have the accomplished and gentlemanly Poitier come to dinner.

Off-screen in the 1960s, Poitier positioned himself squarely in the mainstream of the civil rights movement; he marched with the Reverend Martin Luther King, Jr., and lent his emblematic presence to a number of progressive causes. Yet he never succumbed to the extremes of black militancy in either separatist rhetoric or personal style. As for his own contribution to the struggle for racial equality, he attributed his screen success to "being at the right place at the right time, one in that series of perfect accidents from which Fate fashions her grand design."

In the 1970s Poitier moved behind the camera to direct a series of highly successful comedy, caper, and genre films, including *Buck and the Preacher* (1972), *Uptown Saturday Night* (1974), *Let's Do It Again* (1975), *A Piece of the Action* (1977), and the blockbuster *Stir Crazy* (1980). After playing so many of what he called "saintly unreal" blacks, Poitier the auteur seemed to luxuriate in lighthearted fare featuring lovable rogues. "I wanted to make fun movies in which black people could sit in a theater and laugh at themselves without restraint—and feel good about it," Poitier recalled. After divorcing his first wife in 1965, Poitier married the actress Johanna Shimkus on 23 January 1976; they had two daughters.

Poitier's talent as an actor was inseparable from his color: he was a black man who played black men, and often black men who had been created by white screenwriters. As such, later generations of African-American activists came to see Poitier as too much the "good Negro" of the white liberal imagination: well spoken, well behaved, and white featured. Especially in the 1960s, when phrases like "a credit to his race" and "role model" became epithets, not compliments, Poitier was derided as a "paradigm of tokenism" and sneered at as an Uncle Tom by certain blacker-than-thou elements of the African-American community.

Over time, however, as tempers cooled and the shadings of Poitier's rich portrait gallery endured, the immensity of his artistic achievements was recognized and honored. At the 2002 Academy Awards, Poitier was presented with an Oscar for lifetime achievement, an apt tribute to an artist whose pioneering legacy extended far beyond the motion picture screen.

★

Poitier is the author of two memoirs, *This Life* (1980) and *The Measure of a Man: A Spiritual Autobiography* (2000). Critical studies of his work include Lester J. Keyser, *The Cinema of Sidney Poitier: The Black Man's Changing Role on the American Screen* (1980), and Samuel L. Kelley, *The Evolution of Character Portrayals in the Films of Sidney Poitier* (1983).

THOMAS DOHERTY

PORTER, Katherine Anne (*b.* 15 May 1890 in Indian Creek, Texas; *d.* 18 September 1980 in Silver Spring, Maryland), prize-winning short-story writer and novelist who was in the forefront of the "women's literature" of the 1960s.

Born Callie Russell, Porter was the fourth of five children of Harrison Boone Porter, a farmer, and Mary Alice Jones Porter (who died when Porter was nearly two). The children were reared by their grandmother, Catherine Anne Skaggs Porter, until her death in 1901 and then by a cousin near San Antonio, Texas. Through the fictional Miranda Gay, whom Porter identified as her alter ego, Porter implied that the family of her childhood was more genteel, educated, and wealthy than it was.

After her marriage at age sixteen to John Henry Koontz in June 1906, Porter moved to New York City and, with little formal schooling, worked as a journalist and publicist. In 1915 she legally adopted her grandmother's name with a slight change in spelling. After a divorce (1915) and several years in Mexico, Porter finally began her career as a short-story writer in 1922 with "María Concepción." In 1926 she was briefly married to Ernest Stock. In 1931 Porter received a Guggenheim Fellowship and went to Germany, and in 1933 she married Eugene Dove Pressly, who worked in the U.S. Consulate in Paris. Porter received another Guggenheim in 1938, the year she was divorced from Pressly. That year she married Albert Erskine, but they, too, divorced, in 1942. She was writer in residence or member of the English faculty at several noted universities and in 1959 became the first female faculty member in the history of Washington and Lee University.

Porter's major works, highly praised short stories and novellas, were written from the 1920s to the 1940s, and she became a major figure in the 1960s as a result of the reassessment of her early works. *The Collected Stories of Katherine Anne Porter* (1965) received the 1966 Pulitzer Prize and the 1966 National Book Award as well as the Gold Medal for Fiction of the American Academy of Arts and Letters. The short stories and novellas had long received the highest critical acclaim. Married and divorced several times, with no children, Porter became a public figure of "women's liberation" and was frequently photographed with a succession of men, often considerably younger than she was. Porter often compared the characters and lives of the women in her stories to her own life and experience. Like Porter herself, Miranda in "Old Mortality" "knew now why she had run away to marriage, and she knew that she was going to run away from marriage . . . with anyone that threatened to forbid her making her own discoveries."

Although Porter occasionally commented that she was not sympathetic to all the ideology of modern feminism, many of her women characters are staunch individualists. Most of her female protagonists are hardy survivors, as shown in "The Jilting of Granny Weatherall," which tells the story of a single woman who raises her children alone in a hostile frontier territory. Similarly, Jenny Brown in *Ship of Fools* rejects her fiancé because he attacks her sense of self-worth. "Men are continually accusing women of trying to castrate them by insulting their maleness," Porter wrote in 1958. "When a woman loves a man, she builds him up . . . [but] it is his deepest instinct to destroy, quite often subtly, insidiously, but constantly and endlessly, her very center of being, her confidence in herself as woman." Such themes earned Porter's work a place in the emerging women's studies movement.

A second thread of Porter's work that resonated in the 1960s was the awareness of Mexican culture. As well as growing up in the Southwest and spending time in Mexico, she had met several Mexican artists in Greenwich Village and wrote the story of a Mexican ballet performed in Mexico City in 1923. Porter became deeply immersed in Mexico's culture, especially Aztec and Mayan art and crafts, and was involved in political conflicts, which laid the ground-

Katherine Anne Porter. AP/WIDE WORLD PHOTOS

work for such stories as "Flowering Judas" and "Hacienda." In the late 1920s she fled Mexico when the Mexican government accused her of being a Bolshevik. Porter wrote to the editor of *Century* in July 1923, "My America has been a borderland of strange tongues and commingled races, and if they are not American, I am fearfully mistaken. And, to my mind, this includes Mexico."

Having also lived in Europe in the 1930s, Porter was aware of increasing tensions between Germany and France. She began working on *Ship of Fools* in 1945, and several of her characters attack the way the ship's officers and passengers express overt hostility toward the Jewish Germans. In 1946 she wrote, "I believe that human beings are capable of total evil, but no one has ever been totally good, and this gives the edge to evil." Consistent with that viewpoint, Porter said in April 1962 that the novel's point is "that evil is always done with the collusion of good."

The initial response to *Ship of Fools* (1962) was very positive. Porter wrote in the preface to the novel that the German ship *Vera* was a "simple almost universal image of the ship of this world on its voyage to eternity. . . . I am a passenger on that ship." Although the novel may seem like a pastiche of short stories without a primary character or central plotline, Porter's general focus is on the lesser forms of evil, its pettiness and all-pervasiveness. Even those not actively evil contribute to evil by their tolerance of it or by ignoring it. The novel also observes women at transitional points in their lives: a widow; a political exile, La Condesa; an unattractive young woman travelling with her parents; and two figures comparable to Porter herself, the artist Jenny Brown and an American woman self-exiled to Paris. The novel and its subsequent film (1965) brought Porter critical acclaim and wealth.

During the late 1960s and early 1970s, Porter continued her journalism, gave interviews, and wrote book reviews. In 1972 *Playboy* magazine sent her to Cape Canaveral to cover an Apollo moon mission. Her last major publication, *The Never-Ending Wrong* (1977), was an account of her protest against the verdict in the 1921 Sacco-Vanzetti case. (The political radicals Nicola Sacco and Bartolomeo Vanzetti were accused of robbery and murder in Massachusetts and eventually were executed for their alleged crimes despite conflicting evidence and the confession of another man.) From the late 1970s Porter lived in Maryland, where she died after a series of strokes. Her remains were cremated and buried in a small cemetery in Indian Creek, Texas, beside her mother's grave.

Shortly after Porter's death, the American poet and novelist Robert Penn Warren wrote of her in the *Saturday Review* that she had "created an oeuvre . . . keenly aware of the depth and darkness of human experience . . . and thoroughly committed to a quest for meaning in the midst of . . . ironic complexities." Porter's style is marked by rhetorical beauty and balance; her simple and clear dialogue is appropriate to each speaker. The remarkable range of her fiction reaches from the Mexican landscape to the interior monologue of her character Granny Weatherall. Her focus on independent women in her short stories established Porter as one of the major figures in the rising field of women's literature. Her writing on Mexico, from its crafts to the idiom and lifestyle of its people, is one of the early evocations of the country in American literature. The prizes awarded to her collected short stories, even more than the critical acclaim of *Ship of Fools,* denoted Porter's acceptance by both academia and the reading public of the 1960s.

★

Porter's papers are at the McKeldin Library of the University of Maryland and at the Beinecke at Yale. Perhaps the best biography of Porter is Joan Givner, *Katherine Anne Porter: A Life* (1991). Darlene Harbour Unrue edited Porter's *"This Strange, Old World" and Other Book Reviews* (1991), written between 1920 and 1958. See also Enrique Hank Lopez, *Conversations with Katherine Anne Porter: Refugee from Indian Creek* (1981) and *The Collected Essays and Occasional Writings of Katherine Anne Porter* (1970),

and Isabel Bayley, ed., *Letters of Katherine Anne Porter* (1990). Useful in assessing Porter's impact on the 1960s are Glenway Wescott, "Katherine Anne Porter: The Making of a Novel," *Atlantic Monthly* 209 (April 1962): 43–49, and "Katherine Anne Porter: The Art of Fiction," an interview by Barbara Thompson in the *Paris Review* 29 (winter–spring 1963): 87–114. Obituaries are in the *Washington Post* (10 Sept. 1980), *New York Times* (19 Sept. 1980), and *Newsweek* (29 Sept. 1980).

DESSA CRAWFORD

POWELL, Adam Clayton, Jr. (*b.* 29 November 1908 in New Haven, Connecticut; *d.* 4 April 1972 in Miami, Florida), minister, politician, civil rights leader, and social activist who, through his leadership of strikes, picket lines, and civic demonstrations, and through legislation, improved employment conditions for African Americans.

Powell was the younger of two children born to Adam Clayton Powell, Sr., a Baptist pastor, and Mattie Fletcher (Shaffer) Powell. Soon after Powell's birth his father became the pastor of the Abyssinian Baptist Church in Harlem in New York City. The church became the largest Protestant congregation in America, with nearly 15,000 members.

When Powell was six years old he contracted what was probably tuberculosis, and it took him more than six years to recover. During this period he became close to his sister

Adam Clayton Powell, Jr. AP/WIDE WORLD PHOTOS

Blanche, ten years his senior, who tended him. Powell graduated from Townsend Harris High School in 1925 at the age of sixteen. That year he attended the City College of New York (CCNY), partying more than studying and failing three courses. He was given another chance at the college in 1926, again failing.

In the winter of 1926 Powell's sister died of a burst appendix. The shock to him was such that he spent four years in a profound depression, what he called an "aching void." In 1926 he entered Colgate University in Hamilton, New York. In February 1930, while studying late, he had a religious revelation in which he felt he was "called" to the ministry. Powell graduated from Colgate in 1930 with a B.A., then attended Union Theological Seminary in New York City briefly before quitting over a dispute with the administration about his girlfriend, Isabel Washington, a nightclub dancer. He then attended the Teacher's College of Columbia University, receiving his M.A. in religion in 1932. On 8 March 1933 he married Washington and adopted her child from an earlier marriage; they divorced in 1945.

In 1936 his father retired as pastor of the Abyssinian Baptist Church, and Powell was selected to replace him. Meanwhile he was awarded an honorary doctorate in divinity from Shaw University in 1938. During this period Powell campaigned for stores in Harlem to employ more African Americans, organizing picket lines and strikes to publicize this endeavor. On 23 September 1941 he entered the race for New York City Council, finishing third out of six candidates and earning a seat; he was the council's first African-American member. In 1944 the Harlem congressional district was gerrymandered to ensure the election of an African American; Powell, who had refused to be partisan as a council member, received the endorsement of both the Democratic and Republican parties and ran unopposed in the November election.

The light-skinned Powell immediately made his presence felt in Congress by entering every whites-only establishment and insisting his African-American aides be allowed in also. He challenged segregated establishments throughout Washington, D.C., opening them up for nonwhites. In August 1945 Powell married Hazel Scott, a professional jazz pianist; they had a son, Adam Clayton Powell III. During the 1940s and 1950s Powell persistently tried to add to bills a piece of legislation that became known as the Powell Amendment. This amendment forbade the disbursement of federal money to any organization or private enterprise that practiced racial discrimination. The conservative Democrats in Congress tended to thwart Powell's efforts, resulting in his occasionally threatening to jump to the Republican Party. In 1956 he endorsed President Dwight D. Eisenhower for reelection, forming a working relationship with the president's staff that helped result in

the passage of the Civil Rights Act of 1957. During the 1950s he became known as "Mr. Civil Rights."

In 1960 Powell divorced Hazel Scott, then married his staff secretary, Yvette Marjorie Flores Diago of Puerto Rico; he hoped to make Puerto Rico a state. They had one son and separated in 1966. In 1960 Powell endorsed Lyndon B. Johnson for president during the presidential primary, but in 1961 he allied with President John F. Kennedy and his New Frontier policies. Seniority made him the chair of the House Committee on Education and Labor, and he proved himself an exceptional parliamentarian, wielding the powers of his office with skill. Between 1961 and 1967 the committee passed forty-eight important social bills, including a revised version of the Education Act of 1958, the Civil Rights Act of 1960, the Minimum Wage Bill of 1961, and the Manpower Development Act of 1962. Each bill included the Powell Amendment.

The assassination of Kennedy in 1963 appalled Powell, but he found in the new president, Johnson, a goal-oriented politician with whom he could work closely. When Johnson presented several major pieces of legislation that he wanted passed in only a few months, Powell drove his committee into relentless work. Powell's greatest triumph was passage of the Civil Rights Act of 1964, Title VI of which made the Powell Amendment the standard for all federal laws. Education bills, poverty relief bills, and other social legislation were driven through Powell's committee.

Even so, his brashness, his condescension toward colleagues, and his flirtations with the Republican Party made him powerful political enemies. In 1960, during a televised interview in which Powell named some people in New York who allegedly were involved in graft, he mentioned Esther James as a "bag woman"—that is, someone who took payoffs from gangsters and delivered them to the police. James sued for slander and, in spite of her long criminal record, she won. Powell ignored the judgment, then later appealed it, to no avail.

Powell had a long history of love affairs, often putting his wives and lovers on the congressional payroll. He and his staff often took vacations to exotic locales on taxpayer money. In January 1967 the Democratic leadership moved that Powell not be seated in the House of Representatives; a subsequent vote overwhelmingly denied him his seat. Powell was the first committee chair to be removed from the House in 160 years.

A special election was held in Harlem and Powell again won, without even campaigning. In June 1969 the U.S. Supreme Court ruled that the House of Representatives acted unconstitutionally and ordered Powell to be seated. Even so, the House leadership stripped him of his seniority and fined him $25,000. In 1970 the Harlem congressional district was gerrymandered again so as to include areas of upper west Manhattan that were unfriendly to Powell, and he lost his reelection bid by just over two hundred votes.

Powell, living with his common-law wife, Darlene Expose Hine, since 1966, took up residence in Bimini in the Bahamas for tax purposes. He resigned the pastorate of Abyssinian Baptist Church in April 1971. Powell finished his autobiography, *Adam on Adam* (1971), the same year. He died at the age of sixty-three of complications from surgery for prostate cancer in Jackson Memorial Hospital in Miami. His body was flown to New York and viewed at the Abyssinian Baptist Church. Powell was cremated and his ashes scattered over the waters on Bimini's coast.

Always hostile to Powell, the *New York Times* declared in an obituary that Powell "leaves no lasting heritage"—nonsense even in 1972. Title VI of the Civil Rights Act of 1964 alone has reshaped the American workplace, fostered minority businesses, and increased minority employment. Without Powell's efforts, civil rights legislation of any type might have been another decade in coming.

★

There is no single archive of Powell's papers, but his book *Keep the Faith, Baby!* (1967) is a collection of his sermons and speeches. Powell's autobiography, *Adam by Adam: The Autobiography of Adam Clayton Powell, Jr.* (1971), is the best resource for details about his family background and early life. Biographies include James Haskins, *Adam Clayton Powell: Portrait of a Marching Black* (1974); Robert Jakoubek, *Adam Clayton Powell, Jr.* (1988); and Charles V. Hamilton, *Adam Clayton Powell, Jr.: The Political Biography of an American Dilemma* (1991). Contemporary works on Powell include Claude Lewis, *Adam Clayton Powell* (1963); Neil Hickey and Ed Edwin, *Adam Clayton Powell and the Politics of Race* (1965); Gil and Ann Chapman, *Adam Clayton Powell: Saint or Sinner?* (1967); P. Allen Dionisopoulos, *Rebellion, Racism, and Representation: The Adam Clayton Powell Case and Its Antecedents* (1970); and Kent M. Weeks, *Adam Clayton Powell and the Supreme Court* (1971). Biographical information is also in Andy Jacobs, *The Powell Affair: Freedom Minus One* (1973), and E. Curtis Alexander, *Adam Clayton Powell, Jr.: A Black Power Political Educator* (1983). Wil Haygood, *King of the Cats: The Life and Times of Adam Clayton Powell, Jr.* (1993), is written in an eloquent, vibrant style that suits its subject. Obituaries are in the *New York Times* (5 Apr. 1972), *Washington Post* (6 Apr. 1972), *L'Express* (10 Apr. 1972), and *Time* and *Newsweek* (both 17 Apr. 1972).

KIRK H. BEETZ

POWERS, Francis Gary ("Frank") (*b.* 17 August 1929 in Burdine, Kentucky; *d.* 1 August 1977 in Encino, California), pilot of the ill-fated U-2 reconnaissance flight over the Soviet Union on 1 May 1960 who was captured and later released in the first Soviet-American spy swap.

Powers was the sixth child and only son of Oliver Powers, a coal miner who managed a shoe-repair shop and worked in a defense plant, and Ida Ford, a housewife. He took his first airplane ride at the age of fourteen. Powers attended Grundy High School in Pound, Virginia. His father wanted him to become a physician and had him enroll in a premedical program at Milligan College, a church school near Johnson City, Tennessee. Powers dropped out of the program in his junior year but continued to study biology and chemistry. He graduated in June 1950, then enlisted in the U.S. Air Force, achieving the rank of first lieutenant in 1952.

Powers married Barbara Gay Moore in April 1955. He hoped to pilot commercial airliners after his enlistment expired in December 1955, but he was recruited to work for the Central Intelligence Agency (CIA). In January 1956 the CIA asked Powers to fly the Lockheed U-2 reconnaissance aircraft, which was designed for high-altitude flights to observe foreign military installations. The agency offered him the then-considerable sum of $2,500 a month. Powers flew a U-2 over the eastern Mediterranean in autumn 1956, monitoring the Anglo-French buildup prior to the invasion of the Suez Canal. The body of the shiny aircraft was so thin that a workman who bumped his tool kit against the plane left a four-inch dent. Technicians joked that the aircraft was made from Reynolds Wrap.

The U-2 had a ceiling of 20–21 kilometers, while Soviet fighters could not exceed 15–17 kilometers. Longer-range Zenith rockets had entered the Soviet arsenal in 1960. There were about twenty U-2 flights between 1956 and 1960, with the U-2s flown in circular paths, exiting the Union of Soviet Socialist Republics (U.S.S.R.) at different points. Powers was the first to fly in a line that could be plotted by Soviet radar. On 1 May 1960 he began his most famous mission: a nine-hour, 3,788-mile flight from Peshawar, Pakistan, over the missile launch site at Tiuratom in the Soviet Union. Powers was to pass Sverdlovsk and photograph the missile base under construction at Plesetsk before landing at Bodø, Norway. His aircraft, number 360, had experienced fuel-tank problems and made an emergency landing in Japan in September 1959. During his 1960 flight Powers had problems controlling the pitch of the plane.

Three missiles were fired at Powers's U-2 over Sverdlovsk. The first exploded near the aircraft, causing it to lose altitude, and the second hit the plane. The tail and both wings flew off. Without pressurization, pinned by G forces, and being strangled by his oxygen hoses, Powers somehow managed to bail out. A third missile, shot from a MiG-19, destroyed another Soviet fighter trying to intercept the U-2.

Powers's flight was the last U-2 mission scheduled before a summit between President Dwight D. Eisenhower and Soviet premier Nikita Khrushchev in Paris in May

Francis Gary Powers testifying before the Senate Armed Forces Committee, 1962. © BETTMANN/CORBIS

1960. The leaders had planned to discuss a limited test-ban treaty, the first major agreement of the cold war. On 5 May, Khrushchev told the U.S.S.R. Supreme Soviet that an American plane had been shot down. Although the summit was cancelled, Khrushchev apparently wanted it to go ahead and blamed the spy flight on Pentagon militarists who had acted without Eisenhower's knowledge.

When Powers's U-2 disappeared, U.S. officials wrongly assumed that he was dead and the plane had been destroyed. They did not know Powers had been captured on a collective farm near Sverdlovsk. After sixty-one days of interrogation in Moscow's Lubianka Prison, he went on trial for espionage on 17 August 1960. The audience at the Hall of Trade Unions exceeded 1,000 people. Powers was convicted and sentenced to ten years in prison, and transferred to a jail in Vladimir, Russia, in September 1960. The wreckage of his U-2 aircraft was exhibited in the chess pavilion at Gorkii Park, and later was piled in a corner of the Central Museum of the Armed Forces of the U.S.S.R. in Moscow.

On 10 February 1962 Powers was exchanged for the Soviet spy Rudolf Ivanovich Abel in the first Soviet-American "spy swap." Khrushchev claimed that, because he delayed Powers's release until after the 1960 U.S. presidential election, the Republican candidate Richard Nixon failed to benefit from improved Soviet-American relations, and John F. Kennedy was able to clinch his narrow election victory.

Once back in the United States, Powers found work with the CIA in Virginia, but he soon resigned and later joined Lockheed in Burbank, California. He obtained a divorce from his first wife in January 1963 and married Claudia ("Sue") Edwards Downey, a CIA employee, on 24 October of the same year. Powers adopted his seven-year-old stepdaughter, and the couple had a son in 1965. Powers chronicled his U-2 experience in the book *Operation Overflight* (1970). He lost his job at Lockheed, and in the 1970s worked as a traffic-watch pilot for KGIL radio in Los Angeles, at an aircraft communications company, and as a reporter for KNBC.

Powers died at the age of forty-seven when his aircraft ran out of fuel and crashed on a baseball field in Encino. Boys playing on the field felt he had maneuvered his helicopter to spare their lives. Although Powers had received broad public criticism in 1960 for not committing suicide after he was captured by the Soviets, President Jimmy Carter granted permission for him to be buried in Arlington National Cemetery in Virginia.

Powers has been depicted as unexceptional and unlucky. An obituary characterized him as "a human element necessary only until robot satellites would come along." Indeed, the day Powers was sentenced, the United States recovered the first film from a spy satellite whose cameras had photographed more territory than all the U-2 missions combined. However, reconnaissance from U-2s proved crucial during the 1962 Cuban Missile Crisis, and these aircraft were still in use during the 1991 Gulf War.

The early U-2 flights disclosed that the Soviets did not enjoy superiority in bombers or missiles, allowing U.S. leaders to allocate resources more prudently. The historian Michael Beschloss has written that the flights may have persuaded Moscow to accept arms control, since Soviet leaders could no longer bluff about enjoying a strategic advantage. They also eased fears among Americans that Washington did not know or care what was happening in the Soviet Union. In his memoirs Eisenhower called the U-2 incident involving Powers insignificant compared to the information gained from the flights.

★

The best books about the May 1960 U-2 incident and this period in U.S.–Soviet relations include Francis Gary Powers and Harold H. Burman, trans., *The Trial of the U-2: Exclusive Authorized Account of the Court Proceedings of the Case of Francis Gary Powers, Heard Before the Military Division of the Supreme Court of the U.S.S.R., Moscow, August 17–19, 1960* (1960); David Wise and Thomas B. Ross, *The U-2 Affair* (1962); Dwight D. Eisenhower, *Waging Peace, 1956–1961* (1965); Francis Gary Powers with Curt Gentry, *Operation Overflight: The U-2 Spy Pilot Tells His Story for the First Time* (1970); James Bamford, *The Puzzle Palace: A Report on America's Most Secret Agency* (1982), and *Body of Secrets: Anatomy of the Ultra-secret National Security Agency from the Cold War Through the Dawn of a New Century* (2001). See also John Prados, *The Soviet Estimate: U.S. Intelligence Analysis and Russian Military Strength* (1982), and Michael R. Beschloss, *Mayday: Eisenhower, Khrushchev, and the U-2 Affair* (1986). An obituary is in the *New York Times* (2 Aug. 1977).

JOHN L. SCHERER

Elvis Presley. CORBIS CORPORATION (BELLEVUE)

PRESLEY, Elvis Aron (*b.* 8 January 1935 in East Tupelo, Mississippi; *d.* 16 August 1977 in Memphis, Tennessee), the "King of Rock and Roll," the symbol of youthful rebellion in the 1950s, and one of the most commercially successful singers and movie stars of the 1960s.

Presley was the son of Vernon Presley, a truck driver, and Gladys Smith, a homemaker. His twin brother was stillborn. The family moved to Memphis in 1948, where Presley graduated from L. C. Humes High School in 1953. Blending country, blues, gospel, and bluegrass music, Presley made his first recordings in 1954 for Sun Records. Some of his early songs were regional hits. In 1955 Presley's new manager, Colonel Tom Parker, negotiated a recording contract with RCA Records. With "Heartbreak Hotel," "Don't Be Cruel," and other number-one hits the following year, Presley became an international figure and the first major rock-and-roll star.

Presley's career was at its peak when he was drafted into the U.S. Army in 1958. While he served in West Germany, RCA regularly released songs that he had recorded before his induction. Discharged in March 1960, Presley wondered, as did both fans and critics, whether he would maintain his popularity. He did. His first nationwide appearance after his discharge came that year on a Frank Sinatra tele-

vision special that drew a 67 percent share of the viewing audience. His first new single, "Stuck on You," was a number-one hit in April. "It's Now or Never," "Are You Lonesome Tonight?," and "Surrender" all reached number one on the charts over the next year. "It's Now or Never," adapted from a 1916 recording of "O Sole Mio," by the operatic tenor Enrico Caruso, reflected Presley's musical eclecticism and desire to experiment with new styles.

Despite his continued success, Presley soon turned in a new direction. He made two successful films, *G. I. Blues* and *Flaming Star,* in 1960. After a concert in March 1961, he gave up doing live performances to concentrate on movies. For most of the rest of the decade, films, in which he typically appeared as a bland, unthreatening hero, drove his career. These movies—known as "Elvis films" and a genre unto themselves—appeared to embrace the very mainstream culture that Presley's musical performances had supposedly once threatened. In 1962 U.S. motion-picture exhibitors ranked him the fifth most popular star. Presley was soon earning $500,000 per film plus 50 percent of the profits. By 1964 he was regularly making three pictures a year and was probably the highest-paid performer in Hollywood. Among Presley's twenty-seven films of the 1960s were *Blue Hawaii* (1961), *Follow That Dream* (1962), *Kid Galahad* (1962), *Viva Las Vegas* (1964), and *Frankie and*

Johnny (1966). Made quickly and on tight budgets, the films were usually profitable, although not distinguished. Each movie produced a soundtrack album. Nine were gold records, but Presley's singles, which were taken from the soundtracks, were less successful. Twenty-five Presley singles appeared on the *Billboard* pop charts from 1963 through 1968, but only three of them reached the top ten.

Presley married Priscilla Beaulieu on 1 May 1967. A daughter, Lisa Marie, was born on 1 February 1968. In 1968 Presley taped a television special that included his first performances before a live audience in seven years. Airing in December, it was the top-rated show of the year and helped revitalize Presley's recording career. "In the Ghetto"—an atypical (for Presley) song of social conscience—reached number three in the summer of 1969. "Suspicious Minds," Presley's last number-one song, topped the pop chart in November. He was the only performer to have number-one songs in both the first and last years of the 1960s. According to *The Billboard Book of Top 40 Hits,* Presley's chart success in the 1960s was second only to that of the Beatles.

The triumphant television special, especially Presley's energetic performance before a live audience, pointed the way to a new phase in his career. After a decade making movies, in which the public was increasingly less interested, he turned to concerts. His month-long engagement in Las Vegas in July 1969 earned him more than $1 million. Presley made no movies after 1969, except for two concert documentaries. One of them, *Elvis on Tour* (1972), won a Golden Globe Award for best documentary. During the 1970s Presley's career was marked by frequent public performances and increasing reclusiveness. He and Beaulieu separated in 1972 and divorced the next year. Presley died at Graceland, his Memphis home, as a result of various physical ailments, including obesity and heart disease, which had been exacerbated by drug abuse. Although he avoided hard drugs, he had taken large quantities of prescribed pills for years. Presley is buried at Graceland.

To say, as many critics do, that Presley's cultural significance waned in the 1960s says as much about one's standards for cultural significance as it does about Presley's achievements. It is more precise to say that his cultural significance changed with the times. In the 1950s, as the first great rock star, Presley and his music suggested rebellion against blandness and conformity. In the 1960s he seemed increasingly irrelevant to those who wanted to push cultural boundaries further and to use music as a form of political protest. Yet mainstream and conservative America—to which Presley's music and movies often appealed—was as much a part of the 1960s as the counterculture. Presley himself recognized and, to an extent, embraced his new cultural position. He took pride in his selection by the Junior Chambers of Commerce (Jaycees)

in 1970 as one of the ten most outstanding young men in America.

Meeting with President Richard M. Nixon that same year, Presley expressed his aversion to hippies, drugs, and the radical groups Students for a Democratic Society and Black Panthers. He affirmed his patriotism and his support of the president, and volunteered to become an undercover narcotics agent for the U.S. government. Presley's most influential period came in the mid-1950s, when he, more than any single performer, helped make rock and roll the most popular form of music of the latter half of the twentieth century. The Elvis of the 1960s demonstrated how thoroughly this supposedly dangerous music, and its greatest star, could be absorbed by mainstream culture.

★

The first volume of Peter Guralnick's definitive biography, *Last Train to Memphis: The Rise of Elvis Presley* (1994), covers Presley's early years. On Presley's life in the 1960s and 1970s, see Peter Guralnick, *Careless Love: The Unmaking of Elvis Presley* (1999). Ernst Jorgensen, *Elvis Presley: A Life in Music* (1998), has an exhaustive discussion of Presley's recorded music. Joel Whitburn, *The Billboard Book of Top 40 Hits,* available in several editions, provides information on Presley's charted singles. For information on Presley's films, consult Steve and Boris Zmijewsky, *Elvis: The Films and Career of Elvis Presley* (1991). An obituary is in the *New York Times* (17 Aug. 1977).

FRED NIELSEN

PRIDE, Charles Frank ("Charley") (*b.* 18 March 1938 in Sledge, Mississippi), the first African American inducted into the Country Music Hall of Fame (2000), who had thirty-six number-one hit singles and sold over twenty-five million albums.

Pride was one of eleven children born to Mack Pride, Sr., and Tessie B. Stewart, who were poor sharecroppers. Pride's hometown was a small cotton town sixty miles south of Memphis, Tennessee, in an area famous for its cultivation of blues music. Pride's father worked a forty-acre farm, where the five-year-old Pride labored in the cotton fields, following the rhythmic routine of chopping and picking cotton. Weekend recreation was frugal and elemental, the high point being near the family radio listening to the Saturday night live broadcasts from the home of country-and-western music, the Grand Ole Opry in Nashville, Tennessee. Pride adored this style of music and eagerly sought to model the melodies and technical skills of stellar country-and-western performers, especially Hank Williams, Ernest Tubb, Roy Acuff, and Eddie Arnold.

By the time he was fourteen Pride had enough money in his savings account to order a $10 Silvertone guitar from

Charley Pride, 1966. ASSOCIATED PRESS AP

the Sears, Roebuck catalog. Years later he recalled the excitement of receiving the package from Sears: "I opened it up, lifted it in my hands and strummed my first chords. That minute, I was the happiest kid in Mississippi."

Pride explored various avenues to escape the drudgery of the cotton field. The year he received his guitar was the same year he determined to launch his career as a high school baseball player. His hero and role model was Jackie Robinson, who broke Major League Baseball's color barrier in 1947 by joining the Brooklyn Dodgers. The teenager, perhaps unconsciously, may have seen more opportunities in baseball—even if it was only the Negro Leagues—than in music. In the early 1950s the Grand Ole Opry was exclusively white, and entertainers of color, such as the blues harmonica player De Ford Bailey, did not have their contracts renewed.

Pride graduated from Sledge Junior High School. In 1955 he headed for Memphis and the Negro American League, in which African-American entrepreneurs created an informal network of clubs and set them to work within well-organized leagues. The league's urban stadiums drew packed audiences, white and black, and Pride was one of many young African-American men who, during the years of segregation, saw in sports one of the few activities that offered the chance to win fame and riches. Pride played for Detroit, the Birmingham Black Barons, and Memphis, and did well, with ten home runs and a hitting average of .367. His career in baseball was interrupted by military service from 1956 to 1958, and by his marriage to Rozene Cohran

on 28 December 1956, but resumed with the Memphis Red Sox. In 1959 Pride resigned over a pay dispute, but a year later signed with a semiprofessional team in Great Falls, Montana. Then, after an unsuccessful tryout for the Los Angeles Angels in February 1961, Pride returned to Montana.

In some respects the early 1960s must have reminded Pride of his hard days in the cotton fields. To survive he worked in a Helena, Montana, zinc smelter, played semiprofessional ball in the Pioneer League, and did occasional stand-up one-man musical shows at local bars. Ann Malone comments: "He became very popular with the locals, singing straight country without a back-up band, developing an easy, low-key style, and chatting about baseball with the cowboys between sets."

Pride's breakthrough came at a 1963 show in Helena, when the country-and-western stars Red Savine and Red Foley heard him sing "Heartaches by the Number" and told him to take his act to Nashville. Although Pride still dreamed of a career in baseball, his tryout at a New York Mets training camp in the spring of 1963 was a disaster.

Pride's attempts throughout the 1960s to launch a music career have to be seen against a national backdrop of civil rights demonstrations. Pride did not seek to perform in his home state, which in 1964 saw the murder of three young civil rights workers who were part of a voter-registration drive in the South. That same year Pride signed with the Cedarwood Publishing Company and started to record music tapes, testing the waters to see if his sound and songs could be a commercial success. Racism thwarted Pride's career. Even after a successful recording session with RCA Victor in 1965, and despite astute direction from musical entrepreneurs, Pride received favorable responses only up to the point at which "[his] picture [photograph] was produced." One adviser even suggested that Pride should promote himself as a singer of color, change his name to George Washington Carver III, wear a fancy outfit, and label himself not as country-and-western but as a one-of-a-kind novelty act.

Pride persevered, rejecting such advice. Nevertheless, the manner in which he advanced his career is in no small part due to the astute skills of his manager Jack Johnson and the record producer Jack Clement. In 1965 they persuaded RCA executives to sign Pride to a recording contract by playing down Pride's race. During the early months of his recording career, songs like "Snakes Crawl at Night" and "Atlantic Coastal Lane" were promoted as traditional country songs from a typical, albeit unknown, singer. By the time Pride was revealed to be an African American, music fans had already come to enjoy his rich, smooth baritone.

Pride's acceptance by a vast white audience was facilitated to a greater rather than a lesser extent by the fact that Pride produced a careful, middle-of-the-road form of entertainment. Pride's stage performance threatened no one; he seemed refreshingly all-American; he joked about his "permanent tan" and acted deferentially to his conservative, mostly white audiences.

By 1966 Pride was able to give up his job at the smelter and had a Grammy nomination for "Just Between You and Me." On 7 January 1967 Ernest Tubb, one of the founding fathers of country-and-western music, introduced Pride to an enthusiastic capacity crowd at the Grand Ole Opry, and that same year the Country Music Association voted him the most Promising Male Artist. As the decade ended a national group of disc jockeys voted Pride Number One Male Artist of the Year (1969).

Between 1969 and 1971 Pride had six consecutive chart-toppers. In 1971 at the Country Music Association award show at the Grand Ole Opry, Pride was named Entertainer of the Year and Male Vocalist of the Year. In 1994 Pride opened the Charley Pride Theatre in Branson, Missouri. His performance of "Roll on Mississippi" was considered the official song of his home state, and a stretch of highway there has been named after him.

Social historians of the 1960s have tended to ignore the place, position, and impact of Pride. He seemed divorced from, and uninvolved with, those African Americans who sought a new social order. However, Pride's accomplishments from 1960 to 1970 mark a milestone in the story of people of color. What Pride did is an important piece of a larger cultural canvas, peopled by African Americans such as the activist Rosa Parks, who challenged discrimination in public transportation; Dr. Martin Luther King, Jr., who marched into Montgomery; and the boxer Muhammad Ali, who railed against U.S. involvement in the Vietnam War. All energized the long march towards racial justice in the United States.

★

Pride's autobiography, *Pride: The Charley Pride Story* (1994), written with Jim Henderson, is especially revealing about his early life and his attempts to break into Major League Baseball. A biographical sketch by Ann Malone, "Charley Pride," is in Bill C. Malone and Judith McCulloh, eds., *Stars of Country Music* (1975). Colin Larkin, ed., *The Guinness Encyclopedia of Popular Music*, vol. 3 (1992), gives an extensive list of Pride's recorded music albums. Pride is listed in Dick Clark and Larry Lester, eds., *Negro League Book* (1994).

SCOTT A. G. M. CRAWFORD

PRYOR, Richard Franklin Lenox Thomas (*b.* 1 December 1940 in Peoria, Illinois), comedian, actor, writer, and director who is one of the most influential American comedians and the first African-American artist to successfully address racial issues in his acts in the 1960s.

Pryor was born to Leroy "Buck Carter" Pryor, a construction worker, and Gertrude Thomas. Pryor's father married Thomas three years after his birth, but their marriage lasted only a few years. Pryor grew up in Peoria with his grandmother Marie Carter Bryant, who owned several brothels. A caring and tough woman, Pryor's grandmother often disciplined him.

Pryor did not achieve much academically. In junior high school he behaved incorrigibly and was a frequent truant. In his autobiography Pryor stated that he was kicked out of Catholic school when school officials learned about his grandmother's occupation. Pryor found a positive role model in Juliette Whittaker, a teacher at Carver Community Center in Peoria. In the eighth grade he left school; some sources say he was expelled from school for striking a teacher, but others say he dropped out of school. He joined the U.S. Army in 1958, serving in West Germany, but was discharged after two years. He then worked briefly at the Caterpillar Tractor Company.

Pryor returned to Peoria in 1960 and married Patricia Price, the first of his five wives. They had a son, Pryor's second child, but split afterward. (His first child, a daughter, had been born three years earlier.) Pryor began his stand-up comic career in a Peoria nightclub, Harold's, in the early 1960s. He was not the first African American to succeed as a stand-up comedian; Bill Cosby and Dick Gregory, among others, had already enjoyed success. Pryor

Richard Pryor (*right*), with Flip Wilson during a comedy sketch on *The Flip Wilson Show*. AP/WIDE WORLD PHOTOS

became a unique comic when he created a bold new comedic character, turning black American life into humorous performance art. In the 1960s, when many black comedians were gently trying to pry open the color barriers, Pryor was rising quickly in the entertainment business.

Pryor moved to New York City, where he performed stand-up comedy in Harlem and Greenwich Village in 1963. Inspired by the success of Cosby, he modeled jokes in the same fashion, avoiding politics and race to appeal to white audiences. In 1964 Pryor made his television debut on *Rudy Vallee's Summer Variety Show,* in the series entitled "On Broadway Tonight." His appearances on *Merv Griffin* (1965) and *Kraft Music Hall* helped him to enter the entertainment mainstream. Pryor was also featured on *The Ed Sullivan Show,* the first of his many performances on the legendary program. By the mid-1960s his reputation as a comic had spread, making him one of the industry's hottest stars.

In 1966 Pryor appeared in his first film, *The Busy Body,* and in early 1968 he worked at the Village Gate in New York City, one of the few clubs that did not object to his new material. Although his professional successes continued to mount, with Grammy Award–winning record albums and critically acclaimed performances in Las Vegas, New York City, and Hollywood, Pryor was becoming increasingly erratic and unstable. His alcohol and drug abuse, along with numerous affairs, had started to take its toll on his stage appearances, leading to a breakdown in Las Vegas in 1967. In 1968 Pryor played bit parts in the movies *Wild in the Streets* and *The Green Berets.* His first album, *Richard Pryor* (1969), is considered a collector's item. Pryor also acted in two films in 1969, *The Young Lawyers* and *Carter's Army,* and continued to perform before live audiences in Las Vegas. The end of the 1960s brought Pryor two more children (with Maxine Silverman) and one more failed marriage (to Shelly Bonus). Pryor was also audited by the Internal Revenue Service (IRS) for nonpayment of taxes between 1967 and 1970, and was sued for battery by his third wife, Deborah McGuire, for shooting bullet holes into her car.

Pryor won his first important movie role in 1970, when he portrayed Billie Holiday's piano player in *Lady Sings the Blues,* a role that earned him an Academy Award nomination for best supporting actor. In the early 1970s Pryor started writing screenplays and contributed his writing talents to the film *Blazing Saddles* (1974) and television shows such as the *Flip Wilson Show* and *Sanford and Son.* His script for the television special *Lily Tomlin* (1973) earned him an Emmy Award, a Writers Guild Award, and an American Academy of Humor Award.

In the mid-1970s Pryor's career was skyrocketing, and he produced three more albums, *That Nigger's Crazy* (1974), *Is It Something I Said?* (1975), and *Bicentennial Nigger*

(1976), which won Grammy Awards. Pryor married Shelley Bonus in 1967 and divorced in 1970, briefly married Deboragh McGuire in 1977 and divorced in 1978, and then married Jennifer Lee in 1979 but divorced in 1981.

In 1980, at the pinnacle of his success, Pryor was critically injured in a fire while freebasing cocaine at his residence. In 1984 he had a son with Flynn BeLaine, whom he married in 1986 but divorced a few months later. The couple remarried in 1990, had another child, and divorced later. His 1986 film *Jo Jo Dancer, Your Life Is Calling,* which Pryor cowrote, directed, starred in, and produced, was a semiautobiographical tale of his troubled life. The onset of multiple sclerosis in 1986 and quadruple heart bypass surgery in 1991 left Pryor debilitated.

Pryor is one of the most honored African-American entertainers in history, having earned four Grammy Awards for comedy albums, one Emmy Award, and two American Academy Humor Awards. He received the inaugural Mark Twain Prize for American humor in 1998, an MTV Films Lifetime Achievement award in 2000, and a star on the Hollywood Walk of Fame in 1993. His hometown, Peoria, honored Pryor by naming a street after him.

Pryor's life is a tragic story of a talented personality who took a path of self-destruction, a comedian who drew laughs from his own misfortunes but was powerless to change his habits. In spite of his checkered reputation, Pryor is an enormously gifted comic, actor, and writer who is remembered for his brilliance, influence, and for breaking barriers in the industry.

★

Pryor's autobiography is *Pryor Convictions and Other Life Sentences* (1995), written with Todd Gold. It details his difficult childhood, career, failed marriages, substance abuse problems, and multiple sclerosis. Biographies of Pryor include: Joseph Nazel, *Richard Pryor: The Man Behind the Laughter* (1981); Ronald Haver, *Richard Pryor: The Legend of a* Survivor (1981); Fred Robbins and David Ragan, *Richard Pryor: This Cat's Got Nine Lives* (1982); Jeff Rovin, *Richard Pryor: Black and Blue* (1983); Jim Haskins, *Richard Pryor: A Man and His Madness, A Biography* (1984); and John A. Williams and Dennis A. Williams, *If I Stop I'll Die: The Comedy and Tragedy of Richard Pryor* (1991). Other biographical information is in David Schumacher, "Richard Pryor in His Own Words," *Entertainment Weekly* (30 Apr. 1993).

NJOKI-WA-KINYATTI

PUSEY, Nathan Marsh (*b.* 4 April 1907 in Council Bluffs, Iowa; *d.* 14 November 2001 in New York City), first non–New Englander to become the president of Harvard University, who facilitated the institution's rapid growth and in 1969 responded to a student takeover of University Hall by having the students forcibly removed by police.

Pusey's father, John Marsh Pusey, died when Pusey was a baby, leaving his mother, Rosa Drake Pusey, to raise three children on a schoolteacher's wages. In the 1920s Pusey won a scholarship to Harvard College in Cambridge, Massachusetts; strapped by the conditions of his grant, he was a dedicated student in the otherwise rowdy and glamorous period of the jazz age. He earned an A.B. from Harvard in 1928, an M.A. in 1932, and a Ph.D. in 1937, specializing in fifth-century Greece and Athenian democracy. Pusey then taught history and literature at Scripps College in Claremont, California (1938–1940), and classics at Wesleyan University in Middletown, Connecticut (1940–1943). He was the president of Lawrence College in Appleton, Wisconsin, from 1944 to 1953 and was appointed as the president of Harvard in 1953, serving in that role until 1971.

As the president of Harvard, Pusey attempted to democratize private higher education by admitting more students from less privileged backgrounds. He strove to improve every facet of Harvard life and spearheaded the college's first major fund-raising effort. His efforts raised national awareness that U.S. colleges were under-funded. During his tenure, Harvard's endowment grew from $304 million to more than $1 billion, and eight new buildings were constructed. Pusey also was a defender of academic freedom. He preferred for teachers to "grow as persons rather than to become educational technicians." He said that, if Americans were to move into global leadership roles, "there will be tragedy and frustration and failure ahead if [they are] anything less than liberally educated [in the classical sense]."

In the early 1960s the Harvard professors Richard Alpert and Timothy Leary tested Pusey's tolerance by introducing LSD, peyote, and psilocybin to students through funded research into induced psychosis and consciousness-raising. They also popularized several themes that outlived the 1960s: challenging conventions and mores; identifying human behavior as "games"; and promoting the right of individuals to internal freedom—the notion of research "cells," communes conceived of as single-family units, and expanding consciousness. While engaging in a tenuous and lengthy dialogue with the administration, health officials, law enforcement, and students, Alpert and Leary stimulated student fascination with and the proliferation of loosely controlled psychedelic substances. They repeatedly flaunted administration warnings until Pusey fired Alpert in 1963 for violating an agreement not to furnish the substances to students. Leary's appointment was allowed to expire. The *Harvard Crimson* said, "In firing Richard Alpert, Harvard has disassociated itself not only from flagrant dishonesty but also from behavior that is spreading infection throughout the academic community."

Pusey supported peaceful and orderly dissent, but he censured a "small group of over-eager young . . . who feel they have a special calling to redeem society." In his president's report for 1966 to 1967, he called these protesters "self-possessed revolutionaries" who were "Walter Mittys of the left." Opposed to any Harvard involvement with the Vietnam War effort or initiatives that appeared to oppress the poor, student protestors conducted a series of demonstrations beginning in the autumn of 1966 and culminating in April 1969. This series of clashes between various factions at Harvard culminated in a violent student takeover of University Hall, the administration building.

In the pre-dawn hours of 9 April 1969, approximately 500 members of Students for a Democratic Society (SDS) and antiwar protesters descended on Pusey's home at Harvard. They shouted anti–Reserve Officers Training Corps (ROTC) slogans and pinned a list of demands to Pusey's front door with a knife. By mid-morning the SDS had taken over the administration building, physically ousting several deans and administrators, and threatened to occupy the building until their demands were met. By 8:00 P.M. Pusey had issued a statement, saying, "Can anyone believe the Harvard SDS demands are made seriously?"

The Harvard student population opposed the methods used by the protesters, but in a controversial move Pusey called in the police. That decision elicited sympathy for the protesters from an otherwise unsympathetic student body. At 5:00 A.M. on 10 April, 400 state and local policemen, armed with riot gear and accompanied by paddy wagons, removed 250 protesters. Forty-five of them were injured, and Pusey's response to the takeover was characterized in the press as panic stricken and extreme. According to the author Roger Rosenblatt, who was an English instructor at Harvard in April 1969, "Mr. Pusey unleashed at least two centuries of town-grown hatred" by calling local police to "bust" the protesters. However, Pusey maintained that student violence could not be allowed to interfere with the university's normal daily functions.

Pusey's declining popularity was evidenced by the fact that only sixty-three seniors attended the 1970 baccalaureate, during which he addressed "extremist splinter groups of the New Left [who] would like to see our colleges and universities denigrated, maligned, or even shut down." Pusey served as the president of Harvard until 1971, when he left to take a post as the president of the Andrew Mellon Foundation. He was appointed as the president emeritus of Harvard in 1971. Pusey died of heart disease in 2001 at the New York Weill Cornell Medical Center. He left his wife, Anne Woodward, two sons, and a daughter.

Rosenblatt described Pusey as "establishment . . . in spades. . . . His face was an institution itself—handsome, monumental, and implacable." He recalled the summation of Pusey's relationship with the student demonstrators given by Martin Peretz, then a Harvard assistant professor of government: that the smug sense of order shown in

Nathan M. Pusey *(center)*, shown with Edward M. Kennedy *(left)* and Robert F. Kennedy *(right)* at a December 1963 press conference announcing the creation of the President John F. Kennedy Memorial Library © Bettmann/Corbis

Pusey's face may have antagonized the rebellion. Rosenblatt said Pusey looked like a "police artist's sketch of a good-looking man." While Pusey's inclination to rise above the fray made him appear distant and unemotional, his colleagues described him as wise, kind, decent, and dedicated to teaching and to Harvard. He was the embodiment of the aspirations and conventions of his middle-class generation, as well as an icon of classical liberalism. Revolutionaries saw him as an unflappable, unyielding, "straight" bureaucrat. In his attempts to preserve the freedom that cultivated independence and inventiveness, Pusey articulated the reality that freedom depended upon certain unyielding constraints.

★

Pusey's observations on teaching and religion may be found in his *The Age of the Scholar: Observations on Education in a Troubled Decade* (1963). Contextual sources include Roger Rosenblatt, *Coming Apart: A Memoir of the Harvard Wars of 1969* (1997). See also Andrew T. Weil, "The Strange Case of the Harvard Drug Scandal," *Look Magazine* (5 Nov. 1963). Obituaries are in the *Harvard Gazette* (15 Nov. 2001) and the *Economist* (24 Nov. 2001).

Leri M. Thomas

PUZO, Mario (*b.* 15 October 1920 in New York City; *d.* 2 July 1999 in Bay Shore, New York), novelist and screenwriter whose book *The Godfather* was not only one of the best-selling novels published in the 1960s, but changed the way Americans thought of organized crime.

Puzo was one of seven children born to railroad trackman Antonio Puzo and Maria Le Conti, both born in Italy.

Growing up in Hell's Kitchen on the west side of Manhattan, he yearned to escape his working-class background, and later said that, while he was tempted to join up with the criminals in his neighborhood, his family kept him out of trouble. He served in World War II with the U.S. Army Air Corps, attaining the rank of corporal.

From the time he was in high school, Puzo had dreamed of becoming a writer. After the war, he made a step toward this dream by taking advantage of the G.I. Bill to take courses at the New School for Social Research and Columbia University, both in New York City. He married Erika Lina Broske, with whom he would have five children, in 1946.

After years of minor jobs and freelance writing, Puzo published his first novel, a tale of postwar Germany called *The Dark Arena,* in 1955. A second work, *The Fortunate Pilgrim,* appeared in 1964. Both books received favorable reviews but earned a total of only $6,500. In debt, with a wife and children to support, Puzo talked an editor at G. P. Putnam's Sons into offering him a $5,000 advance for a novel about the Italian-American underground, a book he correctly saw as his opportunity for fame and fortune.

Published in 1969, *The Godfather* was an immediate success, and spent sixty-seven weeks on the *New York Times* best-seller list. Moreover, Fawcett Books bought the paperback rights for an unprecedented $410,000, and Paramount immediately obtained the film rights.

The book was not merely a best-seller; it was a phenomenon. It offered an apparently authentic look into the secretive world of the Italian-American criminal organization known as the Mafia. Puzo always insisted that he was far from a Mafia insider and that he wrote the book from gossip and research rather than firsthand knowledge.

The Godfather is a multifaceted work. It has many standard best-seller ingredients, including copious violence and a famously explicit sex scene in the very first chapter, as well as a character almost universally thought to be based on Frank Sinatra. Yet it also offers a richness of character, a multiplicity of subplots, and a level of descriptive detail far beyond that expected from the typical popular novel. The book has been accused of glorifying crime, but it unflinchingly describes the violence its characters commit. Rather than treating these criminals as simple villains*, The Godfather* describes them as complex people, motivated by family loyalty and respect, as well as by the desire for material gain.

The title of the book is ambiguous. At the beginning it refers to the old Godfather, Don Vito Corleone. We learn of the don's immigrant origins, living among criminals first in Sicily and then in America, losing his father and some friends to organized crime, finally killing an extortionist in self-defense and being moved to take the man's place and run organized crime right. He steps into the traditional businesses of bookmaking and loan sharking, and when the government is foolish enough to outlaw alcohol, he profits from that. He always starts out trying to reason with people, shunning gratuitous threats or violence, but if that fails, he will kill to protect his interests. He has principles: for instance, he draws the line at participating in the heroin trade, a stand that puts him in opposition to some of the other crime families and thus motivates much of the action in the book.

The Godfather is the tale of a family, as well as of an individual. Corleone has three sons, and he wants them to continue in the business. However, Sonny, the eldest, is rash; Fredo is weak; and the Ivy Leaguer Michael wants no part of organized crime. The father is ambivalent about Michael's feelings. He wants to move the family out of crime, as many billionaires have done—the book's epigraph is Honoré de Balzac's "Behind every great fortune there is a crime"—yet he knows that this cannot be done overnight.

An attempt on the old don's life by rival crime families impels Michael to join the fight, killing another family's leader and a corrupt cop. He is forced to hide out in Sicily for years, but eventually he returns and becomes the Godfather upon his father's death, moving the family closer to the final goal of legitimacy and respectability; nevertheless, he is still willing to kill those he considers threats.

Francis Ford Coppola wound up making *The Godfather* into three movies, with Puzo serving as coauthor for all three screenplays. Puzo also contributed to the screenplays for the first two Superman movies (1978, 1980) and *Christopher Columbus: The Discovery* (1992). He had stated that

Mario Puzo. Mr. Jerry Bauer

the money he made from *The Godfather* would enable him to write a great serious novel, but though *Fools Die* (1978) sold well, it was generally considered a disappointment, badly organized and long-winded. Puzo published two other novels—*The Sicilian* (1984) and *The Fourth K* (1991)—then returned to the scene of his greatest triumph with two last tales of Mafia leaders, *The Last Don* (1996) and *Omerta* (2000), generally considered to have many of the strengths of *The Godfather*. He died of heart failure shortly after completing *Omerta*.

Puzo changed society's view of the Mafia with a single book. Paradoxically enough, this supposed glorification of crime is a conservative, law-and-order tale. The Godfather's values include family, loyalty, and trust, but also vigilante justice and keeping women in their place. It begins with an honest man who had feared the Godfather turning to him because the thugs who had brutally beaten his daughter were not punished by legitimate authority, whereupon the Godfather has them beaten (though not killed). It ends with the proud, intelligent woman Michael married submitting to the traditional role of the Mafia wife: taking care of the children and going to church every morning to pray for her husband's soul.

★

Puzo's papers are kept at Boston University, Boston, Massachusetts. He never wrote a full autobiography, but memoirs of his early life and of the writing and later success of *The Godfather* are found in his essay collection, *The Godfather Papers and Other Confessions* (1972). He was interviewed in *Publishers Weekly* (12 July 1978): 10–12. James Hall discusses *The Dark Arena* in *Rediscoveries,* edited by David Madden (1971). An obituary by Mel Gussow is in the *New York Times* (3 July 1999).

ARTHUR D. HLAVATY

PYNCHON, Thomas Ruggles, Jr. (*b.* 8 May 1937 in Glen Cove, Long Island, New York), award-winning author whose novels exploring the influence of science, technology, racism, and authority on twentieth-century society are among the most important postmodern works written in English.

Very little is known about Pynchon's life. Since the early 1960s he has led a secretive existence, known only to a few friends and his publishers, all of whom refuse to reveal anything about the author. Pynchon's insistence on anonymity may stem simply from shyness; on the other hand, he may want his literature to stand alone, with no opportunity for readers or critics to compare his works and his personal life.

Pynchon, the son of Thomas Ruggles Pynchon, Sr., an industrial surveyor, and Katherine Frances Bennett, was the eldest of three children. The prominent family included historically important ancestors in both England and colonial America. Pynchon graduated from Oyster Bay High School, on Long Island, New York, as salutatorian of his class in 1953; he also received honors in English. His photograph in the high school yearbook was for decades the only known likeness. He entered Cornell University in the fall of 1953 and declared a major in engineering physics. Although he transferred to the College of Arts and Sciences during his sophomore year, Pynchon reputedly retained a strong interest in physics. His determination to maintain personal privacy began during his freshman year, when he refused to be photographed for the school's registry. In 1955 Pynchon enlisted in the U.S. Navy. While ashore at his home base in Norfolk, Virginia, Pynchon dated Anne Cotton. The two may have married, although no evidence for the marriage exists.

In 1957 Pynchon left the navy and returned to Cornell, where he took courses in literature, including at least one from the acclaimed author Vladimir Nabokov, and worked for a school literary magazine. He graduated with honors in 1959 with a bachelor's degree in English. He lived in Greenwich Village in New York City for one year, but moved to Seattle in 1960. In Seattle, Pynchon worked for the Boeing Corporation as a technical writer until Septem-

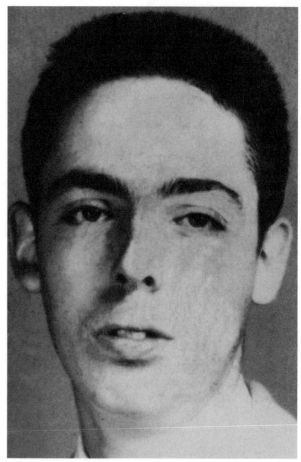

Thomas Pynchon. CORBIS CORPORATION (BELLEVUE)

ber 1962. Since leaving Boeing, Pynchon has been accessible only to the people closest to him, although he is known to have lived for a time in both California and Mexico. Pynchon's short stories and occasional articles won him some critical attention, but his reputation rests on five novels: *V.* (1963), *The Crying of Lot 49* (1966), *Gravity's Rainbow* (1973), *Vineland* (1990), and *Mason and Dixon* (1997). *V.* hit the literary market like a bomb and became one of the most celebrated novels of its time. It fascinated general audiences and puzzled critics with its dazzling humor, intricate narrative structure, and bizarre characters.

The novel takes its title from a woman, the "V." of the title, who never actually appears but is the obsession of the other characters, especially the narrator, Herbert Stencil, and his father, Sidney. V., a treacherous spy involved in various mysterious conspiracies, is dead when the novel opens. As she moved about the world, she became more of a machine than a human being, as her body parts were replaced with artificial ones, including a glass eye with a clock in it. At once absurd, funny, and frightening, *V.* represents the continuing dehumanization of people by their technological culture. A parallel plot describes picaresque moments in the life of Benny Profane, whose lack of focus stands in ludicrous contrast to Stencil's compulsion.

Stencil's quest for V. requires the retelling of several brutal historical events, such as the German genocide of the inhabitants of southwest Africa. Although the timeline for events is confused, it is plain that human cruelty increases during the twentieth century and that, like V. herself, people are increasingly becoming parts of machines. V.'s ambitious scope offers a satirical yet profoundly serious account of the decline of Western civilization. Pynchon links the decline to entropy, one of Isaac Newton's laws of thermodynamics. As society becomes ever more mechanical and people become like objects, so does the physical law of entropy subject them to relentless decay. V. received the William Faulkner Foundation Award for best novel of 1963.

While working on his second novel, Pynchon wrote a short story, "The Secret Integration" (1964), and an essay, "A Journey into the Mind of Watts" (1966). Both works reflect on racism and civil rights. In the short story children invent a fantasy world in which there are no separate races. In the essay Pynchon studies the effects and motivations for the violence that attended the 1965 riots in the Watts neighborhood of Los Angeles, suggesting that the violence was a form of communication.

The Crying of Lot 49, a straightforward narrative, is Pynchon's most generally accessible work. A protagonist with the richly suggestive name of Oedipa Maas stumbles upon the existence of a secret, subversive group, the Tristero, when she is named the executor of an estate. For hundreds of years the Tristero have used their own mail service in an effort to subvert civilization. They drop their mail in special trash cans labeled "Waste" (We Await Silent Tristero's Empire), and they kill people who interfere with them. When an acting company stages an Elizabethan revenge play, *The Courier's Lament,* the director drowns under mysterious circumstances. The plot implies that he was murdered, apparently because the play provides details of Tristero operations during the Elizabethan era. Oedipa Maas glimpses evidence of the Tristero's operations everywhere, especially in San Francisco, where the group's activities pervade all aspects of the city's life.

As in *V.,* entropy signals the decline of society in *The Crying of Lot 49.* Oedipa Maas's limited ability to distinguish reality from illusion symbolizes the decay. Since the Tristero adeptly avoid detection by most people, Oedipa Maas doubts that what she sees is true. Yet Pierce Inverarity, the stamp collector for whose estate Maas is responsible, used to call Oedipa Mass on the telephone and speak to her in different voices each time. His behavior suggests that there is reality behind her strange experiences. The Tristero, if they exist, seem very interested in Inverarity's stamps, and the novel ends with Oedipa Maas attending the auction of the stamps, hoping finally to uncover the

Tristero as they try to obtain the collection. *The Crying of Lot 49* won the Richard and Hilda Rosenthal Foundation Award of the National Institute of Arts and Letters.

Through the 1970s Pynchon seems to have moved back and forth between California and New York, followed by a long stay in California in the 1980s. *Gravity's Rainbow* is considered Pynchon's most accomplished work and has been compared to *Ulysses* and *Moby Dick.* Despite its length and complexity, the book became popular and won the National Book Award, which Pynchon declined. The Pulitzer Prize nominating committee unanimously recommended that *Gravity's Rainbow* receive the award for fiction in 1973, but the editorial board condemned the novel as obscene and refused to give Pynchon the award.

In the 1990s Pynchon continued to move about the United States while writing novels. The *Times* (London) claimed in 1997 to have sighted Pynchon in New York and photographed him, although it is not certain that they found their man. His reputation grew from year to year, with his novels becoming staples of college literature courses. Many literary critics believe that, by the end of the 1960s, Pynchon had already established himself as a major writer and that his publications thereafter made him one of the world's most accomplished novelists. They note how his blending of science and satire deepens his themes. Moreover, they acclaim his insight into how reliance on technology can complicate life without changing fundamental human experience, as in the discovery that the journey is more important than the goal in *V.* Pynchon's wordplay and satire lend a dimension of pleasure to his novels and make reading them a Shakespearean experience—the rare achievement of combining merriment with serious thought.

★

In his introduction to the collection of his short stories *Slow Learner* (1984), Pynchon reveals some of his thinking behind his early fiction. For information about Pynchon's early career, see Mathew Winston, "The Quest for Pynchon," *Twentieth Century Literature* 21 (Oct. 1975): 278–287. Jim Baird's essays "The Crying of Lot 49" (vol. 2) and "V." (vol. 8), in *Beacham's Encyclopedia of Popular Fiction* (1996), offer good explanations of characterization and theme in each novel.

KIRK H. BEETZ

QUILL, Michael Joseph ("Mike") (*b.* 18 September 1905 in Gourtloughera, Kilgarvan, County Kerry, Ireland; *d.* 28 January 1966 in New York City), labor leader and longtime head of the Transport Workers Union who crippled New York City in 1966 by shutting down the subway and bus systems during a mass transit strike.

Born to Roman Catholic farmers, John Daniel Quill and Margaret Lynch, Quill was the second youngest of eight

Michael Quill, December 1961. © BETTMANN/CORBIS

children. After leaving Kilgarvan National School at the age of fourteen, he joined the Irish Republican Army as a dispatch carrier. When Great Britain gave the southern part of Ireland independence, and "The Troubles" ended, Quill decided to emigrate and flipped a coin to pick his new home. America won.

Arriving in New York City in 1926, Quill found a job as a night gateman on the Interborough Rapid Transit (IRT) subway line and soon rose to the position of agent. From 1929 to 1935, when twelve-hour, seven-day workweeks were common, Quill worked in almost every station on the IRT circuit, thereby gaining a wide acquaintance with the subway workers and learning their grievances. In 1934 he helped found the New York–based Transport Workers Union (TWU), a Communist-backed group created to address poor pay and dangerous working conditions. He became president of the union in 1935, a position that he would hold for the remainder of his life. Known for his quick wit and aggressive, outspoken personality, Quill used militant rhetoric to achieve gains for workers. He became a U.S. citizen in 1931, and married Maria Theresa ("Mollie") O'Neill on 26 December 1937; they had one son. After years of taking orders and money from Moscow, Quill publicly repudiated the Communists in 1948. As the TWU expanded, he cemented his position as a labor leader in 1949 by becoming a national vice president of the Committee for Industrial Organizations, or CIO (later AFL-CIO).

When the 1960s opened, Quill was in the twilight of his life. Rank-and-file members had begun to protest his compromises with the New York Transit Authority (TA) by withholding their dues, while splinter unions emerged in New York to challenge his authority. Mollie had died in 1959, and Quill's health had been on the decline since a 1950 heart attack. Now nearly bald, with a gray fringe of hair, blue eyes, and a round face, and a chronic limp from a faulty hip joint, Quill walked with a trademark silver-tipped black cane and spoke with a strong Irish brogue. On 20 January 1961 he married his longtime secretary, Shirley Garry.

Believing that walkouts hurt workers as well as the public, and that they never assured a higher settlement for labor, Quill, despite his rhetoric, always preferred to settle instead of strike. In 1961, however, he led his first strike. In September he shut down the nation's largest rail carrier, the Pennsylvania Railroad, for the first time in its 114-year history, to get better working rules for maintenance workers. Idling over 10,000 miles of track across 13 states, the strike lasted 12 days and prompted 6 governors and 11 mayors to call for its end. After resolving their differences, both sides claimed victory.

Although the TWU had branches in many cities, most of Quill's activity focused on New York City. Every two years, with the New York City TWU contract due to expire, Quill and the mayor of the day would engage in the same charade. Quill would loudly demand the sky for his membership, threaten to shut down the public transportation system, quietly negotiate, and then accept a far less costly settlement.

Unfortunately for New York, changes in the political climate brought an end to this arrangement. In 1965 John Lindsay won the mayoral election. Quill and Lindsay lacked any understanding of each other. To Lindsay, Quill was a corrupt, irresponsible man who periodically bullied the city and needed to be put in line. He wanted to do away with Quill's inflationary and pressure-packed deals every two years. Often booed when visiting union meetings, Quill's hold upon his membership had become tenuous, and he worried about his legacy. He thought that the union's survival could only be assured by the experience of a good strike. Disliking the patrician Lindsay, Quill believed that the new mayor had contempt for the working class.

The TWU contract with the Transit Authority expired at midnight, 31 December 1965. Following the November 1965 election, Quill began contract negotiations with a list of seventy-six demands that included proposals for a four-day work week and a 30 percent pay raise that would cost the city an estimated $250 million over a two-year period. By law, transit expenses could only be covered by fares, and the fare would have to jump from fifteen cents to a politically unacceptable forty-seven cents to satisfy the workers. As usual, Quill's demands exceeded the package that he was willing to accept. Lindsay refused to join the negotiations and sent Quill a telegram urging him to bargain in good faith with the TA commissioners. An insulted Quill publicly categorized Lindsay as a "coward." The TA made one offer, rejected as inadequate by Quill, and the TWU declared a strike to begin on the day Lindsay took office, 1 January 1966.

As scheduled, all buses and subways stopped. New York traffic, normally heavy, became so congested that few commuters could get to work. Schools shut down and business losses were estimated at $100 million a day. With freight trains from the city halted, the strike also had nationwide impact. By this time, Quill's health was in serious decline, but he ignored a doctor's order to go to the hospital. On 3 January New York State Supreme Court Justice Abraham Geller ordered Quill to halt the strike by 11 A.M. the next day or go to jail for civil contempt of court. On 4 January Quill was arrested when he arrived at the bargaining table. While awaiting a medical examination at the jail, he fainted and was moved to Bellevue Hospital for treatment of congestive heart failure. On 13 January the TWU, with a membership of 135,000, won a $62 million settlement with the city that included a 15 percent wage hike recognizing the cost of living increases generated by the Vietnam War. Quill left the hospital and returned to his apartment on 24 January, but died there on 28 January of coronary occlusion. His wake at the Plaza Funeral Home drew about 14,000 mourners. Following a funeral at St. Patrick's Cathedral on 1 February, Quill was buried in the Gate of Heaven Cemetery in Westchester County, next to his first wife.

The man that many loved to hate, Quill is remembered as one of the most controversial labor leaders that the United States has ever produced. In the 1960s he managed to achieve the impossible by bringing New York City to an almost complete stop and, in the process, cemented his legacy as a protector of the American working class.

★

Quill left no collection of personal papers, but union papers and some of Quill's papers and interview transcripts are held at the Transport Workers Union Collection at the Robert Wagner Archives at New York University. Two biographies of Quill are L. H. Whittemore, *The Man Who Ran the Subways: The Story of Mike Quill* (1968), and Shirley Garry Quill, *Mike Quill—Himself: A Memoir* (1985). Biographical information is also in Michael Marmo, *More Profile Than Courage: The New York City Transit Strike of 1966* (1990), and at the TWU Web site at http://www.twu.com. An obituary is in the *New York Times* (29 Jan. 1966).

CARYN E. NEUMANN

QUINN, Anthony Rudolph Oaxaca (*b.* 21 April 1915 in Chihuahua, Mexico; *d.* 3 June 2001 in Boston, Massachusetts), Academy Award–winning actor who was prominent during the 1960s for his work in such landmark films as David Lean's *Lawrence of Arabia* and Michael Cacoyannis's *Zorba the Greek.*

Quinn was the eldest of two children born to Francisco (Frank) Quinn and Manuela (Nellie) Oaxaca. The elder Quinn, son of an Irish father and Mexican mother, had fought for Pancho Villa. After becoming a migrant worker, he relocated the family several times before settling in 1920 in East Los Angeles. After Quinn's father died in a car accident in 1926, his mother eventually married Frank Bowles, but Quinn and his sister preferred to reside with their paternal grandmother.

Quinn took on a variety of jobs and activities, including boxing, and continued schooling off and on at Belvedere Junior High School and Polytechnic High School, where his interest in art and architecture resulted in first prize for a supermarket design. This resulted in a meeting with famed architect Frank Lloyd Wright, who suggested that Quinn undergo corrective surgery to improve his diction. According to Quinn, he himself was unaware of any speech defect until Wright commented that Quinn was stammer-

Anthony Quinn. ARCHIVE PHOTOS, INC.

ing somewhat and on closer observation concluded that Quinn's frenum (the fold of skin under the tongue) was too thick and needed minor, corrective surgery. (A successful architect also must make impressive verbal presentations, Wright had advised.) After the surgery, Quinn began speech therapy with Katherine Hamil at her drama school. After the therapy, Quinn decided to become an actor, and joined the Gateway Players, in which he met Hollywood director George Cukor.

After a role in *Clean Beds* (1934) attracted good notices, Quinn made a brief but impressive appearance in *Parole!* (1936). A part in Cecil B. DeMille's *The Plainsman* (1937) led to a player's contract with Paramount Studios, and ultimately to Quinn's first marriage: near the set, he met DeMille's adopted daughter Katherine, whom he married on 21 October 1937. In 1941 Quinn's two-year-old son Christopher darted from the family property and drowned in W. C. Fields's nearby pool (Zorba experienced a similar tragedy in Kazantzakis's tale).

The brown-eyed, six-foot, three-inch Quinn presented a rugged, vigorous, and dignified demeanor readily adaptable to a variety of ethnic roles. In 1940 Quinn, refusing to renew his contract, tripled his salary with Warner Brothers Studios, where his first film was *City for Conquest* (1940), with James Cagney and Elia Kazan. He became a U.S. citizen in 1947, the year of his Broadway debut in *The Gentleman from Athens*. Major theatrical success developed when Kazan asked him to play Stanley Kowalski on the 1948 national tour of Tennessee Williams's *A Streetcar Named Desire*.

Quinn had several major film successes in the 1950s, as evidenced by his two best supporting actor Academy Awards for his portrayals of Eufemio Zapata in *Viva Zapata!* (1952), and of Paul Gauguin in *Lust for Life* (1956). He won international fame, and a Venice Film Festival award, as the carnival strongman Zampano in Federico Fellini's *La Strada* (1954), and received an Academy Award nomination for best actor in *Wild Is the Wind* (1957).

During the 1960s Quinn appeared in more than a dozen films. He costarred as Andrea Stavros in the World War II action story *The Guns of Navarone* (1961), filmed primarily in Greece. (Quinn, who purchased property on the island of Rhodes, became an honorary Greek citizen). He played the Bedouin Auda Abu Tayi in the award-winning epic *Lawrence of Arabia* (1962), and appeared as a boxer named Mountain Rivera in Rod Serling's *Requiem for a Heavyweight* (1962). Releases in 1964 included *The Visit,* with Ingrid Bergman; *Behold a Pale Horse,* with Gregory Peck; and *Zorba the Greek,* with Alan Bates, Irene Papas, and Lila Kedrova.

The latter, through which Quinn became forever identified with the role of Alexis Zorba, was based on a Nikos Kazantzakis novel that had first been transformed unsuccessfully into a 1968 Broadway work. Quinn's volatile and earthy personality and robust intensity, as well as his acute acting sensibilities and his "ethnic" bearing, credibly transformed him into Zorba. His on-screen Zorba represented the universal archetype of a carefree character surviving life's alternating currents of extreme joys and hardships by recharging himself with a simple dance on the sands of life. Although *Zorba the Greek* won the Academy Award for best picture, and Quinn was nominated for best actor, the latter award went to Rex Harrison for *My Fair Lady.*

Another major role for Quinn in the 1960s was that of *Barabbas* (1962), in a different type of biblical epic, a genre still popular during that decade. During the shooting, Quinn met a young Italian costume designer, Iolanda Addolori, and later publicly acknowledged their first son, born in 1963. After the birth of their second son in 1964, Quinn divorced DeMille in Juarez, Mexico (January 1965), and married Iolanda on 2 January 1966 at his agent's Beverly Hills home. Later that year, their third son was born. By that point, Quinn's primary residence was a villa outside Rome. Some columnists at the time suggested that Quinn's disruptive personal life cost him Academy votes for the Zorba role.

Other films of the 1960s included Quinn as a priest in *Guns for San Sebastian* (1968), as a fictional Russian-born Pope Kiril I opposite Laurence Olivier in *Shoes of the Fisherman* (1968), and as the mayor in *The Secret of Santa Vittoria* (1969). In November 1968 the Museum of Modern Art in New York exhibited a collection of stills from his career. Important Broadway work during the 1960s included Quinn's portrayal of King Henry II opposite Olivier in Peter Glenville's production of Jean Anouilh's *Becket* (1960 to 1961), as well as the frothy *Tchin-Tchin* (1962), with Margaret Leighton. In June 1969 Quinn placed his handprints in the cement walkway outside of Grauman's Chinese Theater in Hollywood.

Quinn continued to work on films—some very popular at the box-office—through the 1990s, and left a legacy of more than one hundred film appearances. He returned to the United States in 1993, and during most of his final years, made Bristol, Rhode Island, his home base. He lived with his young former secretary, Kathy Benvin, eventual mother of two children by him, and divorced Addolori in 1997. Quinn died of respiratory failure in a Boston hospital and was buried on the Quinn estate in Bristol, Rhode Island. At the time of his death, he was survived by four of his five children with De Mille (who died in 1995); three children with Addolori; two with Benvin; one by an unnamed French woman; and two by a German woman.

The mature Anthony Quinn was a film actor whose name assured moviegoers and television viewers of a memorable performance—usually by a forceful, masculine presence whose frequently gruff attitudes sheltered a sensitive core of emotions. At other times, he portrayed a weak, sentimental man who somehow found inner moral fortitude at the moment of crisis. His proficiency as an actor was especially acute during the 1960s, with his flexibility to dominate the screen, with a seemingly effortless manner, in a variety of powerful, virile portrayals. *Zorba the Greek* left its mark upon the film legacy of the 1960s, and Quinn's Zorba towers as a classical figure cast in a contemporary mode.

★

Autobiographies of Quinn are *Original Sin: A Self-Portrait* (1972), and *One Man Tango* (1995), with Daniel Paisner. Biographical works include Alvin H. Marill, *The Films of Anthony Quinn* (1975), and Melissa Amdur, *Anthony Quinn,* Hispanics of Achievement Series (1993). Among many articles and reviews, see Judy Klemesrud, "From Zapata to Zorba to the Pope to . . .?," *New York Times* (20 Sept. 1970). Obituaries are in the *New York Times* and *Washington Post* (both 4 June 2001).

MADELINE SAPIENZA

R

RADO, James (*b.* 23 January 1939 in Los Angeles, California), and **Gerome RAGNI** (*b.* 11 September 1942 in Pittsburgh, Pennsylvania), *d.* 10 July 1991 in New York City), actors, librettists, and lyricists who cowrote the groundbreaking and controversial 1968 musical *Hair: The American Tribal Love-Rock Musical,* the first to show the counterculture to mainstream audiences.

Rado, born James Radomski, was one of two sons of Alex Radomski, a professor and sociologist. Rado began his theatrical career in college and was known as a "consummate musician" who dreamed of becoming a Broadway composer. He moved to New York City when he was in his early twenties and supported himself by writing pop music, performing in summer stock theater, and doing office work. His career blossomed after studying Method acting with Lee Strasberg, and he appeared in a succession of Broadway shows, including *Marathon '33* (1963) and *The Lion in Winter* (1966).

Ragni, the son of Lawrence Ragni and Stephanie Williams, was born into a large Pittsburgh family; he had five brothers and two sisters. A stubborn and creative child, he showed interest in theater in high school and college. Ragni attended both Georgetown University and Catholic University in Washington, D.C., but did not graduate. Determined to become a stage actor, he moved to New York City when in his early twenties and quickly became involved in experimental and traditional theater. He helped organize

the Open Theater from 1962 to 1963 and performed in a number of shows, including *Hamlet* (1964) on Broadway, and *Viet Rock* (1966) off Broadway. In 1963 he received the Barter Theater Award for best young actor and married Stephanie Williams on 18 May; the couple had one son.

Ragni and Rado met while performing in *Hang Down Your Head and Die* (1964) and the Chicago production of *The Knack* (1965). Ragni introduced Rado to experimental theater, and together they yearned to develop stage techniques that would present important social issues to mainstream audiences. As Rado said, "we wanted to create . . . something that translated to the stage the wonderful excitement we felt in the streets." Although both young men were "straight" in appearance—clean-shaven and short-haired—they shared strong antiwar sentiments and were intrigued by the Greenwich Village counterculture. For the next two years, Ragni and Rado spent time observing hippie ways of life in Greenwich Village, a type of research that sociologists call *participant observation,* and from these behavioral observations the seeds of *Hair: The American Tribal Love-Rock Musical* were planted.

By 1966 Ragni and Rado had written the first draft of the musical. Although the show evolved substantially, the central characters and message were apparent. *Hair* was a nearly plotless collection of sketches and songs about a group of New York City hippies. The main characters are Claude Hooper Bukowski, a middle-class dropout; George Berger, the charismatic leader; and Sheila, a New York

University student protester and Berger's erstwhile girlfriend. In the first act, Claude questions whether to evade the draft (for the Vietnam War), and the tribe criticizes representatives of the establishment, including parents and school officials. The second act revolves around a party for Claude, who has decided to go to war. Claude eventually dies in Vietnam, a martyr to the middle-class establishment's mistaken values.

In 1966 Joseph Papp of the New York Shakespeare Festival made *Hair* the opening piece at New York's Public Theater. Galt MacDermot, a Canadian composer, was enlisted to write the electrified score. Director Gerald Freedman, who insisted on considerably editing the script, clashed relentlessly with Ragni and Rado. Although the authors were unhappy with the changes, the show opened on 17 October 1967 as a success. However, its run was limited to six weeks.

By this time, the show had come to the attention of Michael Butler, an experienced theatrical producer who was determined to get *Hair* on Broadway. Avant-garde director Tom O'Horgan replaced Freedman. Ragni, Rado, and MacDermot added thirteen songs, which downplayed the antiwar theme, focusing on the free-love, antiracist, prodrugs, hippie lifestyle symbolized in the song that now opened the show—"Aquarius."

The new show, which used experimental theater techniques unknown on Broadway, premiered at the Biltmore Theatre on 29 April 1968. Ragni, with his crown of brown curls and flashing eyes, took the role of Berger; wispy-blond Rado played Claude; and then-unknowns Diane Keaton and Melba Moore rounded out the racially mixed cast.

Mainstream critics universally praised *Hair*. Michael Smith wrote in the *Village Voice*, "I should simply report that something downtown, dirty, ballsy, and outrageous has hit Broadway at last." *Hair* influenced Broadway musical theater in a variety of ways. As well as being the first rock musical, it was one of the first "concept" musicals, in which a theme, such as hippie life, drives the show rather than a traditional plot. Controversially, it was the first Broadway production to show full-frontal nudity, which embroiled the show in court cases across the country. Most importantly, it was the first to deal with contemporary issues, including the Vietnam War and the generation gap. In contrast to the praise of the mainstream press, the alternative press roundly critiqued *Hair* for sugarcoating hippie life to make it palatable to middle-class tastes.

Hair earned Grammy Awards for best Broadway roadway show album and best score in 1968, and for record of the year for 1969 for Ragni and Rado, who were briefly barred from the show by Butler in 1969 for objectionable onstage behavior. The original cast album for *Hair* and the single "Aquarius/Let the Sun Shine In" both became gold records. *Hair* continued for 1,742 performances on Broad-

way, closing on 1 July 1972 after earning net profits of more than $6 million and using more than 1,000 performers during its run. At the same time as the Broadway run, local companies adapted the show, performing it for an estimated 20 million people worldwide. In 1970 *Newsweek's* Jack Kroll called *Hair* "the greatest global cultural event of the '60s." In 1979 Oscar-winning director Milos Forman adapted *Hair* into a motion picture. Ragni and Rado wrote a screenplay, but Forman chose to use a version by Michael Weller, which added a coherent structure to the musical. Although the film did moderately well, Ragni and Rado both distanced themselves from it, feeling the changes, including having Berber switch places with Claude and dying in Vietnam in Claude's place, had ruined the meaning of the original.

After *Hair*, Ragni and Rado parted ways. In 1972 Rado wrote a musical called *Rainbow* that followed Claude after his death to "Rainbow Land." Ragni's post-*Hair* project, *Dude, the Highway of Life* (1972), was a plotless retelling of the Genesis story (with a 2,000-page script) that closed after sixteen performances. Ragni died of cancer in 1991. Rado was involved in a revival of *Hair* that played at the City Center in New York City in 2001.

Both Ragni and Rado will be remembered as the creators of the quintessential expression of countercultural life, *Hair*. Although the show skewered the politics and mores of the establishment, it was thoroughly popular with audiences, introducing them to the countercultural ideology of free love and peace.

★

For biographical information and a recounting of the history of *Hair*, see Lorrie Davis and Rachel Gallagher, *Letting Down My Hair: Two Years with the Love Rock Tribe—From Dawning to Downing of "Aquarius"* (1973); Stanley Richards, ed., *Great Rock Musicals* (1979); and Barbara Lee Horn, *The Age of Hair: Evolution and Impact of Broadway's First Rock Musical* (1991). Obituaries for Ragni are in the *New York Times* (13 July 1991) and the *Los Angeles Times* (15 July 1991).

MARY RIZZO

RAFFERTY, Maxwell Lewis, Jr. ("Max") (*b.* 7 May 1917 in New Orleans, Louisiana; *d.* 13 June 1982 in Troy, Alabama), prominent conservative educator and California State Superintendent of Public Instruction whose flamboyant oratory during the 1960s stirred education reform.

Rafferty, an only child, was the son of Maxwell Lewis Rafferty, Sr., owner of a paint and wallpaper store, and DeEtta Cox. Growing up in the Great Depression, he learned to read, with the help of his mother, at the age of three. When his father's paint business failed in 1931, the family moved

Max Rafferty. ASSOCIATED PRESS AP

from Sioux City, Iowa, to southern California, where his father found work in an auto plant. Rafferty graduated from Beverly Hills High School when he was sixteen, two years younger than his peers. He attended the University of California, Los Angeles (UCLA), where he managed the football and rugby teams and served as president of the Sigma Pi fraternity. He also belonged to the UCLA Americans, a conservative campus organization that served as a balance to its left-wing counterparts. In 1938 Rafferty graduated with a C + average and a B.A. in history.

After working at a gas station for a short time, Rafferty returned to UCLA to become a teacher. In his view, however, the UCLA School of Education was full of John Dewey's progressives, whose philosophy he viewed as a denial of "positive eternal values," and whose stress on "life adjustment and group acceptance" he believed to be at the expense of individualism and curriculum content. An ardent anticommunist, Rafferty was concerned about the "grim reality of Red military force and the crafty cunning of Red psychological warfare."

Rafferty's first job as an educator was in the Trona Unified School District in California, where he taught English and history and coached the football team from 1940 to 1948. He married Frances Longman in 1944. The couple had a son and two daughters.

After serving as principal of Big Bear High School in Big Bear Lake, California, from 1948 to 1951, Rafferty became superintendent of the Saticoy School District. He meanwhile continued his education, receiving an M.A. from UCLA in 1940 and an Ed.D. in educational administration from the University of Southern California in 1956. In 1955 Rafferty became the new superintendent of the Needles, California, school system, where he raised academic standards, added a new variety of textbook, boosted teachers salaries, instituted programs for gifted students, built a strong athletic program, and raised funds for scholarships for Mexican American and Native American children.

In 1961 Rafferty was hired as the superintendent of La Canada, California, school district. His first speech before the La Canada school board proved to be a turning point in his career. In this speech, "The Passing of the Patriot," he blamed his generation of educators for having been "so busy educating for 'life adjustment' that they forgot that the first duty of a nation's schools is to preserve that nation." As a solution, he proposed returning patriotism to education, making "our young people informed and disciplined and alert—militant for freedom, clear-eyed—to the filthy menace of Communist corruption . . . and happy in their love of country." The speech was widely distributed to right-wing groups including the Citizen's Advisory Committee on Education, which urged Rafferty to run for state superintendent of public instruction in 1962.

Rafferty's opponent, Professor Ralph Richardson of the University of California, had the almost unanimous backing of the educational establishment in California, but Rafferty had strong support from conservative groups, and in public debates he scored heavily over Richardson. Rafferty took the election by a margin of 219,844 votes, and was reelected in 1966 with a landslide of almost three million votes. Rafferty feuded with the liberal state board of education, especially over books that he wanted banned. But his conservative philosophy of education had little real impact because of the checks and balances and local control built into the California school system. The state's schools were never as progressive as Rafferty claimed.

Rafferty's speeches to education groups and civic clubs, as well as his articles written during these years, expressed his contempt for progressive education. In a 1967 speech to the Jaycees at the Yolo County Fairgrounds, Rafferty observed: "We're in the Sick Sixties Syndrome. We are a sick society. We are bored . . . bored stiff. With all the sex stimulants we have, we should be raked up all the time. The faster jets fly, the faster people go crazy. The more LSD we have to war off boredom the more bored we get. It all boils down to apathy." His speeches soon won the admiration of the growing John Birch Society. In accordance with his philosophy, grammar texts were returned to the elementary grades of California's schools, and programs in compensatory education were instituted for potential dropouts. Rafferty's opposition never wavered. He later noted, "After more than two decades in this Alice-in-Wonderland profession, I am more convinced than ever that the fastest and simplest way to learn about Eskimos in Alaska is to read about them and discuss them, not to construct harpoons and eat whale blubber."

In 1967 a Riverside, California, realtor named Dick Darling formed a committee of conservative Republicans interested in unseating liberal senator Thomas H. Kuchel in the 1968 Republican primary. The committee selected Rafferty. Campaigning as an opponent of the "four deadly sins" of violence, pornography, drugs, and lawlessness, Rafferty took fifty percent of the total vote and beat Kuchel by 66,635 ballots. In the general election against liberal Democrat Alan M. Cranston, former controller of California, Rafferty stressed the theme of law and order as "the one great issue." He blamed racial unrest on unemployment and promised to support tax cuts or rebates for businesses providing jobs for inner-city dwellers. Rafferty lost to Cranston.

Rafferty proved to be a great opponent of progressive educational policies, arguing with his "fire and brimstone" style for a return in schools to discipline, patriotism, and the "three Rs." His essays criticizing progressive education were brought together in a book entitled *Suffer, Little Children* (1962). In a stunning upset, Rafferty was defeated in 1970 in his third reelection bid for superintendent by Wilson Riles, a black educator whom he had appointed his deputy. He left California in 1971 to become the dean of education at Troy State University in Troy, Alabama. He drowned as a result of a car accident in 1982 and was buried in Green Hills Memorial Park in Troy.

★

There is one biography on Rafferty: Paul F. Cummins, *Max Rafferty: A Study in Simplicity* (1968). Insight into Rafferty's controversial views on education can be found in his books, including *Suffer, Little Children* (1962), *What They Are Doing to Your Children* (1964), *Max Rafferty on Education* (1968), and *Classroom Countdown: Education at the Crossroads* (1970). An informative article is "School Critic Max Rafferty (1917–1982) and the New Right," *Review Journal of Philosophy and Social Science* 10, no. 2 (1985).

REED MARKHAM

RAGNI, Gerome. *See* Rado, James, and Gerome Ragni.

RAND, Ayn (*b.* 2 February 1905 in Saint Petersburg, Russia; *d.* 6 March 1982 in New York City), author, lecturer, and philosopher whose stories of individualistic heroes in pursuit of personal wealth and happiness made her one of the best-selling writers of the 1960s.

Rand was born Alissa Zinovievna Rosenbaum, daughter of Fronz Rosenbaum, a chemist, and Anna (Borisnova) Rosenbaum, a teacher. As youngsters, Rand and her two sisters witnessed the Russian revolution and its social upheaval. In 1924 at the age of twenty-one, the aspiring writer graduated from the University of Petrograd with a bachelor's degree with honors in philosophy and history and entered the State Institute for Cinema Arts to study screenwriting.

In 1926 Rand moved to the United States and changed her name. *Ayn* she took from the name of a Finnish writer, *Rand* from her Remington-Rand typewriter. In Hollywood she worked as an extra and a scriptwriter. She married Frank O'Connor, an actor, on 15 April 1929.

In the 1930s and 1940s Rand devoted her life to writing novels. Her first novel, *We the Living,* was published in 1936, followed by the novella *Anthem* in 1938. The *Fountainhead* (1943), whose hero, Howard Roark, was the Randian ideal man, a man as "he could be and ought to be," became a best-seller in 1945. Her novel *Atlas Shrugged* (1957) made her a household name in the 1960s.

Atlas Shrugged, at over 1,000 pages long, contains the bases of Rand's philosophy, Objectivism, which she elaborated and publicized throughout the 1960s. Objectivism states that man is a heroic being, with his own happiness

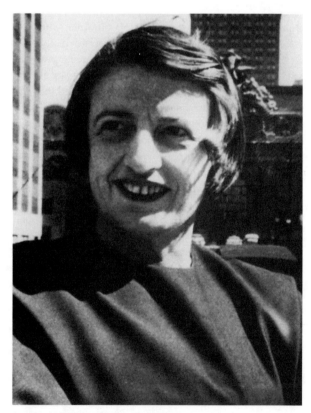

Ayn Rand. AP/WIDE WORLD PHOTOS

the purpose of life, productive achievement his noblest activity, and reason his only absolute. Objectivism preached for the complete deregulation of business and the abolition of welfare and any other institution devoted to altruism. One line from the novel, "Who is John Galt?", became a password for Rand's devoted fans, who called themselves Randroids in the 1960s. The novel gained her international fame and millions of new readers. She became the most successful author of propaganda fiction.

While the reading public was devouring Rand's novels in the 1960s, she gained few admirers in philosophical circles. Most philosophers objected to her belief that selfishness was good and altruism evil, that the good of the group should be subordinated to the self-interest of the individual. Rand thrived on the negative publicity. An unabashed advocate of capitalism, she often wore a gold brooch and pendant in the shape of a dollar sign. At the end of *Atlas Shrugged*, the triumphant antihero John Galt "raised his hand and over the desolate earth" and "traced in space the sign of the dollar." Many critics claimed that Rand's readers had taken on the status of cultists with her as the godhead. Bennett Cerf, the head of Random House, which published *Atlas Shrugged*, recounted in his memoirs how he had advised Rand to cut one speech by John Galt that ran over 35,000 words, to which she replied, "Would you cut the Bible?"

Enriched by the success of *Atlas Shrugged*, Rand wrote about and lectured on her philosophy at Yale University (1960), Princeton University (1960), Columbia University (1960, 1962), Harvard University (1962), and other institutions. She wrote several books exploring her philosophy, including: *For the New Intellectual: The Philosophy of Ayn Rand* (1961), *The Virtue of Selfishness: A New Concept of Egoism* (1965), *Capitalism, the Unknown Ideal* (1966), *Introduction to Objectivist Epistemology* (1967), and *The Romantic Manifesto: A Philosophy of Literature* (1969).

During the 1960s Rand continued a torrid love affair with Nathaniel Branden, who, as a young philosophy student years before, had written her an enthusiastic fan letter and who, with his wife, Barbara, had been a regular visitor at the O'Connors' ranch. Both Branden's and Rand's spouses knew about and agreed to the affair, which the two couples kept among themselves for fourteen years. Rand helped her lover establish the Nathaniel Branden Institute (NBI) in January 1958, a think tank for the propagation of Objectivist principles. Barbara Branden kept the books for NBI, and all three gave lectures and appeared on TV and radio, explaining "Rand–Thought." By the mid-1960s the institute was conducting Objectivist courses in eighty American cities and publishing the magazine *The Objectivist Newsletter*.

NBI quickly took on the fervor of a fanatical religion with Rand as its deity and Branden as its psychotherapist and chief priest. Those who expressed different opinions were expelled and publicly humiliated. In 1968 Branden was attracted to a young Randian groupie and wanted out of his affair with Rand. Retaliation was swift. Branden, author of *The Psychology of Self-Esteem* and later a leader in the self-esteem movement in psychology, was thrown out of his own institute, followed a week later by his wife. The NBI was no more. Rand continued to publicize her ideas, supporting a newsletter devoted to her teachings, the *Ayn Rand Letter*, which was published sporadically from 1971 to 1976.

O'Connor, who had remained with Rand through fifty years of marriage, died in 1979. Rand, being treated for lung cancer, died of heart failure at the age of seventy-seven in her New York City apartment, while working on a screenplay for a projected miniseries of *Atlas Shrugged*. She and her husband are buried in Kensico Cemetery in Valhalla, New York.

Over the years, more than thirty million copies of Rand's books have been sold. In 1991 a survey by the Library of Congress pronounced *Atlas Shrugged* the most influential book in American lives after the Bible. She loved Rachmaninoff and light opera and hated Bach and Shakespeare. Her favorite TV programs were *Charlie's Angels* and *Kojak*. She preferred James Bond to John Steinbeck. Her favorite American author was the early Mickey Spillane.

Rand gave a moral justification for capitalism and showed that a free society is also a productive society. She insisted that what matters most is individual freedom. She withstood attacks from the left for her anticommunist procapitalist politics, by the right for her atheism and civil libertarianism. Her fans who openly admit the influence of her works include Hillary Rodham Clinton, Alan Greenspan, and Clarence Thomas. The Ayn Rand Institute, founded in 1985 by Leonard Peikoff and based in Marina del Ray, California, and The Objectivist Center, founded in 1990 by David Kelley and based in New York City, are the two leading sites dedicated to the propagation of Rand's libertarian views, summed up in a line from *The Fountainhead*: "Great men can't be ruled."

★

Rand's writings have been edited in two books: Michael S. Berliner, *The Letters of Ayn Rand* (1995), and David Harriman, *Journals of Ayn Rand* (1997). Biographies include: Barbara Branden, *The Passion of Ayn Rand* (1986); Nathaniel Branden, *Judgment Day: My Years with Ayn Rand* (1989); Michael Paxton, *Ayn Rand: A Sense of Life* (1998); and Tibor R. Macahn, *Ayn Rand* (2001). Chris Matthews Sciabarra, *Ayn Rand: The Russian Radical* (1995), is a comprehensive examination of Rand's philosophical thought and her place in intellectual history. The film documentary *A Sense of Life* (1997) incorporates conversations with the people who knew Rand best. A lengthy article on Rand's life and her influence is in the *Manchester Guardian* (2 Aug. 1997). An Internet site for Rand's works and thoughts is <http://www.aynrand.org>. Obituaries are in the *New York Times* and *Los Angeles Times* (both 7 Mar. 1982), London *Times* (8 Mar. 1982), and *Time* (15 Mar. 1982).

JOHN J. BYRNE

RATHER, Daniel Irvin ("Dan") (*b.* 31 October 1931 in Wharton, Texas), anchor and managing editor of *CBS Evening News* who covered many of the world's major stories of the 1960s, including the assassination of John F. Kennedy and the tumultuous 1968 Democratic National Convention.

Rather is the son of Irvin Rather, an oil pipeliner, and Byrl Page. He attributes his passion for news to his father, a "voracious reader" who impulsively subscribed to newspapers from all over the United States. The elder Rather was also, according to his son, "a man of sudden angers who would leap from his chair and cancel whichever paper had offended him. . . . Out of that cycle, somehow, grew

Dan Rather at the 1968 Democratic National Convention. CORBIS CORPORATION (BELLEVUE)

my interest in the news, how it was gathered and reported and in what form it reached our home." Rather attended Sam Houston State Teachers College (now Sam Houston State University), where he received a B.A. in journalism in 1953. While in college, Rather found his first major reporting job with a 250-watt radio station in Huntsville, Texas. For forty cents an hour, he was a jack-of-all-trades, putting together newscasts; doing the play-by-play for local junior high, high school, and college football games; and even answering the phone, repairing the equipment, and mowing the lawn.

After being "sidetracked," in his own words, for a year or so following graduation from college, Rather moved on to part-time writing and reporting assignments for the *Houston Chronicle* and spent a year as a journalism instructor. In 1954 he joined the news staff of KTRH, a radio station owned by the *Chronicle*. About KTRH, Rather recalled, "I was doing the one thing I had always visualized myself doing. Not the broadcast part, the reporting, covering City Hall, the courts, the police station. I was learning." He married Jean Goebel, a painter, on 21 April 1957, and they had two children.

In 1960 the twenty-nine-year-old Rather became news director and anchorman of KHOU-TV, the CBS affiliate in Houston. Within a year after his arrival, the station moved from third place to first place in the ratings. When Hurricane Carla struck the Texas Gulf Coast in September 1961, Rather headed a news team that provided unprecedented live coverage of the storm for nearly three days from the offices of the Galveston Weather Bureau. His professional handling of the situation captured the attention of CBS executives in New York who had monitored the reports from Texas.

Rather's subsequent rise through the ranks at CBS was meteoric. In 1962 he was appointed chief of the southern bureau in Dallas, responsible for coverage of news events in the South, Southwest, Mexico, and Central America. During that time he reported on racial conflicts in the South, and the crusade led by Dr. Martin Luther King, Jr. Over the next two years Rather covered the civil rights movement, reporting on such stories as the rioting that followed James Meredith's enrollment at the University of Mississippi in 1962, as well as the assassination of Medgar Evers in 1963.

On 22 November 1963 Rather was in Dallas to coordinate CBS's coverage of President John F. Kennedy's visit to the city and to conduct an interview with the former vice president John Nance Garner (who was celebrating his ninety-eighth birthday) for use as a possible filler piece on the evening news. After completing the interview, Rather volunteered to work with the crew assigned to report on the president's motorcade. Stationed at the end of the route, he noticed a police car and what he thought was the president's limousine suddenly breaking away from the rest of the motorcade and speeding off in the wrong direction. He ran to the CBS affiliate's offices and began monitoring Dallas police communications. After hearing a reference to a local hospital, Rather was immediately in touch with the hospital's switchboard operator, a physician, and a Catholic priest, from whom he learned that the president had been shot and was dead. Rather's unofficial report to CBS Radio constituted the first public announcement of Kennedy's assassination. For the next five days he presented numerous live reports and helped to initiate CBS's coverage of the assassination and subsequent events, including the president's funeral. Rather's impressive work was rewarded with an immediate promotion to Washington correspondent, an assignment that required him to report on the new administration of President Lyndon B. Johnson.

In 1964 Rather was given an overseas assignment in London. From there he traveled throughout Europe, the Middle East, and parts of Asia, covering the Greek and Turkish civil war on Cyprus and Pakistan's invasion of India. In 1965 Rather was sent to Saigon, Vietnam, for a year to cover the American involvement in the military conflict between the north and south Vietnamese. Rather ignored official press briefings that focused on the political aspects of the war and instead reported on actual combat situations. Rather notes: "For the first time . . . war was coming into our homes. For the first time people could watch actual combat scenes while they ate dinner."

In 1966 Rather was assigned to cover the White House. He stayed on after the 1968 election and through the entire Watergate era, when President Richard M. Nixon was forced to resign from office. His aggressive coverage of Nixon made him a nationally recognized figure and earned him the nickname "the Reporter the White House hates." Rather was transferred from the White House beat to New York City in 1974, shortly after Nixon resigned and Gerald R. Ford took office. Rather became the anchorman for the documentary-style *CBS Reports*, and was chosen to serve as anchor for the CBS Saturday and Sunday evening newscasts. In 1981 Rather succeeded Walter Cronkite as anchor and managing editor of *CBS Evening News*, a post he held through the beginning of the twenty-first century. He has also anchored and reported for *48 Hours* from the time of its premiere in 1988. His regular contributions to CBS News Radio include *Dan Rather Reporting*, a weekday news program.

Since 1962, when Rather first joined CBS News, he has handled some of the most challenging assignments in broadcast journalism. Known as an outspoken Democrat, he has sometimes been criticized for inserting his own viewpoints into his reporting. Nevertheless, his day-to-day commitment to substantive, fair, and accurate news re-

porting and his tough, active style have earned him a position of respect among his peers and the public.

★

Rather's autobiographies include *The Camera Never Blinks: Adventures of a TV Journalist,* with Mickey Herskowitz (1977); *Memoirs: I Remember,* with Peter Wyden (1991); and *The Camera Never Blinks Twice: Further Adventures of a Television Journalist,* with Mickey Herskowitz (1994). For additional information about Rather, see Robert Goldberg and Gerald Jay Goldberg, *Anchors: Brokaw, Jennings, Rather, and the Evening News* (1990).

REED MARKHAM

RAUSCHENBERG, Robert (*b.* 22 October 1925 in Port Arthur, Texas), artist whose experimental style resulted in works that anticipated and defined the 1960s avant-garde.

Born Milton Ernest Rauschenberg, the artist was the elder of two children born to Dora Carolina (Matson) Rauschenberg, a homemaker, and Ernest Rauschenberg, a utility employee. He graduated from Thomas Jefferson High School in 1943 and briefly attended the University of Texas at Austin before dropping out (largely due to undiagnosed dyslexia). He was drafted into the U.S. Navy in 1944, was honorably discharged the summer of 1945, and worked in a series of jobs on the West Coast. A friend advised him to go to art school, and in February 1947 Rauschenberg en-

Robert Rauschenberg. ARCHIVE PHOTOS, INC.

rolled in the Kansas City Art Institute (today the Kansas City Art Institute and School of Design) in Missouri, where he changed his name to *Robert*. A year later he went to Paris to attend the Académie Julian, where he met Susan Weil. In October 1948 they enrolled in Black Mountain College, near Asheville, North Carolina, to study with Josef Albers and then moved to New York in fall 1949 to attend the Art Students League. In June 1950 he married Weil; they had one child before divorcing in October 1952.

The *White Paintings* (1949–1951) were Rauschenberg's first serious artistic endeavor. In fall 1950 he took them to the dealer Betty Parsons for a critique, and she offered him a solo show for the next season. Audacious in their simplicity, the starkly white canvases shocked the art world and presaged minimalism by more than a decade. "I did them as an experiment to see how much you could pull away from an image and still have an image," Rauschenberg recalled in a 1987 interview with critic Barbara Rose. He followed with his *Black Paintings* (1952) and *Red Paintings* (1953–1954) before devising a new art form he called *Combines* (1954–1965), because he merged aspects of painting and sculpture.

Between 1955 and 1960 Rauschenberg created more than sixty combines, works that influenced younger artists, such as minimalists, and that were considered forerunners of pop art. *Bed* (1955), one of Rauschenberg's most provocative combines, consists of an old quilt attached to a board over which he poured and dripped paint; he then added a pillow and part of a sheet folded down, followed by more paint. His seminal (and most widely reproduced) work, *Monogram* (1955–1959), is a stuffed Angora goat with a tire around its middle standing on a heavily painted and collaged platform with wheels. Pop artist Roy Lichtenstein said, "[The work] marked the end of the abstract expressionist era. The beginning of something that developed in the 1950s and 1960s—the return of the subject." By 1960 Rauschenberg had established himself as one of the most controversial figures in the art world, largely due to his radical work and irreverent attitude. His reputation as an enfant terrible can be traced back to this time.

Although he continued to make combines until 1965, Rauschenberg had grown tired of them by the end of the 1950s. In 1958 he started a project of illustrating Dante's *Inferno*, which took him more than two years. He made one drawing for each of the thirty-four cantos and combined them with media images he had clipped from magazines, using a process he developed called solvent transfer (a printed image placed face down on paper, soaked in lighter fluid, then rubbed until the image is transferred). To carry the narrative, certain images were reused; Dante, for example, is a male figure wrapped in a towel that came from a golf advertisement in *Sports Illustrated*. Clever, irreverent, and technically inventive, the series received wide

acclaim at the Leo Castelli Gallery in New York City in December 1960.

Rauschenberg's canny appropriation of the media immediately linked him to the pop artists just then emerging—to the extent that he has often called himself "Poppa Pop." He carried his use of media images further in his lithography and silkscreen experiments, beginning in 1962. The thirty-two-foot-long *Barge* (1962–1963) is a jumble of advertising and print images silk-screened directly onto the canvas, to which he added splatters and swipes of paint. It was included in his first retrospective held in spring 1963 at the Jewish Museum. In 1964 Rauschenberg received a second retrospective at the Whitechapel Art Gallery in London, followed by the International Grand Prize in painting at the prestigious Venice Biennale. Rauschenberg was at the height of his fame.

For Rauschenberg the 1960s encompassed mostly collaborative work. His most sustained involvement was with experimental dance and theater, especially with the Merce Cunningham Dance Company, with which he toured from 1961 to 1964. The avant-garde composer John Cage provided the music and Rauschenberg designed the sets, costumes, and lighting. Cunningham's philosophy was that the various elements of a production—dance, music, and design—should function independently. Rauschenberg's experiences led him to work with the Judson Dance Theater, which pushed the definition of dance far afield by exploring the structure of everyday movement. He debuted as choreographer (in addition to performer) with the company in 1963 in *Pelican,* in which he juxtaposed the movements of classical ballet with those of aeronautics. From 1963 to 1968 he choreographed and designed eleven theater pieces.

His theatrical experiments, coupled with his desire to break down the barriers between the arts, led to Rauschenberg's 1967 founding, with research scientist Billy Klüver, of E.A.T. (Experiments in Art and Technology), which sought collaboration between artists and engineers on technical works of art. Rauschenberg demonstrated the possibilities for such collaboration by installing an interactive sculptural environment, *Oracle* (1962–1965), in his studio. *Oracle,* which Rauschenberg made with Klüver's help, uses separate pieces that contain radios operated by remote control and a console unit with which the viewer can scan multiple stations. He made several more interactive, technical works of art; these efforts provided postmodern artists with the starting point for a range of experimentation in machine and light works.

Rauschenberg continued his activism and collaboration into the seventies. He lobbied in Congress on a number of campaigns for the rights of artists, such as retaining copyright to works of art and royalty rights when works of art were reproduced, and he helped found Artists Rights Today

(A.R.T.). In 1984 he organized the ongoing Rauschenberg Overseas Cultural Exchange (R.O.C.I.). In his own work Rauschenberg continued to expand the definition of art, returning in 1970 to collage and assemblage with a series made out of cardboard boxes. His constant challenge of artistic boundaries resulted in work that helped inspire many of the artistic impulses of the 1960s and of postmodern art. "Painting relates to both art and life," explained Rauschenberg. "Neither can be made. (I try to act in that gap between the two)."

★

Calvin Tomkins, *Off the Wall: Robert Rauschenberg and the Art World of Our Time* (1980), is a lively and perceptive study of the artist and of the period. Also good is Mary Lynn Kotz, *Rauschenberg, Art and Life* (1990). The best sources on Rauschenberg and his work are the two exhibition catalogs by Walter Hopps: *Robert Rauschenberg* (1976) and, with Susan Davidson, *Robert Rauschenberg: A Retrospective* (1997), which contains a detailed chronology.

LEIGH BULLARD WEISBLAT

RAY, James Earl (*b.* 10 March 1928 in Alton, Illinois; *d.* 23 April 1998 in Nashville, Tennessee), small-time crook, robber, and the convicted assassin of Dr. Martin Luther King, Jr.

Ray was the oldest of nine children. Ray's father, James Gerald Ray, was a factory worker and a convicted robber. Ray's mother, Lucie (Maher) Ray, was a cleaning woman and an alcoholic. Ray, who had a rough childhood, entered elementary school at the age of seven and was known to be a poor student with a low intelligence quotient. His parents separated when Ray was fifteen years old, and he dropped out of high school at that point.

In 1946 Ray joined the U.S. Army and served for two years in Germany. He was discharged in December 1948 for not adapting to military service. He soon headed to Los Angeles, where he embarked on a life of crime. While serving time at the Missouri State Penitentiary, Ray plotted his escape, and in 1967 he succeeded by hiding himself in a bread truck. Ray soon contacted his brothers and learned from one of them about a $50,000 contract on Martin Luther King, Jr.'s life. Ray knew that killing King would carve his name in history.

No one knows when Ray started stalking King, but in 1968 he traveled from the West Coast to the South, moving through California, Georgia, Alabama, Tennessee, and Texas. On 23 March 1968 he drove to Birmingham, Alabama, and purchased a rifle. On 4 April 1968 he followed King to Memphis, Tennessee, where King was lending support to striking laborers. Ray checked into a Main Street rooming house across from the Lorraine Motel, where King

James Earl Ray, shown during his trial with the House Assassinations Committee, August 1968. HULTON-DEUTSCH COLLECTION/CORBIS

was staying, and that afternoon fired the fatal shot. The bullet struck King's jaw, fracturing his lower mandible, severing the jugular vein, and shattering several vertebrae in his neck and back. King was pronounced dead at Saint Joseph Hospital that evening.

Eyewitnesses said that moments after the shooting, they saw Ray running from the building, carrying a bundle. He remained a fugitive for two months. Ray's fingerprints were found on the rifle, a scope, a pair of binoculars, and a transistor radio with Ray's Missouri inmate number etched into it. He admitted during his trial that he had panicked and thrown these objects away. He was apprehended at London's Heathrow airport. He pleaded guilty in March 1969 to avoid a death penalty.

Days after his sentencing Ray claimed that his guilty plea had been an attempt to avoid the death penalty. He claimed that he was set up by a shadowy gun dealer he met in Montreal who was using him as a pawn in a plot to kill the civil rights leader. Ray tried to persuade the world that the Federal Bureau of Investigation had used him as a fall guy. Even King's family believed Ray's account and supported his plea for a new trial, but despite many appeals, none of Ray's lawyers ever produced enough evidence to convince a court of law to reopen the case. Ray tried unsuccessfully for nearly three decades to bring his case to trial.

While serving his ninety-nine-year prison sentence at Brushy Mountain Penitentiary in Tennessee, Ray made four attempts to escape. He was successful in 1977 but was captured within fifty-four hours. After that Ray was kept in a continuously lit cell, with two armed guards and television cameras watching him.

Many books have been written about Ray's life and about the assassination. In *Killing the Dream: James Earl Ray and the Assassination of Martin Luther King, Jr.* (1998), by Gerald Posner, Ray is described as a racist: "Ray had picked fights with black sailors while in Mexico, tried to flee to segregationist Rhodesia after killing King, and refused to be transferred to an integrated honor farm." William F. Pepper, author of *Orders to Kill: The Truth Behind the Murder of Martin Luther King* (1995), spent eighteen years researching the case and concluded that Ray was duped.

In 1978 Ray married Anna Sandhu, a courtroom artist who believed Ray's accounts. She later admitted that the marriage was a terrible mistake and that she had come to believe in his guilt. They divorced fifteen years later. Ray died on 23 April 1998 at Columbia Nashville Memorial Hospital. His death was attributed to illness and kidney failure. Ray's medical file indicated he was diagnosed with cirrhosis of the liver, caused by a long-term affliction with hepatitis B, which he acquired from a blood transfusion he had received in prison. He lived his last days in an eight-foot cell. His remains were cremated, and the family directed that his ashes be shipped to Ireland.

Although few doubted that Ray had fired the fatal shot, many questioned whether he had acted alone. Even after his death controversy continued to swirl around Ray's trial and the possibility of a larger conspiracy. As far as the courts were concerned, however, Ray was the assassin. The assassinations of John F. Kennedy, Robert F. Kennedy, and Martin Luther King, Jr., marked a defining moment in the history of the United States. The violence, racial clashes, and social turmoil symbolized by these killings forever ended any sense of innocence within the cultural fabric of the nation. Ray's assassination of King removed the most compelling and effective civil rights leader of the twentieth century from the scene and sent parts of the movement spiraling into chaos.

★

Biographical information on Ray can be found in James Robert, ed., *Nash Encyclopedia of World Crime, Criminal Justice, Criminology and Law Enforcement* (1999); Ronald Gottesman, ed., *Violence in America: An Encyclopedia* (1999); and *Britannica* (1992). Obituaries are in *U. S. News and World Report* (4 May 1998) and the *New York Times* (24 Apr. 1998).

YAN TOMA

REAGAN, Ronald Wilson (*b.* 6 February 1911 in Tampico, Illinois), former movie actor who rose to political prominence in the 1960s, was elected governor of California in 1966 and 1970, and became the fortieth president of the United States (1981–1989).

Reagan was the son of John Edward (Jack) Reagan, a shoe salesman, and his wife, Nelle Wilson Reagan. The family, which included an older brother, Neil, moved several times before settling in Dixon, Illinois, in 1920. Following his graduation from Eureka College in Illinois in 1932 with a degree in economics and sociology, Reagan worked as a radio announcer in Iowa. In 1937 he traveled to California, where, after a successful screen test, he signed an acting contract. He married the actress Jane Wyman on 26 January 1940. They had one daughter and adopted a son. The couple divorced in 1948. Reagan married another actress, Nancy Davis, on 4 March 1952. They had two children.

Reagan served several terms as president of the Screen Actors Guild. When his movie career waned in the 1950s, he became the host of a weekly television show sponsored by General Electric (GE). He also traveled around the country making speeches on GE's behalf. Although he had long been a New Deal Democrat, Reagan was coming to believe that people were too dependent on government. In his speeches he called for reductions in the size of government, fewer regulations on business, and lower taxes.

Reagan joined the Republican party in 1962. On 27 October 1964, he spoke on national television in support of the party's presidential nominee, Senator Barry Goldwater of Arizona. "The Speech," as it came to be known, was a reprise of themes Reagan had stressed in his appearances for GE. Although the speech did little to help Goldwater, it catapulted Reagan to national political prominence. The Washington columnist David Broder hailed it as the most successful political debut of the century. Whereas Goldwater scared off many Americans with his bluntness, the affable Reagan seemed less threatening. After Goldwater's overwhelming defeat in 1964, Reagan emerged as the leading conservative spokesman in the country.

Encouraged by Holmes Tuttle, a Ford Motor Company dealer, and other wealthy businessmen, Reagan ran for governor of California in 1966. He confounded the expectations of the Democratic incumbent, Edmund G. Brown, Sr., and others that he would be a weak candidate. While continuing to stress his opposition to big government, Rea-

Governor-elect Ronald Reagan conducting a news conference, 1966. © BETTMANN/CORBIS

gan successfully played on the reactions of many white working-class and middle-class Californians to the bloody Watts (Los Angeles) race riots of 1965 and to continuing student unrest at the University of California—especially the Berkeley campus. Reagan insisted that radical students who disrupted school activities should "observe the rules or get out." Declaring that he was "sick at the sit-ins, the teach-ins, and walk-outs," he promised that as governor he would organize a "throw-out" of Clark Kerr, president of the University of California, on whom he blamed the "mess" at Berkeley. Reagan's conservative message struck a chord with many voters. He won a convincing victory, collecting 3.7 million votes to Brown's 2.7 million.

Kerr was dismissed in the first month of Reagan's term. When, in an effort to balance the budget, Reagan called for an end of free tuition for students at state universities, critics saw it as a further attack on the college system. Reagan made a limited run for president in 1968. Although not an officially declared candidate, his name appeared on the Republican primary ballot in Oregon and California. The first choice of many conservatives, especially from the South, Reagan finally announced his candidacy on the eve of the Republican convention, too late to derail the first-ballot nomination of the former vice president Richard Nixon.

Back in California, the governor and higher education continued to be at odds. The nadir came in 1969, when Reagan responded to a student strike at Berkeley by sending in the National Guard for seventeen days to impose order. Reagan won reelection in 1970, after a campaign in which he stressed the need for reform of the welfare system, which he denounced as requiring working Americans to pay taxes for programs that increased others' dependency on government. As governor, Reagan's policies sometimes belied his conservative words. Confronted by a budget crisis in 1967, he initially proposed a 10 percent across-the-board cut in spending. In the end, he supported increases in the corporate tax, maximum personal income tax, and state sales tax. During his eight years as governor, spending on higher education increased 136 percent, more than the overall 100 percent increase in state spending. Reagan made a second and more serious run for the presidency in 1976, losing the Republican nomination to Gerald Ford. After finally winning the nomination in 1980, he defeated Jimmy Carter to become the fortieth president of the United States. He was reelected in 1984. Reagan dropped from public view in 1994 after revealing that he had Alzheimer's disease.

Reagan reached his political apogee as president in the 1980s, a fact that obscures both the importance of the 1960s to him and his importance in the 1960s. It was in that decade that he was transformed from an actor to a national political figure. The 1960s saw the apparent triumph of liberalism over conservatism, a result that some thought was clinched by Goldwater's poor showing in 1964. California itself became a focal point for cultural and political radicalism, and to many it was the hippies in San Francisco—not the conservative governor in Sacramento—who defined both the state and the nation. Yet Reagan voters were what Nixon called the "Silent Majority": working-class and middle-class Americans who went to work, respected traditional values, and ultimately were much more representative of America than the vocal minority. Reagan was successful precisely because he opposed the political liberalism and cultural radicalism of the era. He was both a beneficiary and a leader of the conservative backlash that defined much of the latter part of the 1960s and helped shape the American political scene for the next three decades.

★

Reagan's autobiography is *An American Life* (1990). It presents Reagan's perspective on the 1960s, although it slights the decade in favor of his early years and especially his presidency. For a fuller view of the period, see Bill Boyarsky, *Ronald Reagan: His Life and Rise to the Presidency* (1981). Also useful is Lou Cannon, *Reagan* (1982).

FRED NIELSEN

REDDING, Otis, Jr. (*b.* 9 September 1941 near Dawson, Georgia; *d.* 10 December 1967 in Madison, Wisconsin), singer who, as a leading pioneer of southern-style soul music, transcended region and race with his music, which became one of the defining sounds of the 1960s.

Redding was the fourth child and first son of Otis Redding, Sr., a sharecropper, and Fannie Mae Roseman, a homemaker. Redding and his five brothers and sisters were born in a sharecropper cabin nine miles from Dawson, Georgia. In 1942 the family settled in Macon, Georgia, where Redd-

Otis Redding. © BETTMANN/CORBIS

ing's father was a maintenance worker and part-time preacher and his mother worked at Woolworth's. Redding had to drop out of Ballard-Hudson High School when he was fifteen years old and in the tenth grade. His father, who had long been in poor health, was no longer able to maintain employment. As the oldest male, Redding had to go to work to support the large family.

Redding began his music career in 1956, singing in amateur spots in local nightclubs, generally using his rough voice on songs by his idol, Little Richard. In 1959 he performed at a local talent show and won. Redding was singing professionally soon after that and working with bands, notably Johnny Jenkins and the Pinetoppers, which he joined in 1959 as manager, driver, and occasional singer. In mid-1960 Redding went Los Angeles for a few months, hoping for a break in his singing career, but the session he recorded there showed little of his promise. He returned to Macon later the same year and joined the unfortunately named Confederate (later Orbit) label, recording "Shout Bamalama," a derivative Little Richard sound that sold only moderately. On 17 August 1961 Redding married Zelma Atwood, a local girl whom he had dated for two years. The couple had two sons and a daughter. (Redding's sons and their cousin Mark Locket formed a successful recording group in the 1980s, the Reddings.)

Through his association with the Johnny Jenkins and the Pinetoppers band, Redding got the opportunity to record again in 1962. The band was contracted to record at Stax Records in Memphis, and at the end of the session, Redding was scheduled to record two songs on speculation. Redding impressed the company with an original, "These Arms of Mine," an achingly sung ballad that captured the emerging new soul style. Stax released the record on its Volt imprint, and the record reached number twenty-nine on the Cash Box rhythm and blues (R&B) chart in 1963. As soul music records came to dominate the R&B charts, Redding rapidly became one of the foremost disseminators of the style. Most of his 1964 hits were slow ballads, notably "Pain in My Heart" and "Chained and Bound," but the more up-tempo "Security" demonstrated a broader range of his abilities as a songwriter and singer. Redding's album *The Great Otis Redding Sings Soul Ballads* (1965) made some of his earliest hits accessible in one popular package.

Redding kept his name on the charts with some up-tempo original compositions in 1965, including "Mr. Pitiful" and "Respect," which reached number four on the Billboard R&B chart and became a number-one hit for Aretha Franklin in 1967. A ballad written with soul singer Jerry Butler, "I've Been Loving You Too Long (to Stop Now)," generated Redding's first notable pop success on Billboard's Hot 100 chart in the spring of 1965. Redding, however, was still not a household name in white America.

Redding sustained his recording success in 1966 with a

remake of the Rolling Stones hit "Satisfaction," "Fa Fa Fa Fa Fa Fa (Sad Song)," and a propulsive remake of a 1933 big band hit, "Try a Little Tenderness." Stax released *Otis Blue/Otis Redding Sings Soul* in 1965 and *Complete & Unbelievable . . . The Otis Redding Dictionary of Soul* in 1966. This second album gathered his 1965 and 1966 hits and combined them with remakes of soul classics.

Beginning in 1965 Redding began to branch out from performing to other areas of the music business. He established a music publishing company, Redwall Music, and a record label, Jotis, and began producing and writing for other artists. His only major success in this area was Arthur Conley's "Sweet Soul Music," a song he recorded and produced; it reached number two on both the R&B and the pop charts in early 1967.

In June 1967 Redding appeared at the Monterey International Pop Festival, which was focused on the big rock acts of the day. His performance was captured for posterity in the film *Monterey Pop*. The audience was unfamiliar with Redding as a live artist, but his stunning performance so enhanced his reputation that the rock world came to view him as the definitive soul artist.

Meanwhile, in late 1966 Stax had teamed Redding with its premier female soul star, Carla Thomas, and the two recorded a duet album, *King & Queen*. The album generated two of Redding's biggest hits during 1967, a Lowell Fulson remake, "Tramp," and an Eddie Floyd remake, "Knock on Wood." Late in 1967 Redding recorded a remarkable song that he had written with Steve Cropper. Representing a radical change of style for Redding, "(Sitting on) the Dock of the Bay" employed almost a folk-song approach. Sadly, he did not live to see the record become a million-selling hit, reaching number one on both the R&B and pop charts in early 1968. Redding and several members of his backup band, the Bar-Kays, died in a plane crash on 10 December 1967 while on their way to a concert date in Madison, Wisconsin. The world had just glimpsed Redding's newly evolved creativity, where under the influence of the decade's flourishing rock music revolution he was improving his lyrics and going beyond his Southern soul style.

After Redding's death Stax continued to release material he had recorded during the last year of his life. Posthumously Redding had nine records on the R&B and pop charts in 1969. The most successful of the releases were "The Happy Song (Dum Dum)," "I've Got Dreams to Remember," and "Papa's Got a Brand New Bag," the last a remake of an old James Brown hit.

Redding emerged as a successful recording artist during the civil rights movement and the urban riots that engulfed the country's large cities, when African Americans were fighting for and winning a more equitable place in American society. As a principal architect of soul music, Redding became emblematic of black gains, becoming a cultural hero to his African-American followers and an icon of black music for the rock generation. For these achievements he was elected to the Rock and Roll Hall of Fame in 1989 and the Songwriters Hall of Fame in 1994. He is buried at his ranch outside Macon.

★

Otis Redding is the subject of two book-length biographies: Scott Freeman, *Otis! The Otis Redding Story* (2001), and Geoff Brown, *Otis Redding: Try A Little Tenderness* (2001). The best magazine feature on Redding is Rob Bowman, "Otis Redding: R-E-S-P-E-C-T," *Goldmine* 16, no. 12 (15 June 1990): 9–14, 102. A four-CD boxed set, *Otis! The Definitive Otis Redding* (1993), includes a complete discography and several biographical essays, including commentary by Redding's widow, Zelma. An obituary is in *Rolling Stone* (20 Jan. 1968).

ROBERT PRUTER

REDFORD, (Charles) Robert, Jr. (*b.* 18 August 1937 in Santa Monica, California), one of America's favorite actors, directors, and producers, who by the end of the 1960s had become one of the world's top movie stars.

Redford is the elder of two sons of Charles Redford and Martha Hart, a homemaker. Charles, who delivered milk, worked long hours during Redford's early years. Because the family went to the library every week, Redford developed a tremendous respect for storytelling. He describes himself as "a funny-looking, freckle-faced kid with too many cowlicks." Following World War II, Redford's father found employment as an accountant with the Standard Oil Company and moved the family to Van Nuys, California, where Redford attended Van Nuys High School and graduated in 1955. Redford called Van Nuys "a cultural mud sea." He climbed buildings and stole hubcaps in the Hollywood area to escape the boredom. Redford excelled in athletics and received a baseball scholarship from the University of Colorado at Boulder. While in college Redford developed a drinking problem and started skipping classes and baseball practice. He was kicked off the baseball team and lost his scholarship.

Redford traveled throughout Europe to study painting with the money he earned working in oil fields for Standard Oil in the 1950s. Disillusioned, he moved to the East Coast but then hitchhiked back to Los Angeles, where he began drinking again. In 1958 Redford married Lola Van Wagenen; their family grew to include three children. Lola encouraged Redford to resume his art studies. In September 1958 they moved to New York City, and Redford began studying painting at the Pratt Institute in Brooklyn. He began his study of theatrical set design and acting at the

Robert Redford *(left)*, with Paul Newman in a scene from *Butch Cassidy and the Sundance Kid*, 1969. AP/ WIDE WORLD PHOTOS

American Academy of Dramatic Arts in New York City. Up to that point Redford had never been to a play and believed that acting was ludicrous.

In 1959 Mike Thoma, stage manager for the Broadway comedy *Tall Story*, started to notice Redford's work. Thoma was responsible for recruiting replacement actors and invited Redford to audition for a small part. Redford was hired for a role in *The Highest Tree* and discovered that he enjoyed acting; he moved back to Los Angeles to try out for acting jobs in television. In 1960 Redford played a dozen roles within six months. His most notable one was on television in the *Playhouse 90* series, as a Nazi lieutenant in *In the Presence of Mine Enemies*. In late 1960 Redford returned to New York to participate in the production of *The Iceman Cometh*. Redford also was cast in the production of *Little Moon of Alban*, which had only twenty performances.

Sunday in New York, a Broadway production, gave Redford his first leading role and in 1961 earned him the Theatre World Award. The production ran until May 1962, but during breaks Redford appeared in the television shows *Route 66, The Twilight Zone, Alfred Hitchcock Presents,* and *Naked City*. Redford made his motion picture debut in 1962 in the film *War Hunt*, an antiwar drama in which he played opposite John Saxon. Despite its low budget, the film won critical acclaim. In 1962 Mike Nichols, who was the director for a production of Neil Simon's new play *Barefoot in the Park*, noticed Redford and demanded that he play the lead role. Redford played opposite Elizabeth Ashley in the com-

edy about a young married couple. The production opened in New York City in October 1963 and was an overnight success.

Redford became bored with the monotony of plays, with having to do the same performance several times a week, and withdrew from the cast in 1964, never returning to the stage. Instead, he decided to focus on making motion pictures. In 1962 he was nominated for a best supporting actor Emmy award for his performance in *The Voice of Charlie Pont*, which aired on *Alcoa Premiere*, an American Broadcasting Company production.

Redford was not successful in his first four motion pictures, but he doggedly perfected his craft and pursued his goals. In 1965 he appeared in *Situation Hopeless—but Not Serious*. In 1966 Redford received a Golden Globe award for new male star of the year for his performance in *Inside Daisy Clover* (1965), a film in which he starred opposite Natalie Wood. In 1966 Redford performed in two other films, *The Chase* and *This Property Is Condemned*. Both films received poor reviews, and the public did not seem interested in them, so Redford decided to take his family to Spain and Crete while he waited for the right role. It came in 1967 with the motion picture version of *Barefoot in the Park*, in which he starred opposite Jane Fonda. The film was a great success, and the critics raved about his performance. In 1968 Paramount cast him in *Blue*, but Redford did not approve of the final script and walked out, resulting in a lawsuit and unemployment for a year.

In 1969 Redford was cast in *Butch Cassidy and the Sundance Kid.* The head of Twentieth Century–Fox initially rejected Redford but offered him the role after arrangements with three other actors did not succeed. The film, now a classic, is based on the real-life adventures of the Wild West's last two famous bandits, who in 1904 fled the United States for Bolivia and its less secure banks. The film, in which Redford plays opposite Paul Newman, resembles *Bonnie and Clyde* (1967), except that in this movie the robbers are humorous and likable. Redford became a household name following the release of *Butch Cassidy and the Sundance Kid,* which is one of the most successful westerns of all time. The film won four Academy Awards and made Redford a sought-after actor in Hollywood.

Redford starred in and co-produced *Downhill Racer* in 1969. The film portrays the world of amateur competitive skiing, starring Redford as an ambitious young man from a small town in Colorado who aspires to be an Olympic champion. Critics praised the film, but the public's approval was not nearly as strong as it had been for *Butch Cassidy and the Sundance Kid.* Redford's next film, *Tell Them Willie Boy Is Here*, was rushed to theaters in December 1969 and earned Redford the British Film Academy's 1970 award for best actor. The public response was about the same as it had been for *Downhill Racer.* This film, written and directed by Abraham Polansky, is a contemporary western focusing on a manhunt for a Piute Indian thought to be guilty of a crime. Some reviewers saw the film as a masterpiece, while others found it pretentious. The critics were unanimous, however, in their praise for Redford in his role as sheriff. He made *Jeremiah Johnson,* still his favorite film, in 1972. His success continued with *The Way We Were* (1973), *The Sting* (1973), *The Great Gatsby* (1974), *All the President's Men* (1976), and many other films in succeeding decades.

In 1981 Redford founded the Sundance Institute, located in Utah, to provide funding for young artists to experiment with cinema. It has grown to include a yearly film festival in Park City, Utah; the success of the Sundance Film Festival has resulted from Redford's unfailing commitment to the independent filmmaker. Redford's passion for his career over family life led to his divorce from Lola in 1985, after nearly thirty years of marriage. He won the Academy Award for best director for the film that marked his directorial debut, *Ordinary People* (1980). In 1994 Redford won the Cecil B. Demille Award, best picture, for the film *Quiz Show.* In 1995 he was given the Screen Actors Guild Lifetime Achievement Award.

Besides his artistic achievements, Redford is also a dedicated environmentalist. He lobbied for the Clean Air Act of 1974 and the Energy and Conservation Act of 1976 and serves on the National Resources Defense Council and the Environmental Defense Fund. Redford's love of the environment led to his work as founder of the Institute for Resource Management. In 1976 he took time off from filmmaking to write *The Outlaw Trail* (1978), which tells about the American West and an old escape route that starts in Canada and ends in Mexico.

Nearly all of Redford's roles in the 1960s were of charming heroes or handsome icons who rarely display emotional extremes. Richard Schickel, in a February 1970 *Life* magazine article, described Redford as "a perennial adolescent who has a way of making even his contemporaries feel old and has long referred to himself, in his many self-satirical moments, as 'the Kid.'" Redford is one of only a few prominent actors who have complete creative control of their films. Throughout his four-decade-long career, he has starred in roles that depict his beliefs and best suit his screen persona. Robert Redford became a movie icon in the 1960s with successful and varied performances in such films as *Butch Cassidy and the Sundance Kid* and *Downhill Racer.* He perpetuated the image of the rugged individualist in his roles as a gunslinger and later as a fiercely competitive Olympic skier. Redford's participation in filmmaking increased the popularity of moviegoing among the American public.

★

Biographies of Redford include Gerard Bardavid, *Robert Redford* (1980); David Downing, *Robert Redford* (1982); Bruce Crowther, *Robert Redford* (1985); Philippe Durant, *Robert Redford* (1985); and Minty Clinch, *Robert Redford* (1989). For an account of the making and content of his films, see James Spada, *The Films of Robert Redford* (1977).

REED B. MARKHAM

REISCHAUER, Edwin Oldfather (*b.* 15 October 1910 in Tokyo, Japan; *d.* 1 September 1990 in La Jolla, California), founder of the Japan Institute at Harvard University and U.S. ambassador to Japan from 1961 to 1966.

Reischauer was the second son of extraordinarily accomplished Christian missionaries. His father, August Karl Reischauer, was a noted scholar of Japanese history and culture and cofounder of Tokyo Women's College; his mother, Helen Sidwell Oldfather, founded the first deaf school in Japan to utilize oral instruction. After a primary and secondary education spent almost exclusively in Japan, Reischauer attended Ohio's Oberlin College, where he graduated with a B.A. in history in 1931. The following year he began graduate work in East Asian studies at Harvard University, where he came under the influence of the professor of Japanese studies Serge Elisseeff, who, according to Reischauer, helped "set the course of my life." Under Elisseeff's direction, Reischauer completed his M.A. in 1932

Edwin O. Reischauer testifying at a Senate hearing, January 1967. WALLY McNAMEE/CORBIS

and his Ph.D. in 1939 and took a position as instructor at Harvard. In 1935 he had married Adrienne Danton, with whom he would have three children. Following her death in 1955, Reischauer married Haru Matsukata, a writer and granddaughter of a Japanese prince, in 1956.

During the summer of 1941 Reischauer served as a State Department consultant in the Division of Far Eastern Affairs and unsuccessfully fought the decision to suspend oil shipments to Japan. In 1942 Reischauer established a school for the Army Signal Corps to train Japanese language translators and cryptologists. After accepting an officer's commission, he served in U.S. Army Intelligence from 1943 to 1945, working on the top-secret MAGIC project, which deciphered Japanese diplomatic codes.

In the autumn of 1945 Reischauer returned to the State Department to help craft policy for the postwar occupation of Japan and Korea, and in the fall of 1946 he returned to Harvard, where he served until his appointment in 1961 as ambassador to Japan. During these fifteen years, Reischauer, along with China expert John K. Fairbank, oversaw the expansion of Harvard's East Asian Studies program. Reischauer's writings on Japanese history during this period broke new ground by rejecting Marxist assumptions in favor of the so-called modernization theory, which posited that Japan's historical development was paralleling that of the United States and other western democracies.

Events in Japan during 1960 soon led Reischauer far from Harvard to the forefront of U.S.–Japanese diplomacy. During May and June, Japanese disapproval of a new security treaty with the United States and growing apprehension over high-handed government tactics to guarantee the treaty's passage led to nationwide strikes and protests,

which culminated on 22 June with a massive protest in which some 6 million Japanese went on strike. In the aftermath of the treaty protests Reischauer penned a penetrating analysis of U.S.–Japanese relations for the journal *Foreign Affairs,* in which he argued that while there existed no rising tide of anti-Americanism among the Japanese, the two nations suffered from fundamentally flawed perceptions of one another that came to a head during the treaty fight. Reischauer noted that the growing perception gap could prove fatal to U.S. defense of noncommunist Asia if it led Japan to adopt a neutralist foreign policy. This article, along with the urging of undersecretary of state Chester Bowles, led to Reischauer's appointment as U.S. ambassador to Japan in 1961.

Reischauer immediately set about repairing what he termed "the broken dialogue" with Japan. He understood that many Japanese saw the United States as an aggressive power that could drag their nation into a nuclear struggle for which no adequate defense existed. Reischauer also believed that his compatriots and its leaders should pay greater attention to Japan and display a greater appreciation for Japan's critical role in the cold war struggle. Although the Japanese military could not decisively influence the outcome of the struggle, Japan's growing economic clout could prove vital. As ambassador, Reischauer encouraged Tokyo to double its foreign aid budget and increase its aid to South Korea. To improve channels of communication, meanwhile, he revamped the embassy staff, bringing in a cadre of Japanese-speaking officers, while keeping up a constant round of public appearances designed to bridge the gap in understanding between the people of Japan and the people of the United States. In the hopes of familiarizing key leaders with conditions in Japan, Reischauer convinced important officials, including Attorney General Robert Kennedy, to visit Japan. During his tenure Reischauer remained an immensely popular figure whose stature increased even more after he survived a 1964 assassination attempt at the hands of a deranged Japanese youth.

Although Reischauer's stock soared in Japan, the same could not be said for his standing in Washington. By 1964 several issues complicated both U.S.–Japanese relations and Reischauer's position within the new administration of President Lyndon B. Johnson. While ably dealing with controversial issues such as the continued U.S. occupation of Okinawa as well as the U.S. Navy's practice of carrying nuclear weapons into Japan, Reischauer found it increasingly difficult to support Washington on certain issues. The ambassador, for example, disagreed with the decision to press for greater tariffs on the bulk of Japanese textile exports to the United States. Reischauer saw that Washington's case for restraints rested on unsupportable ground and urged authorities instead to focus on stimulating U.S. agricultural exports to Japan. He also disagreed with the

Kennedy–Johnson policy of attempting to limit trade between Japan and Communist China. Vietnam, however, proved a greater strain both on U.S–Japanese relations, as well as the ambassador's relations with Johnson. While privately opposing much of Washington's evolving policy in Vietnam, Reischauer publicly supported his government and worked to counteract what he saw as naive Japanese press coverage that heavily favored North Vietnam.

In 1966, after almost six years of service, Reischauer determined that he had achieved what he had set out to do. Much of the misinformation that had clouded earlier relations had cleared, and Japan and the United States were far closer to being equal partners than ever before. Further service in Japan, he concluded, might only undermine all that he had accomplished.

In the summer of 1966 Reischauer returned to Harvard, where he taught until his retirement in 1981. Among his many academic writings, both *Japan: The Story of a Nation* (1970) and *The Japanese Today: Change and Continuity* (1988) remain highly regarded studies in Japanese history.

Despite several severe illnesses, Reischauer kept up a busy schedule of travel, writing, and speaking until shortly before his death of complications from chronic hepatitis acquired from a blood transfusion.

★

Reischauer's autobiography is *My Life Between Japan and America* (1986). As yet there is no authoritative biography. Among Reischauer's many writings, "The Broken Dialogue with Japan," *Foreign Affairs* 39 (Oct.–July 1960–1961), is quite informative and illustrative of the ambassador's views prior to his posting. Obituaries are in the *New York Times* and *Washington Post* (both 2 Sept. 1990) and the (London) *Times* (4 Sept. 1990).

SIDNEY PASH

RESTON, James Barrett ("Scotty") (*b.* 3 November 1909 in Clydebank, Scotland; *d.* 6 December 1995 in Washington, D.C.), journalist who, as the nation's preeminent columnist during the 1960s, raised important questions in the *New York Times* about U.S. institutions, government policy, and the role of the press during a time of international instability and domestic unrest.

Reston was the younger child and only son of James Reston, a machinist, and Johanna Irving, a homemaker. The family emigrated from Scotland to Dayton, Ohio, in 1920; Reston's parents became naturalized U.S. citizens in 1927. Reston graduated from Oakwood High School in 1926 and a year later entered the University of Illinois, from which he received a B.S. degree in journalism in 1932. While at Illinois he met Sara ("Sally") Jane Fulton, whom he married on Christmas Eve 1935; they had three sons.

James B. Reston. CORBIS CORPORATION (BELLEVUE)

Initially a sports writer, Reston began a fifty-year-long association with the *New York Times* in London on 1 September 1939, the day World War II began. He remained in England throughout the Blitz (a concentrated period of German bombardment of London between 1940 and 1941), returning to the United States to write *Prelude to Victory* (1942), a patriotic call to arms filled with the moral imperatives and faith in the American system that were to be the hallmarks of his syndicated columns in later years. Named the paper's diplomatic correspondent in 1944, Reston earned a Pulitzer Prize in 1945 for a series of stories based on confidential memos and policy papers he had obtained from the Chinese delegation to the Dumbarton Oaks conference that created the United Nations.

Over the next fifteen years Reston developed a network of top-level government and diplomatic contacts, and on the strength of the insider information he received, won numerous awards, including a second Pulitzer in 1957 for the quality of his reporting. As Washington bureau chief from 1953 to 1964, he hired and nurtured a stellar corps of young reporters, who figured prominently in the *Times*'s 1960s coverage of the civil rights movement and the war in Vietnam.

Reston's thrice-weekly column began on 1 March 1960, and within months he had become the most influential columnist of his day. He was a Jeffersonian democrat, with a boundless faith in America and the American Dream, as well as in the capacity of the American people to right themselves when they strayed from the national norms of freedom and civic responsibility. Throughout the 1960s he took a slightly left-of-center stance on the civil rights struggle in the South, challenged the growth of presidential power, and opposed first the escalation of military force in Vietnam and then the war itself. A defender of evolutionary change, he faulted the 1960s radicals for their lack of historical understanding and their propensity for violence.

In 1961, when one of Reston's reporters, Tad Szulc, learned that the Central Intelligence Agency (CIA) was training nearly 5,000 Cuban refugees for an invasion of their home island in an effort to topple the Castro regime, Reston faced a serious dilemma—to publish the account or to withhold key elements in the interest of national security. After lengthy debate among the *Times* editors, key details were edited from the story before it was published. The Bay of Pigs disaster occurred eleven days later. Sometime afterward, President John F. Kennedy told the editor of the *Times* that he wished the original story had run in full because he would have foreseen the outcome of the invasion and withdrawn U.S. support. In 1962 Reston withheld publication of critical information during the Cuban Missile Crisis at the president's behest in order not to interfere with the secret negotiations that brought about a diplomatic resolution of the Soviet presence in the Caribbean.

Reston addressed those events and the issues they raised in three lectures to the Council on Foreign Relations in New York City in 1966. Published as *The Artillery of the Press: Its Influence on American Foreign Policy* (1967), the lectures examined the historic role of the press as the gadfly of politics and the defender of the people's right to know in light of changes that had significantly altered the conduct of foreign policy since World War II. Noting that the national press now had a global reach, Reston considered the dilemma of journalists operating in the atmosphere of the cold war, a time, he said, of "half-war and half-peace." Aggressive reporting that revealed the inner workings or hidden goals of the nation's foreign policy might put security at risk, but a failure to report might produce equally damaging results, as had been the case at the Bay of Pigs. It was essential to the security of the nation, Reston said, that a "vigilant and skeptical" press keep up "a steady barrage of facts and criticism," and that it direct its attention to "the causes rather than merely the effects of international strife."

As Washington bureau chief and later executive editor of the *Times,* Reston applied those principles by encouraging his reporters to write clearly labeled analyses that examined such developments as student radicalism, court decisions on civil rights, and the growing opposition to the war in Vietnam. Reston himself had gone to Vietnam in 1965, and on his return began a long assault on the U.S. government's ongoing escalation of what he called "futile brutality." As he wrote in 1967, the Johnson administration's diversion of resources from the "fundamental problems" of overpopulation, hunger, and political instability worldwide was inimical to the best interests of the United States.

Reston played a key role in the *Times* controversial publication in 1971 of the Pentagon Papers, which revealed the extent of the government's manipulation of the press during the build-up and conduct of the Vietnam War. He continued to write his column in his remaining years on the *Times,* but his influence waned. Younger critics argued that, as the quintessential insider, he had lost the capacity to challenge the nation's leaders and was now a mere "presenter of established policy." More significantly, as Reston himself recognized, television had replaced newspapers as the chief purveyor of news and opinion and thus had reduced significantly the impact a single columnist might have. He retired from the *Times* on his eightieth birthday, 5 November 1989. He died of cancer at the age of eighty-six.

In his memoirs Reston wrote that there were three primary influences on his life: the ethical lessons of his parents, the love of his wife, and "the integrity of the *New York Times."* In a long and distinguished career, he served them and his readers well.

★

Reston's papers are in the Archives of the University of Illinois at Urbana-Champaign. His autobiography is *Deadline: A Memoir* (1991). For information about Reston's years on the *New York Times,* see Gay Talese, *The Kingdom and the Power* (1969), and Harrison Salisbury, *Without Fear or Favor: The New York Times and Its Times* (1980). An obituary is in the *New York Times* (7 Dec. 1995).

ALLAN L. DAMON

REUTHER, Walter Philip (*b.* 1 September 1907 in Wheeling, West Virginia; *d.* 9 May 1970 in Pellston, Michigan), local union president, labor leader, civil rights activist, antiwar activist, president of the United Automobile Workers, president of the Congress of Industrial Organizations, and vice president of the American Federation of Labor–Congress of Industrial Organizations.

Reuther was the oldest of three sons of the German immigrants Valentine Reuther, a brewery-wagon driver and union leader, and Anna Stocker, a homemaker. In 1930, while he was a student at Detroit City College (now Wayne State University), Reuther helped organize the local Social

Walter Reuther. CORBIS CORPORATION (BELLEVUE)

Problems Club, an affiliate of the League for Industrial Democracy, which was itself an affiliate of the Socialist Party. Although he attended college, Reuther never graduated. From November 1933 until June 1935 Reuther and his brother Victor worked in the Gorky Auto Works in the Soviet Union. Their other brother, Roy, was also active in labor. Reuther led the first major auto strike in Detroit in 1936. That year he married May Wolf; they had two children. He continued working in labor, and in 1940 he headed the General Motors department of the United Automobile Workers (UAW). Badly beaten by strikebreakers that same year, Reuther sustained crippling injuries to his right hand. Two assassination attempts were also made on his life.

Reuther did much to earn respect for labor unions from management. His career focused on worker benefits, wage raises, guaranteed annual wages, profit sharing, pensions, and holidays. He also advocated civil rights, low-cost housing, health insurance, and environmental protection of air and water. Reuther participated in two marches for social justice and racial equality, the March on Washington and the march from Selma to Montgomery, Alabama. He also supported the struggles of the Mexican farm workers in California, and he opposed the Vietnam War.

Reuther worked hard for civil rights within the automobile industry. In the early 1960s the workforce of the American automobile industry was about 13 percent African American, and in Michigan the figure exceeded 20 percent. While paragraph sixty-three of the UAW-GM contact gave foremen the power to transfer and upgrade production workers, all too often white supervisors continued to practice racism in not promoting a multiracial workforce. Many African-American autoworkers did not know that Reuther worked unsuccessfully for years to reform paragraph sixty-three. Just as many people in the civil rights movement expressed their discontent by forcing integration at lunch counters in North Carolina, African-American workers in Detroit often criticized the racism of the factory, and they blamed labor union leadership and leaders like Walter Reuther for not changing it.

George Meany, president of the American Federation of Labor–Congress of Industrial Organizations (AFL-CIO), did not endorse the 12 August 1963 March on Washington for freedom and jobs; the only AFL-CIO executive council members who did were A. Phillip Randolph and Reuther. Reuther himself participated in the March on Washington, at which some 200,000 people gathered to demonstrate their support for equality for all. Reuther not only participated in the march but also supported it by paying $16,000 for the public address system. Before the march Reuther and Randolph, along with the civil rights leader Martin Luther King, Jr., Roy Wilkins, leader of the National Association for the Advancement of Colored People, and Whitney Young, the executive director of the Urban League, met with President John F. Kennedy. They encouraged him to include a fair employment statute in the proposed Civil Rights Act. In later years the AFL-CIO took perhaps more credit than was its due for supporting the march and influencing civil rights legislation—in reality it was only Reuther who was present at the event.

With the help of Roy Wilkins, Reuther persuaded Randolph, who was the head of the steering committee, to add an additional Protestant, Jew, and Roman Catholic to this group for the Washington march. These additions shifted the social focus of the March on Washington away from racial equality and more toward the Kennedy administration's civil rights bill. Full employment for African Americans and a minimum wage of two dollars per hour were no longer the sole considerations. Attorney General Robert Kennedy's Justice Department wanted a peaceful march, and Reuther, who represented the UAW to both the Justice Department and the march steering committee members, did his best to make the demonstration fall in line with the administration's vision.

Reuther and the Justice Department both received unauthorized, advance copies of the speech of John Lewis, the leader of the Student Nonviolent Coordinating Committee

(SNCC). In it he called for a revolution. When Patrick Cardinal O'Boyle (the Archbishop of Washington who was to offer the invocation at the march) read the speech, he refused to share the same platform with Lewis. With the support of the Justice Department, Reuther convinced Lewis and the other steering committee members that Lewis should rewrite his speech in a manner that would better support the coalition of labor and African Americans. Lewis rewrote the speech, toning down his criticism, and Reuther persuaded O'Boyle to give the invocation on that contingency.

In his own speech that day, Reuther called for full employment and full production for Americans during times of peace, just as in times of war. He criticized Kennedy for defending Berlin, which was at that time being supplied and supported by an airlift from the West, and not defending Birmingham, Alabama. Later that afternoon, when the march leaders met at the White House with President Kennedy, the Reverend Martin Luther King, Jr., modestly deflected Kennedy's compliment on his speech by praising Reuther's speech, but Kennedy noted that King's speech was the major one delivered that day.

Reuther did not always do all that should have been done for civil rights. In the 1950s Horace Sheffield and Willouby Abner, African-American members of the Trade Union Leadership Council, spoke out on the inability of a white man to advocate for African-American autoworkers. Reuther remained as opposed to the Trade Union Leadership Council as he did to the Dodge Revolutionary Union movement, because of the hard Marxist lines of both organizations. The top leadership of the UAW did not actively support Title VII of the Civil Rights Act of 1964, either, which prohibited discrimination based on race, color, religion, sex, or national origin.

Reuther made other efforts for civil rights, however, such as desegregation of the Memphis Harvester local and the inclusion of anti-discrimination in collective-bargaining contracts. Throughout his life Reuther strove to put labor at the center of the social movement for civil rights. As a labor leader who supported racial equality, Reuther was much stronger than Jimmy Hoffa—a convicted felon who was president of the Teamster's Union—David J. Mac-Donald, or George Meany. Unlike his contemporaries, he made labor the core of a dynamic social movement. For Reuther, unions had the power to change the world.

In another dispute with Meaney in 1968, Reuther led the UAW out of the AFL-CIO. The next year Reuther attempted, through his Alliance for Labor Action, to merge the UAW with the Teamsters Union, but he was unsuccessful. Reuther was killed on 9 May 1970 in a plane crash in Pellston, Michigan. He was awarded the Presidential Medal of Freedom posthumously. Reuther, perhaps more than anyone else, demonstrated that, through the labor movement, the improvement of the social conditions for all Americans, black and white, could be improved.

★

Biographical information on Reuther is in Frank Cormier and William J. Eaton, *Reuther* (1970); Jean Gould and Lorena Hickok, *Walter Reuther: Labor's Rugged Individualist* (1972); Irving Howe and B. J. Widick, *The UAW and Walter Reuther* (1973); John Barnard, *Walter Reuther and the Rise of the Autoworkers* (1983); and Nelson Lichtenstein, *The Most Dangerous Man in Detroit: Walter Reuther and the Fate of American Labor* (1995). An obituary is in the *New York Times* (11 May 1970).

LARRY D. GRIFFIN

RICH, Adrienne Cecile (*b.* 16 May 1929 in Baltimore, Maryland), feminist theorist, writer, and poet whose work during the 1960s evolved from formal modernism to radical feminism.

Rich grew up in Baltimore, the elder of two daughters of Arnold Rice Rich, a doctor, and Helen Jones Rich, a composer and pianist, and was educated at home until the fourth grade. Interested in writing from an early age, she

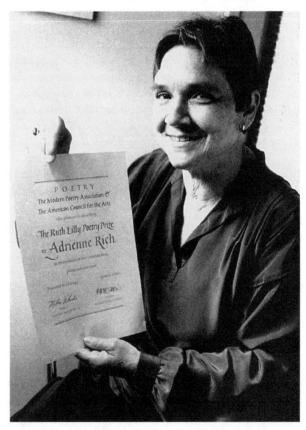

Adrienne Rich. AP/WIDE WORLD PHOTOS

immersed herself in her father's library of Victorian writers. In 1951 Rich graduated from Radcliffe College and published her first poetry collection, *A Change of World*, which won the Yale Series of Younger Poets Prize. Until that time, Rich's reading had consisted mainly of male poets, and she often used a male persona or wrote with a tone of ironic detachment characteristic of male poets she admired. One of those poets, W. H. Auden, wrote in his introduction to the volume that her poems "are neatly and modestly dressed, speak quietly but do not mumble, respect their elders but are not cowed by them, and do not tell fibs." In *Writing like a Woman* (1983), Alicia Ostriker commented that Rich's early reviewers approved of the "good girl" qualities of her poetry, which reflected a sense of caution and propriety.

Upon receiving a Guggenheim Fellowship in 1952, Rich traveled in England and Europe. On 26 June 1953 she married Alfred H. Conrad, a Harvard University economist. She had her first son and published her second poetry collection, *The Diamond Cutters,* in 1955. By 1959 she had three sons and was balancing her roles as writer, wife, and mother. She did not publish another collection until 1963, when *Snapshots of a Daughter-in-Law* appeared. The book examines the roles of women in relationship to men, women, and social institutions and beliefs. Rich wrote in her 1971 essay, "When We Dead Awaken: Writing As Re-Vision," that she underwent a transformation when she wrote *Snapshots*, writing "in a longer, looser mode than I'd ever trusted myself with before. It was extraordinary relief to write that poem."

The title poem describes a young woman's anger and frustration at the limitations placed on her by a male-dominated society. This collection marked a change from formal, traditional poems to the use of free verse and feminist themes. Instead of using stanzas, Rich relied on fragments and segments of various lengths. She also dropped the initial capital letter in each line and used limited rhyme and the cadences of speech instead of more formal meter, thus giving her poems more force and freshness. The themes that eventually would be seen as characteristic of Rich—her interest in history and political issues, the separateness of individuals, and the importance of relationship—began to appear in these poems. Rich later observed, however, that these visible changes did not go deep enough. In *On Lies, Secrets, and Silence* (1979), she wrote, "I hadn't found the courage yet to do without authorities, or even to use the pronoun 'I'—the woman in the poem is always 'she.'"

In 1966 Rich and her family moved to New York City, where Rich became involved with the growing civil rights and antiwar movements and began reading more widely in women's literature and history. She also taught and gave poetry readings and lectures, activities that brought her into prominence as a feminist activist and thinker. During this period she published three poetry collections, *Necessities of Life* (1966), *Leaflets* (1969), and *The Will to Change* (1971). These works are overtly confrontational and antipatriarchal, expressing her personal and political dissatisfaction with a male-run society and a woman's place in it. Rich's commitment to feminism, now a central part of her work, was also a central part of her life. She believed that her role as a poet was to instigate, to question, to challenge society—the poet as revolutionary.

Rich's husband, from whom she had become estranged, committed suicide in 1970. Rich has never discussed his suicide, referring to it only obliquely in her writing. Rich's freedom from marriage seemed to allow her a greater involvement in the women's movement. She had become increasingly interested in feminist ideas and identified herself as a radical feminist when she won the National Book Award in 1974 for *Diving into the Wreck* (1973). In 1976 she "came out" as a lesbian, identifying with female separatists, who wished to live a life without men. The rest of the 1970s were a prolific time, during which she produced *Twenty-One Love Poems* (1977), *The Dream of a Common Language* (1978), and *A Wild Patience Has Taken Me This Far* (1981), as well as the essays in *Of Woman Born* (1976), and *On Lies, Secrets, and Silence* (1979). In the 1980s and 1990s Rich wrote about poverty, racism, and violence. She was a professor of English and feminist studies at Stanford University from 1986 to 1992.

Rich continues to write poetry, essays, and criticism. Because of the outspoken tone of much of her work, she has generated controversy as well as praise; some critics complain of an antimale bias, while others claim that her poetry is merely a vehicle for her political views. Despite this controversy, Rich has received numerous awards, including Guggenheim Fellowships (1952, 1961), the National Institute of Arts and Letters Award for Poetry (1961), a National Endowment of the Arts grant (1970), a National Book Award (1970), the Robert Frost Silver Medal for Lifetime Achievement in Poetry from the Poetry Society of America (1992), a Lambda Book award (1992), and a MacArthur Foundation Fellowship (1994).

In 1997 Rich earned a National Medal of the Arts but declined the award, stating that it was meaningless in the context of the "cynical politics" of President Bill Clinton's administration, which awarded the medal. Rich's keen awareness of political and social issues and her insistence on speaking for oppressed and marginalized people have made her work essential reading for those interested in feminism and the social history of the twentieth century.

★

Discussions of Rich's life and work appear in Barbara Charlesworth Gelpi and Albert Gelpi, eds., *Adrienne Rich's Poetry: A Norton Critical Edition* (1975); Alicia Ostriker, *Writing like a Woman*

(1983); and Claire Keyes, *The Aesthetics of Power: The Poetry of Adrienne Rich* (1986). David St. John discusses Rich in "Brightening the Landscape," *Los Angeles Times Book Review* (25 Feb. 1996). Rich's brief statement declining the National Medal of the Arts is in *Time* (21 July 1997).

KELLY WINTERS

RICKLES, Donald Jay ("Don") (*b.* 8 May 1926 in New York City), stand-up comedian and actor in film and television, known as a master of insult humor, who stretched the envelope of television content during the 1960s in several areas, including ethnic humor, in his appearances on the late-night talk show *The Tonight Show.*

The son of Max Rickles, an insurance salesman, and Etta Feldman, a homemaker, Rickles was born and raised in lower-middle-class Jackson Heights, a community in Queens, a borough of New York City. Rickles performed in class plays while attending public schools and developed a contentious style of humor beyond the confines of the stage. "I loved to perform, but I was really a very shy and frightened kid," he admitted to the *New York Times* in 1980.

After graduating in 1944 from Newtown High School in Elmhurst, New York, Rickles enlisted in the U.S. Navy and served in the Pacific during the last part of World War II. In 1946 he won admission to the American Academy of Dramatic Arts in New York. He graduated in 1948, but success did not come quickly. He all but gave up on

show business and took jobs selling cosmetics, used cars, and life insurance. "I played small resort hotels in the Catskills and cabaret dumps—when I could get the jobs," he recalled. "The customers were . . . always heckling, and I began giving it right back to them." Rickles gradually discovered that audiences were provoking him for the pleasure of being insulted, and that they enjoyed this exchange more than his prepared material. His reputation grew, and he began to get regular bookings around the country, although he was still far from a headliner.

Rickles's major break came in 1957. While substituting at a Los Angeles nightclub, he noticed the singer Frank Sinatra in the audience. "Hey, Frank," he said, "make yourself at home and hit somebody." Sinatra's laughing approval conferred a kind of jester's mantle on Rickles. One night, sighting the entertainer Bob Hope, who was known for taking his all-star shows into battle zones to play for the troops, Rickles asked the audience, "Who let *him* in here? What happened, is the war over?" To Diana Ross: "If you quit show business, don't worry. I'll always have a job for you. Do you do windows?" Notoriety brought Rickles a film role in the war movie *Run Silent, Run Deep* (1958).

By the early 1960s Rickles had become famous for insulting the famous. Like most established club performers, he hoped to take advantage of the more lucrative opportunities for work in film and television. Finding venues in which he could effectively channel the compulsive energy and spontaneity of his work in the context of the prerecorded, highly edited world of mass media was not easy.

Don Rickles *(right)*, with Frank Sinatra at the Academy Awards, 1969. © BETTMANN/CORBIS

In 1964 he appeared in a series of teen pictures, including *Muscle Beach Party* and *Beach Blanket Bingo,* playing foils to the screen idols Frankie Avalon and Annette Funicello and a gaggle of made-for-swimwear extras from central casting.

In 1965 Rickles found his best role on television when he began appearing on *The Tonight Show Starring Johnny Carson.* At the top of his game in terms of energy and talent, the comedian displayed a convincingly neurotic ability to verbally mow down all who crossed his path, whether he was sitting on the talk-show couch with the stars or roaming through the studio, working over the audience. Part of his effect may have been contextual; the mid-1960s was perhaps the blandest period in television history. The comedian's willingness to make ethnic and racial jokes on television, a form of comedy that was otherwise restricted to the most sophisticated big-city nightclubs of the era, shocked many viewers. The overall inclination of the television audience to accept, even to embrace, this kind of humor can be seen as a marker of the end of the cultural assimilationism that dominated the 1950s. It was also a signal of the general reawakening of ethnic and racial consciousness that took place in the United States during the 1960s. Rickles was frequently asked to host *The Tonight Show* when Carson was away.

Rickles appearances in prime time were quite another story. Although he appeared as a guest star on more than thirty top-rated shows during the 1960s, including *The Beverly Hillbillies, The Andy Griffith Show,* and *Rowan and Martin's Laugh-In,* he could not sustain a television series of his own. It was not for want of trying. The first *Don Rickles Show* (1968–1969) was an American Broadcasting Company (ABC) comedy-variety hour, and it was quickly added to the list of aborted attempts to revive that genre. The second *Don Rickles Show,* on the Columbia Broadcasting System (CBS) in 1972, possibly an experiment in surrealism, had him in a situation comedy as a suburban husband and father. (The *Washington Post* recommended the show to "masochists.") *C.P.O. Sharkey,* on the National Broadcasting Company (NBC) (1976–1978) packaged Rickles as a navy chief petty officer screaming at his men. Attempts to find Rickles a successful prime-time show continued into the 1990s.

The lack of a performance space in prime-time television for the compelling psychodrama of which Rickles was capable during the 1960s is more of a comment on the limitations of American television than on the performer. As a live put-down artist, he not only flourished at the nation's top nightclubs, but he also was summoned to the Los Angeles restaurant Chasen's to let loose on Ronald Reagan during his presidency and to Buckingham Palace for a go at the British royals.

Rickles married Barbara Sklar, a secretary, on 14 March 1965, and they had two children. In 1995 Rickles surprised many critics with his stone-faced, mostly silent performance as a pit boss in the film *Casino,* directed by Martin Scorsese. "I'm not just some schmuck who goes around hollering rotten things about people," he had told *Reader's Digest* in 1982.

Achieving popularity on the nightclub circuit as a man that audiences "loved to hate," Rickles was characterized by *TV Guide* as "potentially the funniest comedian on television." The stardom of a television series eluded him, however, owing in large part to the blandness of the medium during the 1960s. Rickles remained a top nightclub performer throughout, and he continued to headline shows in Las Vegas, Atlantic City, and elsewhere into the twenty-first century.

★

Information on Rickles can be found in articles in *Time* (7 Aug. 1995) and the *New York Times Magazine* (25 Aug. 1996). A good sample of Rickles's humor can be found in a comic interview he gave to *Time* (13 Dec. 1999). A more in-depth interview, conducted by Maurice Zolotow, appeared in *Reader's Digest* (Mar. 1982).

DAVID MARC

RIGBY, Cathy (*b.* 12 December 1952 in Long Beach, California), Olympic gymnast whose performances in the late 1960s revolutionized women's gymnastics and popularized the sport in the United States.

Rigby is the third of five children of Paul Rigby, an aeronautical engineer, and Anita Peters Rigby, an aerospace materials analyst. Rigby's gymnastics career began in 1961 when her father signed her up for a trampoline class. Although she was just nine, her fearlessness and talent attracted the attention of Coach Bud Marquette, a gymnastics champion in the 1930s who ran one of the best gymnastics training programs in the United States. In 1963, when Rigby was eleven years old, Marquette invited her to become a member of his Southern California Acrobatic Team (SCATS), located in Long Beach, California. Two years later Rigby was touring and performing in gymnastics exhibitions throughout the United States with SCATS. In 1967 at her first official gymnastics meet, the Midwest Open in Chicago, she placed second in her age group.

Under Marquette's coaching Rigby qualified for the 1968 U.S. Olympic women's gymnastic team that competed in Mexico City. At fifteen she was the team's youngest member. Cute with a radiant smile, Rigby was courted by the media and public. Rigby came in sixteenth in overall scoring, the most points ever scored by an American woman

Cathy Rigby competing at the World Cup Championships, 1971. Asso-CIATED PRESS AP

gymnast. Four feet, eleven inches tall, with blond pigtails, she enthralled the public with her fearless, well-executed moves. Her pixie-like performance changed the face of women's gymnastics. After Rigby, aerobatic, childlike performers such as Russia's Olga Korbut and Romania's Nadia Comaneci would come to dominate Olympic women's gymnastics.

After the 1968 Olympic Games, Rigby competed in international competition in preparation for the 1972 Olympics in Munich, Germany. At the first World Cup held in 1968, she won the gymnastic championship and became a gold medallist with a record score of 38.5 points out of a possible 40. That same year she toured Europe with her SCATS team and became a favorite of the European press. The German media adoringly referred to her as "Cookie," and the Swiss press called her "the American whirlwind."

Still in high school, Rigby was attending classes, competing in gymnastics competitions, and training seven or eight hours a day for the Olympics. This hectic schedule left no time for a social life, but she still managed to graduate from Los Alamitos High School in 1971 with a B average. She then briefly attended Long Beach City College, dropping out to train full-time for the 1972 Olympics.

In 1970 at the U.S. championships Rigby was the All-Around gold medalist. That same year at the World Championships held in Ljubljana, Yugoslavia, she won a silver medal for the balance beam. She also became the first American gymnast, male or female, ever to win a medal in the World Championships. In 1971 she won numerous medals for national and international competition. She earned gold medals for all-around, vaulting, balance beam, floor exercises, and uneven bars, becoming the World Cup Champion. At the Riga Cup in Latvia, she won a gold medal for the balance beam and two bronze medals for all-around and for the uneven bars. At the South African Cup Championship, she won all-around, and at the US-USSR Dual Meet Championships she won the floor exercises. For the first time, it looked as if the United States might be a medal contender at the 1972 Olympic Games.

Affectionately called "Shrimp" and "Peanut" by her coach, and loved by the American public, Rigby's life seemed idyllic. But the reality was very different. Beginning in the late 1960s, she developed an eating disorder. Rigby felt that her coach really did not want her to grow up. She knew that Marquette worried that if her body changed during puberty, the added weight would change her center of gravity and affect her performance. Coach, parental, and public expectations for Rigby to win a medal at the 1972 Olympics put her under tremendous pressure. To win she believed that she had to maintain her girlish, ninety-pound weight. When her weight shot up to 105 pounds, she panicked. Obsessed with losing weight, Rigby began a practice of bingeing on food and then making herself throw up. Unfortunately, little was known about eating disorders in the 1960s, and she suffered from bulimia for twelve years. At one point she weighed only seventy-nine pounds. Twice she was hospitalized with serious health problems. Since 1981 Rigby has shared her story with the public in hopes of educating others about the disease and its health problems.

At the 1972 U.S. Olympic try-outs in Terre Haute, Indiana, all eyes were on Rigby. On the third day of competition, she fell while landing a flip during the floor exercises, twisting her right ankle and pulling the ligaments. She was unable to compete the final day of the trials. In an unprecedented move, the U.S. Olympic gymnastics committee named her to the six-member Olympic team anyway.

Rigby was the focus of media coverage at home and abroad. She made guest appearances on major television shows such as *The Johnny Carson Show, The Dick Cavett Show,* and *What's My Line?* Her picture appeared on the cover of *Life* magazine, and she was the subject of a feature article in *Sports Illustrated.* Rigby's picture also appeared on the front page of European newspapers, where one newspaper referred to her as "one in a million."

At the 1972 Olympics in Munich, the United States came in fourth in all-around competition, the highest ranking ever achieved. Rigby improved her overall performance from sixteenth at the 1968 Olympics to tenth place in 1972, but it was a bitter disappointment for Rigby. Her performance was overshadowed by a new Olympic gymnastics pigtail sensation, Russia's seventeen-year-old Olga Korbut.

Korbut won three gold and two silver medals and made history by being the first person to do a backward somersault on the uneven bars.

The *Los Angeles Times* named Rigby the 1972 Sportswoman of the Year. It is largely due to her that gymnastics became popular in the United States. From 1970 to 1973, high school gymnastics programs doubled in number. After the 1972 Olympics, Rigby retired from competition and formed her own gymnastics academy. She also served as an Olympic sports commentator for American Broadcasting Company (ABC) sports. ABC's *Wide World of Sports,* for its twenty-fifth anniversary in 1986, listed Rigby as one of the twenty-five most influential women in sports. In 1998 she was inducted into the International Gymnastics Hall of Fame. Rigby is involved in charitable work with the Special Olympics, the Boy and Girl Scouts of America, The Will Rogers Institute, Mercy Corps International, and the National Center for the Prevention of Sudden Infant Death Syndrome.

Rigby's acting career began in 1974 when she played Peter Pan in a National Broadcasting Company (NBC) television program of the same name. Since then she has appeared in numerous musicals, but she is probably best known for her Broadway performance in *Peter Pan,* from 1998 to 1999, for which she received a Tony nomination. Rigby has four children: two sons from her 1973–1981 marriage to Tom Mason, a former All-Pro running back for the Washington Redskins, and two daughters with her current husband, Tom McCoy, whom she married in 1982.

In the 1960s Rigby drew worldwide attention for American gymnastics and made the sport popular in the United States. Although she didn't win a medal at the 1968 Olympics, she scored higher than any prior U.S. gymnast. Her aerobatic performance is credited with revolutionizing women's international gymnastics competition.

★

A brief biography of Rigby is Linda Jacobs, *Cathy Rigby on the Beam* (1975). References for Rigby's gymnastics career include Irwin Stambler, *Women in Sports: The Stories of Twelve Great American Athletes* (1975), and Anne J. Johnson, *Great Women in Sports* (1996). Articles about Rigby are "Little Big Women: Catching Up with Cathy Rigby," *Woman Sports* (Oct. 1980), and "Cathy Rigby, Flying High," *People* (6 May 1991). See also "Cathy Rigby," *Life* (5 May 1972); and Anita Verschoth, "Sugar and Spice—and Iron," *Sports Illustrated* (21 Aug. 1972).

GAI INGHAM BERLAGE

RIVERS, Larry (*b.* 17 August 1923 in New York City; *d.* 14 August 2002 in Southampton, New York), painter and mixed-media artist who combined post-war abstract expressionist technique with figurative and pop cultural imagery and thus anticipated and influenced popular art of the 1960s.

Born Yitzroch Loiza Grossberg, Rivers was the eldest of three children of Shiah Grossberg, a plumber and later a trucking-company owner, and Sonya Hochberg, a homemaker. His Jewish parents were immigrants from Poland. When Rivers was seven, he learned to play the piano to accompany his father on the violin. Four years later he switched to the saxophone and became, at age seventeen, a professional jazz musician. For two years Rivers and his combo toured the "borscht belt" of the Catskill Mountains. One night they were introduced as "Larry Rivers and His Mudcats," and the new stage name stuck.

In 1942 Rivers enlisted in the U.S. Army Air Corps and then was given a medical discharge. He continued playing with jazz bands and in 1944 studied composition in New York City at the Julliard School of Music. While touring, he met jazz pianist Jack Freillicher, whose painter wife, Jane, introduced Rivers to her circle of friends. Among them was the painter Neil Blaine, who began giving Rivers informal lessons in drawing and painting. That same year (1945), Rivers married Augusta Burger. They had one son but divorced in 1946.

From 1940 through 1941 Rivers experimented in painting by expressively copying covers and illustrations of art magazines. At Neil Blaine's suggestion, Rivers began to study painting seriously, enrolling in 1947 under the GI Bill at Hans Hofmann's School of Fine Arts. The German-

Larry Rivers. ARCHIVE PHOTOS, INC.

born Hofmann was then one of the foremost painters and art teachers in the United States. As a painter, he was a part of a group known as abstract expressionists, whose work was characterized by hermetic drippings and cryptic slashings, thickly globbed all over large canvases. The group abhorred realistic, blatant subject matter, such as the magazine illustrations of Norman Rockwell and the quaint "Americana" paintings of Thomas Hart Benton. Instead of such obvious realism, Hoffmann's paintings and teaching philosophy concentrated on how thickly applied colors "pushed and pulled" each other optically on a canvas. In class Rivers often debated with Hofmann about abstraction versus representation, and Rivers defiantly painted realistic figures instead of the abstract work done by the other students (and Hofmann).

Rivers wanted to somehow combine the painterly abstract space of abstract expressionism with representational subject matter. His breakthrough came while viewing an exhibition of the turn-of-the-century French painter Pierre Bonnard. Bonnard's brightly colored and loosely painted canvases were mostly figure studies, which Rivers at first freely copied. He then painted his own figures of friends, as well as that of his ex-mother-in-law, Bertie, whose aged, flabby, nude flesh he painted repeatedly until her death in 1958.

Rivers frequented the hangout of the abstract expressionists, the Cedar Bar, where he hotly debated the merits of combining figuration with abstraction. In 1957 he became nationally famous as an authority on contemporary art when he won $32,000 answering questions about the subject on the *$64,000 Challenge* quiz show. He was then featured in *Life* magazine as a sax-playing, "boy wonder" painter. In 1961 he married Clarice Price. They had two daughters before divorcing in 1967.

Rivers visited Paris for eight months in 1950 and wrote poetry while staying there. He spent part of 1957 in Paris as well but soon returned to New York, at which time he began collaborating with poets, especially Frank O'Hara. Rivers combined poetry with images in prints and paintings. His interest in poetry and with words then led him in a new direction. With *Cedar Bar Menu* (1960), Rivers began to use photographic source material with stenciled lettering that labeled the photo source. Then he began a series of textbook vocabulary lesson images in paintings that combined nude figures and stenciled labels with arrows pointing to body parts. These works anticipated the conceptual art of the later 1960s. In part, this later movement emphasized the philosophical contemplation of language but abandoned the traditional painting-on-canvas retained by Rivers.

The hallmark of Rivers's painting is the combination of popular-culture subject matter with the loosely brushed painting style of abstract expressionism. While flattening the space surrounding a subject, he fragmented the image. He also added patches of pure paint that seemed to float on the surface of the canvas. His works bridged the then-dominant abstract expressionist generation and their later 1960s pop art rivals. The pop artists abandoned the loosely painted style and freely floating color patches retained by Rivers.

A notable example of Rivers's style is *Dutch Masters and Cigars, no. 2* (1964). Its fragmented and doubled image was taken from an open cigar box. Inside the lid there is a reproduction of a Rembrandt painting. At the painted hinge between the reproduction's figures and the tobacco product appears the stenciled word "CIGAR." Then the image of the open box is repeated again at the bottom of the canvas, suggesting a close-up view of shelves of a tobacco shop. The figures and cigars are loosely painted, and color splotches are evenly dispersed throughout the canvas.

In an essay written for his 1965 retrospective, Frank O'Hara wrote that Rivers "had chosen to mirror his preoccupations and enthusiasms in an unprogrammatic way." Rivers did evoke eye-catching designs with equal attention to painterly concerns and to popular subject matter.

In 1965 Rivers began work on *History of the Russian Revolution: From Marx to Mayakovsky*, which became a mixed-media work that combined seventy-six canvases mounted onto a wooden construction more than thirty-two feet long and fourteen feet high. With many relatives still living in Russia, Rivers gave this personal topic epic scope. Scenes, personalities, events, and symbols traced historical struggle. Loosely painted figures, photographs, stenciled letters, and found objects (including real weapons) are combined tabloid-like in his passionate perspective of Russia.

From the early to late 1960s, Rivers did collaborations with the Swiss-French sculptor Jean Tinguely. *The Friendship of America and France* works were two-sided paintings on motorized, revolving stands. Images included French currency, cigar boxes, and French/English vocabulary diagrams. Throughout the 1960s, Rivers collaborated on many projects. He did set designs for plays by Le Roi Jones (the African-American poet who changed his name to Amiri Baraka), as well as costume and set designs in 1966 for the New York Metropolitan Opera. In 1968 Rivers collaborated on a film documentary that was set in Nigeria. The Nigerian government mistook the crew for mercenaries, and to escape execution, they fled the country. Later that year Rivers illustrated Terry Southern's novel *The Donkey and the Darling*.

In 1969 the Smith Haven Mall in Smith Haven, Long Island, commissioned Rivers to do a major work that would evoke the shopping experience in the mall. His *Forty Feet of Fashion* was that length and included that number of legs, hands, smiling lips, and dashing figures constructed in mixed media. Encased in clear plastic, it included slide projections of products and mall shops.

After the 1960s, Rivers's work combined the themes of cultural history, clichés of popular culture, art-world gossip, and autobiographical subjects, and he continued to collaborate with writers and to mix media. He died of cancer of the liver at the age of seventy-eight; his remains were cremated.

★

Rivers's autobiographies are *Drawings and Digressions* (1979), written with Carol Brightman; and *What Did I Do?: The Unauthorized Autobiography* (1992), written with Arnold Wenstein. Major studies include Sam Hunter, *Larry Rivers* (1970, rev. ed., 1971), and Helen A. Harrison, *Larry Rivers* (1984). Obituaries are in the *New York Times* (16 Aug. 2002) and the *Manchester Guardian* (17 Aug. 2002).

PATRICK S. SMITH

ROBARDS, Jason Nelson, Jr. (*b.* 26 July 1922 in Chicago, Illinois; *d.* 26 December 2000 in Bridgeport, Connecticut), actor who helped to establish the plays of Eugene O'Neill as masterpieces of American drama and in doing so established his own legacy as an "actor's actor."

Robards was the son of Jason Robards, Sr., a silent-screen movie star, and Hope Glanvilles. His father and mother

Jason Robards, 1962. THE KOBAL COLLECTION

divorced, and at the age of five, Robards went to live with his father and stepmother in Beverly Hills, where he attended Hollywood High School. He graduated in 1939 as a sports star, having rejected acting because of his father's failing career. In 1939, at the age of seventeen, he joined the U.S. Navy and was a radio operator at the time of the bombing of Pearl Harbor in December 1941. Robards served in the South Pacific during World War II, took part in thirteen battles, and was honored with the Navy Cross in 1946 before his discharge with the rank of radioman first class.

Robards married four times. He married Eleanor Pitman in 1948; they had three children. In 1959 he married Rachel Taylor; they divorced in 1961. In 1961 he married the actress Lauren Bacall; they had one child, but divorced in 1969. In 1970 he married Lois O'Connor; they had two children, and divorced in 2000.

After reading some of Eugene O'Neill's plays during the war, and with his father's support, Robards enrolled in the American Academy of Dramatic Arts in New York City. In 1956 the director Jose Quintero unexpectedly cast the thirty-four-year-old Robards in the leading part of Hickey in O'Neill's *The Iceman Cometh.* Robards connected with the broken, disheartened, dark souls whom O'Neill portrayed with more passion than any actor had previously done. He struck the same resounding chord with his 1957 performance as Jamie Tyrone in O'Neill's *Long Day's Journey Into Night.* As a result of Robards's passionate portrayals of his characters, O'Neill was not only rediscovered, but also recognized as one of the greatest American dramatists. In 1959 Robards won a Tony award for his portrayal of a character based on F. Scott Fitzgerald in *The Disenchanted,* written by Budd Schulberg.

During the 1960s Robards's reputation as an actor became as firmly established in films as it had been on the stage. He acted in more than ninety films and television productions during his lifetime, but noted that he only did these to pay the bills—his real love was the theater, appearing in front of a live audience.

Robards's first two marriages, to Eleanor Pitman and then to Rachel Taylor, ended in divorce as the 1950s came to a close. Riding the wave of the election of John F. Kennedy in 1960, with its promise of youth, intellectualism, and social action, Robards was inspired by the Kennedy administration's message of hope, which encouraged each person to make a difference. He took that challenge to his audiences, demanding that they confront social injustice in both their public and private lives. By 1961 he had married Lauren Bacall, and he had found his calling by portraying brutal but honest characters.

Also in 1961, Robards played Dick Diver in the film *Tender Is The Night,* adapted from the F. Scott Fitzgerald novel that chronicles Fitzgerald's divorce from his wife,

Zelda. Here Robards portrayed the character of one of America's most complex writers and brought his own angst and fragile self-confidence to the screen with perfect pitch. Again, Robards brought the importance of the self-examined life to the forefront of American culture.

In 1962 Robards recreated the part of Jamie Tyrone in the film version of *Long Day's Journey Into Night*. As a result of the collaboration of Jose Quintero and Robards, O'Neill's *The Iceman Cometh, Long Day's Journey Into Night, Ah Wilderness, Hughie,* and *A Touch of the Poet,* which had been dismissed as dark and pessimistic during the 1940s and early 1950s, took on new meaning during the 1960s. With numerous social revolutions taking place, Robards's portrayal of O'Neill's characters brought home to the American public the playwright's message about the powerful dichotomies between love and hate, guilt and forgiveness. O'Neill, like other great modern existentialists, was concerned that traditional values lead to meaningless lives. Robards had witnessed his father's fall from famous silent-screen star to a forgotten man, and Robards himself was haunted by alcohol, though he never experienced the alcoholism that O'Neill's characters suffered. But Robards clearly understood the anger, frustration, and self-loathing of these characters. His portrayal of Jamie Tyrone was so convincing that one critic claimed, "Robards is Tyrone." O'Neill's message that the past affects the present reverberates throughout the film version, and some critics give credit to Robards for helping to establish *Long Day's Journey Into Night* as the greatest American play written in the twentieth century.

Through the character of Tyrone, Robards spoke about taking responsibility for the unfolding of events; in the end, people must be true to the better part of themselves. O'Neill's words, spoken through Robards, seemed to foreshadow the American psyche after President Kennedy was assassinated in 1963, when, for many, the idealism of the Kennedy years was shattered along with the president's death. The sullen, drunken men in dark, seedy barrooms that Robards so often portrayed loomed over Americans like warnings.

Although Robards did such lighthearted films as *A Thousand Clowns* (1965), during the latter part of the 1960s, his films reflected the political upheavals that raged during the Vietnam War. The deaths of Dr. Martin Luther King, Jr., and Senator Robert Kennedy seemed to jettison Robards into antiheroic roles in which he could vicariously challenge and strike out at the establishment. He starred as an antihero in *The St. Valentine's Day Massacre* (1967), *The Night They Raided Minsky's* (1968), and *Once Upon a Time in the West* (1969), films that reflect an American psyche that was no longer content to be acquiescent. Americans were angry and vocal, and Robards's hardened characters gave voice to their anger.

Although Robards was very busy during the 1970s, his marriage to Bacall had ended in divorce, and he felt as if he were just "an actor waiting for the phone to ring." He made more than twenty films during this decade, and won two Academy Awards back to back for *All the President's Men* (1977) and *Julia* (1978), but Robards could not wait to return to the stage. When he did, he performed in plays by Arthur Miller, Lillian Hellman, and Harold Pinter; and returned to O'Neill in *Hughie, A Touch of the Poet, Long Day's Journey Into Night, Ah, Wilderness,* and *A Moon for the Misbegotten.* He continued to act the part of the angry man in such films as *Max Dugan Returns* (1983), *Sakharov* (1984), *The Long Hot Summer* (1985), *The Good Mother* (1988), *Philadelphia* (1993), *A Thousand Acres* (1997), and *Magnolia* (1999).

Robards died of cancer in Bridgeport Hospital. He had the extraordinary gift of giving voice to the suffering who search for meaning. Some of Robards's greatest roles were created and recreated during the 1960s when Americans were trying to come to terms with the death of their president, Dr. Martin Luther King, Jr., and Senator Robert Kennedy, as well as the Vietnam War and the civil rights movement. Robards chose roles in which he starkly laid out for Americans, in his sharp, angry voice, what their lives would be like if they neglected and abused important family members and friends.

★

A discussion of Robards's lifelong association with O'Neill's work is in Michael Manheim, ed., *Eugene O'Neill* (1998). Obituaries are in the *New York Times* and *Washington Post* (both 27 Dec. 2000).

JANE FRANCES AMLER

ROBBINS, Jerome (*b.* 11 October 1918 in New York City, *d.* 29 July 1998 in New York City), one of the greatest American choreographers and directors for the Broadway stage and ballet theater.

Born Jerome Rabinowitz, Robbins was one of two children of Russian-Jewish immigrants Harry Rabinowitz and Lena (Rips) Rabinowitz, a homemaker. His father first managed a delicatessen on the Upper East Side of Manhattan, but the family moved in the 1920s, first to Jersey City and later to Weehawken, New Jersey, where Harry Rabinowitz and his brother-in-law ran the Comfort Corset Company. The entire family eventually changed its name to *Robbins* after Robbins started to become well known during the 1940s.

Robbins discovered dance as a teenager. He graduated from Woodrow Wilson High School in 1935 and enrolled that fall at New York University, intending to follow his parents' wishes and study either journalism or chemistry.

Jerome Robbins *(left)*, shown with Gene Kelly in April 1962. Robbins is holding his Academy Award for best director for the film version of *West Side Story*. ASSOCIATED PRESS AP

However, because his family's finances were strained during the Great Depression, and he was markedly unenthusiastic about his studies, Robbins's career in higher education was short-lived. After a year of college, he returned to dancing as an apprentice at Senya Gluck-Sandor's dance center, where his sister Sonia already danced professionally. He made his professional debut in 1937 with the Yiddish Art Theater.

By this time Robbins had begun to study ballet and a wide variety of other dance forms and techniques. He landed small dancing roles, appearing in the chorus lines of four Broadway musicals. His first opportunity to choreograph came when he went to work at Camp Tamiment, a summer resort for adults in the Poconos of Pennsylvania. By 1940 Robbins was dancing with George Balanchine's Ballet Theater in New York City, where he eventually became associate ballet master, a post he held, except for a brief period, until 1983. Despite his early success, Robbins was restless and weary of classical ballet. "Why can't we do ballets about our own subjects," he complained, "meaning our life here in America?"

Robbins's first attempt at breaking with dance conventions came in 1944 with *Fancy Free,* a lighthearted, half-hour celebration about three sailors on shore leave in New York. Robbins's choreography, which drew on dances from the Lindy to the waltz, was an immediate hit with audi-

ences. Eight months later, the play reappeared as the more elaborate musical comedy *On the Town.* After the success of *On the Town,* Robbins went on to choreograph many Broadway shows, including *The King and I* (1950), *Peter Pan* (1954), and *Gypsy* (1959). Unquestionably, his greatest triumph was the 1957 production of *West Side Story,* a contemporary retelling of Shakespeare's *Romeo and Juliet,* for which he won an Antoinette Perry (Tony) award in 1958 for choreography.

During the 1960s Robbins built his reputation, not only as a choreographer, but also as a stage director. He began the decade as choreographer and codirector, with Robert Wise, of the film version of *West Side Story,* for which he won two Academy Awards, a special award for choreography as well as one for directing. Robbins returned to the theater in 1962 with the off-Broadway production *Oh Dad, Poor Dad, Mamma's Hung You in the Closet and I'm Feelin' So Sad,* a play satirizing the conventions of the theater. He followed this effort in 1963 with the more serious antiwar play *Mother Courage and Her Children.*

Although Robbins devoted himself more to directing than choreographing during the early 1960s, he had not completely divorced himself from musical theater. In 1962 he was summoned to heal the musical comedy *A Funny Thing Happened on the Way to the Forum,* which was in danger of being shelved before it opened. Even though the play received a warm reception and enjoyed a long Broadway run, Robbins was never credited for his role in the production. A year later in 1963, Robbins was again approached to help with a musical in trouble. This time the play was *Funny Girl,* which was based on the life of Jewish comedienne and singer Fanny Brice. It was Robbins's decision to cast a relatively unknown singer named Barbra Streisand in the title role. The gamble paid off; *Funny Girl* became a hit and made the twenty-one-year-old Streisand an overnight sensation.

In 1964 Robbins agreed to direct the Broadway production of *Fiddler on the Roof,* the tale of a Jewish family and community living in a small Russian village in 1905. The project quickly became personal for Robbins in many ways. His father had fled from a small town similar to the one portrayed in the play, and the story enabled Robbins to more fully explore his Russian-Jewish heritage. *Fiddler on the Roof* was among the greatest successes of Robbins's career, earning him two more Tony Awards (best director and best choreography), yet the play was also his last original Broadway musical.

After choreographing and directing *Fiddler,* Robbins turned his attention to the creation of several original ballets. In 1966 he received a two-year grant from the National Endowment for the Arts to experiment with lyric theater. For two years, the American Theater Laboratory, a handpicked group of performers, met every day to work on movement improvisations that drew from dance forms and cultural rituals around the world. During rehearsals the performers were sworn to secrecy, and no formal production has ever been performed based on Robbins's work.

In 1969 Robbins, working in conjunction with the New York City Ballet, choreographed what many consider to be his masterpiece, *Dances at a Gathering*. This production marked a clear break with Robbins's choreographic style of the past, as he moved away from "story ballets" to works that were more abstract and neoclassical in form. The ballet included ten dancers in various combinations, expressing a wide range of moods and emotions. Critics praised Robbins's diverse choreography, describing it simply as "a celebration of dance."

For the next twenty years, Robbins entered the most prolific phase of his career, choreographing more than twenty ballets. In 1988 he returned to Broadway after a twenty-five-year absence, reconstructing some of the highlights from his years in musical theater with *Jerome Robbins' Broadway*. The production earned him his fifth Tony award. In July 1998, after suffering a stroke, Robbins died at his home. His remains were cremated, and the ashes were scattered near his beach home in Bridgehampton, New York. He was three months short of his eightieth birthday.

Throughout his distinguished career, Robbins combined what one writer identified as "theatrical savvy with an unerring sense of movement to create potent, moving panoramas." Robbins's creativity knew few bounds; always in search of new challenges, he created a vast and eclectic body of work, often drawing on American themes and issues. However, beneath the diversity and scope of Robbins's work there was always the theme of community and friendship—among sailors on a lark, New York street gangs, Russian-Jewish peasants, or isolated souls linked only by experience, emotion, and time. Robbins's death marked the end of an era in dance, during which American choreographers brought a distinctive vitality to American musical theater.

★

The most complete biography of Robbins is Greg Lawrence, *Dance with Demons: The Life of Jerome Robbins* (2001). Robbins's work is examined in Nancy Reynolds, *Repertory in Review* (1977). Martin Gottfried, *Broadway Musicals* (1979); Otis L. Guernsey, Jr., ed., *Broadway Song & Story* (1985); Christena Schlundt, *Dance in the Musical Theater: Jerome Robbins and His Peers* (1989); and Robert Emmet Long, *Broadway, The Golden Years: Jerome Robbins and the Great Choreographer-Directors 1940 to the Present* (2001), all contain insightful discussions of Robbins's life and career. An obituary is in the *New York Times* (27 Dec. 1998).

MEG GREENE

ROBERTS, Oral (*b.* 24 January 1918 near Ada, Oklahoma), evangelist, faith healer, author, educator, and university founder and president.

Roberts, born Granville Oral Roberts, was the fifth and youngest child of Reverend Ellis M. Roberts, an independent Pentecostal evangelist, and Claudius Irwin Roberts, a homemaker. He claims Native American ancestry. Roberts grew up in poverty and struggled with stuttering. In 1933 he left home to attend school in another town but returned two years later when he was stricken with tuberculosis. He attended a revival meeting and says that he was healed when traveling evangelist George Moncey prayed for him. Roberts delivered his first sermon that evening.

Roberts married Evelyn Lutman on 25 December 1938, and the couple had four children. That same year he finished his first book, *Salvation by the Blood*. Roberts holds honorary law and doctor of divinity degrees from Centenary College of Louisiana and an honorary doctor of divinity from the International Church of the Foursquare Gospel, a master's of divinity from Phillips University in Enid, Oklahoma, and a B.A. from Oklahoma Baptist University in Shawnee.

In the late 1940s Roberts affiliated with the Pentecostal Fellowship of North America (now the Pentecostal/Char-

Oral Roberts. ARCHIVE PHOTOS, INC.

ismatic Churches of North America). In 1948 he preached the final rally of that fellowship in Des Moines, Iowa. Then, in 1949 in Enid, Oklahoma, Roberts, in his fourth Pentecostal Church as pastor, heard God tell him that he had the ability to heal the afflicted. The following month he healed a woman who had been crippled for thirty-eight years. Roberts then resigned as pastor of the Pentecostal Church in Enid and began radio broadcasts from his large tent meetings. By 1950 he was traveling with an 18,000-seat tent and broadcasting his message on sixty-three radio stations. The Baptist evangelist Billy Graham invited Roberts to lead the prayer at the World Conference on Evangelism in Portland, Oregon, in 1950, and the audience gave Roberts a standing ovation. Two years later Roberts was broadcasting from over four hundred television and radio stations. In 1957 he claimed to be reaching an audience of a billion people. By comparison, radio evangelist Carl McIntire's *20th Century Reformation Hour* was carried every day for a half hour in the 1960s on more than six hundred stations in the United States and Canada. Roberts has conducted more than three hundred evangelistic and healing crusades on six continents. He has also written more than 120 books.

The Pentecostal Holiness Church remained divided in their support of Roberts after 1953. Pentecostal leaders such as R. O. Corvin and Oscar Moore worked with Roberts in his evangelistic association. Although the white members of the Pentecostal Fellowship of North America had separated themselves from the African-American members in Des Moines, Iowa, in 1948, Roberts, like Billy Graham, welcomed African Americans to his services and did not segregate them from his white audience. At first Bishop Joseph A. Synan of the Pentecostal Holiness Church opposed Roberts, but he did attend the dedication ceremonies of Oral Roberts University in 1967.

Roberts broadcast his ministry on local television in the 1960s from Tulsa, Oklahoma, where he also established his evangelical organization. Founded by its namesake, Oral Roberts University was first chartered in 1963, and its first students came in 1965. Seven years later, the school's enrollment had grown from 300 to 1,800 students, and it had a $48 million endowment. In 1963 Roberts was named "Indian of the Year" by the American Indian Exposition of Anadarko, Oklahoma. Roberts led a successful revival in Berlin, Germany (26 October to 4 November 1966). He left the Pentecostal Holiness Church in 1968 and joined the United Methodist Church, which then became the First United Methodist Church. Soon thereafter he supported the founding of the Business Men's Fellowship International, and he had access to their membership lists.

Roberts devised his evangelism around the theme of seed-faith. According to Roberts, those listeners and viewers who contributed to his ministry planted a seed that would grow and produce an abundance of spiritual and material dividends within this lifetime. According to his *Miracle of Seed-Faith* (1970), seed-faith's three attributes include making a blessing-pact covenant with God, sowing and reaping, and insisting on giving seed money to God so he can make it multiply and serve one's personal financial needs. Beginning in the 1960s Roberts used his huge computers at the Abundant Life Building in Tulsa to facilitate his mass mailings to supporters. In 1969 he produced a record with Senator Mark O. Hatfield with Hatfield reading "The Incomparable Christ" on one side and Roberts reading "Christ in Every Book in the Bible" on the other (Lexicon Music).

Roberts's family has been touched by tragedy. His daughter Rebecca and her husband were killed in an airplane crash in 1977, and his son Richard divorced his wife in 1979. In 1982 Roberts's son Ronald committed suicide.

After a vision from God, Roberts built the City of Faith Hospital in Tulsa. Roberts later had a vision of a 900-foot Jesus who picked up the City of Faith in his hands to encourage Roberts to complete the project; at the millennium, Roberts was continuing work on the institution. In 1987 God appeared to Roberts in another vision and told him to raise $8 million for Oral Roberts University scholarships within the next year or he would die. Roberts raised the money.

In the 1960s Roberts led the country in the founding of successful radio and television evangelism, and from that he built a state-of-the-art hospital and a major university. He is now retired, but his son Richard continues in his father's roles. Oral Roberts Ministry's magazine, *Abundant Life,* continues to publish articles telling readers that Roberts knows how God creates miracles. In addition to *The Hour of Healing* television show, Richard's wife, Lindsay, hosts the television program *Make Your Day Count.*

★

Roberts's memoir is *The Call: An Autobiography* (1972). Also see David Edwin Harrell, *Oral Roberts: An American Life* (1985) (reviewed in *The New Republic,* 29 Sept. 1986); James Morris, *The Preachers* (1973); and Charles H. Lippy, *Twentieth-Century Shapers of American Popular Religion* (1989).

LARRY D. GRIFFIN

ROBERTSON, Marion Gordon ("Pat") (*b.* 22 March 1930 in Lexington, Virginia), clergyman, broadcasting executive, television personality, and political activist who founded the Christian Broadcasting Network (CBN) in the early 1960s; host of CBN's flagship magazine program *The 700 Club.*

Robertson is the son of A. Willis Robertson, an anti–New Deal southern Democrat who represented Virginia in both houses of Congress for over thirty years. His mother,

Gladys Churchill Willis, was a devout Christian and biblical literalist who counted two U.S. presidents among her ancestors. Robertson received the education of a southern gentleman, attending prep school at the McCallie School in Chattanooga, Tennessee, and college at Washington and Lee University in Lexington, Virginia. He graduated from Washington and Lee with a bachelor's degree in economics in 1950, Phi Beta Kappa and magna cum laude. He then served two years in the U.S. Marine Corps during the Korean conflict, after which he enrolled in Yale Law School, receiving his J.D. degree in 1955. In 1954 Robertson married Adelia ("Dede") Elmer; they have four children.

If the intellectual and spiritual crises of the conformist 1950s can be seen as a source of 1960s cultural radicalism, this analysis is as true of Robertson as it is of any Beat generation writer. As an eligible young man from a wealthy family, he enjoyed the advantages of the high life at Yale and in New York City society. At the same time, however, he found himself suffering the inner pain of what he called "a God-shaped vacuum" that was not relieved by hedonism. Robertson cites a meeting, arranged by his mother, with the Baptist missionary Cornelius Vanderbreggen in 1957 as the turning point in his personal conversion to Christianity. Robertson was working as a financial analyst for W. R. Grace and Company while studying to retake the New York State bar examination. In response to his "born-again" experience, Robertson sold his house in Staten Island, moved his family to a Brooklyn religious commune, and enrolled in the New York Theological Seminary. He received his master of divinity degree in 1959, and in 1961 he was ordained as a Southern Baptist minister.

Robertson described the event that led him from street-corner evangelism to the life of a broadcasting executive: "My mother had received a letter from an old friend who said there was a TV station for sale in Portsmouth, Virginia, and, 'Would Pat be interested in claiming it for the Lord?'" After a period of intense prayer and thought, Robertson left Brooklyn and went to Virginia to buy the station. He formed the Christian Broadcasting Network (CBN) as a non-stock, non-profit corporation on January 11, 1960. Renaming the station WYAH for *Yahweh,* the ancient Hebrew name of God, Robertson refused to sell commercial time, instead appealing directly to viewers for funds, following the model of the left-leaning Pacifica Foundation, which was financing its radio stations in California and New York this way.

During the early 1960s WYAH-TV survived on a shoestring. Its programming consisted of religious-oriented talk and music, along with whatever public-domain material (mostly travelogues) Robertson could find. A toll-free number superimposed on the screen allowed viewers to consult with telephone prayer counselors about their problems and to pledge funds to the television ministry if they wished to

do so. In 1963, with the station in financial crisis, Robertson conducted a telethon asking for 700 viewers to each pledge $10 per month to keep it on the air. The goal was reached, and he later renamed his daily program *The 700 Club* in honor of the event.

By the end of the 1960s, Robertson had stabilized the operation with funds provided by investors. CBN bought three more television stations (including one in Lebanon that reached across the Middle East), as well as five more radio stations. In addition, affiliate agreements were made with scores of television and radio stations to carry *The 700 Club* and other CBN programs. In 1977 Robertson purchased access rights to RCA's Satcom II satellite, a crucial move that secured the success of CBN as a national communications company and established him as a true pioneer of the cable television revolution. Able to beam its signal to every cable system in the United States (and abroad), CBN quickly became one of the most-viewed cable channels in the United States, ranking with Ted Turner's WTBS Superstation and MTV in terms of household penetration and ratings. In a move that disturbed some of his religious followers, Robertson changed the name of the cable outlet to the Family Channel in 1981, introduced commercials, and turned it into a for-profit company. The Family Channel was sold in 1998, but CBN continues to exist as an umbrella for Robertson's television and radio interests.

Robertson's fundamentalist religious beliefs in "gifts of the spirit," such as faith healing and speaking in tongues, draw a combination of mockery and animus from his critics. The same is true of his populist views on subjects ranging from the teaching of natural selection, to the replacement of state welfare programs with religion-based charities. However, it should be noted that racial reconciliation, one of the overriding themes of the 1960s, became an important message in Robertson's television ministry. Ben Kinchlow, an African American who had once considered membership in Elijah Muhammed's Nation of Islam (or "Black Muslims"), was for many years Robertson's co-host on *The 700 Club,* and the friendship and conviviality of the two had a tangible effect on the many unreconstructed segregationists among Robertson's audience.

In 1987 Robertson announced his candidacy for the Republican nomination that was eventually won by George H. W. Bush. Attacked by moderates for his religious beliefs (such as his claim that a hurricane had spared the CBN transmitting station because of prayer) and for inconsistencies with his philosophy in his personal life (such as his revising the date of his marriage anniversary to conceal the birth of his first child), Robertson soon retreated to the role of a powerbroker in the Republican Party, which, as the founding president of the Christian Coalition, he institutionalized. His support was crucial in the Republican primary victories of George W. Bush in the 2000 presidential campaign.

Robertson bristles at being called a "televangelist," which he regards as the equivalent of "calling a black person a 'nigger.'" Clearly his aims have been broader and his achievements more noteworthy than other television preachers whose scandals are conjured by the term. As is often the case with 1960s idealists of all political stripes, Robertson's subsequent career leaves those who have followed it arguing over whether he has successfully "changed the world" or "sold out to the establishment."

★

Robertson's autobiography, with Jamie Buckingham, *Shout It from the Housetops* (1972), gives an account of his life as a young man. Biographies include Gerard T. Straub, *Salvation for Sale: An Insider's View of Pat Robertson's Ministry* (1986); David E. Harrell, *Pat Robertson: A Personal, Religious, and Political Portrait* (1987); and John B. Donovan, *Pat Robertson: The Authorized Biography* (1988). In addition, the transcript of a two-hour videotaped interview conducted by the author in 2000 is held at the Syracuse University Library by the Center for the Study of Popular Television.

DAVID MARC

ROBINSON, Frank, Jr. (*b.* 31 August 1935 in Beaumont, Texas), professional baseball player, coach, Hall of Famer, first professional to win the Most Valuable Player (MVP) crown in both the American and National Leagues, and the first African-American manager in Major League Baseball.

Robinson was the youngest of ten children born to Ruth Shaw and the only child of her third marriage to Frank Robinson, a railroad worker with business interests and real estate in Silsbee, Texas. In 1939 Robinson, his mother, and two brothers moved to Alameda, California. In the fall of 1950 Robinson entered McClymonds High School in West Oakland. There he garnered All-City awards for three consecutive years in baseball and basketball. He graduated in 1953.

Robinson was pursued by the Chicago White Sox, Cincinnati Reds, and St. Louis Browns. Cincinnati made the best offer, and in June 1953 he signed with the team. Assigned to Ogden, Utah (Pioneer League), he batted .348 (20 doubles and 6 triples) and led the team with 17 homers. The Californian also handled the racial prejudice he encountered in de facto segregated Utah.

In 1954 Robinson was initially promoted to Tulsa (Texas League, Class AA) after eight games, but he was reassigned to Columbia, South Carolina (South Atlantic League). Robinson endured racial taunts and threats from fans and opposing players and separate lodging and dining

Frank Robinson. ARCHIVE PHOTOS, INC.

from his teammates. He said, "The South really made me a better ballplayer. I was just determined to get out of there."

On 17 April 1956 Robinson made his major-league debut against the St. Louis Cardinals. During his first season the rookie batted .290, tied Wally Berger's rookie home run (HR) record with 38, made the National League (NL) All-Star team, led the NL with 122 runs scored, was hit by a pitch 20 times (a rookie record), and earned NL Rookie of the Year honors. At the end of the 1957 season he enlisted in the Marines. However, he was honorably discharged after only one month when a doctor found calcium deposits in his right shoulder.

In 1961 Robinson hit .323, knocked out 37 homers, and drove in 124 runs, leading Cincinnati to its first NL title since 1940. He also won the NL's MVP award. Despite these heroics, animosity brewed between Robinson and the Reds front office, in particular the general manager Bill DeWitt. Since 1960, when DeWitt had assumed the job, annual contract negotiations had been a sore point. Robinson felt that DeWitt demeaned the ballplayers when he balked at raising their wages. In 1961 Robinson did receive a then-record salary in excess of $60,000, although not without acrimony. On 28 October 1961 Robinson married Barbara Ann Cole. They had two children.

Robinson opened the 1962 season threatened with possible retirement because of his latest contract rounds with DeWitt. Nevertheless, he earned his third consecutive slugging title and led the NL with 51 doubles and 134 runs. He hit .342 with 39 HRs and 136 runs batted in (RBI), but he missed leading the NL in total bases and batting average. Robinson lost out to the Giants' Willie Mays and Dodgers' Tommie Davis, respectively. In 1963 Robinson played through injuries, and although he had a drop in batting numbers he achieved a career high of 26 steals. In 1964 he was back to his batting form with a .306 average, 29 HRs, and 96 RBI.

On 9 December 1965 DeWitt traded Robinson to the Baltimore Orioles (once the St. Louis Browns) for Milt Pappas, Jack Baldschun, and the outfielder Dick Simpson. DeWitt labeled Robinson "an old 30." The swap led to DeWitt's ouster as general manager. Robinson pushed Baltimore to four pennants and two World Series titles in the next six years.

In 1966 Robinson won baseball's "triple crown," leading the league with a .317 batting average, 49 HRs, and 122 RBI. He was also named AL MVP, becoming the first player to win that title in both leagues. He led Baltimore to its first pennant and a World Series upset sweep of the Los Angeles Dodgers. As an Oriole, Robinson's annual salary was raised to $100,000, and he was featured in many of the club's promotional materials. One particular diamond highlight came during an 8 May 1966 game against the Cleveland Indians, when Robinson hit a home run that completely cleared Baltimore's Memorial Stadium.

Robinson studied Orioles manager Earl Weaver's baseball strategy and in the 1968 off-season inked a contract to manage the Santurce Cangrejeros (Crabbers) of the Puerto Rican Winter League. In early 1969 the team won the Winter League pennant, and Robinson was named Manager of the Year.

In 1971, with his consent, Robinson was traded to the Los Angeles Dodgers. That year Baltimore retired Robinson's number 20, making him the first Oriole to receive that honor.

In 1975 Robinson became the first African American to manage a major-league team. On 7 April of that year, in his first at bat as a player/manager, he crushed a home run to lead his Cleveland Indians to a 5–3 home win over the New York Yankees. In 1982 Robinson was inducted into the National Baseball Hall of Fame and named the NL Manager of the Year with the San Francisco Giants. A trailblazer, Robinson held various Major League Baseball executive posts. In 2002, with the league's takeover of the Montreal Expos franchise, he returned to the field as manager of the Expos.

★

Robinson's three autobiographies are *My Life Is Baseball* (1968), with Al Silverman; *Frank: The First Years* (1976), with

Dave Anderson; and *Extra Innings* (1989), with Berry Stainback. More information is available in Edwin B. Henderson and Editors of SPORT Magazine, *International Library of Afro-American Life and History: The Black Athlete Emergence and Arrival* (1978); Arthur R. Ashe, Jr., *A Hard Road to Glory: A History of the African American Athlete Since 1946* (1988); Norm Macht, *Frank Robinson* (1991); L. Mpho Mabunda, ed., *Contemporary Black Biography: Profiles from the International Black Community,* vol. 9 (1995); David Pietrusza, Matthew Silverman, and Michael Gershman, eds., *Baseball: The Biographical Encyclopedia* (2000); and Dan Schlossberg, *The Baseball Almanac: Big Bodacious Book of Baseball* (2002).

JOHN VORPERIAN

ROBINSON, William, Jr. ("Smokey") (*b.* 19 February 1940 in Detroit, Michigan), singer, songwriter, record producer, and record-company executive who in the 1960s led the Miracles, a popular rhythm and blues (R&B) group, and contributed to the careers of several other R&B artists at Motown Records.

Robinson's father, William Robinson, Sr., worked in a bowling alley; his mother, Flossie Smith Bynum Ligon, was a homemaker. His parents divorced when he was three, and his mother died when he was ten, after which he was

Smokey Robinson (*far left*), and the Miracles. CORBIS CORPORATION (BELLEVUE)

raised in a household containing many family members, including his sister Geraldine and his father. The nickname "Smokey" was applied to him ironically because he was actually quite light skinned. Robinson was interested in singing as early as the age of six and formed his first vocal group in grade school; he also began writing songs at an early age. His voice was a high tenor, and he claimed to use falsetto only rarely to hit high notes. Robinson's high school group, at first called the Five Chimes, was later dubbed the Matadors. This was the group that would evolve into the Miracles. In addition to Robinson, it consisted of Warren "Pete" Moore, Ronnie White, Emerson "Sonny" Rogers, and Rogers's cousin Bobby Rogers. When Sonny Rogers went into the army, he was replaced by his sister Claudette Rogers, who was also Robinson's girlfriend. When Rogers returned from military service, he rejoined the group, and Claudette retired from touring, although she continued to sing with the Miracles in the studio. Robinson and Claudette Rogers married on 7 November 1959; they had two children. They divorced in 1985.

After graduating from high school in 1957 and briefly attending college, Robinson met the songwriter Berry Gordy at an audition. Gordy became the Matadors' manager. Their name changed to the Miracles, the group recorded Robinson's composition "Got a Job," an answer record to the Silhouettes' hit "Get a Job," and Gordy leased it to End Records for their first release. In the winter of 1958 Gordy founded his own label, Motown Records, with the Miracles as one of its flagship acts. He continued to lease their tracks elsewhere at first, and the group scored their first chart entry with Robinson's "Bad Girl" on Chess Records in 1959. On the Motown subsidiary label Tamla, they enjoyed their first major hit in 1961 with Gordy and Robinson's "Shop Around," which topped the R&B charts and just missed topping the pop charts.

Subsequent Miracles' singles were more modest successes over the next few years, but Robinson scored as a writer/producer with other Motown performers. His song "The One Who Really Loves You" was a Top Ten hit for Mary Wells in the spring of 1962, as were his and White's "You Beat Me to the Punch" that fall and his "Two Lovers" in the winter of 1962–1963. In early 1963 Robinson and the Miracles returned to the Top Ten with his "You've Really Got a Hold on Me," and they were back in September with Brian Holland and Lamont Dozier's "Mickey's Monkey." Robinson's "The Way You Do the Things You Do" became the Temptations' breakthrough pop hit when it reached the Top Ten in April 1964, and, continuing to work with Mary Wells, Robinson topped the charts with her in May 1964, writing and producing "My Guy." "My Girl," which Robinson wrote with White, was a number-one hit for the Temptations in March 1965. Also in 1965

he cowrote two Top Ten hits for Marvin Gaye, "Ain't That Peculiar" and "I'll Be Doggone." In recognition of his contributions to Motown, Gordy appointed Robinson a vice president of the company in charge of acquiring new talent.

Robinson's next major hit as a songwriter was "Don't Mess with Bill," which peaked in the Top Ten for the Marvelettes in February 1966, the same month the Miracles' recording of Robinson's cocomposition "Going to a Go-Go" did the same. As of the start of 1967, the group was rebilled as Smokey Robinson and the Miracles in recognition of his increased stature. That year Johnny Rivers reached the Top Ten with his revival of Robinson's "The Tracks of My Tears," which had been a Top Twenty hit for the Miracles in 1965. In December 1967 Robinson and the Miracles had their biggest hit in seven years, when Robinson and Alfred Cleveland's "I Second That Emotion" reached the Top Five. Several lesser hits followed in 1968, but it was not until early 1969 that Robinson and the Miracles returned to the upper reaches of the charts with the Robinson cocomposition "Baby, Baby Don't Cry."

By 1969 Robinson had tired of touring with the Miracles and decided to leave the group. Unexpectedly, however, a track from a 1967 Miracles' album, "The Tears of a Clown," which he had cowritten with Henry Cosby and Stevie Wonder, took off as a single in the fall of 1970 and became the Miracles' first number-one pop hit. As a result Robinson felt obligated to stay with the group until June 1972. At first he intended to retire from performing, but by 1973 he was releasing solo records, and by 1975 he was back to doing concerts. Robinson's later hits as a solo artist included "Cruisin'" (1979), "Being with You" (1981), "Just to See Her" (1987), and "One Heartbeat" (1987). His 1975 album *A Quiet Storm* launched a radio format of romantic R&B ballads. In the early 1990s, after Motown had been sold to a major label, Robinson left the company, but he had returned by the end of the decade.

Robinson's autobiography claims he is the author of 4,000 songs. In addition to those previously mentioned, they include "Ooh Baby Baby," a Top Twenty 1965 hit for the Miracles that became a Top Ten hit in 1979 for Linda Ronstadt; "The Hunter Gets Captured by the Game," a Top Twenty hit for the Marvelettes in 1967; and "Get Ready," a Top Forty hit for the Temptations in 1966, which became a Top Five hit for Rare Earth in 1970. In Joel Whitburn's *Pop Annual 1955–1999,* a compendium of the *Billboard* Hot 100 charts, Robinson is ranked as the eighth most successful songwriter of the forty-five-year period covered, with 123 hits.

★

Robinson tells his own story in *Smokey: Inside My Life* (1989), written with David Ritz, which details not only his songwriting and performing career but also his romantic ups and downs and a late bout with substance abuse. Many accounts of Motown Records are available, with Robinson figuring prominently in the story. The best of these are Nelson George, *Where Did Our Love Go?* (1985), and Don Waller, *The Motown Story* (1985).

WILLIAM RUHLMANN

ROCKEFELLER, David (*b.* 12 June 1915 in New York City), chairman of Chase Manhattan Bank, international financier, and developer of lower Manhattan.

The fifth and youngest son of multimillionaire industrialist John D. Rockefeller, Jr., and Abby Greene Aldrich, Rockefeller received both his elementary and secondary education at the Lincoln School attached to the Teachers College at Columbia University. He graduated from Harvard University with a B.S. in English history and literature in 1936, performed postgraduate work at Harvard and the London School of Economics, and in 1940, earned his Ph.D. in economics from the University of Chicago. On 7 September 1940 he married Margaret McGrath, with whom he has six children.

Rockefeller worked in New York City government from 1940 to 1941, serving as secretary to Mayor Fiorello H. LaGuardia. In World War II Rockefeller enlisted in the U.S. Army as a private in 1942, saw service in North Africa

David Rockefeller. THE LIBRARY OF CONGRESS

and France, and left as a captain in 1945. Returning home, he went to work in 1946 at the Chase National Bank, whose chairman was his uncle, Winthrop W. Aldrich. By 1951 he was senior vice president.

The 1955 merger of Chase with the Bank of Manhattan began a quarter-century in which Rockefeller became one of the most powerful men in New York City, and indeed, all of the United States. First he became executive vice president of Chase Manhattan Bank, with responsibility for the development department, and by 1957 he was vice chairman of the bank's board, with control over administration and planning. In addition, Rockefeller, who had long had an interest in international affairs, served as vice president for a foreign financing subsidiary, Chase International Investment Corporation.

Much greater influence came in 1961, when Rockefeller became chairman of the board at Chase Manhattan, a position he would hold for the next twenty years. From 1961 to 1968 he also served as president and chairman of the executive committee and, from 1969 to 1980, as chief executive officer. During the 1960s, Rockefeller formed the International Executive Service Corps, composed of volunteers whose purpose was to provide businesses in developing nations with the benefit of their managerial experience and technical expertise. In addition, he wrote the book *Creative Management in Banking* (1964).

One legacy of Rockefeller's years at the helm of Chase Manhattan produced quite literally a concrete reminder of his work: the lower Manhattan redevelopment project, which became the site of the World Trade Center towers. As early as 1947, real estate broker and former Florida governor David Sholtz had presented New York governor Thomas E. Dewey with a plan for the revitalization of the New York ports and Washington Market area, but the time was not yet right, and the plan had been shelved. Although it seemed that the lower Manhattan revitalization project had no future, Rockefeller became enamored of it, and during the mid-1950s, heavily invested both Chase Manhattan and private funds in a building at One Chase Plaza. To push through his plan for the Chase Plaza building and the area around it, in 1956 he organized one of the first business improvement districts in New York or any other U.S. city.

The Downtown–Lower Manhattan Association (DMLA), which Rockefeller chaired, spent the next decade attempting to win over opponents. And opposition there was, from the owners of retail stores, as well as the operators of repair shops on "Radio Row," and of various light industrial sites—all of which would be obliterated in the creation of the new business district. These small businesspeople, however, acted too late, and they lacked the political and financial clout of the DMLA, which included not only Rockefeller, but also Henry Alexander of Morgan Guaranty, Robert Lehman of Lehman Brothers, Henry S. Morgan of Morgan Stanley, and many other luminaries of Wall Street. The election of Rockefeller's brother Nelson as governor of New York in 1958 virtually sealed the fate of Manhattan's southwestern corner.

In a July 1960 *New Yorker* article, Rockefeller explained that the DMLA had submitted a report to New York mayor Robert Wagner and others recommending that several thousand buildings "be torn down to make way for improved industrial and commercial structures and middle-income housing, and that many of the smaller streets and lanes be closed." As justification for the demolition, Rockefeller asserted that many of the buildings were more than 100 years old. By that point, One Chase Plaza had been completed, and Rockefeller was clearly winning the war for lower Manhattan. Already he had recommended the creation of a "world trade center," and by the late 1960s, the actual World Trade Center—whose functions had long since become divorced from those implied in its name—was well underway. The twin towers eventually acquired the nickname "Nelson and David," for the two brothers who made them possible.

With interests that went far beyond New York City, Rockefeller has been a member of the Council on Foreign Relations since 1949, and in 1973 founded the Trilateral Commission to promote greater integration and networking between North America, western Europe, and Japan. He also helped establish the Council of the Americas, and served as chairman of the Americas Society. In 1981 Rockefeller retired from active management of Chase Manhattan, but he continued with the bank's advisory committee until 1999.

Rockefeller's status as a citizen of the world is reflected not only in the international organizations with which he has been involved, but the varied honors he has received from dozens of countries: the Order of the Aztec Eagle from Mexico, the Order of the White Elephant from Thailand, the Order of the Humane African Redemption from Liberia, and so on. Rockefeller's philanthropic activities included being a trustee of the Rockefeller Institute of Medical Research (now Rockefeller University), the Rockefeller Brother's Fund, and the Museum of Modern Art. Yet his most significant contribution to American life may well have been his role in creating the business district in southwestern Manhattan.

Assessments of that contribution are mixed. There was an unmistakable strong-arm element behind the Rockefeller brothers' machinations to push through their urban redevelopment plan, and it is hard to imagine such a plan gaining acceptance in today's preservation-conscious environment. Yet they also helped turn an area of small, gray, old buildings into a district of gleaming high-rises, and with the tragedy of 11 September 2001, the once-disputed ground on which the World Trade Center towers stood became forever hallowed.

★

Rockefeller published his *Memoirs* (2002), and there is only one other biography, William Hoffman, *David: Report on a Rockefeller* (1971). Observations on Rockefeller's role in business in the United States can be found in Joseph R. Frese and Jacob Judd, eds., *American Industrialization, Economic Expansion, and the Law* (1981). For insights about the Rockefeller family, see Myer Kutz, *Rockefeller Power: America's Chosen Family* (1974); Peter Collier and David Horowitz, *The Rockefellers: An American Dynasty* (1976); and John E. Harr and Peter J. Johnson, *The Rockefeller Century: Three Generations of America's Greatest Family* (1988). A profile of Rockefeller is in the *New York Times* (10 Dec. 1995).

JUDSON KNIGHT

ROCKEFELLER, John Davison, III (*b.* 21 March 1906 in New York City; *d.* 10 July 1978 in Mount Pleasant, New York), philanthropist, writer, industrialist, social activist, patron of the arts, and member of one of the nation's wealthiest families.

Rockefeller was the eldest son of the six children of John Davison Rockefeller, Jr., and Abby Greene Aldrich Rockefeller. His father, the son of John D. Rockefeller, the founder of the Standard Oil Company, was a philanthropist who gave more than $537 million to educational, religious, cultural, medical, and other charitable projects. His

John D. Rockefeller III. THE LIBRARY OF CONGRESS

271

mother, a philanthropist in her own right, worked to establish charitable organizations and was on the board of many educational and cultural institutions. Rockefeller attended the Browning School in New York City and the Loomis Institute in Windsor, Connecticut. He earned his B.S. with honors in economics from Princeton University in 1929.

In December 1929 Rockefeller embarked on the career for which he had been groomed: taking on the responsibilities for his generation's philanthropic endeavors. At his father's office in New York City he immersed himself in the operations of the many institutions associated with the Rockefeller family. He took his life and job seriously. Many, including his father, felt he was "too sweet" to count for much, but Rockefeller took to heart his father's views about the caretaking of money and the obligation to serve.

During his early career he developed many of his lifelong interests. One of them was his commitment to the issues of population and birth control, which he began in 1928 with his work as a board member of the Bureau of Social Hygiene. On 11 November 1932 Rockefeller married Blanchette Ferry Hooker, and they had four children. They lived primarily in an apartment in New York City and had a second home at Fieldwood Farm in Mount Pleasant, New York. In July 1942 Rockefeller joined the U.S. Navy, serving with the rank of lieutenant commander. His principal work was on an interagency task force devoted to planning postwar policy for Japan. Released from active duty in 1945, he was appointed a cultural consultant to the diplomat John Foster Dulles during the Japanese peace treaty negotiations. This experience helped foster his deep interest in Japan and, indeed, in all of Asia. During the late 1940s he and his wife began collecting Asian art.

During his busy years of institution building in the 1950s, Rockefeller continued to develop and deepen his personal appreciation of the arts. His interest began with Asian cultural programs and was intensified during his leadership in creating the Lincoln Center for the Performing Arts in New York City. Rockefeller revitalized the Japan Society in the early 1950s, and in 1956 he organized the Asia Society. He also helped found the Council on Economic and Cultural Affairs (renamed the Agricultural Development Council in 1963), which provides assistance to Asian farmers, as well as the Population Council, hoping it would bring the problem of overpopulation to global attention.

Rockefeller was convinced of the imperative to devote his influence and wealth to finding solutions to global as well as national problems. The 1960s saw change and expansion in his activities. His interests came together, and he showed himself a man of substance and influence. He persuaded Sherman Lee, the director of the Cleveland Museum of Art and an expert on Asian art, to help him put together a substantial collection. His understanding of

Asian art began to advance under Lee's tutelage. Edgar P. Richardson helped Rockefeller develop his personal collection of American art. Rockefeller always viewed himself as the temporary custodian of the works of art he owned; eventually his collections were intended to serve the public. On his death, his major collections of Asian and American art were donated to the Asia Society in New York City and to the Fine Arts Museums of San Francisco respectively.

In 1963 Rockefeller established the JDR III Fund, which provided grants in four major areas: the advancement of opportunity for Asians, the qualification and preservation of Asian cultural traditions, exhibitions and performances of Asian cultural achievements in the United States, and exhibitions and performances of cultural achievements of the United States in Asia. In sum, the fund encouraged reciprocity in the traffic of ideas. Despite numerous minor initiatives toward the end of the decade, however, Rockefeller's great period of institution building was over. His concerns now turned to ensuring the success of the institutions he had already established and to continuing his leadership in his major fields of concern: the arts, population, Asian affairs, and philanthropy. At this time work in the population field took off, probably because of Rockefeller's participation. In 1970 President Richard Nixon asked him to chair the Commission on Population Growth and the American Future.

As the 1960s progressed, Rockefeller became the leading spokesman on private philanthropy. He undertook a major campaign to influence public policy on philanthropy, particularly private philanthropy, which he viewed as a "unique social force that is indispensable to the continued success of the United States." He lobbied Congress for regulatory and tax laws under which private giving could flourish. In his role as self-appointed caretaker of philanthropy, Rockefeller created the Commission on Foundations and Private Philanthropy (usually known as the Peterson Commission) and the Commission on Private Philanthropy and Public Needs (usually known as the Filer Commission).

Rockefeller began writing in the early 1970s, drawing on his extensive experience for material. In his book *The Second American Revolution* (1973) he was optimistic about the great potential in the civil rights and youth movements of the 1960s. He described his vision of the United States as a pluralistic democracy and emphasized the need for cooperation between public and private institutions. This book set the image for Rockefeller's involvement in planning the U.S. bicentennial celebration. As a member of the National Committee for the Bicentennial Era, he provided funding for many of the projects from the JDR III Fund.

Rockefeller made an important difference in all areas of his concern. He belonged to a wide range of organizations that addressed local, national, and international issues.

These organizations include the American Academy of Political and Social Sciences, the American Association of Museums, the Citizens Committee for Reorganization for the Executive Branch of the Government, the Council in Foreign Relations, the Foreign Policy Association, the Academy of Political Science of New York, the New York State Chamber of Commerce, the New York Zoological Society, the Westchester County Conservation Society, the Historical Society of the Tarrytowns (New York), the Metropolitan Museum of Art, the Museum of Modern Art, the Century Club, and the Metropolitan Club. His numerous awards highlight his many accomplishments in the areas of populations control as well as fine art, music, and education.

Rockefeller was killed in an automobile accident in Mount Pleasant on 10 July 1978. Following a memorial service at the Riverside Church in New York City, his cremated remains were buried in the Rockefeller Family Cemetery, near the family's Westchester County estate in Sleepy Hollow, New York. A quiet, dedicated, and hardworking man, he would perhaps have been happier if his accomplishments had been made anonymously. Born with the grave responsibility to use his inherited wealth wisely and for the benefit of humankind, he devoted his life to finding and implementing ways in which he could best accomplish this goal.

★

Rockefeller's papers are in the archives of the Rockefeller Foundation. See John Ensor Harr and Peter J. Johnson, *The Rockefeller Century* (1988) (Rockefeller's life up to 1952), and *The Rockefeller Conscience: An American Family in Public and in Private* (1991) (his life from 1952 to 1978). See also Peter Dobkin Hall, "What You See Depends on Where You Stand," *Philanthropy Monthly* (Nov. 1991 and Jan./Feb. 1992). Numerous articles are in the *Wall Street Journal, New York Times, Time, Newsweek,* and other magazines, including Frand W. Notestein, "John D. Rockefeller 3rd: A Personal Appreciation," *Population and Development Review* 4, no. 3 (Sept. 1978): 501; T. Mathews and E. D. Lee, "Man of Good Works," *Newsweek* (24 July 1978); and "Shy Philanthropist," *Time* (24 July 1978). An obituary is in the *New York Times* (11 July 1978).

JOAN GOODBODY

ROCKEFELLER, Nelson Aldrich (*b.* 8 July 1908 in Bar Harbor, Maine; *d.* 26 January 1979 in New York City), governor of New York throughout the 1960s who sought and failed to receive the Republican nomination for president in 1960, 1964, and 1968; the scion of the enormously wealthy Rockefeller family.

The second son and third of six children born to philanthropists John Davison Rockefeller, Jr., and Abby Greene Aldrich, Rockefeller grew up with tremendous wealth, power, and prestige as the grandson of the richest man in the world, John D. Rockefeller, and of U.S. senator Nelson Aldrich, who represented Rhode Island as a Republican. He attended the Lincoln School, a progressive coeducational institution in New York City, then graduated from Dartmouth College (1926–1930) with a B.A. cum laude in economics. Rockefeller married Mary Todhunter Clark, a Philadelphia socialite, on 23 June 1930; the couple had five children and divorced in 1962.

Although he knew he would inherit a trust fund of $40 million, Rockefeller was no playboy. He joined the family office in 1931, obtained a real estate broker's license, and began to sell space in the new Rockefeller Center, then the world's largest office complex. Taught from birth that wealth carries an obligation to help others, Rockefeller made his first contribution to public life by serving under President Franklin D. Roosevelt in 1940. As coordinator of the Office of Inter-American Affairs, he attempted to ward off the threat of Nazism by providing Latin Americans with economic assistance. In 1944 he became the assistant secretary of state for Latin American affairs, but his aggressive approach led to conflict with his superiors, and Rockefeller resigned a year later. Determined to help other families benefit from capitalism as his had, he created the American International Association for Economic and Social Development to prevent the spread of Communism in Latin America by using private U.S. funds to improve public health, education, and agriculture. Named by President Dwight Eisenhower in 1952 to reorganize the federal government, Rockefeller recommended the creation of the Department of Health, Education, and Welfare (HEW) and served as its undersecretary from 1953 to 1954. Rockefeller left HEW to serve as Eisenhower's special assistant on cold war strategy, a post he held until his nomination as secretary of defense was blocked in 1955 because of his reputation for heavy spending.

With his federal government career curtailed, Rockefeller looked to his home state of New York and won election as its governor in 1958. He eventually served four terms over fifteen years, from 1959 to 1973. Charismatic, hardworking, and able to relate to people at all rungs on the social ladder, he saw every problem as solvable, but his optimistic spending contributed to New York's financial troubles in the 1970s. Intent on keeping a friendly business climate in the state by lowering business taxes, Rockefeller paid for the expansion of New York government and the accompanying 300 percent jump in the state budget during his tenure by raising individual taxes. He continually argued that the federal government should provide greater subsidies to larger states. To defend his controversial fiscal policies and to measure public opinion, Rockefeller began

Nelson Rockefeller. ARCHIVE PHOTOS, INC.

an innovative ten-year practice in 1961 of holding a series of town meetings around New York.

As socially liberal as he was free-spending, Rockefeller often seemed more like a New Deal Democrat than a Republican. He revitalized Albany, the capital of New York, by building a vast governmental complex; he funded the construction of hospitals and roads, advocated civil rights, supported rent control, and promoted treatment for narcotics abusers rather than strict criminal penalties (a position that changed in the 1970s because treatment failed to have much effect). One of his most creative programs, the Urban Development Corporation (UDC) of 1968, built low- and middle-income housing by mixing four dollars of private capital with one dollar of government aid. Able to override local zoning laws, much to the anger of many New Yorkers, it was the nation's most powerful state agency for urban housing construction. Rockefeller used his personal contacts with the Wall Street financial community, particularly his brother David, head of Chase Manhattan Bank, to keep the agency solvent. After he left office, the UDC defaulted on its loans. Rockefeller's greatest legacy to the state may be the expansion of the state university system, which increased from 38,000 students on 28 campuses to 246,000 students on 71 campuses by the time he left office.

Rockefeller's personal life occasionally made headlines during the 1960s. In 1961 his youngest son, Michael, disappeared on an anthropological expedition in New Guinea. The family's prominence made the disappearance headline news around the globe. Rockefeller immediately flew to assist in a fruitless search for the remains of the young man, who was possibly attacked by crocodiles or, more likely, killed in a racially motivated attack by cannibals.

As governor of the most populous and powerful state in the country, Rockefeller instantly became a major figure in the Republican Party upon his 1958 election; moderate Republicans bandied his name about as a candidate for the presidency in 1960. An ambitious man, Rockefeller had designs on the office and made a nationwide exploratory tour in 1959, but the qualities that made him a successful governor did not make him a good national candidate. Rockefeller typically relied on his staff to conduct massive amounts of research. In 1960 he gave up his pursuit of the nomination, reporting that the "people who were running my campaign said it was hopeless." He simply lacked the fierce determination that propelled other men, like Richard Nixon, to ignore the naysayers. The downing of a U-2 spy plane over Russia in May 1960 prompted Rockefeller to threaten to split the party at the convention by making himself available for a draft unless his advocacy of increased defense spending and stronger support for civil rights were reflected in the Republican Party platform. This blackmail did not endear Rockefeller to party leaders, and his actions hurt him when he again flirted with the nomination in subsequent years.

Rockefeller's presidential campaigns were also constrained by his governorship; unlike the eventual 1960s Republican presidential nominees Nixon and Barry Goldwater, he had a state to run. He did not have the luxury of spending years courting the party faithful, nor, as he acknowledged in his twilight days, would he have been content to sit on the sidelines gathering support while others ran the country. Rockefeller also had to attract diverse, multiethnic urban voters to maintain political power in New York, and the programs that appealed to such an audience did not necessarily meet with the approval of southern or western white suburbanites. Key state and local Republicans around the country preferred a more conservative leader.

In 1964 Rockefeller had an excellent chance of winning the presidential nomination, but his personal life cast too dark a shadow. He had fallen in love with Margaretta "Happy" Fitler Murphy, eighteen years his junior and a married mother of four young children. Both Rockefeller and Happy divorced their spouses; they married on 4 May 1963. Before his remarriage, Rockefeller had been ahead of Goldwater in the polls, but his actions cost him this lead. To add further insult, Goldwater partisans came up with the slogan "We want a leader, not a lover." Rockefeller managed to win the Oregon primary in May 1964, but the first of two sons that Happy bore him arrived with unfortunate timing a week before the California primary. With Rockefeller's morality again on center stage, California voters gave Goldwater the win.

In 1968 a staff analyst told Rockefeller he could not be nominated for the presidency, and he intended to sit out the campaign. Accordingly, he publicly withdrew in March 1968, but he reentered the race at the end of April after appeals from moderates and the business community. Having entered too late to mount a serious challenge to the frontrunner, Richard Nixon, and having antagonized many leading Republicans, Rockefeller's only hope lay in a massive groundswell of support. He spent lavishly on national television advertising to raise his opinion polls, but he could not overcome Nixon's lead.

Despite his differences with Nixon, Rockefeller loyally supported the president. A hawk and a strong anti-Communist, he supported Nixon's Vietnam policy and acted as the president's emissary to Latin America in 1969. Continuing to yearn for the presidency, he renominated Nixon at the 1972 convention in an attempt to better position himself for the 1976 campaign. Chosen as Gerald Ford's vice president when Nixon and Agnew resigned in disgrace, Rockefeller was sworn in on 19 December 1974 and found himself marginalized in the White House and in his own party. He retired from politics in 1975. On a Friday night in 1979 he met privately with a female staff worker in his New York City townhouse and suffered a fatal heart attack, fueling considerable speculation about the exact circumstances of his demise. His cremated remains were buried in the Rockefeller Family Cemetery, near the family's Westchester County estate in Sleepy Hollow, New York.

A liberal and a believer in an activist government, Rockefeller fell out of step with the increasingly conservative Republican Party of the 1960s. Although a much-admired and enormously popular governor who helped millions of New Yorkers with innovative policies, he failed in his lifelong ambition to become president because he did not appeal to voters in the South and West who dominated the Republican ranks.

★

Rockefeller's private and governmental papers are held at the Rockefeller Archive Center, Pocantico Hills, near Tarrytown, New York. He authored a number of books, including *The Future of Federalism* (1962); *Unity, Freedom, and Peace* (1968); and *Our Environment Can Be Saved* (1970). Biographies of Rockefeller include James Desmond, *Nelson Rockefeller: A Political Biography* (1964); Robert H. Connery and Gerald Benjamin, *Rockefeller of New York: Executive Power in the Statehouse* (1979); Joseph E. Persico, *The Imperial Rockefeller: A Biography of Nelson A. Rockefeller* (1982); and James F. Underwood and William J. Daniels, *Governor Rockefeller in New York: The Apex of Pragmatic Liberalism in the United States* (1982). James Poling's *The Rockefeller Record: A Political Self-Portrait* (1960) is a collection of his public utterances. The dominant Rockefeller of his generation, he is covered heavily in Peter Collier and David Horowitz, *The Rockefellers: An American Dynasty* (1976). Nicol C. Rae, *The Decline and Fall of the Liberal Republicans: From 1952 to the Present* (1989), summarizes Rockefeller's presidential runs. An obituary is in the *New York Times* (27 Jan. 1979).

CARYN E. NEUMANN

RODDENBERRY, Eugene Wesley ("Gene") (*b.* 19 August 1921 in El Paso, Texas; *d.* 24 October 1991 in Santa Monica, California), television writer and producer and creator of the legendary science-fiction television and movie series *Star Trek*.

Roddenberry was one of three children of Eugene Edward Roddenberry, a noncommissioned officer in the U.S. Army and a police officer with the Los Angeles Police Department, and Carolyn Glen Goleman, a homemaker. Roddenberry was just three years old when the family moved to Los Angeles. He graduated from Franklin High School in 1939 and from Los Angeles Community College (LACC) in 1941. While earning his associate of arts degree at LACC, he joined the Civilian Pilot Program, which was run by the U.S. Army in an effort to train pilots for the coming conflict. Roddenberry served with distinction during World War II as a pilot in the Pacific theater from 1941 through 1945.

Prior to being sent overseas, Roddenberry married Eileen Anita Rexroat in 1942. The couple had two children. After the war Roddenberry became a pilot for Pan American Airways. He had started writing during his wartime service and continued taking classes even while working for the airline and, later, as a police officer. In 1956 he began writing full time.

From 1956 to 1963 Roddenberry wrote dozens of scripts for some of the most popular television shows of the time, including *Highway Patrol*, *The Virginian*, *Dr. Kildare*, and *Have Gun Will Travel*, where he was the head writer. While writing these scripts, Roddenberry formed the idea for a show that has often been referred to as the "Wagon Train to the stars," a reference to a popular western of the time, *Wagon Train*. Thus was born one of the true cultural phenomenons of the twentieth century, *Star Trek*.

Roddenberry conceived the show as a method for illuminating social issues that would never have been allowed on air except through the medium of science fiction. He assured the show's acceptance and popularity by creating realistic, likable characters confronted with scientific, moral, and ethical dilemmas that required solution through employing a balance of logic and emotion.

Roddenberry worked with fellow scriptwriters Samuel Peeples and Jerry Sohl to polish his program proposal. First he pitched the show to executives at the Colombia Broadcasting System (CBS), who initially seemed interested. However, they ultimately declined, citing their own science-fiction vehicle, *Lost In Space,* then under development. On 11 March 1964 Roddenberry teamed up with Oscar Katz of Desilu Productions to sell the show to the National Broadcasting Company (NBC) television network. The story of Captain Robert April and his crew aboard the SS *Yorktown* intrigued the network executives. They paid Roddenberry $435,000 to shoot the pilot episode, "The Cage." By this time, the Captain's name had changed to Christopher Pike, and the spaceship was renamed the USS *Enterprise.*

Roddenberry worked with assistant art director and former fellow World War II aviator Matt Jefferies to develop a believable look for the starship. He approached many actors to play Pike. Those considered for the role included Lloyd Bridges, Jack Lord, and James Coburn. In the end, he chose Jeffery Hunter, who unlike many motion picture stars, was interested in acting in a television series. He then asked actor Leonard Nimoy, who had appeared in an episode of *The Lieutenant,* to play the role of the alien from the planet Vulcan, Mr. Spock. Nimoy was intrigued by the idea of a regular series, although he was not impressed with the pointed ears he would be required to wear. Roddenberry told him to have faith and made an agreement with him that if after thirteen shows the ears were still not working, they would alter them. This convinced Nimoy that using the pointed ears was worth a try.

"The Cage" revolved around the *Enterprise,* under the command of Captain Christopher Pike and his coolly logical female second in command, "Number One." Mr. Spock was a junior officer in Pike's mostly human crew. Network executives were overwhelmingly positive about the pilot, but NBC rejected it, because they feared their general audience would not understand the show. They also wanted more action in the episodes.

Desilu executive Herb Solow, believing in the concept, asked for a second pilot for Roddenberry's proposal. NBC consented, but insisted that Spock be written out of the script because of concerns about his satanic looks. Roddenberry revamped the premise, but fought to keep Spock, whom he considered essential to the show. "Where No Man Has Gone Before" had plenty of action and featured Spock as second in command to Captain James T. Kirk, played by William Shatner. This time, NBC bought the series and slated it for a September 1966 premier.

NBC executives were not pleased with *Star Trek*'s per-

formance in the ratings and tried to get Roddenberry to alter what they saw as imperfections in the show, but Roddenberry refused. By December 1966 *Star Trek* was in danger of being cancelled, so Roddenberry enlisted the help of the author Harlan Ellison to get the science-fiction community involved in saving the show. The letter-writing campaign they conceived worked, and the show continued into 1967. When faced with possible cancellation a second time, *Star Trek* fans again made NBC realize that the show had a large and loyal viewer base. The show was renewed for a third season.

The crew of the USS *Enterprise* traveled to "strange new worlds" for seventy-nine episodes. But the fourteen-hour days, six-days-per-week, shooting schedules required to complete the episodes took their toll. Roddenberry spent much of his time away from his wife and family, and his marriage, already strained, suffered accordingly. In the third season, the quality of the show also began to wane. Roddenberry himself, angered by NBC's insistence that *Star Trek* be moved to a 10:00 P.M. Friday time slot, stepped down as producer. The final episode of the original *Star Trek* series aired 3 June 1969.

Later that year, Roddenberry and his first wife divorced, and the writer married actress Majel Barrett, with whom he had another child. Following the demise of *Star Trek,* Roddenberry worked on several other projects, including serving as executive consultant to *Star Trek: The Animated Series.*

Star Trek's utopian vision and emphasis on diversity, female equality, and bold exploration had captured the imaginations of an entire group of people, who came to be known as Trekkies. Eventually, recognizing the commercial potential of the *Star Trek* concept, Paramount Pictures underwrote *Star Trek: The Motion Picture,* which premiered on 6 December 1979. Roddenberry also created and consulted on the first of several spin-offs, the highly successful *Star Trek: The Next Generation,* which first aired in 1987. Besides the first two series, there have been three more based on Roddenberry's original vision. Six movies were based on characters in the original version and four on *The Next Generation*'s crew. Countless video games, fanzines, websites, clubs, conventions, and more have spread the myth through U.S. culture. Episodes of the four series still in syndication have broken all records for longevity and commercial appeal. The fact that Roddenberry's imprint can still be seen in every product associated with the *Star Trek* phenomenon attests to the strength and appeal of his original vision.

Roddenberry continued to engender support from the fans and consult on *Star Trek: The Next Generation,* until a series of strokes culminated in his being taken to Santa Monica Medical Center, where he died of a heart attack. His remains were cremated, with part of his ashes being transported aboard Pegasus Rocket Earthview 01—The Founders' Flight and launched into Earth's orbit. The rocket detached from a Lockheed L-1011 over the Canary Islands on 21 April 1997. The rest of the ashes were buried at Forest Lawn Memorial Park.

The man responsible for the catch phrase "Beam me up, Scotty" and for advancing a vision of hopefulness for humanity remains a force in popular culture, with successive generations finding meaning in his creation. This impact was no more strongly felt than when NASA was asked by the White House to rename the first space shuttle test vehicle *Enterprise* due to requests from *Star Trek* fans. Attending the 17 September 1976 rollout ceremony at Rockwell's Air Force Plant 42, Site 1, in Palmdale, California, were Roddenberry and most of the original series cast.

★

Roddenberry's biography is David Alexander, *Star Trek Creator: The Authorized Biography of Gene Roddenberry* (1994). Joel Engel, *Gene Roddenberry: The Myth and the Man Behind Star Trek* (1994), is a less-than-flattering portrait. This is balanced by James Van Hise, *The Man Who Created Star Trek: Gene Roddenberry* (1992). A firsthand account of the *Star Trek* universe is Stephen E. Whitfield and Gene Roddenberry, *The Making of Star Trek* (1968). Obituaries are in the *Los Angeles Times* (25 and 26 Oct. 1991) and the *New York Times* (25 and 26 Oct. 1991).

BRIAN B. CARPENTER

RONSTADT, Linda (*b.* 15 July 1946 in Tucson, Arizona), pop-rock superstar, songwriter, actress, and record producer who came out of the Los Angeles club scene in the 1960s to win Grammy Awards in rock, pop, country, and Latin music, becoming one of the most beloved singers of her generation.

Ronstadt was the third of four children born to Gilbert Ronstadt, a hardware store owner, and Ruthmary (Copeman) Ronstadt, a homemaker who was the daughter of Lloyd Copeman, a well-known inventor. Ronstadt grew up surrounded by music. She spent her free time listening to the radio and to records. When she was fourteen she formed a trio with her brother Mike and sister Suzie, called the New Union Ramblers. Cute and talented, she took center stage as the threesome performed in local clubs and coffeehouses, singing Mexican folk music, country songs, and popular folk songs. Ronstadt attended Catalina High School in Tucson.

In 1964, when she was eighteen, Ronstadt attended the University of Arizona briefly before moving to Los Angeles to launch her singing career at the invitation of Fred Kimmel, a Tucson friend who played rhythm guitar. Ronstadt arrived in the city with thirty dollars and a two-dollar bill with the corner torn off, a gift from her father for good

Linda Ronstadt, 1968. HENRY DILTZ/CORBIS

luck. Naive and optimistic, she would later say that if she had realized how difficult it would be to earn a living as a musician, she would have stayed in Tucson. Still, in 1964 Los Angeles was exactly the right place for her—a mecca for aspiring musicians, attracting many artists who would become successful singers and musicians.

Ronstadt formed a trio with Kimmel and the keyboardist Ken Edwards, and they called themselves the Stone Poneys, after the Charlie Patton song "The Stone Poney Blues." Ronstadt, with her vibrant soprano voice and sexy waiflike beauty, was clearly the group's drawing card. With her raw and powerful voice and her instinct for lyrics, she shone above the others and soon attracted a cult following on the club circuit. Like other struggling musicians, Ronstadt was searching for a musical style and not finding it. A first chance to record came from Mercury Records, but the group turned down the offer, which would have renamed them the Signets and had them playing surfing music. Another offer came just for Ronstadt, but she did not want to sing solo. The Stone Poneys, who began as an acoustic rock band, did not jell as a pure rock act, because the group members were drawn in different directions musically. Ronstadt was more interested in country music, but the others were dubious of that musical style.

The Stone Poneys were booked into the Troubadour in West Hollywood, the "in" club where both rock stars and aspiring artists hung out, mingling with managers and promoters on the lookout for new talent. The band's stint at the "Troub" landed them a contract with Capital Records. In January 1965 the Stone Poneys recorded "Some of Shelley's Blues," their first single, for Capital Records, and the following year they recorded the album *The Stone Poneys,* which featured three Ronstadt solos. Their second album, *Evergreen Volume II* (1967), produced the group's only successful single, Ronstadt's rendition of "Different Drum," which had been written by Mike Nesmith of the Monkees. The song, a sad ode to lost love and breaking up, became the first of many Ronstadt hits.

By 1968 the song made number thirteen on the Billboard charts. At age twenty-one Ronstadt had her first hit record, but psychologically she was not prepared for success. She was insecure and felt that she was not an accomplished musician, and felt that she suffered from a lack of guidance. The group was constantly on the road opening for other bands and artists, such as the Doors, Alice Cooper, the Mothers of Invention, and Neil Young. With audiences unsympathetic to the band's style of music, Ronstadt's self-confidence continued to wither. Artistic differences, dissatisfaction with being an opening act for other bands, and low pay of barely $100 per month were all factors in the breakup of the band. Ronstadt recorded another album, *Linda Ronstadt, Stone Poneys, and Friends, Volume 3* (1968), backed entirely by studio musicians.

Despite suffering from agonizing stage fright, Rondstadt made her first solo appearance at a popular Los Angeles club, the Whiskey-a-Go-Go. In spite of her shyness she established a rapport with the audience, gradually becoming accustomed to solo performances. She continued to make records for Capitol, such as *Hand Sown . . . Home Grown* (1969) and *Silk Purse* (1970), and she had a hit single, "Long, Long Time," in 1970. This tearjerker about romantic yearning and sadness brought her continuing fame as the singer who taught the baby boomers how to cry. Ronstadt recalled these solo years as bleak: she was constantly on the road opening for other bands, had no continuity in terms of backup musicians, and was taking drugs, including cocaine, to help her deal with her insecurities.

Ronstadt was a paradox: a beautiful, sexy singer with low self-esteem who struggled to find her musical style. Her love affairs often were more publicized than her music. Over the years she was linked romantically to her one-time manager John Boylan; the singer/songwriter John David Souther; the actor/producer Peter Brooks; the comedian Steve Martin; California's governor Jerry Brown, Jr.; and the producer George Lucas. She always maintained, however, that her career was her first love and priority. In 1972 Ronstadt found self-confidence and success with the manager/producer Peter Asher, who knew how to provide an instrumental setting for her voice. In 1973, with Asylum Records, the two released *Don't Cry Now,* which included the critically acclaimed "Desperado." Ronstadt was on her

way to superstardom. In 1974 she had her first platinum album, *Heart Like a Wheel.* In 1975 she had her first number-one single, "You're No Good."

Ronstadt had been singing since the early 1960s, but in musical terms the 1970s are remembered as Ronstadt's decade. Her next four albums went platinum, selling more than one million copies each, making her one of the biggest rock stars of the era. Her popularity helped bring an end to the male domination of rock and roll, and she used her success to open doors for other female performers and to improve the status of women within the music industry. Although Ronstadt never married, she adopted two children.

In the following years she would go on to change musical directions many times, singing everything from opera to Mexican folk tunes, from Tin Pan Alley favorites to country-and-western songs, from pop tunes to children's lullabies. She has released more than thirty albums in as many years and has earned nine Grammy Awards.

★

Biographies of Ronstadt include Vivian Claire, *Linda Ronstadt* (1978); Connie Berman, *Linda Ronstadt: An Illustrated Biography* (1980); Mark Bego, *Linda Ronstadt: It's So Easy* (1990); and Melissa Amdur, *Hispanics of Achievement, Linda Ronstadt* (1993). Her place in the baby boom generation is noted in Joel Makower, *Boom! Talkin' About Our Generation* (1985). An interview with Ronstadt concerning her song "Long, Long Time" and her Troubadour days is Ron Rosenbaum, "Melancholy Baby," *Esquire* (10 Oct. 1985). Biographical information and Ronstadt's place in musical history are discussed in Susan Katz, *Superwomen of Rock* (1978); Mary Ellen Moore, *Linda Ronstadt Scrapbook* (1978); and Edith and Frank N. Magill, eds., *Great Lives from History, American Women Series,* vol. 4 (1995). A website with information about Ronstadt and her recording career is <http://www.ronstadt-linda.com>.

JULIANNE CICARELLI

ROSENQUIST, James Albert (*b.* 29 November 1933 in Grand Forks, North Dakota), artist whose billboard-sized painting *F-111* represented the apotheosis of the pop art movement of the 1960s.

The only child of Louis A. Rosenquist, an automotive and aviation mechanic, and Ruth, a homemaker, Rosenquist had a peripatetic early childhood, but in 1944 the family settled down in Minneapolis. He graduated from Roosevelt High School in 1952 and entered the University of Minnesota that autumn. In September 1955 he moved to New York City to continue his education at the Art Students League. After one year, Rosenquist dropped out and took on a variety of jobs, while painting on his own. In 1958 he

James Rosenquist. EXPRESS NEWSPAPER/GETTY IMAGES

began working as a billboard painter for Artkraft Strauss, where he met Mary Lou Adams, a textile designer. The two married on 5 June 1960; they had one son. Also in June 1960, Rosenquist's penchant for publicity was in evidence when he met a reporter while painting billboards in Times Square. "These billboards are snake oil stuff. I'm an artist; I paint miniatures," he said, and an article and photograph of the artist on scaffolding soon followed.

By the end of the 1960s Rosenquist had quit Artkraft to focus on his painting, but drew on his billboard experience to "get below zero" in his paintings, beyond the formalist aesthetics of artists such as Frank Stella. "The only way I knew to do that," he recalled, "was to start using imagery again." Rosenquist turned to the media, especially magazine advertisements, for his subject matter. He chose common, everyday things that were immediately familiar to the viewer, fragmenting them within suggestive groupings. As part of a now famous series of interviews entitled "What Is Pop Art?" that the critic Gene Swenson conducted in 1963 with pop artists, Rosenquist recalled, "So I geared myself like an advertiser or a large company to this visual inflation." He added, "It has such impact and excitement in its means of imagery. Painting is probably more exciting than advertising—so why shouldn't it be done with that power and gusto, with that impact."

Rosenquist's first attempt in his new style was *President Elect* (1960–1961), which pictures, on a large-scaled canvas, a section of President John F. Kennedy's smiling face, a fragment of a woman's hand offering cake, and the side of a nondescript American automobile. Rosenquist was ulti-

mately dissatisfied with this work; he felt that his commentary on the materialism of society was too obvious—too much like an advertisement itself. He brought more subtlety to his next major work, *Zone* (1960), which has fragments of a woman laughing (or is she crying?), drops of water (perhaps tears), and a dark red tomato. The odd combination of a woman with the fruit has an undercurrent of sexual tension, linking the woman with the idea of a hot tomato.

Rosenquist garnered early attention as part of the wave of general interest in pop artists, including Andy Warhol, Roy Lichtenstein, and Claes Oldenburg. In 1961 dealers and curators began visiting Rosenquist's studio, but it was Richard Bellamy of Green Gallery who successfully wooed him. The dealer brought in collectors who wanted to buy Rosenquist's work and set a date for his first solo show. At Green Gallery in February 1962, every painting was sold. Respectability was quickly conferred upon Rosenquist and his colleagues when the gallery owner Sidney Janis included them in his November 1962 exhibition "New Realists," the first major show of these artists as a group. That December, the Museum of Modern Art in New York City held a symposium on pop art (a transcript was published in *Arts Magazine,* April 1963), during which artists and critics took sides in a fierce debate about the merits of pop art that continued to be argued throughout the decade.

In the summer of 1964 Rosenquist began work on a massive painting, *F-111.* Regarded as one of the most important examples of pop art, it is also the largest and most visually jarring. *F-111* is comprised of fifty-one panels that form an eighty-six-foot-long panoramic mélange of disparate images, from that of the fighter jet and its fuselage, which provides the painting's formal structure, to that of the little girl in a hair dryer that resembles the nose of a jet, the mushroom-capped nuclear explosion over which hangs an umbrella, and the field of Franco-American spaghetti in an unappetizing shade of acid orange-red. In his uneasy juxtapositions of imagery, Rosenquist was alluding to more than just the obvious dangers of war and nuclear proliferation; he also was making a point about the ideology of consumption and its ties to the economics of military spending.

Famous even before it was finished, *F-111* was exhibited to great fanfare in April 1965 at the Leo Castelli Gallery. The painting filled all four walls of the gallery and engulfed the viewers. It brought on rabid reactions by many critics, who believed the mural debased fine art. On the last day of the show, Robert Scull purchased all fifty-one panels allegedly for $60,000 (the collector received a hefty discount). The sale made the front page of the *New York Times*. After a three-year international tour that ended at the Metropolitan Museum of Art in 1968, *F-111* aroused more negative commentary from critics who still found it vulgar and superficial. In 1978 the painting was one of the highlights of the Venice Biennale, and in 1984 it was sold at Sotheby's for $2.09 million.

Rosenquist remained within the media glare throughout his subsequent career. After participating in the volatile art market of the 1960s with paintings that commanded high prices, he and other artists found that their early patrons stood to make financial windfalls by selling off their collections during the even hotter art market of the early 1970s. He helped to campaign for resale royalty rights, and the activism of Rosenquist and his colleagues laid the groundwork for later successes with artist copyright laws. In 1976 Rosenquist moved to Aripeka, Florida, a year after his marriage to Adams ended in divorce. On 18 April 1987 he married Mimi Thompson; they had one daughter.

Rosenquist continued to command attention with his work. His 1980 large-scaled mural, *Star Thief,* commissioned for the Miami International Airport, infuriated the retired astronaut and president of Eastern Airlines, Frank Borman, who led a very public fight against its installation. The incident became a cultural embarrassment for the city. As the critic John Russell responded in the *New York Times,* the painting was "a characteristically powerful and paradoxical statement by an artist whose best work is often underrated precisely because it looks to be so plain and direct."

★

The most complete source for biographical information about Rosenquist is Judith Goldman, *James Rosenquist* (1985), published in tandem with the Denver Art Museum traveling retrospective.

The exhibition catalog for IVAM Centre Julio González, *James Rosenquist* (1991), reprints Rosenquist's most important statements and interviews. For his early work, see the exhibition catalog for Gagosian Gallery by Judith Goldman, *James Rosenquist: The Early Pictures, 1961–1964* (1992). See also Susan Brundage, ed., *James Rosenquist, Leo Castelli: The Big Paintings, Thirty Years* (1994), which reprints some of the critical commentary and several interviews.

LEIGH BULLARD WEISBLAT

ROSS, Diana Earle (*b.* 26 March 1944 in Detroit, Michigan), lead singer of the Supremes, who symbolized the success of the Motown sound on pop and rhythm and blues (R&B) record charts as the most popular female vocal group of the 1960s.

Born to Fred and Ernestine Earle Ross in Detroit, Ross grew up on the city's east side with her five siblings. Her father was active in the labor movement through his factory job at the American Brass Company and as a leader of United Auto Workers Local 174. Her mother, a domestic worker for families in the Grosse Pointe suburbs, had recurring bouts with tuberculosis that occasionally sent her

Diana Ross *(right)*, leading the Supremes in concert. AP/WIDE WORLD PHOTOS

away from the family to recover. The Ross children often joined their mother and extended family in Bessemer, Alabama. One such trip in the early 1950s gave Ross her first experience with Jim Crow racial segregation when the children were forced to change seats and move to the back of the bus at Cincinnati, the demarcation between North and South.

Ross studied fashion design and cosmetology at Detroit's premier public high school, Cass Technical, and graduated in 1962. By that time she was already pursuing a professional career as a singer. Acquainted with a number of musicians from her neighborhood on Belmont Street, including William "Smokey" Robinson, Ross began to sing informally with new friends she made after her family moved into the Brewster-Douglass housing project in 1958. With Florence Ballard, Mary Wilson, and Betty McGlowan, Ross formed the Primettes in the spring of 1959 as a girl group to accompany the Primes, later known as the Temptations. McGlowan left the group after a few months and was replaced by Barbara Martin. As a foursome, the Primettes auditioned for Robinson at Motown Records in 1959, but were disappointed when the company's founder and owner Berry Gordy, Jr., advised them to finish high school before pursuing a career in music.

Undeterred, the group achieved its first success as the winners of the Emancipation Celebration talent show in Windsor, Ontario, on 1 August 1960. In January of the following year the women signed a contract with Motown under a new group name, the Supremes. Martin left the group shortly thereafter, and Ross, Ballard, and Wilson carried on as a trio. Between March 1961 and October 1963 the group released a series of singles that failed to make any significant impact outside Detroit. "When the Lovelight Starts Shining Through His Eyes," which hit number twenty-three on the pop charts in early 1964, finally relieved the group of its nickname around Motown, "The No-Hit Supremes." Invited to join the Motortown Revue on a concert tour in the summer of 1964, the group's experience in the South revived Ross's childhood memories of Jim Crow. The tour received threats by the Ku Klux Klan that turned violent when its bus was fired on after a concert in Montgomery, Alabama.

By the time the Motortown Revue was over, the Supremes had the number-one single in the country with "Where Did Our Love Go?" This was followed by four consecutive chart toppers through 1965: "Baby Love," the group's biggest hit, with four weeks at number one; "Come See About Me"; "Stop! In the Name of Love"; and "Back in My Arms Again." With driving drumbeats and bass lines, and arrangements that put Ross's distinctive vocals up front, the Supremes' chart-dominating singles represented the pinnacle of the Motown sound. The mix of R&B and pop elements was designed to appeal to the broadest pos-

sible audience, an approach demonstrated by the slogan that appeared on Motown's record labels, "The Sound of Young America." Although some critics attacked Motown for pandering to mainstream tastes, it became the most successful business owned by African Americans in the United States, and to many it symbolized the gains of the civil rights movement during the 1960s.

Decked out in evening gowns and the latest hairstyles, the Supremes became a staple of television variety shows and youth-oriented music programs. The group made eighteen appearances on *The Ed Sullivan Show* alone between December 1964 and December 1969. After their initial run of five chart-topping singles, they returned to the top of the charts with "I Hear a Symphony" in 1965; "You Can't Hurry Love" and "You Keep Me Hangin' On" in 1966; and "Love Is Here and Now You're Gone" and "The Happening" in 1967. After a name change to "Diana Ross and the Supremes," and the departure of Florence Ballard in mid-1967, Ross and Wilson performed with Cindy Birdsong. Most of the group's hits stayed safely within youthful, romantic territory, but the Supremes ventured into social commentary on illegitimacy with the 1968 number-one single "Love Child." The group returned to romantic balladry for its last number-one hit, "Someday We'll Be Together," released in October 1969. The most successful Motown act and female vocal group of the decade, the Supremes reached the top of the pop charts twelve times between 1964 and 1969.

Ross's career with the Supremes was notable not only for the string of number-one hits, but for her iconic presence as a role model for African Americans during a decade of social change. Indeed, by the end of the 1960s Ross was the most famous African-American woman in the performing arts. Looking back at her achievements with the Supremes in the 1960s, Ross was proud of her contribution to the gains made by the civil rights movement during the decade. As she wrote in her 1993 memoir *Secrets of a Sparrow*, "We were already crossing color lines and breaking racial barriers. . . . Since both blacks and whites were listening to, loving, and enjoying the music, we were actively changing the world by doing what we loved best—singing."

After a farewell concert in Las Vegas, Nevada, on 14 January 1970, Ross pursued a successful solo singing career that achieved six additional number-one pop hits. Ross also debuted as a dramatic actress with her Academy Award-nominated role as Billie Holiday in *Lady Sings the Blues* in 1972. Ross married businessman Robert Silberstein in January 1971. They had two daughters (one daughter, born during their marriage, was fathered by Berry Gordy), and divorced in 1976. On 23 October 1985 Ross married for the second time, to Norwegian shipping magnate Arne Naess, Jr., and they had two sons. Ross and Naess divorced in

February 2000. Ross remains one of the most popular concert performers in Europe and the United States. The Supremes were inducted into the Rock and Roll Hall of Fame in 1988.

★

Ross's autobiography is *Secrets of a Sparrow: Memoirs* (1993). Biographies of Ross include J. Randy Taraborrelli, *Call Her Miss Ross: The Unauthorized Biography of Diana Ross* (1989). Histories of Motown Records include Nelson George, *Where Did Our Love Go?: The Rise and Fall of the Motown Sound* (1985); Suzanne E. Smith, *Dancing in the Street: Motown and the Cultural Politics of Detroit* (1999); and Kingsley Abbott, ed., *Calling Out Around the World: A Motown Reader* (2001). Mary Wilson published a memoir, *Dreamgirl: My Life as a Supreme* (1986). A list of the Supremes' chart singles appears in Joel Whitburn, ed., *The Billboard Book of Top Forty Hits,* 6th ed. (1996).

TIMOTHY BORDEN

ROSTOW, Walter Whitman ("Walt") (*b.* 7 October 1916 in New York City), economic historian of theories of development who served in the administrations of presidents John F. Kennedy and Lyndon B. Johnson as deputy special assistant to the president for national security affairs (1961), chairman of the State Department Policy Planning Council (1961–1966), and special assistant to the president for national security affairs (1966–1969). An enthusiastic hawk on the Vietnam War, Rostow's views carried particular weight in the later years of the Johnson administration.

Walt Rostow. CORBIS CORPORATION (BELLEVUE)

Rostow was the second of three sons of Victor Aaron Rostow, a Russian-Jewish immigrant to the United States who worked as a metallurgical engineer, and Lillian Helman Rostow, a homemaker. He studied economics at Yale University and as a Rhodes scholar at Oxford University, earning a Ph.D. from Yale in 1940. During and after World War II, he served in the Office of Strategic Services (1941–1945), the State Department (1945–1946), and the Economic Commission for Europe (1947–1949). On 26 June 1947 he married Elspeth Vaughan Davies, a professor of political science; they had two children. Returning to the academic world in 1950, for ten years the plump and bespectacled Rostow taught economics at the Massachusetts Institute of Technology and was also an associate of the Institute's Center for International Studies, which was supported by the Central Intelligence Agency (CIA).

During the 1960 election campaign, Rostow provided informal advice and ideas on foreign affairs to the Democratic presidential candidate, Senator John F. Kennedy, to whom he had been close since 1958, and devised two of Kennedy's campaign slogans, "Let's Get This Country Moving Again" and "The New Frontier." Since the mid-1950s Kennedy, a committed foreign-policy activist whose

inaugural speech proclaimed his dedication to winning the cold war, had already devoted much thought to how the United States might gain the loyalties of the developing or "Third World" countries, the often post-colonial nations of Asia, Latin America, and Africa, which Kennedy perceived as the most acute arena of competition between the Soviet Union and the United States. Rostow's academic writings—including *The Process of Economic Growth* (1952) and *The Stages of Economic Growth: A Non-Communist Manifesto* (1960), which centered upon the possibility of providing an alternative to Marxist models and historical theories of economic development and purported to provide a roadmap developing countries could follow in order to achieve modernization without revolution—appealed to the young senator. As president, Kennedy displayed the same confidence as Rostow in his country's ability to remake developing nations in its own image. This outlook characterized programs such as the Alliance for Progress, designed to promote economic development and stave off revolution in Latin America, a particularly pronounced concern of the Kennedy administration after its failure to overthrow Fidel Castro's radical government in Cuba.

Rostow's initial reward for his assistance to Kennedy's campaign was an appointment as deputy to McGeorge Bundy, President Kennedy's special assistant for national security affairs. Rostow almost immediately became involved with Vietnam, whose southern half was often viewed in the late 1950s as a successful model for U.S. modernization efforts in former colonial states. Rostow had long argued that only the use of military force against the outside source could halt externally supported insurgencies. He also believed that the very process of modernization often generated short-term dislocations and dissatisfactions that could facilitate communist challenges, and that these challenges must be held off until full modernization was accomplished. In early February 1961 Rostow passed on to Kennedy and enthusiastically endorsed a report by Brigadier General Edward G. Lansdale, which suggested that a serious crisis was imminent in South Vietnam and recommended a major expansion of U.S. programs in that country. Rostow urged consideration of the options of bombing North Vietnam or occupying its southern regions, an outlook that made him one of the strongest hawks in the Kennedy administration, and he would remain as such until the end of the administration of President Lyndon B. Johnson. In October 1961 Rostow and General Maxwell D. Taylor went on a mission to Vietnam to assess the situation there and to consider the merits of possible U.S. courses of action. Their report recommended that the United States change its existing advisory role to one of "limited partnership" with South Vietnam, increasing U.S. economic aid to and the number of military advisers in the country. A secret appendix to the report also suggested that 8,000 U.S. combat troops be deployed. All but the last of these recommendations were implemented.

In late 1961 Rostow was appointed a State Department counselor and chairman of the department's Policy Planning Council, with wide-ranging responsibilities for long-range analysis and planning. He launched measures to improve the viability of West Berlin, international planning efforts, and initiatives to win Latin American support for a U.S. trade embargo on Cuba. In April 1963 he explored the possibility of a negotiated settlement to the Indian-Pakistani dispute over Kashmir but returned deeply pessimistic. In May 1964 Rostow also became U.S. representative to the Inter-American Committee on the Alliance for Progress, whose mission was to promote economic development and progress, reform, and peaceful change in Latin America.

It was with Vietnam, however, that Rostow's name became indelibly associated. Under Johnson, to whom he enjoyed personal access from June 1964, Rostow remained one of the administration's strongest advocates of an assertive U.S. policy in Vietnam, constantly urging increased military pressure against North Vietnam. By late 1964 he believed that escalating U.S. military actions, including the commitment of ground forces and a naval blockade and bombing of North Vietnam, would convince Hanoi that victory over South Vietnam was impossible. When these

measures were implemented in 1965, Rostow urged their expansion and intensification, and he continued to do so after he was appointed in March 1966 to succeed McGeorge Bundy as special assistant to the president for national security affairs. This appointment alarmed many of his colleagues, who feared that the perennially enthusiastic and optimistic Rostow lacked the balance, judgment, and sophistication essential to that position.

In the final years of the Johnson administration, Rostow's confidence in an eventually favorable outcome in Vietnam remained unshaken by mounting public protests or the war's inconclusive progress. In 1967 he called for the extension of the U.S. bombing program, opposing an unconditional bombing halt, although in late 1967 he did endorse proposals by Secretary of Defense Robert S. McNamara to try to reduce U.S. casualties and shift more of the burden of fighting to the South Vietnamese. In an increasingly divided and demoralized administration, Rostow remained a committed hawk, opposed to the March 1968 decision taken after the Tet Offensive to open negotiations with North Vietnam and withdraw from the war. Rostow also accompanied Johnson to his June 1967 meeting in Glassboro, New Jersey, with Soviet premier Aleksei N. Kosygin. During the July 1967 Arab-Israeli war, Rostow and Johnson worked closely together, and afterward Rostow served on a special group, headed by Bundy, that attempted to manage the immediate crisis and initiate long-range plans for the Middle East.

After his resignation from the State Department in January 1969, Rostow became a professor of economics and history at the University of Texas at Austin. Some of his colleagues in the Johnson administration such as Robert McNamara subsequently admitted their policies were mistaken, but Rostow's voluminous writings after leaving office, such as *The Diffusion of Power: An Essay in Recent History* (1972), consistently defended U.S. actions in Vietnam. In the mid-1990s he argued that U.S. involvement in the war gave other Southeast Asian nations the breathing space they required to develop strong economies and become staunch regional bastions of anticommunism. In volumes such as *Politics and the Stages of Growth* (1971), *The World Economy: History and Prospect* (1978), *Why the Poor Get Richer and the Rich Slow Down: Essays in the Marshallian Long Period* (1980), *Rich Countries and Poor Countries: Reflections on the Past, Lessons for the Future* (1987), *Essays of a Half-Century: Ideas, Policies, and Action* (1988), *History, Policy, and Economic Theory: Essays in Interaction* (1990), and *The Great Population Spike and After: Reflections on the 21st Century* (1998), Rostow also wrote extensively on the economic issues with which he had always been preoccupied. For many, Rostow epitomized the can-do spirit of the "American High" of the early cold war, and they considered his somewhat naive belief in his country's capacity to shape the world to its liking as emblematic of the hubris that ultimately embroiled the United States in Vietnam.

★

Collections of Rostow's papers are in the John Fitzgerald Kennedy Library in Boston and the Lyndon Baines Johnson Library at the University of Texas at Austin. Many of his official writings have also been published in the appropriate volumes of the series *Foreign Relations of the United States*. Rostow's autobiography is *Concept and Controversy: Sixty Years of Taking Ideas to Market* (forthcoming 2003). In addition, several of his works deal in part with his activities in the Kennedy and Johnson administrations. David Halberstam, *The Best and the Brightest* (1972), gives a harshly critical portrait of Rostow. Works focusing on his role in the Kennedy and Johnson administrations include Kimber Charles Pearce, *Rostow, Kennedy, and the Rhetoric of Foreign Aid* (2001); Kevin V. Mulcahy, "Walt Rostow as National Security Adviser," *Presidential Studies Quarterly* 25, no. 2 (1995): 223–236, and "Rethinking Groupthink: Walt Rostow and the National Security Advisory Process in the Johnson Administration," *Presidential Studies Quarterly* 25, no. 2 (1995): 237–250; David Grossman Armstrong, "The True Believer: Walt Whitman Rostow and the Path to Vietnam" (Ph.D. diss., University of Texas at Austin, 2000); and Mark Henry Haefele, "Walt Rostow, Modernization, and Vietnam: Stages of Theoretical Growth" (Ph.D. diss., Harvard University, 2000). Rostow as economist is the subject of Charles P. Kindleberger and Guido di Tella, eds., *Economics in the Long View: Essays in Honor of W. W. Rostow*, 3 vols. (1982); Barry Supple, "Revisiting Rostow," *Economic History Review* 37, no. 1 (1984): 107–114; and Robert Dorfman, "Economic Development from the Beginning to Rostow," *Journal of Economic Literature* 29, no. 2 (June 1991): 573–591. The Kennedy and Johnson libraries hold oral histories recorded by Rostow.

PRISCILLA ROBERTS

ROSZAK, Theodore   (*b.* 1933 in Chicago, Illinois), social philosopher, educator, and prolific writer who was a primary authority of the 1960s American counterculture (a term he coined), and a critic of techno-science society and culture.

The son of Anton Roszak, a cabinetmaker, and Blanche Roszak, a homemaker, Roszak has consistently shunned interviews and any publicity about his life and writings. Apparently, his Roman Catholic parents immigrated to Chicago, where Roszak went to public schools. He received a B.A. in history from the University of California, Los Angeles, in 1955, and a Ph.D. in history from Princeton University in 1958. He taught history at Stanford University from 1959 to 1963, and during 1964 to 1965 he edited the socialist periodical *Peace News* in London, England. Since then he has taught at California State University, Hayward.

Roszak's prolific writing career began in 1966 when he contributed articles to the *Nation*, a liberal weekly, and the *Atlantic*, a monthly. In 1968 he edited the socially committed anthology *The Dissenting Academy*. This book appeared at the cusp of student protests against the Vietnam War. Its academic authors (including the linguist Noam Chomsky and S. M. Rosen) vigorously criticized the decline of educational standards and the slack social consciousness of pedantic teachers. With his wife, Betty, Roszak coedited *Masculine/Feminine: Readings in Sexual Mythology and the Liberation of Women* (1969), an anthology exploring American myths of sex and the women's liberation movement.

Roszak's reputation as a dissenting liberal intellectual became nationally known to the general public with his book *The Making of a Counter Culture: Reflections on the Technocratic Society and Its Youthful Opposition* (1969). A best-seller that quickly went into many printings, it distilled his previous writings and foreshadowed his subsequent fiction and nonfiction.

More than any other single book, *The Making of a Counter Culture* constructed a consistent and coherent map of 1960s radical sensibilities and enabled the values and lifestyles of young people to be understood by their parents. In fact, a *New York Times* review praised the book's reasonable tone, "scrupulous" qualifications, "prudent" reservations, and linear narrative. Although Roszak remained skeptical and ambivalent when detailing the counterculture, he nonetheless concluded his book with a visionary utopia that could be made possible only by such a culture. That is, Roszak coined the term *counterculture*, explained it in this book, and made a career advocating it.

Counter Culture is essentially divided into four areas of argument. The first characterizes the Establishment in its own terms. The bulk of the book describes "the still uncompleted" rebels who counter that culture. A third argument describes further sources of the Establishment's unquestioning ideals: rational criticism, scientific objectivity, emotional discipline, and traditional cultural values. Roszak concludes with a description of his own potential utopia.

In his introduction Roszak characterizes the Establishment as the dominant "culture of white, western masculinity," with an unthinking and all-accepting idolatry of constructing and maintaining an urban industrialization of the world. As a modern, industrial society, Western culture is essentially repressive and destructive to the full range of human(e) thought and feeling. The Establishment is, moreover, dominated by (social) science's mystique of "reason." That is, Roszak argues, it tolerates only the "impassioned ideology handed down to us from our ancestors of the Enlightenment."

Here, "reason" was seen by the counterculture as itself unreasonable. Because of generations of dominance of the

Establishment, "reason" became a repressive rationality. It was now a mystique or "single vision" mindset that was "a total cultural and political program." The only sane reality in the Establishment is the one created by intellectual and technocratic elites and bureaucrats. Thinking individuals lived such absurd, dehumanized lives that their chronic natural and spiritual alienation—"the ideology of objective consciousness," the ideal and method of science—now felt normal.

It was the distinct and separate, or "counter," culture that rebelled against the Establishment's instrumental use of "reason." Roszak presented what he called "the leading mentors of our youthful counter culture," who have "called into question the conventional scientific world view, and in so doing have set about undermining the foundations of the technocracy." The bulk of the book provides narrative sketches of dissenters' intellectual, spiritual, and artistic achievements, including the fractured utopianism of Paul Goodman, the poetic mysticism of Allen Ginsberg, the glossed Buddhism of Alan Watts, among many others.

Roszak admired Beat generation poets like Ginsberg for their roles as mystics, but not their writings per se. He found rock music "too brutally loud and/or electronically gimmicked up." The drug culture of the hippies and of LSD guru Timothy Leary was too decadent for Roszak because a "psychedelic crusade" ended in the absurdity "that personal salvation and the social revolution can be packed in a capsule." He noted, though, that such dissidence provided the only actual social revolution.

Ultimately for Roszak, a countercultural revolution "will free us from our alienation" because essentially it is "therapeutic in character and not institutional." The counterculture of the young was forging new lifestyles and developing a new consciousness that rejected repressive rationality in favor of a new visionary wholeness.

Roszak concluded his book with his own renewing utopia based on the shaman. For Roszak it was the shaman "who enters wholly into the grand symbiotic system of nature, letting its currents and nuances flow through him." This mystical utopia would allow an environmentally friendly new tribe of individuals to live a more simple and free lifestyle. The countercultural fringes of America become central.

Roszak's book became a classic sourcebook and guide to 1960s radical sensibilities. His subsequent fiction and nonfiction repudiated the Establishment and advocated the mystical. *Where the Wasteland Ends* (1972) describes how "the essential religious impulse was exiled from our culture, what effect this has had on the quality of our life and course of politics, and what part the energies of transcendence must now play in saving urban-industrial society from self-annihilation." *The Unfinished Animal* (1976) examines mysticism and occultism as cures for a sick society. Fiction

works like *Pontifex* (1974) and *Bugs* (1981) are morality plays of science fiction in which the magic of an individual battles against the terror of the computer age. Roszak became a leading proponent of mysticism and one of the foremost opponents of techno-science.

Roszak's *The Making of a Counter Culture* was the best known of his sustained critiques of American technocratic society, an authoritative primer of alternative living styles. Its title brought the term *counterculture* into the popular consciousness. It is still useful as a barometer of the period, indicating also the beginning of what today's academics call a postmodern approach to cultural studies. For Roszak himself, his book encapsulates his preoccupations of dissention against rational techno-science and cultural values.

★

There is no biography of Roszak. For the full text of the review of *Counter Culture* referred to in the essay, see the *New York Times Book Review* (7 Sept. 1969). Reviews are also in the *Village Voice* (30 Oct. 1969) and the (London) *Times Literary Supplement* (16 Apr. 1970). See also James Hitchcock, "A Short Course in the Three Types of Radical Professors," *New York Times Magazine* (21 Feb. 1971).

PATRICK S. SMITH

ROTH, Philip Milton (*b*. 19 March 1933 in Newark, New Jersey), award-winning author of *Goodbye, Columbus, Portnoy's Complaint*, a series of novels about the fictional character Nathan Zuckerman, and other controversial works of literature that are vehicles for his trademark satire and comic genius.

The son of Herman Roth, an insurance salesman, and Bess (Finkel) Roth, a homemaker, Roth and his older brother grew up in a working-class, first-generation Jewish neighborhood in Newark. An intelligent, observant boy, Roth realized early in his life that his father carried a special burden as an employee of Metropolitan Life: as a Jew, he would never be allowed to rise as high as middle management in the company hierarchy. This notion that American Jews could be set apart and discriminated against resulted in a lifetime of novels, short stories, and essays that touch on what sets American Jews apart from other citizens and how the American dream promised by the dominant culture has affected American Jews.

Roth attended Weequahic High School, which had a predominantly Jewish student body. By the time he graduated in 1950, he was already wondering what he, coming from a comfortable but insular Jewish neighborhood, would be able to do in a society that seemed determined to limit the possibilities for Jews to experience success. Also by then, he had become a "secular Jew," meaning that he was culturally Jewish but not a believer in the Jewish faith.

Philip Roth. ARCHIVE PHOTOS, INC.

Roth attended Rutgers University, Newark Campus from 1950 to 1951. He transferred to Bucknell University in Lewisburg, Pennsylvania, in 1951. There he edited a literary magazine and began writing satires. In 1954 he graduated magna cum laude, receiving a B.A. in English. He then went to the University of Chicago, where he earned an M.A. in 1955. Although he liked Chicago, he enlisted in the U.S. Army and was assigned to Washington, D.C.; he served only one year instead of the usual two for enlistees because he hurt his back while on duty and was unable to perform physical tasks.

In 1956 Roth returned to the University of Chicago to teach freshman composition courses and to work toward earning a Ph.D. in English. After taking a few courses toward the degree, he lost interest and decided to focus on his writing. His first professional publication was the short story "The Day It Snowed," which appeared in the *Chicago Review* in 1956.

Roth left Chicago in 1958 to travel in Europe. During that year Houghton Mifflin gave him a fellowship of $8,000 for the manuscript of *Goodbye, Columbus, and Five Short Stories* (1959). The novella *Goodbye, Columbus* is a satirical account of the relationship between Brenda Patimkin, a spoiled, rich girl, and Neil Klugman, a working-class man from Newark. The novella comically portrays Brenda as a crass, selfish materialist, and her family, as uncultured

fools. Reviewers in general admired Roth's style and narrative pacing, although some objected to his not portraying the Patimkins in an establishment-approved manner. Perhaps, as Roth speculated, the novel, made up of what he considered to be apprentice stories, would have passed from view after only brief controversy had it not received the 1960 National Book Award for literature and a very disputed 1960 Daroff Award from the Jewish Book Council of America. In 1960 Roth went to Rome on a Guggenheim fellowship, so he was out of the United States when the storm of controversy over *Goodbye, Columbus* began to reach its frantic heights. Roth was stunned by the storm of protest that followed; there were many people, he discovered, who fervently hated him because of the book, and he was labeled an anti-Semite. As far as he was concerned, he had done little more than write about what he knew.

In 1959 Roth married Margaret Martinson Williams, called "Josie," a divorcee with two absent children who was four years older than he. Roth maintained that she was a madwoman who was constantly on the verge of suicide or murder, and he began hiding the kitchen knives in the garage. His life during the 1960s was largely preoccupied with coping with the continuing accusations of anti-Semitism and his bizarre relationship with his wife.

Returning from Rome, Roth taught writing at the University of Iowa from 1960 to 1962. By the end of his teaching stint in Iowa, Roth's marriage had become intolerable, with anger on both sides, and in 1963 he and his wife separated. He wanted a divorce, but the law was such that he could only receive a legal separation, and he had to pay half his income to his wife. He later called this "court-ordered robbery." During this period Roth formed a close relationship with May Aldridge, and they were almost inseparable for five years. She came from a well-to-do background with tastes suited to the upper class, but she and Roth shared political views about the Vietnam War and President Lyndon B. Johnson. Moreover, she possessed a healing warmth that Roth welcomed.

In 1962 his first full-length novel, *Letting Go*, was published. It drew on his experiences at the University of Chicago, presenting a Jewish professor dealing with moral quandaries. Critics greeted it with modest reviews; they admired Roth's ability to convey meaningful details of modern life. Even so, some reviewers criticized it as another example of anti-Semitism because of Roth's portrayal of the professor as a weak character. In 1962 Roth, along with Pietro di Donato and Ralph Ellison, was invited to Yeshiva University in New York to participate in a symposium. From the beginning of the event, Roth was the focus of attention, first fielding loaded questions from the moderator and then hostile polemics from members of the audience who indicated that they despised him. Roth handled himself adequately but was breaking down when Ellison interrupted and defended Roth's work as a universal expression of ethnic minorities coping with a sometimes inhospitable national culture. Roth left the gathering vowing never to write about Jews again. It was a turning point in his career.

Roth later recalled that from that point forward he decided to defy those who hated him and write deliberately controversial books that included characters who were Jews. In the meantime, his anger over his estranged wife's legal hold over him was blighting his life. In an effort to distance himself emotionally from the anguish he was suffering, he wrote a book about his first wife, *When She Was Good*. The protagonist Lucy Nelson lives in a small town. Her angry, manipulative behavior estranges her from her neighbors, and eventually, she freezes to death during one of her senseless moments of rage. The novel can be read as Roth's revenge fantasy, but the motivation for Nelson's death emerges naturally from the narrative. The book was published in 1967.

In May 1968 Josie Roth was killed in an automobile accident in New York's Central Park. The news was liberating for Roth, and he relished feeling free. Strangely, he ended his happy relationship with Aldridge; he later wrote that he just wanted to be free of personal entanglements. By 1976 Roth had once again become involved with a woman, the British actress Claire Bloom, whom he married in 1990. They divorced in 1994.

Random House gave Roth a $250,000 advance for *Portnoy's Complaint* in 1968. In 1969 the motion picture *Goodbye, Columbus,* starring Ali McGraw and Richard Benjamin, was released to both critical and popular acclaim. That same year, *Portnoy's Complaint* appeared. It was deliberately controversial, and in it Roth found the sardonic, authorial voice that is typical of his writings. Roth himself regarded *Portnoy's Complaint* as his first mature novel.

In *Portnoy's Complaint,* Roth experimented with narrative structure and sexual themes. A young man, Alexander Portnoy, gives a confessional to a psychiatrist. The long, sometimes rambling narrative tells of Alexander's oppressive relationship with his mother, his desire for sexual promiscuity, and detailed accounts of his masturbating, both as an act of defiance against social convention and as a release from the pressures of family and society. The masturbation scenes shocked some readers, who considered the novel pornographic, but that was exactly the effect Roth wanted. The portrait of a sexually oppressed young Jew with a symbolically castrating mother was condemned as anti-Semitic. Yet the novel is funny, and its language sparkles. As decades passed, the novel became historically important as an example of the changing literary landscape in the United States in the 1960s and 1970s, a fine character study, and an investigation of sexual repression. The novel sold almost 400,000 hardbound copies, with the royalties

providing Roth with the freedom he needed to focus on his writing.

In the postmodern novel *The Breast* (1972), Roth further developed his ideas about sexual identity. As he grew older, his writing became ever more focused on the psychology of his characters. In 1995 Roth received the National Book Award for fiction for *Sabbath's Theater;* in 1998 he received the Pulitzer Prize for fiction for *American Pastoral.*

Roth is among the most popular writers who started their careers in the 1950s, and he has been remarkably consistent in writing great works that command respect for their brilliant characterization and their insights into the human condition. Although he never fully escaped the accusation of being anti-Semitic, his candid portrayal of the experience of being Jewish in America eventually garnered respect rather than notoriety. By the 1990s Roth had earned a place in the pantheon of great American authors.

★

Roth's *The Facts: A Novelist's Autobiography* (1988) covers his life up to 1970. Roth's *Patrimony: A True Story* (1991) is a splendid account of the life of Roth's father. Claire Bloom's autobiographical *Leaving a Doll's House* (1996) includes an account of her relationship with Roth. Paul Gray's "Philip Roth: He Has Delighted and Infuriated Readers for Four Decades," *Time* (9 July 2001), assesses Roth's literary stature at the turn of the twentieth century.

KIRK H. BEETZ

ROTHKO, Mark (*b.* 25 September 1903 in Dvinsk, Russia [now Daugavpils, Latvia]; *d.* 25 February 1970 in New York City), major abstract artist in the New York School of painting that emerged after World War II.

Rothko was born Marcus Rothkowitz, the fourth and youngest child of the Russian Jews Jacob Rothkowitz and Kate Goldin Rothkowitz. His father, a popular town pharmacist, encouraged secular education over orthodox religious fervor. By 1910, to avoid the tsarist pogroms, Jacob emigrated to Portland, Oregon, sending for his eldest sons first and then the rest of the family. Seven months after the family was united Jacob died, leaving his widow and children struggling to make a living.

An excellent student, Rothko completed his studies at Portland's Lincoln High School in three years. With the promise of scholarships, he entered Yale University in the fall of 1921. Two years later the nonconformist was weary of Yale's anti-Semitism and social stigmas, and he moved to New York City permanently in 1925 "to wander, to bum a bit, and to starve." He enrolled at the Art Students League, where he took painting classes and studied for four months with the modernist painter Max Weber. He always

Mark Rothko. AP/WIDE WORLD PHOTOS

considered himself self-taught, however. During the late 1920s and through the depression of the 1930s Rothko taught children's art and worked for the Federal Art Project of the Works Progress Administration. His early figurative and representational paintings from this project have disappeared. In 1935 he co-founded The Ten, a group of expressionist artists in New York City.

Rothko married Edith Sachar, a jewelry designer, on 12 November 1932; this first marriage was short-lived. After a bohemian life of poverty the marriage ended, and they were divorced in 1944. Rothko became a U.S. citizen in 1938. In 1945 he was featured in a one-man show sponsored by the socialite and benefactor Peggy Guggenheim at her Art of This Century gallery. That March he married Mary ("Mell") Alice Beistle, a children's book illustrator; they had two children. By 1951 postwar prosperity extended into the art world, and art trading experienced a financial boom fueled by the new international millionaires. A *Fortune* magazine article (Dec. 1955) encouraged art buyers to play the market with living artists, suggesting that the pioneers of the New York School—Willem de Kooning, Jackson Pollock, and Rothko—were growth issues. Rothko had been using the shortened form of his name on paintings since 1940, and in 1958 he changed it legally.

Awards, honors, and glowing reviews kept pace with increasing prices for paintings by Rothko and his peers. Unfortunately, the first generation of abstract expressionists was financially naive; they were shamefully exploited and cheated by galleries and dealers. In June 1958 Rothko agreed to provide murals for the elegant Four Seasons restaurant at the new Seagram Building on Park Avenue. The building was designed by Ludwig Mies van der Rohe, assisted by the eminent architect Philip Johnson, in the International style. Rothko, a socialist by political persuasion, was upset at the necessarily wealthy clientele of the restaurant. Further, he was outraged by its opulent theatrical setting, in which his paintings would be but a backdrop; he had imagined diners soulfully communing with his murals only. After two years and nearly forty paintings he returned his commission in a fury of betrayal. The paintings were dispersed to the Tate Gallery in London and the National Gallery of Art in Washington, D.C.

By his own admission, in 1961 Rothko was financially comfortable, with an East Ninety-fifth Street townhouse; a cottage in Provincetown, Massachusetts; and showings in museums and galleries. He was a frequent subject of articles in art magazines as well as in *Time* and *Newsweek*, but he felt misunderstood. In January 1961 he was the first living artist of his generation to be given a one-man show at the Museum of Modern Art. In the following two years the exhibit traveled to Paris, London, Brazil, Amsterdam, and Rome. *Time* and *Newsweek* published interviews and articles before the opening. Previously a "fellow traveler," Rothko became a staunch anti-Communist during the cold war. He and Adolph Gottlieb, cofounder of The Ten, founded the Federation of Modern Painters and Sculptors and decried the Communist Party's influence on art organizations.

The radical abstract expressionists emerged at a point when the United States was seizing the cultural lead after World War II. Politically, the Central Intelligence Agency (CIA) supported and funded efforts like those of the Museum of Modern Art to promote the new art, seizing the opportunity to showcase U.S. culture as modern and progressive compared with that of Western Europe. In 1962 Rothko was encouraged to donate paintings to Harvard's faculty dining room. The arrangement both affirmed Harvard's interest in the influential painting of the decade and allowed Rothko to deduct the gift for tax purposes; he was flattered at the request, differentiating between the dining room of elite academics and the Four Seasons. Rothko explained that his somber canvases were depictions, however abstract, of Christ's suffering and the Easter Resurrection. Nathan Pusey, president of Harvard, was convinced that Rothko had painted his vision of a universal religion. Unfortunately, the use of cheap fugitive colors, sun damage, and destruction consequent to the use of the faculty dining room for parties took a severe toll on the paintings. The works remain in dark storage now, accessible only to scholars.

Although Rothko continued to paint throughout the 1960s, he sold primarily out of his studio. He was inducted into the National Institute of Arts and Letters in May 1968, and in June 1969 Yale awarded him an honorary doctorate. In 1965 Rothko signed a contract for $250,000 to paint murals for a small chapel commissioned by John and Dominique de Menil in a quiet residential neighborhood in Houston, Texas. Philip Johnson was hired to build the chapel under Rothko's direction. It would be the crowning achievement of the artist's work. From 1964 until he finished in 1967 Rothko worked on the project with the expectation that the building would be modest and not detract from the paintings. Controversy arose, however, when Johnson planned a vertical, visually prominent building into which Rothko's paintings would fit, whereas Rothko wanted a building that would fit his paintings. Johnson resigned from the project in 1967, and the architects who replaced him deferred to Rothko's wishes. Rothko never saw the work installed. The building eventually was named the Rothko Chapel.

On 1 January 1969, at the age of sixty-five, Rothko left his family. A year earlier he had suffered an aneurysm of the aorta, adding to the depression he had experienced all his life. Rothko smoked heavily, drank and ate too much, and had high blood pressure. Although he was a millionaire, he spent his last months in his poorly furnished studio, lonely, depressed, and suffering from myriad illnesses, both real and imagined. His studio assistant found him dead on the morning of 25 February 1970; he had committed suicide by cutting the brachial arteries inside his elbows, having first taken a large dose of the antidepressant Sinequan to dull the pain. What may have destroyed Rothko was that his deepest fears about the art world were coming true; close friends, dealers, and advisers, driven by greed, were profiting from the masterpieces he had painted from the depths of his soul. He is buried in East Marion Cemetery in East Marion (Suffolk County), New York.

After the death of their mother not long after, Rothko's children were left with the enormous burden of recovering their father's collection, which was in danger of being stolen and hidden in Europe through the machinations of the executors of his estate. After six years of litigation and millions of dollars in legal fees the case was concluded in the New York State Court of Appeals. In a landmark decision, seven judges imposed fines and damages on Rothko's executors, Francis K. Lloyd and the Marlborough Galleries, for $9.3 million. The paintings were returned to the Rothko children and the Mark Rothko Foundation; they have since been organized, catalogued, and cared for appropriately.

The contradictions, tensions, anger, despair, and sadness of Rothko's life disappear in the quiet solitude and mystical depths of his paintings. Throughout the world viewers find their own serenity in the rich and somber works of his later life.

★

Biographies of Rothko include Dore Ashton, *About Rothko* (1983); James E. B. Breslin, *Mark Rothko: A Biography* (1993); Lee Seldes, *The Legacy of Mark Rothko* (1978); Anna C. Chave, *Mark Rothko: Subjects in Abstraction* (1989); *Mark Rothko 1903–1970,* a catalog of the Rothko exhibition of 17 June–1 September 1987; and London and Frances Stonor Saunders, *The Cultural Cold War* (2000). See also Diane Waldman, *Mark Rothko, 1903–1970: A Retrospective* (1978). An obituary is in the *New York Times* (26 Feb. 1970).

ROSEMARIE S. CARDOSO

ROUS, (Francis) Peyton (*b.* 5 October 1879 in either Texas or Baltimore, Maryland; *d.* 16 February 1970 in New York City), Nobel Prize–winning physician and pathologist whose groundbreaking research on the relationship of viruses to cancer was recognized in the 1960s and led to new advances in understanding and treating the disease.

Rous was one of three children and the only son of Charles Rous, a grain broker who died when Rous was eleven, and

Peyton Rous. THE LIBRARY OF CONGRESS

Frances Anderson Wood. Rous may have been born in Texas, where his father met and married his mother, but he grew up in Baltimore. In the 1890s he enrolled at Baltimore's Johns Hopkins University, but he was not an outstanding student. Early on he wanted to become a naturalist, and he published articles about flowers in a Baltimore newspaper.

After receiving his B.A. in 1900, Rous enrolled in Johns Hopkins Medical School. He received his medical degree in 1905 but during his internship found that he did not actually enjoy treating patients. He went to the University of Michigan, where he developed his interest in and taught pathology and the study of disease. After spending a year studying in Dresden, Germany, Rous accepted an appointment in 1909 at the Rockefeller Institute for Medical Research (later Rockefeller University) in New York City. Soon afterward he began his historic investigations into the pathogenesis of cancer, ignoring advisers who told him not to commit himself to cancer research. Rous remained at the institute for the rest of his life. He married Marion Eckford de Kay on 7 January 1915; they had three children.

Throughout most of his career, Rous worked in relative anonymity. His early research into how cancer develops in the body was largely ignored by other scientists. By the 1950s, however, Rous's work was beginning to gain attention. In 1966 he received the Nobel Prize for physiology or medicine for his discovery that viruses cause cancer. His major breakthrough occurred in 1910, when he began an experiment to determine whether chickens could contract cancer from each other. The idea contradicted what scientists thought about cancer at that time, but Rous proceeded with the experiments.

He began by successfully transplanting naturally occurring connective tissue tumors from one chicken to another, using small numbers of tumor cells. Although this was an accomplishment in itself, it did not reveal anything about the pathogenesis of cancer—that is, how cancer develops. Rous then created cell-free extracts, or filtrates, of the tumors by processing them through a filter with minute pores that even destroyed bacteria. He then injected the submicroscopic extracts into another chicken. Surprisingly, cancer developed in the chicken, and the implication was that the origin of the cancer was viral. The virus became known as the Rous sarcoma virus. Rous went on to show that different viral agents produce specific types of tumor, such as bone, cartilage, and blood vessel tumors, when injected into otherwise healthy chickens.

For the most part, Rous's colleagues refused to accept his findings, which were published in several papers in the *Journal of Experimental Medicine* and the *Journal of the American Medical Association*. One problem was that the findings could not be reproduced in other animals. Rous even failed at extracting similar viral agents from mouse cancers. Furthermore, molecular biology was still in its infancy, and scientists were focusing on numerous areas of research concerning the causes of cancer. In a sense, they could not connect the results of these many avenues of cancer research and related discoveries.

The refusal of the scientific community to take his discoveries seriously led Rous to give up his cancer research for two decades. However, in 1933 he returned to cancer research when his colleague at the institute and good friend Richard Shope found that a wartlike growth on rabbits could progress to cancer and that an agent similar to a virus transmitted the tumor. Excited by the discovery, Rous began to study the biology of the agent that caused the tumor, which became known as the Shope papilloma. Over the next two decades Rous discovered how tumor production speeds up in several ways when chemicals, such as tar and radiation, and tumor-inducing viruses work together. He also found that carcinogenesis, or the production of cancer, begins with an initial phase in which a cell gains malignant "potential" and then proceeds to the "promotion" stage, in which this potential turns into an actively growing cancer.

Rous's demonstration of the viral origin of tumors was one of the most important discoveries in oncology, or the study of cancer. An octogenarian by the time he shared the Nobel Prize with Charles B. Huggins in 1966, Rous nevertheless was gratified to receive one of science's highest honors for his work decades earlier. That work had resulted in the first demonstration of an oncogenic virus—that is, a virus capable of causing cancer. In his Nobel Prize acceptance lecture, Rous commented, "Tumors destroy man in a unique and appalling way, as flesh of his own flesh, which has somehow been rendered proliferative, rampant, predatory, and ungovernable." He went on to point out that after seventy years of research, tumors "remain the least understood. . . . What can be the why for these happenings?" Over the next decades, more and more answers to this question would be found using new tools in molecular biology. The revolution in the understanding of cancer, however, rests on research based on Rous's early discovery of the Rous sarcoma virus. For example, genetic studies of the virus have found that a gene or genes in the virus help transform cells into cancer, revealing that the seeds of cancer lie within us.

Described by Renato Dulbecco, a 1975 Nobel Prize winner, as "rather small in stature with silvery hair and penetrating eyes," Rous was always meticulous in his research and continued to conduct studies until his death at ninety from abdominal cancer. He pioneered research into blood preservation and transfusion, which led to the establishment in 1917 of the world's first blood bank near the front lines in Belgium during World War I. Rous was also a noted editor of the *Journal of Experimental Medicine*. In 1962 Rous was awarded the United Nations Prize from the

World Health Organization, and President Lyndon Johnson presented him with the National Medal of Science in 1966.

★

Two useful books containing information on Rous and his research into cancer are Isaac Berenblum, *Man Against Cancer: The Story of Cancer Research* (1952), and Greer Williams, *Virus Hunters* (1959). George W. Corner, *A History of the Rockefeller Institute, 1901–1953* (1964), contains detailed information on Rous's life and work, as does Renato Dulbecco, "Francis Peyton Rous," *Biographical Memoirs of the National Academy of Science* 48 (1976): 274–307. An obituary is in the *New York Times* (17 Feb. 1970).

DAVID PETECHUK

ROZELLE, Alvin Ray ("Pete") (*b.* 1 March 1926 in South Gate, California; *d.* 6 December 1996 in Rancho Santa Fe, California), longest-running commissioner of the National Football League (NFL), who during the 1960s presided over league expansion and the merger with the American Football League (AFL), created the Super Bowl, developed *Monday Night Football,* negotiated the first league-wide television contract, and helped football eclipse baseball as the national pastime.

Rozelle was the older of two sons of Raymond Foster Rozelle, a grocery-store owner and later a purchasing agent for Alcoa, and Hazel Viola Healey. Nicknamed "Pete" by an uncle at the age of five, Rozelle grew up in the Los Angeles suburb of Compton, California, and played basketball and tennis for Compton High School. He graduated from high school in 1944.

After a U.S. Navy tour from 1944 to 1946, Rozelle attended Compton Junior College, which housed the new practice facility of the Los Angeles Rams of the NFL. He worked in the Rams publicity department until he entered the University of San Francisco (USF). He served as USF athletic-news director, and, after receiving his B.A. in 1950, became assistant athletic director. Rozelle served as the Rams publicity director from 1952 to 1955, before taking a brief position in corporate public relations. He returned to the team in 1957 as general manager on the recommendation of NFL Commissioner Bert Bell, and he generated revenue with an extensive new line of team merchandise and resolved a bitter ownership dispute among Rams stockholders.

Bell died unexpectedly in October 1959, and his position remained vacant for the remainder of the season. In January 1960 NFL owners gathered at the Kenilworth Hotel in Miami to hold their annual meeting and to vote on a new commissioner. After ten days, twenty-three ballots, and a

Pete Rozelle, 1968. © BETTMANN/CORBIS

dozen candidates (most notably, the San Francisco 49ers' polarizing attorney Marshall Leahy), the position remained vacant. On 26 January, the Rams' owner Dan Reeves first recommended the relatively unknown Rozelle, who had accompanied him to Miami, for the position.

At thirty-three Rozelle was thin, unassuming, inexperienced, and seen by many NFL owners as an easily controlled compromise candidate. He was elected that evening, and the sports press hastily nicknamed him "the boy czar." Rozelle's youth and quiet demeanor, however, belied a tenacity and bold vision that would revolutionize the NFL.

Following his relocation of NFL headquarters from suburban Philadelphia to midtown Manhattan, a move designed to lift the profile of the league, Rozelle focused on building unity among the existing twelve NFL teams. Essentially managed as unconnected franchises, the teams were worth about $1 million each in 1960, but many of the smaller markets were floundering and NFL franchises had been going bankrupt as recently as 1952. Rozelle's concept of "League Think" was vital to the NFL's growth and central to his management. As he explained, "When you have unity and harmony and can move basically as one, you can have a successful sports league."

For Rozelle, the key to that success was network television. Until then college football dominated network schedules, and NFL teams had sporadic regional coverage at best. In late 1960 Rozelle introduced his plan to transform the fragmented NFL into a modern corporation, with his new television policy at its center. He proposed that the NFL sell its television rights as a single package and share the revenue equally among all the franchises. For self-interested NFL owners, this concept was a hard sell, but Rozelle's perseverance won their acceptance by early 1961. At the same time he built a partnership with national television networks, attending affiliate meetings and selling the potential profitability of NFL games. Rozelle spent that summer lobbying the U.S. Congress for an exemption to the Sherman Act. Passed on 30 September 1961, this exemption, the Sports Antitrust Broadcast Act, permitted sports leagues to sell their television rights collectively. Later that year the NFL was awarded its first lucrative television contract, a $4.6 million, two-year deal with the Columbia Broadcasting System (CBS) that was worth nearly $330,000 for each franchise. By 1964 the league's broadcast rights had tripled to $14 million.

The NFL also had new competition from the American Football League (AFL), organized and financed by millionaire Lamar Hunt. The AFL had begun operations in 1960. Commissioner Bell had considered expanding the NFL with AFL teams, and this was one way Rozelle could both expand the NFL and eliminate competition. After years of battling with Hunt and lobbying Congress for a second exemption to the Sherman Act, the NFL-AFL merger was achieved in 1966. An expanded NFL of two conferences and twenty-five teams was created, and Rozelle remained commissioner. Rozelle's creation, the AFL-NFL World Championship Game (later renamed the "Super Bowl" by Hunt's son), was first played on 15 January 1967. It has become the most important one-day sporting event in the United States. In 1970 *Monday Night Football,* Rozelle's idea since the mid-1960s, marked the debut of weekly televised professional football games in prime time.

Rozelle was named *Sports Illustrated* Sportsman of the Year in 1963. By then he had brought professional football to Dallas and Minnesota and had restructured the players' pension plan. Following a three-month investigation, he suspended and fined popular players Paul Hornung and Alex Karras in April 1963 for betting on league games and galvanized respect for himself around the NFL. However, Rozelle was also criticized the following November for allowing games to resume two days after President John F. Kennedy's assassination. He later considered this "the most regrettable decision I ever made." In 1969 Rozelle forced the New York Jets quarterback Joe Namath to sell his interest in a Manhattan nightclub, Bachelors III, because of its alleged association with gamblers.

Rozelle was elected to the Pro Football Hall of Fame in 1985 while still active in the NFL, a rare honor as selections are traditionally reserved for retired candidates. He resigned as commissioner of the NFL in 1989 after serving for twenty-nine years. Rozelle was named one of *Time*'s most influential people of the twentieth century in 1998. He died of brain cancer at his home and was buried at El Camino Memorial Park in La Jolla, California. He was survived by his wife, Carrie (Cooke), whom he had married in December 1973. The couple had one daughter. Upon Rozelle's death, the New York Giants' owner Wellington Mara reflected that Rozelle "did more for professional football and the NFL than any sports executive has ever done."

★

There is no full-length biography of Rozelle. A concise biography by R. Jake Sudderth is included in *Scribner Encyclopedia of American Lives: Sports Figures* (2002). An absorbing look at his career and the evolution of the NFL is found in David Harris, *The League: The Rise and Decline of the NFL* (1986). A discussion of his early accomplishments is featured in *Sports Illustrated* (6 Jan. 1964). Michael Lewis's overview of Rozelle's career appears in *Time*'s "Time 100: Twentieth Century's 100 Most Influential Builders and Titans" (7 Dec. 1998). An obituary is in *The New York Times* (8 Dec. 1996).

TRACY L. EDDY

RUBIN, Jerry Clyde (*b.* 14 July 1938 in Cincinnati, Ohio; *d.* 28 November 1994 in Los Angeles, California), 1960s radical and antiwar demonstrator who organized the 1967 March on the Pentagon, cofounded the Youth International Party with Abbie Hoffman, and gained notoriety as one of the "Chicago Seven" tried for protesting at the 1968 Democratic National Convention.

Rubin was the eldest of two sons born to Robert Rubin, a truck driver who became a union organizer, and Esther (Katz) Rubin, a homemaker. He graduated from Walnut Hills High School in 1956. That same year he entered the University of Cincinnati and also began working as a reporter at the *Cincinnati Post*. In 1961 he graduated with a B.A. and ended his newspaper career. Following the deaths of his parents in 1960 and 1961, Rubin became the guardian of his thirteen-year-old brother, Gil. He took his brother to Israel and spent a year studying sociology at Jerusalem's Hebrew University.

In January 1964 Rubin entered graduate school at the University of California, Berkeley, and succumbed almost immediately to its radical student culture. Six weeks after arriving he dropped out of graduate school to become a full-time activist. Rubin found his calling when Berkeley's Free Speech Movement (FSM) broke out in December 1964. He participated in all of its events, and later called the FSM his political training ground. Rubin became locally famous as an organizer of the Vietnam Day Committee, which in 1965 conducted a giant teach-in and demonstrated against troop trains passing through Berkeley. In a four-way race for the mayor of Berkeley in 1966, Rubin came in second, a great disappointment as he had expected to win.

Jerry Rubin *(center)*, appearing before the House Un-American Activities Committee with a toy gun, October 1968. ASSOCIATED PRESS AP

Rubin dropped his former clean-cut look in favor of a beard, long hair, and hippie dress. However, when he was called before the House Un-American Activities Committee (HUAC) in 1966 to testify about his activities in Berkeley, Rubin wore the full uniform of a Revolutionary War soldier. HUAC canceled the Washington, D.C., hearings before he could speak, but Rubin's costume attracted the press and made him a celebrity overnight. He won further notoriety in January 1967 when, with the activist Abbie Hoffman and others, he dropped dollar bills on the floor of the New York Stock Exchange. Rubin met Hoffman for the first time at this demonstration and, as the project director of its planned March on the Pentagon, he brought Hoffman into the National Mobilization Committee to End the War in Vietnam (Mobe).

Rubin and Hoffman drew on the emerging counterculture to make the March on the Pentagon the decade's most spectacular manifestation of political street theater. The Mobe included traditional pacifists, and the march itself featured celebrities such as the pediatrician Benjamin Spock, the novelist Norman Mailer, and the poet Robert Lowell. Rubin, Hoffman, and the New Left, especially members of Students for a Democratic Society (SDS), provided the color. On 21 October 1967 between 50,000 and 75,000 people gathered in Washington, D.C., and crossed the Arlington Memorial Bridge. The older marchers believed they were leading a peaceful protest before the Pentagon, while the leftists intended to storm it.

Armed troops and military police met the marchers at the Pentagon. Hoffman described what happened next as, "Homecoming Day at the Pentagon and the cheerleaders

chant, 'Beat Army! Beat Army!' It's SDS at the thirty-yard line and third down. Rubin cuts the rope with a hunting knife and the Charge of the Flower Brigade is on." Some marchers broke through the police lines and managed briefly to enter the Pentagon. Demonstrators then staged an exorcism and attempted to levitate the massive building, which failed to rise. Ultimately police arrested about 800 marchers, but not before they reaped a harvest of publicity. Mailer's account of the event in the *Armies of the Night* (1968) marvelously captured the spirit of the moment and enhanced the leftist protestors' mystique.

Rubin, Hoffman, and their followers staged their last major theatrical events in August 1968 during the Democratic National Convention (DNC) in Chicago. They began planning for the convention in January, opening an office in New York City and forming the Youth International Party so they could call themselves Yippies. Upon arriving in Chicago they flooded the city with rumors that Yippies were going to put LSD in the water supply and perform many lewd and nefarious acts. They nominated their candidate for president, Pigasus, an actual pig, among other antics, some of which provoked the police to beat and arrest them. The police arrested Rubin, Hoffman, and leaders of the SDS and Mobe, who had been holding parallel and sometimes joint demonstrations against the DNC.

HUAC subpoenaed Rubin again for his role in the Chicago protests, but, after he had waited days to testify, guards denied him entry to the hearing room for wearing a Santa Claus suit in honor of the holiday season. The Justice Department indicted Rubin and seven (later six) others for having conspired to incite violence during the

Democratic convention. The Chicago Seven's trial began in September 1969 and dragged on until mid-February of the following year. Unlike some defendants who fell into deep depressions as a result of the trial, Rubin called it the highlight of his life and reveled in its publicity. The trial ended with five of the defendants, including Rubin, being found innocent of conspiracy but guilty of crossing state lines in order to riot. An appeals court subsequently overturned their convictions.

Rubin's reputation faded away with the end of the 1960s. A child of the times, Rubin never quite managed to find a place for himself in the conservative decades that followed. After a period of despair Rubin devoted himself to self-improvement, fitness, and health. In 1978 he married Mimi Leonard Fleischman; they had two children and divorced in 1992. In the 1980s and 1990s Rubin worked briefly on Wall Street, led an executive networking firm, and eventually moved back to California and began peddling nutrition products. He was one of the few New Leftists to renounce his old beliefs, publicly embracing and defending the capitalist system. In 1994 Rubin was hit by a car while jaywalking; he died of the resulting injuries two weeks later. Rubin is buried at Hillside Memorial Park in Culver City, California.

Mailer once called Rubin "the most militant, unpredictable, creative—therefore dangerous—hippie-oriented leader available to the New Left." Rubin helped to define the 1960s through his energy, playfulness, and ability to attract attention with shocking performances and demonstrations. Only Hoffman rivaled him as an impresario of the New Left.

★

Rubin, *Growing Up at Thirty-Seven* (1976), is interesting and remarkably candid. His "Guess Who's Coming to Wall Street," *New York Times* (30 July 1980), explains his conversion to capitalism. Paul Krassner, *Confessions of a Raving, Unconfined Nut: Misadventures in the Counterculture* (1993), has a chapter on the Yippies. William L. O'Neill, *Coming Apart: An Informal History of America in the 1960s* (1971), puts the Yippies in context. For more information on Rubin's background and later years see the *Scribner Encyclopedia of American Lives,* vol. 4 (2001). Obituaries are in the *Los Angeles Times* (29 Nov. 1994) and *Newsweek* (12 Dec. 1994).

WILLIAM L. O'NEILL

RUBY, John ("Jack") (*b.* 25 March 1911 in Chicago, Illinois; *d.* 3 January 1967 in Dallas, Texas), nightclub owner who murdered Lee Harvey Oswald, the presumed assassin of President John F. Kennedy, in 1963.

Ruby, born Jacob Rubenstein, was the fifth of eight living children of Joseph Rubenstein, a Polish immigrant carpen-

Jack Ruby at the Dallas County Jail, January 1964. ASSOCIATED PRESS AP

ter, and Fannie Turek Rutkowski, a homemaker. Although the exact month and day of his birth are somewhat vague, the date Ruby most often cited was 25 March. Ruby grew up in a series of poor Jewish neighborhoods in Chicago. By the age of eleven Ruby was showing antisocial tendencies in the form of truancy and misconduct at home; the Jewish Social Service Bureau referred him to the Institute for Juvenile Research. Characterized as "quick tempered" and "disobedient," Ruby was placed temporarily in foster homes but eventually returned to his family. Ruby's only legal difficulty as a youth, however, resulted from an altercation with a policeman about ticket scalping. Ruby attended several schools in Chicago and is believed to have completed the eighth grade, but he probably did not attend high school.

After leaving school, Ruby drifted, working for a while in San Francisco, where he made money selling "tip" sheets at Bay Meadows racetrack and newspaper subscriptions door-to-door. He eventually returned to Chicago and started the Spartan Novelty Company. He was inducted into the U.S. Army Air Force on 21 May 1943 and spent his military career at bases in the South until he was honorably discharged on 21 February 1946. After the war he briefly went into the novelty business with his brother Earl and then moved to Dallas in late 1947. Over the next fifteen years, Ruby made his living primarily by operating nightclubs and dance halls.

On 22 November 1963, President John F. Kennedy was assassinated as his motorcade traveled through Dallas. Within two hours of the assassination, police arrested Lee Harvey Oswald outside a Dallas movie theatre and charged him with the crime. On 24 November 1963 Ruby made his way up an auto ramp into the basement of the Dallas City Jail and placed himself among the reporters, photographers, and others who had gathered to witness Oswald's transfer to the county jail. As the police walked Oswald through the basement, Ruby emerged from the crowd and shot and killed Oswald as millions watched on national television.

By the early 1960s, Ruby had gained a reputation as a man with a violent temper. According to the Warren Commission, which was charged with investigating the Kennedy assassination, Ruby's relationships with his employees were often violent; records show that he often hit or beat people with whom he had disagreements. He was also reported to have beaten, pistol-whipped, or blackjacked unruly patrons at the two strip clubs in which he held interests, the Carousel Club and the Vegas Club. During an incident in February 1963, Ruby badly beat someone who had made some remarks about a woman accompanying him, but he was acquitted of assault charges. By 1963 Ruby's record included eight arrests for a variety of reasons, including disturbing the peace, carrying a concealed weapon, and violating state liquor laws. On 12 February 1963, Ruby was arrested on a charge of simple assault but was found not guilty. He was also arrested on 14 March 1963 for ignoring traffic summonses.

Noted attorney Melvin Belli defended Ruby with a temporary insanity plea, arguing that Ruby had "psychomotor epilepsy," which allowed him to function physically while he was, for all intents and purposes, unconscious. The jury convicted Ruby of murder on 14 March 1964 and sentenced him to death. However, in October 1966 the Texas Court of Criminal Appeals reversed the conviction, citing improper admission of testimony and saying that a change of venue should have been ordered. Although a new trial was scheduled to take place in Wichita Falls, Texas, Ruby contracted pneumonia and was admitted to Parkland Hospital in Dallas on 9 December 1966. Further tests revealed that he had terminal lung cancer, and he died in the hospital from a blood clot in his lungs. He is buried in Chicago.

With the death of Oswald, it did not take long for con-

spiracy theories about the president's assassination to begin developing. Ruby vehemently denied any involvement in a conspiracy aimed at silencing Oswald so that the accused assassin could not reveal information about possible coconspirators in Kennedy's assassination. Conspiracy theorists point to the fact that Ruby was supposedly involved in organized crime and had visited Cuba in 1959, which was construed as suspicious, since the Kennedy Administration had severely strained relations with the Castro government. The Bay of Pigs invasion on 17 April 1961 and the Cuban Missile Crisis in October 1962 assured at best an armed truce between the two countries.

Nevertheless, the 1964 Warren Commission report stated that no evidence existed that Ruby was part of a larger conspiracy. As for Ruby, he always maintained that he shot Oswald partly from grief and outrage. The Rockefeller Commission, which was established to investigate the Central Intelligence Agency (CIA) in 1975, also found no evidence of an association between the CIA and either Ruby or Oswald, which some conspiracy theorists had maintained.

Many of Ruby's family and friends who testified before the Warren Commission told of his unusual generosity and described him as an extremely emotional person who often overreacted to people in distress. He was also described as a "publicity hound," "glad hander," and "name dropper" who always wanted to be the center of attention. Ruby was at the offices of the *Morning News* to place an advertisement for his club when he heard of Kennedy's assassination; he became upset and turned his advertisement into a tribute to the president. Although conspiracy theories have never died out completely, most experts agree that Ruby, who was capable of abrupt and violent reactions and who was obviously upset after the president's assassination, acted on an irrational impulse when he shot Oswald.

★

Two biographies of Ruby are Garry Wills and Ovid Demaris, *Jack Ruby* (1968), and Seth Kantor, *Who Was Jack Ruby?* (1978). Detailed information about Ruby's murder of Oswald in relation to President Kennedy's assassination can be found in the Warren Commission records, which are housed in the National Archives in Washington, D.C. An obituary is in the *New York Times* (4 Jan. 1967).

DAVID PETECHUK

RUDOLPH, Wilma Glodean (*b.* 23 June 1940 in Saint Bethlehem, Tennessee; *d.* 12 November 1994 in Brentwood, Tennessee), the "fastest woman in the world" and the first American woman to win three gold medals in a single Olympics.

Born into poverty in 1940 in the racially segregated South, Rudolph's opportunities seemed limited. She was the twentieth of twenty-two children of her father's first and second marriages. Her father, Ed Rudolph, was a railroad porter, and her mother, Blanche (Pettus) Rudolph, was a domestic. Their home in Clarksville, Tennessee, had neither electricity nor indoor plumbing. Rudolph's life was a struggle from birth. Born two months premature, she weighed only four and a half pounds. By age four she had contracted measles, mumps, chicken pox, pneumonia, scarlet fever, and polio. Polio left her with a crooked left leg and a foot that turned inward.

Defying all odds, Rudolph began her stellar athletic career at age twelve. Finally free of the leg brace she had worn for support after her bout with polio, she participated in school sports. By the time she was in high school Rudolph was winning every race she entered, yet she knew she needed expert training. At the end of her sophomore year she had been selected to compete against the top runners in the South at a track meet in Tuskegee, Alabama. She expected to win, but to her horror she lost every race, which caused her to conclude she needed intensive training to reach the competitive level she envisioned for herself.

That summer Rudolph attended coach Ed Temple's high school girls' track program at Tennessee State College. The team trained five days a week and ran twenty miles a day. The goal was for the team to win the junior division championship at the Amateur Athletic Union (AAU) national meet in Philadelphia. At the end of the summer Rudolph and the team were the national junior champions. Rudolph won the 75-meter and 100-meter races and the 400-meter relay. That day she competed in nine races and won all of them—yet there was no mention of these achievements in the newspapers because at the time the public had little interest in women's track and field events. Rudolph recalled, "I won nine races that day, and our team won the junior title, and none of us even thought about looking in the sports pages . . . because we knew . . . nobody would bother to write it up." At that meet she had her photo taken with Jackie Robinson of the Brooklyn Dodgers, the first African-American player in major league baseball, who became her hero and inspiration.

Under Temple's coaching and through her hard work, Rudolph qualified at age sixteen to become the youngest member of the 1956 U.S. Olympic women's track and field team. At the Olympic Games in Melbourne, Australia, she lost in the 200-meter race but won a bronze medal as part of the 400-meter relay team. She dedicated herself to doing even better at the 1960 Olympics in Rome.

Rudolph's career was almost sidetracked when she became pregnant in fall 1957, her senior year in high school. So Rudolph could attend college, her family offered to raise

Wilma Rudolph displays her three gold medals, 1960.

her daughter while she pursued her academic and athletic careers. In 1958 Rudolph graduated from high school and received a full scholarship to attend Tennessee State University as a member of Coach Temple's Tigerbelles track team. Tennessee State was one of the few schools that offered women's athletic scholarships prior to the passage of Title IX in 1972.

At the AAU national meet in Corpus Christi, Texas, just before the 1960 Olympic trials, Rudolph set a world record, 22.9 seconds in the 200-meter race; the record stood for eight years. At the Olympic trials in Emporia, Kansas, she easily qualified in three events, the 100- and 200-meter races and the 400-meter relay. To her delight, Temple was named coach of the 1960 U.S. women's Olympic team.

At five feet, eleven inches tall and weighing 132 pounds, Rudolph was a slim and graceful sprinter with amazing speed. At the 1960 Rome Olympics she won the 100-meter race in a world record time, 11 seconds; however, because of a strong following wind, the record remained unofficial. She set an Olympic record in the opening heat of the 200-meter race with a time of 23.2 seconds and went on to win the gold medal with a time of 24.0 seconds. In the 400-meter relay, despite a poor baton pass, she caught up with and passed the German runner to take the gold. The 44.5-second time was one-tenth of a second over the teams' semifinal time of 44.4 seconds, a world record. Rudolph became the first American woman to win three gold medals in a single Olympics and the most celebrated female athlete in the world. The Italian press dubbed her La Perla Nera (the black pearl), and the French press called her La Gazelle Noire (the black gazelle).

After the Olympics the team had an audience with Pope John XXIII, then competed in the British Empire Games in London. Rudolph won the two events in which she competed, the 100-meter race and the 400-meter relay. The U.S. Olympic Committee arranged for Rudolph and three of her teammates to tour several European cities. People everywhere came out to see her. *Sports Illustrated* reported that mounted police had to hold back the crowds in Cologne, Germany.

When Rudolph returned to the United States, her hometown of Clarksville welcomed her with a victory parade and banquet. The occasion was especially notable because it was the first integrated event in the town's history. Nashville also held a parade in her honor. In Chicago mayor Richard J. Daley honored her by giving her the keys to the city, an event repeated in other cities throughout the United States. President John F. Kennedy invited Rudolph and her parents to the White House, and she was a guest on the *Ed Sullivan Show*.

In 1962 Rudolph retired from track and field, explaining she wanted to be remembered at her best. That year she was divorced from her first husband, William Ward, whom she had married in 1961. In 1963 she graduated from Tennessee State University with a degree in elementary education and in July married her high school boyfriend, Robert Eldridge. Their family grew to include four children (the couple divorced in 1981).

Rudolph became a celebrity in the wake of her spectacular performances at the 1960 Olympic Games. In 1963 the U.S. State Department asked her to be a goodwill ambassador to the Friendship Games in Senegal. A devoted Baptist, she joined evangelist Billy Graham's Baptist Christian Athletes tour in Japan. Over the years Rudolph held various teaching positions. She dedicated her life to helping others and gave selflessly of her time to various community endeavors. In 1967 Vice President Hubert Humphrey asked her to be part of Operation Champion, a government athletic program designed to aid underprivileged children in sixteen ghetto communities. In 1982 she founded the Wilma Rudolph Foundation, a nonprofit organization that promotes amateur athletics.

Rudolph received many honors. In 1960 European sportswriters voted her Sportswoman of the Year, and both United Press International and the Associated Press named her Female Athlete of the Year. In 1961 she received the James E. Sullivan Award for the top amateur athlete, and in 1962 the Babe Zaharias Award. In 1987 she became the first female to be given the NCAA Silver Anniversary Award, and in 1993 President William J. Clinton presented her with a National Sports Award.

Rudolph was inducted into the Black Athletes Hall of Fame in 1973, the National Track and Field Hall of Fame in 1974, the Afro-American International Hall of Fame in 1980, the U.S. Olympic Hall of Fame in 1983, and the National Women's Hall of Fame in 1994. Following her death at age fifty-four from a brain tumor, her alma mater, Tennessee State University, established the Wilma Rudolph Residence Center in her honor. She is buried at Edgefield Missionary Baptist Church in Clarksville.

Rudolph overcame seemingly insurmountable obstacles, including poverty, racism, sexism, and a crippling bout with polio, to achieve athletic excellence. Her life serves as a model of courage and dedication for all Americans and proof of the veracity of the American dream.

★

A collection of news clippings documenting Rudolph's achievements, photographs, and her Tigerbelle trophies are in the Special Collections Department of the Tennessee State University Library. Rudolph's autobiography, written with Martin Ralbovsky, is *Wilma* (1977). Other good sources for information about her life and career are Tom Biracree, *Wilma Rudolph* (1988); Michael Davis, *Black American Women in Olympic Track and Field* (1992); and Anne Janette Johnson, *Great Women in Sports* (1996). Helpful articles include Frank Litsky, "Wilma Rudolph," *New York Times*

(13 Nov. 1994), and Susan Reed, "Born to Win," *People Weekly* (28 Nov. 1994). An obituary is in the *New York Times* (13 Nov. 1994).

GAI INGHAM BERLAGE

RUFFIN, David Eli (*b.* 18 January 1941 in Meridian, Mississippi; *d.* 1 June 1991 in Philadelphia, Pennsylvania), lead singer of the Temptations, a Motown group, known for its onstage dynamism, that first hit the top of the charts with "My Girl" and later recorded such classic 1960s tunes as "Ain't Too Proud to Beg" and "I Wish It Would Rain."

Ruffin grew up in a family led by his strict Baptist preacher father, Eli Ruffin. His mother died shortly after his birth, leaving him and his two older brothers and sister to be raised by their father and stepmother. The family toured the South as a gospel group throughout Ruffin's childhood. When he was fourteen he left his family to perform with the Dixie Nightingales and other gospel groups; his touring eventually took him to Detroit, where his cousin, Melvin Franklin, was singing with the Distants, an R&B vocal group.

Ruffin's tenor voice—by turns soulful, pleading, and gruff—made him into one of the hottest singers on the Detroit R&B scene with the Voice Masters while he was still in his teens. Around 1960 Ruffin recorded a couple of singles as a solo artist for Anna Records, run by Berry Gordy's older sister, Anna Gordy. Two years later he tried to jump-start his solo career with some releases on Check-

David Ruffin (*bottom right corner, in glasses*), and the Temptations. CORBIS CORPORATION (BELLEVUE)

Mate Records but, like his earlier releases, they went nowhere. While Ruffin's career stalled, his cousin succeeded as a member of the Temptations on Motown's Gordy Records subsidiary. Franklin had founded the group along with two of his partners from the Distants, Otis Williams and Elbridge Bryant, and two members of the Primes, Eddie Kendricks and Paul Williams. In 1962 and 1963 the Temptations released a number of singles that reached the top forty on the R&B chart but failed to match the success that other Motown artists like Mary Wells, the Miracles, and the Marvelettes were having on the pop charts.

In 1963 a fight between Bryant and Williams led to Bryant's ouster by the band. Ruffin, who had already made an impromptu appearance that year with the Temptations when he jumped on stage during a concert in Ann Arbor, Michigan, filled Bryant's place. With the addition of Ruffin, the Temptations immediately scored the band's first pop hit, "The Way You Do the Things You Do," which narrowly missed the top ten in the spring of 1964. Two other singles reached the pop top thirty that year, but it was their January 1965 release, "My Girl," that gave the group its first number-one single on the pop and R&B charts. Written and produced by Smokey Robinson, the song's clever lyrics and catchy tune typified the Motown sound of the mid-1960s. So too did the band's live performances, which typically featured the band members, in evening dress, performing smooth choreography by Cholly Atkins, best remembered for the synchronized "Temptation Walk." The group's stage presence—particularly Ruffin's emotional delivery on songs such as the 1966 hits "Beauty Is Only Skin Deep" and "(I Know) I'm Losing You"—made the Temptations the most popular concert act on Motown's roster.

The group's run of hits continued into 1967 with the release of "All I Need" and "You're My Everything," which went into the top ten, and "(Loneliness Made Me Realize) It's You That I Need," which was another top-twenty hit. Yet the strong personalities that made the Temptations such dynamic performers on record and on stage were pulling the group apart. While Otis Williams considered himself the group's leader, Ruffin wanted recognition as the group's primary lead singer. Although Eddie Kendricks had sung lead vocals on the group's 1966 classics "Ain't Too Proud to Beg" and "Get Ready," Ruffin demanded that the group change its name to "David Ruffin and the Temptations" to reflect his status. He began to travel separately from the other members of the group in a limousine lined with mink upholstery and adorned with his name on the side. His desire for a solo career was also fueled by the success of his older brother, Jimmy Ruffin, who had a top-ten hit with "What Becomes of the Brokenhearted" in 1966 on Motown's Soul label.

After leading the group on the top-five pop and number-one R&B hit "I Wish It Would Rain" in 1968, Ruffin was voted out of the Temptations by its other four members after he missed a concert date in Cleveland. The last Temptations single to feature Ruffin's voice, "Cloud Nine," was released late that year and became the group's seventh top-ten hit in four years. It also won the 1969 Grammy Award for best R&B performance by a group. With Dennis Edwards taking Ruffin's place, the Temptations recorded three more chart-topping hits with a more aggressive sound—"I Can't Get Next to You" in 1969; "Just My Imagination (Running Away with Me)" in 1971; and "Papa Was a Rolling Stone" in 1972—as well as the classic soul hits "Run Away Child, Running Wild," "Psychedelic Shack," and "Ball of Confusion (That's What the World Is Today)." Ruffin's long-anticipated solo career got off to a rocky start after he battled unsuccessfully to be released from his Motown contract. His first single, "My Whole World Ended (The Moment You Left Me)" hit the top ten in early 1969, but it was Ruffin's last chart appearance until 1975, when he entered the top ten again with "Walk Away from Love."

Ruffin battled drug dependency from the late 1960s onward, which contributed to his personal and career troubles. In 1982 he served time in a federal penitentiary for tax evasion and in 1988 was convicted of using crack cocaine. A 1991 Temptations reunion tour in England with Eddie Kendricks and Dennis Edwards put Ruffin back into the spotlight, but he continued to struggle with drug addiction. On 1 June 1991 Ruffin died from a drug overdose after visiting a West Philadelphia crack house; his funeral in Detroit brought together most of his former Motown colleagues in tribute to his life and career as one of the most talented singers and performers of his generation. He is buried in Woodlawn Cemetery in Detroit. The most successful male vocal group on the Motown label during the 1960s, the Temptations were inducted into the Rock and Roll Hall of Fame in 1989.

★

Ruffin's career is covered in the memoir by Tony Turner and Barbara Aria, *Deliver Us from Temptation: The Tragic and Shocking Story of the Temptations and Motown* (1992). Otis Williams co-authored *The Temptations: African American Achievers* (2002) with Patricia Romanowski. Histories of Motown Records include Nelson George, *Where Did Our Love Go? The Rise and Fall of the Motown Sound* (1985); Suzanne E. Smith, *Dancing in the Street: Motown and the Cultural Politics of Detroit* (1999); and *Calling Out Around the World: A Motown Reader* (2001), edited by Kingsley Abbott. Ruffin's later years were profiled by Duane Noriuki in the *Detroit Free Press* (26 May 1988). Obituaries are in the *Detroit Free Press* and *Rolling Stone* (both 11 June 1991) and *Newsweek* (17 June 1991). A list of the Temptations' chart singles is in *The Billboard Book of Top Forty Hits*, 6th ed. (1996), edited by Joel Whitburn.

TIMOTHY BORDEN

RUSK, (David) Dean (*b.* 9 February 1909 in Cherokee County, Georgia; *d.* 20 December 1994 in Athens, Georgia), president of the Rockefeller Foundation (1952 to 1960), U.S. secretary of state in the administrations of Presidents John F. Kennedy and Lyndon B. Johnson (1961–1969), an advocate for winning the war in Vietnam, and a target for war protesters.

Rusk was the son of Robert Hugh Rusk, an ordained Presbyterian minister, small farmer, schoolteacher, and mail carrier, and Elizabeth Frances Clotfelter, a schoolteacher. He was raised in Atlanta and graduated from Boys' High School in 1925. He graduated Phi Beta Kappa and magna cum laude from Davidson College in 1931 and was a Rhodes scholar, receiving an M.A. in political economics and philosophy at Saint John's College, Oxford University, England, in 1934. During those formative years at Oxford, Rusk observed Britain's passive attitude toward the rise of fascism in Europe.

From 1934 to 1940 Rusk taught government at Mills College, Oakland, California. He married Virginia Wynifred Foisie on 19 June 1937; they had two sons and a daughter. On 15 December 1940 he was called to active duty as a reserve officer in the U.S. Army. He served in the China-Burma-India theater and eventually attained the rank of colonel. Between 1946 and 1951 Rusk served in

Dean Rusk. CORBIS CORPORATION (BELLEVUE)

various State Department posts, culminating with his 1950 appointment as deputy undersecretary of state for Far Eastern affairs. From 1952 until 1960 he was president of the Rockefeller Foundation.

In 1960 John F. Kennedy was elected president and appointed Rusk secretary of state. During his first press conference Rusk discussed "revolutionary" change and "a world in turmoil." A liberal internationalist, he saw aggression as the world's most serious problem and recognized the need for a strong defense. That year an American U-2 spy plane had been downed by the Soviets, Cuban president Fidel Castro signed an economic agreement with Moscow, eighteen new African nations were organized, and the Republic of the Congo entered a civil war. The Soviet presence in the Western hemisphere and the emergence of so many new African nations as a result of revolution suggested to Rusk the upsetting of the balance of world power. Less fearful than future-oriented, he articulated this philosophical conviction: "One must be prepared to make war in order to avoid war." Further, he said, "I think that we, and others nations of the West, can dramatically abridge the process [of democratic development] by providing leadership training, technical aid, material aid. We must increase our effort in Africa, both relatively and absolutely."

Rusk's idealism was matched with realism. He said, "Across the world the winds of change are blowing; awakening peoples are demanding to be admitted to the promise of the twentieth century." During the Cuban Missile Crisis, from 16 to 28 October 1962, Kennedy agreed with Rusk that a peaceful solution between the superpowers would prevent nuclear disaster. Concerning the Cuban blockade, Rusk commented, "We were eyeball to eyeball, and the other fellow just blinked." He regretted his earlier reluctance to voice his skepticism about the 1961 Bay of Pigs operation, which had resulted in what he deemed Kennedy's "darkest hour" and, ultimately, the severance of U.S. relations with Cuba.

Kennedy largely acted as his own Secretary of State. He approved a counterinsurgency plan for Vietnam and announced support for a multilateral nuclear force in a plan he, Rusk, and Vice President Lyndon Johnson initiated, the goal of which was to assert the primacy of the Atlantic Alliance over Franco-German leadership. French President Charles de Gaulle would have no part in it, and Congress was also reluctant to relinquish the command of nuclear missiles; as a result, the multinuclear force plan died. Rusk's fear of Communist aggression increased in response to three events: the 30 October 1961 detonation by the Soviets of the largest bomb in history, the erection of the Berlin Wall, and Chinese premier Mao Tse-tung walking out of the Twenty-second Congress of the Soviet Communist Party.

Rusk was among the first U.S. secretaries of state to promote respect for human rights wherever abuse of power and discrimination occurred. He was dedicated to strengthening the Third World and dismayed by brutality against Buddhists by the South Vietnamese army under President Diem. Rusk was haunted by the idea that the United States might be tied to a "losing horse" in Vietnam. Three weeks after Diem's assassination in 1963 Kennedy was also assassinated; his defense of South Vietnam was bequeathed to the new president, Johnson.

Rusk had a particularly heavy diplomatic schedule during 1964. He visited South Vietnam. He warned Turkey and Russia about aggression in Cyprus. U.S. bombing increased following the Gulf of Tonkin incidents and the Gulf of Tonkin Resolution. China detonated her own nuclear weapon. Johnson was elected president. As the number of North Vietnamese troops in the South increased, Rusk spent long days at his desk, chain-smoked, ate poorly, downed scotches, and exercised rarely. He repeatedly invoked the SEATO (Southeast Asia Treaty Organization) Pact, intended to endorse the American commitment in Vietnam and to prevent the spread of Communism, but it was too weak to be effective; it neither required military action from its members and nor received more than token aid.

The United States war effort increased in 1965. Pleiku was attacked, Operation Rolling Thunder was initiated, and marine battalions were dispatched to Da Nang. According to William Bundy, the Assistant Secretary for Far Eastern Affairs, in 1961 Rusk was skeptical about the importance of support for South Vietnam, but by the end of 1965 he had "concluded that to walk away from an American commitment . . . would pose the gravest possible danger to world peace." General William C. Westmoreland requested an increase in troops, but Rusk argued there were sufficient numbers to prevent a U.S military defeat. Exhausted, he told Johnson, "These days are an exercise of sheer spirit."

There were occasional rifts between the press and Rusk, but they liked him because he never played favorites. He was agreeable and even-tempered, but he was a mystery—an enigma. The press always waited for him to show outrage over some event, but this never occurred, and his reserve disappointed them. Johnson praised his Secretary: "[Rusk] has the compassion of a preacher and the courage of a Georgia cracker," he said. Another time, Johnson said of Rusk, "When you're going in with the Marines, he's the kind you want at your side."

As the number of U.S. casualties in Vietnam increased, protests against U.S. involvement escalated. The first teach-in—a forum or alternative course on antiwar subjects—was held in 1965 at the University of Michigan, where 3,000 students and faculty discussed the war. The following day (21 May 1965) several hundred students at the University of California, Berkeley, staged an antiwar demonstration. In Uruguay, Rusk barely escaped being spit upon by a youth. A six-day bombing halt was imposed in Vietnam while Johnson decided whether to send additional troops. After Rusk presented his fourteen-point peace plan in December 1965 a Christmas bombing halt was extended into the following year.

The Senate Foreign Relations Committee (SFRC) met with Rusk in hearings during 1966 and again in 1968. Committee members interrogated him about the administration's position on the war in Vietnam. Mao's "cultural revolution" began. A treaty banning nuclear tests in outer space was signed, but fear for the world situation heightened as China tested her first hydrogen bomb in 1967. That year Rusk spoke at Cornell University amid students donning death's-head masks. His son Richard, a student there, heard protesters call Vietnam "Rusk's War."

Johnson, discouraged by failure to negotiate peace in Vietnam, was urged by Rusk to withdraw from the 1968 presidential race. Although Rusk achieved the Nuclear Non-Proliferation Treaty with the Soviet Union in the closing days of the Johnson administration, the Vietnam conflict continued.

Rusk left the State Department on 20 January 1968 to reenter private life—a broken man in health and spirit. Rusk said, "I leave office as a hawk. And basically I am an idealist and a man of peace." He had difficulty finding work; even some of his old friends despised him. When he was appointed Sibley Professor of International Law at the University of Georgia, Athens, in 1970, Rusk was overjoyed. "When I studied law at Berkeley before World War II, I wanted to be a teacher of international law. Now, after some interruptions, I have finally made it."

Rusk died of congestive heart failure at his home in Athens, Georgia; he is buried at Oconee Hill Cemetery there. Four years earlier the cold war had ended, and in 1995 the United States restored diplomatic relations with Vietnam. Upon reflection, Rusk, a liberal ideologue, explained his old-fashioned views: "I felt that the free world cannot afford to have the communist world picking it to pieces by various forms of aggression and pressure." As secretary of state, Rusk believed that history held the key to unlock the present, and that foreign policy in the turbulent 1960s would open the door to the future.

★

Rusk's autobiography is *As I Saw It* (1990), as told to his son Richard and edited by Daniel S. Papp. Thomas J. Schoenbaum, *Waging Peace and War: Dean Rusk in the Truman, Kennedy, and Johnson Years* (1988), is a fair and extensive biographical study of Rusk's efforts for the U.S. cause in Vietnam. Thomas W. Zeiler, *Dean Rusk: Defending the American Mission Abroad* (2000), provides an excellent biographical review of Rusk's vision of foreign policy. Some of the best articles about Rusk and his career during

the 1960s are "The Painful Search," *Newsweek* (19 Dec. 1960); "Rusk: New Tempo," *Newsweek* (6 Feb. 1961); "Quarterback of the Cabinet," *Saturday Evening Post* (22 July 1961); "Secretary Rusk: Close-Up of Washington's Busiest Man," *U.S. News World Report* (11 Sept. 1961); "Evolution of Our No. 1 Diplomat," the *New York Times Magazine* (18 Mar. 1962); "The Quiet Man," *Time* (6 Dec. 1963); "The Mild Mr. Rusk," *The New Republic* (11 Apr. 1964); "The Enigma of Dean Rusk," *Harper's Magazine* (July 1965); "Professor Rusk's Problem," *Time* (5 Jan. 1970); and "Rusk Goes Home," *Newsweek* (12 Jan. 1970). Obituaries are in the *New York Times* (22 Dec. 1994) and *Time* (9 Jan. 199).

SANDRA REDMOND PETERS

RUSSELL, Richard Brevard, Jr. ("Dick") (*b.* 2 November 1897 in Winder, Georgia; *d.* 21 January 1971 in Washington, D.C.), conservative Democratic U.S. Senator from Georgia for more than half his lifetime, from 1933 to 1971, and leader of the southern Bloc in the Senate.

Russell was the fourth of thirteen children of Richard Brevard Russell, Sr., a judge and businessman, and Blandina (Dillard) Russell, a teacher. Russell's father served as Chief Justice of the Georgia Supreme Court from 1922 until 1938. Russell, who grew up near Atlanta, graduated from Gordon Military Institute in Barnesville, Georgia, in 1915 and earned an LL.B. degree from the University of Georgia in 1918. On 12 September 1918 Russell enlisted in the U.S. Naval Reserves, serving for only three months of active duty but content thereafter to be referred to as a "veteran."

After practicing law briefly with his father in Winder, Russell spent the remainder of his life in public office. He served as a Democrat in the Georgia House of Representatives from 1921 to 1931, being Speaker his last two terms, from 1927 to 1931, and was elected as the youngest governor in Georgia's history, serving from 1931 to 1933. When Senator William Harris of Georgia died in April 1932, Russell was elected easily that November to complete the remainder of his term. He defeated Governor Eugene Tallmadge in the bitter 1936 Democratic primary and was reelected every six years from 1942 to 1966 without opposition.

Russell served on the powerful Appropriations Committee in the U.S. Senate, heading its Defense Appropriations Subcommittee. He joined the newly formed Armed Services Committee in 1947 and directed that prestigious group from 1951 to 1953 and from 1955 to 1969. He resigned that chair in 1969 to replace Carl Hayden of Arizona as head of the Appropriations Committee. His strong personality, integrity, fairness, wisdom, and ability to arrange compromises made him a dominant figure. During the Great Depression, Russell vigorously supported most of President Franklin D. Roosevelt's early New Deal legislation. He pioneered agriculture, conservation, forestry, and

Richard B. Russell. THE LIBRARY OF CONGRESS

rural electrification programs; originated the school lunch program, feeding more than eighteen million American children; favored strict immigration laws; and advocated national defense preparedness. Russell grew increasingly conservative on social legislation, opposing most of President Harry Truman's Fair Deal program in the 1940s and 1950s. He supported American military intervention in Korea in 1950 and chaired the special committee that investigated Truman's dismissal of General Douglas MacArthur as commander of the United Nations forces during the Korean War. In 1952 he unsuccessfully sought the Democratic nomination for the presidency.

Russell planned strategy for the southern-led filibusters against the Civil Rights Acts of 1957 and 1960, calling those measures unconstitutional, a violation of state's rights, politically inspired, and punitive against the South. The Senate was deadlocked for nearly two months on the 1960 measure, holding more than a week of record-breaking, around-the-clock sessions. Russell believed in the superiority of the Anglo-Saxon (white) culture, which informed his politics. He viewed himself as the voice of the Old South and firmly believed in institutionalized racial segregation and opposed special laws designed to protect the freedom of African Americans.

Russell served on the Warren Commission investigating the 1963 assassination of President John F. Kennedy. The commission concluded in September 1964 that Lee Harvey Oswald alone committed the crime by firing three shots from the sixth floor of the Depository Building in Dallas. Russell termed the commission's task a "sad and morbid experience" in the "most strenuous year of my life." He had opposed most of Kennedy's New Frontier programs and went on to oppose President Lyndon B. Johnson's Great Society programs. He did not accept racial equality, objecting to the Civil Rights Act of 1964 and the Voting Rights Act of 1965. Southern Senators, led by Russell, led a filibuster of the 1964 civil rights legislation for eighty-three days before the Senate invoked the cloture rule, ending the filibuster by calling for a vote. Russell warned that the 1964 civil rights legislation was "vote bait" that would destroy more civil rights than it would protect.

During the 1960s Russell secured large defense appropriations and championed the development of major weapons systems. He believed that America's military should be so strong that no other nation would dare attack the United States, and he advocated the development of the Anti-Ballistic Missile Program. He strongly urged Kennedy to invade Cuba during the 1962 Cuban Missile Crisis, when the Soviet Union positioned missiles in Cuba, only a few miles from the United States, and he supported American military intervention in the Dominican Republic in 1965 to 1966. (Prompted by exaggerated reports of a Communist threat in the Dominican Republic, Johnson sent American troops to unseat a left-leaning president and install a government more favorable to U.S. economic interests.)

Russell was a foreign aid critic who did not believe that the United States should serve as the world's police. He initially opposed American military involvement in Vietnam and denied that the country possessed anything of strategic or economic value. He warned as early as 1954 that the Vietnam conflict would be "a long drawn-out affair costly in both blood and treasure."

Russell reluctantly supported the 1964 Tonkin Gulf Resolution authorizing Johnson to use armed force against aggression in Southeast Asia, and he remained cool to the escalation of the war in 1965. He questioned whether the United States could fund such a war effort and continue to support domestic spending programs. Russell claimed that the South Vietnamese could not be relied upon to fight for themselves, expected conditions to deteriorate, and believed that the American people would oppose sending troops to Vietnam. Once American troops came under fire in Vietnam, however, Russell became more hawkish. If the United States left Vietnam, he feared that American prestige would diminish, the confidence of the free world in American dependability would be shaken, and American enemies would be emboldened. Russell advocated the bombing of North Vietnam and the blockading of its ports. He denounced military desertions, draft-card burnings, and antiwar sit-ins. Record-breaking defense appropriations bills swept through his committees and the Senate with little or no debate.

Russell, a bachelor and member of the Methodist Church of Winder, did not have many close friends. He maintained a rigorous Senate work schedule and read the *Congressional Record* daily from cover to cover. Russell mastered parliamentary maneuver, knew Senate rules well, and debated effectively. He served as president pro tempore of the Senate from January 1969 until his death, putting him third in line for succession to the presidency, behind the vice president and the Speaker of the House. He died at Walter Reed Hospital in Washington, D.C., from respiratory problems brought on by emphysema. Russell is interred in a family gravesite at Russell Memorial Park in Winder, Georgia.

Russell's service in the U.S. Senate was the longest in Georgia's history. A defender of the Old South, he did not appreciate the central paradox of the nation in the 1960s: how the "Land of the Free" could deny freedom to its own citizens. His inability to accept racial equality and full civil rights for all, in accordance with the change in national sentiment, prevented Russell from attaining true national greatness. Nevertheless, he left many legislative legacies in agriculture, defense, foreign affairs, and the school lunch program, and he passionately defended the institutional integrity of the Senate. In 1972 his Senate colleagues named the Russell Senate Office Building in his honor.

★

The Russell papers are located in the Richard B. Russell Library for Political Research and Studies at the University of Georgia in Athens. The Johnson papers at the Lyndon B. Johnson Library in Austin, Texas, have additional material on Russell's Senate career. The definitive biography is Gilbert C. Fite, *Richard B. Russell, Jr., Senator from Georgia* (1991). Biographical information is also in John A. Goldsmith, *Colleagues: Richard B. Russell and His Apprentice Lyndon B. Johnson* (1993); Robert Mann, *The Walls of Jericho: Lyndon Johnson, Hubert Humphrey, Richard Russell, and the Struggle for Civil Rights* (1996); and Calvin MacLeod Logue and Dwight L. Freshley, eds., *Voice of Georgia: Speeches of Richard B. Russell, 1928-1969* (1997). See also the dissertation studies of David D. Potenziani, "Look to the Past: Richard B. Russell and the Defense of Southern White Supremacy," (Ph.D. diss., University of Georgia, 1981), and Karen K. Kelly, "Richard B. Russell: Democrat from Georgia," (Ph.D. diss., University of North Carolina, 1979). Obituaries are in the *Atlanta Constitution* and *New York Times* (both 22 Jan. 1971).

DAVID L. PORTER

RUSSELL, William Felton ("Bill") (*b.* 12 February 1934 in Monroe, Louisiana), basketball player who shifted dominance in the sport to rebounding and defense as he led college, Olympic, and professional teams to championships over a fifteen-year period.

Russell, one of two sons of Charles Russell, a factory worker, and Katie Russell, a homemaker, moved from Louisiana to West Oakland, California, with his family at the age of nine. He entered McClymonds High School in 1948 and graduated in 1952, with a minimal impact on high school basketball. He enrolled at the University of San Francisco (USF) when he was offered a basketball scholarship by Coach Phil Woolpert. In Russell's last two years at USF, the team was 57–1 and won back-to-back NCAA championships in 1955 and 1956. Russell was voted Most Outstanding Player in the 1955 NCAA tournament and USA Player of the Year in 1956, the same year that he received his B.A. degree from USF. In his college career he averaged better than 20 points and 20 rebounds per game. He was acquired by the Boston Celtics through a trade of players for him as a draft pick, but he did not report to the team until late October 1956, instead opting to play for the U.S. Olympic Basketball team. The games were in Melbourne, Australia, and were not held until the fall, delaying Russell's entry into professional basketball. Led by Russell and K. C. Jones, Russell's USF teammate, the United States finished 8–0 in the Olympics and won the gold medal.

From the beginning of Russell's tenure with the Celtics, they were winners. Coach Red Auerbach emphasized team defense and fast-breaking offense and Russell, with his uncanny shot blocking ability, anchored the defense. Along with Russell himself, Russell's teammates—Bob Cousy, Bill Sharman, Jim Loscutoff, Frank Ramsey, and Tommy Heinsohn—all averaged double figures in points per game, and the Celtics won their first NBA Championship in 1957. Russell led the league in rebounds for both the regular season and the playoffs, the finals of which went seven games until the Celtics defeated the St. Louis Hawks. Over the next twelve years, until his retirement as a player after the 1969 playoffs concluded, Russell and the Celtics won ten more championships. Their only losses were in 1958 to the St. Louis Hawks (when Russell suffered an ankle injury in game three and was not able to play in two games and was severely limited in a third) and in 1967 to the Philadelphia 76ers. These facts only begin to describe the dominance of the Celtics and Russell. Between 1957 and 1969 Russell led the league in rebounding average five times and finished second four times. More impressive is that in the playoffs, Russell led in rebounds ten of those years. For his career, Russell averaged 22.5 rebounds per game and just over 15 points a game, highlighted by a 51-rebound performance in one game in 1960. He was voted All-NBA First Team

Bill Russell *(left)*, battles Wilt Chamberlain. CORBIS CORPORATION (BELLEVUE)

three times (1959, 1963, 1965), Second Team eight times (1958, 1960–1962, 1964, 1966–1968), Most Valuable Player five times (1958, 1961–1963, 1965), and was a twelve-time NBA All-Star. In 1980 he was voted Greatest Player in the History of the NBA by the Professional Basketball Writers of America.

Russell was instrumental in making the NBA a "major" major league. In the mid-1960s the NBA finally succeeded in landing a national television contract with ABC, whereby an NBA game would be shown every Sunday afternoon. It was the success of these games that solidified the NBA as a professional league. The ratings grew and the NBA and its owners made more money. In order to ensure a well-received product, the NBA and ABC invariably selected either the Celtics with Russell or the Philadelphia 76ers with Wilt Chamberlain as one of the teams to screen. As often as possible the Celtics-76ers struggles were scheduled for Sunday afternoons, and the battles between Russell and Chamberlain were titanic. From 1959 when Chamberlain entered the league until 1969 when Russell retired, the two met on 142 occasions. Chamberlain outscored Russell, averaging 28.7 points to Russell's 23.7, and outrebounded him, 28.7 to 14.5, but Russell's Celtics won the most important statistic, games won, an edge of 88–74. Four times they met in seventh games in the playoffs, and the Celtics won each time. During this time period Russell was an outspoken critic of a quota system for African Americans that the NBA tacitly promulgated. This had to do with a set number of African Americans who could be on the floor for a team at any one time as well as the number of African Americans on a team's roster.

In 1966 Auerbach announced his retirement as the coach of the Celtics after sixteen seasons, and the Celtics surprised the sports world as well as American society by selecting the first African-American coach in a major professional league—Russell. He came to the position with a great advantage—he would remain as a player and be player-coach. The Celtics improved their record by six games from the previous year but finished eight games behind the 76ers, who cruised to the title behind Wilt Chamberlain. The next year, however, the Celtics under Russell managed to win another NBA title despite having only the third best record in the league during the year. The following year, a thirty-five-year-old Russell did it again. The Celtics finished fourth in the Eastern Division but defeated the 76ers and the New York Knicks in the playoffs to face Chamberlain and the Los Angeles Lakers (who had moved from Minneapolis in 1960) in the finals. In a grueling seven-game series, the Celtics won, nipping the Lakers 108–106 in what was Russell's final game. He announced his retirement as a player and coach after the game.

In 1973 Russell returned as an NBA coach and general manager with the Seattle Supersonics, a position he held until 1977. His overall coaching record in the NBA was 341–290. He is still a fixture at Celtic playoff games.

Russell married Rose Swisher in 1956 and had three children with her. They were divorced in 1969, and he married Didi Anstett on 8 June 1977.

In 1970 Russell was voted the Sporting News Athlete of the Decade of the 1960s. He was voted to the NBA 25th Anniversary All-Time team in 1970 as well the 35th in 1980 and the 50th in 1996. In 1975 he was enshrined in the Basketball Hall of Fame.

★

Russell's first autobiography, written with William McSweeney, is *Go Up in Glory* (1966). His second autobiography, written with Taylor Branch, is *Second Wind: The Memoirs of an Opinionated Man* (1979). It provides factual data and great insight into Russell's varied interests and complex personality. In 2001 Russell and David Faulkner published *Russell Rules: Lessons on Leadership from the Twentieth Century's Greatest Winner*. Terry Pluto, *Tall Tales* (1992), provides a chapter on the Russell-Chamberlain "battles" that relies on the recollections of former colleagues in the NBA. A number of histories of the Celtics have been published with at least two, Bob Ryan, *The Boston Celtics* (1989), and Jeff Greenfield, *The World's Greatest Team: A Portrait of the Boston Celtics 1957–1969* (1976), having great emphasis on Russell and his teams.

MURRY R. NELSON

RUSTIN, Bayard Taylor (*b.* 17 March 1910 in West Chester, Pennsylvania; *d.* 24 August 1987 in New York City), distinguished African-American civil rights activist who helped to organize the massive August 1963 March on Washington for Jobs and Freedom, the largest civil rights demonstration the United States had ever seen.

One of nine children, Rustin was raised as the son of Janifer Rustin, a caterer, and Julia (Davis) Rustin, a social worker and caterer, just southwest of Philadelphia. At the age of eleven, he discovered that the people he had thought were his parents were actually his grandparents. His real mother, he learned, was a woman named Florence, who he had been told was an older sister. His father, Archie Hopkins, was a native of the West Indies with whom Florence had had a brief relationship. His grandmother, Julia, a Quaker, early on instilled in young Rustin a commitment to social justice.

The family lived in a poor section of West Chester, which had been an important way station on the Underground Railroad, a fact that helped shape Rustin's decision to become a social activist. Of his hometown, Rustin wrote in his *Strategies for Freedom* (1976), "The antislavery sentiment of the inhabitants was revealed in the town's architecture, for beneath its aging, Colonial homes ran hidden passageways which had concealed runaway slaves from [their] southern plantation owners."

As a student at West Chester Senior High School, Rus-

Bayard Rustin. AP/WIDE WORLD PHOTOS

tin excelled in both academics and athletics. After his graduation, Rustin drifted around the country, working at odd jobs and studying briefly when he could scrape together the funds for tuition. Although he never received a college degree, over the years he took courses at Wilberforce University in Ohio (1930–1931), Cheyney State Normal School (later Cheyney State College) in Pennsylvania (1931–1933), and the City College of New York (1933–1935). He moved to New York City in 1931 to live with a relative and worked irregularly, singing with a variety of musical groups performing in Greenwich Village.

In 1936 Rustin became affiliated with the Communist Party, a connection that would come to haunt him later in life. He joined the Young Communist League (YCL) and was quickly put to work as a recruiter. When the Communists backed off on their push for U.S. racial reform after the outbreak of World War II, Rustin quit the YCL in 1941, the same year that he cofounded the Congress for Racial Equality. During the war Rustin, who was a conscientious objector, was imprisoned for twenty-eight months in a federal penitentiary in Ashland, Kentucky (1943–1945).

Rustin worked for a time with A. Philip Randolph's March on Washington Movement and, through Randolph, he was introduced to A. J. Muste, the head of the Fellowship of Reconciliation (FOR), an international pacifist organization. Rustin was hired as FOR's youth secretary. In 1942 he and James Farmer were named as the directors of FOR's newly established Department of Race Relations. In the early 1950s after Rustin, an admitted homosexual, had a few brushes with the law because of his sexual orientation, he was warned that any further negative publicity would force his dismissal from FOR. After being arrested on morals charges in Pasadena, California, in 1953, he quietly resigned from FOR.

As the civil rights movement gathered momentum in the latter half of the 1950s and early 1960s, Rustin was quick to offer his services. Many African-American leaders feared, however, that his political past and personal life might bring discredit upon the movement. As a consequence, Rustin's primary role in the civil rights campaign was behind the scenes, as an organizer, strategist, liaison, and speechwriter. Although Rustin had helped to found the Southern Christian Leadership Conference (SCLC) in the late 1950s, he was forced to resign from the organization in 1960 when the Harlem congressman Adam Clayton Powell threatened to expose Rustin's personal and political past. His resignation from the SCLC did not sever Rustin's close ties to the Reverend Martin Luther King, Jr., with whom he had worked on the 1955 bus boycott in Montgomery, Alabama. Behind the scenes, Rustin remained a close adviser to King and other members of the SCLC leadership for many years. In 1953 Rustin was appointed as the executive secretary of the War Resister's League, a large pacifist organization, and he planned and executed a series of antinuclear demonstrations and the San Francisco to Moscow Peace Walk in the late 1950s.

Without question, Rustin's crowning achievement was the organization and coordination of the August 1963 March on Washington, which earned him the nickname "Mr. March." The idea for such a massive civil rights demonstration had originated with A. Philip Randolph, the founder of the Brotherhood of Sleeping Car Porters union. Randolph had already planned a march on the nation's capital as a labor rally for his union members. King, meanwhile, believed that the civil rights movement was on the verge of a breakthrough and badly needed a "mass protest" to win greater popular support. Rustin and other advisers suggested to King that Randolph might be willing to see his rally expanded into a broader civil rights demonstration, giving King and the civil rights cause the national publicity it needed to achieve its ultimate goals.

Randolph agreed to the suggestions for a broader-based march and asked Rustin to organize the massive demonstration, naming him the deputy director of the march committee. Rustin's particular genius lay in his ability to draw together all the disparate elements of the civil rights movement, creating what became one of the largest protest events in the history of the United States. The march drew about 250,000 civil rights supporters to Washington, D.C., but the truly remarkable achievement of the demonstration was the extraordinary climate of dignity, order, and peacefulness in which the event was staged. Critics had predicted confidently that such a massive protest would spark violence and widespread disorder. In the event, however, Washington police recorded only four march-related arrests, all of white people.

The historian Taylor Branch, writing in *Pillar of Fire* (1998), observed that, in the wake of the peaceful staging of the March on Washington, Rustin was credited as an unparalleled social engineer who had managed to pull off what many had thought impossible. "Overnight, Rustin became if not a household name at least a quotable and respectable source for racial journalism, his former defects as a vagabond ex-Communist homosexual henceforth overlooked or forgiven." So highly did King value Rustin's counsel that in the spring of 1964 he strongly considered hiring him to replace the outgoing Wyatt Walker as the SCLC executive director. Other King advisers cautioned the civil rights leader against such a decision, arguing that not even the success of the March on Washington could wash away the political liabilities of Rustin's political past and sexual orientation. In the end, Rustin was not offered the SCLC job, but he continued to serve as a trusted adviser to King until the latter's assassination on 4 April 1968. Rustin was part of the delegation that accompanied King to Oslo, Norway, for the presentation to King of the 1964 Nobel Peace Prize. Although Rustin and King continued to maintain close ties, their political ideologies diverged more and more after 1964, as they disagreed on such issues as the Vietnam War and King's decision to take the civil rights struggle north, using Chicago as a hub for its activity.

In 1965 Rustin was appointed as the executive director of the newly founded A. Philip Randolph Institute (APRI). In this position he directed APRI's day-to-day operations, which included the sponsorship of voter registration drives and civil rights conferences as well as endorsement of political candidates. Rustin continued to travel and lecture extensively across the country. In addition to his efforts in the struggle for civil rights, Rustin was a longtime supporter of workers' rights. A staunch ally of organized labor, he took part in a number of strikes and, in the mid-1960s, helped form the Recruitment and Training Program (R-T-P, Inc.), launched to increase minority participation in the building and construction trades.

Rustin's organizational skills were responsible for numerous successful civil rights demonstrations during the 1960s, including a 1964 boycott, attended by more than 400,000 students, of New York City's school system to protest the school board's foot-dragging on classroom integration. He also organized the Poor People's Campaign of 1968, which drew thousands of civil rights supporters—black and white—to Washington, D.C., to set up a "Resurrection City" on the grounds of the Lincoln Memorial.

In the early 1970s Rustin stepped down as the executive director of APRI, becoming the organization's honorary president. He remained involved in APRI policy-making and other activities, serving as the organization's chair from 1979 to 1987. He lectured widely on social issues throughout the United States and abroad. One year before his death, Rustin founded Project South Africa to generate financial support for the country's full democratization. After a fact-finding mission to Haiti in the summer of 1987, Rustin returned to New York and shortly thereafter fell ill. After a series of misdiagnoses, he was found to have a perforated appendix. He died at the age of seventy-seven of a heart attack following surgery for acute appendicitis. Rustin's memorial service was held on 1 October 1987 at the Community Church in Manhattan. He was cremated and his ashes are interred at a private residence in upstate New York.

Rustin's contributions to the advancement of social causes—most notably civil rights—in the United States are difficult to calculate since much of his work was done behind the scenes. Enormously gifted, Rustin would have enjoyed a much higher profile in the monumental civil rights struggle of the 1960s were it not for concerns about his personal and political past. As a consequence, he worked out of the glare of the spotlight for much of his career. Rustin, however, will be forever remembered for his genius in organizing the August 1963 March on Washington—a mass demonstration of great majesty and dignity that captured the imagination of the American public and helped to pave the way for the passage of key civil rights legislation.

★

Rustin provides an insightful overview of his role in the civil rights movement in his books *Down the Line: The Collected Writings of Bayard Rustin* (1971) and *Strategies for Freedom: The Changing Patterns of Black Protest* (1976). A comprehensive profile of Rustin's life is Jervis Anderson, *Bayard Rustin: Troubles I've Seen—A Biography* (1997). More about Rustin's contributions toward the struggle for civil rights is in James Haskins, *Bayard Rustin: Behind the Scenes of the Civil Rights Movement* (1997), and Taylor Branch, *Pillar of Fire: America in the King Years, 1963–1965* (1998). Obituaries are in the *New York Times* and *Washington Post* (both 25 Aug. 1987).

DON AMERMAN

RYUN, James Ronald ("Jim")   (*b.* 29 April 1947 in Wichita, Kansas), track and field runner who, after becoming the first high school runner to break the four-minute mile in 1964, emerged as the greatest middle-distance runner in the history of the sport during a decade notable for producing great running stars.

Ryun was the middle child born to Gerald Ryun, an aircraft manufacturer parts inspector, and Wilma Strutton, a department store clerk; he had an older brother and younger sister. Ryun had a strict religious upbringing, as his parents were members of the Church of Christ, which had many social taboos, including dancing, drinking, and smoking. When Ryun was an infant, a high fever permanently damaged his inner ear, leaving him with only 50 percent of his hearing and causing him to suffer from occasional dizziness and equilibrium problems. He also suffered from asthma. Throughout grade school, the thin and sickly Ryun showed no gift for any athletic endeavor.

When Ryun entered Wichita East High School as a sophomore in the fall of 1962, the school's track and cross-country coach Bob Timmons encouraged him to go out for cross-country, the activity where athletes who are not talented in team sports tend to gravitate. His surprise sixth-place finish in the state cross-country meet helped Wichita East win the state team title. Coach Timmons saw in Ryun's early performances the possibility that he could be the first high schooler to break four minutes in the mile, and he put Ryun through a grueling, 100-mile-a-week training regimen with that aim in mind. By the end of the summer of 1963, Ryun had broken national sophomore

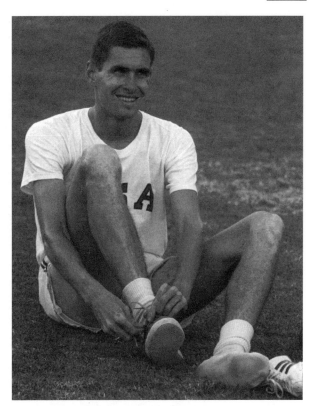

Jim Ryun, 1966. AP/WIDE WORLD PHOTOS

records for the 880-yard, 1-mile, and 2-mile races, and he was being hailed as the brightest running prospect in the nation. In the fall of 1963, he won the state high school cross-country championship. During these years, Ryun developed his classic race strategy of running behind the pack for most of the race, and then, with 200 to 300 yards to go, suddenly spurting to the front with an amazing burst of speed.

In June 1964, seventeen-year-old Ryun became the first schoolboy runner to break four minutes, with a time of three minutes, fifty-nine seconds (3:59) at the Compton Invitational. In competition against the best of his peers in the United States, he finished in eighth place. That eight runners broke four minutes stunned the country, but no achievement was more electrifying than that of Ryun, whose awkward gait and side-to-side, flopping head belied the possibility of racing greatness. Later in the year Ryun qualified in the Olympic Trials in the 1,500-meter run for the Tokyo Olympics. However, at Tokyo a severe cold slowed him, and he failed to reach the finals.

Coach Timmons moved to the University of Kansas to coach track in the fall of 1964, at the end of Ryun's junior year, and was replaced by J. D. Edmiston. Despite the change in coach, Ryun's running career continued spiraling upward. In the state high school cross-country championship, Ryun again led Wichita East to the state title, setting a course record of nine minutes, eight seconds. In the spring, Ryun won his third consecutive state high school one-mile championship, setting the national high school record of 3:58.3. After graduating from high school in 1965, eighteen-year-old Ryun entered a meet in San Diego in the one-mile event against Olympic champion Peter Snell from New Zealand. Ryun defeated Snell while running the distance in 3:55.3, setting a record for a schoolboy that lasted thirty-six years. (Ryun's record was finally surpassed in 2001, when Alan Webb, of South Lakes High School in Reston, Virginia, ran the mile in 3:53.43.)

After high school, Ryun went to the University of Kansas, where Timmons had advanced to the position of head track coach. The spring 1966 track season was an extraordinary one for the freshman. On 13 May, in the Coliseum Relays in Los Angeles, Ryun set a new U.S. record in the two-mile event with a time of 8:25.2. Then on 10 June, in Terre Haute, Indiana, he set a world record in the 880 yards of 1:44.9; and finally in July, in Berkeley, California, he set a new world record in the mile run, at 3:51.3. As of September 2002, he was still the youngest runner ever to hold the world record in this event. At the end of this spectacular year, the nineteen-year-old Ryun was the world record holder in three events. He capped his achievements by winning the Amateur Athletic Union's Sullivan Award as the nation's best amateur athlete and the *Sports Illustrated* Sportsman of the Year award, the youngest person ever to receive this accolade.

In 1967, Ryun lowered his world record in the mile to 3:51.1 at the national Amateur Athletic Union (AAU) meet on 23 June 1967 when he won his third consecutive AAU title in the event. On 9 July, in the U.S. versus the Commonwealth meet, Ryun out-kicked his toughest rival in the event, Kipchoge Keino of Kenya, to set a new world record of 3:33.1 in the 1,500-meter race.

In the 1968 Olympic Games in Mexico City, Ryun faced two obstacles going into the competition. First, his training had been hampered by a siege of mononucleosis. The second challenge was one faced by all the athletes accustomed to low altitudes; they had to compete in a high altitude where the thin air can cause severe oxygen deprivation.

Nonetheless, Ryun won a Silver Medal, losing only to Keino, who had grown up in the Kenyan highlands.

On 25 January 1969, shortly before graduating from Kansas University, Ryun married Anne Snider; they had four children. Ryun finished out his senior season at Kansas, attempting to help the school win the 1969 National Collegiate Athletic Association (NCAA) championship. He lost the mile run to Marty Liquori, however, the first mile run Ryun had lost in four years, and Kansas missed the title by a few points. Nonetheless, while at Kansas, Ryun helped lead the school to national indoor track titles in 1966 and 1969, while winning five individual collegiate titles, four of them indoors.

Ryun was losing his competitive fire in 1969, and in a national AAU meet that year he stepped off the track in the middle of a race and announced his retirement from the sport. In 1971, however, he returned to running to prepare for the 1972 Olympic Games in Munich, but his medal hopes were dashed when he fell in a semifinal race. From 1973 to 1976 Ryun competed on the professional track circuit. In 1980 he was elected to the National Track and Field Hall of Fame. Ryun entered politics in 1996, winning election as a Republican from Kansas's Second Congressional District.

The decade's fabulous sports story of the ungainly, unprepossessing Ryun, who through incredible grit and determination beat the greatest runners in the world in a spate of world-record performances, cut through the din of a tumultuous era of social upheaval. His achievements gave the United States something positive to cheer about, and provided not only the country but also the world with an authentic athletic hero.

★

Although it overlooks many important races, Ryun tells the story of his running career and his born-again Christian conversion in his autobiography, *In Quest of Gold: The Jim Ryun Story* (1984). Cordner Nelson, *The Jim Ryun Story* (1967), was the first biography of Ryun and provides a detailed examination of his track career up to 1967.

ROBERT PRUTER

S

SAARINEN, Eero (*b.* 20 August 1910 in Kirkkonummi, Finland; *d.* 1 September 1961 in Ann Arbor, Michigan), one of the foremost architects of his generation, who designed some of the most distinctive American buildings of the late 1950s and early 1960s.

Saarinen emigrated from Finland to Evanston, Illinois, and then to Detroit in 1923, with his father, Eliel Saarinen, a well-known architect, his mother, Louise ("Loja") Gesellius, an artist, and his two sisters. He was educated in public schools in Michigan, but he and his sisters also helped their father with his designs. The whole family would become involved with designing furniture, fabrics, and wall coverings for their father's buildings. Saarinen began his career by separating himself from his father's influence, studying sculpture in Paris in 1929, before studying architecture at Yale University in 1931, graduating with honors with a B.F.A. in 1934. He received an M.A. from Yale in 1949. Saarinen began his professional career as an architect in Finland, where he designed the Helsinki Post Office (1934). He married Lily Swann and became a naturalized U.S. citizen in 1939. The couple had two children, but divorced in 1953. On 8 February 1953 Saarinen married Aline B. Louchheim; they had one son.

While in Europe, Saarinen came under the influence of leading modernist architects such as Erich Mendelsohn and Alvar Aalto. By the time he returned to the United States to work with his father in 1936, Saarinen had a well-developed sense of his own approach to architecture. He broke away from modernist influences, including his father's, to create designs that better represented the dynamic culture of the late 1950s and 1960s. Even in the years before World War II, Saarinen developed each building as a unique and self-contained project, designing for the immediate context, rather than architectural progression. This repeated breaking with the past pushed modernist architecture to its natural limits and beyond in buildings such as the Columbia Broadcasting System (CBS) Headquarters in New York (1960–1964), and in Saarinen's masterpiece, the terminal building at Dulles International Airport in Washington, D.C. (1958–1963).

Except for a brief period of wartime service as a government adviser in the Office of Strategic Services in Washington, D.C., between 1942 and 1945, Saarinen worked in the family firm (which became Eero Saarinen and Associates in 1950) for most of his adult life. He won many prizes in his early career, including the Smithsonian competition in 1939, and, collaborating with his friend Charles Eames, two first prizes in the Organic Design Competition for furniture at the Museum of Modern Art, New York City in 1940. Winning the Jefferson National Expansion Memorial competition in 1948, however, established his name, and heralded a new direction for American architecture. His grand arch, built in stainless steel between 1961 and 1966 at Saint Louis, Missouri, is both a monument to Thomas Jefferson, a founding father of the United States,

Eero Saarinen. ARCHIVE PHOTOS, INC.

and a symbolic gateway to the future. At 630 feet, the arch is the tallest memorial in the United States.

All of Saarinen's important buildings were constructed after World War II, and his greatest work was not completed until after his death in 1961. He created designs for the campuses of Yale University and Harvard University in the 1950s, and the twenty-five buildings of the General Motors Technical Center at Warren, Michigan, all of which are suggestive of his background in sculpture. Other projects he began in the late 1950s include: the U.S. Embassy at Grosvenor Square, London (1955-1960), the Trans World Airlines (TWA) terminal at Kennedy Airport, New York (1956–1962), the Terminal Building at Dulles International Airport, Washington, D.C. (1958–1963), the John Deere and Company Administration Building at Moline, Illinois (1957–1963), and the CBS Headquarters in New York City (1960–1964). These buildings made regular appearances in the press, in movies, and on television shows, and they came to represent the nation's dynamic, modern attitudes and beliefs. In effect, Saarinen helped design the landscape of 1960s America.

Both Saarinen and his work are enigmatic. He skipped from one architectural influence to another, and few of his designs are of the sort that could be developed by others. Yet his visionary approach was far from haphazard or unplanned. Although the Dulles terminal building is cluttered in comparison with the airy TWA terminal, Saarinen carefully considered the process of moving people through the building and onto the planes, eventually settling on an innovative "mobile lounge" system. The exterior of the Dulles terminal garnered Saarinen the most praise. Its vast suspended roof with its high front and swooping downward curve give the impression of flight, and makes it arguably the most distinctive airport building in the world. Saarinen avoided designing skyscrapers until 1960, possibly because he shared his father's dislike of them, but when he finally did so, it was with characteristic flair. The CBS Headquarters building is considered to be one of the most architecturally distinctive skyscrapers in the United States.

It was not only in the appearance of his designs that Saarinen broke new ground. He pioneered many building techniques that would offer new possibilities for architects in the 1960s and after. Perhaps the most important of these is the "shell" technique, in which the outer shell of a building is constructed independently of its internal structures. Although it became one of the most common building techniques of the 1960s, the first shell construction in the United States was Saarinen's Kresge Auditorium and Chapel at the Massachusetts Institute of Technology, in Cambridge, Massachusetts (1953–1956).

In 1961 Saarinen was diagnosed with a brain tumor, and he died following brain surgery at Ann Arbor. Often criticized by other architects as a showman, Saarinen is considered by many to have died before completing his best work. His influence on the architecture of the 1960s and after is profound. He was elected a Fellow of the American Academy of Arts and Sciences in 1960, and posthumously awarded the Gold Medal of the American Institute of Architects in 1962, the profession's highest honor.

★

Some of Saarinen's personal papers are kept in the Manuscripts and Archives Department at the Sterling Memorial Library at Yale University. Books about his life and work are Allan Temko, *Eero Saarinen* (1962), and Rupert Spade, *Eero Saarinen* (1971). Further biographical information is in Muriel Emmanuel, *Contemporary Architects* (1980); Robert C. Judson, *Design in America: The Cranbrook Vision* (1983); and Dennis Sharp, ed., *The Illustrated Encyclopedia of Architects and Architecture* (1991). An article about Saarinen is in *Architecture and Urbanism* (Apr. 1984). Obituaries are in the *New York Times* and (London) *Times* (both 2 Sept. 1961), *Time* (8 Sept. 1961), *Newsweek* (11 Sept. 1961), and *Architectural Design* (Dec. 1961).

CHRIS ROUTLEDGE

SABIN, Albert Bruce (*b.* 26 August 1906 in Bialystok, Russia [now Poland]; *d.* 3 March 1993 in Washington, D.C.), virologist who developed the first polio vaccine offering life-long protection against the disease.

Sabin was the son of Jacob Sabin and Tillie Krugman, and was fifteen years old when his family immigrated to the United States, where his father worked in the textile business. Sabin graduated from Paterson High School in Paterson, New Jersey, in 1923 and earned his B.S. degree from New York University (NYU) in 1928. He then enrolled in medical school at NYU, where he earned his M.D. degree in 1931. He performed his residency at Bellevue Hospital in New York City.

In 1932, while still an intern, Sabin isolated the B virus from the body of a colleague who had suffered a fatal bite from a monkey, and was able to prove the relationship between the B virus and the herpes simplex virus. Following one year at the Lister Institute of Preventive Medicine in London from 1934 to 1935, Sabin accepted a fellowship at the Rockefeller Institute for Medical Research, where he became deeply involved in research regarding poliomyelitis, commonly known as polio. Working with Peter K. Olitsky, Sabin in 1936 proved that polio was primarily an infection of the alimentary tract, thus opening up the possibility of an oral vaccine.

During World War II, Sabin served with the virus committee of the U.S. Army Epidemiological Board, earning

Albert Sabin. ARCHIVE PHOTOS, INC.

the rank of lieutenant colonel. From 1939 to 1943, he had worked as an associate professor of pediatrics at the University of Cincinnati College of Medicine and Children's Hospital Research Foundation, and in 1946 he returned as a professor of research in pediatrics at the same institution. He spent the next decade working on a polio vaccine, concentrating on the isolation of a mutant, avirulent (harmless) form of the virus that would displace the more common virulent strains in the alimentary tract.

In 1954 Jonas Salk developed his own polio vaccine, which used a killed form of the virus (which could revert to a virulent state), and had to be supplemented by regular booster shots. Initially accepted by the medical community with unqualified praise, the Salk vaccine suffered a setback on 26 April 1955, when five children in California contracted polio as a result of receiving vaccines containing virulent strains. At the same time, Sabin continued to develop his own vaccine, and tested it relentlessly. The first human subjects were Sabin himself, along with members of his family and his research associates; then, from 1955 to 1957, Sabin and his team administered the vaccine to hundreds of prison inmates.

Recognizing that the success of Salk's vaccine owed as much to public relations as to medicine, Sabin in the late 1950s and early 1960s set out to wage a public-relations war of his own, traveling extensively and promoting his vaccine through newspaper editorials, press releases, and speeches at scientific meetings. Then, late in the 1950s, he got the chance to prove the efficacy of his vaccine among a huge population—not of Americans, but of their cold war foes behind the iron curtain. In 1957, as the Soviet Health Ministry faced a polio epidemic that was infecting 18,000–20,000 people each year, they turned to Sabin, who in the next two years administered the vaccine to millions in the Soviet Union, Poland, East Germany, Czechoslovakia, and Hungary.

News of his success in vaccinating large populations helped sway opinions in the West, and by late 1959 smaller groups in Sweden, England, Singapore, and even the United States received the Sabin vaccine. In 1960 some 180,000 schoolchildren in Cincinnati were thus vaccinated, and the U.S. Public Health Service approved the manufacture of the vaccine in large quantities. Even then, however, the U.S. Public Health Administration remained reluctant, as a body, to actively support the use of the Sabin vaccine. As a result, the Salk vaccine remained dominant in the United States as a whole during 1960 and 1961.

In those years, however, Sabin found an ally in Richard Johns, a pediatrician in Phoenix who became an enthusiastic supporter of his vaccine. Launching his own personal crusade, Johns entreated the Phoenix political leadership and the county medical society, as well as the local newspapers and radio and television stations, to support a vaccination drive. On a particular Sunday, the community supplied free vaccines, with Johns and other colleagues providing their services for free as well. With the success of the first such Sunday vaccination, the city began making them a somewhat regular event, with large numbers of doctors and their assistants providing their time and expertise as a public service. Other towns began to duplicate the approach of Johns and others, and thus was born the idea of the "Sabin Sunday," a practice later applied with great success in the cities and towns of Latin America. By 1962 the tide had turned in Sabin's favor, and his method finally replaced Salk's as the vaccine of choice for the U.S. Public Health Service, which oversaw the vaccination of some 100 million Americans in the period between 1962 and 1964.

Whereas the Salk vaccine had required painful shots, the Sabin vaccine could be delivered in a much more pleasant package, a sugar cube. During the 1960s, the "Sabin sugar cube" became a symbol of public health, and the ease of administration, combined with the fact that it required no boosters and carried much less risk of infection, led to widespread international acceptance of the vaccine.

Sabin was a distinguished service professor at the University of Cincinnati College of Medicine and Children's Hospital Research Foundation from 1960 to 1971, after which he continued as an emeritus distinguished professor. From 1965 until his death, he served on the board of governors of the Weizmann Institute of Sciences in Rehovot, Israel, and as president of that institution from 1970 to 1972. He also sat on the board of governors of Hebrew University in Jerusalem from 1965 until his death and served as a trustee of NYU from 1966 to 1970.

In 1935 Sabin married Sylvia Tregillus; they had two children. Tregillus died in 1966, and late in the 1960s, Sabin married Jane Warner. The two later divorced, and on 28 July 1972, he married for the third and last time, to the journalist Heloisa Dunshee de Abranches.

Awards for Sabin's achievements began to roll in during the 1960s and early 1970s, when he received the Antonio Feltrinelli prize in medicine and surgical science from the Accademia Nazionale dei Lincei in Rome (1964), the Albert Lasker Award for Clinical Medical Research (1965), the gold medal from the Royal Society of Health in London (1969), the United States National Medal of Science (1971), and the Distinguished Civilian Service medal from the U.S. Army (1973). Yet even as he continued to accrue honors, the battle of words with Salk raged.

In 1973, for instance, Salk wrote a blistering guest editorial for the *New York Times* in which he denounced Sabin and his method. It was true that, as use of the Sabin vaccine spread, virologists discovered that about one in 1 million children administered the Sabin sugar cube contracted the disease. Yet by 1991, there were only six reported cases of poliomyelitis in the United States, and at the time of

Sabin's death in 1993, health organizations throughout the Western Hemisphere attested to the near-extinction of polio—thanks to Sabin's vaccine—in the Americas.

By the time the 1960s came to a close, Sabin had reached the age at which most people retire, but he remained as vigorous as ever, traveling the world to promote his vaccine and continuing his public debate with Salk. He also continued to work in the laboratory, devoting much of his time in the 1970s to the search for viral causes of certain types of cancer. Only in 1986, the year he earned the Presidential Medal of Freedom from President Ronald W. Reagan, did Sabin officially retire from medicine; but even then, he remained an active commentator on medical affairs.

Sabin died of congestive heart failure at the Georgetown University Medical School and is buried at Arlington National Cemetery in Virginia. Following Sabin's death, Salk (who died in 1995) issued a statement praising the work of his former adversary.

As a man, Sabin presented two sides. In most social situations, he tended to be quiet, unassuming, mild-mannered, and even self-effacing. Within the laboratory and the world of virology, by contrast, he was an autocrat, and many of his colleagues described him as egotistical and possessive regarding his work. He pursued his vaccination crusade with the passion of a missionary or a political revolutionary, and was so committed to his cause that he routinely insisted on the complete safety of his vaccine, even in the face of data showing that it could sometimes cause infection. Yet the vaccine itself remains one of the great achievements of medicine during the 1960s. Thanks to Sabin, millions of children's lives were saved, and millions of children and adults were saved from the wheelchair and the iron lung.

★

There are no biographies of Sabin. However, aspects of his life and achievements are treated in Theodore Berland, *The Scientific Life* (1962); Richard Carter, *Breakthrough: The Saga of Jonas Salk* (1965); and Roger Rapoport, *The Super-doctors* (1975). Obituaries are in the (London) *Guardian* (4 Mar. 1993), the *Lancet* (13 Mar. 1993), and *JAMA: The Journal of the American Medical Association* (28 Apr. 1993).

JUDSON KNIGHT

SACKLER, Howard Oliver (*b.* 19 December 1929 in New York City; *d.* 14 October 1982 in Ibiza, Spain), dramatist, director, and screenwriter whose play and film *The Great White Hope* became a classic commentary on the uneasy interpenetration of race, society, and boxing within American society.

Sackler was the son of real estate salesman Martin Sackler and Ida Rapaport. He spent his teenage years in Florida before returning to New York. He graduated from Brooklyn College with a B.A. degree in 1950.

While at college he wrote his first screenplay and had the good fortune to have another, *Desert Padre,* filmed by another young craftsman just beginning his career, the incomparable Stanley Kubrick. Sackler and Kubrick had much in common. They were born just one year apart, they both felt sustained by the energy and animation of New York, especially the Bronx, and they were desperate to succeed. With a Sackler script, Kubrick virtually single-handedly made *Fear and Desire* (1953). He financed the project with monies he borrowed, and he was the one-man crew—he directed, shot the camera, edited, and produced. With similar passion and focus between 1950 and 1953, Sackler committed himself to his vision of being a full-time writer. Thanks to writing grants from the Rockefeller and Littauer Foundations, he succeeded.

In 1953 Sackler founded Caedmon Records. Although today the company is all but forgotten, at the time it was a leader in the recording industry. Based in London, Sackler worked as Caedmon's production director for the next fifteen years. London was especially attractive to Sackler for three reasons: much of the most innovative recording work in the 1950s was being done there; the political climate was relatively liberal and devoid of the anticommunist witch-hunting that tarnished Hollywood's reputation; and, for a young man captivated by the theater, London was an inspiring base. Sackler produced more than two hundred recordings for Caedmon. His forte was full-length treatments of Shakespeare, and during his tenure a "Who's Who" of luminary British actors recorded at his studio. During this time he continued to write, winning the Maxwell Anderson Award for verse drama in 1954 with *Uriel Acosta,* a one-act play. His next short work, *The Yellow Loves* (1959), received the Sergel Award. Sackler married Greta Lynn Lungren in 1963; they had two children.

In the mid-1960s Sackler's career blossomed with the production of an anthology of four one-act plays titled *A Few Enquiries* (1965) as well as the staging of *The Pastime of Monsieur Robert* (1966). In an interview Sackler explained how his work at the recording studio helped to shape his rare ability to listen to voices and then to get those voices to be listened to by a theater audience: "One can't learn about plays by reading them nearly as well as one can by getting inside them, conducting them, directing them."

Sackler's crowning glory, and the work that both defines him and sets him apart from his contemporaries, is *The Great White Hope,* which reached out to many constituencies. It was a popular box office hit; normally curmudgeonly critics were generous in their praise; social historians relished its realism; and black activists of the 1960s saw in the script, and especially in the character of boxer Jack Jefferson, an individual whose angst resonated with the dis-

content and discomfort of the civil rights movement and of more extreme black militant groups.

The Great White Hope not only ran for 556 performances on Broadway, beginning in 1968, but in the 1968–1969 drama season swept the New York Drama Critics Award, the Tony Award, and the Pulitzer Prize. The play is based on Jack Johnson, who in 1908 became the first black heavyweight champion of the world. Sackler's title nicely captures an agitated white community, desperately seeking a challenger to tame, thump, and destroy the "uppity" boxer. The antihero Jack Jefferson is a brooding, enigmatic figure who struts around the stage but is ever mindful of the perils that surround him.

The real Jack Johnson, as a boxer, was seen to be a threat to the dominant white culture. Civic leaders, boxing authorities, and white supremacists saw him as a figure of Armageddon. Jackson was railed against because he had a penchant for taunting his opponents and then because he married a much younger white woman just months after his first wife committed suicide. Convicted of transporting a woman across state borders for "immoral purposes," Jackson was sentenced to a year in prison. In Jack Johnson, therefore, Sackler had a remarkable individual to chronicle. Although on one level a powerful analysis of tensions between black and white, *The Great White Hope* is, more profoundly, a singular psychological thriller about a man trapped and made impotent by social forces. Sackler said about the play: "What interested me was not the topicality but the combination of circumstances, the destiny of a man pitted against society. It's a metaphor of struggle between man and the outside world."

Although Sackler played down the view of *The Great White Hope* as a thesis on racial conflict, some critics disagreed. The essayist Julius Novick, writing in 1968, wondered if Sackler was catering to what he termed "Negro paranoia," but added, "the play demands of us, in urgently, dramatic terms, that we examine the whole question [of racism] and our stake in it." James Earl Jones starred in the stage play and in the 1970 Twentieth Century–Fox film, for which Sackler wrote the screenplay. Sackler's other plays were *Semmelweiss* (1977) and *Goodbye Fidel* (1980). He collaborated on several screenplays for several films, among which were *Bugsy* (1973), *Jaws II* (1976), *Gray Lady Down* (1978), and *Saint Jack* (1979). Sackler was found dead at the age of fifty-two in his studio in Ibiza, Spain; the cause of death was pulmonary thrombosis.

Sackler's leadership role at Caedmon—during his tenure he mentored such luminaries as the actors Rex Harrison, Albert Finney, and Paul Scofield—marks his considerable cultural contribution to the history of the spoken word. A good case can be made that the launch of *The Great White Hope* at the Arena Stage in Washington, D.C. (1967), was a pivotal point in American drama. The themes of racism, African-American sexuality, and justice gone wrong shocked theater-going audiences.

★

Douglas T. Putman, *Controversies of the Sports* (1999), gives a thorough review of Johnson's troubled and controversial boxing career. Obituaries are in the *New York Times* (15 Oct. 1982), *Washington Post* (16 Oct. 1982), and (London) *Times* (18 Oct. 1982).

SCOTT A. G. M. CRAWFORD

SAINTE-MARIE, Buffy (*b*. 20 February 1941 in Piapot Cree Reserve, Craven, Saskatchewan, Canada), composer, singer, actress, visual artist, teacher, and political advocate of Native Americans.

Sainte-Marie was born Beverly Sainte-Marie to full-blooded Cree parents. They died suddenly, and she was adopted in infancy by an American couple, Albert Sainte-Marie, a mechanic, and Winifred Kendrick, a proofreader. The couple, originally from Maine, moved to Wakefield, Massachusetts, where Sainte-Marie grew up. The nickname "Buffy" was given to her by her adoptive parents.

A shy child, Sainte-Marie spent much of her time alone. She started to write poetry very early, and at age four began setting her poems to music, having taught herself to play the used piano that her parents had bought. When she was sixteen or seventeen years old, she taught herself to play the guitar, which eventually became her instrument of choice. Sainte-Marie's playing technique was unusual, and she invented thirty-two ways of tuning the guitar, which enabled her to coax new sounds out of it.

The only native child in white schools, Sainte-Marie felt isolated, and later confessed that she had wanted to be blonde like many of her schoolmates. In her mid-teens, she started to research her Native American heritage, and at sixteen, she made a trip to the Piapot Reservation, where she was welcomed by her relatives. She felt accepted as she had never before, and thereafter, she visited the reservation regularly.

Sainte-Marie entered the University of Massachusetts in 1959 to study veterinary science, but changed her studies to education and Eastern philosophy. Among her college activities were practice teaching, theater, and singing. She was encouraged by friends to perform off-campus in local venues. She graduated in 1963 with a B.A. in philosophy, and was voted one of the ten outstanding members of her graduating class.

Shortly after graduation, during the summer of 1963, Sainte-Marie appeared at the Gaslight Café in Greenwich Village. She was heard by folk-music critic Robert Shelton of the *New York Times,* who wrote about her singing during that summer. Other appearances at Greenwich Village ven-

Buffy Sainte-Marie. CORBIS CORPORATION (BELLEVUE)

ues resulted in concert bookings and recording contracts. After some reflection, Sainte-Marie decided to pursue a career in folk singing.

Sainte-Marie signed a contract with the Vanguard Records, and released her first album, *It's My Way,* on 9 November 1964. Commercial successes came with the albums *Many a Mile* (1965), *Little Wheel Spin and Spin* (1966), *Fire and Fleet and Candlelight* (1967), *I'm Gonna Be a Country Girl Again* (1968), and *Illuminations* (1969). She continued to record in subsequent decades, but not as frequently.

Recordings and performances in various media resulted in Sainte-Marie gaining national and international attention. She appeared at Carnegie Hall, Philharmonic Hall in Lincoln Center, the Royal Albert Hall in London, and at the Newport Folk Festival. She has performed not only in the United States and Canada, but also Mexico, France, Finland, and other countries.

Most of the songs Sainte-Marie sings are her own compositions. Her best-known works of the 1960s were protest songs such as "The Universal Soldier" (informally adopted by some as an antiwar anthem during the Vietnam War and which Sainte-Marie was banned from singing on television and radio programs), "Now That the Buffalo's

Gone," and "My Country 'Tis of Thy People You're Dying." (The last two songs are about the plight of Native Americans.) Highly prolific, Sainte-Marie has written love songs such as the popular "Until It's Time for You to Go," blues songs, country ballads, and "Cod'ine," about her codeine addiction. Her compositions were appreciated and sung by others, including Elvis Presley, Barbra Streisand, Bobby Darin, Donovan, Mick Jagger, Sonny and Cher, Glen Campbell, and Tracy Chapman.

Despite her busy concert schedule in the 1960s, Sainte-Marie invested a great deal of time helping the causes of Native Americans. She served as editor of the Canadian publication *Native Voices,* and as a member of the advisory council for the Upward Bound Project in 1966. She also founded the Native North American Women's Association. In 1969 Sainte-Marie founded the Nihewan Foundation. Its purpose is to provide education and scholarships for Native American students by directing funds to Native American studies programs, and by seeking to educate others about the plight of indigenous peoples.

On 16 September 1967 Sainte-Marie married Dewain Kamaikalani Bugbee; they divorced in 1972. She married Sheldon Peters Wolfchild on 4 September 1974, and together they had a son, Dakota Wolfchild Starblanket, who appeared with his mother on *Sesame Street.* Sainte-Marie and Wolfchild divorced in 1978, and she married Jack Nitzsche on 19 March 1981.

Sainte-Marie continued to compose and sing after the 1960s, and won an Academy Award in 1982 for the song "Up Where We Belong," from the film *An Officer and a Gentleman.* She also wrote the film scores for *Stripper* (1985), *Harold of Orange* (1986), and *Where the Spirit Lives* (1989).

Sainte-Marie has also acted. She was in a well-received episode of the television show *The Virginian,* and appeared in the television film *The Broken Chain.* She also narrated the documentary *Broken Arrow.* Perhaps her best-known television appearances were on the Public Broadcasting Company's *Sesame Street.* She was a member of the cast of the PBS children's show from 1976 to 1981.

Sainte-Marie has worked as an adjunct professor at York University in Toronto, and at Indian Federated College in Saskatchewan, among other places, and has lectured on an array of topics such as songwriting, Indian women's issues, art (she is a notable digital artist), and electronic music. She has also been involved in the Cradleboard Teaching Project, which was designed for elementary and secondary curricula, and emphasizes the contributions that Native Americans have made to science, music, and other fields of endeavor.

The recipient of numerous awards and honors, Sainte-Marie can count among them the Billboard Award (1965), Outstanding Artist of the Year from the National Associ-

ation of FM Broadcasters (1975), the aforementioned Academy Award, and Best International Artist of 1993 (France). She was inducted into the Canadian Music Juno Hall of Fame in 1996.

Sainte-Marie's activism was unique in the 1960s, as it focused more on the plight of Native Americans and the history of their maltreatment by the United States, rather than on the Vietnam War. As well as championing Native Americans, she also emphasized environmental issues, including the near extinction of the buffalo.

★

An interview with Sainte-Marie can be found in E. K. Caldwell, *Dreaming the Dawn: Conversations with Native Artists and Activists* (1999). A profile of Sainte-Marie appears in the *Los Angeles Times* (20 Apr. 1986). Information about Sainte-Marie's current interests and activities is available at her Web site at http://www.creative-native.com.

JENNIFER THOMPSON-FEUERHERD

SALINGER, J(erome) D(avid) (*b.* 1 January 1919 in New York City), author of numerous short stories and four books, including the classic *The Catcher in the Rye,* who rose to fame in the late 1950s and early 1960s, only to become a recluse intensely possessive of his privacy.

The son of Solomon Salinger, a successful cheese merchant, and Miriam Jillich, a homemaker, Salinger and his older sister grew up in financial comfort in Manhattan. In 1934 his father enrolled him in Valley Forge Military Academy near Wayne, Pennsylvania, where Salinger pursued writing and acting. Despite an average academic performance, Salinger graduated in 1936. He was admitted to New York University for a semester and acted in several New York theatrical productions. He then spent a semester at Ursinus College in Collegeville, Pennsylvania, probably to humor his parents. Salinger did average work; reported for the school newspaper, the *Ursinus Weekly;* and wrote short stories. That spring he enrolled in a writing class taught by Whit Burnett, the editor of Columbia University's *Story* magazine.

In April 1942 Salinger was drafted into the U.S. Army and sent to Fort Dix in New Jersey. There he started and finished a draft of his most well-known work, *The Catcher in the Rye,* the timeless story of Holden Caulfield, a young man coming of age. Salinger served overseas after training with the Counter-Intelligence Corps in England. He was involved in the invasion of Normandy and the liberation of France and later hospitalized for combat-related stress. In September 1945 he married a Frenchwoman named Sylvia; they divorced in 1947. Discharged in 1945, Salinger took a break from writing and even turned down an offer from

J. D. Salinger. AP/WIDE WORLD PHOTOS

Simon & Schuster to publish a collection of his stories. From 1945 to 1947 he drifted, visiting bars in Greenwich Village with other literary figures.

The Catcher in the Rye, published in July 1951 by Little, Brown, and Company, received excellent reviews and was even called "brilliant" by reviewers, despite a few criticisms for the vulgar language used by the main character. Salinger, always considered a loner, wanted no part of promoting the work. He did not want any advance galleys or review copies of the book sent to the press, and demanded that his picture be removed from the dust jacket, which it eventually was. Salinger even left for England when the book was released. During the mid-1950s, the so-called teenage revolution gave *The Catcher in the Rye* a second wind and elevated the novel to cult status. An outsider and rebel against the adult establishment, Caulfield's character appealed to the young, and, along with Marlon Brando and James Dean, Caulfield became a student favorite and made Salinger the voice of a generation. By 1956 the book had caught the attention of academics, and by 1961 it had sold 1.25 million copies. *The Catcher in the Rye* was available in nine countries, translated into thirty languages, and became an international best-seller in the mid-1960s. Its universal appeal and critical success is evidenced by its acceptance as an American classic and its place on high school and college reading lists.

In 1953 Salinger moved to Cornish, New Hampshire, and became a member of the community. Teenagers loved Salinger and visited his house in droves. Also in 1953 *Nine Stories,* a collection of previously published short stories, was published, just as *The Catcher in the Rye* was released in paperback. *Nine Stories* generally received good reviews and was a best-seller for three months. Then in the fall, two local students asked Salinger if they could interview him for the high school page in the (Claremont) *Daily Eagle.* Salinger agreed, but when the story appeared it did so as a feature in the *Eagle,* not on the high school page. Salinger responded by barricading himself behind a wooden fence and refusing to grant any more interviews.

Salinger married Claire Douglas, a young Radcliffe student, on 17 February 1955, and they had two children. They divorced in October 1967, shortly after Salinger retreated in seclusion to their New Hampshire farm.

During the first part of the 1960s, Salinger continued to write and publish short stories, but he never published another novel. The material for his two books in the 1960s originally appeared as short stories in magazines during the 1950s. *Franny and Zooey* (1961), which was on the best-seller list for six months, and *Raise High the Roof Beam, Carpenter and Seymour: An Introduction* (1963), chronicled the life and relationships of the Glass family. In *Franny,* the story examines Franny's attempt to achieve religious purity and her resulting nervous breakdown. In the sequel, Zooey tries to help his sister out of her emotional and spiritual crisis.

Both *Franny and Zooey* and *Raise High the Roof Beam, Carpenter and Seymour: An Introduction* are narrated by Buddy Glass and deal with the death of his older brother Seymour Glass. The new works also showed the influence of Salinger's interest in Eastern religion, mostly Zen Buddhism. Although both books became best-sellers, the critical reviews were extremely negative. Critics found Salinger's writing self-indulgent and wordy. Critics were also disappointed that Salinger had failed to develop something new, and that even though he spent ten years on the Glass family, the characters had not evolved and remained static. With both Glass books, Salinger again wanted no prepublication deals.

At least part of Salinger's draw was his reclusive lifestyle. *Time, Life,* and *Newsweek* all did features on Salinger during the 1960s, but throughout the decade, Salinger became more of a hermit and recluse, refusing any and all interviews. Reporters tried staking out places where Salinger was known to shop and eat in an effort to make contact with him. Salinger's last published work was "Hapworth 16, 1924," which appeared in the *New Yorker* (19 June 1965). The Hapworth story took the form of a letter, found by Buddy Glass, written from camp by a young Seymour

Glass. By all accounts Salinger continued to write, sometimes spending weeks at a time in his studio, but he decided not to publish. He even returned a $75,000 advance that Little, Brown, and Company had paid him for a new book of fiction.

Salinger has refused to allow any publication, collected or otherwise, of his work. In 1974 a pirated work, *The Complete Uncollected Stories of J. D. Salinger,* was published. Salinger called it "a terrible invasion" of his privacy. Then in 1986 he attempted to block the publication of Ian Hamilton's unauthorized biography, stating that Hamilton violated copyright by paraphrasing his letters that recipients had donated to various libraries. In 1988 Hamilton's book was published without the letters.

★

Biographies of Salinger include Warren French, *J. D. Salinger* (1963), and *J. D. Salinger, Revisited* (1988); Ian Hamilton, *In Search of J. D. Salinger* (1988); and Paul Alexander, *Salinger: A Biography* (1999). Works on Salinger by his daughter, Margaret Ann Salinger, include *Dream Catcher: A Memoir* (2000) and *Dream Catcher: Reflections on Reclusions* (2001).

LISA A. ENNIS

SALISBURY, Harrison Evans (*b.* 14 November 1908 in Minneapolis, Minnesota; *d.* 5 July 1993 in Providence, Rhode Island), reporter, writer, and authority on the Soviet Union.

Salisbury, the only son and older of the two children of Percy Pritchard and Georgianna (Evans) Salisbury, was born in a decaying section of Minneapolis. His father worked in the office of a company that manufactured flour and feed bags. His mother was a homemaker.

In 1925 Salisbury matriculated at the University of Minnesota and joined the staff of the school newspaper. Dropping out of school for financial reasons, he became a reporter for the *Minneapolis Journal.* By 1929, he was back in college but was expelled the following year for protesting administrative policies (he did earn his degree in 1930). Salisbury joined the United Press in St. Paul, moving to the Chicago bureau the next year, and finally to Washington, D.C.

After the outbreak of World War II, Salisbury covered the war in New York and in London; he was then assigned to Moscow until late in the war. Back in Moscow for the *New York Times* in 1949, his reporting was far more perceptive than that of other journalists, but professional anti-Communists, not specifically informed that his dispatches were heavily censored, tried to tarnish his reputation. Salisbury's fourteen-piece series on Russia, written after he returned home, earned him a Pulitzer Prize in 1955. In *To Moscow and Beyond: A Reporter's Journal* (1960) and *Mos-*

cow Journal: The End of Stalin (1961), he described the trials and tribulations of a working journalist in Stalin's Russia and in the transition period following the dictator's death.

One of Salisbury's major aims was to produce a history of Leningrad under siege in World War II. Frustrated by lack of access to necessary data and people, he settled for a novel, *The Northern Palmyra Affair* (1962). By the end of the decade, Salisbury was finally able to publish his magnum opus, *The 900 Days: The Siege of Leningrad* (1969). In between, he wrote two other works on Russia and edited memoirs of Marshal Georgi Zhukov, the heroic commander of Soviet forces in the war (*Marshal Zhukov's Greatest Battles*). He also looked at growing tensions between the two Communist giants in *War between Russia and China* (1969).

Focusing on America as well as the Soviet Union in the period from the late 1950s to the early 1970s, Salisbury wrote *The Shook-Up Generation* (1958), which looked at tensions faced by youths in a time of change and the cold war, and the upbeat *The Many Americans Shall Be One* (1971). The *Times* named him editor of the op-ed page in 1970, and he served as an assistant managing editor from 1964 to 1972.

Harrison Salisbury. ARCHIVE PHOTOS, INC.

On more than one occasion, Salisbury himself became the source of news. In the spring of 1960, he wrote a series of articles on the growing civil rights movement. His blunt stories on Birmingham, Alabama, depicted it as a city living in fear, under siege from racist police. Businessmen and city officials insisted that he exaggerated grossly and had never interviewed those who represented the forces of stability. The mayor, police commissioner, and public service commissioner quickly sued him and the *Times* for libel. Within days they were joined by officials from Bessemer, Alabama, and at least one police detective, all of whom filed additional suits. In all, Salisbury was charged with forty-two counts in state and federal courts, with a total liability of more than $7 million. In 1964 both Salisbury and the *Times* were vindicated when all of the suits were dismissed.

Over Christmas of 1966, Salisbury was invited to visit Hanoi. He documented civilian casualties from bombing raids that American officials had always described as strikes only on military targets. This early description of what would later be known as "collateral damage" further lessened the credibility of the American government. Salisbury was attacked as a dupe of America's enemies by such journals as *Time* and *Newsweek*, which still supported U.S. military involvement. The latter added that he had been demoted at the *Times,* where staffers found him autocratic and quixotic. But Salisbury's stories led to increased activity by both supporters and opponents of American involvement.

As a foreign correspondent, Salisbury was seldom able to enjoy family life. He married Mary Hollis on 1 April 1933; the couple were the parents of two sons, but the stormy marriage finally ended in divorce in 1955. In 1964 he married Charlotte Young Rand.

As the 1970s dawned, Salisbury became more interested in China. After the visit by President Richard M. Nixon in 1972, he was invited with other journalists to visit that country. Over the next two decades, he produced a number of books on the transition from the age of Mao Zedong to the crushing of the student movement at Tiananmen Square in 1989, including *The Long March* (1985), *China: 100 Years of Revolution* (1983), and *The Great Black Dragon Fire* (1989).

During the 1980s, Salisbury worked on his memoirs. He died of heart failure in Providence, Rhode Island, on 5 July 1993.

Salisbury was a durable reporter whose active career spanned more than sixty years. His strengths were persistence, an analytical mind, a way with words, and even his arrogance. A measure of the brilliance of Salisbury's lyrical prose is his description of ballerina Galina Ulanova in *To Moscow—and Beyond*. His arrogance made him a great reporter. Though he was aware early in his career that the truth is not always welcome, his sense of his own reputation impelled him to present even unpleasant truths. He was outstanding in his ability to uncover information under adverse conditions by employing his eyes and ears and using the reaction of censors to confirm his discoveries.

★

The massive Salisbury papers are in the library of Columbia University. His bluntly honest, though sometimes self-serving, autobiography was begun in *A Journey for Our Times: A Memoir* (1983). Many of his other works include enough personal materials to make them significantly autobiographical. Examples of these are *To Moscow—and Beyond: A Reporter's Narrative* (1960), *Moscow Journal: The End of Stalin* (1961), *Orbit of China* (1967), *Behind the Lines—Hanoi* (1967), *To Peking—and Beyond* (1973), *Travels around America* (1976), *A Time of Change* (1988), and *Tiananmen Diary* (1989). An obituary is in the *New York Times* (17 July 1993).

ART BARBEAU

SAMORA, Julian (*b.* 1 March 1920 in Pagosa Springs, Colorado; *d.* 2 February 1996 in Albuquerque, New Mexico), college professor and sociologist whose research in the 1950s and 1960s influenced government policies toward Mexican Americans and Mexican immigrants.

Samora disliked speaking about himself, which is why his early life is only known in vague terms. In later life he said that he grew up amid intense discrimination against Mexican Americans. For example, he was embarrassed by failing first grade because he could not speak English well. In elementary school, if he spoke in Spanish in class, he would be sent to the principal's office, where the principal would hit him with a ruler. Children were forbidden to speak Spanish even during recess or in the school's playground, and these slights stayed with him throughout his life. He had a moment of triumph in 1971, when a new law, as he put it, made it "illegal to prohibit children from speaking Spanish in the school yard."

Samora said that his drive to achieve reform stemmed from his desire "to prove I was equal." It was tough going. When he was chosen to play the lead in a high school play, what should have been a triumph was soured when the other youngsters in the play quit rather than accept a Hispanic leading man. In 1938, he entered Adams State College in Alamosa, Colorado, graduating with a B.A. degree in 1942. From 1942 to 1943 he taught high school in Walsenburg, Colorado, and from 1944 to 1945 he was an instructor at Adams State College.

Samora had a strong desire to learn how Hispanic Americans came to be the targets of discrimination, and he pursued his education in social studies at Colorado State University, where he received his M.S. degree in 1947. He later said that during the 1940s, African Americans knew they were being segregated, but that Hispanics often did not recognize that they were as well. As an example, he recalled trying to find a hotel room in an unfamiliar city; all hotels seemed full except for a seedy one in a bad neighborhood. In the morning, he discovered he had only been given even that room because it was assumed he was Indian, not Hispanic.

From 1948 to 1949, Samora studied sociology at the University of Wisconsin; he then attended Washington University in St. Louis, where he received his Ph.D. in sociology in 1953. For his dissertation, he studied folk medicine among Mexican-American communities in the Southwest. He taught at the University of New Mexico as a visiting professor in 1954, at the School of Medicine of the University of Colorado as an assistant professor of preventive medicine and public health from 1955 to 1957, and at Michigan State University as an assistant professor of sociology and anthropology from 1957 to 1959, before accepting an appointment as professor of sociology at the University of Notre Dame in 1959. In addition to teaching and research, he was put in charge of recruiting Hispanic students and began shepherding these students through graduate school, with his home serving as a student hangout.

From 1963 to 1966 Samora served as head of Notre Dame's sociology department. By then, he had earned a reputation for expertise on Hispanic American culture and social needs, and was often consulted by government agencies about the civil rights of Hispanic Americans. In 1966 the University of Notre Dame Press published Samora's book *La Raza: Forgotten Americans,* which discussed how Mexican Americans were marginalized by American society and how their civil rights issues were ignored. Samora credited the civil rights movement with helping the cause of civil rights for everyone, not just African Americans, and for providing avenues for other ethnic minorities to make their cases for equal rights.

La Raza was a landmark study, and it, more than Samora's other achievements, led to his being dubbed the "father of Hispanic sociology." To many sociologists, Samora had seemed to be laboring almost by himself in Hispanic studies, but in the 1960s, his work began defining the study of Hispanic society as a new field of research. He was soon appointed to federal commissions such as Upward Bound and the Commission of Rural Poverty. He also served on the Indiana Civil Rights Commission and the Colorado Anti-Discrimination Commission.

Samora coauthored, with Richard A. Lamanna, *Mexican Americans in a Midwest Metropolis: A Study of East Chicago* (1967). This book introduced research into the lives of urban Hispanic Americans and was pioneering in moving its focus of inquiry from Southwestern states to the Midwest.

Thereafter, Samora did much fieldwork along the Mexico–United States border, resulting in the publication of *Mexican Americans in the Southwest* (1969), which he coauthored with Ernesto Galarza and Herman Gallegos. While researching this book, Samora became especially interested in the lives of immigrants from Mexico. This resulted in another landmark book, *Los Mojados: The Wetback Story* (1971), which suggested that Mexican farm workers were exploited on both sides of the border.

In 1972 Samora established the Mexican-American Graduate Studies Program at Notre Dame, which he directed until his retirement in 1985. From 1981 to 1984 he served as Notre Dame's Director of Graduate Studies. The most important book of his later years was *A History of the Mexican American People* (1977), which he coauthored with Patricia Vandel Simon. The book was revised in 1993 and remained the standard book on its subject into the twenty-first century.

Samora's wife, Betty, with whom he had four children, died in the mid-1980s; Samora died from a rare disease of the nervous system. On 13 April 1996, a memorial service featuring Mexican and American customs was held at Notre Dame. Samora is noted for having pioneered studies in Hispanic American culture, for laying the scholarly foundations for modern research into the lives of Hispanic Americans, and for helping numerous Hispanic-American students earn advanced college degrees.

★

Samora's papers are in the Nettie Lee Benson Latin American Collection at the University of Texas at Austin, Texas. A good interview of Samora is Rosemary Horvath, "Voice in the Wilderness," *South Bend Tribune* (10 Nov. 1990). Obituaries are in the *New York Times* (6 Feb. 1996) and *Los Angeles Times* (17 Feb. 1996).

KIRK H. BEETZ

SAMUELSON, Paul Anthony (*b.* 15 May 1915 in Gary, Indiana), Nobel Prize–winning economist, *Newsweek* columnist, author, economics professor, and adviser to presidents John F. Kennedy and Lyndon B. Johnson.

Samuelson was born to Frank, a pharmacist, and Ella (Lipton) Samuelson. He enrolled at the University of Chicago when he was sixteen, before he finished high school, and completed a B.A. in economics in 1935. He was the first person to be awarded an economics fellowship by the Social Science Research Council, which provided financial support for his continuing studies in economics at Harvard University. He earned an M.A. from Harvard in 1936 and his Ph.D. in 1941, both in economics. During World War II, Samuelson was a consultant to the National Resources

Planning Board from 1941 to 1943 and the War Production Board and the Office of War Mobilization and Reconstruction in 1945.

Samuelson was renowned even before completing his graduate studies at Harvard. His first major published work, *Foundations of Economic Analysis* (1947), was developed from his dissertation. The work demonstrated his promise as a scholar, and he was honored with the American Economic Association's John Bates Clark Medal in 1947, awarded to promising scholars under the age of forty.

He married Marion E. Crawford on 2 July 1938; they had six children. Crawford died in 1978; Samuelson married Risha Eckaus in 1981. Samuelson joined the economics department at the Massachusetts Institute of Technology (MIT) in 1940. He was named associate professor in 1944, was promoted to full professor in 1947, and received a Guggenheim Fellowship the following year. He was awarded a Ford Foundation Research Fellowship in 1958. In his years at MIT, Samuelson helped create what he would later describe as "a leading world center for economics." He was named institute professor and chairman of the economics department in 1966.

John F. Kennedy made the sluggish rate of U.S. economic growth vis-à-vis the Soviet Union the leading issue in his successful presidential campaign in 1960. Samuelson, who began advising Kennedy during the 1950s, was instrumental in shaping Kennedy's economic arguments. Samuelson declined Kennedy's offer to become chairman of the Council of Economic Advisers, recommending University of Minnesota economist Walter Heller in his place. Samuelson's influence within the Kennedy administration was as great, however, as that of Heller and the other members of the Council.

The president-elect gave Samuelson the job of drafting a transition report on the economy to serve as a policy roadmap for the new administration. The report reflected Samuelson's belief that measures taken during the Eisenhower administration to hold down prices might also be stifling economic growth. "Avoiding inflation," he later wrote, "is not an absolute imperative, but rather is one of a number of conflicting goals that we must pursue and that we may often have to compromise." Accordingly, he envisioned a constant struggle, necessitated by growth at or near inflationary levels, that would enable the economy to grow without the uncertainty of volatile price shifts.

In his report Samuelson advocated aggressive action to boost the economy. During his first few months in office Kennedy called for a 10 percent increase in defense spending. This move reflected the Kennedy administration's view that Eisenhower's efforts to control defense expenditures out of concern for the domestic economy were neither warranted nor wise. Samuelson endorsed this position by maintaining that defense expenditures ought not "be kept

Paul Anthony Samuelson. CORBIS CORPORATION (BELLEVUE)

below the optimal level needed for security because of the mistaken notion that the economy is unable to bear any extra burdens." While the White House argued that the defense-spending increases were predicated on their strategic merit, Samuelson observed that "any stepping up of [defense] programs that is deemed desirable for its own sake can only help rather than hinder" the health of the economy.

Samuelson labored to convince the president of the merits of Keynesian economics, and he was instrumental in convincing Kennedy to drop plans for a tax increase during the summer of 1961. By the summer of 1962 Kennedy's opposition to deficit spending had softened, and his support for a Keynesian-style tax cut in 1963 reflected Samuelson's success in promulgating these ideas within the White House.

Samuelson's influence was not restricted to policymaking in the 1960s. He also shaped professional and popular attitudes toward economics through his regular columns in *Newsweek* magazine from 1966 to 1981. Meanwhile, he continued to influence economic theory at a professional level, and his peers repeatedly recognized him as a leader in the field. He was president of the American Economic Association in 1961 and served as president of the International Economic Association from 1966 to 1968.

Samuelson helped train a generation of students through his introductory textbook, *Economics*. First published in 1948, the book reached the pinnacle of its influence in the 1960s as a new generation of economics professors used Samuelson's simple yet sophisticated description of the basic principles of economics to teach hundreds of thousands of undergraduates. The editions published during the 1960s sold over 1.1 million copies.

In his writings Samuelson established the key features of post-Keynesian economics, a framework characterized as the postclassical or neoclassical synthesis. The central features of this synthesis combined many of the macroeconomic principles of Keynesianism—especially faith in the use of government fiscal policy to maximize economic performance—with classical theory, which celebrated the operation of the free market and focused especially on consumer behavior.

Samuelson rejected the libertarianism of contemporaries, such as Milton Friedman, in part because he doubted the morality of a strictly laissez-faire economic system that tolerated great disparities in wealth between the rich and the poor. Instead, he believed the government had a role to play in ensuring high levels of employment, and he was an enthusiastic supporter of the welfare programs embodied in President Lyndon B. Johnson's War on Poverty of the mid- to late-1960s.

In 1970 Samuelson was awarded the Nobel Prize for economics, the first American to be so honored. In awarding the prize the Swedish Royal Academy of Sciences praised him for his contributions "covering nearly every area of economic theory," concluding that Samuelson "had done more than any other contemporary economist to raise the level of scientific analysis in economic theory." Samuelson also was awarded the Medal of Science in 1996.

Samuelson's influence during the 1960s contributed to, and was reflective of, the ascendancy of Keynesian economic theory. Through the hundreds of columns and articles he published for both scholarly and popular audiences, Samuelson facilitated a dramatic transformation in the way in which political leaders and the public thought about government spending and taxes, budget deficits, inflation, and economic growth. By the end of the 1960s Keynesian principles dominated economic discourse and served as the foundation for the government's economic policies.

★

Samuelson's scholarly writings are published in five volumes in Joseph E. Stiglitz, ed., *The Collected Scientific Papers of Paul A. Samuelson* (1966–1986). Many of his *Newsweek* columns from the 1960s are in *The Samuelson Sampler* (1973), and others are in MaryAnn O. Keating, ed., *Economics From the Heart: A Samuelson Sampler* (1983). Samuelson reflects on his career in William Breit and Roger W. Spencer, eds., *Lives of the Laureates: Seven Nobel Economists* (1986). In addition to his classic textbook, *Economics:*

An Introductory Analysis (1948), Samuelson's approach to economics during the 1960s is described in *Problems of the American Economy: An Economist's View* (1962); *Stability and Growth in the American Economy* (1963); and, with Arthur F. Burns, *Full Employment: Guideposts and Economic Stability* (1967). See also Mark Skousen, "The Perseverance of Paul Samuelson's *Economics*," *Journal of Economic Perspectives* (spring 1997): 137–152. Biographical information about Samuelson and analyses of his writings are in George R. Feiwel, ed., *Samuelson and Neoclassical Economics* (1982); C. Cary Brown and Robert M. Solow, eds., *Paul Samuelson and Modern Economic Theory* (1983); Stephen Martin, "Paul A. Samuelson," in *Thinkers of the Twentieth Century* (1987): 670–672; John C. Wood and Ronald Woods, eds., *Paul A. Samuelson: Critical Assessments* (1989); and K. Puttaswamaiah, ed., *Paul Samuelson and the Foundation of Modern Economics* (2001).

CHRISTOPHER A. PREBLE

SANDERS, Harland David ("Colonel") (*b.* 9 September 1890 in Henryville, Indiana; *d.* 16 December 1980 in Louisville, Kentucky), Midwestern farm boy and grade school dropout whose special recipe fried chicken business grew into the largest fast-food franchise in the United States by the mid-1960s.

Sanders was born to Margaret Ann Dunlevy and her farmer-turned-butcher husband, Wilbert Sanders. Wilbert Sanders died in 1895, leaving behind his widow and three small children, when Harland, the eldest, was five years old. His mother taught him both how to care for his younger siblings and how to cook because she had to work long hours at a local tomato cannery. She later remarried and moved to Greenwood, Indiana, with her new husband, William Broaddus. Twelve-year-old Sanders was often at odds with his stepfather, and at his mother's urging he left home to preserve the peace.

Sanders's childhood thus ended abruptly, and he dropped out of school and worked as a farmhand and later as a conductor on the New Albany streetcar line before joining the U.S. Army in November 1906 on a four-month tour of duty. Sanders took correspondence courses for a law degree from Southern University. This was followed by a series of jobs with the railroad before he set up a law practice, sold insurance and tires, and managed a gas station for Standard Oil. When fallout from the Great Depression forced him to close the doors of the station in 1929, he found a Shell Oil station to manage in Corbin, Kentucky, at the junction of U.S. Routes 25 and 25E. He opened a tiny, one-table diner in the back room of the station, eventually expanding his business across the street, where he built a seventeen-room motel complex in 1937. During these early years he met and married Josephine King in

Harland D. Sanders. KFC

1908. The couple had three children, but divorced in 1947. Sanders married his second wife, Claudia Ledington, a former employee, in 1949.

The motel and restaurant business at Corbin generated a healthy income for Sanders and became the first Kentucky Fried Chicken restaurant, but a Route 25 bypass outside of Corbin in 1955 prompted Sanders to liquidate the operation. Already sixty-five years old and reduced to an income of $105 per month from Social Security, Sanders banked his future on the franchising of his famous fried chicken. He purchased a home in Shelbyville, near Louisville, Kentucky, where he set up a makeshift headquarters and peddled his product under the brand name Colonel Sanders Recipe Kentucky Fried Chicken. In 1952 Sanders had established a franchise with restaurateur Pete Harman in Salt Lake City, Utah, and Harman expanded the franchise into Utah and Montana while Sanders focused on selling franchises in Indiana and Illinois.

Along with a precise method of pressure-cooking the chicken and a secret combination of eleven herbs and spices, Sanders lent a unique persona to the new venture.

As a member of the Honorary Order of Kentucky Colonels, he cultivated an image as the quintessential gentleman of the antebellum South. He accordingly accessorized his wardrobe of white linen suits, adding black string ties and dapper walking sticks, and let his silvery gray hair, goatee, and mustache whiten naturally to enhance his kindly, photogenic face. Sanders assumed this new identity with serendipity, evolving gracefully into the grandfatherly colonel. He traveled the country in a white Cadillac, with his pressure cooker and precious seasonings on board, stopping at selected restaurants where he prepared samples of Kentucky Fried Chicken and generous bowls of succulent gravy. He offered restaurant owners the rights to serve the special recipe chicken for a franchise fee of five cents per chicken. Claudia Sanders prepared and shipped packages of the special ingredients to franchises and sometimes accompanied her husband to demonstrations, where she mingled with customers dressed in a hoop skirt, while the colonel, outfitted in white coattails with vest and gold watch chain, complemented her appearance. Within three years Sanders had established dozens of outlets throughout the Midwest, making personal appearances and passing out free chicken at franchise openings. Amid the success he initiated his first fast-food take-out service in Jacksonville, Florida, as a wedding present for his daughter. He established a spin-off company, Colonel's Foods, to distribute special recipe products.

By 1960 Kentucky Fried Chicken (KFC) encompassed approximately 200 franchises across North America, with pretax profits of $100,000. At five cents per chicken, over 2 million chickens were fried annually. Sanders upgraded from his classic white Cadillac to a gold Rolls-Royce Silver Cloud. The company grew to 600 franchises by 1963; profits tripled proportionally to $300,000. KFC by then was the largest fast-food franchise in the United States. Sanders prepared to deal with John Y. Brown, Jr., to serve KFC chicken through Brown's barbecue outlets; Brown instead made a bid for KFC in its entirety.

In 1964 Sanders agreed to transfer ownership to Brown and a partner, Jack Massey, for $2 million and exclusive rights to the company's Canadian operation. The deal guaranteed Sanders a lifetime annual salary of $40,000 plus commercial residuals to continue as goodwill ambassador. Although hotheaded in private and prone to pepper his speech with profanity, Sanders was a charismatic spokesman, and the company contracted a series of television commercials featuring Colonel Sanders touting "Finger Lickin' Good" chicken. Brown recalled, "[Sanders] wasn't just a trademark . . . that an adman had made up. He was real, . . . colorful, . . . a great actor . . . [who] made things look easy." With his easy Southern charm, Sanders in fact earned guest appearances on more than thirty national television shows, including such popular talk shows as Johnny

Carson and Merv Griffin, during a three-year period in the mid-1960s, as well as a cameo appearance in the Jerry Lewis feature film *The Big Mouth* in 1967, all of which contributed to make KFC the fastest growing company in the United States.

By 1967 the carry-out business had grown to comprise 30 percent of KFC business. Soon afterward the freestanding, red-and-white-striped KFC carry-out stores dotted the landscape in the United States, and fast-food franchise restaurants symbolized the freewheeling American culture during the final quarter of the twentieth century. When Brown and Massey sold KFC to Heublein, Inc., in 1972, the franchise had increased in value to $273 million.

Sanders died at age ninety after a bout of pneumonia, and is buried in Louisville's Cave Hill Cemetery.

★

Sanders's autobiography is *Life as I Have Known It Has Been "Finger Lickin' Good"* (1974). Edward G. Klemm, Jr., discusses Sanders in *Claudia, the Story of Colonel Harland Sanders Wife* (1980), and John Ed Pearce documents the colonel's life in *The Colonel: The Captivating Biography of the Dynamic Founder of a Fast-Food Empire* (1982). Obituaries are in the *New York Times* and *Louisville Courier-Journal* (both 17 Dec. 1980).

GLORIA COOKSEY

SASSOON, Vidal (*b.* 17 January 1928 in London, England), trend-setting hairstylist and entrepreneur who promoted the wash-and-go, easy-to-manage, "Sassoon bob" hairstyle of the 1960s and whose hair-care products are used worldwide.

Sassoon was the second son of Nathan Sassoon, a carpet salesman, and Betty (Bellin) Sassoon, a homemaker. The family lived in London's working-class East End. When Sassoon was five years old, his father abandoned the family for another woman, and his now-impoverished mother placed her sons in an orphanage. When she remarried eight years later, her sons rejoined her and began attending public school. Poor at schoolwork, Sassoon dropped out when he was fourteen.

Inspired by a dream of her son styling her hair, his mother apprenticed Sassoon to a hairdresser, Adolf Cohen. For two years he cleaned the shop, shampooed hair, and practiced barbering. In another shop he shampooed and dressed the hair of war-prosperous prostitutes of London's Soho area. During the 1940s and 1950s, hairstyling was elaborate and labor-intensive, often featuring a permanent wave done with intricate wiring, with thin, aluminum curlers used in the process.

Realizing his thick Cockney accent prevented any advancement, Sassoon frequented London's West End thea-

ters to learn better English; he also began taking elocution lessons. At night he attended meetings of antifascist and Zionist groups. In 1948 he joined the Palmach army group and fought in Israel's War of Independence. He returned to London and to hair styling and opened his first salon in a small, third-floor room on Bond Street. By 1954 Sassoon had opened another salon in a renovated, first-floor space he had designed himself. The salon featured an open floor plan with shampoo and cutting stations in plain view, rather than the traditional layout of individual stylists working in cubicles.

Also in 1954 Sassoon befriended couturier Mary Quant. "She cut clothes with a brilliant flair," Sassoon later wrote, "and I tried to match her style with hair." For the next several seasons, he styled Quant's hair and that of her models. Eventually, he began to specialize in a hairstyle that was short-cropped in the back (so that no fuzz would be caught in the collar) and longer at the sides, the hair falling forward with an upward flip at the cheeks.

The 1963 fashion season featured Quant's miniskirt sported by models wearing Sassoon's short, geometric crop, which the British press dubbed "the Sassoon bob." By 1964 Britain's *Queen* and France's *Elle* fashion magazines had adopted this hairstyle. That year Sassoon was featured at the Intercoiffure convention in New York City and fell in love with the United States. "I love it," he told the *New York Times.* "It switches me on."

In 1965 Sassoon opened a salon in New York City's posh Charles of the Ritz makeup studio. Within hours of its opening, appointments were booked months in advance. Like his London shops, the New York salon employed young, energetic stylists (the average age was twenty-two) working in an open floor plan layout. Sassoon's clients, the with-it "mod" set, would be photographed at discothèques such as Ondine and Arthur. Within a year *Vogue* and *Harper's Bazaar* featured articles on the jet-setting Sassoon, who now commuted between swinging London and New York.

Because of his international fame Sassoon was initially allowed to operate without a New York cosmetology license, but he was finally required to take the certification exam in 1966. With much publicity, he refused to do so, insisting that the required techniques were outmoded. In interviews and talk shows he promoted "Sassoon's Philosophy: Short Is Good." With Sassoon barred from cutting hair himself, his New York salon began to lose business even as he became nationally known by publicizing his noncertification. Business prospered again, however, when he submitted to taking the exam and passed.

In 1965 Sassoon featured squared curls achieved by winding hair on wooden blocks. For the 1966 season he reversed this style, with a long, asymmetrical bob cut covering one eye in the manner of actress Veronica Lake's

Vidal Sassoon (*left*), styling the hair of actress Mia Farrow, March 1967. © BETTMANN/CORBIS

peek-a-boo style of the 1940s. The following year he returned to a short look featuring "the curly geometric" perm, which was complemented by Charles of the Ritz makeup with a bright red, cupid's-bow mouth, reminiscent of the 1920s flapper style of actress-vamp Clara Bow.

For Mia Farrow's hairstyles in Roman Polanski's *Rosemary's Baby* (1968), Sassoon created two influential and startlingly different looks. There was a long hairpiece for early scenes when Farrow's naive character falls in with a witch's coven. Then, while pregnant with the devil's child, Farrow's character suddenly sports an extremely short pixie cut. Typically for Sassoon, he fashioned the gamine haircut with much publicity. In front of an audience of 40 fashion stylists, 110 photographers, and 5 television crews, Farrow's hair-as-spectacle became a major media event.

That same year Sassoon featured a "little boy" cut, longer at the sides and nape of the neck, with a short and shaggy top. Another highly influential hairstyle was the "Greek Goddess," with hair tightly permed on top and cropped very short at the back.

Sassoon's business began to attract young men who visited the salon after hours, and Sassoon believed that these new clients needed a separate venue for daytime cuttings. Parting with Charles of the Ritz in 1968, Sassoon opened two salons, one for women on Madison Avenue and another for men in the chic department store Bonwit Teller.

By the late 1960s, Sassoon had opened a chain of salons in the United States and in Europe. To train his stylists, he opened the Vidal Sassoon Academy, first in New York, then later in London and in San Francisco. The training program was complemented by the development of hair products such as shampoos and conditioners, which initially were sold exclusively at his saloons. Later the hair products were manufactured, and then owned, by the Procter and Gamble Company.

In the 1970s and 1980s, Sassoon actively promoted his hair care products on talk shows and commercials ("If you don't look good, we don't look good.") Eventually, his products included styling combs and brushes, curling irons, and a pioneering, hand-held, portable plastic hairdryer for use at home or when traveling. Also during this time, he ventured, with moderate success, into designer jeans and a radio talk show.

Sassoon became a naturalized U.S. citizen in 1972. Sassoon and his first wife, the actress Beverly Adams, had four children. In 1975 Sassoon and Adams, along with the former *Vogue* editor Camille Duhé, wrote a best-selling beauty and natural health book, *A Year of Beauty and Health*. After divorcing Adams, Sassoon married the interior designer Rhonda Holbrook.

Sassoon's career as hairstylist and entrepreneur featured the 1960s "mod" look of a short and geometric bob style with low maintenance. He pioneered the open salon layouts and salon venues for men that are now industry standards. He was the first hair stylist who both created and produced complete hair care product lines used internationally.

★

Sassoon's autobiography is *Sorry I Kept You Waiting, Madam* (1968). Diane Fishman and Marcia Powell, *Vidal Sassoon: Fifty Years Ahead* (1993), a retrospective catalog, details his career and influence on the field of hairdressing. See also Angela Taylor, "Coiffeur 'Switched On' in New York," *New York Times* (16 Mar. 1964).

PATRICK S. SMITH

SAVIO, Mario (*b.* 8 December 1942 in New York City; *d.* 6 November 1996 in Sebastopol, California), civil rights activist and student leader of the 1964 Free Speech Movement at the University of California, Berkeley.

Savio's parents emigrated from Sicily to the borough of Queens in New York City, where his father, Joseph, worked as a machine-punch operator. They were devout Catholics who instilled in their two altar boy sons a strong sense of morality and an understanding of the importance of education. Savio, called "Bob" for most of his youth, graduated first in his class of 1,200 at Martin van Buren High School and was a finalist in the Westinghouse Science Talent Search Scholarship before going on to Manhattan College, a Catholic school, in the Bronx, and later Queens College. In the summer of 1963 he worked for a Catholic relief organization, building a laundry near Taxco, Mexico. When his parents moved to Los Angeles that year, Savio enrolled at the University of California, Berkeley, as a philosophy major. He began calling himself "Mario."

In his first year at Berkeley, Savio quickly gravitated to civil rights activism and was first arrested for taking part in a sit-in at the Sheraton Palace Hotel in San Francisco, where protesters demanded that African Americans be hired for positions other than maids. At the end of the school year he took part in Freedom Summer, teaching a freedom school for black children in McComb, Mississippi. His parents supported his activism and commitment to social justice. Administrators at the Berkeley campus, however, were not as supportive. For decades the school had prohibited political activity on campus but had allowed students to set up card tables to distribute leaflets on the edge of campus, at the corner of Bancroft Way and Telegraph Avenue. In September 1964 administrators unilaterally issued new rules banning the tables from the campus. This outraged civil rights activists, including Savio, who had returned to Berkeley from Mississippi to lead the campus chapter of Friends of the Student Nonviolent Coordinating Committee. "I spent the summer in Mississippi," he said. "I witnessed tyranny. I saw groups of men in the minority working their wills over the majority. Then I came back here and found the university preventing us from collecting money for use there and even stopping us from getting people to go to Mississippi to help."

The organization that became known as the Free Speech Movement (FSM) began when angry students, frustrated by the harassment of school officials, moved their leaflet tables to Sproul Plaza, well inside the campus perimeter. Eight students, including Savio, were suspended indefinitely, but when university police drove onto the plaza and arrested the civil rights activist Jack Weinberg, hundreds of students surrounded the car before it could drive away. A standoff continued as Weinberg sat in the car for thirty-two hours. During the standoff Savio established himself as a leader of the protests in several thoughtful, spontaneous addresses delivered from the top of the police car (police had given the students permission to place

Mario Savio speaking at a political rally at the University of California, Berkeley, in December 1964. © BETTMANN/CORBIS

a microphone on the roof), beginning on 1 October 1964. Although Savio frequently stuttered in private conversation, he spoke forcefully and articulately to crowds.

Negotiations between students and the university president, Clark Kerr, ended the plaza sit-in with promises of a reexamination of the student suspensions and negotiations for a new policy on campus political activity. In late November, however, when negotiations began to unravel and the students asserted their First Amendment right to free speech and set up tables again, Kerr responded by sending out disciplinary letters marking Savio and three others for further punishment. In response, the FSM made plans for a massive sit-in of Sproul Hall, home to administration offices.

In anticipation of the event, on 2 December, Savio spoke his most memorable words, extemporaneously, to a crowd of thousands: "There is a time when the operation of the machine becomes so odious, makes you so sick at heart, that you can't take part; you can't even passively take part, and you've got to put your bodies upon the gears and upon the wheels, upon the levers, upon all the apparatus and you've got to make it stop. And you've got to indicate to the people who run it, to the people who own it, that unless you're free, the machines will be prevented from working at all." Here Savio captured the sense of alienation and powerlessness felt by so many students at the modern university (called the "knowledge factory" by Kerr) and in American society, inspiring the famous FSM slogan "Human Being—Do Not Fold, Spindle, or Mutilate." Two days later police arrested 773 students who had occupied Sproul Hall, the largest mass arrest in California history. The entire campus then went on strike, with fewer than 18 percent of students attending classes. The following week the Berkeley faculty voted overwhelmingly to allow freedom of expression on campus. Although Savio spent four months in jail and was suspended from the university, Kerr was defeated.

Weary of media attention, Savio left Berkeley with his wife, the FSM leader Suzanne Goldberg, with whom he later had two children. In 1966 Savio was arrested again at Berkeley—this time as a nonstudent—for protesting an armed forces recruiting table. In 1969 he ran for state senate on the Peace and Freedom Party ticket and in 1980 helped found the Citizen Party. After his first marriage ended in divorce, Savio in 1980 married another FSM activist, Lynn Hollander; they had one son. Twenty years after the Free Speech Movement, in 1984, Savio earned his B.S. degree in physics from San Francisco State University; he earned a master's degree in 1989. He taught physics, mathematics, philosophy, and poetry at Sonoma State University from 1990 until 1996, when, while moving furniture, he suffered heart fibrillation and slipped into a coma from which he never recovered. Savio died at the age of fifty-three at Palm Drive Hospital. At the time he had been advising Sonoma State students fighting a fee increase and working against Proposition 209, an anti–affirmative action initiative.

Although he eschewed celebrity, Savio's highly publicized role in the Free Speech Movement inspired student activists in the New Left, civil rights, antiwar, and women's liberation movements and beyond. Draft resisters who openly defied Selective Service laws found strength in his description of the machine's operation and the sacrifice required to stop it. He personified the New Left quest for authentic human relations in a society numbed by the alienation of modern institutions, wounded by racism and discrimination, and threatened by the cold war arms race. Although he received hate mail in 1964 and Kerr at times detested him, following his death Berkeley officials held a memorial service for Savio in December 1996 and renamed the steps of Sproul Hall the Mario Savio Memorial Steps on 3 December 1997.

★

Savio's role in the Free Speech Movement is chronicled in Hal Draper, *Berkeley: The New Student Revolt* (1965), for which Savio wrote the introduction; Bettina Aptheker, Robert Kaufman, and Michael Folsom, *FSM: The Free Speech Movement at Berkeley* (1965); W. J. Rorabaugh, *Berkeley at War: The 1960s* (1989); and David Lance Goines, *The Free Speech Movement: Coming of Age in the 1960s* (1993). Mark Kitchell's documentary film, *Berkeley in the '60s* (1990), showcases Savio's personality and oratorical skills. The Free Speech Movement's archives are housed at the Bancroft Library at Berkeley. Obituaries are in the *San Francisco Chronicle* and *San Francisco Examiner* (both 7 Nov. 1996), the *New York Times* and *Washington Post* (both 8 Nov. 1996), the *Los Angeles Times* (10 Nov. 1996), *U.S. News and World Report* (18 Nov. 1996), and *Time* (25 Nov. 1996).

MICHAEL S. FOLEY

SCHECHNER, Richard (*b.* 23 August 1934 in Newark, New Jersey), avant-garde theater director, writer, editor, and the director of the Performance Group, whose *Dionysus in 69* explored the ritual and communal roots of drama.

The third of four sons of Sheridan, a corporate president and then a banking director, and Selma Schwarz Schechner, a homemaker, Schechner was born into wealth and privilege. Not until he was twelve did he realize that not everyone has servants. As a child he studied the Talmud with his rabbi grandfather. His family moved to South Orange, New Jersey, and there he attended Columbia High School and began an ardent interest in social issues.

While majoring in English literature at Cornell University in Ithaca, New York, Schechner was the news editor of the student newspaper, which featured his editorials blasting Joseph McCarthy's Communist-baiting Senate hearings of 1952 and compulsory ROTC. After graduating with honors in 1956 he won a teaching fellowship at Johns Hopkins University, which he left the following year for Iowa State University, where his interests turned to theater. After completing his master's degree in 1958 he served two years in the army as an information specialist, lecturing to officers about current affairs and editing the army base's newspaper.

Schechner decided to return to graduate school to study the history of theater, and he chose Tulane University in New Orleans; his dissertation analyzed theater of the absurd playwright Eugene Ionesco. After spending a research year in Paris, he returned and completed his degree (1962). He was then invited to become the new editor of the *Tulane Drama Review*.

Previously, the journal had published traditional articles about pre-twentieth-century drama. Schechner transformed it into a forceful and dynamic advocate of contemporary debates of performance. Groundbreaking issues became thematically devoted, for example, to the first translations of surrealist and theater of the absurd playwrights or to psychoanalytic explications of a play's inner character motivations ("subtext") and of stage fright. One 1965 issue contained the earliest academic consideration of artists doing performance art ("Happenings" or "Painter's Theater"). Two issues of the journal concerned Konstantin Stanislavsky's Moscow Art Theater and his "Method" of training actors by emphasizing their psychological motivations in forming characters, as well as how the Actors Studio in New York deliberately distorted the Method to ensure commercial success. Such uncoverings led to national publicity and surging subscriptions.

In 1966 New York University (NYU) assumed control of the publication, and Schechner moved to New York City to continue editing the journal, now titled the *Drama Review*, and to teach performance, theory, and theater history at NYU. The journal continued addressing cutting-edge issues in contemporary performance, such as radically political and communal troupes of Off-Off Broadway (the Living Theatre, the Open Theater) and African-American playwrights. When still in New Orleans, Schechner had cofounded (1964) the Free Southern Theater to advance African-American drama projects in the rural South, and he was codirector (1965–1967) of the New Orleans Group, which presented avant-garde plays. Schechner's NYU performance workshops explored the ritualistic and communal roots of Greek theater, leading him to found and direct the Performance Group (1967–1980).

Schechner's Performance Group put into practice the concerns of new theater explored in the *Drama Review*. How can one not just reform both theater and society and make them refreshingly meaningful to contemporary life but also construct a model community that is at once intensely personal and mystically communal? Traditional notions of the playwright as author and authority, separation of stage and audience, and resolved linear plots with actors playing psychologically motivated characters were, for new theater advocates like Schechner, dead issues. Instead, truly meaningful and alive performance included an open-ended process of images/events, audience participation, multifocused scenarios, and a transformative communal ritual. For Schechner, to make performance radical is to reroot it, literally.

Dionysus in 69 (1969) was the landmark production of Schechner's Performance Group. First performed in workshops and then at the Performing Garage on Wooster Street in New York, it made contemporary Euripides's *The Bacchae* (405 B.C.). The play concerns the power of the darkly primitive and ecstatically irrational forces within us, personified in a distraught young king of Thebes. His, and the audience's, conventional restraints, including clothing, are to be released. The audience was perched on scattered cowhides under rough-hewn wooden platforms on which the scenario of the king of Thebes was enacted. The audience also participated as the Greek chorus, but not as just commentators on the action.

As the Theban king is tormented by his inner demons, so, suddenly, was the audience by followers of the god Dionysus in eye-to-eye confrontations ("Feel pain, it's a gas!"). The evening concluded with inviting, but not forcing, the audience to be psychically reborn in a nude feast and to be the dancing followers of Dionysus. "I left with the feeling," wrote one critic, "that I had come closer to the guts of the play—to, in Freudian terms, its unconscious—than a polite traditional version could ever have taken me."

When it was performed later that year at the University of Michigan, the troupe was arrested for public nudity. Back in New York, Schechner upstaged the Living Theater's production of *Paradise Now* by stripping in the audience as that performance began. He received further publicity in *Life* magazine on 29 April 1969.

Later Performance Group productions included an adaptation of Shakespeare's *Macbeth* (1969), *Commune* (1970–1972), *Oedipus* (1977), and Jean Genet's *The Balcony* (1980). Each project investigated the possibilities of expanding performance as an open field of theatrical ritual and communal practice, just as the *Drama Review* continued to redefine the criticism and theory of new theater.

★

Schechner's collected writings on new theater and the Performance Group include *Public Domain* (1968), *Environmental Theater* (1973), *Essays on Performance Theory, 1970–1976* (1976), and *The Future of Ritual: Writings on Culture and Performance* (1993).

Also see Dan Sullivan, "Theater: *Bacchae* Updated in Garage," *New York Times* (7 June 1968).

PATRICK S. SMITH

SCHELL, Jonathan Edward (*b.* 21 August 1943 in New York City), columnist for the *New Yorker* whose detailed descriptions of the systematic annihilation of a Vietnamese village and U.S. military criteria for identifying Vietcong raised public awareness of the irrationality of U.S. policy in Vietnam.

Schell is one of two sons of Orville H. and Marjorie Bertha S. Schell. He attended the Dalton School and the Putney School. Schell graduated from Harvard University with honors with a B.A. in 1965, and then studied Japanese in an intensive, one-year course at the International Christian University in Tokyo, Japan. He then enrolled in graduate study in Far Eastern history at Harvard in 1967.

Schell's second book, *The Military Half*, is dedicated to his brother Orvill, who, "against everybody's better judgment, suddenly dropped out of his junior year in college to set out for the Far East as third cook—or vegetable peeler—on a Norwegian dynamite freighter," which set the tone for many impulsive trips East they both made since. However erratic his inspiration to travel East, Schell developed a reputation for tenacity in consistently describing the Vietnam War in such a way as to characterize U.S. intervention as inane and arbitrary.

At the age of twenty-four, Schell published *The Village of Ben Suc* (1967), the story of the January 1967 evacuation and leveling of a Vietnamese village thirty miles north of Saigon. The village was an instrumental part of a forty-square-mile jungle "iron triangle" stronghold of the Vietcong. Schell flew with the first sixty helicopters and witnessed the invasion, the evacuation of 3,500 Vietnamese civilians, and the annihilation of the village. John Dillon of the *Christian Science Monitor* aptly explained the source of power in Schell's writing style, "(Schell) lets the events speak." In relentless, uncomplicated description Schell illustrated the nature of the destruction. By using simple observations and by pointing out the contradictions in American assumptions about Vietnamese culture and life, he illustrated the U.S. military's ignorance of guerrilla warfare.

The power of Schell's straightforward writing style is further manifested in *The Military Half* (1968), which originally appeared in serial form in the *New Yorker,* and was introduced as a book "about what is happening in South Vietnam." Schell limited his observations to the criteria used by the U.S. military to identify the enemy and the extent of destruction of a specific area in South Vietnam. Schell believed that, in a democracy, everyone participates in the decisions; therefore, everyone should be informed

immediately. He wrote, "All of us must share the responsibility for this war." He hoped that by recording what he witnessed, " . . . it would help us all to understand better what we are doing."

Beginning in January 1969, Schell contributed some of his most persuasive editorials about Vietnam and the Nixon administration to the "Notes and Comment" section of the *New Yorker*. Schell addressed a lag in the underlying political assumptions of presidential administrations dating back to President John F. Kennedy, pointing out that the containment theories of the post–World War II era were driving U.S. policy in Vietnam. The United States, he said, was more interested in its international image or credibility within the context of the nuclear age than it was in any honest effort to save Vietnam from oppression or promote democracy. In the early 1970s Schell observed that U.S. administrations favored credibility—"the image of the truth"—over candor. He said they "referred not to anything tangible but to an image: an image of vast national strength and of unwavering determination to use that strength in world affairs." Obsolescent assumptions, coupled with the "domino theory," which described the potential chain reaction of toppling small governments by Communism, were the root causes of the destruction of the very country that Americans professed to be rescuing. Schell added that the existence of a South Vietnamese government depended solely upon U.S. support, and that the South lacked the support of the people. He wrote that, while policymakers warned that the South would fall within a month of a U.S. withdrawal, it had already succumbed.

Schell claimed that every aspect of American life in the 1960s had been consumed by the escalation of the U.S. intervention in Vietnam. President Lyndon B. Johnson's so-called guns and butter proposals had drained social programs of funding in favor of the war effort. Watergate, the antiwar demonstrations, campus unrest, war propaganda, and the intimidation of the American press posed direct threats to the U.S. Constitution and the republic. Schell was part of a generation and subculture whose assumptions were informed by a televised popular culture. In addition, the precursors of unscripted television—nightly broadcasts of the Vietnam War—only compounded the effects of the daily threat of nuclear destruction that baby boomers had grown up with. The promises and hopes generated by World War II victories and subsequent social programs to rebuild U.S. society were crushed during the most vulnerable years of adolescence for baby boomers. The betrayal of the public trust, the assassination of a president, and a series of drug- and alcohol-induced deaths of their popular heroes had eroded the confidence of their generation.

Bearing those orientations in mind, Schell's ability to constrain his reporting to reasonable observation was remarkable. He did not conceal the fact that he believed the

Vietnam War was a mistake and morally wrong, but neither did he entertain sensationalism or accusations in order to make his point. There was no need. The gruesome nature of the war, the paradoxes faced by U.S. troops and society in general, and the massive contradictions between what the establishment espoused and what it actually did furnished him with ample material. In the preface to Schell's *Observing the Nixon Years,* William Shawn wrote in 1988, "What to me is most characteristic of Schell's writing is the unexpectedness of his turn of thought. He is constantly saying what has not been said before."

Schell was awarded the National Institute and American Academy of Arts and Sciences award in literature in 1973. His book *The Fate of the Earth* garnered the *Los Angeles Times* Book Prize, the National Book Critics Prize nomination, and a Pulitzer Prize nomination in 1982. He wrote for the *New Yorker* from 1967 to 1988, and became a staff writer for *Newsday* and *NY Newsday* beginning in 1990. In 1989 Schell was awarded a Guggenheim Fellowship, and in 1990 a MacArthur Foundation Grant for Writing on Peace and Security. Schell has taught at Princeton University, the New York University School of Journalism, Emory University, and Wesleyan University. A life-long resident of New York City, he lives with his wife Elspeth and their three children.

★

Biographical information is found in Schell's own works, *The Village of Ben Suc* (1967), *The Military Half: An Account of the Destruction of Quang Ngai and Quang Tin* (1968), *The Time of Illusion, an Historical and Reflective Account of the Nixon Era* (1976), and *Observing the Nixon Years: "Notes and Comment" from the New Yorker on the Vietnam War and the Watergate Crisis, 1969–1975* (1989). Articles about Schell and his work include those in: *Time* (17 Nov. 1967), the *Christian Science Monitor* (2 Dec. 1967), the *National Review* (25 Mar. 1969), *Newsweek* (12 Jan. 1976), the *Christian Science Monitor* (9 Mar. 1976), the *New Republic* (28 Apr. 1982), and the *National Review* (22 July 1988).

LERI M. THOMAS

SCHIRRA, Walter Marty, Jr. ("Wally") (*b.* 12 March 1923 in Hackensack, New Jersey), U.S. Navy fighter pilot and test pilot who became one of the first seven U.S. astronauts and was the only astronaut to fly in all of America's first three spaceflight programs—Mercury, Gemini, and Apollo.

Schirra was born to an engineer and stunt pilot, Walter Marty Schirra, Sr., and a stuntwoman, Florence (Leach) Schirra. His father had been a U.S. Army pilot during World War I. After the war Schirra, Sr., and his wife traveled the United States performing stunts at fairs, with Florence often walking on a wing while her husband put the plane through its paces.

Walter M. Schirra. AP/WIDE WORLD PHOTOS

Schirra loved working with his hands, building model airplanes and even a kayak. His father taught him to fly, and Schirra was flying solo by age sixteen. He graduated from Dwight W. Morrow High School in Englewood, New Jersey, in 1940 and entered the Newark College of Engineering (later the New Jersey Institute of Technology) to study aeronautical engineering. In 1942 he entered the U.S. Naval Academy in Annapolis, Maryland, enlisting in an accelerated three-year matriculation program. He graduated with a B.S. in 1945, but World War II ended before he saw action.

On 23 February 1946 Schirra married Josephine Cook Fraser, the stepdaughter of Admiral James L. Holloway; the couple had two children. Schirra attended pilot's school in Pensacola, Florida, and in 1948 he became a navy pilot. He served with Fighter Squadron Seventy-one for three years, and then in 1951 was temporarily assigned to the U.S. Air Force 154th Fighter Bomber Squadron in Korea, where he flew ninety bombing and close-ground support missions. Schirra spent the years from 1952 to 1954 at the China Lake Naval Ordnance Training Station in California, where he was a test pilot. In 1954 he became a flight instructor for the F7U-3 Cutlass and the FJ-3 Fury. Then in 1956 he served on the aircraft carrier *Lexington* as the operations officer. By 1959 he was a test pilot at a base in Patuxent River, Maryland.

Lieutenant Commander Schirra applied to be one of the first U.S. astronauts. After much testing, on 9 April 1959 he was named as one of the Mercury Seven. A relaxed, friendly prankster who took his duties seriously, Schirra made it seem as though he were breezing through the intense astronaut training. He established himself as an expert on life-support systems for the Mercury, Gemini, and Apollo programs, most notably helping to develop and test space suits.

The fifth manned Mercury mission was assigned to Schirra. There were problems with *Sigma 7*'s launch rockets and a fuel valve that delayed the launch from 28 September to 3 October 1962, when the craft was launched from Cape Canaveral, Florida. To determine whether long space-flights in the Mercury capsule were possible, he tested maneuvering the craft manually, even turning off all of the controls and letting it drift for three hours, twenty-six minutes. About three-fourths of the craft's fuel was still unspent when it splashed down near Midway Island, making that part of the mission successful. However, Schirra's space suit had overheated during the flight and thus required design changes. He remained inside the capsule while it was fished out of the water, becoming the first astronaut not to leave his craft prior to recovery. Schirra was hailed for his accomplishments on *Sigma 7* and visited with President John F. Kennedy.

With his successful maneuvering and fuel management on his Mercury flight, Schirra was assigned to one of the space program's most perilous missions. He and Thomas Stafford, one of the second group of astronauts, or New Nine selected in September 1962, were to test the feasibility of docking spacecraft together in space. The navy promoted Schirra to captain in 1965, a year in which the members of the troubled *Gemini 6* mission faced their worst problem: an explosion, before it reached orbit, of the unmanned rocket with which Schirra's craft was supposed to dock. Therefore, about an hour before launch on 25 October 1965, the *Gemini 6* mission was halted. The event underscored the dangers of Schirra and Stafford's mission.

The mission was changed to be a rendezvous between *Gemini 7* and *Gemini 6*. Part of the *Gemini 7* mission was to test the effects of long spaceflights on astronauts, and it had already been in orbit for eleven days before *Gemini 6* was finally launched on 15 December 1965. Six hours into their flight, Schirra and Stafford maneuvered their craft within six feet of *Gemini 7* and kept it there, proving that spacecraft could be controlled well enough to dock with each other.

The Apollo Moon mission program also was fraught with problems, with astronauts unhappy with poor systems designs and a badly designed hatch to the main capsule. On 27 January 1967 three astronauts were killed when the

interior of *Apollo 1* caught fire during testing. It was not until *Apollo 7* was launched on 11 October 1968 that the three-in-one craft was fully tested in outer space. Schirra commanded that mission, sharing the spacecraft with Donn Eisele (who piloted the command module) and Walter Cunningham (who piloted the lunar module). Schirra and his crew performed a wide variety of maneuvers and tests of the ship's engines to ascertain the craft's ability to function in the complex rendezvous and docking that would be required in an actual flight to the Moon. This flight was the first to have a full-time, fully functioning television camera to reveal the astronauts' activities.

After this successful flight, Schirra retired from both the space program and the navy in 1969. He moved to Colorado and served as a business executive and board member for a series of industrial companies in the 1970s and 1980s. He also provided television commentary for several space missions.

Schirra earned many honors during his years of military service, including three Distinguished Flying Crosses, two Air Medals, both the navy's and NASA's Distinguished Service Award, and an Exceptional Service Medal. In 1987 he was inducted into the National Aviation Hall of Fame. Schirra was one of the best-liked U.S. astronauts, with his quick wit and affable demeanor defusing tension in many difficult situations. His work in the 1960s on life-support systems helped to make the Apollo Moon missions more comfortable by eliminating unnecessary noises, making temperature controls easier to use, and making space suits not only safe but also flexible. His testing of ways to conserve fuel was essential to the eventual success of the Moon missions.

★

Schirra with Richard N. Billings, *Schirra's Space* (1988; rev. ed., 1995), offers the astronaut's own highly opinionated view of the history of America's space programs. Schirra is profiled in M. Scott Carpenter, et al., *We Seven, by the Astronauts Themselves* (1962). *Current Biography Yearbook* (1966) provides an adequate account of Schirra's early life. See the NASA website, "Walter M. Schirra," *Astronaut Bio*, for a brief summary of Schirra's accomplishments. This website also offers access to Courtney G. Brooks, James M. Grimwood, and Loyd S. Swenson, *Chariots for Apollo: A History of Manned Lunar Spacecraft* (1979), which includes an informative account of the *Apollo 7* flight.

KIRK H. BEETZ

SCHLAFLY, Phyllis Stewart (*b.* 15 August 1924 in St. Louis, Missouri), conservative political activist and author who rose in the ranks from local political agitator to influential player in national campaigns, where she brought the agenda of social conservatives to national attention as part of a resurgent New Right.

Schlafly is the elder of two children of John Bruce Stewart, a salesman, engineer, and staunch Republican, and Odile Dodge, a librarian. Schlafly attended mostly public schools until seventh grade, when she enrolled in the Sisters of the Sacred Heart's City House where she learned French, Latin, proper etiquette, and discipline in a challenging and academically rigorous environment. She earned her B.A. degree from St. Louis's Washington University in 1944, an education she financed by working forty-eight hours a week in a World War II ordnance plant, where she fired machine guns at night. Upon graduation she rejected a fellowship from Columbia University for a smaller stipend from Radcliffe College, Harvard University's sister school for women. Earning a M.A. degree in political science in 1945, she chose not to continue toward a Ph.D. but rather to move to Washington, D.C., where her interest in political science could take a more activist approach. Soon disillusioned by the size and scope of the federal government, Schlafly returned to St. Louis in 1946, where she ran the congressional campaign of a local Republican, Claude Bakewell, who beat the New Deal incumbent John Sullivan in an upset victory. On 20 October 1949 she married Fred Schlafly, a successful lawyer and political conservative; they have six children.

After marrying and moving to Alton, Illinois, Schlafly continued to immerse herself in civic and community organizations. In 1952 she ran for U.S. Congress from the Twenty-fourth Illinois District, a heavily Democratic county in which no woman had ever been a political candidate. In a campaign in which the press condescendingly focused almost exclusively on her gender, Schlafly won the April Republican primary but lost the election. She served as a 1956 delegate to the Republican National Convention, where she pledged her support to the reelection of Dwight D. Eisenhower and Richard M. Nixon, although she was sorry that Robert Taft had not earned the nomination four years earlier. Throughout the decade, Schlafly's anticommunist zeal intensified, although the 1950s were a mere prologue for what was to come. Schlafly's popularity and influence grew apace during the next two decades as she gained national notoriety.

In 1960 Schlafly attended the Republican National Convention as an alternate delegate pledged to Nixon. As president of the Illinois Federation of Republican Women (1956–1964) in the state hosting the convention, Schlafly picked Arizona senator Barry Goldwater as the keynote speaker at a convention luncheon honoring the fiftieth state, Hawaii. Disappointed by Nixon's compromises with the Republican Party's more liberal, Northeastern wing, Schlafly sought in Goldwater an unapologetic conservative to head the ticket in 1964. Getting the Grand Old Party (GOP) to agree that the Arizona senator represented the future for Republicans posed a major challenge. Seeking to bolster his chances, Schlafly wrote her first book, a history

Phyllis Schlafly. AP/WIDE WORLD PHOTOS

of Republican National Conventions entitled *A Choice Not an Echo* (1964). She began with the assertion, "Since 1936 the Republican presidential nominee has been selected by a small group of secret kingmakers who are the most powerful opinion makers in the world." In 1964, she argued, the kingmakers must be repudiated. "The Republican Party has one obvious, logical, deserving, winning candidate," Schlafly continued, Barry Goldwater, a candidate who "combines the integrity of Robert A. Taft, with the glamour of Dwight Eisenhower." The book, published and distributed by Schlafly, sold millions of copies (she claims that it is one of the ten best-selling conservative books of all time). More importantly, it helped invigorate the conservative wing of the GOP and paved the way for Goldwater's nomination. Shortly thereafter, more books followed on anticommunism and U.S. foreign policy, which demanded that policy makers take an uncompromising, unapologetic, hard line against the Soviet Union. Schlafly wrote twenty books on topics such as politics, education, gender studies, and foreign policy.

In 1967 Schlafly herself became the victim of the kingmakers. She had hoped to be elected president of the National Federation of Republican Women (NFRW) but was opposed by party leaders who, responding to Goldwater's embarrassing defeat, hoped to purge uncompromising ideologues from leadership. They built a strong anti-Schlafly movement, and, most likely with the help of rigged voting machines, ensured her defeat in the first-ever NFRW election. Disappointed, Schlafly returned to Alton, where in 1967 she began printing the *Phyllis Schlafly Report,* a monthly newsletter for her grassroots supporters around the country, which kept them abreast of current political events and encouraged them to become politically active. In 1968 she attended the GOP convention again, as a Nixon delegate. Running for Congress again in 1970, she was defeated—a defeat that ushered in a new phase of her career as the nation's foremost antifeminist.

Joining the battle over the ratification of the Equal Rights Amendment (ERA), Schlafly devoted her superb organizing and speaking skills to STOP-ERA, a lobbying group that she organized to defeat ratification. Mobilizing thousands of traditionally apolitical women through her newsletter and, later, her national volunteer organization, the Eagle Forum (founded in 1975), she worked tirelessly and ultimately successfully to bury the amendment. Schlafly also earned a law degree from the Washington University Law School in 1978 and has continued to speak out on numerous issues such as foreign policy, education, immigration, and "family values."

Schlafly's life is emblematic of many trends in post-war, twentieth-century politics. A devout Catholic and a devoted mother, few would have guessed during the 1950s that she would become an influential conservative leader. Helping

bring Goldwater to the front of the GOP in 1964, Schlafly contributed to both the GOP's shift to the right and to the political and ideological realignment that characterized U.S. politics in subsequent decades. A brilliant populist, she serves as the champion of those women who believe the two sexes are fundamentally different and that feminism is a threat to the norms and values that lend meaning to their lives. And as a beneficiary of the long tradition of progressive women leaders who created the space in American society that allowed her to emerge as a public figure, Schlafly used that space to argue that women's skills are best used in their traditional role as nurturer rather than achiever. Yet she has refused to set such limits on her own ambitions and abilities as she has embraced the causes in which she believes. Despite major ideological differences, Schlafly's own life represents a model of the growth, empowerment, and possibilities that feminists sought for all women.

★

Biographies of Schlafly include Carol Felsenthal, *The Sweetheart of the Silent Majority: The Biography of Phyllis Schlafly* (1981), and Peter N. Caroll, *Famous in America: The Passion to Succeed* (1985). Biographical information is also in Kevin Markey, *100 Most Important Women of the 20th Century* (1998). On Schlafly and the ERA see Jane Sherron DeHart and Donald G. Mathews, *Sex, Gender, and the Politics of ERA: A State and the Nation* (1990). Articles about Schlafly are in *Rolling Stone* (26 Nov. 1981), *Ms.* (Jan. 1982) and (Sept. 1982), and the *National Review* (19 Oct. 1992).

MATTHEW A. SUTTON

SCHLESINGER, Arthur Meier, Jr. (*b.* 15 October 1917 in Columbus, Ohio), historian, educator, liberal spokesperson, and author of two Pulitzer Prize–winning histories who served as a special adviser to President John F. Kennedy and is considered by many as the most notable public intellectual of the 1960s.

Schlesinger was one of two sons born to Arthur Meier Schlesinger, Sr., and Elizabeth Bancroft, a homemaker and descendant of the historian George Bancroft. His father was a noted historian who became a professor at Harvard University in Cambridge, Massachusetts. Schlesinger was educated at Phillips Exeter Academy in Exeter, New Hampshire, from 1931 to 1933. He then attended Harvard, studying history and graduating summa cum laude with a B.A. in 1938. After a year in England as a Henry Fellow at Peterhouse College at the University of Cambridge, Schlesinger was made a member of the Society of Fellows at Harvard. Since this award allowed him to teach at Harvard, he never earned a Ph.D. On 10 August 1940 he married Marian Cannon; they had four children and divorced in 1970.

Arthur M. Schlesinger, Jr. CORBIS CORPORATION (BELLEVUE)

During World War II, Schlesinger worked first for the Office of War Information from 1942 to 1943, and then for the Office of Strategic Services from 1943 to 1945. He was discharged from the U.S. Army in late 1945 with the rank of corporal. At the end of the war, Schlesinger's book *The Age of Jackson* (1945) was published; it became a best-seller and won the 1946 Pulitzer Prize for history. A year later Schlesinger was offered a tenured position in the history department at Harvard. He remained on the Harvard faculty until 1962, but lived in Washington, D.C., from early 1961 until Kennedy's assassination in 1962. Between 1957 and 1960 he published a three-volume history of the policies of President Franklin D. Roosevelt, *The Age of Roosevelt.*

In keeping with his liberal political views (referring to himself as "an unrepentant New Dealer"), Schlesinger helped to found Americans for Democratic Action in 1947 and became an influential figure in the Democratic Party. In the 1950s he served as a political adviser to Adlai Stevenson's presidential campaigns. In the early days of the 1960 presidential campaign, Schlesinger offered advice to three contenders for the nomination: Stevenson, Hubert Humphrey, and John F. Kennedy. Although he preferred

Stevenson, he decided to back Kennedy in view of the Massachusetts senator's strong showing in the primaries. In support of Kennedy's campaign, Schlesinger wrote *Kennedy or Nixon: Does It Make a Difference?* (1960). His basic precepts of liberalism were clearly spelled out in this short polemic: that political leadership belongs to those who truly understand the issues facing the United States; that these issues are health, education, equal opportunity, and environmental protection; and that people of education and wealth should be concerned with "the sufferings of the poor and the inequities of society."

In 1961, after Kennedy's victory, the new president asked Schlesinger to become a special assistant at the White House. Schlesinger took a two-year leave of absence from Harvard, and, when the two years were up, he resigned from his academic position in order to remain in Washington, D.C. Schlesinger performed several functions at the White House. He was Kennedy's liaison with Stevenson, the U.S. ambassador to the United Nations. Schlesinger also served as the president's contact with intellectuals and cultural figures. One Kennedy adviser, Theodore Sorensen, saw Schlesinger as a "lightning rod" to attract Republican attacks, deflecting them from the president. In addition, Schlesinger served as an adviser on Latin American affairs and was one of the few in Kennedy's inner circle to argue against U.S. involvement in the Bay of Pigs invasion in Cuba in April 1961, an early foreign policy debacle for the Kennedy administration. All accounts indicate that Kennedy appreciated Schlesinger's intellectual honesty and sense of humor.

In 1963 Schlesinger published a collection of essays, *The Politics of Hope,* in which he expressed the view that Kennedy, as a result of "his deep desire to improve the quality of life and opportunity in the United States," was having a positive and dynamic effect on the country. Kennedy's assassination on 22 November 1963 was a severe blow to Schlesinger, and he resigned from his White House post two months later. After the Bay of Pigs episode, Kennedy had asked Schlesinger to keep a journal of his White House experiences, and this record became the basis for his book on the Kennedy presidency, *A Thousand Days: John F. Kennedy in the White House* (1965). This best-seller, which deals mainly with foreign policy, earned Schlesinger the 1966 Pulitzer Prize for biography and a National Book Award.

Given his intimate involvement in U.S. political life, Schlesinger participated in the debate that erupted in the 1960s over the war in Vietnam. Although he initially opposed the withdrawal of U.S. influence, by the mid-1960s he came to support de-escalation, and expressed this view in *The Bitter Heritage: Vietnam and American Democracy, 1941–1966* (1966). Schlesinger supported Robert F. Kennedy's bid for the Democratic presidential nomination in 1968, serving as his political adviser until the New York senator's assassination in June 1968. A decade later Schlesinger published *Robert Kennedy and His Times* (1978), another National Book Award winner and best-seller.

Not surprisingly, Schlesinger was critical of the administration of Republican president Richard M. Nixon, and in 1973 he published *The Imperial Presidency,* an analysis of how power had come to be accumulated by presidents, particularly during the terms of Lyndon B. Johnson and Nixon. In *The Cycles of American History* (1986), Schlesinger argued, perhaps wishfully, that there were cycles of conservatism and liberalism in U.S. history, and that a trend toward liberalism was due. Although his prediction was not entirely accurate, the book reflected his deep insight into the political psyche of the American people. It also reflected Schlesinger's persuasive, yet graceful, writing style.

A slender man of average height known for his love of films, Schlesinger was immediately recognizable by his ever-present bow tie. He returned to university teaching in 1966, becoming the Albert Schweitzer Professor of Humanities at the City University of New York, a position he held until his retirement in 1995. Schlesinger served as president of the American Institute of Arts and Letters from 1981 to 1984, and was awarded a National Humanities Medal in 1998. After his divorce, he married Alexandra Emmet on 19 July 1971; they had two sons.

Many observers, including his political enemies, consider Schlesinger to be one of the leading political commentators and intellectuals of the twentieth century. Although it is occasionally difficult to distinguish in his writings where the neutral historian ends and the politically engaged intellectual begins, there is no doubt that his sixteen books on U.S. history and modern politics made important contributions to the public debates of his time. Certainly he was one of the foremost defenders of liberalism. In particular, in the early 1960s his advocacy of that ideology in the highest circles of power made Schlesinger the most politically influential intellectual of that decade.

★

Schlesinger's papers are at the John F. Kennedy Presidential Library at Columbia Point, Boston, Massachusetts. Schlesinger has published the first volume of his autobiography, *A Life in the Twentieth Century: Innocent Beginnings, 1917–1950* (2000). For studies of Schlesinger's ideology, see Stephen P. Depoe, *Arthur M. Schlesinger, Jr., and the Ideological History of American Liberalism* (1994); and John Patrick Diggins, *The Liberal Persuasion: Arthur Schlesinger, Jr., and the Challenge of the American Past* (1997). For biographical information, see Alejandro Benes, "The Guardian of Liberalism," *Cigar Aficionado* (1995); and William E. Leuchtenburg, "What Makes Arthur Tick?," *American Prospect* 12, no. 2 (29 Jan. 2001): 33–35.

ROBERT HENDRICK

SCHULLER, Gunther Alexander   (*b.* 22 November 1925 in New York City), composer, conductor, and musicologist who almost single-handedly forged "third stream" music, a combination of jazz and traditional western music.

Schuller was the son of Arthur E. Schuller, a violinist for the New York Philharmonic Orchestra, and Elsie Bernartz. As a boy he sang soprano in the St. Thomas Choir School in 1937, learned flute and French horn, and studied music theory at the Manhattan School of Music. He played the horn for the New York Philharmonic Orchestra, directed by Arturo Toscanini in 1942; the Ballet Theatre Orchestra in New York City in 1943; the Cincinnati Symphony Orchestra from 1943 to 1945; and New York City's Metropolitan Opera Orchestra from 1945 to 1959. Schuller also taught music at the Manhattan School of Music from 1950 to 1963. He married Marjorie Black on 8 June 1948; they had two children.

In 1959, after holding the position of principal French horn with the Metropolitan Opera Orchestra for fourteen years, Schuller became its musical composer. The first work he presented in this capacity, *Seven Studies on Themes of*

Gunther Schuller, 1967. ASSOCIATED PRESS AP

Paul Klee (1959), applied the principles of serial music—a style based on a series of tones in a particular pattern, chosen without consideration of traditional tonality—to the bold, surreal canvases of the expressionist artist. His "Twittering Machine" and "The Arab Village" are especially vivid passages within the larger work.

As the 1960s dawned, Schuller's work showcased a concept he had long been considering in his capacity as a music theorist and teacher: the idea of "third stream" music, a combination of jazz (an American music form with African roots) and western styles from classical to serial composition. In Schuller's mind, western music could benefit from the rhythms and the improvisational, impromptu techniques of jazz, while jazz would be well served by incorporating the discipline and structure of western styles. His career has been largely devoted to the synthesis of these styles.

During the early 1960s, Schuller received numerous grants and awards—two Guggenheim fellowships (1962, 1963), a Brandeis University Creative Arts award (1960), and others—that made it possible for him to pursue his compositions and his "third stream" ideas without concern for earning a secondary income as a teacher. During this time he sharpened his knowledge of jazz by working with John Lewis of the Modern Jazz Quartet. Among his other work during the 1960s, Schuller served as music director of the First International Jazz Festival in Washington, D.C., in 1962; as acting director from 1963 to 1965, and as head of the composition department from 1965 to 1969 at the Berkshire Music Center in Boston University's Tanglewood Institute; associate professor of composition at Yale University; and organizer and conductor for the "Twentieth Century Innovations" concert series at Carnegie Hall from 1963 to 1965.

In 1965, while serving briefly as a composer in residence in Berlin, Schuller completed *The Visitation,* an opera first produced in Hamburg the following year. The libretto was a double adaptation; taken from Franz Kafka's novel *The Trial,* it was recast with African-American characters in the southern United States. Perhaps because of the underlying racial themes and the existing tensions over segregation and civil rights in the United States, the opera—a classic example of "third stream" music—did not fare well when subsequently presented in that country. Other Schuller compositions of the 1960s and early 1970s include *Spectra* (1960), *Six Renaissance Lyrics* (1962), *String Quartet No. 2* (1965), *Symphony* (1965), *The Fisherman and His Wife* (opera, 1970), *Capriccio Stravagante* (1972), *The Power Within Us* (1972), and *Tre Invenzioni* (1972).

Although Schuller's first published book focused on a highly specialized topic—*Horn Technique* (1962)—his second was a 401-page tome on the early history of jazz, with emphasis on its African roots. Of *Early Jazz: Its Roots and Musical Development* (1968), Frank Conroy wrote in the *New York Times Book Review,* "Here, at last, is the definitive work" on the subject. Two decades later, Stanley Crouch was even more effusive. The book, he maintained, "brought a sometimes Olympian precision to writing about an art that has often languished in the whale's belly of sociology, obscured by pretension and blubbery thinking." The occasion of Crouch's observations was the publication of *The Swing Era: The Development of Jazz, 1930–1945* (1989), which Schuller has promised will be followed by another work to complete the history as a trilogy.

Although he left the Metropolitan Opera Orchestra in 1967, Schuller stayed very busy. He served as director of the Berkshire Music Center from 1969 to 1984 and as president of the New England Conservatory of Music from 1967 to 1977. In the latter capacity, he presented the conservatory's ragtime ensemble in 1972, catalyzing a revival of ragtime music. As founder, in 1975, of Margun Music, a publishing company devoted to the principal that "all musics are created equal," Schuller has continued to pursue his goal of synthesizing musical styles.

Additionally, Schuller worked as music director of the Spokane Symphony in Spokane, Washington, from 1985 to 1986, and as artistic director of the Festival at Sandpoint, Idaho, from 1985. He has been a regular feature on the weekly radio series *Contemporary Music in Evolution* on WBAI-Radio in New York City and has made guest appearances as conductor for ensembles that include the British Broadcasting Corporation (BBC) Symphony, the Berlin Philharmonic, the French Radio Orchestra, and the Tonhalle Orchestra in Zurich. In 1994 he published *The Compleat Conductor,* a detailed examination of the varying interpretations of eight symphonic works. Schuller also won the 1994 Pulitzer Prize in music for *Of Reminiscences and Reflections.*

The presentation accompanying the Alice M. Ditson Award from Columbia University in 1970 aptly characterizes the scope of Schuller's career. "You have already achieved distinction in six careers," it said, "as conductor, as composer, as horn virtuoso and orchestral musician, and as author and educator." With his vast musical knowledge, his boundless energy, and his ever-inventive wellspring of creativity, Schuller has contributed immeasurably to the American musical lexicon.

★

The only full-length book on Schuller is Norbert Carnovale, *Gunther Schuller: A Bio-Bibliography* (1987). Also noteworthy are Gilbert Chase, ed., *The American Composer Speaks: A Historical Anthology, 1770–1965* (1966); David Ewen, *The World of Twentieth-Century Music* (1968) and *American Composers: A Biographical Dictionary* (1982), which contain short biographical sketches and analyses of the composer's work; and Schuller's own work, *Musings: The Musical Worlds of Gunther Schuller* (1986). *Down Beat* (Sept. 1993) profiled Schuller when it bestowed on him its Hall of Fame and Lifetime Achievement awards.

JUDSON KNIGHT

SCHWERMER, Michael Henry. *See* Chaney, James Earl, Andrew Goodman, and Michael Henry Schwerner.

SCHWINGER, Julian Seymour (*b.* 12 February 1918 in New York City; *d.* 16 July 1994 in Los Angeles, California), physicist and educator whose pioneering work in quantum electrodynamics (QED) successfully reconciled quantum mechanics with special relativity and earned him (along with Richard Feynman and Sin-Itiro Tomonaga) the Nobel Prize for physics in 1965.

Raised in a middle-class family in the Jewish Harlem section of New York City, Schwinger was the younger of two sons born to Benjamin Schwinger, a dressmaker, and Belle Rosenfeld, both Eastern European Jewish immigrants. As a youth, he was curious and bright, reading books on physics and math and attending Townsend Harris High School for gifted students, where he skipped three grades and graduated at the age of fourteen. Schwinger began at the City College of New York in 1934, but with the help of Isidore I. Rabi, he graduated with a B.A. from Columbia University in 1936 at the age of seventeen. Schwinger received a Ph.D. from Columbia in 1939, and subsequently began teaching at the University of California, Berkeley, under the tutelage of J. Robert Oppenheimer. He accepted a job at Purdue University two years later, but took leave in 1943 to research microwaves in pursuit of radar at the Massachusetts Institute of Technology's (MIT) Radiation Laboratory and the Metallurgical Laboratory in Chicago. After being recruited to Harvard University in 1945, Schwinger found both prestige and love in 1947, becoming one of the youngest full professors in Harvard history and marrying Clarice Carrol of Boston. They had no children.

Schwinger began reaping the rewards of his monumental efforts as he received the Nature of Light Award of the National Academy of Sciences (1949) and the first Einstein Prize (1951), which he shared with Kurt Gödel. He was granted honorary doctorates from Purdue (1961) and Harvard (1962) and given the National Medal of Science (1964) by President Lyndon B. Johnson. On 11 December 1965 Schwinger received the Nobel Prize for physics with fellow QED pioneers Feynman and Tomonaga.

The 1960s were prolific years in which Schwinger published nearly a third of his 150 total articles. In one article of 1964 titled "The Future of Fundamental Physics," he offered some thoughts on the role of science in society. The author reiterated key questions in nuclear physics and argued that experimental techniques must play a role in the study of the properties of matter. If not, the United States risked the intellectual fate of China in the fifteenth century when it halted its maritime adventures and lost ground to the West when Portuguese ships rounded the Cape of Good Hope.

A four-article series, "Field Theory of Matter," exemplified Schwinger's commitment to innovative scientific methods. In these essays, as well as in books such as *Field Theory of Particles* (1965), *Field Theory of Matter* (1966), *Discontinuities in Waveguides* (1968), *Particles and Sources* (1969), and *Quantum Kinematics and Dynamics* (1970), Schwinger advocated a new paradigm for the study of the magnetic fields created by charged particles. Unsatisfied with quantum field theory (a principle he and his colleagues had formulated), he hypothesized the new source theory. With intellectual support only from his own students, he argued that mathematical measurements of physical properties are not just measurements of the created field but are in fact measurements of the particles and of the particle interaction that engender the field. In short, the hypothesis held that the properties of the magnetic field are a product as much of the interaction between individual particles as of the particles themselves.

In addition, Schwinger penned works on the quantum action principle (also known as Schwinger's action principle) and measurement algebra, two techniques he created to make better sense of the quantum world. Closing out his work on source theory, he also published papers on quantum gravitation and magnetism.

Schwinger traveled extensively, seeing Belgium in 1961, and then visiting Mayan ruins in Mexico to satisfy his interest in archeology in 1962. Also in 1962, he taught in Leningrad for three weeks as an exchange professor before traveling to Moscow. Schwinger went on sabbatical to Paris in 1963 and also visited Italy, Yugoslavia, Austria, and Switzerland before arriving in Sweden in 1965.

?In the activist decade of the 1960s, Schwinger was politically conscious but not politically active. He was a member of the American Civil Liberties Union, the National Academy of Sciences, and a sponsor of the *Bulletin of Atomic Scientists,* a publication created by former Manhattan Project scientists to advocate nuclear arms control. Yet only three petitions bear his name and all were signed in 1975. One called for the awarding of the Nobel Peace Prize to Russian physicist Andrei Sakharov, another condemned astrology, and the last resisted the proliferation of nuclear power.

Through the 1960s Schwinger's views paralleled those of other politically aware scientists, including Albert Einstein. Like Einstein, he hoped that humankind was moving away from war as a means of deciding issues, evidenced by the growing public dissent over U.S. involvement in Vietnam. Moreover, Schwinger found little difference between Western and Communist scientists during his brief stay in the Soviet Union in 1962. From this experience, he thought intellectual freedom was a point on which the superpowers could agree, precipitating a lessening of tensions and instilling hope for a peaceful end to the cold war.

In his leisure time, Schwinger read science fiction, played tennis, enjoyed swimming and skiing, played the piano, and savored time with his wife and his cats (including one named Galileo).

Schwinger left Harvard in 1972 and accepted his final position at the University of California, Los Angeles (UCLA). The department of Physics and Astronomy at UCLA has a fellowship named after Schwinger. A meticulous and brilliant lecturer, he trained around seventy graduate students, three of whom won Nobel Prizes of their own. Despite his monumental contributions to physics, as a scientist he has typically been overshadowed by Feynman, whose outgoing personality starkly contrasted with Schwinger's shy, reserved, and unassuming ways. His well-known solitary work habits grew more acute in his final years as he moved from QED into studies of cold fusion. Working until the very end, Schwinger died of pancreatic cancer at his home in the Los Angeles neighborhood of Bel-Air.

★

Schwinger's papers are held in the Department of Special Collections, University Research Library, University of California, Los Angeles. The only full-length biography of Schwinger is Kimball A. Milton and Jagdish Mehra, *Climbing the Mountain: The Scientific Biography of Julian Schwinger* (2000). James Gleick, *Genius: The Life and Science of Richard Feynman* (1992), has biographical information about Schwinger. Another fine biographical source is Silvan S. Schweber, *QED and the Men Who Made It: Dyson, Feynman, Schwinger, and Tomonaga* (1994). For less technical information, see Jeremy Bernstein, "Julian," *American Scholar* (1995): 241–246, and a collection of articles by Schwinger's acquaintances edited by Y. Jack Ng, *Julian Schwinger: The Physicist, the Teacher, and the Man* (1996). An obituary is in *The Scientist* (5 Sept. 1994).

BRIAN MADISON JONES

SCOTT, George C(ampbell) (*b.* 18 October 1927 in Wise, Virginia; *d.* 22 September 1999 in Westlake Village, California), film, television, and stage actor whose career reached its apex in the decade between the films *The Hustler* (1961) and *Patton* (1970).

Born in the mining country of western Virginia, Scott was one of two children of George C. and Helena Scott. The coming of the Great Depression forced a move to Detroit, where his father worked in the Buick automobile plant.

George C. Scott as General Patton in the movie *Patton,* 1969. © BETT-MANN/CORBIS

Scott's mother, an amateur poet, died when he was eight, and his sister helped raised him. In 1945 Scott graduated from Detroit's Redford High School and joined the U.S. Marines. However, the war was nearing its conclusion, so the marines put him to work burying the dead at Arlington National Cemetery in Arlington, Virginia.

Discharged in 1949, Scott enrolled on the GI Bill in the journalism program at the University of Missouri, Columbia. There Scott first discovered his abilities as an actor, appearing in a student production of Terence Rattigan's *The Winslow Boy.* Later he would say of acting that, for him, it "clicked, just like tumblers in a safe." Soon he realized that he cared more for the stage than for journalism, so he left school in 1950. During the next six years, Scott appeared in more than 125 stock theater productions in Toledo, Ohio; Ontario, Canada; and Washington, D.C. In 1956 Scott moved to New York City, where he paid his bills by working as an operator of a check-sorting machine in a bank while he searched for acting jobs.

Although his life in those early days on the road might have been better suited to a single man, Scott was actually married twice. In August 1951 he married actress Carolyn Hughes, a union that lasted until March 1955. At some point during the late 1950s (biographies of Scott are vague on the matter of his first two marriages), he was married to another actress, Patricia Reed, with whom he had three children. Scott also had a child who was born out of wedlock while Scott was in college.

Scott's breakthrough came in 1957 with a title role in Joseph Papp's Shakespeare Festival stage production of *Richard III*. Parts in *As You Like It* and *Children of Darkness* followed in 1958, the year of his Broadway debut in *Comes a Day*. Already seasoned by his performance as Shakespeare's sociopathic king, Scott again displayed his talent for playing malevolent characters with his Tydings Glenn, who tortures birds. That performance earned him his first Tony Award nomination, followed by a second for *The Andersonville Trial* (1959). His stage performances in the late 1950s won him an Obie and Theatre World awards, but these would be some of the only ones he was to accept: by the beginning of the 1960s, if not earlier, Scott had come to believe that awards were a farce that encouraged cutthroat competition between actors.

In 1958 Scott emerged on the national scene with several television performances, most notably "A Tale of Two Cities" on the *Dupont Show of the Month* for the Columbia Broadcasting System (CBS). The following year marked his film debut with *The Hanging Tree* (1959), in which he played Dr. George Grubb, an enraged alcoholic who incites his neighbors to hang a man. He followed this with an even more significant supporting role as Claude Dancer in Otto Preminger's *Anatomy of a Murder* (1959), in which he was pitted against Jimmy Stewart in blistering courtroom scenes that earned him his first Academy Award nomination.

A second Academy Award nomination followed for *The Hustler* (1961), in which Scott played a memorable supporting role as Bert Gordon, a pool shark. Although this was his most well-known performance of the early 1960s, Scott stayed active in film, on television, and on stage in the years from 1960 to 1962. During this time he performed on television as Gordon Cross in "The Burning Court" on the National Broadcasting Company's (NBC) *Dow Hour of Great Mysteries* (1960); as the devil in "Don Juan in Hell" on the syndicated *Play of the Week* (1960); as Lord Henry Wotton in CBS's *The Picture of Dorian Gray* (1961); and as a police lieutenant in the CBS miniseries *The Power and the Glory* (1961). Additionally, he appeared in episodes of *Ben Casey* (1961), *Naked City* (1962), *The Virginian* (1962), and *The Eleventh Hour* (1962). The *Ben Casey* role earned him an Emmy nomination. Scott's stage performances in New York City include appearances as Dolek Berson in *The Wall* at the Billy Rose Theatre (1960); in the title role in *General Seeger* at the Lyceum (1962); and as Shylock in *The Merchant of Venice* at the Delacorte Theatre during the New York Shakespeare Festival (1962).

Another memorable film role came in 1964, when Scott played General "Buck" Turgidson in director Stanley Kubrick's *Dr. Strangelove; or, How I Learned to Stop Worrying and Love the Bomb*. Not only did his performance show that Scott had a talent for comedy, but Scott had fun with the role and later said that he enjoyed making *Dr. Strangelove* so much that he almost felt guilty getting paid for his work. Additionally, the film marked his first significant performance as a military figure, giving him experience that would contribute to his most important motion picture six years later.

Scott's other film appearances during the mid-1960s include his first leading role in *The List of Adrian Messenger* (1963), a mystery directed by John Huston; *The Yellow Rolls-Royce* (1964), written by Rattigan; Huston's *The Bible* (1966), in which Scott played Abraham; and Norman Panama's *Not With My Wife You Don't!* (1966). Scott had his first regular role on a television series in the highly acclaimed but short-lived *East Side, West Side* (1963–1964), and he appeared in "A Time for Killing" on NBC's *Bob Hope Presents the Chrysler Theatre* (1965), and one episode of *The Road West* (1966). Also during the period from 1963 to 1966, Scott performed on the New York stage in *Desire Under the Elms* (1963) and in the London debut of *The Three Sisters* (1965).

Both *The Yellow Rolls-Royce* and *Not With My Wife You Don't!* were comedies, and with *The Flim-Flam Man* (1967), Scott once again displayed his comedic talents to good advantage, this time as a con artist named Mordecai. Other film work from the late 1960s includes performances in *Petulia* (1968), alongside Julie Christie, and in *This Savage Land* (1969), which brought together several episodes of *The Road West* television series. Scott played John Proctor on CBS's *The Crucible* (1967) and appeared on *Johnny Carson's Repertory Company* special (1969). On the New York stage he acted in *The Little Foxes* at the Vivian Beaumont Theatre (1967) and played three different roles in *Plaza Suite* at the Plymouth Theatre in 1968.

The greatest role of Scott's career came in 1970, when he played General George S. Patton. Coming as it did at a time when antiwar sentiment was at its height, *Patton* might at first have seemed ill timed, but in fact the opposite proved to be the case. The film spoke not only to establishment figures—it was supposedly President Richard M. Nixon's favorite movie, and stories of repeated solitary screenings at the White House became legendary—but to the counterculture as well. This appeal to youth is not surprising, given the fact that the Patton of the film is a rebel, a visionary, and a dreamer, who even believes in reincarnation.

Even Patton's militarism, set against the backdrop of a war that took place twenty-five years earlier, comported with the views of those who opposed the war in Southeast Asia. On a superficial level, of course, his strident speeches present a call to arms for those who sought victory in Vietnam and the restoration of order at home. But from another perspective, Patton seems to be saying, over and over, that war is hell, and that if one is to fight in a war at all, one had best be entirely committed to the cause.

Under Scott's masterful treatment, the character was at once a soldier and a nonconformist, and he played both aspects of Patton's personality to such a height that the resulting characterization might have seemed hyperbolic in the hands of a lesser actor. Scott's Patton could be intimidating, as in the opening speech before a U.S. flag; brutal, as in the scene in which he slaps a soldier who claims to have battle fatigue; tender, as when he kisses the cheek of a dead combat soldier; and even charming, as when speaking to a group of ladies in London. Seldom has an actor so fully inhabited a character as Scott did Patton, and even the similarity of their names—George C. and George S.— bespoke an affinity that seemed to destine Scott for the role.

Given the brilliance of his performance, Scott was a virtual shoo-in for the best actor Academy Award in 1970, which he won. Scott, however, refused the award, the first actor ever to do so. Scott chose instead to stay home in bed, and in so doing, he set the stage for Marlon Brando's rejection of the Oscar for *The Godfather* two years later. Scott later called the Academy Award ceremonies "a two-hour meat parade, a public display with contrived suspense for economic reasons." His snub, however, did not stop Academy members from nominating him for the award again the following year, this time for his performance in Paddy Chayevsky's *The Hospital* (1971).

Throughout the 1960s, Scott was married to actress Colleen Dewhurst—twice. The first union, from 1960 to July 1965, brought two children, including Campbell (born 19 July 1961), who became a famous actor in his own right. Then, after being divorced for two years, Scott and Dewhurst remarried on 4 July 1967, only to divorce again for a second and final time on 2 February 1972. Not long afterward, on 14 September, Scott married another actress, Trish Van Devere, who was nearly sixteen years his junior.

Scott made more than two dozen feature films after *Patton*, including *They Might Be Giants* (1971); *Rage*, which he also directed (1972); *The Day of the Dolphin* (1973); *The Hindenburg* (1975); *Islands in the Stream* (1977); *Hardcore* (1979); and *The Changeling* (1980). As General Harlan Bache in *Taps* (1981), he worked with unknowns, most notably Tom Cruise and Sean Penn, who would dominate film in the next decades. Scott made another two dozen television movies and miniseries, including a performance as Benito Mussolini in the NBC miniseries *Mussolini: The Untold Story* (1985). He also reprised his most famous role with *The Last Days of Patton* on CBS in 1986. Additionally, Scott had numerous appearances on television specials and episodic series and had a regular role on the short-lived Fox series *Mr. President* (1987–1988). He also won an Emmy

in 1997 playing Juror #3 in the television remake of *12 Angry Men*.

Scott died from a ruptured abdominal aortic aneurysm just after completing a television version of the courtroom drama *Inherit the Wind* (1999). In recognition of Scott, who had continued to appear in and direct stage plays during the last three decades of his life, Broadway dimmed its lights for one minute. He is buried at Westwood Memorial Park in Los Angeles.

No one who has ever seen the electrifying opener of *Patton* can forget Scott's performance. What is remarkable is that the entire scene consists of just one actor with minimal props: his full military regalia, complete with swagger stick and star-bedecked helmet, and behind him a gargantuan U.S. flag. Against this backdrop, Scott proceeds to address the viewer as a drill sergeant would a recruit, and the message is clear—sit up and take notice of what you are about to see. This was Scott at his most intimidating, a role he perfected off-screen as well. A heavy drinker, he had his nose broken in multiple barroom fights, and once, when an actress complained to director Mike Nichols that she was afraid of Scott, Nichols replied, "My dear, *everyone* is scared of George." Yet Scott could also be sensitive, both on-screen and off, and with his passing, actors of all generations were aware of a great loss. In eulogizing Scott, Tony Randall called him "the greatest actor in American history," while Jack Lemmon said of him, "George was truly one of the greatest and most generous actors I have ever known."

★

The sole biography of Scott is W. Allen Harbinson, *George Scott: The Man, The Actor, and the Legend* (1977). An article on Scott by Rex Reed appears in Elizabeth Weis, ed., *The Movie Star* (1981). Obituaries are in the *New York Times* and *USA Today* (both 23 Sept. 1999); the *Washington Post, Chicago Tribune*, Manchester (England) *Guardian* (all 24 Sept. 1999); *Variety* (27 Sept. 1999); and *Science Fiction Chronicle* (Feb./Mar. 2000).

JUDSON KNIGHT

SEABORG, Glenn Theodore (*b.* 19 April 1912 in Ishpeming, Michigan; *d.* 25 February 1999 in Lafayette, California), nuclear chemist, cowinner of the 1951 Nobel Prize in chemistry, longtime chair of the Atomic Energy Commission, and the only scientist to have an element named after him (seaborgium) while still alive.

Seaborg's parents were the Swedish immigrants Herman Theodore, a machinist, and Selma Erickson Seaborg. When Seaborg was ten, his mother urged the family to move to southern California, where she believed Seaborg and his sister could get a better education than in the iron-mining town in the Upper Peninsula of Michigan where

Glenn T. Seaborg. THE LIBRARY OF CONGRESS

they were born. Seaborg graduated from David Attar Jordan High School in Los Angeles in 1929, the valedictorian of his class. Educated at the University of California, Los Angeles, where he originally enrolled as a literature major, Seaborg received a B.A. in 1934 and did his graduate work at the University of California, Berkeley, where he received his Ph.D. in chemistry in 1937 under the direction of Gilbert N. Lewis.

At Berkeley he was a research associate to Lewis from 1937 to 1939, and they published a number of scientific papers together. In 1939 Seaborg and Emilio Segrè were the codiscoverers of technetium 99m, a radioisotope used extensively in nuclear medicine. That same year Seaborg was made an instructor, then an assistant professor in 1941, interrupted by his participation in the Manhattan Project in Chicago, and became a full professor of chemistry in 1946. That year he was also named as the director of nuclear research at the Ernest Orlando Lawrence Berkeley National Laboratory. Seaborg married Helen L. Griggs, Lawrence's secretary, on 6 June 1942; they eventually had six children.

From 1940 to 1957 Seaborg and his coworkers added ten new elements to the periodic table (atomic numbers 94

to 102 and 106). Seaborg discovered plutonium in February 1941 after bombarding a sample of uranium with deuterons and transmuting it to plutonium, using the 60-inch cyclotron built by Lawrence. Plutonium is the best known of the elements Seaborg discovered because of its use as a nuclear explosive and for nuclear power. The plutonium 238 isotope was discovered in 1940; the fissionable plutonium 239 isotope in 1941.

Beginning in April 1942, Seaborg's extensive knowledge of radioactive materials prompted his participation during World War II in the Manhattan Project (the U.S. effort to create an atomic bomb) as a section chief at the University of Chicago Metallurgical Laboratory. There he was responsible for isolating plutonium from the reaction products of the newly devised uranium reactors. However, he opposed dropping the bomb on Japan, foreshadowing his later advocacy for the peaceful use of nuclear energy.

Seaborg's research group also discovered americium (atomic number 95) in 1944; curium (96) in 1944 to 1945; berkelium (97) in 1949; californium (98) in 1949; einsteinium (99), identified from nuclear explosion debris, in 1952; fermium (100), identified in 1955 from the decay of nuclear explosion products; mendelevium (101) in 1955; nobelium (102), discovered in 1957 at the Nobel Institute of Physics in Stockholm; and seaborgium (106) in 1974, created by a team at Berkeley. Seaborgium was officially named in 1997, the first time an element had been named for a living person. All of these elements are radioactive, and none occurs to any appreciable extent in nature; they are synthesized by transmutation reactions in a laboratory setting.

Seaborg worked extensively on reorganizing the periodic table to show the relationship of the new elements to those already known. In 1944 he enunciated the actinide concept, which states that the fourteen elements heavier than actinium belong in a separate group in the periodic table, forming a transition series analogous to the rare earth series of lanthanide elements. This concept had great impact on predicting the chemical properties and placements of heavy elements on the table, and it was one of the most significant changes in the design of the periodic table since its creation. Seaborg and his group were also responsible for identifying more than 100 isotopes of elements through the periodic table.

The information assembled in Seaborg's laboratory had made possible the prediction of radioactive characteristics of isotopes and elements yet to be found. Not only that, whole new bodies of methodology and instrumentation developed during that research became a cornerstone of nuclear chemistry.

From 1947 to 1950 Seaborg served on the first General Advisory Committee for the Atomic Energy Commission (AEC), chaired by Robert Oppenheimer. He shared the 1951 Nobel Prize in chemistry with Edwin McMillan for research into the transuranium elements. He was Berkeley's chancellor from 1958 to 1961, overseeing an extensive building program that included the new College of Environmental Design and the Space Sciences Laboratory, and he served as a member of the President's Science Advisory Committee (1959–1961). President Dwight D. Eisenhower selected him for the National Science Foundation's National Science Board (1960–1961). In 1961 President John F. Kennedy appointed him to the chairmanship of the AEC (later the U.S. Department of Energy). He held that position from 1961 to 1971 under the administrations of presidents Kennedy, Lyndon Johnson, and Richard Nixon, longer than any other chair. During this time Seaborg lived in Washington, D.C., on leave from Berkeley. He encouraged both the rapid growth of the U.S. nuclear power industry and the peaceful uses of nuclear energy.

In 1971 Seaborg returned to the Berkeley campus as the associate director of the Lawrence Radiation Laboratory until 1975. He was named the University Professor of Chemistry and appointed as the first chair of the Lawrence Hall of Science (which he cofounded) in 1984. A champion of science education, Seaborg was a member of President Ronald Reagan's National Commission on Excellence in Education, which produced the 1983 landmark report *A Nation at Risk: The Imperative for Educational Reform*. He was a primary mover for the Internet resource for science teachers, "Great Exploration in Math and Science."

Seaborg was an advocate for nuclear arms control, international cooperation in science, and conservation of natural resources. He wrote more than five hundred scientific articles, including comprehensive reviews, compilations, and books, including his autobiography, *A Chemist in the White House: From the Manhattan Project to the End of the Cold War* (1988). He held more than forty patents, including the only patents issued for chemical elements, americium and curium. His honors included the American Chemical Society Award in Pure Chemistry (1947), Perkin Medal of the American Section of the Society of Chemical Industry (1957), AEC Enrico Fermi Award for outstanding work in the field of nuclear chemistry and for his leadership in scientific and educational affairs (1959), Franklin Medal (1963), and National Medal of Science (1991). He also received more than fifty honorary degrees.

A former president of the American Association for the Advancement of Science (1972) and the American Chemical Society (1976), Seaborg was also a fellow of the American Institute of Chemists, a member of the National Academy of Sciences, and a fellow of the American Physical Society, among others. Seaborg remained an active figure in the science and education fields until his death at age eighty-six from complications of a stroke. The Lawrence Berkeley National Laboratory named its IBM supercomputer Seaborg in his honor in August 1999.

Seaborg made significant contributions to the field of chemistry and to science education throughout his career. In particular in the 1960s, he worked to improve the quality of science teaching, interest young people in science careers, promote greater scientific literacy, and encourage scientists' understanding of social problems.

★

Seaborg's diaries are held by the University of California, Los Angeles Library, Department of Special Collections. Documents pertaining to the period when he was the chancellor of the University of California, Berkeley, are in the University Archives of the Bancroft Library at Berkeley. In addition to Seaborg's autobiography, *A Chemist in the White House: From the Manhattan Project to the End of the Cold War* (1988), see also his *The Transuranium Elements* (1958), *Education and the Atom* (1964), *Man and Atom* (1971), and *Kennedy, Khrushchev, and the Test Ban* (1981). H. Peter Metzger, *The Atomic Establishment* (1972), discusses Seaborg's leadership of the AEC; see also Rae Goodall, *The Visible Scientists* (1977). Obituaries are in the *New York Times* and *Washington Post* (both 27 Feb. 1999).

MARIA PACHECO

SEALE, Robert George ("Bobby") (*b.* 22 October 1936 in Dallas, Texas), cofounder of the Black Panther Party for Self-Defense, author, and revolutionary.

Seale was the eldest of three children, with one sister and one brother. His father, George, worked as a carpenter and his mother, Thelma, was a homemaker. The Seale family moved from Dallas to Port Arthur, Texas, and then to San Antonio, before finally settling in Oakland, California, during World War II. Seale attended Oakland High School, but left before graduating and joined the U.S. Air Force. He was dishonorably discharged in 1958 after three years and four months. Returning to Oakland, he worked as a sheet-metal mechanic at Kaiser Aerospace Electronics for eighteen months, earning his high school diploma through night school. In 1962 he enrolled at Oakland City College (now Merritt College). At college, he joined the Afro-American Association (AAA), a campus organization that stressed black separatism and self-improvement, where he met the activist Huey P. Newton in September 1962. Seale married his first wife, Artie, in 1965; they had one child and later divorced. He married Leslie Johnson in approximately 1974.

Seale's role in the creation and popularization of the Black Panther Party for Self-Defense (BPP) was complementary to that of Huey P. Newton's. While Newton's writing focused on the theoretical and ideological aspects of the BPP, Seale specialized in narrative and description. His 1970 book, *Seize the Time: The Story of The Black Panther Party and Huey P. Newton,* uses the voice of the

Bobby Seale. CORBIS CORPORATION (BELLEVUE)

African-American community in its vernacular and its turns of phrase. Seale, who was beginning to make a name for himself in local productions as an actor and comedian, had an awareness of audience and an ability to hold a person's attention that Newton lacked. Newton recognized this talent early on and realized its value in persuasion. In his autobiography, *Revolutionary Suicide,* Newton said of Seale that he was an excellent mimic who could "do" several celebrities as well as members of local rival organizations. "I would crack my sides laughing not only because his imitations were so good, but because he could convey certain attitudes and characteristics so sharply."

Seale also shared fellow Black Panther Eldridge Cleaver's respect and admiration for Newton. The title of his book is an indication of his tendency to put Newton above himself and to give him his due as the true motivating force behind the formation of the Black Panther Party. (The phrase "for Self-Defense" was dropped soon after the Party's founding.) His accounts of the creation of the Ten Point Platform and Program and of the conduct of the confrontations with the police always give Newton credit for all the ideas and their articulation. One time when Seale was the center of attention, however, was the Panther visit to the California legislature on 2 May 1967. He read a

statement written by Newton and corrected by Cleaver. Newton received full credit for "Executive Mandate Number One," though, and Seale relates that "Huey P. Newton had ordered me to take [it] to the Capitol." This event first put the Black Panthers in the national news, and Seale was the Panther the entire country saw on television, as well as the one who was arrested. He served time from 8 August until 8 December 1967.

While Seale was in jail, Huey Newton had a confrontation with two Oakland police officers that left Newton and one officer wounded, and the other officer dead. Newton was charged with murder. From that moment, Seale devoted himself to planning how to help his fellow Panther. When he was released, he worked tirelessly with Eldridge Cleaver in the "Free Huey" campaign, refusing even to hold down a job so he would have more time available for the cause. During this period he began the tape recordings that became his book, *Seize the Time.* He billed it as "the true story of the Black Panther Party." Its major goal was to create sympathy for Huey Newton, who is held up as a role model and inspiration throughout the work.

On 17 February 1968, Seale and Cleaver organized a "birthday party" rally for Huey Newton at the Oakland Coliseum, located in full view of the Oakland County Jail in which Newton was being held. The speakers included not only Panthers, but also Student Nonviolent Coordinating Committee (SNCC) figures H. Rap Brown and Stokely Carmichael. This event was intended to demonstrate black unity, but whether there was to be a "merger" or a "coalition" between the two groups was unclear. Cooperation between the two organizations was brief because of a fundamental difference in philosophies: under Carmichael, SNCC had become a black separatist organization, whereas the Black Panthers, while rejecting white oppression, did not reject white people.

The need for Huey's defense led Seale and Cleaver to select a radical white lawyer named Charles Garry, who was willing to work without a retainer, in order to get the defense started. Their coalition with the mostly white Peace and Freedom Party (PFP), which offered $3,000 for the defense fund as well as the loan of sound equipment in return for black voters registering under their party name, created negative feelings among some in the black community. Many, especially lawyers, wanted a black lawyer to represent the BPP and anyone associated with it; further, they thought that a black nationalist group such as the Panthers should stay separate from white groups.

In accord with their professed beliefs, however, Seale and Cleaver stuck with these decisions and worked together to defy racism of all varieties. Seale condemned those with "their little racist hang-ups." Cleaver published the speech he had given to the Peace and Freedom Foundation Convention earlier that year, entitled "Revolution in the White

Mother Country and National Liberation in the Black Colony," in a 1968 issue of the *North American Review,* a mainstream, liberal, intellectual publication. Both Seale and Cleaver were cynical about the commitment of opportunistic black radicals as compared with idealistic white revolutionaries. In 1968 Seale ran for the California State Assembly, and Newton ran for Congress from the Seventh Congressional District on the PFP ticket.

Because he was briefly present to make a speech in Chicago during the Democratic National Convention in August 1968, Seale was arrested for conspiracy to incite a riot. Thus, he became one of the Chicago Eight, and was arrested in August and put on trial in September 1969, along with such luminaries of the left as Abbie Hoffman, Jerry Rubin, David Dellinger, and Tom Hayden. Seale wanted Garry to represent him, but the Panthers' lawyer was in the hospital for a minor operation, and the judge would not extend the trial, so Seale insisted he wanted to defend himself. The judge refused to allow him this option. Instead, he ruled that radical lawyer William Kunstler, who was defending all of the white activists, would be his lawyer as well. Seale's repeated protests led to his being bound and gagged and tied to his chair. Drawings of Seale thus silenced were distributed through the underground press all over the country, further delegitimizing a trial that liberals and activists had never accepted in the first place. Finally, Seale was separated from the group, which then became the Chicago Seven, and sentenced to four years in prison for sixteen counts of contempt of court, each count equaling a time he tried to assert his right to defend himself. He was later exonerated from the conspiracy charge and served a total of two years for contempt of court.

In the spring of 1969 Seale visited the Black Panther group in New Haven, Connecticut. Soon after he left, a Party member and accused informer, Alex Rackley, was tortured and killed. In August 1969, immediately after he posted bail for his Chicago arrest, Seale was rearrested and charged with having ordered Rackley's death, thus becoming one of the "New Haven Fourteen." He contended that "CIA-FBI infiltration" into the Party had been responsible for the crime. Seale was acquitted of all charges related to Rackley's death in 1971.

Seale spent his time after 1971 working on the party paper *The Black Panther* and running the Party Survival Programs in Oakland, which included free clinics. As part of this work, Seale created the first free breakfast program for children in Oakland, as well as successful food giveaways in big grocery bags printed with the Party emblem of the stalking black panther. In 1972 he ran for mayor of Oakland and placed second in the balloting. In 1974 Seale resigned from the declining Black Panther Party.

For a number of years Seale has worked with Temple University in Philadelphia as a community liaison person.

He devotes much of his energy to making Panther history and his views concerning world brotherhood and peace accessible to all. When *Seize the Time* was reissued in 1991, Seale wrote an introduction renewing his commitment to the need for civil and human rights for everyone, regardless of race or religion, and called on new generations of youth to advocate for the original objectives of the Black Panther Party.

★

Seale's psychological state during his childhood and his years as an activist are explored in *A Lonely Rage: The Autobiography of Bobby Seale* (1978). *Seize the Time: The Story of the Black Panther Party and Huey Newton* (1970) is Seale's testament to the ideals on which the BPP was founded. For more information about the BPP, see Gene Marine, *The Black Panthers* (1969).

KAY KINSELLA ROUT

SEARLE, John Gideon ("Jack") (*b.* 18 March 1901 in Sabula, Iowa; *d.* 21 March 1978 in Hobe Sound, Florida), pharmaceutical manufacturer with G. D. Searle, Inc., the company that developed the first effective and inexpensive oral contraceptive ("the Pill") for women in 1957, which was integral to the 1960s sexual revolution.

The second of two sons of Claude Searle, a physician and pharmaceutical manufacturer, and Marion Titus Searle, a housewife, Searle represented the third of what is now four generations of drug manufacturers. His grandfather, Gideon Daniel, founded G. D. Searle, Inc., in 1888. (It merged with Monsanto Company in 1985.) Searle worked for the family business during summer breaks from Howe (Indiana) Academy and New Trier Township (Illinois) High School. A champion swimmer, he enlisted (though he was underage) in the U.S. Naval Reserve forces during World War I and taught swimming; he graduated from high school in 1918, while he was serving in the reserves (1918–1919). After the war Searle attended the University of Michigan from 1920 to 1923, where he played quarterback for the football team. After graduating in 1923 with a B.S. in pharmacy, Searle worked as a buyer and later as an office manager for the family's firm. He married Frances Crow on 25 April 1925; they had three children.

By 1931 Searle had become general manager and vice president of the family firm. He eliminated unprofitable products from the line during the Great Depression, and he reoriented the company's research efforts to develop unique products that could be marketed profitably worldwide. Among the new products were the laxative Metamucil; Aminophyllin, for treatment of respiratory disorders; and Dramamine, which was developed as an antihistamine but was discovered to be the most effective remedy for motion sickness. The company's fortune rested, however, on developing the first effective and inexpensive oral contraceptive for women.

The social activist Margaret Sanger had pioneered family planning and birth control in America. In 1923 she opened the first family planning clinic in New York City. During the 1920s Sanger organized medical conferences concerning hormonal contraceptives, while fundamental research was sponsored by the philanthropist Mrs. Page McCormick. The principle of oral contraceptives, using artificially synthesized derivatives of natural steroid hormones, was understood theoretically in the 1920s. Estrogen and progesterone are natural steroid hormones. Estrogen makes possible the growth of the endometrium, a membrane that lines the womb. It is present in the early stage of the menstrual cycle. Progesterone produces a mucus substance in the lower lining of the womb and inhibits the passage of sperm. It is present in the late part of the menstrual cycle.

In 1937 researchers noted that synthetic progesterone could inhibit ovulation during the early menstrual cycle in rabbits, but at $200 a gram the synthetic progesterone was very expensive. During the early 1950s it was discovered that progesterone could be simulated with synthetic steroids made from a wild Mexican yam. Margaret Sanger urged Mrs. McCormick to fund further research at the Rock Reproductive Clinic in Brookline, Massachusetts. There, John Rock had been studying the promotion of fertility. Meanwhile, the physicians M. C. Chang and Gregory Pincus, at the Worchester (Massachusetts) Foundation for Experimental Biology, were researching estrogen. Rock found that when hormones to induce fertility over months of treatment were stopped, a significant percentage of women became pregnant ("the Rock rebound"). Chang and Pincus discovered that progesterone was effective in inhibiting pregnancy. The three researchers then collaborated on experiments that combined dosages of estrogen and progesterone. In animal tests even a low dosage effectively controlled menstrual bleeding. Moreover, by starting the dosage five days after the menstrual period began and ending it on the twenty-fourth day, ovulation was effectively inhibited. In 1956 Rock's collaborator, Celso Ramon Garcia, conducted extensive clinical trials.

Searle then developed a sequential dosage of estrogen, followed by a dosage of combined estrogen and progestrogen. The sequential dosage was first marketed in 1957 under the trade name Enovid, packaged in a round plastic tray so that the proper pill would be taken during each day of a menstrual cycle. In 1966 Searle marketed Ovulen, which reduced the dosage of estrogen while remaining equally effective. When the pills were discontinued, fertility returned rapidly. G. D. Searle, Inc., boosted its sales from $37 million in 1960 to almost $89 million in 1965. Almost half its business came from Enovid, which cost $2.50 retail

per month. A prescription lasted six months, and doctors monitored women for any side effects. During the early 1960s minor side effects (weight gain, headaches, nausea) were noted in a tiny percentage of users. By the mid-1960s there were many press reports of rare major side effects (among them, blood clots leading to strokes, especially in older smokers). At the same time, the press reported on the finding that certain cancers and pelvic infections were less likely to develop among contraceptive users.

Searle's Enovid quickly became known simply as "the Pill." There was a sudden and profound effect on the social and emotional lives of the population. Effective and independent of the sex act, the Pill was hailed by women because it emancipated them from unwanted pregnancies. Sanger's dream for birth control was at last a reality, and discussion of sexual matters had become front-page news. Conservatives railed against looser moral standards, and the Roman Catholic Church roundly condemned the Pill. Nonetheless, by 1966 about 20 percent of American Catholic wives were Pill users.

The American birthrate had been climbing in the 1950s, even after the postwar "baby boom," to a 1957 peak of twenty-five births per 1,000 in population. By 1966 this number fell to 19.1 per 1,000. Federal birth-control program clinics had a 50 percent increase in use of the Pill between 1960 and 1965 alone. Now, poor or disadvantaged women could have prescriptions of the Pill for very little or no cost. Abortion rates, too, fell dramatically. In 1964 four other companies marketed a version of the Pill, and in 1966 two companies marketed "morning-after" progesterone pills. During the 1960s the media proclaimed a "sexual revolution." Family planning became more precise. With the Pill, newlyweds felt confident that a first child would not catch them emotionally and financially unprepared. Middle-aged couples were better protected against late-life "accidents."

Much media attention focused on teenagers, and many questions were asked: Just how old should a teenager be before being allowed to take the Pill? Did parents have the right to prevent their daughters from seeking a prescription for the Pill? Discussions on these moral issues, among others, still revolve around the Pill. Moreover, the media still questions whether the Pill initiated the sexual revolution of the 1960s or whether it was simply a by-product of the times. Nonetheless, by 1975 there were thirty million Pill users worldwide. In 2001 there were one hundred million users.

After Searle retired in 1966, his eldest son became president, and his second son and son-in-law became vice presidents of the family's firm, continuing another generation of what is now a Fortune 500 pharmaceutical giant. At the age of seventy-eight, Searle died of natural causes in his winter home in Hobe Sound, Florida. He was buried in the churchyard of Christ Episcopal Church, Winnetka, Illinois.

★

There is no book-length biography of Searle. Oral contraceptives are discussed regularly in the bimonthly *Family Planning Perspectives*. See also Lawrence Lader, "Three Men Who Made a Revolution," *New York Times Magazine* (10 Apr. 1966) and Jane E. Brody, "The Pill: Revolution in Birth Control," *New York Times* (31 May 1966). Obituaries are in the *Chicago Tribune* and the *Chicago Sun Times* (both 23 Jan. 1978).

PATRICK S. SMITH

SEAVER, George Thomas ("Tom") (*b.* 17 November 1944 in Fresno, California), National Baseball Hall of Fame pitcher, a hardworking, consummate professional whose intelligence on the mound matched his physical talents, and the charismatic young leader of the 1969 "Miracle Mets," a New York team that captured the scruffy, underdog spirit of the late 1960s.

Seaver is the son of Charles H. and Betty Lee (Cline) Seaver. Growing up in southern California, Seaver excelled in athletics and academics and was a fan of the Los Angeles Dodgers pitching great Sandy Koufax, often going to games with his father to see Koufax pitch. "I learned about pitching from watching Koufax, even when he lost," Seaver told James Mauro in a 1992 interview. "But it was more—it was seeing someone do what they love, and do it so well."

Seaver served with the U.S. Marine Corps Reserves in

Tom Seaver. AP/WIDE WORLD PHOTOS

1963 before attending Fresno City College in 1964, then transferring to the University of Southern California (USC). While at USC he married Nancy Lynn McIntyre; they have three daughters. While a senior at USC, Seaver was illegally signed to a contract by the Atlanta Braves' Richmond, Virginia, farm club. (Major league clubs are not allowed to sign players to professional contracts while they are in college.) He was declared ineligible to play his final college season, and the Braves were forbidden to draft him. Any club willing to match Atlanta's $40,000 contract offer was allowed to enter a lottery. Three teams entered, and on 3 April 1966 the New York Mets of the National League (NL) were drawn out of a hat in the baseball commissioner's office.

It would prove to be the luckiest day in the Mets' history. During the 1960s the Mets were a team of bumbling, ordinary guys with whom fans sympathized. They attracted a cult following as the proletarian antithesis to their crosstown rivals, the Yankees, baseball's patrician dynasty. Fitting into the Mets culture with his work ethic, Seaver instantly became a team leader, pitching his initial game on 13 April 1967. At six feet, one inch and 206 pounds, the right-handed pitcher was a commanding figure on the mound. In his first season he won sixteen of the team's sixty-one victories and was named 1967 NL Rookie of the Year.

Mets fans had never seen such a terrific player on their side. "Here was the ball club's entire future hopes wrapped up in one sensational arm and in an athlete who was wise far beyond his years in the craft of pitching," wrote the Mets historian Peter C. Bjarkman. "Indeed, never has it been any more crystal clear that a single player held the key to an entire franchise's future." Seaver, mature beyond his years, would meet or exceed all the inflated expectations.

In 1968 Seaver boosted the team to seventy-three wins, one game ahead of the last-place Houston Astros. It was the best season in the Mets laughable seven-year history. Nobody expected much improvement in 1969. The Mets were essentially the same team as in 1968 and were 100-to-1 underdogs to win the pennant. Yet, with Seaver piling up win after win, the team's fortunes soared. On 9 July Seaver came within two outs of a perfect game, beating the first-place Chicago Cubs. Eventually, the Mets overtook the Cubs, and Seaver went through nearly two months of the pennant drive without losing a game. He finished the season with twenty-five wins against only seven losses, and a 2.21 earned run average. He won the Cy Young Award as the National League's best pitcher and narrowly lost in the voting for Most Valuable Player, an honor rarely bestowed on a pitcher.

Seaver won one game in the NL championship series against the Braves and another in the World Series, as the Mets beat the Baltimore Orioles to cap their incredible season—a year in which Seaver and the Mets seemed perfectly in tune with the antiestablishment spirit of the times. Seaver also won the 1969 *Sports Illustrated* Sportsman of the Year award.

"It was right when Vietnam was going on," Seaver recalled in a 2000 on-line interview sponsored by the National Baseball Hall of Fame. " . . .You know that with all the tension that's going on in New York City you're giving some sort of relief."

After the Mets' World Series victory, Shea Stadium resembled the landmark music festival, Woodstock, held just a few months earlier in upstate New York. Delirious fans climbed the railings and tore up the turf, and the exuberant but peaceful celebration spilled over into the city streets. "It was an eruption of joy not surpassed in New York City since the Times Square celebrations that rang out World War II," recalled Bjarkman.

From this memorable beginning Seaver went on to greater achievements during a twenty-year career with the Mets and Cincinnati Reds in the NL, and the Chicago White Sox and Boston Red Sox in the American League (AL). On 22 April 1970 he struck out a record-tying nineteen batters in a game, including a record ten in a row to end the game. He was named to the All-Star team eleven times, and led the NL in victories three times. He won the Cy Young Award again in 1973—when he again pitched in the World Series—and in 1975. He finished his career with 3,640 strikeouts; at the time, only two other pitchers had ever struck out more batters. Seaver was the seventeenth pitcher in Major League Baseball history to win at least 300 games, finishing with 311 wins and 205 losses with a career earned run average of 2.86. Seaver compiled 4,782 and two-thirds innings pitched, 231 complete games, and 61 shutouts in all.

After his retirement Seaver became a Yankees broadcaster and a national television baseball commentator for the National Broadcasting Company (NBC). During and after his playing career, Seaver authored many books, including: *Pitching to Win* (1971); *Pitching with Tom Seaver* (1973), with Steve Jacobson; *How I Would Pitch to Babe Ruth: Seaver vs. The Sluggers* (1974), with Norman Lewis Smith; *The Art of Pitching* (1984), with Lee Lowenfish; *Tom Seaver's All-Time Baseball Greats* (1984), with Marty Appel; *Great Moments in Baseball* (1992), also with Appel; and even a murder mystery, *Beanball: Murder at the World Series* (1989), with Herb Resnicow.

Seaver, known by fans as "Tom Terrific," was an icon in late 1960s New York, one of the athletic embodiments of a youth culture that seemed to defy received wisdom and break down barriers. His poise and maturity—and the intelligence evident in his deep study of the game and his concentration on the mound—reflected the thoughtful, intense spirit of the times. Seaver's contributions to American

sports broadened after his playing days, as he became a recognized authority on baseball and one of the most respected and well-known athletes of his era. Seaver was elected to the National Baseball Hall of Fame on 7 January 1992, being named on a record 98.84 percent of the ballots.

★

Seaver collaborated on three autobiographical books: *The Perfect Game: Tom Seaver and the Mets* (1970), with Dick Schaap; *Baseball Is My Life* (1973), with Steve Jacobson; and *Tom Seaver: Portrait of a Pitcher* (1978), with Malka Drucker. Biographies of Seaver include George Sullivan, *Tom Seaver of the Mets* (1971); John Devaney, *Tom Seaver: An Intimate Portrait* (1974); Paul J. Deegan, *Tom Seaver* (1974); Dick Belsky, *Tom Seaver: Baseball's Superstar* (1977); Gene Schoor, *Seaver: A Biography* (1986); and Norman L. Macht, *Tom Seaver* (1994).

MICHAEL BETZOLD

SEEGER, Peter R. ("Pete") (*b.* 3 May 1919 in New York City), folk singer, folklorist, environmentalist, and social and political critic whose words and music during the 1960s decried U.S. involvement in the Vietnam War.

Seeger was one of three sons born to Charles Louis Seeger, a noted musicologist and college professor, and Constance de Clyver (Edson) Seeger, a violinist and teacher. He also had three half brothers and one half sister from his father's subsequent marriage to the musicologist Ruth Crawford. Seeger received his primary education at public schools in Nyack, New York, and at the Spring Hill School in Litchfield, Connecticut. He then entered Avon Old Farms, a private boarding school in Connecticut.

His interest in grass roots music and the five-string banjo began in 1935, when he attended a folk festival in Asheville, North Carolina. In 1936 he entered Harvard University in Cambridge, Massachusetts, to study sociology. In 1938 Seeger left school to perform as a singing troubadour in migrant camps and on street corners across the country; he also joined the Communist Party in 1941. On 20 July 1943 Seeger married Toshi-Aline Ohta. They raised a son and two daughters in a two-room, hand-built log cabin near Beacon, New York, overlooking the Hudson River.

During the 1940s Seeger performed with Lee Hays, Woody Guthrie, and other members of the Almanac Singers. He served in the U.S. Army Special Services from 1942 to 1945, entertaining troops stateside and in the South Pacific, and attained the rank of corporal. Seeger founded and directed People's Songs, Inc., in 1945 to encourage folk music. In 1948 the Weavers (with Seeger, Hays, Ronnie Gilbert, and Fred Hellerman) debuted at the Village Vanguard. The group disbanded temporarily in 1952, then reunited in 1955, with Seeger finally leaving the group in

Pete Seeger entertaining the Peace Moratorium crowd in Times Square, 1969. © BETTMANN/CORBIS

1957. Seeger also performed solo during the 1950s, before capacity crowds at Carnegie Hall and Town Hall.

In 1952 the Communist informant Harvey Matusow testified before the House Un-American Activities Committee (HUAC) that Seeger, Gilbert, and Hellerman were members of the American Communist Party. Although Matusow later admitted to giving false testimony, the Weavers were blacklisted and banned from radio and television performances. In 1955 Seeger was called to testify by the HUAC. Rather than answer questions, he cited his freedom of speech under the First Amendment to the Constitution, but was indicted on ten counts of contempt of Congress and sentenced to ten years' imprisonment. He went to trial in March 1961 and was found guilty, but the sentence was overturned on appeal in May 1962. The blacklist, however, continued and Seeger pursued a solo career in Europe and periodically performed at U.S. college campuses. Seeger resented his treatment, saying, "I have never in my life supported or done anything subversive to my country. I am proud that I have never refused to sing for any organization because I disagreed with its beliefs."

Seeger claimed that most of his songs were adapted from older melodies. He chose themes demonstrating the strength of the working class, forbearance of indigents, and power to overcome injustices. In 1961 he signed a contract with Columbia Records, while continuing his thirteen-year partnership with Folkways Records and Service Corporation. That year his song "Where Have All the Flowers Gone?" was a popular hit. He collaborated with Lee Hays to write "If I Had a Hammer," and joined with the Weavers to write "Kisses Sweeter Than Wine," all in the same year.

Seeger and his wife also produced short educational films through Folklore Research Films. In 1963 the Seeger family performed in twenty-one countries on a world tour. During an interview that year, Seeger stated, "I feel I'm building a healthy musical life for people who seem to have lost it somewhere in the machine age." Seeger's cabin, with its small woodlot, garden, workshop, and fireplace, was a peaceful retreat for his family and friends during the political upheaval of the 1960s. It provided a contrast of rustic spirituality against a national atmosphere of physical and intellectual violence.

During the 1960s Seeger sang for the peace and civil rights movements. In February 1968 he sang his antiwar song "Waist Deep in the Big Muddy" (which the Columbia Broadcasting System had censored in 1967) on the *Smothers Brothers Comedy Hour.* Also in 1968, when civil rights and antiwar activists were advocating revolutionary violence, Seeger, his wife, and his daughter Tinya camped out with protestors in Resurrection City, the tent encampment on the National Mall in Washington, D.C. They led the crowd, singing songs of the poor and dispossessed.

Seeger told the biographer David King Dunaway, "I am a product of my family and my childhood. One thinks that one creates one's own life. So there I was at nineteen . . . going out to what I thought needed to be done. To my surprise, thirty-five years later, I found that I was practically carrying out what my family had trained me to do." Seeger inherited a legacy of old New England Calvinism. The radicals of 1968 thought Seeger had lost touch with their struggle, but they viewed him only superficially, failing to see his inward need to correct an imperfect society.

In 1969 Seeger launched a seventy-six-foot sloop, the *Clearwater,* on the Hudson River. Clearwater also was the name of what became a 12,000-member Hudson River restoration organization, symbolized by the boat. Shortly after the launch, Seeger organized a local environmental group, the Beacon Sloop Club, in a ramshackle ex-diner. Members met the first Friday of each month to plan waterfront cleanup activities and fundraisers. His words from "Rainbow Race" embraced the top of the building: "One blue sky above us, one ocean, lapping all our shores / One Earth so green and round, who could ask for more?"

Seeger's wife helped him to stay organized and directed. Without her and Harold Leventhal, his agent since 1950, Seeger was likely to start a project, then move on to create another. At six feet, six inches tall and 165 pounds, with thin and balding brown hair and blue eyes, Seeger's body provided the physical frame for the boyish, fun-loving dreamer inside. Donned in mismatched socks—a longtime trademark—Seeger confessed that he first wore the socks to protest dressing in a tuxedo for a Weavers concert. Seeger received a National Medal of the Arts in 1994 and was inducted into the Rock and Roll Hall of Fame in Cleveland, Ohio, in 1996. On 26 February 1997 Seeger won a Grammy Award for best traditional folk album of 1996 for *Pete*.

Seeger's recordings from the 1960s include *American Game and Activity Songs for Children* (1962), *I Can See a New Day* (1964), *Strangers and Cousins* (1965), *God Bless the Grass* (1966), *Abiyoyo and Other Story Songs* (1967), *Waist Deep in the Big Muddy and Other Love Songs* (1967), and *Young vs. Old* (1969). Other songs from that period appear on *World of Pete Seeger* (1973), *The Essential Pete Seeger* (1978), *Circles and Seasons* (1979), *Carry It On: Songs of America's Working People* (1987), *Pete Seeger's Greatest Hits* (1987), *American Industrial Ballads* (1992), *Waist Deep in the Big Muddy* (1993), and *If I Had a Hammer: Songs of Hope and Struggle* (1998).

Provided the advantages and opportunities of an upper-class lifestyle, Seeger refused a life of leisure to represent people caught up in the struggles of oppression. His wide-ranging recordings include songs for children, free speech, human rights, protecting the environment, promoting peace, and furthering social justice. During the upheaval of the 1960s, Seeger remained grounded in his own system of morality, and targeted a misdirected political system and its materialist culture, which he believed threatened to destroy the basic rights that all Americans deserve.

★

Seeger's books applicable to the 1960s are, with Robert S. Reiser, *Carry It On!: A History in Song and Picture of the Working Men and Women of America* (1985), and *Everybody Says Freedom: The Civil Rights Movement in Words, Picture, and Song* (1989). See also Seeger with Peter Blood, *Where Have All the Flowers Gone?* (1996). David King Dunaway, *How Can I Keep from Singing: Pete Seeger* (1981), gives an in-depth biography, including a bibliography and discography. Biographical information is also in Ray M. Lawless, *Folksingers and Folk Songs in America: A Handbook of Biography, Bibliography, and Discography* (1960); Larry Sandberg and Dick Weissman, *The Folk Music Sourcebook* (1976); and George T. Simon, *The Best of the Music Makers* (1979). Articles relating to Seeger's experiences in the 1960s are "A Minstrel with a Mission," *Life* (9 Oct. 1964); "Big and Muddy," *Newsweek* (25 Sept. 1967); "Keeping the Faith," *Horizon* (Oct. 1981): 42–47; "Pete Seeger's Homemade Music," *The Progressive* (Apr. 1986); "Pete Seeger: Keeping the Dream," *Sierra* (Mar./Apr. 1989); and "He Shall Overcome: Pete Seeger," *New England Review* (fall 1990).

SANDRA REDMOND PETERS

SEGAL, George (*b.* 26 November 1924 in New York City; *d.* 9 June 2000 in South Brunswick, New Jersey), sculptor and painter who placed plaster casts made from live models within real environments.

Segal was the younger son of Jacob Segal, a butcher and chicken farmer, and Sophie Gerstenfeld Segal. He attended Public School 70 in the Bronx and Stuyvesant High School, a public school with competitive entrance exams, in Manhattan. There he majored in art and graduated in 1940. That year Segal moved with his family to South Brunswick, New Jersey, to the family chicken farm. In 1949 Segal bought the chicken farm across the road and ran it until 1958, thereafter continuing to maintain his home and studio in that location. In 1946 he married Helen Steinberg; they had two children.

In 1956 Segal was given his first one-person show at the Hansa Gallery in New York, and in 1962 he was included in the New Realists show of mainly pop artists at the Sidney Janis Gallery in New York, where he exhibited often after 1965. He taught English at Jamesburg High School (1957–1958) and a summer adult painting class in New Brunswick (1961). From 1961 to 1964 he taught at Roosevelt Junior High School. Segal studied at Rutgers University

George Segal. ARCHIVE PHOTOS, INC.

from 1962 to 1963, when he received an M.F.A. He taught at Hunter College in New York City in 1964. That year long articles on him and his work appeared in *ArtNews*, *ArtForum*, and *Art International*. In 1968 he was given his first solo museum exhibition at the Museum of Contemporary Art in Chicago. For the 1968–1969 academic year he was appointed lecturer in sculpture at Princeton University. In 1970 he received an honorary doctorate from Rutgers University.

Segal's first venture in direct casting with white plaster was *Man Sitting at a Table* (1961), made from his own body. He explained that we are "left with a white and somewhat abstracted surface—showing . . . little distinguishing detail to identify it as a portrait of a particular man—the figure became a generalized sign for a person." One motivation for this kind of art, the first example of which was presented on his farm in 1958, was his experience of the avant-garde artist Allen Kaprow's Happenings (a form of theater without plots and without character development, in which people perform a number of unrelated actions). Critics referred to his early sculptural assemblages as "frozen happenings."

Segal's skill in building chicken coops quickly transferred to skill in constructing his assemblages. Although his work in this vein had no direct precedent, he felt indebted to European sculptors of the late 1800s to the mid-1900s, among them Auguste Rodin, Medardo Rosso, Germaine Richier, and Alberto Giacometti. The settings encompassing his plaster figures suggested small-town American life from the 1940s through the 1960s, the kind of life he experienced in and about South Brunswick. One would not find, for example, a setting suggestive of a modernistic Manhattan skyscraper. His models were typically his neighbors and friends.

Segal's *Gas Station* (1963), measuring eight feet high by twenty-two feet wide by five feet deep, was his largest assemblage of the 1960s. It contained real-life objects—cans of motor oil, a wall clock, a Coca-Cola dispensing machine, and cases for Coca-Cola cans—and two white plaster figures. The figure striding and carrying an oilcan was cast from a man who operated a gas station about a mile from the artist's home. The other figure, sitting lethargically on an empty upturned Coca-Cola case, derived from the artist's sculptor friend Gary Kuehn, who was not the loafer he appeared to be. *Bus Driver* (1962), with its figure encased tightly in the front steering section of a bus, was inspired directly by a ride Segal caught on the last bus from New York City at 1:00 A.M. The driver, portly and pompous, was cast from Segal's brother-in-law, whom Segal characterized as being "a kind of moral, dogmatic, convinced guy, sure of where he is going." The pieces for the bus came from a junkyard and were put together with the cast of the driver

in such a way as to convey "a massive strong man surrounded by massive strong machinery and yet basically a very unheroic man trapped by forces larger than himself that he couldn't control and least of all understand."

Segal's simple material, white plaster, lent itself to a wide variety of settings. His own mother, shown hacking off the head of a chicken, posed for *Butcher Shop* (1965). The words "kosher meat" in Hebrew letters, part of the assemblage, stood in for the artist's father, who had operated a kosher meat store in the Bronx. The rectilinearity of the table, the glassless windows, and the purposefulness of the woman's gesture suggest something akin to a religious rite. Other tableaux had to do with ordinary acts of everyday life—people sitting at a diner counter, a woman fastening her bra, and so on.

Although Segal is best known as a sculptor, in the 1960s he worked in oil and in pastels, producing vigorously handled paintings mostly of female nudes or parts of their torsos. Especially noteworthy is the *Nude Behind Shower Curtains* (1963), with its adroit combination of flesh tones with violets for the curtains, blue for the tub, and tans for the bathroom wall. In *Upside Down Man* (1960), the male figure (a departure from Segal's usual choice of female nude) is set beside an imposing large round table; the motif anticipates the upside-down figures of the German neo-expressionist Georg Baselitz.

After the 1960s, as Segal's reputation spread, he received important national as well as international commissions. The former included *The Steelmakers* for the Federal Plaza Mall in Youngstown, Ohio, and *Three Figures on Four Park Benches* for the Justice Center in Cleveland. The latter included the *Sacrifice of Isaac* for the Tel Aviv (Israel) Foundation for Literature and Art. Without changing his format, Segal broadened his basic idea by sometimes coloring all or parts of a figure. One example is the blue that pervades his portrait of the art historian Meyer Schapiro (1977). He also sometimes made political statements, as with *In Memory of May 4, 1970, Kent State: Abraham and Isaac* (1978), which expressed his dissatisfaction with U.S. involvement in Vietnam. Segal died at his New Jersey home of cancer at the age of seventy-five.

Segal sometimes is grouped with the pop artists, who produced art based on the commonplace objects of modern twentieth-century life (like the soup cans of Andy Warhol and the comic-strip characters of Roy Lichtenstein), but he fits neatly into no category, except for the general one of assemblage. His ghostlike figures in real settings of the 1960s suggest the alienation of the modern human being. The critic Lawrence Alloway wrote that "a pathos emanates" from the work, but Segal himself argued that he was "try[ing] to capture the subject's gravity and dignity. . . . I'm dependent on the sitter's human spirit."

★

See Jan Van Der Marck, *George Segal* (1979), for excellent illustrations and long discussions of individual works. The author sometimes makes exaggerated claims for the artist. A reliable and informative text containing statements by the artist and critics is Phyllis Tuchman, *George Segal* (1983). Useful for photographs showing step-by-step casting of a plaster sculpture is Sam Hunter, *George Segal* (1989). Valuable for its illustrations of Segal's little-known paintings is Marco Livingstone, *George Segal Retrospective: Sculptures, Paintings, Drawings* (1997). An obituary is in *Who's Who in American Art* (2002–2002).

ABRAHAM A. DAVIDSON

SELBY, Hubert, Jr. (*b.* 23 July 1928 in New York City), novelist whose harrowing depictions of drug addiction and street life shocked, disturbed, and outraged readers, making him a cult figure among "underground" writers and readers.

Selby was born and raised in middle-class Brooklyn, New York, the son of Hubert Selby, an engineer and apartment building manager, and Adalin Layne. He dropped out of Peter Stuyvesant High School in 1944 at age fifteen to serve with the U.S. Merchant Marine. In 1947 he developed nearly fatal tuberculosis while stationed in Europe, and spent most of the next four years in New York hospitals. Doctors expressed little hope for his recovery, and he suffered treatments that left him asthmatic, with ten ribs and half of one lung removed. Selby admitted that the obsession with death that colors his writing developed during those years, as did his addiction to narcotics. Out of the hospital and back at home in New York, Selby switched from morphine, Demerol, and codeine to heroin and alcohol.

He married Inez Taylor in 1953 and had a son and a daughter. Unable to work, Selby stayed home with the children while his wife worked at Macy's department store. In 1950, despite his lack of education, Selby began associating with a group of young rebel writers, including Gilbert Sorentino (who became a lifelong friend and mentor), LeRoi Jones (later Amiri Baraka), Joel Oppenheimer, and Robert Creely. He began publishing in "underground" literary magazines; eventually, these obscure publications caught the attention of Grove Press, which signed a contract with Selby. Collected, culled, and revised, these stories would become the basis for Selby's first novel, *Last Exit to Brooklyn*.

Selby worked on his novel for six years while he went back to work as an insurance clerk to support his family and struggled with his drug habit. Upon its publication in 1964, the book sparked a wave of controversy, and Selby emerged as a voice for American counterculture. With six interwoven tales depicting hopelessness, violence, and human isolation in Brooklyn's Red Hook district, the book is a "journey into

hell," a horrific and brutal study of violence and sexuality, criminality and self-loathing on the cruel streets of New York. Critics reacted strongly both for and against it, but most agreed that Selby, with his energetic and uninhibited style, was a master of his material. *Time* magazine attacked it, but *Newsweek* and the poet Allen Ginsberg praised and publicized it enough that the first edition sold out before its publication date. The book was censored in Britain by the Obscene Publications Act and was banned in Italy, but these facts only increased its street credibility. The work quickly escalated to "underground classic" status, selling 750,000 copies and giving the high-school dropout a dramatic entry into the literary world. It is considered a forerunner of virtually every "streetwise" novel written in the years that followed.

Divorced from his first wife in 1960, Selby married Judith Lumino in 1964. That marriage, too, ended in divorce, and he married Suzanne Shaw, with whom he had two children, in 1969.

The success of *Last Exit* was a mixed blessing for Selby: still drug-dependent, he now had money to feed his habit. This led to his arrest in 1967 for heroin possession, followed by a stint in jail, where he was able to end his heroin addiction. After two more years spent weaning himself from alcohol, Selby began to write again. The resulting novel, *The Room* (1971), forgoes a traditional plot and is written from the perspective of an anonymous, incarcerated criminal. The character's desperate and claustrophobic stream-of-consciousness narrative traverses his issues of pride, hatred of himself and others, misogyny, rage, and powerlessness. The boredom of incarceration drives him to sadistic fantasies of revenge upon his captors, episodes so horrific that Selby himself later admitted that the book was too disturbing for even him to read. Selby's most shocking insight in *The Room* is that such cruelty is quite human. He was able to convey the prisoner's lifetime of psychological damage with as much complexity as it deserves, while keeping the character free of intellectual depth, personifying an urban "Everyman." *The Room* met with favorable reviews but did not receive the kind of promotional backing it needed to be commercially successful.

Selby later published *The Demon* (1976), *Requiem for a Dream* (1978), a collection of short stories entitled *Songs of the Silent Snow* (1986), and *The Willow Tree* (1998). He also wrote two screenplays, *Day and Night* (1985) and *Soldier of Fortune* (1990). The film version of *Last Exit to Brooklyn* (1988) revived interest in the book, while the writer, rocker, and independent publisher Henry Rollins introduced Selby's work to a younger generation in the 1990s through a series of spoken-word recordings and tours. Selby's career has been a cycle of success and obscurity, feast and famine; he had separated from his wife, Suzanne, and was living on welfare in 1999 before *Requiem for a Dream* was adapted into a successful film by director Darren Aronofsky.

In the six years it took Selby to write *Last Exit to Brooklyn,* he later recalled, he truly learned how to write. He also discovered that he was able to find inspiration within himself. As a New Yorker, he was also able to convey the "music" of the speech he heard on the New York streets, patterns he considered unique to New York. Selby used that distinctive dialogue in such a way that the dialogue itself becomes part of the emotional experience of the story.

★

A biography and critical study of Selby is James R. Giles, *Understanding Hubert Selby, Jr.* (1998). Other sources include John O'Brien, "Interview with Hubert Selby, Jr.," *Contemporary Fiction* (summer 1981); Michael Wood, "30 Years Ago This Week: On the Shelf," *Sunday Times* (London, 28 Jan. 1996); Hubert Selby, Jr., "Why I Continue to Write," *L.A. Weekly* (26 Feb.–4 Mar. 1999); Jonathan Rendall, "Last Exit to Welfare: Other Writers Compare Hubert Selby to Dante and Whitman. So Why Can't He Get Published?" *Independent Sunday* (London, 18 Apr. 1999); and Jory Farr, "Savage Vision: Hubert Selby Lived the Addictions He Wrote About in *Requiem for a Dream,*" *Dallas Morning News* (24 Nov. 2000).

BRENNA SANCHEZ

SENDAK, Maurice Bernard (*b.* 10 June 1928 in New York City), prolific illustrator and author of children's books who is most noted for *Where the Wild Things Are,* which first startled the publishing world with its honest portrayal of childhood fears and then transformed children's publishing.

Sendak was the youngest of three children of Philip Sendak, a dressmaker, and Sarah Schindler Sendak, Polish Jews who left their home villages outside Warsaw before World War I and moved to New York City. Throughout his childhood, Sendak was influenced both by the vibrant life of New York City and by his parents' memories of Poland. From his parents, Sendak received a rather pessimistic view of life, which he struggled against, and a sense of his Jewish heritage, which later influenced his work. Sickly and overweight as a child and disrupted by his family's financial troubles and his parents' frequent moves to various locations in New York City, Sendak was lonely and isolated and hated school, but he loved drawing and decided at a young age to become an illustrator.

After graduating from high school in 1946, Sendak moved to Manhattan and found a job in the warehouse of a window display company, where he worked until 1948. In 1948 he was promoted to a different department of the company, where he was deeply unhappy because his coworkers were uncongenial. After quitting the job because

Maurice Sendak. ARCHIVE PHOTOS, INC.

of his unhappiness, Sendak moved back to his parents' home and spent his time drawing the children he saw outside the window; these sketches continued to inspire him throughout his later career. In his acceptance speech for the Caldecott Medal, which he won in 1964 for *Where the Wild Things Are,* he said of the sketchbooks that he kept during this time, "There is not a book I have written or a picture I have drawn that does not, in some way, owe them its existence."

During that same summer, he and his brother Jack built model toys and took them to the toy store F.A.O. Schwarz. The toys were too expensive to mass-produce, but the store's window-display director was impressed with Sendak's sense of design and hired him as an assistant window dresser. While at Schwarz he took night classes in art and met Ursula Nordstrom, who launched his career as an illustrator. Nordstrom was a children's book editor at Harper and Brothers, and she immediately offered him a contract to illustrate Marcel Ayme's *The Wonderful Farm* (1951). Nordstrom continued to choose works for Sendak to illustrate and carefully nurtured his career as it grew. Between 1951 and 1962 Sendak illustrated dozens of books and wrote seven. Trying different styles and techniques, he experimented and learned. Although he studied the work of many artists, his style, with its intricacy and cross-hatching, was more akin to that of nineteenth-century artists than to artists of the twentieth century; even more important than the nineteenth-century artists was the influence of the Romantic poet and engraver William Blake.

Sendak's long apprenticeship ended with the publication of *Where the Wild Things Are* (1963). The book stars Max, an unruly boy who is sent to bed without supper by his mother, who calls him a "Wild Thing." Max imagines that he travels to the land of the monstrous Wild Things, where he becomes king. Later, however, he returns from his fantasy to find that his mother has left his warm supper in his bedroom. The book contains numerous pen-and-ink drawings, washed with watercolors; amusingly, Sendak has commented that the frightening Wild Things resemble relatives he disliked as a child.

Where the Wild Things Are aroused a great deal of controversy among parents, teachers, and librarians, who believed that the potentially frightening depiction of the Wild Things was unsuitable for children, who should be protected. In the *Journal of Nursery Education,* for example, one critic wrote, "We should not like to have it left about where a sensitive child might find it to pore over in the twilight." Another critic, the well-known psychoanalyst Bruno Bettelheim, who had not read the book, nevertheless commented that it would provoke fears of abandonment and anxiety in children when they read about Max's being sent to bed without supper. Because of this critical response, the book was initially unpopular, but soon the pleasure that it gave readers of all ages outweighed the critics' warnings, and in 1964 Sendak was awarded the Caldecott Medal.

In his acceptance speech for the Caldecott Medal, Sendak placed himself squarely against the traditional view of children and their tolerance for anxiety. He noted that "from their earliest years children live on familiar terms with disrupting emotions," and through fantasy, "children achieve catharsis. It is the best means they have for taming Wild Things." He also said that the "truth and passion" of his work came directly from his understanding of the "awful vulnerability of children and their struggle to make themselves King of all Wild Things." Despite the initial controversy surrounding it, the book was soon embraced by readers everywhere and has since sold more three million copies in English alone. It has been published in sixteen languages and has had a lasting influence on children's literature through its honest view of children and their emotions.

In 1967 Sendak's mother became ill with cancer, and in the same year Sendak himself had a heart attack while being interviewed on television in England. During his recovery he had a friend send his parents postcards from all over Europe so that they would not know that he was ill. When he returned to the United States, his beloved terrier, Jennie, fell ill and had to be put to sleep. Sendak's mother

died in 1968. Before these events, Sendak had felt that he would live long and happily as long as he worked to recall his childhood as honestly as possible, but in the wake of so much illness and loss, he lost that sense of immunity.

In *Higglety Pigglety Pop! Or, There Must Be More to Life* (1967), Sendak immortalized Jennie, who had been his companion for fourteen years. The book tells the story of a terrier that thinks there must be more to life than having everything she wants. She undergoes various trials to gain experience and finally is chosen as the leading lady of the Mother Goose Theatre's production of the nursery rhyme "Higglety Pigglety Pop!" The book received favorable reviews and was popular with adults as well as children.

Sendak has said that his two other major books, *In the Night Kitchen* (1970) and *Outside over There* (1981), form a trilogy with *Where the Wild Things Are.* Although they do not have any obvious similarities, he claims that all three examine how children deal with frustration, boredom, anger, and other strong feelings. In addition to the Caldecott Medal (1964), Sendak received the Hans Christian Andersen Award (1970), the Laura Ingalls Wilder Medal (1983), and the Empire State Award for excellence in literature for young people (1990).

Sendak believes that illustrators should not merely draw what is in the text but should move beyond the text and enlarge the story. His insistence on emotional honesty resulted in a profound change in children's book publishing; after the success of *Where the Wild Things Are,* critics began citing it as a model to be emulated. Sendak has had a lifelong commitment to helping other artists launch their careers, working with them and teaching at the Parsons School of Design in New York City. He also has worked as artistic director at the Sundance Children's Theater in Utah. According to Amy Sonheim in *Maurice Sendak,* Sendak said, "My great editor at Harper, Ursula Nordstrom . . . was able to bring me along gradually. I'd like to do that for others." Sendak resides in New York City; he has never married.

★

Amy Sonheim, *Maurice Sendak* (1991), is a detailed biography of the illustrator. A lengthy profile of Sendak appears in the *Dictionary of Literary Biography*, vol. 61: *American Writers for Children Since 1960: Poets, Illustrators, and Nonfiction Authors* (1987). Sendak's acceptance speech for the Caldecott Medal appears in his *Caldecott & Co.: Notes on Books and Pictures* (1988).

KELLY WINTERS

SERLING, Rodman Edward ("Rod") (*b.* 25 December 1924 in Syracuse, New York; *d.* 28 June 1975 in Rochester, New York), television and film writer, producer, host, commercial spokesman, and social critic who created *The Twilight Zone* and cowrote *The Planet of the Apes.*

Serling was the second of two sons of Samuel Lawrence Serling, a secretary, grocer, and butcher, and his wife, Esther (Cooper) Serling, a homemaker. The family moved to Binghamton, New York, in 1926. After graduating from Binghamton Central High School in 1943, Serling enlisted in the army and joined the 511th Parachute Infantry Regiment of the 11th Airborne Division. Wounded twice during action in the Philippine Islands, his wartime experiences caused nightmares and flashbacks for the rest of his life. The experiences also provided inspiration for some of his stories and informed his later antiwar stance.

After the war, Serling enrolled at Antioch College in Ohio. While a student, he converted from Judaism to Unitarianism to marry Carolyn Kramer on 31 July 1948; the couple eventually had two daughters. After graduating with a B.A. in 1950, he wrote scripts for both a radio and a television station in Cincinnati, Ohio. He began selling television scripts for various anthology dramas to New York–based networks and moved to New York City to work as a freelance writer. Serling won Emmys for three early teleplays, including *Requiem for a Heavyweight* in 1956.

Disappointed by television's shift away from live dramatic programs in the late 1950s, Serling publicly criticized television's failure to address social issues. But his success led the Columbia Broadcasting System (CBS) to offer him a job writing a fantasy anthology series. He agreed only

Rod Serling. ARCHIVE PHOTOS, INC.

after the network gave him total creative control of the show, which he called *The Twilight Zone*. Serling wrote more than ninety of the 156 episodes that aired during the show's five seasons, produced the series, and also served as the show's off-screen narrator-host during the first season. The show premiered on 2 October 1959.

Although a critical hit, *The Twilight Zone* developed only a small though loyal following, especially among teenagers. Serling used the show to comment discreetly on humanity and human behavior. As Carolyn Serling later explained, "Rod felt that drama should be an assertion of social conscience. He found that in *The Twilight Zone* . . . he could make the same point that he wanted to make with straight drama." Consequently, Serling used alien beings, magical machines, or time travel to address such controversial topics as prejudice, censorship, or nuclear war. He won two more Emmys for his work.

Before the debut of the second season, two important changes took place. One was the eerie new theme music and visually surreal opening credits. The second was the decision to have Serling host the show by providing the on-screen introduction and closing statement for each episode as a way to tie the episodes together. The move made the diminutive writer (he stood only five feet, four inches tall) an instant star and quickly turned him into a cultural icon. He added to his fame by publishing his television scripts in book form and appearing on other shows to parody himself. The name of the show itself became a catchphrase around the world. With *The Twilight Zone*, Serling reached the peak of his success, although he always felt that *Requiem for a Heavyweight* was his best piece of work.

Success, though, came at a price. After three seasons, the relentless writing and production pace caught up with Serling. Exhausted, he turned most of the writing chores over to a stable of writers. In the fourth season Serling wrote only seven episodes, but the show still placed strong demands on him when it switched to a one-hour format. Looking for a break, Serling took a one-year position as writer in residence at Antioch College beginning in September 1962. There he taught writing, drama, and a survey course about the "social and historical implications of the media." The light teaching load left him time for other projects, including the screenplay for *Seven Days in May*, a story about nuclear disarmament and the power of the military. In 1963 he won his sixth and final Emmy for the teleplay *It's Mental Work*. At the end of its fifth season, the final episode of *The Twilight Zone* aired in May 1964. That same month, Serling was elected president of the National Academy of Television Arts and Sciences, a position he held for two years. His attempts to revamp the awards system did not survive his tenure.

In the fall of 1965, CBS premiered Serling's *The Loner*, a half-hour, post-Civil War western about a wandering, introspective cowboy in search of life's meaning. The series garnered poor ratings and lukewarm reviews. When CBS demanded less talk and more gunfights, Serling refused to comply. *The Loner* was canceled in April 1966. Serling next turned to film, but most projects either failed to reach the screen or were critical disappointments. The one notable exception was his 1968 movie adaptation of Pierre Boulle's *The Planet of the Apes,* in which he tackled racism and anthropocentrism.

That same year Serling, an outspoken critic of the Vietnam War, publicly supported antiwar candidate Eugene McCarthy's presidential bid. Having no television show as an outlet for social commentary, Serling, a longtime political activist, continually wrote letters to newspapers and had his opinions published throughout the country. He also toured the college lecture circuit in 1968 and 1969. He spoke on racism, television, the government, and other subjects that angered him. Much to his surprise, he encountered receptive audiences at colleges because of the popularity of *The Twilight Zone* in syndication. But having sold off the rights to the show, he found himself working as a spokesman for products such as Anacin and Crest and even hosting a game show in order to maintain his lifestyle. It was a bitter irony for the man who had spent years criticizing the effect of sponsors on programming.

Serling returned to television in 1969 with a pilot for an American Broadcasting Company (ABC) series called *The New People* (1969–1970), a show about an assorted group of young Americans stranded on a South Pacific atoll. He delivered his script but criticized the series. Serling next agreed to serve as host of the National Broadcasting Company's (NBC) horror-fantasy anthology *Night Gallery* (1970–1973). He received two Emmy nominations for episodes he wrote, but he was never satisfied with the show, in large part because he did not have creative control over it. After *Night Gallery* was canceled, he opted to teach writing at Ithaca College, in upstate New York. A lifelong heavy smoker, he suffered a heart attack in May 1975 and died a month later in Rochester, New York, during open-heart surgery. Serling is buried at Interlaken Cemetery in Interlaken, a small town in upstate New York.

★

Serling's personal papers can be found in the Special Collections department at the UCLA Research Library in Los Angeles, California, and at the University of Wisconsin Center for Film and Theatre Research in Madison. Two biographies of Serling are Joel Engel, *Rod Serling: The Dreams and Nightmares of Life in the Twilight Zone* (1989), and Gordon Sander, *Serling: The Rise and Twilight of Television's Last Angry Man* (1992). Marc Scott Zicree, *The Twilight Zone Companion* (1982), includes a synopsis of all the show's episodes. Peter Wolfe, *In the Zone: The Twilight World of Rod Serling* (1997), is a full-length thematic, artistic, and technical analysis of the show. Short stories adapted from scripts are widely available in mass-market paperback editions. An obituary is in the *New York Times* (29 June 1975).

JAMES G. LEWIS

SESSIONS, Roger Huntington (*b.* 28 December 1896 in New York City; *d.* 16 March 1985 in Princeton, New Jersey), one of the most influential composers and teachers of the twentieth century.

Sessions's parents were Archibald Lowery Sessions, a lawyer, and Ruth Gregson Huntington, a writer and musician. When Sessions was four years old, his father quit his law practice to become a writer. The family was plunged into dire financial straits, and Sessions's mother took her four children to Hadley, Massachusetts, to live with her relatives, beginning a twenty-five-year separation from her husband.

A child prodigy, Sessions started playing the piano at age five and began formal lessons with his mother three years later. In 1906 he was sent to Cloyne, a boarding school in Newport, Rhode Island, but he left after three months because he found the school too regimented. In 1908 he enrolled at the Kent School in Kent, Connecticut. He wrote his first opera, *Lancelot and Elaine,* inspired by Alfred Tennyson's *Idylls of the King,* in 1910. After graduating from high school in 1911 at age fourteen, he enrolled at Harvard University. He received his B.A. from Harvard in 1915, then enrolled at Yale University, receiving his B.Mus. in

Roger Sessions. CORBIS CORPORATION (BELLEVUE)

1917. While at Yale he studied with composer Horatio Parker.

From 1917 to 1921 Sessions taught music composition at Smith College in Northampton, Massachusetts, where he met Barbara Foster, whom he married in 1920. His first important composition, *The Black Maskers,* incidental music for Leonid Andreyev's play, had its premiere at Smith in June 1923. Sessions worked as composer Ernest Bloch's assistant at the Cleveland Institute of Music until 1925. He then went to Europe, living on money from his father and various grants.

In August 1933, with the rise to power of the Nazis in Germany, Sessions left Berlin and returned to the United States, where he tried to warn Americans about the threat of Nazism. Sessions and his first wife divorced in September 1936. He then married librarian Sarah Elizabeth Franck on 26 November 1936; they had two children.

Until 1935 Sessions taught in Boston at the Boston Conservatory, the Dalcroze School of Music, and the Malkin Conservatory. He took an instructor's position at Princeton University in 1935, working his way through the academic ranks, and then in 1945 became professor of music at the University of California, Berkeley, only to return to Princeton as the William Shubael Conant Professor of Music in 1953.

During the 1940s and 1950s Sessions published several books about music, including *Reflections on the Music Life in the United States* (1956). In 1957 the Boston Symphony Orchestra performed his Symphony no. 3, a commission to celebrate the orchestra's seventy-fifth anniversary. The symphony marked the beginning of a very productive period for Sessions and helped cement his creative reputation.

Sessions had worked on his opera *Montezuma* periodically for twenty-eight years. After his librettist Antonio Borghese died in 1952, Sessions rewrote the libretto. The opera had its premiere in 1964 in West Berlin's Deutsche Oper. According to various accounts, the opera was either a great success or there were riots in the streets because of it. The subject of *Montezuma* was the conquest of the Aztecs by Cortez. Sessions was gripped by the idea of the futility of conquest and made it the theme of the opera. Told in three acts, *Montezuma* is very ambitious, incorporating Sessions's experimentation with twelve-tone music. Sessions greatly admired Verdi, and his lush orchestration in *Montezuma* reflects the Italian's influence.

The Japanese Philharmonic Orchestra recorded Sessions's Symphony no. 1 in 1960. It was well received by the critics and also marked the beginning of popular interest in Sessions's works. The Fromm Music Foundation of Chicago (January 1961) and the Museum of Modern Art in New York City (October 1961) both presented Sessions's works, the latter to commemorate his sixty-fifth birthday.

That same year he was made a member of the American Academy of Arts and Sciences.

In 1964 he finished Symphony no. 5, and it was well received as an accessible piece from a composer noted for the difficulty of his works for both musicians and audiences. Sessions was unapologetic about his music's complexity. He said that once audiences became accustomed to his style, his works were usually easy for both musicians and listeners. Despite that, many violinists have pronounced his Violin Concerto unplayable.

In 1965 Sessions was forced to leave Princeton because he had passed the mandatory retirement age of sixty-eight. Harvard University made him Charles Eliot Norton Professor from 1966 to 1969; he also taught at the Julliard School in New York City from 1966 to 1983. He finished three more symphonies: no. 6 (1966), no. 7 (1967), and no. 8 (1968). Each successive work became more complex, featuring his usual inventiveness and long passages without repetition. Critics complained Symphony no. 8 was awkward, noisy, flashy, and incomprehensible.

The 1960s were memorable for the creation of several major works in a short period. Although never immensely popular, during the decade Sessions won a following that appreciated the complexity of his works and admired their thoughtfulness. In 1974 the Pulitzer Prize committee awarded Sessions a special citation for the excellence of his musical career, and in 1982 he received a Pulitzer Prize for *Concerto for Orchestra.* He composed over forty works in all, including nine symphonies, two string quartets, several concertos and piano sonatas, two full-scale operas, and a cantata, *When Lilacs Last in the Dooryard Bloom'd* (1964–1970), which some consider his most appealing work.

In February 1985 Sessions suffered a stroke; he died in March of pneumonia. He was cremated and his ashes returned to Hadley, Massachusetts, where they were interred in Old Hadley Cemetery.

★

Session's biography is Andrea Olmstead, *Roger Sessions and His Music* (1985). Sessions's essays are in Edward T. Cone, ed., *Roger Sessions on Music* (1979). An obituary is in the *New York Times* (18 Mar. 1985).

KIRK H. BEETZ

SEXTON, Anne (*b.* 9 November 1928 in Newton, Massachusetts; *d.* 4 October 1974 in Weston, Massachusetts), Pulitzer Prize–winning poet and performer, popular in the 1960s for her dramatic flair and controversial confessional writing.

Born Anne Gray Harvey, Sexton was the youngest of three daughters born to Mary Gray Staples, a homemaker with unfulfilled literary aspirations, and Ralph Churchill Harvey, the owner of a successful woolen mill. Although the family was wealthy, Sexton had a painful home life (including possible sexual abuse) as a child and gravitated toward her great-aunt ("Nana" Anna Dingley) for comfort and security.

Sexton attended public schools in Wellesley, Massachusetts, and then Rogers Hall, a girls' preparatory school in Lowell, Massachusetts, from which she graduated in 1947. Hoping to transform their disobedient daughter into a proper lady, Sexton's parents sent her to the Garland School in Boston, a finishing school for women. There Sexton met and, on 16 August 1948, eloped with Alfred Muller "Kayo" Sexton II. The Sextons later bought a home in Newton Lower Falls, Massachusetts, and had two daughters.

The Sextons may have appeared to be an idyllic 1950s suburban family, but Sexton's continuing anxiety and depression were never far from the surface. During her husband's service in Korea, she engaged in occasional infidelities (which continued throughout their marriage) and abuse of the children. In 1955 she began psychiatric treatment for what was initially diagnosed as postpartum depression. Although managed at times, her condition worsened through her short life, leading to several suicide attempts and intermittent institutionalization. In 1956 her psychiatrist, Dr. Martin T. Orne, encouraged Sexton to use poetry writing as part of her therapeutic process. This was the beginning of Sexton's remarkable career as a so-called confessional poet.

Sexton always saw a close relationship between writing and psychotherapy. Her most successful poetry translates her "private terrors" (as she put it) into public forms. The unusual beginnings of her work, on the analyst's couch, portended not only her poetry's range but also the ways in which it was received. On the one hand, it was praised for its raw feeling, gutsy candor, and confessional intimacy. On the other hand, it was condemned for its lack of decorum, both personal and poetic. Sexton's work appeared just at the right time. With its dramatic secrecy, its flamboyant gestures, and its willingness to address taboo issues (particularly women's sexuality), her poetry was perfectly calibrated for the 1960s.

In the late 1950s and early 1960s, Sexton set out to transform herself from a suburban housewife and part-time model into a serious poet. She enrolled in writing courses and joined workshops around Boston where she met poets such as George Starbuck, John Clellon Holmes, and Maxine Kumin. Sexton's work progressed with help from W. D. Snodgrass (whose autobiographical poem "Heart's Needle" is generally considered the first confessional work) and Robert Lowell (perhaps the most respected contemporary poet in America at the time). Through Lowell's writing seminar at Boston University, Sexton also met Sylvia Plath, to whom her personal subjects, biting tone, and dark ob-

Anne Sexton. AP/WIDE WORLD PHOTOS

sessions are often compared. Indeed, when Plath committed suicide in 1963, a decade before she did, Sexton reportedly remarked to her doctor, "That death was mine!"

Lowell was instrumental in helping Sexton publish her first book, *To Bedlam and Part Way Back* (1960), a poetic treatment of her descent into, and partial recovery from, madness. This first book establishes Sexton's most identifiable persona, the "mad housewife," and also one of her primary themes: the death impulse. "Suicides have a special language," she writes in "Wanting to Die," "Like carpenters they want to know *which tools. / They never ask why build.*" As with Plath and other so-called extremist artists, the insistent closeness of death is part of what gives the work its charge. As Sexton wrote in a 1963 letter, "The soul is . . . a human being who speaks with the pressure of death at his head."

Having little academic background, Sexton continued to professionalize herself through her appointment, in 1961, as an artist/scholar at the newly founded Radcliffe Institute. Here she was first exposed to feminist thought, reading work from Virginia Woolf's *A Room of One's Own* to Betty Friedan's controversial 1960s manifesto of the women's movement, *The Feminine Mystique*. This education was crucial to the kind of poetry Sexton would produce throughout the 1960s, with its assertive focus on female experience. Characteristic poems with titles such as "The Abortion" and "Menstruation at Forty" unabashedly treated the secret subjects of women's lives—from marital and family relations to incest, adultery, and abuse. Her forthrightness made Sexton extremely popular in some circles and equally reviled in others. Whatever the judgment, one of her legacies was to give women's experience an important place in contemporary poetry. In this respect, Sexton paved the way for much of the feminist poetry of the coming decades. While other writers were concentrating on overtly political themes centered on the Vietnam War, Sexton proved her assertion that "poems of the inner life can reach the inner lives of readers in a way that anti-war poems can never stop a war."

All My Pretty Ones (1962), Sexton's second collection, was another popular success, and, like her first volume, it was nominated for the National Book Award. It continues her confessional themes and deals movingly with personal experiences of loss. This was a subject of some urgency to a poet who had lost not only her beloved great-aunt in 1954, but also both her parents to unexpected illnesses in 1959.

In May 1963 Sexton was awarded a traveling fellowship by the American Academy of Arts and Letters, which she used to tour Europe for three months. Her popularity spread quickly, and in 1964 Britain's prestigious Oxford University Press published *Selected Poems*. This led to her election as a fellow of the Royal Society of Literature, London, in 1965. Among Sexton's other awards and honors during the decade are the Levinson Prize (1962), the Shelley Memorial Prize (1967), and the Pulitzer Prize (1967) for her third volume, *Live or Die*. She was also the recipient of several honorary doctoral degrees and professorships at Colgate University and Boston University.

Despite all these successes, Sexton's mental condition worsened. In the mid-1960s her psychiatrist began audiotaping their therapy sessions as a way of helping the patient recall material she might later repress. The tapes became important raw material for Sexton's poetry, which continued to push the boundaries of privacy. As well, the tapes, which were released by her doctor after Sexton's death, became the centerpiece of a controversy surrounding Diane Wood Middlebrook's *Anne Sexton; A Biography* (1991). The decision to release the tapes, which contain intimate revelations about Sexton's many extramarital affairs (including one with her second psychiatrist), her alcoholism, and her sexual abuse of her own daughter, sparked controversy in both literary and psychiatric circles for its perceived disregard of doctor-patient privilege.

Therapy informed not only Sexton's poetry but also her decade-long work on a play that uses the psychoanalytical process as its model and incest as its central image. This work went through three distinct drafts: "The Cure" (1962), "Tell Me Your Answer True" (1964), and finally *Mercy Street* (1969)—the only version actually produced. Performed at the American Place Theatre in New York, the play was praised for its lyrical language but criticized for its weak theatrical form.

In a more successful mixture of poetry and performance, Sexton began adding music to her already extremely popular readings. Anne Sexton and Her Kind, a chamber rock group that began when one of Sexton's students set several of her poems to music, was an attempt to capitalize on the huge audience for the popular poets of the 1960s such as Bob Dylan and Janis Joplin. Decked out in glamorous evening wear, Sexton chanted her poetry to the accompaniment of a five-piece band. The group's first performance in Boston (July 1968) was a benefit for Eugene McCarthy's bid for the presidency. In the late 1960s, the poetry circuit of American university campuses had become a booming and lucrative business, and Sexton had become a star of the circuit, to the consternation of more academic and serious-minded friends such as Kumin. As Sexton reached for an ever larger audience, the quality of her work declined, according to many critics. Her last books of the decade, *Love Poems* (1969) and *Transformations* (1971), were best-sellers but received little critical attention.

The 1970s saw a worsening of Sexton's mental and physical health. Her alcoholism and addiction to prescription drugs isolated her from friends and family. In 1973, after her children had departed for college, she asked her husband for a divorce. It had long been evident from public and private records that Sexton was planning her own death, and despite the efforts of many people close to her to prevent such an act, she committed suicide. On 4 October 1974, after a lunch with Kumin during which they corrected the galley proofs of Sexton's final book, *The Awful Rowing Toward God,* Sexton returned home, closed the door of her garage, and asphyxiated herself with carbon monoxide. She was cremated, and her ashes were interred in August 1976 at the Sexton family plot at Forest Hills Cemetery in Jamaica Plain, Massachusetts.

Although Sexton's importance as a cultural figure of the 1960s seems assured, her status as a major poet and innovator is somewhat less certain. Critics have argued that the confessional label has unfairly confined Sexton, but the fact is her success was crucially tied to the self-revelation and self-performance at the heart of confessional writing. In a memorial essay, Erica Jong described Sexton as "a woman without skin" who "had so little capacity to filter out pain that everyday events often seemed unbearable to her." The ability to turn pain into print, to embody this odd skeletal figure, part witch, part helpless child, will likely be the final legacy, the achievement and the tragedy, of Sexton's art.

★

All of Sexton's papers are held by the Harry Ransom Humanities Research Center, the University of Texas at Austin. Her correspondence, *Anne Sexton: A Self-Portrait in Letters* (1977), is edited by Linda Gray Sexton, her daughter (and literary executor), and Lois Ames. Linda Gray Sexton has also published a telling personal memorial, *Searching for Mercy Street: My Journey Back to My Mother, Anne Sexton* (1994). Diane Wood Middlebrook's *Anne Sexton: A Biography* (1991) is an extremely readable and useful authorized biography. The major critical work is Diana Hume George, *Oedipus Anne: The Poetry of Anne Sexton* (1987). Collections of essays include J. D. McClatchy, *Anne Sexton: The Artist and Her Critics* (1978); Frances Bixler, *Original Essays on the Poetry of Anne Sexton* (1988); Steven E. Colburn, *Anne Sexton: Telling the Tale* (1988); Diana Hume George, *Sexton: Selected Criticism* (1988); and Linda Wagner-Martin, *Critical Essays on Anne Sexton* (1989). The only extensive bibliographic source is Cameron Northouse and Thomas P. Walsh, *Sylvia Plath and Anne Sexton: A Reference Guide* (1974). *No Evil Star: Selected Essays, Interviews and Prose* was edited by Steven E. Colburn (1985). Sexton's *Complete Poems* were published in 1981, and *Selected Poems* was edited by Diane Wood Middlebrook and Diana Hume George in 1988. Obituaries are in the *New York Times* and the *Washington Post* (both 6 Oct. 1974) and in *Time* (14 Oct. 1974).

MARK SILVERBERG

Albert Shanker. ARCHIVE PHOTOS, INC.

SHANKER, Albert ("Al")   (*b.* 14 September 1928 in New York City; *d.* 22 February 1997 in New York City), educator, labor union organizer, labor leader, and civil rights activist, whose leadership of New York City's public school teachers in the 1960s gained collective bargaining rights for them and national recognition for himself.

Shanker was born to Russian immigrant parents on Manhattan's Lower East Side. His father, Morris, studied to be a rabbi and worked as a union newspaper deliveryman, and his mother, Mamie (Burko) Shanker, was a garment worker. Both parents, Orthodox Jews who spoke only Yiddish, were staunch Roosevelt Democrats and ardent trade unionists.

When Shanker was a toddler, the family moved to Ravenswood, Queens. Shanker, the only Jewish boy in this Irish and Italian neighborhood, was constantly beaten up by local bullies. A prisoner in his own house, he listened to the radio and collected stamps.

The gangly, six feet, three inches tall youngster was in constant competition with his younger sister, Pearl, a star student. In 1944 he passed the entrance exam for Stuyvesant High School, an intensely competitive school in Manhattan, where he flourished, heading the school's debating team. He graduated in the top fifth of his class.

Shanker enrolled in the University of Illinois at Urbana-Champaign, where he encountered rampant anti-Semitism. He was not allowed to live on campus and was forced to live on a farm miles outside of town. In college, he joined the recently formed Congress of Racial Equality (CORE) and participated in local civil rights demonstrations. Surprised by the racism and anti-Semitism he encountered at Urbana, Shanker found some acceptance in left-wing circles. He joined the Young People's Socialist League and became chair of the campus democratic Socialist Study Group.

In 1949 Shanker graduated *cum laude* with a B.A. degree in philosophy. He returned to New York to attend Columbia University's graduate school of philosophy. There he earned an M.A. and enrolled in the doctoral program, intending to become a college professor. While at Columbia, Shanker married his college sweetheart, Pearl Sabath, in 1949. The couple had one son, Carl Eugene, whom they named after the socialists Karl Marx and Eugene V. Debs.

To earn money to complete his doctoral dissertation, Shanker became a *per diem* substitute, teaching sixth-grade mathematics at Public School (PS) 179 in East Harlem in 1952. He detested this job, which left no time for even a lunch break. Equally annoying was the near-absolute power of the principal. The following year, Shanker moved into a regular substitute-teaching job at Junior High School

(JHS) 126 in Long Island City, Queens. He joined Local 2 of the New York Teachers Guild, an affiliate of the American Federation of Teachers (AFT).

In 1959, at age thirty-one, Shanker quit his job as mathematics teacher at Manhattan's JHS 88 in East Harlem to become a full-time organizer for the Teacher's Guild, which in March 1960 merged with the High School Teachers Association to become the United Federation of Teachers (UFT). Shanker visited more than 700 schools, preaching the gospel of teacher unity, but he was greeted with apathy and anti-union sentiments from teachers and politicians alike. He later related a conversation he had in 1960 with Robert F. Wagner, New York's mayor at the time: "I asked . . . why it was that . . . [there was no money for teacher salaries] yet when a hurricane came, he found millions of dollars. He said that was a disaster . . . . From that day we decided to become a disaster."

On 7 November 1960, 5,600 members of the UFT conducted a one-day strike, the nation's first teachers' strike, to demand collective bargaining rights. They won even though the strike violated current law. Moreover, only one in ten teachers participated, and striking teachers could have been fired for their illegal action.

After the strike, the UFT began to grow. Shanker had divorced his first wife, and on 18 March 1960, when New York City teachers chose the UFT as their collective bargaining agent, Shanker married Edith (Eadie) Gerber, a teacher he met while organizing the UFT. They had four children. In 1962 Shanker was elected UFT secretary, and in 1964 he succeeded Charles Cogen to become the union's second president. He served in this capacity until 1986.

In 1967 Shanker was jailed for fifteen days for organizing a three-week strike over smaller classes and the demand for more money for education. Shanker gained national prominence in 1968 when he was jailed for fifteen days after a conflict erupted in a Brooklyn district called Ocean Hill–Brownsville. A month-long strike, the longest teachers' strike in U.S. history, centered on a local school board's attempt to dismiss teachers without due process. A series of three violent strikes, the third of which affected the district's one million students for two months and cost the city more than $7.8 billion, divided the city along racial lines.

Shanker himself was routinely branded a racist in the conflict, to the amazement of those who knew his background. Influenced by his college activism, Shanker had made union involvement in civil rights a priority for the UFT during his presidency. In the early 1960s he had formed alliances with A. Philip Randolph, head of the predominantly black Brotherhood of Sleeping Car Porters, and Bayard Rustin, director of the A. Philip Randolph Institute (APRI), which was founded to foster alliances between blacks and labor. Shanker was treasurer of the APRI, and

he served on the Board of Directors of APRI from 1965 to 1997.

Shanker had marched for civil rights in the South in the 1960s, sent hundreds of union members south to register black voters, and lobbied for passage of major civil rights legislation. In 1963 he saw to it that the union endorsed and sent representatives to the March on Washington for Jobs and Freedom. Under his leadership the executive board of the UFT voted in 1965 to place funds in a bank free from dealings with South Africa's apartheid government. He publicly favored a civilian complaint board to investigate charges of police brutality in black communities.

In the end, the union won the struggle in Ocean Hill–Brownsville, resulting in victories for the teachers, who emerged with an even stronger contract. Shanker had forever changed the image of the docile, compliant teacher. Shanker's reputation as a militant union leader was immortalized by Woody Allen in the movie *Sleeper* (1973), in which Allen's character, awakening in the year 2173 after being frozen, explains the cause of the destruction of civilization: "A man by the name of Albert Shanker got hold of a nuclear warhead."

In 1969 Shanker organized thousands of classroom paraprofessionals, many of them minority group members from Ocean-Hill Brownsville, and began a career ladder program so that they could receive a college education and eventually become teachers.

A national figure because of his role in the strikes, Shanker attempted to balance the public image of a union fanatic by launching a weekly paid advertisement column, "Where We Stand," in the Sunday *New York Times* in 1970. In 1972 he helped create the New York State United Teachers (NYSUT), which became the largest statewide union in the country. In 1974 he was elected president of the AFT, which had over 700,000 members. During New York City's fiscal crisis in 1975, Shanker asked the Teachers' Retirement System to save the city from bankruptcy by buying $150 million of untested Municipal Assistance Corporation bonds.

In the 1980s Shanker turned to educational reform. He proposed school restructuring, a voluntary national certification board for teachers, and high national standards for student assessment. From 1987 to 1990 he served as visiting professor at Harvard University.

In 1994 Shanker was diagnosed with cancer. For most of his life he smoked heavily, and he had had a lung removed in 1951. He died at the age of sixty-eight at Memorial Sloan-Kettering Cancer Center in New York City; he had a private interment.

★

An analysis of Shanker's contributions to national labor unionism is in "The Education of Al Shanker," *Teacher Magazine*

(19 Feb. 1996). Obituaries are in the *New York Times* and the *New Leader* (both 24 Feb. 1997), *Time* (10 Mar. 1997), and *The New Republic* (17 Mar. 1997).

JOHN J. BYRNE

SHAPIRO, Karl Jay (*b.* 10 November 1913 in Baltimore, Maryland; *d.* 12 May 2000 in New York City), noted poet, critic, professor, and editor who was named consultant in poetry (the position now called U.S. poet laureate) at the Library of Congress in 1946. His work won the prestigious Bollingen Prize for poetry in 1969.

Born Carl Jay Shapiro, Shapiro was the second son of Joseph Shapiro, a businessman, and Sara Omansky. His given name was legally changed to Karl in 1920. He attended the University of Virginia for one semester in 1932 and Johns Hopkins University from 1937 to 1939. In 1940 he attended the Pratt Library School in Baltimore. Early in 1942, during World War II, Shapiro left for the southwest Pacific aboard a troopship. He had just begun to write poetry. When he returned home in 1946, he was famous, having won the Pulitzer Prize in 1945 for his second book, *V-Letter and Other Poems.* Three years later he figured dramatically in the awarding of the first Library of Congress Bollingen Prize, which was given to the writer Ezra Pound for *The Pisan Cantos* in 1948. Shapiro was a member of the jury and voted against the "traitor poet." (Pound was arrested and jailed for treason in 1945 because he had made public broadcasts in Italy supporting fascism and anti-Semitism during World War II.) Shapiro's statement read, "I voted against Pound in the belief that the poet's political and moral philosophy ultimately vitiated his poetry and lowered its standard as literary work." A national debate ensued, with most siding with Shapiro.

From 1950 to 1955 he edited *Poetry: A Magazine of Verse* in Chicago. He edited *Prairie Schooner* at the University of Nebraska from 1956 to 1966 and was professor of English at the Chicago Circle Campus of the University of Illinois from 1966 to 1968. Shapiro married Evalyn Katz in March 1945; they had three children and divorced in January 1967. His other marriages were to Teri Kovach (married 31 July 1967; divorced July 1982) and Sophie Wilkins (married 28 April 1985).

While Shapiro surfaced early on the American poetry scene, at age thirty-two, his staying power was significant in the 1960s, witness the 1969 Bollingen Award for his 334-page *Selected Poems.* His selected collection of critical essays, *In Defense of Ignorance,* was published in 1960. It contained some of his most enduring essays—on the writers T. S. Eliot, Pound, William Butler Yeats, Dylan Thomas, W. H. Auden, William Carlos Williams, Walt Whitman, and Henry Miller. His breakthrough book of prose poems,

Karl Shapiro. AP/WIDE WORLD PHOTOS

The Bourgeois Poet, appeared in 1964. Another U.S. poet laureate, Stanley Kunitz, regarded it as Shapiro's finest book, reflecting the full flower of his creativity as well as the influence of the Beat poets. The Beat poets, among them Allen Ginsberg and Laurence Ferlinghetti, espoused writing based on authentic individual experience; their adoption of free verse as opposed to formal verse captured Shapiro's attention for some years in the 1960s. Abandoning meter and rhyme, he gave new life to the prose poem, a form originally conceived by the nineteenth-century French poet Aloysius Bertrand. Shapiro's book was greatly influential in the 1960s and arguably influenced later prose poems by Robert Bly, James Wright, David Ignatow, and others.

In *The Bourgeois Poet,* Shapiro wrote in a form that he had created, poems in the shape of a paragraph with a panhandle on the left. One began:

> This is a paragraph. A paragraph is a sonnet in prose.
> A paragraph begins where it ends. A paragraph may
> contain a single word or cruise for pages. Good
> writing rids itself of style, sanctifies no grammar, is
> silent more than it speaks . . .

Shapiro published his only novel, *Edsel,* in 1971. It is an irreverent and moving book that takes an angry look at university life (reflecting his own years at the University of Nebraska) and at the chaotic rage of students in the 1960s and the self-seeking pretensions of their elders. One unforgettable scene occurs during a faculty brawl honoring the self-proclaimed guru of modern poetry (a character based upon Ginsberg) and his bearded chanters. Another character in the novel, called Dylan McGoon, resembles the writer Rod McKuen, a mawkish, pop-culture "poet" who gained a wide audience in the 1960s. Shapiro claimed to have written the novel on the beach one summer, passing pages to friends as he finished them.

Among his other important books from the 1960s are *White-Haired Lover* and *To Abolish Children and Other Essays,* both published in 1968. *White-Haired Lover* marked a return to formal poetry after the experimentation of *The Bourgeois Poet.* In the second volume of his autobiography, *Reports of My Death* (1990), Shapiro gives an account of himself in the 1960s. He was teaching at the University of California, Davis, at the time of the assassinations of President John F. Kennedy and his brother, Senator Robert Kennedy, and the civil rights leader the Reverend Martin Luther King, Jr. He felt that the 1960s would be a landmark decade, "a turning point of history, a moment of irreversible dissolution for the old order, a wild warping of the social crust of the earth, as violent in its way as the war decade of the Forties but with its own war against war."

Shapiro claimed to have understood the 1960s before anyone else. He had read Zen books before they were available in America and talked about Zen and astrology to his students, even asking his poetry students under which zodiac sign they were born. (Zen is an important school of Buddhism in Japan. It claims to transmit the spirit or essence of Buddhism, which consists of experiencing the enlightenment achieved by Buddha. The fad of astrology made its debut at this time.) Shapiro also believed that he was part of the revolution in the defense of obscenity, since he had written an essay in defense of Henry Miller and his sexually explicit novel *Tropic of Cancer,* which was written in 1934 but not published in the United States until 1961. This essay, titled "The Greatest Living Author," appeared as the foreword to the 1961 edition and helped get Miller sanctioned by the Massachusetts Supreme Court. Shapiro also helped promote Ginsberg's collection of poems *Howl* (1959), considered the poetic manifesto of the Beats, and the cause of homosexual rights. He claimed that the revolutions of the 1960s had made a patriot of him, and he took to flying a big silk American flag before his home on the proper holidays. The one "revolution" he did not espouse was the institution of creative writing courses, which began at the University of Iowa in the 1930s but became widespread in the 1960s. He had taught at Iowa for a time but resigned, saying that he could not tolerate it. One of his

poems, titled simply "Creative Writing," begins, "English was in its autumn when this weed / Sprang up on every quad."

By the mid-1980s Shapiro was a less influential figure, but he made a "comeback" by publishing two volumes of autobiography, *The Younger Son* (1988) and *Reports of My Death,* followed by a solid selection from his lifework in poetry, *The Wild Card: Selected Poems, Early and Late* (1998). Shapiro died of natural causes. His body was cremated and his ashes stored with his widow, Sophie Wilkins, in a ceramic vase made by a former student. After his death an entire manuscript of uncollected poems was found in his desk in New York, and plans were made to publish it.

★

There are important manuscript collections at the Library of Congress and the Harry Ransom Center at the University of Texas at Austin, with a smaller collection at the University of Maryland. An in-depth interview with Robert Phillips, "The Art of Poetry," is in the *Paris Review* (spring 1986). See also the book-length study by Joseph Reino, *Karl Shapiro* (1981); a festschrift by Sue B. Walker, ed., *Seriously Meeting Karl Shapiro* (1993); and the dissertation of Diederik Oostidijk, *Karl Shapiro and Poetry: A Magazine of Verse (1950–1955),* Katholieke Universiteit Nijmegen (submitted in Sept. 2000). See also the videotape Arthur Hoyle and Karl Shapiro, *Karl Shapiro's America* (1976). An obituary is in the *New York Times* (17 May 2000).

ROBERT PHILLIPS

SHEEHAN, Cornelius Mahoney ("Neil") (*b.* 27 October 1936 in Holyoke, Massachusetts), journalist, Pulitzer Prize–winning author, and one of the first war correspondents to report that the Vietnam War was going badly; his 1988 book, *A Bright Shining Lie,* is often called the best book about America's involvement in Vietnam.

Sheehan's parents were Cornelius Joseph Sheehan and Mary (O'Shea) Sheehan, farmers and Irish immigrants to America. Sheehan graduated from Northfield Mount Hermon High School in Northfield, Massachusetts, in 1954. He then attended Harvard University, majoring in Middle Eastern history, and received his bachelor's degree in 1958. During the summers of his college years Sheehan worked on highway construction crews. From 1959 to 1962 he served in the U.S. Army as a military journalist and was assigned to cover Korea and Japan, receiving the Army Commendation Medal for his service. In Korea he moonlighted for United Press International (UPI), then one of America's two major wire-service news companies. He credited the army with teaching him a lesson that he applied to his work as a journalist: "It may be raining, it may be snowing, the sun may be shining, but you get up and YOU MARCH."

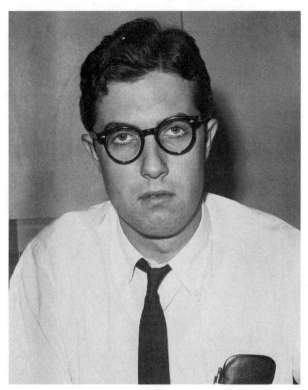

Neil Sheehan. CORBIS CORPORATION (BELLEVUE)

After Sheehan left the army in 1962, UPI hired him as bureau chief for Saigon, South Vietnam. He then believed that the war in Vietnam was "a glorious adventure." At that time the United States had approximately 3,200 military advisers in South Vietnam. The South Vietnamese had long sought independence from North Vietnam, finally achieving it in the early 1950s, only to have France yoke them into a colony, Indochina. The American advisers found the South Vietnamese Army unprepared for war. At first Sheehan glamorized going into combat with South Vietnamese troops, with bullets zinging past him. His reports for UPI were enthusiastic about America's participation in the war.

This enthusiasm began to wane when he was fooled into reporting a decisive South Vietnamese victory in which two hundred enemy troops were killed. It turned out to be a lie, and he had to submit a retraction to UPI. He expected to be fired but was not; he did, however, learn to verify everything the military told him. Later he surveyed the gory aftermath of the 2 January 1963 battle at Ap Bac, which left corpses scattered in rice paddies, and he lost his belief in the glory of battle.

In 1962 he met Lieutenant Colonel John Paul Vann, an adviser to the South Vietnamese government. Vann was critical of how the war was being conducted. He believed that indiscriminate bombing with B-52s was killing civilians; he argued that the war had to be fought and won on the ground, with rifles and knives. Sheehan and other journalists found Vann's views refreshingly honest, and they admired his courage in battle. Vann retired in 1963. By then Sheehan's reports for UPI were focusing on the weak leadership of the South Vietnamese Army, the corrupt nature of the South Vietnamese government, and the lack of popular support among South Vietnamese civilians for their government. UPI censored Sheehan's reports on the grounds that they were too emotional.

In June 1964 Sheehan left UPI to work for the *New York Times*. That year he was awarded the Louis M. Lyons Award for integrity in journalism. In January 1965 the *New York Times* transferred Sheehan to Indonesia. On 30 March 1965 Sheehan married Susan M. Margulies, a journalist for the *New Yorker* magazine, who later published several books under the name Susan Sheehan, including *Ten Vietnamese* (1967). They had two daughters. In June 1965 Sheehan was sent back to Vietnam at the request of the *New York Times* bureau chief for Saigon, Charles Mohr. The United States was escalating its involvement in the Vietnam War, and Mohr wanted Sheehan to help him report the changes.

In 1966 the *New York Times* called Sheehan back to Washington, D.C., to cover the Pentagon. In 1968 he was made the newspaper's White House correspondent, but in 1969 he focused on investigative reporting. By this time he was an opponent of America's involvement in the war, but he earned a reputation for fairness. Sheehan wrote an exhaustive review of thirty-three books on Vietnam for the *New York Times*, and a government official named Daniel Ellsberg read it. Ellsberg was a Defense Department analyst who, among others, had been commissioned by Defense Secretary Robert McNamara to write a history of Vietnam covering the years 1945–1967. The resulting history comprised forty-seven volumes. Ellsberg smuggled an archive of documents out of the Pentagon and gave it to Sheehan. When Sheehan reported what he had to A. M. Rosenthal, the editor of the *New York Times*, Rosenthal unhesitatingly decided to publish it.

In April 1972 Sheehan and eleven other *New York Times* staff members, calling themselves Project X, took seven weeks to organize what became the notorious Pentagon Papers. On 13 June 1971 the first installment of the Pentagon Papers was published on the front page of the *New York Times*. After two more installments were printed, the U.S. government obtained an injunction, on 15 June 1971, against the *Times* forbidding further publication of the Pentagon Papers, but other newspapers, such as the *Boston Globe*, continued to publish fragments. The *New York*

Times and the *Washington Post* sued the government for the right to publish the material. On 30 June 1971 the U.S. Supreme Court ruled in favor of the newspapers.

The *New York Times* received a 1972 Pulitzer Gold Medal for public service for publishing the Pentagon Papers. In December 1971 Sheehan received the Drew Pearson Prize for excellence in investigative reporting. In 1972 he was given the Page One Award from the Newspaper Guild of New York, the Sidney Hillman Foundation Award, and the Columbia Journalism Award. At that time Sheehan began writing a biography of Vann, who in 1964 had returned to South Vietnam as a civilian adviser but ended up directing the military operations of an entire province as if he were a general, moving from concern about civilian casualties to wanting to turn Vietnam into a moonscape of desolation. Vann died in Vietnam in a helicopter crash in 1972. It took Sheehan sixteen years to write *A Bright Shining Lie: John Paul Vann and America in Vietnam* (1988); it was hailed as the best book ever published about the Vietnam War. The length of the writing project prompted Sheehan's friends to joke that Sheehan was "the last casualty of Vietnam." For the biography Sheehan received the 1988 National Book Award, the 1989 Pulitzer Prize for general nonfiction, and the 1989 Robert F. Kennedy Book Award.

Sheehan, an outstanding journalist, possessed formidable physical courage, and his reports from the field have become significant historical documents. His Vietnam reporting helped inform Americans about their country's successes and failures in Southeast Asia. Likewise, his editing of the Pentagon Papers helped reveal the hidden history of America's involvement in Vietnam. Through dogged determination Sheehan conducted almost four hundred interviews for a classic study of Vietnam, *A Bright Shining Lie*.

★

Sheehan's *A Bright Shining Lie: John Paul Vann and America in Vietnam* (1988) offers insights into his own activities, as does *After the War Was Over: Hanoi and Saigon* (1992). *Reporting Vietnam: American Journalism 1959–1969*, vol. 1 (1998) presents some of Sheehan's Vietnam journalism. Biographical information is also in William Prochau, *Once Upon a Distant War: David Halberstam, Neil Sheehan, Peter Arnett—Young War Correspondents and the Early Vietnam Battles* (1996), which examines how Sheehan's views evolved in the early 1960s; and Fred Inglis, *People's Witness: The Journalist in Modern Politics* (2002), which discusses how Sheehan's journalism helped shape history. Articles on Sheehan include "Literary Lights: Branch, Sheehan, Caro," *U.S. News and World Report* (9 July 1990); and "A Bright Shining Lie," *Variety* (25 May 1998).

KIRK H. BEETZ

SHEPARD, Alan Bartlett, Jr. (*b.* 18 November 1923 in East Derry, New Hampshire; *d.* 21 July 1998 in Monterey, California), U.S. Navy test pilot, astronaut, and businessman who in 1961 became the first American to be launched into outer space and in 1971 became the fifth man to walk on the Moon and the first to play golf there.

Shepard's father, Alan Bartlett Shepard, Sr., was a U.S. Army lieutenant colonel who later worked in insurance. His mother, Renza (Emerson) Shepard, was a homemaker. The elder child in the family, Shepard attended rural East Derry's one-room school. For high school he attended Pinkerton Academy in nearby Derry, leaving in 1940 to attend Admiral Farragut Academy in Toms River, New Jersey, for a year. He then entered an accelerated three-year program at the U.S. Naval Academy in Annapolis, Maryland, graduating with a B.S. in 1944. Although Shepard served on a destroyer in the closing months of World War II, he found time to marry Louise Brewer on 3 March 1945; they had two daughters.

Once World War II ended, Shepard attended naval flight training school at Corpus Christi, Texas, and Pensacola, Florida. He simultaneously attended a civilian flight school, earning a civilian flying license before finishing his naval flying studies in March 1947. For three years he was assigned to Fighter Squadron Forty-two, stationed in Norfolk, Virginia, and served on aircraft carriers in the Mediterranean Sea. In 1950 he began attending the test pilot school in Patuxent River, Maryland.

As a test pilot he researched U.S. weather conditions at different altitudes and then tested methods for in-flight refueling of jet aircraft, the suitability of the F2H3 Banshee fighter for landing on and taking off from aircraft carriers, and the use of angled decks on aircraft carriers. He was stationed for a short period at Moffett Field in California, becoming the operations officer for Fighter Squadron 193, which sailed on the aircraft carrier *Oriskany* in the Pacific. Thereafter he tested several cutting-edge aircraft before becoming an instructor at the test pilot school in Patuxent River, finishing in 1956. Shepard then studied at the U.S. Naval War College in Newport, Rhode Island, graduating in 1958. During Shepard's long military career he was honored with the Distinguished Flying Cross, the Distinguished Service Medal, the Congressional Space Medal of Honor, and several other awards.

Shepard's career took a twist and a turn in 1959, when 110 test pilots from all of the services were asked to try out to become astronauts. Because Shepard's orders had been misplaced, he entered the testing program a bit belatedly, but he still was named as one of the first U.S. astronauts, the Mercury Seven. Shepard was assigned to develop the tools needed to track spacecraft, as well as to train the peo-

Alan B. Shepard. ARCHIVE PHOTOS, INC.

ple who would retrieve astronauts and recover spacecraft. There was constant speculation about whether John Glenn, Gus Grissom, or Shepard would be the first human pilot in a Mercury capsule.

In late April 1961 the National Aeronautics and Space Administration (NASA) announced that Shepard would be the first U.S. astronaut to fly into outer space. On 12 April 1961 the Russian Yuri Gagarin had become the first human in space, although he had no control over his capsule. Unlike Gagarin, who was only a passenger, Shepard would be able to maneuver his craft during the flight. Bad weather caused the launch of Shepard's *Freedom 7* to be delayed from 2 May until 5 May 1961.

From 5:20 A.M. to 9:34 A.M., Shepard sat uncomfortably in his capsule atop its launch rockets, waiting while technicians uncovered and corrected one problem after another; then *Freedom 7* was launched. Once in outer space, Shepard took over manual control of the craft and practiced some maneuvers. He reported that weightlessness was actually pleasant and did not make him sick. The descent of *Freedom 7* was too fast, but Shepard was able to maneuver it enough to put it on the desired landing trajectory. For his historic fifteen-minute flight, Shepard was honored by President John F. Kennedy and by congratulations from all over the world.

He soon returned to work and was scheduled for another Mercury flight, but that launch was scrubbed in favor of the new Gemini program, which featured two-seater capsules. Shepard was assigned to one of the Gemini flights, but he soon began to suffer from bouts of nausea and dizziness. He would feel fine for several days and then become sick again, with ringing in one of his ears. In 1963 Shepard was diagnosed with Ménière's syndrome, or too much fluid pressure in the inner ear. Because of this disease, he was no longer allowed to fly aircraft and his seat on the Gemini mission was given to another astronaut. From 1965 to 1974 Shepard served as the director of NASA's astronaut office.

In 1968 Shepard had a tube surgically inserted in his ear to drain the excess fluid that was causing the damaging pressure. The operation was a success, and on 7 May 1969 he regained his flight status and returned to the astronaut-training program. He was assigned as the commander of *Apollo 14,* with the crew of Edgar Mitchell, who would join Shepard in walking on the Moon, and Stuart Roosa, who, as the pilot of the command module, would orbit the Moon until the spacewalkers' return. They were launched from Cape Kennedy on 31 January 1971. In spite of the scientific work completed by the astronauts, most people remembered the third lunar landing for Shepard's golfing demonstration in the dust of the lunar surface, which was broadcast live on television all over the world.

After his return to Earth, in 1971 Shepard was made a delegate to the United Nations General Assembly and was promoted to rear admiral. He retired from the navy and from NASA on 31 July 1974. During the 1960s Shepard had made good investments in real estate and banking, and he was likely already a millionaire before his Apollo flight. After his retirement he pursued a successful business career in Houston, Texas, as the chair of a construction company and the president of a beer distributor. He also chaired the Mercury Seven Foundation for many years. In the 1990s Shepard moved to California. He died of leukemia in Monterey at age seventy-four; his remains were cremated and the ashes were scattered over the Pacific Ocean.

Shepard will long be remembered as the first U.S. astronaut in space and as the first true pilot of a space vehicle. He brought a sense of humor and joy to his work that caught the imaginations of 1960s audiences and gave space travel a human perspective. By encouraging others to view his adventures as their own, he helped the U.S. public to believe space was a place where humans belonged.

★

Shepard and Deke Slayton, with Jay Barbree and Howard Benedict, *Moon Shot: The Inside Story of America's Race to the Moon* (1994), describes the 1960s space program. A profile of Shepard is included in M. Scott Carpenter, et al., *We Seven, by the Astronauts Themselves* (1962). *Current Biography Yearbook* (1961) presents details about Shepard's life and indicates some of the breathless excitement inspired by his Mercury flight. For significant insights into Shepard's life, see Tara Gray, "Alan B. Shepard, Jr.," *Fortieth Anniversary of the Mercury Seven,* on the NASA website. This website also offers access to Loyd S. Swenson, Jr., James M. Grimwood, and Charles C. Alexander, *This New Ocean: A History of Project Mercury* (1989), which includes a detailed account of Shepard's 1961 flight. Obituaries are in *Time* (3 Aug. 1998) and *People Weekly* (10 Aug. 1998).

KIRK H. BEETZ

SHOEMAKER, William Lee ("Bill") (*b.* 19 August 1931 in Fabens, Texas), American jockey who amassed 8,833 wins from 40,350 mounts with purse wins in excess of $123 million. While the United States has a pantheon of distinguished jockeys, a good case can be made that Shoemaker was the best of them.

Shoemaker was the elder of two sons of Bebe Shoemaker, a cotton mill worker, and Ruby Harris, a homemaker. His astonishingly long and successful athletic career had a rocky start. Shoemaker was born prematurely; at birth he weighed a fraction under two pounds, and he was fortunate to survive. Joan Goodbody, in her short biography, emphasizes that Shoemaker himself is convinced he would not have survived had it not been for the loving ministrations of a doting grandmother. When he was ten his parents divorced.

Bill Shoemaker. AP/WIDE WORLD PHOTOS

For a time Shoemaker lived with his grandparents on a farm on the outskirts of Abilene, Texas; it is said he regularly rode a farm horse to pick up the daily mail. He later relocated to the San Gabriel Valley in California to live with his father, who had remarried. *Current Biography* observes of Shoemaker that despite "his bantam size he distinguished himself as a high school athlete." He attended El Monte Union High School but dropped out at age fifteen. Goodbody points to his development, as a preteen, of just the sort of physical and psychological strengths that turned him into an extraordinary jockey. Despite weighing only eighty pounds he was undefeated as a wrestler in the flyweight division and also won a Golden Gloves boxing championship. The challenges and accomplishments of individual sports helped develop Shoemaker's extraordinary athletic focus.

He rode his first race on 19 March 1949, and by the end of the season he had amassed 219 victories, making him the runner-up as champion jockey. In his second year of riding he was first equal jockey (tied with one other rider) with 388 wins. He was the top money-winner on no fewer than ten occasions, and he had a run of years—1958 to 1964—in which he earned the most purse money. In 1951, even though the United States was the leading country in terms of prize monies awarded in sports like tennis, golf, and auto racing, the actual amounts involved were in the low thousands. Massive salaries for baseball, basketball, and football players were unheard of at that time. Yet in 1951 and 1954 Shoemaker's purse earnings were $1,329,890 and $1,876,760 respectively. These were astonishing amounts of money for the four-foot, eleven-inch and 100-pound jockey.

The 1960s marked the apotheosis of Shoemaker's career. On 19 May 1961 he won his 4,000th race on Guaranteeya at Hollywood Park, California. In the same year the Arlington-Washington Futurity race advertised itself as the richest horse race of all time. Shoemaker, riding Candy Spots, won the race and took the prize money of $142,250. A year later, racing at Belmont, he set a national record for the distance of one and three-eighths miles with a time of 2 minutes and 13.2 seconds. The acme of the decade may have been 24 January 1964, when Shoemaker rode Braganza to success on the Santa Anita track. He became the all-time leading money-winning thoroughbred rider with $30,040,005, beating the former record held by the retired Eddie Arcaro. Then, in October, he won his 5,000th race, aboard Slapstick at Aqueduct. In 1965 Shoemaker won his third Kentucky Derby on the mount Lucky Debonair. Elite racing is a cutthroat business, and any assessment of Shoemaker either during the 1960s or over his total career has to recognize he was a resilient competitor who bounced back from adversity. For example, in 1965 Shoemaker lost his top-money-winner spot to Braulio Baeza, and at the start of the 1966 season he had a run of zero wins in twenty starts on the Aqueduct track in New York.

Horse racing takes a heavy toll on riders. In January 1968, in a race on the Santa Anita track in California, Shoemaker took a heavy fall, resulting in a broken leg. While legs mend relatively quickly, the skills of the jockey's craft evaporate at an alarming rate in the absence of daily saddling, training, and racing. Jockeys need to race and race hard to stay on the cusp of elite competition. It took Shoemaker all of thirteen months to resume his racing career. Just over three months later a horrifying spill in a paddock accident nearly terminated his life. Shoemaker suffered a fractured pelvis, a ruptured bladder, and nerve damage in a leg. His courage and grit in rehabilitating himself stand as a remarkable testament to a little man possessed of a huge heart and rare pluck.

In an Entertainment and Sports Programming Network (ESPN) essay, Rob Flatter analyzes the reasons for Shoemaker's genius in the 1960s. He points out that although Shoemaker was strong enough to control an animal fifteen times his weight, the real explanation for his success was his finesse and gentle control. Flatter makes the analogy of the powerful quarterback who can throw a touch pass or the explosive snooker player who can also score with a gentle and slow shot. With Shoemaker, his jockey craft was based on "soft hands." Flatter quotes the jockey Chris McCarron, who said of Shoemaker, "His smooth, calm style was deceiving."

In the 1960s Shoemaker won the Belmont Stakes in 1962, the Preakness in 1963, and both the Belmont and the Preakness in 1965. Then, on 7 September 1970, at not quite forty years of age, Shoemaker, with 6,033 victories, broke Johnny Longden's all-time winning record. *Current Biography* makes the point that Shoemaker, despite being an intense competitor, was revered by his fellow jockeys. Eddie Arcaro called Shoemaker the "Little Champ" in the 1960s and thought he was "the cleanest rider" he had ever seen. Just as Ted Williams is baseball's purest striker of the ball, Shoemaker qualifies as the most consummately elegant jockey. Arcaro recalls Shoemaker's urging him to get "into" a horse. By this Shoemaker did not mean driving hard or using the whip; instead, he referred to the business of communicating and becoming one with a horse. Shoemaker, arguably, was racing's modern centaur—a man who fused with a legion of charging horses. In the same month Shoemaker passed Longden's record (September 1970), Willie Mays joined Babe Ruth in baseball's 600 homers club and Rocky Marciano, the undefeated former heavyweight boxing champion, was killed in a plane crash. In every sense of the word Shoemaker was as skilled and tough and at the top of his form as were Mays and Marciano in their heydays.

Shoemaker married in 1950; he and his wife adopted two children, then divorced in 1960. In 1961 he remarried and adopted his new wife's son; the couple divorced in 1978. He married for the third time that same year, divorcing in 1994 after having one daughter. Shoemaker's amazing career stretched through the 1970s. On 27 May 1981 at Hollywood Park he won his record 8,000th career race. Shoemaker's swan song was on 3 February at Santa Anita. The fifty-eight-year-old rode Patchy Groundfrog before an ecstatic crowd of 63,200. A fourth-place finish could not erase Shoemaker's contribution to racing. He had amassed 8,833 wins, more than $123 million in purse money, four Derby wins, five wins in the Belmont Stakes, and two wins in the Preakness. On 8 April 1991 Shoemaker's car went off the road. His neck was broken, and he was rendered a quadriplegic. In recent years Shoemaker's greatest passion has been his involvement with Paralysis Project; he serves as honorary chair.

★

Current Biography (1966) has an extensive essay on Shoemaker that is especially useful on the 1960s. Ralph Hickok profiles Shoemaker in the *Encyclopedia of North American Sports History* (1992). Ron Smith, *The Sporting News: Chronicle of Twentieth Century Sport* (1992), has a series of vignettes on Shoemaker's accomplishments. Joan Goodbody wrote a brief biographical sketch of Shoemaker for *Scribner's Encyclopedia of American Lives, Sports Figures,* vol. 2 (2002). Ron Flatter, "Shoemaker Made Racing History," a special ESPN piece, is available at <http://espn.go.com/sport-scentury/features/>.

SCOTT A. G. M. CRAWFORD

SHORE, Dinah (*b.* 1 March 1917 in Winchester, Tennessee; *d.* 24 February 1994 in Beverly Hills, California), singer and television host who claimed nineteen gold records and ten Emmy Awards.

Dinah Shore.

Frances Rose Shore was the younger of two daughters born to Solomon and Anna Stein Shore. Her father ran a dry goods store after immigrating to Tennessee from Europe. When she was about eighteen months old, Shore's life was marked by a bout of polio. With constant massages and exercise, she made a nearly full recovery by the time she was eight years old. The Shores were the only Jewish family in Winchester, and her experience with polio added to her sense of being an outsider.

In about 1932 the Shores moved to Nashville, Tennessee, where Solomon Shore invested in a department store. That same year Anna Shore was stricken with a heart attack and died; the older daughter, Elizabeth, returned home with her physician husband to help care for her sister, who was then about sixteen years old. After graduating from Hume-Fogg High School in 1934, Shore attended Vanderbilt University in Nashville. She also adopted a new name, "Dinah," taken from a song she had performed at an audition for Nashville's WSM radio station. The newly christened Dinah Shore completed her degree in sociology in 1938 and traveled to New York City to pursue a career as a singer.

Her radio appearances led to a recording contract, and in 1942 Shore had her first of nineteen million-selling singles, "Blues in the Night." Among her other best-sellers during the 1940s were "I'll Walk Alone" (1944), "The Anniversary Song" (1947), and "Buttons and Bows" (1948). She made several cameo appearances in such films as *Up in Arms* (1944) and *'Til the Clouds Roll By* (1946), but even after being glamorized with blonde hair and cosmetic surgery on her nose and teeth, Shore seemed out of place in the elaborate musicals. Her transition to television, a far better vehicle for her engaging and enthusiastic personality, proved much more successful. The fifteen-minute *Dinah Shore Show,* a music program sponsored by Chevrolet that aired twice a week on the National Broadcasting Company

(NBC) from 1951 to 1957, earned its star two Emmy Awards for best female singer, in 1954 and 1955.

In 1956 Shore also began hosting the *Dinah Shore Chevy Show,* a one-hour variety program that aired until 1961. As on her earlier program, Shore ended each broadcast with the theme song "See the U.S.A. in Your Chevrolet" and an exaggerated goodnight kiss directed to the television audience. The show was also notable for its host's warm regard and obvious admiration for African-American entertainers, such as Ella Fitzgerald. Shore picked up three more Emmys for the *Chevy Show,* and its popularity put her on the Gallup poll list of the ten most admired women in the late 1950s and early 1960s. Years later the *New York Times* summed up her appeal by describing Shore as "a symbolic Everywoman of the 1950s and 1960s."

Chevrolet ended its sponsorship in 1961, and the *Dinah Shore Show* continued as a monthly program until 1963. Shore had married the actor and businessman George Montgomery on 5 December 1943; they were divorced in 1962. The couple had two children, a daughter born in 1948 and an adopted son born in 1954. Shore married for a second time in 1963, to Maurice F. Smith, but the union lasted less than a year. For a performer whose press coverage routinely referred to the importance of her home life—a 1960 *Life* cover story headlined "The Dual Lives of Dinah: TV's

Sunny Top Lady Harmonizes Job and Home"—the events seemed uncharacteristic.

With television specials and concert tours in the mid-1960s, Shore stayed in the public eye as one of the most recognizable, yet outwardly down-to-earth celebrities of the decade. She reemerged with a daily television talk show on NBC, *Dinah's Place,* in 1970. The show ran for four years and coincided with Shore's most scrutinized period as a celebrity, owing to her relationship with the actor Burt Reynolds. Given that Reynolds, then in his mid-thirties, was nineteen years younger than Shore, the couple endured some good-natured ribbing from their celebrity friends during their courtship. After twenty years on television, Shore's popularity with the public did not falter, despite the potential for criticism over the relationship. Indeed, Shore gained the admiration of many women for dating Reynolds, who was not only much younger but also reaching the peak of his matinee-idol status in the early 1970s. The couple lived together in Shore's Beverly Hills home through the mid-1970s, when their relationship ended.

Shore picked up two Daytime Emmy Awards for *Dinah's Place* and another for *Dinah!,* a ninety-minute daily talk show that aired in syndication from 1974 to 1979. From 1989 to 1991 Shore hosted *Conversation with Dinah* on the Nashville Network. She also published three cookbooks from 1971 and 1990 and turned her love of golf into a major event on the Ladies Professional Golf Association (LPGA) tour, the Dinah Shore Classic, beginning in 1972. In 1992 Shore was honored with an induction into the Academy of Television Arts and Sciences Hall of Fame; she was inducted into the LPGA Hall of Fame in 1994. After a brief bout with cancer, Shore died in her Beverly Hills home just before her seventy-seventh birthday.

From torch singer to television host to sports philanthropist, Shore was a constant presence in America's cultural life over six decades of social change. In his 1994 memoir, *My Life,* Burt Reynolds offered her this tribute: "She didn't gossip. She wasn't judgmental. Her sense of decency, of right and wrong, was impeccable. Her insight into people was as sharp as anyone's and her advice was always on target."

★

For more information on Shore's life, see Bruce Cassiday, *Dinah!: A Biography* (1979). Burt Reynolds recalled his relationship with Shore in *Burt Reynolds: My Life* (1994). A list of Shore's chart singles in the 1950s appears in Joel Whitburn, ed., *The Billboard Book of Top Forty Hits, Sixth Edition* (1996). For a typical article on Shore during her television heyday, see "The Dual Lives of Dinah: TV's Sunny Top Lady Harmonizes Job and Home," *Life* (1 Feb. 1960). Obituaries are in the *New York Times* (25 Feb. 1994) and *Billboard* (12 Mar. 1994).

TIMOTHY BORDEN

SHOUP, David Monroe (*b.* 30 December 1904 near Battle Ground, Indiana; *d.* 13 January 1983 in Alexandria, Virginia), World War II Medal of Honor recipient, Commandant of the U.S. Marine Corps from 1960 to 1963, and outspoken opponent of the Vietnam War.

Shoup was one of four children of John Lamar Shoup, a farmer, and Mary Layton, a homemaker. Shoup graduated from DePauw University in Greencastle, Indiana, in 1926 with a B.A. in mathematics. Although he was a college wrestler, football player, and record-setting marathoner, financial circumstances forced Shoup to wait tables, wash dishes, and work in a cement factory to pay for his education. Participation in the Reserve Officers Training Corps provided additional funds.

In no better financial straits at graduation, Shoup enrolled in the U.S. Army Infantry Reserve. By July 1926 Shoup had received a commission as a second lieutenant in the Marine Corps. He remained in the corps until retiring as commandant and general in December 1963. On 15 September 1931 Shoup married Zola De Haven; they had two children.

As a colonel in World War II, Shoup was awarded the Medal of Honor for his command of the 20–23 November 1943 attack on the island of Betio in the Tarawa atoll. Although Shoup sustained eight shrapnel wounds on the first day of the assault, his "conspicuous gallantry and intrepidity" are credited in the fall of the heavily fortified island.

After the war Shoup continued to rise through the ranks. However, he was still a major general when he was advanced by President Dwight D. Eisenhower over other officers to the position of Commandant of the Marine Corps in 1959. His promotion to four-star general became effective when his four-year term as commandant began on 1 January 1960.

Shoup grew up in rural poverty but was proud of his "Indiana farm boy" roots. Five feet, eight inches tall and of stocky build, he was a demanding leader, not averse to coarse language to make a point. As commandant, Shoup emphasized internal reforms to improve the combat readiness of the corps, including reorganization of the supply system. He eliminated the use of "swagger sticks" and defended the corps from assertions by Senator Strom Thurmond of South Carolina that marines knew too little about communism.

Shoup was disturbed by the disastrous Bay of Pigs invasion of April 1961, believing that military leaders had not been adequately included in planning. Eighteen months later, when the Cuban Missile Crisis raised the specter of invasion of the island, Shoup was determined to prevent another miscalculation. He presented to the Joint Chiefs of Staff a map of Cuba overlaid on a map of the United States, showing the island stretching from New York to Chicago.

David M. Shoup testifying before the Senate Armed Services Committee, 1959. © BETTMANN/CORBIS

He added a tiny red dot, representing the island of Betio, which, Shoup reminded, took 18,000 marines three days to subdue.

Shoup's belief in the scarcity and expense of military resources extended to Vietnam. A brief 1962 tour confirmed for him his conviction that the United States should not undertake a land war in Asia. In 1963, when an officer obtained an increase in the Marine Corps advisory role in Vietnam, Shoup disparaged the mission as a "rat hole."

Still, Shoup was a favorite of President John F. Kennedy. In 1962 Shoup stirred the president's passion for history with an invitation to the marine barracks, advising that while the Washington, D.C., location had been selected by Thomas Jefferson, an actual presidential inspection was long overdue. Kennedy subsequently directed Shoup to a Theodore Roosevelt memorandum requesting Marine Corps officers to demonstrate their fitness with fifty-mile hikes. When Shoup called present-day officers to the task, fifty-mile hikes became a national fad. Despite his affinity with Kennedy, Shoup declined an offer of reappointment, believing it unfair to lower-ranking officers who might otherwise vie for the position.

Shoup's stark view of Vietnam grew in retirement as he watched the U.S. commitment escalate. His feelings erupted in a 14 May 1966 speech to students at the Tenth Annual Junior College World Affairs Day in Los Angeles. Using incendiary language, Shoup told students that, with respect to the safety and freedom of the American people,

the whole of Southeast Asia was not "worth the life or limb of a single American." Shoup asserted his belief that "if we had and would keep our dirty, bloody, dollar-crooked fingers out of the business of these nations so full of depressed, exploited people, they will arrive at a solution of their own." He believed that the exploited people of the world had the right to pursue violent revolution if they deemed it necessary.

In his speech to the students, Shoup encouraged them to demonstrate. Professing a belief that communism would inevitably fade into capitalism, he nevertheless told the students that the most noble effort of humanity was to free humankind from the affluent who gorged on delicacies, while some children starved for lack of milk and bread.

In 1967 Shoup reiterated his opposition in a nationally televised interview, calling for negotiations with the North Vietnamese. His speech and the interview were inserted into the *Congressional Record* but also earned him investigation by the Federal Bureau of Investigation (FBI). Nevertheless, Shoup brought credibility to the antiwar movement, since, as it was observed, it was "difficult to cast doubt on the patriotism of a military man, and doubly so when he has [a] record of gallantry and leadership."

On 20 March 1968 Shoup testified before the Senate Committee on Foreign Relations, chaired by Senator J. William Fulbright of Arkansas. Although Shoup felt privileged, he pointedly noted that he had been called a dissenter and traitor, and had been accused of giving aid and comfort to the enemy. Shoup told the committee that military victory was impossible, no matter how many troops were sent to Vietnam. The conflict, he believed, was essentially a civil war, pitting the unpopular South Vietnamese government against the revered North Vietnamese leader Ho Chi Minh.

Shoup declined many invitations to speak at antiwar rallies. However, he expressed concern over a perceived militarization of the country in his writings, suggesting that intraservice rivalry and career ambition created momentum for military engagements. Later Senate testimony by Shoup in 1971 disparaged President Richard M. Nixon's "Vietnamization" plan and called upon Congress to take action to end the war.

Shoup spent his retirement in Alexandria, Virginia, where he died of a heart condition. He is buried in Arlington National Cemetery in Arlington, Virginia. On 24 February 2001 the U.S. Navy christened the AEGIS guided-missile destroyer *Shoup* in his honor.

Known as the "marine's marine," heroism in World War II made Shoup one of the most highly decorated in that service. Duty beckoned him in retirement to speak out against a war he considered foolhardy. As a voice from the 1960s establishment, he gave weight to the rising swell against the U.S. involvement in Vietnam.

★

Shoup's papers are at the Hoover Institution on War, Revolution, and Peace at Stanford University, Palo Alto, California. For a journal of his tour of duty in China, see Shoup, *The Marines in China, 1927–1928: The China Expedition Which Turned out to Be the China Exhibition; A Contemporaneous Journal* (1987), edited by Howard Jablon. See also Howard Jablon, "General David M. Shoup, U.S.M.C.: Warrior and War Protester," *The Journal of Military History* 60, no. 3 (1996): 513–538; Robert Buzzanco and Leigh Fought, "David Shoup: Four-Star Troublemaker," in *The Human Tradition in the Vietnam Era* (2000), edited by David L. Anderson; and Allen Mikaelian, *Medal of Honor: Profiles of America's Military Heroes from the Civil War to the Present* (2002). Obituaries are in the *Washington Post* (15 Jan. 1983) and *New York Times* (16 Jan. 1983).

DENNIS WATSON

SHRIVER, Eunice Mary Kennedy (*b.* 10 July 1920 in Brookline, Massachusetts), civic worker and activist who helped to establish numerous programs in the 1960s focusing on mental retardation and physical fitness, including the Special Olympics.

Shriver, a Roman Catholic, was the fifth of nine children of the businessman and financier Joseph P. Kennedy, Sr., a successful entrepreneur, and Rose Fitzgerald Kennedy. She attended Roman Catholic convent schools and graduated from a British boarding school during her father's tenure as the U.S. ambassador to England. She graduated from Stanford University in California with a B.S. in sociology in 1943. From 1943 to 1945 she worked with the U.S. Department of State's special war problems division, helping former World War II prisoners of war adjust to civilian life. She was a social worker from 1947 to 1954 at a Virginia federal penitentiary and at a Chicago youth shelter and juvenile court.

She married Sargent Shriver on 23 May 1953 and gave up paid employment with the birth of their first child in 1954. In 1956 she became the executive vice president of the Joseph P. Kennedy, Jr., Foundation, created in 1946 to honor the memory of Shriver's oldest brother, who was killed in a plane crash during World War II. She also worked on the political campaigns of her brothers John, Robert, and Edward ("Ted"), including John's successful 1960 presidential campaign.

Established by Joseph Kennedy, Sr., the Joseph P. Kennedy, Jr., Foundation focused primarily on supporting various Catholic organizations and institutions for the mentally handicapped, including the Saint Coletta institution in Wisconsin, where Shriver's mentally handicapped sister, Rosemary, lived. By the early 1960s Shriver had changed the foundation's focus to emphasize research into preventing retardation and toward various efforts aimed at educating the public about mental retardation. In 1961 she persuaded President John F. Kennedy, her brother, to es-

Eunice Kennedy Shriver photographed during a news conference announcing plans for an International Conference on Abortion, 1967. © BETTMANN/CORBIS

tablish the Presidential Committee on Mental Retardation. The committee's recommendations led to the establishment in 1962 of the National Institute for Child Health and Human Development.

That same year Shriver helped to create the Joseph P. Kennedy, Jr., Awards in mental retardation and convinced her family that they needed to go public with the story of her mentally handicapped sister. The result was an article by Shriver in the *Saturday Evening Post* that revealed how the mildly handicapped Rosemary had undergone brain surgery to mitigate her violent tendencies, only to have her overall condition worsen. The article represented a major step forward in removing the veil of secrecy and shame that surrounded mental retardation.

With the help of her husband, Shriver began a summer day camp in 1963 at Timberlawn, a summer home they rented that included 200 acres and a Civil War–era mansion. At the camp, mentally challenged children and adults could enjoy normal summer vacation activities. The camp was especially successful in demonstrating that the mentally challenged could participate in and benefit from recreational programs and the same sports that those without handicaps played. Shriver, who taught a gym class at the camp, quickly realized that many of the children were extremely capable athletes. As a result, she implemented the establishment of fitness standards and tests for individuals with mental retardation as well as further research to develop these standards. These tests were similar to the physical fitness program established by President Kennedy that targeted U.S. schoolchildren.

After so many accomplishments, many people might have rested on their laurels, but Shriver was just getting started. In 1964, again through the foundation, she initiated a five-year public information campaign by the National Advertising Council to promote acceptance and understanding of people with mental disabilities. Shriver was also instrumental in influencing the passage of key bills aimed at combating retardation, including the 1964 changes in civil service regulations to employ persons with mental retardation based on their ability rather than artificial test scores.

One of the major participants in a camp program that evolved from Shriver's efforts at Timberlawn was the Chicago Park District. In 1968, through a foundation grant to the park district, Shriver expanded the program by establishing the first Special Olympics Games. One thousand handicapped athletes from throughout the United States and Canada attended the games. They competed in events similar to the regular Olympics. Since Shriver started the Special Olympics, the program has grown to involve more than 1.5 million athletes from 130 nations competing in twenty-two sports. When asked in an article for the *Milwaukee Journal Sentinel* (17 Dec. 2001) whether she was surprised at the growth of the program, Shriver replied, "I am surprised. Not at the Special Olympians, because I think they have enormous . . . gifts. . . . I think the growth comes from them. And that doesn't surprise me."

The Eunice Kennedy Shriver Center was founded in 1969 at the University of Massachusetts Medical School to focus on research into the biological and environmental influences on human development, with a special focus on human disabilities. Shriver kept up her activities in the decades following the 1960s, including heading the foundation and many of its programs. In 1971 she helped to create major centers for the study of medical ethics at Harvard University and at Georgetown University, which named its center the Kennedy Institute of Ethics. Other important programs initiated by Shriver and the foundation include the 1990 establishment of the Community of Caring programs in 450 public and private schools. She has received numerous awards, including the 1984 Presidential Medal of Freedom, the nation's highest civilian award, and the 2002 Theodore Roosevelt Award, the highest honor bestowed to an individual by the National Collegiate Athletic Association. She and her husband had five children, including Maria Shriver, a news broadcaster and the wife of the actor Arnold Schwarzenegger.

Shriver's work throughout the 1960s and beyond reflected not only her own devotion to improving the lives of those with mental retardation but also a decade in which social consciousness and the rights and abilities of others, whether they were racial minorities or the handicapped, came to the forefront in America. Adamant and hard-driving in her efforts, Shriver also was noted for her wit and sensitivity. Her efforts on behalf of the mentally handicapped served as a precursor to the larger movement to secure rights for people with all types of disabilities. Perhaps Shriver summed up her philosophy and her contributions best when, at the first Special Olympics, she said, "What you are winning by your courageous efforts is far greater than any game. You are winning life itself, and in doing so you give to others a most precious prize—faith in the unlimited possibilities of the human spirit."

★

Rarely is a book written about the Kennedy family without mentioning Shriver and her many accomplishments. Among them are Harrison Rainie and John Quinn, *Growing Up Kennedy: The Third Wave Comes of Age* (1983), and Peter Collier and David Horowitz, *The Kennedys: An American Drama* (1984). For a look at Shriver in relation to the Special Olympics, see Doug Single, *Skill, Courage, Sharing, Joy: The Stories of Special Olympics* (1992). A good overview of Shriver and her works can be found in the *Encyclopedia of World Biography Supplement,* vol. 19 (1999).

DAVID PETECHUK

SHRIVER, (Robert) Sargent, Jr. (*b.* 9 November 1915 in Westminster, Maryland), journalist and first director of the Peace Corps; John F. Kennedy's brother-in-law and campaign manager; and an outstanding 1960s public servant who symbolized the best qualities of the Kennedy era.

Shriver was the son of Robert Sargent Shriver, Sr., who owned a variety of mills and tanneries in Maryland, and Hilda Shriver, a homemaker. The Shriver family included a long list of public servants, including David Shriver, signatory on the Stamp Act and the Bill of Rights. Shriver's wealthy upbringing enabled him to attend the Canterbury School in New Milford, Connecticut, as a youth. He remained in the Northeast after completing his secondary education and attended Yale University, where he graduated cum laude in 1938, and went on to attend Yale Law School.

Much like his predecessors, Shriver was committed to the idea of public service. After he graduated from Yale Law School in 1941, he enlisted in the navy during World War II. Following the war, he turned away from a career in law and began working as a journalist for *Newsweek*. Shriver relocated to Chicago, a move that created the conditions that determined the course of his life and allowed him to express his public ambitions to their fullest.

Shriver soon served on many public boards and committees. He was president of Chicago's board of education and a member of the city's Council on Foreign Relations. With a growing reputation for being circumspect and diligent, Shriver soon captured the attention of Ambassador Joseph P. Kennedy, Sr., the patriarch of the Kennedy family. Ambassador Kennedy hired Shriver to manage a recent business venture in Chicago. Shriver's work for the elder Kennedy produced more than long-lasting business ties; it also introduced him to Eunice Kennedy, who later became his wife, attaching him indelibly to the Kennedy clan.

Shriver came to assume a prominent role in the political side of the Kennedy business, serving as John F. Kennedy's midwestern campaign manager during the 1960 presidential campaign. Once Kennedy was in office, Shriver took on the daunting task of making his campaign promise of an international volunteer corps a reality. The volunteer corps, officially titled the Peace Corps, was a cornerstone of Kennedy's New Frontier, billed as an improvement over Truman and Eisenhower's unimaginative cold war policy.

True to his reputation, Shriver made the Peace Corps idea a testament to mid-twentieth century development, goodwill, and international cooperation. With meager appropriations from a reticent and highly partisan Congress, and uneven support from the Kennedy administration, Shriver fashioned an organization independent of the political wrangling of the time. In the unforgiving political climate of the cold war, the Peace Corps was a testament to the notion of development and Shriver's lobbying ability.

In the face of sobering international crises—the Bay of Pigs, the Berlin Crisis, the Cuban Missile Crisis, and a fledgling conflict in Southeast Asia—he kept the Peace Corps committed to idealism, even though the program could very well have been a casualty of domestic politics.

The first project that the Peace Corps undertook was in Tanzania, and all sides of the arrangement considered it a resounding success. The agency established strong relationships with developing countries in Africa, Asia, Latin America, and the Middle East.

Shriver also used the Peace Corps to tap into the spirit of volunteerism among recently graduated college students and professionals in the United States. The group promoted a brand of development in developing nations aimed at defeating not only structural and intellectual deficiencies, but also their cultural antecedents. Shriver promoted a program of self-improvement with Americans serving as the catalyst.

When drafted by Kennedy's successor, Lyndon B. Johnson, to design the Office of Economic Opportunity (OEO), yet another rhetorical piece that was more idealism than substance, Shriver in 1964 adopted a similar approach. In the case of the OEO, the governing notion was that the poor needed training, legal resources, access to employment, and adequate education to improve their lot. To this end, the OEO became an umbrella organization that over-

Sargent Shriver, 1967. WALLY MCNAMEE/CORBIS

saw a loose constellation of programs: Head Start, Volunteers in Service to America (VISTA), Community Action Program (CAP), Job Corps, and Upward Bound. As with the Peace Corps, Shriver tried to navigate an autonomous path for the agencies that became the backbone of the War on Poverty. The OEO was a courageous attempt that proved unrealistic as the nation witnessed rioting, student demonstrations, and an increasingly disastrous Vietnam conflict.

Near the close of the decade in 1968, Shriver's public career took a more dramatic turn. In that year he moved from the OEO to an ambassadorship in France, where he served in President Richard M. Nixon's administration. His service ended in 1970, and in 1972 he served as Senator George McGovern's running mate in McGovern's failed bid to unseat Nixon as president. Since the 1980s Shriver has continued inspiring liberal idealism through his work with the Special Olympics International and the Washington, D.C., law firm of Fried, Frank, Harris, Shriver, and Jacobson.

To Washington insiders Shriver was a catalyzing force with a talent for navigating uncharted administrative territory and a shrewd decision-maker with a sharp intellect. For the American public, Shriver represented a charming leader who could make others believe in spite of themselves. During his career as a public servant he flirted with a run at the White House and laid the foundation for America's policy on poverty at home and throughout the world. To many, Shriver represented the last vestige of Kennedy's highest ideals and Camelot mystique in the cold-war era. Shriver embodied the principles that endeared the Kennedy administration to the nation at a time when America was in the throes of tremendous civil and political upheaval.

★

There is no definitive biography of Shriver. Much of his public work can be gleaned from the prominent studies of the Peace Corps and Lyndon Johnson's War on Poverty, including Shriver's own *Point of the Lance* (1964); Gerard T. Rice, *The Bold Experiment: JFK's Peace Corps* (1985); Fritz Fischer, *Making Them Like Us: Peace Corps Volunteers in the 1960s* (1998); Michael Latham, *Modernization as Ideology: American Social Science and "Nation Building" in the Kennedy Era* (2000); and James T. Patterson, *America's Struggle against Poverty in the Twentieth Century* (2000).

CHRISTOPHER T. FISHER

SHULTZ, George Pratt (*b.* 13 December 1920 in New York City), politician and statesman who served as U.S. Secretary of Labor (1969–1970), first director of the Office of Management and Budget (1970–1972), Secretary of the Treasury (May 1972–May 1974), and Secretary of State (July 1982–January 1989).

Shultz is the only child of Birl E. Shultz, founder and director of the New York Stock Exchange Institute, and Margaret Lennox (Pratt) Shultz. He grew up in Englewood, New Jersey, and attended a private school in Windsor, Connecticut. Shultz received his bachelor degree cum laude in economics from Princeton University in 1942. Later that year Shultz enlisted in the U.S. Marine Corps and served as an artillery officer in the Pacific theater through 1945, earning the rank of captain. On 16 February 1946 he married Helena Marie O'Brien, with whom he had five children. After his service, he earned his Ph.D. in industrial economics from the Massachusetts Institute of Technology (MIT) in 1949.

Shultz taught economics at MIT until the then little known University of Chicago Graduate School of Business (GSB) hired him in 1957 as a professor of industrial relations. Shultz served in the first of his government posts when he was appointed as a senior staff economist to President Dwight Eisenhower's Council of Economic Advisors in 1957. In 1962 Shultz was appointed dean of the GSB and served until 1968. While at Chicago, his fellow economist Milton Friedman's monetarism theories greatly influenced Shultz. Later, Friedman's theories and Shultz's application of them were crucial to the economic policies of President Richard M. Nixon.

Shultz was involved as both a writer and editor for several books and articles on industrial and labor relations during his tenure at Chicago, including *Strategies for the Displaced Worker: Confronting Economic Change* (1966), co-written with Arnold R. Weber. The material for the 1961 book *Management Organization and the Computer*, edited with T. A. Whisler, came from the proceedings of a 1959 seminar sponsored by GSB and the McKinsey Foundation. Shultz described this work as a "wake-up call" on the coming paradigm shift in management practices that technology would cause. "But no one paid any attention," recalled Shultz. Also, *Guidelines, Informal Controls, and the Market Place: Policy Choices in a Full Employment Economy* (1966), edited with Robert Z. Aliber, detailed a GSB conference in response to the growing trend of the executive branch to influence labor and industry by offering wage-price guidelines. Such guidelines and federally ordered "freezes" were Nixon's prescription for containing unemployment and inflation.

One of Shultz's personal accomplishments at GSB was the integration of the M.B.A. program. As dean, he worried about the absence of minority representation. Shultz visited many of the major African-American universities to find out why none of their students applied to GSB. "I was told that the school was too expensive," he later said, "and none of the candidates believed they'd be hired into management positions after graduation." Shultz then recruited several major corporations to underwrite fellowships that guaranteed summer jobs between the M.B.A.'s first and second

George Shultz, shown following his December 1968 nomination as secretary of labor by President Richard Nixon. © BETTMANN/CORBIS

years. "This was something of a breakthrough," said Shultz.

Shultz continued his personal research on labor market problems, specifically the effect of strikes on major industries. The period from 1963 to 1973 saw a marked rise in labor contract rejections, and unauthorized "wildcat" strikes reached a post–World War II high. Industry tried to contain wages, and union leaders struggled to overcome member apathy and the growth of racial and feminist activism within their ranks. The John F. Kennedy and Lyndon B. Johnson administrations practiced an interventionist policy by invoking the 1947 Taft-Hartley Act and declaring a strike a "national emergency" to compel the parties to the negotiating table. (The Taft-Hartley Act outlawed a "closed shop," where all employees must be union members; allowed the president to delay strikes by ordering a "cooling off" period; and restrained labors' political and economic power.) Shultz, however, believed that labor and management differences were best resolved when left alone. Political reality tested Shultz's academic theories once he was inside the Nixon White House.

Shultz garnered his secretary of labor post on 11 December 1968 by successfully heading up a Republican task force to develop economic proposals and recommendations for Nixon to implement if elected president. If Nixon's cabinet was colorless, then, according to *Newsweek* magazine, Shultz was "the grayest of the gray." Soft-spoken, physically stiff, and yet with Marine Corps discipline, Shultz was Nixon's choice for the difficult tasks, such as the Job Corp reorganization of 1969 and the settling of the postal workers' strike of 1970. Shultz had the respect of all for his principles, flexibility, and intelligence. Some even called him an "intellectual conglomerate."

As labor secretary, Shultz resolved the inherited 1968 international longshoreman strike. The Labor Department's eighty-day Taft-Hartley injunction, issued under Johnson, was about to expire. The national press corps asked Shultz, "Now, what are you going to do, Professor?" Nixon accepted Shultz's noninterventionist recommendation, and the parties soon settled. As he had at GSB, Shultz continued to work on racial equality. He effectively established goals for minority employment at federally subsidized construction sites, a program called the Philadelphia Plan. Moreover, he quietly ended the racially sensitive Charleston, South Carolina, hospital strike. Later Nixon appointed Shultz to chair the Cabinet Committee on School Desegregation, to ensure that school districts in the Deep South complied with federal regulations. Little did Shultz realize that Nixon's economic policy had a political objective: building a coalition of conservative white southerners and northern blue-collar workers by appealing to racial and cultural fears. Nixon saw the American Federation of Labor–Congress of Industrial Organizations (AFL-CIO) president George Meany and his union as a crucial ally in this plan. Shultz was Nixon's unofficial ambassador to the AFL-CIO.

From his post at the Labor Department, Shultz was Nixon's most trusted economic adviser. When Nixon created the Office of Management and Budget, he named Shultz its first director in the hope that he might run the economy from there. However, Shultz's Friedmanesque gradualist monetary policies exacted a political price as the economy slowed. Ever the team player, Shultz served the Nixon administration even though he opposed all three phases of the New Economic Policy of Nixon and Treasury Secretary John Connally. The policy included intervention-ist wage and price controls and involved Connally's support of Nixon's suspension of the Bretton Woods agreement that allowed the dollar's convertibility into gold, which Shultz philosophically opposed. Nonetheless, in May 1972, Nixon appointed Shultz as secretary of the treasury. Even as Nixon and Shultz tried to forestall the Great Recession that lasted into 1975, the Watergate scandal preoccupied Nixon. (Watergate was the name for the political scandal sur-rounding the break-in of the Democratic Party headquar-ters at the Watergate office complex, which was subse-quently traced back to the White House and the Committee to Re-elect the President.) Shultz counseled the President to "tell all" about his participation, but in May 1974, William Simon replaced Shultz, who reentered the business community, becoming executive vice president of Bechtel Corporation in San Francisco.

Later, Shultz accepted another cabinet position when President Ronald Reagan replaced Alexander Haig with Shultz as secretary of state. Sworn into the cabinet on 16 July 1982, Shultz served until January 1989, becoming the only man ever to have held four cabinet-level posts. After his last stint of public service, Shultz returned to academia in January 1989 at Stanford University's Hoover Institu-tion, where he was named the Thomas W. and Susan B. Ford Distinguished Fellow. Shultz also received the Pres-idential Medal of Freedom, the highest award given to a civilian, on 19 January 1989.

★

Shultz wrote a 1,184-page best-selling memoir, *Turmoil and Triumph: My Years as Secretary of State* (1993). Other accounts of Shultz's life and political career are in Dan Rather and Gary Paul Gates, *The Palace Guard* (1974); William Safire, *Before the Fall: An Inside Look at the Pre-Watergate White House* (1975); and Lau-rence I. Barrett, *Gambling with History: Reagan in the White House* (1983). See also Allen J. Matsuow, *Nixon's Economy: Boom, Busts, Dollars, and Votes* (1998). Articles about Shultz are in *Time* (5 July 1982), *Newsweek* (5 July 1982 and 7 Feb. 1983), the *New Republic* (15 Dec. 1986); the *Economist* (2 Apr. 1988 and 3 Dec. 1988), and *Newsweek* (31 May 1993).

ROBERT VELLANI

SILLS, Beverly (*b*. 25 May 1929 in New York City), Amer-ican operatic coloratura soprano, television host, and arts ad-ministrator.

Sills, born Belle Miriam Silverman, was the only daughter of three children born to Morris Silverman, an agent for Metropolitan Life Insurance, and Shirley Bahn Silverman, a musician and homemaker. Born with a bubble of saliva in her mouth, the obstetrician dubbed her "Bubbles" and the nickname stuck. Sills began her career in radio at the age of three, singing on a children's show called *Uncle Bob's Rainbow House* (1932). In 1936 she auditioned for Estelle Liebling, a scholar of early Romantic operas, labeled by the press as the best vocal coach of the time. Liebling described Sills as the "first 7-year old with a trill," and took her on for abbreviated lessons. Liebling remained Sills's only vocal coach until Liebling's death in 1970. Sometime after the audition, Sills appeared on *Major Bowes' Capitol Family Hour,* a show that spawned a number of talents in early television, and she later received a permanent spot on his weekly program. She retired at the age of twelve to con-centrate on schooling and graduated from the Professional Children's School in 1945.

Sills was engaged in a series of musical theater roles and then took parts with lesser companies. She made her op-eratic debut with the Philadelphia Civic Opera in 1947 as Frasquita in Bizet's *Carmen*. She also toured as Violetta in *La Traviata* (1951), singing the role more than fifty times while traveling from city to city in a bus; she endured a similarly grueling touring schedule the next year, perform-ing as Micaela in *Carmen* more than sixty times.

Sills began her long association with the New York City Opera on 29 October 1955, singing Rosalinde in *Die Fle-dermaus*. By 1958 she was important enough to the com-pany to be given the title role in the New York premier of Douglas Moore's *The Ballad of Baby Doe*. On 17 November 1956 Sills married Peter B. Greenough, the associate editor of the *Cleveland Plain Dealer*. She became stepmother to Greenough's three children and later gave birth to a daugh-ter, who was born with a serious hearing impairment and who now has multiple sclerosis, and to a son, who has autism.

These family problems prompted Sills to retire briefly from the stage; she told New York City Opera director Julius Rudel she was too distracted to sing. Sills's strength as a singer was not so much her voice quality as her acting ability. She appeared at the end of the era of the big singer who would stride to the front of the stage and belt out the aria. Sills, who had been a singing cowgirl in a radio soap opera in her youth, had also learned to act. She studied her voice roles like a method actor reading history books to assimilate a character. She would carefully study the libretto and could converse well in French.

With these strengths in mind, Rudel, perhaps the most effective opera administrator of his time, coaxed Sills out of retirement. She did not like her first new role—Queen of the Night in Mozart's *The Magic Flute*. In February 1964

Beverly Sills. AP/WIDE WORLD PHOTOS

Sills first performed *The Tales of Hoffman*, in which she appeared in all three soprano roles. Later that year she debuted as Donna Anna in *Don Giovanni*, a role also performed by both of her great rivals of the period—Birgrit Nilsson and Joan Sutherland.

October 1966 saw the New York opening of two new opera houses at Lincoln Center, on the West Side of New York. The Metropolitan Opera Company (the Met) acquired its own building, replacing an antiquated one located further downtown, while Rudel's City Opera had shared the New York State Theater with the ballet. Lincoln Center was the City Opera's first permanent home. A more intense (if mostly friendly) rivalry could scarcely be imagined. The Met chose to open with the world premier of Samuel Barber's *Antony and Cleopatra*. Leontyne Price played the role of Cleopatra, thus smashing the Met's color barrier. Rudel mirrored the Met's choice with the odd selection of Handel's period opera *Julius Caesar*. Sills told Rudel, "If I don't get the Cleopatra, I will resign," but she was awarded the role.

In the battle of the debuts, City Opera won. Barber's piece was considered too avant-garde, and it suffered from opening night technical horrors, such as a breakdown of the new mechanical stage. By contrast Sills, who is not reticent, called the City opening, "One of the great performances of all time in the opera house."

In 1968 Sills introduced perhaps her finest role—the title role in *Manon*. Sills liked the role because the changes take place "on the stage, not between scenes . . . I can develop Manon in full view of the audience." The next year saw Sills in the title role in *Lucia di Lammermoor,* the first of her great bel canto performances. The *Saturday Review* critic Irving Kolodin had some problems with Sills's approach, but "she put together some choice examples of almost any kind of technical discipline one could think of [including] high notes up to E-flat." Kolodin complained, however, that Sills engaged more in action than acting.

In the 1970s Sills went on to explore further Donizetti and Bellini roles, studying Elizabeth in *Roberto Devereaux* and Mary Stuart in Donizetti's opera of the same name. She went on to sing at the Met (ending a long feud), La Scala, and at Covent Garden. She announced her retirement from singing during a nationally televised concert in 1980, and assumed administrative roles with City Opera, the Met, and the Lincoln Center. She remains a spokesperson for the hearing impaired and mentally challenged, serving as a national chairperson for the March of Dimes "Mothers March" on Birth Defects. Sills also received the Presidential Medal of Freedom in 1980 from President Jimmy Carter.

Sills was not quite as commanding on an international level as the Wagner specialist Birgit Nilsson or Joan Sutherland, who sang a similar repertoire, but during the 1960s she represented not only the best in American operatic performance, but also the hope of an American cultural ascendancy in classical European music.

Sills has written three autobiographies: *Bubbles: A Self-Portrait* (1976), *Bubbles: An Encore* (1981), and *Beverly: An Autobiography* (1987), written with Lawrence Linderman. A biography is Bridget Paolucci, *Beverly Sills: Opera Singer* (1990). Martin Mayer, *The Met: One Hundred Years of Grand Opera* (1983), describes Sills's controversial relationship with the Metropolitan Opera. Periodical citations include "Beverly Sills," *Opera* (Dec. 1970), and the cover story of *Time* (22 Nov. 1971).

JOHN DAVID HEALY

SIMON, (Marvin) Neil (*b.* 4 July 1927 in New York City), playwright and screenwriter whose works, such as *Barefoot in the Park* and *The Odd Couple,* became classics of 1960s stage and film.

Simon's father, Irving, was a salesman of piece goods, or fabric for dresses. He had an uneven temperament and often abandoned his family and then returned. Simon's mother, Mamie (Levy), made money by running poker games, taking in boarders, and working at Gimbel's department store. Simon attended Woodside High School and DeWitt Clinton High School, graduating in 1944. Briefly, in 1944, he attended New York University, hoping to major in engineering, but he was a member of the reserves and was called to duty in the Army Air Corps. He was sent to Biloxi, Mississippi, for training and then to Lowry Field, Colorado, where he served as editor for the base newspaper and where he briefly attended the Univer-

sity of Denver. He never earned a college degree. In 1946 Simon was discharged from the army, and his brother, Danny, helped him get a job in the mailroom of Warner Bros.

He and Danny eventually found jobs writing comedy for radio shows, usually as a team. During the 1950s they began writing for television shows as well. Simon married the dancer Joan Baim on 30 September 1953; they had two children, and he settled into what seemed to be a comfortable career of writing for Sid Caesar and other television stars. Even though he received Emmy nominations in 1957 and 1958 as a writer for the series *Caesar's Hour,* Simon decided that he had to try to break free of the constraints of television.

Simon's first play, *Come Blow Your Horn,* went through perhaps forty producers, each one liking the play and suggesting changes while declining the chance to stage it. Finally, in New Hope, Pennsylvania, the Bucks County Playhouse agreed to put on his play in August 1960. Simon took his wife and children to Pennsylvania with him. The producers of the play were Michael Ellis and William Hammerstein, the son of Oscar Hammerstein. The play had a first-time director, Stanley Prager, with the game-show host Gene Rayburn in the lead. Simon listened to audience responses to his play about his own family and made seemingly endless rewrites in an effort to eliminate dead spots in the performances.

The play was brought to the Brooks Atkinson Theater on Broadway on 22 February 1961 and ran for eighty-four weeks, a very good run. It would become a staple of rep-

Neil Simon, 1967. © BETTMANN/CORBIS

ertory theaters, yet the success was not easy. After the first night, the producers were ready to close the show in a week, because the audience had been small and not particularly responsive. Instead of quitting, the producers, Simon, and others connected with the play distributed free tickets everywhere they could think of, building interest by word of mouth. After a week or so, this began to work. The play was funny, and people liked it. The veteran character actor Davey Burns, who milked his every line for all the laughs it could receive, played Simon's father. Irving Simon, who saw the play a few days after it opened on Broadway, told his son that the play was very funny, especially the character of the father—apparently not realizing that he himself was the basis for the father.

During the run of *Come Blow Your Horn,* Simon and Joan worried that fame and fortune would ruin their marriage—that constant public attention would prove too great a strain on their private family life. As it turned out, their marriage remained strong. Another anxiety for Simon was that he would prove a one-play wonder and that failure lay just ahead. While struggling to write a new play, Simon received a call from the producer Ernest Martin, who asked him to write the dialogue for a musical, *Little Me,* based on a book by Patrick Dennis. In it, a poor girl marries seven men successively, each husband richer than the previous one; eventually she reaches the man who had loved her many years earlier, when she was still poor. One of Simon's contributions to the musical was the idea to have one actor play all seven husbands, and he suggested that Sid Caesar be cast for the part. The musical opened first in Philadelphia to good reviews, but Simon was not satisfied and revised sections of the dialogue. On 17 November 1962, *Little Me* opened in the Lunt-Fontanne Theater on New York's Broadway. Simon was still not satisfied with the tone of the show, which he thought was uneven, tilting back and forth from farce to satire, but reviews were excellent.

Simon's next play was *Barefoot in the Park.* Like *Come Blow Your Horn,* it had a first-time director, Mike Nichols, who launched his brilliant directorial career with Simon's play. Again, Simon revised the play many times while it ran in the Bucks County Playhouse. It was inspired in part by Joan and the early years of their marriage. In it, Paul and Corie Bratter argue almost the whole time, even though they are in love. Corie wants warmth and companionship, but Paul is too absorbed in his work as a lawyer. In casting the play, Simon, Nichols, and the producer Saint Subber settled on Robert Redford, who was then just beginning to build a name for himself, to play Paul. Elizabeth Ashley played Corie.

The pair was electrifying, the actors delivering their lines with conviction, as if the words were their own. The comedy was character-driven, meaning that the humor came out of what the audience learned about the characters' lives. When *Barefoot in the Park* opened in the Biltmore Theater on Broadway on 23 October 1963, theater reviewers loved the production. Still insecure about his success, Simon fretted that the play would be his last, that he would never have another success. *Barefoot in the Park* ran for more than fifteen hundred shows on Broadway and became an international hit. Simon wrote the screenplay for the 1969 motion picture version, in which Redford again played Paul, and Jane Fonda played the part of Corie. The movie was popular and helped extend Simon's fame beyond Broadway.

It was with his next play, *The Odd Couple,* inspired by Simon's brother, Danny, and one of his roommates, that Simon secured his place in literary history. The main characters—Oscar Madison, an incorrigible slob, and Felix Unger, a fanatic for neatness and order—quickly became icons of popular culture, known to hundreds of millions of people through the play, the motion picture, and the television series. The premise was that these two divorced men lived together and irritated each other with the personal qualities that had caused their divorces.

The Odd Couple debuted in Wilmington, Delaware, where problems with the third and final act became apparent. The play next appeared in Boston, with a new third act that still proved neither funny nor well organized. The Boston theater critic Elliot Norton helped Simon by suggesting that the Pigeon sisters of the second act be included in the third. The possibilities for character development and comedy in the suggestion struck Simon right away. On 10 March 1965 the play opened with Walter Matthau as Oscar and Art Carney as Felix, with Mike Nichols directing and Saint Subber producing, at the Plymouth Theater on Broadway. Simon received a Tony for best author for the play, which ran on Broadway for two years. Simon's screenplay version of *The Odd Couple* became a 1968 Paramount motion picture starring Walter Matthau and Jack Lemmon. The film was a hit, but, unfortunately, Paramount persuaded Simon to sell the licensing rights for $125,000. Paramount then made the television series, from which Simon received nothing. Simon believed that he lost more than $20 million in the deal.

Simon was not satisfied with his next two productions, *Sweet Charity* and *The Star-Spangled Girl.* Bob Fosse directed *Sweet Charity,* and Simon loved his work, but the play was based on a fairly serious work, *The Nights of Cabiria,* by Federico Fellini. Simon thought the depth of characterization of the original was lost during revisions of his script for the musical. It opened at the newly remodeled Palace Theater on Broadway on 29 January 1966 to standing room only and became the most popular of Simon's musicals. Simon believed that he made numerous mistakes with *The Star-Spangled Girl* that ended up making the characters too shallow. The play opened 21 December 1966 in the Plymouth Theater to mostly friendly reviews. This opening gave Simon the distinction of having four shows on Broadway at the same time.

Simon's next play was *Plaza Suite,* which began as a series of four one-act plays that he reduced to three because he thought the fourth was not to up his standards. Each short play tells a story of an event that takes place in a hotel. Mike Nichols directed the production, and George C. Scott and Maureen Stapleton starred in each play. Scott suffered from bouts of profound depression, and one problem in producing *Plaza Suite* was that Scott disappeared more than once, the second time vowing that he was quitting for good. About a week later he showed up, put on his makeup, and went on stage as if nothing had happened. *Plaza Suite* began its Broadway run on 14 February 1968 in the Plymouth Theater and was a triumph. Simon wrote the screenplay for the 1971 motion picture version, which was also a popular success.

Simon's wife, Joan, died in 1973. Later that year he married the actress Marsha Mason. The couple had no children and divorced in 1982. In January 1987 Simon married Diane Lander, and they adopted a daughter. They divorced in 1988, remarried in February 1990, and divorced again in 1998. Simon married Elaine Joyce in September 1999.

Simon finished the 1960s with the plays *Promises, Promises* (1968), a reworking of the film *The Apartment,* and *Last of the Red-Hot Lovers* (1969), about a middle-aged man's love affairs. His next big hit was *The Sunshine Boys* in 1972. In 1985 he won a best drama Tony Award for *Biloxi Blues* (1984), and in 1991 he repeated the Tony win with *Lost in Yonkers,* for which he also received the Pulitzer Prize for drama. Simon is recognized not only as America's most prolific playwright but also as one of the country's most consistently good playwrights—and probably the most loved. Millions of people attend his plays and view his motion pictures simply because they associate his name with high-quality writing and entertaining comedy.

★

Simon's *Rewrites: A Memoir* (1996) is a brilliantly written account of his life up to the mid-1970s and is entertaining reading. *The Play Goes On: A Memoir* (1999) is somewhat more diffuse than *Rewrites,* but it, too, is entertaining. In "I Try to Walk a Fine Line Between Laughter and Tears," an interview in *U.S. News & World Report* 98 (22 Apr. 1985), Simon tells about what he hopes to achieve in a play. Alec Foege and Michael Fleeman outline Simon's private life in "What's Up, Doc?" in *People Weekly* (8 Nov. 1999). William A. Henry III offers details of Simon's family relationships in "Reliving a Poignant Past: Neil Simon's Best Comedy Looks Homeward" in *Time* (15 Dec. 1986).

KIRK H. BEETZ

SIMON AND GARFUNKEL (Simon, Paul Frederic, *b.* 13 October 1941 in Newark, New Jersey, and Arthur Ira Garfunkel, *b.* 5 November 1941 in Forest Hills, New York), folk-rock duo whose poetic lyrics and evocative vocal harmonies made them a definitive musical act of the 1960s, with such hits as "The Sound of Silence" and "Mrs. Robinson."

Simon, the diminutive singer and guitarist, wrote the duo's songs, but Garfunkel, the tall vocalist with the head of golden curls, had the better singing voice. Born within a month of each other, Simon and Garfunkel grew up three blocks apart in a middle-class neighborhood in Queens. Simon's father was a bass player and his mother a teacher; Garfunkel's parents were a traveling salesman and a homemaker. The two attended elementary school together, getting to know each other when they costarred in a school play, *Alice in Wonderland* (Simon was the White Rabbit, and Garfunkel was the Cheshire Cat). As teenagers they recorded harmonies together on a portable tape recorder, and at age fourteen they copyrighted their first cowritten song.

On 22 November 1957, shortly after their sixteenth birthdays, they appeared on the popular television show *American Bandstand,* billed as Tom and Jerry. The song they performed, "Hey, Schoolgirl," became a modest rock-and-roll hit, but their attempts to follow its success failed. By 1959, with their fifteen minutes of fame presumably over, Simon and Garfunkel went their separate ways. Simon received a degree in English from Queens College and briefly attended law school, while Garfunkel attended Columbia University, where he earned degrees in architecture and mathematics.

Simon worked his way through college writing and producing songs for other artists, and Garfunkel became a draftsman and a carpenter. In the early 1960s a chance meeting on the street led the two to rekindle both their friendship and their singing act. By this time Simon, without Garfunkel's assistance, was writing literary songs influenced both by the folk-rock singer Bob Dylan and by the poetry Simon had studied in college. "We wrote rock-and-roll songs together, but suddenly one of us could write poetic folk songs," Garfunkel recalled. Simon may have written the songs, but Garfunkel had the superior voice and was indispensable in arranging the duo's perfect vocal harmonies. Soon the two were playing regularly in the folk clubs of Greenwich Village in New York City. In 1963 Simon's song about a slain civil rights worker, "He Was My Brother," caught the attention of Tom Wilson, a producer at Columbia Records, and the duo was signed to a recording contract. Although the singers wanted to record under aliases because they feared their Jewish names would discourage record sales, Columbia insisted that their real names be used.

Art Garfunkel *(left)* and Paul Simon. AP/WIDE WORLD PHOTOS

Simon and Garfunkel's first record, *Wednesday Morning 3 A.M.*, was a commercial failure despite the inclusion of "The Sound of Silence," a haunting masterpiece that eventually became the pair's signature tune. Simon had written the famous opening lines ("Hello darkness, my old friend / I've come to talk with you again") as a teenager, but the rest of the song did not materialize until after the assassination of President John F. Kennedy in 1963, when he completed it in a burst of creativity. Wilson, the Columbia producer, thought the solemn acoustic track could be a hit if it were a bit more energized. On 15 June 1965 Wilson borrowed Bob Dylan's studio band, which had recorded "Like a Rolling Stone" earlier that day, and recorded a new backing track for "The Sound of Silence." The new folk-rock track, with drums, bass, and electric guitar added to the previous vocals, was released without Simon and Garfunkel's knowledge or consent. Simon initially disliked the new version, but in November 1965 the song reached number one on the pop charts, propelling Simon and Garfunkel to stardom. In 1966 their second album, *Sounds of Silence*, also became a hit.

During the mid-1960s Simon spent most of his free time in England, where he performed solo shows at folk clubs and spent time with Kathy Chitty, the British girlfriend who became the inspiration for many of his most beautiful songs, including "Kathy's Song," "America," and "Homeward Bound." Simon and Garfunkel's commercial success enabled them to exercise more creative control over their third album, *Parsley, Sage, Rosemary, and Thyme*, released in October 1966. Almost every song was a mini-master-

piece, including "Scarborough Fair/Canticle," a lush adaptation of a folk song from medieval England, and "The 59th Street Bridge Song (Feelin' Groovy)," a happy-go-lucky, drug-influenced tune that became a 1960s anthem of sorts.

By 1967 Simon, along with Dylan, was one of the two most acclaimed songwriters in the United States. The beautiful imagery of his lyrics led many to describe his songs as poetic, but Simon resisted the label. "The lyrics of pop songs are so banal that if you show a spark of intelligence they call you a poet," he said. That year the film director Mike Nichols asked Simon to write the soundtrack for *The Graduate*, starring Dustin Hoffman. The film was released in early 1968 with five Simon and Garfunkel songs, but only one, the still incomplete "Mrs. Robinson," was written specifically for the film. The songs, like the film, captured the imagination of young people alienated from the establishment, and the result was perhaps the most perfect blending of song and film in the history of American cinema. *The Graduate* became the third most-profitable movie of all time, and Simon and Garfunkel's soundtrack sat atop the Billboard charts for nine weeks in 1968.

In April 1968 Simon and Garfunkel released *Bookends*, their most personal and ambitious album to date. The songs included "America," a wistful tune about young lovers on a cross-country road trip, and a fleshed-out version of "Mrs. Robinson" that included the now famous yearning, "Where have you gone, Joe DiMaggio? / A nation turns its lonely eyes to you." Both the album and the new version of "Mrs. Robinson" were wildly successful, with the latter spending three weeks at number one on the charts and winning the Grammy Award for record of the year. Meanwhile, *Bookends*, with most of its songs about people growing old and growing apart, indicated what was happening in Simon and Garfunkel's personal relationship.

Once the best of friends, the singers now spent much of their time apart, and their separation was exacerbated by Simon's jealousy of Garfunkel's new career as a film actor. While Garfunkel devoted most of his time and attention to filming *Catch-22* in Mexico, Simon continued to write songs about the alienation between them. The resulting album, *Bridge over Troubled Water*, would ironically become their best-known work. When it came time to pick the album's twelfth and final song, the two reached an impasse. Garfunkel wanted a Bach chorale, but Simon insisted on the political song "Cuba Sí, Nixon No." When they could not reach an agreement, the album was released with only eleven songs. "It's a Simon and Garfunkel record, but not really," Simon said. "There are many songs where you don't hear Simon and Garfunkel singing together. It became easier to work by separating." One of the album's most intriguing songs was "The Boxer," an allegorical ballad that many speculated was about Dylan, although Simon insisted it was about himself. But the undisputed jewel of the album was the title track, a soaring, gospel-influenced anthem of devotion, sung solo by Garfunkel. The song became an international phenomenon, spending six weeks at number one, and *Bridge over Troubled Water* became one of the best-selling albums in recording history.

With their popularity at an all-time high but their rapport at low ebb, Simon and Garfunkel embarked on a concert tour in the spring of 1970. Every night Simon would retire to the side of the stage as Garfunkel took the spotlight to sing "Bridge over Troubled Water" by himself. "People would stomp and cheer when it was over," Simon said. "And I would think, 'That's my song, man. Thank you very much. I wrote that song.'" He added, "In the earlier days when things were smoother I never would have thought that, but towards the end when things were strained, I did." Although they did not talk about it, both musicians realized their partnership had come to an end. "It had lost its sense of fun," Garfunkel said. "The juices weren't flowing." They never made formal announcement, but for all practical purposes, the duo of Simon and Garfunkel had ceased to exist.

Garfunkel married Linda Grossman in October 1972; they divorced in 1975. In September 1988 he married Kim Cermak; they have a son. Simon married Peggy Harper in 1970; they had one son and divorced in 1975. His second wife was the actress and novelist Carrie Fisher; they married on 16 August 1983 and divorced in April 1984. Simon married the singer Edie Brickell on 30 May 1992; they have three children.

Since the 1960s Garfunkel's solo recording efforts were largely unremarkable, but Simon continued to make acclaimed albums, such as *Still Crazy After All These Years* (1975) and *Graceland* (1987). In addition to making music, Garfunkel acted in films, wrote poetry, and taught high school mathematics. On 19 September 1981 the two reunited for a highly publicized free concert in Central Park, attended by an estimated 500,000 people. Simon and Garfunkel were inducted into the Rock and Roll Hall of Fame as a duo in 1990, and Simon was elected as an solo performer in 2001.

Along with Dylan and the Beatles, Simon and Garfunkel were among the handful of musical acts that defined the 1960s. But unlike Dylan and the Beatles, they appealed to a broad spectrum of listeners. Their clean-cut appearance and nonthreatening sound made them acceptable to adults, but their literate songs and themes of alienation appealed to younger audiences as well. Unlike most popular music, their work has gracefully stood the test of time. "The Sound of Silence" is considered a songwriting masterpiece, and "Bridge over Troubled Water" and "Mrs. Robinson" remain poignant and evocative anthems of the late 1960s.

★

Several biographies cover Simon and Garfunkel as a duo, including Joseph Morella and Patricia Barey, *Simon and Garfunkel: Old Friends* (1991), and Victoria Kingston, *Simon and Garfunkel: The Biography* (1998). Stacey Luftig, ed., *The Paul Simon Companion: Four Decades of Commentary* (1997), is an outstanding anthology covering Simon's career with and without Garfunkel. Significant articles are in *Rolling Stone* (20 July 1972) and *Playboy* (Feb. 1984).

ERIC ENDERS

SINGER, Isaac Bashevis (*b.* 14 July 1904 in Radzymin, Poland; *d.* 24 July 1991 in Surfside, Florida), Yiddish-language fiction writer, possibly the last major author to work in that language, who received the Nobel Prize for literature for his "impassioned narratives, which, with roots in a Polish-Jewish cultural tradition, bring universal human conditions to life."

Singer was the descendant of rabbis. Both of his grandfathers, as well as his father, Pinchos Menachem Singer, were rabbis; his father was also the author of several religious texts. Singer's mother, Bathsheba Zylberman Singer, clearly intended for him to follow suit. She sent the boy away at age eight to the shtetl (or rural Jewish settlement town) of Bilgoray to be raised by his grandmother and to receive a Jewish education unencumbered by the worldly distractions of Warsaw, the family's home. Singer dutifully returned as a teenager and enrolled in rabbinical seminary.

Isaac Bashevis Singer. MR. JERRY BAUER

tional magazines. Works published during the 1960s include short-story collections (*The Spinoza of Market Street, Short Friday,* and *The Séance*), novels (*The Magician of Lublin, The Slave, Scum, The Manor,* and *The Estate*), and a memoir (*In My Father's Court*). Most of his writings were serialized in the Yiddish-language newspaper the *Jewish Daily Forward* before being translated into English and other languages.

Singer's reputation and popularity burgeoned in the 1960s along with the startling revival of American ethnic consciousness that took place during the decade. One of the cultural events of the period was the literary celebration of the "Jewish-American novel," which included the works of such best-selling and highly regarded authors as Bernard Malamud, Saul Bellow, Grace Paley, and Phillip Roth. Singer was deeply appreciated by these writers (Bellow was among his translators) as a kind of "missing link" between their tales of American assimilation and the vanished culture of European Jewry. Although he was proficient enough in English to translate his own works when he cared to, Singer's insistence on continuing to write primarily in Yiddish functioned as living proof that the perpetrators of the Holocaust had been less than fully successful in their aims.

Beyond these historical implications, and beyond the literary craftsmanship of his characters and narratives, Singer was especially appreciated during the 1960s by many American Jewish readers for introducing or reintroducing them to the mysticism of Yiddish folklore. This had been a salient feature of secular Jewish culture, obscured for most of a century by a combination of politically motivated promotions of social realism on the one hand and disdainful religious orthodoxy on the other. The dybbuks (wandering souls), golem (artificial humans endowed with life), and other pagan-like spirits of Singer's shtetl tales caught the imagination of a generation that otherwise had come to associate "Jewishness" with abstract polemics of either a socialist or a religious nature.

Moreover, the vital, almost uncontrollable, sexuality found in some Singer characters seemed very much in step with what was being called "the sexual revolution." *The Slave,* one of his best-selling novels, explores a sexual relationship between a Jewish man and the daughter of a Polish noble in seventeenth-century Poland. It was described in the *New Republic* as "a story of . . . forbidden love." Kalman Jacoby, a character who appears in the sequential novels *The Estate* (1967) and *The Manor* (1969), develops insatiable sexual appetites late in life that become the obsession of his old age. Several Singer stories even appeared in *Playboy.* "Sex, of course, is nothing new," he commented during one of the many talks he gave on the college lecture circuit. "But to write freely and truthfully about such a subject without causing headaches for yourself with an editor . . . is maybe a kind of revolution."

At the age of twenty-two, however, largely owing to the influence of his older brother, the writer Israel Joseph (known as "I. J.") Singer, he quit his clerical studies, declaring his intention of becoming a secular writer. His first novel, *Satan in Goray,* was completed in 1931 and published in installments in the Yiddish literary magazine *Globus,* where he was also employed as an editor. (The novel was published in book form in 1935.) Once again following the lead of his brother, Singer immigrated to the United States in 1935 in the face of the growing threat of Nazi Germany. This occasioned his separation from his common-law wife, Rachel Zamir, who chose to immigrate to British Palestine with their son. Singer had no contact with his son, Israel Zamir, for twenty years, but the two were later reconciled, and Zamir translated many of his father's short stories into Hebrew.

Arriving in New York during the depths of the Great Depression, Singer's brother helped him find work as a staff writer for the *Jewish Daily Forward.* In 1940 he married Alma Haimman Wasserman, and in 1943 he became a U.S. citizen. By the 1950s Singer had become a well-established figure and was gaining familiarity among English-language readers for his translated stories, which appeared in the *New Yorker,* the *Atlantic Monthly,* and other leading na-

The widespread acceptance of Singer by both readers and critics can be seen as a milestone in the general reinterpretation of American literature during the 1960s. This reinterpretation rejected the notion of a monolithic canon of homogenous "great works" written in an anglophile tradition, in favor of an understanding of American culture as a sum of distinct parts, identifiable by ethnicity, race, and other cultural affinities. Singer's election to the National Institute of Arts and Letters in 1964 was a precedent-setting milestone in this regard, in that he was the first writer working primarily in a language other than English to be so honored. The publication of *Short Friday and Other Stories* earlier that year, which contained the writer's first pieces set in the United States, was helpful in gaining his inclusion.

In the mid-1960s Singer branched out in a new direction, publishing the first of his translated children's books, *Zlateh the Goat and Other Stories.* This one was followed by several others, including *A Day of Pleasure* (1969), for which he received the National Book Award in 1970. "You can't be a big faker when you write for children," he told an interviewer, expressing pleasure with his success in the genre. He received a second National Book Award in 1974 for *A Crown of Feathers,* a short-story collection for adult readers. By the end of the decade, Singer found himself elevated to the status of a grand literary figure, a status confirmed in 1978 when he was awarded what many consider the greatest honor that can be bestowed on a writer, the Nobel Prize for literature. During his acceptance speech in Stockholm, he abruptly switched from English to Yiddish, thanking the Swedish Academy for honoring not just him, but *"a loshon fun golus, ohn a land, ohn grenitzen, nisht geshtitzt fun kein shum meluchoch,"* translating this description of the tongue he had spoken in as "a language of exile, without a land, without frontiers, not supported by any government." In the 1980s the writer went into semiretirement in Surfside, Florida, continuing to write stories, some of them set in the nearby Jewish neighborhoods of Miami Beach, until he was disabled by a series of strokes, which led to his death.

★

Singer's manuscript archive is located at the Harry Ransom Humanities Research Center at the University of Texas at Austin. He declined invitations to write a comprehensive autobiography, but he did complete several books about his childhood. They include *In My Father's Court* (1967), *A Day of Pleasure: Stories of a Boy Growing Up in Warsaw* (1969), and *A Little Boy in Search of God: Mysticism in a Personal Light* (1976), which is illustrated with photographs by Roman Vishniac. Grace Farrell, *Isaac Bashevis Singer: Conversations* (1992), is part of the University of Mississippi Press's series of transcribed interviews with writers. Lester Goran, *The Bright Streets of Surfside* (1994), paints a picture of the author's retirement years in Florida. As a Nobel laureate, Singer is the subject of much critical commentary and is included in virtually all biographical reference works concerning world literature, American literature, and Jewish and Jewish-American culture. Obituaries are in most major newspapers in the United States and Western Europe, including the *New York Times* (26 July 1991).

DAVID MARC

SIRHAN, Sirhan Bishara (*b.* 19 March 1944 in Jerusalem, Palestine), Arab nationalist serving a life sentence in San Quentin State Prison in California for the assassination of Senator Robert F. Kennedy on 5 June 1968.

Very little is known about Sirhan's early beginnings, and details on his family background are sketchy. No one really knows what motivated the twenty-four-year-old Sirhan to kill Robert F. Kennedy, younger brother of President John F. Kennedy, at a campaign rally in Los Angeles. Sirhan himself, when his eighth plea for parole was rejected, said, "I wish it had never happened." One thing is clear from his testimony during his trial—Sirhan deeply hated the West for its support of Israel. Growing up, Sirhan witnessed the suffering of Palestinian refugees in the aftermath following the creation of the state of Israel. Palestinians were removed from the land they called home in order to make room for the Jewish state. Sirhan saw this as unjust. He

Sirhan Sirhan outside a Los Angeles courtroom, July 1968. ASSOCIATED PRESS AP

pointed out that Israel was "no underdog," and that in fact it was the Palestinians who were the underdogs and deserved the support of the West. When Sirhan saw his people struggling to survive without a home, he blamed Jews and Zionists for "beating away at them." The whole situation, he said, "burned the hell out of me."

Sirhan longed for fame. For much of his life, the Arab immigrant had suffered failure. He was not outstanding in school or at work, and he had little success with romantic relationships. To achieve notoriety, he fixed on assassinating Kennedy. In a notebook recovered after Kennedy's murder, Sirhan had written repeatedly that Kennedy must die.

The location was the Ambassador Hotel in Los Angeles. At 12:16 A.M. (Pacific Standard Time) on 5 June 1968, Kennedy was shot three times. One bullet ripped into the right side of his head, damaging his brain. Kennedy never came out of the resulting coma, and after brain surgery was pronounced dead the next day at 1:44 A.M. Found in the hotel's pantry with the murder weapon still in his grasp, Sirhan was charged with Kennedy's murder, tried, and sentenced to death. However, the sentence was commuted to life imprisonment in 1972 when the Supreme Court ruled against capital punishment.

For many the crime seemed to be an open and shut case. Kennedy was shot; close by was his assassin, still holding the gun. Witnesses had seen Sirhan aim his .22-caliber pistol at the senator and fire. As for motive, Sirhan claimed that he killed Kennedy out of political protest, out of love for his country. It seemed as if there was no reason to probe further for an unknown assailant. But for some there were puzzling questions to be answered. Who was the woman reportedly seen with Sirhan before the murder? Why did Sirhan's notebook have references about promises of money in connection with the murder? Why did he seem to have no memory of the actual shooting? Certainly Sirhan was no help. Apprehended at the scene of the crime, he lied about being at a Kennedy rally on 2 June and also lied about his movements on 3 June. Apparently he had driven his car 350 miles on that day, but as to why or where, the only clue Sirhan would give was that "The FBI doesn't know everything."

Even though Sirhan was caught with the weapon, questions remained about what had actually happened. In *Shadow Play: The Murder of Robert F. Kennedy, the Trial of Sirhan Sirhan, and the Failure of American Justice* (1997), journalist William F. Klaber and Kennedy Assassination Archives curator Philip H. Melanson look at inconsistencies in the case. They believe that Sirhan may have been lying when he said he had no accomplice. According to Klaber and Melanson, ballistic evidence suggested a second gun may have been fired during the murder.

The truth seems elusive because puzzling factors cast doubt on what actually took place. Experts say the bullet that killed Kennedy came from behind, but witnesses saw Sirhan shoot Kennedy from the front. Bullet markings from Sirhan's gun appeared not to match the markings on the bullet that killed Kennedy. Also, Sirhan's gun held only eight bullets, but nine were said to have been fired. Furthermore, a security guard near the senator disliked the Kennedys; some witnesses saw him fire his weapon, but his gun was not checked.

However puzzling these factors, they can perhaps be explained. Kennedy turned his head before Sirhan fired, and this may be why the bullet hit him from behind. Also, Sirhan's gun was apparently fired by police officers who wanted souvenirs, and the residue may have affected slug markings. The presence of a ninth bullet may be explained because a police officer could have improperly identified a bullet hole. As for the security guard, there seems to be no way of telling what part he played. Photographs taken by photographer Jamie Scott Enyart during the assassination were never recovered after the police seized his camera.

One theory discussed by conspiracy theorists was that Sirhan had been "programmed" to shoot Kennedy by someone who could use hypnosis to direct Sirhan's actions. No doubt Kennedy—a proponent of civil rights and a crusader of organized crime—had his share of enemies. But if Sirhan was used as a tool to commit the murder, it has never been confirmed.

Anticonspiracy theorist Dan Moldea talked to Sirhan's family and friends, looked at the FBI files, and visited Sirhan in his San Quentin cell. In *"R. F. K. Must Die!": A History of the Robert Kennedy Assassination and its Aftermath* (1970), Moldea tells Robert Blair Kaiser that the police bungled the investigation because evidence that Sirhan may not have acted alone was lost. But in Moldea's book, *The Killing of Robert F. Kennedy: An Investigation of Motive, Means, and Opportunity* (1995), he suggests that the inconsistencies were caused by investigators' human error and incompetence. Talks with Sirhan had convinced Moldea that Sirhan was merely toying with those who wanted to believe he was innocent or that others had been involved.

Despite the debate over his role in the killing, Sirhan remained incarcerated. He became a model prisoner, earning high marks in college extension courses and performing his duties as a food server to the satisfaction of his guards. Nevertheless, Sirhan's pleas for parole, including his eighth attempt in 1986, were never granted.

★

Books that discuss the mystery behind Sirhan's case include Robert Blair Kaiser, *"R. F. K. Must Die!": A History of the Robert Kennedy Assassination and its Aftermath* (1970); John Seigenthaler,

A Search for Justice (1971); Godfrey H. Jansen, *Why Robert Kennedy Was Killed: The Story of Two Victims* (1971); and William Klaber and Philip H. Melanson, *Shadow Play: The Murder of Robert F. Kennedy, the Trial of Sirhan Sirhan, and the Failure of American Justice* (1997). An article regarding Sirhan's rejected parole is in *Time* (7 Apr. 1986). *People Weekly* gives eyewitness accounts of the assassination in "In the Night Kitchen" (7 June 1993). A documentary released by William Klaber, "The R. F. K. Tapes" (1993), claims that Sirhan may not have been the killer.

A. E. SCHULTHIES

SLICK, Grace Wing   (*b.* 30 October 1939 in Chicago, Illinois), lead singer and songwriter for Jefferson Airplane, a band whose acid-rock sound personified the counterculture milieu of San Francisco in the 1960s.

Slick was born Grace Barnett Wing, the elder of two children of Ivan Wing, an investment banker, and Virginia Barnett, a singer and actress and later a homemaker. Slick's father was transferred to California, and the family lived initially in San Francisco before moving to Palo Alto in the early 1950s.

Slick described her childhood and adolescence as a rather normal middle-class existence in postwar America. Just as her mother had, Slick developed a passion for music. Somewhat of a loner as a child, she escaped her conventional lifestyle by visiting museums and dressing in costumes. During her high school years Slick gained a repu-

tation for challenging the authority of her teachers, so her mother moved her from Palo Alto High School to the Castilleja School for Girls.

Following high school graduation in 1957, Slick attended Finch College in New York City. In the fall of 1958 she enrolled at the University of Miami, where she briefly studied art. Returning to California, Slick became a fashion model for I. Magnin's department store, and on 26 August 1961 she married her childhood friend Jerry Slick. The couple moved to San Francisco, where he studied cinematography and she continued her modeling work. In 1963 Slick gave up her modeling career to help her husband prepare his senior film, which won first prize at the Ann Arbor Film Festival.

Meanwhile, Grace and Jerry Slick became involved with the evolving counterculture scene in San Francisco, associating with musicians and experimenting with drugs such as peyote, mescaline, and LSD. After viewing a 1965 performance by the Jefferson Airplane at the Matrix, a club on Fillmore Street in San Francisco, the Slicks were inspired to form their own musical group, which they called the Great Society, a reference to President Lyndon B. Johnson's name for his strategic plan of social and economic reform. The band consisted of Jerry Slick on drums, his brother Darby on guitar and sitar, Brad DuPont on bass, and Grace Slick on keyboards and vocals. The Great Society played at various San Francisco venues including the Matrix, Mother's, the Coffee House, and Fillmore Auditorium, gathering a following based upon the experimental lyrics

Grace Slick *(third from right)*, and the members of Jefferson Airplane. AP/WIDE WORLD PHOTOS

of such songs as "Somebody to Love," "White Rabbit," "Often as I May," and "Father Bruce." The group was rife with dissension, however, as Grace Slick believed the band was not talented enough musically and lacked a tight sound. Accordingly, when vocalist Signe Anderson left the Jefferson Airplane in September 1968, Slick seized the opportunity to replace Anderson, and departed the Great Society.

Jefferson Airplane, with its combination of folk, blues, and psychedelic rock, had a large following in San Francisco and had already released a debut album, *Jefferson Airplane Takes Off* (1966), before Slick joined the group. The band consisted of Marty Balin on vocals and harmonica, rhythm guitarist Paul Kantner, lead guitarist Jorma Kaukonen, bassist Jack Casady, and drummer Spencer Dryden. Slick brought to the group a powerful voice and sensuality that had a riveting effect on audiences. According to the *San Francisco Chronicle* columnist Herb Caen, "When she performed her lyrics like an intricate soliloquy you had to put down your drink and sit up and listen." Slick also brought with her the Great Society songs "Somebody to Love" and "White Rabbit," which became major hits for Jefferson Airplane. "White Rabbit," written by Slick, uses *Alice in Wonderland* and the rhythm of Ravel's *Bolero* to attract the growing drug culture with its refrain of "feed your head." These songs appeared on the album *Surrealistic Pillow* (1967), which was on the *Billboard* charts for over twenty weeks, rising to the number-three slot.

After Bathing at Baxter's (1968), the group's third album, did not sell as well as the platinum *Surrealistic Pillow,* in part due to radio censorship in reaction to the explicit sexual lyrics of Slick's "Rejoyce." The group returned to platinum status with *Crown of Creation* 1968), featuring hit singles "Crown of Creation" and "Greasy Heart," and *Volunteers* (1969). The album *Bless Its Pointed Little Head* (1969) and the compilation *The Worst of Jefferson Airplane* (1970) also made *Billboard's* Top One Hundred.

Meanwhile, the band continued to play throughout the San Francisco area, exemplifying the counterculture values of rebellion, free love, peace, and drugs. The rock impresario Bill Graham, who operated the Fillmore West and East, became the manager of Jefferson Airplane, booking the group nationally and internationally. While on tour Jefferson Airplane played to overflow crowds, and Slick established a reputation for sexuality and explicit language onstage that often provoked local law enforcement. Slick and fellow band members were arrested for drug violations and profanity in various places throughout the United States.

Jefferson Airplane's centrality to the counterculture is evidenced by the band's appearance at some of the quintessential cultural events of the 1960s. In 1967 Jefferson Airplane played at the nation's first major outdoor rock festival in Monterey, California, which drew an audience of more than 300,000 people and sparked a film celebrating the concert. Monterey was described as "three days of music, love, and flowers," but it also marked the increasing commercialization of the rock scene. Slick and Jefferson Airplane were also present at the Woodstock festival (1969), which the singer described as the highlight of the counterculture's possibilities. But the dark side of the 1960s also became evident later that year when Slick and the Jefferson Airplane joined the Rolling Stones for the Altamont concert outside of San Francisco. Members of the Hell's Angels motorcycle gang, hired to provide security for the concert, accosted the Airplane's Balin when he attempted to intervene with an overly aggressive and inebriated group of Hell's Angels, and one spectator was killed amid the chaos surrounding the concert.

By the late 1960s Slick and the Airplane were becoming increasingly disenchanted and angry with the political establishment. The song "Volunteers" (1969) called for a violent revolution in the United States. As a Finch College alumnus, Slick was asked to a 1969 White House reception sponsored by President Richard M. Nixon's daughter Tricia, who was celebrating her connection with the school. According to Slick, she invited the radical Yippie leader Abbie Hoffman as her escort, and they planned to spike the White House tea with LSD. The Secret Service, however, denied Slick and Hoffman access to the presidential mansion.

Slick also epitomized the 1960s sexual revolution. The dark-haired former fashion model exuded sexuality on the stage, and though she was officially still married, she pursued numerous sexual liaisons—including relationships with members of the band. Her husband, however, did seek a divorce in 1971 after Slick gave birth to Kantner's child, a daughter they named China. She married Skip Johnson on 29 November 1976; they divorced in 1994.

In the early 1970s, as the counterculture movement splintered, Jefferson Airplane also began to disintegrate. The group's founder, Balin, left the band, while Kaukonen and Casady formed the group Hot Tuna. Kantner and Slick continued to record with Jefferson Airplane, including the albums *Long John Silver* (1972) and *30 Seconds over Wonderland* (1973). Seeking to alter its image, the band changed its name to Jefferson Starship in 1974 and convinced Balin to rejoin the group. With a more mellow sound, Jefferson Starship recordings such as *Red Octopus* (1975) were more commercially successful than even the Airplane's best-selling *Surrealistic Pillow*. Battling problems with alcohol, Slick left the group after a disastrous concert appearance in Germany on 17 June 1978.

In 1981 Slick rejoined the band, now known simply as the Starship, but she departed again in 1989, touring briefly with the original members of Jefferson Airplane in the early

1990s. She also recorded four solo albums, all of which were commercially unsuccessful.

★

For more information on Slick see her autobiography (with Andrea Cagan), *Somebody to Love?: A Rock and Roll Memoir* (1998), and an authorized biography by Barbara Rowes, *Grace Slick: The Biography* (1980). For information on Jefferson Airplane and the San Francisco music scene see Ralph Gleason, *The Jefferson Airplane and the San Francisco Sound* (1969), and Charlie Gillett, *The Sound of the City: The Rise of Rock and Roll* (1970).

RON BRILEY

SMITH, David Roland (*b.* 9 March 1906 in Decatur, Indiana; *d.* 23 May 1965 near Bennington, Vermont), artist whose abstract metal sculptures and innovative use of welding both influenced and served as a catalyst to younger sculptors, especially during the 1960s.

Smith was one of two children born to Harvey Martin Smith, a telephone engineer and inventor, and Golda

David Smith. CORBIS CORPORATION (BELLEVUE)

Stoler, a schoolteacher and strict Methodist. In 1921 the Smiths moved to Paulding, Ohio, where he attended Paulding High School, graduating in 1924. Smith attended Ohio University in Athens, Ohio, for one year, but the summer of 1925 found him at the Studebaker automobile factory in South Bend, Indiana, working as a spot welder and riveter. That fall he entered Notre Dame University in Indiana but dropped out after only two weeks and began working for the Studebaker Finance Agency. In 1926 he was transferred to Washington, D.C., then to New York City, where he was introduced to cubism and constructivism during evening classes in painting at the Art Students League. He chose the league on the advice of a young art student, Dorothy Dehner. Smith became a full-time student the fall of 1927 and married Dehner on Christmas Eve that year.

Smith created his first welded sculpture in the fall of 1933, prompted in part by Pablo Picasso's and Julio González's welded examples of the late 1920s. He had seen examples of Picasso's welded work reproduced in the art magazine *Cahier d'Art*. However, from the beginning Smith's works reflected his antipathy towards the prevailing understanding of sculpture as a monolithic object. Smith eliminated or incorporated the pedestal into his work. He preferred to disperse his forms across the plane so that there was usually no "spine," or single orientation, to his sculpture. Smith welded rods and forms together to create what the critic Clement Greenberg later described as "drawings in air." In 1934 Smith rented studio space from Terminal Iron Works, a metal shop in Brooklyn, even helping out the workmen to improve his facility with welding techniques. He later appropriated the name for his factory-like studio at his farm in Bolton Landing near Lake George, New York, which he and Dehner had purchased in 1929.

In 1940 Smith moved permanently to Bolton Landing, although he continued to exhibit with the Marian Willard Gallery, where his first solo show was held in 1938. He further honed his welding skills during World War II, when he worked for two years in a factory. In his own sculpture, Smith began to incorporate symbolic forms that were ambiguously personal, even autobiographical. His work reflected aspects of surrealism, as well as the prevailing tendencies of the emerging New York School, and for this reason Smith is often associated with the abstract expressionists.

Smith's mature work is usually considered to have begun around 1951. He received the Guggenheim Foundation Fellowship in 1950, renewed in 1951, and began a sustained commitment to working in series, beginning with the *Agricolas* (1951–1959). These sculptures are composed of farm machinery pieces, hence the title, which is Latin for "farmer." Smith welded the parts together so that the original function of the implements was obscured, transforming the sculpture into an abstract construction. In 1952 the artist began the *Tanktotems* (through 1960), which were anthropomorphic in character, and in 1956 the *Sentinels* (through 1961), so named for their extreme verticality and watchful air. Smith achieved a new monumentality in terms of scale and sculptural power in the *Zigs* (1961–1964), each of which shares an interest in reductive geometry (both planar and modular) and in surface texture.

Smith's personal life suffered upheavals during this period. He divorced Dehner in 1952 and on 6 April 1953 married Jean Freas, with whom he had two children. They divorced in 1961. Nevertheless, his career enjoyed several boosts. In 1957 the Museum of Modern Art in New York held his first retrospective, which confirmed Smith's status as a major sculptor after years of relative isolation, and in 1958 he and three of his colleagues represented the United States in the Venice Biennale. The entire February 1960 issue of *Arts Magazine* was devoted to Smith, with photographs illustrating his factory-like working process. In 1962 he was invited to participate in the Fourth Festival of Two Worlds in Spoleto, Italy, where he was given access to the contents of several factories. Over the course of a month, Smith produced twenty-seven sculptures made out of the materials he had found there. He called them *Voltri,* after the name of the town in which he worked, and had the found remnants shipped back to Bolton Landing, where he created twenty-five more, known as the *Voltri-Boltons.*

Smith began his final series, the *Cubis,* in 1961, although he did not return to the series until 1963. The title is a reference to their main compositional element—solid squared units, usually rectangular boxes, made out of stainless steel. These sculptures differ from his earlier work in that Smith now directly acknowledged the volume of the form, rather than metaphorically referring to it with planes or rods. He arranged these cubes by stacking them, tilting them to form a diamond shape, and combining them with other geometric shapes, such as cylinders, disks, and plinths. The sculptures were designed to be set outdoors, and the natural daylight on the polished sheen of the cubes made them seem to dissolve, their three-dimensionality effectively countered by the effects of the light. The series was unfinished at the time of Smith's death in an accident in which his truck rolled over. At the time of his death, Smith had eighty-nine of his sculptures, many of them *Cubis,* in the fields around his home at Bolton Landing.

With their frank acknowledgement of austere, geometric forms, emphasis on industrial materials, and process of welding, the *Cubis* struck a responsive chord with many artists of the 1960s, despite the philosophical differences that went into their creation. Among younger artists there was a strong interest in elemental, standard shapes, especially the minimalists, from Tony Smith's single cubes to Robert Morris's blocks of six unequal sides. When Donald

Judd created his famous and often reproduced 1966 untitled sculpture of seven galvanized iron boxes arranged vertically, but each separately attached to the wall, he was undoubtedly reflecting in part an awareness of—or a reaction to—Smith's *Cubis.*

Smith's work provided an example against which younger artists had to respond, both formally and philosophically. Over the course of his career, Smith transformed the definition of sculpture so completely that the use of metals and welding as part of the creative process had become commonplace, demonstrating in the process the many open-ended possibilities available to the artist. "Art has its tradition, but it is a visual heritage," stated Smith in 1959. "It is an inner declaration of purpose, it is a factor which determines artist identity."

★

Smith's papers are at the Archives of American Art, Smithsonian Institution, Washington, D.C. For biographical information, see Candida N. Smith, *The Fields of David Smith* (1999), the catalogue for an exhibition at Storm King Art Center, New York, that year. For Smith's mature work, see E. A. Carmean, *David Smith* (1982), the catalogue for the exhibition at the National Gallery of Art, Washington, D.C. For a discussion of thematic and symbolic aspects in Smith's work, see Rosalind E. Krauss, *Terminal Iron Works: The Sculpture of David Smith* (1971), and for artistic process, see Stanley E. Marcus, *David Smith: The Sculptor and His Work* (1983). For a general overview, see Karen Wilkin, *David Smith* (1984). An obituary is in the *New York Times* (25 May 1965).

LEIGH BULLARD WEISBLAT

SMITH, Hazel Brannon   (*b.* 4 February 1914 in Alabama City, Alabama; *d.* 14 May 1994 in Cleveland, Tennessee), activist, newspaper publisher, editor, and Pulitzer Prize–winning writer in the South who increasingly opposed segregation through her four weekly southern newspapers.

Born Hazel Freeman Brannon, Smith was the eldest child of a middle-class Baptist couple, Dock Boad and Georgia Parthenia Brannon. Her father was a wire inspector for the steel industry who also owned his own small wiring company, Brannon Electric. Raised in Alabama, Smith was proud of her Confederate ancestry and, at a young age, was captivated by the mystique of the antebellum South. She even dreamed one day of being mistress of a *Gone with the Wind*–style mansion. Although the Brannons instilled in their children a respect for other races and religions, they accepted the typical southern way of life before the civil rights era as the norm: blacks were "different" and so were to be treated differently.

Considered by her mother to be too young to head off

Hazel Brannon Smith, October 1964. GETTY IMAGES

to university after her high school graduation at age sixteen, Smith took a job as an ad salesperson for the *Etowah Observer,* in Etowah County, Alabama. During her two years at the *Observer,* she became determined to one day own her own newspaper. She enrolled as a journalism student at the University of Alabama at Tuscaloosa, where she worked on the *Crimson–White.* After graduating with a major in journalism in 1935, Smith sought a newspaper for sale and found the *Durant News* in Durant, a small town in Holmes County, Mississippi. The newspaper industry was struggling as a result of the Great Depression, but Smith borrowed $3,000 and became a committed publisher and editor at age twenty-two.

Smith's treatment of blacks in the paper fell in line with that of her peers in the South: news was separated into "white" and "colored" sections, though she avoided the use of derisive terms such as "darkies, "pickaninny," and "mammy." The paper contained mostly parochial items: announcements, city council meetings, county news, and obituaries. Smith was well liked among white society members and was elected secretary of the Holmes County Democratic Executive Committee. In time, however, in her own column, "Through Hazel Eyes," she prompted a minor furor by commending the work of a group supporting a venereal disease clinic. Smith raised eyebrows again when

she suggested that the historically Democratic South would do well to establish a strong Republican Party, which she believed would put the South on a par politically with the other states of the Union. Her editorials exposing local gambling and bootlegging earned her the top award from the National Federation of Press Women. Smith was very clear about her future: acquisition of more newspaper properties would come before marriage and family. She would buy three more Mississippi papers: the *Lexington Advertiser, Banner Country Outlook,* and *Northside Reporter* in Jackson. She married Walter Smith in 1950.

The shift in Smith's civil rights awareness began in 1946, when she was held in contempt of court after interviewing the widow of a black man who had been whipped to death. Her life changed permanently in 1954 when she witnessed a Holmes County sheriff shooting a fleeing black man in the thigh. She wrote an editorial calling for the sheriff's resignation, and the sheriff won a $10,000 libel suit against her, which later was overturned by the state supreme court. The sheriff organized white citizens against Smith, and she came out against the White Citizens' Council as a racist and dictatorial group. The council supported the founding of a rival weekly, the *Lexington Herald,* and led an advertising boycott against her that would linger for the next three decades. Pressure from the council also cost Smith's husband his job as a hospital administrator.

Although Smith continued to speak out against unfair treatment of blacks, she was not an integrationist. In fact, when the *Herald* reported that an honor given Smith by the University of Southern Mississippi was awarded for her support of integration, she considered the charge a smear. She simply believed that blacks and whites should be allowed to live in peace, but separately. Still, a cross was burned in her front yard, and she was accused of involvement with black leaders, including Medgar Evers, the secretary of Mississippi's National Association for the Advancement of Colored People. She was portrayed as a shrewd, scheming woman who was trying to undermine Holmes County policies and tradition.

Smith was unsympathetic in 1961 after the arrest of the freedom riders, civil rights protestors who rode into Jackson. She preferred, she wrote, that they not ride to the South, yet she defended their right to do so as protected by federal law. She was unenthusiastic in 1962 when the student James Meredith attempted to integrate the University of Mississippi at Oxford, but she criticized Mississippi's governor for the bloodshed that ensued. Smith published an account critical of the police after the unprovoked killing of a black man in downtown Lexington. Again the police sued her for libel, and even her friends warned her against starting a riot by publicizing the matter. She brought the South to task for the murder of President John F. Kennedy, blaming southerners' election of bigots and extremists to leadership positions for fostering the atmosphere in which Kennedy was killed. "First Lincoln, Now Kennedy," the headline on her editorial read, "The South Kills Another President." Her editorial offices were firebombed after she appeared on a biracial panel in Washington, D.C., to discuss the case of three missing civil rights workers in Neshoba County, Mississippi. In addition to a slew of civil rights, public service, and journalism awards, Smith won a Pulitzer Prize in 1964 for her "steadfast adherence to her editorial duty in the face of great pressure and opposition."

By 1965, Smith and her papers were suffering for the cause. As racial tension and violence increased, she was $100,000 in debt. She mortgaged the plantation-style home of her childhood dreams and received donations from journalistic peers across the United States. She also had taken a radical turn from her 1954 statement that interracial marriage was a sin against God. In an interview with the *Boston Globe,* she said she supported the individual right to intermarry, despite the fact that it violated Mississippi law. In the spirit of fair play, she allowed her facilities to be used to print black publications.

During the 1970s, Smith struggled to keep her newspapers alive as she faced the onset of Alzheimer's disease. Her husband died in 1982, and she printed the last edition of the *Lexington Advertiser* in 1985. She lost her home and died penniless in a nursing home in 1994 following a lengthy illness. *A Passion for Justice: The Hazel Brannon Smith Story,* a made-for-television movie starring Jane Seymour, was produced in 1994. Throughout the turbulent 1960s, Smith kept journalistic freedom clearly in view, once saying, "When I am no longer able to print the truth unafraid, you are no longer able to speak the truth without fear."

★

Further readings on Smith include a biography by John Whalen, *Maverick Among the Magnolias* (2000), and David R. Davies, "Mississippi Journalists, the Civil Rights Movement, and the Closed Society, 1960–1964," a paper Davies presented at the 1994 convention of the American Journalism Historians Association. Obituaries are in the *New York Times* and the *Washington Post* (both 16 May 1994) and the *Masthead* (fall 1994).

BRENNA SANCHEZ

SMITH, Robert Weston. *See* Wolfman Jack.

SMITH, Walter Wellesley ("Red") (*b.* 25 September 1905 in Green Bay, Wisconsin; *d.* 15 January 1982 in Stamford, Connecticut), sportswriter known for his crisp writing and keen observations.

The middle child of Walter Philip Smith, a grocer, and Ida Richardson, a homemaker, Smith was raised in Green Bay,

Wisconsin. After graduating from East High School in Green Bay, Smith entered Notre Dame University, where he wrote for the school paper and edited the college yearbook.

Upon graduating from Notre Dame in 1927, Smith took his first job in journalism as a cub reporter for the *Milwaukee Sentinel.* The following year he went to work as a copy editor at the *St. Louis Star,* where within a few months he was offered a job as a sportswriter. Smith married Catherine "Kay" Cody, with whom he had two children, on 11 February 1933. In 1936 Smith went to work for the *Philadelphia Record,* where he first became known as "Red" Smith. Smith never served in the armed forces.

He remained with the Philadelphia newspaper until 1945, when he joined the staff of the *New York Herald Tribune,* where he worked until 1965. After the death of Grantland Rice in 1954, Smith's "Views of Sport" column, which appeared six times weekly, became the most widely read sports column in America and would remain so throughout much of the 1950s and 1960s.

During the 1950s and mid-1960s, Smith won millions of fans with his obvious love of sports, especially baseball, combined with his skeptical, sometimes bemused, approach to the subject and its place in the grand scheme of things. Typical of his writing from this period was a 7 February 1965 tribute to recently deceased St. Louis Cardinals slugger John Leonard "Pepper" Martin. A passing comment about Martin "brought memories back in a flood—a hundred memories of the cutting, slashing desperadoes who were the Cardinals of 1931." Discussing Martin at work, Smith wrote, "he'd go busting down to second base with one of those headlong, belly-whopping sides and up he'd come out of the dusty whirlwind that was his native habitat with his sweat-soaked haberdashery blacked with loam, a glistening film of grime on the homely face with its great, beaked prow."

In keeping with his attitude of pure love for the game, Smith refused to take sides in fan disputes or on any other issues involving sports, although he always tended to side with players against owners. Still, he remained rather subdued about his views, until the late 1960s. That period, and the years leading up to it, marked a transitional period in several ways for Smith.

On a personal level, liver cancer claimed Kay on 19 February 1967, and on 2 November 1968, Smith married Phyllis Warner Weiss, an artist and widow with five children. Professionally, he had to deal with the loss of his job at the *Herald Tribune,* which closed its doors in August 1965. Its former owners started a new paper, the *New York World Journal Tribune,* in late 1965, but in less than two years, that paper also folded. Smith supported his family during this period by writing for the Publishers-Hall Syndicate, also owned by the former *Herald Tribune* owners.

Only in 1971 did he finally secure another regular position, this one with the *New York Times,* which published his "Sports of the Times" column four days a week until just before his death.

Perhaps in part because of his recent experiences at the hands of big business, Smith became much more vocal in his support of players against owners during the late 1960s and early 1970s. For instance, he championed the cause of center fielder Curt Flood, who had recently been traded from the St. Louis Cardinals to the Philadelphia Phillies. At issue was baseball's reserve clause, which provided that a team could decide a player's fate without allowing him to choose a new team for himself. This was an example of the machinations that led Smith to bestow the nickname of "the slave trade" on professional baseball. Writing on 1 January 1970 about Flood's fight, which led to a Supreme Court battle and ultimate victory for the players in the mid-1970s, Smith noted that Flood "is a man of character and self-respect. Being black, he is more sensitive than most white players about the institution of slavery as it exists in professional baseball." He characterized one baseball official's response to Flood's efforts against the reserve clause thusly: "You mean that at these [salaries] they want human rights too?" Reviewing a letter to Flood by baseball commissioner Bowie Kuhn, Smith concluded, "Thus the commissioner restates baseball's labor policy: 'Run along, sonny, you bother me.'"

In 1972 Smith took on a more powerful entity in the realm of sports as big business, the International Olympic Committee (IOC). The occasion was the Summer Olympics in Munich in September, memorable for the bloodshed that occurred when Palestinian terrorists captured and killed eleven Israeli athletes. After that incident, Smith maintained, the IOC should have declared the Games concluded and sent everyone home. "Walled off in their dream world," he wrote, " . . . the aging playground dictators who conduct this quadrennial muscle dance ruled that a little bloodshed must not be permitted to interrupt play." Smith called for a U.S. boycott of the Moscow Games in 1980 as a protest of the Soviets' invasion of Afghanistan, and soon afterward, President Jimmy Carter declared that American athletes would stay home that year. Many observers credit Smith with influencing the boycott.

In addition to writing an estimated ten thousand newspaper columns, Smith published a number of books, including *The Best of Red Smith* and *Red Smith on Fishing Around the World* (both 1963), the latter an homage to his favorite pastime. A man of contrasts and balances, Smith was devoted to his family but loved drinking with friends. He was also a devout Roman Catholic. He died of congestive heart failure at Stamford Hospital in Stamford, Connecticut, and his ashes are buried at Stamford's Long Ridge Union Cemetery.

Smith, who in 1976 became only the second sportswriter in history to win a Pulitzer Prize, attracted the notice of no less a figure than Ernest Hemingway, who in *Across the River and into the Trees* (1950) wrote that a character "was reading Red Smith, and he liked him very much." Smith achieved such renown with his clear writing and emphasis on facts, characteristics that served to distinguish his work from the often high-blown, overly stylized writing of many sports columnists. His work influenced an entire generation of young writers, and not just sportswriters; among the figures he impacted were the poet and critic Donald Hall and his own son, Terry Fitzgerald, who became a reporter for the *New York Times.*

Despite his abilities, Smith never found writing easy; or, as he put it, "Writing is easy. I just open a vein and bleed." It was this skepticism, which he directed as much toward the world of sports and the politics of it as toward himself, that made Smith a truly keen and insightful observer not just of sports, but of life.

★

The definitive biography of Smith is Ira Berkow, *Red: A Biography of Red Smith* (1986). Also notable is Jerome Holtzman, *No Cheering in the Press Box* (1974). Significant profiles of Smith include Roger Kahn, "Red Smith of the Press Box" in *Newsweek* (21 Apr. 1958), and Donald Hall, "First a Writer, Then a Sportsman" in the *New York Times Book Review* (18 Jul. 1982). A tribute by colleague Dave Anderson and an obituary by Berkow are in the *New York Times* (both 16 Jan. 1982).

JUDSON KNIGHT

SMOTHERS, Thomas ("Tom") (*b.* 2 February 1937 in New York City), and **Richard ("Dick") SMOTHERS** (*b.* 20 November 1939 in New York City), folk-singing and comedy duo whose 1960s television show *The Smothers Brothers Comedy Hour* enjoyed a controversial three-year run before cancellation because of its political content.

The Smothers brothers (along with their younger sister) were the children of Major Thomas Bolyn Smothers, Jr., and Ruth Smothers. In 1941 Major Smothers was assigned to the Philippines. His family accompanied him, but they were evacuated to the United States with the outbreak of World War II. The major was captured at Bataan, and he died aboard a prisoner-of-war ship destined for Japan. Ruth Smothers moved the family to her hometown of Redondo Beach, California, where she found employment in an aircraft factory. Busy at work and reportedly married five times, she had little time for her children, who grew up largely unsupervised.

Both Tom and Dick Smothers graduated from Redondo

The Smothers Brothers. THE KOBAL COLLECTIOIN

Beach Union High School. Tom attended San Jose State College, where he was joined by his younger brother in 1957. More interested in music than academics, guitar-strumming Tom taught Dick to play the double bass. They played before college crowds at local venues before getting their first major break at the Purple Onion, a nightclub in San Francisco. In April 1959 they were scheduled to open for a flamenco dancer, but when the dancer suffered a twisted ankle shortly before showtime, the folk singers filled in with a comedy routine that delighted patrons, resulting in a thirty-six-week run.

By early 1961 the Smothers brothers were drawing crowds and positive notices for their performances at the Blue Angel in New York City. Jack Paar, the host of National Broadcasting Company (NBC) television's *The Tonight Show*, caught their act and booked them for an appearance. This led to a series of early 1960s guest spots on television variety shows, such as *The Steve Allen Show*, *The Garry Moore Show*, *The Andy Williams Show*, *The Ed Sullivan Show*, and *The Jack Benny Show*. Meanwhile the brothers continued a successful recording and touring career with their blend of folk music and self-effacing humor in which Dick played the straight man to his stammering brother Tom, who always claimed that Mom loved his younger brother best.

Their commercial success, especially with the college crowds television executives wanted to entice, led Columbia Broadcasting System (CBS) television to create *The Smoth-*

ers Brothers Show. The situation comedy premiered on 17 September 1965 and featured Tom as an angel whose well-intended divine interventions made life difficult for his brother, Dick. After a successful beginning the show's ratings deteriorated, the brothers feuded with the producer, Phil Sharp, and Tom developed an ulcer. The series was not renewed for a second season, but CBS executives still believed the Smothers brothers had television potential if afforded the proper vehicle.

Accordingly, the brothers were given an opportunity to host a variety show to air on Sunday evenings opposite *Bonanza*, NBC's popular Western. The thought among officials at CBS was that the Smothers brothers might be able to attract youthful viewers not drawn to the more traditional *Bonanza*. The executives received more than they expected on 5 February 1967, when the premier of *The Smothers Brothers Comedy Hour* pulled 36 percent of the available audience to *Bonanza*'s 26 percent share. Although ratings slipped somewhat during ensuing weeks, *The Smothers Brothers Comedy Hour* was one of the top twenty shows on television.

During this initial season the Smothers brothers played it safe, seeking the approval of both younger and older viewers on opposing sides of the growing cultural division in America during the 1960s. This was perhaps best symbolized by the show's closing credits, which featured both a traditional uniformed marching band playing John Philip Sousa tunes and a group of shaggy-haired protesters carrying signs. Guest stars included conventional vocalists such as Jim Nabors as well as the voices of alienated youth such as the band Buffalo Springfield. An admiring *Time* magazine piece praised the Smothers brothers as "hippies with haircuts."

However, during the show's second season, Tom, the major creative force behind the series and the more politicized of the brothers, began to push the envelope, incorporating more political satire into each episode. Tom's identification with the youth culture and antiestablishment views became increasingly apparent. For the second-season premiere on 10 September 1967 the brothers invited former blacklisted folk singer Pete Seeger to perform. Seeger sang "Waist Deep in the Big Muddy," an allegorical commentary on the Vietnam War that included the lyrics "We're waist deep in the Big Muddy / and the big fool says to push on." CBS executives insisted the lyrics were disrespectful to President Lyndon Johnson, and the performance was censored. Following a public outcry Seeger was invited back to perform the song without network interference.

Nevertheless, during the second season the Smothers brothers continued to battle network censors. In addition to finding a sketch on sex education unacceptable, the network guardians of morality axed a skit in which Tom and guest star Elaine May played motion picture censors objecting to the use of the word *breast* in a dinner table conversation scene. Recurring characters on the show also caused censors discomfort. The comedian David Steinberg antagonized some CBS affiliates with a series of "sacrilegious" sermonettes. The comedian Leigh French created the "hippie chick" character Goldie O'Keefe who, with her "Share a little tea with Goldie" segment, parodied television advice shows for women. The sketches were full of innuendoes dealing with drug use, including drug code words such as *tea*, *roaches*, and *goldie*. Yet there was little censorship of this material, perhaps because the censors from an older generation failed to comprehend the hipster humor. CBS officials seemed much more threatened by overt political material. The network took the unprecedented step of requiring the Smothers brothers to make advance copies of each episode available for review by affiliate stations.

Sprouting moustaches and longer hair, the Smothers brothers again tangled with the network on the show's third-season premiere in September 1968. Guest star Harry Belafonte's calypso piece "Don't Stop the Carnival" was a critical account of the violence at the Chicago Democratic National Convention in August. While Belafonte performed, footage of the violent convention confrontations played in the background. CBS refused to air the five-minute segment. Instead, the network sold this extra five minutes of advertising time to the Republican Party, which ran a spot for Richard Nixon's presidential bid. Another famous

spot on the show featured the perennial presidential candidate Pat Paulsen. His parody of campaign shenanigans struck a nerve with many viewers.

The third season also witnessed frequent sketches critical of television censors, creating a more confrontational environment between CBS and the Smothers brothers. On 9 March 1969 CBS pulled the entire episode of *The Smothers Brothers Comedy Hour* when guest star Joan Baez dedicated a song to her husband, David Harris, who was serving a prison term for draft resistance. The network relented and aired the episode with Baez's introduction deleted. But CBS wanted no more of the Smothers brothers. On 3 April 1969 Robert D. Wood, the president of CBS, informed Tom Smothers that because an acceptable broadcast tape was not submitted in time for review by the Program Practices Department and affiliated stations, the contract between the Smothers brothers and the network was terminated. Failing ratings made the decision easier for CBS. By overtly identifying with the antiestablishment youth culture the Smothers brothers had evidently lost older viewers. After starting the 1968–1969 television season as the seventh most popular show with a 37 percent share of the audience, *The Smothers Brothers Comedy Hour* had dropped to twenty-fourth place by March 1969, and *Bonanza* had rebounded to third place in the Nielsen ratings. Despite a public uproar led by Tom, the network was unrelenting, although the Smotherses did eventually win a lawsuit for wrongful dismissal.

Although the Smotherses continued a lucrative recording and concert career, they were never able to recoup their position in prime-time television. In 1970 they were given a summer variety series on the American Broadcasting Company (ABC) television network. However, the controversy with CBS seemed to have taken something out of the brothers, who lacked their political edge, and the series was not picked up for the fall season. A 1975 variety show on NBC did not last a full season. Twenty years after their cancellation, CBS aired a *Smothers Brothers Comedy Hour* special that enjoyed decent ratings, and the Smothers were rewarded with a new series that was canceled after the 1990 season. While unable to regain a slot in prime time (an area still closed to political satire), *The Smothers Brothers Comedy Hour* (1966–1969) paved the way for such television parody as *Saturday Night Live* and *Politically Incorrect*.

Dick Smothers has been married three times. In September 1959 he married the former Linda Miller, and they had three children. His second wife was Lorraine, whom he married in 1986, and his third Denby Franklin, whom he married on 4 January 1997. He has six children in all. Tom Smothers was married in 1963 to Stephanie Owen; the couple had one child before a 1967 divorce. He married a second time, then most recently married Marcy Carriker, a television producer, on 9 September 1990; they had two children. Tom and Dick share an enthusiasm for automobiles and auto racing.

★

The confrontation between the Smothers brothers and CBS television is well developed in Aniko Bodroghkozy, "*The Smothers Brothers Comedy Hour* and the Youth Rebellion," in Lynn Spigel and Michael Curtin, eds., *The Revolution Wasn't Televised: Sixties Television and Social Conflict* (1997); Robert Mertz, *CBS: Reflections in a Bloodshot Eye* (1975); and Bert Spector, "A Clash of Cultures: The Smothers Brothers vs. CBS Television," in John E. O'Connor, ed., *American History/American Television* (1983). All episodes of *The Smothers Brothers Comedy Hour* are available at the UCLA Film and Television Archive in Los Angeles, California.

RON BRILEY

SONDHEIM, Stephen Joshua (*b.* 22 March 1930 in New York City), composer and lyricist who met with both success and failure during the 1960s and found himself in 1970 the new voice of the American musical theater.

The only child of Herbert Sondheim, a dress manufacturer, and Etta Janet "Foxy" (Fox) Sondheim, a dress designer, Sondheim began life in Manhattan but moved with his mother to Pennsylvania at the age of ten when his parents separated. After a couple of years in military school, he

Stephen Sondheim. ARCHIVE PHOTOS, INC.

attended the George School, a preparatory academy in Pennsylvania, and graduated from Williams College with a major in music in 1950. He went on to study privately with composer Milton Babbitt.

Sondheim's relationship with his mother was conflicted, but he found a spiritual home in his teenage years with the family of lyricist Oscar Hammerstein II, who served as a substitute parent. "I wrote for the theater in order to be like Oscar," Sondheim later said. "I have no doubt that if he'd been a geologist, I would have been a geologist." His mentor taught Sondheim about the construction of musical comedy and continued to advise him until Hammerstein's death in 1960.

Sondheim's first job was as writer for the television series *Topper* in 1953. His first professional score was for the unproduced play *Saturday Night* in 1954. When its producer died, so did the project, but this work led Sondheim to a stunning Broadway debut in 1957, penning lyrics to Leonard Bernstein's music for *West Side Story*. Sondheim also served as lyricist for *Gypsy* (1959), with music by Jule Styne. Both are considered first-rate, classic, Broadway musicals; both included non-traditional subject matter that attracted Sondheim; and both helped him shape himself as an artist. *West Side Story*'s Romeo-and-Juliet tale and *Gypsy*'s saga of motherhood run amok were less comforting, less light, than what many theatergoers were used to.

Sondheim was able to present himself as composer as well as lyricist in his next Broadway project, *A Funny Thing Happened on the Way to the Forum* in 1962. Burt Shevelove and Larry Gelbart adapted material by the ancient Roman playwright Plautus into a humorous romp involving a slave who wants to be free. Audiences and critics responded to the bawdy yet benign spectacle, which fitted nicely into popular tastes of the early 1960s.

The composer later noted that his score for *Forum* represented the beginning of his move away from the tradition of the integrated musical comedy pioneered and sustained by his beloved Hammerstein in such productions as *Show Boat* (1927) and *Oklahoma!* (1943). In an integrated musical, a number stems naturally from the action of the play and furthers the plot. In contrast, Sondheim saw the songs in *Forum* as respites from the frantic pace of the play.

As the decade progressed, Sondheim began to exhibit an intellectuality and a social consciousness that much of Broadway's musical fare lacked. His next show, *Anyone Can Whistle* (1964), closed after nine performances. Nevertheless, this work, with a book by Arthur Laurents, forged new ground for the musical theater, embracing controversial subject matter. Set in a town with a corrupt mayor and a prominent mental institution, it played with the boundaries between sanity and insanity. Like those in *Forum*, its songs departed in function from established tradition.

"They commented on the action instead of advancing it," Sondheim later explained.

His next play taught Sondheim what he did not want to do. Before his death, Hammerstein had urged his protégé to work with the lyricist's partner, Richard Rodgers. When Rodgers was asked to compose for a musical adaptation of Laurents's play *The Time of the Cuckoo* (1952), Sondheim agreed to serve as lyricist for the project, titled *Do I Hear a Waltz?* (1965). Sondheim later commented that the play should probably never have been adapted. Beyond that difficulty and his reluctance to return to mere lyric writing, he experienced great constraints working with Rodgers. He would never again settle for less than full participation in a musical project.

After *Waltz,* Sondheim worked on a variety of projects that did not develop fully. In 1966 he and playwright James Goldman adapted a John Collier short story for the television anthology *ABC Stage 67.* A fantasy about a group of people who hide out from the world in a department store but live in fear of "dark men" who punish emotionalism and nonconformity, "Evening Primrose" did not quite manage to make the transition to the small screen successfully. It nevertheless signified a stepping stone in Sondheim's career and another case in which he embraced what many would consider depressing subject matter.

The remainder of the decade was one of trial and error for Sondheim, including a stint in which the veteran games player composed crossword puzzles for *New York* magazine. He returned to Broadway in 1970 with a production that put him on the map as far as critics and scholars were concerned. *Company* built on Sondheim's past work at conveying mood with his music. The first of the "concept musicals" he pioneered with producer Harold Prince, it is a play based on theme rather than plot, exploring the ins and outs of marriage in New York as seen through several couples who befriend a bachelor. It speaks and sings of love, accommodation, fear of commitment, and the excitement and alienation of living in the city.

In the years after 1970, Broadway became decreasingly fertile ground for musical theater. In the 1950s and 1960s it had lost its connection with American popular music as the recording market fragmented and rock music became dominant. Escalating costs in the 1970s made it riskier to fund new works, and producers relied increasingly on rehashes and revivals of old material.

In this new climate, Sondheim proved the primary—sometimes the only—serious American theater composer. "The biggest challenge for me is the opportunity to constantly try new things," he told *New York* in 1974. "It's the writer's job . . . to bring [the audience] things they would never have expected to see." His knowledge of the traditions of musical theater, combined with his desire to explore new techniques and themes, took him from an homage to the great musical revues of the past in *Follies* (1971) to an exploration of Japanese response to western culture in *Pacific Overtures* (1976), and from a rewriting of fairy tales in *Into the Woods* (1987) to an exploration of the impulse to kill presidents in *Assassins* (1991). He never lost the passion he displayed in the 1960s for exploring new techniques, forms, and subject matter.

★

There are several books about Sondheim, including Joanne Gordon, *Art Isn't Easy: The Achievement of Stephen Sondheim* (1990); Martin Gottfried, *Sondheim* (1993); and Meryle Secrest, *Stephen Sondheim: A Life* (1998). Craig Zadan, *Sondheim and Co.* (1986), collects quotations from colleagues to round out the picture of Sondheim's work. There is also a journal devoted to the composer, *The Sondheim Review.*

TINKY "DAKOTA" WEISBLAT

SONNY (Bono, *b.* 16 February 1935 in Detroit, Michigan; *d.* 5 January 1998 in South Lake Tahoe, California) **AND CHER** (*b.* 20 May 1946 in El Centro, California), pop music duo who brought a counterculture look to mainstream America with a string of hit records and television appearances.

Salvatore ("Sonny") Phillip Bono was born to Santo and Jean Bono, a working-class family of Sicilian immigrants, in Detroit in 1935. When the boy was seven, the Bono family relocated to the Los Angeles area, where his father worked as a truck driver. After finishing high school, Bono married Donna Rankin, with whom he had a daughter, and took a series of menial jobs to support his family. Breaking up the boredom by writing songs on the job, Bono began auditioning his songs for producers and artists around Los Angeles. One such encounter led to his first job in the record industry as an artists and repertoire director at Specialty Records, where he worked as a producer, talent scout, and songwriter. In 1962 Bono started working for producer Phil Spector, best known for his string of hits featuring distinctive and elaborate "Wall of Sound" arrangements. Divorced that year from his first wife, Bono met Cherilyn Sarkisian ("Cher"), then a sixteen-year-old high school dropout living with friends in Hollywood.

Born in the southern California desert town of El Centro in 1946 to John and Georgia Holt Sarkisian, Cher's home life was marked by poverty and instability as her mother, who married eight times, struggled to work as an actress and model in Hollywood. Self-conscious about her dark features in contrast to her mother's blonde, all-American looks, Cher grew up wanting to be famous but not knowing how she would accomplish that objective. Encouraged by her mother, she took acting lessons, although her formal education, hampered by dyslexia, ended when she dropped out of high school in the tenth grade. Going from one job to another, Cher had just been fired from her job at a candy shop when she met Bono in 1962.

The two remembered different versions of their first meeting. Bono recalled that Cher was part of a double date that matched them with different partners; weeks later, they happened to meet again when Bono moved into the apartment building where Cher was living. In her memoir, *The First Time* (1998), Cher described her first memory of seeing Bono as he walked into a Hollywood coffee shop: "I was fascinated by Son from the moment he walked through the door. And I actually thought to myself, 'Something is different now. You're never going to be the same.'" Bono agreed that their relationship marked a turning point in both their lives; in his autobiography, *And the Beat Goes On* (1991), he remarked, "Basically, we were two lost kids who found direction in each other."

Cher began accompanying Bono on his trips to Spector's sessions at Goldstar recording studios and sang back-up vocals on classic tracks such as "Be My Baby," "Da Doo Ron Ron," and "You've Lost That Lovin' Feeling." She also made her recording debut under the name "Bonnie Jo Mason" on Spector's novelty record dedicated to the Beatles, "Ringo, I Love You," in 1964. Billed as "Cesar and Cleopatra," Bono and Cher began to perform in small clubs around Los Angeles, playing cover tunes and some of Bono's own compositions. The appearances were originally planned as solo showcases for Cher, but she was too nervous to go out on stage alone and insisted that Bono appear with her. "Cesar and Cleo" also recorded three singles for Reprise Records, but the releases sank without a trace. The couple's first three releases as "Sonny and Cher" in 1965 did little better, but the duo's fourth release that year, a song written by Bono that summed up his relationship with Cher, turned the couple into a pop music sensation.

With a hummable melody, simple lyrics, and a radio-friendly, Wall of Sound arrangement, "I Got You, Babe" hit number one for three weeks in August 1965 in the United States and repeated the feat a few months later in Great Britain. Sonny and Cher had two more Top Ten hits during the rest of the decade, "Baby Don't Go" in 1965 and "The Beat Goes On" in 1967. As solo artists, Bono also scored a solo Top Ten hit with "Laugh at Me" in 1965, while Cher entered the Top Ten with "Bang Bang (My Baby Shot Me Down)" in 1966 and "You Better Sit Down, Kids" in 1967. While the hits made them pop stars, it was their appearances on music and variety shows such as *Hullabaloo* and *The Ed Sullivan Show* that made Sonny and Cher into household names. Sometimes the duo wore matching fur vests with ankle boots and turtlenecks; at other times, Cher sported widely flared, embroidered, bell-bottom slacks while Sonny wore shirts with psychedelic designs or patterned trousers. Combined with their string

Sonny *(left)* and Cher. AP/WIDE WORLD PHOTOS

of Top Ten hits, the couple's unconventional appearance and flippant attitude toward the press blurred the line between mainstream popular tastes and the emerging hippie subculture.

After the summer of love in 1967, however, Sonny and Cher no longer seemed as hip as when they debuted on the scene in 1965. As their singles stumbled on the charts, the two starred in the poorly received films *Good Times* in 1967 and the self-financed *Chastity* in 1969. Facing bankruptcy, Sonny and Cher refocused on their concert act on "The Nightclub from Hell Circuit," as Cher called it. These appearances kept the duo in the public eye and in 1971 led to an offer for a six-week summer variety show series based on their act, which had incorporated banter between the couple as part of its appeal. An immediate hit, *The Sonny and Cher Comedy Hour* stayed on the air until 1974 and helped revitalize Cher's recording career, which included three number-one singles between 1971 and 1974. After living together since 1964 and marrying in 1969 (their daughter, Chastity, was born 4 March of that year), Bono and Cher divorced on 27 June 1975. Bono later married his third wife, Susie Coehlo, in 1982, but the union ended in divorce in 1984. Cher was briefly married to the rock star Greg Allman, with whom she had one child.

Bono and Cher reunited for *The Sonny and Cher Show*

in 1976–1977 but pursued different career paths after that. Cher remained one of the most popular entertainers of her era. She revitalized her acting career in the 1980s and won the Academy Award as best actress for her performance in *Moonstruck* in 1987. An enduring presence on the music charts, her single "Believe" became the biggest-selling track of 1999 and won the 2000 Grammy Award for best dance recording. Bono opened up a chain of restaurants in southern California in the 1980s and entered politics as the Republican candidate for mayor of Palm Springs in 1988. He served as mayor until 1992 and was elected as the U.S. representative from California's Forty-fourth Congressional District in 1995. During his second term in Congress, Bono died in a skiing accident on 5 January 1998 while on vacation with his fourth wife, Mary (Whitaker) Bono, and their two children in South Lake Tahoe, California. Featuring a eulogy by Cher, Bono's funeral attracted worldwide media attention not only for his accomplishments as a politician but also for his place in the popular culture of the 1960s and 1970s.

★

Bono published his autobiography, *And the Beat Goes On* (1991), and Cher wrote a memoir with Jeff Coplon, *The First Time* (1998). Their daughter, Chastity Bono, published *Family Outing* (1998) with Billie Fitzpatrick. Biographies of Cher include Lawrence J. Quirk, *The Life and Wild Times of Cher* (1991), and Mark Bego, *Cher: If You Believe* (2001). Bono's obituary by Bernard Weinraub appeared in the *New York Times* (7 Jan. 1998). A list of Sonny and Cher's chart singles in the United States appears in Joel Whitburn, ed., *The Billboard Book of Top Forty Hits, Sixth Edition* (1996). For their singles on the U.K. charts, see Dave McAleer, ed., *The All Music Book of Hit Singles,* (1994).

TIMOTHY BORDEN

SONTAG, Susan (*b.* 16 January 1933 in New York City), critic, essayist, novelist, and radical New York intellectual who emerged during the 1960s as a provocative commentator on avant-garde art, popular culture, and leftist politics.

Born Susan Lee Rosenblatt, Sontag was the eldest of two daughters of Jack Rosenblatt and Mildred Jacobson, both descendants of European Jewish immigrants. Sontag was born in a Manhattan hospital but spent her early childhood in China, where her father headed a fur-trading business until his death from tuberculosis when Sontag was five. Shortly thereafter, Sontag began experiencing bouts of asthma, prompting her mother to move the family from their American residence in New York to Miami. When the Florida climate failed to improve Sontag's condition, her mother relocated to Tucson, Arizona, in 1939. There Sontag, already recognizably precocious and serious-minded, began elementary school in the third grade.

Sontag has described her childhood as a period of "imprisonment" during which her advanced intellectual development and, later, her disdain for postwar conformist culture chafed against the mediocrity and superficiality of her peers. The early loss of her father and ambivalent relationship with her mother, a vain and distant woman prone to melancholia and alcoholism, further heightened Sontag's sense of isolation. Turning to books for solace and much needed stimulation, Sontag became a voracious reader, adopting as her first literary heroes the adventure writer Richard Halliburton and Edgar Allan Poe.

Sontag's mother married Nathan Sontag, a convalescing Air Force pilot and decorated war hero, in 1945, and the next year the family moved to Southern California. There, Sontag devoted herself to reading nineteenth-century European classics, the avant-garde fiction of the French writer André Gide, and *Partisan Review,* then the leading intellectual journal of the American Left, which she discovered at age thirteen and to which she dreamed of one day being a contributor. While in high school, Sontag and a friend managed to arrange a visit with the German novelist Thomas Mann at his California home, a formative, if somewhat demystifying, experience that shaped her conception of the literary life. In January 1949 Sontag graduated early

Susan Sontag. MR. JERRY BAUER

from North Hollywood High School and, to placate her mother, enrolled at the University of California, Berkeley, for the spring semester.

In the fall of 1949 she transferred to the University of Chicago, her first choice, where she completed the rigorous undergraduate curriculum in two years, graduating in 1951. While at Chicago, Sontag met David Rieff, a sociology instructor and doctoral candidate, whom she married in December 1950 after a mere ten-day courtship. Sontag was seventeen and Rieff twenty-eight. She gave birth to their son, David, on 28 September 1952. During their eight-year marriage, Sontag collaborated with Rieff on his book *Freud: The Mind of a Moralist* (1959), although she did not receive credit as coauthor.

In 1953 Sontag began a graduate English program at the University of Connecticut but left the next year for Harvard University, where she completed a master's degree in philosophy in 1957. With a recommendation from the philosopher Paul Tillich, Sontag received a fellowship to study at Oxford University in England the next academic year. Leaving her husband and son behind, she traveled alone to Europe. Dissatisfied with the dominance of A. J. Ayer's analytical philosophy at Oxford, however, in 1958 Sontag moved to Paris and enrolled at the Sorbonne with the intention of completing her dissertation; she never did. In Paris, Sontag befriended the American writer Alfred Chester and his circle and immersed herself in the French intellectual milieu, then under the spell of Jean-Paul Sartre and existentialism.

Returning to the United States at the end of 1958, Sontag requested a divorce from Rieff. She had come to regard her husband as overly conventional and regretted having married him at such an early age. She collected her six-year-old son and moved to New York to support herself as a writer, even refusing alimony from Rieff. Sontag worked briefly as an editorial assistant for *Commentary* and taught philosophy at Sarah Lawrence College and City College during 1959 and 1960 before securing a position in the religion department at Columbia University beginning in 1960. During this time, Sontag became romantically involved with the playwright María Irene Fornés. Though Sontag has remained silent about her sexuality, her longtime relationship with the photographer Annie Liebovitz, initiated in the late 1970s, reduced the matter to an open secret.

In 1963 Sontag published her first novel, *The Benefactor,* which she dedicated to Fornés. Sontag's challenging book, influenced by the French *nouveau roman,* was championed by the renowned editor Robert Giroux at Farrar, Straus (subsequently Farrar, Straus, and Giroux) and received mixed but respectful reviews. Through Giroux and his publishing partner, Roger Straus, Sontag gained entrée to the upper circles of the New York literati and made an im-

mediate impression. The allure of Sontag's superior mind and statuesque beauty, featured in striking photographs that graced the jackets of her books, proved irresistible to many, while inciting the envy of others.

In 1962 Sontag realized her aspiration of writing for *Partisan Review* with a published review of the Polish-born writer Isaac Bashevis Singer's *The Slave.* Over the next two years Sontag wrote additional critical pieces for *Partisan Review, Evergreen Review,* the *Nation,* and the newly established *New York Review of Books,* together forming the core of her highly regarded first collection, *Against Interpretation* (1966). Among these was "Notes on Camp," published in the autumn 1964 issue of *Partisan Review,* in which Sontag attempted to distill the essential characteristics of "camp" sensibility in both highbrow and popular artistic forms.

Camp, Sontag noted, is predominantly found in the performing and decorative arts, and its hallmarks are unabashed extravagance, sentimentality, theatricality, self-parody, and the primacy of style over content. In contrast to kitsch or art that is merely bad, Sontag argued that the flamboyance and corniness of camp—displayed, for example, by opera, art nouveau, the British writer Oscar Wilde's dandyism, and such film stars as Greta Garbo—can result in an awfulness that is genuinely admirable. This essay in particular—along with writings on such Continental luminaries as Albert Camus, György Lukács, Claude Lévi-Strauss, Eugène Ionesco, Nathalie Sarraute, and Jean-Luc Godard—attracted notice in the mainstream press, leading to a *Time* magazine feature and widening interest in Sontag's dynamic intelligence and self-styled aesthetic principles. In other essays, notably "Against Interpretation" and "On Style," Sontag delineated her corrective view of criticism as an act of passion and sensuous appreciation rather than a "philistine" obsession with deciphering the content of a work.

While establishing herself as a talented literary polemicist, Sontag began work on a second novel, *Death Kit* (1967). Like *The Benefactor, Death Kit* is a novel of ideas, fashioned after experimental French forms, that explores the paradoxical nature of dream, reality, and perception. Although the fanfare surrounding its publication enhanced Sontag's fame, the book was poorly received and invited a backlash against the author's celebrity, including charges of pretentiousness, aesthetic detachment, and hypocritical self-promotion. All these criticisms would become the staples of Sontag's detractors and the subject of various literary feuds throughout her career.

In 1967 Sontag's political consciousness, dormant since adolescence, was reawakened by escalating American military action in Vietnam. In January 1968 Sontag was arrested, along with the writers Allen Ginsberg and Grace Paley, during an antiwar demonstration in New York. In

May of that year Sontag accepted an invitation from the Communist government of North Vietnam to visit Hanoi. Sontag recorded her cultural disorientation and observations of the North Vietnamese people, whose foreign demeanor and morality she naively struggled to understand, in "Trip to Hanoi." Sontag's self-described "neo-radicalism," conveyed in spirited Marxist declamations of American-style capitalist imperialism, also extended to commentaries on Cuba during the late 1960s, leading to a visit to that country in December 1968 and support for Castro's Communist revolution. More than a decade later, however, after these regimes proved repressive rather than democratic, Sontag reversed her position. In a notorious speech, given at Manhattan's Town Hall in February 1982, she condemned Communist tyranny and denounced Communism itself as "fascism with a friendly face." The speech and Sontag's apostasy were sharply criticized by members of the American Left.

By the late 1960s Sontag was an international star. She traveled to Sweden in the spring of 1968 to begin work on her first feature film, *Duet for Cannibals,* which premiered in 1969. Though the film was well received at Cannes and the New York Film Festival, Sontag's subsequent work as filmmaker failed to live up to its promise. Like her fiction, it was relegated to the periphery of her creative endeavors, vastly overshadowed by the acclaim of her critical proclamations and the inseparable mystique of her celebrity persona.

Sontag's second essay collection, *Styles of Radical Will* (1969), included "Trip to Hanoi" and essays previously printed in *Partisan Review* and other journals. Among these are two landmark essays: "Aesthetics of Silence," a philosophical argument for silence as a valid mode of resistance and transcendence in modern art, and "The Pornographic Imagination," a defense of literary pornography as a radical art form, exemplified by *The Story of O* and certain erotic works by Georges Bataille. The volume also contains "What's Happening in America (1966)," Sontag's dire diagnosis of contemporary American politics and culture, and masterly critiques of Ingmar Bergman's *Persona* and of Godard that reveal Sontag's sophisticated understanding of cinema.

Hailed during the 1960s as a model of the new, independent woman—glamorous, wildly brilliant, outspoken, and, above all, self-defined—Sontag established herself as an audacious and prescient authority on matters of culture and style. Her high-profile appearances in glossy women's magazines and her willingness to treat belittled subjects of popular art with serious critical attention leveled distinctions between high and low culture, encouraging others to do the same and adumbrating the omnivorous approach of cultural studies in the coming postmodern age. Likewise, her affinity for postwar Continental literature, which she showcased in much of her writing, precipitated, if not directly influenced, the influx of French literary philosophy into the American academy during the 1970s and 1980s.

Over the next several decades Sontag remained a preeminent woman of letters, renowned for her verve, intellectual commitment, and complex, often self-contradictory engagement with controversial issues of the day. She continued to produce important collections of critical essays, including *On Photography* (1977); *Illness as Metaphor* (1978), inspired by her near-death experience with breast cancer in the mid-1970s; and *AIDS as Metaphor* (1989). Her novel, *In America* (2000), received the National Book Award.

★

Sontag's semi-autobiographic stories in *I, etcetera* (1978) offer insight into her formative experiences. *Conversations with Susan Sontag* (1995), edited by Leland Poague, contains interviews with Sontag dating from 1969 through 1993. *Susan Sontag: The Making of an Icon* (2000), by Carl Rollyson and Lisa Paddock, is a highly informative biography that does much to counter Sontag's reticence on personal matters. Critical studies include Sohnya Sayres, *Susan Sontag: Elegiac Modernist* (1990); Kennedy Liam, *Susan Sontag: Mind as Passion* (1995); and Carl Rollyson, *Reading Susan Sontag: A Critical Introduction to Her Work* (2001).

JOSH LAUER

SORENSEN, Theodore Chaikin ("Ted") (*b.* 8 May 1928 in Lincoln, Nebraska), President John F. Kennedy's chief adviser and speechwriter, who translated Kennedy's political philosophy into New Frontier programs and policies.

Sorensen's attraction to public service and his liberal/pacifist views were rooted in his family background. Raised a Unitarian, he was one of four children of Christian Abraham and Annis (Chaikin) Sorensen. His lawyer father was born in a prairie sod house to Danish immigrants and served as state attorney general of Nebraska. He became a crusading Republican and political ally of the progressive senator George Norris. Ted's mother was of Russian-Jewish background and was a feminist and pacifist. As youths, Ted and his older brother Tom were active campaigners for civil rights before this became a national political cause. After receiving a law degree in 1951 from the University of Nebraska, where he was first in his class, Ted headed for Washington, D.C., to work as an attorney for the Federal Security Agency and then as a researcher for a congressional subcommittee on railroad retirement before joining John F. Kennedy's staff.

In 1953 first-year Senator John F. Kennedy recruited the twenty-four-year-old Sorensen as his legislative assistant. He became an indispensable aide on both legislative and political matters. In the mid- to late 1950s, he planned Kennedy's speaking tours and accompanied him in his travels. It was Sorensen who researched and wrote a profusion of speeches and articles that showcased Kennedy's understanding of domestic and foreign issues and historical perspectives, all of which contributed to Kennedy's rising national stature. Although never taking credit for it, Sorensen is widely acknowledged to have been a shaping force behind Kennedy's Pulitzer Prize–winning *Profiles in Courage*. Sorensen also played a leading role in Kennedy's nearly successful bid for the Democratic vice-presidential nomination in 1956.

So important was Sorensen to Kennedy that as special counsel he became the president-elect's first appointee in November 1960. Kennedy delegated to him considerable responsibility for screening people and ideas and for fleshing out policy; cabinet and agency officials typically dealt with Sorensen rather than the president on most domestic matters. In totally dedicating himself to Kennedy, Sorensen worked long hours, often alone; as a result, both his health and marriage suffered. In August 1963 he was divorced from Camilla (Palmer) Sorensen, whom he had married on 8 September 1949. She returned to Nebraska with their three sons. Sorensen remarried in 1964, but that union also ended in divorce within five years.

Tall and angular, with a square, somber face set off by dark-rimmed glasses, Sorensen's appearance underscored a reputation as a no-nonsense intellectual. His demeanor was stiff, his personal habits prudish, and his attitude aloof, though it may have masked a natural shyness. When charm was required, however, Sorensen could rise to the occasion, and his colleagues reported that he had a wry wit.

Kennedy valued Sorensen's advice as a generalist. Insiders confirmed his contributions both to domestic policy and international issues. His voice counterbalanced more politically conservative and militarily aggressive pressures, as in his support for using a blockade instead of an air strike against Cuba during the missile crisis of October 1962. Sorensen was a major force behind Kennedy's persistent pursuit of the August 1963 nuclear test ban treaty despite repeated Soviet rebuffs and delays.

Sorensen captured in speeches and in other writings the content and emotional emphasis required at each critical point of the Kennedy administration. The most noteworthy of Sorensen's speeches included the inaugural address; the announcement of the blockade of Cuba on 22 October 1962; the American University foreign-policy address of 10 June 1963; and the eloquent civil rights speech televised nationally on 11 June 1963. The drafts were perfectly attuned to Kennedy's clipped, emphatic delivery. The messages were lofty, but the language and syntax were simple, making frequent use of short sentences, staccato phrasing, parallelisms, and alliteration. Though some critics ex-

Ted Sorensen. CORBIS CORPORATION (BELLEVUE)

pressed irritation over the mannered oratorical style, none challenged the impact that the Kennedy-Sorensen speeches had on listeners at home and abroad.

Following the Kennedy assassination, Sorensen stayed on with President Lyndon Johnson only long enough to assist with the transition. His departure in early 1964 was criticized by some as an abandonment of Kennedy's programs and ideals. Instead, Sorensen felt compelled to write *Kennedy,* published in 1965, which he described as a "substitute for the book [Kennedy himself] was going to write." In that sense it remains the closest thing possible to a Kennedy memoir. Sorensen has written or edited seven other books, mostly dealing with the Kennedys and the presidency. Sorensen returned to Kennedy service as an unofficial consultant to Senator Robert F. Kennedy and as a full-time member of Robert Kennedy's staff during his aborted 1968 presidential campaign. Ironically, Sorensen had advised Kennedy to wait until 1972 to seek the presidency.

In the decades following the 1960s, Sorensen remained active in Democratic Party politics in New York and the nation. He served in a number of appointed positions and unsuccessfully ran for the U.S. Senate from New York in 1970. Although endorsed by the state Democratic committee in the primary, he finished a distant third for the nomination, evidence that he lacked the charisma to capture public support. In 1977 President-elect Jimmy Carter considered Sorensen for director of the Central Intelligence Agency, but Sorensen withdrew his own name following opposition from the Senate Intelligence Committee, due partly to his registration for the draft in 1945 as a noncombatant.

On 28 June 1969 Sorensen married Gillian Martin. They have a daughter and continue to live in New York City. Sorensen practices international law as senior counsel with Paul, Weiss, Rifkind, Wharton and Garrison, the firm he joined in 1966. Sorensen also writes commentaries for the national press and scholarly journals on foreign issues and the American political scene.

Sorensen was important to the 1960s for his central role as special counsel in the Kennedy White House. Over the decade of his relationship with John Kennedy, he impacted Kennedy's thinking and implemented Kennedy's political agenda to as great a degree as any other individual. Although they came from contrasting backgrounds and rarely socialized, the two formed an effective and powerful team. Sorensen had a liberalizing effect on Kennedy's political philosophy. In turn, Sorensen absorbed a keen pragmatism that he directed toward protecting the political interests of his chief. They united on the middle ground of what was politically possible. Sorensen became so attuned to the thoughts, desires, speech patterns, and mannerisms of Kennedy that he was dubbed the president's "alter ego." In the years since the 1960s, he has remained one of the most ardent apologists for the Kennedy presidency. By his own admission, no day passes without his thinking of John Kennedy.

★

The Sorensen papers and oral history transcripts are found in the John Fitzgerald Kennedy Library, Boston, Massachusetts. Sorensen's books, especially *The Kennedy Legacy* (1969), record his perceptions and provide insight on his participation in events. Analysis of Sorensen's background and influence on John Kennedy can be found in Patrick Anderson, *The Presidents' Men: White House Assistants of Franklin D. Roosevelt, Harry S. Truman, Dwight D. Eisenhower, John F. Kennedy and Lyndon B. Johnson* (1968); Herbert S. Parmet, *Jack: The Struggles of John F. Kennedy* (1980); and *JFK: The Presidency of John F. Kennedy* (1983). For further information see Arthur M. Schlesinger, Jr., *A Thousand Days: John F. Kennedy in the White House* (1965); James N. Giglio, *The Presidency of John F. Kennedy* (1991); and Laurence Leamer, *The Kennedy Men* (2001).

JOANNE SCHENK PAULL

SOUTHERN, Terry Marion, Jr. (*b.* 1 May 1924 in Alvarado, Texas; *d.* 29 October 1995 in New York City), satiric novelist, screenwriter, and journalist whose penchant for attacking authority and smugness in any and all forms made him a hip icon and 1960s countercultural hero.

Although he was born on 1 May, Southern's birth was recorded the following day, leading some sources to cite 2 May as his birthday. The only child of Terrance Marion Southern, a pharmacist, and Helen (Simonds) Southern, a dressmaker and housewife, Southern was raised in Oak Cliff, a suburb of Dallas, Texas, where he hunted, fished, and played outdoor sports. He also enjoyed less wholesome diversions, such as visiting freak shows and reading the tales of Edgar Allan Poe. He attended the Winnetka primary school and graduated from Sunset High School in June 1941. That fall he enrolled in North Texas Agriculture College but transferred to Southern Methodist University in 1942. After serving as a lieutenant in the U.S. Army from 1943 to 1945, Southern resumed his studies first at the University of Chicago and then at Northwestern University, where he received his B.A. in English in 1948.

Southern began classes at the Sorbonne on the GI Bill in September 1948. In Paris the tyro writer was befriended by George Plimpton and Peter Matthiessen, who published his story "The Accident" in the inaugural issue of their *Paris Review*. He also met Pud Gadiot, a model, whom he married in 1953; the couple divorced in 1954 after returning to New York City. In October 1955 Southern met Carol Kauffman at a party in the photographer Robert Frank's studio. They married on 14 July 1956 and had one son. Southern and Kauffman separated in the mid-1960s, after Southern began what was to become a lifelong relationship with Gail Gerber, a dancer he met on the set of the *Loved One* (1965). He and Kauffman's divorce was finalized in 1972.

In the fall of 1956 Southern and Kauffman left for Europe, where Southern worked on his first novel, *Flash and Filigree* (1958), a satire on the medical profession. That same year Maurice Girodia's Olympia Press published a parody of Voltaire's *Candide* called *Candy,* a novel that Southern co-authored with Mason Hoffenberg, working together under the pseudonym Maxwell Kenton. Parodying Voltaire's *Candide,* it recounts the adventures of Candy Christian, a naive, all-American girl whose virtue is assailed at every turn. Candy's sexual generosity and her involvement in Eastern mysticism would come to typify a generation of "flower children" (as the hippies were called) in 1967's Summer of Love, when some 100,000 young people descended on the Haight-Ashbury neighborhood of San Francisco. Published in the United States in 1964, *Candy* remained on the best-seller list for more than seventy weeks. It went on to sell more than five million copies.

After returning to the United States in 1959, Southern and Kauffman purchased a colonial farmhouse on twenty-seven acres in East Canaan, Connecticut. A year later Random House published *The Magic Christian* (1960), the story of Guy Grand, an eccentric billionaire who spends millions of dollars a year playing practical jokes on people in an effort to "make it hot for them." Stanley Kubrick liked the book so much that he invited Southern to work on the

Terry Southern. CORBIS CORPORATION (BELLEVUE)

screenplay for *Dr. Strangelove, or How I Learned to Stop Worrying and Love the Bomb* (1964). Kubrick made a good choice. Southern took *Red Alert* (1958), Peter George's melodramatic novel on America's fail-safe system, and turned it into a hilarious black comedy on the arms race, the cold war, and the military. The film, which helped promote antiwar sentiments, received the Writers Guild Award and the British Screen Writers Award in 1964 as well as an Academy Award nomination for best adapted screenplay.

Southern's success with *Dr. Strangelove* made him one of Hollywood's most sought-after screenwriters. From 1964 to 1967, he worked on *The Loved One* (1965), *The Cincinnati Kid* (1965), *The Collector* (1965), *Casino Royale* (1967), and *Barbarella* (1968). He commanded scriptwriting fees of more than $100,000, enjoyed a jet-set lifestyle, and hobnobbed with the likes of Ringo Starr and the Rolling Stones. His appearance on the album cover of the Beatles's *Sgt. Pepper's Lonely Hearts Club Band* in 1967 made him a pop icon. That same year Random House published *Red Dirt Marijuana and Other Tastes,* a collection of essays and stories revolving around drugs and violence. Southern continued to explore these themes in *Easy Rider* (1969). The film, written with Dennis Hopper and Peter Fonda, received an Academy Award nomination for best screenplay. The final words of Captain America, played by Peter Fonda, sum up the feelings of many 1960s radicals at the close of the tumultuous decade: "We blew it."

The notion that the counterculture was dead grew more widespread after the National Democratic Convention in Chicago in August 1968, when Mayor Richard Daley's police clashed with Yippie demonstrators in bloody confrontations. Southern covered the event for *Esquire* with William Burroughs and Gene Genet and participated in demonstrations with his fellow journalists and with the poet Allen Ginsberg. He later testified on behalf of the Chicago Eight, a group of demonstrators that included the Yippie activist Jerry Rubin and the Black Panther leader Bobby Seale, who were charged with crossing state lines to incite a riot.

Southern spent the next two years working on the film script for John Barth's *End of the Road* and on *Blue Movie* (1970), his own novel on Hollywood and pornography. Over the next twenty-five years he would produce very little, though he worked on numerous failed projects, including a screen adaptation of his friend William Burroughs's novel *Junkie*. He toured with the Rolling Stones in 1972 and wrote for *Saturday Night Live* in the early 1980s. From 1985 to 1990 Southern joined Harry Nillson at Hawkeye Productions, where he served as vice president of literary and script development. Tax problems and poor business decisions strained his finances, but he continued to scrape by, supplementing his income by teaching courses at New York University and Columbia University. On his way to class at Columbia on 25 October 1995, Southern collapsed and was taken to Saint Luke's Hospital, where, four days later, he died of respiratory failure. His ashes were scattered over a pond on his East Canaan farm. He was remembered at a memorial service at the Unitarian Church of All Souls in New York City on 16 December 1995.

Often compared to Mark Twain and Nathanael West, Southern was a gifted satirist with a sharp ear for dialogue. His reputation reached its height in the 1960s, a decade particularly suited to his fierce iconoclasticism and flamboyant lifestyle. Over the last twenty-five years of his life, Southern produced only one major work, *Texas Summer* (1992), a poorly received novel set in his Texas childhood. Whether Southern's decline can be attributed to drug and alcohol abuse, unsound business decisions, or changing artistic and political attitudes remains uncertain. What is certain is that his contributions in film, the new journalism, and "the quality lit game," a term he coined to describe the literary establishment, helped extend the boundaries of artistic freedom and topple cultural and political barriers to free speech. As he told *Newsweek* in 1964: "The assumption has always been that there are limits. But we now know there are no limits."

★

Southern's life and work is archived by his son Nile at <http://www.terrysouthern.com>. Nile Southern and Josh A. Friedman, eds., *Now Dig This: The Unspeakable Writings of Terry Southern*

1950–1995 (2001), contains some autobiographical material, including letters and interviews as well as journalism and fiction. Lee Hill, *A Grand Guy: The Art and Life of Terry Southern* (2001), is the only full-length biography. An interview Hill conducted with Southern is in Patrick McGilligan, ed., *Backstory 3: Interviews with Screenwriters of the Sixties* (1997). Profiles are in *Newsweek* (22 June 1964) and in *Life* (21 Aug. 1964).

"Groovin' in Chi," *Esquire* (Nov. 1968), recounts Southern's experience at the National Democratic Convention. The *Paris Review* (spring 1996) includes tributes by George Plimpton, Henry Allen, William Styron, and Caroline Marshall; an interview with Mike Golden; an account of Southern's last hours by his son Nile; and a brief autobiographical piece titled "Making It Hot for Them." A longer tribute by Plimpton is in *Harper's Magazine* (Aug. 2001).*"Give Me Your Hump!" The Unspeakable Terry Southern Record* (2001) is a CD featuring Southern and friends Marianne Faithful, Allen Ginsberg, and Michael J. Pollard, among others, reading from the author's works. Southern appears in video clips in *Burroughs: The Movie* (1985) and *The NY Beat Generation Show*, vol. 3: *Music Moves the Spirit* (1995). Obituaries are in the *New York Times, Los Angeles Times, Washington Post,* and the *Guardian* (London) (all 31 Oct. 1995).

WILLIAM M. GARGANA

Phil Spector. FRANK DRIGGS COLLECTION/GETTY IMAGES

SPECTOR, Philip Harvey ("Phil") (*b.* 26 December 1940 in New York City), regarded as rock music's most influential and distinctive record producer, songwriter, and director, whose internationally known "wall of sound" musical invention and style had a prominent effect on rock and roll during the 1960s and beyond.

Spector was the only son and second child of Benjamin, an ironworker, and Bertha Spector. His father died when he was nine years old, and his mother moved with him and his sister to Los Angeles in 1953. There, Spector attended Fairfax High School, but he had little interest in academic studies. He became interested in music, studied guitar and piano, and later excelled in drums, bass, and French horn. He was especially drawn to the rhythm-and-blues sound of the rock-and-roll explosion that was playing constantly on radio stations. He dreamed of one day making his own records, and while spending time around recording studios, he persuaded the independent record producers Lester Sill and Lee Hazlewood to teach him the recording business.

While he was still in high school, the seventeen-year-old Spector debuted in the music industry, writing and producing his first hit, "To Know Him Was to Love Him" (1958) for the Teddy Bears, a vocal trio he put together with two of his classmates. The title of the song was inspired by the inscription on his father's tombstone. This record sold more than a million copies and remained in the number-one position on the *Billboard* pop chart for twenty-three weeks.

In the spring of 1958 Spector graduated from Fairfax High School and started taking courses to become a court reporter, but soon he decided that was not the direction in which he wanted to go. He enrolled for one year at the University of California, Los Angeles, but left in 1960 for New York City, where he worked with the songwriters Jerry Leiber and Mike Stoller on a variety of projects, trying to get experience and make a name for himself. He wrote and co-wrote songs and was a freelance producer for several famous musicians, including Ben E. King, Ray Peterson, Gene Pitney, and the Paris Sisters. Spector became head of the artists and repertoire division of Atlantic Records at the age of nineteen.

The 1960s marked an important stage in Spector's life. In 1961 he was offered a partnership in Philles Records with Lester Sill, whose slogan was "Tomorrow's sound today." In late 1962 Spector bought out his partner and became sole owner of Philles Records, where he and his arranger, Jack Nitzsche, and later, Larry Levine, began to develop the Spector sound, or the "wall of sound," and turning out numerous hits. His most original and influential work came after he had full ownership of the label, which gave him creative and financial control. He left an indelible impression on every record he produced, and his style had a powerful impact on rock-and-roll artists over the years.

Spector's record-producing vision was artistic and expansive, and he worked closely with various artists to create the "wall of sound" effect. To achieve this new art form, he used a variety of techniques, including the integration of guitarists, bass players, pianists, drummers, strings, percussionists, and vocalists as well as the manipulation of tape speeds and overdubbing to weave a musical texture that was both winning and exhilarating. He was involved throughout the recording production process, from co-writing the materials to getting the very best work out of the artists. He often seemed obsessed, spending weeks or months on individual tracks until he was satisfied that the record was perfect. Spector maintained that the work he was trying to create was a serious art form, in which he used the recording studio to create distinctive and relevant masterpieces in sound—regardless of the critics' views.

During the years 1962–1965, Spector did his most renowned work, producing a number of rock classics—singles as well as albums—and making stars of such groups as the Crystals, the Ronettes, the Righteous Brothers, Ike and Tina Turner, Darlene Love, and Bob B. Soxx and the Blue Jeans. It was during this period that Spector had twenty-one consecutive hits, including "He's a Rebel," "Then He Kissed Me," "Be My Baby", "You've Lost That Loving Feeling," "Da Doo Ron Ron," and "Walking in the Rain," some of the most recognizable hits of the 1960s, which sold more than thirteen million copies. It was the Crystals' "He's a Rebel" and subsequent hits that introduced the "wall of sound" to international prominence. His Christmas album collection, *A Christmas Gift for You* (1963), is still popular. In 1963 Spector married Annette Merar; they divorced in 1965.

When the Beatles were to appear on the *Ed Sullivan Show* in American in 1964, they asked Spector, who was in London at the time, to tell them about New York City and what they could expect. Indeed, they even asked Spector to join them on the flight to the United States. When they arrived at John F. Kennedy Airport, Spector was able to observe at firsthand the crowds of screaming fans welcoming the Beatles and the beginning of rock's new age. In 1966 Spector closed Philles Records and went into a period of isolation. Some critics claimed that this was because Ike and Tina Turner's "River Deep, Mountain High" failed to be as successful as he had wished and that as British rock, notably the Beatles, came into prominence, Spector's influence declined. It was also believed that the music industry was changing and that listeners were becoming interested in full-length albums instead of singles.

In 1968 Spector married Veronica (Ronnie) Bennett of the Ronettes; they adopted three children and divorced in 1974. In 1969 and into the 1970s Spector reentered the music scene with a series of releases for A&M, with albums for Sonny Charles and the Checkmates, John Lennon, and

George Harrison, among others. He also established the Warner-Spector outlet and formed Phil Spector International, which undertook new recordings. Spector produced the Beatles' album *Let It Be* (1970), widely regarded as the weakest release of their career as a group, but he rebounded strongly with George Harrison's *All Things Must Pass* (1970), which is thought to be both his and Harrison's finest work.

Spector became detached from music and reclusive throughout the latter part of the 1970s and the 1980s. His projects and behavior were increasingly controversial, owing to the many stories about him. Spector has been described as a mad genius and an eccentric megalomaniac known for throwing tantrums in the studio. Among his many awards are induction into the Rock and Roll Hall of Fame (1989) and the Songwriters Hall of Fame (1996) and the Lifetime Achievement Award from the Philadelphia Music Alliance (1994). His four-disc box set, which includes sixty of his most famous recordings and the 1963 Christmas album, was released in 1991 as *Phil Spector: Back to Mono (1958–1969)*.

A pop music legend, Spector was credited with revolutionizing the recording industry. A successful entrepreneur at the age of seventeen, he was a millionaire at the age of twenty-one and a multimillionaire by the time he was twenty-five—far from his first hurdle of raising the initial forty dollars to book a recording session. He also captured the new wave in pop music—the girl groups, as they were called—and was dubbed the "Tycoon of Teen." He described his records as "symphonies for the kids," and many of them became classics, from his first hit with the Teddy Bears to his work in the late 1960s and early 1970s.

★

For further information on Spector, see Richard Williams, *Out of His Head: The Sound of Phil Spector* (1972); Rob Fennis, *The Phil Spector Story* (1975); and Mark Ribowsky, *He's a Rebel* (1989). John J. Fitzpatrick and James E. Fogerty, *Collecting Phil Spector: The Man, the Legend and His Music* (1991), documents in words and pictures Spector's influence and legend up to the present. There is also an informative interview with Spector by Robert Hilburn, *Los Angeles Times* (10 Nov. 1991).

HOPE E. YOUNG

STARZL, Thomas. *See* Moore, Francis Daniels, and Thomas Earl Starzl.

STEIGER, Rodney Stephen ("Rod") (*b.* 14 April 1925 in Westhampton, New York; *d.* 9 July 2002 in Los Angeles, California), actor whose notable motion-picture performances during the 1960s included *In the Heat of the Night*, for which he won the Academy Award in 1968.

Steiger, who was known professionally as Rod Steiger, was the son of Frederick Steiger and Lorraine Driver, both of whom were entertainers. His home life was not a happy one, and often he had to slip away from school to retrieve his mother, an alcoholic, from the local saloon. This experience contributed to a toughness of attitude that, combined with his physical strength, gained him the nickname "Rodney the Rock" from his classmates. After attending various public schools in Irvington, Bloomfield, and Newark, New Jersey, Steiger dropped out of high school to join the U.S. Navy in 1941. He served in the Pacific, and after his discharge in 1945, he worked briefly at a Veteran's Administration office.

Living in New York City during the mid- to late 1940s, Steiger became interested in acting, which he studied for two years at the New School for Social Research. In the course of his study, which took him also to the Dramatic Workshop and the Actors Studio, he became intrigued with a revolutionary concept known as the Stanislavski Method.

Named after Russian director Konstantin Stanislavski, "the Method," as it came to be called, represented a complete reversal of the ideas that had virtually dominated the stage since the time of the Greeks. Hitherto, it had been understood that an actor was simply playing a role, and

Rod Steiger. THE KOBAL COLLECTION

that there could be no confusing the performer with the character being portrayed. As a result, acting tended to be, quite literally, theatrical, involving a great deal of shouting, dramatics, and gesturing very different from the behavior of real humans. By contrast, the Method dictated that an actor personalize and individualize a role as much as possible. Ideally, according to Stanislavski and American disciples such as Lee Strasberg, the actor would *become* the character in a sense. Indeed, the actor served as a sort of cowriter for his or her role, seeking to find nuances that, while true to the character, went beyond what the playwright or screenwriter had envisioned.

Of all the American actors to emerge in the postwar years, no two names are more closely associated with the Method than those of Steiger and Marlon Brando, who portrayed brothers in *On the Waterfront* (1954). His role in the film, only his third, earned Steiger an Academy Award nomination. Other notable examples among Steiger's dozen or so films from the 1950s are *Oklahoma!* (1955) and *Al Capone* (1959). Reviewing the first of these, many critics faulted Steiger for playing the role of Jud Fry with much more intensity than the part required. The other film, in which he played the title role, illustrated a facility for playing famous men, a talent Steiger put to use many times during his career.

Already by 1947, Steiger had made his debut in the newest of all dramatic media, television. The 1950s saw numerous appearances on the small screen, none more notable than his lead in Paddy Chayevsky's *Marty* (1953), a production that helped to show that television could also serve as a legitimate medium for art. On a personal front, Steiger spent much of the 1950s (1952–1958) married to actress Sally Gracie; then, in 1959, he began a ten-year marriage to actress Claire Bloom, with whom he had his first child, Anna.

Early 1960s movies featuring Steiger included *Seven Thieves* (1960), *The Mark* (1960), *The World in My Pocket* (1960), *Thirteen West Street* (1961), *The Longest Day* (1962), *Convicts Four* (1962), and *Hands Across the City* (1963). Most notable among these is *The Mark*, a strikingly modern tale. The story follows a former child molester who has been released from prison and attempts to start a new life, only to find himself hounded by a reporter. One of his few sympathizers is Dr. Edmund McNally, played by Steiger. Reminiscing on the role years later, Steiger observed that "in the fifties, everybody went to a psychiatrist because if you didn't, you'd have nothing to talk about at cocktail parties." Since he, too, had an analyst, Steiger—true to his roots in the Stanislavski Method—spent a great deal of time studying the therapist. Influenced by the image of his apparently overworked analyst, he created a character who chain-smokes, drinks coffee relentlessly, and walks around looking unkempt, with rolled-up sleeves and a five o'clock shadow. His performance was so compelling that the American Psychiatric Association invited him to deliver a lecture.

The mid-1960s saw even more significant performances from Steiger in *The Pawnbroker* (1964) and *Doctor Zhivago* (1965), as well as his highly acclaimed portrayal of Willy Loman in *Death of a Salesman* (1966) for television. *The Pawnbroker,* in which Steiger played the lead role of Sol Nazerman, was one of the first major films to explore the effects of the Holocaust on concentration camp survivors. As the title suggests, Nazerman operates a pawnshop, and as he becomes immersed in a new Jewish ghetto—that of New York City—he begins to flash back to his experiences in the Nazi death camps. Steiger's performance earned him an Academy Award nomination, as well as the Berlin Film Festival Bear Award and the British Film Academy BAFTA Award.

Steiger played a supporting role as the lecherous Victor Komarovsky in *Doctor Zhivago.* He later explained that he had read the novel by Boris Pasternak but was still surprised when director David Lean invited him to play the role, because the cast was composed primarily of British actors. The prospect of performing alongside Omar Sharif, Alec Guinness, and Julie Christie both excited and intimidated him, he said, because audiences tended to assume that an American actor would be unable to hold his own against British performers. "My happiest thing about that picture," he recalled in an interview upon the occasion of the film's re-release on DVD in 1999, "is that I proved that American actors can speak as well [as British actors] and also fit in with an ensemble like that."

One of the remarkable aspects of Steiger's performance in *Doctor Zhivago* is that he manages to turn Komarovsky, a profiteer who seduces a mother and daughter, into a sympathetic character. Yet Steiger, once again true to the method-acting philosophy of the actor as cowriter, managed to expand on Komarovsky's character. In Steiger's view, Komarovsky was not a louse; he was a man of culture, an art dealer, who starts out simply wanting to sleep with Lara (Christie), but ultimately falls in love with her. In the end, Komarovsky proves his good faith by saving not only her life, but that of the man she loves, Zhivago (Sharif).

From playing a Russian art dealer in *Doctor Zhivago,* Steiger went on to play a prejudiced southern sheriff in what proved to be his greatest performance of the 1960s, and indeed of his career. When Norman Jewison invited him to play opposite Sidney Poitier in *In the Heat of the Night* (1967), he characterized Sheriff Bill Gillespie by saying "he chews gum." Steiger's first reaction was to tell Jewison that this was the basest of clichés; but as he settled into the role, he found that the gum chewing provided an extraordinary medium for letting the audience in on Gillespie's thought processes. "If you see the picture," he observed many years later, "when things get exciting, he

chews faster. When he gets really shocked, *everything* stops, including the chewing."

As with earlier Steiger films, *In the Heat of the Night* confronted social issues with which audiences were not entirely comfortable. The story concerns Virgil Tibbs (Poitier), a Philadelphia homicide detective visiting his mother in rural Sparta, Mississippi. After a wealthy white man is murdered, the local police arrest Tibbs simply because he is a well-spoken black man from out of town, but soon they discover that he is a police officer and release him. The critical plot point occurs when Tibbs's superiors in Philadelphia order him to assist in the investigation, since Gillespie has little experience with homicide cases.

At the time of the film's release, African Americans in the South had only recently gained the right to vote without fearing intimidation; therefore, the racial tension in the film is palpable in a way that it would not have been just a few years later. The change in attitudes is illustrated by the relationship of Gillespie and Tibbs portrayed in an enormously popular television series based on the film that the National Broadcasting Company (NBC) aired from 1988 to 1995. Whereas the latter-day Gillespie and Tibbs (Carroll O'Connor and Howard Rollins) are close friends, the characters in the movie are at best wary allies.

In fact, Steiger and Poitier were close friends off-screen. At a time when racial tensions in the South still ran very high, Steiger later recalled, the actors making the film had reason to fear reprisals. "One of my conditions to [making] that picture," he explained, "was that I had to be next to Sidney all the way in case some fanatic . . . tried to do anything." To ensure Poitier's safety, Steiger insisted that the door connecting their two hotel suites remain open at night. Illustrative of the racial situation in 1967 is the fact that Poitier was not even nominated for an Academy Award, whereas Steiger won the Oscar, as well as BAFTA, Golden Globe, Laurel, National Society of Film Critics, and New York Film Critics Circle awards.

Three other performances from the late 1960s, all of them lead roles, are also notable. In the thriller *No Way to Treat a Lady* (1968), Steiger played Christopher Gill, a theatre manager and serial killer pursued by a police detective (George Segal), whose girlfriend (Lee Remick) Gill begins stalking. *The Sergeant* (1968) is a complex drama in which Steiger's Master Sergeant Albert Callan finds himself deeply attracted to a private, played by John Phillip Law. Though the tale is set in the aftermath of World War II, the anti-Vietnam sentiment is clear. Finally, in *The Illustrated Man* (1969), Steiger plays a character, known simply as Carl, whose body is covered in tattoos. In the course of his search for the woman who placed the tattoos on him, he discovers that each tattoo contains a story of the future. The film, which seems to have influenced *Memento* (2001), also starred Bloom.

In the years following the 1960s, Steiger played an almost dizzying array of roles and showed a special penchant for portraying famous men and world leaders. He even played Benito Mussolini twice. Yet he had one major regret: that he had turned down the title role in *Patton* (1970), which proved to be an enormous success for George C. Scott. (Interestingly, Scott also played Mussolini.) Notable films by Steiger in the period since the 1960s include *Lucky Luciano* (1975), *W. C. Fields and Me* (1976), *The Amityville Horror* (1979), *The Chosen* (1982), *American Gothic* (1987), *Ballad of the Sad Cafe* (1991), *The Specialist* (1994), *Mars Attacks!* (1996), and *The Hurricane* (1999). Divorced from Bloom in 1969, he was married to Sherry Nelson (1973–1979) and then to Paula Ellis (1986–1997), with whom he had a son. On 10 April 1997 Steiger was awarded a star on Hollywood Boulevard. On 10 October 2000 he wed actress Joan Benedict, who survives him. He died on 9 July 2002 after being hospitalized for pneumonia and kidney failure.

In a career that has been a monument to versatility, Steiger embodied the Stanislavski Method in portrayals that run the gamut in terms of characters' nationality and social class. His penchant for exploring roles and accents won him praise and sometimes ridicule, but Steiger continued to explore his seemingly limitless range as an actor. In keeping with his chameleon-like stage persona, his appearance changed over the years and from role to role, but by the late 1990s he had taken on the look of a seasoned veteran, complete with a bald head, piercing eyes, and square jaw. Noted for his pithy wisdom, he shared a number of his sayings in an October 1998 *Esquire* interview, which included this observation: "Curiosity will lead you to many little deaths and many little happinesses. The day your curiosity dies, your life is over."

★

The only notable biography of Steiger is Tom Hutchinson, *Rod Steiger: Memoirs of a Friendship* (1998). Interviews are in the *Boston Globe* (3 Nov. 1991), *Back Stage West* (6 Aug. 1998), and *Esquire* (Oct. 1998). Additionally, profiles of Steiger are in the *Washington Times* (23 May 1991) and the *Christian Science Monitor* (2 July 1999). An obituary is in the New York Times (10 July 2002).

JUDSON KNIGHT

STEIN, Herbert (*b.* 27 August 1916 in Detroit, Michigan; *d.* 8 September 1999 in Washington, D.C.), economist and adviser to President Richard M. Nixon.

Stein was born the son of David Stein, an automotive machinist, and Jessie (Segal) Stein, a homemaker. He attended Williams College in Williamstown, Massachusetts, on scholarship and earned an A.B. in economics (magna cum

Herbert Stein. CORBIS CORPORATION (BELLEVUE)

laude) in 1935. He then began work on his Ph.D. at the University of Chicago, though he did not actually receive the degree until 1958. Stein married Mildred Sylvia Fishman on 12 June 1937, and they had two children, Rachel and Benjamin. Benjamin became famous as a pundit, actor, and television game show host.

In 1938 Stein became an economist at the Federal Deposit Insurance Corporation (FDIC) in Washington, D.C., where he lived for most of his career. With war looming, he went to work in 1940 for the National Defense Advisory Commission, and in 1941 he took a job with the War Production Board. He remained on the board until 1944, the same year he received first prize in the Pabst Postwar Employment Awards, a national contest to devise a plan for full employment after the war. He had joined the United States Naval Reserve after the attack on Pearl Harbor and in 1944 reported for active duty. By the time his service was over, in 1945, he had attained the rank of lieutenant junior grade.

Following his wartime service, Stein began a long and important relationship with the Committee for Economic Development (CED), an organization that is engaged in research on matters of national economic policy and is funded by business rather than government. He served on

407

the CED for twenty-two years, successively as economist (1945–1948), associate director of research (1948–1956), director of research (1956–1966), and vice president and chief economist (1966–1967).

At the CED Stein distinguished himself with a 1947 paper on national economic policy in which he recommended setting tax rates in such a way as to provide for small surpluses at times of full employment; otherwise, budgets should not be tampered with in response to short-term economic needs. This was a keystone concept for Stein, later embodied in "Stein's law," an example of his pithy wit: "If something cannot go on forever, it will stop." The "law" was a response to observers who maintained that efforts should be taken to stop unfavorable economic trends that they believed could not continue.

From 1965 to 1966 Stein was a fellow at the Center for Advanced Study in the Behavioral Sciences in Palo Alto, California. After leaving the CED in 1967, he served for two years as a senior fellow at the Brookings Institution in Washington, D.C. Meanwhile, his ideas attracted the attention of President Richard M. Nixon, who in 1969 appointed him to the Council of Economic Advisors (CEA).

In taking a position on the three-member council, Stein found himself in the midst of an ongoing debate involving the greatest economic minds in America. Robert Mundell, chief international economist for the International Monetary Fund and pioneer, with Arthur Laffer, of what later became known as supply-side economics, published a seminal text in 1960. According to Mundell, for every economic target, there is an economic instrument: for the employment target, fiscal policy was the instrument, whereas for inflation, monetary policy was the instrument. However, James Tobin, a member of the CEA under President John F. Kennedy, took an opposite and more conventional position, holding that monetary policy should be targeted toward employment and that fiscal policy should be the instrument against inflation.

Tobin's ideas, known among economists as "the policy mix," fell out of favor in the administration of President Lyndon B. Johnson, but Nixon and Stein revived them. As a CEA member, Stein recommended that Nixon raise taxes in order to balance the budget, a measure that would supposedly put the brakes on inflation. Stein and the other members of the CEA also advised Nixon to tighten credit and reduce the money supply. They predicted that unemployment would remain low and that inflation, then at 4 percent, would drop. Acting on this advice, Nixon in 1969 proposed an increase in the capital gains tax, which Congress passed. Recession soon followed, fueled by a number of factors, not the least of which were the continued costs of the Vietnam War. However, the capital gains tax in-

crease, which served to discourage investment, certainly had a share of the blame.

With unemployment on the rise, Nixon took a measure that Stein had expressly warned against, ordering an increase in the money supply. The president's thinking was that, in keeping with the policy mix approach of using monetary policy to address employment problems, an infusion of dollars would expand the economy. This, of course, meant that the value of the dollar itself would have to drop, and in 1971 the Nixon administration severed all remaining links between the value of the dollar and that of gold. Nixon's advisors, including possibly Stein, had recommended the devaluation measure, probably as a corrective to problems resulting from the increase in the money supply.

On the advice of the Federal Reserve Bank chairman Arthur Burns and others, in August 1971 Nixon instituted wage and price controls, meaning that wage increases would be contingent on gains in productivity. Stein later described this as "Nixon's one serious mistake in economic policy." This may have been a generous statement, considering that Nixon's economic decisions probably did more damage to the nation than did the fallout from the Watergate scandal. At any rate, wage and price guidelines were certainly the worst aspect of Nixonian economics, and even though Nixon lifted them on the advice of Stein and others, inflation soared to 11 percent by 1974. The result was an economic recession that lasted until the early 1980s, which prompted President Ronald Reagan to cut taxes and the Federal Reserve to lower interest rates.

Stein served as chairman of the CEA from January 1972 until August 1974, the month in which Nixon left office. He continued for a few weeks under the administration of President Gerald R. Ford but resigned at the end of the month. From 1974 to 1984, he served as the A. Willis Robertson Professor of Economics at the University of Virginia. For most of his last three decades, Stein was heavily involved with the American Enterprise Institute (AEI), another conservative economic think tank. Stein was an adjunct scholar at the AEI from 1975 to 1977 and a senior fellow in 1977.

A prolific writer, Stein was a member of the *Wall Street Journal* board of contributors in 1974, a weekly columnist for the *Economy Today* and Scripps Howard newspapers (1974–1980), and a contributor to the Internet journal *Slate* in the 1990s. He wrote more than a dozen books and AEI pamphlets, including *The Fiscal Revolution in America* (1969); with Benjamin Stein, *Moneypower: How to Make Inflation Make You Rich* (1979); *Presidential Economics: The Making of Economic Policy from Roosevelt to Reagan and Beyond* (1984); *Washington Bedtime Stories: The Politics of Money and Jobs* (1986); *Tax Policy in the Twenty-First Cen-*

tury (1988); *Governing the $5 Trillion Economy* (1989); with Murray F. Foss, *An Illustrated Guide to the American Economy* (1991); and *What I Think: Essays on Economics, Politics, and Life* (1998). He also coauthored a novel, *On the Brink* (1977), with his son Benjamin.

In addition to his other work, Stein served the Reagan administration as a member of the President's Economic Policy Advisory Board (1981–1989) and the President's Blue Ribbon Committee on Defense Management (1985–1986). Under the administration of President Bill Clinton, he was a member of the President's Committee to Study Capital Budgeting (1998). Stein also acted as consultant to the Congressional Budget Office (1976–1989) and the U.S. Department of State (1983–1992). He died of heart failure in Washington in 1999.

As an economic advisor to the Nixon administration, Stein found himself in a difficult position, one in which his name could potentially become associated with the disastrous economic policies he had opposed. That it did not, and that he remained a respected economic thinker, is a tribute to his forthrightness and intellectual independence. Although he had distinct political and economic ideas, he never allowed ideology to govern his thinking. As a critic of his own fellow conservatives, Stein remained an opponent of supply-side economics, and in the social realm, decried the use of the phrase "family values," saying that such things do not exist; there are only human values.

He also distinguished himself by calling for greater action on behalf of the poor: "The children growing up in wretched families, in unsafe schools, and in vicious streets," he wrote, "are also 'our' children. A decent respect for family values calls for . . . more commitment to them." By remaining intellectually independent, Stein won the admiration of both conservatives and liberals. Among the latter was E. J. Dionne, who in a *Washington Post* obituary praised "the many bits of contrarian wisdom offered by a smart, puckish, and exceptionally honest commentator who, alas, will no longer be around to prick our intellectual balloons."

★

Biographical information on Stein is scarce. A good source of information on his career prior to the Nixon appointment is the congressional document *Nominations of Paul W. McCracken, Hendick S. Houthakker, and Herbert Stein: Hearing, Ninety-first Congress, First Session, January 27, 1969* (1969). For a more personal view, see Stein, *What I Think* (1998), as well as various writings by his son Benjamin, including *Financial Passages* (1985) and *Tommy and Me: The Making of a Dad* (1998). Obituaries are in the *New York Times* (9 Sept. 1999); the *Los Angeles Times* (10 Sept. 1999); the *Washington Post* (14 Sept. 1999); *The American Enterprise* 10, no. 6 (Nov. 1999): 12; *Business Economics* 35, no. 1

(Jan. 2000): 4; and the *Southern Economic Journal* 66, no. 4 (Apr. 2000): 1,009–1,010.

JUDSON KNIGHT

STEINBECK, John Ernst (*b.* 27 February 1902 in Salinas, California; *d.* 20 December 1968 in New York City), Nobel– and Pulitzer Prize–winning American writer, noted as a champion of the ordinary working person and for his moral commitment to the traditional ideals of American democracy.

Born and raised in the rural community of Salinas, California, the third of four children and the only son of John Ernst Steinbeck, the county treasurer, and Olive Hamilton Steinbeck, a schoolteacher, Steinbeck attended Stanford University following graduation from high school but dropped out before earning a degree. He moved to New York City in 1925 to find work. With the help of relatives, he worked first as a laborer and then as a reporter for the *New York American*. Finding journalism too sordid for his tastes, he worked his way back to California and settled in Lake Tahoe to write. His first three novels went unpublished, and his first two published novels were dogged by the publishers' financial woes.

In 1935, however, Steinbeck's star began to rise with the publication of *Tortilla Flat,* which depicted the lives of

John Steinbeck. ARCHIVE PHOTOS, INC.

Mexican Americans in Monterey, California. Readers liked Steinbeck's depiction of impoverished but noble characters, and Steinbeck's reputation soared even higher with the publication of *Of Mice and Men* (1937), a tale of two ranch hands who hope to buy a place of their own, and *The Grapes of Wrath* (1939). The latter novel tells the story of migrant workers who travel to California in search of a better life but find only degradation and starvation. Steinbeck won the 1940 Pulitzer Prize for *The Grapes of Wrath*, firmly establishing him as a great American writer.

Steinbeck tried to enlist in the Army Air Corps during World War II but was prevented from serving because of false charges that he was a Communist. (These accusations arose from the controversy surrounding his depiction of the California fruit growers in *The Grapes of Wrath.*) Instead, Steinbeck worked from June to December 1943 as a special correspondent in the European theater and wrote propaganda pieces for the U.S. government. In 1945 he moved to New York, eventually coming to feel at home there and considering himself a successful transplant to the city.

Steinbeck published *East of Eden,* a retelling of the biblical Cain and Abel story, in 1952. Although he intended this to be his masterpiece, it was not well received by critics, who compared it unfavorably with *The Grapes of Wrath.* Throughout the 1950s, his career seemed to be fading, and his antimaterialistic, pro-labor stance, as well as his anger at big business, further alienated a society that was increasingly nervous about socialist and Communist infiltration. Indeed, *The Grapes of Wrath* was one of the most frequently banned books in the United States in the mid-twentieth century.

Steinbeck was a private person, a loner from his adolescent years, and he based most of his works on people and events he observed, rather than on his own experiences. By 1960, however, he apparently felt that he had lost touch with the ordinary working Americans whose lives he had always celebrated, so he set off on a journey to renew his acquaintance with them. Equipping a three-quarter-ton pickup with a cabin similar to that on a boat, he set out on a three-month, ten-thousand-mile trip with an elderly French poodle named Charley. He documented his journey in *Travels with Charley: In Search of America* (1962). In addition to describing the people and places he saw, the book also contains musings on topics of the time, such as racial tensions, the exodus of people from small towns to cities, the growth of superhighways, and the disappearance of local dialects and customs. Most critics considered the book light and pleasant reading, and the public agreed; it sold well and won the Paperback of the Year Award in 1964.

In 1962 Steinbeck was awarded a Nobel Prize for literature, ostensibly for his novel *The Winter of Our Discontent* (1961). Most reviewers panned the book, and many critics believed the prize had been awarded mainly because of the quality of Steinbeck's early work. According to Warren French, Steinbeck himself told reporters that he did not think he deserved it. Other critics disagreed. F. W. Watt wrote of Steinbeck, "Like America itself, his work is a vast, fascinating, paradoxical universe: a brash experiment in democracy; a naive quest for understanding at the level of the common man; a celebration of goodness and innocence; a display of chaos, violence, corruption and decadence." In his acceptance speech for the Nobel Prize, Steinbeck summed up his view of the writer's mission: "The writer is delegated to declare and to celebrate man's proven capacity for greatness of heart and spirit—for gallantry in defeat, for courage, compassion and love." He also said, "I hold that a writer who does not passionately believe in the perfectibility of man has no dedication nor any membership in literature."

The Nobel Prize win aroused renewed public interest in Steinbeck's work, and sales of his books soared. In recognition of his status, he was chosen to make a nine-week tour of Europe by the Department of State's Cultural Exchange Program in 1963. In the same year, he was appointed an honorary consultant in American literature to the Library of Congress. Steinbeck campaigned for the reelection of President Lyndon B. Johnson in 1964, and on 14 September 1964 Johnson awarded him the Presidential Medal of Freedom. Following the 1964 election, Steinbeck remained one of Johnson's intimate advisers, even spending a weekend at the presidential retreat, Camp David. In 1966 Johnson appointed Steinbeck to the National Arts Council.

In 1965 Steinbeck began writing a weekly column for *Newsday* in which he decried the turbulence and lack of respect for law and order that he saw among younger Americans, who were increasingly rebelling against traditional values. Steinbeck originally wrote the column from his Sag Harbor, New York, home, but later he reported from Ireland, Israel, and South Vietnam. While in Vietnam, he strongly supported President Johnson's increasingly unpopular war policies, a view opposed by almost every other major American writer.

Steinbeck was married three times and had two children. His first wife, Carol Henning, played an important role in his initial literary success, but they were divorced in 1943 after thirteen years of marriage. He married the singer Gwyn Conger, who gave birth to their two sons, on March 29 of the same year. Following a bitter divorce in 1948, Steinbeck married Elaine Scott on 29 December 1950. Steinbeck died of a heart attack in New York City on 20 December 1968. He is buried in Salinas, California.

★

The most important collections of Steinbeck's papers are in the Stanford University Libraries; the University of California,

Berkeley, Bancroft Library; the Harry Ransom Humanities Research Center at the University of Texas, Austin; the Morgan Library in New York City; the National Steinbeck Center in Salinas, California; and the Steinbeck Research Center at San Jose State University. Biographies of Steinbeck include F. W. Watt, *John Steinbeck* (1962); Warren G. French, *John Steinbeck* (1975); and Jackson J. Benson, *True Adventures of John Steinbeck, Writer: A Biography* (1984). Critical examinations of Steinbeck's work include Joseph R. McElrath, Jr., Jesse S. Crisler, and Susan Shillinglaw, eds., *John Steinbeck: The Contemporary Reviews* (1996), and John Ditsky, *John Steinbeck and the Critics* (2000). An obituary is in the *New York Times* (21 Dec. 1968).

KELLY WINTERS

STEINEM, Gloria Marie (*b.* 25 March 1934 in Toledo, Ohio), journalist, political activist, and founder of *Ms.* magazine, who became one of the leading spokespersons for the feminist movement.

Steinem endured an unsettled childhood during the Great Depression in Toledo, Ohio. She is the younger of two daughters of Leo Steinem, an antiques dealer (in the winters) and owner and manager of Ocean Beach Pier, an entertainment hall at Clark Lake, Michigan (in the summers), and Ruth Nuneviller Steinem, a reporter and editor. Steinem's grandmother, Pauline Perlmutter Steinem, was the president of the Ohio Women's Suffrage Association (1908–1911) and traveled to the 1908 conference of the International Council of Women. Five years after her marriage, Ruth Steinem was hospitalized for a nervous breakdown (what might be described today as an anxiety disorder and agoraphobia). Although she coped with daily life, she struggled with psychological problems for decades afterward. The arrival of her daughter Gloria, combined with her husband's failed business schemes, added to her instability. After their older daughter, Susanne, left for college, Leo Steinem divorced his wife in 1944 and turned over her care to his ten-year-old younger daughter.

For the next several years, Steinem and her mother lived on the working-class east side of Toledo in an increasingly dilapidated house that had belonged to her maternal grandparents. The adolescent struggled to balance her schoolwork with the demands of caring for her mother. In 1951 Leo Steinem agreed to live with his former wife for a year so that Steinem could move in with her older sister and finish her senior year at Western High School in Washington, D.C. Although the reunion between her parents was brief, Steinem's mother eventually received the psychiatric treatment she needed and lived semi-independently until her death.

Steinem attended Smith College in Northampton, Massachusetts, and completed her degree in government in

Gloria Steinem. © BETTMANN/CORBIS

1956 magna cum laude. She spent the next two years in India on a fellowship and wrote her first book, *A Thousand Indias,* about the experience. Returning to the United States in 1958, Steinem worked for the Independent Research Service in Boston before moving to New York City and a job at *Help!* magazine in 1960. She quickly picked up assignments for *Esquire* and *Show* as well; her 1963 investigative piece for the latter magazine, "I Was a Playboy Bunny," established her as a well-known journalist and celebrity figure. For the next few years, Steinem's freelance work appeared in *Vogue, McCall's, Cosmopolitan, Life,* and the *New York Times Magazine;* she also edited *The Beach Book,* a 1963 publication of photos and essays on sunbathing. On a more serious note, Steinem worked as a scriptwriter on the television news satire *That Was the Week That Was,* from 1964 to 1965. In 1968 Steinem joined the staff of *New York* magazine as a political writer with a weekly column, "The City Politic," in which she covered the careers of the agricultural labor leader Cesar Chavez, the black radical Angela Davis, Senator Eugene McCarthy, and Senator Robert F. Kennedy.

Steinem won the Penney-Missouri Journalism Award in 1969 for her article "After Black Power, Women's Liberation," one of the first serious looks at the new feminist movement. On 21 March 1969 she attended an abortion-rights rally held by a New York feminist group, the Redstockings, that changed the focus of her career and the course of her life. Inspired by the uncompromising stance of the group, which held its forum on abortion after being barred from public hearings to revise New York laws, Steinem developed a feminist outlook that immediately informed her "City Politic" column. In addition to using feminist analysis in her essays, Steinem helped found the National Women's Political Caucus (NWPC) in 1971 with the feminist leaders Betty Friedan, Congresswoman Bella Abzug, and Shirley Chisholm. A political action committee that supported female candidates in their runs for elective office, the NWPC was just one of a number of projects that Steinem supported. The Women's Action Alliance, a grassroots political organizing committee, cofounded with Brenda Feigen in 1971, was another of Steinem's contributions to the feminist political landscape of the era.

Despite these accomplishments, mainstream media coverage often focused on Steinem's sense of style and quick wit. One widely publicized quote had her dismissing the concept of marriage by saying she could not "mate in captivity." Another saying attributed to Steinem, "A woman without a man is like a fish without a bicycle," became a catchphrase of the feminist movement in the 1970s. Although some feminist activists were critical of Steinem's high public profile, her media savvy and sense of humor made her the best-known leader of the women's movement by the early 1970s. Part of Steinem's appeal was her ability to communicate the basic objectives of economic, social, and legal equality for women in plain, commonsense language. At a time when the women's movement was beset by internal political tensions, Steinem also was able to help unite the movement across its political, economic, racial, generational, and sexual-orientation divisions.

Steinem's best-known contribution to the feminist movement came with the publication of *Ms.* magazine. With the support of the *New York* publisher Clay S. Felker, Steinem and Pat Carbine published the inaugural issue as a supplement in *New York* in December 1971. The following month the first stand-alone issue of *Ms.* was an instant success that sold out its first run of 300,000 copies in just over a week. As a monthly magazine with Steinem as its editor, *Ms.* claimed a subscriber base of half a million readers by the mid-1970s. Steinem also kept a high profile as a media pundit and political activist throughout the decade, particularly in support of the Equal Rights Amendment; the proposed constitutional amendment to outlaw gender discrimination failed to gain ratification, however. Steinem's role as America's best-known feminist also generated criticism on the part of some feminists who disagreed with her tactic of working for political change within the existing system or resented her high visibility.

In addition to her contributions to *Ms.*, Steinem published a collection of her past work in the best-selling *Out-rageous Acts and Everyday Rebellions* (1983), a feminist analysis of the life of Marilyn Monroe in *Marilyn: Norma Jeane* (1986), a consciousness-raising memoir in *Revolution from Within: A Book of Self-Esteem* (1992), and a series of essays exploring various aspects of gender in *Moving Beyond Words* (1994). A contributing editor to *Ms.* after its sale in 1987, Steinem remained a leading social commentator, journalist, and activist at the millennium. She emerged from her battles with conservative opponents and detractors within the feminist movement with her integrity and sense of humor intact. In 2001 Steinem married David Bale, an entrepreneur and political activist who was born in South Africa. They have no children. She released a statement to the press saying, "I hope this proves what feminists have always said—that feminism is about the ability to choose what's right at each time of our lives."

★

Biographies of Steinem include Carolyn G. Heilbrun, *The Education of a Woman: The Life of Gloria Steinem* (1995); Sydney Ladensohn Stern, *Gloria Steinem: Her Passions, Politics, and Mystique* (1997); and Caroline Evensen Lazo, *Gloria Steinem: Feminist Extraordinaire* (1998). Among the many interviews that Steinem has granted over the years are discussions with Cynthia Gorney in *Mother Jones* (Nov.–Dec. 1995) and Toddi Gutner in *Business Week* (17 Sept. 2001).

TIMOTHY BORDEN

STELLA, Frank Philip   (*b.* 12 May 1936 in Malden, Massachusetts), artist whose austere, geometric paintings and articulate statements about his aesthetics established him as a leader of the 1960s art scene.

Stella was one of three children of first-generation Sicilian Americans, Constance Aida (Santonelli) Stella, a homemaker with a background in art, and Frank Stella, a gynecologist. In recognition of his lively intelligence, his parents sent him to the nearby Andover preparatory school, Phillips Academy, which he attended from 1950 to 1954. He received his first concentrated art study under the guidance of the abstract painter Patrick Morgan. In the fall of 1954 Stella entered Princeton University, receiving an A.B. degree in history in 1958. While there he studied with the renowned art historian William Seitz and artist in residence Stephen Greene, both of whom had a decisive effect on the artist's understanding of modernism. The summer after graduation, Stella moved to New York City, settling in a storefront studio on the Lower East Side, then in a loft on West Broadway. He worked as a house painter a few days a week, making just enough money to support himself while he painted as an artist.

By late 1958 Stella had embarked on his now famous

Frank Stella. ASSOCIATED PRESS AP

Black Paintings series (1958–January 1960), his response to the pictorial challenges presented by Jasper Johns's target and flag paintings, which he had seen earlier that year in January. He used commercial enamel paint in a design of thin black stripes separated by strips of unpainted canvas. Through his eradication of color and insistence on patterning and nonrelational symmetry, Stella sought to remove from his compositions any spatial references, explaining in a 1960 lecture at the Pratt Institute that "the solution I arrived at forces illusionistic space out of the painting at constant intervals by using a regulated pattern." He added, "The remaining problem was simply to find a method of paint application which followed and complemented the design solution," which for him was housepainter's techniques and tools. During the summer of 1959 Stella showed the paintings both to Leo Castelli, who asked him to join his gallery, and Dorothy Miller, who invited him to participate in her "Sixteen Americans" exhibition opening that December at the Museum of Modern Art in New York City. Because Stella's *Black Paintings* seemed so radically anti-expressionistic, they were among the most controversial works, and the resulting publicity helped catapult Stella to fame.

Stella's first one-person exhibition in New York, held at the Leo Castelli Gallery in September 1960, featured his next major series, his *Aluminum* paintings. He used commercial silver radiator paint, because, as Stella recalled, "you couldn't penetrate it, both literally and, I suppose, visually. It would appear slightly reflective and slightly hard and metallic." Again he adopted a pattern of thin stripes achieved by applying lines of metallic paint separated by strips of raw canvas left in reserve. But he gave the overall design of the stripes slight jogs that left empty areas at the canvas's edge. Stella decided to cut the empty areas out, resulting in his first shaped canvases. This pictorial solution was quickly adapted by a number of other artists throughout the decade and further explored by Stella in his next series, the *Copper* paintings, exhibited at Castelli's in 1962.

On 3 November 1961 Stella married Barbara Rose, with whom he had two children. Rose was developing a formidable reputation in her own right with her critical writings and became a renowned art historian and author. Their home was a kind of salon for a diverse group, including artists, gallery dealers, critics, academics, and even graduate students.

By the mid-1960s, Stella was a leading figure of the art scene, with work that touched upon its main artistic impulses, from minimalism and pop to post-painterly and hard-edged abstraction. His work had been included in ten museum group exhibitions in 1964 alone, including the Whitney Annual and the Venice Biennale, and he had already had over ten solo exhibitions both in the United States and Europe.

In February 1964 Stella and the minimalist sculptor Donald Judd attempted to explain their artistic goals in a broadcasted interview, edited for publication in 1966 by the critic Lucy R. Lippard, titled *New Nihilism or New Art*. Stella's statement about his work seemed to speak for the period: "My painting is based on the fact that only what can be seen there *is* there. It really is an object." He concluded, "All I want anyone to get out of my paintings . . . is the fact that you can see the whole idea without any confusion . . . . What you see is what you see."

Just at the moment when Stella was closest in intent to that of the minimalist artists, he began to incorporate color and rely less on symmetry in his work. In his *Notched V* series, begun in 1964, Stella painted stripes on canvases that were already wedge- or chevron-shaped. He then joined the canvas sections, each in a different color, so that the stripes were fused at the point of contact, forming a "V" pattern. Each shaped area became in essence a color field of stripes that appeared to vibrate. He moved immediately into his *Irregular Polygons* (fall 1965–summer 1967), the first paintings in which he used large geometric areas of color unbroken by stripes, although he left a strip of raw canvas as an outline around the forms to give visual breathing room. Stella maintained his goal of the elimination of pictorial illusionism, however, and the structure of the composition—the interpenetration of the irregularly shaped canvas sections—was still his primary aesthetic issue, with the interaction of the color fields being second in importance.

The *Protractor* series, begun in the summer of 1967 and completed in 1971, was Stella's final major series of the decade. They were his largest paintings to date, each work nearly wall-sized, and the most decorative in terms of color and design. When the paintings were first shown at Castelli's in December 1967, buyers lined up, even for future paintings, which they purchased on the basis of Stella's preliminary drawings. The title comes from the basic shape used in many of the ninety-three canvases, the half-circle or protractor. Stella established thirty-one different canvas formats, each of which he made into three paintings, eventually relying on his instinct for his selections of bright, flat colors, which he laid out in broad bands and geometric fields. Stella overlapped the color bands to deny the suggestion of pictorial illusion suggested by the color either advancing or receding into space. "My main interest," explained Stella about this series, "has been to make what is called decorative painting truly viable in unequivocal abstract terms." The artist made this statement as part of a series of conversations with William Rubin, the chief curator of the Museum of Modern Art, in preparation for his 1970 retrospective, a watershed in Stella's career.

In 1970 Stella stated to Rubin that he was "coming to the end of something," meaning not only the direction of abstraction in his own work but for the whole era as well. Confined to his bed after knee surgery, Stella began the drawings for his *Polish Village* series (completed in 1973), a new direction in his pictorial investigations. For the first time, Stella began to infuse real space into his paintings by constructing each one out of various materials collaged onto a stretcher, which was in later examples a wooden base. Now Stella incorporated aspects of sculpture and architecture in his work, testing how far he could push the boundaries between the arts and still produce paintings. Critics have described this and his later series as a turn from minimalist to maximalist painting, and Stella has certainly become expressionistic and spatially inventive in his later work, from his first all-metal *Brazilian* series (1974–1975) to his *Cones and Pillars* (1984–1986) and his *Moby Dick* series (1986–1992).

Stella's marriage to Rose ended in divorce in 1969, and in 1978 he married Harriet McGurk, with whom he had two children. Between marriages, Stella had a relationship with Shirley Wyse, and they had one daughter.

As an innovative painter and articulate theorizer on abstraction, Stella has been a powerful force in the art world, especially during the 1960s. The attitudes of the period towards materials, method of execution, pictorial solutions, and aesthetic experience were manifested in his work.

Stella's desire for the viewer to understand his paintings in one shot emphasized the concreteness of the object, an idea that was crucial to minimalism, but he also sought to increase the sense of flatness in their design. Honored by Harvard University as the Charles Eliot Norton Professor of Poetry for the 1983–1984 academic year, Stella chose for the six-part lecture series to address issues of pictorial space in postmodern art. The lectures were published in 1986 as *Working Space*.

For Stella, space has remained at the heart of his artistic explorations. During the 1960s he eschewed illusionism, and in his later series, he incorporated actual space within his paintings, going beyond mere illusionism.

★

Stella's papers are in the Archives of American Art, Smithsonian Institution, Washington, D.C. The standard texts on the artist are the 1970 and 1987 exhibition catalogues for the Museum of Modern Art by William S. Rubin: *Frank Stella* and *Frank Stella, 1970–1987*. Useful discussions of Stella's aesthetics and philosophy for the 1960s are Michael Fried, *Three American Painters: Kenneth Noland, Jules Olitski, Frank Stella* (1965), and Robert Rosenblum, *Frank Stella* (1971). For biographical and anecdotal information, see Sidney Guberman, *Frank Stella: An Illustrated Biography* (1995).

LEIGH BULLARD WEISBLAT

STEVENSON, Adlai Ewing (*b.* 5 February 1900 in Los Angeles, California; *d.* 14 July 1965 in London, England), politician and diplomat who made an unsuccessful bid for a third Democratic nomination for president in 1960 and, as United Nations ambassador during the John F. Kennedy and Lyndon B. Johnson administrations, worked to advance the causes of nuclear disarmament, international peace, and Third World development.

Stevenson grew up in Bloomington, Illinois, one of two children of two prominent families. His paternal grandfather and namesake was a veteran Democratic officeholder who served under Grover Cleveland as vice president from 1893 to 1897. His maternal great-grandfather, Jesse Fell, was a close friend and supporter of Abraham Lincoln. Stevenson's father, Lewis Green Stevenson, mixed farming with politics, while his mother, Helen Louise Davis Stevenson, raised her son with a love of learning. Despite this, he was only a fair student and entered Princeton University in 1918 after failing its entrance examination three times. Following a short stint in the navy during World War I, he worked for his mother's family's Bloomington-based newspaper before earning a law degree from Northwestern University. Stevenson married Ellen Borden in Chicago in 1928. The couple had three sons, one of whom, his father's

Adlai Stevenson. THE LIBRARY OF CONGRESS

namesake, represented Illinois in the U.S. Senate from 1970 to 1981. The couple divorced in 1949.

Stevenson began his career in government as a lawyer for the administration of President Franklin D. Roosevelt in the 1930s. In 1941 he became special assistant to Secretary of the Navy Frank Knox, which in turn led to service under the secretaries of state Edward Stettinius and James Byrnes. Most notably, he was a key U.S. representative to the formative sessions of the United Nations (UN) from 1945 to 1947. Returning to Illinois, he was elected the state's governor on the Democratic ticket in 1948.

After resisting calls to run, Stevenson finally accepted the Democratic nomination for president in 1952. Vowing to "talk sense to the American people," he conducted a gallant campaign against his highly popular opponent, the Republican Dwight Eisenhower. Stevenson inspired millions through his ready wit, eloquent speeches, and idealistic approach to politics. Although he lost to Eisenhower by a landslide, he retained his stature as the leader of the Democratic Party's liberal wing. He remained a public figure after his defeat, decrying anti-Communist extremism and advocating a less confrontational foreign policy. After a bruising primary campaign, he won a second Democratic nomination against Eisenhower in 1956. During the fall campaign, he came out in favor of a nuclear test ban, federal aid to education, and a Medicare-like health program. Stevenson suffered a crushing second defeat that November; still, he lived to see many of his proposals become law in

the following decade. Moreover, his attack on the conservative complacency of the Eisenhower administration anticipated John F. Kennedy's call to "get this country moving again" during the 1960 presidential campaign.

Many urged Stevenson to try for a third nomination in 1960. Though tempted, he recognized Kennedy's strength and hesitated to mount a campaign against him. Even on the sidelines, he continued to retain the support of many liberal party activists, who worked on his behalf. At the 1960 Democratic convention in Los Angeles, his supporters packed the galleries and loudly cheered his name, proclaiming themselves "Madly for Adlai." Delivering a memorable and dramatic speech, Senator Eugene J. McCarthy nominated Stevenson to be the Democratic nominee for president, eliciting a wild demonstration. Although Stevenson actively made a last-minute bid for delegate support, the party nominated Kennedy on the first ballot. Stevenson campaigned for Kennedy and held expectations of being chosen as secretary of state. After his narrow victory, though, Kennedy picked Dean Rusk for the post instead and asked Stevenson to become the United States Permanent Representative to the United Nations, a cabinet-level position. Disappointed, Stevenson took his time in agreeing to accept the appointment.

The relationship between Kennedy and Stevenson proved to be less than comfortable. The president and his closest advisers found Stevenson long-winded and unrealistic at cabinet meetings; Stevenson in turn found Kennedy and his inner circle to be overconfident and sometimes ruthless. On a number of issues, such as representation of Communist China at the UN, Stevenson was more forward-looking than most of Kennedy's advisers. Despite these differences, Kennedy benefited from his UN ambassador's worldwide prestige, even if he gave his old rival little decision-making authority. He grew to respect Stevenson's coolness under pressure and willingness to defend policies he did not always fully support. For his part, Stevenson loyally supported Kennedy in public, though old friends detected frustration and unhappiness under the surface. He continued to surround himself with a loyal band of longtime aides and supporters, turning particularly to the planning expert Barbara Ward for advice on Third World issues.

In April 1961 Stevenson's diplomatic credibility was put to the test during the Bay of Pigs invasion. Continuing plans set in motion by Eisenhower, Kennedy agreed to support military action by Cuban exiles against Fidel Castro's regime. Briefing Stevenson shortly before the operation began, Kennedy's aides misled him as to the extent of U.S. involvement. On 14 April, during UN Security Council meetings called by Cuba, Stevenson passed on this deception to the world, claiming that "there will not be under any conditions . . . any intervention in Cuba by the United States armed forces." Events proved otherwise—the U.S. Central Intelligence Agency played an active part in the exiles' assault on Cuba, which was routed by Castro's forces at the Bay of Pigs on 16 April. Stevenson also had spread the false story that Castro's air force was in revolt, displaying photos at the Security Council of "Cuban" planes (actually repainted U.S. aircraft) supposedly flown to Miami by defecting pilots. When it became clear that the administration had misled him, he felt humiliated. "Now my credibility has been compromised, and therefore my usefulness," he told one friend. "Yet how can I resign at this moment and make things worse for the president?" In the end, he swallowed his misgivings and stayed on.

In late 1961 Kennedy helped persuade Stevenson to forgo a bid for the U.S. Senate and remain at his UN post. Simmering conflicts in India (involving the Portuguese colony of Goa) and what was then the Belgian Congo kept him occupied into the early months of 1962. Many of these issues had cold war implications, and Stevenson frequently was opposed by his Soviet counterpart, Valerian Zorin, at Security Council meetings.

Tensions between the two superpowers escalated dramatically in October of that year, when the Kennedy administration learned that Soviet missiles armed with nuclear warheads were en route to Cuba. Stevenson participated in cabinet discussions about how to respond to this threat, arguing in favor of a diplomatic rather than a military response. While supporting the idea of a Cuban blockade, he also advocated making conciliatory gestures,

including the removal of obsolete American missiles from Turkey and Italy and the evacuation of the U.S. base at Guantanamo Bay in Cuba. Stevenson's overall goal was to link the solution of the Cuban crisis to larger arms control issues with the Soviets. Kennedy's inclination, though, was to take a harder line. On 22 October the president made the crisis public, announcing a "quarantine" of Cuba and harshly warning the Soviets of the risk of nuclear war.

Stevenson vigorously advanced this position at UN Security Council meetings that followed. Mindful of the tainted evidence presented by the U.S. during the Bay of Pigs affair, he still presented a convincing case to the world that the Soviets were equipping bases in Cuba for offensive missile capability against the American mainland. In measured but firm language, tinged at times with anger, he submitted a resolution demanding the withdrawal of all missiles from Cuba. Angered by evasive answers from Zorin during a Security Council session, he stated that he would wait for a clear-cut response "until Hell freezes over." Ultimately, the missiles were withdrawn. Stevenson's performance during the crisis won considerable praise, including personal thanks from Kennedy.

Despite his tough talk to the Russians, Stevenson still drew criticism from some quarters as an "appeaser" who was soft on Communism. Reports that he had favored trading "U.S. bases for Cuban weapons" during cabinet meetings appeared in the press, causing Stevenson to doubt Kennedy's continued support. Loathed by the extreme Right, he was spat upon during a visit to Dallas, Texas, in the fall of 1963. The incident was ugly enough for him to consider warning Kennedy to postpone his own visit to the city. (Three weeks later, the president was assassinated in Dallas.)

Remaining at his UN post under President Lyndon B. Johnson, Stevenson grew increasingly isolated from foreign policy decision-making. Although he was a believer in the containment of Communism, he felt uneasy with the direction of Johnson's policies in Vietnam. In late 1964 he attempted to initiate negotiations between North Vietnam and the United States; these efforts were stymied by the Johnson administration, which then blamed Stevenson for not keeping diplomatic channels open. Once again, the UN ambassador considered quitting and then elected to stay. His doubts about American involvement in Southeast Asia increased during early 1965, though he refrained from speaking out publicly.

On 14 July 1965 Stevenson collapsed from a massive heart attack during a visit to London. His body was taken to the National Cathedral in Washington, D.C., and placed in the Bethlehem Chapel, where thousands of mourners came to pay their respects. His body also lay in state in Springfield, Illinois, under the capitol dome, before burial at Evergreen Cemetery in Bloomington, Illinois. Five days before his death, he had delivered a memorable speech in

Geneva at a UN conference. Pleading for world unity, he spoke of Earth as "a little space ship . . . preserved from annihilation only by the care, the work, and, I will say, the love we give our fragile craft." It proved a fitting epitaph to a career largely dedicated to promoting international peace. Stevenson was mourned as a brilliant, inspiring statesman who, despite being denied the presidency, exemplified the highest ideals in public service.

★

Stevenson's papers are available in Walter Johnson, *The Papers of Adlai E. Stevenson,* 8 vols. (1972–1979). Manuscript material is held by the Princeton University Library. Papers from Stevenson's term as governor of Illinois are at the Illinois State Historical Library. Among Stevenson biographies, John Bartlow Martin, *Adlai Stevenson of Illinois* (1976) and *Adlai Stevenson and the World* (1977), are the most thorough. Jean H. Baker, *The Stevensons: A Biography of an American Family* (1996), offers a more critical, revisionist view. Also valuable are Kenneth S. Davis, *The Politics of Honor* (1967), and Porter McKeever, *Adlai Stevenson: His Life and Legacy* (1989). The events of the 1960 Democratic convention are detailed in Theodore H. White, *The Making of the President, 1960* (1961). An obituary is in the *New York Times* (15 July 1965).

BARRY ALFONSO

STEWART, Ellen (*b. c.* 1920 in Alexandria, Louisiana), founder of the La Mama Experimental Theater Club, which has nurtured avant-garde off-Broadway playwrights since 1962.

Stewart's life before moving to New York City in 1950 is, at best, sketchy and vague. Her interviews always vary her origins. Apparently, her African-American family's origin is either Creole or Geechee (slaves who settled along the Ogeechee River in Georgia). "Some of my people were in vaudeville and burlesque," she told one interviewer. Her father was perhaps a laborer or a tailor, and her mother was perhaps a schoolteacher. Their names are unknown. Her birth year is given as 1920 in several sources, and some sources list her birthplace as Chicago.

As children, Stewart and her brother (who was perhaps her foster brother), Frederick Lights, had a miniature theater constructed from a shoebox and used thread spools to represent actors. Lights studied theology at Howard University, then drama at Yale University. Stewart has said that his difficulty in finding a producer for his first play led her into theatrical production.

Stewart later lived in Chicago, working as a seamstress and dressmaker, and she was married several—perhaps as many as five—times. She moved in 1950 to New York City and worked there as a seamstress, then as a designer for Edith Lances's custom corsetiere salon at Saks Fifth Avenue (1950–1957). After working freelance for several years, she designed sport dresses and beach wraps for Victor Bijou's custom salon, also at Saks. Throughout the 1960s Stewart's daytime dress designing supported her productions of avant-garde theater.

In 1962 Stewart met two theater people, Jim Moore and Paul Foster, and they decided to open a combined boutique (an outlet for her own line of dresses) and theater. The first locale was in a basement space at 321 East Ninth Street in New York City's East Village. A building inspector, who was a former actor and sympathetic to them, suggested opening with a restaurant license to make the operation legal, creating Café La Mama ("Mama" was Stewart's nickname). Workshop productions began in the summer of 1962 with an adaptation of Tennessee Williams's short story *One Arm* (1948), followed by Michael Locasio's *In a Corner of the Morning* and the first New York staging of Harold Pinter's *The Room.*

In 1963 a zoning inspector closed the space on East Ninth Street. The next venue, a loft space at 82 Second Avenue, was similarly closed after Foster's play *Balls* was produced. The third space, also on Second Avenue (number 122), was turned into a private nonprofit club in order to avoid any further building violations. Patrons paid a nominal membership fee for a week's admission to the newly named La Mama Experimental Theater Club.

The following year (1964) began a new policy, which was retained. Previously, a chosen playwright would hold auditions for an individual production. Because Stewart wanted to produce as many plays by aspiring playwrights as possible, she began an ensemble troupe of young actors. For Stewart, "the playwright is the inspiration, the beginning, the germ," she told a reporter. "All things must serve him in their particular way." With new plays by new playwrights to run for one week, Stewart believed an acting ensemble was essential.

During the early 1960s young actors and playwrights flocked to New York City's Greenwich Village area. In addition to La Mama, Joe Cino's Caffè Cino, Julian and Malina Beck's Living Theater, Joseph Chaikin's Open Theater, and the Judson Poet's Theater were venues supporting the latest new theater projects. Workshop productions of the Open Theater were often staged at La Mama. A young playwright might stage a piece at the Caffè Cino and then a revised production would open later at La Mama. Consequently, these performance spaces were fluid. That is, actors and playwrights could be and often were associated with all of these performance spaces. Stewart's La Mama is the only one that remained as of 2002.

Between 1962 and 1966 alone, La Mama presented more than 200 different plays. In addition to a resident acting troupe, Stewart retained directors. The playwright-director

Ellen Stewart. AP/WIDE WORLD PHOTOS

Tom O'Horgan directed more than fifty plays between 1964 and 1968, including a revised production of Rochelle Owens's *Futz!* in 1967. Among the many aspiring playwrights nurtured by Stewart during the 1960s were Ross Alexander, Tom Eyen, Paul Foster, Tom O'Horgan, Sam Shepard, David Starkweather, and Lanford Wilson.

Whatever the play, an evening at La Mama retained a communal atmosphere. After Stewart cooked soup to feed the acting troupe, director, and playwright, the audience would enter and settle into their seats. Stewart would ring a cowbell to start the performance, greeting the audience with these words: "Welcome to La Mama, dedicated to the playwrights and all aspects of the theater." For Stewart, theater was a family, and she was the mama.

Not only did Stewart provide a physical and spiritual home for aspiring playwrights, she wanted their work published. When she approached various publishers, she was told that only reviewed works would be seriously considered. Only two New York City publications, the *Village Voice* and the *East Village Other,* covered La Mama's productions with any regularity. Undeterred, Stewart asked others for advice, and she was told that European newspapers reviewed everything. The Becks' Living Theater, during its exile in Europe (1964–1968), had been receiving critical acclaim. Following this example, Stewart sent O'Horgan and an acting troupe on a European tour. The plays presented there in 1965 included Adrienne Kennedy's *Black Mass,* Shepard's *Chicago,* and Wilson's *This Is the Rill Speaking.* Reviews of the twenty-one plays were highly enthusiastic, and twelve were eventually published.

Since 1965 foreign tours have been a routine of the La Mama schedule. These tours have been so successful that La Mama branches are thriving in Canada, Colombia, England, and Japan. The La Mama theaters regularly book each other's productions so that playwrights around the world have international exposure.

By 1967 Stewart's finances were severely strained, and she applied for and received grants from the Ford and Rockefeller foundations, the Kaplan Fund, and the National Endowment for the Arts. That year La Mama was able to purchase a six-story building at 74A East Fourth Street, which remains its present location. The first floor is its repertory theater, and above it are spaces for workshops and storage. Stewart's apartment is on the top floor. An ensemble troupe regularly develops works by new playwrights. An annex at 66–68 East Fourth Street was purchased in 1974.

Since 1962 Stewart's La Mama Experimental Theater Club has fostered emerging playwrights by providing a workshop atmosphere in which to develop a production, and a performance space in which to stage new theater.

★

There is no biography of Stewart. Interviews and profiles of her include Josh Greenfeld, "Their Hearts Belong to La Mama," *New York Times Magazine* (9 July 1967), and George W. Anderson, "Visiting La MaMa's Founder," *America* (8 Feb. 1997). See also Stuart W. Little, *Off-Broadway: The Prophetic Theater* (1972); Ellen Stewart, "Finding Ways to Survive," *Backstage* (21 Dec. 1990); and John Heilpern, "La Mama Courage," *Vogue* (Aug. 1992).

PATRICK S. SMITH

STILLS, Stephen. *See* Crosby, Stills and Nash.

STOKES, Carl Burton (*b.* 21 June 1927 in Cleveland, Ohio; *d.* 3 April 1996 in Cleveland, Ohio), lawyer, state legislator, newscaster, labor lawyer, and municipal court judge who was the first African-American mayor of a major American city.

Stokes, the great-grandson of a slave, grew up in Cleveland's first federally funded housing complex for the poor. He was the younger of two sons of Charles, a laborer, and Louise Stokes. After his father died when Carl was two, his mother worked as a domestic to support the family. Stokes also helped at a young age by working as a newspaper carrier and in neighborhood stores. He dropped out of East Technical High School to help support the family and took a job in a foundry.

After a short period in the army (1945–1946), Stokes received an honorable discharge and was able to return to his studies. Using the GI Bill, he finished high school and was educated at West Virginia State College (1947–1948), Western Reserve University (1948–1950), and earned his B.S. in law at the University of Minnesota in 1954, finally ending at Cleveland's Marshall School of Law, where he received his J.D. (1956).

Stokes was married four times. His first wife was Edith

Carl B. Stokes. THE LIBRARY OF CONGRESS

Smith, whom he divorced in 1953. He had three children with his second wife, Shirley Edwards (married 30 January 1958 and divorced in 1973). He married Raija Kostadinova in 1981. After a divorce the couple remarried in 1993, and Stokes had an adopted daughter and a stepson from the fourth marriage.

In pursuing the law as a career, Stokes was mindful of the events around him. The 1960s saw the beginning of political turmoil nationwide. Cleveland was no different from other U.S. cities. The climate in the nation was one of unrest. Many factors contributed to the political instability for the country and the region. Unlike the southern states, violence was not always the primary action. Although simmering just beneath the surface was a cry for change, Cleveland's population dropped to 876,050 because of white flight to the suburbs. In 1963 Ohio launched a giant economic development program to attract more industry. The Supreme Court ruled in 1964 that Ohio must reapportion its House of Representatives to provide more equal representation based on population. The plan developed, however, was not voted on until 1967.

After receiving his law degree, Stokes worked as a probation officer in Cleveland Municipal Court and as the assistant city prosecutor. He left the court in 1962 to open a law practice with his older brother, Louis.

Stokes's career during the 1960s was marked with many firsts. Beginning his political career as the first African-American Democratic member of the Ohio General Assembly in 1962, he served three terms in this capacity until 1967. His voting record established him as a moderate, strongly favoring civil rights and aid measures as well as the use of National Guard troops in the event of serious rioting.

In 1965 Stokes made his first bid for mayor of Cleveland on an independent ticket. He lost to the Democratic mayoral candidate, Ralph Locher, by a narrow margin. Stokes then launched a second bid for the mayoral position. This time running as a Democrat, he was able to beat Locher in the primary and then Seth Taft, the grandson of President William H. Taft, in the general election in 1967. Stokes, who became the first African American to be elected mayor of a major American city, won the election with 50.5 percent of the vote at a time when Cleveland's black population was only 37 percent of the total. He was able to win his electoral campaign with a coalition of black and white votes garnered through the force of his personality. His strong convictions attracted talented and idealistic people to his administration, thus leaving a memorable impact on local politics in Cleveland. He emphasized jobs and housing. He believed the crisis of the city "threatens to strangle and destroy our entire urban civilization. We need to mobilize our brain power, our talents and our human responses without delay."

He was elected to a second term in 1969 with the same

zeal and conviction. Once again the coalition held fast. His second term focused on expanding public housing and revitalizing the police department. His term ended in 1971; he decided not to run for a third term based on the political damage he suffered from the 23 July 1968 shoot-out in the Glenville neighborhood that claimed the lives of six black civilians and three white police officers. In his autobiography, *Promises of Power,* he states, "The aftermath of that night was to haunt and color every aspect of my administration for the next three years. Glenville killed much of my public support and gave nonsupporters a chance to emerge from the woodwork." This incident overshadowed any improvements that his administration had made in welfare, repair and maintenance of city streets, and water purification.

Although Stokes was able to calm the city successfully with the help of other black leaders after the assassination of Dr. Martin Luther King, Jr., in April 1968, he did not have the same good fortune with the incident in Glenville in July. Calm was only achieved by requesting that National Guardsmen be called in to patrol the streets and restore peace. Understanding the frustrations of the black community, Stokes ordered the white police and guardsmen out of the area and patrolled the neighborhoods with a hundred black policemen and about five hundred black volunteers from among the black leadership and militant groups. Although looting occurred, the rioting stopped and there were no further casualties.

Criticism of his handling of the incident lingered, however, and Stokes began to take a more conservative approach to dealing with urban unrest. In 1969 he noted it was the responsibility of law-abiding black people to report wrongdoing in their neighborhoods to the police.

To demonstrate his commitment to better living conditions for all and to advance the theme of improving U.S. cities, Stokes in 1968 wrote the book *The Quality of the Environment* and the articles "The Urban Crisis," "Summer Progress and Social Progress," and "What's Ahead for Race Relations."

Stokes left Cleveland and politics in 1972 to become a newscaster at the National Broadcasting Company (NBC) in New York City. Returning to Cleveland in 1980, he served as general counsel to the United Auto Workers. In 1983 he was elected municipal court judge and served two terms as head of the court. He served as ambassador to the Seychelles, islands in the Indian Ocean off the African coast, from 1994 to 1995. He died in Cleveland of esophageal cancer and is buried in the city's Lake View Cemetery.

★

Stokes's autobiography is *Promises of Power* (1983). For additional biographical data see I. Cloyd, *Who's Who Among Black Americans,* 6th ed.; W. Augustus Low and Virgil A. Clift, *Ency-*clopedia of Black America* (1981); H. O. Lindsey, *A History of Black America* (1994); and Jamilah Salim, *Interpretive History of African American Education 1950–1990s: Political Frustration and Accomplishment in Cleveland, Ohio* (2001). Also see Kenneth G. Weinberg, *Black Victory: Carl Stokes and the Winning of Cleveland* (1968), and Estelle Zannes, *Checkmate in Cleveland: The Rhetoric and Confrontation During the Stokes Years* (1972). Obituaries are in the *New York Times* and *Washington Post* (both 4 Apr. 1996).

ANN E. PHARR

STONE, Edward Durell (*b.* 9 March 1902 in Fayetteville, Arkansas; *d.* 6 August 1978 in New York City), innovative modern architect whose distinctive style, seen in buildings from New York's Museum of Modern Art to Washington, D.C.'s John F. Kennedy Center for the Performing Arts, has been the subject of both praise and condemnation.

Stone was the son of Benjamin Hicks Stone and Ruth Johnson. After studying art at the University of Arkansas for three years, Stone joined his older brother, a practicing architect, in Boston. There he took courses at night through the Boston Architectural Club while pursuing an apprenticeship with the firm of Coolidge, Shepley, Bulfinch, and

Edward Durell Stone. CORBIS CORPORATION (NEW YORK)

Abbott. In 1926 Stone won a competition entitling him to study architecture, first at Harvard and then at the Massachusetts Institute of Technology (MIT). He proceeded to win a second MIT competition, the reward for which was two years' study and travel in Europe.

Upon his return to the United States in 1929, Stone obtained immediate employment helping to design the interior of the Waldorf-Astoria Hotel in New York City and then the fabled interior of Radio City Music Hall. Several years of journeyman work followed, enabling him to open his own firm in 1936 with a major commission: the Museum of Modern Art (1937), which was praised as an embodiment in glass and concrete of the art it was intended to house. The building displayed the motifs for which he would become known: circular windows, overhanging flat roofs, and decorative concrete facades.

Stone built hangars and other utilitarian structures for the U.S. Army Air Corps during World War II, an experience that influenced his postwar designs. After the war he built a number of resort hotels incorporating the cantilever methods he had learned in the military. In 1954 he designed the American Embassy in New Delhi, India, featuring a pierced concrete grillwork and an overhanging roof that protected the interior from direct sun and heat. The building, set on a platform over a sheltered parking area, seemed to float above its site.

As Stone's reputation grew during the 1960s, he repeated these motifs in numerous commissions. In a controversial action, he renovated his Manhattan townhouse in 1964, covering the entire facade with a four-story pierced screen. For the headquarters of the National Geographic Society, erected in Washington, D.C., in 1964, Stone employed a two-story base with overhang and a second overhang on the main roof. For the Center for Continuing Education at the University of Chicago (now a graduate-student residence hall), he imposed bold geometric patterns on the concrete of the exterior walls and the overhanging roof and extended the preternaturally thin columns (which had become another recurring motif) to the full height of the structure. Perhaps Stone's finest work in this vein was a pair of libraries, one for the University of South Carolina and the other for the city of Davenport, Iowa, in which the roof overhang served a functional purpose similar to that performed in New Delhi: protecting the interior (and its books) from the effects of direct sun. The South Carolina library won the American Institute of Architects' First Honor Award in 1963.

Stone's designs brought him equal amounts of praise and criticism. The extreme thinness of his columns, made possible by Stone's mastery of cantilever design, was attacked as masking the true form of his buildings; the columns, however, contributed to the illusion of a "floating" building, which was particularly valuable in either a lush or unattractive landscape, as Stone demonstrated with the Huntington Hartford Museum (now the property of the New York City Department of Cultural Affairs). The pierced-concrete facade appears to hover on structural piers that are split into large circular voids at the second-story level, decisively separating the beauty of the building from the bustling traffic and intrusive signs at street level. Some critics recommended the building for landmark status; Ada Louise Huxtable, however, called it "a Venetian palazzo on popsicle sticks."

Inevitably, Stone was approached to do ever larger projects. Between 1964 and 1972 he designed two campus master plans, one for the University of Alaska in Anchorage and the other for the State University of New York at Albany; a headquarters building for General Motors in midtown Manhattan; a headquarters building for the Standard Oil Company (now the Aon Center) in Chicago; the PepsiCo World Headquarters in Purchase, New York; and the John F. Kennedy Center for the Performing Arts in Washington, D.C., whose three performance halls and associated public areas total some 1.5 million square feet.

At large scales the delicacy of Stone's vision could be overwhelmed by the sheer magnitude of concrete and marble; the lobbies of the JFK Center are one hundred feet high, and the four-hundred-acre campus in Albany remains unfilled decades after its inception. But on the more human scale of the PepsiCo headquarters, in particular, Stone fused metal, glass, and natural materials to achieve an architecture that works both visually and functionally. And even when he failed in the view of critics, he did so in some cases because his materials were not adequate to the realization of his vision. A visitor to Chicago sees the Aon Center reaching for the sky while the nearby Sears Tower clutches the ground, and the fact that the Corten steel of the latter has better withstood the brutal Chicago winters does not invalidate Stone's choice of marble.

Stone married Orlean Vandiver on 5 December 1931; they had two children. They were divorced in 1951, and on 24 June 1953 Stone married Maria Elena Torchio. The architect often said that it was she who infected his designs of the late 1950s and 1960s with their famous "romanticism." Nevertheless, that marriage did not last, and Stone married for the third time, to Violet Campbell Moffat, in 1972. Stone died after a brief illness in New York City on 6 August 1978.

Stone gained fame as an architect working in the international modern style, but transformed in the late 1950s and became the world's foremost proponent of romanticism in large structures. Although his greatest work undoubtedly is found in his more modest structures, his large buildings have proved to be extremely efficient in operation, praised for their sensuous good looks yet condemned as examples of "architectural populism."

★

Stone's autobiography is titled *The Evolution of an Architect* (1962). Additional information on his architectural vision can be found in his *Recent and Future Architecture* (1967). An obituary is in the *New York Times* (8 Aug. 1978).

HARTLEY S. SPATT

STONE, I. F. (*b.* 24 December 1907 in Philadelphia, Pennsylvania; *d.* 18 June 1989 in Boston, Massachusetts), radical journalist and publisher of *I. F. Stone's Weekly* from 1953 to 1971.

Born Isidor Feinstein, Stone in 1937 changed his name, arguing that he would influence more readers if he seemed "less Jewish"; thereafter he was known as I. F. Stone. He was the eldest of four children born to Bernard Feinstein, a dry goods merchant, and Katherine ("Katy") Novack. The parents, immigrants from Russia, had settled in Haddonfield, New Jersey, where at age fourteen Stone started his first publication, *The Progress.*

In high school Stone worked as the local correspondent for the *Camden Evening Courier.* After graduating in 1924

I. F. Stone. AP/WIDE WORLD PHOTOS

he enrolled as a philosophy major at the University of Pennsylvania while supporting himself by working part-time for local papers. In his junior year Stone dropped out of school to become a full-time journalist. He married Esther Roisman, with whom he had three children, on 7 July 1929, and in 1933 they moved to New York City. In the years that followed he published his first books and wrote editorials for the *New York Post* until 1938, at which point he resigned to protest the paper's increasingly anticommunist tone.

Drawn from an early age to socialism, Stone developed politics that relegated him to working mostly for left-wing publications such as the *Nation,* where he served as associate editor (1938–1940) and Washington editor (1940–1946). He also worked for *PM,* a small radical newspaper that sent him in 1946 to report on the status of Jewish refugees. He joined a group that dodged a British blockade and landed in Palestine, where he remained for a time, sending out further dispatches. These experiences led to the books *Underground to Palestine* (1946; revised edition, 1979) and *This Is Israel* (1948). During the period from 1942 to 1952 Stone worked variously for *PM,* the *Post,* the *New York Star,* and the *Daily Compass.* The latter had been founded in 1949 after *PM* folded, but when it, too, closed its doors in 1952, he found himself with few prospects for work.

In postwar America, charged as it was with anticommunist sentiment, Stone, whose *Hidden History of the Korean War* (1952) questioned the motivation behind U.S. involvement in the Korean War, found himself more marginalized than ever. Therefore, he decided to start his own independent publication. Using the mailing lists of *PM* and the *Daily Compass,* Stone signed up some 5,300 advance subscribers, including Albert Einstein and Eleanor Roosevelt, for five dollars a year. This helped him offset the initial cost of $6,500, and with help from his wife, he launched *I. F. Stone's Weekly* on 17 January 1953.

From the beginning the paper, a four-page newsletter, was as conservative in appearance as its content was radical. Because he had chosen a place for himself far outside the mainstream, Stone could not undertake the ordinary journalistic practice of developing sources and contacts. This was especially the case inasmuch as *I. F. Stone's Weekly* concerned itself with the activities of the federal government, and the latter took an extremely dim view of Stone. In 1994 the Federal Bureau of Investigation (FBI) would reveal that for a period of thirty years, from 1941 to 1971, Stone was under investigation at the behest of the FBI director J. Edgar Hoover. Although Stone had no direct knowledge of the FBI probe, he was certainly aware that Washington viewed him as persona non grata, and therefore, instead of cultivating contacts in the government, he simply used official documents as his sources.

By that point the Stones had moved to Washington, D.C., from New York City, and this location would prove essential to the work that occupied Stone for the next eighteen years. To do the type of research he needed to do, in that era long before the advent of the Internet, it was necessary to obtain bulky paper documents from the U.S. Government Printing Office and pore over thousands of pages of text. Putting to work his great capacity for remembering details, Stone read over this often quite dull material, and he managed to catch the government in errors, contradictions, and outright lies. Throughout the 1950s and 1960s Stone used the *Weekly,* which he referred to affectionately as a "little flea-bitten publication" and "the journalistic equivalent of the old-fashioned Jewish momma-and-poppa grocery store," to spread his views on everything from segregation to the cold war. Using the government's own material against it, he set out to show that Washington was not being forthright with its own citizens and to make a case for radical changes in racial and economic policy at home as well as military efforts overseas.

From the beginnings of U.S. involvement in Vietnam in 1954, Stone had been an outspoken critic of the war, and as the conflict escalated, so did his attacks on it in the *Weekly.* "You can't go on pouring napalm on villages and poison on crops," he wrote in 1963, "uprooting the people and putting them in prison-like compounds, and expect to be liked." He became one of the only American journalists to challenge President Lyndon B. Johnson's account of events in the Gulf of Tonkin in early August 1964, an incident in which the North Vietnamese torpedoed an American craft on a spy mission. In addition to investigating public records on the war, Stone visited South Vietnam in 1966. His positions on Vietnam and other issues won him a new generation of admirers, and Stone soon became a counterculture icon on the nation's campuses. He thus fulfilled a prediction he had made once to his wife: "I'm going to graduate from a pariah into a character, and then if I last long enough, I'll be regarded as a national institution." By the end of the 1960s his subscriber base had climbed to more than seventy thousand, and, for the first time, Stone had a measure of economic security and freedom.

By the mid-1960s Stone was reaching a vastly larger audience with articles in the *New York Review of Books,* pieces that collectively reveal much about both their author and the time. In discussing conservatives or military leaders, naturally, Stone tended to strike a note somewhere between derisive and disgusted, but closer to the former. He called the conservative Republican senator Barry Goldwater, for instance, "Arizona's leading political scientist" and referred to the cowritten memoirs of General Curtis E. LeMay, the former air force chief of staff and an outspoken "hawk" on Vietnam, as "the account [LeMay] helped prepare of his life." As a radical, however, Stone reserved his sharpest criticism for liberals and Democrats. Reviewing two books by Hubert Humphrey in September 1964, he wrote that "during the Democratic convention, they could be read in rolling chairs on Atlantic City's boardwalk, by big business men, without their suffering the slightest ill-effect."

At least as telling as Stone's writing on domestic affairs in the *New York Review of Books* is his work on international affairs in the same publication. He joined with a host of intellectual celebrities in July 1967 to call for the release of Regis Debray, a wealthy French radical and proponent of violent revolution being held by the government of Bolivia for his activities in their country. The list of signatories was much shorter, just six names, including Stone's, on a January 1969 letter condemning the Soviet invasion of Czechoslovakia, much of which was taken up by caveats making clear the authors' condemnation of U.S. imperialism and undimmed admiration for Communism. With those disclaimers established, they let it be known that "the Soviet invasion of Czechoslovakia is a severe setback for world socialism. It gravely impedes the anti-imperialist struggle . . . [and] dishonor[s] the Soviet Union."

Some of the old intellectual fashions were changing, and it was now possible for a dedicated leftist to criticize the Soviets, at least for the right reasons. Stone also exemplified the shift in the wind taking place with regard to the Middle East when he reviewed a record of an Arab-Israeli symposium in 1967. For the preceding twenty years, when Israel looked more to the Soviet Union than to the United States for assistance, Stone's and other leftists' support of Israel had still been strong. Things had begun to change, however, after the Six-Day War in 1967 (the third of the wars fought between the Arabs and Israelis over territorial and strategic issues related to the creation of the Israeli state). Stone, who had once strongly identified with Israel, now referred to Israel's "supra-nationalist dream" while condemning "Zionist propaganda."

Stone rounded out his successes of the 1960s with a series of widely read essay collections: *The Haunted Fifties* (1963), *In a Time of Torment* (1967), *Polemics and Prophecies, 1967–70* (1970), and *The Truman Era.* It was indicative of Stone's changing fortunes that the last of these volumes, published originally in 1952 to limited response, was reissued in 1972 by Random House, publisher of all his books from 1963 to 1973. In addition, Stone published *The Killings at Kent State: How Murder Went Unpunished* (1971) and *The I. F. Stone's Weekly Reader* (1973). By the time of the last book, an anthology of his best work from the *Weekly,* Stone had closed down his newsletter. Although he had long suffered from poor eyesight and deafness, he had continued to work, but heart trouble in the late 1960s forced him to go to a biweekly schedule; then, in 1971 he ceased publication of the *Weekly* altogether. In 1971 Stone received the George Polk Memorial Award.

Stone did not remain idle in the last two decades of his life. Long fascinated with ancient Greece, he taught himself Greek in his seventies and applied this knowledge in the research and writing of *The Trial of Socrates* (1988), a *New York Times* best-seller. Also during the 1980s he published opinion pieces criticizing the administration of President Ronald Reagan in the *Nation* and *New York Times*. Stone died after suffering a heart attack and undergoing surgery in a Boston hospital.

Ignored in the 1950s, Stone lived long enough to become a highly admired grandfatherly figure, affectionately known as "Izzy," in the 1960s and thereafter. To a greater extent than almost any other American intellectual, he served as a bridge between the Old Left of the 1930s and the New Left of the 1960s, and he managed to do so without endorsing the sexual and pharmaceutical adventurism of the latter. He exerted an enormous influence on a rising generation of liberals and radicals, many of whom would later take important positions in government, media, and education.

The ultimate impact of Stone's ideas is open to interpretation. Of particular concern is the revelation, which emerged in the late 1990s, that he accepted money from the Soviet government. The information comes from the Venona intercepts of the National Security Agency, which published information gathered and deciphered some fifty years earlier. Communiqués by Soviet agents refer to Stone by the code name *Blin* ("Pancake"), and one such dispatch, dated 23 October 1944, indicates that "he would not be averse to having a supplementary income." Certainly, the Soviets had reason to believe he would be sympathetic, because he had defended the Stalinist show trials a few years earlier. Records indicate that Stone refused to receive further monies from the Soviets only after the invasion of Czechoslovakia.

★

There are two notable biographies of Stone: Andrew Patner, *I. F. Stone: A Portrait* (1988), and Robert C. Cottrell, *Izzy: A Biography of I. F. Stone* (1992). Stone's own work, particularly *Underground to Palestine* (1946), provides numerous insights regarding his life and ideas. For information on FBI surveillance of Stone, see the *Los Angeles Times* (25 Sept. 1994). Stone's secret relationship with the Soviet government is discussed in Herbert Romerstein and Eric Breindel, *The Venona Secrets: Exposing Soviet Espionage and America's Traitors* (2000). Obituaries are in the *New York Times* and *Washington Post* (both 19 June 1989); *The Progressive* 53, no. 8 (Aug. 1989): 4; *Mother Jones* 14, no. 7 (Sept. 1989): 17; and the *Utne Reader* (Sept.–Oct. 1989).

JUDSON KNIGHT

STOOKEY Paul. *See* Peter, Paul and Mary.

STREISAND, Barbra (*b.* 24 April 1942 in New York City), singer and actress noted for her Broadway performances, top-selling albums, and comedy films.

Barbara Joan Streisand (she later changed the spelling of her first name) was one of two children born to Emanuel Streisand, a high-school English literature teacher, and Diana (Rosen) Streisand. Hers was an unhappy childhood, an influence Streisand often has cited as the source of her determination to succeed as well as the perfectionism that marks her work. Her father died of an epileptic seizure when she was just fifteen months old, leaving Streisand's mother to raise two children by herself. The family was so poor that Streisand had only one "doll," a hot-water bottle wrapped in a sweater.

Eventually, her mother found employment as a secretary in the New York City public school system and married a used-car salesman named Lou Kind. Streisand felt rejected by her mother and her new stepfather, and she began increasingly to rely on her intelligence and talent to create a better life for herself. In 1959, when she was only sixteen years old, she graduated with honors from Erasmus High School in Brooklyn. The only additional formal education she received consisted of a few classes at Brooklyn's Yeshiva University in preparation for the making of her 1983 film

Barbra Streisand. ARCHIVE PHOTOS, INC.

Yentl. By the end of the 1950s, Streisand had moved to Manhattan, where she shared an apartment with friends and tried to find work as a musician. When someone said that her last name sounded "too Jewish," she responded by changing the spelling of her first. This defiance exemplified an attitude that would have a profound effect on American culture once Streisand became a star: rather than cover up her Jewish identity, she embraced it, and by emphasizing that which differentiated her from the mainstream, she forced a change in American concepts of what was acceptable and even beautiful.

Streisand performed in obscure nightclubs and bistros during the lean days of 1960, often literally singing for her supper. Things began to change, however, in 1961. First, she won a talent contest at a bar in Greenwich Village, an achievement that secured her the first regular engagement of her career, at the Village's Bon Soir club. Then, on 21 October, she made her off-Broadway debut in *Another Evening with Harry Stoones,* a show that closed the same night it opened. Throughout late 1961 and early 1962, she performed in a variety of off-Broadway productions, while continuing to sing at the Bon Soir. There she developed a reputation for placing her unique stamp on songs ranging from "Happy Days Are Here Again" to "Who's Afraid of the Big Bad Wolf?"

Her choice of material was also a signature aspect of Streisand's work during that time. Though she was younger than the folk singer Bob Dylan and the Beatle John Lennon, she never belonged to their musical era, and her music from the 1960s contains barely a hint of the troubles afoot in the nation at the time. In the grand tradition of the chanteuse, the diva, and the crooner, she sang songs written by others, and most often the songs themselves dated to the time before she was born. Only in the 1970s did she begin to release pop hits. Typical of her fascination with the pre–World War II era was Streisand's interest in Fanny Brice, a Ziegfeld Follies star of the 1910s and 1920s. The actor Barry Dennen, whom she met in 1961 (they were involved romantically for a time), shared that interest and helped her create a nightclub show built around songs that Brice had made famous.

By then Streisand had begun working at the Blue Angel, a well-known incubator of young talent, and there a Broadway producer discovered her in early 1962. He signed her to the part of Miss Marmelstein, a frumpy secretary in *I Can Get It for You Wholesale,* which opened in March 1962. The show ran for nine months, and by the time it ended, Streisand found herself greatly in demand. She had always wanted to be an actress, not a singer, but the biggest opportunities at first were chiefly musical. Signed by Columbia Records in late 1962, she released *The Barbra Streisand Album* and *The Second Barbra Streisand Album* in February

and October 1963, respectively. Both sold well, and the first of them won Streisand her first Grammy awards, for album of the year and best female vocal. Also in 1963, on 21 March, Streisand married the actor Elliott Gould, with whom she later had her only child, Jason.

The year 1964 brought still more successes, beginning with *Barbra Streisand/The Third Album,* released in February. Then, thanks in large part to her experience portraying Fanny Brice, Streisand bested such experienced performers as Anne Bancroft and Mary Martin to secure the lead in *Funny Girl,* a Broadway show based on Brice's career. The production, which called on her to act, sing, and combine comedy with drama, ideally suited Streisand's gifts and won her the first of many Golden Globe Awards. A successful album, based on the musical, appeared late in the year. September 1964 saw the release of *People,* her biggest-selling album yet, which won her another Grammy Award.

In 1965 Streisand appeared in a one-woman television special, *My Name Is Barbra,* which was followed by an album of the same name. The album won her another Grammy, and the television special garnered her two Antoinette Perry (Tony) awards. *My Name Is Barbra,* the album cover of which features a picture of Streisand as a little girl, is not to be confused—even though the titles mean the same thing—with *Je M'appelle Barbra,* a 1966 album. Also in 1966 Streisand made another television special, *Color Me Barbra,* which was accompanied by an album as well. A third TV special, *The Belle of 14th Street* (1967), aired in Europe as well as in North America. Although this show did not spawn an album, two more recordings, *The Christmas Album* and *Simply Streisand,* were released that year.

Streisand continued to release albums throughout the late 1960s and early 1970s, including *A Happening in Central Park* (1968), a recording of a show also broadcast on television; *What About Today?* (1969); *On a Clear Day You Can See Forever* (1970); *Greatest Hits* (1970); *Barbra Joan Streisand* (1971); and *Stoney End* (1971). The title song of the latter gave Streisand her first pop hit, but by the early 1970s, an attack of stage fright, combined with concerns for her safety—she had received a death threat in 1967—brought an end to touring. (More than twenty years later, in the early 1990s, Streisand came out of seclusion and again performed live.)

Even as Streisand the singer retreated from the stage—though she continued to turn out dozens of studio albums in the years that followed—the late 1960s offered more opportunities to Streisand the actor. In 1968, the same year she read the book that would later become *Yentl,* Streisand made her film debut—fittingly enough—in *Funny Girl.* Her Fanny Brice established a prototype for the character she would develop in many other motion pictures: an unattractive but intelligent Jewish woman who, through sheer determination and inherent moral superiority, triumphs over circumstances and wins the love of a handsome gentile man. *Funny Girl* won Streisand the first of several Academy Awards.

After *Funny Girl*, Streisand made two more musicals, *Hello Dolly!* (1969) and *On a Clear Day You Can See Forever* (1970). Then she ventured into new territory with *The Owl and the Pussycat* (1970), in which she played a foul-mouthed prostitute, as well as the zany *What's Up, Doc?* and the feminist comedy *Up the Sandbox* (both 1972). Other notable Streisand pictures include *The Way We Were* (1973), often cited as a career high point; *Funny Lady* (1975), in which she reprised the role of Brice; *A Star Is Born* (1976); *Nuts* (1987); and *The Prince of Tides* (1991), which Streisand directed.

Divorced from Gould in 1971, Streisand married the actor James Brolin on 1 July 1998. Her successes in the 1960s and thereafter present a stunning record of achievement, with lifetime earnings that exceed $100 million. She has received countless awards and sold a staggering number of recordings, as reflected by several facts about her career. Not only has she won more Golden Globe Awards than any other entertainer, but she also was the first performer ever to win Academy, Emmy, Grammy, *and* Tony Awards. She is also the only person to win Academy Awards for both acting and songwriting, and her *Higher Ground* (1997) set the record for the longest time between a performer's first and most recent number-one albums: thirty-three years.

All of these superlatives, however, still fall short of identifying the contribution to the national culture that Streisand made in the 1960s. At a time when Americans equated success and acceptability with a waspish background, and people of noticeable ethnicity—especially Jews—went to such lengths as changing their names or even their appearances, Streisand took exactly the opposite approach. In becoming a star, she did so on her own terms, and it was a hallmark of changing attitudes in the 1960s that by the end of the decade, *Hello Dolly* depicted Streisand, once the ugly duckling, as a woman of beauty.

★

Among the countless biographies covering Streisand's entire career, one that particularly addresses her life in the early 1960s is Barry Dennen, *My Life with Barbara* (1997). Notable early biographies include James Spada, *Barbara, the First Decade* (1974), and René Jordan, *The Greatest Star* (1975). Later biographies of note are Randall Riese, *Her Name Is Barbra* (1993); Spada, *Streisand: Her Life* (1995); and Anne Edwards, *Streisand: A Biography* (1997).

JUDSON KNIGHT

STYRON, William Clark, Jr. (*b.* 11 June 1925 in Newport News, Virginia), award-winning novelist who created a storm of controversy with his fictionalized account of an 1831 slave insurrection, *The Confessions of Nat Turner* (1967), and whose other works examine pain, self-knowledge, and evil through a masterly control of diverse points of view.

Styron was the only child of William Clark Styron, an engineer at the Newport News shipyards, and Pauline Margaret Abraham Styron, a musician who died after a ten-year struggle with breast cancer when her son was barely fourteen. Styron then boarded at Christchurch, an Episcopal boys' school in Virginia, and continued as a self-described "indifferent student" at Davidson College from 1942 to 1943. He served in the United States Marine Corps from 1944 through 1945; he was briefly recalled to active duty in 1951 during the Korean conflict. Styron completed his education at Duke University, earning a bachelor's degree in 1947.

Critical acclaim followed the publication of Styron's first novel, *Lie Down in Darkness* (1951), which owed much to the influence of William Faulkner. Styron sailed to Europe, where he became a founding member of the literary journal the *Paris Review* and wrote the statement of purpose in its first issue. On 4 May 1953 he married Rose Burgunder, a poet and social activist. They moved to Roxbury, Connecti-

William Styron. THE LIBRARY OF CONGRESS

cut, in October 1954 and began raising a daughter, the first of their four children.

From 1954 Styron worked on his second novel, *Set This House on Fire* (1960). Early in the novel the American narrator in Italy, Peter Leverett, articulates a perspective that may account for the behavior of many Americans in the restless decade of the 1960s: "[W]e Americans are . . . nervous and driven [because] . . . our past is effaced almost before it is made present; . . . almost nothing remains for us to feel or see, or to absorb our longing." Although the novel was only moderately successful in the United States, its French translation (*La proie des flammes*) was highly praised and hugely successful.

Publication of *The Confessions of Nat Turner* (1967) was both an effect and a cause of racial unrest, which Styron called "the storm center of the most inflammatory public issue in the U.S." As a child, he had seen a commemorative plaque referring to the 1831 slave rebellion; as an adult, he reflected on the segregated society in which he had grown up. His intellectual curiosity inspired his interest in researching the Turner rebellion, and with perceptive sensitivity he created a fictionalized spokesman for the Negroes both in the 1830s and in the present time. Styron wrote in *Harper's* (April 1965) that he wanted "to break down the old law, to come to *know* the Negro," a knowledge that is "the moral imperative of every white Southerner." He received the 1968 Pulitzer Prize for *Nat Turner* and an honorary degree from the historically African-American Wilberforce University. Many black writers, however, resented Styron's choice to speak from Turner's point of view; they attacked the numerous details he created in describing the motivations and background of Nat Turner, about whom little is known. The African-American novelist James Baldwin, however, affirmed Styron's approach when he wrote, "He has begun the common history—ours." Styron remembers being influenced by the American civil rights leader and writer W. E. B. DuBois's statement in *The Souls of Black Folk* (1903) that "the color line" would be the central problem of the United States in the twentieth century. "I believed it when I wrote *Nat Turner* and I still believe it," Styron said in 1992.

Calling himself a "dissenting Democrat," Styron contributed five words to President Lyndon Baines Johnson's 1964 civil rights speech: "our unending search for justice." He traveled to the famously confrontational August 1968 Democratic convention to argue the case that one candidate, Senator Eugene McCarthy, deserved more official delegates. A committee, however, denied the point, thus preventing Styron and others from being those pro-McCarthy delegates. He did, however, remain in Chicago and witnessed the rioting that ensued when police tried to break up antiwar demonstrations in the streets outside the convention. Further, he acted as a witness for Abbie Hoffman, one of the famous Chicago Eight who stood trial for inciting a riot. J. Edgar Hoover, head of the Federal Bureau of Investigation, had started a file on Styron as early as 1961, when he and James Baldwin wrote a public letter protesting Hoover's defense of the death penalty. The file was kept current at least through April 1970; it included references to the 1968 Democratic convention and Styron's "associations with people of leftist sympathies."

Styron epitomized the sixties in his themes—racial unrest and self-knowledge—and in his actions. From slavery and segregation to the Holocaust, he focused on subjects carrying great emotional weight in the turbulent decade. His first extended article on a social issue, "The Death-in-Life of Benjamin Reid," published in *Esquire* in February 1962, maintained that the death penalty was illogical and inappropriate. He wrote, "As for Ben Reid, in arbitrarily inflicting upon him the sentence of death, in denying him even the chance of rehabilitation that we have just as arbitrarily granted others, we have committed a manifest injustice; and the death penalty, once again, reveals its ignoble logic." In 1970 Styron received the William Dean Howells Medal from the American Academy of Arts and Letters, concluding the decade in which he was both heavily attacked and greatly praised.

Styron first compared American slavery and the Nazi death camps in a magazine article he wrote in 1963. He wrote a *New York Times* op-ed article in 1974, "Auschwitz's Message," reflecting on anti-Semitism, Christian guilt, and Hitler's gentile victims. His broader interpretation was that the death camps were not merely anti-Jewish; they were "anti-human. Anti-life." This idea became a guiding theme in *Sophie's Choice* (1979), which was made into a successful film. The narrator is Stingo, a New Yorker who comes to know Sophie Zawistowska and finally to understand her anguished response to imprisonment by the Nazis.

Styron's third major work resulted from an encounter at age sixty with a major depressive episode that neither therapy nor drugs relieved. He described the experience of his illness in the memoir *Darkness Visible* (1990). Since that time he has advocated tirelessly to erase the stigma attached to depression and other mental illnesses.

Perhaps the most significant of Styron's contributions is his daring use of the narrative persona. He has made all of us see the world through the eyes of the Reverend Nat Turner and the eyes of Stingo and of anyone going through the horrors of depression. Styron continues to work on his novel in progress, *The Way of the Warrior,* dividing his time between homes on Martha's Vineyard and in Roxbury. He and his wife still pursue their long-term advocacy of Amnesty International.

★

Styron's papers are collected at Duke University and the Library of Congress. The excellent 1998 biography by James L. W.

West III, *William Styron: A Life,* is supplemented by West's edited texts in *Conversations with William Styron* (1985), some of which are translated from French interviews. Critical works about *The Confessions of Nat Turner* include John Henrik Clarke, ed., *William Styron's Nat Turner: Ten Black Writers Respond* (1987), and James Baker, *Nat Turner: Cry Freedom in America* (1998). For critical appraisal of all of Styron's works, see Samuel Coale, *William Styron Revisited* (1991); Daniel William Ross, *The Critical Response to William Styron* (1995); and Abigail Cheever, "Prozac Americans: Depression, Identity, and Selfhood," *Twentieth Century Literature* 46 (Fall 2000): 346.

DESSA CRAWFORD

SULLIVAN, Edward Vincent ("Ed") (*b.* 28 September 1902 in New York City; *d.* 13 October 1974 in New York City), television variety show host who is forever remembered for introducing and making household names of Elvis Presley and the Beatles on his extraordinarily successful *Ed Sullivan Show.*

Sullivan's parents were Peter Arthur Sullivan, a customs inspector, and Elizabeth Smith Sullivan, an amateur painter. He had six siblings, two of whom died. Sullivan's family moved to Port Chester, Westchester County, New York, in 1907, when he was five years old. He studied at Saint Mary's Parochial School and graduated from Port Chester High School in 1917. In athletics he was gifted and versatile. His

Ed Sullivan (*left*) and Jackie Mason on *The Ed Sullivan Show.*

other passion was journalism, and as a teenager he wrote a regular sports column for the *Port Chester Daily Item.* After a brief stay in Chicago, where he tried to join the navy but was turned down because of his youth and lack of a birth certificate, he rejected an offer from his uncle to pay his college tuition and decided on a career in journalism.

Subsequently he worked for several newspapers, including the *New York Evening Mail, Philadelphia Ledger, New York World,* and *New York Evening Graphic.* By 1930 Sullivan was the Broadway editor for the *Graphic,* and in 1932 he became a columnist for the *New York Daily News.* His column was a regular feature of the paper for many years, appearing under the byline "Little Old New York." He married Sylvia Weinstein on 28 April 1930, and they had one daughter.

In 1947 a senior Columbia Broadcasting System (CBS) manager was impressed with Sullivan, who was acting as master of ceremonies of the Harvest Moon Ball at Madison Square Garden, and signed him as the front man for a new one-hour show called *Toast of the Town.* The program was launched on 20 June 1948 and immediately captured the interest of the nation.

Why Sullivan became both beloved and hugely popular continues to be a mystery. His large head and big smile made him quickly recognizable. Moreover, his absence of affectation and an abundance of traits that made audiences identify with him created a new sort of celebrity figure. Here was the epitome of an ordinary man who could seem gauche and awkward. However, millions of Americans embraced him because he seemed like one of them.

Profile upon profile of Sullivan talks of an "awkward, wooden, word-mangling newspaper man," but, as Tim Brooks notes, this simple-sounding man, although the antithesis of the polished television host, was "a sort of twentieth century P. T. Barnum who not only had his finger on the pulse of what was hot at the moment but could get his whole hand on it." Despite mediocre ratings in the 1950s, Sullivan's astonishing weekly appeal allowed the CBS network to demand and expect higher fees for their program advertisers.

In the 1950s Sullivan showcased the likes of Victor Borge, Margaret Truman, Hedy Lamarr, Gloria Swanson, and Bob Hope. He launched his initial program with a pair of wacky unknown comedians with the names of Dean Martin and Jerry Lewis. Then on 9 September 1956 Sullivan introduced a young truck driver from Memphis, Tennessee (originally Tupelo, Mississippi), named Elvis Presley. Sullivan spluttered and looked half-puzzled and half-dumbfounded by the gyrating hips of a white musician who somehow combined rock, blues, and folk. Presley's career was emphatically launched, and Sullivan's status as premier impresario was firmly embedded in the national mindset.

Sullivan was the genius behind not just the selection of

the acts shown on the show but the sequencing and the duration of each segment. By the time *Toast of the Town* metamorphosed into *The Ed Sullivan Show* in 1955, Sullivan, as executive producer, was not just America's most famous television personality. He had assumed the role of a cultural conduit. Sullivan crafted a variety program that was so artfully packaged that the aesthetic and athletic merged seamlessly, and American households were transformed into miniature theaters into which Italian opera, British ballet, German classical music, and Broadway dramas were introduced as wholesome divertissements.

Ron Simon, for example, describes Sullivan as a combination muse and Renaissance man who relished the opportunity to elevate popular tastes and captivate plebeian America. Sullivan presented the prima ballerina Margot Fonteyn in 1958 and then teamed her with Rudolf Nureyev in 1965. He promoted stellar American performers such as the pianist Van Cliburn and the opera sensation Roberta Peters. Exotic European divas such as Maria Callas were featured as were Pearl Bailey, Richard Burton, Julie Andrews, Sammy Davis, Jr., Yul Brynner, and Barbra Streisand. Henry Fonda read Abraham Lincoln's Gettysburg Address, and, as the 1960s progressed, Sullivan stayed up with the times and hosted the new and famous: musical acts such as the Rolling Stones, the Doors, Janis Joplin, and Martin Gaye.

Unequivocally, 9 February 1964 was Sullivan's defining moment. On that date he hosted the first of three live Beatles performances. The *Encyclopedia of Television* (1997) says it was an exclamation point in popular culture, in every sense "the beginning of a revolution in music, fashion, and attitude." Paul McCartney, in a British Broadcasting Corporation interview with Michael Parkinson (2002), said that although going to America launched the group, it was Ed Sullivan who catapulted them to fame and fortune.

Sullivan was an intense individual who wrestled with several demons. He steadfastly supported African-American entertainers during a period when there were Americans, and portions of America, committed to a policy of being separate and unequal. The tenor of the times can be gauged by Alabama governor George Wallace's 1963 statement, "I say segregation now, segregation tomorrow, segregation forever," which was roundly applauded in many quarters. The top television shows of 1965 give some sense of the whiteness of American entertainment: *Bonanza, Gomer Pyle, Bewitched, The Andy Griffith Show,* and *The Red Skelton Hour.* So Sullivan has to be seen as an activist in that he welcomed onto his show Bill "Bojangles" Robinson, Ethel Waters, Louis Armstrong, and Diana Ross. A major negative is that he was rabidly "anti-red" and a supporter of Senator Joseph McCarthy, not reticent about the public naming of entertainment people with any supposed Communist allegiance.

Although Sullivan remains best known for showcasing Presley and the Beatles, his support of homegrown comedy (people like Woody Allen, Richard Pryor, and George Carlin) and his easy rapport with sports folk heroes (Mickey Mantle and Ben Hogan) widened the appeal of his variety show and helped it reach every American constituency.

The Ed Sullivan Show reflected an era of network television when a mass audience and even a national consensus seemed possible. Sullivan became a talent scout and cultural commissar for the entire country, introducing more than ten thousand performers throughout his career. His show implicitly recognized that Americans should have an electronic exposure to all forms of entertainment, from juggling to opera.

In the late 1960s Sullivan's Nielsen ratings dropped, and the show was canceled in 1971. Sullivan's wife, Sylvia, died suddenly on 16 March 1973, and Sullivan died in New York City a year later from cancer. He is buried in Ferncliff Cemetery in Hartsdale, New York.

At the show's peak in the mid-1960s, advertisers paid $162,000 for a minute of advertising time, and Sullivan's honorarium was $20,000 a week. Until almost the end of his life he wrote two weekly columns for the *New York Daily News.* In 1971 the National Academy of Television Arts and Sciences presented Sullivan with a special Emmy Award. They spoke of him as "pioneering," commended him for his "showmanship, taste, and personal commitment," and saved the most fulsome praise for his position on race. He demonstrated "foresight and courage to provide network exposure for minority performers." On 10 December 1967 CBS renamed its studio at Broadway and Fifty-third Street the Ed Sullivan Theater.

★

For more information about Sullivan see Michael D. Harris, *Always on Sunday* (1968), Jerry Bowles, *A Thousand Sundays: The Story of The Ed Sullivan Show* (1980), and Ron Simon's excellent essay, "The Ed Sullivan Show," in Horace Newcomb, ed., *Encyclopedia of Television* (1997). Obituaries are in the *Los Angeles Times* and *New York Times* (both 14 Oct. 1974). Paul McCartney's interview with Michael Parkinson was shown on *BBC America* (16 June 2002).

SCOTT A. G. M. CRAWFORD

SUSSKIND, David Howard   (*b.* 19 December 1920 in New York City; *d.* 22 February 1987 in New York City), energetic producer of television programs, theatrical plays, and feature films, best known to the public during the 1960s as a controversial talk-show host and show business maverick.

Susskind, the son of Benjamin Susskind, an insurance sales agent, and Frances Lear Susskind, a homemaker, was one of three children. Benjamin Susskind provided a comfort-

David Susskind. AP/WIDE WORLD PHOTOS

able life for the family in Brookline, Massachusetts, and instilled in his son a strong desire for learning. Susskind was a straight-A student in high school. His natural intelligence enabled him to excel without spending long hours studying, which also freed him to engage in extracurricular activities. He worked on the school paper, belonged to the debate team, and wrote a column every week for the hometown newspaper. Susskind enrolled at the University of Wisconsin following his graduation from Brookline High School in 1938. Within a year, on 23 August 1939, the eighteen-year-old Susskind married seventeen-year-old Phyllis Briskin. The couple had three children. Susskind transferred to Harvard University in 1940 to study political science and received a B.S. degree in 1942, graduating with honors. Susskind then served in the U.S. Navy as a communications officer during World War II, stationed in the Pacific.

Upon military discharge in April 1946, Susskind accepted a job with the publicity department of Warner Bros. in New York City, where he quickly ascertained the importance of talent agents in show business. Being a talent agent was a profession he enjoyed, and after a short stint with Warner Bros., he went to work for Century Artists, an agency representing star performers. When the company

went out of business, Susskind entered a partnership with another agent, Al Levy, and they formed Talent Associates in 1948, handling primarily writers and directors. Talent Associates evolved into a creative organization that packaged and also produced television programming, films, and plays.

Live drama on television and Susskind's productions in the genre reached their pinnacles in 1957. During every week of that television season, a Susskind-produced show appeared on the air. By the late 1950s, however, the business of New York television production began to shift to Hollywood. Westerns and action-adventure series recorded on film were replacing live drama. It was an alarming trend to Susskind, who became a vociferous critic, angrily declaring, "TV is going down the drain like dirty water."

Susskind's reputation as an iconoclast was bolstered when he began hosting the syndicated talk show *Open End* in 1958. *Open End* was a weekly program of undetermined length. In other words, the show stayed on the air for as long as the host thought the conversation interesting. *Open End* attracted big-name and powerful guests from all walks of life, and Susskind proved to be a tireless inquisitor. In May 1960, for instance, he interrogated Vice President Richard Nixon for nearly four continuous hours. Often, though, his interviews sparked controversy, as when he interviewed Soviet Premier Nikita Khrushchev during his 1960 visit to the United States. Critics complained that Susskind gave the Russian leader a propaganda platform. Throughout the 1960s *Open End* was a sophisticated forum on culture and politics. America's racial crisis, the war in Vietnam, and the sexual revolution were frequent subjects.

Susskind's short, curly hair had started to gray by the time he reached his forties. His disdain for sleep was apparent in the puffy bags under his eyes, which tended to dominate his face. Even though he was not overweight, Susskind's compact stature gave the impression of stockiness, about which he was sensitive. The talk show remained his avocation while Susskind continued to be a full-time producer. Among his most critically acclaimed projects in the 1960s were the feature films *A Raisin in the Sun* (1961) and *Requiem for a Heavyweight* (1962). The debut of *East Side/West Side* in 1963, a dramatic series produced by Talent Associates, was a television landmark—representative of the kind of experimentation that marked the decade. Although the series lasted only a single season, *East Side/West Side* is a significant program in television history because of its socially controversial subject matter—such as poverty, prejudice, drug addiction, abortion, and capital punishment—and the casting of the black actress Cicely Tyson in a recurring lead role.

The stark realism of the series disconcerted viewers and sometimes made them uncomfortable. They did not know what to make of a hero (the social worker Neil Brock, played by George C. Scott) who often was dazed by moral complexities. For the Columbia Broadcasting System (CBS), the series was a bust; in fact, one-third of the advertising time went unsold. A few years later Susskind reflected on the ratings problems of *East Side/West Side*: "A gloomy atmosphere for commercial messages, an integrated cast, and a smaller, Southern station lineup, all of these things coming together spelled doom for the show. I'm sorry television wasn't mature enough to absorb it and like it and live with it." Susskind's most celebrated special of the 1960s was an innovative television presentation of Arthur Miller's *Death of a Salesman*. With Lee J. Cobb and Mildred Dunnock as Willy and Linda Loman, the production was shot in five, uninterrupted sequences staged in the round on a 360-degree set. The CBS broadcast was hailed as a video masterpiece.

Following a long separation, Susskind and his first wife divorced in 1966. That same year, on 22 April, he married the Canadian television personality Joyce Davidson, with whom he had one child. *Open End* was retitled *The David Susskind Show* in 1967, and the format changed to a standard, two-hour program taped before a studio audience. By then Susskind was a fixture in American popular culture. His flamboyant language skills and feisty demeanor were the stuff of parody. In the prehistoric animated town of Bedrock, for example, the Flintstones' local TV station carried David Rockkind—a talk-show host who was never at a loss for words.

Throughout the 1970s and well into the 1980s Susskind continued to develop prestige programming. Among his later projects were the acclaimed miniseries *Eleanor and Franklin* and nine *Hallmark Hall of Fame* specials. Suss-

kind and his second wife were divorced in 1986, and he died the following year of heart failure. Susskind won twenty-seven Emmy awards and three Peabody awards over the course of his long television career. In 1988 he was inducted into the Academy of Television Arts and Sciences Hall of Fame. In 1990 the Producers Guild of America presented the first David Susskind Lifetime Achievement Award.

Susskind was a difficult man. Even people who loved and admired him acknowledged his mercurial personality. Still, he was embraced by performers, artists, and political figures, who respected his commitment to high standards of culture and thoughtful conversation. Susskind believed that America could be uplifted through television. His legacy is a remarkable body of work, especially that produced during the 1960s, and an unrelenting quest for excellence.

★

The personal and professional papers of Susskind, including correspondence, scripts, production materials, and clippings, are housed at the State Historical Society of Wisconsin. No full-length biographies of Susskind had been produced by 2002, but many contemporaneous articles examine his career, including Thomas B. Morgan, "David Susskind: Television's Newest Spectacular," *Esquire* (Aug. 1960). For an examination of his contributions in a historical context, see two articles by Mary Ann Watson, "Open End: A Mirror of the 1960s," *Film and History* 21, nos. 2 and 3 (May and Sept. 1991): 70–76, and "Continental Rift: David Susskind's Futile Fight to Keep TV Drama in New York," *Television Quarterly* 25, no. 4 (1992): 55–50. An obituary is in the *New York Times* (23 Feb. 1987).

MARY ANN WATSON

T

TANDY, Charles David (*b.* 15 May 1918 in Brownsville, Texas; *d.* 4 November 1978 in Fort Worth, Texas), major industrialist and entrepreneur who, during the 1960s, transformed a family leather business into an international conglomerate that included Pier One Imports and RadioShack.

Tandy was the first of two children of David, a leather merchant, and Carmen (McClain) Tandy, a housewife. He attended public schools in Brownsville and Fort Worth and started work at the age of twelve, helping his father sell shoe bindings to repair shops. His father and a partner co-owned the Hinckley-Tandy Leather Company. Tandy graduated from Texas Christian University in 1940 and entered Harvard Business School.

In 1941 Tandy joined the navy and became a supply officer stationed in Hawaii. He noticed sailors being taught knitting and needlepoint as part of recuperative therapy. Believing that the men would prefer leatherwork to needlework, he established a system of leather craft for hospitalized service personnel. In letters to his father, he noted that leather craft not only was useful in military hospital units but also could be marketed in postwar civilian recreational centers. In 1945 Tandy married Gwendolyn Purdy Johnson, a widow with two children.

Tandy was discharged as a lieutenant commander in 1947, and he and his family returned to Fort Worth. His father made him the manager of his company's leather craft division. After the war American companies entered a new era of producing a vast supply of consumer goods for families with more time for hobbies and do-it-yourself activities. Tandy's career has made handicraft almost synonymous with "Tandycraft."

After buying out his partner, Tandy's father gave his son more control of the business. In 1950 Tandy opened two leather craft retail stores and began an aggressive mail-order business. Advertisements appeared in such national magazines as *Popular Science*. Whenever there were at least one thousand mail-order customers in a concentrated area, he contracted with a local partner to start a retail business. The partner put up 25 percent of the capital. Tandy took a personal interest in store managers and encouraged employees through profit sharing. As more retail stores opened, his market share expanded, and by the early 1960s, the newly named General American Industries, Inc., had 175 retail leather craft supermarts throughout North America.

When Tandy became the company's president in 1955, he fundamentally pioneered diversification. He acquired new divisions outside the leather business and then sold them by 1960 if they were unprofitable. The most successful new division was Tex Tan, which sold various finished leather goods and Western clothes. In 1961 the company was renamed Tandy Corporation, with its headquarters in downtown Fort Worth. Eventually, the Tandy Center occupied eight blocks and included shopping areas, offices, and an ice-skating rink.

As president and chairman of the corporation's board,

Tandy further diversified throughout the 1960s. In 1961 he bought Corral Sportswear, Cleveland Crafts, and Merribee Art Embroidery Company. His Tandy Marts expanded craft and hobby merchandise. His philosophy was "You can't sell from an empty wagon," and thus his retail stores carried high inventories and short delivery times. In 1962 he founded Pier One Imports, based on the San Francisco importer Cost Plus. A strong U.S. dollar allowed Pier One to import furniture and knickknacks at rock-bottom prices. That division supplied a national audience of students and other first-time buyers with furniture and other household items, and the exotic appeal of its merchandise reflected the fashions of the 1960s.

Also in 1962 and into 1963 Tandy expanded into electronics. During those years Tandy acquired two smaller firms, Electronics Crafts of Fort Worth and RadioShack of Boston. RadioShack had been a bankrupt, nine-store chain supplying ham radio equipment. (When early wireless equipment was first installed on ships, the wooden structure built on the open upper decks was known in navy slang as the "radio shack.") As he had previously done with leather goods, craft items, and inexpensive furniture, Tandy aggressively expanded the potential of the industrial and consumer electronics industry. In 1966 he sold the Pier One chain to its division management and concentrated on building up RadioShack.

By the end of the 1960s, Tandy had diversified his conglomerate's portfolio even further. Craft and hobby divisions now manufactured and sold mosaics, needle crafts, wood, ceramic tiles, metalwork, jewelry, plastics, plaster, glass, and basketry. Tandy also sold the tools for each craft. Divisions included Craftool Co., Clarke and Clarke Ltd., and ColorTile stores. In addition, Tandy bought and expanded Wolfe Nurseries and Leonard's Department Stores.

Tandy's major success internationally was RadioShack. By the end of the 1960s Tandy had bought or built twenty manufacturing plants in Asia and North America. First nationally and then globally, Tandy's supplying divisions equipped several hundred stores by the late 1960s with a full range of electronic products. RadioShack radios, televisions, and audiotape and, later, videotape recorders were complemented by supplies for the goods. Batteries became the leading auxiliary product. By 1969 Tandy had increased the number of RadioShack outlets to 530, and the chain had become a household name. Moreover, Tandy stressed customer satisfaction and guaranteed complete refunds for defective models or service.

Still later, in the 1970s and 1980s, RadioShack sold citizen-band radios. RadioShack was also one of the first corporations to enter into the field of microcomputers. In the mid-1970s, Tandy's TRS-80 Model 100 portable computer was hugely successful. Low pricing and repair service through any RadioShack outlet assured distribution and

reassured service. Tandy's success with RadioShack led Tandy Corporation into becoming the largest and most profitable network of thousands of electronic specialty outlets in the world. Beginning in the late 1960s Tandy furthered expansion in electronics into more divisions of the corporation. RadioShack was itself complemented by McDuff Electronics, Computer City Super Centers, and the Incredible Universe electronic entertainment chain. Tandy's wife died in 1967, and in 1969 he married Anne Burnett Windfor. Tandy died of a heart attack in 1978; he is buried in Greenwood Cemetery, River Oaks, Texas.

Tandy transformed a small family leather business into a multibillion-dollar international conglomerate. Yet its heritage is based on his family's first company, which featured high-quality products retailed and serviced in networks of outlets whose managers are motivated by profit sharing.

★

There is no biography of Tandy. Important studies of his entrepreneurial success are James L. West, *Tandy Corporation: "Start on a Shoe String"* (1968), and Irvin Farman, *Tandy's Money Machine* (1992). An obituary is in the *New York Times* (6 Nov. 1978).

PATRICK S. SMITH

TAYLOR, Maxwell Davenport (*b.* 26 August 1901 in Keytesville, Missouri; *d.* 19 April 1987 in Washington, D.C.), U.S. Army officer, presidential adviser, chairman of the Joint Chiefs of Staff, and U.S. ambassador to South Vietnam, who helped shape U.S. foreign and military policy during the Vietnam War.

Taylor was the only child of John E. M. Taylor, an attorney, and Pearle Davenport, a homemaker. He attended public schools in Kansas City, Missouri, where, through accelerated studies, he graduated from Northeast High School at age fifteen. Taylor spent summers on the farm of his maternal grandparents, Milton and Mary Eliza Davenport, where his grandfather regaled him with stories of his service in the Confederate cavalry during the Civil War. As his interest in the military grew, Taylor falsified his age by one year in order to register for the draft in 1918. When World War I ended before he was drafted, Taylor secured an invitation to take the entrance exams for both the U.S. Military Academy and the U.S. Naval Academy. He failed the geography portion of the naval exam but passed the army exam and enrolled at West Point in the fall of 1918. Taylor later joked, if the Strait of Malacca had been in the Mediterranean, he might have ended up an admiral instead of a general. As he did with his high school studies, Taylor distinguished himself as an excellent student at the military

Maxwell Taylor. NATIONAL ARCHIVES AND RECORDS ADMINISTRA-TION

academy, particularly in the field of foreign languages, and he graduated in 1922, fourth in a class of 102 cadets. On 26 January 1925 he married Lydia "Diddy" Gardner Happer, whom he had met at a Saturday evening dance in 1920. They had two sons.

From 1922 until 1941 Taylor continued his military training at the Army Engineers School at Camp Humphreys, Virginia; the Artillery School at Fort Sill, Oklahoma; the Command and General Staff School at Fort Leavenworth, Kansas; a Japanese-language training program at the U.S. embassy in Tokyo, Japan; and eventually the Army War College in Washington, D.C. He also briefly served as a military attaché in Peking, China, and returned to West Point for five years (1927–1932) to teach French and Spanish.

When World War II erupted, Taylor helped organize the army's first airborne division, the 82nd, at Camp Claiborne, Louisiana. Commissioned a brigadier general, he traveled overseas in 1943 to participate in the Allied forces landings at Sicily and Italy. While in charge of the 101st Airborne Division in 1944, Taylor became the first major general to land at Normandy on D-Day. Although wounded in Holland later that year, he subsequently led his "Screaming Eagle" paratroopers in the defense of the Bastogne during the Battle of the Bulge in December 1944. Upon returning to the United States in 1945, Taylor be-

came the thirty-seventh superintendent of the U.S. Military Academy at West Point, where he revised the curriculum to include more courses in the humanities. In 1949 he relinquished the post to become the U.S. military governor in Berlin for two years, followed by two years of service as deputy chief of staff for operations and administration of the army. In 1953 he took charge of the Eighth Army in South Korea and led them in the last major battle of the Korean War, as well as assisting in the postwar reconstruction effort.

For Taylor, the 1960s began five years early, as the U.S. military commitment in Vietnam began to escalate following the French defeat in the region in 1954. He served as U.S. Army chief of staff from 1955 to 1959, during which time he became a vocal critic of President Dwight D. Eisenhower's "New Look" defense strategy, which stressed the development of an overwhelming nuclear arsenal, as opposed to conventional forces, as the centerpiece of U.S. military might. Although loyalty to his branch of service no doubt colored his opinions, Taylor harbored serious concerns that reliance on nuclear weapons would leave the United States without a conventional option to fight in smaller, regional conflicts that might pose a significant threat to the nation's security, such as the one unfolding in Vietnam. He also emphasized that the Soviet Union's recent development of atomic capabilities diminished the advantage once held by the United States and required a renewed emphasis on developing a stronger conventional armed force. Specifically, Taylor proposed maintaining a well-manned conventional force equipped and trained in the use of tactical nuclear weapons. He explained his view on national security in his book *The Uncertain Trumpet* (1960). "Flexible Response," he wrote, enabled the U.S. military to handle a variety of threats, from counterinsurgency brush wars to Communist national liberation fronts, as well as nuclear conflicts. Angered by Eisenhower's refusal to consider his proposals fully, Taylor retired from the army when his term as chief of staff ended in 1959.

Following a short-lived stint as president of the Lincoln Center for the Performing Arts in New York City from 1960 to 1961, Taylor reemerged on the military and political scene as an adviser to President John F. Kennedy in 1961. Kennedy, who had read Taylor's book and incorporated several of his military proposals concerning regional conflicts and conventional forces into his presidential campaign, saw in the retired general a perfect addition to the "best and the brightest" who surrounded him in the White House, a military intellectual who was as adept in the classroom or with a pen as he was on the battlefield or leaping from a plane. Still suffering from the sting of an embarrassing defeat in the Bay of Pigs fiasco, Kennedy asked Taylor in April 1961 to head an investigation of the failed effort to unseat Fidel Castro from power in Cuba. After issuing his final report, in which he recommended that the Central Intelligence Agency avoid such major operations in the future, Taylor formally became the special military adviser to the president. Mindful of Eisenhower's previous efforts to brush aside his views, Taylor at first requested the title of "the military adviser to the president." However he settled for the title of "special adviser" and set about his duties.

For his first official task as Kennedy's military adviser, Taylor led a fact-finding mission to South Vietnam. In October 1961 he traveled to Saigon with Deputy National Security Adviser Walt V. Rostow and counterinsurgency expert Col. Edward G. Lansdale to evaluate the threat that Ho Chi Minh's Communist forces posed to the stability of the South Vietnamese government, as well as to offer recommendations for U.S. foreign policy in the embattled region. Taylor subsequently reported that he found the morale among the South Vietnamese army to be very low, President Ngo Dinh Diem's political effectiveness questionable, and the state of military intelligence highly unreliable. Increased U.S. involvement was necessary, he concluded, in order to allow South Vietnam "room to breathe." In short, Taylor described the entire Southeast Asian perimeter as facing a turning point, at which it could easily fall to Communist influences or, with U.S. intervention, weather the storm and deliver a stern warning to the Soviet Union and China in the process. A "limited partnership" was necessary, he stressed, in which the United States would assume a measure of responsibility for the survival of the South Vietnamese government. Specifically, Taylor recommended that Kennedy increase economic and military aid to the Diem regime, send additional support troops and military advisers to the region, and detach a "logistical task force" of 8,000 soldiers. Ostensibly, this force would help with flood relief in South Vietnam, but the more important reason for their presence was to improve morale among the embattled army of the Republic of Vietnam, as well as to serve in combat missions should such a step become necessary. Kennedy approved all the recommendations except for the detachment of a task force, and on 22 November 1961 he initiated the "First Phase of Vietnam Program," which marked a significant escalation in the U.S. commitment to the region, a commitment based largely on Taylor's views.

On 1 October 1962 Kennedy appointed Taylor chairman of the Joint Chiefs of Staff, the highest-ranking uniformed military post in the country. During his first month in that capacity, he closely advised Kennedy on the Cuban Missile Crisis. Although not adopted, his initial recommendation was that the president should order the air bombing of the missile sites before they were fully operational, as well as enact a naval blockade to prohibit the shipment of any further offensive weapons to the region. In 1963 Taylor's influence as chairman was more keenly

felt when he helped garner crucial military support for passage of the Limited Nuclear Test Ban Treaty, on a promise from the president that he would continue underground testing and, should the Soviet Union abrogate the treaty, immediately resume atmospheric testing.

During a second fact-finding mission to South Vietnam in September 1963, undertaken with Secretary of Defense Robert S. McNamara, Taylor concluded that a victory over the Communist insurgents could be complete by the end of 1965, provided the political situation did not deteriorate further. Specifically, Taylor recommended that Kennedy stay the course with Diem and, while simultaneously urging Diem to end his repressive tactics, assure him of U.S. commitment to his struggle to eliminate the Communist threat in South Vietnam. Neither recommendation bore fruit. Diem remained reluctant to bend to the will of the United States and eventually fell victim to a military coup that resulted in his death in November. Three weeks later Kennedy was assassinated, and Taylor found himself serving as chairman of the Joint Chiefs of Staff for the new president, Lyndon B. Johnson. Two subsequent visits to South Vietnam in March and May 1964 convinced Taylor of the growing difficulties the United States faced there. After each visit, he recommended that Johnson increase the U.S. military commitment to the region short of sending combat troops, and suggested initiating a limited bombing campaign over North Vietnam. By July 1964 Johnson decided to station Taylor in Saigon as the U.S. ambassador to South Vietnam for one year, in an effort to better coordinate U.S. diplomatic and military efforts in the region, as well as to oversee the work of the 16,000 U.S. military "advisers" stationed there.

During his year of service as ambassador, Taylor continued to support a counterinsurgency campaign to defeat the Communist Vietcong and to win the hearts and minds of the villagers. He also renewed his recommendation to conduct a systematic bombing campaign of Hanoi and other strategic sites in the North. He never believed the United States would become entangled in a major ground war because Hanoi presented such an ideal and vulnerable bombing target. Johnson eventually adopted Taylor's proposals, and in February 1965 the president initiated Operation Flaming Dart to bomb select installations around Hanoi, and a few weeks later Operation Rolling Thunder, a sustained, long-term bombing campaign that lasted for the next three years. Despite his reluctance to send combat forces to Vietnam, by July 1965 Taylor reluctantly realized the necessity of such a move, and in his last act as ambassador supported General William C. Westmoreland's request for 100,000 ground troops.

When he concluded his mission in Saigon, Taylor was anxious to return to the United States and continue to work as a military consultant to the president. In his letter of resignation to Johnson, he professed "the essential rightness" of U.S. policy in Vietnam and his faith in "the ultimate success" of the strategy employed. From July 1965, until the end of Johnson's presidency in January 1969, Taylor remained unwavering in his support of the president's decisions and U.S. conduct of the war. During that time he delivered over 125 public addresses in support of the war effort, including a rancorous appearance before the U.S. Senate Foreign Relations Committee in February 1966. Even in the wake of the disastrous Tet offensive in 1968, which shattered most of the lingering public support for U.S. military involvement in Vietnam, Taylor encouraged Johnson to maintain troop levels and continue the fight in order to force North Vietnam to the negotiations table.

In June 1966 Taylor assumed the presidency of the Institute for Defense Analysis (IDA), a military research organization affiliated with the Joint Chiefs of Staff. During his three-year tenure with the IDA, Taylor supervised numerous projects and wrote his second book, *Responsibility and Response* (1967), which included several essays on national security. Although he did not serve as a military consultant for the new president Richard M. Nixon, he continued as a member of the president's Foreign Intelligence Advisory Board in 1969 before retiring. Three years later he published his autobiography, *Swords and Plowshares* (1972), to mixed reviews, and he continued to speak publicly on issues of foreign policy, as well as remaining active on the boards of several organizations. In his final book, *Precarious Security* (1976), Taylor presented a series of essays in which he dismissed the threat of Soviet expansion, chastised Congress for its interference in foreign affairs, and identified unchecked overpopulation as the next big threat facing global security.

Taylor died at the Walter Reed Army Medical Center in Washington, D.C., of amyotrophic lateral sclerosis (ALS), also known as Lou Gerhig's disease. He is buried in Arlington National Cemetery in Arlington, Virginia.

★

Taylor's papers are at the National Defense University Library, Fort McNair, in Washington, D.C., although several diplomatic and military memoranda remain classified. Taylor's autobiography, *Swords and Plowshares* (1972), provides a detailed account of his life through the Vietnam War. Subsequent biographies by Taylor's son John M. Taylor, *General Maxwell Taylor: The Sword and the Pen* (1989); and former army general Douglas Kinnard, *The Certain Trumpet: Maxwell Taylor and the American Experience in Vietnam* (1991), continue the story to his death. Obituaries are in the *New York Times* and *Washington Post* (both 21 Apr. 1987).

TODD J. PFANNESTIEL

TERRY, Megan (*b.* 22 July 1932 in Seattle, Washington), prolific writer of plays and musicals best known for *Viet Rock* (1966), the first play and the first rock musical about the Vietnam War.

Terry was born Marguerite Duffy, the only child of Harold Joseph, a businessman, and Marguerite (Henry) Duffy, a housewife. After attending a theater production at the age of seven, Terry wanted to be involved with all aspects of theatrical production. She would write, direct, and design sets for productions in her family's backyard and avidly took part in school theatricals. During her senior year in high school, Terry became a member of the local community theater company of the Seattle Repertory Playhouse under the direction of Florence and Burton James. Their liberal politics tinged their works and influenced Terry's later use of political commentary within plays. The Jameses also believed that rehearsing and producing plays should be occasions for actors not just to perform a part in a play but also to experience an intense involvement within a theatrical community. This philosophy would become a hallmark of Terry's career.

While attending college in Alberta, Canada, Terry met the comedienne Myra Benson, whose caustic sense of humor and impeccable timing contributed to Terry's later use of absurd comic moments counterposed with dramatic tension. In Alberta, she earned certificates in directing, design, and acting at the Banff School of Fine Arts (1952–1953). Banff housed all the disciplines of art under one roof and emphasized collaboration between the arts as a total work of art. Terry decided to become a playwright at that time, because then she could be responsible for the entire staging and environmental effect on an audience, as reflected in early works like *Beach Grass* and *Go out and Move the Car* (both 1955). She finished her education in Seattle, earning a B.Ed. at the University of Washington (1956). While she was there, Terry taught drama at the Cornish School of Allied Arts and formed the acting troupe called the Cornish Players (1954–1956). She experimented in allowing the troupe to use improvised techniques in class and to prepare scripted scenes. Terry intensified the use of improvisation when she moved to New York City in 1956.

Terry's first years in New York City involved acting and writing. She supported herself by acting in television serials, and she began writing short pieces with naturalistic plot constructions and with themes of sardonic pathos (*Ex-Miss Copper Queen on a Set of Pills,* 1956). Her work became increasingly influenced by the theater of the absurd, and she would juxtapose a conventional plot with interpolations of nonsense language and bits of pantomime (*The Magic Realists,* 1960). In 1963 she met Joseph Chaiklin, the founder of the Open Theater (1963–1973). He had been until then a member of Julian Beck and Judith Malina's radically political and communal group, the Living Theatre. Chaiklin intensified the idea of the cooperative nature of an ensemble acting troupe initiated by Beck and Malina. He premised that the Open Theater would be a completely democratic ensemble that collectively interacted to create works without regard to any traditional boundaries of author, actor, or member of the crew. In 1964 the Internal Revenue Service closed the Living Theater, and that troupe went to Europe for a four-year self-imposed exile. With Beck and Malina gone, the resolve of the Open Theater intensified.

Chaiklin invited Terry to be the Open Theater's resident writer and director of the troupe's weekly acting workshops. Terry's earlier experiments in allowing actors to improvise during rehearsals became, within the context of the Open Theater, a radical program of communal engagement in the nonhierarchical and collaborative ensemble of a theater troupe. As such, a "play" was to be created and presented as a continuing process, not as an end product. Improvised performances were to depict responses by actors to exercises in workshops and then to more settled compositions of those exercises by a "playwright." Moreover, themes were to reflect a profound social engagement that questioned assumed perceptions and acceptances of American culture.

Terry provided collaborative exercises designed to prompt and inspire the actors. For Terry the most important of these exercises was "transformation," in which the actors, using improvised dialogue and actions, would transform into characters coping with various predicaments, such as dealing with moments of aggravated or neurotic family life or with predicaments of an increasingly depersonalized society. These exercises fueled Terry's works for several years (*Keep Tightly Closed in a Cool Dry Place* and *Gloaming, Oh My Darling,* both from 1965). The works were performed by the troupe at the Sheridan Square Theater or the Martinique Theater.

Terry's *Viet Rock* (1966) represents the Open Theater's landmark production. It grew out of earlier workshop improvisations as a communal theatrical practice, and it provided radical social engagement as a commentary. Moreover, it was the first play and the first rock musical dealing with America's involvement in Vietnam. *Viet Rock* was presented first at Ellen Stewart's La Mama Experimental Theater Club, then at the Yale School of Drama, and finally at the Off-Broadway Martinique Theater. Before it opened at Yale, Terry told a newspaper reporter that *Viet Rock* was about the "futilities and irrelevancies" of war in general and the "nightmares, fantasies, regrets, terrors, confusions" of the Vietnam War specifically. *Viet Rock* conveys "the bombardment of impressions we get from the mass media" as well as firsthand testimonials about the war. The production was conceived as a "folk war movie." It staged startlingly juxtaposed intimate scenes (a boy crawling on his belly lifting his head and saying, "I can't wait till I get there and make a killing on the black market!") on a stage filled with actors performing rock numbers ("Let's go gay with L.B.J.!"). Like channel surfing, unexpected moments collide. As with the transformation exercises done earlier in workshops, *Viet Rock* transformed personal stories into an-

tiwar testimonials and rock and roll into bitter satire. Reviews were mixed, but *Viet Rock* became Terry's most well-known work.

Terry left the Open Theater group after this production and became the resident writer for the Minneapolis Firehouse Theater and then the Omaha Magic Theatre, where she has remained as playwright in residence and literary manager (from 1974). She periodically returned to New York City for individual projects for public radio or television (*Home: Or Future Soap,* 1968), the La Mama troupe (*Changes,* 1968), and the Open Theater's final production (*Nightwalk,* 1973). From the 1970s Terry's works have examined the life of the early-twentieth-century French philosopher Simone Weil (*Approaching Simone,* which received the 1970 Obie Award for best off-Broadway play), family issues (*Goona Goona,* 1979), and feminist issues (*American King's English for Queens,* 1978). In fact, Terry is an early and extremely influential feminist playwright and played an important role in the development of the genre for thirty years.

For Terry, transformation is a structural principle for actors in training and a montage effect for scenes within a play in order to provoke social engagement. A play or musical is an intense involvement between actors and audience and among actors and other members of a theatrical group or community. Theater is artistic and rhetorical, personal and communal, feminist and humanist.

★

Terry's manuscripts are in the collections of the Lincoln Center Library of the Performing Arts, New York City, and the Omaha (Nebraska) Public Library. There is no book-length biography of Terry. Collections of Terry's plays include *Viet Rock and Other Plays* (1967), *Three One-Act Plays* (1971), and *Right Brain Vacation Photos: New Plays and Production Photographs, 1972–1992* (1992). Terry wrote "Who Says Only Words Make Great Drama?" for the *New York Times* (10 Nov. 1968). About her work, see Robert Pasolli, *A Book on the Open Theater* (1970), and James Wallace Larson's dissertation, *Public Dreams: A Critical Investigation of the Plays of Megan Terry, 1955–1986* (University of Kansas, 1988). Also see Dan Sullivan, "Play on Vietnam to Open at Yale," *New York Times* (26 Sept. 1966).

PATRICK S. SMITH

THOMAS, David R. ("Dave") (*b.* 2 July 1932 in Atlantic City, New Jersey; *d.* 8 January 2002 in Fort Lauderdale, Florida), fast-food entrepreneur and founder of Wendy's restaurants.

Thomas, an adopted child, lived for the first five years of his life in Kalamazoo, Michigan, with his adoptive parents, Rex, a construction worker, and Auleva, a homemaker. After Auleva died of rheumatic fever in 1937, Rex remarried, moving his family to various locations in the Midwest and South, where he could find employment. Thomas spent most of his summers with his adoptive grandmother, Minnie Sinclair, whom he described as a compelling and uncompromising religious woman who gave him the one thing his father had not, a refuge from his isolation. Still, by 1947, Thomas estimated that his family had moved at least twelve times as jobs appeared in various towns. He never really felt as if he belonged with his family and came to find security in work.

The seeds of Thomas's interest in the food-service industry came from his early work experiences helping his adoptive father pay the bills. Thomas began his career at the Hobby House, a local restaurant in Fort Wayne, Indiana. When the family relocated yet again, Thomas decided to stay at his job and work his way up. Living at the local Young Men's Christian Association, he even dropped out of school to focus on his work. His career goals were delayed temporarily by his entry into the army during the Korean War. Thomas went to Fort Benning, Georgia, where he attended the army's Cooks and Bakers School. Sent overseas to Germany, he served as a staff sergeant and a cook.

After his military service, Thomas returned to the Hobby House, working as a short-order cook. When his boss, Phil Clauss, opened a second restaurant, Thomas became the assistant manager there. In the mid-1950s, Clauss began working with Harland Sanders (later known as Colonel Sanders). Thomas was taught how to prepare chicken using Sanders's recipe and how to sell it to customers. In the latter half of the 1950s Clauss bought four Kentucky Fried Chicken (KFC) franchises in Columbus, Ohio. But the restaurants failed to make a profit, so he offered to sell 45 percent of his ownership to Thomas if he was able make them solvent. Thomas had married Lorraine Buskirk in 1954, and by that time they had four children to support, with a fifth, their last, on the way—he was determined to succeed.

In 1962 Thomas moved his family to Columbus so he could run the four restaurants. Under his leadership, the four not only became solvent but also made a profit. Sanders became Thomas's mentor, and he took advantage of the experience, learning everything he could from the fried chicken entrepreneur about the quickly evolving fast-food industry. Thomas helped create the new famous revolving Kentucky Fried Chicken sign, and according to Nancy Millman of the *Chicago Tribune,* he helped persuade Sanders to appear in his own commercials. It was a move that boosted profits for KFC and made Sanders a familiar face in the late 1960s and early 1970s. Having made his four franchise shops profitable, Thomas sold them back to KFC in 1968. The move made him a millionaire, and he was invited to take a position at the parent company. Thomas stayed only briefly at KFC headquarters, because of a business conflict with John Y. Brown, Jr., another executive. Brown and Jack Massey had bought KFC from Sanders in the mid-1960s.

Thomas then took his money and used part of it to build his own chain of restaurants, whose specialty was fresh-cooked made-to-order hamburgers, not ones made from frozen meat patties. For his freshly cooked hamburgers he offered customers a variety of toppings. Sandwiches were never prepared in advance, and diners always got a hot, fresh, and juicy sandwich on a square bun. The original menu at his new restaurant consisted of made-to-order hamburgers, chili, french fries, soft drinks, and the Frosty Dairy Dessert. To make his restaurants even more inviting, Thomas created a relaxed, homey atmosphere with carpeting, Tiffany-style lamps over the tables, and Bentwood chairs. As a final touch, Thomas used the face of a little freckled, red-haired girl in ponytails as the logo for his new business. This image was the likeness of his eight-year-old daughter, Melinda Lou, nicknamed Wendy. The first Wendy's Old Fashioned Hamburgers restaurant opened in Columbus on 15 November 1969. Thomas's new enterprise began to make a profit within six weeks of its opening.

By 1973 Thomas began to expand his restaurants across the country. He negotiated with entire cities and geographic regions, rather than selling single franchises to individual buyers. Wendy's restaurants became familiar sights in cities across the United States. Then Thomas decided it was time to step aside and let his corporate office run the business. Serving as senior chairman, he invested in other smaller businesses as his restaurant business continued to boom. In the late 1980s, however, quality began to slide, and Thomas was asked to return to a leadership position in the company. Until his death in January 2002, Thomas made folksy humorous commercials stressing the difference between Wendy's and its leading competitors. The campaign worked. By 2002 Wendy's had five hundred franchise stores for a total of more than six thousand restaurants worldwide.

Thomas in his later years came to terms with being adopted and became an advocate for foster parent and adoption programs. In 1979 he received the Horatio Alger Award for his business efforts. He also wrote his autobiography and a follow-up book that explained his restaurant business philosophy. Thomas spoke frequently to teenagers and young adults, urging them to stay in school. To prove the benefits of an education, he earned his general equivalency diploma in 1993 from Coconut Creek High School in Fort Lauderdale, Florida. Thomas continued to be active and outgoing, despite being diagnosed with cancer in the early 1990s. He died at home in Fort Lauderdale of liver cancer and is buried in Union Cemetery in Columbus.

★

Thomas's autobiographical work, *Dave's Way: A New Approach to Old-Fashioned* Success (1991), and Ron Beyma and Dave Thomas, *Well Done! Dave's Secret Recipe for Everyday Success* (1994), provide invaluable background information. The *Chicago Tribune* (2 Mar. 1993), *Forbes* (5 Aug. 1991), and *People Weekly* (2 Aug. 1993) had important articles on milestones in Thomas's career. An obituary is in the *New York Times* (9 Jan. 2002).

BRIAN B. CARPENTER

THOMAS, Marlo   (*b*. 21 November 1938 in Detroit, Michigan), actor, civil activist, and feminist, best known for her role as Ann Marie, America's "sweetheart of the sixties," in the television situation comedy *That Girl*.

Margaret Julia Thomas is the eldest child of Danny Thomas, an actor and comedian, and Rose Marie Cassaniti Thomas, a homemaker. Margo was her nickname, but she was unable to pronounce the "g," so she became Marlo. Thomas grew up in Beverly Hills, California, with her younger sister and brother. In a 1966 interview in the *New York Times,* Thomas stated that she could not think of a time when she did not want to be an actress. At age six she printed programs, announcing the next performance of "Miss Margaret Thomas." Both parents were opposed to her following her father into show business.

Marlo Thomas, 1967. © BETTMANN/CORBIS

The roots of Thomas's feminism reach back to her childhood. In a 1973 interview, also in the *New York Times,* Thomas reflects on her parents, saying that while "they encouraged me to be myself, they raised me to be a stereotype woman." At age ten she wrote a book titled "Women Are People, Too." Her father encouraged her to go to school to become a teacher. Consequently, she graduated from the University of Southern California with a B.A. in education but spent her summers working at film studios and acting in summer stock. During her last year in college, when it seemed as if everyone she knew wanted to get married and have a baby, Thomas wondered why. She felt she would never marry because she would "lose" herself if she did.

Following graduation Thomas tried to get acting jobs. For seven years, as she stated in a 1967 interview in *Look* magazine, "everyone just kept saying no." Although as a child she was "bounced on every famous show-business lap in Hollywood," Thomas could not get a decent part. "I could've made it in Bikini Goes Crazy movies," she once said, but that was not what she wanted. Her family was not happy when she went to New York to study acting with Sanford Meisner at the Neighborhood Playhouse School of Theater. In 1965, as the star of the London production of Neil Simon's *Barefoot in the Park,* Thomas won acclaim as a "great new comic actress." Thomas returned to New York to star in an American Broadcasting Company (ABC) television pilot, but the network declined to pick up the show. Although she was offered other roles, Thomas had her own ideas about what she wanted to do.

The concept for the comedy *That Girl* was Thomas's own. Television roles for young women were as "daughter of," "wife of," or "assistant to" and always were defined by men. Thomas wanted to do a show about a young woman who defined herself, lived in her own apartment, and was trying to start a career without the help of family. Both the Columbia Broadcasting System and the National Broadcasting Company television networks turned her down, but ABC took a chance on the bold proposal. Capitalizing on the new women's movement and the youth revolution during the mid- to late 1960s, the network began offering shows targeting the young female audience. Although the producers, all male, predicted failure, *That Girl* was an immediate success from its first episode in September 1966 through the final episode in September 1971.

That Girl was the first television show to focus on a single, career-minded young woman. Thomas, with her distinctive crackly voice, her flipped-up hairdo, and her stylish clothes, was a hit. Her character, Ann Marie, an aspiring actress, had left her family in Brewster, New York, and moved into her own apartment in New York City. To support herself while seeking success on the stage, she worked at a number of different jobs, providing a multitude of comic scenarios. Ann Marie also had a boyfriend, Donald Hollinger, played by Ted Bessell. The network was adamant that the relationship be chaste, and Thomas was urged continually to have her character marry Hollinger. The character of Ann Marie reflected the young women of the day in their struggle in both the male-dominated workplace and society in general. They were pressured from all sides to marry and fulfill traditional roles. Through her television character, Thomas modeled a young, attractive woman who successfully fought against these pressures. Although they became engaged during the final season, Thomas resisted network pressure to have Ann Marie and Donald marry on the last show. Instead, she dragged him to a women's liberation meeting.

Thomas was amazed by the amount of mail the show generated and the content of the mail. Questions such as "I'm seventeen and pregnant, and I can't tell my parents. Where do I go?" were not uncommon. Likewise, there were letters from women asking how to get out of abusive relationships and where to get help. Thomas and her staff tried to respond, but Thomas soon discovered that there was nowhere for these troubled women to go. She remarked in her 1999 *New York Times* interview, "It totally politicized me as a feminist." She met the feminist activist Gloria Steinem and began traveling across the country for the women's movement.

During the run of *That Girl*, Thomas won the Golden Globe for best television actress in 1967 and Emmy nominations each year from 1967 to 1970. Despite good ratings, the show was cancelled in 1971. Thomas was tired of playing a character that did not change or develop. She continued her acting career, appearing in and producing several made-for-television movies, including *It Happened One Christmas* (1977); *Nobody's Child* (1986), for which she won an Emmy; and *Ultimate Betrayal* (1994). Thomas also has appeared in numerous plays, including *Thieves* (1974), her Broadway debut; *Six Degrees of Separation* (1992–1993); and *The Vagina Monologues* (2000). Her concern for how girls were supposed to behave and how they were portrayed spurred her to put together the anthology *Free to Be . . . You and Me* (1974). Other books Thomas has compiled and edited are *Free to Be . . . a Family* (1987) and *The Right Words at the Right Time* (2002). Thomas produced television programs of both *Free to Be* books that won Emmys. She was a member of the 1968 Democratic National Committee and is a member of the National Women's Political Caucus. Following in her father's footsteps, Thomas has been involved with Saint Jude Children's Research Hospital, which was founded by Danny Thomas. She married the talk show host and political activist Phil Donahue on 22 May 1980 and helped raise his four adolescent sons from a previous marriage.

In the 1990s cable viewers were introduced to *That Girl* via reruns on the Nickelodeon cable television network, and Thomas became known to television audiences as Rachel Green's mother on the situation comedy *Friends*. She remarked in a 1996 interview, "In my last show, I was playing 'That Girl.' Now I'm playing the mother of 'That Girl.'" It was Thomas who introduced television audiences to the concept that a woman could choose to pursue a career rather than marry, live away from family without benefit of roommates, and celebrate the single life.

★

Articles on Thomas's life and career are in Judy Stone, "And Now—Make Room for Marlo," *New York Times* (4 Sept. 1966); Betty Rollin, "Marlo Thomas: That Girl Is Some Girl," *Look* (17 Oct. 1967): 124; and Katie Kelly, "Marlo Thomas: 'My Whole Life I've Had My Dukes Up'," *New York Times* (11 Mar. 1973). More recent articles, reflecting on Thomas as a trendsetter, are Jean Prescott, "'That Girl' Really Was Independent," *Tampa Tribune* (2 May 1996); Peter M. Nichols, "Television/Radio; Feminism's Unlikely Heroine," *New York Times* (30 May 1999); and Robin Finn, "Public Lives; Who Thought 'That Girl' Would Go There?" *New York Times* (17 Mar. 2000).

MARCIA B. DINNEEN

THOMPSON, Hunter S(tockton) (*b.* 18 July 1939 in Louisville, Kentucky), leading practitioner of New Journalism during the 1960s who wrote for the *National Observer* and the *Nation* before completing *Hell's Angels: A Strange and Terrible Saga* in 1966 and then establishing his unique style, known as "Gonzo journalism," as a columnist for *Scanlan's Monthly*.

Thompson is the oldest of three sons of Jack Robert Thompson, an insurance agent, and Virginia Davidson Ray. He entered I. N. Bloom Elementary School during World War II and later wrote about the local air-raid drills and the family's "victory garden." (Victory gardens began to be cultivated soon after rationing took effect during the war, to supplement the diet and to show civilian support of the war effort.) In 1954 Jack Thompson died, and his oldest son began to drift into juvenile delinquency. Thompson's rebelliousness resulted in several incidents with local law enforcement. Still, many considered the teenager charming and gifted. "He was obviously intelligent—what other juvenile delinquent carried around Plato's *Republic*?—and could be friendly, polite, and intensely loyal to friends," noted William McKeen in *Hunter S. Thompson*. Nonetheless, Thompson found himself in serious trouble when he and two friends robbed a service station. He received a sixty-day sentence. Although Thompson did graduate from high school, his prison term prevented him from receiving his diploma with his classmates.

When Thompson was released in 1956, he joined the

U.S. Air Force at the urging of the court. He was assigned to Eglin Air Force Base in Florida, and he got his first writing job as a sports editor of the *Command Courier.* While Thompson's superiors noted his talent as a reporter, they found it necessary to expunge controversial content from his articles. They also noted his disrespect for military dress and authority. When they learned that he was moonlighting for Fort Walton Beach's *Playground News* under the pseudonym of Sebastian Owl, he was honorably discharged two years before his enlistment was finished. In 1958 Thompson traveled to New York and worked temporarily for *Time* and the Middletown *Daily Record.* In 1959 he moved to Puerto Rico to write for *El Esportivo,* a bowling magazine. He also began *The Rum Diary,* a novel he would sporadically work on for many years. In the early 1960s Thompson lived for a short time in Big Sur, California, and then traveled to South America, where he became a correspondent for the *National Observer,* the sister publication of the *Wall Street Journal.* He returned to the United States in 1963 and on 19 May married Sandra Dawn Conklin. The couple moved to San Francisco, and Thompson continued writing for the *National Observer* until a dispute over the Berkeley Free Speech Movement, a 1964 protest by students against the university's prohibition of student organizations' advocacy of political causes or candidates, led him to resign. Thompson and Conklin had one child, a son, and later divorced.

Thompson returned once again to his novel until he received a letter from Carey McWilliams of the *Nation,* offering him an assignment. McWilliams wanted Thompson to write a balanced article about the motorcycle gang the Hell's Angels to counter a number of sensational articles that had appeared in *Newsweek, Time,* and the *New York Times.* With no other prospects, he agreed. After Thompson convinced the Hell's Angels that he wanted to write a truthful account of the organization, he received their cooperation. The article appeared in the *Nation* on 17 May 1965. Soon afterward, Thomson received several offers for a book about the Hell's Angels, and he accepted one from Random House.

While gathering information for the book, Thompson used part of his advance to buy a motorcycle. Like other New Journalists, he was determined to see the world from his subject's point of view. He rode with the Hell's Angels and attended events, and some Angels began visiting his house at all hours for readings from the latest installment of the book. Thompson used these visitors to his advantage by asking them to answer the door when the landlady arrived to collect the overdue rent. Thompson was also instrumental in introducing many of the Hell's Angels to Ken Kesey, the author of *One Flew over the Cuckoo's Nest* (1962), a biting commentary of life in a mental institution. The journalist and author Tom Wolfe would later recount

Kesey's adventures with the Angels in another New Journalist milestone, *The Electric Kool-Aid Acid Test* (1967).

Thompson collected material for the book over the next six months, but he fell behind the completion date. In an interview with Criag Vetter in *Playboy,* he recalled checking into a quiet hotel to write the second half of the book in four days. He bought four quarts of Wild Turkey, took amphetamines to stay awake, and ate a McDonald's hamburger each morning. Although Thompson's method was highly unorthodox, it nonetheless brought a looser, wilder quality to his prose, which he developed into a personal style. When *Hell's Angels: A Strange and Terrible Saga* was published in the summer of 1967, it became a best-seller.

Thompson began writing about politics for *Pageant* during the 1968 presidential race. He was granted an interview with Senator Richard M. Nixon with the stipulation that he avoid talking about politics. Instead, the two men discussed football for an hour. Thompson became disillusioned with election politics, however, after violence erupted in the streets during the Democratic convention in Chicago. He returned to his new home in Woody Creek, Colorado, and in 1970 he ran for sheriff in nearby Aspen. His campaign proved as unconventional as his writing style: he promised to use the office of sheriff to harass land developers. Although Thompson lost the race, he met Jann Wenner of *Rolling Stone* during the election, leading to a fourteen-year association with the rock-and-roll magazine.

Thompson is an exhilarating if controversial writer. Unlike Wolfe, who is often invisible as a narrator, Thompson thrusts himself into the center of the story. While many found his Gonzo style refreshing, others were bothered by the loss of objectivity. In 1970 Thompson began writing for *Rolling Stone,* where he worked on two of his most noted books, *Fear and Loathing in Las Vegas* (1972) and *Fear and Loathing on the Campaign Trail '72* (1973). In the 1990s he published *The Rum Diary: The Long Lost Novel* (1998) and two volumes of correspondence, *The Proud Highway: The Saga of a Desperate Southern Gentleman, 1955–1967* (1997) and *Fear and Loathing in America: Brutal Odyssey of an Outlaw Journalist, 1968–1976* (2000). In 2000 Thompson began writing an Internet column for the Entertainment Sports Network (ESPN).

★

Biographies of Thompson include William McKeen, *Hunter S. Thompson* (1991), and Peter Whitmer, *When the Going Gets Weird: The Twisted Life and Times of Hunter S. Thompson* (1993). New Journalism is discussed in the introduction to Tom Wolfe, ed., *The New Journalism* (1973). A lengthy review of *Hell's Angles: A Strange and Terrible Saga* is in the *New York Times Book Review* (29 Jan. 1967), and an interview with Thompson is in *Playboy* (Nov. 1974): 75.

RONNIE D. LANKFORD, JR.

THOMPSON, Llewellyn E., Jr. ("Tommy") (*b*. 24 August 1904 in Las Animas, Colorado; *d*. 6 February 1972 in Bethesda, Maryland), diplomat who played a key role in resolving several U.S.–Soviet crises during the 1960s.

Thompson was born the son of Llewellyn E. Thompson, Sr., a sheep rancher, and Lula L. Butcher. He graduated from Bent County High School in 1922 and afterward spent two years earning money for college. During this period he met a retired diplomat who instilled in him the dream of serving his government overseas. Thompson went on to work his way through the University of Colorado at Boulder, where he earned a B.A. in economics in 1928.

After attending a foreign-service training program at Georgetown University in Washington, D.C., while working as an accountant for Price, Waterhouse, Thompson received an appointment as a foreign-service officer in January 1929. After a posting to Colombo, Ceylon (now Sri Lanka), that lasted through 1933, he was sent to Geneva, Switzerland, where he spent the remainder of the 1930s. In 1940 he attended the Army War College in Washington, D.C., and was sent to the Soviet Union as second secretary and consul in 1941.

Arriving in Moscow during the prolonged German siege of World War II, Thompson elected to stay in the capital even as many other diplomats and dignitaries evacuated for the safety of eastern Russia. This act earned him the admiration and respect of the Russians who knew him, a

Llewellyn Thompson, following his nomination as ambassador to Russia, October 1966. ASSOCIATED PRESS AP

benefit of his experience in 1941 and 1942 that would prove at least as valuable as his knowledge of the Russian language, which he acquired at this time. A posting to London followed (1944–1946), after which he returned to Washington. On 2 October 1948 he married Jane Monroe Goelet, with whom he had two children. Thompson also had a stepchild, a daughter from his wife's first marriage.

In the immediate aftermath of the war, Thompson gained valuable experience as a diplomatic liaison. For example, he was present at the Potsdam conference in July 1945, where the Allied leaders Winston Churchill, Joseph Stalin, and Harry S Truman met to discuss the postwar structure of Europe. He attended virtually every major U.S.–Soviet conference thereafter. Postings to Rome (1950) and Vienna (1952) followed. In Austria, Thompson helped make possible two important pieces of cold war diplomacy: the Trieste settlement of 1954, which ended a border dispute between Italy and Yugoslavia, and the Austrian State Treaty of 1955, which ensured Austrian independence. The Austrian accord marked the first time in postwar history that the Soviets had willingly withdrawn their troops from territory they had gained during World War II.

Thompson's career entered an important new phase with his appointment, by President Dwight D. Eisenhower, to serve as ambassador to the Soviet Union in July 1957. There he developed a professional and personal relationship with Nikita S. Khrushchev, and he was instrumental in arranging the first visit by a Soviet leader to the United States. Khrushchev's 1959 tour of the country was a success, and on the heels of it, Thompson arranged a summit with Eisenhower, which was scheduled to occur in Paris in mid-May 1960.

Just eleven days before the summit, however, the Soviets shot down an American U-2 spy plane, piloted by Francis Gary Powers, over Russian airspace. An angry Khrushchev demanded that Eisenhower apologize, but when the president merely stated that the United States had discontinued the U-2 flights, the Soviet leader called off the summit. It was indicative of Thompson's relationship with Khrushchev that the latter publicly exonerated the U.S. ambassador for any responsibility with regard to the spy-plane incident. Appointed career ambassador in June 1960, Thompson further gained the trust of the Soviets by his refusal to grant interviews to the U.S. media or to write about his insights on the Soviet leadership.

A new international crisis emerged in August 1961, when the East Germans built the infamous Berlin Wall around West Berlin. A new U.S. president, John F. Kennedy, called on the aid of his Moscow ambassador, seeking Thompson's advice regarding how to deal with the Soviets. For his part, Thompson kept a close watch on his hosts, maintaining open lines of communication to ensure that neither side misinterpreted the comments of the other.

Once again, his handling of the situation won the admiration of Khrushchev, who praised Thompson for his efforts and even drank a toast to him at a gathering of Soviet leaders.

In the summer of 1962 the career of the fifty-eight-year-old Thompson seemed to be winding down. He left Moscow and returned to Washington, where in June he received the President's Award for Distinguished Federal Civilian Service, the highest civilian honor granted by the federal government. He planned to retire thereafter, but at Kennedy's request he agreed to remain in Washington as ambassador at large. This was a decision that would have repercussions for the entire world.

Among cold war crises, none compares to the Cuban Missile Crisis of October 1962, which began with the building of Soviet missile sites in Cuba. As a result of this act, which would place Soviet warheads just ninety miles off the U.S. coast, the two superpowers came closer to open war than ever before or since. As leaders in Washington scrambled to make a response, Kennedy proposed to his advisers—including Thompson—that he demand Soviet withdrawal of the missiles and offer in return the U.S. withdrawal of outmoded warheads in Turkey. Thompson advised against this, maintaining that while the president should by all means call for the removal of the Soviet missiles, he should not offer the abandonment of the silos in Turkey as a quid pro quo. In the end the Soviets withdrew their missiles, a superpower war was averted, and the United States ultimately did remove its missiles from Turkey—but not as a contingency to any agreement with the Soviets.

In the period leading up to the Cuban Missile Crisis, Kennedy had come to believe that Thompson had grown too close to the Soviets and would always urge concessions. Therefore, Thompson's aggressive response to the Cuban crisis helped the Moscow ambassador regain trust with the White House. His knowledge of Khrushchev's personality stood Thompson in good stead; by advising the National Security Council Executive Committee that Khrushchev would not willingly take on the risk of nuclear war, he may have helped avert World War III. Furthermore, Thompson wisely advised the U.S. leadership to allow the Soviets to save face in the aftermath of the incident and therefore not to make a great show of celebrating a diplomatic victory.

After Kennedy's assassination, President Lyndon B. Johnson kept Thompson on as ambassador at large and, in 1965, appointed him deputy undersecretary of state for military-political affairs. Then, in 1966, Johnson named him ambassador to the Soviet Union. Back again in his old post, Thompson found a much different situation from the one he had faced a decade earlier. Khrushchev was gone, ousted in large part because of his handling of the Cuban Missile Crisis; in his place Thompson found a much less

amicable figure. Unlike his predecessor, Leonid I. Brezhnev was not inclined to spend long hours with the U.S. ambassador, and therefore Thompson found himself shut out of the Soviet inner circle. This change of leadership, combined with rancor over the U.S. participation in Vietnam, made it difficult for Thompson to do business in Moscow. He did, however, manage to arrange a March 1967 meeting between Johnson and the Soviet Premier Aleksey N. Kosygin. Although as general secretary of the Communist Party, Kosygin played a secondary role to that of Brezhnev, the meeting was an important one. As a result of discussions with Johnson, Kosygin indicated a willingness to begin talks for strategic arms limitation, a move that helped pave the way for détente in the 1970s.

Thompson ended his second term as ambassador to the Soviet Union in January 1969, having served longer than any U.S. ambassador in Moscow up to that point. He then retired but continued to remain active in diplomacy during the years that remained. President Richard M. Nixon appointed him a delegate to the Strategic Arms Limitation Talks (SALT), in part an outgrowth of the earlier Johnson-Kosygin summit. Thompson was present at SALT talks in Helsinki, Finland, during November and December 1969 and again in Vienna in April 1970. A series of meetings thereafter in Helsinki and Vienna led to the SALT accords of May 1972, which marked the first U.S.–Soviet agreements to limit nuclear armaments. Ironically, Thompson died of cancer at the National Institutes of Health in Bethesda, Maryland, just three months before the SALT accords. He is buried at Las Animas Cemetery in his hometown.

In a career that spanned the most desperate days of the cold war, Thompson saw at least three phases of that conflict: the sullen antagonism of the late 1940s and 1950s; the risky brinksmanship of the early 1960s; and the exhaustion of the late 1960s, which led to the nuclear accords and uneasy peace of the 1970s. At least once, and probably many more times, he helped avert serious conflict between the two superpowers. It is indicative of his contribution to U.S. national security that he spent his last days attempting to bring about a reversal of the mad escalation in arms development that had characterized so much of the period in which he lived and worked.

★

Papers relating to Thompson's role as diplomat are housed in the National Archives in Washington, D.C., as well as in the libraries of the presidents under whose administrations he served: the Harry S Truman Library in Independence, Missouri; the Dwight D. Eisenhower Library in Abilene, Kansas; the John Fitzgerald Kennedy Library in Boston, Massachusetts (which also contains an oral history transcript); the Lyndon Baines Johnson Library and Museum in Austin, Texas; and the Richard M. Nixon Library and Birthplace in Yorba Linda, California. Tributes by

Charles Bohlen (11 Feb. 1972) and Dean Rusk (24 Feb. 1972) are in the *New York Times,* and obituaries are in the *New York Times* and *Washington Post* (both 7 Feb. 1972).

JUDSON KNIGHT

TOURÉ, Kwame. *See* Carmichael, Stokely.

TOWNES, Charles Hard (*b.* 28 July 1915 in Greenville, South Carolina), physicist and engineer who dedicated his life to applications of microwave generation and amplification and invented the maser and its optical descendent, the laser.

Townes was one of two sons of Henry K. Townes, an attorney, and Ellen Sumter Townes, who helped run the family farm. He attended elementary school, high school, and Furman University in Greenville, graduating with a dual bachelor's degree in physics and modern languages in 1935. Townes finally left his hometown to attend graduate school, obtaining a master's degree from Duke University in Durham, North Carolina, in 1936 and a Ph.D. from the California Institute of Technology, in Pasadena, in 1939, both in physics. He would have liked to go straight into academia, but given the depressed economy, he was grateful to get a job with Bell Telephone Laboratories in Murray Hill, New Jersey, earning $3,016 a year. Townes married Frances H. Brown of Berlin, New Hampshire, in the spring of 1941, and the couple had four daughters. He continued to work at Bell throughout World War II, focusing on the development of radar bombing systems; his findings eventually were incorporated into the B-52 bomber. As radars were shifted to shorter wavelengths, they became less effective; Townes discovered that the radar energy was being absorbed by ammonia and water vapor in the atmosphere. This led him to investigate microwave spectroscopy.

Townes joined the faculty of Columbia University in New York City in 1948 and soon obtained a grant from Union Carbide to do research into microwave generation. In April 1951, unable to sleep, he had an inspiration: "One should be able to put enough excited . . . molecules through a cavity to produce an oscillator. . . . The signal, I also knew, would be coherent." It took him three years to turn his vision into reality, amplifying and generating microwaves in ammonia gas by stimulated emission of radiation. He coined a term for his process: microwave amplification by stimulated emission of radiation, or MASER.

Microwaves vibrate with a relatively long wavelength— Townes was working at 1.25 centimeters, or half an inch; to achieve the same results with energy in the visible wavelengths would require working with waves only thousandths

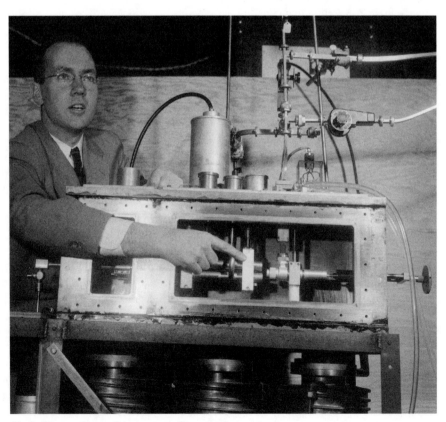

Charles Townes. CORBIS CORPORATION (BELLEVUE)

of an inch long. Nevertheless, in an article in the December 1958 issue of *Physical Review,* Townes and his associate Arthur Schawlow showed how their maser could be transformed into an optical maser, or laser. They applied for, and received, a patent for their invention on 25 March 1960, just about the same time that Theodore Maiman of Hughes Aircraft Company built the first practical laser. In 1964 Townes shared the Nobel Prize with Aleksandr Prokhorov and N. G. Basov of the Lebedev Institute in Moscow, who had independently envisioned a similar method of microwave amplification shortly after Townes's inspiration.

Townes moved his academic affiliation to the Massachusetts Institute of Technology in 1961, serving as provost for five years. During this time he also directed a special session on coherent light at the Enrico Fermi International School of Physics in Varenna, Italy, and delivered the Scott Lectures at the University of Toronto. In 1967 he became a professor at the University of California at Berkeley; his research interest since then has been the application of quantum electronics to astronomy. He became professor emeritus in 1986.

One of the highlights of Townes's career occurred in 1969, when the Apollo 11 astronauts placed reflector panels on the moon and astronomers from the University of California and the University of Texas bounced laser beams off the panels and back to Earth, measuring the distance accurately within less than one inch. A second highlight had occurred the previous year, when he detected ammonia in Sagittarius B2, near the center of the galaxy; Townes's discovery demonstrated that interstellar gas exists at much higher densities than had been thought. When radio astronomers, excited by Townes's discovery, turned their antennas toward the constellation of Orion, they found traces of water at such intensities that there was only one explanation: natural masers must occur on an astronomical scale. As Townes boasted, "A single astrophysical water maser can put out much more power than the total radiation from the sun, all at a single . . . frequency." Since then a number of such masers have been found, lending strong experimental support for the existence of black holes. After 1982 Townes shifted his focus to the infrared spatial interferometer, a device that uses a complex system of mirrors and lasers to measure the size of stars and to discover clouds of dust and gas that are invisible to normal telescopes.

Throughout his career Townes has displayed a special talent for administration. On leave from Columbia between 1959 and 1961, he served as vice president and director of research at the Institute for Defense Analysis, and he established "Jason," a regular gathering of academic scientists and industry representatives whose purpose was to make recommendations to Washington on important scientific topics, such as the development of nuclear energy, control of thermal pollution, and chemical and biological warfare.

In 1966 he was appointed to the President's Scientific Advisory Committee (a position he continues to hold) and later served as chair of both the Strategic Weapons Panel of the Defense Department and the Science and Technology Advisory Committee for Manned Space Flight of the National Aeronautics and Space Administration; in this last capacity he made the initial suggestion for the Lunar Rover. He also served as president of the American Physical Society in 1967 and on the Technical Advisory Committee for General Motors.

In addition to the Nobel Prize and numerous honorary degrees, Townes has received medals from the American Academy of Arts and Sciences, the Franklin Institute, the Institute of Physics, and the National Academy of Sciences. In 1967 he received the Institute of Electrical and Electronic Engineers' Medal of Honor "for his significant contributions in the field of quantum electronics which have led to the maser and the laser." Townes has had a brilliant academic career as a professor, administrator, and researcher, but his name always will be associated with a single innovation: the technique of wave amplification through internal reflection, leading to the stimulated emission of radiation—the laser. In *Life* magazine's 1997 poll naming the most influential people of the last millennium, Townes was 819th on the list.

★

For additional information about the development of the laser, see Charles H. Townes, *How the Laser Happened: Adventures of a Scientist* (1999).

HARTLEY S. SPATT

TOWNSEND, Lynn Alfred (*b.* 12 May 1919 in Flint, Michigan; *d.* 17 August 2000 in Farmington Hills, Michigan), accountant who became head of Chrysler Corporation during one of its periodic financial crises, guided it to profitability and stability in the 1960s, and resigned in the mid-1970s when it again approached collapse.

The only child of Lynn A. and Georgia E. Crandall, Townsend moved at an early age to Los Angeles, where his father opened an auto repair shop. His mother, a gifted teacher, home-schooled him until he entered a Beverly Hills school as a second grader. His mother died when he was nine; five years later so did his father. As a result he went to live with an uncle in Evansville, Indiana, graduating in 1935 at age sixteen from high school there. After a brief stint as a bank clerk, in fall 1936 Townsend entered the University of Michigan at Ann Arbor, sustaining himself with a series of odd jobs. A top student (his accounting professors found him "gifted"), he earned a B.A. in 1940 and an M.B.A. (with distinction) in 1941.

Townsend married Ruth M. Laing on 14 September 1940. They had three sons. In 1941 Townsend joined the accounting firm Ernst and Ernst in Detroit, leaving in 1944 to serve as a disbursing officer on the aircraft carrier *Hornet* in the Pacific. In 1946 he returned to Ernst and Ernst and the next year went along as a supervising accountant when one of its partners left to start a firm. When that firm merged into what became Touche, Niven, Bailey, and Smart (soon one of the nation's largest accounting firms) he continued as a supervising accountant, later becoming a partner as well. He was in charge of the audits of one of the firm's major clients, the Chrysler Corporation, and became an expert on its finances. In 1957 he became Chrysler's controller and in 1958 group vice president in charge of international operations.

Chrysler had serious economic problems because of administrative infighting, purchasing scandals involving the company's president, staggering overhead costs, declining market share, and an aging plant. In December 1960 Townsend was named administrative vice president of Chrysler, in effect running it on a day-to-day basis, and on 27 July 1961 he became its president, the first "bean counter" to hold the job—that is, his background was in numbers rather than manufacturing. He was, as such, a trailblazer in this new style of auto executive.

Lynn Townsend, August 1964. GETTY IMAGES

Characterized as a "smart, facile, and abrasive" executive who "brooked no interference," Townsend dramatically cut Chrysler's bloated overhead, laying off 25 percent of its white-collar employees, who nicknamed him "The Brute." He closed obsolete plants, shut down an office building, and sold off company planes. He reorganized staff and line operations, oversaw complete restyling of Chrysler's product (improving quality to the point that he could implement the industry's then most extensive warranty, which was five years or 50,000 miles on power train components), and revamped the company's dealer system. Townsend also internationalized Chrysler, buying parts of foreign companies and taking over others outright. Under his direction the company's nonautomotive activities, such as space and defense, expanded. A *Fortune* profile found that "scarcely a corner of the company has not been transformed by the Townsend regime."

Initially Townsend produced marvelous results. Chrysler's share of the U.S. automobile market, which had fallen to less than 10 percent, nearly doubled by 1967. In just three years (1961 to 1964) the company's sales rose more than 100 percent. Annual sales continued to rise dramatically (23 percent between 1964 and 1965), as did profits (for eleven of Townsend's fourteen years at Chrysler's helm, the company was profitable). By 1965 Chrysler's net income had risen almost 2,000 percent. Until 1969, each year brought improved financial results. The company's stock appreciated, becoming for a time "a Wall Street pet"; during Townsend's second year as president, the price of a share of Chrysler stock rose from $38.00 to $74.00.

In 1967 Townsend became chair of the company. He soon faced a new set of problems arising in part from what automotive journalist Brock Yates has described as the "over-riding passion" of executives "rewarded on the bonus system based on annual profits . . . to pump up sales over the short haul." Chrysler (as well as various other American manufacturers) had become more concerned with numbers than with product. For Chrysler one result was "the sales bank," a business trend that began in the early 1960s. Instead of producing cars as a result of dealers' orders, the company manufactured cars in anticipation of orders, stacking them like "cans of beans on a shelf." A limited number early in the decade (66,000 at one point) by 1969 had risen to over 400,000 vehicles stored all over Detroit in the ruinous winter weather. Quality was affected because the company rushed production in order to keep up the numbers. Cash flow was affected because dealers increasingly could acquire cars at a substantial discount and because unordered cars were assigned to the Chrysler Financial Corporation "to give . . . the semblance of . . . something that could pass for an order sheet."

When Townsend took over in 1961, despite the company's parlous state, it had been debt-free. But in 1970

Chrysler owed nearly $800 million. The recession of the early 1970s and the 1974 oil embargo severely hurt the company's finances. It lost $52 million in 1974 and $260 million in 1975. The company faced a possible shutdown. Mass layoffs took place; investment in research and development was much reduced. In July 1975 Townsend resigned as chair, supposedly at the urging of the board, although he asserted the decision was made on his own.

Townsend died at the Botsford Continuing Health Center in Farmington Hills, Michigan. The cause of death was not disclosed. He is buried in Fairview Cemetery in Linden, Michigan.

Townsend was not a car guy but rather one of the first "numbers men" who took over the U.S. auto industry. He became the president in 1961 of a distressed company and did what was necessary, if unpleasant. He had a good run during the 1960s but miscalculated severely in the 1970s and ultimately, under other management, the company had to be bailed out by the federal government.

★

There is no biography of Townsend. Interesting comments on his role at Chrysler are in Robert Sheehan, "Success at Chrysler," *Fortune* (Nov. 1965); Brock Yates, *The Decline and Fall of the American Automobile Industry* (1983); and David Halberstam, *The Reckoning* (1986). Townsend is the subject of a *Time* cover story (28 Dec. 1962). Obituaries are in the *Detroit News* (21 Aug. 2000), the *New York Times* (22 Aug. 2000), and *Automotive News* (28 Aug. 2000). See also *Current Biography* (1966) and *Who Was Who in America,* vol. XIII.

DANIEL J. LEAB

TRAVERS, Mary. *See* Peter, Paul and Mary.

TRILLING, Lionel (*b.* 4 July 1905 in New York City; *d.* 5 November 1975 in New York City), influential literary critic, novelist, and Columbia University professor whose mandarin-like prose and judgments cast a spell over the literary establishment.

The son of the Jewish immigrants David W. Trilling, a manufacturer of men's coats, and Fannie Cohen, Trilling attended New York's De Witt Clinton High School before entering, at the age of sixteen, Columbia University, from which he graduated with a B.A. in English in 1925 and an M.A. in English in 1926. On 12 June 1929 he married Diana Rubin, who also became a prominent literary intellectual. They had one child. After brief teaching stints at the University of Wisconsin–Madison and Hunter College, Trilling was offered an instructorship at Columbia in 1932. He remained at Columbia for the rest of his career. He received his Ph.D. in English literature from Columbia in 1938, following the completion of a dissertation on Mat-

Lionel Trilling. ARCHIVE PHOTOS, INC.

thew Arnold, which was published as his first book, *Matthew Arnold,* in 1939. Other critical books followed, and with such notable exceptions as *E. M. Forster* (1943) and *Sincerity and Authenticity* (1972), the majority of these came in the form of essay collections.

Resisting the tide of New Criticism, Trilling's engagement with literature was that of one especially interested in cultural and moral concerns. In the 1920s and early 1930s Trilling encountered intellectual socialism, which was centered in Greenwich Village. His interest in morality led him to rethink the prevailing dogmatic and political liberalism. He wrote in *Matthew Arnold* that liberalism should be thought of as an awareness "of the contradictions, paradoxes and dangers of living the moral life." It was a notion that finds its most articulate expression in *The Liberal Imagination: Essays on Literature and Society* (1950) and that came to be identified with the most influential period of Trilling's work.

Trilling experienced a vexed relationship with the 1960s and its upheavals. On the one hand his work helped lay the groundwork for the decade's adversarial spirit. On the other hand he was not especially pleased by what had been wrought; he openly wondered whether the 1968 campus uprisings at Columbia University and elsewhere might not be understood as evidence that civilization was now at the end of its tether. If it was, Trilling conceded, it was because thinking such as his own had helped to move it to that point. The note of concession is especially apparent in Trilling's influential 1965 collection of essays *Beyond Culture: Essays on Literature and Learning*. The phrase "beyond culture" suggests that individuals might "extricate themselves from the culture into which they were born." Doing so, in fact, was at the heart of modernism, a movement that Trilling saw as dating from the late eighteenth century, having "its apogee in the first quarter of the twentieth century," and continuing into Trilling's own day. He noted that a historian of this period "will take virtually for granted the adversary intention, the actually subversive intention, that characterizes modern writing—he will perceive its clear purpose of detaching the reader from the habits of thoughts and feeling that the larger culture imposes." Trilling argued that culture was hopelessly philistine but that one might pass beyond it by posing the questions, Is it true? Is it true for me? Living out the answers to those questions would not be easy, but success would find individuals living in harmony with their own truths.

Trilling's take on modernism would be eroded by a movement that began essentially with such Romantic artists as William Wordsworth, Samuel Taylor Coleridge, and Percy Bysshe Shelley. The movement delineated "a situation in which the artist is alone and in which his audience is small and made up of isolate individuals." The adversarial impulse of modernism had become legitimized, and the old questions were displaced by new questions: Is it true? Is it true for us? Trilling did not believe the new questions would "yield the same results as the first question," and they might "even make it harder for anyone to ask the first question." Thus, when Trilling introduced his students to modernism's most individual, most abyss-fronting texts, they came away not terror struck but complacently satisfied, mindful that in enhancing their cultural capital, they were also enhancing their social capital, something that would serve them in the real world: "I asked them to look into the Abyss, and, both dutifully and gladly, they have looked into the Abyss, and the Abyss has greeted them with the grave courtesy of all objects of serious study, saying: 'Interesting, am I not?'"

To Trilling's great chagrin, he found not one but two philistine cultures. There was mainstream culture, "satisfied with its unexamined, unpromising beliefs," and there was a culture that defined itself as mainstream's opposite, professing an allegiance "to the imagination of fullness, freedom, and potency of life," but that was, in fact, as comfortably established and welcoming as the first. Moreover, as the intent to examine, embrace, and experience freedom became fashionable, civilization, which is predicated on acts of renunciation, became increasingly taxed. Trilling,

acknowledging his debt to Sigmund Freud, wrote that fewer people were now prepared to suffer "the pain that civilization demands, . . . to say with Freud that the loss of instinctual gratification, emotional freedom, or love, is compensated for either by the security of civilized life or by the stern pleasures of the masculine moral character."

The belief that civilization had lost its mooring—itself symbolized for Trilling by the student revolts of the late 1960s—became a conviction in the critic's last works, *Mind in the Modern World* (1972) and *Sincerity and Authenticity* (1972). In the latter essays, first delivered as "The Charles Eliot Norton Lectures, 1969–1970," Trilling argued that the long tradition "of being true to one's own self" (that is, sincerity) now found itself "usurped by the darker and still more strenuous modern ideal of authenticity," which was defined by society's prescriptions. The consequence was a furthering of our sense of being fallen, or as Trilling wrote, "That the word [authenticity] has become part of the moral slang of our days points to the peculiar nature of our fallen condition, our anxiety over the credibility of existence and of individual existences." It was on the note of a "dying fall" that Trilling's career ended. He died of pancreatic cancer at the age of seventy.

★

Studies of Trilling's work include Robert Boyers, *Lionel Trilling: Negative Capability and the Wisdom of Avoidance* (1977); Mark Krupnick, *Lionel Trilling and the Fate of Cultural Criticism* (1986); D. T. O'Hara, *Lionel Trilling: The Work of Liberation* (1988); and John Rodden, ed., *Lionel Trilling and the Critics: Opposing Selves* (1999). An obituary is in the *New York Times* (7 Nov. 1975).

CHRISTOPHER J. KNIGHT

TURÉ, Kwame. *See* Carmichael, Stokely.

TURNER, Izear Luster ("Ike") (*b.* 5 November 1931 in Clarksdale, Mississippi), and **Tina TURNER** (*b.* 26 November 1938 in Brownsville, Tennessee), leaders of the Ike and Tina Turner Review who contributed to the integration of traditional blues and gospel elements in the 1960s transformation of rock and roll.

Ike Turner was the son of a preacher and a seamstress. He got his first piano at the age of seven or eight and taught himself to play, with early influence coming from Pinetop Perkins's boogie-woogie style. While he was still in high school he formed a local band of some acclaim, the Tophatters.

Tina Turner, born Anna Mae Bullock, was the daughter of Floyd Bullock, a migrant worker, sharecropper, and Baptist deacon, and Zelma Currie, a part-time domestic. As a child, she worked the fields alongside her family and sang along with the radio and the church organ. By her mid-

Ike and Tina Turner. ARCHIVE PHOTOS, INC.

teens, her parents had moved away, leaving their two daughters in Tennessee with their grandparents and other relatives. Eventually, in 1956, she and and her sister, Alline, moved to St. Louis.

After the Tophatters split up (some members preferring the big band style to Ike's style, which became known as rhythm and blues), Ike formed a new band called the Kings of Rhythm in 1947–1948. While performing locally with the Kings of Rhythm, Ike also worked as a disc jockey and studio musician for WROX radio in 1947, and in 1950 he met the record producer Sam Phillips in Memphis, Tennessee. In 1951 the Kings of Rhythm moved to Memphis to record with Phillips. Their single "Rocket 88" often is referred to as the first-ever rock-and-roll record. Accidentally, credit for the song was given to Jackie Brenston and his Delta Cats instead of the Kings of Rhythm. Brenston was the Kings' saxophone player.

Turner's money troubles started early. He earned a reputation for being hardnosed and insisting on up-front payments. He worked as a talent scout for Modern Records, and in 1956 Turner moved the Kings of Rhythm to St. Louis and learned to play guitar. By the late 1950s the Kings of Rhythm were a local success in St. Louis. Anna Mae Bullock met Ike at the Manhattan, the hottest club in St. Louis and begged him to let her sing. When he finally agreed, she was a hit. From 1958 to 1960 Anna performed

with the Kings of Rhythm. Ike, recognizing her marketability, gave her the stage name "Tina" and began buying her clothes and grooming her as a front person. The band made the "chittlins' circuit" of black juke joints and bars in the South. Their style featured Tina's characteristic shouting and singing combined with traditional blues, gospel, and call-and-response music. Tina's rattling blues sound and flamboyant stage presence set them apart. Tina and Ike were married around 1960 in Mexico. They had no children, though Tina had had a child by Ike's saxophone player in the late 1950s.

"A Fool in Love" was the first hit for the Ike and Tina Turner Revue; released in 1960 on Sue Records, it peaked at number two on the rhythm and blues chart and number twenty-seven on the pop charts. The Ike and Tina Turner Revue performed the song on the television show *American Bandstand,* and the song sold one million copies. Other popular songs at that time included Brenda Lee's "I Want to Be Wanted." In contrast, Tina sang, "I'm Gonna Keep Him Satisfied." Her raunchy, provocative delivery marked a distinct departure from accepted sentiments in songs by 1960s female vocalists.

In 1962 free-form dances like the twist overtook dance floors across the country. Ultimately, such dances influenced performances by such artists as Ike and Tina Turner. "It's Gonna Work Out Fine" reached number two on the rhythm-and-blues charts and number fourteen on the pop charts, selling more than a hundred million copies. Other chart hits included "I Idolize You," "Poor Fool," "Tra-La-La-La-La," "I Can't Believe What You Say," and "You Shoulda Treated Me Right."

Ike, who early on in his career recognized that he could earn additional income by dodging contracts and jumping from record label to record label, had songs on Sue, Sonja, Innis, Kent, Loma, Modern, Tangerine, Cenco, Philles, Pompeii, Blue Thumb, and Minit in the 1960s. One of the disadvantages to this approach, which he soon realized, was that records sometimes did not get the quality of promotion they deserved and thus were not as successful as they might have been. The quick money earned by his dodging technique, in the long run, contributed to money problems that would plague most of his career and contribute to later legal difficulties.

In 1966 Tina recorded "River Deep, Mountain High" with the famed producer Phil Spector. Ike was banned from the sessions. By all accounts, Tina was "electric," and everyone, including a studio full of the musicians required to create Spector's "wall of sound," expected a hit from this endeavor. While it was popular in Europe (thirteen weeks in the charts in the United Kingdom, peaking at number three), the very pop sound of the record was too white for Ike and Tina's established black audience and too black for the white fans of Herman's Hermits and the Dave Clark Five. The song was not a success in the United States.

That same year, Mick Jagger invited the Ike and Tina Turner Revue to tour with the Rolling Stones in Europe as the opening act. During those twelve dates, Ike and Tina were treated as stars in a way to which they were not accustomed in the United States. Tina's dancing, rhythm, and stage presence, especially, provided inspiration for Jagger on the tour. The Revue had few hit records from 1966 to 1969, but they did perform on the *Ed Sullivan Show* and began to play in better venues after the 1966 Stones tour. They toured with the Stones again in 1969, also playing gigs at Fillmore Auditorium in San Francisco and the Fillmore East in New York City and at the Newport Rock Festival with fellow artists, including Jimi Hendrix (rumored to be a one-time member of Ike's Kings of Rhythm), Joe Cocker, Creedence Clearwater Revival, and the Byrds. Tina was featured in an article in *Vogue* magazine.

In 1971 Ike and Tina had their greatest chart success with John Fogerty's "Proud Mary." It reached number four on the pop charts. Another important success was "Nutbush City Limits," written by Tina and released in 1973. Ike was physically and emotionally abusive to Tina throughout their marriage, and on 2 July 1976, Tina left him to build a new life and career on her own. By 1983 Tina had established herself as a solo artist. *Private Dancer,* her album released in 1984, was extremely successful. The Ike and Tina Turner Revue was inducted into the Rock and Roll Hall of Fame in 1991. In 1993 *What's Love Got to Do with It?,* a screen adaptation of Tina's 1986 autobiography, was released in theaters. Ike, after trouble with money, drugs, and violence, released two solo albums and wrote *Taking Back My Life.*

★

Tina Turner's autobiography, *I, Tina* (with Kurt Loder, 1986), is the source for the 1993 movie *What's Love Got to Do with It?* Ike Turner, with Nigel Cawthorne, has his say in *Takin' Back My Name: The Confessions of Ike Turner* (1999). Also see Bart Mills, *Tina* (1985).

COURTNEY S. DANFORTH

U-V

UNITAS, John Constantine ("Johnny") (*b*. 7 May 1933 in Pittsburgh, Pennsylvania; *d*. 11 September 2002 in Timonium, Maryland), college and professional football player, chosen by the Associated Press as the National Football League Player of the Decade for the 1960s.

Unitas was the third of four children of Leon and Helen Unitas. His father owned a small coal-delivery business, and his mother was a homemaker. When Unitas's father died in 1938, his mother briefly took over the business and then worked at a succession of odd jobs while taking night classes in bookkeeping. She eventually gained employment with the City of Pittsburgh and sold insurance. While his mother struggled to support the family, Unitas began a successful football career. At Saint Justin's High School in Pittsburgh, he won All-Catholic League honors as a quarterback. He graduated from Saint Justin's in 1951. Despite his success on the field, most college recruiters were unimpressed. Unitas weighed only 135 pounds as a freshman. His only scholarship offer came from the University of Louisville. Unitas grew to six feet, one inch and 195 pounds at Louisville and played extensively. During his senior season of 1954 he led the Cardinals to a record of 7–2 and married his high school sweetheart, Dorothy Jean Hoelle; they had five children.

Passing for 3,007 yards and twenty-seven touchdowns during his career at Louisville brought Unitas to the attention of the pro scouts. He was selected in the ninth round of the National Football League (NFL) draft by the Pittsburgh Steelers. As one of four quarterbacks in training camp Unitas had few opportunities to play and was cut before the season began. He returned to Pittsburgh and worked as a pile driver on a construction crew. To stay in football shape, he earned $6 per game by playing for the Bloomfield Rams of the Greater Pittsburgh League. In the spring of 1956 Unitas was offered a tryout by the Baltimore Colts and made the team as a backup to George Shaw. When Shaw broke his leg during the fourth game of the season Unitas had his chance. His first game was a disaster. Coming in with the Colts ahead 21–20, he fumbled three times and threw an interception. Baltimore wound up losing 58–27. Soon, though, his talent began to show itself. In 1957 Unitas led the NFL in passing yardage and touchdowns and began a streak in which he would throw a touchdown pass in forty-seven consecutive games.

More important, with Unitas at quarterback the Colts began to gel. In 1958 Baltimore won the Western Conference title and met the New York Giants in the league championship. With the Colts trailing 17–14 with 1:56 to go, a large television audience saw Unitas complete seven consecutive passes to set up a Steve Myhra field goal and send the game into sudden-death overtime. In the extra period Unitas led the Colts on another long drive, to secure a 23–17 victory. The 1958 championship game often is considered the greatest game of professional football ever played. It also is considered vital to the growth of the sport.

Johnny Unitas. AP/WIDE WORLD PHOTOS

Before 1958 pro football lagged behind both the college game and major league baseball in popularity.

The drama of sudden-death overtime, the almost made-for-TV ending, and Unitas's own rags-to-riches story changed that. By the 1960s professional football had become America's dominant televised sport. The influx of television money encouraged expansion. The NFL added teams in Dallas, Minnesota, New Orleans, and Atlanta during the 1960s, while the oil billionaire Lamar Hunt started the successful American Football League (AFL). More exposure and the competition of rival leagues for players drove salaries upward and made media celebrities of the stars. As the quarterback who led the Colts to the championship in 1958 and again in 1959, Unitas was uniquely positioned to represent the game during the ensuing decade.

Unitas remained the Colts' starting quarterback throughout the 1960s, missing only the bulk of the 1968 season with injuries. He led Baltimore to the playoffs in 1964 and 1965 and watched them reach the Super Bowl in 1968. Throughout he remained one of the most feared players in the game. Unitas's most noted talent was his ability to understand defenses. The Green Bay Packers coach Vince Lombardi said, "He is uncanny in his abilities, under the most violent pressure, to pick out the soft spot in a defense."

During 1968's Super Bowl III, with the Colts hopelessly behind the New York Jets, a hobbled Unitas entered the game. The Jets defensive back Johnny Sample remembered that even though his team had the game in hand, Unitas's appearance was disconcerting. "He scared grown men just by taking the snap and looking your way," Sample said.

Beyond his skill Unitas was known for the style with which he played. Throughout his career he wore old-fashioned high-top football shoes and styled his hair in a crew cut. He was a team player, never seeking attention or celebrity. As the 1960s went on, the increase in player salaries and media attention, along with the flamboyant youth culture of the day, made Unitas seem like a throwback to an earlier time. The Jets quarterback during Super Bowl III, Joe Namath, sometimes wore a full-length mink coat on the sideline and was known for his wild social life and panty-hose commercials. Unitas saw such showmanship as detrimental to team unity.

Unitas remained with the Colts through the 1972 season; he led the team to victory in Super Bowl V in 1970. In June 1972 he and his wife divorced and he remarried, to Sandra Lemon; they had one child. In 1973 Unitas finished his career with the San Diego Chargers. He retired with 40,239 passing yards and 290 touchdowns. Both were records at the time. His streak of forty-seven consecutive games with a touchdown pass is still unequalled. Unitas was inducted into the Pro Football Hall of Fame in 1979.

Following his retirement Unitas worked several years as a broadcaster for the Columbia Broadcasting System. He coauthored three books, *The Athlete's Handbook: How to Be a Champion in Any Sport* (1979) and *Improving Health and Performance in the Athlete* (1979), with George Dintiman, and *Playing Pro Football to Win* (1968), with Harold Rosenthal. Unitas also became involved in several business ventures. Among the more successful were the Golden Arm Restaurant in Baltimore; the Unitas Management Corporation, a real estate development firm in Florida; and the Johnny Unitas Golden Arm Educational Foundation. Since 1987 the best college quarterback in America has received the Johnny Unitas Golden Arm Award. In 2002 Unitas became minority owner of the Wilkes-Barre/Scranton Pioneers of the Arena Football 2 (AF2) League. He died of a heart attack at age sixty-nine.

During the 1960s Unitas was regarded as the best player in the most popular spectator sport in America. His passing abilities made the Baltimore Colts regular candidates for the NFL playoffs, while his quiet demeanor and uncanny understanding of the game made him the epitome of team play.

★

Newspaper clippings and memorabilia are in the Pro Football Hall of Fame in Canton, Ohio. Unitas's autobiography, *Pro Quar-*

terback: My Own Story (1965), was written with Ed Fitzgerald. Lee Greene, *The Johnny Unitas Story* (1962), is a juvenile biography. Unitas is interviewed in Vince Bagli and Norman L. Macht, *Sundays at 2:00 with the Baltimore Colts* (1995), and Dave Klein, *The Game of Their Lives* (1976). A brief, but good biographical treatment is in Dave Anderson, *Great Quarterbacks of the NFL* (1965). An obituary is in the *New York Times* (12 Sept. 2002).

HAROLD W. AURAND, JR.

UPDIKE, John Hoyer   (*b.* 18 March 1932 in Reading, Pennsylvania), novelist, short story writer, poet, essayist, and critic who first came to literary prominence in the 1960s with such novels as *Rabbit, Run* and *Couples*.

Updike, of Dutch and German descent, is the only child of Wesley Russell and Linda Grace (Hoyer) Updike. In 1945, after living in Shillington, Pennsylvania, where his father was a public school mathematics teacher, Updike's family moved to the maternal grandparents' six-room sandstone farmhouse near Plowville, Pennsylvania. Encouraged by his mother, herself a writer, Updike pursued parallel interests in art and writing. Updike became editor of the Shillington High School newspaper, the *Chatterbox*, and was elected senior class president. After graduation in 1950 Updike worked as a copy boy for the *Reading Eagle* and then entered Harvard on a tuition scholarship in the fall

John Updike, 1960. © BETTMANN/CORBIS

of 1950. An English literature major, he wrote and drew cartoons for the *National Lampoon*. He graduated summa cum laude in 1954, the same year the *New Yorker* published his story "Friends from Philadelphia" and a poem, "Duet with Muffled Brake Drums." In 1953 Updike married Mary E. Pennington, a Radcliffe fine arts major, whom he divorced in 1976. The Updikes had four children. In 1977 he married Martha Ruggles Bernhard.

After attending the Ruskin School of Drawing and Fine Arts at Oxford University, Updike was hired by Katharine White as a staff writer for the *New Yorker*. Leaving the magazine in 1957 to concentrate on his poetry and fiction, Updike moved with his family to Ipswich, Massachusetts. In 1958 his volume of poems, *The Carpentered Hen and Other Tame Creatures*, was published. Updike's first novel, *The Poorhouse Fair*, and a collection of short stories, *The Same Door*, were published in 1959. In this period Updike—a Lutheran—was experiencing a spiritual crisis and reading the works of the existentialist Søren Kierkegaard and the neo-orthodox theologian Karl Barth. By the end of the 1950s Updike had achieved status as a writer of "typical" *New Yorker* stories and as a master of lyrical realism. The 1960s, for Updike, was a prolific period in which he ascended into the top rank of American novelists and was on his way to becoming one of the seminal writers of the twentieth century.

The publication of *Rabbit, Run* in 1960 introduced Updike's most enduring character, Harry "Rabbit" Angstrom. Using a third-person, present-tense style of narration, Updike drew on his small-town Pennsylvania roots in telling the story of the twenty-six-year-old former high school basketball star's impulsive flight from a stifling marriage and nowhere job selling dime-store vegetable peelers toward a future that tempts him with the promise of transcendence. Set in the late 1950s, *Rabbit, Run* addresses sex and religion in the broader context of the American themes of transience, loss, and dislocation. Updike imbues Rabbit with the modernist spiritual hunger bridging T. S. Eliot's poem "The Waste Land" to the counterculture of the Vietnam War period and the prosperity of the Reagan era. Like Sinclair Lewis's George Babbitt in the 1920s, Updike's Rabbit Angstrom personifies the middle American spiritual angst that accompanied the materialism of postindustrial, mass society. To underscore this theme Updike richly peppers his narrative with details of popular culture, current history, advertising, and politics.

Updike has acknowledged that an impetus for *Rabbit, Run* was the publication of Jack Kerouac's signature novel of the Beat Generation, *On the Road*. Yet Harry Angstrom is no Sal Paradise or Dean Moriarty. As his nickname implies, Rabbit is a creature of impulse: sex-obsessed, reckless, and instinctual. But this "beautiful brainless guy" is also patriotic, familial, and full of guilt. From his abortive car trip south listening to AM radio to his final flight from his daughter's grave, Rabbit realizes that "the thing that has left his life has left irrevocably; no search would recover it. No flight would reach it." Rabbit's quest, after all, is an inward journey away from chaos and toward an individualistic, almost inchoate kind of faith. In subsequent Rabbit novels, *Rabbit Redux* (1971) and *Rabbit Is Rich* (1981), Updike's protagonist, still running, circles back into the mainstream, encountering black nationalism and white backlash, the gasoline lines of the Carter administration, acquired immune deficiency syndrome (AIDS), and uneasy affluence as a Toyota dealer in the Reagan-era 1980s. Updike's final novel in the tetralogy, *Rabbit at Rest* (1990), explores Rabbit's retirement and death in Florida. In sum, the Rabbit quartet is Updike's magnum opus about a protagonist, according to Updike, "meant to be a Kierkegaardian man, as his name Angstrom hints."

Also in 1960 came the publication of Updike's essay "Hub Fans Bid Kid Adieu," an epic tribute to the artistry of the Boston baseball great Ted Williams. After the phlegmatic Hall of Famer refused to take a curtain call for his final home run in his last game for the Boston Red Sox, Updike wrote, "Gods do not answer letters." The poet Donald Hall writes that Updike's essay marks the beginning of the "High Belletristic Tradition" of baseball writing, which "represents the fan's view from the stands, glorified by good prose."

Updike's output in the 1960s included three volumes of short stories: *Pigeon Feathers* (1962), *Olinger Stories* (1964), and *The Music School* (1966). *Assorted Prose* was published in 1965. A second volume of poems, *Midpoint* (1969), and three more novels—*The Centaur* (1963), *Of the Farm* (1965), and *Couples* (1968)—completed the decade.

The Centaur and *Of the Farm* represented the culmination of Updike's use of his Shillington, Pennsylvania, background until the appearance of his memoirs, *Self-Consciousness*, in 1989. *The Centaur*, which won a National Book Award, focuses on three days in the lives of teacher George Caldwell and his son, Peter, in January 1947. This first-person retrospective narrative is juxtaposed with the mythological story of Chiron the centaur's wounding to release Prometheus from imprisonment. The novel serves as Updike's homage to his father, the model for Caldwell. The *Washington Post* called *The Centaur* "Updike at his angel-tongued best" in reference to his rich style. But Updike's painterly use of imagery, expressed in Peter Caldwell's love of Vermeer, was problematic for some readers. The novelist John Barth called Updike the "Andrew Wyeth of literature." The critic Alfred Kazin wrote that Updike's works lacked "depth." Norman Podhoretz complained that Updike had nothing to say. Yet in its narrative shifts and rhetorical variety, *The Centaur* foreshadowed Updike's movement toward fabulism in later novels such as *The*

Coup (1978), *The Witches of Eastwick* (1984), *Roger's Version* (1986), and *S* (1988).

Of the Farm is an extension of *The Centaur*, focusing on the return of the Peter Caldwell character, now called Joey Robinson, to the family farm a year after the death of his father and his remarriage to a woman his mother clearly resents. Updike's linear narrative avoids the experimentalism of *The Centaur* in shaping a psychological drama with piquant dialog and a plausibly ambiguous conclusion. *Of the Farm,* in its treatment of domestic and marital disharmony, seemed to be Updike's response to the critics' charges of irrelevancy. The novel is a finely crafted minor classic that ranks with the best work of Updike's contemporary Edward Albee, whose realistic plays of the 1960s penetrated the facade of Eisenhower-era family life in such works as *Who's Afraid of Virginia Woolf?* and *A Delicate Balance.*

In 1964 Updike, at age thirty-two, became the youngest person elected to membership in the National Institute of Arts and Letters. That year he was invited by the State Department to tour Eastern Europe and the Soviet Union as part of a cultural exchange program. Later he signed, along with other writers, a letter drafted by Robert Penn Warren urging Soviet writers to use their writing to help restore Jewish cultural institutions. In a 1967 letter to the *New York Times,* Updike explained his moderate position on the Vietnam War, including his hope for a negotiated settlement. He also suggested that President Lyndon B. Johnson not run for reelection in 1968. The letter was his last public statement about the war until his chapter "On Not Being a Dove" was published in *Self-Consciousness.* Updike describes himself as a liberal Democrat with a "hardened antipathy to Communism" and a distrust of orthodoxies, "especially orthodoxies of dissent." In *Self-Consciousness,* Updike confesses that his "disposition to take contrary positions and to seek for nuances within the normal ill-suited" him for national debate.

Updike "found the country so distressing in its civil fury" that he took his family to London during 1968 and 1969. Describing the contrasts of the time, Updike writes, "what with Woodstock and *Barbarella* and *The Joy of Sex* and the choral nudity in *Hair,* there was a consciously retrieved Edenic innocence, a Blakeian triumph of the youthful human animal, along with napalm and defoliation."

Between 1962 and 1968 Updike's marriage was under stress. A self-described period of "grayness" followed in which Updike explored the subject of adultery and its consequences. During this time he wrote the draft of a novel that was eventually published as *Marry Me: A Romance* in 1976; it included material from a story titled "Couples" that was rejected by the *New Yorker.* His short stories from this period, as found in *The Music School* (1966), are brooding and meditative. In "The Stare," wrote the critic William H. Pritchard, Updike is "at his most Hawthornesque, at moments making us think of Poe, a writer to whom he seems otherwise alien."

Updike appeared on the best-seller lists and on the cover of *Time* magazine in 1968 with the publication of his novel *Couples*. Set in the years 1963 and 1964, the novel details the sexual relationships among the young married set in a New England town called Tarbox. Published in the first flowering of the sexual revolution, *Couples,* in its explicitness, seemed to capture the wife-swapping hedonism of a new age, one that *Time* called "the adulterous society." Yet in a deeper sense the novel is about the spiritual quest of its Calvinist protagonist, Piet Hanema, and the ways in which America has fallen from grace. Dismissed by some critics as an upper-middle-class version of the popular 1960s television series *Peyton Place, Couples* seemed to be the major novel that critics had predicted for him. Arthur Mizener had called him "the most talented writer of his generation." Yet in the year of the Tet offensive, the assassinations of Dr. Martin Luther King, Jr., and Senator Robert Kennedy, and continued urban violence, Updike's centrist politics and his focus on the white suburban upper middle class brought criticism from the left. In reviewing *Couples,* Alfred Kazin described Updike as "someone who can brilliantly describe the adult world without conveying its depth and risks, someone wholly literary, dazzlingly bright, the quickest of quick children."

Updike's precocity invited such judgments, though they seem overheated now. The contemporary novelist Joyce Carol Oates thoughtfully connects Updike to the tradition of nineteenth-century French realism. Of Rabbit Angstrom, she writes: "One thinks of Flaubert and his doomed fantasist Emma Bovary, for . . . Updike . . . mesmeriz[es] us with his narrative voice even as he might repel us with the vanities of human desire his scalpel exposes."

In *Midpoint and Other Poems* (1969) Updike concludes "Midpoint," an extended five-part poem, with the lines "Born laughing, I've believed in the Absurd, which brought me this far; henceforth, if I can, I must impersonate a serious man." Clearly, Updike, at thirty-seven, was taking stock and pointing toward new challenges. The immediate results were *Bech: A Book* (1970), and a return to Pennsylvania in *Rabbit Redux* (1971). The character Bech, a Jewish novelist suffering from writer's block, is a comic alter ego that Updike would assume again in *Bech Is Back* (1982) and *Bech at Bay: A Quasi-Novel* (1998). Echoing the influence of the character Humbert from Vladimir Nabokov's novel *Lolita, Bech: A Book* won critical praise for its wit and mockery of late 1960s morals and manners.

Rabbit Redux was Updike's most extensive exploration of the turbulence of the Vietnam era. Set against the Moon landing of 1969 and the urban decay of Brewer, Pennsylvania, the novel traces Rabbit's estrangement from his wife, Janice, and his cohabitation with Jill, a nineteen-year-old

runaway hooked on drugs. Skeeter, a black Vietnam veteran and self-styled prophet, joins Rabbit's household, where he is trying to raise his adolescent son, Nelson. Updike devotes portions of the novel to Skeeter's militant raps and revisionist rants on American history. Throughout, Rabbit's reflections drip with dissonance between his traditional past and the new world revealed in the events unfolding on the television news each night. Events build toward a holocaust. Rabbit's suburban house is torched by vigilantes, Jill dies in the fire, and Rabbit helps Skeeter escape. The novel ends in a literal anticlimax when Rabbit and Janice are reconciled in a motel room, where they simply fall asleep.

The 1960s was, for Updike, a formative and productive decade. He won Pulitzer Prizes in 1982 for *Rabbit Is Rich* and in 1992 for *Rabbit at Rest*. In 1996 he revisited the 1960s once again in *In the Beauty of the Lilies*, a 500-page novel tracing the course of an American family over four generations. On publication of *More Matter* (1999), Updike's fifth collection of prose essays and criticism, the critic William Pritchard made a strong case for Updike's placement as "our preeminent man of letters." The beginning of the new century found Updike at work on his twentieth novel. His place in the American literary pantheon is secure.

★

The most comprehensive literary biography on Updike is William H. Pritchard, *Updike: America's Man of Letters* (2000). Pritchard's explication of Updike's oeuvre is superb. James Yerkes, *John Updike and Religion: The Sense of the Sacred and the Motions of Grace* (1999), is a collection of essays on Updike as a Christian writer. "View from the Catacombs," *Time* (26 Apr. 1968), presents a portrait of the writer after the publication of *Couples*. "Perennial Promises Kept," *Time* (18 Oct. 1982), is also essential reading. The chapter "On Not Being a Dove," in *Self-Consciousness* (1989), is essential to understanding Updike's position on Vietnam. Dennis Farney, "Novelist Updike Sees a Nation Frustrated by Its Own Dreams," *Wall Street Journal* (16 Sept. 1992), presents a useful thematic overview of the Rabbit novels.

DOUG COLLAR

VAN ANDEL, Jay. *See* DeVos, Richard Marvin, and Jay Van Andel.

VANCE, Cyrus Roberts (*b.* 27 March 1917 in Clarksburg, West Virginia; *d.* 12 January 2002 in New York City), statesman who worked to settle several international and domestic conflicts in the 1960s, managed the crisis of the Detroit riots of 1967, and in 1968 was one of the central figures at the Paris Peace Talks to end the Vietnam War.

Vance was the younger of two sons of John Carl Vance, a wealthy insurance executive who died when his son was very young, and Amy (Roberts) Vance. His uncle, John W. Davis, President Woodrow Wilson's ambassador to England and runner-up to President Calvin Coolidge in 1924, provided the fatherless Vance with his first introduction to the legal and political world. Vance excelled in academics and athletics at Kent School in Connecticut. He earned a B.A. in economics at Yale in 1939, where his classmates included such men as McGeorge Bundy and R. Sargent Shriver, who later would work with him in the John F. Kennedy and Lyndon Baines Johnson administrations. He continued studies at Yale and earned his law degree with honors in 1942. Vance then joined the U.S. Navy in 1942 and served in the Pacific theater during World War II. Following the war, and after a year with Mead (paper) Corporation, Vance began a career in which he alternated his time between his duties as partner (by 1956) in the Wall Street law firm of Simpson, Thatcher and Bartlett and as a government official in Washington, D.C. He married Grace Elsie Sloane on 15 February 1947, and they had five children.

Vance's years in government began in 1957, when he was asked by Senator Lyndon Johnson to serve as a legal counsel on several Senate committees. On one of those committees Vance helped draft the National Space Act of 1958, by which the National Aeronautics and Space Administration (NASA) was created. In part this was an effort to counter the world's first man-made satellite, *Sputnik*, and the perceived missile gap between the Soviet Union and the United States. If the exclamation point on the 1960s was the moon landing of 1969, Vance was there at the beginning. Vance moved from Senate committees to the Defense Department, first as general counsel in 1961, assisting President John F. Kennedy in fashioning foreign policy in Cuba after the U.S.-sponsored failed Bay of Pigs invasion of Cuba by Cuban exiles. He then aided Defense Secretary Robert McNamara in reorganizing the Pentagon. In 1962 Kennedy appointed Vance as secretary of the army, and in 1964 President Johnson named him deputy secretary of defense. During this period Vance visited several cold war hot spots to reassert American influence and to settle conflict. These conflicts were embedded in the larger cold war conflict, in which the United States supported regimes that opposed Communism. Vance visited Panama in 1964 and the Dominican Republic in 1965. The most significant cold war hot spot in the 1960s, of course, was Vietnam. In 1966 Johnson sent Vance to Vietnam to assess the prosecution of the war. Vance initially recommended military intensification as a way to end the war quickly, but he later modified that position at the Paris Peace Talks.

Back in the heart of America, Vance's conflict-management skills were put to the test in the Detroit riots of 1967. Called by President Johnson to deal with the situation, Vance coordinated a response that involved federal, state, and local forces. Quickly stemming the violence, which had included nearly five thousand cases primarily of looting and arson, was only part of the response. Vance's written summary and analysis of the riots, known as the "Detroit Report," carefully detailed the security, social, economic, and legal dimensions of the riots. The report came to be accepted as the guidebook for future responses to such emergencies. At the state level Vance spelled out the legal precedent that limits federal intervention in domestic conflict.

Cyrus Vance *(right)*, posing with President Lyndon B. Johnson *(left)* and Averell Harriman *(center)*, May 1968. © BETTMANN/CORBIS

At the individual level he described measures that would help ensure the availability of legal representation for the accused and the long-term social and economic reconstruction of the lives of the people of Detroit. The following year Vance assisted in settling social unrest in Washington, D.C., in the wake of the assassination of the civil rights leader Reverend Martin Luther King, Jr. In April 1968 Johnson made Vance a trustee of the Urban Institute, whose mission was to solve the problems of America's cities.

In one of his notable successes, Vance returned to the international stage in 1967 in shuttle diplomacy between Greece and Turkey over the politically and culturally divided island country of Cyprus. His efforts are responsible for having averted a larger war between the Greeks and the Turks. In February 1968 Vance was sent once more to a lingering cold war hot spot, Korea, where the North Koreans had gained Western military intelligence by seizing the American ship the *Pueblo* and where South Korea's President Chung Hee Park had survived an assassination attempt. Vance helped cool tensions and revitalized the South Korean–American alliance.

The Vietnam War would eventually end for the United States by way of the Paris Peace Talks, begun in May 1968. The four central figures in these talks were Ambassador W. Averell Harriman and Cyrus Vance on the American side and Mai Van Bo and Xuan Thuy on the North Vietnamese side. Public hopes were raised through the prospect of these discussions. Vance had tried in vain to involve the South Vietnamese in the talks, but they refused to participate. His remaining efforts were directed at the protocol of the discussions, including seating arrangements and the shape of the table. Following the changeover from the administration of Johnson to that of Richard M. Nixon, Henry Kissinger took over diplomacy for the Americans. The Vietnam War continued until the Watergate era replaced the Vietnam era in America's popular imagination.

One might think of Vance's work in the 1960s as an apprenticeship for his years as secretary of state under President Jimmy Carter. The seeds of Vance's idealism and of the humanism that characterized the Carter years were sown in his work as negotiator and crisis manager under Johnson. Vance's legacy is typified in the conflict between his steadfast idealism and the realpolitik espoused by Carter's National Security Adviser Zbigniew Brzezinski. Vance resigned in 1980 as secretary of state in opposition to a proposed (and, later, failed) rescue attempt of Americans held hostage in Iran. During his later years he continued to mediate disputes, primarily in the private sector. He also was active as an elder statesman in organizations such as the Council on Foreign Relations and the Palme Commission on Disarmament and Security Issues. He died at the age of eighty-four after a long battle with Alzheimer's disease and is buried in Arlington National Cemetery.

★

The Cyrus R. Vance and Grace Sloane Vance Papers are in the Yale University Library. Vance's autobiography is *Hard Choices: Critical Years in America's Foreign Policy* (1983). A series of oral history interviews with Vance and the "Detroit Report" ("Final Report of Cyrus R. Vance, Special Assistant to the Secretary of Defense, Concerning the Detroit Riots, July 23 through August 2, 1967") are among the documents available at the Lyndon Baines Johnson Library in Austin, Texas. David S. McLellan's biography, *Cyrus Vance* (1985), includes two chapters on Vance's Kennedy/Johnson years. An obituary is in the *New York Times* (13 Jan. 2002).

BRIAN McCORMACK

VAN DYKE, Richard Wayne ("Dick") (*b.* 13 December 1925 in West Plains, Missouri), entertainer in television, film, and theater, known for his versatility and individual style as an actor, physical comedian, and song-and-dance man.

Van Dyke was one of two children born to Loren "Cookie" Van Dyke, a truck dispatcher, and Hazel Van Dyke. His brother, Jerry, later became a well-known actor. Van Dyke

Dick Van Dyke. ARCHIVE PHOTOS, INC.

grew up in Danville, Illinois, and attended public schools. In 1944 he joined the U.S. Army Air Corps, intending to become a pilot. But at six-feet, one-inch tall and weighing just 147 pounds, the gangly teenager was ruled underweight for flight school and served out his time on a ground crew. While he was in the service, he won a job as an announcer on *Flight Time,* an armed forces radio program. Byron Paul, a fellow GI, saw potential in the performer and encouraged him to become a professional entertainer. Paul would become Van Dyke's personal manager.

Van Dyke returned to Danville in 1946 and went into the advertising business with a childhood friend, hoping to use his army radio experience to write, produce, and perform broadcast commercials. When the business failed in less than a year, he went on the road with Philip Erickson, another Danville friend, in a comedy pantomime act known as the Merry Mutes. Eventually, they obtained cross-country bookings. Van Dyke married Marjorie Willett in 1948. The couple had four children and divorced in 1984. Since that time his companion has been Michelle Triola Marvin.

In 1953 Van Dyke found his way into television as a local program host in Atlanta. A hit with his largely female afternoon audience, he was courted away by a New Orleans station in 1955 and less than a year after that by the Columbia Broadcasting System (CBS) television network, with whom he signed an exclusive seven-year contract. His early network assignments in New York included hosting duties on *CBS Cartoon Theater* and the *Morning Show.* But when network executives decided they could make better use of him in prime time, Van Dyke balked and was released from his contract in 1958. "I want to stay with the housewives," he told a reporter. "I can't think of a more delightful way to make a living."

Once free of the CBS contract, Van Dyke moved his career along on several fronts at once. To hold on to his daytime audience, he made a deal with the American Broadcasting Company (ABC) to host both a television game show and a daily radio series. Meanwhile, he expanded his audience by making multiple appearances in prime time, including the *Ed Sullivan Show,* where he performed his song-and-dance and pantomime comedy routines, and *Sgt. Bilko,* where he got his first exposure as a comic actor. He took roles in several dramas as well.

If all this were not enough, Van Dyke captured a part in a 1959 Broadway musical revue, *The Boys Against the Girls.* The show was a flop, but Van Dyke won positive notices from several critics, including Kenneth Tynan of the *New Yorker,* who lauded him for giving "color to an otherwise drab production." Within a year the mostly self-trained actor, singer, and dancer had a starring role in the hit Broadway musical *Bye Bye Birdie.* His performance as a small-time promoter out to exploit a rock-and-roll teen idol won him

the Tony Award for best actor in 1961, and he went on to play the part in the Hollywood film adaptation.

Van Dyke now had his pick of offers for stage, screen, and television projects. Confident that he was ready for the big time, he dropped his other commitments and focused on what in the early 1960s had become the great brass ring for a hot young performer: a television series. He auditioned for the role of Rob Petrie in a situation comedy then titled *Head of the Family,* which concerned a New York comedy writer who commutes between a serene suburban family life in New Rochelle, New York, and the frenetic show-business world of midtown Manhattan. Carl Reiner, the show's creator-producer, originally had written the lead role for himself and performed it in a pilot episode. Advised by the veteran producer Sheldon Leonard that the show might stand a better chance of reaching prime time if it were recast with a less "ethnic" (that is, less Jewish) and more "mainstream" (that is, more WASPish) male lead, Reiner held auditions to replace himself. Van Dyke won the role over another up-and-coming performer, Johnny Carson, and with his star rising he negotiated title billing and a partnership in the show's production company.

The Dick Van Dyke Show premiered on CBS in the fall of 1961. Because the show devoted few of its story lines to the parent-child morality tales that otherwise dominated the genre, its treatment of home and work relationships seemed mature by contrast. As a "backstage" comedy about the writers of a mythical television variety show, the show supplied setups for Van Dyke and the cast to present musical numbers and comedy routines, something that the genre had not seen since the heyday of *I Love Lucy.* At a time when popular situation comedies were often idyllic tales of 1950s suburban family life (for example, *Father Knows Best* and *Leave It to Beaver*), the *Van Dyke* show effected a distinct Kennedy-era look, with Rob, the youngest of the comedy writers, as head of the team, and his beautiful wife, Laura (played by Mary Tyler Moore), sporting an unmistakable "Jackie" (Kennedy) hairdo. During the show's five-year run, Van Dyke won three Emmy Awards, and the show took "outstanding comedy series" honors four times. In the spring of 1966, however, CBS, the last of the networks to air black-and-white programs, decreed that all shows, new and returning, must be in color for their September premieres. With Van Dyke and Moore both eager to move on to other projects, the producers chose to call it quits rather than gear up for color production.

While appearing in what many were calling the only "adult sitcom" on television during the 1960s, Van Dyke simultaneously emerged as one of the decade's great stars of family-oriented and children's movies. He appeared in featured or starring roles in such international hits as *Mary Poppins* (1964), *Lt. Robin Crusoe, U.S.N.* (1966), *Fitzwilly* (1967), and *Chitty Chitty Bang Bang* (1968), displaying his considerable talents as a mime and a song-and-dance artist. His other film efforts, including *The Comic* (1969), which was based loosely on the life of the entertainer Buster Keaton, were less successful at the box office.

Van Dyke continued to be a popular figure on television during the 1970s, appearing in a new situation comedy as well as in comedy-variety and dramatic programs. He admitted to being plagued by alcoholism problems and cut down his frantic work schedule toward the end of the decade. In 1993 he surprised both critics and audiences with a new dramatic series, *Diagnosis Murder,* in which he played a murder-sleuthing medical doctor. The show, which ran for a decade, was heavily weighted with baby boomers, who have remained loyal Van Dyke fans since childhood.

★

There are two fan books devoted to Van Dyke's "classic" 1960s sitcom, both of which contain a surfeit of biographical material and trivia: Vince Waldron, *The Official Dick Van Dyke Show Book: The Definitive History and Ultimate Viewer's Guide to Television's Most Enduring Comedy* (1994), and Ginny Weissman and Coyne Steven Sanders, *The Dick Van Dyke Show* (rev. ed., 1993). Biographical articles appear in *Newcomb's Encyclopedia of Television* and *Current Biography* (1963). An interview with the performer was audiotaped in 1980 as part of the Encyclopedia Americana/CBS News Audio Resource Library.

DAVID MARC

VANN, John Paul (*b.* 2 July 1924 in Norfolk, Virginia; *d.* 9 June 1972 in the Republic of Vietnam), career U.S. Army officer and, later, ranking civilian adviser in South Vietnam who, during the Vietnam War, advocated counterinsurgency, pacification, and social revolution while criticizing U.S. dependence on armed forces and massive firepower.

Vann was born out of wedlock to John Spry, a trolley-car operator, and Myrtle Tripp, a prostitute who later married Aaron Frank Vann, a bus driver, factory worker, and carpenter. His mother and stepfather had three more children. Vann grew up in a working-class neighborhood in Norfolk. Early humiliations and deprivation shaped Vann's combativeness and determination. After attending Ferrum Training School and Junior College, south of Roanoke, Virginia, for four years on a scholarship, Vann joined the U.S. Army Air Corps in 1943 but completed training as a navigator for the B-29 bomber just after the end of World War II. He married Mary Jane Allen on 6 October 1945; they had five children.

When the air corps split away from the army in 1947 to form the U.S. Air Force, Vann opted to return to the army, and despite standing only five feet, six-and-a-half inches and weighing 125 pounds (five feet, eight inches and 150

John Paul Vann. ASSOCIATED PRESS AP

pounds in later years) he joined the paratroopers. In the Korean conflict he showed courage when he initiated a risky aerial supply mission to U.S. soldiers who were surrounded by Communist forces. He taught Reserve Officers Training Corps at Rutgers University in New Brunswick, New Jersey, and completed a bachelor's degree in business administration in 1955. He served at various posts as a logistical officer, graduated from the U.S. Army Command and General Staff College in Fort Leavenworth, Kansas, in 1958; earned a master's degree in business administration from Syracuse University in New York in 1959; and received the rank of lieutenant colonel in 1961.

In 1962 Vann volunteered to serve in South Vietnam as the senior adviser to the Seventh Division of the Army of the Republic of Vietnam (ARVN). There he witnessed the endemic corruption of the Saigon regime and its debilitating effects on the South Vietnamese armed forces. In January 1963 his ARVN unit fought the Vietcong at the battle of Ap Bac, where the ARVN showed incompetence and reluctance to engage the enemy, allowing the Vietcong to slip away while costing the lives of U.S. advisers and many ARVN soldiers. The U.S. command in Saigon claimed a victory, although Vann and news reporters at the scene knew the truth. After the U.S. Army brushed aside Vann's reports calling for a new strategy to win the war, he leaked information to journalists in Vietnam and developed close relationships with the the U.S. reporters David Halberstam and Neil Sheehan. This was the beginning of Vann's criticism of the manner in which America conducted the war in Vietnam. Upon the completion of his tour of duty in March 1963, Vann returned to the Pentagon for a debriefing that was denied. Frustrated, he retired from the army on 31 July 1963 and began to speak out publicly on the war.

In March 1965 Vann returned to Vietnam as a pacification representative of the Agency for International Development and was assigned to a province near Saigon that had been written off as controlled by the Vietcong. Capable of getting by on one or two hours of sleep at a time, Vann threw himself into his work, driving highways that no one else would use for fear of ambush to visit provincial and village leaders, organizing the distribution of food and supplies to Vietnamese peasants, and training community-defense teams.

In September 1965 Vann issued "Harnessing the Revolution in South Vietnam," a ten-page proposal that argued the South Vietnamese could prevail against the Communist insurgency through the assistance of U.S. military and civilian advisers. These advisers would win the "hearts and minds" of the Vietnamese peasants by capturing the social revolution from the Communists and incorporating it as part of America's anti-Communist crusade. The immediate goal was to utilize peasant support to destroy the Vietcong. The long-term goal was to foster a national government responsive to a social revolution and stable enough to survive after U.S. troops left South Vietnam. As the United States rapidly began to increase its number of combat troops in Vietnam starting in 1965, however, Vann feared that the ARVN would lose any incentive to pursue an aggressive campaign against the Communists, while U.S. troops would alienate the peasants by the indiscriminate use of firepower that would kill and wound civilians and destroy their homes. U.S. military leaders in South Vietnam viewed Vann as a renegade and dismissed his ideas as impractical.

Daniel Ellsberg, an influential intelligence analyst, a protégé of Vann's in Vietnam, and the person who leaked the top-secret Pentagon Papers to the *New York Times* in 1971, persuaded Secretary of Defense Robert McNamara in 1966 to appoint Vann as the director of the entire civilian pacification program for the III Corps region. The massive Tet offensive launched by the Vietcong and North Vietnamese armies in January 1968 caught U.S. and South Vietnamese forces off guard and undermined the credibility of U.S. leaders who claimed that the enemy was in retreat. While many U.S. civilian and military leaders wrung their hands in dismay, Vann seized the moment to push his plan, calling for sustained military action against what he saw as a weakened enemy and phased military withdrawal to mollify demands at home for an end to the war. The combination of U.S. firepower and increased numbers of South Vietnamese troops could win the war, he argued. This position represented a reversal of his earlier belief in winning the hearts and minds of the Vietnamese peasants.

Vann's ideas caught the attention of the Republican presidential candidate Richard Nixon, who seized upon the strategy, calling it "Vietnamization." On 15 May 1971 Vann received command of the U.S. military operations in the II Corps region, becoming the first civilian in U.S. history to assume a position equivalent to a two-star general and to command military forces in a combat zone. Even as more U.S. forces withdrew and the North Vietnamese put pressure on a crumbling South Vietnamese army, Vann, blinded by personal ambition and commitment to a war that had become his life, remained optimistic that the United States would prevail. On 9 June 1972 Vann, who had shown reckless disregard for his life on many occasions, died when his helicopter crashed while flying at night in bad weather. Many U.S. military and civilian leaders attended his funeral and interment at Arlington National Cemetery in Virginia on 16 June 1972. Afterward, Vann's family went to the White House to receive the Presidential Medal of Freedom from President Nixon.

Vann spent nearly the entire decade of the 1960s in South Vietnam. In the early 1960s he called for a social revolution to overthrow the corrupt government of South Vietnam, a pacification program to win the support of the peasant majority, and counterinsurgency to defeat the Communists. He opposed the buildup of U.S. military forces until the Communist Tet offensive in 1968 and then supported U.S. military efforts to defeat the Communists. Vann was both a critic and architect of U.S. policy in South Vietnam, but he, like many Americans, never wavered in the belief that the U.S. involvement in Vietnam was a necessary part of cold war strategy.

★

Vann's papers (1964–1972) are held by the U.S. Army Military History Institute, Carlisle Barracks, Pennsylvania. Neil Sheehan, *A Bright Shining Lie: John Paul Vann and America in Vietnam* (1988), provides the most comprehensive examination of Vann and his involvement in the Vietnam War. Bruce Wetterau, *The Presidential Medal of Freedom: Winners and Their Achievements* (1996), provides the citation and an overview of Vann's career. An obituary is in the *New York Times* (10 June 1972).

PAUL A. FRISCH

VENTURI, Robert (*b.* 25 June 1925 in Philadelphia, Pennsylvania), prominent architect who in the 1960s helped formulate the postmodern revolt against the simplicity and functionalism of modern architecture, instead emphasizing buildings rich in symbolism and history.

The only child of the Italian immigrants Robert Charles Venturi, a fruit produce merchant, and Vanna (Lanzetta) Venturi, a housewife, Venturi credits his father with his early exposure to and appreciation of architecture. By the

Robert Venturi. AP/WIDE WORLD PHOTOS

time he was four years old, Venturi knew that he wanted to be an architect. His parents' pacifism led them to convert to the Quaker religion, and Venturi spent much of his childhood attending Quaker meetings. He attended private schools and graduated from the Episcopal Academy in Merion, Pennsylvania.

In 1943 Venturi entered Princeton University in New Jersey to study architecture. Under the direction of Jean Labatut, who had trained at the prestigious Ecole des Beaux Arts in Paris, Venturi learned not only how buildings are imagined in the mind of the architect but also how the average person perceives them. Venturi also studied architectural history with the noted scholar Donald Drew Egbert, taking his course four times. As Venturi later recalled, Egbert's course steered away from the then popular philosophy that modern architecture was not just a style but an ideology. Instead, Egbert stressed architecture as evolution, suggesting that modern architecture would continue to develop and change. Venturi's keen knowledge of architectural history proved a vital inspiration for his own works. In 1947 Venturi graduated with a B.A., summa cum laude; he earned an M.F.A. from Princeton in 1950.

Between 1950 and 1954 Venturi worked as a designer in the offices of Oscar Stonorov, Louis I. Kahn, and Eero Saarinen. In 1954 he won the Prix de Rome, which enabled

him to spend two years studying at the American Academy in Rome. Venturi was particularly drawn to mannerist and baroque buildings and admired the work of Michelangelo and Francesco Borromini. During his time in Rome, Venturi began to formulate ideas about reinterpreting the traditional architectural vocabulary of columns, arches, and pediments to create structures of great originality. He later referred to Rome as his "Mecca," stating that the city was "where I proved that my architectural fathers were wrong when they said that history was bunk."

Within two years of his return to Philadelphia in 1956, Venturi had established his own architectural firm of Venturi, Cope, and Lippincott. In 1961 he entered into a brief partnership with William Short and in 1964 went into business with John Rauch. The Zambian-born designer Denise Scott Brown, whom Venturi married on 23 July 1967, became the third partner in Venturi, Rauch, and Scott Brown in 1977. The couple had one son.

During the 1960s Venturi began teaching courses on architectural theory at the University of Pennsylvania in Philadelphia. These courses formed the basis of his first book, *Complexity and Contradiction in Architecture,* which was published by the Museum of Modern Art in 1966. The book encouraged architects to turn away from the rigid "form follows function" doctrines of the modernist movement. Instead, Venturi argued, architects should look to the rich architectural traditions of the past, from the classically executed works to the vernacular architecture that reflected local and popular culture. Deriding Ludwig Mies Van der Rohe's famous maxim "less is more," Venturi wrote, "Less is a bore." He confirmed, "I am for messy vitality over obvious unity. I am for richness of meaning rather than clarity of meaning." Venturi's book marked a watershed in American architectural history and was hailed as the most important writing on architecture since Le Corbusier's *Rise of Architecture* (1923). *Complexity and Contradiction* became a guidebook for young architects the world over who had become disillusioned with the modernist movement.

Venturi practiced what he preached. His first major work, the Guild House, constructed between 1960 and 1963 as an apartment building for the elderly in Philadelphia, combined high-art aesthetics with motifs drawn from popular culture. The six-story brick building appeared at first glance to be a quite ordinary. A closer look revealed a small main entranceway, marked by a massive black granite column, in a large frame of white glazed brick. A sign done in giant supermarket-style lettering completed the building's facade. For a time, a gold television antenna was displayed prominently on top of the building directly over the entrance as a symbol, according to Venturi, "of the aged, who spend so much time looking at TV." The inclusion of such commonplace elements, which Venturi intended to be viewed as high art, combined with the design of the Guild House, produced an unexpected symmetry.

Venturi's best-known building from the1960s was the house he designed for his mother in Chestnut Hill, Pennsylvania. For Mother's House, which he completed in 1962, Venturi again created a building that mixed contradictory elements, including a simple exterior with a complex interior plan. The symmetry of the house was disrupted by unbalanced windows and an off-center chimney. Although Venturi conceived the scale to be small, he also incorporated oversized interior doors, chair rails, and fireplace mantels.

Unfortunately, Venturi's innovative forays and his attacks on modernist orthodoxy did not win him many commissions during the 1960s. He continued to teach and from his courses came his next book, *Learning from Las Vegas* (1972), which he coauthored with Steven Izenour and Denise Scott Brown. Venturi's argument was as audacious as it was original. The gaudy explosion of neon that characterized the Vegas strip was not an architectural abomination, he insisted, but an important vernacular art form worthy of serious study. Venturi thought that the so-called Decorated Shed and other types of roadside buildings offered lessons in design that architects could no longer ignore.

When Venturi's business began to prosper in the early 1970s, he devoted his attention more to design than to teaching and writing. Throughout the last half of the twentieth century, Venturi's buildings continued to illustrate his architectural philosophy by combining the vernacular, the historical, and the artistic. Venturi published his third book, *A View from the Campidoglio: Selected Essays, 1953–1984*, in 1985, and that same year Venturi, Rauch, and Scott Brown won the architectural firm award of the American Institute of Architects. In 1991 Venturi was awarded the Pritzker Architecture Prize, one of the highest honors an architect can receive. Since that time, his work has been the subject of museum retrospectives and exhibitions. Venturi's designs continue to challenge architects to rethink their theory and practice.

Venturi's groundbreaking writings and designs of the 1960s illustrated for architects all over the world that "the commonplace and everyday built environment cannot be willed out of existence and is 'almost alright.'" Venturi's deft handling of conventional and everyday elements in his architecture, while shocking at first to many, also demonstrated that the everyday could become the extraordinary if done thoughtfully. Instead of embracing the credo of modernists, who felt it necessary to educate and elevate public taste, Venturi showed architects how to accept and improve it.

★

There is no biography of Venturi. Overviews of his work often contain some biographical information. See Philip and John Cook

Johnson, *Conversations with Architects: Philip Johnson, Kevin Roche, Paul Rudolph, Bertrand Goldberg, Morris Lapidus, Louis Kahn, Charles Moore, Robert Venturi* (1975); Diane Maddox and Roger K. Lewis, *Master Builders: A Guide to Famous American Architects* (1986); Christopher Mead, ed., *The Architecture of Robert Venturi* (1989); and David B. Brownlee, David G. Delong, and Kathryn B. Hiesinger, *Out of the Ordinary: Robert Venturi, Denise Scott Brown, and Associates: Architecture, Urbanism, Design* (2001). In addition to Venturi's books mentioned in the text, see Robert Venturi, *Complexity and Contradiction in Architecture* (2002).

MEG GREENE

VERNON, Lillian (*b.* 1927 or 1929 in Leipzig, Germany), chief executive officer and president of a mail order corporation she started at her kitchen table and developed into an empire that earns approximately half a billion dollars in sales annually.

It is difficult to pin down exactly when Vernon was born. Interviewers and profilers are evenly divided between 1927 and 1929 as the year of her birth. She was born Lillian Menasche, the daughter of Erna and Herman, a German industrialist. In 1933 her family moved to Amsterdam in the Netherlands. Years later she recollected that she did not understand why they made the move; she had a vague sense that it was to keep her only sibling, a brother, out of the army. Another possibility is that, being Jewish, the family moved to escape Germany's Nazi regime. In 1937 Vernon's parents foresaw the advent of World War II and fled Amsterdam for New York City, where they could live free of persecution. Vernon's brother died in combat in World War II, in service to the United States.

Vernon's father had the ability to conjure businesses out of nothing and did so by refurbishing zippers for the American war effort; he then built a small but successful company that made leather goods. He often asked his daughter for her opinion about new products or revisions to old ones, and he always took her views seriously, building her confidence in her own judgment and showing her how to manage a business at the same time. Vernon entered New York University in 1947 but left after two years. In 1949 she married Samuel Hochberg, a manager of a women's clothing store, and they settled in Mount Vernon, New York; the couple had two children. By the time she married, Vernon was thoroughly Americanized and spoke English without a trace of accent. She soon became bored with being a homemaker, and she wanted a more comfortable life than her husband's $75 per week afforded. She figured that an additional $50 per week would provide what she desired.

Thus in 1951, while four months pregnant, she decided to figure out a way to make money while staying at home, where young mothers of the time were expected to stay.

She hit on the idea of monogramming matching handbags and belts. Her father agreed to sell her sets of handbags and belts for $3, and she decided to offer them at $7 after monogramming them at her kitchen table. Much has been made of her starting her multimillion-dollar corporation with only $2,000 of wedding gift money, but in 1951 that sum was actually quite large; $4,000 per year was considered a good middle-class income in those days and was about what her husband earned. Vernon spent $495 to place an advertisement in *Seventeen* magazine, and in three weeks she had $16,000 in orders; a few weeks later the amount had doubled.

This initial success established the hallmark that still characterizes her company. Vernon sold feel-good items, such as pendants, rings, combs, and buttons, priced to be affordable for people with average incomes, and she chose items she would want for herself. She named her business Vernon Specialties, after Mount Vernon. By 1954 her business had outgrown her home, so she rented buildings in Mount Vernon—one for a warehouse, another for monogramming, and a third for shipping. In 1956 Vernon expanded her line to include men's items, such as cufflinks and collar pins, and created a sixteen-page catalog and mailed it to 125,000 customers. The response to the catalog was so great that Vernon Specialties tripled its income, and "Lillian Hochberg" became "Lillian Vernon" in the minds of her customers.

During the 1960s Vernon published catalogs that presented her products without categorization, a trait that persisted in her main catalog throughout her career, even though she created specialty catalogs in the 1970s. Vernon was a tough businesswoman who dickered fiercely with suppliers. She may have enjoyed surprising male suppliers with her competitiveness; she liked recalling how men trivialized her and how shocked some of them were to discover that a woman named Lillian really was running the company. In the 1960s Vernon found a growing customer base composed of women who were joining the workforce and who did not have time to shop for the treats Vernon offered—women who, therefore, found Vernon's catalog and around-the-clock customer service convenient.

Vernon branched into manufacturing in the 1960s, making items like lipstick cases and charm bracelets. In 1963 Revlon contracted with Vernon to supply it with specialty goods, and Avon, Elizabeth Arden, Max Factor, and Maybelline signed on to purchase goods wholesale. By 1965 Vernon's company was not only a mail order business but also an industrial enterprise, and Vernon incorporated it as Lillian Vernon Corporation. Years later Samuel Hochberg explained that the company broke up their marriage. He liked relaxing and having fun and did not take the corporation as seriously as did his wife. Vernon asserted that he treated her business like a hobby; Hochberg said that she

was more devoted to the company than he was and that their differences in management approaches drove them apart. In 1969 they divorced. The manufacturing segment of Lillian Vernon Corporation went to Hochberg, with Vernon keeping the mail order business. She poured her creative energy into her wounded company, and in 1970 it posted $1 million in sales for the first time.

In 1970, the same year that she married Robert Katz, Vernon visited Germany for the first time since her family had fled Leipzig in 1933. She reported that just visiting Germany made her break out in hives; even so, she was determined to find suppliers of specialty goods as well as new customers in Europe. By then she had developed a reputation for a bad temper; she defended her outbursts by pointing out that the money to be made or lost was hers.

She brought both of her sons into her business, with Fred eventually replacing her as company president (she remained chief executive officer) and David becoming head of public relations. In 1987 Lillian Vernon Corporation was placed on the American Stock Exchange, with 35 percent of the company's shares made available to the public. The sale of the shares brought in $28 million, $12 million of which was distributed among Vernon and her sons. The other $16 million was invested in a new computerized distribution center in Virginia Beach, Virginia. In 1990 Vernon and Katz divorced, and Vernon legally changed her name to Lillian Vernon. In June 1998 she married Paolo Martino.

Vernon was a trailblazer for women in business, sometimes remarking that she lived the feminist life others only talked about. She lived life primarily by her own rules. Through talent and intensely focused determination, she built one of the world's most prosperous mail order businesses. She expressed just one major regret: that she should have taken more vacations.

★

Lillian Vernon's autobiography, *An Eye for Success* (1997), emphasizes her business career and makes building a business seem like an entertaining adventure. Lisa Coleman, "I Went Out and Did It," *Forbes* (17 Aug. 1992), is the best profile available. Martha I. Finney, "The Treasure of Her Company," *Nation's Business* (Feb. 1987) is a key source for other publications about Vernon.

KIRK H. BEETZ

VIDAL, Gore (*b.* 3 October 1925 in West Point, New York), novelist, playwright, scriptwriter, and essayist who became a well-known liberal political commentator in the 1960s through television appearances, articles in *Esquire* magazine, and debates with conservative William Buckley during the 1968 Democratic and Republican conventions.

Vidal, whose full given name is Eugene Luther Gore Vidal, is the only child of Eugene Luther and Nina (Gore) Vidal.

Vidal's father taught aeronautics at the U.S. Military Academy, founded several airlines, and served as director of air commerce under President Franklin D. Roosevelt from 1933 to 1937. Vidal attended several private high schools and in 1943 graduated from Phillips Exeter Academy in Massachusetts, at which time he shortened his name to Gore Vidal. He enlisted in the army in July 1943 and served as a warrant officer aboard a ship in the Pacific Theater. Shortly after his discharge in 1946 his first novel, *Williwaw,* was published. Vidal had begun the novel at the age of nineteen while serving on a ship and finished it while being treated for rheumatoid arthritis in a hospital. His next novels were *In a Yellow Wood* (1947) and *The City and Pillar* (1948), which gained him widespread notoriety for its account of a homosexual man's self-discovery. In the 1950s Vidal began writing plays as well as movie and television scripts to augment his income. Perhaps his most successful effort in these genres was *Visit to a Small Planet*, which was televised in 1955 and then staged on Broadway.

By 1960 Vidal was earning several thousand dollars per television script, and his play *The Best Man* (1959), a cynical political drama, was doing well on Broadway. That same year Vidal, whose grandfather, Thomas Prory Gore, had been a U.S. senator from Oklahoma, ran for Congress in upstate New York, but he lost the election. In 1962 a number of essays on literary and political topics Vidal had written in the 1950s and early 1960s were published in *Rocking the Boat*. The book gained Vidal a reputation as an incisive and provocative commentator on American politics and society. He followed up *Rocking the Boat* with two plays, *On the March to the Sea* (1961), a Civil War drama based on a television script he wrote in the 1950s, and the 1963 play *Romulus*, a historical comedy about the fall of Rome, adapted from a play by Friedrich Dürrenmatt. The comedy featured familiar themes in Vidal's works—history, politics, and power. In 1964 Vidal received a Screen Writers Annual Award nomination and the Cannes Critics Prize for his screenplay adaptation of *The Best Man*.

In 1964 Vidal published his first novel in a decade. *Julian* told the story of a Roman emperor, circa 360 A.D., who tried to turn his people and country away from the growing religion of Christianity. The book's publication received good reviews, introduced Vidal's talent for historical fiction, and firmly established him as a best-selling novelist. Vidal followed up with the script for the movie *Is Paris Burning?* (1966), the 1967 political thriller *Washington, D.C.*, and *Sex, Death, and Money* (1968).

Vidal's play *Weekend* opened on 13 March 1968 at the Broadhurst Theater in New York but closed after just twenty-two performances. A story of political ambition and amorality, the play included acerbic references to the Vietnam War and President Lyndon Johnson.

Gore Vidal, 1968. © Bettmann/Corbis

Despite the play's disastrous run, Vidal rebounded that same year with his book *Myra Breckinridge* (1968), which took the critics and the public by surprise. The sexually daring novel told the story of Myra, who was called Myron before a sex-change operation. The book revealed Vidal's camp sensibility via a black comedy about a transsexual woman who wants to dominate men. Although shocking to many, the novel garnered Vidal widespread acclaim and admiration.

Vidal's wit and willingness to speak his mind also gained him wide notoriety throughout the decade as he freely commented on politics and society. He was recognized by the general public because of his guest appearances on television programs and his hosting of a syndicated panel discussion show, *The Hot Line,* in 1964. Vidal also had connections to the White House. After divorcing his father, Vidal's mother was married briefly to Hugh Auchincloss, a stockbroker who eventually divorced her and married Jacqueline Bouvier's mother. Bouvier became the wife of President John F. Kennedy. As a result of this connection and Vidal's reputation as a liberal Democrat, Vidal enjoyed insider status on the political scene for a brief time during the Kennedy administration until he had a confrontation with Robert Kennedy at a White House reception in 1961. His association to the Kennedys eventually led to several essays in *Esquire* about the family. Vidal's 1970 novel, *Two Sisters*, also contained an irreverent, fictionalized account of the mystique surrounding the former First Lady.

In 1968 Vidal participated in a series of ten debates during the Republican National Convention in Miami and the Democratic National Convention in Chicago. Set up by American Broadcasting Company (ABC) television, the debates highlighted the opposing left-wing liberal and right-wing conservative views of the time as represented by Vidal and William Buckley, respectively. The long-time ideological enemies did not disappoint. The debates reached a crescendo on 22 August 1968 as the two confronted each other in Chicago during the Democratic convention, which became known more for its Vietnam War protests and the violent police efforts to suppress them than for what occurred within the convention itself. During the debate Vidal called Buckley a "pro-crypto-Nazi." The enraged Buckley countered with "Now listen, you queer, stop calling me a crypto-Nazi or I'll sock you in your goddamn face and you'll stay plastered." The two men completed the last of their debates the next night. The battle continued, however, with mutual lawsuits and the publication in *Esquire* in 1969 of competing versions of the encounter.

Vidal ended the 1960s with another collection of essays, *Reflections upon a Sinking Ship* (1969), and the screenplay *The Last of the Mobile Hotshots* (1970), based on Tennessee Williams's *The Seven Descents of Myrtle*. During the decade he not only solidified his skills as a novelist but also became known as a controversial and acid-tongued provocateur. He was, for example, an early supporter of legalizing illicit drugs, which had reached the middle class in epidemic proportions by the late 1960s. Vidal, who never went to college, is a respected novelist but has never achieved the reverence accorded other novelists of his generation, like John Updike and Saul Bellow. He may be best remembered for his contributions to American literature via his essays, which cover numerous topics from literary criticism to national issues.

★

Robert F. Kiernan's biography, *Gore Vidal*, was published in 1982 and contains extensive information on Vidal's works and life in the 1960s. To learn about Vidal's life in his own words, read *Palimpsest: A Memoir* (1995). Several good interviews with Vidal during the 1960s can be found in Eugene Walter, "Conversations with Gore Vidal," *Transatlantic Review* (summer 1960): 5–17; Eve Auchincloss and Nancy Lynchi, "Disturber of the Peace: Gore Vidal," *Mademoiselle* (Sept. 1961); and "Playboy Interview: Gore Vidal," *Playboy* (June 1969). Critical studies of Vidal's works of the 1960s include Bernard F. Dick, *The Apostate Angel: A Critical Study of Gore Vidal* (1974).

DAVID PETECHUK

VILLELLA, Edward Joseph (*b.* 10 January 1936 in Bayside, Long Island, New York), first American male ballet star.

Villella, the only son of Joseph and Mildred (DeGiovanni) Villella, grew up in a working-class neighborhood in New York City. His father was a truckdriver, and his mother was a homemaker. To keep him off the streets and out of trouble, his parents in 1946 enrolled him in ballet classes at the School of American Ballet, where his older sister, his only sibling, was also a student. Villella was a natural and began thinking seriously of becoming a professional dancer. The instructors were so impressed with his talent that they told him to apply for a scholarship. Villella auditioned and was immediately accepted as a scholarship student. When his sister decided to quit dancing, Villella was expected to do the same, for his parents had other plans for him. Although Villella attended Maritime College, in the Bronx, earning a B.S. in maritime transportation in 1957, he never gave up his dream of becoming a dancer. After completing his education he returned to dancing classes. He had to work hard, however, to compensate for the four years he had lost. His progress was nothing short of extraordinary. In 1957, just one year after he returned to dance, Villella was accepted into the New York City Ballet (NYCB) under the directorship of the famed George Balanchine.

By his own admission, Villella spent most of his time at the NYCB "on the outs with Mr. B." Balanchine was the wrong teacher for Villella. Almost from the beginning Villella began to suffer severe cramps as a result of Balanchine's training methods, which were better suited for taller female dancers than for Villella's shorter, more muscular body. With the help of Stanley Williams, a member of the faculty at the School of American Ballet, Villella discovered a way to survive Balanchine's regime. Williams worked with Villella to build up his endurance, strength, and flexibility, considerably diminishing the risk of serious injury.

During the 1960s Villella became a featured dancer in Balanchine's troupe and, hailed as the greatest American-born male dancer in history, rocketed to national prominence. Villella debuted in the title role of *The Prodigal Son*, a work Balanchine personally disliked but revived for Villella during the 1959–1960 season. The role established Villella as a dancer of great power, finesse, and skill, and his performance remains one of the defining moments in the history of American ballet.

In 1961 Ballanchine promoted Villella to principal dancer in the NYCB. That year Villella danced at President

John F. Kennedy's inaugural celebration. Throughout the 1960s Villella created roles in nearly a dozen of Balanchine's works but came to be most strongly identified with the memorable roles of Oberon in *A Midsummer Night's Dream* (1962) and Harlequin in *Harlequinade* (1965). During the 1960s he also appeared in Broadway musicals, including *Brigadoon* (1962).

With its sharply defined proportions, Villella's physique appeared to have been tailor-made for Balanchine's choreography. Dancing the roles of cavaliers and princes, Villella captured the essence of the gentleman, albeit one with a bit of the rascal in him. Villella's athleticism also made him an excellent partner. As one critic noted, Villella "shone as beautifully as the women with whom he was paired." Villella commanded attention in his performances with facial expressions that were as powerful and memorable as his leaps and turns. Many ballet aesthetes found his style too brash and earthy, but his good looks and charismatic presence, both on and off the stage, made him popular with audiences.

Part of Villella's immense popularity arose from his pioneering efforts to bring dance to television. In the 1960s he appeared as a guest on a number of television variety programs, including *The Ed Sullivan Show*, *The Bell Telephone Hour*, and *The Mike Douglas Show*. The National Broadcasting Company (NBC) produced a documentary about his career in 1968, titled *Man Who Dances*. Through television Villella reached audiences that might never have had the inclination or the opportunity to attend live ballet programs. Even on the small screen his performances conveyed energy, bravado, and excitement. In addition Villella demonstrated for many Americans that ballet was not only a permissible activity for heterosexual males but also was a way to display male power and sensuality.

By the early 1960s Villella attained international stardom. One of the most unforgettable moments of his career came in 1962 when he was invited to perform an encore at the famed Bolshoi Theatre in Moscow, making him the first American male dancer ever to do so. It was also a first for a member the New York City Ballet. The significance of the event, which occurred at the height of the cold war, during the Cuban Missile Crisis, was not lost on Villella. In his autobiography Villella wrote that he was "dancing for my country." He later became the first American male dancer to perform with the Royal Danish Ballet.

Peter Martins, who later became a member of Balanchine's company, recalled seeing Villella in 1969 when Villella was still at the peak of his form. Martins found the experience electrifying. Years afterward, he wrote, "What I saw was rough-edged, overwhelming energy, full-out brio and excitement. . . . Here was someone with city street energy, who hadn't been brought up in the tradition-bound, sheltered, directed, somewhat protected environment."

Villella tried his hand at choreography, but without success. He continued to dance until 1979, when his numerous injuries at last forced his retirement. Since then Villella has spoken to audiences around the United States in an effort to promote an interest in dance. He has also served as artistic director for two ballet companies and in 1986 started his own in Miami, Florida. Villella and his wife, Janet Greschler, with whom he had one child, divorced in November 1980; they had been married since 1962. He married Linda Carbonetta, a figure skater, in April 1981. They have three children.

Although he no longer performs, Villella has never lost his love of ballet. His place in American dance history is secure, unrivaled, and in some ways reflective of the American dream. For the son of working-class Italian immigrants to rise to the pinnacle of the dance world was no mean feat. His accomplishment also brought recognition to ballet as an American art form.

★

With Larry Kaplan, Villella coauthored his autobiography, *Prodigal Son: Dancing for Balanchine in a World of Pain and Magic* (1992). Villella's place in the history of American ballet is documented in Olga Maynard, "Edward Villella Talks to Olga Maynard," *Dance Magazine* (May 1966). Igor Youskevitch, et al., *The Male Image* (1969); John Gruen, *The Private World of Ballet* (1975); Brett Shapiro, "One Ballet Dancer: Edward Villella," *Dance Scope* (1981); and "Villella Speaks on Balanchine," *Dance Teacher Now* (Mar. 1985), are all useful sources.

MEG GREENE

VOIGHT, Jon (*b.* 29 December 1938 in Yonkers, New York), actor who became a star in his first major film, *Midnight Cowboy* (1969), which expressed the angst and social rebellion that permeated much of American society at the end of the 1960s.

Voight was the second son of Elmer Voight, a professional golfer at the Sunningdale Golf Club in Westchester County, and Barbara Camp. As a child Voight had a talent for doing impersonations and learned much from his father, who greatly enjoyed participating in routines, telling fairy stories and creating spy scenarios. To this day Voight's genius is inextricably tied up with character roles rather than starring ones. Voight was mentored in dramatics by Father Bernard McMahon at Stepinac High School in White Plains, New York, from which he graduated in 1956. One of Voight's roles during his high school years was that of an eighty-year-old German playboy. His success revealed his enormous potential as an actor.

Voight began college in 1956 at Catholic University of America in Washington, D.C. Once again a priestly inter-

Jon Voight in a scene from *Midnight Cowboy,* 1969. THE KOBAL COL-LECTION

vention, this time from Father Gilbert Hartke, saw to it that Voight focused on drama. Upon graduating with a B.F.A. in 1960, Voight was determined to pursue a career in acting. He went to New York City and studied for the next four years with Stanford Meisner at the Neighborhood Playhouse. Parental support allowed Voight the time and resources to concentrate on learning how to act.

During the 1960s Voight had a varied apprenticeship on the stage and screen. He had a small part in the hugely successful Broadway production of *The Sound of Music,* then a major role in Arthur Miller's *View from the Bridge.* In 1967 Voight received a Theatre World Award for a star-ring role in *That Summer—That Fall,* Frank Gilroy's adaptation of *Phèdre.* Although the play only ran for twelve performances, Voight's performance was well received by critics.

Voight was always eager to try new roles. He played the lead in *Romeo and Juliet* (1966) and Ariel in *The Tempest* (1966), appeared in seven television shows (including the Westerns *Gunsmoke* and *Cimarron Strip*), then found himself in an educational television production of a Howard Pinter play called *The Dwarfs* (1967).

In 1966 Voight read the screenplay for *The Midnight Cowboy,* by James Leo Herlihy. He was desperate to win the role of Joe Buck, the handsome, boyish drifter from Texas who heads for New York convinced that his cowboy persona will transform him into a high-class gigolo. He campaigned energetically with the film's producer, Jerome Hellman, and its director, John Schlesinger, to win the role.

When United Artists released *Midnight Cowboy* in 1969, the movie enjoyed spectacular box-office success despite nude scenes and other bold content that caused it to receive an X rating. This was eventually downgraded to R. The story follows the unglamorous, dismal, and often hopeless odyssey of two homeless hobos who somehow become close companions. The film critic Tim Dirks sees the story as a modern version of John Steinbeck's novel *Of Mice and Men.* *Midnight Cowboy,* for some, was a morality tale fitfully placed in an ugly and depersonalized metropolis. The film critic Leonard Maltin argues that Voight's role of the male prostitute and hustler helped define the sensitive, as opposed to macho, male character for American movie audiences in the 1960s, 1970s, and 1980s.

Voight's six-foot, three-inch build, plus the muscle he acquired as he trained for the Joe Buck role, allowed him to adroitly carry off the appearance of a Texan peacock. Clad in a fringed leather jacket, a flamboyant Stetson hat, and shiny cowboy boots, Buck is full of fanciful dreams as he departs Texas and heads north to make his fortune.

Voight earned only $17,000 for his Joe Buck role (costar Dustin Hoffman reportedly earned $700,000), but critics uniformly applauded his performance. The film earned three Oscars, one each for best adapted screenplay, best director, and best picture. Voight was nominated for the best actor Oscar and received a New York Film Critic's Award and a National Society of Film Critics Award, both for best actor.

Voight's post–*Midnight Cowboy* career entails his selection of a series of roles that reprise the character Joe Buck. Searching for a denouement and hoping to find meaning or salvation in a cluttered and uneven cultural landscape, Voight's characters are seldom one-dimensional heroic figures. In *Catch 22* (1970) Voight played Milo Minderbinder, a scheming provisions officer who makes a fortune by selling "chocolate-covered cotton." Two years later Voight was the sensitive, cerebral man caught unawares and exposed in John Boorman's harrowing outdoor adventure *Deliverance* (1972). To carry off the role of Ed Gentry, Voight mastered a series of stunts, including riding a canoe through whitewater, climbing a slippery cliff, and shooting a bow and arrow. Vincent Canby, in his review, praises Voight's portrayal of a "thoughtful, self-satisfied business-man who rather surprisingly meets the challenge of the wilderness." In *Conrack* (1974) Voight played a school-teacher who deeply affects African-American pupils on an isolated island off the coast of South Carolina. Then, with *Coming Home* (1978), a drama about the effects of the Viet-nam War, Voight, once again the sensitive and compassionate man, transforms from driven warrior to paralyzed soldier. The film secured for Voight a 1979 Oscar for best actor and awards from the New York Film Critics, the Los Angeles Film Critics, and the Cannes Film Festival.

In 1985 Voight's portrayal of a brutal escaped convict in *Runaway Train* earned him his third Academy Award nomination. In a 1992 Home Box Office (HBO) special, *Last of His Tribe*, Voight explored the issue of land rights for Native Americans. Other especially interesting Voight performances have been an Irish policeman in *The General* (1998) and the demonic football coach in *Varsity Blues* (1999). In *Pearl Harbor* (2001) Voight's depiction of President Franklin D. Roosevelt was mesmerizing. He followed with a priceless, pitch-perfect rendering of broadcaster Howard Cosell in *Ali* (2001), which earned him a fourth Academy Award nomination.

Voight's 1962 marriage to the actor Lauri Peters ended in divorce in 1967. His 1971 marriage to the actor Marcheline Bertrand also ended in divorce. He had two children with Bertrand. One is the film director James Haven Voight; the other is the actress Angelina Jolie.

Voight's intriguing depiction of Joe Buck in *Midnight Cowboy* was much more than artful caricature. The challenged and flawed character of Buck, desperately trying to make sense of a topsy-turvy world, epitomized the changing moral landscape of the 1960s.

★

Current Biography (1974) contains a full and richly textured profile of Voight. *The World Almanac Who's Who of Film* (1987), *Leonard Maltin's Movie Encyclopedia* (1995), and *Earl Blackwell's Celebrity Register* (1998) have short entries on Voight. Vincent Canby's review of *Deliverance* is in the *New York Times* (31 July 1972). The same writer discusses Hollywood Vietnam movies in the *New York Times* (19 Feb. 1978). Tim Dirks's review of *Midnight Cowboy* is extensive—see <www.filmsite.org> and <www.greatestfilms.org>.

SCOTT A. G. M. CRAWFORD

VON BÉKÉSY, George. *See* Békésy, Georg von.

VON BRAUN, Wernher (*b.* 23 March 1912 in Wirsitz, Germany; *d.* 16 June 1977 in Alexandria, Virginia), astrophysicist and engineer, "the father of space travel," who played a vital role in rocket design and space exploration and who developed the launch system used in the Apollo space program.

Von Braun was the second of three sons born to Baron Magnus Alexander Maximilian von Braun, a magistrate and minister of nutrition and agriculture in the Weimer Republic, and Emmy von Quistorp, a homemaker. Von

Wernher Von Braun, 1958. ASSOCIATED PRESS AP

Braun's mother was a well-educated woman who fostered her son's interests in outer space by introducing him to the "science fiction" writers Jules Verne and H. G. Wells.

Von Braun graduated from the Berlin-Charlottenburg Institute of Technology in 1932 with a B.S. in mechanical engineering and aircraft construction. While in school he became involved in the German Society for Space Travel, organized by Hermann Oberth, a group that experimented with launching small liquid-fuel rockets. After funding ran out, von Braun accepted an offer from the German army to join their ordnance department. The military was interested in rockets because they were unregulated by the Treaty of Versailles, the 1919 peace agreement that ended World War I. Von Braun used the information he gained to write his doctoral dissertation in physics, which he completed at the University of Berlin in 1934.

The Nazi regime financed rocket development, and von Braun was a part of their program. Although some V-1 and V-2 rockets were launched, they were too late and ineffective to be of strategic value to the German war effort. Rather, the value was in the rocket technology, for the work of von Braun and his team was more advanced than that of any other country. As it became obvious that Germany was losing the war, von Braun and his group decided to be captured by the Americans rather than the Russians. Therefore, they moved to a Bavarian resort and surrendered to the Americans on 2 May 1945. About 120 of the scientists went to the United States to continue their research in a rocket project called Operation Paperclip. Von Braun returned to Germany to marry his cousin Maria Louise von Quistorp on 1 March 1947; they had three children.

Originally, von Braun and other scientists tested, assembled, and supervised the launching of captured V-2 rockets in White Sands, New Mexico. In 1952 von Braun moved to the Redstone Arsenal near Huntsville, Alabama, as technical director of the U.S. Army's ballistic weapons program. On 15 April 1955 von Braun and forty of his associates became U.S. citizens. During the 1950s he actively promoted space flight, including the launching of an earth satellite, on television, and in books and magazines. After the Soviet Union launched *Sputnik* and the U.S. Navy's Vanguard rocket exploded in 1957, the von Braun group launched the first U.S. satellite, *Explorer I,* on 31 January 1958. The federal government began funding space exploration to increase national pride, as well as to gain scientific knowledge, and Presidents Dwight D. Eisenhower, John F. Kennedy, and Lyndon B. Johnson gave the space program their complete support. Von Braun and his team became part of the National Aeronautics and Space Administration (NASA).

As the space race continued, von Braun assumed a pivotal role. By late 1961 he was director of the Marshall Space Flight Center and controlled 40 percent of NASA's budget. He became responsible for supplying NASA with booster rockets. Von Braun and his team at Huntsville conceived the *Saturn I* using the latest advances in technology. By 1962 NASA could estimate the size of the booster needed for a manned space mission. To determine its exact requirements, a decision had to be made from three operational concepts—direct ascent with no intermediate stages; earth orbit rendezvous which combines payloads from craft in earth orbit; and lunar orbit rendezvous (LOR), in which a single rocket launches separable spacecraft. After the spacecraft is in orbit, the lunar module detaches and lands on the moon. Although von Braun did not originally favor LOR, he later supported it as a way to win the cooperation of the Houston Manned Space Center and continue to be part of the space race.

Von Braun was forced to accept a different approach to rocket testing. In 1963 George Mueller, the new head of the office of Manned Space Flight, calculated that at the rate the program was progressing, it would be impossible to land a man on the moon before 1970. He recommended using "all up" testing instead of step-by-step testing, which meant testing all the components of the *Saturn V* together. This approach was heresy to the German engineers, who had been testing components individually since the 1930s

and had witnessed numerous rocket failures. The Apollo missions, using the *Saturn IB* rocket (Apollo 7) and the *Saturn V* rocket (Apollo 8, 10, and 11), were key engineering successes that acted as a precursor to the manned moon landing.

Von Braun was lauded as a national hero. He received numerous awards, such as the Robert H. Goddard Memorial Trophy (1958), the Distinguished Federal Civilian Service Award (1959), and the National Medal of Science (1977). After the successful moon landing, there were no new space projects on the horizon. Von Braun moved on to NASA administration in Washington, D.C., in 1970. As funding ended for new projects, he left for private industry in 1972, working for Fairchild Industries in Maryland on satellite development and deployment.

Von Braun enjoyed being in the limelight. After *Sputnik* landed, he was a common sight on Capitol Hill testifying before Congress, mesmerizing them with his knowledge and charm. From 1958, when the *Explorer I* was launched, until 1966, he received nineteen honorary doctorate degrees and joined eighteen professional organizations. He wrote several hundred articles, although few were technical or scientific pieces. He produced monthly articles for *Popular Science* for ten years and coauthored *History of Rocketry and Space Travel* in 1966 with Frederick I. Ordway.

Von Braun has been accused of knowing that slave laborers and workers from the Dora concentration camp produced the V-2s, and that the Nazis abused the workers. Throughout his life, von Braun continued to deny any knowledge of the conditions in the concentration camps. Many critics feel, however, that he knew the conditions of the camps but chose to ignore them to continue producing rockets at the Nordhausen facility—his blinding passion. His failures appear to be indirect—not protesting about the camp conditions rather than inflicting them. Von Braun died of cancer and is buried at Ivy Hill Cemetery in Alexandria, Virginia.

★

The Manuscript Division of the Library of Congress has many of von Braun's papers from the period of 1950 to 1970, and the NASA History Division in Washington, D.C., has other papers, along with von Braun's writings, speeches, interviews, and newspaper clippings. Biographies of von Braun include Helen B. Walters, *Wernher von Braun: Rocket Engineer* (1964); John C. Goodrum, *Wernher von Braun: Space Pioneer* (1969); Erik Bergaust, *Wernher von Braun* (1976); Christopher Lampton, *Wernher von Braun* (1988); Ernst Stulinger and Frederick I. Ordway, *Wernher von Braun: Crusader for Space* (1994); Diane K. Moser and Ray Spangenburg, *Wernher von Braun: Space Visionary and Rocket Engineer* (1995); and Dennis Piszkiewicz, *Wernher von Braun: The Man Who Sold the Moon* (1998). Biographical information is also in Walter Dornberger, *V-2* (1954); Frederick I. Ordway and Mitchell R. Sharpe, *The Rocket Team* (1979); and Frank H. Winter, *Rockets into Space* (1990). Obituaries are in the *Washington Star* (17 June 1977), *New York Times* and *Washington Post* (both 18 June 1977); and *Time* and *Newsweek* (both 27 June 1977).

SHEILA BECK

VONNEGUT, Kurt, Jr. (*b.* 11 November 1922 in Indianapolis, Indiana), novelist and essayist whose offbeat characters and dark comedy echoed the disillusionment of a generation sullied by war, corporate greed, and government corruption, and who rose to prominence with the publication of *Slaughterhouse-five* (1969), a novel about the U.S. bombing of Dresden, Germany, during World War II.

Vonnegut, the third child of Kurt Vonnegut, an architect, and Edith Lieber, a homemaker, began writing at Shortridge High School (1936–1940), working as a columnist and editor for the *Shortridge Daily Register*. His journalistic interests continued at Cornell University (1940–1942) in

Kurt Vonnegut, Jr., 1971. ASSOCIATED PRESS AP

Ithaca, New York, where he managed and wrote for the *Cornell Sun* while majoring in biochemistry. At Cornell, Vonnegut felt "marginal [and] somehow slightly off-balance all the time," a feeling he credits with making him a writer, and which led to his literary style that emerged in the 1960s. He did not graduate from Cornell.

Vonnegut served in the U.S. Army (infantry) during World War II and received the Purple Heart. Several events occurred during 1944 and 1945 that further shaped Vonnegut's writing and the direction of his life. In May 1944 his mother committed suicide. In December 1944 he was captured by the Nazis during the Battle of the Bulge and sent to a prisoner of war camp in Dresden, Germany, where, on 13 February 1945 he survived the infamous fire-bombing of the city by Allied forces. The city was decimated in the attack—more than 50,000 civilians were killed—and Vonnegut's captors forced him to remove corpses from the resulting rubble. In May 1945 he was freed by Russian soldiers. Three months later, on 6 August, the U.S. dropped an atomic bomb on Hiroshima, Japan, resulting in the deaths of more than 200,000 people. Much of Vonnegut's disillusionment with humanity and human systems—government, business, religion, science—is traceable to these early experiences. Vonnegut said of the Hiroshima bombing, "I was a great believer in truth, scientific truth, and then . . . truth was dropped on Hiroshima. . . . I was hideously disappointed."

After the end of the war, Vonnegut married Jane Marie Cox on 1 September 1945, enrolled at the University of Chicago, and began working toward a master's degree in anthropology. He continued to write, taking a job as a police reporter for the Chicago City News Bureau. When his master's thesis was rejected by the university, Vonnegut took a job as a publicist for the General Electric Company in Schenectady, New York, to support his wife and two children, a son born in 1947 and a daughter born in 1949. He also began writing short stories. Vonnegut's first published story, "Report on the Barnhouse Effect," appeared in the 11 February 1950 edition of *Colliers* magazine; he vowed to quit his job at General Electric when he sold four or five more stories.

Writing turned out to be a lucrative enterprise, and Vonnegut soon moved to Provincetown, Massachusetts, to write full time. He published more than fifty short stories between 1950 and 1966. His first novel, *Player Piano,* was published in 1952. The book, a postmodern version of Aldous Huxley's *Brave New World* (1932), was dismissed by critics who categorized it as science fiction. It was reprinted in 1954, the year his second daughter was born, with the title *Utopia 14.* Between 1954 and 1956 Vonnegut worked a number of jobs to support his growing family while struggling to establish himself as a writer. He was employed at an automobile dealership and an advertising agency and also taught English. Meanwhile, he faced the death of more family members: his father died in 1957, and in 1958 his beloved sister died of cancer within twenty-four hours of her husband's death in a train accident. Vonnegut adopted three of their children.

After the publication of *The Sirens of Titan* in 1959, Vonnegut began to garner a cult following of hip, young readers in search of alternative literary works and writers. Baby boomers, who were center stage during the 1960s, found that Vonnegut's writings mirrored their own search for self apart from war, racism, sexism, capitalist greed, and corrupt politics. Vonnegut's prose, like his audience, was playfully irreverent, critical of corporate and political monoliths, fresh, innovative, funny, and intimately focused on the individual.

Vonnegut's early novels addressed issues similar to those reshaping U.S. culture in the 1960s. While America's youth rebelled against tradition and struggled to make sense of their lives and their world, Vonnegut published *Mother Night* (1962), a story of war-crime tribunals and fascism that questions our ability to distinguish good from evil; *Cat's Cradle* (1963), a story of worldwide apocalypse that critiques the indifference of science and the arbitrariness of religion; and *God Bless You, Mr. Rosewater* (1965), a story of inherited wealth that exposes the absurdity of materialism and the inhumanity of greed. In particular, the publication of *Cat's Cradle* extended Vonnegut's appeal and helped to establish him as a major figure in American literature and the avuncular voice of a disillusioned generation.

By 1965 Vonnegut's reputation as a writer had grown enough for him to land a resident teaching position with the acclaimed writer's workshop at the University of Iowa in Iowa City. In 1967 he stopped teaching at Iowa and returned to Germany on a Guggenheim Fellowship to research a new book, *Slaughterhouse-five*. Published in 1969, the novel fuses a true accounting of Vonnegut's experiences in Dresden with the fantastic tale of a man who is kidnapped by aliens and becomes "unstuck in time." This story outlining the senselessness and unavoidability of war captivated popular audiences and gained critical attention, conflating the categories of literature and popular fiction. Laudatory reviews in the *New York Times Book Review* and other influential periodicals cemented Vonnegut's reputation as an important American author. According to Jerome Klinkowitz, an English professor and noted authority on Vonnegut's work, *Slaughterhouse-five* so "perfectly caught America's transformative mood that its story and structure became best-selling metaphors for the new age." Ironically, Vonnegut at first thought the book was a failure, but in light of its warm reception he amended his opinion.

After the publication of *Slaughterhouse-five*, Vonnegut briefly taught creative writing at Harvard University in Cambridge, Massachusetts, where he worked on *Happy*

Birthday, Wanda June, a play based on *Penelope,* which he had written around 1960. *Happy Birthday, Wanda June* debuted on Broadway in March 1971, the same year the University of Chicago accepted *Cat's Cradle* as Vonnegut's long overdue thesis and awarded him a master's degree in anthropology. In 1972 *Slaughterhouse-five* was made into a popular movie, and Vonnegut's reputation grew. In 1973 he published *Breakfast of Champions,* his second most popular work, and became the distinguished professor of English prose at the City University of New York. He published two more novels and a collection of essays during the remainder of the 1970s, but none achieved the success and critical attention of his previous works. In 1979 Vonnegut divorced his first wife; he married the photographer Jill Krementz on 24 November 1979, and the couple adopted a daughter. In 1982 Vonnegut published *Deadeye Dick*. In 1984, suffering from severe depression, he attempted suicide with alcohol and sleeping pills.

Vonnegut's next three novels, *Galápagos* (1985), *Bluebeard* (1987), and *Hocus Pocus* (1990), recapture the insight of his work during the 1960s, but with an added maturity. During the 1980s and 1990s Vonnegut was frequently asked to comment on events in popular culture. As a spokesperson for the children of the 1960s, Vonnegut opposed government appropriation of the rights of the individual and was adamantly against nuclear proliferation. After *Slaughterhouse-five* was banned by a number of school libraries—and even burned at a school in Drake, North Dakota—Vonnegut became an unassuming voice for the First Amendment rights of individual expression, calling such acts of censorship "ignorant, dumb, superstitious . . . [and] cowardly."

Despite the dark and serious subject matter of his work, Vonnegut, like the audience that embraced him, never sacrificed his sense of humor. Although his works confront irresolvable issues about war, wealth, politics, bureaucracy, death, insanity, and identity in their search for humanity and basic decency, they are always witty and often hilarious. In the 1960s Vonnegut's literary technique challenged traditional forms and paralleled similar movements in art and music. Like the art of Andy Warhol and the music of the Beatles, his novels threw into question notions of high and low art. Vonnegut eventually became, in the fashion of Mark Twain, a gentleman of American letters, one whose perception of the human condition awes us in its concision and whose message for a disillusioned generation is simply to "respect one another." His writings repeatedly return to the same request: to behave with common courtesy, act humanely, and be kind to one another.

★

No book-length biographies of Vonnegut exist, but several of his works are autobiographical, such as *Wampeters, Foma, and*

Granfalloons (1974), *Palm Sunday: An Autobiographical Collage* (1981), and *Fates Worse than Death: An Autobiographical Collage of the 1980s* (1991). Information about Vonnegut is also in Jerome Klinkowitz, *The American 1960s: Imaginative Acts in a Decade of Change* (1980), and William R. Allen, *Conversations with Kurt Vonnegut* (1988).

KEVIN ALEXANDER BOON

VREELAND, Diana (*b.* c. 1903 in Paris, France; *d.* 22 August 1989 in New York City), legendary fashion editor, author, and arbiter of taste.

The date of Vreeland's birth is somewhat obscure; various sources record it as taking place in 1901, 1903, and 1906. What is more certain is that Vreeland was the first child born to an American mother, Emily Key Hoffman, and a Scottish father, Frederick Y. Dalziel, who was a stockbroker. Vreeland first became aware of the fashion and art world during a childhood spent in Paris, where her parents entertained such notables as Vaslav Nijinsky, Sergei Diaghilev, Ida Rubenstein, and Vernon and Irene Castle.

With the outbreak of World War I in 1914, the family moved to New York City. Here Vreeland and her younger sister, Alexandra, attended private school, practiced ballet, and took horseback riding lessons. In 1922 Vreeland made her social debut. Like many young women of her social circle, she never attended college. Two years later, while vacationing in Saratoga, New York, she met banker T. Reed Vreeland. The two married later that year and had two sons. Vreeland lived in Albany, New York, for four years (she became a naturalized citizen in 1925) and then moved to London, where she managed a lingerie shop. By 1936 she was back in New York and writing for *Harper's Bazaar*. Her column, "Why Don't You . . . ?," offered readers beauty and fashion advice. Vreeland's success as a writer lay in her ability to combine whimsy and fantasy with an almost unerring eye for fashion. Within a year she was promoted to fashion editor, shaping the magazine into an influential arbiter of high fashion and good taste.

Vreeland's full ascent into the vanguard of style did not begin until she left *Harper's Bazaar* in 1962 to become associate editor of *Vogue*. Her time in that position was short-lived; a year later she became editor in chief, a position she held until her departure in 1971. During this period Vreeland proved to be far more than a fashion editor. "Far surpassing a fashion editor's role of reporting fashion," observed another fashion writer, "Vreeland predicted it, set it, personified it. . . . She was 'seen' wherever she went, listened to whenever she spoke, and quoted endlessly."

Vreeland's keen eye was more than a match for the riotous changes that took place in fashion during the 1960s. Her style dictates were obeyed by all who wished to appear hip. Under her direction *Vogue* moved from being a showcase of haute couture to promoting Vreeland's emphasis on the offbeat and the youthful. She coined the phrase "beautiful people" and "pizzazz," both of which became catchwords used to describe individuals who were trendsetters. Her comments on the state of fashion and world affairs were hot copy for newspapers and magazines around the world. She became famous for such statements as "pink is the navy blue of India" and "the bikini's only the most important invention since the atom bomb."

Vreeland also used *Vogue* to push her own cultural agenda. An early advocate of physical fitness, she devoted ample space in the magazine to exercise regimens as well as to skin and hair care and other aspects of personal grooming. Her conversation was filled with unrivaled hyperbole. Even her handwritten memos were the stuff of conversation and were routinely circulated, copied, and cherished.

Vreeland's foresight created some of the trademark styles of the 1960s. Vreeland popularized boots, costume jewelry, and pants for women, as well as see-through tops and the "peasant look," which consisted of loose, patterned blouses and full skirts. When Vreeland believed in a "look," she not only reported on it but also promoted it endlessly until it took hold in the popular imagination.

As part of her unconventional approach to make *Vogue* the fashion magazine of the 1960s, Vreeland also experi-

Diana Vreeland inspecting a coat by Balenciaga, March 1973. © BETT-MANN/CORBIS

mented with fashion photography, employing such innovative photographers as Richard Avedon. She also moved away from the sophisticated and feminine fashion models, instead championing models who exemplified an unconventional look. She helped launch the careers of model Lauren Hutton and designer Roy Halston. She helped to make pop artist Andy Warhol a cult figure and graced the pages of *Vogue* with images of the English model Twiggy and the rock star Mick Jagger. One reporter concluded that Vreeland "not only chronicled fashion, she influenced it, transforming what she saw through the use of daring photography and originating the deft, inimitable descriptions that became her signature."

Vreeland practiced what she preached, cultivating her own distinctive style. Instantly recognizable with her jet-black hair, bright red nail polish and lipstick, rouged cheeks, forehead, and earlobes, Vreeland wore simple yet dramatic all-black ensembles. Both her Manhattan apartment and her office at *Vogue* were painted red.

Critics suggest that Vreeland's energy might better have been applied to subjects other than that of fashion trends. She disagrees. "People always say there are more interesting things than fashion. But show me a fashionably dressed woman and I'll show you someone who accomplishes something."

By 1971 the kaleidoscopic whirl that marked the fashions of the 1960s had ended. Vreeland was "released" from her position as editor in chief, though she remained with *Vogue* as a consulting editor. Never one to wax sentimental, Vreeland that same year began a new job as a consultant to the Costume Institute of the Metropolitan Museum of Art (Met). Multicultural fashions, so much a part of her legacy during the 1960s, were showcased at the Met, with exhibits featuring Chinese mandarin robes, Russian peasant outfits, and gypsy caftans. During the 1970s Vreeland wrote five books on fashion and style and was repeatedly honored for her contributions to the fashion world. Among her numerous awards were an honorary doctorate in 1977 from the Parsons School of Design as well as recognition from the Italian fashion industry and the Rhode Island School of Design. Vreeland died of a heart attack at Lenox Hill Hospital, Manhattan, in 1989.

Five years before she died Vreeland summed up her views on fashion, stating that "fashion . . . is a social contract. . . . Designers keep proposing something new, but whether their ideas come to fruition depends ultimately on whether the society that counts accepts them or rejects them." For many, Vreeland helped bridge the gap between a designer's vision and the public taste, without sacrificing a sense of fantasy and daring that has seldom been rivaled.

★

There is no biography of Vreeland, but she wrote an autobiography, *D. V.: Give 'Em What They Never Knew They Wanted* (1984), which was edited by George Plimpton and Christopher Hemphill. Biographical information on Vreeland can be found in Anne Stegemeyer, ed., *Who's Who in Fashion,* 3d ed. (1996). See also Hilton Als, "D. V. on Display," *The New Yorker* (22 Sept. 1997). Obituaries of Vreeland are in the *New York Times,* the *Chicago Tribune,* and the *Times* (London) (all 23 Aug. 1989).

MEG GREENE

W

WALD, George (*b.* 18 November 1906 in New York City; *d.* 12 April 1997 in Cambridge, Massachusetts), biochemist, teacher, and political activist who won the 1967 Nobel Prize in physiology or medicine for his research on the role of vitamin A in vision and on the light-absorbing molecules in the retina.

Wald was the son of Isaac Wald, a Polish immigrant tailor, and Ernestine (Rosenmann) Wald, a housewife, who came from a small village in Bavaria. Shortly after his birth, the family moved from lower Manhattan to Brooklyn, where Wald attended Brooklyn Technical High School. The training he received there allowed him to modify and even build the scientific instruments later needed in his research. Wald did his undergraduate work at the Washington Square College of New York University, completing his B.S. in zoology in 1927. He then enrolled as a graduate student in zoology at Columbia University, earning an M.A. in 1928, and worked with Selig Hecht, who studied the physiology of vision.

Wald received a Ph.D. in 1932 and went to Europe on a National Research Council Fellowship in biology. He was accompanied on this trip by Frances Kingsley, whom he had married on 15 May 1931 and with whom he had two children; this marriage later ended in divorce in 1957. Wald did research in the laboratories of three noted European biochemists, beginning with Otto Warburg in Berlin. Working in Warburg's lab, Wald discovered that vitamin A plays a role in the functioning of the light-sensitive pigment rhodopsin, which is found in the retina of the eye. In Paul Karrer's lab at the University of Zurich, Wald confirmed the presence of vitamin A in the retinas of cattle, sheep, and pigs. At his third stop, Otto Meyerhof's laboratory at the Kaiser Wilhelm Institute in Heidelberg, Germany, Wald did research indicating that light splits rhodopsin into a protein called opsin and a molecule ultimately called retinal, a derivative of vitamin A. The reverse process occurs in the dark, thus regenerating rhodopsin. Wald discovered the biochemical explanation for the fact that when a person goes from a brightly lit room into a dark one, there is a temporary difficulty in seeing, called night blindness. The bright light splits rhodopsin into opsin and retinal. The pigment rhodopsin detects light in the cells of the retina, called rods. It takes a few moments to re-form the rhodopsin, thus making it possible to detect what little light there is in a darkened room.

After returning from Europe in 1934, Wald began his association with Harvard University in Cambridge, Massachusetts, ultimately becoming a professor of biology there in 1948. For the next forty years Wald continued to study the biochemistry of the visual pigments. He discovered that the cones, the cells that work in bright light and are responsible for color vision, also contain pigments with retinal attached to opsins. But the opsins of each of the three pigments in cones are different, and each responds to different wavelengths of light.

George David Wald. THE LIBRARY OF CONGRESS

In 1958 two students arrived in Wald's laboratory who had a huge impact on the work done there in the 1960s. One was Paul K. Brown, who discovered how the cone pigments function and found that each form of color blindness is due to the absence of one of the three pigments. In the 1980s other researchers discovered the genes that determine the structure of the opsins in these pigments. The other student was Ruth Hubbard, who came as a graduate student and married Wald in 1958, while continuing to do research with him. They had two children. With Hubbard and Brown, Wald discovered that light causes a structural change in the retinal in rhodopsin. This change leads to the separation of the retinal from the opsin.

In 1965 Wald published a significant paper in the field of the biochemistry of visual systems. His research led him to speculate that a single photon or particle of light, initially splitting one rhodopsin molecule in a retina cell, could trigger a cascade of reactions that amplify the trigger, leading to the initiation of a nerve impulse going to the brain. He likened such a cascade or amplification process to that found in blood clotting. Wald's article stimulated research that established the validity of his view.

The 1960s were a busy time for Wald. In 1967 he was awarded the Nobel Prize in physiology or medicine for his

research on visual pigments; he shared the prize with Ragnar Granit and Haldan Keffer Hartline. Also in the 1960s Wald became a political activist. The Vietnam War, which he opposed, initially stimulated his interest in civic matters. He was active in antinuclear causes and was supportive of the political uprisings in Nicaragua, the Philippines, Guatemala, and elsewhere. On 4 March 1969 Wald gave a speech at Harvard entitled "A Generation in Search of a Future," which attracted national attention to anti–Vietnam War sentiment and thereafter was referred to as "The Speech." After his retirement from Harvard in 1977, he devoted himself to political activism until the last two years of his life.

In addition to teaching his highly regarded biochemistry course, Wald began teaching a biology course for nonscience majors in 1960 and continued to do so until his retirement. In 1966 *Time* magazine cited him as one of the ten best college teachers in the United States. Wald was known as a brilliant lecturer, and his presentations on the origin of life and the evolution of the visual pigments were particularly popular. Wald's impact on the field of vision studies was immense. His work on the visual pigments took the study of vision down to the molecular level, describing how the molecular changes caused by light create electrical impulses that are sent to the brain. His 1967 Nobel Prize testified to the importance of these discoveries, and his work as a teacher and political activist indicated how science is not an isolated field but is tied intimately to the larger culture. Wald died of natural causes at his home in Cambridge at the age of ninety.

★

Wald's scientific papers, speeches, and correspondence are held by the Harvard University Archive. Biographies of Wald include "George Wald," in *Modern Scientists and Engineers* (1980); Marc Kusinitz, "George Wald," in *Notable Twentieth-century Scientists* (1995); and John E. Dowling, "George Wald," in *Biographical Memoirs of the National Academy of Sciences* (2000). See also "George Wald," *New Yorker* (1966); articles about Wald in *Time* (6 May 1966) and *Science* (27 Oct. 1967); and "George Wald: The Man, the Speech," *New York Times Magazine* (17 Aug. 1969). Obituaries are in the *New York Times* (14 Apr. 1997), *Harvard University Gazette* (17 Apr. 1997), and *Time* (28 Apr. 1997).

MAURA C. FLANNERY

WALLACE, George Corley, Jr. (*b.* 25 August 1919 in Clio, Alabama; *d.* 13 September 1998 in Montgomery, Alabama), four-term governor of Alabama, three-time presidential candidate, leading segregationist, and spokesman for southern Democrats.

Wallace was one of four children born to George Corley Wallace, Sr., and Mozell (Smith) Wallace in rural Barbour

George Wallace. THE LIBRARY OF CONGRESS

County, Alabama. George Wallace, Sr., was a slightly successful farmer who suffered terribly from a host of physical ailments, while Mozell Wallace was a homemaker and farm wife. Wallace's father died when Wallace was eighteen years old. In his autobiography, *Stand Up for America,* Wallace assesses his father: "He was typical of the solid, hardworking, God-fearing people who . . . inhabit rural Alabama, and whose combination of faith and sinew helped to make the state strong and prosperous." Wallace worked alongside his father in the fields and did odd jobs to earn extra money to help out his family. During his school years Wallace was an athlete, in particular a boxer. He attended the University of Alabama at Tuscaloosa from 1937 to 1942, earning a degree in law. During World War II he married Lurleen Burns, on 23 May 1943, and from 1942 to 1945 he served in the Army Air Corps in the Pacific; he was involved in the 1945 bombing raids over Japan. He and Lurleen had four children.

Wallace was a tenacious politician who served in a variety of state offices. He was a populist who believed in tough campaigns and going door-to-door, talking with the people and earning their trust slowly through honesty and determination. During the 1940s and 1950s Wallace had a fledgling law practice while he served in the Alabama attorney general's office, as a delegate to Democratic conventions, and as a state judge. Wallace believed in protecting

the rights of the common (white) people and in conservative Christianity. He was branded a racist during these years, which in his autobiography he denies, claiming that as a judge he was colorblind and that his growing racist tag derived from his dogged determination to protect states' rights in the face of growing federal power. Wallace ran for governor of Alabama in 1958 on a platform of bringing industry to the state and revitalizing the state's public schools. Although he lost to John Patterson, he immediately began preparing to run again. He was elected governor in 1962.

As governor from 1963 to 1967 Wallace tried to reconstruct the political and social philosophy of the southern confederacy and apply it to modern conditions. His inaugural address was forthright in its devotion to the ideals of a previous century. "From this Cradle of the Confederacy," said Wallace, "this very Heart of the Great Anglo-Saxon Southland . . . we sound the drum for freedom as have our generations of forebears before us." The tyrants were liberals who sought to spread Communism throughout America, who sought "to persecute the *international* white minority to the whim of the *international* colored majority" dominated by the United Nations. Wallace called upon African Americans to join him in working for a social structure based on the assumption of a "separate racial station," preserving "our freedom of race." Segregating the races was the only way to preserve their respective freedom, he argued. Integration represented a tyrannical response to Wallace's own motto for Alabama: "Segregation today, segregation tomorrow, segregation forever."

This was quite an astonishing speech for the man the National Association for the Advancement of Colored People (NAACP) had supported in his 1958 run for governor. Yet Wallace was singular in his independence from the many interest groups that would have liked to put him in their pocket, such as the Ku Klux Klan, a prominent white supremacist group. Wallace's ideals of white supremacy were moderated by his Christian beliefs, his devotion to honor and duty, his respect for the elderly, sick, and helpless. If Wallace was a segregationist, he was at the same time committed to helping African Americans enjoy rights and peace within their own sphere.

Such a sphere was no longer tenable in America, but Wallace refused to see it. Historical events were moving faster than he was willing to accept. In the spring of 1963 demonstrations, riots, and brutality broke out in Birmingham, Alabama, in response to desegregation. The city and the state were unable to control the violence and protect civil rights; President John F. Kennedy called for federal troops. Wallace responded to the federal intervention by filing court papers to repudiate unwanted federal force in the state of Alabama and "to declare the Fourteenth Amendment unconstitutional by virtue of its illegal ratification." Wallace objected to the attempted enrollment of two African-American students at the University of Alabama. A year earlier a similar incident in Mississippi had resulted in death and destruction. Wallace declared that the university would remain segregated even if he was forced to "be present to bar the entrance of any Negro who attempts to enroll." To this and his later attempt in 1963 to resist court-ordered integration of Alabama's public schools, Wallace claimed that his actions had nothing to do with race but rather were in response to the liberal agenda of weakening state government in the face of rising federal government control.

Wallace's foray into national politics began when he ran for the Democratic nomination for president of the United States in 1964. He campaigned for no government interference in state and local education, for allowing business owners to choose their employees, and for giving people the freedom to act within their "sphere." Wallace proclaimed in *Stand Up for America* that his platform attracted support from those "little people who feared big government in the hands of phony intellectuals and social engineers." He garnered respectable numbers in the Wisconsin, Indiana, and Maryland primaries before bowing out of the election, proclaiming that he had accomplished his goal of defending and promoting the philosophy of states' rights on the national scene.

Wallace's response to the Civil Rights Act of 1964 and the Voting Rights Act of 1965 was consistent with his stated beliefs. Both of these acts, pushed by the Lyndon B. Johnson administration, were aimed at destroying the Jim Crow laws of the South, laws that promoted the old "separate but equal" dogma, set restrictions on African-American suffrage, and attempted to keep African Americans in their place by providing them with the lowest-paying jobs and by restricting their access to good education. Wallace compared the attempts by the Johnson administration to create an America of complete equality with a Communist agenda along the lines of the Soviet Union, where the executive branch of government imposed its will on the people. During one face-to-face meeting Wallace told President Johnson that the Voting Rights Act was a federal imposition on state control, which violated the Tenth Amendment and threatened to destroy federalism as set forth under the Constitution.

Under Alabama law Wallace could not seek a successive term as governor. Wallace avoided this restriction by supporting his wife's campaign for governor. She won easily. Wallace turned his attention to the presidential contest of 1968. But joy for her victory was countered by her health problems. During fall 1967 she began a battle against cancer. As the disease grew worse by the end of 1967, Wallace reconsidered whether or not he should run for president, but Lurleen wouldn't think of his breaking "a promise to

the people of Alabama . . . to bring a message to the American people." When she died in May 1968 Wallace channeled his overwhelming grief into an exhausting presidential campaign.

Wallace in 1968 became the candidate of the American Independence Party for president of the United States; his running mate was Curtis LeMay. Wallace and LeMay promoted a platform based on supporting American troops in Vietnam by aggressively pursuing the war, lowering taxes to bring about reduction of government spending, bringing inflation under control, and ending forced integration of American schools. Wallace appealed to the conservative, white, middle class, who responded with a surprising degree of support. He appealed to some conservative Democrats, particularly because the Democrats were reeling from disaster and disagreement—the assassination of Senator Robert F. Kennedy and the uncertainty about whether to continue or abandon Johnson's policy toward Vietnam. Wallace's platform was similar to Republican beliefs, even if he did state them with more force and bluntness. In the end, however, Wallace's message was seriously considered only in his home base. In the 1968 election he garnered forty-six electoral votes, winning five states of the Deep South—Arkansas, Louisiana, Mississippi, Alabama, and Georgia. He won 13.5 percent of the popular vote.

After the election Wallace toured Vietnam and considered his political options. Having been out of the governorship for a term, he decided to reenter the Alabama gubernatorial race, once again embracing the Democratic Party; he won reelection handily. Wallace remarried in January 1971 to Cornelia Ellis Snively. They were divorced in January 1978. Cornelia was an important resource for her husband during his second term as governor, during his run for the Democratic nomination in 1972, and after he had been struck down and paralyzed by the would-be assassin Arthur Bremer in May 1972 in Laurel, Maryland. Bound to a wheelchair, Wallace rebounded to run again for governor of Alabama. In September 1981 he married Lisa Taylor, but they divorced in January 1987.

Wallace served as governor of Alabama for four terms; he ran for president of the United States three times. During these campaigns he assumed the role of the twentieth-century spokesman for the ideals of the Old South and the confederacy. He was a complicated man who lived in complicated times. He never departed from the traditional beliefs and values of his native Alabama. During the 1960s Wallace represented stability to the millions of southern white-collar and blue-collar whites who saw surrounding them a variety of threats, such as the spread of Communism throughout the world and in America, the increasing power of the federal government, the cultural extremes in America, and the civil rights movement. He died of cardiac and respiratory arrest in Jackson Hospital. He is buried in Greenwood Cemetery in Montgomery.

★

Wallace's autobiography is *Stand Up for America* (1976). Biographies include E. Culpepper Clark, *The Schoolhouse Door: Segregation's Last Stand at the University of Alabama* (1993); Stephan Lesher, *George Wallace, American Populist* (1994); and Dan T. Carter, *The Politics of Rage: George Wallace, the Origins of the New Conservatism, and the Transformation of American Politics* (1995). An obituary is in the *New York Times* (15 Sept. 1998).

RUSSELL M. LAWSON

WALLACE, Mike (*b.* 9 May 1918 in Brookline, Massachusetts), award-winning journalist who revolutionized news journalism by using hard-hitting, insightful interviewing techniques. It was during the 1960s that Wallace began to concentrate solely on serious news journalism and, primarily because of a television show called *60 Minutes,* became universally known and respected as television's "Grand Inquisitor."

Wallace was born Myron Leon Wallace, the son of Russian Jewish immigrant parents. His father, Frank Wallace, was an insurance broker and his mother, Zina (Sharfman) Wal-

Mike Wallace, 1964. HULTON ARCHIVE

lace, was a homemaker. After graduating from high school, Wallace attended the University of Michigan with the intent of becoming either a lawyer or an English teacher. But after wandering into the university's broadcast center, he changed his major to speech and broadcasting.

Wallace graduated from the University of Michigan in 1939 and became a radio newscaster, first at WOOD in Grand Rapids (1939 to 1940) and later at WXYZ in Detroit (1940–1941). While in Detroit, Wallace married Norma Kaphan; the marriage produced two sons, Peter and Christopher, but the couple divorced in 1948. (Chris Wallace followed in his father's footsteps and at the millennium is the chief correspondent for the American Broadcasting Company's news show *Nightline.*)

In 1941 Wallace moved to Chicago as a radio broadcaster for *Air Edition* for the *Chicago Sun* (1941 to 1943 and 1946 to 1948) and later with the radio station WMAQ. During World War II Wallace served in the U.S. Navy as a communications officer. In 1951 Wallace moved to New York City to host an interview show for the Columbia Broadcasting System (CBS) entitled *Mike and Buff.* The show's other host was his second wife, the actress Buff Cobb, whom he married in 1949. When their turbulent marriage ended in 1954, so did the show. On 21 July 1955 he married his third wife, Lorraine Perigord, who had two children from a previous marriage. She divorced Wallace in 1985; the couple had no children of their own.

Aside from his regular broadcasting jobs, Wallace did freelance radio announcing, television commercials, and entertainment shows, such as *All Around Town* (1951 to 1952), *I'll Buy That* (1953 to 1954), and the *Big Surprise* (1956 to 1957). Wallace even appeared on Broadway in the play *Reclining Figure* in 1954. In 1956 Wallace became the host of an innovative talk show called *NightBeat,* which employed a hard-edged format using pointed questions, close-up images of (usually perspiring) guests, and solid background research. The studio's dark backdrop and the drifting smoke of Wallace's cigarette further enhanced the mood. Originally broadcast 9 October 1956 on the DuMont's network New York affiliate Channel 5 (WABD), the show moved to the American Broadcasting Company (ABC) network in 1957 as *The Mike Wallace Interviews.* It proved too controversial for the network, however, and was cancelled in 1958. Wallace later hosted the chat show *PM East* (1961 to 1962), a nightly news program called *News Beat* (1959 to 1961), and the television documentary *Biography* (1959 to 1961).

The year 1962 marked a significant turning point in Wallace's personal and professional life. In August 1962 Wallace's son Peter was killed in a hiking accident in Greece. Grief stricken, Wallace vowed to make a dramatic change in his life. He decided to shun all advertising and entertainment jobs and concentrate on hard news, even if it meant a drastic cut in pay. When Wallace was rehired by CBS in 1963, the network's veteran news reporters initially snubbed him because of his reputation for doing commercials and talk shows. By virtue of his impressive work ethic, however, he won their respect. Starting in 1963 Wallace hosted the *CBS Morning News* but left the show after three years to become a general news correspondent.

Wallace reported on many major events during the turbulent decade of the 1960s. He logged various tours of duty reporting on the Vietnam War, and his stories dealing with the war ranged from coverage of the My Lai massacre (in which a U.S. infantry platoon killed more than one hundred unarmed civilians) to stories about U.S. military deserters living in Canada. Wallace also covered the Arab-Israeli Six-Day War in 1967.

Wallace reported on the militant aspect of the civil rights movement during the 1960s. In 1959 Wallace had produced the controversial but powerful documentary on the Black Muslims entitled "The Hate That Hate Produced" for his program *News Beat*. A little more than ten years later, Wallace interviewed the Black Panther leader Eldridge Cleaver, who was living in exile in Algiers. The story aimed to show that the Panthers had ceased to be a legitimate threat to society, but Cleaver's threat of shooting his way into the White House and "taking off" President Richard M. Nixon's head alarmed not only viewers but also the Justice Department. They later demanded materials concerning the interview from CBS.

Wallace began covering the national political conventions starting in 1960, reporting freelance for a chain of Westinghouse-owned stations. In later conventions, Wallace was part of the solid CBS team that included Roger Mudd, Dan Rather, and Morton Dean. As floor correspondent at the volatile 1968 Democratic National Convention in Chicago, Wallace found himself in the middle of the violence that underscored the event. In an attempt to investigate the expulsion of a delegate from the convention floor, Wallace took a punch in the jaw from a police officer and was arrested and held briefly. In 1966 Wallace started covering the campaigning of Richard Nixon for CBS, and his admiration for the future president grew. When Nixon offered Wallace a job as press secretary, however, Wallace turned him down to remain at CBS.

Soon afterward, the CBS producer Don Hewitt approached Wallace about hosting a different type of new television magazine show called *60 Minutes*. The program debuted 24 September 1968 with the team of Mike Wallace and Harry Reasoner, total opposites in personality. The teaming proved to be fortuitous; it was an excellent opportunity for Wallace to concentrate on tough political stories while Reasoner could excel on the lighter pieces. It took approximately five years for *60 Minutes* to become a hit; viewership continued to grow throughout the 1970s. On *60*

Minutes, Wallace used his tough interviewing style not only with a Who's Who of famous personalities but also on notorious criminals, gaining him the nickname of "America's District Attorney."

Wallace faced adversity after his 1982 interview of General William Westmoreland, the former commander of American forces in Vietnam. His *CBS Reports* documentary, "The Uncounted Enemy," led to a libel suit, which later was dropped. This was also the beginning of Wallace's publicized battle with depression. Wallace rebounded, however, and in 1986 he married a fourth time, to Mary Yates. Entering the twenty-first century, Wallace continued to be a correspondent for *60 Minutes*.

★

Autobiographical material can be found in Mike Wallace and Gary Paul Gates, *Close Encounters: Mike Wallace's Own Story* (1984); additional material on Mike Wallace is available in Gary Paul Gates, *Air Time: The Inside Story of CBS News* (1978). Articles on Wallace include Steve Lopez, "Mike Wallace: At 79, the 60 Minutes Man Has Beat Depression and Gained New Perspective," *People* (1 Dec. 1997): 109–113; Lynn Hirschberg, "Mike Wallace: The Grand Inquisitor of 60 Minutes Remembers the Days When TV Had a 'Real Reality,'" *Rolling Stone* (19 Sept. 1997): 83–86. Additional articles are "The Mellowing of Mike Wallace," *Time* (19 Jan. 1970); A & E Network, "Mike Wallace: TV's Grand Inquisitor" (1998); and Fox and CBS Video, "*60 Minutes: 25 Years*" (1993).

STEVEN WISE

WALTON, Samuel Moore ("Sam") (*b.* 29 March 1918 in Kingfisher, Oklahoma; *d.* 5 April 1992 in Little Rock, Arkansas), retail merchant who transformed mass merchandising and revolutionized the shopping habits of the American consumer in the 1960s. Walton, president of Wal-Mart, Inc.—the largest retail chain in America—founded his first superstore in the 1960s.

Walton was one of two sons born to Thomas Gibson and Nancy Lee Walton, a farm couple living near Kingfisher. Thomas Gibson was a banker and a farmer and became a farm loan appraiser in 1923. To earn much-needed money during the Great Depression, Walton's mother bottled milk, which Walton delivered. Having learned early the value of a dollar, he sold magazine subscriptions from the age of seven and had paper routes throughout his college years. Walton also raised and sold rabbits and pigs.

In 1936 Walton graduated from Hickman High School in Columbia, Missouri, and then studied at the University of Missouri, where he earned a B.A. in economics in 1940. He began his career in retailing that same year by going to work for J.C. Penney in Des Moines, Iowa, as a manage-

Sam Walton. AP/WIDE WORLD PHOTOS

ment trainee for a salary of $85 a month. During World War II he served in the U.S. Army from 1940 to 1945, where he achieved the rank of second lieutenant. In 1943 he married Helen Robson of Claremore, Oklahoma; they had four children.

In 1945 Walton became a retail store owner by opening the first of several Ben Franklin five-and-dime franchises in Arkansas. The lease was not renewed, because the landlord saw the success of the store and wanted it for his own son. With his pride only a little damaged, Walton started a store in Bentonville, Arkansas, where he negotiated a ninety-nine-year lease. It was also a Ben Franklin franchise, but he called it Walton's Five and Dime. Walton was a poor boy from a poor state, but through hard work, ingenuity, and a commitment to provide customers with low-priced, high-quality merchandise, his small business in rural Arkansas began to grow.

In March 1962 the S.S. Kresge Company opened its first Kmart discount store in Garden City, Michigan. In May the Dayton Corporation opened its first Target discount store in Roseville, Minnesota. Arkansas City Products Corporation, the parent company of the Ben Franklin chain of variety stores, rejected Walton's franchise proposal for a discount store in Arkansas. Undaunted, he took on the project himself. Walton opened his first Wal-Mart store, naming it Walton's Family Center, in Rogers, Arkansas, in 1962. In July he opened the first Wal-Mart Discount City, a larger

variety store, in Rogers. The Rogers outlet was a sixteen-thousand-square-foot building. Spelled out in huge letters across the building was "Wal-Mart," an amalgam of Walton's name and the word "mart," which means a "place where goods are sold." The grand opening attracted tens of thousands of consumers. He had demonstrated that a store in a small town could attract a large number of customers from a significant distance and generate a substantial volume of business, if it offered a wide variety of goods at reasonable prices. His first store specialized in providing consumers with name-brand products at low prices.

By 1962 Walton and his brother, James, owned and operated sixteen variety stores in Arkansas, making theirs the largest independent variety store chain in the nation. From 1960 to 1962 Walton, presenting himself as the "little country boy from Arkansas," traveled the nation, examining the successful practices of the nation's leading retail enterprises. From this effort Walton realized that he could succeed by using a practice of modest overhead expenses with low retail prices and efficient distribution. In 1964 Walton opened his second unit in Harrison, Arkansas. He located the store in a building that had been used as a cattle-auction yard. The grand opening took a downward turn when the day's heat (115 degrees) caused the promotional watermelons to pop, thus frightening the donkeys that were part of the ride promotion and causing them to flee. The grand opening was not a complete disaster; numerous shoppers came to the store because the prices were 20 percent below those of competitors. The success of the Harrison store provided the funding needed to build several other stores and served as the training ground for future managers. Some analysts believe that without the success of the Harrison store, there would not be a Wal-Mart company today.

Although many poorly managed retail firms failed in the early 1960s, by 1965 the discount industry continued to expand and capture the attention of the majority of America's shoppers. In the mid-1960s discount merchandising included many small retail businesses, but their importance was declining as the industry became dominated by larger chains. By 1964 Walton was worried that other discount chains would adopt his concept of discounting in small towns and began to establish Wal-Marts as rapidly as financing would permit. He opened one store in 1965, two stores a year in 1966 and 1967, and five a year in 1968 and 1969, for a total of nineteen Wal-Marts by the end of the decade. Eleven of the stores were in Arkansas, and the others were located in Missouri and Oklahoma. In 1969 Walton's firm incorporated.

Walton's success with expansion in the 1960s was matched by continued growth in the discount industry, which caught up with and exceeded the growth of department stores nationwide. By the end of the decade Walton's total workforce numbered 650 full-time and 150 part-time employees, including competent executives to assist in managing the company's increasingly diverse interests. Walton's company performed well during the 1960s. The number of units in his variety and discount store chains had doubled from fiscal year 1966 to 1970, and both net sales and net income had shown gains of about 400 percent. Walton's success in the 1960s retail industry can be attributed to his strategy of copying successful business practices of competitors; using small-town locations; pushing to expand business interests; employing innovative business techniques; and demonstrating a willingness to share the profits with managers. Walton's decision to shift the focus of his company away from his variety store chain to his expanding discount store chain and the consolidation of business interests into a single, publicly held corporation provided the means of facilitating future growth in the decades to come.

Wal-Mart stores spread across rural America. Walton's employee-oriented management style helped fuel growth as Wal-Mart went public in 1970. A decentralized distribution system created further growth in the 1980s. Wal-Mart's "superstore" concept was successful in competing against smaller, traditional mom-and-pop stores. By the early 1990s Wal-Mart became the largest retailer in America, with 1,700 stores. Walton was known by many as a modest, simple family man who devoted endless hours to his family, community, employees, and customers. He once reflected on whether he made the right choices in life: "I am absolutely convinced that the only way we can improve another's quality of life . . . is through what we call free enterprise—practiced correctly and morally." Walton was active in managing the company as the chief executive officer and president until 1988 and was chair until his death. Walton died from complications arising from a bone disease and leukemia. He is buried in Little Rock. Walton left his family a fortune estimated at $23.5 billion.

★

Biographies and autobiographies of Walton include Austin Teutsch, *The Sam Walton Story* (1991); Sam Walton and John Huey, *Sam Walton: Made in America* (1992); Sandra S. Vance and Roy V. Scott, *Wal-Mart: A History of Sam Walton's Retail Phenomenon* (1994); and Bob Ortega, *In Sam We Trust* (1998). Obituaries are in the *Detroit Free Press* (6 Apr. 1992) and *Time* (20 Apr. 1992).

REED B. MARKHAM

WANG, An (*b.* 7 February 1920 in Shanghai, China; *d.* 24 March 1990 in Boston, Massachusetts), inventor of the first efficient computer memory and founder of Wang Laboratories, manufacturer of the first electronic calculators and word processors.

Wang was one of five children born to Yin-lu Wang and Z.-W. Chien. Because Wang was the eldest son (of four siblings), Wang's father, an English teacher, pushed the boy to excel academically. At Shanghai Provincial High School and, later, at Chiao Tung University, from which he graduated in 1940 with a bachelor's degree in science, most of his textbooks were in English, and his mathematics curricula were modeled directly on those of American colleges. The Japanese invasion of China threatened his dreams of becoming an electrical engineer, and Wang fled to central China to join those fighting against the Japanese. By 1945 his work in building radio equipment earned him entry into an American program designed to train Chinese engineers in the United States and then return them to their homeland after the war.

Living on a meager stipend of $100 a month, Wang studied briefly at Georgetown University and then at Harvard, where he earned an M.S. in applied physics in 1946. By then the fellowship program had collapsed, but Wang earned a Benrus Time Fellowship, enabling him to gain a Ph.D. in applied physics and engineering in 1948. After graduation Wang worked at the Harvard Computation Laboratory under Howard Aiken, designer of America's computer. There Wang designed a series of toroid-shaped magnetized nickel-iron (later ferrite) coils, which provided a new way to store information. These memory units, or Pulse Transfer Controlling Devices, as they were called in Wang's 1949 patent application, would serve as the dominant form of computer memory storage for the next two decades. In 1949 Wang married Lorraine Chiu; they had three children. In 1951 he founded Wang Laboratories.

IBM's purchase of Wang's patent rights, in 1955, was a classic win-win situation: Wang used the capital from the deal to start designing and building his own line of digital electronic products, and IBM, using the densely packed memory-storage unit in its 360 series computers, which contained 250,000 ferrite cores, was able to dominate the mainframe computer market throughout the 1960s. Combined, Wang's electronic calculators and IBM's computers—both introduced in 1964—made Wang famous. Wang Laboratories's early products were successful but only within severely limited market niches. Several dozen transistorized logic boards for scientific work, seventy or eighty digital controllers for machine tools, and about twenty phototypesetting machines might be sold per year. Certainly this was impressive—in 1964 the company's gross income reached a million dollars—but it was only the beginning. The true breakthrough came with the electronic calculator.

Wang's early calculators, the LOCI and the WANG 300, were hardly hand-held. The LOCI took up most of a desktop and used a teletype keyboard; it sold for $6,700. The WANG 300, a "breakthrough" model, employed some

An Wang. CORBIS CORPORATION (BELLEVUE)

three hundred transistors and featured a numerical keypad and a small desktop display. It sold for $1,700; by 1971 its price had dropped to $600. The success of Wang's calculators was made possible by the use of what we now call software. To multiply or divide two numbers, the calculator read the logarithm of each number, added or subtracted as needed, and converted the result back to a natural number. However, all operations of Wang's early machines had to be hardwired; even when the later WANG 360 calculated trigonometric functions, the operation employed a software-like sequence of existing hardwired functions. The WANG 380, introduced in 1968, was the first programmable calculator, which for $3,800 offered a choice of magnetic tape or punched card input and output; all it lacked to be considered one of the first personal computers was a usable memory. That breakthrough had to wait for the development of semiconductor-based memory systems, which was introduced to the market in 1971.

Perhaps Wang's greatest inspiration was his recognition that these new integrated circuits would spell the end of the electronic calculator as a profit source; he aggressively shifted Wang Lab's resources into the development of minicomputers and word-processing systems. The first Wang computers, the model 4000 and the model 3300 BASIC, designed to take advantage of the first programming language to use all-English instructions, were introduced in 1968. The next year, Wang began shipping the model 700, a programmable calculator that could be, and was, used as a computer; it was the last Wang product to use the ferrite-core memory system on which the company's fortunes had been founded. The same electronics powered the model 1200 word processor, introduced in 1971. By 1978 the company became the largest North American supplier of computers for small businesses.

In 1964 Wang Laboratories moved from rented space to a new headquarters complex in Tewksbury, Massachusetts, on Route 128—the 1960s version of Silicon Valley. That year, Wang Laboratories sold just twenty LOCI calculators; the next year they sold 120; and in 1966, when they introduced the model 300, Wang sold 340 in just six months. Sales quickly rose from $1 million in 1964 to $2.5 million in 1965 and to $6.9 million in 1967; by 1970 the company recorded $25 million in sales. In these three years, Wang Labs grew from thirty-five employees to four hundred; at its height, in the 1980s, it would have thirty thousand. Wang's rise was capped in 1967, when Wang Labs went public. Initially priced at $12.50 per share, the stock ended its first day at $40.50. Wang, who had retained 64 percent of the stock, ended the day worth nearly $50 million.

Wang's last years were darkened by struggles to preserve his company and his life. He succumbed to cancer of the esophagus in 1990 and was buried in Lincoln, Massachusetts. His company, which could not withstand a nationwide recession, filed Chapter 11 bankruptcy a year later. He was mourned throughout Boston, his adopted city, to whose institutions he had given generously over the years. The Wang Center for the Performing Arts and the Wang outpatient care unit of Massachusetts General Hospital are but two visible signs of that support.

Wang exemplified the American dream. Arriving in the United States a nearly penniless immigrant in June 1945, he won a series of scholarships and academic appointments.

By 1951 he was able to found his own company, Wang Laboratories. Four years later he assigned one of his patents to IBM for $500,000; and at his company's height, in the 1980s, Wang Labs had a gross income of more than $2.5 billion. Throughout, the modest Dr. Wang continually asserted, "Success is more a function of consistent common sense than it is of genius."

★

Wang's autobiography, *Lessons: An Autobiography* (1986), was written with Eugene Linden. For information about Wang's contributions to computer development, see Eric A. Weiss, "Eloge: An Wang, 1920–1990," *IEEE Annals of the History of Computing* 15, no. 1 (1993): 60–69. An obituary is in the *New York Times* (25 Mar. 1990).

HARTLEY S. SPATT

WARHOL, Andy (*b.* 6 August 1928 in Pittsburgh, Pennsylvania; *d.* 22 February 1987 in New York City), artist, filmmaker, and entrepreneur whose pop art works of the 1960s, featuring such icons as Campbell's soup cans, Marilyn Monroe, and Elvis Presley, made him one of the world's most influential and popular artists.

Born Andrew Warhola, Warhol was the youngest of three boys born to Ondrej Warhola, a laborer for the Eichleay Corporation, and Julia (Zavacky) Warhola, a homemaker and folk artist. Warhol attended Schenley High School in Pittsburgh, graduating in 1945, and then undertook a lengthy apprenticeship in commercial art. After graduating from Carnegie Institute of Technology (now Carnegie Mellon University) in 1948 with a B.F.A. in pictoral design, Warhol moved with fellow artist Philip Pearlstein to New York City. There, Warhol dropped the last letter of his family name and poured himself into his art. His spare, evocative sketches quickly captured attention and helped him become one of the top commercial artists in the city. By 1955 he was earning over $100,000 annually, though his mother, who had moved in with him in his apartment on Lexington Avenue, pointed out that he was spending $125,000 each year.

Warhol loved the clandestine but culturally rich gay life of New York City and began to collect important works of art, which he piled in his home alongside mounds of American kitsch art. He had larger ambitions and gradually created an individual style of artistic expression. His first efforts stemmed from his commercial work and included sketchbooks of gold leaf shoes, cats, and flowers. His work was featured in galleries, and he published limited edition books containing reprints of his sketches. Still, he lacked recognition. The *New York Times* labeled his Wild Raspberries show, which opened on 1 December 1959, as "clever frivolity *in excelsis.*" Even though the pop artists Jasper Johns and Roy Lichtenstein were lampooning abstract expressionism, this art form still dominated the scene. As a result critics viewed Warhol's commercial work with horror. Nevertheless, Warhol had by the close of the 1950s sustained a large cadre of contacts, even if many in the New York art world despised him.

As the 1960s dawned Warhol needed a gallery and a distinctive style. He began drawing such childhood cartoon heroes as Dick Tracy, Popeye, and Nancy, and a series of "crummy, cheap ads," though Lichtenstein had already appropriated cartoon imagery in his brutal satires of the artist Jackson Pollock. Warhol began inviting Ivan Karp, an assistant in the Leo Castelli gallery, to view his newer work. Warhol was reinventing his persona as a combination of Marilyn Monroe's vulnerability and Marlon Brando's monosyllabic, punk style. Karp liked one of Warhol's paintings, which presented elaborate, smeared lines of Coca-Cola bottles. Warhol also played inane pop songs for Karp about a hundred times a day until he "understood what it meant." Warhol's sublime, satirical humor helped create this new persona of the artist as pop symbol, a persona he expanded enormously over the next decade. Karp convinced Castelli to sign Warhol to his illustrious stable of pop artists.

Warhol's major notoriety came with his meticulous recreation of a series of Campbell's soup cans. His mother had served him the instant soup daily for lunch during the Great Depression. *Campbell's Soup Cans* did especially well in Los Angeles, where the pop movement was becoming sovereign.

Warhol began to attract a cadre of artists, assistants, lovers, and sycophants to his home, which served as a salon. There, he discovered the method of silk screening, which, as the author Victor Bockris explains, is a "stencil process in which a photographic image transferred to a porous screen can be quickly duplicated on canvas by laying the screen on the canvas and applying paint or ink over it with a rubber squeegee." Warhol immediately realized the commercial and artistic possibilities of this method. Coincidentally, the actor Marilyn Monroe committed suicide on 4 August 1962, and Warhol decided to paint a series of images of her as an homage. Borrowing a lush still of her from the movie *Niagara* (1953), he used the outline to frame harsh, almost neon colors. Using the silk-screen method, he reproduced this painting with color variations dozens of times, and then applied the method to another pop icon, Elvis Presley. He then reproduced the *Mona Lisa* and boxes of Brillo brand soap, and made a controversial mural for the 1964 World's Fair. The mural, which covered a huge wall, featured mug shots of the Federal Bureau of Investigation's thirteen most-wanted men. Angrily, Governor Nelson Rockefeller and the fair's sponsors ordered it to be

Andy Warhol. CORBIS CORPORATION (BELLEVUE)

painted over. Ironically, the next day the *New York Times* ran an article about the spate of robbing at the fair.

Warhol's image appropriations made him the most notorious pop artist of the decade. Shrewdly, he associated himself with global icons and with controversy. In an era when American cultural dominance was controversial, his inscrutable gloss on media fame won adherents in Europe and across America. As his notoriety grew, the monetary values of his paintings soared, and Warhol became a blue-chip artistic commodity, a reputation he enjoyed.

Ever expanding his artistic vision, Warhol moved into filmmaking, which was a natural outgrowth of his fascination with Hollywood and fame, and a good way to use the squads of characters who now fawned on him. Warhol eschewed commercial production techniques by using a hand-held camera to create his "movies." Immediately, he created controversy with his films, which included a six-hour film of a man sleeping, a lengthy film of the Empire State Building from dawn to dusk, and a film of couples engaged in various forms of sex. In 1966 he identified a number of wayward society debutantes as superstars in *Chelsea Girls,* which won him a wider audience and praise for innovation. Warhol also began recording hundreds of hours of conversation with various people, all of whom he

labeled superstars, though no Hollywood producer would ever touch them. He also hired a large Ukrainian hall to showcase Lou Reed's rock band, The Velvet Underground. Warhol, who produced records for the band, designed the cover of their first album with a peel-off image of a banana on the front.

Warhol's studio on Union Square West was named the Factory. Its walls were covered with aluminum foil, giving it a look of cheap pretension. As the painter's fame grew, the Factory became a must-visit spot for any hip tourist in New York City. Each night, Warhol's entourage moved across the square to Max's Kansas City, a phenomenally popular restaurant and bar, where Warhol held court to a shifting array of rock stars, petty nobility, and Hollywood starlets, along with his coterie of drag queens, boyfriends, and druggies. Warhol's openness and his exploitation of misfits backfired tragically on 3 June 1968. Valerie Solanas, an aspiring East Village playwright, and founder and sole member of SCUM (the Society for Cutting Up Men), had become angry with Warhol for losing a pornographic manuscript she had submitted to him. At the Factory, Solanas shot Warhol several times, hitting him in the chest and stomach, nearly killing him. Warhol was in the hospital for seven weeks, and he suffered from the wounds the rest of his life. Solanas, who declared herself mentally incompetent to stand trial, was sent to an insane asylum. The feminist spokeswoman Ti-Grace Atkinson declared that Solanas would surely go down in history as a hero for the women's movement. A local radical group denounced Warhol as a "plastic fascist" and applauded Solanas.

Warhol returned to work slowly. His near-death experience only amplified his fame. He produced a major movie called *Trash* (1970), which featured sodomy and drug injection yet played at movie houses all over the country. His first retrospective was held at New York City's Museum of Modern Art, where he wallpapered the gallery with purple and yellow cow's heads; a similar show opened in Germany, and Rainer Crone published the first serious monograph on Warhol. Always the entrepreneur, he started a magazine, *Inter/View* (later *Interview*), which was still prosperous at the beginning of twenty-first century.

After 1970 Warhol's fame grew exponentially. He created a major work in 1972 by appropriating and silk screening a political image of the Chinese leader Mao Tse-tung. He started a lucrative portrait business, charging $25,000 to $50,000 per work. During the late 1970s he became a social star of the disco era, presiding over the dance club Studio 54 and appearing at virtually every social event of note. Warhol attempted to cultivate the shah of Iran before that dictator was deposed in 1978. Warhol also created thousands of party-scene images, which he published in a series of illustrated books in the 1970s and 1980s. He also published barely edited transcripts of his taped conversations.

Warhol's originality was never as great as it was in the mid-1960s, though anything he produced was immediately purchased. His wealth and reputation were still growing when he died of cardiac arrest after a gall bladder operation in 1987. Today, with retrospectives, a constant stream of monographs written on him, and his influence apparent everywhere, Warhol's enormous reputation is secure. Warhol is buried in the Warhola family plot in Saint John the Baptist Catholic Cemetery, Byzantine Rite, in Bethel Park, a suburb of Pittsburgh.

★

Comments from Warhol on his life and work in the 1960s can be found in Andy Warhol and Pat Hackett, *Popism: The Warhol 1960s* (1988). For a good biography on Warhol, see Victor Bockris, *Warhol: The Biography* (1997). Information about Warhol's creative work can be found in Patrick S. Smith, *Andy Warhol's Art and Films* (1986). Obituaries are in the *New York Times* and *Los Angeles Times* (both 23 Feb. 1987).

GRAHAM RUSSELL HODGES

WARREN, Earl (*b.* 19 March 1891 in Los Angeles, California; *d.* 9 July 1974 in Washington, D.C.), three-term governor of California and distinguished American jurist who served for sixteen years as chief justice of the U.S. Supreme Court (1953–1969) during one of the most turbulent periods in U.S. history.

Earl Warren. SUPREME COURT OF THE UNITED STATES

Warren was the only son of Methias H. (Matt) Warren and Christine Hernlund. Matt Warren, a railroad worker, had immigrated to the United States from Norway as a teenager. Christine Warren, a homemaker, was of Swedish ancestry. In 1894 the family, including Warren's older sister, moved to Bakersfield, California, where Matt Warren found work in a repair yard of the Southern Pacific Railroad. During his school years in Bakersfield, Warren worked summers for the Southern Pacific as a "call boy," notifying crew members when they were scheduled to go on duty. This proved an eye-opening experience for the young Warren, who witnessed firsthand the ability of large corporations to dominate the lives of their employees, as well as the powerlessness of minorities in the face of discrimination. Living in Bakersfield, a rough-and-tumble frontier town in the late nineteenth and early twentieth centuries, also exposed Warren to "crime and vice of all kinds countenanced by a corrupt government," he recalled.

After graduating from Kern County High School in Bakersfield, Warren headed to Berkeley, where he studied law at the University of California, earning his bachelor's degree in 1912 and his law degree in 1914. He joined the law firm of Robinson and Robinson, working there for a couple

of years, and was about to launch his own law practice when the United States entered World War I in 1917. After a brief stint in the U.S. Army, Warren in 1920 joined the district attorney's office in Alameda County in the hope that the experience would broaden his legal expertise. He spent the next eighteen years with the office, including three four-year terms as district attorney. In October 1925 Warren married a widow, Nina Palmquist Meyers, and adopted her young son. The couple later had five children.

During his twelve-year tenure as district attorney, Warren developed a reputation as a tough, no-nonsense prosecutor, although he remained sensitive to the rights of the accused and fought personally to ensure that all those accused received a competent defense regardless of their ability to pay. He ran his office in nonpartisan fashion, strongly supporting the autonomy of county law enforcement agencies. In 1938 Warren was elected attorney general of California. Near the end of his term, in 1942, he supervised the forcible relocation of more than 110,000 Japanese Americans on the grounds that they posed a threat to the security of the United States in the wake of the Japanese attack on Pearl Harbor. Although for most of his life Warren defended the internment as the correct action in view of the military situation at the time, in his memoirs he acknowledged that the relocation was a mistake.

Warren was elected governor of California in a landslide victory in 1942, his first of three terms in the state's highest office. Republican presidential candidate Thomas A. Dewey tapped Warren as his running mate in 1948. Although Warren campaigned vigorously for the Republican (conservative) ticket, Dewey was upset at the polls by incumbent Harry S Truman. A strong supporter of Dwight D. Eisenhower's presidential bid in 1952, Warren was rewarded in 1953 when Eisenhower nominated him as chief justice of the U.S. Supreme Court.

The Court that Warren took over in 1953 was deeply divided between those justices in favor of judicial restraint and those who advocated a more active role for the Court. Almost from the outset Warren proved uncommonly effective in securing consensus among the justices, as evidenced in one of his first major cases as chief justice, *Brown* v. *Board of Education of Topeka,* the 1954 case in which the doctrine of "separate but equal" public education was struck down. The Court's school desegregation decision laid the groundwork for the accelerated civil rights movement of the 1950s and 1960s.

Although some observers questioned Warren's lack of judicial experience, whatever deficiencies he may have had as a jurist were more than made up for by his political acumen. His ability to forge majorities in support of major decisions quickly made Warren the chief justice not just in name but in fact. This perception was further enhanced by Warren's willingness to call upon the expertise of other justices when he felt his own lack of experience might impede the Court's progress. In his first days on the Court he asked Hugo Black, senior associate justice of the Supreme Court, to preside over its private deliberative conferences until Warren could become more familiar with the process.

In 1962, over the objections of conservative justice Felix Frankfurter, perhaps the Court's leading legal scholar, Warren agreed that questions arising from malapportionment in state legislatures were subject to judicial resolution. Rural interests for years had deprived city dwellers of equal representation in state legislatures. While Frankfurter argued that the Court would never be able to determine a straightforward formula to guide lower courts in the flood of lawsuits almost certain to follow, Justice William O. Douglas put forward the simple formula of "one man, one vote." In handing down the Court's opinion on a number of such apportionment cases in *Reynolds* v. *Sims* in 1964, Warren observed, "The weight of a citizen's vote cannot be made to depend on where he lives. This is the clear and strong command of our Constitution's Equal Protection Clause."

Frankfurter had suffered a stroke before the apportionment decisions were handed down and was replaced by Arthur Goldberg, giving Warren the fifth vote he needed to prevail on reapportionment. An even closer ally among the Court's liberals was William Brennan, a 1956 Eisenhower appointee. The two complemented each other perfectly; Warren's political savvy meshed well with Brennan's extraordinary legal skills and knowledge. The two conferred privately to map their strategy in advance of the Court's deliberative conferences. Many consider the Warren Court's decisions on reapportionment its greatest success story, even more significant than its ruling on school integration.

Although the Warren Court's decisions on desegregation and reapportionment were well received by the majority of Americans, the public was far less receptive to Warren's so-called due process revolution in the area of criminal justice. The chief justice's background as a prosecutor had led many to believe that he would have little sympathy for the rights of the accused, but even in his days as district attorney in Alameda County, Warren had always insisted on fair play. The passion with which Warren believed in fair treatment for the accused was apparent in the Court's decisions, including 1963's *Gideon* v. *Wainwright,* which guaranteed indigent defendants the right to legal counsel, and *Mapp* v. *Ohio* (1961), which barred prosecutors from using evidence seized in illegal searches. Undoubtedly the most widely publicized of the due process decisions, *Miranda* v. *Arizona* (1966), probably best summed up Warren's philosophy of criminal justice. The *Miranda* decision compelled law enforcement officers to advise criminal suspects of their constitutional rights before they could be interrogated. Any thought that Warren was soft on criminals, however, was dispelled by the Court's decision in *Terry* v. *Ohio* (1968), which gave police considerable leeway to stop and search those they suspected of carrying weapons.

Warren and the Court weathered a firestorm of criticism for the 1962 decision in *Engel* v. *Vitale,* which outlawed mandatory school prayer. However, Warren and his fellow justices believed strongly in the Bill of Rights, as the Court proved repeatedly in numerous decisions that applied the national standard outlined by those rights to individual states. In 1965 in *Griswold* v. *Connecticut,* the Court set forth a constitutionally protected right to privacy.

Despite his considerable political savvy, Warren took a critical misstep in 1963 when he succumbed to President Lyndon B. Johnson's powers of persuasion and agreed to head the governmental panel investigating the assassination of President John F. Kennedy. Warren initially resisted the job, believing that his acceptance would pose a threat to the separation of powers. However, Johnson's appeals to Warren's sense of patriotism eventually wore him down, and he reluctantly accepted the assignment. Because of the sensitive nature of the investigation, Warren felt strongly that the panel's final report should be unanimous. To achieve such unanimity, it became necessary for Warren to compromise on a number of key issues. Although many

Americans accepted the general conclusion of the Warren Report—that Lee Harvey Oswald, acting alone, killed the president—almost no one was fully satisfied with specifics of the end product, which was criticized for overlooking or distorting key evidence.

Against the backdrop of the unpopular war in Vietnam and the growing likelihood that the Democrats would lose the presidency in the fall of 1968 to Warren's longtime California rival, Richard M. Nixon, the chief justice told President Johnson that he wanted to step down. Warren agreed, however, to remain on the job until Johnson could find a successor. According to a White House memorandum, Warren asked Johnson "to appoint as his successor someone who felt as (he) did." Johnson's decision to elevate Justice Abe Fortas to the position of chief delighted Warren, but the joy was short-lived, for revelations about Fortas's financial affairs doomed the nomination. Fortas asked that his name be withdrawn from consideration and stepped down from the Court altogether in 1969. In the absence of a successor, Warren presided over the Court's term beginning in October 1968 and stayed on until the spring of 1969, when Nixon named Warren Burger to succeed him.

In his final term as chief justice, Warren presided over the Court's decision in *Powell* v. *McCormack* (1969), which rejected an attempt by the House of Representatives to exclude New York congressman Adam Clayton Powell from membership simply because a majority disliked the way he conducted his personal affairs. As in the apportionment cases of the early 1960s, the *Powell* decision reaffirmed Warren's unshakeable belief in democracy.

After stepping down as chief justice in 1969, Warren spent most of his time writing, traveling, and lecturing. He also worked passionately to oppose a proposal to establish an intermediate court of appeals to cut the workload of the Supreme Court. Suffering from painful heart disease, Warren was hospitalized a number of times after leaving the Court. His health began to fail rapidly in early 1974, and he died on 9 July of cardiac arrest at Georgetown University Hospital in Washington, D.C. He is buried in Arlington National Cemetery, in Arlington, Virginia.

Although some legal experts were critical of Warren's lack of judicial experience, he displayed a startlingly effective ability to administer the high court's deliberations and to find consensus among justices with sometimes widely diverse views. Even more impressively, Warren managed to effect this magic during a period of sweeping changes in U.S. constitutional law, particularly in the realms of criminal justice, race relations, and legislative apportionment. Perhaps unfairly, he is best remembered for engineering the decision in *Brown* v. *Board of Education,* which found that "separate but equal" public education facilities were inherently unequal and therefore in violation of the Constitution.

Some would argue that Warren's most lasting contribution to the U.S. judicial system came from his unflagging push for improved court administration. For much of his career in the legal profession, Warren had been disturbed by what he considered the courts' lack of attention to administrative problems, which had resulted in overcrowded court dockets, a shrinking trial bar, and a degradation, in his view, of criminal law in general. Summing up his view of the problem, Warren in June 1969 told the American Law Institute: "We have never come to grips with . . . court administration. . . . We should make bold plans to see that our courts are properly managed to do the job the public expects." Warren put his words into action, transforming the Judicial Conference of the United States from a social club for chief judges of the courts of appeal into an effective general administrator for the federal courts.

★

Warren's autobiography, *The Memoirs of Earl Warren* (1977), provides valuable insight into his career before he joined the Supreme Court as chief justice. To learn more about Warren's years as chief justice, as well as his earlier life and career, read Jack Harrison Pollack, *Earl Warren* (1979); G. Edward White, *Earl Warren* (1982); and Bernard Schwartz, *Super Chief* (1983). An obituary is in the *New York Times* (10 July 1974).

DON AMERMAN

WARWICK, Dionne (*b.* 12 December 1940 in East Orange, New Jersey), singer who served as the mouthpiece for the sophisticated pop songs of Burt Bacharach and Hal David, resulting in a string of hits in the 1960s.

Born Marie Dionne Warrick, Warwick acquired her stage name when her name was misspelled on an early record release. She is the daughter of Mancel Warrick, a gospel record promoter for Chess Records, and Lee Drinkard, who managed the gospel group the Drinkard Singers, consisting of Warwick's aunts and uncles. Steeped in gospel music, Warwick got her first singing experience in church. She studied the piano as a child, and, with her sister Dee Dee, Warwick formed a vocal group, the Gospelaires. The group began to get work singing background vocals on records in New York.

Warwick began attending the Hartt College of Music in Connecticut on a music scholarship in 1959, but she continued to work in New York recording studios. There, at a Drifters session in 1961, she met songwriter Burt Bacharach, who was impressed with her unusual alto voice and extensive range, and hired her to sing on demonstration records he was making with his songwriting partner Hal David. They played one of these demos for Florence Greenberg, head of the small independent Scepter Records,

Dionne Warwick, 1969. ASSOCIATED PRESS AP

and Greenberg signed Warwick as an artist to the label. Scepter released her debut single, "Don't Make Me Over"—written and produced by Bacharach and David, and inspired by a comment the singer herself had made to them—in the fall of 1962. It became a top-twenty pop and a top-five rhythm and blues (R&B) hit. Despite her success, Warwick managed to continue her schooling, completing her bachelor's degree and in 1976 earning a master's degree in music from Hartt.

During this period, Warwick married musician/actor Bill Elliot. They divorced after less than a year of marriage, but reconciled and remarried. They had two sons, but divorced again in the 1970s.

Warwick's follow-up singles to "Don't Make Me Over" were not as successful, but in early 1964 "Anyone Who Had a Heart" peaked in the top ten of the pop, R&B, and easy-listening charts, as did its follow-up, "Walk On By." The British invasion led by the Beatles temporarily sidelined the work of songwriters such as Bacharach and David, but some of Warwick's less-popular recordings of the mid-1960s have weathered well, particularly her summer 1964 single pairing "You'll Never Get to Heaven (If You Break My Heart)" and "A House Is Not a Home." Although American artists often were robbed of hits in Britain by covers of their records that were quickly released by native singers, Warwick was able to mount her own invasion of Europe, taking "Walk On By" into the top ten of the U.K. charts. She followed this with numerous other chart entries, and performed successfully on the Continent. Her concert at the Olympia Theater in Paris on 18 January 1966, at which she was introduced by Marlene Dietrich (for whom

Bacharach had served as musical director), was captured on the album *Dionne Warwick in Paris.*

Warwick finally returned to the U.S. Top Ten in 1966 with "Message to Michael." Follow-ups "Trains and Boats and Planes" and "I Just Don't Know What to Do with Myself" were less successful, but have since joined the list of Bacharach and David standards. In the spring of 1967, Warwick finally launched a sustained period of success with her top-twenty recording of the philosophical "Alfie." The theme song from a motion picture of the same name released the previous year, it had already been recorded without notable success by others. There followed a string of top-ten hits: "I Say a Little Prayer" later in 1967; the million-selling "(Theme From) Valley of the Dolls" (written by André and Dory Previn but produced by Bacharach and David); and "Do You Know the Way to San Jose" (which won her a Grammy Award for best female contemporary pop vocal performance, the first of her five Grammys) in 1968; and "This Girl's in Love with You" and "I'll Never Fall in Love Again" in 1969. The last of these won her a second Grammy Award for best female contemporary vocal performance. She also earned gold-record certifications for her albums *Here Where There Is Love* (1966), *Valley of the Dolls* (1968), and *Dionne Warwick's Greatest Motion Picture Hits* (1969). In 1968 she launched a film career, acting in the movie *Slaves,* but it was not a success, and she took on only occasional acting assignments thereafter.

In 1971 Warwick temporarily changed her name to Warwicke on the advice of a numerologist, and moved from Scepter to Warner Bros. Records in a deal that included Bacharach and David. *Dionne,* their first album together under the new deal, was only a moderate seller in 1972. Unfortunately, the songwriting team then broke up in the wake of their work on the disastrous film remake of *The Lost Horizon* in 1973, and Warwick was forced to sue them for failing to write and produce for her. The parties eventually reached a legal settlement. Warwick topped the charts in 1974, singing with the Spinners on the million-selling "Then Came You" and had another gold record in 1979 with "I'll Never Love This Way Again," which brought her another Grammy Award for best female pop vocal performance. The latter song came from her million-selling Arista Records debut (also called *Dionne*) produced by Barry Manilow, which also featured "Deja Vu," a Grammy winner for best rhythm and blues vocal performance, female. In 1983 she returned to the top ten with "Heartbreaker," written for her by the Bee Gees and coproduced by Barry Gibb. A reconciliation with Bacharach led in 1986 to the number-one single "That's What Friends Are For," which she recorded as "Dionne & Friends" with Elton John, Gladys Knight, and Stevie Wonder. Together, they won the Grammy Award for best pop performance by a duo or group with vocals. During the 1980s she served as a host on the *Solid Gold* television

491

series. In 1994 she hosted television infomercials for the Psychic Friends Network, later quitting the network after it tarnished her image. She continued to record and perform into the early twenty-first century.

★

No biography of Warwick has yet been written. A good biographical article is Clarence A. Moore, "Dionne Warwick: Forever Gold," *Goldmine* (26 Jan. 1990). Also useful are David Nathan's liner notes to the album *From the Vaults* (1995).

WILLIAM RUHLMANN

WATSON, James Dewey   (*b.* 6 April 1928 in Chicago, Illinois), molecular biologist, educator, codiscoverer of the double helical structure of DNA, author of *The Double Helix: A Personal Account of the Discovery of the Structure of DNA* (1968), and corecipient of the Nobel Prize in physiology or medicine (1962).

Watson's father, James Dewey, was a businessman, and his mother, Jean (Mitchell), a secretary at the University of Chicago. He has one sister. At the age of twelve Watson appeared on the radio program *Quiz Kids* and at fifteen was admitted to a special program at the University of Chicago. While an undergraduate he developed an interest in the gene. He graduated in 1947 with a B.S. degree in zoology.

James D. Watson. CORBIS CORPORATION (NEW YORK)

He received a fellowship to study zoology at Indiana University, Bloomington. Here his advisor and mentor was Salvador Luria, a biologist who was a founding member of the important Phage Group, an informal organization of scientists who were interested in viral reproduction. Watson eventually became a member of this group. In 1950 he received his Ph.D. in zoology for work on X-ray inactivation of bacteriophages.

Watson spent the 1950–1951 academic year doing postdoctoral work in Copenhagen, Denmark. In the spring of 1951, at a scientific meeting in Naples, Italy, he attended a lecture by Maurice Wilkins, a physicist turned molecular biologist. Wilkins displayed an X-ray diffraction image of crystalline deoxyribonucleic acid (DNA). Watson was deeply impressed by the fact that DNA was not amorphous and decided that it might be the crucial part of the gene, one that he wanted to study.

Watson spent the next two years at the Cavendish Laboratory of the University of Cambridge, England. Here he met Francis Crick, another physicist turned microbiologist. Watson and Crick immediately became close friends and collaborators, spending many hours discussing scientific ideas. Both were obsessed with the importance of the structure of DNA.

Watson and Crick were aware of the recent work of Linus Pauling, perhaps the greatest chemist of the twentieth century, showing that some proteins have helical structure. They obtained information from Wilkins concerning his and Rosalind Franklin's work on X-ray diffraction of DNA done at King's College, London. They consulted with mathematicians and chemists at Cambridge. After several false starts they were able to construct a model of DNA as a double helix, which satisfied all the known chemical and physical properties of the molecule and elegantly implied the manner in which reproduction and mutations can occur. They described their model in the 25 April 1953 issue of *Nature*.

Watson was a senior research fellow at the California Institute of Technology from 1953 to 1955. He was appointed an assistant professor at Harvard in 1955 but immediately took a leave of absence to spend the 1955–1956 academic year back at the Cavendish Laboratory working with Crick. He started his career at Harvard in 1956 and was promoted to associate professor in 1958 and to professor in 1961. During this period he worked on the role of ribonucleic acid (RNA) in protein synthesis.

In 1962 Watson, together with Crick and Wilkins, was awarded the Nobel Prize in physiology or medicine for his work on the structure of DNA. In 1965 Watson published *The Molecular Biology of the Gene,* a much admired undergraduate text that earned him about as much as his Harvard salary.

The manuscript of *The Double Helix,* begun in 1962,

was finished in 1966. Harvard refused to publish it because several scientists described in it had raised objections. After a few changes were made the book was published by Athenaeum Press (1968) and became a best-seller. It has been described as a scientific memoir, the first of its kind, illustrating how scientists work and how they are subject to the same foibles and competition as nonscientists. It has also been criticized as misleading and not typical of the way science is done, and for describing unverified and incorrect motives and thoughts of participants. However, in the Preface, Watson stated that he wanted to recreate his impressions of the events and personalities involved in the story. He succeeded in writing a memoir that can be read as if it were a lively and suspenseful novel.

The central issue that Watson described was the race to be the first (with Crick) to come up with the structure of DNA. At the time, the best work on X-ray diffraction had been done at King's College by Rosalind Franklin and Maurice Wilkins. Unfortunately Franklin, new to King's College, and Wilkins became bitter enemies over whether Franklin was hired to assist Wilkins or to work independently. Watson described Franklin in a very negative manner but appreciated her skill as a scientist. Wilkins shared his own results and, without her knowledge, some of Franklin's results with Watson and Crick. In particular, Wilkins informed them of Franklin's discovery that DNA changed form depending on how much water was present—a fact that was crucial in determining the structure of DNA.

Word reached Watson and Crick that Pauling had constructed a model of the DNA molecule. Pauling's son, Paul, was at the Cavendish Laboratory and received a preliminary report on his father's work. Paul Pauling showed it to Watson, who found a fundamental chemical flaw in the proposed model. Instead of informing Linus Pauling of his error, Watson and Crick decided that they were close to a solution and had six weeks to complete a model before Pauling's work was published and the error spotted.

Succeed they did! In an exciting climax to the book, Watson describes how they finally came up with their model and notes that even Franklin thought it was correct.

The problem with the scenario as described by Watson is that although he thought of the endeavor as a race for priority, Pauling did not, nor did Wilkins or Franklin. Two of Franklin's student-collaborators describe her temperament quite differently from Watson. Unfortunately she died in 1958 and thus was not eligible to be considered for a Nobel Prize. In the Epilogue to *The Double Helix,* Watson pays homage to Franklin's superb accomplishments as a scientist in a male-dominated environment not very welcoming to women.

On 28 March 1968 Watson married Elizabeth Lewis. They have two sons. Also in 1968 Watson became part-time director of the Cold Spring Harbor Laboratory on Long Island, New York. In 1978 he resigned from Harvard to work full-time at Cold Spring Harbor. In 1988 he was appointed associate director and later director of the Human Genome Project of the National Institutes of Health; he resigned from that position in 1992. In 1994 he became President of the Cold Spring Harbor Laboratory, a position created for him to relieve him of administrative duties.

In addition to the Nobel Prize, Watson has received many honors and awards, including the Albert Lasker Award of the American Public Health Association (1960), the Presidential Medal of Freedom (1977), the Copley Medal of the British Royal Society (1993), and the National Medal of Science (1997).

★

Watson has published two scientific memoirs, *The Double Helix: A Personal Account of the Discovery of the Structure of DNA* (1968) and *Genes, Girls, and Gamow: After the Double Helix* (2002). The Norton Critical Edition of *The Double Helix* (1980) includes the original text, commentaries, contemporary reviews, and original papers. Additional biographical material may be found in Robert C. Olby, *The Path to the Double Helix* (1974), a scholarly work; Anne Sayre, *Rosalind Franklin and DNA* (1975); Horace Freeland Judson, *The Eighth Day of Creation: Makers of the Revolution in Biology* (1979), from the perspective of a historian of science; John Gribbin, *In Search of the Double Helix: Darwin, DNA, and Beyond* (1985), written for the general reader; and Francis Crick, *What Mad Pursuit: A Personal View of Scientific Discovery* (1988).

HOWARD ALLEN

WATSON, Thomas John, Jr. (*b.* 8 January 1914 in Dayton, Ohio; *d.* 31 December 1993 in Greenwich, Connecticut), businessman whose foresight and decisiveness built International Business Machines (IBM) from a prosperous $700-million-per-year general business supplies and keypunch machine company into "Big Blue," a multibillion-dollar-per-year company that dominated the world market for computers.

Watson's father, Thomas John Watson, Sr., was the chief executive who built International Business Machines (IBM) into the dominant manufacturer of keypunch machines; his mother, Jeanette Mary Kittredge, was the daughter of an industrialist. Watson was the eldest of four children. Watson, Sr., always expected his son to follow him as president and chief executive officer (CEO) of IBM. Young Watson felt the pressure when he was very young and was intimidated by the thought of following in the footsteps of the father he revered. Even at age ten, he expressed doubts about his own abilities; he did poorly in school and often managed to get himself into trouble. He would eventually shed his childish irresponsibility to become a dynamic, brilliant leader.

Thomas J. Watson, Jr. (*far left*), demonstrating an IBM copy machine, April 1970. © BETTMANN/CORBIS

Watson applied to enter Princeton University but was rejected for poor grades. A friend of the family got him admitted to Brown University, from which he graduated with a B.A. degree in 1937, after a college career more notable for parties than for studies. That same year Watson became IBM's sales representative to Wall Street and neighboring parts of Manhattan. In 1940 Watson joined the National Guard and was called up to the U.S. Army Air Corps in September of that year. He trained as a pilot and became a second lieutenant. On 15 December 1941 he married Olive Field Cawley; they had six children. Watson served in several areas of conflict during World War II, earning the United States Air Medal. He was one of the pilots chosen to pioneer the lend-lease ferry air route between Alaska and Russia and was made a lieutenant colonel in 1946.

Watson credited his military service with teaching him self-discipline. Even so, as he returned to IBM in January 1946, he was still very insecure about his ability to measure up to his father. Watson believed that his father never fully trusted him, even when he replaced him as IBM president in January 1952 and immediately began urging that the company enter the then very young electronic machines market.

During the Korean War, IBM developed the 701 Data Processing Machine (also known as the Defense Calculator) for the U.S. military, and in 1954 it offered a business version of the machine, the IBM 702, which pioneered the use of transistors instead of vacuum tubes for calculating. The senior Watson retired in May 1956, and Watson became CEO of IBM. Under his leadership, IBM undertook the SAGE (Semi-Automatic Ground Environment) project for the U.S. Air Force, which involved setting up radar stations across North America and linking them via computers; this was the beginning of real-time data processing. Although SAGE was not especially profitable, IBM was able to apply what it learned to SABRE (Semi-Automatic Business-Related Environment), which went online in 1964, serving airline companies by allowing them to build networks with travel agents that allowed the agents to confirm airline reservations almost instantly.

Watson considered himself a liberal Democrat and took some pleasure in annoying other business leaders by suggesting that corporations had social responsibilities. By 1960 he was concerned about the people his computers were putting out of work, but he thought that retraining laid-off workers was impractical and unrealistic for people in their forties and fifties who had worked at only one kind of job all their lives. This concern may have been one reason why he supported social welfare programs. He especially favored the ideas of John F. Kennedy, with whom he met often, even after Kennedy became president of the United States.

By 1961 there were slightly more than 6,000 computers in the United States; more than 4,000 of them were manufactured by IBM. Up until that time, computer manufacturers had built specific computer systems for specific clients. One of IBM's big selling points was the service that it provided for its machines and the software programs that were unique to its various clients. Watson thought there should be a better way to meet clients' needs; his company was beginning to be overwhelmed by the demands of meeting the differing requirements of various systems scattered across the country as well as the world. He settled on the idea behind System/360, the most revolutionary change in the designing and marketing of computers before the development of the Apple personal computer. The System/360 was to be standardized; it would come in the form of five sizes (eventually clients' needs increased the number to seven), would use hard disks for storing information, and would be internally compatible—Watson's key innovation. All peripherals, all data-storage units, all programs designed for one computer would work on all the other computers. This innovation spawned a vast industry of independent companies making peripherals and writing software that would be compatible with IBM computers.

The System/360 faced significant obstacles. One was that it took years to develop. The initial cost in development, job training, and factory building was more than $5 billion before any of the computers began bringing in money. Another obstacle was Watson's own deep depression after his friend John F. Kennedy was assassinated. He announced the development of the System/360 on 7 April 1964, before it was ready to go to market. That year he was suggested as a candidate for the vice presidential nomination on President Lyndon B. Johnson's Democratic ticket, but he declined. In 1965 IBM was one of the top ten manufacturing companies in the United States, but despite the company's success, Watson felt that his life was out of control. His effort to get System/360 into production was eating him up.

In 1967 Watson declared his support for Senator Robert Kennedy's potential bid to become president, expecting that that opportunity would come in 1972, after Johnson had served another term. When Kennedy announced that he was running for president in 1968, Watson was invited to run for his senatorial seat in New York, but by then he had lost whatever interest he had had in becoming a politician. When Kennedy, like his brother, was assassinated, Watson lost another good friend. He was asked by the Kennedy family to take Kennedy's place in the presidential race, but he declined.

During the 1960s IBM's revenues had risen by 30 percent per year, an achievement probably unequaled in U.S. business. In December 1968, Control Data, then developing what would be known as the Cray ultrafast computers, sued IBM for trust violations, contending that IBM was using its vast size to discourage companies from buying Crays from Control Data, a small company. At the time, companies were constantly suing IBM, and since Watson had decided that superfast computers like the Crays did not fit into IBM's view of building broadly compatible machines, the suit seemed just another nuisance.

Creating software for the System/360 had cost $500 million by 1966, making it more expensive than any other aspect of developing the system. By 1968, smaller companies with much smaller development teams were producing cheaper computer programs faster than IBM. IBM always had sold what Watson called "bundled" services: hardware, peripherals, software (or keypunch cards), and support services, such as repair services. With the System/360, computers were bundled with software as well as with all the services that IBM traditionally provided those who bought or leased its equipment. By 1969 IBM computers accounted for about 70 percent of all computers sold. On "Black Friday at IBM," the United States Justice Department, using Control Data's lawyers and research, filed an antitrust lawsuit against IBM, demanding that the $7.5 billion giant be broken up into seven different companies. In June 1969 IBM unbundled its products, selling each aspect of its computer products separately and allowing small specialty companies to compete.

IBM was being pressed hard by the Japanese manufacturers Fujitsu and NEC, and Watson feared that the ability of its individual divisions to compete against these giants would be lost if IBM was broken up. In any case, he foresaw IBM's market share shrinking as the market expanded. In this expectation Watson seems to have been correct; by 1980 IBM had vigorous competition from numerous U.S. companies. In 1972 IBM settled with Control Data out of court by giving Control Data IBM's computer services division. The Justice Department case lingered on until 1981, when it was abandoned.

Watson was inducted into the National Business Hall of Fame in 1976. He served as ambassador to the Soviet Union from 1979 to 1981. In its 31 August 1987 issue, *Fortune* magazine said, "If creating wealth for shareholders is the best measure of a businessman's success, Thomas J. Watson Jr. is the greatest capitalist who ever lived." He died of a stroke, and is buried at Sleepy Hollow Cemetery, in Sleepy Hollow, Westchester County, New York.

★

Watson's autobiography, *Father, Son & Co.: My Life at IBM and Beyond* (1990), is an outstanding account of his relationship with his father and how he and many others built the modern manufacturing giant IBM. Watson's *A Business and Its Beliefs* (1963) offers insight into his thinking when IBM was growing by as much as 30 percent in wealth per year. Robert Sobel, *IBM: Colossus in Tradition* (1980), discusses the changes in IBM made by Watson. Emerson W. Pugh, *Memories That Shaped an Industry: Decisions Leading to IBM System/360* (1984), tells of the project initiated by Watson that reshaped the computer industry and laid the foundation for IBM PC compatibles. Obituaries are in the *Los Angeles Times, New York Times,* and *Washington Post* (all 1 Jan. 1994); the *Chicago Tribune* (2 Jan. 1994); and the (London) *Times* (3 Jan. 1994).

KIRK H. BEETZ

WATTS, André (*b.* 20 June 1946 in Nuremberg, Germany), Hungarian/African-American concert pianist who received overnight acclaim in 1963 and crossed the racial barrier by captivating classical music audiences with his virtuosity.

Watts is the only child of Herman Watts, a black American career soldier, and Maria Alexandra Gusmits, a Hungarian and his first piano teacher. He studied violin at four, switching to piano at six. When he was eight, the family

André Watts. MR. ALIX B. WILLIAMSON

moved to the United States and settled in Philadelphia, where he attended the Lincoln Preparatory School and the Philadelphia Academy of Music, studying under Genia Robinor, Doris Bawden, and Clement Petrillo. At age nine he substituted as soloist for his first public performance, playing a concerto by Franz Joseph Haydn with the Philadelphia Orchestra's Children's Concerts. His parents divorced in 1962, and Watts lived with his mother. He graduated from the Philadelphia Academy of Music in 1963.

Watts's big break came on 24 January 1963, at age sixteen, when illness forced the Canadian pianist Glenn Gould to cancel two scheduled performances with the New York Philharmonic under the baton of Leonard Bernstein. Seeking a substitute, Bernstein recalled the young teenager from *Young People's Concert,* televised on the Columbia Broadcasting System (CBS) on 15 January 1963. Watts was the first classical musician to make an initial public impact through television and the first black instrumental soloist since the turn of the twentieth century to play with the Philharmonic in a regular concert. Before a concert audience of two thousand, Watts executed a stunning interpretation of Franz Liszt's Concerto no. 1 in E-flat Major. Afterward, fans and critics pressed into his dressing room doorway. When asked whether he would join the classical concert circuit, Watts calmly responded, "That would be foolish. I have so much to learn." Bernstein called him "a natural, a real pro." Watts even made the front page of the *New York Times,* while *Newsweek* discussed his "pyrotechnics . . . and lyricism." The next week, ticket requests for his student recital at the Philadelphia Academy of Music exceeded the number of seats available.

In January 1968 Bernstein welcomed Watts back to the hall to play Johannes Brahms's Piano Concerto in B-flat on the fifth anniversary of his debut. Bernstein commented, "If he goes on this way, he will become one of the world's major pianists." Harold Schonberg, the music critic for the *New York Times,* wrote that Watts "matured in the right direction," and Harriett Johnson, music critic of the *New York Post,* said that he was "ageless before he has grown up." Watts's schedule included a fall 1967 European tour with the conductor Zubin Mehta and the Los Angeles Philharmonic and sixty-nine concerts in 1968, each earning $6,000 to $7,000. But Watts agonized over his popularity, trying to limit his expanding concert schedule. Meanwhile, he studied piano with Leon Fleisher and worked part-time toward a bachelor's degree at the Peabody Conservatory of Music in Baltimore. (He graduated in 1972). At age twenty-one Watts described the bridge from youth to mature musicianship: "I don't think you're really aware of it until you've crossed over." In 1969 Watts lived in a roomy apartment across the street from Carnegie Hall. He practiced as much as eight hours daily, mastering the music of Beethoven, Schubert, Liszt, and Chopin, stomping his feet when not pedaling, and adding vocalization to completed rhythm. To "add vocalization" means that like all masterful pianists, he initiates rhythm, adds content, and then concludes with interpretation of the music he is adding to his repertoire. After practice he relaxed his 145-pound body with yoga and a good cigar.

In May 1969 Watts performed Liszt's Piano Concerto no. 1 under the Boston Symphony conductor Erich Leinsdorf for the Inaugural Concert in Constitution Hall. An elderly lady, who turned out to be Jane Beeson of Lindsay, California, leaned over to her nephew and former music student and said, "If you only had practiced more, you could have been up there on that stage yourself, instead of sitting just here." Her nephew was Richard Milhous Nixon, president of the United States.

A black critic for the *Saturday Review* critiqued Watts's interpretation of Beethoven's Sonata no. 24 in F Sharp Major, op. 78. "I thought the greatest pleasure of the evening would be the novel sight of hearing a brother playing the piano . . . but before he got two feet into his program, . . . who he was or what he looked like had no part in his accomplishment. He became a pianist without race." Watts himself rejected the idea of a black aesthetic or a black ideology. "I share both the black and the white worlds. . . . I think I'm qualified to criticize both sides." Black militants resented Watts for "making it on their money but keeping too quiet on the Cause scene, that he must have a hole in his soul," and some musical critics accused Watts of careless musicianship. Despite negative commentary, Watts was a symbol for the civil rights movement, a quiet fighter "who lets his good example as a famous artist have the effect of a thousand protesters," according to Norman Darden, writing in the *Saturday Review* (26 July 1969). By 1969 Watts had played with nearly every major orchestra in the United States, Asia, and Europe, with a growing list of recordings to his credit.

As the decade of the 1960s closed, Watts was compared to Van Cliburn, Artur Rubinstein, and Vladimir Horowitz. Watts believed "in fidelity of the mind" and chose to live a solitary life, admitting, "I suppose when I'm old I'll be very lonely." Around his neck hung a gold medallion, a gift from his mother. On it, his motto was inscribed: "Even this shall pass away."

★

Notable Black American Men (1999) covers Watts's development as a concert pianist. Linda J. Noyle, ed., *Pianists on Playing: Interviews with Twelve Concert Pianists* (1987), contains a personal interview with Watts about his technique and practice habits. Numerous periodicals discuss his life, including "A Real Pro," *Newsweek* (11 Feb. 1963); "Prodigies," *Esquire* (May 1964); "Beautiful Innocence," *Newsweek* (29 Jan. 1968); "André Watts: A Giant Among Giants at Age 22," *Ebony* (May 1969); "My Man André," *Saturday Review* (26 Jul. 1969); "I'm Doing All Right, I'm Never Good Enough, But I'm Not Standing Still," *New York Times Magazine* (19 Sept. 1971); "André Watts," *American Music Teacher* (Apr. 1972); "Ten Outstanding Single Men: André Watts," *Ebony* (Aug. 1972); "Watts Plays for the Millions," *New York Times* (26 Nov. 1976); and "Concert: André Watts Plays Mozart," *New York Times* (13 Aug. 1987).

SANDRA REDMOND PETERS

WEAVER, Robert Clifton (*b.* 29 December 1907 in Washington, D.C.; *d.* 17 July 1997 in New York City), statesman, college professor, and economist who was the first African-American member of a New York State cabinet, the first African-American member of a presidential cabinet, and the first secretary of the U.S. Department of Housing and Urban Development (1966–1968).

Weaver was the son of Mortimer Grover Weaver, a postal clerk, and Florence E. Freeman. His mother instilled in Weaver his love of learning, and he had a very strong work ethic and a notable independent streak in his personality that were manifested during his time at Dunbar High School in Washington. During his junior year he held a full-time job as an electrician; in his senior year he ran his own electrical repair service.

Weaver graduated from Dunbar High School in 1925 and entered Harvard University, where he majored in economics, graduating with a B.S. degree in 1929 and then continuing at Harvard to earn an M.S. degree in economics in 1931. From 1931 to 1932 he taught economics at the Agricultural and Technical College of North Carolina, but he received a scholarship to continue his education at Harvard and returned there in 1932, receiving his Ph.D. in economics in 1934. By then he was already having an effect on the social policies of the U.S. federal government.

In 1933 the newly elected president Franklin D. Roosevelt recruited young, college-educated people to serve in his administration, and Weaver was among them. In 1934 he became an adviser to Secretary of the Interior Harold L. Ickes, developing special expertise in the economics of housing, redevelopment, and racial segregation. On 18 July 1935 Weaver married a college professor, Ella V. Haith. They adopted a son, who died in 1962. Although he was years away from being known to the general public, Weaver may well have been the most influential African American in Roosevelt's administration by the time the president formed the Federal Council on Negro Affairs in 1936, nicknamed the "Black Cabinet" by journalists. By the time he left his position with the Department of the Interior in 1938 to join the U.S. Housing Authority, Weaver was the man Roosevelt turned to first for advice on policies involving African Americans.

Robert C. Weaver. AP/WIDE WORLD PHOTOS

In 1940 Weaver joined the National Defense Advisory Commission; in 1942 he became chief of African-American employment affairs in the Office of Production Management; from 1942 to 1943 he focused on African-American labor issues for the War Production Board; and from 1943 to 1944 he was the director of the Negro Manpower Services for the War Manpower Commission. In 1940 Roosevelt was leaving New York City from Pennsylvania Station when his press secretary Stephen T. Early was blocked from entering the station by police officers. After Early angrily bowled over an African-American police officer to gain admittance, Roosevelt and those close to him worried about the effect the incident would have on African-American voters in an election year. As he had become accustomed, Roosevelt asked Weaver for advice, and Weaver sent a message to the president that resulted in the promotion of Benjamin O. Davis, Jr., who would become the first African-American general of the U.S. Army; the move also resulted in the appointment of William H. Hastie, the first African-American aide to the secretary of war; and the appointment of Campbell C. Johnson, the first African-American aide to the director of the Selective Service.

In 1946 Weaver served as a representative of the United Nations Relief and Rehabilitation Administration in the Ukraine. That same year his book *Negro Labor: A National Problem* was published, and as a result Weaver began to develop an influence outside government. His 1948 book *The Negro Ghetto* was a pioneering effort to analyze housing segregation, which Weaver believed to be at the root of all other forms of racial segregation. From 1947 to 1955 Weaver served in several academic positions, while writing numerous articles about economics.

In 1955 Weaver was appointed New York State's deputy rent commissioner, and in December 1955 New York governor W. Averell Harriman appointed him director of the State Rent Commission, making Weaver the first African American to become a member of the New York cabinet. He left the position in January 1959. In 1960 Weaver chaired the board of directors of the National Association for the Advancement of Colored People (NAACP). On 31 December 1960 President-elect John F. Kennedy announced the appointment of Weaver as director of the Housing and Home Finance Agency (HHFA); Weaver was officially sworn in on 11 February 1961.

In 1961 Weaver helped draft the Housing Act of 1961, which focused on creating public housing units for poor people and on revitalizing inner cities. That year Kennedy tried to create a new cabinet post and a new federal government department focusing on urban affairs, and he wanted Weaver to head the agency, but Congress refused to authorize the new department. During his years as director of the HHFA, Weaver tried to expand the federal government's role in providing housing for the poor, as well as to expand the government's influence on urban renewal projects, which he believed tended to ruin inner-city neighborhoods and to drive African Americans from their homes. In addition, he wanted the government to encourage the racial integration of suburbs. Weaver's book *The Future of the American City* was published in 1962; *The Urban Complex: Human Values in Urban Life* was published in 1964; and *Dilemmas of Urban America* was published in 1965. These books established Weaver as one of the foremost experts on the problems of U.S. cities.

In 1966 President Lyndon B. Johnson won congressional approval for the creation of a new federal department, Housing and Urban Development (HUD). On 13 January 1966 Johnson appointed Weaver as the secretary of HUD, making Weaver the first African American to be a member of a presidential cabinet. As secretary, Weaver sought to expand the department's powers and to have the federal government invest in housing in inner cities, winning a $2.5 billion congressional authorization for this purpose in 1966. Weaver left his cabinet post after Richard M. Nixon was elected president.

From 1969 to 1970 Weaver served as the first president of the new Bernard M. Baruch College, part of the New York University system. From 1971 to 1978 he was distinguished professor of urban affairs at Hunter College. Weaver died at the age of eighty-nine.

During his years of government service, Weaver helped open new economic opportunities for African Americans and guided the racial policies of three presidents. His books and essays helped give an authoritative foundation to efforts to improve life in America's cities, and his ideas and work helped reshape those cities during the 1960s.

★

Harvard Sitkoff, *A New Deal for Blacks: The Emergence of Civil Rights as a National Issue* (1978), mentions Weaver's early career. *Notable Black American Men,* edited by Jessie Carney Smith (1999), offers fairly complete coverage of Weaver's career. The entry on Weaver in *Current Biography Yearbook* (1961) presents a detailed summary of his career to 1961. Obituaries are in the *New York Times* and *Chicago Tribune* (both 19 July 1997).

KIRK H. BEETZ

WEBB, James Layne ("Jimmy") (*b.* 15 August 1946 in Elk City, Oklahoma), songwriter whose compositions, including "By the Time I Get to Phoenix," "Up, Up and Away," and "MacArthur Park," dominated the mainstream pop music of the late 1960s.

Webb was the son of Robert Lee Webb, a Baptist minister who moved his family around the Southwest when Webb was a child. The boy showed an early interest in music, taking his first piano lesson at age six and later serving as the organist in his father's church. By age thirteen he was writing songs. In 1964 his father was appointed pastor of the First Southern Baptist Church in Colton, California, and the family moved there. Later, Webb began attending San Bernadino Valley College. After a year he dropped out of college and moved to Los Angeles to pursue songwriting. He was hired by Jobete Music, a song-publishing company associated with Motown Records, and began getting cuts on Motown albums, such as "My Christmas Tree," which appeared on the 1965 Supremes album *Merry Christmas.*

Jimmy Webb, 1968. HENRY DILTZ/CORBIS

In 1966 Johnny Rivers became the first artist to record "By the Time I Get to Phoenix," a loosely autobiographical Webb ballad in which the narrator describes his plan to leave his lover. Rivers did not release the song as a single, but he did hire Webb to his Soul City record label and had him write for a new group, the 5th Dimension. Webb wrote five songs in addition to arranging, conducting, and playing keyboard on the group's debut album, named after one of his tunes, *Up, Up and Away.* The effervescent song, released as a single in the spring of 1967, became the 5th Dimension's first hit, reaching the Top Ten. The group's follow-up singles "Paper Cup" and "Carpet Man," also Webb's compositions, reached the Top Forty.

Webb wrote, arranged, and conducted most of Rivers's Top Twenty 1967 album *Rewind* and then did the same work on the next 5th Dimension album, *The Magic Garden,* released at the end of the year. Although it was not as successful as its predecessor, the album featured the Webb song "Worst That Could Happen," recorded for a million-selling Top Five hit by the Brooklyn Bridge a year later. Meanwhile, Glen Campbell had recorded a remake of "By the Time I Get to Phoenix," which was released as a single in the fall of 1967. It became a Top Forty hit, a statistic that does not do justice to the success the song achieved over time. By the end of the century BMI, the performance rights organization, listed "By the Time I Get to Phoenix" as the third-most-performed song of the previous fifty years. Both it and "Up, Up and Away" were nominated for Grammy Awards for 1967 song of the year, with the latter winning out. Campbell became a favored singer for the songwriter, going on to record Top Five, million-selling versions of "Wichita Lineman" and the soldier's lament "Galveston" as well as a Top Forty rendition of "Where's the Playground, Susie" in 1968 and 1969.

Webb began working with the Irish actor and singer Richard Harris, producing and writing all the songs on Harris's spring 1968 album, *A Tramp Shining*. The album's single was the unusually long, multipart epic "MacArthur Park," which just missed topping the charts. (It finally hit number one when it was revived by Donna Summer in 1978.) The LP, which reached the Top Five and was nominated for an album of the year Grammy (while winning Webb a Grammy for arranging), also featured "Didn't We?," which went on to become a much-covered standard. Before the end of 1968 Webb had written and produced Harris's follow-up album, *The Yard Went On Forever . . .*, which reached the Top Forty.

Still only twenty-three years old by the end of the 1960s, Webb already had written a handful of pop standards. He had been embraced by an adult pop audience and had seen his songs recorded frequently by middle-of-the-road pop singers. But he longed to be taken seriously by his own generation and, in keeping with the common aspirations of songwriters his age, to achieve success as a performer of his compositions rather than as a writer for others. As early as 1968 Epic Records had acquired a collection of his demos, added overdubs, and released it without his authorization under the title *Jim Webb Sings Jim Webb*. His more official debut was the single "One of the Nicer Things," also released in 1968. He made his performing debut in June 1969 as an opening act for Connie Stevens at the Desert Inn in Las Vegas. Webb attracted favorable reviews but shunned further work in Las Vegas, fearing that it would add to his reputation as an easy-listening artist.

Rejecting the trappings of pop success and seeking legitimacy as a rock singer-songwriter, Webb formed a band and began touring clubs. In 1970 he released his first album recorded as such, *Words and Music*. Like its seven successors released over the next quarter century, it did not sell well enough to reach the charts, but Webb persevered in trying to establish himself as a performer. He also continued to write for others on occasion. In 1972 he produced, arranged, and wrote half the songs on the album *The Supremes*, made by the group after the departure of the lead singer, Diana

Ross. That year he married Patsy Sullivan; they had five children.

In 1973 Art Garfunkel (who formerly had teamed with Paul Simon) scored a Top Ten hit with Webb's affecting ballad "All I Know." "The Moon Is a Harsh Mistress," introduced on Joe Cocker's 1974 album *I Can Stand a Little Rain* and also appearing that year on the Glen Campbell album *Reunion (The Songs of Jimmy Webb)*, which Webb arranged, has earned several recordings over the years. In 1975 Webb had another reunion, this one with the 5th Dimension, for its *Earthbound* album, producing, arranging, and contributing five songs to the LP. Garfunkel's 1978 album *Watermark* was another LP dominated by Webb's songs. In the 1980s Linda Ronstadt put four of Webb's songs on her album *Cry Like a Rainstorm, Howl Like the Wind*, and his Grammy-winning song "Highwayman" topped the country charts for the quartet of Waylon Jennings, Willie Nelson, Johnny Cash, and Kris Kristofferson and received the Country Music Association's award for single of the year. In the 1980s and 1990s Webb spent much of his time working on stage musicals.

★

Jimmy Webb, *Tunesmith* (1998), is a songwriting instruction book, but it contains anecdotes and reminiscences that reflect on his life. There are useful entries on Webb in Mark White, *"You Must Remember This . . .": Popular Songwriters 1900–1980* (1985), and in Nigel Harrison, *Songwriters: A Biographical Dictionary with Discographies* (1998). An excellent magazine article tracing Webb's career in detail is Jeff Bleiel, "Jimmy Webb: The Song Goes On," *Goldmine* (20 Dec. 1996).

WILLIAM RUHLMANN

WELCH, Raquel (*b.* 5 September 1940 in Chicago, Illinois), actress and sex symbol who took the worldwide media by storm after the 1966 release of a movie poster featuring her natural assets in a wild and woolly prehistoric bikini.

Welch, born Jo-Raquel Tejada, moved with her family in 1942 to the tiny Pacific Coast village of La Jolla, California. She was the oldest of three children of Armand C. Tejada, a Bolivian structural engineer of Castilian origins, and Josephine Sarah (Hall) Tejada, a statistical clerk at an aircraft factory who was of English and Scottish descent. Her parents divorced when Welch was in high school. Welch studied ballet for seven years and by adolescence was well proportioned and naturally poised—she stood five feet, six inches tall and weighed 118 pounds, with an hourglass figure. She earned a spot on her La Jolla High School cheerleading squad and at age fourteen entered a beauty contest, winning first prize out of a field of 150 contestants.

Raquel Welch, 1967. THE KOBAL COLLECTION

At age fifteen she was crowned Miss La Jolla, Miss San Diego, and Maid of California.

Welch was married by age sixteen (some sources say age eighteen) but nonetheless finished high school in 1958 as vice president of her graduating class. Her husband, James Westley Welch, two years her senior, was a tuna fisherman; he remained away from home for months on end, leaving her continually alone, even after the birth of their first child, a son, in 1959. After the birth of their daughter in 1961, faced with two children to raise, Welch parted ways abruptly with her absentee husband. As a student in La Jolla, Welch had apprenticed at the local playhouse and participated in actors' workshops, and after high school she won a college scholarship for theater arts, which she declined because she was married with children. She did study acting for one year at San Diego State College but later moved to Dallas, Texas, where she easily found work as a Neiman-Marcus store model and secured a job on television, reporting the weather on a morning talk show. After six months in Dallas, she moved to Los Angeles, California, in 1963 in search of a film career. Her divorce was finalized in 1964.

Upon her arrival in Hollywood, Welch hired an agent and spent her days visiting film studios searching for work.

Among the hordes of Hollywood hopefuls, Welch's extraordinary good looks and photogenic proportions caused her to stand out among her peers. Initially, she accepted bit parts and eventually secured a job as a spokesmodel on a variety show, called *Hollywood Palace*. She took an uncredited role in an Elvis Presley film called *Roustabout* and walk-on roles in *Do Not Disturb* and *A House Is Not a Home* in 1964. *Life* magazine featured Welch in an article about Hollywood starlets that year, and she was presented at the Deb Star Ball at the Hollywood Palladium on 21 November 1964.

This early exposure was a mere prologue to the pending media blitz that would surround Welch in 1966, largely as a result of the efforts of Patrick Curtis, a one-time child actor who became both manager and lover to Welch. After the two consolidated under the name of Curtwel Productions in 1964, Curtis promoted Welch to the couple's mutual profit, obtained a Screen Actors Guild card for Welch, and distributed pinup photos to studios and media outlets. Her first milestone was a small role in *A Swingin' Summer* in 1965; it was a musical debut also for Welch, who contributed a song to the film's soundtrack.

Her first major role was in the 1966 science fiction fantasy *Fantastic Voyage,* from Twentieth Century–Fox. She played the scientist Cora Peterson, shrunken to the size of a microbe and sent to perform emergency brain surgery on a man while traveling through his bloodstream in a boat. The movie co-starred Stephen Boyd. Critical reception was lukewarm, but the media exposure proved invaluable to Welch's career. That same year she starred as the cavewoman Loana Shell in *One Million Years B.C.* The role, which had been rejected by the film siren Ursula Andress, made Welch a superstar when, through a fortuitous marketing ploy during filming, Curtis released a photo of Welch as Loana, wearing a costume that was little more than a tattered rag of animal skin fashioned like a skimpy bikini. It was a dramatic shot of Welch in a broad-legged stance, pulling her long, wild mane of hair from her face, awakening figuratively—if not literally—to the dawn of man. The photo campaign achieved its desired effect, and by the movie's release, Welch was a bona fide international star and an earthy new sex symbol in distinct contrast to her predecessors from Hollywood's glamour era in the 1940s.

Welch and Curtis were married for a time, from 14 February 1967 to 1972, and they adopted two children. Curtis took Welch to Europe, where she starred in three films in 1967, including *Shout Loud, Louder, I Don't Understand,* with the Italian heartthrob Marcello Mastroianni. Stateside that year Welch starred in Twentieth Century–Fox's *Fathom* and *Bedazzled* and in Metro-Goldwyn-Mayer's *The Biggest Bundle of Them All.* Despite her outspoken refusal to appear naked in films, she remained in demand for her voluptuous appearance, and she spent the rest of the decade in roles that emphasized her physical assets. Welch appeared in other films in the 1960s, including *The Queens: The Oldest Profession* (1968), *Bandolero* (1968), *Lady in Cement* (1968), and *Flare-Ups* (1969). Her controversial interracial love scenes with the former football player Jim Brown in *100 Rifles* (1969) fueled the image of Welch as an icon of unbridled sex appeal.

At the end of the decade Welch took on the challenging role of portraying the female version of a transsexual named Myra/Myron in *Myra Breckinridge,* a 1970 movie release of Gore Vidal's novel of angst and depravity. Although the movie was panned, public lust for Welch's beauty failed to subside. She remained committed to her goal of becoming a serious actress but had to wait to win a major industry award until after the release of Richard Lester's *Three Musketeers* (1973), in which she portrayed the comedic Mademoiselle Bonancieux. Welch received a Golden Globe Award for her part in the tongue-in-cheek film.

Welch's career endured well beyond the 1960s. Among her many movie roles, she starred as a Roller Derby queen in *Kansas City Bomber* (1972) and as Jennifer "Jugs" Jurgens in *Mother, Jugs, and Speed* (1976). She appeared in a one-woman televised variety show, *Raquel!*, and performed a stint in Las Vegas. In 1982 she was seen on Broadway in *Woman of the Year,* the same year that the National Broadcasting Company aired her dramatic television debut, *The Legend of Walks Far Woman.* From 1980 to 1990 Welch was married to the photographer Andre Weinfeld; on 17 July 1999 she married a fourth time, to Richard Palmer, a restaurateur. Welch, who continued as an entertainer into the twenty-first century, was honored with a star on the Hollywood Walk of Fame on 8 June 1996.

★

A biography of Welch is Peter Haining, *Raquel Welch: Sex Symbol to Superstar* (1984). Other biographical information is in *Current Biography Yearbook* (1971); "Raquel Welch," in *Dictionary of Hispanic Biography* (1996); and Gary D. Keller, *A Biographical Handbook of Hispanics and United States Film* (1997). Articles about Welch are in *Playboy* (Dec. 1979); *Life* (July 1982): 74-78; *Cosmopolitan* (May 1983): 250-256 and (May 1990): 320-324; *People* (2 Aug. 1999): 52; and *Interview* (June 2001): 68, wherein Welch contrasts herself with Marilyn Monroe.

GLORIA COOKSEY

WELLEK, René Maria Eduard   (*b.* 22 August 1903 in Vienna, Austria; *d.* 10 November 1995 in New Haven, Connecticut), literary critic, theorist, and educator in comparative literature whose theories of literary criticism have been highly influential.

Wellek was the son of Bronislav and Gabriele von Zelewsky, both born to families of the minor aristocracy in what is now the Czech Republic. Wellek's father worked as a government lawyer in Vienna; he was also a man of the arts, who wrote reviews for the opera and biographies of famous Czech artists. Wellek's mother was born in Rome and was fluent in German, Italian, French, and English. After the fall of the Austro-Hungarian Empire following World War I, Wellek's parents moved back to Prague, Czechoslovakia, when he was fifteen. He attended the University of Prague, where he studied Germanic philosophy, English literary history, and comparative literature and met a group of professors known as the Prague Linguistic Circle. He graduated with a Ph.D. in 1926. Wellek married Olga Brodska on 22 December 1932; they had one son.

In 1939 Wellek immigrated to the United States, and he became a naturalized U.S. citizen in 1946. He spent some time at the University of Iowa, where he met many of the so-called New Critics—William Wimsatt, Cleanth Brooks, Allen Tate, and Robert Penn Warren. At Iowa he contributed to a collection of essays found in *Literary Scholarship: Its Aims and Methods* (1941). There he also met Austin Warren, with whom he wrote the celebrated *Theory of Literature* (1949). Unfortunately, it was with this same work that Wellek became forever associated with the New Criticism movement, but he denied the connection, saying that he had developed his theory long before he read the work of other New Critics. There were two more editions of *Theory of Literature* published, the third appearing in 1963, when it was again regarded as an important text for graduate students.

The most famous part of the book is the chapter on the intrinsic approach to literature. This approach requires the reader to look at the work of art as autonomous, a place where form and content merge as one, free from all inquiry, except as a linguistic system with its own aesthetic life. The book also has a chapter on the extrinsic approach. Wellek was concerned that his work might be misinterpreted. He insisted that only after having used the intrinsic method could one begin to interpret the work using an extrinsic approach, an approach that might use some outside source, for example, biography, history, philosophy, or psychology. The artwork, he insisted, must first be analyzed, interpreted, and evaluated before it can be compared to other systems and their aesthetic qualities.

During the 1960s Wellek's work became better known because of the publication of the third revised edition of *Theory of Literature.* In 1960 he became chair of the department of comparative literature at Yale, a department he built almost entirely on his own. He also was part of several important associations. He served on the editorial board and the executive council of the Modern Language Association (MLA) and was vice president of the MLA; in addition he was president of the International Comparative Literature Association, the American Comparative Association, and the Czechoslovak Society of Arts and Sciences. He completed the first two volumes of the *History of Modern Criticism* in 1955; the work grew to eight volumes published between 1955 and 1992. He also published five other books during the 1960s: *Essays on Czech Literature* (1963), *Concepts of Criticism* (1963), *Confrontations* (1965), *History of Modern Criticism: 1750–1950* vols. 3 and 4 (1965), and *Discriminations* (1970). Two of his books were reprinted, *Theory of Literature* (1949, 1956, 1966, 1973, 1984, and 1996) and *The Rise of English Literary History* (1966). He also published numerous lectures, essays, and reviews.

Critics praised him for the attention he gave to his subject and for not compromising his own values and beliefs by making his work popular. Wellek was also a defender of the tradition that made possible his theories and methods. He began to read from a range of literary perspectives, each with their own different philosopher—Plato, Aristotle, Saint Thomas Aquinas, Immanuel Kant, Georg Wilhelm Friedrich Hegel, Karl Marx, and Friedrich Nietzsche. Through these studies he became concerned that criticism had moved away from the literary object. He emphasized the need for a more formalistic approach and wondered when and how criticism would return to the analysis, interpretation, and evaluation of literature. Wellek did not minimize the importance of such subjects as history, but he considered them secondary to literary analysis and evaluation, where the true essence of literature can be best found.

Perhaps the most ambitious of his projects was *History of Modern Criticism: 1750–1950*. In justification of this work, he wrote that theory needed a history of criticism, which itself requires a comparative approach. Critics claimed that this enterprise would serve the needs of future critics and scholars; it would become for these future scholars a standard reference source. Wellek's *History of Modern Criticism: 1750–1950* was an attempt "to illuminate and interpret our present situation . . . [which is] comprehensible only in the light of a modern literary theory." As a comparatist, he contended that no work could be studied in isolation. Instead, he believed in the "interdependence" of all literature. He went so far as to claim that there is a "supernational" history of literature. *History* was divided into English, German, French, Italian, Russian, and American criticism. Wellek attempted to illustrate how each critic offered a particular method and framework for understanding the literary object and for discovering new approaches to the understanding of literary criticism. Wellek's own method viewed the work of art as the experiences of the author, both conscious and unconscious. The reader can never know or interpret this object completely; instead, through its various readings, the work takes on a life of its own. From these readings, certain "standards" or "norms" emerge as important literary qualities. These norms come out of the trained reader's attempts to understand the work that exists in each of these readings. These attempts to understand the object become an "inter-subjective" reading of trained readers.

Wellek's first wife died on 11 September 1967; he married Nonna Dolodarenko Shaw on 21 May 1968; the couple had one son. During the 1960s his work was filled with renewed energy, but it and the work of the New Criticism came to an end in the 1970s, when other forms of literary theory, such as structuralism and deconstruction, emerged. In fact, Wellek ended his work, *History of Criticism: 1750–1950*, in the 1950s because he foresaw the rise of these newer theories. In the 1970s he defended his methods against what he called "the new barbarism." In *The Attack on Literature* (1982) he described Marxist views of literature as the product of current ideologies and the structuralist's view of literature as being indecipherable. Through it all, he argued, "I hold to it [his own methodology] tenaciously and defend it as a basic category of the life of the mind."

★

Steve Lynn's essay on Wellek in the *Dictionary of Literary Biography*, vol. 63: *Modern American Critics, 1920–1955* (1988) is a good source for a summary of important books and articles and a statement of Wellek's literary theories. Martin Bucco, *René Wellek* (1981) in Twayne's United States Authors Series 410, offers valuable information on Wellek's life and works. An obituary is in the *New York Times* (16 Nov. 1995).

JAMES VARN

WESTMORELAND, William Childs (*b.* 26 March 1914 in Spartanburg, South Carolina), career military officer who was from 1964 to 1968 commander in chief of the Military Assistance Command in Vietnam, the American establishment formed to help South Vietnam in its battle against Communist forces; he was instrumental in expanding the U.S. military involvement in the Vietnam War.

The son of James Ripley Westmoreland, a prosperous manager of a textile plant, and Eugenia Childs, Westmoreland showed a military bearing from his earliest days. He was a serious, well-behaved boy who showed leadership qualities and excelled in extracurricular activities, becoming president of his senior class in high school, and an Eagle Scout. He particularly enjoyed the camaraderie of the Boy Scouts and took pride in wearing a uniform. A scout trip to Europe during high school stoked his desire to see the world.

That journey began, ironically, within his home state of South Carolina, at The Citadel, the prestigious military college in Charleston. Westmoreland was a good but un-

William Westmoreland. NATIONAL ARCHIVES AND RECORDS ADMINISTRATION

exceptional student who was nevertheless viewed by his fellow students and instructors as a "prototype military man" with a bright future in the armed forces. He felt at home in the discipline and regimentation of The Citadel, and planned to dedicate his life to the military. With the help of family friend, James Byrnes, a U.S. Senator from South Carolina, Westmoreland won an appointment to the U.S. Military Academy at West Point, New York. There he won the Pershing Award for military proficiency and leadership and was named captain of cadets, the highest honor available to a cadet. His closest friends believed he would rise to become army chief of staff, and Westmoreland proved them right.

After graduating from West Point in 1936 with a second lieutenant's commission, Westmoreland decided to enter field artillery, the military discipline concerned with large mounted firearms. After stints in Oklahoma and Hawaii, he was posted to Fort Bragg, North Carolina, where he was promoted to the rank of major. During World War II, he fought Rommel's forces in North Africa and landed at Normandy on D-day, leading the 9th infantry. After the war, Westmoreland's star was in ascendance, and he was rumored to be on President Dwight D. Eisenhower's "rocket list" for promotion. In 1947 he married Katherine Stevens Van Deusen, the daughter of his first commanding officer at Fort Sill, Oklahoma. They had three children.

Westmoreland sought to make himself a well-rounded soldier, alternating his assignments between field opera-

tions and the more intellectual pursuits of high strategy and military policy. To bolster his combat skills, he enrolled in paratrooper and glider training at Fort Benning, Georgia, and was chief of staff of the 82nd Airborne at Fort Benning from August 1947 to July 1950. He also served as a faculty member at the Army War College in Carlisle Barracks, Pennsylvania, for a year before becoming commander of the 187th Airborne Regimental Combat Team in Korea. By 1953 he was promoted to brigadier general and took over the army's manpower office at the Pentagon. In December 1956 he received his second star, becoming the youngest major general in the U.S. Army. Westmoreland was a soldier's officer, committed to troop morale; the men knew that "Westy," as he was called, would look out for them.

In July 1960, after two years as commander of the 101st Airborne Division "Screaming Eagles" at Fort Campbell, Kentucky, Westmoreland was appointed superintendent of West Point. At forty-seven, he was the second-youngest commandant ever, after General Douglas MacArthur, who took over at just thirty-nine. It was through West Point that Westmoreland met President John F. Kennedy. The two men discovered that they shared the same goal with respect to Vietnam: increasing the military presence of the United States in South Vietnam as necessary to prevent the expansion of Communism in Southeast Asia.

The men also shared a mutual friend in General Maxwell D. Taylor, who served as Kennedy's personal military adviser, and who later became President Lyndon B. Johnson's ambassador to South Vietnam. Taylor and Westmoreland had met in Sicily in World War II. At that time, Taylor was a brigadier general, and Westmoreland an aggressive young officer known for venturing alone into enemy territory to identify potential targets. They forged a life-long friendship, and their careers advanced somewhat congruently, with Westmoreland at one point serving as secretary to the general staff when Taylor was army chief of staff.

When Kennedy came into office, he had been determined to counter Communist aggression anywhere in the world, on any terrain. He instructed Defense Secretary Robert McNamara to develop a counterinsurgency force, known as the Special Forces of "Green Berets." In 1962 and 1963 Vietnam was beginning to look like a test case for Kennedy's policy. After Kennedy's assassination in November 1963, President Johnson maintained Kennedy's policy, but accelerated the pace of events, determined to win the war. Taylor was dispatched to Vietnam as ambassador, and Westmoreland joined him in December 1963 as commander of the Eighteenth Airborne Corps. Shortly thereafter, Johnson handpicked Westmoreland to command the growing contingent of U.S. military advisers in Vietnam. The president had a simple charge: "Don't pull a MacArthur on me," a reference to MacArthur's defiance of President Harry Truman during the Korean War.

Initially, Westmoreland was a media darling. When he first arrived in Vietnam, Americans were there only in an advisory capacity, and he was a handsome man with a military bearing straight out of central casting. His favorable press coverage culminated in recognition as Man of the Year by *Time* magazine in 1965. Westmoreland continued to cultivate the press throughout the Vietnam conflict, organizing a daily press briefing at command headquarters peppered with kill ratios, body counts, and other statistics designed to portray the war effort in a positive light. The honeymoon would not last, however. As the conflict in Vietnam drew on, the media began to view the military-supplied statistical information as a farce, and the daily briefing became known as the "five o'clock follies."

On 2 August 1964 Johnson received reports that U.S. destroyers had been attacked by North Vietnamese torpedoes in the Gulf of Tonkin. Johnson seized the opportunity to push a resolution through Congress. This resolution, which became known as the Gulf of Tonkin Resolution, effectively gave Johnson a blank check to broaden the war effort as he saw fit, without congressional interference. In late 1964 and early 1965 the U.S. began air strikes against North Vietnam. This was the first major escalation of the conflict—but not the last. On 7 February 1965 Vietcong troops attacked the U.S. air base at Pleiku, killing eight U.S. soldiers and destroying six helicopters and a transport plane. McGeorge Bundy, national security adviser to Pres-

ident Johnson, went to the scene for an inspection. He urged a retaliatory strike, a recommendation supported by Ambassador Taylor and Westmoreland. Within twelve hours, retaliation was ordered.

As the pressure mounted to introduce ground troops, the issue divided Taylor and Westmoreland. The two men were the senior U.S. political and military officials in Vietnam, respectively, and their counsel would be influential with President Johnson. Prior to the initial air strikes, Westmoreland advised Taylor that he did not believe the strikes would be militarily effective. He believed that the real battleground was in South Vietnam, and that ground troops would be required. Taylor was growing increasingly wary of bringing in more troops, and argued for the political benefits of striking by air. Westmoreland deferred to Taylor's political judgment, as he always had before, but he felt that a ground war was both desirable and inevitable. As early as August 1964, shortly after the Tonkin incident, he began planning the logistics necessary to accommodate an influx of combat troops.

The introduction of ground troops would have another effect; it would elevate Westmoreland to the status of commander of chief of the Military Assistance Command. He relished the chance, not merely because he had been training for it all his life, but because he was troubled by the fact that official Washington remained deeply divided by the war. The determination to send combat troops, Westmoreland believed, would settle the question, committing the United States once and for all to the job at hand. This would in turn ensure that he would have access to the means necessary to properly prosecute the war; surely, he reasoned, the politicians would not endanger the welfare of the troops.

After much internal debate, on 8 June 1965 Johnson authorized U.S. troops to engage in ground combat. Soldiers began to embark for Vietnam, and their arrival was made virtually seamless by Westmoreland's advance work on logistics—a monumental effort that remains a textbook case since studied at West Point and other military colleges. It was an auspicious beginning to the ground war. But the presence of combat troops in Vietnam did not, as Westmoreland had hoped, stop the dithering within the U.S. government over tactics and goals. Nor did it provide him with any certainty when it came to resources.

Militarily, Vietnam would prove a difficult test. It was necessary to fight the war on two fronts, employing a conventional defense against North Vietnamese units infiltrating the south, while developing a new set of tactics to hold off guerrillas (the Vietcong, or Vietnamese Communists) attacking South Vietnam from within. This would be a proving ground for the Green Berets, the counterinsurgency force developed by Kennedy and McNamara, and a chance for Westmoreland to flex his strategic muscles.

Westmoreland needed a way to pin down a mobile and elusive enemy, and he and his staff developed the so-called search and destroy mission, which took the fight to the enemy. Helicopter gun ships carried troops deep into the jungle, their trails blazed by heavy bombs and Agent Orange, a defoliating chemical.

Search and destroy was effective as a tactic, but not as a strategy, as short-term successes failed to translate to long-term strategic gains. Vietcong casualties were extraordinarily high, but there seemed no end to the enemy's will. Much of the military establishment, Westmoreland included, had held as an article of faith that the Vietnamese would surrender once they had a full taste of superior troops, training, and firepower. Yet despite ever-increasing body counts, the Vietcong were as fierce and determined as ever. The American public was less cavalier about casualties, and as the military commitment mounted in terms of dollars, troop levels, and lives lost, opinion began to turn against the war. But Westmoreland would remain committed to the war in Vietnam, believing in the rightness of the cause and the prospects for victory until the bitter end—and beyond.

In late 1967, Johnson recalled Westmoreland to the United States to sell the president's rosy projections—a role that had previously fallen to McNamara, until he appeared to lose faith in the war effort. In a speech at the National Press Club in Washington, D.C., Westmoreland boldly declared, "I am absolutely certain that whereas in 1965 the enemy was winning, today he is certainly losing." He predicted victory within two years, insisting that the success of the U.S. war effort was both possible and necessary.

Just a few months later, in January 1968, came Tet, a Vietnamese religious holiday, when Communist forces launched a surprise offensive. The attacks were swift and brutal, and the Americans and their South Vietnamese allies were driven from the countryside into the cities. In one fell swoop, the optimism of Johnson and Westmoreland had been shown to be a lie. The administration tried gamely to suggest it was a last-ditch offensive, but the success of President Johnson's opponents in the Democratic presidential primaries suggested that few Americans believed it. Westmoreland, who was apparently among the few true believers, requested 200,000 more additional troops. From Johnson's perspective, this would have necessitated two politically untenable actions: calling up the reserves and expanding the draft. Shocked by this confluence of events, Johnson announced on 31 March 1968 that he was abandoning the bombing campaign in North Vietnam and withdrawing from the presidential race.

With little if any credibility left, in July 1968 Westmoreland was sworn in as U.S. Army Chief of Staff and left Vietnam. He returned to Washington to assume his new position; the role he had once dreamed of as a young West Point cadet was now thrust on him as a demotion.

He retired from the army after thirty-six years of service on 30 June 1972. He moved back to South Carolina and, at the urging of President Gerald R. Ford, ran for the Republican nomination for governor in 1974. He was soundly defeated in the primary.

Westmoreland has continued to insist that Vietnam was a winnable war, had Johnson not restrained the military from the full application of its capabilities. Speaking to a reporter more than twenty years after he left Vietnam, Westmoreland said: "One can make a case for the proposition that we should have never made the political commitment to the people of South Vietnam. But, having made it, we should have made good our pledge."

★

Westmoreland's memoirs are *A Soldier Reports* (1976). He has also been the subject of two full-length biographies: Ernest B. Ferguson, *Westmoreland: The Inevitable General* (1968), and Samuel Zaffiri, *Westmoreland: A Biography of General William C. Westmoreland* (1994). Westmoreland is also featured in a number of books about the Vietnam War, including Colonel Harry G. Summers, Jr., *On Strategy: A Critical Analysis of the Vietnam War* (1982); David Halberstam, *The Best and the Brightest* (1983); General Bruce Palmer, Jr., *The 25 Year War: America's Military Role in Vietnam* (1984); Stanley Karnow, *Vietnam* (1984); and Neil Sheehan, *A Bright Shining Lie: John Paul Vann and America in Vietnam* (1988).

TIMOTHY KRINGEN

WHARTON, Clifton Reginald, Jr. (*b.* 13 September 1926 in Boston, Massachusetts), international development economist and adviser on human resource development during the 1950s and 1960s to Southeast Asian and Latin American countries, who later became a prominent leader in higher education and business and served as U.S. Deputy Secretary of State. Several of his accomplishments and positions were firsts for an African American.

Although he was born in the United States, Wharton spent much of his early childhood abroad while his father, Clifton Reginald Wharton, Sr., served as a career foreign-service officer and diplomat for the U.S. State Department. Wharton's earliest education occurred during the family's residence in the Canary Islands, Spain, with his mother Harriette (Banks) as teacher. He had two younger brothers and a sister. He returned to the United States to attend the historic Boston Latin School and afterward completed undergraduate studies (1947) in history at Harvard University. During his sophomore year he met Dolores Duncan, a native of New York City, and they were married in 1950 and had two sons.

Wharton's earliest career interest was to follow his father

Clifton R. Wharton, Jr. AP/WIDE WORLD PHOTOS

into the foreign service. However, inspired at his commencement by the speech of Secretary of State George C. Marshall, in which Marshall described his plan for the postwar reconstruction of Europe, Wharton determined to pursue international development as a career. He completed an M.A. in international affairs at Johns Hopkins University (1948), the first African American to do so, and took a position in a philanthropic organization headed by Nelson Rockefeller. Later, he earned another M.A. (1956) and in 1958 became the first African American to receive a Ph.D. in economics from the University of Chicago.

In 1957 Wharton began a thirteen-year stint in a second Rockefeller philanthropic organization, the Agricultural Development Council (ADC). ADC's primary mission was to help developing countries, through research and teaching, to establish the technical, economic, and social infrastructure that complemented agricultural development using high-yield crop varieties. This combination of human resource development and advances in creating high-yielding crop plants became known in the 1950s and 1960s as the "Green Revolution." Wharton occupied several successively more responsible positions in the ADC. As associate director of Southeast Asian operations, in addition to Malaysia where he was based, he oversaw the council's services to Cambodia, Laos, Thailand, and Vietnam. He was also active as a university lecturer and conducted economic research on the region.

Wharton's focus was on developing human capital, on cultivating local technical expertise and leadership, an approach he described as "rice-roots" development. "We wanted Asians to work on the agrarian problems, not experts from the outside who would help for a couple of years and then leave," Wharton said. Although it was not ADC policy, his personal view was to advocate for changing U.S. foreign policy toward Southeast Asia, which was motivated largely by military objectives.

In 1964 Wharton returned to the United States to assume the position of director of the ADC's American University Research Program. The program's mission was to provide overseas experiences for U.S. scholars and scientists to stimulate their interest and research on the problems of developing Asian countries. As the Vietnam War escalated, the ADC found that its work was concentrated in a hot spot of U.S. military activity. Wharton himself was a critic of U.S. military policy: "The military solution is no longer viable," he wrote. "Our military policy has become little more than a simple-minded policy of force. Military policy has virtually become our sole foreign policy." In spite of the contradiction between U.S. policy and ADC's mission, the ADC enjoyed considerable success in support of the developing economies and agriculture in Southeast Asia.

Wharton became executive director of the ADC in 1966 and vice president the next year, a position he held until 1969. At the end of that year his career entered its second important phase when he was appointed president of Michigan State University (MSU) and became the first African American in the post. Assuming office at the beginning of January 1970, Wharton found himself in the midst of what was arguably the most tumultuous period of the twentieth century for higher education administrators. College students had grown ever more restive, their discontent fueled especially by the war in Vietnam. Wharton knew the cultures and economies of Southeast Asia as well as only a handful of U.S. experts; he opposed U.S. military policy there; and he had been a founding officer of the U.S. National Student Association during his college days. He thus understood fully the context of student dissent, but he faced the immediate and formidable challenge of assuring the safety of 35,000 MSU students during potentially violent times. Events on college campuses reached a feverish pitch after the announcement by President Richard Nixon on 30 April 1970 that the war was being expanded to Cambodia. On 4 May 1970, four students were killed by National Guardsmen during a protest demonstration at Kent State University in Ohio.

In the heat of student demonstrations that led to considerable damage on the MSU campus, some observers, including the Michigan Senate, and media were critical of Wharton's handling of the situation. But his demeanor and style, his empathy with the students' complaints, and his outspoken opposition to the destructive tendencies of a small minority of anarchic students, quickly won him near universal praise, unlike many of his contemporary U.S. university presidents. The prominence on campus of his wife, Dolores, during the student unrest was recognized as helpful in diminishing tensions.

Just as Wharton became a respected voice on U.S. foreign policy toward Southeast Asia, he became a national spokesperson and leader during the 1970s for universal access to college education. College, he said in a speech, "is considered to be a right today," not the "privilege" it was in previous years. On this view he was promptly—and prominently—derided by Vice President Spiro Agnew, who called for a return to the "Jeffersonian concept of a natural aristocracy." Wharton responded that to attack universal access to higher education, as Agnew had done, was "an argument of unbecoming arrogance."

In 1977 he became the first black chancellor of the State University of New York, and in 1987 he embarked upon his third career, as chairman and chief executive officer of the Teachers Insurance and Annuity Association-College Retirement Equities Fund. In doing so, he became the first African-American head of a Fortune 500 company. In 1993 Wharton made history for African Americans again when he accepted the position of deputy secretary of state in the administration of President Bill Clinton. He resigned within a year, however, for reasons that the news media described as early disorganization and mistakes by administration officials that were inaccurately attributed through news leaks to Wharton.

The approach and style that Clifton Wharton, Jr., brought to human resource development in Southeast Asia and Latin America during the 1950s and 1960s were essential complements to the success of the Green Revolution. His determination and consistently held beliefs about fairness, equality, and the development of human potential led to other widely recognized successes in a diverse array of prominent leadership positions. Considerable emphasis has been placed on the several "firsts" in Wharton's career, and he recognizes the significance of his accomplishments for African Americans. He has emphasized that he is interested in seeing "the seconds, the thirds and fourths."

★

George R. Metcalf, *Up from Within: Today's New Black Leaders* (1971), provides an account of Wharton's early life through the critical first year of his presidency at Michigan State University.

Wharton's report, *The U.S. Graduate Training of Asian Agricultural Economists* (1959), is his exposition of the problems faced by Southeast Asian graduate students pursuing the Ph.D. in U.S. universities. His paper in *Foreign Affairs* (April 1969) is an analysis of the challenges of developing human resources to facilitate agricultural and economic improvements in developing countries.

A library of audiotapes of his speeches from 1969 to 1979 is in the Michigan State University library.

W. HUBERT KEEN

WHEELER, Earle Gilmore (*b.* 13 January 1908 in Washington, D.C.; *d.* 18 December 1975 in Frederick, Maryland), army officer who, as chairman of the Joint Chiefs of Staff, was the highest-ranking military officer during the peak of America's participation in the Vietnam War.

The only son in a family with three children, Wheeler's parents were Clifton F. Wheeler, a dentist, and Ida Gilmore, a homemaker. Wheeler graduated from Eastern High School in Washington, D.C., in 1928 and received an appointment to the U.S. Military Academy, from which he graduated in 1932. He was commissioned a second lieutenant in the infantry. On 10 June 1932 he married Frances Rogers Howell; they had one son. During World War II, Wheeler served as commander of an infantry battalion and as operations officer of the Ninety-ninth Infantry Division before becoming chief of staff of the Sixty-third Infantry Division in May 1943. Holding the rank of colonel, he helped oversee the division's training program and then, in the final months of the war, participated in its drive across Germany to the Danube River.

Following the war Wheeler served primarily in staff positions, rising to the rank of general. Urbane, modest, intelligent, and articulate, he earned a reputation as a hardworking professional who understood the Washington bureaucracy, leading to his appointment as army chief of staff in October 1962. In this post he handled the deployment of troops during the Cuban Missile Crisis and during the civil rights disturbances in Mississippi and Alabama, gave vital support to the 1963 Limited Nuclear Test Ban Treaty with the Soviet Union, and forged a good working relationship with Secretary of Defense Robert McNamara, who was impressed with Wheeler's low-key style and readiness to defer to civilian authority. As a result, President Lyndon B. Johnson named him chairman of the Joint Chiefs in July 1964.

The Vietnam War dominated Wheeler's tenure as chairman of the Joint Chiefs. From the outset he believed that only the swift application of overwhelming military power would compel North Vietnam to cease its "aggression" against South Vietnam. Faced with the possible collapse of South Vietnam, Johnson in 1965 agreed to a bombing campaign against North Vietnam and the dispatch of American ground troops to South Vietnam. But concerned about the impact of the war on his domestic political program and the possible intervention of China if the United States waged all-out war, he adopted an ad hoc strategy, placing

Earle Wheeler, 1967. © BETTMANN/CORBIS

restrictions on the bombing of North Vietnam and deploying troops in small increments. Johnson's piecemeal escalation fell far short of what Wheeler thought was required. However, imbued with the military's "can-do" spirit and not wanting to appear disloyal to civilian authority, he did not contest Johnson's actions. Displaying his negotiating skills, Wheeler also kept the other members of the Joint Chiefs, who were more obstreperous than Wheeler and vehemently favored a powerful blow against North Vietnam, in line, avoiding a major confrontation with the White House. Apparently, Wheeler believed that once the war had been Americanized, he could maneuver Johnson into giving the military the strategic freedom to fight the war on its terms.

During the next two years Wheeler issued optimistic statements about the prospect of victory in Vietnam. Privately, however, he increasingly feared that Johnson's "gradualism" gave the enemy time to adjust to American pressure and ultimately would fail. Either unwilling or unable to develop a strategy that conformed to Johnson's desire to fight a limited war, Wheeler pressed for an expanded bombing campaign against North Vietnam, attacks against enemy sanctuaries in Laos and Cambodia, and the mining of North Vietnamese harbors. As the war dragged on, Johnson lifted some of the bombing restrictions and sent more troops to South Vietnam. But he still placed limits on the operations of American units, prompting the Joint Chiefs in August 1967 to consider resigning en masse to protest his policies.

Wheeler made his major effort to change the war's strat-egy at the time of the Tet offensive, an effort on the part of the Vietnamese Communists to capture cities in South Vietnam in early 1968. While Tet was a disastrous defeat for the Communists, he saw it as an opportunity to get Johnson to mobilize reserve forces to build up the strategic reserve, which had been depleted severely by the demands of Vietnam, and eliminate the remaining restrictions on American operations. During a visit to South Vietnam in February 1968 he and General William Westmoreland, commander of American forces in Vietnam, agreed to ask Johnson for 206,000 additional troops, an action that would necessitate calling up the reserves. Westmoreland wanted the troops to follow up on the victory in Tet and win the war by extending ground operations into Cambodia, Laos, and the Demilitarized Zone between North and South Vietnam. Wheeler, knowing of Johnson's reluctance to expand the war, did not inform Johnson of Westmoreland's plans and instead accompanied the request with a pessimistic appraisal of the situation in South Vietnam in the hope that he could frighten Johnson into providing the troops. Wheeler's request prompted a fierce debate within the administration over the war's strategy, and in a rebuke to the military, Johnson, at the end of March, refused to mobilize the reserves and decided to deescalate the war.

Doubting that the war now could be won on American terms and suffering from health problems, including a heart attack in 1967, Wheeler looked to retire when his four-year term as chairman of the Joint Chiefs expired in July 1968. But holding Wheeler in high regard and accustomed to his nonconfrontational manner, Johnson extended his term for another year. When Richard Nixon became president in 1969, Wheeler again wanted to retire; however, Nixon persuaded him to stay an additional year, implying that he would listen more closely to military advice than Johnson had. Although Nixon agreed to Wheeler's proposal to go after the Communist sanctuaries in Cambodia, his strategy centered on withdrawing American troops from South Vietnam and turning over the ground war to the South Vietnamese. While skeptical that Nixon's policies would ensure the survival of South Vietnam, Wheeler endorsed them out of concern that the American army was disintegrating under the strains of Vietnam. He retired in July 1970 after serving as chairman of the Joint Chiefs for an unprecedented six years. Wheeler died of heart failure and was buried in Arlington National Cemetery.

Wheeler placed much of the blame for America's eventual defeat in Vietnam on Johnson's makeshift approach to the war. While there is much to criticize about Johnson's strategy, Wheeler is not above reproach. Under his leadership the Joint Chiefs never forcefully challenged Johnson with their conviction that the United States should go all out to win. At the same time, they failed to articulate a strategy that fit with the war Johnson wanted to fight. In this way Wheeler helped enmesh the nation in a strategy that was doomed to failure.

★

Wheeler's chairmanship of the Joint Chiefs and civil-military relations during the Vietnam War are discussed in Mark Perry, *Four Stars* (1989), George C. Herring, *LBJ and Vietnam: A Different Kind of War* (1994), Robert Buzzanco, *Masters of War: Military Dissent and Politics in the Vietnam Era* (1996), and H. R. McMaster, *Dereliction of Duty: Lyndon Johnson, Robert McNamara, the Joint Chiefs of Staff, and the Lies That Led to Vietnam* (1997). An obituary is in the *New York Times* (19 Dec. 1975). Oral histories by Wheeler are in the John F. Kennedy Library in Boston and the Lyndon B. Johnson Library in Austin, Texas.

JOHN KENNEDY OHL

WHITE, Edward Higgins, II (*b.* 14 November 1930 in San Antonio, Texas; *d.* 27 January 1967 in Cape Kennedy [now Cape Canaveral], Florida), U.S. Air Force test pilot and one of the second group of U.S. astronauts (the New Nine) who in 1965 became the second person to walk in space and the first spacewalker to control his movements and maneuver around the outside of the spacecraft.

White was the son of Edward Higgins White and Mary (Haller) White. His father, a major general, had pioneered balloon flight and heavier-than-air flight for the U.S. Army Air Corps. In addition, two of his uncles had distinguished

Edward H. White II. NASA JOHNSON SPACE CENTER

themselves in the army and the Marine Corps. Perhaps because of his father's interest in flying, the young White developed an early fascination in aircraft; as a treat, his father took him on a flight in an AT-6 training plane when he was twelve years old.

White's family moved to Washington, D.C., before he reached secondary school, and there he attended Western High School. He excelled in athletics, especially track and field. After graduating from Western in 1948 he attended the U.S. Military Academy at West Point, New York, graduating in 1952 with a B.S. in military science. In 1951 he married Patricia Eileen Finegan; they had two children. At West Point he was an athletic standout; he was invited to the U.S. qualifying meet for the 1952 Olympic Games and barely missed going to the games to compete in the 400-meter hurdles.

Following his graduation from West Point, White transferred from the army to the new U.S. Air Force to pursue his interest in flying. In flight school in Florida he qualified as a jet pilot and then was sent to Bad Tolz, Germany, to attend survival school. He was stationed in Germany for three-and-a-half years, flying the fighter craft F-86 Sabres and F-100s.

From reading a magazine in 1957, White learned that the United States might soon be looking for astronauts, so he transferred stateside to attend graduate school at the University of Michigan in Ann Arbor, believing an advanced engineering degree would enhance his chances of joining the space program. At Michigan he met the future astronaut James McDivitt. After graduating with an M.S. in aeronautical engineering in 1959, White trained to be a test pilot at Edwards Air Force Base in California. He received his test pilot credentials in 1959 and was sent to Wright-Patterson Air Force Base in Ohio, where he tested a wide variety of cutting-edge aircraft and equipment. He flew some of the first seven U.S. astronauts (the Mercury Seven) in large cargo aircraft in which they experienced weightlessness when he sent his planes into steep dives.

The National Aeronautics and Space Administration (NASA) began looking for nine more astronauts, and White underwent numerous unpleasant tests to become one. On 17 September 1962 he was named as one of the New Nine. He loved his work and threw himself into his mission assignment: the designing of the controls for the Gemini and Apollo programs, which put him in the company of the second American in space, Gus Grissom. When the NASA command center was relocated to Houston, Texas, White moved his family to El Lago, a Houston suburb.

In July 1964 NASA designated Major McDivitt as the commander of the second Gemini spaceflight, with White as his partner. They worked well together. Indeed, White's upbeat outlook was welcomed by Grissom and the other Mercury Seven astronauts. White's craft, the *Gemini 4,* was launched on 3 June 1965. During this flight, White took his famous space walk. Several weeks earlier, on 18 March 1965, the Russian cosmonaut Alexi Leonov had entered a space lock in *Voskhod 2* and, after the lock was depressurized, had exited the craft and floated in space for ten minutes. While the Americans did not have the space lock, they did have a small "gun" that shot gas and could be used to maneuver in space. When White exited *Gemini 4,* after the entire cabin had been depressurized, he maneuvered joyously in space while hundreds of millions of people listened to the transmissions among Grissom on the ground, McDivitt, and him. He climbed all over the spacecraft, but his gun quickly ran out of fuel and he had to use the cord that attached him to the ship for maneuvering; it took a seemingly long time to get him back inside *Gemini 4.* In June 1965 White was promoted to lieutenant colonel for his exploits.

White was named to be a pilot on *Apollo 1,* the prototype Moon voyager that was to be tested by flying it in Earth orbit. Grissom was the commanding officer, and both were very concerned about numerous badly designed systems in the craft. White insisted that all of the controls be the same on each of the interlinked capsules that made up an Apollo craft. On 27 January 1967 he slipped into the center seat of *Apollo 1,* between the astronauts Grissom and Roger Chaffee, to test the craft's equipment and systems. After several hours of testing, a fire broke out from an electrical short

circuit. NASA used pure oxygen in its spacecraft (the Russians used ordinary air), and the fire consumed all of the oxygen in twenty-two seconds, killing White and his companions. The escape hatch was over and behind White's head, and he required a minimum of ninety seconds to lift a ratchet up over his head to unfasten its bolts. Thereafter, the hatch was redesigned. White is buried in the West Point U.S. Military Academy Post Cemetery in New York.

White was among the most promising of America's astronauts. His exceptionally high intelligence, enormous capacity for taxing work, and sense of duty seemed likely to result in his becoming a notable leader. He turned his 1965 space walk into a true test of a human being's ability to work in space. His insistence on making all of the Apollo craft have the same controls may have saved lives; the consistent controls were especially valuable during the *Apollo 13* crisis, when that mission's three astronauts had to switch among the various components of their craft and control their return to Earth with vehicles not intended for that purpose.

★

Current Biography Yearbook (1965) offers information on White's family heritage and his life. "A (Long) Walk in Space," *Washington Post* (4 June 1999), provides a reprinted account of White's behavior during his space walk. Jamie Murphy, Benjamin W. Cate, and James O. Jackson, "It Was Not the First Time," *Time* (10 Feb. 1986), describes how White died. Gregory P. Kennedy, "Jet Shoes and Rocket Packs: The Development of Astronaut Maneuvering Units," *Space World* (Oct. 1984), offers a lively account of how White's maneuvering "gun" contributed to the development of maneuvering units for spacewalkers. See also Mary C. Zornio, "Ed White," *Detailed Biographies of Apollo 1 Crew,* on NASA's website. An obituary is in the *New York Times* (28 Jan. 1967).

KIRK H. BEETZ

WHITE, Theodore Harold ("Teddy") (*b.* 6 May 1915 in Boston, Massachusetts; *d.* 9 May 1986 in New York City), foreign correspondent, journalist, and author whose books on presidential elections reshaped political reporting in the United States.

White was one of four children of David Vladefsky, a lawyer, and Mary Winkeller White, both Russian immigrants. His father adopted the name "White" from a prominent Boston department store. The elder White used his law degree to support radical causes and represent poor clients, and the family was never well off; after his death in 1931, his widow and children were forced to go on welfare. White graduated from Boston's prestigious Latin High School, and by selling newspapers on streetcars, along with gaining

Theodore H. White. AP/WIDE WORLD PHOTOS

a newsboys' scholarship and assistance from the university, he was able to enter Harvard a year later in 1934.

Majoring in history with an emphasis on China, White earned an A.B. summa cum laude in 1938. Before sailing to China on a Frederick Sheldon traveling fellowship after graduation, he made arrangements to submit stories to the *Boston Globe.* En route, he earned his first money as a journalist when the *Globe* published his article on conflicts between Jews and Muslims in Palestine.

In March 1939 White was hired by the Chinese Ministry of Information. Over the next nine months, he filed stories with the *Globe,* the British *Manchester Guardian,* and the Australian Broadcasting Company in addition to fulfilling his official duties. As a stringer for *Time* magazine, he came to the attention of the publisher Henry Luce. White's report of fighting on the Shaanxi front was the first story in *Time* to carry a byline. With enough journalistic assignments to keep him busy, White ended his connection with the Chinese government in 1940.

Luce brought White to New York in 1941 to do a series of articles for *Fortune.* Following the Japanese attack on Pearl Harbor, Hawaii, in December, White returned to China as a war correspondent and was later awarded an Air Medal for his participation in combat flights. His criticism of the removal of General Joseph Stilwell and an un-

flattering story on China's Chiang Kai-shek resulted in White being ordered back to the States. He took a leave of absence from *Time* so that he and Annalee Jacoby could complete *Thunder Out of China* (1946). This book, and his continued support of the State Department's "old China hands," led to his departure from *Time,* whose staff soon referred to him as a "pinko" or Communist.

On 29 March 1947 White married Nancy Bean; they had two children. That same year Stilwell's widow asked White to edit her husband's papers. The general's testy views, and White's continued criticism of the Chinese government, made it difficult for him to find work with mass-circulation journals in the United States, so in 1948 he and his family moved to Europe where he had found work with the independent Overseas News Agency.

From Paris, White reported on the Marshall Plan (by which the United States provided economic assistance to European countries recovering from World War II) and the beginnings of the postwar European community. Returning to the States in 1953, he was briefly on the staff of the *Reporter* and then joined *Collier's* just before its demise. With the collapse of *Collier's,* White wrote two novels. *The Mountain Road* (1958), set in China during the war, was well received and became a selection for various book clubs. *The View from the Fortieth Floor* (1960) was a fictionalized account of the death of *Collier's.*

As the new decade opened, it appeared that White had come to the end of his journalistic career. Shifting ground, however, he set out to report on the presidential campaign of 1960. During the primaries, he spent time with the front-runners Richard Nixon and John F. Kennedy, as well as with other candidates. After the national conventions, he cast the race for the world's most powerful position as a sort of medieval joust. Going behind the headlines, White created a new way of looking at American politics by high-lighting what he felt were the roots of the candidates' political ambitions.

The manuscript for *The Making of the President* was rejected by several publishers who felt there would be little market for a political book several months after the end of the campaign. When the book did appear in 1961, it was a phenomenal success, selling more than four million copies and earning White the Pulitzer Prize. Undoubtedly, the key to its success was White's intellectual insights combined with a compelling narrative.

Although critics generally praised White's work, some questioned his objectivity, arguing that he had become too enamored of the Kennedy charm, and had portrayed the new president more sympathetically than Kennedy's opponents. As a result, White may have overstated the significance of what was a razor-thin margin of victory. His article in *Life* following Kennedy's assassination in 1963 appeared to continue the myth of Camelot. Despite this criticism, many political reporters adopted White's style in covering subsequent political campaigns.

The 1960s constituted the high point of White's political reporting. The overwhelming success of *The Making of the President* almost guaranteed that the next presidential campaign would see a successor volume. But *The Making of the President: 1964* was less successful in its sale and reception than its predecessor. The fault lay not only with White, but with the fact that the 1964 election was less interesting than that of 1960. The candidates Lyndon Johnson and Barry Goldwater did not inspire the same enthusiasm as Kennedy and Nixon; the issues seemed lackluster and lacking in focus; and over it all hung the pall of Kennedy's death. On the other hand, perhaps White's reporting skills may have been somewhat sharper the second time around.

In some respects, White's next attempt, *The Making of the President: 1968,* was a failure despite, or perhaps because of, the turmoil and tragedies with which the year began. These included the Tet offensive, the stunning announcement that President Johnson would not seek reelection, and the assassinations of Martin Luther King, Jr., and Robert Kennedy. There were many elements of potential high drama: the disruption of the Democratic convention in Chicago, George Wallace's candidacy, and growing dissension over the war in Vietnam. These events overshadowed the candidates and their personalities, the critical elements of White's previous books.

National politics had simply become too complicated and confusing to be covered by one individual. By now, too, it appeared that White had become an "insider." His strength had always been in interpreting character, but this was an approach that had been outgrown by events. White's last foray into political reporting following the 1972 election was not well received. His views were too colored by his ready access to people in positions of power, and with numerous other journalists delving into elections, his post-election analyses were no longer novel.

In 1971 White divorced his wife, and in March 1974 he married Beatrice Kevitt Hofstadter. Following Nixon's resignation that year, White's *Breach of Faith* examined the president's political fall. *In Search of History* (1978) was the first of a planned two-volume work in which White hoped to trace his path as a professional journalist. He was working on the second volume when he died of a stroke in New York City, just three days after his seventy-first birthday.

Known for his lucid and dynamic style, White was a journalist who was committed to in-depth analysis of the headlines. Trained as an historian, he tried to fit the events and figures of his time into an historical framework. As a foreign correspondent White made China understandable to his readers; as a political reporter he forever changed the way Americans look at candidates and elections. He was passionate and involved, traits he never attempted to hide.

He cared about outcomes. His narrative style ensured that his work would be a slice of history in the making rather than an ephemeral catalog of passing events.

★

White's personal papers, notes, and correspondence are in the library of Harvard University. He began to tell his own life story in *In Search of History* (1978). Edward T. Thompson, ed., *Theodore White at Large* (1992), provides a collection of some of his major articles. Joyce Hoffmann, *Theodore H. White and Journalism as Illusion* (1995), is critical of his role as an "insider," but recognizes the strengths of his work and gives appropriate credit to his reshaping of American journalism. An obituary is in the *New York Times* (17 May 1986).

ART BARBEAU

WIESNER, Jerome Bert (*b.* 30 May 1915 in Detroit, Michigan; *d.* 21 October 1994 in Watertown, Massachusetts), scientific statesman, educator, and engineer who, as a science adviser to President John F. Kennedy, established the U.S. Arms Control and Disarmament Agency.

Wiesner was born to Joseph and Ida Wiesner. His father ran a dry goods store in Dearborn, Michigan, where the boy grew up. At the University of Michigan at Ann Arbor, studying mathematics and electrical engineering, Wiesner worked as a cook and dishwasher at a local restaurant to earn his meals. At Michigan, he also met Laya Wainger, a fellow mathematician from Johnstown, Pennsylvania, whom he married in 1940. Wiesner received a B.S. in 1937 and an M.S. in electrical engineering in 1938.

After working as the chief engineer at the Library of Congress from 1940 to 1942, he was recruited to work on the war effort at the radiation laboratory located at the Massachusetts Institute of Technology (MIT) in Cambridge. After the end of World War II, Wiesner continued his government service at the University of California's laboratory in Los Alamos, New Mexico, from 1945 to 1946, helping to develop electronic components for the Bikini Atoll atomic weapon tests in 1946. That same year he returned to MIT as an assistant professor of electrical engineering and worked on his Ph.D., which he completed at the University of Michigan in 1950. He also began a long service to the Research Laboratory for Electronics (RLE), beginning as its assistant director in 1947 and serving as its director from 1952 until 1961, when he was asked to serve the government once again.

In January 1961 John F. Kennedy, the president-elect, chose Wiesner to serve as his special assistant for science and technology, a position established by President Dwight D. Eisenhower in 1957 as a result of the Soviet *Sputnik* satellite launch. The public surprise at the Soviets' achieve-

Jerome Wiesner testifying before the Senate Labor Committee, July 1962. ASSOCIATED PRESS AP

ment had forced Eisenhower to respond to growing criticism that the United States was behind the Soviet Union in science and technology. Eisenhower had great respect for the scientific community, which had worked diligently in the mid-1950s on various government committees, advising on national security issues. Establishing the prominent position was an easy decision for Eisenhower, and it did much to alleviate the public's concern. Wiesner was the third scientist to hold the position, following James Killian and George Kistiakowsky.

The scientific community had gained overnight respect and elevation after the atomic bombings of Hiroshima and Nagasaki ended World War II. But in 1954 the preeminent physicist Robert Oppenheimer, who had headed the Manhattan Project, was denied security clearance in a public hearing, largely because of his vocal opposition to the American development of a hydrogen bomb. This severely damaged the relationship between the government and the scientific community. Bridges were quickly mended, largely through the work of Killian and the President's Science Advisory Committee (PSAC). Science advising to the government reached its golden age in the late 1950s and into the early 1960s.

Wiesner had served with Killian in the 1950s on the

PSAC and had a deep respect for the PSAC and its work. He headed a task force in 1960 that reviewed American missile and space programs and reported to Kennedy in January 1961 that both programs lagged far behind their Soviet counterparts. Wiesner persuaded the president-elect to consider reorganization of the programs rather than increased funding. The two men had known each other for a long time and shared an intellectual curiosity. Wiesner, like Kennedy, made his home in Massachusetts. He was a Democrat and had run and won a race for the Watertown planning board. He did not relax often, but when he did, he enjoyed sailing and cooking Sunday breakfast for the family. His work ethic was exemplary: he stated once that if a professor did not see students often, that professor might as well be working in industry. He also made time to serve as the chair of the technical committee of the American Foundation for the Blind, after having become interested in books for the blind while working at the Library of Congress. Like the new president, Wiesner was young and ambitious. Together they were a good fit, and Wiesner was very influential in shaping national policy as a scientific statesman.

After the rapid changes in nuclear technology in the 1950s, which included the hydrogen bomb, ICBM technology, and the miniaturization of warheads, the 1960s did not see many scientific and technological achievements in the arms race. What dominated the 1960s were the issues of space, defense, and arms control. Wiesner was passionate about arms control. He had traveled to the Soviet Union a number of times and felt that the Soviets, too, wished to achieve some kind of limit on the arms race. He helped to establish the U.S. Arms Control and Disarmament Agency, and worked to prevent the deployment of the antiballistic missile (ABM) system in the early 1960s. The high point in his career in Washington came when the Soviet Union, Great Britain, and the United States signed the Limited Test Ban Treaty in 1963, which limited the testing of nuclear weapons in the atmosphere and underwater. Although the treaty had major limitations, it is generally considered the stepping-stone to more meaningful arms-control agreements, and represented a major turning point in U.S.–Soviet relations during the cold war.

Wiesner also had strong opinions about the American space program. Believing that the United States was unlikely to be the first to put a man in orbit, he was critical of the attention the press was giving the Mercury program, which in his view falsely raised the hopes of the American public. However, Wiesner did believe that putting a man in orbit was the first step to Moon exploration and a space station. Therefore, he recommended that the National Aeronautics and Space Administration (NASA) be reorganized so that top scientists and engineers could be recruited. His efforts proved successful as NASA enjoyed many triumphs, culminating in the 1969 landing on the

Moon. In June 1962 Kennedy had reorganized various government agencies as part of his plan to encourage and coordinate research. As part of that reorganization, the new Office of Science and Technology (OST) was created. Upon Wiesner's recommendation, the special assistant to the president for science and technology would head the OST and thus be able to testify before Congress as needed.

After serving briefly in the same two positions for President Lyndon Johnson, Wiesner returned to MIT as the dean of the School of Science in 1964. He reflected upon his experiences in Washington in his book *Where Science and Politics Meet* (1965), in which he warned, "Only by agreeing to effective disarmament measures and employing the resources thus made available for constructive purposes can we have any hope of ultimate survival." He remained outspoken about issues regarding arms control, and was a founding member of the International Foundation for the Survival and Development of Humanity, a group of Soviet and American scientists who worked together to raise money for research on global issues. He was also a vocal critic of Johnson's policies in Vietnam. As the provost of MIT (1966–1971), he led 4,000 antiwar protesters on a peace march between MIT and the Boston Common in 1969.

Wiesner became the thirteenth president of MIT in 1971, retiring in 1980. He had a stroke in 1989 and died in 1994 due to heart failure at his home in Watertown. His wife and four children survived him.

Wiesner's mark on the 1960s was his ability to educate policymakers, scientists, and the general public about the dangers involved in weapons production and testing and the consequences of an unrestrained arms race. In the words of a National Academy of Engineering memorial tribute to Wiesner, his gift was "his ability to elucidate complex issues and to explain the effects of policies and their technical and political consequences." In doing so, Wiesner was able to convince policymakers in the United States and the Soviet Union that restraint was needed in arms control. The Limited Test Ban Treaty was the direct result of his dedicated work.

★

A good memorial tribute to Wiesner can be found in the *National Academy of Engineering Journal*, vol. 8 (1996).

VALERIE L. ADAMS

WIGNER, Eugene Paul (*b.* 17 November 1902 in Budapest, Hungary; *d.* 1 January 1995 in Princeton, New Jersey), Hungarian-American professor of mathematical physics and recipient of the 1963 Nobel Prize in physics for his pioneering work in quantum mechanics.

Wigner, born Jenó Pál Wigner, was the second of three children and the only son of Anthony Antal Wigner, a

Eugene Wigner. ARCHIVE PHOTOS, INC.

leather-tanning factory director, and Elizabeth Erzsébet Einhorn, a housewife. Doctors incorrectly diagnosed a childhood illness as tuberculosis. While Wigner was recuperating in a sanatorium, he pondered mathematics problems. "I had to lie on a deck chair for days on end, and I worked terribly hard on constructing a triangle if the three altitudes are given," he later said. Wigner attended Lutheran High School, Budapest (1915–1920), and met the Hungarian-born mathematician and mathematical physicist John von Neumann who, he said, "was a much better mathematician than I was and a better scientist. But I knew more physics." He enrolled at Technische Hochschule, Berlin, in chemical engineering, studying physics and mathematics during his spare time. He also attended colloquia at the University of Berlin with the physicists Albert Einstein and Max Planck.

In 1925 Wigner obtained his doctorate under fellow Hungarian Michael Polyani, a physical chemist, economist, and philosopher. Wigner was invited back to Technische Hochschule as an assistant professor in the physics department. He immigrated to the United States in 1930, joined the faculty at Princeton University, and devoted himself to the study of atoms and their applications. He was naturalized as an American citizen in 1937. From 1935 to 1937 he taught at the University of Wisconsin and then returned to

Princeton, where he spent the remainder of his career. He was named Thomas B. Jones Professor of Mathematical Physics in 1938 and emeritus professor in 1971. During his years at Princeton, he also spent time at the University of Chicago Metallurgical Laboratory and directed a civil defense project for the National Academy of Sciences (1963) and a similar project for the Oak Ridge National Laboratory (1964–1965).

Wigner's 1933 statement "The problem of modern physics is now: What is the structure of the nucleus?" indicated his serious interest in atomic particles. He helped develop the first nuclear reactors and the first nuclear bomb. For his detailed design of the reactors, Wigner was called "the first nuclear engineer." At a National Academy of Sciences award ceremony in Washington, D.C., on 18 May 1960, Chairman James R. Killian, Jr., said, "The trustees believe the development of the nuclear reactor is one of the great advances in man's capability for using atomic energy for peaceful purposes."

One of Wigner's favorite sayings was "The optimist regards the future as uncertain." At times, however, he was not an optimist. As an early refugee from Nazi Germany, he worried, during the late 1930s, that the United States did not take Hitler seriously enough. Later he worried about Stalin's aims in the Soviet Union. During the 1950s he seemed certain that nuclear war was imminent. In 1939 Wigner advised Einstein to warn President Franklin D. Roosevelt of the threat of the Nazi's nuclear weapons. In 1941 Roosevelt established the University of Chicago Manhattan Project to construct an atomic bomb. Wigner worked on that project (1942–1945) and was Director of Research and Development at Clinton Laboratories (1946–1947).

At Princeton, Wigner developed the ideas that eventually resulted in his receiving the 1963 Nobel Prize in physics. His Nobel lecture on December 12—"Events, Laws of Nature, and Invariance Principles"—was a discussion of the general role of symmetry and invariance in modern and classical physics. Wigner supported his thesis that the laws of nature form the raw material in all natural sciences and said that the success of physics was its explanation of the regularities of nature. Wigner's Nobel Prize was representative of the 1960s' emphasis on quantum mechanics and its focus on the study of the microcosm.

During debates on the Princeton campus over the American incursion into Laos, Wigner argued that scientists should be advisers to the government. Others believed that scientists should rise above the political fray and keep themselves separate from political ends. Wigner, however, believed in a strong civil defense, and many liberals of the 1960s saw his outlook as outdated and bleak. Politically, he was a conservative, and he was accused of being a hardliner on the war in Vietnam. Hostile faculty and students at-

tacked his views in 1969. Generally, however, his priority was physics, and he was largely divorced from social issues. Wigner's name was synonymous with scientific discovery: the Wigner-Eckart theorem in group theory; the Wigner coefficients in the quantum theory of angular momentum; the Wigner effect, the Wigner correlation energy, and the Wigner crystal in solids; the Wigner force and the Breit-Wigner formula in nuclear physics; and the Wigner distribution in quantum chaos. What Wigner called his "precious field" was the application of fundamental principles of symmetry in physics.

He coauthored numerous books on nuclear reactors and nuclear structure, including more than five hundred papers published in eight volumes. Official recognition for his nuclear research included the U.S. Medal for Merit (1946); the Enrico Fermi Prize (1958); and the Atoms for Peace Award for 1959, shared with fellow scientist Leo Szilard. Wigner also received the Franklin Medal (1950), the Max Planck Medal of the German Physical Society (1961), the George Washington Award of the American-Hungarian Studies Foundation (1964), the Semmelweiss Medal of the American-Hungarian Medical Association (1965), and the National Medal of Science (1969), among others. He received honorary degrees from more than twenty colleges and universities in the United States and Europe. Wigner was a member of the General Advisory Committee to the U.S. Atomic Energy Commission from 1952 to 1957, was reappointed in 1959, and served until 1964.

Wigner married Amelia Zipora Franck, also a physicist, on 23 December 1936. She died tragically in 1937, a few months after their marriage. Four years later, on 4 June 1941 he married Mary Annette Wheeler, a professor of physics at Vassar College. They had a son and a daughter. Following Mary's death from cancer in 1977, Wigner married Eileen C. P. Hamilton in 1979 and became stepfather to her child. In an article written by Erich Vogt for *Physics Today* (December 1995), Wigner was described as "always genuinely solicitous of people's feelings. . . . It was essentially impossible to follow him through any door."

In 1960 Wigner said, "The enormous usefulness of mathematics in the natural sciences is something bordering on the mysterious." He gave extensive interviews, but he remained as elusive as his subject matter. Dr. Abraham Pais, a fellow physicist, wrote, "He was a very strange man and one of the giants of twentieth-century physics." Wigner helped build the edifice of quantum mechanics. During an interview with the editor Andrew Szanton, he shared his belief in the duty of physics "to provide a living picture of our world, to uncover relations between natural events, and to offer us the full unity, beauty and natural grandeur of the physical world."

★

Wigner's memoir is *The Recollections of Eugene P. Wigner,* as told to Andrew Szanton (1992). For a biography, see F. S. Wagner, *Eugene P. Wigner: An Architect of the Atomic Age* (1981). Tyler Wasson, ed., *Nobel Prize Winners* (1987), provides chronological details of Wigner's career. See also "Eugene Wigner—A Tribute on His Seventieth Birthday," *Physics Today* (Oct. 1972); "A Conversation with Eugene Wigner," *Science* (10 Aug. 1973); "Bargmann and Wigner Honored," *Physics Today* (Nov. 1978); "Eugene Paul Wigner: A Towering Figure of Modern Physics," *Physics Today* (Dec. 1995); "Eugene Wigner (1902–1995)," *Nature* (26 Jan. 1995); and "Symmetry in Physics: Wigner's Legacy," *Physics Today* (Dec. 1995). An obituary is in the *New York Times* (4 Jan. 1995).

SANDRA REDMOND PETERS

WILKINS, Roy (*b.* 30 August 1901 in St. Louis, Missouri; *d.* 8 September 1981 in New York City), civil rights leader in the 1960s who was instrumental in securing voting rights for African Americans and who eventually served the National Association for the Advancement of Colored People for forty-six years.

Wilkins's father, William, fled St. Louis prior to his son's birth to escape being lynched for refusing to allow his civil rights to be abused; the boy's mother, Mayfield Edmondson, died when he was four years old. Wilkins and his younger sister and brother were raised by an aunt and uncle in Saint Paul, Minnesota, in a poor, integrated neighborhood. Wilkins attended the integrated Mechanic Arts High School. After earning a B.A. in sociology, economics, and journalism in 1923 from the University of Minnesota, he joined Kansas City's African-American newspaper, the *Call,* as a reporter and soon became the managing editor. In 1926 he began dating Aminda "Minnie" Badeau, and they were married on 15 September 1929. Although the couple had no biological children, they raised Wilkins's brother's son.

As a journalist Wilkins's interest in writing overlapped with his participation in civil rights events and organizations. In 1931 he was appointed as the assistant executive secretary of the National Association for the Advancement of Colored People (NAACP), and in 1934 he replaced W. E. B. Dubois as the editor of *Crisis,* the NAACP's official magazine, a position he held until 1949. He was appointed as the executive director of the NAACP in 1955.

During his long tenure in this position, Wilkins served on the U.S. Commission on Civil Rights. He and Senator Edward W. Brooke of Massachusetts were the only African Americans on the commission, which was chaired by Otto Kerner, the governor of Illinois. Being a member of the commission was very important for the levelheaded and respected leader during the racial turmoil of the 1960s.

The year 1963 was a critical time for the civil rights movement, with the historic March on Washington taking place on 28 August. Wilkins initially was reluctant to participate in the march, for he feared reprisal from the administration of President John F. Kennedy, which was divided over its support. However, he joined the leadership forces of A. Philip Randolph, Martin Luther King, Jr., and

Roy Wilkins, February 1969. © BETTMANN/CORBIS

Whitney Young, Jr., to march for the desegregation of all public schools and better housing, legal rights, and employment opportunities for African Americans. This demonstration was larger than any in the annals of the nation's capital: more than 250,000 African Americans joined with white labor and civil rights supporters. After the march the key figures in its success, including Wilkins, were invited to the White House to meet with Kennedy to discuss and work on strategies for African-American labor to acquire equality.

A year later Wilkins's life was threatened through an anonymous letter, postmarked 5 January 1964 at Saint Petersburg, Florida, which was received at the Federal Bureau of Investigation headquarters in Washington, D.C. The letter stated that Wilkins, King, and Ivan Allen, the mayor of Atlanta, would be killed, as would Robert Kennedy and Lyndon Johnson, who was now the president. While there were suspects, no one was ever indicted for sending the letter. Also in 1964, following riots in northern urban areas, Wilkins asked the U.S. Department of Justice to initiate a full-scale investigation, because he felt there were outside forces influencing these violent activities.

In 1967, when King spoke emphatically against U.S. participation in the war in Vietnam, Wilkins, a conservative, refused to support him. In fact, Wilkins did not want the NAACP to be part of the opposition of the war and grumbled publicly about King's stance. With this activity, as well as plans to ease racial tensions in Cleveland, Wilkins felt King was going to "stir up trouble." Wilkins believed the primary causes of urban racial friction were slums, lack of jobs, and poor public schools in the South. He felt Congress's refusal to pass open-housing legislation and civil rights bills was "creating the atmosphere" for violence.

Wilkins was steadfast about defining civil rights as an ongoing issue, whether in war or peace. By the late 1960s his belief that nonviolence would attain better results for African Americans was seemingly becoming history, however, especially with the rise of the Black Muslims and Black Panthers. Stokely Carmichael's "black power" slogan echoed throughout all civil rights activity during the turbulent, hot summer of 1966. That slogan swiftly traveled across the United States and hit every historically African-American college and university, as well as high schools and some major academic centers. The new movement was well on its way.

At the annual NAACP convention in Los Angeles on 5 July 1968, Wilkins announced that he opposed the black power concept. "No matter how endlessly they try to explain it, the term 'black power' means anti–white power. . . . It has to mean 'going it alone.' It has to mean separatism."

Other civil rights advocates, including the "young turks" of the NAACP, did not equate black power with black supremacy. They perceived it as a unified black platform of self-esteem in a heterogeneous society. This controversy split the organization, and many African Americans lost respect for Wilkins and the NAACP. They began to view the association as a platform for white politicians. Regardless, Wilkins was clear about his goal, which was to obliterate legal segregation throughout the United States. He stood before the Equal Opportunity in an Urban Society Subcommittee of the Republican Platform Committee in Miami on 31 July 1968 and said the nation needed a social and economic bill of rights that guaranteed basic rights for every American.

Wilkins's workable strategies and humane efforts led to national and international recognition of his contributions to the civil rights movement. In 1964 he received the NAACP's most prestigious award, the Spingarn Medal. In addition, he was awarded honorary doctorates from more than thirty institutions of higher learning throughout the United States. In 1981, just four years after retiring from the NAACP, Wilkins died of kidney failure at the age of eighty. He is buried in Farmingdale, New York.

The 1960s was a critical period for Wilkins and the civil rights movement. It was the zenith of protest, radicalism, freedom train rides, marches, and demonstrations. Wilkins, from the old school of thought, firmly believed in integration and nonviolence and was criticized for being too cautious and old-fashioned. His speeches primarily dealt with voter registration, school desegregation, and federal civil rights legislation. He was able to achieve positive results in integrating public schools, improving employment levels, gaining voting rights, and providing greater opportunities for all. Regardless of the controversy over Wilkins's ideology concerning the Black Power movement, his gentle, unwavering spirit, hope, and intellectual skills brought together a society that was in political pain and social turmoil.

Whenever Wilkins was asked for whom he worked, he always responded, "I work for Negroes." His contributions to civil rights created a progressive path to a better society.

★

Wilkins's papers are held by the Library of Congress. Wilkins left a large body of writing, including many articles and an autobiography, with Tom Mathews, *Standing Fast: The Autobiography of Roy Wilkins* (1982). For additional biographical data on Wilkins, see Herbert Aptheker, ed., *A Documentary History of the Negro People in the United States, 1933–1945* (1951); Albert P. Blaustein and Robert L. Zanrendo, *Civil Rights and African Americans* (1968); Peter M. Bergman, *Chronological History of the Negro in America* (1969); Norman Coombs, *The Black Experience in America* (1972); Lenwood G. Davis, *A Paul Robeson Research Guide* (1982); Harry A. Ploski and James Williams, *The Negro Almanac: A Reference Work on the African American* (1989); and Leon T. Ross and Kenneth A. Mimms, *African American Almanac* (1997). Obituaries are in the *New York Times* and *Washington Post* (both 9 Sept. 1981)

OTIS D. ALEXANDER

WILLIAMS, William Appleman (*b*. 12 June 1921 in Atlantic, Iowa; *d*. 5 March 1990 in Waldport, Oregon), educator and historian.

Williams was the son of William Carleton Williams, a pilot killed during military exercises in Texas in 1929, and Mildrede (Appleman) Williams, a schoolteacher. Growing up in Iowa, Williams, an only child, excelled in sports and music and was a drummer in a jazz band. He entered Kemper Military Academy in Booneville, Missouri, in 1939 on a basketball scholarship. Two years later he received an appointment to the U.S. Naval Academy in Annapolis, Maryland. Enamored with the works of Spinoza, Marx, and Freud, Williams read voraciously. He graduated from the academy in 1944 and spent the remainder of World War II serving as an officer on an amphibious landing craft. He married Emma Jean Preston in December 1945. He received a medical discharge from the Navy in 1947 due to a back injury. Williams entered the University of Wisconsin and earned his Ph.D. in 1950. Labeled a leftist and pro-Communist because of his Ph.D. thesis on America's "open door imperialism" and his 1952 book, *American-Russian Relations, 1781–1947,* Williams came under the scrutiny of the Federal Bureau of Investigation and the House Un-American Activities Committee. Williams taught at Washington and Jefferson College, Ohio State University, and the University of Oregon before returning to the University of Wisconsin in 1957. He divorced his first wife in 1956 and married Corrine Croft Hammer, whose two children he adopted. They later had three children together.

In 1960 Williams was becoming the leader of the cold war revisionists, who were attacking the orthodox view of this period of competition, tension, and conflict (mostly nonviolent) between Communist and non-Communist nations, especially the United States and the Soviet Union. Williams's reputation as a revisionist was solidified with the 1959 publication of his book *The Tragedy of American Diplomacy.* The book, which became one of the most influential works ever written about the history of U.S. diplomacy, ushered in the new decade with a call for an honest appraisal of the foreign policy of the United States. Williams contended that American leaders had subverted their own ideals because of economic forces, which led them to impose capitalistic, liberal, economic standards on Eastern Europe. He said this effort frightened the Soviet Union's leader, Joseph Stalin, who wanted to have friendly regimes on Russia's borders and restore the Russian economy, which had been devastated by the war. In essence, Williams argued that Presidents Franklin D. Roosevelt and Harry S Truman were to blame for the cold war, not the Russians. Williams was criticized for putting too much emphasis on economic factors as the cause of the cold war while being lenient in his analysis of Stalin and the Soviet

Union. Following the book's publication, accusations that he was a Communist resurfaced.

Williams's next book, 1961's *Contours of American History,* was eventually named to the Modern Library's List of the "100 Best Nonfiction Books of the Century." Focusing on the many aspects of capitalism in the United States throughout the country's history, Williams presented a unified picture of U.S. foreign policy as it reflected the character of its society. In the book Williams broke down U.S. history into three ages, "Mercantilism," relative "Laissez Faire," and "Corporate Syndicalism." As did his previous books, *Contours of American History* objected to many aspects of American life, in particular its imperialistic tendencies as first expressed by its constant move westward. This theme was continued in his 1969 book *The Roots of the Modern American Empire,* in which Williams also documented what he saw as the imperialist role of agricultural businessmen and explained his view of why America acquired an empire.

Williams is credited as the founder of the "Wisconsin School" of revisionist historians, whose students included noted historians Walter LaFeber, author of numerous books on foreign relations, and Lloyd Gardner, considered one of America's leading diplomatic historians. Throughout the 1960s, many of the Wisconsin School teachers and graduate students figured prominently in "teach-ins" in protest of the Vietnam War. To Williams and his fellow revisionists, the Vietnam War was merely a part of American politicians' efforts to pursue a policy of economic imperialism due to America's insatiable appetite for new markets. Williams, in particular, saw the United States's involvement in the Vietnam War as a tragic result of a misguided cold war policy.

Williams's other books published in the 1960s were *The United States, Cuba, and Castro: An Essay on the Dynamics of Revolution and the Dissolution of Empire* and *The Great Evasion: An Essay on the Contemporary Relevance of Karl Marx and on the Wisdom of Admitting the Heretic into the Dialogue about America's Future.* Despite his academic success, Williams's domestic life was becoming stressed. He was drinking heavily, and his marriage was falling apart. In 1969 he left Wisconsin and accepted a position at Oregon State University, where he focused on teaching undergraduates.

Throughout the 1960s, Williams's ideas on American imperialism, the cold war, and corporate liberalism brought forth the ire of both liberals and conservatives. Despite his largely unorthodox views and his somewhat "leftist" politics, his books and articles were surprisingly conservative, and his views often ran contrary to the prevailing thoughts of the decade's "New Left." Even if one did not agree with his belief that socialism was a viable alternative to the course that America was on, his books provided keen insights and a fundamental understanding of the nation's growth. Instead of taking a simplified, pro-American view of the country's history, Williams broke new ground as he exhorted other historians to analyze it honestly. He wrote that historians should focus on "a searching review of the way America has defined its own problems and objectives, and its relationship with the rest of the world."

In 1971 Williams's marriage to his wife, Corrine, ended, and on 8 December 1973 he married Wendy Margaret Tomlin. Williams was granted sole custody of his three children from the marriage. Although he continued to teach and publish, including *History as a Way of Learning: Articles, Excerpts and Essays* (1973) and *Empire as a Way of Life: An Essay on the Causes and Character of America's Present Predicament* (1980), his most groundbreaking work was behind him. He died of cancer in 1990, and his ashes were scattered near Waldport on the Oregon coast.

★

The William Appleman Williams Papers can be found in the Oregon State University Special Collections. The *Dictionary of Literary Biography, Volume 17: Twentieth-Century American Historians* (1983) contains a comprehensive bibliography. For a retrospective review of Williams's views and impact on history and political thought during the 1960s, good sources include John Lewis Gaddis, "The Tragedy of Cold War History: Reflections on Revisionism," *Foreign Affairs* (Jan.–Feb. 1994): 142–154, and Jacob Heilbrunn, "The Revision Thing: Who Is to Blame for the Cold War? A New Quarrel," *The New Republic* (15 Aug. 1994): 31–38. Obituaries are in the *New York Times,* (9 Mar. 1990), *Chicago Tribune,* (12 Mar. 1990), and *Los Angeles Times,* (10 Mar. 1990).

DAVID PETECHUK

WILLIAMS, William Carlos (*b.* 17 September 1883 in Rutherford, New Jersey; *d.* 4 March 1963 in Rutherford, New Jersey), author and physician whose lifelong commitment to poetic innovation and the creation of a uniquely American form had a major influence on the direction of poetry in the 1960s, at which time he began to be acknowledged as one of the most significant poets of the twentieth century.

Williams, whose poetry candidly represented the multiculturalism of America, came from a richly diverse background. His father, William George Williams, was a New York businessman, born in Britain, who grew up in Saint Thomas, Virgin Islands. His mother, Raquel Hélène Rose Hoheb, was from Puerto Rico and of French, Dutch, Spanish, and Jewish ancestry. Williams and his younger brother, Edgar, were raised speaking Spanish and French as well as English. He attended school in Rutherford until 1897, when he was sent to Switzerland and Paris to study until 1899. He graduated from Horace Mann High School in

William Carlos Williams. ARCHIVE PHOTOS, INC.

New York City in 1902. Williams attended the University of Pennsylvania Medical School from 1902 to 1906. There he received his M.D. and also developed crucial friendships with poets Ezra Pound and H. D. (Hilda Doolittle), and painter Charles Demuth. Williams studied medicine, but his heart was equally devoted to literature. He published his first collection, *Poems,* in 1909.

After completing internships at hospitals in New York and an advanced study of pediatrics in Leipzig, Germany, Williams returned to Rutherford in 1910 and opened the practice where he treated local, working-class patients for the rest of his career. On 12 December 1912 he married Florence "Flossie" Herman; they had two sons. The Williams family settled into the house at 9 Ridge Road (now an official state monument) where they remained, and where Williams practiced medicine, for the rest of their lives. Williams developed his own unique brand of American modernism, writing poetry, fiction, essays, plays, and sketches whose true importance would only achieve recognition near the end of his life.

By the 1960s Williams had reached the end of his career. A series of debilitating strokes and other medical problems from the preceding decade left him with the use of only one hand, unable to read, and limited speech and mobility. He retired from medical practice in March 1951, after his first stroke, but continued to write until his death. While Williams's health in the 1960s was in rapid decline, he nonetheless became a vital influence on the writers and writing of the decade.

Williams's particular contribution to contemporary poetry was the creation of a form that reflected the actual speech and experience of the people around him. His lifelong goal was to create, as Walt Whitman had done, a democratic poetry "in the American grain" (the title of Williams's collection of historical essays on great American figures). While Whitman developed a language of prophetic expansiveness, with a long verse line to match, Williams's poems were simple, spare, and restrained, frequently composed of very short, two- or three-line haiku-like stanzas. His most famous poem, "The Red Wheelbarrow," is a classic example:

so much depends
   upon

a red wheel
   barrow

glazed with rain
   water

beside the white
   chickens.

Williams's poetry abstains both from the drama of Whitman and from the intellectualizing of contemporary high modernists such as Ezra Pound and T. S. Eliot, and instead abides by a principle of "objectivism" in which local things are treated with close attention and quiet respect. This poetic dictum is set forth with typical lucidity in *Paterson*, Williams's important, five-book poem of the American experience: "no ideas but in things."

While Williams was committed to forging a native tradition, he was far from provincial. Part of his attraction for writers of the 1960s was not only the homegrown values he promoted but also his ability to move between the worlds of the local and the international, the populist and the avant-garde. While he lived a humble rural life and focused his poetry on the local scene, he also remained constantly in touch with the latest developments in art in New York City and Europe. Like colleagues such as Pound, Wallace Stevens, and Gertrude Stein, Williams was committed to the contemporary visual arts, and his writing was influenced by movements such as cubism and by artists such as Pablo Picasso, Marcel Duchamp, and Henri Matisse. Williams's interest in the visual arts as an important complement to poetry was renewed in the 1960s by poets such as John Ashbery, Frank O'Hara, and Barbara Guest of the so-called New York School of poets.

Williams was virtually ignored for most of his life in favor of supposedly more sophisticated writers such as T. S. Eliot, whose *The Waste Land* Williams called "the great catastrophe . . . which gave the poem back to the academics." By the 1960s, however, many young writers who also reacted strongly against the politics and impersonality of Pound and Eliot began looking to Williams as a poetic, intellectual, and moral role model. One poet who turned to Williams for advice and encouragement was another New Jersey native named Allen Ginsberg. Ginsberg and Williams corresponded for years, and Williams eventually wrote a laudatory introduction for Ginsberg's groundbreaking book *Howl* (1956)—which became something of a 1960s poetic manifesto. This led to more contact with Beat writers and a famous visit by Ginsberg, Jack Kerouac, Gregory Corso, and Peter Orlovsky to Williams's home. "Doc" Williams's influence and "paternity" extended far beyond the Beat writers, however, and throughout the last decades of his career he kept up correspondences, offering friendship and advice to other such important American writers as Denise Levertov, Charles Olson, Robert Creeley, Theodore Roethke, and Robert Lowell, as well as Canadian poets such as Irving Layton and British poets such as Charles Tomlinson.

Williams continued to write throughout his last years, though his work slowed dramatically. His last poetry collection, *Pictures from Brueghel and Other Poems* (1962), won the Pulitzer Prize for poetry posthumously in 1963. During his final years he edited and organized earlier unpublished work, including *Yes, Mrs. Williams: A Personal Record of My Mother* (1959); his collected short stories, *The Farmers' Daughters* (1961); and his collected plays, *Many Loves and Other Plays* (1961). Though his mobility was limited, he was able to attend productions of two of his plays in New York City, *Many Loves* (1959) and *A Dream of Love* (1961). He also kept up correspondence with, and received occasional visits from, many of his artistic contemporaries and younger protégés. Williams died peacefully at home in Rutherford and was buried at the local Hillside Cemetery.

Williams's importance to the poetry of the 1960s cannot be underestimated. His work helped provoke a major reassessment of what counted as appropriate poetic form, diction, and content. While Pound and Eliot succeeded in internationalizing American literature, many writers felt they did so at the expense of the American experience. Williams, on the other hand, created an American form of international standard. The outward simplicity of his work meant that it went unnoticed for many years. It was not until the 1950s and 1960s, when the values it tacitly promoted—casual openness, frankness, an honest appreciation for the here and now through close attention to its details—became the key values of the era, that his full achievement began to be appreciated.

★

The majority of Williams's manuscripts and letters are held by three libraries: the Beinecke Library, Yale University; the Lockwood Memorial Library, State University of New York at Buffalo; and the Harry Ransom Humanities Research Library, University of Texas at Austin. Williams's *Autobiography* (1951) deals with both his careers as doctor and poet and with the crucial relationship between the two. Reed Whittemore wrote the first biography, *William Carlos Williams: Poet from Jersey* (1975). This was followed by Paul L. Mariani, *William Carlos Williams: A New World Naked* (1981), a meticulously detailed eight-hundred-page biography. There are many important full-length critical studies of Williams's work, including James Breslin, *William Carlos Williams: An American Artist* (1970); Joseph N. Riddel, *The Inverted Bell: Modernism and the Counterpoetics of William Carlos Williams* (1974); Stephen Tapscott, *American Beauty: William Carlos Williams and the Modernist Whitman* (1984); and Peter Schmidt, *William Carlos Williams, The Arts, and Literary Tradition* (1988). Of particular interest for Williams's influence on postmodern poetry is John Lowney, *The American Avant-Garde Tradition: William Carlos Williams, Postmodern Poetry, and the Politics of Cultural Memory* (1997). Bibliographical information can be found in Emily Mitchell Wallace, *A Bibliography of William Carlos Williams* (1968), and Linda W. Wagner, *William Carlos Williams: A Reference Guide* (1978).

MARK SILVERBERG

WILLS, Garry (*b.* 22 May 1934 in Atlanta, Georgia), renowned essayist, historian, professor, critic, and Catholic layman whose work in the 1960s addressed many of the most controversial issues of the era, from the Vietnam War to civil rights.

Wills was the son of John H. and Mayno (Collins) Wills. He went to school in Wisconsin and spent six years in a Jesuit seminary before deciding voluntarily to leave hopes for the priesthood behind. He earned a B.A. degree from St. Louis University in 1957, an M.A. degree from Xavier University in Cincinnati in 1958, another M.A. degree from Yale University in 1959, and a Ph.D. from Yale in 1961.

The culmination of Wills's education coincided with the beginning of the decade of the 1960s. He was completing his M.A. at Xavier in Cincinnati when William F. Buckley of the *National Review* brought him to New York to discuss further writing prospects. The Buckley enterprise was virtually a Catholic cell of conservatives, some of whom, like Buckley, had served in the Central Intelligence Agency (CIA). Wills, who was beginning doctoral studies at Yale, felt privileged to be working with a national publication. However, he found that the magazine was an enabler of its friends and was reluctant to allow harsh criticism of its

own. For example, Wills wrote an unfavorable review of Whitaker Chambers's *Cold Friday,* which Buckley refused to print. While contributing to the magazine, Wills began to explore writing opportunities with other publications.

Bob Hoyt, the editor of the *National Catholic Reporter,* contracted with Wills to appear as conservative counterpoint to John Leo. Wills found himself espousing liberal viewpoints on civil disobedience, the civil rights movement, and the U.S. war in Southeast Asia. Wills did not see how combating Communism in Vietnam was in the nation's interest. In 1962 he had taken a position as an assistant professor at Johns Hopkins University with the hope of embarking on an academic career. He soon found that his articles in the *National Catholic Reporter* were being syndicated to diocesan publications. One of his articles espoused the candidacy of Spiro Agnew for governor of Maryland over George Mahoney, whom Wills castigated as a racist. This article appeared in the Baltimore *Catholic Review,* and Wills's department chair ordered him to stop publishing locally or risk losing his tenure. Wills refused to stop and was fired despite his argument that his scholarly work equaled that of his peers. The department charged him with not sticking to his discipline.

Wills moved to a position as adjunct professor in the Johns Hopkins Humanities Center. He declined invitations to return to his old department when the administration changed. Nevertheless, he retained ties to academia while pursuing work as a professional writer. A friend from graduate school and also a former seminarian, Neil McAffrey, offered him an advance of $7,000 to write a biography of Buckley. McAffrey was an editor with Doubleday and had previously hired Wills to write short religious booklets. Wills began his Buckley book with a chapter dealing with Buckley's debate with the Reverend William Sloane Coffin, the radical Yale campus minister. Buckley was impressed and urged Wills to send the piece to Harold Hayes, the editor of *Esquire.* Hayes hired Wills as a contributing editor at a salary higher than what he earned at Johns Hopkins. Wills subsequently dropped the biography, alienating McAffrey, who demanded a return of the advance after reading Wills's attack in the *National Catholic Reporter* on Alabama Governor George Wallace, who was actively fighting against racial integration in his state.

The *Esquire* experience in the 1960s was an epiphany for Wills. Hayes was a daring and demanding editor who spared neither expense nor people in seeking out good stories. Wills was assigned work on Jack Ruby, the killer of the John F. Kennedy assassin Lee Harvey Oswald. Wills's partner was Ovid DeMaris, a smart, determined investigative journalist with connections within the justice system. Wills wrote a piece on Ruby's motives for killing Oswald and another on the Ruby trial. From both, he determined that there was no larger conspiracy regarding the assassination of President Kennedy. Wills followed with another collaboration with Demaris on Soviet leader Josef Stalin's daughter, which gave Wills insight into the CIA and domestic surveillance techniques.

Hayes now turned Wills to Detroit and Los Angeles to study the growing urban turmoil and government plans to combat social unrest. Wills collected his articles in his book *The Second Civil War: Arming for Armaggeddon* (1968). The book also included his observations during the 1968 Democratic National Convention in Chicago, which he covered for the *National Review*. He exposed the stupidity of both police and military in creating a riot with their arbitrary tactics. Wills followed with another piece criticizing the Vietnam War on the grounds that the United States was not fighting in self-defense. His arguments were to reappear in his book *Nixon Agonistes* in a chapter entitled "Our Country." McAffrey accused him of "going over to the militants," and the *National Review* cover superimposed Wills's head on the body of the activist and Black Panther leader Huey Newton. His break with the magazine and with Buckley was a foregone conclusion as Wills's thinking moved decidedly left of center.

A virtual wunderkind of the conservative revival, Wills was now attacking racism in reviews of works such as James Baldwin's *The Fire Next Time*, which he praised in the *National Review*. In running the review, the magazine suggested that it had an enlightened view of racial issues. Wills was again accused of having "gone liberal," for in 1964 he had suggested that a system of preferential hiring be used to compensate blacks for historic grievances. Buckley repeated the suggestion in a column of his own, and he, too, was attacked for selling out to liberalism.

Wills had also written in the *National Catholic Reporter* that historic guilt for racial wrongs was part of the conservative heritage. He argued that those who prided themselves on inherited values and traditions had to admit to accountability for historic wrongs. He went so far as to declare that "the new Negro . . . would rather be feared than patronized and he is getting his way, and he should."

In Wills's illuminating personal study *Confessions of a Conservative* (1979), he takes up much of his activities during the 1960s. His reflections on student riots, antiwar rallies and sit-ins, campus unrest, the intransigence of the government on Vietnam policy, civil rights, and the assassinations of John and Robert Kennedy and of the Reverend Martin Luther King, Jr., can be found here as well as in the several other books he has published.

Wills has shown himself to be a master writer of analogies among and between often seemingly disparate personalities or situations. As a conscientious Catholic, he has risen as a veritable conscience of the church in all its variables. As a thinker, a writer, an academic, and a critic, Wills has always been willing to take action on behalf of his

beliefs. His concerns for social unrest are founded on an abiding faith in American institutions such as the Declaration of Independence, the Constitution, the Gettysburg Address, and the pathbreaking assertions of respected leaders both within and without the government. Wills was not hesitant about allowing himself to be arrested in protest gatherings against government policy. He also openly refused to pay income taxes in protest against Vietnam policies, the thought of which chastened him later in life as he felt he had been caught up in the cynicism of the American critic H. L. Mencken.

A recurring theme in many of Wills's works is the alienation of portions of society from the government and their subsequent reaction to that government. Another is the infatuation of political figures with power and its uses. His book *The Kennedy Imprisonment: A Meditation on Power* (1982) displays the perils that awaited the Kennedy family, whose desire for power in the 1960s shadowed all the policies of subsequent administrations. Wills is enamored of leaders and leadership, and he is dismayed and disaffected by those who fail to measure up to the demands of the time. His *Certain Trumpets: The Call of Leaders* (1994) counterpoises various historical personalities against one another. Recalling the 1960s, he poses the civil rights leader Andrew Young against the controversial University of California, Berkeley, president Clark Kerr, Young being a proactive agent of healing during racial unrest while Kerr absented himself from the student clamorings for guidance. Kerr alienated those he was charged to help while Young reached out a calming and hopeful hand to his people. Dr. Martin Luther King, Jr., is a personal favorite of Wills, because Wills sees King as a leader who exploited the system for lawful purposes to aid his cause. Rather than tear down and alienate the institutions of the nation, King compelled society and its leadership to examine themselves in the glare of his cause. Wills uses some of the same arguments on those who brandish the Second Amendment as a defense of the right to bear arms. He is a fervent believer in the structure of governmental authority, yet he comprehends the failure of government to do right by its people and to some extent the world at large. In Wills's eyes bureaucracy, incompetence, secrecy, inefficiencies, and hubris too often combine to prevent clarity of thought and a courage to alter course whether it be military policy, civil rights, social policies, or political change.

An inveterate writer, Wills has alternated at university positions, holding positions at Johns Hopkins University and at Northwestern University, where he has been since 1980, first as Henry Luce Professor of American Culture and Public Policy, and, since 1988, adjunct professor of history. Fellowships, lectureships, and titled appointments have been awarded from Yale, Notre Dame University, the

University of California, Princeton, Union College, and Edinburgh University.

He has honorary degrees from colleges and universities such as Yale University, College of the Holy Cross, Spring Hill College, and Siena Heights University. He has also won such awards as the 1993 Pulitzer Prize for nonfiction for *Lincoln at Gettysburg*; the Organization of American Historians Merle Curti Award; the George Foster Peabody Award; two National Book Critics Circle awards; the John Hope Franklin Award; and the National Humanities Medal. Wills married Natalie Cavallo on 30 May 1959. They have three children.

★

Much information on Wills and his relationship to the 1960s is found in his writings during the decade in the *National Review* and the *National Catholic Reporter* as well as in *Esquire*. See also his books *Politics and Catholic Freedom* (1964); *Jack Ruby* (1968), with Ovid Demaris; *The Second Civil War: Arming for Armageddon* (1968); *Nixon Agonistes: The Crisis of the Self-Made Man* (1970); *Confessions of a Conservative* (1979); *Lead Time: A Journalist's Education* (1983); *A Necessary Evil: A History of American Distrust of Government* (1999); and *Why I Am a Catholic* (2002). See also Wills as editor of the *New York Times* compilation of articles *Values Americans Live By* (1973).

JACK J. CARDOSO

WILSON, Brian Douglas (*b.* 20 June 1942 in Inglewood, California), rock and roll composer and vocalist who was the musical genius behind the Beach Boys band and whose music was a major artistic force that fueled the surf music craze of the 1960s.

Wilson was the oldest of three children. His parents, Murry, a leaser of heavy machinery, and Audree Neva (Korthof) Wilson, a homemaker, moved to Hawthorne, California, after the birth of their second son, Dennis, in 1944. A third son, Carl, was born in 1946. Murry Wilson was an amateur songwriter himself and ultimately managed the Beach Boys' career.

Wilson graduated from Hawthorne High School in 1960 and enrolled briefly in a psychology and music curriculum at a local community college, El Camino. He never earned a degree, however. Although deaf in one ear, he was a self-taught pianist, enamored of popular music and the works of George Gershwin. Wilson also nurtured a fascination for the vocal harmonies popular in the 1940s and 1950s. He and his cousin, Mike Love, began performing as vocalists at local parties, and by 1961 they had added Wilson's two younger brothers on drums and guitar along with a schoolmate, Al Jardine, on electric bass, to form a quintet called the Pendletones. Under that name they taped their first single, a song called "Surfin'." Candix Records picked

up the recording and released the song two months later, billing the five musicians as the Beach Boys. "Surfin'," which was written by Wilson for a high school music project, was released on 8 December 1961; it achieved Top Forty play in the Los Angeles area by January 1962 and peaked at number seventy-five on the *Billboard* chart in February. Wilson and the band signed a recording contract with Capitol Records and released a double-sided single, "409"/"Surfin' Safari," four months later. They first penetrated the Top Ten chart with a Chuck Berry adaptation, a single called "Surfin' U.S.A.," in May 1963. A number-one hit album, *Beach Boys' Concert*, was released in 1964. By the end of the decade, the Beach Boys were a well-established chapter in the annals of rock and roll.

Wilson, because of his partial deafness, was classified as exempt during the Vietnam draft. As a result he found the time to compose over 120 songs from 1962 to 1968. He arranged the unforgettable harmonies for the group, produced fourteen albums, and contributed a distinctive falsetto to the Beach Boys sound in the early 1960s. After suffering an emotional breakdown in 1964 and two relapses within sixteen months, Wilson ceased appearing in live performances with the Beach Boys. He was replaced by a succession of vocalists, including Glen Campbell and Bruce Johnston. Despite these setbacks, Wilson composed a number-one single in 1965, "Help Me, Rhonda," and other classic hits, including "California Girls" and "I Get Around," each of which has aired millions of times on radio. With his episodes of breakdown interspersed by marijuana- and LSD-induced intoxication, Wilson entered an introspective era of soul-searching, an attitude that emerged visibly in his work. As he descended into this unabashed, psychedelic period in his life, he ordered yards of sand to be brought into his living room, which he converted into a sandbox. There he kept his piano, which he played barefoot. In this unusual mental state, Wilson began work on an ambitious album called *Smile* but eventually scrapped the project. A drastically diluted version of *Smile*, called *Smiley Smile*, appeared in 1967, taped with studio pianist and lyricist Van Dyke Parks.

According to many critics, Wilson's creative genius is most evident on a 1966 album called *Pet Sounds*. The recording, conceived as a cohesive entity, featured tunes of alienation, analytical in their perspective of love. Because of a series of marketing miscalculations, *Pet Sounds* in its initial release failed to achieve the success of Wilson's other projects with the Beach Boys, and fewer than one million copies were sold. The album's "Sloop John B," however, an adaptation of "The Wreck of the John B," was selected for prerelease as a single in December 1965 and appeared on the Billboard Hot 100 chart on 3 April 1966. Another track, called "Caroline No," was positioned as the closing track on the completed album and appeared as a prerelease single in March 1966. This ill-fated single was credited to

Brian Wilson *(upper left)* and the other members of the Beach Boys. AP/WIDE WORLD PHOTOS

Brian Wilson, without mention of the Beach Boys, a decision that proved unfortunate because Wilson at that time lacked name recognition as a solo artist apart from the Beach Boys. "Caroline No," as a result, barely made an appearance on the Top Forty chart, peaking at an unimpressive number thirty-two. Regardless, *Pet Sounds* appeared in its entirety in the spring of 1966 and entered the Billboard Hot 100 in August, rising to number ten on that chart.

Earlier, in February 1966, Wilson directed the Beach Boys in recording a song called "Good Vibrations," which was released the following October after dozens of retakes. "Good Vibrations" was hailed as Wilson's finest single effort, a seemingly endless blend of juxtaposed rhythms and harmonies. The song, according to Timothy White of *Billboard* magazine, "Was the biggest selling number 1 hit . . . it became the variegate but coherent statement that Brian had endeavored to make with the self-conscious *Pet Sounds*."

Wilson by 1968 was also addicted to cocaine. *Pet Sounds* and "Good Vibrations" notwithstanding, the members of the Beach Boys had become annoyed by the psychedelic undertones and liberal profanity that characterized his compositions in the mid-1960s; they placed a strain on his relationship with the band. He settled with his wife of four years, Marilyn Rovell, into an historic Bel Air, California, mansion once owned by Edgar Rice Burroughs; there the couple set out to raise their two daughters. Wilson ebbed

quickly from professional prominence; he owned and operated a health food store from 1969 to 1970 and became a pupil of the Eastern mystic Maharishi Mahesh Yogi. The 1970s for Wilson was a blur of drugs and ineffectual rehabilitation. His wife divorced him in 1979.

After being ejected from the Beach Boys organization in 1982, Wilson underwent intensive rehabilitation therapy and embarked on a solo career, releasing albums in 1988 and 1998. He married Melinda Ledbetter in 1995; the couple adopted two daughters.

★

Wilson's autobiography, written with Todd Gold, is *Wouldn't It Be Nice: My Own Story* (1991). Composer Paul Williams pays tribute to Wilson with a series of short essays in *Brian Wilson & The Beach Boys: How Deep Is the Ocean? Essays and Conversations,* (1997); Timothy White chronicled Brian Wilson and the Beach Boys in *Nearest Faraway Place: Brian Wilson, the Beach Boys, and the Southern California Experience* (1994).

GLORIA COOKSEY

WILSON, Joseph Chamberlain (*b.* 13 December 1909 in Rochester, New York; *d.* 22 November 1971 in New York City), business executive who in the 1960s transformed the tiny Haloid Company into the Xerox Corporation, which changed the American office environment forever.

The son of Joseph R. Wilson and Katherine M. Upton, Wilson grew up to become a third-generation president of the Haloid Company. His grandfather, Joseph C. Wilson, founded the corporation in 1906, and his father served as its president from 1938 to 1945. So named because of the halogen salts used in photography, Haloid produced paper used for making photographic copies of documents, then an expensive, marginal process.

After attending local public schools, Wilson enrolled at the University of Rochester, from which he graduated in 1931. He went on to Harvard University, where he received an M.B.A. in 1933. Two years later he married Marie B. Curran, with whom he had six children. Training for leadership, he started at the bottom rung of Haloid, working his way through a succession of positions (1933–1936) before becoming secretary and, in 1938, secretary-treasurer.

By the time Wilson became president of Haloid in 1946, company executives had become aware of a promising new process. Developed in the 1930s and 1940s by Chester Carlson, electrography represented a vast improvement over copying processes then in use. In 1947 Wilson purchased rights to the process, which he renamed "xerography," from Greek words meaning "dry writing." During the 1950s Haloid invested heavily in xerography, which paid off with

Joseph C. Wilson. ARCHIVE PHOTOS, INC.

the success of the Copyflo 11 machine, introduced in 1955. Three years later the company changed its name to Haloid Xerox, and in 1959 Wilson became chairman as well as president.

Yet another name change occurred in 1960, as Haloid Xerox became the Xerox Corporation and introduced the Xerox 914 copier. By modern standards it was bulky and slow, producing only seven copies a minute, but for the time the 914 was a revolutionary product, constituting the first automatic, plain-paper copier. Equally important was the method Xerox used for marketing: instead of selling machines, it leased them, and after giving customers a certain base number of copies for free, it charged them for each additional copy. Though the price per copy was somewhat higher than with American Photocopy, or Apeco, the quality of Xerox copies was vastly better. By the end of the decade Apeco, formerly the dominant player in office copiers, was gone from the scene, with Xerox replacing it. In the process the performance of Xerox, as a product and a company, exceeded all expectations.

In 1959, on the eve of the 1960s, due to the changes brought about by the introduction of the 914, Haloid Xerox had profits of $2 million on sales of $32 million. Two years later, profits had jumped 175 percent, to $5.5 million, and revenues had increased by more than 90 percent, to $61 million. This staggering performance was accompanied by an equally impressive climb in the value of common shares, from four to thirty-four. Xerox introduced the 813, a desktop version of the 914, in 1961 and in 1962 undertook its first significant foreign joint venture, combining forces with Fuji Photo Film of Japan—then a small company—to form Fuji Xerox Company. The mid-1960s saw more expansion, in the form of added product lines, corporate acquisitions, and an increased foreign presence.

Xerox acquired Multi-Systems and Electro-Optical Systems in 1963, and in 1965 took over Basic Systems (renamed Xerox Learning Systems) and American Education Publications (renamed Xerox Education Publications), publisher of the *Weekly Reader* and other educational periodicals. Still more acquisitions followed: Professional Library Service and Learning Materials Inc. (both 1966); R. R. Bowker Company, owner of *Books in Print, Publishers Weekly,* and *Library Journal,* and Cheshire, Inc. (both 1967); and Ginn and Company (1968). With the purchase of marketing rights to Central and South America from the Rank Organization in 1964, Xerox spread throughout the Western Hemisphere, while the 1965 opening of a Rank Xerox plant—Haloid had formed a joint venture with the Rank Organization in 1956—in Venray, Holland, expanded the company into Europe.

In 1964 Xerox presented its 2400 model, which could produce 2,400 copies an hour. Such speed in copying was unheard of at the time; in just three years Xerox had produced a copier nearly six times as fast as the 914. The year 1964 also saw the introduction of long-distance xerography, a forerunner of the concept that would become widely used in facsimilie (fax) machines a quarter-century later. These early facsimile machines were large, slow, and expensive, but the Xerox Magnafax Telecopier, which made its debut in 1966, was smaller, faster, and more user-friendly than any other fax machine on the market at the time.

With Wilson at the helm, Xerox grew at a dizzying rate. In some weeks, the company hired more than a hundred production personnel at a time, even as it recruited executives from other leading companies, practically on a daily basis. By 1967 profits were at $97 million, or about 50 percent more than *revenues* had been just six years earlier; revenues themselves, meanwhile, had skyrocketed to $701 million, more than eleven times their value in 1961. It seemed that the growth of Xerox could never stop, but it did—just as Wilson stepped down from his leadership position. By the late 1960s Wilson was entering his seventh decade and was beginning to look toward retirement and a position on the company board. No doubt he had worked himself to the point of exhaustion during those days of hyperactive growth, and judging by his activities after retirement, he must already have been planning a second career in service to the community. In 1968 he named Peter McColough to succeed him as president and chief executive officer.

In 1969, the same year that Xerox moved its corporate headquarters from Rochester, New York, to Stamford, Connecticut, Wilson and McColough together engineered the acquisition of Scientific Data Systems. The latter was a data-processing company, and the $1 billion that Xerox invested in its acquisition indicates the company's degree of interest in the emergent computer industry. Scientific Data Systems, however, proved to be a failure, and by 1975 it had ceased to exist. In the meantime Xerox formed Xerox Computer Services in 1970. A number of important innovations arose from the computer services company, including what may have been the world's first personal computer, but Xerox corporate leadership failed to take notice of it. At the same time, competition from IBM and such Japanese companies as Canon and Ricoh conspired to remove Xerox from its position of leadership. The company suffered throughout the 1970s and 1980s and only began to bounce back in the late 1980s—much too late to acquire a substantial portion of the home-computing market it had helped create.

By then Wilson, who had only a few years to enjoy his retirement, was long dead. After stepping down in 1968 he took a position on the company's board of trustees and served as honorary chairman. He then turned his attention to public service, which was in keeping with a statement he once made regarding the role of a leading corporation

such as Xerox: "Technological companies are at the center of social change and therefore have a responsibility. Those in the inner city have derived little benefit from technology and no profit from it." This view of public service contrasts with the usual image of the hard-driving corporate executive, but Wilson not only expressed such ideas but also lived them. He made Xerox the first company in America to give workers as much as a year's paid leave to devote themselves to worthy causes. When a stockbroker complained about his generosity with corporate funds, Wilson said, "You can sell your stock or try to throw us out, but we are not going to change." He also personally granted the University of Rochester 90,000 Xerox shares in an irrevocable trust in 1965 and in 1967 gave another 50,000 shares to his alma mater.

Wilson served as trustee for the Alfred Sloan Foundation, the Sidney Hillman Health Center, the Carnegie Endowment for International Peace, the George Eastman House, the Committee for Economic Development, and the Rochester Savings Bank. He also sat on the boards of several corporations, most of them based in Rochester. In addition, he served, in 1971, as chairman of both President Richard M. Nixon's Committee on Health Education and New York governor Nelson Rockefeller's Steering Committee on Social Problems. While lunching with Rockefeller, Wilson suffered a heart attack and died.

As president of Xerox in the 1960s, Wilson had the rare opportunity to oversee a company at the height of its powers, when growth occurred at a massive rate and seemingly everything Xerox touched turned to gold. Nor was his leadership merely a passive honor bestowed on a figurehead. More than any other figure in the company—and there were several important leaders, such as research director John H. Dessauer, who discovered Carlson's process—Wilson was responsible for the exponential growth of Xerox in the 1960s. In addition to his sage corporate leadership, however, he did something perhaps even more remarkable: he proved that a corporation and its president can be not only great but also good.

★

There are no biographies of Wilson, but information on his life and impact can be garnered from works by other leading figures at Xerox: John H. Dessauer, *My Years with Xerox* (1971), and David T. Kearns and David Nadler, *Prophets in the Dark: How Xerox Reinvented Itself and Beat Back the Japanese* (1992). Also useful are these corporate histories: Gary Jacobson, *Xerox, American Samurai* (1986), and Douglas K. Smith and Robert C. Alexander, *Fumbling the Future: How Xerox Invented, Then Ignored, the First Personal Computer* (1988). An obituary is in the *New York Times* (23 Nov. 1971).

JUDSON KNIGHT

WISEMAN, Frederick (*b*. 1 January 1930 in Boston, Massachusetts), influential filmmaker who used a "direct cinema" style to produce often controversial documentaries about the interactions between ordinary citizens and social institutions.

Wiseman was the only child of Jacob Leo Wiseman, an attorney, and Gertrude Leah (Kotzen) Wiseman, an administrator at Children's Hospital in Boston. Wiseman attended Rivers Country Day School, graduated with a B.A. from Williams College in 1951, and received an LL.B. from Yale University School of Law in 1954. He married Zipporah Batshaw on 29 May 1955; they had two children. Wiseman worked in the Massachusetts attorney general's office before being drafted into the army. After his discharge in 1956, he and his wife moved to Paris, where he studied at the Sorbonne. While in Paris he became interested in making short films, using an 8-mm camera.

Returning to the United States in 1958, Wiseman worked as a research associate and then lecturer in family and criminal law at Boston University's Law School. In 1961 he was awarded a Russell Sage Foundation grant to study in Harvard's Department of Social Relations. Then, in 1962, he joined the sociology department at Brandeis University as a research associate. Wiseman's continuing interest in film led him to purchase the film rights to *The*

Frederick Wiseman. THE KOBAL COLLECTION

Cool World, a novel by Warren Miller about Harlem street youth. With Wiseman as producer and Shirley Clarke as director, *The Cool World* (1964) was filmed on location with nonprofessional actors. The *New York Times* critic Bosley Crowther attributed the "dynamism of this picture" to the "brilliant, brutal picturing of the community as it is . . . and of the tough youths who range its streets and slums."

Learning from his experience working with Shirley Clarke, Wiseman decided both to produce and direct his next film. His subject was the Bridgewater State Hospital for the Criminally Insane, in Massachusetts, one of the places he had visited with his law students to acquaint them with the institutions their future clients might face. After a year of corresponding and meeting with the superintendent of the facility and other state officials, Wiseman secured permission to make a documentary about the Bridgeport facility. He began filming in the spring of 1966 with lightweight cameras and synchronized sound systems, like those the Robert Drew Associates had used in their television documentaries in the early 1960s, to develop the documentary style called "direct cinema."

Wiseman, along with the photographer John Marshall and one assistant, spent weeks at Bridgewater talking with the warden and, accompanied by a guard, observing daily life in the institution. The scenes captured on film were unrehearsed and unplanned. When filming ended, Wiseman sat down with some forty hours of footage to edit. For a title, he used the name of the annual revue staged by patients and staff, *Titicut Follies*. (Titicut was the Indian name for the Bridgewater area.) Scenes from that show open and close the film. In between are scenes of interactions between the patients and the guards and staff: the force-feeding of an elderly man intercut with images of preparing his body for burial; an inmate's arguing that he be returned to prison because at Bridgewater he was only getting worse; guards taunting a naked man in his room; and a psychiatrist interviewing a child molester. No narration, no interview, no titling explains these and other scenes. The viewer is left to interpret the stark conditions under which the inmates are housed, fed, counseled, and medicated.

In 1967 *Titicut Follies* was shown at film festivals in Mannheim, Germany (where it was named best documentary feature), in Florence, Italy (where it won the critic's prize and award for the film best illustrating the human condition), and in New York City. In Massachusetts, however, the attorney general's office petitioned the Superior Court of Suffolk County (Boston) to prevent distribution of the film, claiming that it violated patients' right of privacy and the state's right to approve the final film. Another petition was filed with the New York Supreme Court to stop a showing of the film at the New York Film Festival. The New York court denied the petition, and the festival showing as well as a short commercial run of the film followed.

In Massachusetts, in the midst of a politicized discussion about conditions in the state's correctional facilities, the debate over *Titicut Follies* continued in legislative hearings, in the press, and in the courts. In May 1969 the Massachusetts Supreme Judicial Court modified a lower court's total ban of the film to allow screenings limited to people with a professional interest in the subject, such as doctors, social workers, lawyers, and psychiatrists. Even though an earlier U.S. Supreme Court ruling, *Burstyn* v. *Wilson* (1952), was believed to have established that film had some protection under the First Amendment, the Massachusetts Supreme Court was successful in prohibiting the showing of a film on grounds other than obscenity or national security. Not until 1991, twenty-four years after *Titicut Follies* was completed, did the Massachusetts courts lift that restriction and allow general distribution of the film. As Wiseman said to the *Boston Globe* reporter Paul Langner, "Naturally, I am very pleased . . . pleased not just for myself, but because it is an affirmation of the value of the First Amendment."

For his second documentary, *High School* (1968), Wiseman took the photographer Richard Leiterman and one assistant to Northeast High School, one of the best high schools in Philadelphia. Most of the students were from Philadelphia's white, upper-middle class. Wiseman has said on several occasions that the process he observed during the four weeks of filming reminded him of a factory. The film, as edited, seems to reflect that view. It begins as the camera approaches the industrial-looking school building and continues with glimpses of "daily life" as administrators and teachers work to instill social values and norms of behavior to produce useful citizens. The students, however, often seem caught between contradictory demands to follow rules but at the same time to develop their independence. The film ends with an ironic scene: During a faculty meeting, the principal reads a letter from a recent graduate who is headed for a combat zone in Vietnam. The graduate writes that, in case of his death, his insurance money will go to a scholarship fund at the school, and comments that he is not worth worrying about, that he is "only a body doing a job." The principal then says, "When you get a letter like this, to me it means we are very successful at Northeast High School. I think you can agree with me." *High School* was broadcast by WNET, New York's public broadcasting television station. Responding to viewers' critical reaction to the school as portrayed in the film, school administrators threatened to sue. To avoid legal action, Wiseman chose not to show the film in Philadelphia.

For *Law and Order* (1969) Wiseman and his crew spent six weeks following the work of officers in the Kansas City Police Department shortly after television viewers had watched police clash with demonstrators on the streets of Chicago during the 1968 Democratic convention. In the film Wiseman presents the complexity of police work in situations ranging from life-threatening ones to mundane ones, in an environment filled with racial tension and expectations from citizens for solutions to problems about which the officers often can do nothing. Broadcast on public television, *Law and Order* received an Emmy for best news documentary of 1968–1969.

During the 1960s Wiseman worked on several policy research projects through the Organization for Social and Technical Innovation, Inc., a private company he formed in 1966 with a partner, Donald Schon. Wiseman withdrew from the company in 1970 and years later referred to policy research work in the 1960s as a "grand boondoggle." His interest in the effect of institutions on the individual, however, continued to find expression in the documentaries he produced—*Hospital* (1970), which won Emmys for best news documentary and best director, *Juvenile Court* (1973), *Near Death* (1989), *High School II* (1994), and others. Reflecting on his experience with *Titicut Follies,* Wiseman acknowledged that one cannot expect a single film to produce social change. In an interview with Cynthia Lucia for *Cineaste* magazine, however, Wiseman expressed hope that "the films provide people with information and experience to draw upon when they're asked to make decisions about what they want in their community."

In talking about his films, Wiseman often refers to them as "reality fiction." What is real is what the viewer sees on the screen. Using a lightweight, hand-held camera, a synchronized audio recorder, and natural light, he is able to follow events as they actually unfold. Because he spends considerable time on location, talking with people and getting to know the institution, most people ignore the presence of the camera as they go about their normal routines. There is no attempt from Wiseman or his photographer to interfere with or influence their behavior. The film's dramatic structure is created as Wiseman edits the film. For Wiseman, editing is a way of summarizing what he has learned about the institution during the process of filming. Although no narration is added to interpret scenes for us, his point of view does emerge.

From his first films in the 1960s, Wiseman has created an important body of work documenting everyday life in the United States across a broad spectrum of economic and social institutions. Through the images his films provide, viewers are invited to reexamine themselves, their experiences, and their relationship to their society.

★

An interview with Wiseman about the making of *High School* appears in Alan Rosenthal, *The New Documentary in Action: A Casebook in Film Making* (1971). Liz Ellsworth provides a shot-by-shot description of Wiseman's early films in *Frederick Wiseman:*

A Guide to References and Resources (1979). Thomas W. Benson and Carolyn Anderson detail the legal and ethical issues surrounding *Titicut Follies* and other Wiseman films in *Reality Fictions: The Films of Frederick Wiseman* (1989). *Voyages of Discovery: The Cinema of Frederick Wiseman* (1992), by Barry Keith Grant, is a useful critical analysis of Wiseman's films. The films are available through Zipporah Films, One Richdale Avenue, Unit 4, Cambridge, Massachusetts 02140.

LUCY A. LIGGETT

WOLFE, Thomas Kennerly, Jr. ("Tom") (*b.* 2 March 1931 in Richmond, Virginia), journalist, illustrator, and novelist who was the greatest of the New Journalists of the 1960s and 1970s.

Wolfe's father, Thomas Kennerly Wolfe, Sr., was a professor of agronomy for Virginia Polytechnic Institute, a businessman who ran the Southern States Cooperative, and a journalist who edited the *Southern Planter*. His mother, Helen Perkins (Hughes) Wolfe, was a homemaker. As a youngster Wolfe enjoyed reading picture books and remembered being especially enamored of *Honey Bear* by Dixie Wilson, which told a story that blended narrative verse with illustrations in a manner he imitated as an adult author. In his teens he was attracted to Emil Ludwig's biographies and the writings of James T. Farrell, James M.

Tom Wolfe. AP/WIDE WORLD PHOTOS

Cain, John Steinbeck, Thomas Wolfe (the 1930s novelist), and William Faulkner. He edited the newspaper for Richmond's Saint Christopher's School, from which he graduated in 1947. In the same year he entered Washington and Lee University in Lexington, Virginia, where he helped edit the college newspaper.

Wolfe graduated cum laude in 1951 with a B.A. in English. He had pitched for the university's baseball team, and in 1952 he had a tryout with the New York Giants. He did not receive a contract offer, so he entered graduate school at Yale University, where he earned a Ph.D. in American studies in 1957. Tired of the academic life, he looked for work outside of academe. In December 1956, when he had completed his coursework, he found it at the Springfield, Massachusetts, *Union,* where he worked as a cub reporter for six months before becoming a full-time reporter. He loved the work.

In June 1959 Wolfe was hired by the *Washington Post.* He covered local and Latin American news, winning a Washington Newspaper Guild award for his coverage of Cuba and another for his humorous coverage in writing and drawings of United State Senate debates, both in 1961. Wolfe's editors liked his work, but Wolfe believed he was being asked to write overly detailed accounts of inconsequential events. He left the newspaper in April 1962 for a job as a writer and illustrator for the New York *Herald Tribune,* where he began making contributions to what was then the *Herald Tribune*'s Sunday magazine, *New York,* which survived the *Herald Tribune*'s eventual bankruptcy.

The *Herald Tribune* was beset by a strike in 1963, putting Wolfe temporarily out of work. While researching another story, he had become interested in the hobby of modifying cars that seemed to be a way of life for some people in California, and he persuaded *Esquire* magazine to send him to California to research an article about them. After a few months in California, Wolfe returned home with copious notes and no idea how he would write the story. As his deadline for the article approached, he told *Esquire* editor Byron Dobell that he could not write the story, but illustrations for the piece were already in press and Dobell had to have the story. Thus, he told Wolfe to type up his notes for another writer to use to construct a story. Wolfe spent the night typing his notes, and Dobell ran the typescript exactly as Wolfe had produced it, full of digressions, impressionistic descriptions, and stream-of-consciousness commentary. It became the publication that launched Wolfe's literary career and was one of the most influential works of its time, imitated by numerous writers continually for decades thereafter.

The story became the title piece in *The Kandy-Kolored Tangerine-Flake Streamline Baby* (1965), a selection of twenty-three from the more than forty articles Wolfe wrote during the two years following the *Esquire* publication; the book included eighteen of Wolfe's illustrations. He had found his authorial voice while writing the original article and then poured out articles for *New York, Esquire,* and *Harper's Bazaar.* They featured bizarre punctuation, mellifluent displays of exotic language, side issues, and a pop culture diction—discomfiting for many critics, although careful readers found that Wolfe's stories had logical underpinnings that held together his flights of colorful vernacular.

In 1968 Wolfe published *The Electric Kool-Aid Acid Test,* an account of the Merry Pranksters, a group of people crossing America on a bus with author Ken Kesey. The book exhibits the solid journalistic experience Wolfe brings to his work. Even though on its surface it is a sensational account of social dropouts abusing drugs and themselves amid the social conflicts of the 1960s, the book covers the history of LSD use during the 1960s and how drug use fit into a cultural search for altered consciousness. The book sold very well. Also published in 1968 was a second gathering of essays, *The Pump House Gang,* which featured Wolfe's high-flying prose style and trenchant observations on American society.

At the end of the 1960s Wolfe solidified his place as a perpetual irritant to social elitists. In 1969 members of the Black Panther party, a high-profile group of African Americans who advocated the use of violence to change society, were charged with plotting to plant bombs. Believing the charges bogus, composer and symphony conductor Leonard Bernstein and his wife held a fund-raiser for the Black Panthers in their New York apartment. Wolfe attended the party, taking shorthand notes of what he saw and heard. One of the uncomfortable aspects of Wolfe's article on the party for those who attended would be the accuracy of his quotations. Entitled "Radical Chic," the article filled the entire issue of the 8 June 1970 *New York.* In it he portrays the rich and well-connected people who attended the party as confused, self-indulgent, and more concerned with appearing socially correct than actually caring about the Black Panthers. They write checks to the Black Panthers who attend the party, but the Black Panthers appear demeaned just by being present in a group of people lacking real regard for them or their cause. This article and one on street gangs were combined in the book *Radical Chic and Mau Mauing the Flak Catchers* (1970).

Some readers were angry that Wolfe had revealed so much about the pretensions of rich liberals. A reputation for cruelly revealing too much about his subjects remained with him through the rest of his career. Even so, by the 1970s he had won a huge popular audience that not only purchased his journalistic books but his scholarly books on the arts, including *From Bauhaus to Our House* (1981). Also in the 1970s Wolfe became a family man. He married

Sheila Berger, an art director of *Harper's* magazine, in 1978; they have two children.

In 1980 Wolfe won the National Book Award for *The Right Stuff* (1979), an account of America's Mercury space program of the early 1960s, which was made into a critically and commercially successful motion picture (1983). His 1987 novel *Bonfire of the Vanities* was made into a motion picture in 1990, but the movie fared poorly with critics and audiences. His latest work is *A Man in Full* (1998), a novel set in the center of the New South, Atlanta, Georgia. Throughout Wolfe's career, each of his publications has found an eager audience, and his reputation as a great man of letters continues to grow.

★

"Wolfe, Tom" in *Current Biography Yearbook* (1971) summarizes Wolfe's early life, with particular attention to his stature by 1971. "Wolfe, Thomas Kennerly, Jr.," in *Contemporary Authors,* New Revision Series, vol. 70, (1999) offers details of Wolfe's life but devotes most of its space to how his writings enhanced his stature in American literature. Barbara Lounsberry, "Tom Wolfe," in *Dictionary of Literary Biography, Volume 152: American Novelists Since World War II, Fourth Series* (1995) provides a comprehensive overview of Wolfe's life, work, and literary contributions. Tom Wolfe and E. W. Johnson, eds., *The New Journalism* (1973) is an anthology of the art form pioneered by Wolfe; it remains a staple in some college journalism classes. Critical studies include Doug Shomette, ed., *The Critical Response to Tom Wolfe* (1992) and William McKeen, *Tom Wolfe* (1995), a work in the Twayne United States Authors Series.

KIRK H. BEETZ

WOLFMAN JACK (Robert Weston Smith) (*b.* 21 January 1938 in New York City; *d.* 1 July 1995 in Belvidere, North Carolina), graveled-voiced radio disc jockey who helped to turn rhythm and blues (R&B) soul music into a Top Forty commercial commodity.

Bob Smith the broadcast entrepreneur and Wolfman Jack the disc jockey were two distinct personalities. Robert Weston Smith was one of two children of Weston Smith, a sometime shoe salesman and would-be magician, who worked for the *Financial World* newspaper, and Rosamund Smith. His parents divorced and both remarried, and he moved with his father and sister to Brooklyn when he was about ten. Nicknamed "Smitty," he was captivated as a child by a powerful, shortwave radio receiver his father gave him. Smith loved to listen to radio; his favorite music was rhythm and blues, and he was drawn to the intimate "rap" style patter of 1950s disc jockeys like Alan Freed.

Smith quit high school after completing his sophomore year. His father and stepmother moved to New Jersey in

1956 and enrolled him in a school for electricians, but he spent his days hanging around WNJR radio in Newark and by age sixteen was employed at the station. Angered, his parents threw him out of the house, and he moved to Alexandria, Virginia, where he sold encyclopedias and Fuller Brushes before enrolling at the National Academy of Broadcasting in Washington, D.C. There he made straight As and after completing a one-year course was hired at WYOU in Newport News, Virginia, where he worked under the pseudonym Daddy Jules. WYOU changed format when it was sold and renamed WTID. The new owner fired the African-American disc jockey and insisted that Smith lose his accent and become "white sounding." Smith complied and thereafter was heard under a new identity, Roger Gordon. In 1961 he moved to KCIJ in Shreveport, Louisiana, to become "Big Smith with the Records."

After Smith conceived the character of Wolfman Jack in the early 1960s, he produced a demonstration tape of the fictitious personality and brought the Wolfman to life as a disc jockey. On a whim in December 1963, Smith traveled with his colleague Larry Brandon to station XERF, a 250,000-watt radio transmitter in the middle of the Mexican desert across the border from Del Rio, Texas. For a young and infatuated radio jockey like Smith, the site of the powerful transmitter was an unprecedented thrill. The radio tower radiated five times the signal allowed legally from U.S. stations, a vibration so powerful that birds fell dead from the skies, according to Smith in his memoir, and the headlights of parked automobiles glowed spontaneously, merely from the vibration of the output. Smith was in awe.

Within twenty-four hours of his arrival at XERF Smith and Brandon joined with the station employees and hijacked the radio station from its owners, who were operating under government receivership. Smith, a streetwise entrepreneur, claimed he began with an unauthorized loan of $15,000 from KCIJ in Louisiana, and within days of his arrival in Mexico turned the illicit investment into $350,000 worth of working capital with the help of the mutineers. After commandeering the station for an entire weekend and upstaging the prepaid programming with a free sample of the *Wolfman Jack Show,* Smith obtained legal operating papers for the pirated station by the week's end. He passed out $1,000 bonuses to the station employees and threw a party to celebrate the takeover.

According to Smith, he had smuggled dozens of rifles, pistols, rounds of ammunition, and a sixty-millimeter machine gun with a turret tripod into Mexico. He and his crew used these weapons to successfully defend the tower from an ambush by the station's former owners. Thereafter, the unorthodox ranting of the highly spirited Wolfman Jack was broadcast throughout the Western Hemisphere from XERF. When Smith returned within the year to Shreveport and resumed work at KCIJ, he kept Wolfman alive by shipping pretaped *Wolfman Jack* shows to XERF.

At the Peppermint Lounge in Bossier City, Louisiana, Smith later gave substance to the faceless voice of Wolfman Jack for the first time. For his stage debut as the Wolfman, Smith donned a wig, fake goatee, black fingernails, and cape. A live recording of the event, *Wolfman Jack—Live at the Peppermint Lounge,* sold modestly.

In 1964 Smith moved north to Minnesota, where he entered into a business venture with George's Record Shop to produce a signature series of Wolfman albums featuring oldies tunes. There he nurtured another station venture, a small, 1,000-watt Minneapolis station called KUXL, featuring a lucrative format of religious sermons. While in Minnesota, Smith simultaneously plastered the international airwaves with the irreverent persona of Wolfman Jack transmitted from tapes at full force from XERF at the Mexican border. With cleverly coined euphemisms like "skinny-dippin' in the oil of joy!," he taunted, "Wolfman comin' atcha!" and "Get nak-kid!" While purveying snake oil and glow-in-the-dark posters of himself, Wolfman Jack brought the sound of R&B to new audiences and lent his name to weekend music reviews.

Soon the *Wolfman Jack Show* aired on border stations XERB in Tijuana, Mexico, and XEG in Monterrey, Mexico. In January 1966 Smith moved to southern California to take control of XERB. He established a Sunset Boulevard business office for the operation, filled XERB program time with content local to Los Angeles, and successfully integrated R&B into the station lineup.

One year later, the flesh-and-blood Wolfman reemerged for his second-ever public appearance. Smith hired a professional makeup artist, who spared no expense in transforming the clean-cut broadcast executive into a yowling Wolfman with furry fangs. As the hairy monster, Smith took the *Wolfman Jack Review* on the road, with all the pomp and regalia of a Barnum and Bailey advance team. Traveling by limousine, the Wolfman was accompanied by an entourage of slinky women dressed in sleazy cat suits and perfume-pumping attendants carrying gaudy atomizers. The Wolfman was dressed to the ghoulish nines and behaved like the pope of the damned, administering fake blessings like a devil priest and otherwise creating a stir. Wolfman Jack offered comedic relief for a nation torn by postwar growing pains and the civil unrest of a turbulent decade. His trademark exclamations like "Have Mercy!" and his wolf howl (AaaoooOOOWW!) became a staple of the contemporary culture, offering youthful audiences a refreshing alternative to beatnik poets, maudlin folksingers, and doom-wielding activists of the 1960s.

As Wolfman Jack, Smith made live appearances in Las Vegas during the 1970s and was heard regularly on armed services radio throughout that decade. With his naturally deep-set eyes and thick wavy hair, Smith grew a goatee as he matured and looked the part of the Wolfman all the time. In 1973 he appeared as Wolfman Jack in the George Lucas retro film *American Graffiti*. Wolfman Jack's televised rock and roll review, called *The Midnight Special*, aired regularly for nine years beginning in the mid-1970s.

Near the end of 1961 Smith married Lou Elizabeth Lamb. The couple had two children. He died of a heart attack and is buried in a private cemetery on his family's property Belvidere, Perquimans County, North Carolina.

★

Smith's autobiography is *Have Mercy!* (1995), written with Byron Laursen. A biographical essay is John A. Garraty and Mark C. Carnes, "Wolfman Jack," *American National Biography* (1999). A lengthy essay on Wolfman Jack is included in Wes Smith, *The Pied Pipers of Rock 'n' Roll: Radio Deejays of the 50s and 60s* (1989). An obituary is in the *New York Times* (2 July 1995).

GLORIA COOKSEY

WONDER, Stevie (*b.* 13 May 1950 in Saginaw, Michigan), singer, composer, and musician who transcended his early days as a child prodigy at Motown Records in the 1960s to fuse soul, jazz, pop, and "world music" into a wide-ranging and popular musical legacy that ranges from love ballads to insightful social commentary.

Born Steveland Judkins Morris, Wonder was the middle of five children. A premature baby, he was blind from birth because he did not receive enough oxygen while in an incubator and suffered a dislocated nerve in one eye and a cataract in the other. His father left the family when he was a toddler, and his mother, Lula Mae Morris, remarried and moved the family to Detroit's east side. His stepfather, Paul Hardaway, was a baker. Wonder later said he was raised in "upper-lower-class circumstances" in a mostly black urban neighborhood.

Wonder began playing the piano at age four. He also quickly mastered the harmonica and drums. By age nine he was singing solos in the choir at the Whitestone Baptist Church. At the same age he formed a duo with his best friend, John Glover, whose cousin Ronnie White was a member of the Miracles, the top group at Detroit's fledgling Motown Records. Wonder began hanging around the Motown studios. Known as the "boy wonder," he could write songs, sing, and play almost every instrument.

By 1962 Motown's founder, Berry Gordy, had named his young prodigy Little Stevie Wonder, and his first record was released just after he turned twelve. *I Call It Pretty Music but the Old People Call It the Blues* did not break through as a hit, and two subsequent records also flopped. But at a live concert at the Regal Theater in Chicago,

Stevie Wonder, 1965. HUTTON-DEUTSCH COLLECTION/CORBIS

Wonder was being led offstage when he broke free from his producer's grasp and returned to the stage to sing "Fingertips." The recording of that spontaneous moment, dubbed "Fingertips Part Two," featured Wonder playing harmonica solos and shouting gospel-style wails. It spent three weeks at the top of the Billboard charts in 1963 and sold more than a million copies. With the success of "Fingertips," Wonder became a part of the Motown family. He spent two weeks a month touring with the other acts in the Motown Revue. He continued his work in the Detroit Public Schools aided by a tutor who traveled with him and eventually got his high school diploma from the Michigan School for the Blind, in Lansing.

It took until 1966 for Wonder to enjoy his second big hit, "Uptight (Everything's Alright)," which reached number three. During the rest of the 1960s Wonder had a string of top-ten hit songs—a remake of the Bob Dylan folk anthem "Blowin' in the Wind" and Wonder's original compositions "A Place in the Sun," "I Was Made to Love Her," "I'm Wonderin'," "Shoo-Be-Doo-Be-Doo-Da-Day," "For Once in My Life," "My Cherie Amour," and "Yester-Me, Yester-You, Yesterday." During the 1960s Motown had become one of the most successful record labels by grooming talented young musicians to produce infectious, danceable rhythm-and-blues tunes whose popularity crossed over from black audiences to mainstream radio stations. From the beginning of his career, Wonder both fit into the Motown sound and transcended it. As one of the label's few solo artists, Wonder experimented from the start with blues, gospel, and jazz influences. His songs included finger-snapping tunes and lushly orchestrated love ballads.

In the 1960s Wonder embodied the ambitiousness of young black musicians who had achieved mainstream popularity but sought to explore further the many forms of soul and pop genres. By the end of the decade Wonder was no longer "little" in any way: he was a mature man, six feet tall, who was emerging as one of the most talented musicians of his generation. He also was speaking out increasingly on the social issues of the day. "I have to say that Vietnam was something I was interested in, the racial situation that still existed, the violence that happened within the inner cities," he explained to *Billboard* magazine in a 1995 interview.

In 1970, with his wife, the singer-songwriter Syreeta Wright, Wonder wrote all the songs on the ambitious album *Where I'm Coming From.* That year he also recorded the hits "Signed, Sealed, Delivered (I'm Yours)" and "Heaven Help Us All." In 1971, when he turned twenty-one, Wonder left Detroit for his own New York recording studio, where he produced the innovative album *Music of My Mind,* on which he played almost all the instruments. He renegotiated his contract with Motown to give him more creative freedom. It was the beginning of a period in which Wonder broke free completely from the packaged Motown sound and released a string of more free-form singles and albums, including five more number-one hits: "Superstition" (1972), "You Are the Sunshine of My Life" (1973), "You Haven't Done Nothin'" (1974), "I Wish" (1976), and "Sir Duke" (1977). His "one-man" albums included the innovative, popular, and legendary *Talking Book* and *Innervisions,* in which he fully realized his expanded musical creativity and gave voice to his deepening political sentiments and spiritual vision. In 1975 alone Wonder won four Grammy Awards. In 1980 he released the album *Hotter Than July,* capping a second decade of exceptional productivity.

In the decades to follow, Wonder continued to expand and refine his career. A prolific singer-songwriter, he produced new recordings on a regular basis, won Grammys and other awards, and often played a large part in benefit concerts and humanitarian enterprises. Among the causes he championed was making 15 January a national holiday in honor of the assassinated civil rights activist Martin Luther King, Jr. In 1989 Wonder was inducted into the Rock and Roll Hall of Fame, and he continued to produce new albums and give concerts worldwide. By age forty-five he had released twenty-five albums. He won an Oscar in 1985 for best original song, "I Just Called to Say I Love You," for the movie *The Woman in Red.* He also wrote the soundtrack for the Spike Lee film *Jungle Fever* (1991) and several other movies. In the fall of 2001 he performed in a nationally televised fund-raising concert for the victims of the terrorist attacks of 11 September.

★

Biographies include William Sanford and Carl Green, *Stevie Wonder: Center Stage* (1986); Martin E. Horn, *Innervisions: The Music of Stevie Wonder* (2000); and Dennis Love and Stacy Brown, *Blind Faith: The Miraculous Journey of Lula Hardaway and Her Son, Stevie Wonder* (2002).

MICHAEL BETZOLD

WOOD, Natalie (*b.* 20 July 1938 in San Francisco, California; *d.* 29 November 1981 off Santa Catalina Island, California), popular film actress known as "Hollywood's youngest veteran," who achieved star status following her performance in *West Side Story* (1961).

Wood was born Natasha Virapaeff, one of three daughters of her Russian immigrant parents, Nicholas Gurdin, a set designer, and Maria Kuleff, a former ballerina. She was educated at public schools in California, but a more significant education for her future career came through a series of childhood movie appearances. Wood's parents ag-

Natalie Wood. THE KOBAL COLLECTION

gressively pushed her into movies at an early age. She took her first screen test at the age of five and made her first appearance in Irving Pichel's *Happy Land* (1943) as an extra who had to drop her ice cream and then cry. By 1946 she was a big-screen regular, appearing opposite the famed actor and director Orson Welles in *Tomorrow Is Forever* and in 1947 starring in the hit *Miracle on 34th Street*. One of the most remarkable features of Wood's career was its consistency. She appeared in at least one film every year between 1946 and 1966.

Like many child stars, Wood struggled to break free from her pigtailed childhood image and win respect as an adult actress. She finally achieved this goal playing alongside James Dean in *Rebel Without a Cause* (1955) and, like Dean, was idolized by the teenage audience. More than any other, this film identified Wood with the fears and desires of her generation; she became a role model for millions of teenage girls. She was nominated for the best actress Oscar for her part in *Rebel Without a Cause* and during the rest of the 1950s continued to play girls who set an example through their struggle with growing up. Off-screen, Wood was involved in highly publicized romances with such teenage idols as James Dean, Elvis Presley, and Nicky Hilton. In the 1960s she was linked with Dennis Hopper and Warren Beatty. She married the actor Robert Wagner for the first time in 1957, but they divorced in 1962. She was married to Richard Gregson between 1969 and 1972, and the couple had a daughter. Wood remarried Robert Wagner in 1972, and they had one daughter.

Although her first real success as an adult actor was as Judy in *Rebel Without a Cause*, it was in the 1960s that Wood reached her peak as a professional and as a major star. Wood's acting roles changed with the tastes of her generation. In 1961 she made two films that established her as "the face of the 1960s" and confirmed her as a major talent. As Maria in *West Side Story* (1961), Wood's formerly unnoticed dancing ability was quite a revelation, although her singing was dubbed by Marni Nixon. The huge success of *West Side Story*, a contemporary *Romeo and Juliet* story set in late 1950s New York City, brought Wood to a more mature audience. She also became the 138th actor to leave a handprint in the sidewalk outside Mann's Chinese Theater. But Wood was not really suited to musicals, although audiences loved her big-eyed prettiness and lively performance as Maria. In *Gypsy* (1962), a musical scored by Stephen Sondheim and Jule Styne, Wood performed a dramatic closing striptease, but the film exposed the truth about her dancing skills. In *West Side Story* her limitations as a dancer were concealed by clever camera work.

Wood's second film of 1961, *Splendor in the Grass*, earned her an Academy Award nomination and generally was regarded as the best performance of her career thus far. Working alongside Warren Beatty, who made his debut in this film, Wood played a young woman in 1920s Kansas whose sexual passion for her boyfriend was countered by strict social mores. The parallels with 1960s youth culture are obvious; Wood's character is driven to madness by her parents' oppressive moral code. In a series of films that followed, Wood played the vulnerable, troubled young woman struggling to cope with changing times. In *Love with the Proper Stranger* (1963) she played yet another character faced with a very modern problem: whether to marry or remain independent. Critics considered it her best-ever screen performance, and she won a third Academy Award nomination for the part. Other, similar roles brought critical acclaim, such as *Inside Daisy Clover* (1965), in which she played a girl pushed to attempt suicide by the overbearing demands of her ambitious mother.

But as the 1960s progressed, the personal moral struggle Wood portrayed so well became less interesting for audiences and less marketable. After a failed marriage, a string of broken romances, and with her career in the doldrums, Wood attempted suicide. Nevertheless, she appeared in the slapstick comedy *The Great Race* in 1965 and in 1969, after a period of recuperation, returned to comedy in *Bob and Carol and Ted and Alice*. The movie is a slick, contemporary farce about two California couples who confess in couples therapy sessions to having extramarital affairs. Looking very dated today, the film is nevertheless a cinema landmark for its frankness about sex and promiscuity. After 1970 Wood's fame declined, although she made a notable Golden Globe–winning appearance in the television miniseries *From Here to Eternity* (1979).

Despite her death at the age of forty-three, Wood's professional acting career lasted almost forty years; she appeared in more than fifty movies. Almost all of her best performances are from the 1960s, when she was one of the best-known stars in Hollywood, appearing in many popular movies, some of which fit the mood of the time with an uncanny resonance. She received many awards and nominations. Her huge celebrity in the 1960s and the problems it caused her are perhaps reflected by the fact that she was awarded "Sour Apple" awards for least cooperative actress by the Hollywood media in 1961 and 1966. Wood drowned in a mysterious accident on 29 November 1981 while enjoying a break on the yacht *Splendour* with her husband, Robert Wagner, and her friend and fellow actor, Christopher Walken. She is buried in Westwood Memorial Park, Los Angeles.

★

Biographies of Wood include Lana Wood, *Natalie: A Memoir by Her Sister* (1984) and Christopher Nickens, *Natalie Wood: A Biography in Pictures* (1986). Warren G. Harris, *Natalie and R. J.: Hollywood's Star-Crossed Lovers* (1988), and Kirk Crivello, *Fallen Angels: The Lives and Untimely Deaths of Fourteen Hollywood*

Beauties (1988), take a rather sensational approach to the star's short life. An obituary is in the *New York Times* (30 Nov. 1981).

CHRIS ROUTLEDGE

WOODEN, John Robert   (*b.* 14 October 1910 in Hall, Indiana), professional basketball player and college coach who was elected to the Naismith Memorial Basketball Hall of Fame as both a player (1961) and a coach (1973).

Wooden was one of four sons and two daughters of Joshua Hugh Wooden, a farmer and postal carrier, and Roxie (Rothrock) Wooden, a homemaker. The family moved to Martinsville, Indiana, in 1924; Wooden won four letters in basketball at Martinsville High School and led his team to the state title game in three straight years (1926–1928), with Martinsville triumphing in 1927 and finishing runner-up the other two years. He was voted All-State in basketball all three of those years.

Wooden enrolled at Purdue University in 1928, and in three years of varsity basketball earned All–Big Ten and All-America honors while playing for the coach Ward Lambert. In 1932 he was named the Helms Athletic Foundation Player of the Year and captained Purdue, which was named by many as the mythical national champion of college bas-

John Wooden *(left)* with Lew Alcindor after beating Saint John's University to win the NCAA championship, 1968. © BETTMANN/CORBIS

ketball. Wooden graduated with a bachelor of science degree in 1932, after which he married his high school sweetheart, Nell Riley, with whom he had a son and daughter. He began teaching English and coaching basketball at Dayton High School in Dayton, Ohio. He then coached and taught at South Bend Central High School in South Bend, Indiana, until 1943. Wooden's overall high school coaching record was 218–42. He also played professional basketball (mostly on weekends) for the Indianapolis Kautskys and Whiting Ciesars.

Wooden served in the U.S. Navy from 1942 to 1946. The year of his discharge he entered the ranks of college coaching at Indiana State Teachers College in Terre Haute, where he earned a master's degree. In his two years at Indiana State, the Sycamores won forty-five games and lost fifteen. Wooden's success led to his being offered the head coaching position at the University of California, Los Angeles (UCLA).

Wooden's success at UCLA is unparalleled in college basketball history. He won 620 games for the Bruins while losing only 147. His teams won ten Pac-10 championships and ten national championships, including seven in a row from 1967 to 1973. In the course of those years they also won eighty-eight consecutive games and thirty-eight straight National College Athletic Association (NCAA) tournament games. He was named NCAA Coach of the Year in 1964, 1967, 1969–1970, and 1972–1973. These figures, however, fail to capture Wooden's integrity and drive or the respect with which he was viewed as the UCLA coach. His principles and intelligence were noted and admired by players, rival coaches, the media, and the public.

Wooden's teams were outstanding, but what made him proudest was that his players, like their coach, were men of character. The list of outstanding players that he recruited to UCLA and who graduated to professional careers in either basketball or other areas is probably his most enduring legacy. However, this did not come easily or right away. When he took the helm at UCLA, Wooden had to overcome a losing record that the Bruins had established over the previous twenty years as well as the general indifference of the local and student populace toward basketball. In addition, the budget for basketball at the school was minimal. Wooden persevered, and his first team won twenty-two games after going 12–13 the year before his arrival. Still, it took fifteen years before his UCLA squads won a national title and before he inspired the sobriquet "The Wizard of Westwood" for his winning ways. Through those years Wooden endured cramped office space, a lack of a home-court gymnasium, and league recruiting sanctions against the university because of football violations.

Wooden's major success began in the 1960s with his first great team, led by Walt Hazzard. In 1960 UCLA went 14–

12, but Hazzard's arrival made a huge difference. Hazzard was recruited in 1961 from Santa Monica City College but was from Philadelphia, and his dynamic passing was the key to the new success of the Bruins. His inventive passes often left his teammates as surprised as his opponents, but once the team adjusted to his play they became conference champions in the Pacific Coast league. The Bruins then beat both Utah State and Oregon State to win the West Regional and advance to the NCAA Final Four. Led by the scoring of Johnny Green and Gary Cunningham and the passing of Hazzard, the Bruins battled the University of Cincinnati down to the wire before losing 72–70. Expectations were high the next year, but after defeating Stanford in a playoff for the conference championship, UCLA lost in the first round of the NCAA tournament to Arizona State. The next year Wooden installed a devastating full-court zone press on a nearly full-time basis, and this became one of the hallmarks of his teams for the rest of his UCLA years.

The Bruins swept through the season undefeated and then beat Seattle and the University of San Francisco in the NCAA Tournament to advance to the Final Four. There they defeated Kansas State and, in the championship game, beat Duke, 98–83, to earn the first NCAA championship for the Bruins and for Wooden. The next season the Bruins repeated as champions, led by Keith Erickson, Edgar Lacey, and Gail Goodrich. They lost two games in the year but were unbeaten in the league and defeated Brigham Young and San Francisco to return to the Final Four. There the Bruins overwhelmed Wichita State and defeated top-ranked Michigan in surprisingly easy fashion, 91–80. Their success enabled them to attract the top prospects nationally, and in 1965 Lew Alcindor (known later as Kareem Abdul-Jabbar) from New York City and Lucius Allen from Kansas City, two of the most highly rated high school players in the nation, enrolled at UCLA. Freshmen were not eligible for the varsity at that time, but the freshman team, led by Alcindor, defeated the varsity, the defending NCAA champions, by a 75–60 score. The varsity went on to stumble to an 18–8 record, looking forward to the Alcindor era beginning in the next season When Alcindor became available as a sophomore, they won three consecutive NCAA titles. Following his graduation the Bruins won four more consecutive titles, the last two with Bill Walton, the dominant force. After losing in the semifinals in 1974, the Bruins came back to win in 1975. UCLA was the finest team of this era.

Wooden retired in 1975, but he remained active in basketball, attending UCLA games and many other charity contests into the twenty-first century. The death of his wife in 1985 was the greatest loss of his life, but he continues to live by and follow his "Pyramid of Success," a formula for life, not just basketball. It combines ambition, adaptability,

resourcefulness, fight, and the faith to succeed. Clearly he was an excellent example. Each year since 1977 the top college basketball player in the country has been given the John R. Wooden award by the U.S. Basketball Writers Association—an award that Wooden stipulated would entail that the recipient be a good student as well as an athlete.

★

Wooden's autobiography, *They Call Me Coach,* written with Jack Tobin, was published in 1972 and revised in 1988. *The Wizard of Westwood,* a biography by Dwight Chapin, was published in 1973. *Wooden: A Lifetime of Observations and Reflections on and off the Court,* written with Steve Jamison, was published in 1997.

MURRY R. NELSON

WOODWARD, C(omer) Vann (*b.* 13 November 1908 in Vanndale, Arkansas; *d.* 17 December 1999 in Hamden, Connecticut), renowned historian from Yale University who challenged conventional thinking about southern history and race relations.

Woodward was born in 1908 in Vanndale, Arkansas, a town his ancestors had built and named after his mother's family. He was the only son of Hugh Alison, a school principal and Latin teacher, and Bessie Vann Woodward, a homemaker. He lived in Vanndale during most of his childhood, before the family moved to nearby Morrilton, where Wood-

C. Vann Woodward. OSCAR WHITE/CORBIS

ward attended high school. Then he enrolled at Henderson-Brown College in Arkadelphia, Arkansas. After completing two years there, he transferred to Emory College in Atlanta, Georgia. He graduated with a B.A. in philosophy in 1930. Woodward began his academic career teaching English at Georgia Technical University and reviewing books for the *Atlanta Journal*. In 1932 he moved to New York City and earned his M.A. in political science at Columbia University. There Woodward met the black poet Langston Hughes and other members of the Harlem Renaissance, a remarkable flowering of the arts among African Americans in the years between the two world wars.

Woodward's experiences led him to explore southern dissent as a historical topic. He chose Tom Watson, a noted racist demagogue and populist who advocated black participation in political and economic reform, as the basis for his first book. He entered the University of North Carolina at Chapel Hill in 1934 on a research grant secured for him by the sociologist and family friend Howard W. Odum, known for his work that embraces a view of the South that favors both success and equal opportunity. Chapel Hill, whose curriculum was that of southern liberalism rejecting racism, was an ideal setting for Woodward. He met and worked with various intellectuals, including Robert Penn Warren and Howard K. Beale, who served as his mentor. *Tom Watson: Agrarian Rebel* (1938, 1955) also served as his dissertation under Beale and earned him a Ph.D. in 1937. The book was the first of many in which Woodward set about to shatter the myth of the "Solid South," as he later called it. This same year, on 21 December, he married Glenn Boyd MacLeod. They had one son.

During the late 1930s and early 1940s Woodward held a number of academic posts before joining the U.S. Navy. He served for three years, and as a result of his naval service in the Pacific theater during World War II, he wrote *The Battle of Leyte Gulf* (1947), published after the war. At Johns Hopkins University, he wrote three more books. In the first two, Woodward again strove to show historians a new way to look at the post-Reconstruction South. The Reverend Martin Luther King, Jr., called the third, *The Strange Career of Jim Crow* (1955), the "historical bible of the civil rights movement."

Despite the success of his books, Woodward decided he was not reaching a large enough audience, so he began writing book reviews and essays on issues other than race. His first effort, "The Age of Reinterpretation," was published in 1960 in the *American Historical Review* and discussed how America had been able to focus almost exclusively on economic development rather than having to build a military force to ward off external threats. In light of this relationship, the dynamics between America and the rest of the world had changed since 1945, and now the United States also needed to build up militarily. This article, now seen as an important interpretation of the U.S. position in the postwar world, was at the time largely overlooked. His book *The Burden of Southern History* (1960), a collection of essays, also made a notable contribution. In 1961 Woodward joined the history department at Yale University.

Woodward continued to examine racial issues and the relevance of the southern experience. During the 1960s he looked at the first and second Reconstructions and hoped the nation would make good on its commitment to equality. But he was becoming pessimistic and came to believe that Reconstruction's aim was not equality after all. However, he hoped the South's experience and his education about what had happened would benefit America by showing that racial inequality was only hurting the country. He continually took on and defeated northern notions that they had saved the South and fostered civil rights. Woodward repeatedly told his fellow historians that this was simply not the case, but at the same time he still held fast to beliefs that the South was not blameless in denying basic rights to African Americans. Still, he thought any change in southern attitude was more likely to succeed if it came from within.

Woodward called on his fellow historians to make good their theory of history as literature with an engaging story to be told so that the proposed argument would stand a better chance of being heard. "Professor Woodward's books and other works were popular among historians and nonhistorians alike due to his talent as a storyteller," according to Howard R. Lamar, former Yale president and Sterling Professor Emeritus of History. Woodward himself admitted that love of writing was what propelled him into the field of history, because he wanted to write about a historical topic. His efforts at Johns Hopkins and Yale attracted gifted graduate students who have made major contributions to the field. Among his notable students are Wille Lee Rose, James M. McPherson, and William S. McFeely. His former students later paid him homage in a 1982 tribute, *Region, Race and Reconstruction*. In 1969 his peers honored him by electing him president of both the Organization of American Historians and the American Historical Association.

In 1971 Woodward published a second collection of essays, *American Counterpoint: Slavery and Racism in the North-South Dialogue*. In this book he reviewed his deepening pessimism about the fate of civil rights and white America's fading commitment to racial equality. During the Watergate political crisis that brought down the presidency of Richard M. Nixon, he supervised a team of historians researching corruption in the presidency. His retirement from Yale in 1977 did not affect his activism. He won the Pulitzer Prize in 1982 for his editing of *Mary Chestnut's Civil War* (1981). Woodward lived in Hamden, Connecticut, until his death at home on 17 December 1999 at age ninety-one.

★

John Herbert Roper, *C. Vann Woodward, Southerner* (1987), and *Directory of American Scholars,* 9th ed., vol. 1: *History* (1999), provide a good look at this southern historian. David Potter, "C. Vann Woodward," in Marcus Cunliff and Robin Winks, eds., *Pastmasters: Some Essays on American Historians* (1969) and Theodore Rosengarten and C. Vann Woodward's "South-by-Northeast: The Journey of C. Vann Woodward. The Noted Chronicler of the South Looks Back on His Own History," *Doubletake* (summer 1999) give Woodward's view on his life. The *New Yorker* (15 Apr. 1972), the *American Historical Review* (June 1973), and *South Atlantic Quarterly* (winter 1978) provide biographical material on Woodward. An obituary is in the *New York Times* (19 Dec. 1999).

BRIAN B. CARPENTER

WOODWARD, Joanne Gignilliat (*b.* 27 February 1930 in Thomasville, Georgia), Academy Award–winning actress known for taking on difficult character roles. She became famous in the early 1960s as the wife and frequent costar of the actor Paul Newman.

Woodward is the daughter of Wade and Elinor Trimmier Woodward. She grew up in Georgia and South Carolina; she

Joanne Woodward, 1960. THE KOBAL COLLECTION

attended Greenville High School, in Greenville, South Carolina; and was a member of the Greenville Little Theatre Group. She graduated from high school in 1947 and attended Louisiana State University from 1947 to 1949. When her father went to work for the Charles Scribner's Sons publishing house, Woodward left college and moved with the family to New York City, where she began to pursue acting, joining the Actors' Studio and the Neighborhood Playhouse. It was another forty years before she received a degree, graduating alongside her youngest daughter, Clea, at Sarah Lawrence College, New York, in 1990. Her professional career began in earnest in 1953, when she understudied in William Inge's play, *Picnic,* during its Broadway run. Also involved in the production was her future husband, the actor Paul Newman.

Woodward's early career was in television, beginning in 1952 with her appearance in "Penny," a drama for the popular *Robert Montgomery Presents* series. By 1955 Woodward had landed a contract with Twentieth Century–Fox, and her career took off quickly. That same year she made her movie debut in *Count Three and Pray* (1955), a low-key Western set in the post–Civil War period. Two years later she appeared in *The Three Faces of Eve* (1957). Within a few years Woodward's versatility, professionalism, and delicate beauty made her one of the most bankable stars in Hollywood. Her performance in *The Three Faces of Eve* as a woman with three personalities won her an Oscar for best actress in 1958. It was the beginning of an intense ten-year period in which Woodward enjoyed worldwide fame, yet managed to achieve it playing difficult, often challenging roles.

Woodward had already proved herself a capable actress in her own right, but when she teamed up with Paul Newman in *The Long Hot Summer* (1958), she became part of one of Hollywood's most productive and enduring partnerships, both on-screen and off-screen. Woodward and Newman married on 29 January 1958 and have three daughters. *The Long Hot Summer* was the first in a series of highly successful films in which the pair co-starred. In the 1960s they were the dream Hollywood couple, appearing on screen together five times between 1958 and 1963. Not only were their performances of the highest quality, but the movies they starred in also were among the most popular of the decade. Woodward had a star placed on the Walk of Fame on Hollywood Boulevard on 9 February 1960.

In *Paris Blues* (1961), regarded as one of the couple's best performances together, Newman and his jazzman buddy, Sidney Poitier, meet up with the innocent tourists Woodward and Diahann Carroll. With Paris as the backdrop and a Duke Ellington score for accompaniment, Woodward and Newman charmed audiences of the day. But the film has sufficient style to survive its period dialogue and is considered one of the best jazz movies ever made. Even in films that lacked the panache of *Paris Blues,* Woodward and Newman were able to satisfy their eager audiences. *A New Kind of Love* (1963) is the story of a writer who finds success writing about a young Frenchwoman and her private life and ends up falling in love with her. In an otherwise disappointing film, Woodward and Newman shine with an appealing, comic-romantic, double act.

In 1968 the couple began a new phase in their professional relationship. Newman directed Woodward in the title role of the film *Rachel, Rachel* (1968), drawing out one of Woodward's finest performances as the naive, frustrated schoolteacher Rachel Cameron. At a time when female stars struggled to find complex, difficult roles, Newman provided Woodward with material that allowed her to demonstrate the impressive range of her acting talent. He has directed her three times more to great critical acclaim, and they have continued to act together, most notably in *Mr. and Mrs. Bridge* (1990).

Despite the attention the couple received in the 1960s from the entertainment press, Woodward also showed that she had the ability to strike out on her own. Going against her usual choice of movie, she won the title role in *The Stripper* (1963), originally planned as a vehicle for the sexy star Marilyn Monroe, who died of a drug overdose in 1962. Yet even as a young actress, Woodward generally shied away from fashionable, glamorous roles. In many ways she had a dual career in the 1960s. On the one hand, she was a sought-after celebrity, yet she also was interested in popular 1960s causes, such as raising public awareness of women's lives at a time when their needs were often ignored. Beginning with her debut in *Count Three and Pray,* in which she plays a "wild" girl who is "civilized" by an attractive parson, Woodward was drawn to spirited characters. In the 1960s she often played women whose inner lives remain hidden from the outside world. As in *Rachel, Rachel,* these are often women whose spirit has survived an otherwise monotonous and conventional life.

During the 1960s Woodward built a reputation as an actress capable of sustaining mood through accurate, detailed characterization. She has won or been nominated for many awards. Her performance in *Rachel, Rachel* won her the New York Film Critics' best actress award and the Golden Globe. Since then she has won best actress accolades from the Cannes Film Festival, the British Academy, and twice more from the New York Film Critics. Woodward and Newman undeniably have benefited professionally from their relationship. They starred in some of the biggest movie hits of the 1960s, and *Rachel, Rachel* and *The Effect of Gamma Rays on Man-in-the-Moon Marigolds* (1972) are representative of Newman's finest work as director. In 1992 they were jointly awarded the Kennedy Cen-

ter honors for lifetime achievement in the performing arts. Both Woodward and Newman have long been concerned with charitable causes, such as Save the Children and research into Alzheimer's disease and diseases of childhood. Woodward is artistic director of the Westport County Playhouse in her hometown of Westport, Connecticut.

★

Biographical information about Woodward is available in Joe Morella and Edward Z. Epstein, *Paul and Joanne: A Biography of Paul Newman and Joanne Woodward* (1988), and Susan Netter, *Paul Newman and Joanne Woodward* (1989). Biographical articles include David McGillivray, "Joanne Woodward," in *Films and Filming* (Oct. 1984); Maureen Dowd, "Paul Newman and Joanne Woodward: A Lifetime of Shared Passions," in *McCall's* (Jan. 1991); and Steve Vineberg, "Joanne Woodward: From *The Stripper* to *Mrs. Bridge,* a Master Manipulator of Mood," in *American Film* (Nov.–Dec. 1991).

CHRIS ROUTLEDGE

WOODWARD, Robert Burns (*b.* 10 April 1917 in Boston, Massachusetts; *d.* 8 July 1979 in Cambridge, Massachusetts), chemist and winner of the Nobel Prize in chemistry (1965), best known for his synthesis of complex organic substances, including quinine, cholesterol, cortisone, and vitamin B_{12}.

The only child of Arthur Chester Woodward, who died when Woodward was very young, and Margaret (Burns) Woodward, an accountant and realtor, Woodward entered the chemistry degree program at the Massachusetts Institute of Technology (MIT) in 1933 at age sixteen. By the spring of 1934 he had been suspended for a semester owing to his "inattention to formal studies." He spent one semester as an employee of MIT's biology department before being readmitted to study at the school in the fall of 1935. After this rocky start, Woodward went on to receive his B.S. degree in 1936 and his Ph.D. in 1937, both degrees in chemistry. By 1934 he had published his first paper, with W. J. Hall, on the precipitation of barium in a qualitative analysis scheme.

Woodward married Irja Pullman on 30 July 1938; they had two children and were divorced n 1946. On 14 September 1946 he married Eudoxia Muller; the couple had two children and divorced in 1972. After receiving his degree, Woodward taught summer chemistry at the University of Illinois. He joined Harvard University that same year and remained associated with that institution for the rest of his life. From 1937 to 1939 he held a postdoctoral fellow position under the direction of Elmer P. Kohler, from 1938 to 1940 he was a junior prize fellow of the Harvard Society of Fellows, and from 1941 to 1944 he held the title of instructor of chemistry. From 1944 to 1946 he was assistant

Robert B. Woodward (*left*). THE LIBRARY OF CONGRESS

professor, and from 1946 to 1950 he was associate professor. In 1950 he was promoted to professor, a title he held until 1953, when he was named Morris Loeb Professor of Chemistry. Finally, in 1960, he was named Donner Professor of Science, a title he held until his death. The Donner professorship allowed him to devote all his time to research.

In the early 1940s Woodward worked on correlating the ultraviolet spectra of steroid compounds with their molecular structure through a series of rules (Woodward's Rules) later presented in a series of four papers published from 1940 to 1942. One of his first synthetic achievements was the total synthesis of quinine in 1944, starting with simple materials, which he achieved in collaboration with William Doering. During World War II he participated in war-related research on quinine and penicillin, two drugs in short supply because of wartime conditions. Although his work did not produce synthesis that could be scaled up, this experience made his name known throughout the world.

For his research, Woodward chose problems that had practical applications—mainly the synthesis of natural products—but whose solutions were generally regarded as virtually impossible. He recognized that physical measurement had greater power than did chemical reactions in providing information on chemical structure. He was one of the major contributors to the instrumental revolution that

extensively used instruments and techniques (including infrared spectroscopy, nuclear magnetic resonance, and mass spectroscopy) after World War II. The combination of instrumental techniques and classical chemical methods allowed the identification and characterization of organic substances that had been impossible or very difficult to analyze before.

Woodward chose to synthesize compound after compound of increasing complexity, becoming a legendary architect of molecules. By the time of his death he was generally regarded as the greatest figure in American organic chemistry and as the father of modern organic synthesis, as his achievements are unparalleled by those of any organic chemist of the twentieth century. Woodward did not limit his work to the area of organic synthesis. His achievements in the field of structure determination were demonstrations of new approaches and reasoning that have guided others in the field. He was the first to propose and show the fused-ring structure of the penicillins (1945), and he established the structures of the broad-spectrum antibiotics terramycin and aureomycin, as well as other compounds, such as strychnine (1947), calycanthine (1960), oleandomycin (1960), streptonigrin (1963), and tetrodotoxin (1964).

Although his research work started in the 1930s, Woodward's contributions to the field of organic chemistry continued at a strong pace in the 1960s and even later on. In 1963 Woodward assumed the directorship of the Woodward Research Institute at Basel, Switzerland, named after him and founded by the Ciba Ltd. pharmaceutical company, a unique honor for a research scientist. From that point on he directed research activities in both Cambridge, Massachusetts, and Basel. The institute closed shortly after his death.

In 1965 he produced what the majority regard as his most significant contribution to organic chemistry. Together with Roald Hoffmann (Nobel Prize winner in 1981) he proposed the principle of conservation or orbital symmetry. The Woodward-Hoffman rule was used to predict and explain the course and stereochemistry of certain types of organic reactions, and profoundly changed the thinking of chemists. This has remained the most frequently cited of his publications.

Woodward demonstrated that the understanding of chemical reaction mechanisms made possible the planning and successful execution of extended sequences of reactions to build up complex compounds in the laboratory. He proposed the correct biosynthetic pathway to the steroidal hormones in living organisms and also synthesized cholesterol and cortisone (1951), chlorophyll (1960), tetracycline (1962), cephalosporin C (1965), and vitamin B_{12} (1971). This last synthesis followed a sequence of more than one hundred intermediate reactions. Many of his syntheses have worked out so well that they have become the basis for the commercial manufacture of synthetic products that are less expensive and more accessible than the natural ones.

From 1966 to 1971 Woodward was a member of the Corporation of MIT, and from 1973 to 1974 he was Todd Professor of Chemistry and a fellow of Christ's College in Cambridge. He was also a member of the National Academy of Sciences and the Royal Society and an honorary member or fellow of several other scientific societies in various countries. He held more than twenty honorary degrees, including those from the University of Cambridge (1964), Brandeis University (1965), Israel Institute of Technology (1966), and Université de Louvain (1970). He received the Davy Medal of the Royal Society (1959), the National Medal of Science (1964), the Nobel Prize (1965), and Japan's Order of the Rising Sun (1970).

Woodward died of a heart attack in 1979. Keeping active in research, Woodward at the time of his death was working on the synthesis of erythromycin A. The synthesis was completed in 1980 by Yoshito Kishi, who had taken Woodward's place as principal investigator in the project.

★

Biographical works are Alexander Todd and John Cornforth, "Robert Burns Woodward," *Biographical Memoirs of Fellows of the Royal Society* 27 (1981); and Mary Ellen Bowden and Theodor

Benfey, *Robert Burns Woodward and the Art of Organic Synthesis* (1992). An obituary is in the *New York Times* (10 July 1979).

MARIA PACHECO

WYNETTE, Tammy (*b.* 5 May 1942 in Itawamba County, Mississippi; *d.* 6 April 1998 in Nashville, Tennessee), country music singer and songwriter who during the late 1960s and early 1970s was known as the First Lady of Country Music.

Born Virginia Wynette Pugh, on her grandfather's farm, Wynette was the only child of William Hollice Pugh and Mildred Faye Russell. Nine months after her birth, her father, a guitar player, died of a brain tumor; the Wynette part of her name honored the nurse who cared for him. Wynette's mother remarried, and Wynette, at odds with her new stepfather, chose to live for some of the time with her maternal grandparents, Flora and Chester Russell. She had childhood lessons on piano, played the flute in high school, and knew accordion. She learned to play guitar from a one-armed uncle when she was twelve. She attended both the Providence Baptist Church and the Oakgrove Church of God as a child and began playing piano for services at Providence when she was eight years old. While working

Tammy Wynette (*left*) with Johnny Cash, 1971. © BETTMANN/CORBIS

in the cotton fields, Wynette daydreamed about singing onstage and sang with friends on two local radio programs.

Wynette picked cotton on the family farm from the age of six, and left school in 1959 at seventeen to marry Euple Byrd, her high school sweetheart; they had one daughter in 1961 and another in 1962. The marriage was troubled by unemployment, and Wynette, pregnant again, filed for divorce while working for her Mississippi beautician's license. She moved to Birmingham, Alabama, and worked to obtain a license there before giving birth to her third child, a daughter, in 1965. Soon after, Wynette began to perform on WBRC's *Country Boy Eddie* morning television program. Porter Wagoner, a country music superstar and Grand Ole Opry member, included her as a warm-up act for ten dates, but offered no further assistance in the launch of her career.

In 1965 the country singer Patsy Cline was selling big, and the songstress Loretta Lynn was making a start on the charts. Ten years after the release of Kitty Wells's "It Wasn't God Who Made Honky Tonk Angels," men were still considered the moneymakers in country music. Nevertheless, after many weekend trips that failed to yield a contract, a job, or any other advancement in the music business, Wynette moved with her daughters to Nashville in 1966.

Soon after, Wynette auditioned for Billy Sherrill, a producer/songwriter with Epic Records, who gave her the stage name "Tammy Wynette." With his help, she signed a contract with Epic and recorded "Apartment #9" in August 1966. The song was immediately successful. After "Your Good Girl's Gonna Go Bad," her next three songs, "My Elusive Dreams," a duet with David Houston; "I Don't Wanna Play House"; and "Take Me to Your World" all reached number one on the country charts. She won a Grammy for best female country vocal performance in 1967 for "I Don't Wanna Play House." The very popular "D-I-V-O-R-C-E" was also released in 1967, and in 1969, "Stand By Your Man" won for her another Grammy for best female country vocal performance. The song, which portrayed the ideal woman as a wife and homemaker who should endure the failings of her husband, drew criticism from feminists, although Wynette had arguably advanced the role of feminism in the country-music community.

After divorcing Byrd in 1965, Wynette married Don Chapel, a would-be country star, in 1967. Her performances brought in several thousand dollars a week, and her fame was escalating, but her marriage was unhappy because of Chapel's failed musical career and his dependency on her. Wynette and Chapel divorced in 1968. Chapel had introduced Wynette to the superstar country singer George Jones, and for more than seven years, Wynette lived and worked with Jones. They married in 1969, and their turbulent relationship included many drunken rages and separations; the construction of "Old Plantation Music Park" in Lakeland, Florida; numerous attempts to overcome Jones's alcoholism; a miscarriage; and the birth of a daughter in 1970. They also recorded an array of successful duets, including the number-one hits "Golden Ring" and "Near You." Jones was unable to resolve his drinking problem, and the couple divorced on 13 March 1975, although they continued to make music together. In 1976 Wynette married Michael Tomlin, a Nashville real estate executive, but they were divorced within a month and a half. Wynette married for the fifth and final time in 1978 to George Richey, a producer, arranger, and songwriter, who also served as her manager.

During the late 1960s and early 1970s, Wynette dominated the country music charts with seventeen number-one singles. Wynette won the Country Music Association (CMA) award for female vocalist of the year in 1968, 1969, and 1970, and was the Academy of Country Music top female vocalist in 1969. Wynette published her autobiography, *Stand by Your Man,* in 1979, and continued recording into the two next decades.

She died at her home in Nashville, and is buried in Woodlawn Memorial Park. She was survived by her husband, Richey, six children, and seven grandchildren.

★

Wynette's autobiography is *Stand by Your Man* (1979), written with Joan Dew. See also Jackie Daly (Wynette's daughter) with Tom Carter, *Tammy Wynette: A Daughter Recalls Her Mother's Tragic Life and Death* (2000). Mary A. Bufwack and Robert K. Oermann, *Finding Her Voice: The Saga of Women in Country Music* (1993), does a wonderful job of examining Wynette's contribution in the context of her fellow performers. An obituary is in the *New York Times* (8 Apr. 1998).

COURTNEY S. DANFORTH

Y-Z

YARROW, Peter. *See* Peter, Paul and Mary.

YASTRZEMSKI, Carl Michael, Jr. (*b.* 22 August 1939 in Southampton, New York), slugging outfielder who won baseball's Triple Crown and led the underdog Boston Red Sox to the American League pennant in the "impossible dream" season of 1967.

Yastrzemski was the older of two sons of Carl Yastrzemski, a potato farmer, and Hedwig ("Hattie") Skonieczny, a homemaker. He grew up in a close-knit Polish-American family in the largely agricultural community of Bridgehampton, New York, near the eastern tip of Long Island. His father, an accomplished semiprofessional shortstop, had been forced to decline a minor league contract offer from the Brooklyn Dodgers because of growing family responsibilities. When his son Carl displayed a similar enthusiasm for baseball, the elder Yastrzemski devoted himself to preparing the boy for a career in the game. He pitched tennis balls to him at an early age and only gave him farm chores that strengthened his hands and wrists. On his own, the younger Yastrzemski developed a smooth, quick swing, practicing for hours with baseballs attached to pipes and hanging from a string in the barn.

A left-handed batter who threw right-handed, Yastrzemski played shortstop, pitched, and caught for Little League and Babe Ruth League All-Star teams that won Long Island and New York State championships respectively. As a senior at tiny Bridgehampton High School, he compiled a .650 batting average and pitched a no-hit game in the Suffolk County schoolboy finals. Yastrzemski also impressed big league scouts playing summer ball with his father on local amateur and semipro teams (most notably the Bridgehampton White Eagles, founded by his father and made up primarily of Yastrzemskis and Skoniecznys).

An all-around athlete who had also starred in basketball, Yastrzemski was courted by major colleges and began receiving professional baseball contract offers in 1957, the year he graduated from high school. When a New York Yankees scout ridiculed his father's demand for a $100,000 bonus, Yastrzemski went off to play freshman baseball and basketball at the University of Notre Dame. His father subsequently rebuffed advances from six more major league ball clubs before settling upon the Boston Red Sox, whose scout (Frank "Bots" Nekola) he liked and whose ballpark (Fenway Park) he viewed as best suited to his son's hitting style. Yastrzemski's contract called for a $108,000 bonus, a two-year, Triple A minor league contract at $5,000 per year, and the remainder of his college expenses. After leaving Notre Dame, he completed the requirements for his B.S. in business administration at Merrimack College in North Andover, Massachusetts, and graduated in 1966.

Although signed as a shortstop, the five-foot, eleven-inch, 170-pound Yastrzemski played second base at Class B Raleigh in 1959. After winning the Carolina League bat-

Carl Yastrzemski. AP/WIDE WORLD PHOTOS

ting title with a .377 average, leading his team to the league championship, and being voted the Most Valuable Player (MVP), he was promoted to Triple A Minneapolis. There he moved to the outfield and was groomed as a replacement for the Red Sox star Ted Williams, who retired in 1960. Easily making the transition from the infield, he led the American Association in outfield assists, finished second in the batting race with a .339 average, and won another MVP award. He married Carolann Casper, a receptionist from Pittsburgh, on 30 January 1960; they had four children.

Yastrzemski floundered at the plate during the first half of his rookie year with Boston. With his batting average hovering around .230, he was compared unfavorably with Ted Williams. Yastrzemski returned to form following an emergency session with the legendary Williams, in his new role as a special batting instructor for the Red Sox, and ended the 1961 season with a more acceptable .266 average. He continued to show improvement, winning the American League (AL) batting title with a .321 average in 1963 and finishing second with a .312 mark in 1965. He also became one of the best defensive outfielders in baseball and the acknowledged master at playing the "Green Monster," the imposing, thirty-seven-foot-high left-field wall at Fenway Park. Possessing the strong, accurate arm of a shortstop, he led AL outfielders in assists four times between 1961 and 1966.

Although Yastrzemski had built up solid baseball credentials in his first six seasons with Boston, he was not yet considered a star. The fact that the lackadaisical Red Sox

had finished no higher than sixth place after he joined the team did not help. But what kept Yastrzemski from the upper echelon of big league outfielders was his lack of power. A line-drive hitter who sprayed the ball to all fields, he averaged only sixteen home runs and seventy-seven runs batted in (RBI) per year. When Ted Williams got him to turn his hips and shoulders and pull the ball more in 1965, Yastrzemski reached the twenty-homer mark for the first time. But he reverted to his old style in 1966 and regressed to sixteen homers and a modest .278 average. After the Red Sox finished in ninth place for the second straight year, rumors had him being traded.

Seeking to become more of a home-run threat, Yastrzemski committed himself to a strenuous, off-season workout program directed by Gene Berde, a former coach of the Hungarian Olympic boxing team. When he reported for spring training, a stronger, fitter Yastrzemski was eager to follow the direction of Ted Williams and swing for the fences. Later, the coach Bobby Doerr, another Red Sox great, advised him to hold his hands higher to increase his power.

During the 1967 season, everything fell into place for Boston and Yastrzemski. A new, demanding manager, Dick Williams, shook the Red Sox from their lethargy, and Yastrzemski contributed a dominating, all-around performance that propelled the team to its first pennant in twenty-one years. He led the AL with forty-four home runs (tied with Harmon Killebrew of the Minnesota Twins), 121 RBI, and a .326 batting average to become the fourteenth Triple Crown winner in major league history. He also was the league leader in hits (189), runs scored (112), and total bases (360).

The tense, four-team pennant race with the Chicago White Sox, Detroit Tigers, and Minnesota Twins brought out the best in Yastrzemski. In the last two weeks of the season, he collected twenty-three hits in forty-four at bats for a .523 average, hit five home runs and four doubles, drove in sixteen runs, and scored fourteen. During this crucial stretch, Yastrzemski hit a home run into the upper deck at Tiger Stadium in the ninth inning to tie a game with Detroit, 5–5, on 18 September (the Red Sox won, 6–5, in the tenth inning). He had four hits, including a homer, and scored the winning run as the Red Sox edged the Indians in Cleveland, 5–4, on 20 September. And, in the pennant-clinching sweep of the Twins (6–4, 5–3) in Boston on the last two days of the season (30 September–1 October), he went seven for eight (including a homer that won the first game) and had six RBI. Equally spectacular in the field, Yastrzemski backhanded a base hit by Bob Allison of the Twins in the left field corner and threw out Allison at second base to end an eighth-inning rally and preserve the last Boston victory. He went on to hit .400 with three homers in the anticlimactic World Series, which the Red Sox lost to the heavily favored St. Louis Cardinals in seven games. At season's end he easily captured the AL MVP award and signed a new contract that made him the second player in Red Sox history to earn $100,000 per year (Ted Williams had been the first).

Although Yastrzemski never again reached the heights of 1967, he remained a productive player. He won his third batting title, hitting .301 in 1968, a year in which pitching was dominant and AL batters collectively averaged .230, and clouted forty homers in 1969. By the time he retired in 1983, Yastrzemski had compiled 3,419 hits, 452 home runs, and 1,814 RBI, and had won seven Gold Gloves for his work in the outfield. He was elected to the National Baseball Hall of Fame in 1989.

Yastrzemski had many notable achievements in a long career, but he is remembered chiefly for his heroics in the heat of the exciting pennant race of 1967. As Roger Angell wrote in the *New Yorker:* "Other fine hitters . . . had finished with comparable statistics. But no other player in recent memory had so clearly pushed a team to such a height in the final days of a difficult season."

★

Yastrzemski wrote two informative memoirs with sportswriters: with Al Hirshberg, *Yaz* (1968), and with Gerald Eskenazi, *Yaz: Baseball, the Wall, and Me* (1990). Other notable works that cover Yastrzemski and the Red Sox in the 1960s are Roger Angell, *The Summer Game* (1972); Al Hirshberg, *What's the Matter with the Red Sox?* (1973); Ken Coleman and Dan Valenti, *The Impossible Dream Remembered: The 1967 Red Sox* (1987); Peter Golenbock, *Fenway: An Unexpurgated History of the Boston Red Sox* (1992); Bill Reynolds, *Lost Summer: The '67 Red Sox and the Impossible Dream* (1992); and Glenn Stout and Richard A. Johnson, *Red Sox Century: One Hundred Years of Red Sox Baseball* (2000). The National Baseball Hall of Fame Library in Cooperstown, New York, has a clipping file on Yastrzemski.

RICHARD H. GENTILE

YOUNG, Andrew Jackson, Jr. (*b.* 12 March 1932 in New Orleans, Louisiana), civil rights leader who served as executive director of the Southern Christian Leadership Conference for much of the 1960s; later he became a U.S. congressman and ambassador to the United Nations during the presidency of Jimmy Carter.

Young's parents were Andrew Jackson Young, Sr., a dentist, and Daisy Fuller Young, a teacher. Born into a position of privilege within African-American society in New Orleans, Young nevertheless faced much of the degradation unique to a southern black American in the segregated South. An exceptional student, Young graduated early from the private Gilbert Academy at the age of fifteen, and at his par-

ent's insistence he spent his freshman year at Dillard University in New Orleans. Young then transferred to Howard University in Washington, D.C., graduating in 1951 with a degree in biology.

The summer after graduation, on a visit to a religious retreat in North Carolina, Young met a white minister who was preparing to go to Angola on a mission. He viewed this encounter as his first step toward searching for his true purpose in life, leading him to the belief that it was his responsibility to help those less fortunate than he. Turning away from his undergraduate focus on biology, Young began a program of study at Hartford Theological Seminary in Connecticut in 1951, while simultaneously working as a youth organizer for the Connecticut Council of Churches. In June 1954 he married Jean Childs in Marion, Alabama. They had four children.

After his graduation from Hartford in 1955, he was called as pastor of the Bethany Congregational Church in Thomasville, Georgia. Young's civil rights work began in Thomasville when he led a move to register local black voters in that rural Georgia community in 1956. Once he had embarked upon an activist career, Young continued on this path, working in connection with mainstream and established civil rights groups across the nation. In August 1957 he joined the executive staff of the youth division of the National Council of Churches, headquartered in New York City.

In 1961 Young became director of a project organized by the United Church of Christ to run a voter registration drive based in Alabama. Young moved his family to Atlanta late that year to work with the Alabama project as well as to continue the work he had begun with the Southern Christian Leadership Conference's (SCLC) Citizenship School in Atlanta. In 1962, working closely with the esteemed Septima Clark, Young merged these two projects into the Voter Education Project, under the auspices of SCLC. He headed this project until February 1963. As part of the Student Nonviolent Coordinating Committee's (SNCC) Freedom Summer project in 1964, Young coordinated the establishment of schools throughout the rural South dedicated to preparing black voters to exercise their right to vote.

SCLC work dominated Young's life during the 1960s. He served as executive director of the organization from 1964 to 1970, and executive vice president, as well, from 1967 to 1970. Young served as one of the Reverend Martin Luther King, Jr.'s closest aides, advisers, and travel companions from the end of his work with the Voter Education Project in 1963 until King's death in 1968. During his tenure in the leadership of SCLC, Young was viewed by many on the staff as representative of the conservative element within the organization—undoubtedly one legacy of his privileged background—and the one most likely to appeal

Andrew Young *(center)*, February 1965. ASSOCIATED PRESS AP

to the conservative white portion of the American South. Aware of this reputation himself, Young considered himself more of a mediator than a facilitator, an assumption that propelled him into political work during the 1970s and 1980s.

Once Young's work with the Voter Education Project had ended, he worked as a march coordinator during Birmingham's 1963 Children's Crusade, supervising marches during the campaign itself and in the wake of the deaths of four young girls at a bombing of Birmingham's Sixteenth Street Baptist Church. Young's reputation as a mediator shone through; he encouraged participants to remain nonviolent, although Birmingham's police chief, Bull Connor, instructed his men to persist in their brutality toward demonstrators.

Present at many of the seminal events of the civil rights movement, Young accompanied King on his fateful trip to Memphis, Tennessee, in April 1968 to support the striking sanitation workers in that city and to launch the SCLC's Poor People's Campaign. After King's assassination on 4 April, Young struggled to continue King's work in shifting SCLC's focus away from racial discrimination and toward economic inequality. Frustrated with the violence that had characterized the decade of the 1960s, as well as delays in implementing the federal legislation that President Lyndon B. Johnson had pushed through the Congress in 1964 and 1965, Young began to look for potential avenues for African Americans to achieve political success. He recognized the need to put forward black candidates for political offices in the South in an attempt to challenge the white southern power structure and, thus, implement the promises contained within the 1964 Civil Rights Act and 1965 Voting Rights Act.

Young's political career, which undoubtedly brought him more recognition than any of his religious endeavors and work within the civil rights movement, began in 1970 when he resigned his position with SCLC to launch a campaign for nomination for U.S. Representative in Atlanta's Fifth Congressional District. Although he won the Democratic nomination for the seat, he lost the general election to the Republican candidate, Fletcher Thompson. Two years later Young became the first black representative from the state of Georgia to the U.S. House of Representatives since the Reconstruction period. He remained in that position until 1977.

Young was one of the first black politicians to openly endorse the presidential bid of Jimmy Carter in 1976. In so doing, he helped attract the critical black Georgia vote that eventually catapulted Carter into the White House. Carter appointed Young to be U.S. ambassador to the United Nations in 1977. When he took his seat on 31 January 1977—he served until 1979—Young became the first African American to occupy that position. As an outspoken supporter of human rights while working in the United Nations, Young transcended his conservative reputation within the civil rights movement by standing consistently on the side of countries fighting for self-determination and freedom from colonial rule.

Young's political career continued into the 1980s, when he succeeded Maynard Jackson as mayor of Atlanta in 1982. He remained in that office for eight years. He later served as cochairman of the Atlanta Committee for the 1996

Olympic Games. Young made an unsuccessful bid for the Democratic nomination for governor of Georgia in 1992 and remained an active figure within the human rights movement and Democratic Party in the new millennium.

★

Young is the author of *A Way Out of No Way: The Spiritual Memoirs of Andrew Young* (1994) and *An Easy Burden: The Civil Rights Movement and the Transformation of America* (1996). Accounts of his role in the civil rights movement of the 1960s are included in Howell Raines, *My Soul Is Rested: Movement Days in the Deep South Remembered* (1977), and Taylor Branch's monumental *Parting the Waters: America in the King Years, 1954–1963* (1988) and *Pillar of Fire: America in the King Years, 1963–1965* (1998).

KIM LITTLE

ZAPPA, Francis Vincent ("Frank") (*b.* 21 December 1940 in Baltimore, Maryland; *d.* 4 December 1993 in Los Angeles, California), musician, composer, social critic, and leader of the progressive 1960s rock band the Mothers of Invention.

Zappa, a Roman Catholic of Italian, Greek, Sicilian, Arab, and French descent, was the oldest of four children of Francis Vincent Zappa, Sr., a University of North Carolina graduate who worked as a meteorologist, metallurgist, and mathematician, and his wife, Rose Marie, a homemaker. The family moved to southern California in 1950. Zappa began learning drums in 1953 and was the drummer in his first band, the Ramblers, in 1955. For the next nine years he played in numerous bands, and by 1958 he had switched to guitar, thereafter his preferred instrument. Among his band mates in the Black-Outs, one of his high school bands, was Don ("Captain Beefheart") Van Vliet. After graduating from Antelope Valley High School in Lancaster, California, in 1958, Zappa dropped in and out of Antelope Valley Junior College in Lancaster and Chaffey Junior College in Alta Loma, California. At Chaffey in 1959 he met and married Kay Sherman, whom he divorced in 1964; the couple had no children.

In 1961 Zappa began writing film scores. His first few ventures failed, but by 1964 his royalties provided him with enough capital to open Studio Z, his own recording studio in Cucamonga, California. Among its products was a pornographic audiotape that earned Zappa a misdemeanor conviction, ten days in jail, three years' probation, ineligibility for the draft, and the demise of Studio Z. Blunt sexuality, most of it more "obscene" than that for which he was convicted, would characterize his lyrics, prose, and general attitude throughout his career. Soon after his release from jail in 1964 he joined a bar band called the Soul Giants, took over its leadership, and renamed it first the Muthers and then, in late 1965, the Mothers of Invention. After seeing them at the Whiskey-a-Go-Go in Los Angeles early in 1966, the producer Tom Wilson signed them to Verve Records.

The first Mothers of Invention album, *Freak Out!,* was released in July 1966, but most of its material was written

Frank Zappa. AP/WIDE WORLD PHOTOS

in 1965. It did not sell well, yet was instantly acclaimed as an underground masterpiece. "Underground rock"—progressive rock music recorded on albums or bootleg tapes, never as singles, and underpromoted by the record companies—existed from about 1965 to 1972. Since the album received almost no radio airplay except on college stations, its popularity, which became substantial in its heyday from 1967 to 1969, was mainly through word of mouth. The lineup at the Woodstock Festival in Bethel, New York, in August 1969 consisted largely of underground musicians, although many of them subsequently achieved mainstream commercial success. A strong case could be made that Zappa invented underground rock and that *Freak Out!* was the first significant underground rock album. It started a dedicated cult around Zappa that persisted even after his death.

Typical Zappa lyrics are sarcastic and mocking. In mid-1960s youth slang, "plastic" meant phony, conformist, or Babbitt-like (after the title character in the book by Sinclair Lewis). Most rock bands of the time attacked this plastic element of society, but none so scathingly as the Mothers, especially on their first two albums. Zappa also saw hippies as plastic. Most of America had not even heard of hippies before the 1967 "Summer of Love," the earliest national expression of the 1960s youth counterculture of recreational drugs, free love, long hair, and unconditional peace. Zappa had already figured them out and lampooned them several times on *Absolutely Free* (May 1967). He turned his full attention to them on his third album, *We're Only in It for the Money* (January 1968), thoroughly savaging them as hypocrites, naive ignoramuses, and shallow thrill seekers, especially in the song "Who Needs the Peace Corps?". Zappa married Gail Sloatman in 1967. They had four children, two of whom, Moon Unit and Dweezil, achieved fame in their own right.

Other albums from this era include the mainly instrumental *Lumpy Gravy* (May 1968); *Cruising with Ruben and the Jets* (November 1968), an extended parody of doo-wop music; *Mothermania: The Best of the Mothers* (March 1969), a "greatest hits" compilation; the jazz-influenced *Uncle Meat* (April 1969); the virtuoso tour de force *Hot Rats* (October 1969); and three highly experimental albums that many consider his best work, *Burnt Weeny Sandwich* (October 1969), *Weasels Ripped My Flesh* (August 1970), and *Chunga's Revenge* (October 1970). In 1969 he briefly disbanded the Mothers and concentrated on discovering and producing new acts, notably Captain Beefheart and Alice Cooper.

In many senses, the American 1960s as a cultural, especially musical, phenomenon ended when Bill Graham closed the Fillmore East in New York City on 27 June 1971. The three weeks before the closing were a grand celebration of the Fillmore's heritage. The final acts were the Mothers, the Hampton Grease Band, and Head over Heels (5–6

June); the Byrds and McKendree Spring, with a surprise appearance by Elton John and his band as Reggie and the Frankensteins (9 June); Bloodrock, Glass Harp, and Alice Cooper (11–12 June); B. B. King, Moby Grape, and Grootna (18–19 June); Johnny and Edgar Winter (24 June), and the Allman Brothers and J. Geils (25–27 June). The Mothers' live album, *Fillmore East, June 1971,* released in September 1971, clearly marks the end of Zappa's 1960s period. In 1967 Zappa began publishing short articles of satire and social criticism. The most poignant and perceptive of these is "The Oracle Has It All Psyched Out" in *Life* (28 June 1968). In it Zappa eloquently, almost poetically, expounds upon one of his favorite themes, the inseparability of sex and rock and the personal liberation afforded by both.

Zappa looked grungy, acted sleazy, and was certainly eccentric, but in stark contrast to the stereotype of scruffy, long-haired 1960s rock musicians, Zappa did not take drugs or drink alcohol and, while on the road, did not allow members of his bands to indulge in these substances. Onstage he was completely uninhibited, and off-stage he was a tireless, shameless champion of free speech, dirty speech, and sexual content. The stand-up comic Lenny Bruce, noted for his crude attacks on establishment hypocrisy, made his last public appearance with Zappa and the Mothers at the Fillmore Auditorium in San Francisco on 24 June 1966. Around 1969 Zappa satirized college fraternities by sitting naked on a toilet for a poster captioned "Phi Zappa Krappa." His libertarian, anti-censorship stance led to his notorious confrontation with Vice President Al Gore's wife, Tipper Gore, and the Parents Music Resource Center in the late 1980s.

Zappa's musical influences were as diverse as the avant-garde classical composer Edgard Varèse, the guitarist Wes Montgomery, and the torrid rhythm-and-blues musician Hank Ballard. Rather than call himself a rock musician, he always described himself as a classical composer working in the milieu of rock. Active in music as long as possible, he lost a three-year fight against prostate cancer at the age of fifty-two. He is buried in an unmarked grave next to the 1930s film star Lew Ayres in Westwood Memorial Park, Los Angeles.

★

John Rocco's article on Zappa in *Scribner Encyclopedia of American Lives*, vol. 3 (1991–1993), lists the most important biographical and critical works. To focus on the 1960s, the 1972 first edition of David Walley's *No Commercial Potential: The Saga of Frank Zappa and the Mothers of Invention* is more valuable than the 1996 rewrite. Also useful are two of Zappa's own articles in *Hit Parader*: "The Incredible History of the Mothers" (June 1968) and "What Ever Happened to the Mothers of Invention?" (Apr. 1970).

ERIC V. D. LUFT

DIRECTORY OF CONTRIBUTORS

ABRAMSON, RUDY P.
Journalist, Reston, Va.
   Harriman, William Averell

ADAMS, VALERIE
Embry-Riddle Aeronautical University
   Phillips, Kevin Price
   Wiesner, Jerome Bert

AGNEW, BRAD
Northeastern Oklahoma State University
   Ashmore, Harry Scott, and William Calhoun ("Bill")
     Baggs
   Momaday, N(avarre) Scott

ALEXANDER, OD
Southeastern University
   Wilkins, Roy

ALFONSO, BARRY
Historical Society of Western Pennsylvania
   Humphrey, Hubert Horatio, Jr.
   McCarthy, Eugene Joseph
   Stevenson, Adlai Ewing

ALLEN, HOWARD
Brooklyn College of the City University of New York
     (Retired)
   Watson, James Dewey

ALLENBAUGH, MARK
Montedonico, Belcuore & Tazzara, P.C.
   Hoffman, Julius Jennings

AMERMAN, DON
Freelance Writer, Saylorsburg, Penn.
   Bancroft, Anne
   Burnett, Carol
   Fonda, Henry Jaynes
   Fortas, Abraham ("Abe")
   Friedman, Milton
   Hersh, Seymour M.
   Jacobs, Jane
   Marshall, Thurgood
   Mercer, John Herndon ("Johnny")
   Nichols, Mike
   Rustin, Bayard Taylor
   Warren, Earl

AURAND, HAROLD W., JR.
Pennsylvania State University, Schuylkill Campus
   Unitas, John Constantine ("Johnny")

BAKER, THERESE DUZINKIEWICZ
Western Kentucky University
   Halston

BARBEAU, ART
West Liberty State College
   Fossey, Dian
   Salisbury, Harrison Evans
   White, Theodore Harold ("Teddy")

BARFIELD, LAURA
Freelance Copyeditor and Writer
   Hargis, Billy James

BECK, SHEILA
Queensborough Community College
   DeBakey, Michael Ellis
   Von Braun, Wernher

BEETZ, KIRK H.
Author and Educator
   Ash, Roy Lawrence
   Buckley, William Frank, Jr.
   Bunker, Ellsworth
   Carpenter, (Malcolm) Scott
   Dick, Philip K(indred)
   Dirksen, Everett McKinley
   Dulles, Allen Welsh
   Fogarty, Anne Whitney
   Gay, Peter ("Jack")
   Grissom, Virgil Ivan ("Gus")
   Hendrix, James Marshall ("Jimi," "Jimmy," "Maurice
     James")
   Hewlett, William Redington ("Bill"), and David
     Packard
   Hope, Leslie Townes ("Bob")
   Jones, Quincy Delight, Jr.
   Kerner, Otto, Jr.
   LeMay, Curtis Emerson
   Lodge, Henry Cabot, Jr.
   McCovey, Willie Lee
   Mantle, Mickey Charles

Mays, William Howard, Jr. ("Willie")
Mitchell, John Newton
Morrison, James Douglas ("Jim")
O'Hair, Madalyn Murray
Oates, Joyce Carol
Odetta
Oliphant, Patrick Bruce ("Pat")
Pauling, Linus Carl
Percy, Walker
Perot, H(enry) Ross
Peter, Laurence Johnston
Powell, Adam Clayton, Jr.
Pynchon, Thomas Ruggles, Jr.
Roth, Philip Milton
Samora, Julian
Schirra, Walter Marty, Jr. ("Wally")
Sessions, Roger Huntington
Sheehan, Cornelius Mahoney ("Neil")
Shepard, Alan Bartlett, Jr.
Simon, (Marvin) Neil
Vernon, Lillian
Watson, Thomas John, Jr.
Weaver, Robert Clifton
White, Edward Higgins, II
Wolfe, Thomas Kennerly, Jr. ("Tom")

BERLAGE, GAI INGHAM
Iona College
Rigby, Cathy
Rudolph, Wilma Glodean

BETZOLD, MICHAEL
Freelance Journalist, Ann Arbor, Mi.
Carmichael, Stokely (Kwame Touré, Kwame Turé)
Clemente, Roberto Walker
Dellinger, David
Illich, Ivan
Killebrew, Harmon Clayton, Jr.
Seaver, George Thomas ("Tom")
Wonder, Stevie

BIELAKOWSKI, RAE SIKULA
Loyola University Chicago
Hesburgh, Theodore Martin

BLOOM, ALAN
Valparaiso University
Hatcher, Richard Gordon

BOON, KEVIN ALEXANDER
*Pennsylvania State University and Harrisburg Area
    Community College*
Capote, Truman Garcia
May, Elaine
Vonnegut, Kurt, Jr.

BOON, LESLIE
*Harrisburg Area Community College, Gettysburg Campus
    and Penn State University, Mount Alto*

Giovanni, Nikki
Kozol, Jonathan

BORDEN, TIMOTHY
Toledo, Ohio
Diller, Phyllis Ada
Fleming, Peggy Gale
Gordy, Berry, Jr.
Ross, Diana Earle
Ruffin, David Eli
Shore, Dinah
Sonny and Cher
Steinem, Gloria Marie

BOSKY, BERNADETTE LYNN
Freelance Writer and Instructor
Kosinski, Jerzy Nikodem
Manson, Charles Milles
Mauldin, William Henry ("Bill")

BRILEY, RON
Sandia Preparatory School, Albuquerque, N.Mex.
Eastwood, Clinton, Jr. ("Clint")
Fall, Bernard B.
Heller, Joseph
Huston, John Marcellus
Lowenstein, Allard Kenneth
Penn, Arthur Hiller
Slick, Grace Wing
Smothers, Thomas ("Tom"), and Richard ("Dick")
    Smothers

BRITTON, KATHARINE FISHER
Freelance Writer, Norwich, Vt.
Cunningham, Mercier Phillip ("Merce")
Nikolais, Alwin Theodore ("Nik")

BURKE, MARGARET G.
Hofstra University
Abzug, Bella
Nevelson, Louise

BYRNE, JOHN J.
Bronx Community College
Beatty, (Henry) Warren
Davis, Sammy, Jr.
Dylan, Bob
Rand, Ayn
Shanker, Albert ("Al")

CAMPBELL, JIM
Bucknell University (Retired)
Blough, Roger Miles
Brown, James Nathaniel ("Jim")
Namath, Joseph William ("Joe")

CARDOSO, JACK J.
*Professor Emeritus, State University of New York College at
    Buffalo*
Gavin, James Maurice
Hofstadter, Richard

Maris, Roger Eugene
Wills, Garry

CARDOSO, ROSEMARIE S.
Artist and Retired Art Educator
Baez, Joan Chandos
de Kooning, Willem
Rothko, Mark

CARPENTER, BRIAN B.
Texas A&M University Libraries
Roddenberry, Eugene Wesley ("Gene")
Thomas, David R. ("Dave")
Woodward, C(omer) Vann

CARRIKER, ANDREW J.
Columbia University
Burger, Warren Earl

CHEN, JEFFREY H.
Cambridge University Press
McCullers, Carson

CICARELLI, JAMES
Roosevelt University
Kroc, Raymond Albert ("Ray")

CICARELLI, JULIANNE
Freelance Writer, Arlington Heights, Ill.
Ronstadt, Linda

COLLAR, DOUGLAS E.
Heidelberg College
Updike, John Hoyer

CONE, ROBERT TEMPLE C., JR.
University of Wisconsin-Madison
Bishop, Elizabeth

COOKSEY, GLORIA
Freelance Writer, Sacramento, Calif.
Brown, Hubert Gerold ("H. Rap")
Gregory, Richard Claxton ("Dick")
Hammer, Armand
Hayakawa, S(amuel) I(chiye)
Hofstadter, Robert
Jones, James Earl
Onassis, Jacqueline Lee Kennedy ("Jackie")
Oswald, Lee Harvey
Sanders, Harland David ("Colonel")
Welch, Raquel
Wilson, Brian Douglas
Wolfman Jack (Robert Weston Smith)

CRAWFORD, DESSA
Delaware County Community College
Castaneda, Carlos César Salvador Arana
Porter, Katherine Anne
Styron, William Clark, Jr.

CRAWFORD, SCOTT A. G. M.
Eastern Illinois University
Ashe, Arthur Robert, Jr.
De Varona, Donna

Fischer, Robert James ("Bobby")
Liston, Charles ("Sonny")
Pride, Charles Frank ("Charley")
Sackler, Howard Oliver
Shoemaker, William Lee ("Bill")
Sullivan, Edward Vincent ("Ed")
Voight, Jon

CROWLEY, GWYNETH H.
Levy Economics Institute of Bard College
Boulding, Kenneth Ewart

DAMON, ALLAN L.
Horace Greeley High School (retired), Chappaqua, N.Y.
Cerf, Bennett Albert
Kunstler, William Moses
Reston, James Barrett ("Scotty")

DANFORTH, COURTNEY S.
University of Maryland
Turner, Ike Izear Luster ("Ike"), and Tina Turner
Wynette, Tammy

DAVIDSON, ABRAHAM A.
Tyler School of Art, Temple University
Lichtenstein, Roy
Oldenburg, Claes Thure
Segal, George

DINNEEN, MARCIA B.
Bridgewater State College
MacLaine, Shirley
Manchester, William Raymond
O'Connor, Flannery
Thomas, Marlo

DOBSON, MELISSA A.
Freelance Writer, Bristol, R.I.
Plath, Sylvia

DOHERTY, THOMAS
Brandeis University
Fonda, Jane Seymour
Poitier, Sidney

DORINSON, JOSEPH
Long Island University, Brooklyn Campus
Bruce, Lenny
Lewis, Jerry

DROBNICKI, JOHN A.
York College, City University of New York
Meader, (Abbott) Vaughn

DYER, LEIGH
Charlotte Observer, N.C.
Cunningham, Harry Blair
Moore, Mary Tyler

EDDY, TRACY L.
Rutgers University
Haldeman, H(arry) R(obbins) ("Bob")
Rozelle, Alvin Ray ("Pete")

EDELMAN, PETER
Georgetown University Law Center
Kennedy, Robert Francis

ENDERS, ERIC
Historian, Cooperstown, N.Y.
Chávez, César Estrada
Ochs, Philip David
Simon and Garfunkel

ENNIS, LISA A.
Georgia College & State University
Aaron, Henry Louis ("Hank")
Banks, Dennis J.
Cash, John R. ("Johnny")
Salinger, J(erome) D(avid)

EVENSEN, BRUCE J.
DePaul University
Brubeck, David Warren ("Dave")
Garland, Judy
Hepburn, Audrey
Hitchcock, Alfred Joseph
Hoffman, Dustin Lee
Lemmon, John Uhler, III ("Jack")
Newman, Paul Arthur

FERRARA, ADI
Freelance Medical and Science Writer, Bellevue, Wash.
Hershey, Alfred Day
Holley, Robert William
Nagel, Ernest

FISCHEL, JACK
Millersville University
Bell, Daniel
Cox, Harvey Gallagher, Jr.
Peckinpah, David Samuel ("Sam")
Podhoretz, Norman Harold

FISHER, CHRISTOPHER T.
The College of New Jersey
Baldwin, James Arthur
Shriver, (Robert) Sargent, Jr.

FLANNERY, MAURA
St. John's University, New York
Khorana, Har Gobind
Luria, Salvador Edward
Nirenberg, Marshall Warren
Wald, George David

FOLEY, MICHAEL S.
College of Staten Island, City University of New York
Chomsky, (Avram) Noam
Clark, (William) Ramsey
Coffin, William Sloane, Jr.
Hayden, Thomas Emmett ("Tom")
Savio, Mario

FORD, KATRINA
Freelance Writer
Dickerson, Nancy

FRISCH, PAUL A.
Library, Our Lady of the Lake University, San Antonio, Tex.
Drysdale, Donald Scott ("Don")
Genovese, Eugene Dominick
Vann, John Paul

GAAR, GILLIAN G.
Freelance Writer, Seattle, Wash.
Avalon, Frankie, and Annette Joanne Funicello
Checker, Chubby
Collins, Judy
Dunaway, (Dorothy) Faye
Kesey, Kenneth Elton ("Ken")

GARGAN, WILLIAM M.
Brooklyn College of the City University of New York
Burroughs, William S(eward)
Southern, Terry Marion, Jr.

GEE, SHALEANE
University of Chicago
Mailer, Norman Kingsley

GENTILE, RICHARD H.
Independent Scholar, South Easton, Mass.
Brooke, Edward William, III
Yastrzemski, Carl Michael, Jr.

GERSTEIN, CHRISTINE W.
Hofstra University
Bumbry, Grace

GOLDBERG, ROBERT ALAN
University of Utah
Goldwater, Barry Morris

GOODBODY, JOAN
Texas A&M University
Allen, Stephen Valentine Patrick William ("Steve")
Morris, Robert
Murrow, Edward Roscoe
Pike, James Albert, Jr.
Rockefeller, John Davison, III

GOODFOX, JULIA
University of Kansas
Gell-Mann, Murray

GOODHAND, GLEN R.
Society for International Hockey Research
Orr, Robert Gordon ("Bobby")

GORDON, W. TERRENCE
Dalhousie University
McLuhan, (Herbert) Marshall

GRIFFIN, LARRY D.
Dyersburg State Community College
Muhammad, Elijah
Reuther, Walter Philip
Roberts, Oral

GRIFFITH, JEAN W. JR.
Pittsburg State University
Hoover, John Edgar

HARMOND, RICHARD P.
St. John's University, New York
Alsop, Joseph Wright, V
Muskie, Edmund Sixtus

HARRIS, JENNIFER
York University
Brown, Claude
Hansberry, Lorraine Vivian
Meredith, J(ames) H(oward)

HARRISON, JENNIFER
The College of William and Mary
Farrell, Suzanne

HEALY, JOHN DAVID
Drew University
Brennan, William Joseph, Jr.
Cooley, Denton Arthur
Lewis, (Joseph) Anthony
Nizer, Louis
Sills, Beverly

HENDRICK, ROBERT
St. John's University
Dine, James ("Jim")
Indiana, Robert
Schlesinger, Arthur Meier, Jr.

HLAVATY, ARTHUR D.
Independent Scholar
Barth, John Simmons
Hefner, Hugh Marston
Leary, Timothy Francis
Macdonald, Dwight
Puzo, Mario

HODGES, GRAHAM RUSSELL
Colgate University
Brown, James Joe, Jr.
Chamberlain, Wilton Norman ("Wilt")
King, B. B.
Orbison, Roy Kelton
Warhol, Andy

HOWELL, KENNETH WAYNE
Texas A&M University
Bailyn, Bernard
Glenn, John Herschel, Jr.

HOWLETT, CHARLES F.
Adelphi University
Berrigan, Daniel Joseph, and Philip Francis Berrigan
Cremin, Lawrence A(rthur)

INGRAM, JANET
Freelance Writer, Pittsburgh, Penn.
Carson, Rachel Louise

JALENAK, NATALIE B.
Playhouse on the Square, Memphis, Tenn. (Retired)
Arendt, Hannah
Kahane, Meir

JONES, BRIAN MADISON
Kansas State University
Schwinger, Julian Seymour

KALB, PETER R.
Independent Scholar
Johns, Jasper

KEEN, W. HUBERT
System Administration, State University of New York
Wharton, Clifton Reginald, Jr.

KINDER, SEAN
Western Kentucky University
Nin, Anaïs

KINYATTI, NJOKI-WA-
York College Library, City University of New York
Carroll, Diahann
Chisholm, Shirley Anita
Pryor, Richard Franklin Lenox Thomas

KNIGHT, CANDICE MANCINI
Writer, Missoula, Mont.
Chall, Jeanne Sternlicht
Koontz, Elizabeth Duncan ("Libby")

KNIGHT, CHRISTOPHER J.
University of Montana
Bellow, Saul
Trilling, Lionel

KNIGHT, JUDSON
Freelance Writer
Burns, Arthur Frank
Cline, Patsy
Gardner, Edward George
Geneen, Harold Sydney
Goodman, Paul
Heller, Walter Wolfgang
Holt, John Caldwell
Joplin, Janis Lyn
Kahn, Louis Isidore
Kohler, Foy David
McCain, John Sidney, Jr.
McCarthy, Mary Therese
Mies van der Rohe, Ludwig
Monroe, Marilyn
Moynihan, Daniel Patrick
Neustadt, Richard Elliott
Rockefeller, David
Sabin, Albert Bruce
Schuller, Gunther Alexander
Scott, George C(ampbell)
Smith, Walter Wellesley ("Red")
Steiger, Rodney Stephen ("Rod")
Stein, Herbert
Stone, I. F.
Streisand, Barbra
Thompson, Llewellyn E., Jr. ("Tommy")
Wilson, Joseph Chamberlain

KRINGEN, TIMOTHY
Portland, Oreg.
  McNamara, Robert Strange
  Westmoreland, William Childs
LAIRD, KIM
Library of Michigan
  Békésy, Georg von ("György")
  Delbrück, Max Ludwig Henning
LANKFORD, RONNIE D. JR.
Freelance Writer, Appomattox, Va.
  Hentoff, Nathan Irving ("Nat")
  McGovern, George Stanley
  Mills, C(harles) Wright
  Thompson, Hunter S(tockton)
LAUER, JOSH
Philadelphia, Penn.
  Sontag, Susan
LAWLOR, WILLIAM
University of Wisconsin-Stevens Point
  Jones, Everett LeRoy (Amiri Baraka, "LeRoi")
LAWSON, RUSSELL
Bacone College
  Wallace, George Corley, Jr.
LEAB, DANIEL J.
Seton Hall University
  Howe, Irving
  Huntley, Chester Robert ("Chet"), and David McClure
    Brinkley
  Townsend, Lynn Alfred
LEWIS, JAMES
Independent Scholar
  Serling, Rodman Edward ("Rod")
LEWIS, JANE FRANCES AMLER
Manhattan College
  Armstrong, Neil Alden
  Robards, Jason Nelson, Jr.
LI, SHAOSHAN
Board of Education of the City of New York
  McNamara, Margaret Craig
LIGGETT, LUCY A.
Eastern Michigan University (Emeritus)
  Wiseman, Frederick
LITTLE, KIM
Ohio University
  Young, Andrew Jackson, Jr.
LO BRUTTO, VINCENT
Sohool of Visual Arts, New York City
  Fonda, Peter Seymour
  Hopper, Dennis
  Kubrick, Stanley
  Lumet, Sidney
  Paik, Nam June

LONGHURST, JAMES
Carnegie Mellon University
  Ling, James Joseph
LOVE, JOHNNIEQUE B.
University of Maryland Libraries
  Haley, Alexander Murray Palmer ("Alex")
  Moses, Robert Parris
  Parks, Gordon, Sr.
LUFT, ERIC V. D.
State University of New York Upstate Medical University
  Masters, William Howell, and Virginia Eshelman
    Johnson
  Moore, Francis Daniels, and Thomas Earl Starzl
  Zappa, Francis Vincent ("Frank")
MCCLELLAN, KEITH
Freelance Historical Writer
  Jackson, Jesse Louis
  Johnson, Rafer Lewis
MCCORMACK, BRIAN
Arizona State University
  Vance, Cyrus Roberts
MCCULLOUGH, STEPHEN
University of Alabama
  Martin, John Bartlow
MCLEAN, MICHAEL
Independent Scholar, New York City
  Hopper, Edward
  Lowell, Robert Traill Spence, IV ("Cal")
MCQUEEN, LEE
Texas A&M University
  Dee, Ruby
MALONEY, SEAN
Siena College Library
  Franklin, John Hope
MALONEY, WILLIAM J.
Writer, New York City
  Day, Doris
  Della Femina, Jerry
  Gernreich, Rudolph ("Rudi")
MALVASI, MARK G.
Randolph-Macon College
  Barzun, Jacques Martin
  Davis, David Brion
  Davis, Miles Dewey, III
  Foote, Shelby Dade, Jr.
  Frazier, Joseph William ("Joe")
  Lasch, (Robert) Christopher
  Niebuhr, Reinhold
  Patterson, Floyd
MALVASI, MEG GREENE
Midlothian, Va.
  Champion, Gower

Crumb, Robert
Joffrey, Robert
Papp, Joseph
Robbins, Jerome
Venturi, Robert
Villella, Edward Joseph
Vreeland, Diana

MARC, DAVID
Syracuse University
Chayefsky, Sidney Aaron ("Paddy")
Cooney, Joan Ganz
Moore, Garry
Newhart, George Robert ("Bob")
Rickles, Donald Jay ("Don")
Robertson, Marion Gordon ("Pat")
Singer, Isaac Bashevis
Van Dyke, Richard Wayne ("Dick")

MARKHAM, REED B.
California State Polytechnic University, Pomona (Emeritus)
Gardner, John William
Getty, Jean Paul
Kerr, Clark
Rafferty, Maxwell Lewis, Jr. ("Max")
Rather, Daniel Irvin ("Dan")
Redford, (Charles) Robert, Jr.
Walton, Samuel Moore ("Sam")

MARKLEY, PATRICIA L.
Librarian, Siena College
Carson, John William ("Johnny")

MARQUSEE, MIKE
Freelance Writer
Ali, Muhammad (Cassius Clay)

MILLER, MICHAEL C.
Dallas Public Library
Karnow, Stanley
Kissinger, Henry Alfred
Krulak, Victor Harold

MOBERG, VERNE
Translator and Lecturer, The Swedish Program
Auden, W(ystan) H(ugh)

MORALES, RUBIL
Brooklyn, N.Y.
Guthrie, Arlo Davy

MORAN, DOROTHY L.
Freelance Writer, Brooklyn, N.Y.
Moreno, Rita

MORAN, JOHN
Queens Borough Public Library, New York
Clifford, Clark McAdams

MURPHY, CHARLES EDWARD
Freelance Writer
Aubrey, James Thomas, Jr.

Brewster, Kingman, Jr.
Johnson, Claudia Alta Taylor ("Lady Bird")
Mott, Stewart Rawlings

MURRAY, PAUL T.
Siena College
Barnett, Ross Robert
Bond, (Horace) Julian
Chaney, James Earl, Andrew Goodman, and Michael
    Henry Schwerner
Evers, Medgar Wylie
Groppi, James Edmund
Lewis, John Robert

NAGEL, MIRIAM C.
Freelance Writer
Ash, Mary Kay
Glaser, Donald Arthur
Harrington, (Edward) Michael
Hartline, Haldan Keffer
Lippmann, Walter
Onsager, Lars

NELSON, MURRY R.
Pennsylvania State University
Bradley, William Warren ("Bill")
Koufax, Sanford ("Sandy")
Russell, William Felton ("Bill")
Wooden, John Robert

NEUMANN, CARYN E.
Ohio State University
Agnew, Spiro Theodore
Dohrn, Bernardine Rae
Friedan, Betty Naomi
Garrison, Earling Carothers ("Jim")
Harkness, Rebekah West
Hoffman, Abbott Howard ("Abbie," "Barry Freed")
Quill, Michael Joseph ("Mike")
Rockefeller, Nelson Aldrich

NIELSEN, FRED
University of Nebraska at Omaha
Fogerty, John Cameron
Nader, Ralph
Presley, Elvis Aron
Reagan, Ronald Wilson

OHL, JOHN KENNEDY
Mesa Community College
Abrams, Creighton William, Jr.
Clay, Lucius DuBignon, Sr.
Hilsman, Roger
Lansdale, Edward Geary
Wheeler, Earle Gilmore

O'NEILL, WILLIAM L.
Rutgers University
Rubin, Jerry Clyde

PACHECO, MARÍA
Buffalo State College
   Alvarez, Luis Walter
   Calvin, Melvin
   Libby, Willard Frank
   Mulliken, Robert Sanderson
   Seaborg, Glenn Theodore
   Woodward, Robert Burns
PASH, SIDNEY
Fayetteville State University
   Reischauer, Edwin Oldfather
PAULL, JOANNE
Freelance Writer and Editor
   Sorensen, Theodore Chaikin ("Ted")
PAULSON, LINDA DAILEY
Freelance Writer
   Arbus, Diane
   Brown, Helen Gurley
   Davis, Angela Yvonne
   Garson, Barbara
   Hewitt, Don S.
PETECHUK, DAVID
Freelance Writer
   Bloch, Konrad E(mil)
   Conrad, Paul
   Cousins, Norman
   Dullea, Keir
   Farmer, James Leonard, Jr.
   Goeppert-Mayer, Maria
   Haynsworth, Clement Furman, Jr.
   Hunt, H(aroldson) L(afayette), Jr.
   Katzenbach, Nicholas de Belleville
   Kennedy, Edward Moore ("Ted")
   McNally, Terrence
   O'Horgan, Thomas ("Tom")
   Rous, (Francis) Peyton
   Ruby, John ("Jack")
   Shriver, Eunice Mary Kennedy
   Vidal, Gore
   Williams, William Appleman
PETERS, SANDRA REDMOND
Southwest Missouri State University
   Fulbright, J(ames) William
   MacDermot, (Arthur Terence) Galt
   Marcuse, Herbert
   Monk, Thelonious Sphere
   Rusk, (David) Dean
   Seeger, Peter R. ("Pete")
   Watts, André
   Wigner, Eugene Paul
PFANNESTIEL, TODD J.
Clarion University
   Taylor, Maxwell Davenport

PHARR, ANN E.
Southeastern University
   Stokes, Carl Burton
PHILLIPS, ROBERT
University of Houston
   Herlihy, James Leo
   Shapiro, Karl Jay
PIERCE, MATTHEW J.
Columbia University
   Franklin, Aretha Louise
PINSKER, SANDY
Shadek Professor of Humanities at Franklin and Marshall College
   Allen, Woody
PORTER, DAVID L.
William Penn University
   Lombardi, Vincent Thomas ("Vince")
   Morse, Wayne Lyman
   Russell, Richard Brevard, Jr. ("Dick")
PREBLE, CHRISTOPHER
Independent Scholar
   Kennedy, John Fitzgerald
   Samuelson, Paul Anthony
PRONO, LUCA
University of Nottingham
   Baker, Carroll
   Nicholson, Jack
PRUTER, ROBERT
Lewis University
   Dion
   Pickett, Wilson, Jr.
   Redding, Otis
   Ryun, James Ronald ("Jim")
PUGH, WILLIAM WHITE TISON
University of Central Florida
   Ginsberg, (Irwin) Allen
RAUSCH, DAVE
West Texas A&M University
   Ehrlichman, John Daniel
   O'Brien, Lawrence Francis, Jr. ("Larry")
REGALADO, MARIANA
Brooklyn College of the City University of New York
   DeVos, Richard Marvin, and Jay Van Andel
   Johnson, Haynes Bonner
RICHARDSON, KIM
University of Texas, Austin
   Connor, Theophilus Eugene ("Bull")
   Gruening, Ernest
RIZZO, MARY
University of Minnesota
   Kirk, Grayson Louis
   Rado, James, and Gerome Ragni

ROBERTS, PRISCILLA
University of Hong Kong
    Ball, George Wildman
    Bohlen, Charles Eustis ("Chip")
    Bowles, Chester Bliss ("Chet")
    Bruce, David Kirkpatrick Este
    Bundy, McGeorge
    Kennan, George Frost
    Rostow, Walter Whitman ("Walt")

ROBINSON, GREGORY K.
JazzTimes Magazine
    Coltrane, John William

ROUT, KATHLEEN KINSELLA
Michigan State University
    Cleaver, (Leroy) Eldridge
    Newton, Huey Percy
    Seale, Robert George ("Bobby")

ROUTLEDGE, CHRIS
Freelance Writer and Editor
    Berryman, John Allyn
    Fariña, Richard George
    Farrow, Mia
    Frankenheimer, John Michael
    Galbraith, John Kenneth
    Giancana, Salvatore ("Sam")
    Hackman, Eugene Alden ("Gene")
    Johnson, Philip Cortelyou
    Matthau, Walter
    McMurtry, Larry Jeff
    Nabokov, Vladimir
    Pei, I(eoh) M(ing)
    Saarinen, Eero
    Wood, Natalie
    Woodward, Joanne Gignilliat

ROYCE, BRENDA SCOTT
Freelance Writer and Editor
    Duke, Anna Marie ("Patty")
    Hudson, Rock

RUHLMANN, WILLIAM J.
Pop Editor, Baker's Biographical Dictionary of Musicians
    Bennett, Tony
    Crosby, Stills, and Nash
    Haggard, Merle Ronald
    Mancini, Henry
    Martin, Dean
    Peter, Paul and Mary
    Phillips, John Edmund Andrew
    Robinson, William, Jr. ("Smokey")
    Warwick, Dionne
    Webb, James Layne ("Jimmy")

SANCHEZ, BRENNA
Freelance Writer, Los Angeles, Calif.
    Ailey, Alvin

    Albee, Edward Franklin, III
    Ashbery, John Lawrence
    Drucker, Peter Ferdinand
    Gordone, Charles
    Haas, Walter A., Jr., and Peter E. Haas, Sr.
    Halberstam, David
    McQueen, Steve
    Peale, Norman Vincent
    Selby, Hubert, Jr.
    Smith, Hazel Brannon

SAPIENZA, MADELINE
Independent Scholar
    Heston, Charlton
    McCloy, John Jay
    Quinn, Anthony Rudolph Oaxaca

SCHERER, JOHN L.
Minneapolis, Minn.
    Powers, Francis Gary ("Frank")

SCHLUETER, JUNE
Lafayette University
    Miller, Arthur Asher

SCHMIDT, RAYMOND
Journalist and Author, Ventura, Calif.
    Block, Herbert Lawrence ("Herblock")
    King, Billie Jean Moffitt
    Nicklaus, Jack William

SCHULTHIES, APRIL
California State University, Fresno
    Daley, Richard Joseph
    Deloria, Vine, Jr.
    Hirsch, Eric Donald, Jr.
    Hoffa, James Riddle ("Jimmy")
    Huggins, Charles Brenton
    Jackson, Henry Martin ("Scoop")
    Lindsay, John Vliet
    Perkins, James Alfred
    Sirhan, Sirhan Bishara

SHOR, RACHEL
Queens Borough Public Library, New York City
    Brooks, Gwendolyn Elizabeth
    Kohl, Herbert R.

SILVERBERG, MARK
Dalhousie University
    Sexton, Anne
    Williams, William Carlos

SINGH, ANNMARIE
Hofstra University
    Ephron, Nora Louise
    McGill, Ralph Emerson
    McGinniss, Joseph ("Joe")

SMALL, MELVIN
Wayne State University
    Nixon, Richard Milhous

SMALLWOOD, JAMES M.
Oklahoma State University
  Johnson, Lyndon Baines
SMITH, PATRICK
Freelance Writer, Pittsburgh, Penn.
  Blass, William Ralph ("Bill")
  Cavett, Richard Alva ("Dick")
  Grooms, Charles Rogers ("Red")
  Hassenfeld, Merrill Lloyd
  Klein, Anne
  Klein, Calvin
  Lauren, Ralph
  Marisol (Marisol Escobar)
  Rivers, Larry
  Roszak, Theodore
  Sassoon, Vidal
  Schechner, Richard
  Searle, John Gideon ("Jack")
  Stewart, Ellen
  Tandy, Charles David
  Terry, Megan
SPATT, HARTLEY S.
State University of New York, Maritime College
  Feynman, Richard Phillips
  Noyce, Robert Norton
  Stone, Edward Durell
  Townes, Charles Hard
  Wang, An
SPRAYBERRY, GARY
University of Alabama
  Clayton-Thomas, David
  Leonard, Sheldon
STANNISH, STEVEN M.
State University of New York, Potsdam
  Campbell, Joseph John
STRINGER-HYE, RICHARD
Librarian, Vanderbilt University
  Garcia, Jerome John ("Jerry")
SU, DI
York College, City University of New York
  Cage, John Milton, Jr.
SUSSER, MARGALIT
Queens Borough Public Library System
  Aiken, George David
  Beck, Julian
  Browne, Malcolm Wilde
SUTTON, MATTHEW
University of California, Santa Barbara
  Schlafly, Phyllis Stewart
TAKOOSHIAN, HAROLD
Fordham University
  Clark, Kenneth Bancroft

  Genovese, Catherine ("Kitty")
  Jensen, Arthur Robert
TAMBORRINO, VICTORIA
St. John's University, New York
  Kelsey, Frances Kathleen Oldham
THOMAS, LERI
Independent Scholar
  Bate, Walter Jackson
  Pusey, Nathan Marsh
  Schell, Jonathan Edward
THOMPSON, MARIE
Freelance Writer
  Coleman, James Samuel
  Connell, Evan Shelby, Jr.
THOMPSON-FEUERHERD, JENNIFER
New York Institute of Technology
  Sainte-Marie, Buffy
THORNTON, JOYCE K.
Texas A&M University Libraries
  Calley, William Laws, Jr.
  Davis, Raiford Chatman ("Ossie")
  Kahn, Herman Bernard
TODMAN, ANTHONY
St. John's University, New York
  Gaye, Marvin Pentz, Jr.
TOMA, YAN
Queens Library, N.Y.
  Ray, James Earl
TRAFLET, JANICE
Columbia University
  Martin, William McChesney, Jr.
VANDOREN, SANDRA SHAFFER
Malvern, Penn.
  Balanchine, George
VARN, JAMES
Johnson C. Smith University
  Wellek, René Maria Eduard
VELLANI, ROBERT
University of Houston
  Shultz, George Pratt
VORPERIAN, JOHN
Attorney, White Plains, N.Y.
  Robinson, Frank, Jr.
WATSON, DENNIS
Attorney, Ann Arbor, Mich.
  Shoup, David Monroe
WATSON, MARY ANN
Eastern Michigan University
  Goode, Malvin Russell ("Mal")
  Minow, Newton Norman
  Susskind, David Howard
WEBB, CLIVE
University of Sussex
  King, Martin Luther, Jr.

WEISBLAT, LEIGH BULLARD

Independent Art Historian

Rauschenberg, Robert
Rosenquist, James Albert
Smith, David Roland
Stella, Frank Philip

WEISBLAT, TINKY "DAKOTA"

Independent Journalist, Scholar, and Singer

Andrews, Julie
Cronkite, Walter Leland, Jr.
Sondheim, Stephen Joshua

WENDT, SIMON

JFK Institute for North American Studies, Free University of Berlin

Malcolm X (Malik El-Shabazz)

WINTERS, KELLY

Freelance Writer

Bradbury, Ray
Kaufman, Bel
Lee, (Nelle) Harper
Rich, Adrienne Cecile
Sendak, Maurice Bernard
Steinbeck, John Ernst

WISE, STEVEN

Our Lady of the Lake University

Wallace, Mike

YOUNG, HOPE E.

York College, City University of New York

Lewis, Oscar
Spector, Philip Harvey ("Phil")

OCCUPATIONS INDEX, VOLUMES 1–5 AND THEMATIC VOLUMES

See also the Alphabetical List of Subjects beginning on p. 619.

Actor (Television)

	Volume		*Volume*
Circus Executive		Henry, Aaron Edd Jackson	5
Feld, Irvin	1	Higginbotham, A(loysius) Leon, Jr.	5
North, John Ringling	1	Holland, Jerome Heartwell ("Brud")	1
Civic Worker		Huie, William Bradford	2
Boyer, Ernest LeRoy, Sr.	4	Jackson, Jesse Louis	1960s-1
Chandler, Dorothy Buffum	5	Kahane, Meir	2
Cohen, Audrey C.	4	Kelman, Wolfe	2
Duke, Angier Biddle	4	King, Martin Luther, Jr.	1960s-1
Furness, Elizabeth Mary ("Betty")	4	Kunstler, William Moses	4
Ginsberg, Mitchell Irving	4	Lamont, Corliss	4
Horton, Mildred Helen McAfee	4	Lelyveld, Arthur Joseph	4
Hughes, Harold Everett	4	Lewis, John Robert	1960s-1
Johnson, Rachel Harris	1	McKissick, Floyd B.	3
McNamara, Margaret Craig	1	Malcolm X (Malik El-Shabazz)	1960s-2
McQueen, Thelma ("Butterfly")	4	Meredith, James Howard	1960s-2
Rouse, James Wilson	4	Moses, Robert Parris	1960s-2
Rudolph, Wilma Glodean	4	Muhammad, Elijah	1960s-2
Shriver, Eunice Mary Kennedy	1960s-2	Murray, Anna Pauline ("Pauli")	1
Civil Rights Activist		Nabrit, James Madison, Jr.	5
Abernathy, Ralph David	2	Newton, Huey Percy	1960s-2
Baker, Ella Josephine	2	Prinz, Joachim	2
Baldwin, Roger Nash	1	Rauh, Joseph Louis, Jr.	3
Banks, Dennis J.	1960s-1	Rustin, Bayard Taylor	2, 1960s-2
Bates, Daisy Lee Gatson	5	Scott, Hazel Dorothy	1
Blackwell, Randolph Talmadge	1	Seale, Robert George ("Bobby")	1960s-2
Bond, (Horace) Julian	1960s-1	Shabazz, Betty Jean	5
Boudin, Leonard B.	2	Wheeler, Raymond Milner	1
Brown, Hubert Gerold ("H. Rap")	1960s-1	Wilkins, Roy	1, 1960s-2
Brown, James Nathaniel ("Jim")	1960s-1	Young, Andrew Jackson, Jr.	1960s-2
Carmichael, Stokely (Kwame Touré; Kwame Turé)	5, 1960s-1	**Clergy (Baptist)**	
Chaney, James Earl, Andrew Goodman, and Michael Henry Schwerner	1960s-1	Cox, Harvey Gallagher, Jr.	1960s-1
		King, Martin Luther, Jr.	1960s-1
Chávez, César Estrada	1960s-1	King, Martin Luther, Sr. ("Daddy King")	1
Chisholm, Shirley Anita	1960s-1	Powell, Adam Clayton, Jr.	1960s-2
Cleaver, Eldridge	1960s-1	Robertson, Marion Gordon ("Pat")	1960s-2
Davis, Angela Yvonne	1960s-1	**Clergy (Conservative Judaism)**	
Dee, Ruby	1960s-1	Kelman, Wolfe	2
Delany, Annie Elizabeth ("Bessie")	4	**Clergy (Dutch Reformed)**	
Deloria, Vine, Jr.	1960s-1	Peale, Norman Vincent	3
Diggs, Charles Coles, Jr.	5	**Clergy (Eastern Orthodox)**	
Dohrn, Bernardine Rae	1960s-1	Meyendorff, John	3
Evers, Medgar Wylie	1960s-1	**Clergy (Episcopalian)**	
Farmer, James Leonard, Jr.	5, 1960s-1	Allin, John Maury	5
Garcia, Hector Perez	4	Murray, Anna Pauline ("Pauli")	1
Golden, Harry	1	Pike, James Albert, Jr.	1960s-2
Gordone, Charles	1960s-1	Stokes, Anson Phelps, Jr.	2
Groppi, James Edmund	1, 1960s-1	**Clergy (Jewish)**	
Harris, Patricia Roberts Fitzgerald	1	Finkelstein, Louis	3
Hatcher, Richard Gordon	1960s-1	Kahane, Meir	2, 1960s-1
Hayden, Thomas Emmett ("Tom")	1960s-1	Kelman, Wolfe	2
Hays, Lee	1	Lelyveld, Arthur Joseph	4

	Volume
Myer, Dillon Seymour	1
O'Brien, Lawrence Francis, Jr. ("Larry")	2, 1960s-2
Pendleton, Clarence Mclane, Jr.	2
Prichard, Edward Fretwell, Jr.	1
Raborn, William Francis, Jr. ("Red")	2
Ray, Dixy Lee	4
Reischauer, Edwin Oldfather	1960s-2
Richardson, Elliot Lee	5
Rosenberg, Anna Marie Lederer	1
Rostow, Walter Whitman ("Walt")	1960s-2
Rusk, (David) Dean	4, 1960s-2
Samuels, Howard Joseph	1
Shriver, (Robert) Sargent, Jr.	1960s-2
Shultz, George Pratt	1960s-2
Snyder, John Wesley	1
Stans, Maurice Hubert	5
Terry, Luther L.	1
Tully, Grace	1
Vance, Cyrus Roberts	1960s-2
Volpe, John Anthony	4
Weaver, Robert Clifton	1960s-2
Webb, James Edwin	3
Wharton, Clifton Reginald, Jr.	1960s-2
Wiesner, Jerome Bert	1960s-2
Williams, G(erhard) Mennen	2
Ylvisaker, Paul Norman	3
Young, Andrew Jackson, Jr.	1960s-2
Zacharias, Jerrold Reinach	2

Historian

Albion, Robert G.	1
Arrington, Leonard James	5
Bailey, Thomas A.	1
Bailyn, Bernard	1960s-1
Bainton, Roland Herbert	1
Baron, Salo Wittmayer	2
Barzun, Jacques Martin	1960s-1
Bettmann, Otto Ludwig	5
Billington, Ray Allen	1
Brodie, Fawn McKay	1
Butterfield, Lyman Henry	1
Byrnes, Robert Francis	5
Clarke, John Henrik	5
Cochran, Thomas Childs	5
Commager, Henry Steele	5
Cremin, Lawrence A(rthur)	2, 1960s-1
Cunliffe, Marcus Falkner	2
Curti, Merle Eugene	4
Dabney, Virginius	4
Dangerfield, George	2
Davis, David Brion	1960s-1
Dawidowicz, Lucy Schildkret	2
Deloria, Vine, Jr.	1960s-1

	Volume
Durant, Will(iam) James, and Ariel Durant	1
Eliade, Mircea	2
Ellis, John Tracy	3
Fairbank, John King	3
Fehrenbacher, Don Edward	5
Foner, Philip Sheldon	4
Foote, Shelby Dade, Jr.	1960s-1
Franklin, John Hope	1960s-1
Gay, Peter ("Jack")	1960s-1
Genovese, Eugene Dominick	1960s-1
Gilbert, Felix	3
Goldman, Eric Frederick	2
Hartz, Louis	2
Hexter, J. H. ("Jack")	4
Hofstadter, Richard	1960s-1
Howe, Irving	3
Hughes, H(enry) Stuart	5
Kennan, George Frost	1960s-1
Kuhn, Thomas Samuel	4
Lasch, (Robert) Christopher	4, 1960s-1
Link, Arthur Stanley	5
Logan, Rayford Whittingham	1
Lynes, (Joseph) Russell, Jr.	3
Malone, Dumas	2
Manchester, William Raymond	1960s-2
Mitchell, (John) Broadus	2
Moos, Malcolm Charles	1
Morison, Elting Elmore	4
Morris, Richard Brandon	2
Nef, John Ulric	2
Nisbet, Robert Alexander	4
Padover, Saul Kussiel	1
Perkins, Dexter	1
Pogue, Forrest Carlisle	4
Quarles, Benjamin Arthur	4
Reischauer, Edwin Oldfather	2
Sachar, Abram Leon	3
Schlesinger, Arthur Meier, Jr.	1960s-2
Schoenbrun, David Franz	2
Smith, (Charles) Page (Ward)	4
Smith, Henry Nash	2
Sterling, J(ohn) E(wart) Wallace	1
Stone, Lawrence	5
Tuchman, Barbara Wertheim	2
Ward, John William	1
Wellek, René Maria Eduard	4
Williams, William Appleman	2, 1960s-2
Wills, Garry	1960s-2
Woodward, C(omer) Vann	5, 1960s-2

Horse Trainer

Stephens, Woodford Cefis ("Woody")	5

	Volume
Snelling, Richard Arkwright	3
Stevenson, Adlai Ewing	1960s-2
Vanderbilt, William Henry	1
Volpe, John Anthony	4
Wallace, George Corley, Jr.	5, 1960s-2
Warren, Earl	1960s-2
Williams, G(erhard) Mennen	2
Williams, John Bell	1

Politician (Mayor)

Alioto, Joseph Lawrence	5
Bono, Salvatore Phillip ("Sonny")	5
Bradley, Thomas ("Tom")	5
Celebrezze, Anthony Joseph	5
Clark, Joseph Sill, Jr.	2
Collins, John Frederick	4
Corning, Erastus, 2d	1
Daley, Richard Joseph, Sr.	1960s-1
DiSalle, Michael Vincent	1
Hatcher, Richard Gordon	1960s-1
Hofheinz, Roy Mark	1
Lee, J(oseph) Bracken ("Brack")	4
Lindsay, John Vliet	1960s-1
Loeb, Henry, III	3
Rizzo, Frank Lazzaro	3
Seasongood, Murray	1
Stanford, Sally	1
Stokes, Carl Burton	4, 1960s-2
Wagner, Robert Ferdinand	3
Washington, Harold	2
Yorty, Samuel William	5
Young, Coleman Alexander	5

Politician (Party Leader)

Bernard, Anna Jones	1
Bliss, Ray Charles	1
Brown, Ron(ald) Harmon	4
Brownell, Herbert, Jr.	4
Gates, John	3
Kahane, Meir	1960s-1
Kuhn, Margaret Eliza ("Maggie")	4
Lovestone, Jay	2
O'Brien, Lawrence Francis, Jr. ("Larry")	2, 1960s-2
Scott, Hugh Doggett, Jr.	4
Yarborough, Ralph Webster	4

Politician (President of the United States)

Johnson, Lyndon Baines	1960s-1
Kennedy, John Fitzgerald	1960s-1
Nixon, Richard Milhous	4, 1960s-2
Reagan, Ronald Wilson	1960s-2

Politician (Presidential Adviser)

Brownell, Herbert, Jr.	4
Bundy, McGeorge	4, 1960s-1
Celebrezze, Anthony Joseph	5

	Volume
Clifford, Clark McAdams	5, 1960s-1
Connally, John Bowden, Jr.	3
Ehrlichman, John Daniel	5, 1960s-1
Finch, Robert Hutchinson	4
Haldeman, H(arry) R(obbins)	3, 1960s-1
Heller, Walter Wolfgang	2
Janeway, Eliot	3
Krim, Arthur B.	4
Larson, (Lewis) Arthur	3
Mitchell, John Newton	2
O'Brien, Lawrence Francis, Jr. ("Larry")	2, 1960s-2
Pauley, Edwin Wendell	1
Ribicoff, Abraham Alexander	5
Scali, John Alfred	4
Smith, William French	2
Taylor, Maxwell Davenport	2, 1960s-2
Weaver, Robert Clifton	5
Wiesner, Jerome Bert	4

Politician (Presidential Candidate)

Chisholm, Shirley Anita	1960s-1
Goldwater, Barry Morris	5, 1960s-1
Humphrey, Hubert Horatio, Jr.	1960s-1
Kennedy, Robert Francis	1960s-1
McCarthy, Eugene Joseph	1960s-2
McGovern, George Stanley	1960s-2
Muskie, Edmund Sixtus	4
Rockefeller, Nelson Aldrich	1960s-2
Stevenson, Adlai Ewing	1960s-2
Tsongas, Paul Efthemios	5
Wallace, George Corley, Jr.	5, 1960s-2

Politician (Representative)

Abzug, Bella	5, 1960s-1
Arends, Leslie Cornelius	1
Aspin, Les(lie), Jr.	4
Bingham, Jonathan Brewster ("Jack")	2
Bono, Salvatore Phillip ("Sonny")	5
Bowles, Chester Bliss ("Chet")	2
Brown, George Edward, Jr.	5
Burdick, Quentin Northrop	3
Burton, Phillip	1
Celler, Emanuel	1
Chisholm, Shirley Anita	1960s-1
Cotton, Norris Henry	2
Diggs, Charles Coles, Jr.	5
Dirksen, Everett McKinley	1960s-1
Fascell, Dante Bruno	5
Fenwick, Millicent Hammond	3
Fish, Hamilton	3
Furcolo, (John) Foster	4
Gore, Albert Arnold, Sr.	5
Green, Edith Starrett	2
Halleck, Charles Abraham	2

ALPHABETICAL LIST OF SUBJECTS, VOLUMES 1–5 AND THEMATIC VOLUMES

See also the Occupations Index beginning on p. 563.

Subject	Volume
Daniel, Price Marion	2
Daniels, Jonathan Worth	1
Daniels, William Boone ("Billy")	2
Danilova, Alexandra Dionysievna ("Choura")	5
Daugherty, Hugh ("Duffy")	2
Davenport, Lindsay	Sports-1
Davies, John Paton, Jr.	5
Davis, (William) Allison	1
Davis, Al(len)	Sports-1
Davis, Angela Yvonne	1960s-1
Davis, Bette	2
Davis, David Brion	1960s-1
Davis, Glenn Woodward ("Junior")	Sports-1
Davis, John Henry	Sports-1
Davis, Martin S.	5
Davis, Miles Dewey, III	3, 1960s-1
Davis, Raiford Chatman ("Ossie")	1960s-1
Davis, Sammy, Jr.	2, 1960s-1
Davison, William Edward ("Wild Bill")	2
Dawidowicz, Lucy Schildkret	2
Day, Dennis	2
Day, Doris	1960s-1
Day, James Lewis	5
Day, Leon	4
Dean, Arthur Hobson	2
Dean, Jay Hanna ("Dizzy")	Sports-1
Dean, Paul ("Daffy")	1
DeBakey, Michael Ellis	1960s-1
DeBartolo, Edward John, Sr.	4
Debus, Kurt Heinrich	1
Dedmon, Emmett	1
Dee, Ruby	1960s-1
Deford, Frank	Sports-1
DeGaetani, Jan	2
de Kooning, Elaine Marie Catherine	2
de Kooning, Willem	5, 1960s-1
Delacorte, George Thomas, Jr.	3
Delany, Annie Elizabeth ("Bessie")	4
Delany, Sarah Louise ("Sadie")	5
Delbrück, Max Ludwig Henning	1, 1960s-1
Della Femina, Jerry	1960s-1
Dellinger, David	1960s-1
Deloria, Vine, Jr.	1960s-1
Delvecchio, Alex Peter ("Fats")	Sports-1
de Man, Paul	1
Demara, Ferdinand Waldo ("Fred")	1
Demaret, James Newton ("Jimmy")	1
de Menil, Dominique Schlumberger	5
de Mille, Agnes George	3
Deming, W. Edwards	3
Dempsey, William Harrison ("Jack")	1, Sports-1
De Nagy, Tibor	3
Denby, Edwin Orr	1
Dennis, Sandra Dale ("Sandy")	3
Denver, John	5
Dessauer, John Hans	3
Deutsch, Helene Rosenbach	1
De Varona, Donna	1960s-1, Sports-1
DeVos, Richard Marvin, and Jay Van Andel	1960s-1
De Vries, Peter	3
Dewhurst, Colleen	3
Diamond, Selma	1
Dichter, Ernest	3
Dick, Philip K(indred)	1, 1960s-1
Dickerson, Eric Demetric	Sports-1
Dickerson, Nancy	5, 1960s-1
Dickey, James Lafayette	5
Dickey, John Sloan	3
Dickey, William Malcolm ("Bill")	4, Sports-1
Didrikson Zaharias, Mildred Ella ("Babe")	Sports-1
Diebenkorn, Richard Clifford	3
Dietrich, Marlene	3
Dietz, Howard	1
Diggs, Charles Coles, Jr.	5
Dillard, Harrison	Sports-1
Diller, Phyllis Ada	1960s-1
DiMaggio, Joseph Paul ("Joe"; "The Yankee Clipper")	5, Sports-1
Dine, James ("Jim")	1960s-1
Dion	1960s-1
Dirac, Paul Adrien Maurice	1
Dirksen, Everett McKinley	1960s-1
DiSalle, Michael Vincent	1
Ditka, Mike	Sports-1
Divine, (Harris Glenn Milstead)	2
Dixon, Jeane Lydia	5
Dixon, Willie James	3
Dmytryk, Edward	5
Doby, Lawrence Eugene ("Larry")	Sports-1
Dodd, Robert Lee ("Bobby")	2
Dohrn, Bernardine Rae	1960s-1
Doisy, Edward Adelbert	2
Dolgun, Alexander Michael	2
Donner, Frederic Garrett	2
Donovan, Anne	Sports-1
Donovan, Hedley Williams	2
Doolittle, James Harold	3
Dorati, Antal	2

Subject	Volume
Faulk, John Henry	2
Favre, Brett Lorenzo	Sports-1
Faye, Alice	5
Fears, Thomas Jesse ("Tom")	Sports-1
Feather, Leonard Geoffrey	4
Fehrenbacher, Don Edward	5
Feininger, Andreas Bernhard Lyonel	5
Feld, Irvin	1
Feldman, Morton	2
Feller, Robert William Andrew ("Bob")	Sports-1
Fender, Clarence Leonidas ("Leo")	3
Fenwick, Millicent Hammond	3
Ferguson, Homer Samuel	1
Ferrer, José	3
Festinger, Leon	2
Fetchit, Stepin	1
Feyerabend, Paul Karl	4
Feynman, Richard Phillips	2, 1960s-1
Fidler, James Marion ("Jimmy")	2
Fielding, Temple Hornaday	1
Finch, Robert Hutchinson	4
Fine, Reuben	3
Fingers, Roland Glen ("Rollie")	Sports-1
Finkelstein, Louis	3
Finley, Charles Oscar ("Charlie")	4
Finney, Walter Braden ("Jack")	4
Fischer, Robert James ("Bobby")	1960s-1
Fish, Hamilton	3
Fisher, Avery Robert	4
Fisher, M(ary) F(rances) K(ennedy)	3
Fitzgerald, Ella Jane	4
Fitzgerald, Robert Stuart	1
Fitzsimmons, Frank Edward	1
Fitzsimmons, James Edward ("Sunny Jim")	Sports-1
Fixx, James Fuller	1
Fleming, Peggy Gale	1960s-1, Sports-1
Flesch, Rudolf Franz	2
Fletcher, Harvey	1
Fletcher, Joseph Francis, III	3
Flexner, Stuart Berg	2
Flood, Curt(is) Charles	5, Sports-1
Flory, Paul John	1
Fogarty, Anne Whitney	1960s-1
Fogerty, John Cameron	1960s-1
Folsom, James	2
Fonda, Henry Jaynes	1, 1960s-1
Fonda, Jane Seymour	1960s-1
Fonda, Peter Seymour	1960s-1
Foner, Philip Sheldon	4
Fontanne, Lynn	1

Subject	Volume
Foote, Emerson	3
Foote, Shelby Dade, Jr.	1960s-1
Forbes, Malcolm Stevenson	2
Ford, Edward Charles ("Whitey")	Sports-1
Ford, Ernest Jennings ("Tennessee Ernie")	3
Ford, Henry, II ("Hank the Deuce")	2
Foreman, Carl	1
Forrest, Helen	5
Fortas, Abraham ("Abe")	1, 1960s-1
Forte, Fulvio Chester, Jr. ("Chet")	4
Fosbury, Richard Douglas ("Dick")	Sports-1
Fosse, Robert Louis ("Bob")	2
Fossey, Dian	1, 1960s-1
Foster, Andrew ("Rube")	Sports-1
Foster, Vincent William, Jr.	3
Fowler, William Alfred	4
Fox, Jacob Nelson ("Nellie")	Sports-1
Foxx, James Emory ("Jimmie")	Sports-1
Foxx, Redd	3
Foyt, A(nthony) J(oseph), Jr.	Sports-1
France, William Henry Getty, Sr. ("Bill")	3, Sports-1
Francis, Sam(uel) Lewis	4
Frankenheimer, John Michael	1960s-1
Franklin, Aretha Louise	1960s-1
Franklin, John Hope	1960s-1
Fraser, Gretchen Claudia	Sports-1
Frazier, Joseph William ("Joe")	1960s-1, Sports-1
Frazier, Walt, II ("Clyde")	Sports-1
Frederick, Pauline	2
Fredericks, Carlton	2
Fredericks, Sara	2
Freleng, Isadore ("Friz")	4
Freund, Paul Abraham	3
Frick, Ford Christopher	Sports-1
Frick, Helen Clay	1
Friedan, Betty Naomi	1960s-1
Friedman, Benjamin ("Benny")	1
Friedman, Milton	1960s-1
Friedrich, Carl Joachim	1
Friend, Charlotte	2
Friendly, Fred W.	5
Friendly, Henry Jacob	2
Frisch, Frank Francis ("Frankie")	Sports-1
Frowick, Roy Halston. *See* Halston.	
Fulbright, J(ames) William	4, 1960s-1
Fulks, Joseph Franklin ("Joe")	Sports-1
Fuller, R(ichard) Buckminster	1
Fuller, S. B.	2
Fuller, Samuel Michael	5

Subject	Volume
Marks, John D. ("Johnny")	1
Marriott, J(ohn) Willard	1
Mars, Forrest Edward, Sr.	5
Marshall, E(dda) G(unnar)	5
Marshall, George Preston	Sports-2
Marshall, Thurgood	3, 1960s-2
Marston, Robert Quarles	5
Martin, Alfred Manuel, Jr. ("Billy")	2
Martin, Dean	4, 1960s-2
Martin, Freddy	1
Martin, John Bartlow	2, 1960s-2
Martin, Mary Virginia	2
Martin, William McChesney, Jr.	5, 1960s-2
Martinez, Pedro Jaime	Sports-2
Marvin, Lee	2
Mas Canosa, Jorge	5
Mason, (William) Birny J., Jr.	5
Massey, Raymond Hart	1
Masters, William Howell, and Virginia Eshelman Johnson	1960s-2
Mathewson, Christopher ("Christy")	Sports-2
Mathias, Robert Bruce ("Bob")	Sports-2
Matson, James Randel ("Randy")	Sports-2
Matson, Oliver Genoa, II ("Ollie")	Sports-2
Matsunaga, Spark Masayuki ("Sparkie")	2
Matthau, Walter	1960s-2
Matthews, Burnita Shelton	2
Mature, Victor John	5
Mauldin, William Henry ("Bill")	1960s-2
Maxwell, Vera Huppé	4
May, Elaine	1960s-2
May, Rollo Reece	4
Mayer, Maria Goeppert. See Goeppert-Mayer, Maria.	
Mayfield, Curtis Lee	5
Maynard, Don(ald) Rogers	Sports-2
Maynard, Robert Clyve	3
Mays, Benjamin Elijah	1
Mays, William Howard, Jr. ("Willie")	1960s-2, Sports-2
Meader, (Abbott) Vaughn	1960s-2
Meadows, Audrey	4
Means, Gardiner Coit	2
Medeiros, Humberto Sousa	1
Medina, Harold Raymond	2
Meeker, Ralph	2
Meisner, Sanford	5
Mellon, Paul	5
Menninger, Karl Augustus	2
Menuhin, Yehudi	5
Meola, Tony	Sports-2
Mercer, John Herndon ("Johnny")	1960s-2
Mercer, Mabel	1
Meredith, (Oliver) Burgess	5
Meredith, James Howard	1960s-2
Merman, Ethel	1
Merriam, Eve	3
Merrill, James Ingram	4
Merrill, John Putnam	1
Metcalfe, Ralph Horace	Sports-2
Meyendorff, John	3
Meyers, Ann Elizabeth	Sports-2
Meyner, Robert Baumle	2
Michener, James Albert	5
Middlecoff, (Emmett) Cary ("Doc")	5
Middleton, Drew	2
Mies van der Rohe, Ludwig	1960s-2
Mikan, George Lawrence, Jr.	Sports-2
Mikita, Stan	Sports-2
Milanov, Zinka	2
Milgram, Stanley	1
Milland, Ray	2
Millar, Kenneth. See Macdonald, Ross.	
Miller, Arnold Ray	1
Miller, Arthur Asher	1960s-2
Miller, Carl S.	2
Miller, Cheryl DeAnn	Sports-2
Miller, Marvin Julian	Sports-2
Miller, Reginald Wayne ("Reggie")	Sports-2
Miller, Roger Dean	3
Miller, Shannon Lee	Sports-2
Miller, William Mosely	2
Mills, C(harles) Wright	1960s-2
Mills, Wilbur Daigh	3
Milstein, Nathan	3
Minnelli, Vincente	2
Minnesota Fats (Rudolf Walter Wanderone, Jr.)	4
Minow, Newton Norman	1960s-2
Mitchell, (John) Broadus	2
Mitchell, Joan	3
Mitchell, John James, Jr.	1
Mitchell, John Newton	2, 1960s-2
Mitchell, Joseph Quincy	4
Mitchell, Robert Cornelius, Sr. ("Bobby")	Sports-2
Mitchum, Robert Charles Durman	5
Mitford, Jessica ("Decca")	4
Mize, John Robert ("Johnny")	3
Mizener, Arthur Moore	2
Mohr, Charles Henry	2
Molnar, Charles Edwin	4

Subject	Volume
Momaday, N(avarre) Scott	1960s-2
Monette, Paul Landry	4
Monk, Thelonious Sphere	1, 1960s-2
Monroe, Earl Vernon, Jr	Sports-2
Monroe, Marilyn	1960s-2
Monroe, Marion	1
Monroe, Rose Leigh Will	5
Monroe, William Smith ("Bill")	4
Montagu, Ashley	5
Montana, Joseph Clifford, Jr. ("Joe")	Sports-2
Montgomery, Elizabeth	4
Montgomery, Robert	1
Moody, Helen Wills. *See* Wills (Moody), Helen Newington.	
Moore, Archibald Lee ("Archie")	5, Sports-2
Moore, Francis Daniels, and Thomas Earl Starzl	1960s-2
Moore, Garry	3, 1960s-2
Moore, Jack Carlton ("Clayton")	5
Moore, Mary Tyler	1960s-2
Moore, Stanford	1
Moos, Malcolm Charles	1
Moreno, Rita	1960s-2
Morgan, Henry (Lerner von Ost)	4
Morgan, Henry Sturgis ("Harry")	1
Morgan, Joe Leonard	Sports-2
Morganfield, McKinley. *See* Waters, Muddy.	
Morison, Elting Elmore	4
Moross, Jerome	1
Morris, Richard Brandon	2
Morris, Robert	1960s-2
Morris, William Weaks ("Willie")	5
Morrison, James Douglas ("Jim")	1960s-2
Morse, Wayne Lyman	1960s-2
Morton, Thruston Ballard	1
Mosbacher, Emil, Jr. ("Bus")	Sports-2
Mosconi, William Joseph ("Willie")	3
Moses, Edwin Corley	Sports-2
Moses, Robert	1
Moses, Robert Parris	1960s-2
Motherwell, Robert	3
Motley, Marion	5, Sports-2
Mott, Stewart Rawlings	1960s-2
Mourning, Alonzo Harding, Jr.	Sports-2
Moynihan, Daniel Patrick	1960s-2
Mueller, Reuben Herbert	1
Muhammad, Elijah	1960s-2
Muldowney, Shirley Roque	Sports-2
Mullen, Joseph ("Joey")	Sports-2
Mulligan, Gerald Joseph ("Gerry")	4

Subject	Volume
Mulliken, Robert Sanderson	2, 1960s-2
Mumford, Lawrence Quincy	1
Mumford, Lewis Charles	2
Murchison, Clint(on) Williams, Jr.	2
Murphy, Calvin Jerome	Sports-2
Murphy, George Lloyd	3
Murphy, Joseph Samson	5
Murray, Anna Pauline ("Pauli")	1
Murray, Arthur	3
Murray, James Patrick ("Jim")	5, Sports-2
Murray, Kathryn Hazel	5
Murrow, Edward Roscoe	1960s-2
Musial, Stanley Frank ("Stan the Man")	Sports-2
Muskie, Edmund Sixtus	4, 1960s-2
Myer, Dillon Seymour	1
Nabokov, Vladimir	1960s-2
Nabrit, James Madison, Jr.	5
Nader, Ralph	1960s-2
Nagel, Ernest	1, 1960s-2
Nagurski, Bronislau ("Bronko")	2, Sports-2
Nagy, Steve	Sports-2
Naismith, James	Sports-2
Namath, Joseph William ("Joe")	1960s-2, Sports-2
Nash, Graham. *See* Crosby, Stills, and Nash.	
Nathans, Daniel	5
Navratilova, Martina	Sports-2
Nearing, Helen Knothe	4
Nearing, Scott	1
Nef, John Ulric	2
Negri, Pola	2
Nelson, (John) Byron, Jr.	Sports-2
Nelson, Eric Hilliard ("Rick")	1
Nelson, Harriet Hilliard	4
Nemerov, Howard	3
Neumann, Vera Salaff ("Vera")	3
Neustadt, Richard Elliott	1960s-2
Nevelson, Louise	2, 1960s-2
Nevers, Ernest Alonzo ("Ernie")	Sports-2
Newell, Allen	3
Newell, Peter ("Pete")	Sports-2
Newhall, Beaumont	3
Newhart, George Robert ("Bob")	1960s-2
Newhouser, Harold ("Prince Hal")	5
Newman, Paul Arthur	1960s-2
Newton, Huey Percy	2, 1960s-2
Neyman, Jerzy	1
Nichols, Mike	1960s-2
Nicholson, Jack	1960s-2
Nicklaus, Jack William	1960s-2, Sports-2

ISBN 0-684-31222-0

90000

9 780684 312224